The Speed Seekers

THE SPEED SEEKERS

Thomas G. Foxworth

MACDONALD AND JANE'S
LONDON

Copyright © 1975 Thomas G. Foxworth

First published in 1975 by
Macdonald and Jane's (Macdonald
& Co. (Publishers) Ltd), Paulton House,
8 Shepherdess Walk, London N1 7LW

Designed by Jacqui Apthorpe
Filmset in 10/11pt Photina by Filmtype
Services Limited, Scarborough
Printed in Great Britain by
Hazell Watson & Viney Ltd,
Aylesbury, Bucks

ISBN 0356 08123 0

CONTENTS

PART ONE

ACKNOWLEDGEMENTS, *ix*

1   RAISON D'ETRE, *3*

2   THE COMPASS OF AIR CONDUCT, *6*
      The Prophets, *7*
      Conditions Elsewhere, *19*
      The FAI, *21*

3   THE GREAT RACES—THEIR PATRONS AND
PROMOTERS, *23*
      Early Long Distance Affairs, *23*
      Newspapermen Stimulate Air Races, *25*
      James Gordon Bennett, *26*
      The Pulitzers, *29*
      The English Aerial Derbies, *41*
      Industrialist Patrons: Henry Deutsch de la
        Meurthe, *45*
      Louis D. Beaumont, *47*
      Jacques Schneider, *49*

4   AN ERA OF TECHNOLOGICAL INNOVATION, *57*
      Propulsion: the Heart of the Aeroplane, *57*
        The Aero Engine, *57*
        The Prop Grows Up, *72*
        Flying Radiators, *75*
      Airframe: Transforming the Aeroplane, *78*
        Rebirth of the Monoplane, *78*
        The Move from Wood to Metal, *80*
        The Bite of Flutter, *84*
        Hiding the Landing Gear, *87*

PART TWO

France

5   SPEEDY SPADS, *91*
        The Spad-Herbemont Racers, *91*

6   QUEST FOR VITESSE, *107*
        The Nieuport Biplane Racers, *107*

7   QUEST FOR VITESSE, *119*
        The Nieuport-Delage Sesquiplan Racers, *119*

8   BERNARD AND THE UNSUNG BREAKTHROUGHS, *129*

9   FRENCH FREAKS AND OTHER FASTBACKS, *139*
        The Louis Clement-Moineau Racer, *139*
        The Borel-Boccaccio Racer, *141*
        The Lumiere-de Monge Racer, *142*
        The Hanriot Racer, *146*
        The Tailless Racers of 1922, *147*
        The Gourdou-Leseurre Racer, *151*
        The Salmson-Bechereau Racer, *153*
        French Flying Boat Racers, *154*

United States

10   A STRANGER IN THEIR MIDST, *161*
        The Dayton-Wright Racer, *161*

11   THE ARMY'S BLOCKBUSTER, *169*
        The Verville VCP Racer, *169*

12   WILDCAT AND KITTEN, *177*

13   THE GOLDEN THOROUGHBREDS, *193*
        The Curtiss CR Racers, *193*

14   THE GOLDEN THOROUGHBREDS, *205*
        The Curtiss R-6 Racers, *205*

15   THE GOLDEN THOROUGHBREDS, *217*
        The Curtiss R2C Racers, *217*

16 THE GOLDEN THOROUGHBREDS, *226*
        The Curtiss R3C Racers, *226*

17 THE MYSTERY RACERS, *243*
        The Navy-Wright Racers, *243*

18 THE THOMAS-MORSE RACERS, *258*

19 PORTRAIT OF THE FUTURE, *277*
        The Verville R-3 Racers, *277*

20 OTHER AMERICAN EFFORTS, *288*
        Loening, *288*
        The Bee-Line Racers, *294*
        The Navy TS and TR, *296*
        Gallaudet, *299*
        Dare, *300*

Great Britain

21 EARLY BRITISH SPORTING EFFORTS, *305*
        The Bantams, *305*
        Avro, *309*
        The Martinsyde Semiquaver, *315*
        Airco and de Havilland, *320*

22 FOLLAND'S FLYING FASTBACKS, *323*
        The "British Nieuport" and Gloucestershire
            Racers, *323*

23 HARRY HAWKER AND THE SOPWITH RACER, *345*

24 THE BRISTOL RACERS, *353*

25 BOATS, FLOATS, BRITANNIA, *367*
        The Supermarine and Blackburn Racers, *367*

Italy

26 THE FEROCIOUS FIAT OF BRACK-PAPA, *383*
        The Ansaldo and Fiat Racers, *383*

27 ITALY GOES TO SEA, *391*
        The Savoia and Macchi Racers—and Others, *391*

POSTSCRIPT, *417*

APPENDIX TABLES

CALENDARS, *421*

CONVERSION TABLES, *422*

1   PROGRESS OF SPEED, *423*
        Notable Speed Flights—Records and Attempts, *423*

2   RACE TABLES, *428*
        Gordon Bennett 1920, *428*
        Prix Deutsch de la Meurthe 1919/1920, *430*
        Coupe Deutsch de la Meurthe 1921/1922, *432*
        The Aerial Derby 1919–1923, *434*
        Coupe Louis D. Beaumont 1923–1925, *443*
        The Pulitzer 1920–1925, *451*
        Curtiss Marine Flying Trophy 1922, *460*
        The Schneider 1919–1926, *463*

3   AEROPLANE SPECIFICATIONS, *490*

4   AERO ENGINE SPECIFICATIONS, *514*

NOTES TO APPENDICES, *531*

ILLUSTRATION CAPTIONS CREDITS CODE, *547*

INDEX, *549*

ACKNOWLEDGEMENTS

The seed of this effort was planted more than a dozen years ago when I first became enamored with the pure aesthetic appeal of the racers and speed planes of the 1920s. The drama of early aerial speed events is self-evident; I suspected that the human drama behind the headlines would be equally — if not more — fascinating. Intensive research into the events described began in 1964, and off and on over the intervening years, by means of thousands of documents, books, blueprints, engineering records, letters and countless interviews (many with people now dead), the story took shape. I soon found that in several instances I had to piece together information from multiple, often diverse sources, and that frequently the amount of conflict — in stories, reports, "reliable" documents — was astonishing. Indeed, the magnitude of conflict threatened at times to overwhelm me. Somehow I have prevailed, and while no one would dare state that detailed information concerning aviation in the 1920s such as that included is infallible, I have gone to sometimes ridiculous lengths to check and verify. What is included is in almost all cases in excess of just the most reasonable; it is the most probable. Conversations are as personally remembered or documented. I have indulged in no flights of imagination: the speed seekers provided fable enough in their actual flights.

There needs to be mentioned my attitude toward footnotes; the kind, that is, which document source material. I fully realize and acknowledge their importance. But this is intended

ix

to be an informal — if accurate — history, and I chose not to bombard the reader with endless attributions. The available evidence for what I included is in many instances voluminous. Indeed, it would be possible in the extreme literally to footnote not once but several times virtually every single sentence in this book. I would rather list the fine people who both gave me and helped me locate the material for this story.

My special thanks go first and foremost to Paul R. Matt, artist *extraordinaire* capable of divining an aeroplane's *essence* with the power only a lover commands, the endlessly patient perfectionist responsible for the lovely full-color art renditions on the endpapers of this volume. His counsel over the half-dozen years since he published my first article in his *Historical Aviation Album* has been invaluable as both stimulant and counterbalance, and his rich lode of aviation lore and memorabilia has provided many brilliant additions to these pages. Another whose counsel has been priceless is Hugo Byttebier of Buenos Aires, who ranks in my estimation as the world's pre-eminent living expert on the early aero engine. Countless times has he with warm hospitality at his home or by means of incredibly detailed correspondence come to my aid to provide from his vast archives not only patient explanations of an engine's innards but how it pointed the course of events. I enjoyed the rare gift of Hugo's typed manuscript on the D-12 engine as reference three years before it was published by the Smithsonian Institution. I owe more of a debt than can be properly expressed to Ann C. Tilbury, indefatigable librarian of *Flight* magazine's incomparable photographic library in London, for her astonishing efforts. Lovely illustrations I would have thought long since lost surfaced as the result of her research. Henry C. Kavelaars of The Hague, Netherlands, also deserves special mention for permitting me to draw on the vast resources he has compiled over decades

relating to the Schneider Trophy races. Much of the accuracy of my accounts is possible only because of "Henk." Writer Ralph Barker of London assisted mightily in my quest of Schneider Trophy data and provided helpful information on the changing British regard for the contest. To my former faculty adviser and aerodynamics teacher at Princeton, Professor David C. Hazen, now as then a highly respected friend, I owe a deep debt for his invaluable technical assistance, including hours of reading and criticizing much of the technical information. The remarkable accuracy of the fifteen maps would not have been possible without the efforts of Marvin Stine and the cartographers of Jeppesen & Company, Denver, who produce thousands of precision aeronautical charts used by most airline pilots (including me) worldwide, and whose enthusiasm about the early days was unexpected and is appreciated. I must also mention Kenn C. Rust of Los Angeles, who over many years as editor of the American Aviation Historical Society *Journal* and the magazine *Aero Album* respectively helped more than he realizes when some of the material in the book appeared in article form under his tutelage. My editors, Stewart "Sandy" Richardson, assisted by Emily Varkala and Ray Waitkins who contributed enormous energy, at Doubleday and Sidney Jackson assisted by Paul Ellis at Macdonald, have my heartfelt thanks for their unfailing enthusiasm and support which sustained me over months of arduous effort. Alex Gottfryd, Doubleday's art director, provided tremendous help and encouragement in assisting my efforts to complete nearly eighty of the aeroplane drawings included. I must also acknowledge the superb job done by the copy editor, Harold Grabau. And Peter Endsleigh Castle deserves thanks for his excellent jacket design.

Others that deserve particular mention in the development of each section are:

France: At the top of the list I place Viscount Louis P. de Monge, who has my deep gratitude for spending long hours with me, providing insights into the life and times — the feelings and motivations — of that band of early French aircraftsmen; then checking and giving his blessing to the manuscript. In the same esteem I hold S. Georges Bruner, renowned French aeronautical engineer, who graciously made me welcome in his Paris home and gave me free access to his treasured material, offering reminiscences on the 280-mph Bernard racer of 1924 which was his pet. Pilot Fernand Lasne in correspondence gave invaluable aid on his own remarkable feats, his flying mate Sadi Lecointe, and conditions at Nieuport during the 1920s. I owe a special debt to Air France Captain Pierre Henry de Guerke for making the long trek to La Ferté personally to visit M. Lasne on my behalf. The personnel at the Musée de l'Air Documentation Center in Paris were remarkable in their unflagging efforts on the occasions of my many grinding day-long visits; they unstintingly dug into the darkest recesses of their files locating to my delight long-unseen glass plate photographic negatives, letters of Spad racer dimensions in Herbemont's own hand, the odd test report and weight schedule — and much more. Henri Beaubois, French aero historian emeritus, also added his personal touch to my efforts. B. Duperier, president of l'Aéro-Club de France, was extremely helpful with extraordinary efforts in confirming some very obscure aspects of the early French aero scene. In addition, the files of the Fédération Aéronautique Internationale, housed in the same elegant Aéro-Club building just a few blocks from the Arc de Triomphe, were thrown open at my disposal. I received generously offered assistance from Les Amis de Delage, an organization of exclusive French auto lovers, in the pursuit of an interesting aspect of the story. The Columbia University Engineering Library in New York City was

the scene of hours of effort when they generously made available to an outsider their precious collections of French documents including complete runs of *l'Aérophile* and *l'Aéronautique.* Especial thanks is reserved for two Pan Am colleagues, vintage aeroplane lover Jerry Marchadier of Paris and fellow pilot Allan Ligas, who gave uncounted hours of their time to translate thousands of words of precise French material. I can never adequately repay them.

The United States: One hardly knows where to begin; assistance from countless sources was essential in framing an effort of this magnitude. Perhaps outstanding in my estimation were the generous and detailed personal interviews, many now preserved in my files on hours' worth of tape, afforded by speed seekers such as Commander Harold "Hap" Brow, USN (Ret.); Captain A. W. "Jake" Gorton, USN (Ret.); Commander Rutledge Irvine, USN (Ret.); engine builder Doctor Arthur Nutt, who also checked extensive portions of the manuscript; aeroplane builder Grover C. Loening; the Reverend Lester Maitland, Brigadier General, USAF (Ret.); Major General Francis P. Mulcahy, USMC (Ret.); former Curtiss test pilot Roland Rohlfs; Major General Lawson H. Sanderson, USMC (Ret.); Brigadier General Donald F. Stace, USAF (Ret.); Curtiss designer William Wait; Doctor Jerome C. Hunsaker of the Massachusetts Institute of Technology. Also Heber Olson, boyhood friend of Russell Maughan; Frank H. "Sonny" Harris, barnstormer who grew up with Roosevelt Field; Hallock "Buck" Ketcham, former Curtiss employee; Major Alexander P. de Seversky. I am also deeply indebted for quantities of unique and invaluable material received in extensive correspondence provided by General James H. Doolittle, USAF (Ret.); the late Alfred V. Verville, whose personal handwritten corrections to the first-draft manuscript of Chapter 19 have provided me with a priceless document;

Professor Nicholas Hoff of Stanford University, who made available much from his study of the aeroplane's infancy; Eugene E. Wilson, wartime head of United Aircraft; George Shestak, copy editor of the Omaha *World-Herald*, exceptional journalist whose dogged sleuthing uncovered the complete 1921 Pulitzer story, supplemented by the personal mementoes of Earl W. Porter, the event's organizer; the late Randolph F. Hall and Paul D. Wilson, both formerly of Thomas-Morse and directly involved in building and flying their racers; the late Theodore P. Wright, the late Charles B. Kirkham, George C. Page, and Frank H. "Diz" Dean, who all provided extensive perspective on Curtiss events; Mrs. Harriet Fladoes, Mrs. Kenneth N. Gilpin, and Mrs. Lewis E. Pillsbury, General Billy Mitchell's sister, daughter, and niece respectively; James Horgan, who made available to me portions of his unpublished Ph.D. dissertation concerning aviation history in St. Louis; military aviation historians Robert Casari and Major Truman C. "Pappy" Weaver, USAF (Ret.); W. F. Maughan with insights on his father — he was the child born at the moment his father was winning the 1922 Pulitzer; Major J. Elliott, USMC, with help on Marine racer participation; and Jesse D. Thompson, who provided insight and balance on early McCook Field activities. Organizations and men deserving special note are Royal Frey and the U. S. Air Force Museum at Wright-Patterson AFB, Ohio; Louis S. Casey and Robert Wood of the National Air Museum, Smithsonian Institution, Washington; Lee M. Pearson, Historian, Naval Air Systems Command; John Sloan and the American Aviation Historical Society; R. J. Williard, Naval Supply Depot, Mechanicsburg, Pennsylvania, a source of rare (in many cases the only surviving) blueprint drawings of early racers; Garry D. Ryan, Assistant Director, Old Military Records Division, The National Archives; Colonel George V. Fagan, USAF, Director, USAF Academy Library; Master Sergeant Walter F. Gemeinhardt, NCOIC, Marine Corps Museum, Quantico MCAS, Virginia; The Library of Congress; Norman Polmar, The U. S. Naval Institute, Annapolis, Maryland; Warden's Office, Leavenworth Federal Penitentiary, Kansas (helpful with data regarding S. E. J. Cox); St. Louis Historical Society (helpful with data regarding Louis D. Beaumont); The Milwaukee Historical Society (helpful with data regarding Billy Mitchell); The Long Island Early Fliers Club and the Nassau County (New York) Historical Society (helpful with data regarding Long Island aeronautical activities); The James V. Forrestal Library of Princeton University, which contains the entire technical literature of NACA (today NASA) and other useful documents; J. C. Kilmartin, Chief, Map Information Service, U. S. Geological Survey, and Captain J. O. Phillips, USESSA, Chief, Geodesy Division, Coast and Geodetic Survey, for information helpful in determining race courses; finally, an especially warm note of thanks to the many helpful people at that incredible institution, the New York Public Library — both at the main library (Fifth Avenue and Forty-second Street) and the newspaper annex (Eleventh Avenue and Forty-third Street), my second home for weeks. Elmo N. Pickerill, late secretary of the Early Birds, an organization of men who soloed before 1917, made available to me his vast personal files, giving especially valuable assistance on Bert Acosta. I also owe deep thanks to Charles G. Mandrake of Ashtabula, Ohio, for coming to my aid with his extensive photographic collection, as did Stephen J. Hudek of Detroit, John Underwood of Glendale, California and Anthony Yusken of Chicago.

Great Britain: Long, involved correspondence with test and race pilot Frank T. Courtney was instrumental in establishing the tone of events in Britain during the 1920s. Eric Folland, son of "HPF", provided important personal reminiscences regarding his father. Hugh Burroughes, for over forty years a director of Gloster Aircraft Corporation, also afforded much helpful firsthand information. Through Ralph Barker I was able indirectly to glean much of a personal nature from pilot Hubert Broad. I am also deeply indebted to John Blake, former editor of the Royal Aero Club *Gazette* and Club competitions manager, who gave me valuable *entrée* into the historical files of the RAeC and provided encouragement and help from his own large collections over many years; to James D. Oughton of British Aircraft Corporation, who provided monumental help on the Bristol racers; to Oliver J. "Ollie" Tapper, now retired, who helped with the Hawker story; and to Phillip Jarrett of the Royal Aeronautical Society. Also to Tony A. Andrews, who went out of his way to locate rare data on "British Nieuport" and Gloster for me; to Steve Birdsall of Sydney, Australia, who was most helpful in tracking down the activities of Frank S. Barnwell; to Edward Eves of IPC Publications who provided useful Supermarine data. A special note of thanks is due to Mrs. Zofia Kortas Millie, former Technical Secretary at the International Federation of Air Line Pilots Associations in London, for hours of spare-time research in museums, the patent office, and elsewhere on my behalf. An interview with Professor Kurt Weil, former designer at Junkers, added dimension to my appreciation of events taking place in Britain during those days. Certain records from the Imperial War Museum and RAE Farnborough were also most helpful. Finally, several years of my own participation in English sport aviation, joyfully flying vintage aeroplanes over that ancient and timeless land, have graced the whole with a patina of understanding as to what it was all about.

Italy: I owe more than I can convey to the warm generosity of Contessa Maria Fede Caproni for making available to me the astonishing and wonderful resources of her Museo Aeronautico Caproni di Taliedo in Rome, and also for contacting Francesco Brack-Papa on my behalf. Dott. Ing. Giuseppe de Angelis of the Registro Aeronautico Italiano, my fellow colleague on the Airworthiness Committee of the International Civil Aviation Organization, with his charming wife Jean helped mightily by securing photos and data and translating quantities of Italian documents for me. Extremely helpful was information from Dott. Ing. Ermanno Bazzocchi, successor to Castoldi as chief engineer of Aeronautica Macchi, and from Muzio Macchi himself. Giorgio Apostolo of the Italian Aviation Historical Society has also provided excellent and comprehensive assistance. Finally, I am deeply indebted to my sister-in-law, Mrs. Nancy A. Brown, for invaluable aid in translation.

It must be emphasized that no one listed should be held accountable for any errors which may have crept in — these are entirely my own; nor should anyone be considered accessory to my opinions or conclusions. Of the hundreds of collaborators, contributors, and citable sources it is inevitable that I have inadvertently omitted important names. I apologize for such oversight where it may exist, and to all visible and invisible I give my sincere and deepest thanks.

THOMAS GORDON FOXWORTH
Huntington, New York
June 1974

Part One

RAISON D'ÊTRE

1

This chronicle quite simply is a story about speed and the men who, during little more than a half-decade span of time following World War I, sought it in the air.

Speed has always been the aeroplane's *raison d'être*. Every new advance in aviation, every additional milestone posted along the journey to conquer time and space has had the quest for speed as its basis.

The question has been posed, why write about the years 1919–26, years of difficult postwar readjustment, years of economic malaise, political upheaval, social depression, seemingly bleak years when people were in many ways backing away from what was happening, plagued by a dearth of enthusiasm, adjusting the lid on an underlying element of hysteria? The answer is because such periods always mark the great leaps in technology. Because the people of the 1920s were caught up in a great technical revolution when more than at any other time they were beginning to be aware – to see and feel even if they did not fully comprehend – the disintegration not only of time and space but of ideas and conventions long taken for granted. The speed seekers were creating achievements that fifty years earlier would have loosed the hysteria, achievements leading to possibilities that were truly incredible and to a degree more visceral, more felt, than for perhaps any other generation. The speeds being achieved for the first time in history during those years were far beyond all previous human experience, yet they were still within the scope of public imagination.

It had taken several thousand human generations for man to reach his top speed of 1918, but without stopping for breath he would *double* this value in little more than half a decade. Never before or since has man made proportionately as long a leap in so short a time. By 1925 he had established an aerodynamic watershed. Cathedrals represented the most advanced technology at the time they were built, so that prayers might rise more easily to heaven; sharp-nosed speedplanes became the cathedrals of the speed seekers, and their prayers became physical.

This is a story rooted in Western civilization. Imperative in the Western soul is the eternal struggle to cross new frontiers, the deep need to keep moving. Ever since Gottlieb Daimler's first practical internal-combustion engine coughed and spit its smoky hello to the world, Western man has been beside himself to go faster. In the nineteenth century a set of wheels was placed astride this mechanical monster. When the twentieth century dawned a prop was stuck on its end and the air race was born.

Before World War I the world's fastest aviator was the Frenchman Maurice Prevost, who in 1913 hurtled through the sky at the amazing speed of 126·59 mph in a cigar-shaped Deperdussin monoplane. Not too many years before that, in 1906, Glenn Curtiss blared across the Florida sands of Ormond Beach at 136·47 mph on what was then the world's fastest vehicle, his terrifying eight-cylinder motorcycle strongly resembling an artillery cannonade. Three years later Curtiss won the world's first aeroplane race — at a paltry 47·65 mph! Prevost's 1913 aerial speed record also fell short of the mark set by a Benz automobile which in 1911 was gunned over a "flying kilometer" by the German driver Burman at 141·73 mph. Indeed, if prewar flying machines had

been noted for anything in particular, it was not speed. For the most part, wheezing, frail contraptions wobbled uncertainly over curious crowds at lazy county fairs; they were novelties, nothing more, and most people ridiculed the idea that the aeroplane would ever amount to anything useful — why, less than ten years before the whole idea of flying had seemed preposterous.

Still, over the upturned heads of robust Americans or stylish Europeans the raucous buzzing from the transparent bamboo and linen aeroplanes signaled an insistent portent for the future. Then the war came with all its fury and aeroplanes suddenly matured into nimble projectiles that ripped the air with smoke and thunder, even as many people could still pretend they did not exist. Curiously, although the aeroplane's utility expanded enormously during World War I, its speed did not rise remarkably. The swiftest operational pursuits were capable of just 140 mph in 1918, hardly more than Prevost's 1913 record. Wartime aeroplanes had to be hurriedly mass-produced; the penalties of tampering with fragile-enough reliability, the need for a cheap product, and the need for front-line maintenance simplicity prohibited any but fairly straightforward, pedestrian designs. On November 11, 1918, when the Armistice put an end to the holocaust, it was still quite easy to be heedless of any of the momentous implications the aeroplane's very existence held for mankind.

But a transformation in motive occurred soon after the war. The incentive shifted to achieving pure speed rather than combat superiority. Speed itself became a simple measure of technical prowess. Many ideas that were generated during the war did not see application until peacetime when for a brief period the established aviation houses indulged in fashioning one-of-a-kind maximum-performance aeroplanes which proudly took their banners into peaceful competition. Such hallowed names as Spad and

Nieuport, almost universally sure to conjure romantic images of swirling dogfights over the scarred fields of Flanders, were perpetuated by ex-aces and ace designers as the hallmarks of progressive peacetime speed developments. After the Armistice many aircraft-manufacturing houses pocketed their wartime profits and turned to other products. Some tried valiantly to continue but went under. But there were those who would continue with energy and momentum kindled by the war, charged by faith, vision, gritty stubbornness, the drive for prestige, and an occasional spark of true genius. It was not a game for the fainthearted. And there was no such thing as tradition or example to go by in this lively endeavor. Every forward step was being taken in uncharted regions.

Aviation in the 1920s, to be sure, was gaudy. It was an age of ambitious, often extraordinary protagonists. At the same time many people did not have telephones or automobiles or refrigerators or even electric lights. The North Pole was as remote as the moon, and plodding, majestic ocean liners meant days — even weeks — still separated nations. It was before noise abatement or air traffic control or even the most rudimentary regulations of any kind existed to govern these spirited, irrepressible men of the air. They were regarded with incredulity and awe, and it took enormous faith to believe their tiny racers, crawling up the graph of speed kilometer by kilometer, could really *change* any of this. But they improved their art more rapidly through these years — and certainly more colorfully — than during any comparable time period, and they enjoyed themselves immensely while doing it.

It cannot be ignored that after the war men also needed a strong financial incentive to stimulate aviation's development. Ultimately, of course, the commercial growth of the world's great airlines provided this need, but in 1919 aviation was not yet ready for

such mundane enterprise and the day when aeroplanes would be hauling profit-making loads reliably over great distances was still in the dim future. While speedplanes seemed to have little redeeming commercial value, the importance of doubling man's speed in a half-dozen years eventually led to important applications of technology and design to commercial activities. At the same time the military could use speed racers directly as prototypes for fighter planes. The specter of Armageddon reawakening was still real enough to frighten military thinkers into using the quest for speed as a crucible to concoct impregnable fighting fleets. Speed records assumed the importance of national prestige. These years mark the only point in time when the military mixed into essentially sporting affairs for their own gain, using the race course as an aeronautical laboratory. And whatever the motivation, speed records and air races always made good news copy. Soon prizes, prestige, and professionalism imbued speed seeking with its own magic aura. Elegant racing aeroplanes with flowing lines appeared in rapid succession, speed records fell in almost daily confusion, and many interesting technical experiments, some with far-reaching consequences, were done for the first time.

The accompanying tables indicate that most organized events could hardly qualify as races. Many competitors did not finish the grueling courses; moreover, competing aeroplanes were usually tested against the clock, not each other. The entry lists were almost always more interesting than the contests, and while formal competitions provided prizes and status, the real stimulus was ultimately the simple, pure essence of adventure, of pushing into regions where man had never gone before, of getting there first. *To be fastest* — that was the spur.

These years were a period of intense human drama in aviation — they provide a story not only of heady success but often of deep frustration as men groped, realized certain hopes and abandoned others, relished great starts and suffered the occasional failures to finish what was started. It took a passion for engineering detail and boldness in design, inevitably evoking objection and restraint which we can appreciate from their parallels today in the all too frequent failure to anticipate, to establish, to pursue; in the wrong trends unrecognized and right trends unappreciated. Only the technical details differ. Despite these occasional setbacks, 1925 was a year when man could look back only five years and comment, the aeroplane built then is now an outdated relic. At no other time has man been caught up in such a heady rush of improvement. In modern times the speed performance of transports, fighters, even spaceships does not change by an order of magnitude in ten or even twenty years. We compare an aeroplane built five years ago to one today and see detail improvements, more sophistication, but not the revolutions common to the speed seekers.

More importantly these men of the early 1920s somehow had more personal communion with the elemental effort to go faster than any other men before or since. There was magic in what those racers did to a man. They were fashioned by imaginations that distilled and concentrated the very meaning of flight into their oily, leathery windy cockpits. The *aeroplanes* — and the men who built and flew them — are the important elements of this story. In this introductory section, background events are described to provide a framework for the story of the great aeroplanes that follows.

The momentum lasted through the first half of the 1920s. Then it began to falter; a barometer of progress toward absolute speed is provided by the changing character of the classic air races, which became increasingly provincial and finally died out — with the exception of the Schneider seaplane contest — by mid-decade. Because the technical formula was by then largely solved, this makes a convenient cutoff point for our chronicle.

The first reason for this decline was money. Technical expertise acquired over the speed course had to be translated into profit. But there was little similarity between a souped-up sprint plane and a feasible commercial product, especially in a hostile market glutted with war surplus and plagued by economic recession. Manufacturing houses and even governments increasingly could not afford to send their specialized speed craft long distances, and the races lost the flavor of international competition. And without vigorous sales the money to continue high-speed research ceased to exist.

Secondly, pure technical advance had far surpassed its immediate applicability to commercial growth. The speed seekers had reached their speed plateau in one great leap. The 140 mph of wartime had been doubled to 280 mph by 1924, and soon thereafter men were exceeding 300 mph in short bursts. Although a couple of Schneider seaplane racers pushed into the 400 mph regime over the next ten years, it was by sheer brute force and not aerodynamic finesse. Expensive, sophisticated research was required to make the next quantum jump into the realm of supersonic speeds and jet propulsion. Unable to afford such

luxury, frontier development languished until the ominous incentive of World War II renewed the cycle.

After 1930, aeroplane racing for the most part moved out of the factory laboratory and into the amateur workshop. Myriad pylon-dusting "horse races," thrilling for spectators, were conducted, columns of increasingly meaningless decimal-point gibberish were added to the books, but in truth the builder of a post-1930 racing aeroplane was no longer an innovator in the grand sense but merely a modifier, a rearranger. Mostly he tortured his engine, and by 1939, predictably, the same basic 1925 aerodynamic shape was being pushed through the air at about 350 mph.

The pilot of a post-1930 racing aeroplane had one additional advantage over his counterpart of the 1920s, a subtle advantage but most important. He *knew* his physical speed limit would depend only on his individual mechanical ability; that it was not also predestined by some greater force had already been determined by the pre-1925 speed seekers. One must understand this essential aspect of aviation history to appreciate fully the speed seekers. When compared to the speeds our modern world has grown accustomed to in a short half-century, the 1925 speed frontier which stood at 300 mph may not seem exceptional. But in absolute terms their feat of 300 mph is truly remarkable, not only because it was achieved in an astonishingly short time span, but because speed seekers during the 1920s were pushing aviation's frontier directly into the face of doubt, misunderstanding, and myth, retardation forces

applied with an intensity that would be incomprehensible today. To our generation, burgeoning technological success has come to be taken for granted. Yet even as recently as the third decade of the twentieth century, as the industrial hegemony of Western civilization solidified, many serious scientists — and even some speed-seeking participants — were convinced there was an impenetrable *upper limit* to speed. Their skepticism stood as a dare, an extra measure of piquancy that impelled the visionary to go on. Eventually, over the intervening years, an attitude toward technology peculiar to the twentieth century was established, for today virtually all doubt in mankind's ability ultimately to master any technological challenge he accepts has been banished. Thus, for the first time in man's evolution, his governing issue is not one of simply proving he can do the job — as it was for the speed seeker of 1920 — but the vastly more sophisticated need to apply wise discrimination in selecting the jobs he should undertake.

We are interested in examining the exploits of airmen at a time when the irritant of skepticism still abounded. When men in aviation were still considered eccentric by the polite and damn fools by the plebeian. When the conditions and quality of life conspired against the success they wrested. Their faces which peer at us today from faded photographs were once animated by the sweet exhilaration of *la vitesse pure* — and this was indeed *raison d'être* enough! So let us go back to the classic, revolutionary times just after World War I and get to know the speed seekers.

THE COMPASS OF AIR CONDUCT

2

Into what sort of world did the speed seekers stride? A groggy world to be sure, a world prostrate from fifty-two months of relentless slaughter and devastation. Almost *30 million* soldiers, one complete link in the hereditary chain of Western manhood, lay maimed or dead; yet the world still burned with bitterness, intolerance, and extreme nationalism. Most of northern France had come under harsh Prussian rule, and virtually every farmhouse between Verdun and Toulon mourned its crippled or perished kinsmen. The Central European tribes, finally beaten, now lay helpless in turn before the Allies. Inarticulate masses everywhere, with one collective shudder of relief, ardently expected their leaders to impose a peace secure for all time.

And so, in January 1919 the leaders of thirty-two nations assembled in the mirrored halls of the Versailles Palace to forge the peace. France sent "The Tiger," rugged Premier Georges Clemenceau, eager to rub Germany's nose in her own evil-doing and guarantee complete French security from future Teuton hordes. From Great Britain came Prime Minister David Lloyd George, the irascible Welsh solicitor intent on preserving the supremacy of the British Empire which in 1919 still contained a quarter of the world's population scattered over a vast area where "the sun never set," but which had felt its close-knitted ties severely loosened. Italian Premier Vittorio Orlando came to enlarge his nation by securing "unredeemed Italy" — *Italia Irredenta* — from pieces left after the breakup of the Austro-Hungarian Empire. And from the United States, newly emerged and reluctant world power, came President Woodrow Wilson, the idealist, convinced his Fourteen Points and concept of a League of Nations would guarantee lasting tranquillity. Cheered as no other conqueror was ever cheered, the French lit candles for him, the English covered his path to Charing Cross Station with flowers.

When the Versailles Treaty was signed on June 28, 1919, Allied troops still occupied the Central European wasteland, their bridgeheads reaching all the way to the Rhine, the frontier France so desperately sought. But this was not to be. Opportunism, greed, vanity, an aura of unreality had gripped those at Versailles. Despite the anguished echoes from a thousand dearly won battlefields, the diplomats carved the world at their whims. Journalist Ralph Pulitzer remarked, "If the Peace Conference is allowed to remain a conference between governments instead of between peoples it is apt to degenerate into a saturnalia of statesmanship which will crown a war to end war with a peace to end peace." France's Rhine frontier was refused by promises of mutual defensive aid from the United States and Great Britain. So Germany, the vanquished, remained intact even as President Wilson's promise was subsequently repudiated by the U. S. Senate. Marshal Ferdinand Foch, Allied generalissimo, snorted his ominous prophecy, "This is not peace. It is an Armistice for twenty years."

Economically the Treaty of Versailles foisted unmanageable conditions on the world. Germany was forced to pay $5 billion in war indemnity to the Allies, and in vengeance the outraged Germans printed stacks of paper money in order to pay with worthless currency. Later the sum was almost entirely returned as foreign aid from the United States in an absurd turn of affairs which Winston Churchill termed "complicated idiocy." Heavy war reparations stiffened tariffs and caused

huge dislocations in industry. Between 1919 and 1923 German economy collapsed and the British economy was rocked, giving rise to strong British sympathy for German suffering even as Britain and France grew apart. In Italy ruinous inflation and widespread unemployment hampered recovery. And in the United States, beneath the surface gaiety and lightheartedness that nostalgically have popularized the 1920s, life had grave undertones. World economy eventually came unhinged, the common man faced heavy taxation and lower living standards which ultimately led to massive European industrial strikes and world depression.

Politically the world had been irreversibly transformed beyond any semblance of the halcyon prewar years. Three dynasties — the German Hohenzollerns, the Austro-Hungarian Hapsburgs, and the Russian Romanovs — had been toppled, leaving voids soon to be filled with cruel dictatorships. Clemenceau was ignominiously cast away and the French Third Republic fell prey to scandals, corruption, a weary parade of governments and ministers. In England the capable if sedate Baldwin-MacDonald regime, which essentially began with the ouster of Lloyd George in 1922, would last until May 1937. In Italy nationalism remained strong — highlighted by the feud between the Nitti government and Gabriele D'Annunzio — and the way for Mussolini's fascism was paved. Even though Americans desired world peace, U. S. foreign policy wavered between a course of international cooperation and one of isolation. In spite of naval disarmament and support for the League's humanitarian activities, isolation continued to dominate and the League of Nations was severely weakened by U. S. refusal to join. President Wilson, fighting for his vision of international brotherhood and cooperation, whistle-stopped the nation to drum up popular support for the League, but was felled by a paralytic stroke during his trip. He lay motionless

for almost two years behind chained White House gates, his dreams of internationalism in agonizing limbo until swept away by the Harding/Coolidge ticket's isolationism and "return to normalcy" in 1920.

Yet the seeds of the whirlwind were in reality sown in what was to Germany the ultimate outrage, and what became the ultimate folly, the arms clauses of the Versailles Treaty. Intended to emasculate Germany for all time, these clauses later proved to be totally unenforceable. Section III, Article 198, specified *"The armed forces of Germany must not include any military or naval air forces."* Thus, through the 1920s, those remarkable German qualities of scientific efficiency which during two world wars generated so many decisive aerodynamic developments were rendered largely inconsequential.

Meanwhile, men in other nations were already feeding the young but faltering eagle loosed by war. There was a severe postwar slump in aviation as heavy wartime contracts were canceled abruptly; moreover, a vast oversupply of surplus aeroplanes and engines existed. As Robert Blackburn, pragmatically optimistic English aeroplane builder, put it, "The problems of present-day industrial life . . . [are] of no small magnitude. Add to them the peculiar problem of a war-swollen [aviation] industry, highly developed on its production side and practically undeveloped on its distributive side . . . In many respects the war had left matters twenty peace-years ahead of 1914; in respect of market organization it has meant a loss of five years. The result is [inevitable] economic instability . . . *The situation will call for abundant faith in those who hold tight to aviation.*" Men with Blackburn's abundant faith were at hand. Resolutely they applied the meager dividends from the beginnings of commercial success together with limited and sporadic military support as the resources to develop the new technology. The favorite and most visible means, it

turned out, was through the use of speedplanes.

After the holocaust, however, anything that smacked of war tended to be abhorrent to many. And many looked upon speedplanes as not only impractical, but uncomfortable reminders of war. Yet to the men of vision who peered ahead into the threatening future, it was clear that the quiet years of peace, the lull before a bigger storm, should be years of building preparedness.

The Prophets
The quest for speed was played against a backdrop of great passion among a few men struggling for air power in a sea of disbelief and indifference. Speedplanes in the 1920s seemed to have direct application to military use, and concepts of air power with which they were thus associated were then almost purely military concepts. The indomitable belief centered in a few strong men; two who were extraordinarily visionary — indeed, prophets of air power whose names will continue to ring down through time — were both at their prime during this period. As architects of their respective air services, their faith and perseverance affected the destinies of whole peoples — and the speed seekers were at the very edge of the swords they forged. Despite their parallels, they had great differences. The two stormy petrels were Boom Trenchard and Billy Mitchell.

Hugh Montague, Viscount Trenchard, Marshal of the Royal Air Force, seemed an unlikely candidate for the role or air prophet. He had attended neither Sandhurst nor Woolwich nor even a staff college. A militiaman in India at twenty with the Royal Scots Fusiliers, he also served with the Nigerian Rifles, Canadian Scouts, and Bushmen's Corps in the South African (Boer) War, during which he was grievously wounded. The career of this strange irregular seemed doomed by ill health as he approached his fortieth birthday in 1912 when he applied for service in the Macedonian Gendarmerie — but a friend's death in an aeroplane crash suddenly made him resolve to master this new fancy. The War Office age limit was forty and the parchment-skinned major had but a fortnight left. He quickly sought out Tommy Sopwith at Brooklands and ten days later on July 31, 1912, he had his brevet (Royal Aero Club [RAeC] number 270) with four days to spare. Enigmatic and somber with blue lights piercing from the depths beneath his forbidding brow, Trenchard — like Pushkin's Prophet — seemed through some dark magic to gather unto him the Will to set free the message now straining to be released. Of massive stature with majestic bearing and a thunderous voice (source of his nickname "Boom"), Trenchard was a man of indomitable convictions,

Boom Trenchard, premier Air Marshal, RAF
(F)

The Flying General, Billy Mitchell   *(USAF)*

8

called fanatic by many, crusader by those more charitable, and the prophet's soul burned within him.

Like Trenchard, William Mitchell (he had no middle name) was of Scots ancestry. Like Trenchard, he had not attended the proper military school; indeed, Mitchell was very conscious of not having attended West Point. And like Trenchard, Mitchell learned to fly late in his career. Beyond that, the externals diverge. Mitchell, seven years younger than Trenchard, was scion of a Milwaukee dynasty, grandson of self-made railroad baron Alexander Mitchell who built the Chicago, Milwaukee, and St. Paul Railroad, son of U. S. Senator John Lendrum Mitchell, anti-imperialist, Bryan democrat, reasoned, cultured, tolerant, deeply anti-war, father of seven including two sons. Young Mitchell came from his birthplace Nice speaking French to the family's 400-acre estate Meadowmere, where he galloped with his boyhood friend Douglas MacArthur (one month younger), whose grandfather had followed Alexander Mitchell to Wisconsin and who dated Billy's sisters. Despite the fervent pronouncement of his father on the Senate floor — "No soldier should be mustered in for the purpose of shooting our ideas of liberty and justice into an alien people" — young Bill longed for action in the Spanish-American War then flaming. He was a rebel and a prophet in his own right. He already sensed warfare's eternal role as mother of the machine; he had also read William Seward: "The Pacific Ocean, its shores, its islands and vast regions beyond, will become the chief theater of events in the world's great hereafter." His father sought General Adolphus W. Greely to sponsor the eager teen-ager. Greely also knew Samuel P. Langley and had sponsored Langley's version of the supreme machine — the flying machine.

So it passed that while Doug MacArthur was a freshman at West Point, Bill Mitchell ("young Willy" to his mother) served as lieutenant and chief signal officer under Doug's father, General Arthur MacArthur, in the Philippine war zone, where they hunted the dreaded insurrectionist Emilio Aguinaldo. Mitchell with marvelous derring-do personally captured "Aggie's" aide. He also laid the first telegraph lines in the Luzon jungle and learned the language of the head-hunting Iggorrohotes and other primitive tribes.

Mitchell's stirring career next took him to Alaska, where — again thanks to General Greely's doing — he was sent to lay the first telegraph line. He spent two years in Alaska and laid 2,200 miles of line across trackless territory. One bitter pre-dawn he left the head of Good Pasture River and trudged twenty-three continuous hours with but one twenty-minute stop, covering 150 icy miles, to this day the longest one-day dog-team trip ever made there.

He came home in 1903, the Army's youngest captain. He also had become the victim of malaria and inflammatory rheumatism (perhaps rheumatic fever), which weakened his heart. He then became a pioneer in military photography, and when he was twenty-five gave lectures at Fort Leavenworth that became standard texts of field signal communications. He also became a master equestrian and was a fixture at competitions astride his horse "Peanuts," the cavalry's best jumper for eleven years. Eventually he returned to the Pacific, a powerful magnet that drew him inexorably, toured the Orient, befriended Chinese war lords, and formed portentous opinions: ". . . if the uncounted millions of Chinese could be organized, equipped, and led properly, and if they were imbued with a national spirit, there is nothing they could not accomplish." At thirty-two Mitchell became the youngest officer assigned to the General Staff, where he first became aware of the aeroplane — and shockingly, that the United States owned only 50 of the world's 2,400 aeroplanes on the eve of World War I. In 1913 when called to testify on a separate air force bill before Congress he deemed the idea premature but added, "Some people think of aeroplanes as an adjunct to the lines of information; the lines of information may grow to be an adjunct of the aeroplane, and very probably will." In 1916 at the age of thirty-six he enrolled at the Curtiss school, Newport News, Virginia, where Walter Lees was his instructor. He cracked up on his third solo, an event he considered invaluable training, and soon found himself a major in charge of Army aviation, then under the Signal Corps.

By that time Boom Trenchard was in charge of the English air service — called Royal Flying Corps (RFC). He had been appointed the first general officer commanding on August 19, 1915, as England's involvement in the war deepened. Trenchard did not spare himself or his men in the desperate struggle. His aide-de-camp Maurice Baring remembered Trenchard, "tall, straight as a ramrod, covering the ground quickly with huge strides and forcing his shorter aide to move in a quaint kind of turkey trot . . . trying to keep up . . ." An insight into Trenchard's demand for perfection in morale is provided by his prohibition of parachutes: just as a naval captain was expected not to abandon his ship, no RFC pilot would be given the opportunity to desert his aeroplane. ("Bloody murder" muttered Sholto Douglas, then a major commanding 84 Squadron.) Yet the pilots worshiped him. He visited squadron after squadron shot almost to scrap and gruffly told the men to "Stick it." They must "maintain a *moral ascendancy* by keeping at it . . ." The voice boomed out. Somehow they did.

The unopposed bombing of London during 1917 which so enraged Prime Minister David Lloyd George gave birth to the demand for a *separate* air force, then seen as a means to reverse the "lamentable state" of English air defense. The plan was to marry the scattered military and naval air services under a single Air Ministry answerable to the harried P.M., an idea he embraced. Just as Mitchell had done at his first brush with the idea, Trenchard opposed it, afraid it would weaken his forces in France. He was overruled and newspaper baron Lord Northcliffe was offered the job as Air Minister, but spurned it, not wanting to be "gagged by a loyalty [to Lloyd George] . . . I do not feel." The P.M. then turned to Northcliffe's brother, Lord Rothermere, who accepted. Totally ignorant of air service needs, he set up headquarters in his private suite at the Hotel Ritz, later moved to Hotel Cecil in the Strand, unofficially called "Bolo House" since activities within supposedly retarded the war. Trenchard and Rothermere bristled with an immediate and mutual dislike which soon came to a head in March 1918 when Trenchard was hamstrung as 1 million Germans poured over the Tommy lines along the Somme. On April 1 the Royal Air Force (RAF) came into existence as a separate entity; to Trenchard the date seemed perversely well chosen.[1] Twelve days later Rothermere accepted Trenchard's resignation: "In getting rid of Trenchard I flatter myself that I did a great thing for the RAF. With his dull and unimaginative mind and attitude of *je sais tout* he would within twelve months have brought death and destruction to the RAF." The gloomy iron eagle moved to his bachelor flat in Berkeley Square and at age forty-five asked to return to the Royal Scots Fusiliers as a major. This was not to be. On June 5 Trenchard, retained as a major general, was placed in charge of the Independent Air Force, a five squadron unit to bomb "strategic targets" deep within Germany. Trenchard had wanted sixty squadrons and began to accomplish what sixty ordinary squadrons might have. As Winston Churchill put it, "[Trenchard] can't write and he can't speak but we can't do without him."

[1] An amalgamation of the RFC, in existence since May 13, 1912, and Royal Naval Air Service (RNAS), originally formed from the naval wing of the RFC on July 1, 1914, organizations which had long since feuded.

On April 27 the unfit Rothermere, himself under certain duress, had "resigned."

Meanwhile, Billy Mitchell, a lieutenant colonel in May 1917, was sent to France as an "observer," bypassed objections, and became the first military man in U. S. service to fly over the front lines under hostile fire. He peered down upon the millions of men burrowed into the ravaged earth, locked immobile by steel and mud with no relief in sight from the relentless insanity of slaughter, and as his aeroplane in brief moments covered more distance than armies had covered in three years, he was intensely aware of being part of the most mobile mode of warfare ever conceived. Mitchell also toured the British sector, where he met Trenchard. Their first meeting was characteristic: Mitchell barged in brashly but with captivating charm; the gruff Trenchard soon perceived Mitchell was "the sort who usually gets what he wants in the end." The three days the airmen spent together had profound influence on the American. Trenchard had developed a complete philosophy of air power; it was the aeroplane's function to strike directly at the enemy's heart, disrupt his supply lines, destroy his resistance, control his territory, indeed to project a total offense. Mitchell noted Trenchard's maxim, "The great captains are those who think out new methods and put them into execution. Anybody can always use the same old methods." Both were already convinced of air power's eventual supremacy over sea power.

Mitchell accepted the philosophy totally and his keen mind sharpened and refined it. Trenchard later said of Mitchell, "He is a man after my own heart. If only he can break his habit of trying to convert opponents by killing them, he will go far." On July 15, 1918, Ludendorff had massed seventy divisions for his grand and final assault to breach the Front and enflank Paris forty miles away. Mitchell drove from Paris in his personal Mercedes (the Lyon 1914 Grand Prix winner),[2] took off on his own solo air patrol, soon spied hordes of Germans pouring toward five pontoon bridges across the Marne. He appreciated at once the dire enormity of the situation where a lesser strategist might not have, raced his aeroplane to the nearby field at Rheims, where he ordered Harold Hartney's 1st Pursuit Group airborne to attack the bridges. He also alerted Allied ground forces for counterattack. Seizing the initiative, the airmen also attacked the German rear. ("What we could do with one thousand aeroplanes instead of a measly two hundred and fifty," bemoaned Mitchell.) The German attack was repulsed and Mitchell's patrol was hailed as the greatest individual flight of the war, earning him the Distinguished Service Cross.

Nevertheless, to a General Staff preoccupied with moving ponderous armies and largely ignorant and indifferent to aviation matters, Mitchell's insistence on reforms was an irritant and more than once got him into trouble. "Black Jack" Pershing, America's senior general, while grudgingly admitting Mitchell's plans might have merit, installed others above Mitchell, refusing to consider his brilliant *enfant terrible* for the post of air operations chief. In the spring of 1918, Mitchell and the stiff Benny Foulois, his current superior, bucked heads because by then, to Foulois' helpless fury, Mitchell was accepted by the French and British as the *de facto* leader of U.S. air forces.[3] Their discord was quieted, and twelve days after his remarkable flight over the Marne, Mitchell was made air chief of the First Army. At once he boldly proposed consolidating all Allied air power under one supreme command for the upcoming St.-Mihiel offensive. By September both Field Marshal Foch and General Pershing approved; Mitchell's sustained planning and brilliant management shaped a giant, well-oiled air armada of 1,500 aeroplanes and 30,000 men which marked the true beginning of great strategic air operations.[4]

Hartney's group among others moved from French to Mitchell's command, and Hartney after conferring with his zealous boss related, "I was fascinated . . . it was like toy soldier stuff but in deadly earnest." Mitchell compared the attacks by his air force to the routs effected by the swift horsemen of Genghis Khan. His aeroplanes in long echelons battered first the left side of the battle's salient, then the right — then the rear. The Germans were obliterated and Trenchard — who to Mitchell was still the master — was effusive with unabashed praise, calling the operation "the most terrific exhibition I have ever seen — you have cleaned out the air." Thus in October 1918, Billy Mitchell, only thirty-eight, splendid in his pink breeches and blouse with non-reg patch pockets, moving at top speed, was appointed brigadier general and given supreme command of the air forces of the Group of Armies, equivalent for air to Foch on land and Beatty at sea.

Mitchell instituted effective night pursuit, massed bombardments, and other innovations in the use of air power. He still overflew the Front in his lone fighter, not to hunt but to observe. The inspired plan he drafted for the Allies' proposed spring 1919 offensive combined dive bombers together with thousands of parachute troops which would be dropped behind enemy lines by no less than sixty squadrons of Handley Page bombers; these had already been authorized for Mitchell when in November 1918 the war ended.[5] Suddenly, in the afterlight, Mitchell's plan seemed absurd. For both Trenchard — who had organized a daring raid to bomb Berlin on November 20 — and Mitchell the war had in a sense ended too soon. Their grand claims for air had never been fully tested. The fact of air power had not been properly established. Mitchell visited London on his way home, once again visited Trenchard, and commented on the RAF, "Everywhere the British are, there is a system, and this is shown distinctly in their air force. It is the best-organized force of its kind in the world . . . if we could have the air organization in the United States that the British have, we would be so far ahead of the rest of the world that there would be no comparison." But for him to convince others of this . . .

Mitchell returned to a land tired of war, a land where the need for a rational air policy was scarcely recognized and where lofty pronouncements met with skepticism and scorn, disbelief and derision. To Mitchell's dismay, Air Service size was slashed to a tiny fraction of its wartime strength as thousands of men were returned to civilian life and hundreds of aeroplanes

---

[2] True to form, the dashing and cultivated Mitchell was lavished in Paris. He quickly befriended James Gordon Bennett, James Hazen Hyde, and the Marquise de Brantes of the Schneider arms-making family, the "Bertha Krupp of France." He lived in Paris briefly as the guest of Major Randolph Churchill, but later moved to a chateau on the Marne near Chaumont which had once been a hunting lodge of Louis XV. His captured Mercedes racer became legendary; once it stalled and a passing Army driver quickly put it in order. Mitchell, impressed, elicited that he was a former racing driver who wanted to fly, and helped him. His name: Eddie Rickenbacker.

[3] Foulois was the third senior U.S. military aviator, having flown since July 1908, but, a latecomer to the war zone, he was considered an incompetent carpetbagger by his tactically gifted junior. A famous and lasting struggle for command grew out of this clash, from which, as has been described (not altogether accurately), "everyone lived happily ever after except Foulois." Foulois later refused to testify for Mitchell at his celebrated court-martial.

[4] Mitchell's force was comprised of forty-nine squadrons from four nations, including twenty-nine U.S. squadrons flying mostly French-built aeroplanes. Although Mitchell directed all Allied air coordination, Trenchard led eight squadrons of British night bombers and later insisted he "never" relinquished control of his squadrons to Mitchell.

[5] Mitchell's startling plan was published in the March 8, 1919, New York *Herald* and May 16, 1926, New York *American*; it was closely studied by the Germans themselves, who copied it precisely some twenty years later — and called it *Blitzkrieg*.

were scrapped.[6] Mitchell expected to be made Director of Military Aeronautics, but this hope evaporated in the harsh postwar reorganization. Instead, on March 1, 1919, Mitchell as a colonel was placed in charge of G-3 (training and operations) under General Charles T. Menoher, an infantry officer who had commanded the gallant Rainbow Division in combat but who knew little of aviation. It would be almost a year until he was made assistant chief of the Air Service and his temporary rank of brigadier general restored. Mitchell's swagger soon inflamed jealousy, his views engendered fear among the entrenched, his talk of a unified air command echoed of heresy in Navy halls,[7] but his vision alone was not enough. He needed vivid demonstrations of air power to wake up America; he would *sensationalize* aviation. Already the press loved his heroic antics, his dash. Confrontation was inevitable, as was the changing nature of his bitter struggle, which required him to stay on the front page.

[6] Officer strength was initially reduced to only 6 per cent of its wartime level. The National Defense Act of 1920 pared the Air Service to 1,516 officers and 16,000 men — including only 232 pilots — in a total army of 280,000. The War Department was then headed by Secretary Newton D. Baker, a Cleveland reformer who was anti-aviation; Assistant Secretary of War, however, was Benedict Crowell, pro-aviation. (The Crowell Mission to Europe had been strongly influenced by Trenchard.) Mitchell had requested $83 million for 1920, but only $25 million was appropriated and Crowell quit in disgust. Secretary of the Navy was then North Carolina newspaper editor Josephus Daniels, a devout temperance man who banished Navy grog — and was thereafter called "the Grape-Juice Admiral." He had no grasp at all of aviation's potential.

[7] Mitchell, invited by Assistant Secretary of the Navy Franklin D. Roosevelt to appear before the Navy General Board, found Admiral Albert G. Winterhalter agreeing with him that aviation was vital — but Winterhalter was hushed and Mitchell never reinvited. FDR later published an article which dismissed many of Mitchell's views on the offensive nature of air power as "pernicious." In some mitigation of FDR, he considered Mitchell's intimations largely premature at that time.

For Trenchard, who was reinstalled as Chief of Air Staff on January 11, 1919, the looming battle would also turn on personalities, but Trenchard did not possess the personal glamour of Mitchell. Moreover, the nature of his struggle had important differences: where Mitchell fought to create, Trenchard fought to preserve. Somehow, pressed by the weight of centuries of regal tradition that had been solidified by the two senior services, Trenchard in mere months had to prove his RAF was equally inviolate. He was terribly needled by irreverent jibes at RAF "stunts" and offended by the casual demeanor assumed by his "fighter boys," tunic top button invariably undone, taking nothing very seriously. Though such nondescript style manifested a need to establish their own tradition, Trenchard was non-sensational by nature and shrank from any publicity about RAF antics; indeed, the entire British military establishment was anti-press. Only rogues appeared in English newspapers and Trenchard resisted the pressure of the press, which instead of idolizing aviation he felt cheapened it. At that very moment his RAF offered a bleak life in cold huts on desolate aerodromes far from towns, an existence without regimental *esprit*, and Trenchard toiled to elevate its quality, to humanize it. He did not waver.

The cornerstone of Trenchard's philosophy was "The air is one and indivisible." But Lloyd George, preoccupied that January with the Peace Conference, told Winston Churchill, "make up your mind whether you would like the War Office or the Admiralty. You can take Air with you in either case. I'm not going to keep it a separate department." Churchill on January 15 became Secretary of State for War *and* Air with the dissolution of the RAF a foregone conclusion. By May the RAF had shriveled to 23 squadrons (only 10 were operational), down from a 1918 peak of 185. Churchill adroitly postponed the fate of the condemned service, but even

King George V harbored a natural prejudice against Air, especially since it jeopardized the traditional doctrine of naval supremacy as the foundation of British defense. Moreover he disliked the noise aeroplanes made, and craning his neck to stare up into the sky. To make matters worse, First Sea Lord David Beatty, youngest admiral since Nelson, hero of Jutland, archetype bulldog British sailor at the peak of his power and wealth, jealous of Senior Service prerogatives, and to whom it was inconceivable anything aboard ship should not be naval, together with Trenchard's own brother-in-law Admiral Roger Keyes, who was Deputy Chief of Naval Staff, began a concerted attempt to cut the naval air squadrons away from the RAF. They allied with voluble, scheming Chief of the Imperial General Staff Henry Wilson, arrogant and patronizing, who squinted with ill-concealed disdain through his monocle at all who flew. This attempt to split the RAF between the Army and Navy was to Trenchard "a sin against the light"; to him the idea of separate air arms was pure folly because (a) it made no difference whether an aeroplane was aloft over dry land or salt sea; (b) it would be wasteful to duplicate training schools, air bases, supply sources, and the like; but mostly (c) if the Navy carved out its own air arm the remainder would go to the Army and his foundling RAF would surely die.

A showdown erupted in Beatty's office during December 1919. Pacing in opposite directions in the pale winter sunlight Boom and the bulldog after an acrimonious hour finally agreed to a year's standoff. But Trenchard faced an uphill battle. He returned to his spare office in Adastral House, Kingsway, and dusted off a memo composed ten months before, a profound document of just eight hundred words — seven paragraphs covering one and a half sheets of foolscap — outlining the *Permanent Organization of the RAF*. It was redrafted into a slightly longer white

paper which on December 11 Winston Churchill presented to Parliament. Its lukewarm reception there belied its historic importance, for Trenchard in one stroke had laid down the entire constitution of a fighting service. His memo became the doctrine for most air forces of the world and fifteen years later, unchanged, it provided in detail for the immense expansion of the RAF as it entered World War II. The simple clarity of Trenchard's document was even more remarkable since he was often inarticulate when speaking, easily becoming impatient, his fluid mind moving faster than his tongue, the judgments hopping between strategic points too fast to follow, the arguments garbled but the insistence intolerant, and finally one was sure he must be right, not from his spoken points but from the sheer force of his personality; *il savait vouloir* — he knew how to will.

Billy Mitchell on the other hand was glib, garrulous, easily persuasive with words. And he faced a battle with the Navy too — but with a difference. Where Trenchard was trying to keep a hostile Navy from splitting his service, Mitchell was trying to amalgamate two distinct air arms into one, but the U. S. Navy balked because it had its own brilliant air champion: William Adger Moffett.

Born in South Carolina in 1869, Moffett spoke in the soft accents of the southern aristocrat, was an 1890 Naval Academy graduate, and wore the Congressional Medal of Honor for heroism during the occupation of Vera Cruz. He was ardent in his conviction that the Navy must retain its own exclusive air arm — "I am unqualifiedly and unalterably opposed to an . . . [independent] air service in this country" — and he buttressed such broadsides with a distinct flair for PR. His edicts issued from the corner office at the extreme end of the top deck, third wing, of the World War I–vintage "temporary" wooden-frame Navy Department home overlooking the Mall and Tidal Basin; there "The

Rear Admiral William Adger Moffett, U. S. Navy *(NA)*

South Carolina Gamecock" peered at papers through pince-nez and signed them while standing at an old-fashioned high desk, a relic of sailing days, incessantly smoking more matches than pipe tobacco. Moffett, too, had a battle: he labored against many of his own colleagues, but always operated from the premise that "the aeroplane in the U. S. Navy is being developed as an adjunct to the fleet and not as a substitute for the capital ship." Mitchell did not believe in the aircraft carrier, foreseeing a Pacific war developing by means of land-based air power through Alaska and the Kuriles whose "flank could not be turned." To Trenchard the aircraft carrier was a valuable strategic weapon — as long as the air arm aboard was RAF. Moffett struggled in the United States for aircraft carrier funding.

Yet until 1921 Navy aeroplanes came under the Bureau of Construction and Repair! Moffett's own boss, Admiral Benson, Chief of Naval Operations, snorted a foghorn blast: "The Navy doesn't need aeroplanes. Aviation is just a lot of noise." He told Moffett he was "wasting his time" and quietly set about to sabotage Navy air.[8] Nevertheless, in September 1921 a new Naval Bureau of Aeronautics came into being (its organization had begun as early as March) and Moffett, raised to rear admiral on July 18 by President Harding, became its first chief.[9] Moffett, who to engine builder Eugene Wilson was "not long on logic," kept no organization chart; to Moffett organization was based purely on personal loyalty, and he was remembered as a "personal ignition system." Already he anticipated the monumental fight with Billy Mitchell, whom he considered excessively belligerent, and Moffett, the astute diplomat, prepared to exploit Mitchell's two tragic flaws: his aggressiveness and his impatience. Moreover, Moffett was afraid that Mitchell's zealous pronouncements were not the inspired declarations of a visionary but the shrill harangue of a dangerous, power-mad demagogue who would monopolize all aviation (including civil) — and perhaps more. Mitchell, on the other hand, was suspicious that the virulence of obstructionism he struggled against was the result of an Army-Navy conspiracy.

Mitchell's fire-breathing, however, fulfilled the vicarious fantasies of millions as he "told off the boss" — and did it with such audacity he got away with it. The press and public loved the hell-for-leather swashbuckling of their handsome air hero: "Billy might pose for a statue of Caesar only he's not bald enough." Picture the impetuous, dynamic general brandishing his Malacca swagger stick, poised in his fire-engine-red Stutz Bearcat, top down, cutouts open, careening through wakes of worshipers. Others cautioned "stop this madman."[10] Mitchell left naval officers fuming helplessly with his taunt, "Keep working, Commander, and someday you may catch up with the Army." Young Air Service pilots would gladly fly to hell and back for him, but among the senior officers of both services — the "groundhogs" — Mitchell would reap implacable enmity. Mitchell was already well under way in his campaign of pushing the aeronautical frontier by means of several wonderful flying feats: a transcontinental air derby in 1919; a return flight

[8] On September 12, 1919, Assistant Secretary of the Navy Franklin D. Roosevelt was deeply embarrassed before Senator James W. Wadsworth's Sub-Committee on Military Affairs when Mitchell divulged an intercepted copy of Benson's order to liquidate Navy air, an order FDR himself had not been made privy to.

[9] Moffett's superior, installed March 1921 in the new Harding administration, was Secretary of the Navy Edwin Denby from Michigan. The new Secretary of War was John W. Weeks from Massachusetts.

[10] Somewhat unfair since at that time the Air Service had another firebrand, Benny Foulois, who drew up a bill of indictments against the General Staff and just managed to avoid a court-martial.

to Nome, Alaska, in 1920;[11] a model airway between New York and Dayton in 1921; endurance records to prove the feasibility of in-flight refueling; more transcontinental flights in 1923 and 1924 to perfect long-range mobility – one was the first non-stop, one the first "dawn-to-dusk"; even a round-the-world flight, conceived in 1919 but which did not take place until 1924 when, in 175 days, two of the original four Douglas Cruisers completed a remarkable 27,534-mile voyage. All these headline-making projects and more – Mitchell outlined almost a hundred – were eminently practical and constructive. And no one could deny his organizing ability and drive.

Yet these items were small fry compared to the real demonstration of air power's possibilities Mitchell planned, for he was out to prove once and for all that the battleship was obsolete. To Mitchell dreadnoughts were dreadful "sitting ducks," and his objective was to shift the nation's first line of defense from sea to the air. He expected objection and his timing in many ways could not have been less opportune. Battleship advocates were already clawing for their life amid the growing forces of pacifism and economy. On August 11, 1921, President Harding issued invitations to the Washington Conference on the Limitation of Armaments. The Balkanization of Europe had been completed in 1920 and the League of Nations installed; now, in 1921, the United States in a kind of morality play made momentous proposals at the conference relating to naval disarmament resulting in agreements among the United States, Great Britain, Japan, France, and Italy to stop building capital ships for ten years and to maintain capital ships in the ratio 15/15/9/5/5 respectively;[12] this in turn meant the United States, to the chagrin of Navy brass, must scuttle several battleships.[13] In addition the Navy had received from Germany several naval vessels as war prizes and these, too, had to be sunk.

Mitchell now seized the opportunity to declare his insolent offer: the Air Service will gladly sink them. Preposterous! scoffed the old-line admirals – but uneasily. Just months before, during the week of the 1920 presidential election when the nation's attention was elsewhere, the Navy in a test had placed aerial bombs aboard an old veteran of Santiago, the USS *Indiana*, hoping the results would prove the battleship's invincibility and give them the goods to quiet Mitchell. The test, directed by Captain Chester Nimitz, backfired and might have been forgotten, but the cat was let out of the bag when the December 11, 1920, *London Illustrated News* published a top-secret Navy photo depicting the badly damaged ship.[14]

Furthermore, the Navy had its own "defectors," notably the "Three Musketeers of the Sea," Sims, Fiske, and Fullam. Rugged Admiral William S. Sims, wartime commander of U. S. naval forces in Europe and then president of the Naval War College, believed in Mitchell and commented on his own colleagues, "The average man suffers very severely from the pain of a new idea."[15] Admiral Bradley Fiske, the Navy's greatest inventor, rebel in his own right, and strong advocate of the torpedo-carrying aeroplane, certainly supported the fight for air power. And Admiral William F. "Quarterdeck" Fullam, perhaps Mitchell's greatest friend in the Navy, predicted "a complete revolution in naval architecture due to the advent of the aeroplane and the submarine," and commenting further on the aeroplane, noted "this new weapon menaces the old Army quite as much as the old Navy." These officers were told quietly but forcibly from topside to pipe down. Yet in the Royal Navy, too, Mitchell found strong support. Admiral Sir Percy Scott, father of modern naval gunnery: "Will you help me with my ignorance? I cannot get an accurate answer to my question, 'what is the use of the battleship?' . . . The battleship is dead. The future is with the aeroplane." And peppery Admiral Jack Fisher, who himself had done much to develop the dreadnought yet who had warned Britain of the submarine menace before World War I, during which he served as First Sea Lord, chimed in with ". . . the approaching aircraft development knocks out the present fleet, makes invasion practicable, cancels our country being an island, transforms the atmosphere into a battleground of the future. There is only one thing to do to the ostriches who are spending these vast millions on what is as useful for the next war as bows and arrows. Sack the lot."

Secretary of the Navy Josephus Daniels was so enraged with the brash Army general that he railed sarcastically, "I will be glad to stand bareheaded . . . on any battleship while Mitchell takes a crack at it from the air." Mitchell said, fine, let the experiment proceed. He was quite willing to stake his career on the outcome.

On February 7, 1921, the Navy agreed to the tests, but slyly imposed several drastic handicaps, such as limiting the size and number of Mitchell's hits. To counter this, Mitchell planned to have an ace up his own sleeve and ordered his best armament experts to design a 1-ton bomb, then an unheard-of size. Under the duress of strict deadline they succeeded admirably.[16] A last-minute clumsy effort by Air Service chief Menoher to have Mitchell booted occurred early in June in the wake of a tragic Army plane crash, but the press defended their darling and Secretary of War Weeks retreated, making an uneasy truce between the two generals. Mitchell continued to assemble and gird his forces as if for all-out war. By June 21 all was in readiness for the month-long tests. There would be five targets, but only one really counted.

---

[11] Four D.H.4 aeroplanes and eight fliers under Lieutenant St. Clair "Wingbone" Streett left July 15, 1920, for Nome and returned August 24, flying more than 9,000 miles, mostly over uncharted country. Mitchell was convinced that Alaska was the strategic key to control of the Pacific, and this flight, tending to prove the feasibility of aircraft operations there, particularly pleased him. In fact, only State Department intervention prevented Mitchell from sending Streett across the Bering Strait to Russia – and perhaps around the world! He also proposed aerial explorations of Grinnell Land and Grant Land – Iceland and Greenland – whose strategic importance he appreciated.

[12] Japan appreciated as early as 1921 that the traditional dominance of the battleship had been upset; moreover, she realized that the United States and Britain had stacked the deck against her at the conference. So she gave in at the talks, meanwhile importing aviation technology from wherever she could find it to establish an *aviation* base line for the future.

[13] In one testy exchange which gives insight into the personal battle then brewing, Mitchell, attending the technical committee on aviation as the Army's expert, was in the chair when Moffett, the Navy's expert, showed up late. "Since when does a brigadier general in the Army rank a rear admiral in the Navy?" he rumbled, and stalked out. Mitchell was soon thereafter replaced by his chief, General Patrick.

[14] It was a worldwide scoop. Source of the leak remains unknown to this day.

[15] Sims had more than once jeopardized his career; on one occasion, working to improve U.S. gunnery, he recklessly claimed one British ship could outshoot four or five U.S. ones, prompting the House of Representatives to pass a resolution barring him from U.S. soil! He had also spurned the award of the D.S.C.

[16] The finless 2,000-pound bombs Mitchell used (11 feet 6 inches long, 18½ inches in diameter) were marvels of ordnance design; even by 1943, twenty-two years of subsequent refinements had increased their original design effectiveness by less than 10 per cent. Responsible for this marvel of ordnance was Captain C. H. M. Roberts, who had learned much from observing the 1920 *Indiana* tests, and had tested his shapes in the wind tunnel. With the deadline approaching, Roberts poured melted TNT into his bombs, force-cooling it with ice water and electric fans to finish on time! In the meantime, under Mitchell's urging, one-legged Russian émigré Alexander P. "Sasha" de Seversky culminated two years' work – mostly secret – in Sperry's Long Island plant on the earliest successful gyroscope-stabilized automatic bombsight – used in the tests.

This was the great 27,000-ton German battleship *Ostfriesland*, unscathed survivor of eighteen gunfire strikes in the Battle of Jutland, tending to bear out Admiral von Tirpitz' boast that the four-skinned monster was "unsinkable." To Mitchell, "looking down at her [from an aeroplane overhead] she appeared like a bulldog where the *Frankfurt* [a smaller ship sunk by his forces three days earlier] had looked like a swan. She was sullen and dark and we knew we had a tough old nut to crack . . . [all we had done] would be forgotten if we failed to kill, bury, and cover up the *Ostfriesland*." Mitchell need not have fretted. The test was a rout.[17]

As Mitchell, his white scarf flying, roared low by the observer ship *Henderson*, which was loaded with reporters and dignitaries, most experts were speechless. Many admirals sobbed openly. The incredible vision of the proud dreadnought obscenely upended, her belly ripped with gaping wounds, represented "the end of an era that began when Rome crossed the high seas and smote Carthage." The press inevitably made it into a personal victory for the forty-one-year-old flying general, but to his impatience; Mitchell wanted it seen simply as an important step in the broad evolution of warfare. His persistent jackhammering that even one thousand aeroplanes required fewer defense dollars than one ineffective battleship now seemed on the verge of success. But the determined complacency of military planners proved tougher to crack than the *Ostfriesland*'s steel plates. Mitchell's "wild assertions" — and unexpected success — sent shudders through the entire steel and armaments industry. From their corner the Joint Army-Navy Board upheld the battleship (Assistant Navy Secretary Roosevelt remarked, "I once saw a man kill a lion with a 30-30 rifle — but that doesn't mean a 30-30 is a lion gun") and Mitchell's conclusions were pigeonholed. The Navy was at least alerted to the crying need to beef up their own air arm, and the beleaguered aviation industry — now eying two potential customers — did not take sides.

In England Mitchell was compared to the outspoken Noel Pemberton Billing, whose acid criticism in 1916 was considered crucial in the creation of the RAF, but the American's style was "not such as would be considered proper for an officer of the British Army." Trenchard on the other hand was acutely conscious of propriety and strived to avoid unnecessary confrontation. Simultaneously with Mitchell's trumpet calls and drumming bomb blasts, the Middle East exploded. In 1919 Trenchard had called Egypt "the Clapham Junction of the Middle East"; in 1920 the British government spent £40 million maintaining their influence in Mesopotamia (soon to be called Iraq).[18] At stake were control of the Persian Gulf and the future of Palestine, but Lloyd George's coalition government was under heavy pressure from an aroused populace horrified at the folly of spending great amounts of national treasure and wasting vast numbers of British troops in alien deserts so far from English shores. Trenchard saw his opportunity and pounced: he promised "control without occupation," a scheme to turn the ground war over to the local Iraqis and provide them British air support. Army brass ridiculed the idea that flimsy aeroplanes would be useful in the harsh desert, but Churchill, now feeling the pinch as Chancellor of the Exchequer, saw merit in Trenchard's daring and in those days completely unprecedented plan and astutely supported him. Thus in the summer of 1922 the C-in-C of British forces in the Middle East was appointed from the RAF and the local Army garrisons cut by 80 per cent. Trenchard's aeroplanes proved very effective in exerting military control. For Trenchard it was not so vivid a display as Mitchell's bombs, but it was a considerable victory. Still, the future of the RAF was far from secure and Trenchard had yet to weather several skirmishes.

Trenchard, the "air crank," had burst his own bombshell in March 1921 when to the wrath of Beatty he declared the RAF should take over from the Navy the prime role of home defense. Future threats to the British Isles, he predicted, would come "not from a landing . . . but from repeated incursions on a large scale by hostile aircraft." Arthur Balfour, summoned to mediate the deepening Trenchard-Beatty conflict, saw merit in Trenchard's claims and agreed "the Air Force must be autonomous." A trick for Trenchard.

Sir Eric Geddes, head of a commission charged by the government to reduce expenditure drastically, succumbed to brazen Army and Navy insistence that he should direct his scrutiny at the RAF as the obvious target for military cuts; but Churchill forced Geddes' probing glare onto the Army and Navy themselves. Army chief Wilson intensified his vitriolic attacks on the RAF, even to decrying the junior service as no more than a means "for killing women and children" at a solemn regimental memorial in France in a speech which disgusted Trenchard. Admirals Beatty and Keyes, in an inept attempt to sabotage Geddes' findings, sponsored a diatribe called "Chaos in the Air Force" published in the January 5, 1922, *Pall Mall Gazette*. Geddes concluded in fact just what Mitchell and Trenchard had both maintained: that an independent air force, far from being an extravagance, fostered economies. Churchill on March 11 refused to be coerced by

---

[17] In summary the celebrated tests proceeded as follows:

Target 1: June 21.
    German submarine *U-117* 50 miles off Cape Charles lightship. Twelve 63-pound bombs dropped from 1,100 feet. Boat sunk in sixteen minutes.

Target 2: June 29.
    U.S. battleship USS *Iowa*, to be located — she was radio-controlled in an area 160×160 miles. Mitchell's forces found her in just two hours, upholding his contention that a ship at sea is far easier for an offensive raid to spot than an object on land. Navy air units dropped eighty small bombs but scored only two hits.

Target 3: July 13
    German destroyer *G-102* adrift 100 miles east of Langley Field. Mitchell led sixteen Martin bombers, each with six 300-pound bombs. Forty-four bombs dropped from 1,500 feet. Ship sunk in nineteen minutes.

Target 4: July 18
    German light cruiser *Frankfurt* (5,100 tons), to Mitchell a "graceful swan." Army and Navy air units alternated in ten rounds of bombing; bomb size limited to 300 pounds for first six rounds, after which her hull remained intact. Limit increased to 600 pounds for last four rounds. On seventh round the Navy dropped 520-pound bombs ineffectively and Navy umpires ordered her sunk by gunfire. Just then Mitchell's forces appeared overhead. Fourteen 600-pound bombs dropped by air sunk the ship in thirty-five minutes.

Target 5: July 20/21
    German battleship *Ostfriesland*. Sixty miles off Cape Charles in 300 feet of water. She was built in 1911, 546 feet long, totally watertight, her internal bulkheads not pierced even by phone lines; normal draft 35 feet, but now unloaded she drew only 28 feet. Test began July 20. The Navy had first crack at her from the air; this was ineffective due to large number of duds and windy (30 knots) weather. Tests called off but Mitchell's forces already en route led by Lieutenant Clayton Bissell. Fifty-two 600-pound bombs were dropped from 1,500 feet. No major damage. Aeroplanes in returning to Langley Field were disrupted by violent thunderstorms, which scattered them all over Virginia and Maryland. It took all night to reassemble the hectic group for the next day's key test in which Mitchell would be allowed "two direct hits with the largest bombs he had." On July 21 eight Martin bombers, each with two 1,000-pound bombs, scored three direct hits (one more than the rules allowed) but still caused no major damage to the hull. Then seven more bombers arrived (one was down at sea), each with one of the new 2,000-pound bombs. Mitchell's theory: a near-miss with its crushing "water-hammer" effect would be more destructive than a direct hit. Six 2,000-pound bombs were dropped "close by" in twelve minutes — and the battleship sank.

[18] Great Britain had accepted the Mandates of Iraq and Palestine from the League of Nations, and was fighting to retain them at risk of war with Turkey. Their ultimate objective was withdrawal of British forces from the area and freedom from obligation of the Mandates.

the senior services into opposing the RAF and appealed to the Cabinet to muzzle Army and Navy leaders, reminding them that only the repeal of an Act of Parliament could abolish the RAF. Another trick for Trenchard.

To emphasize the point, on March 16, 1922, Austen Chamberlain, temperate, august Lord Privy Seal, said in Commons that it would be a "retrograde step" to disband the Air Ministry, and reiterated forcefully, "the Air Force must be autonomous." It was a stunning public announcement which had the effect of a battering ram in the Admiralty, the service regarded by the Air Minister's Parliamentary Private Secretary Lieutenant Colonel J. T. C. Moore-Brabazon, holder of RAeC pilot certificate number 1, as "the spoilt darling of this nation for a hundred years . . . If the Channel had dried up the defense of England would have passed to the Army. But a larger miracle has happened. The air has been conquered . . ." When the true extent of postwar RAF emasculation was made widely known, *The Observer* called it "The Supreme Blunder since the Armistice." Others called it "a great betrayal." At last the press, which for so long had pilloried the RAF with "any stick that came in handy," seemed coming around to Trenchard's side in a manner he could countenance. Add another trick.

On November 2, 1922, a new Secretary of State for Air took office. One of the architects with Lord Beaverbrook of the Bonar Law premiership (Law's Tories threw out the Lloyd George coalition government in October 1922), he was Lieutenant Colonel Sir Samuel J. G. Hoare, a conservative from the days of Kipling and Milner, Harrovian classmate of Moore-Brabazon, steeped in the golden age of classics and cricket, on which his life had once seemed set. Hoare emerged from his schooling a narrow and self-centered young man to whom anything with an engine was "indecent [and] horrible . . . scarcely to be tolerated." The dour Prime Minister,

Canadian-born Andrew Bonar Law, rigid economist, product of a frugal Scots upbringing, told Hoare in no uncertain terms that "two fighting services are quite enough" and to expect to preside over the execution of the RAF. But then a strange and wonderful transformation occurred: Hoare fell totally under the almost hypnotic spell of Trenchard. He sat captivated by the heathen but oddly exciting visions of the master, nodding even if he did not always completely understand. "Trenchard's words discovered for me a new world," Hoare has written. "Not a better or happier world": Trenchard felt intensely that the invention of flying was a calamity for the human race ("If I had the casting vote I would say 'Abolish the Air.' It is an infinitely more harmful weapon than any other") but with no lament, accepting its existence and at once its full strategic significance: "The aeroplane is the most offensive weapon that has ever been invented. It is a shockingly bad weapon of defense." Trenchard, like Mitchell, foresaw the horror — and powerful deterrent value — of strategic bombing forces, even in a day when "large" aeroplanes were miserably inefficient contraptions. Trenchard, never very much concerned with the technical details of flying machines, perceived from the beginning that whatever their state of development, they must be used by those trained to understand their power, not blunted by those who did not believe in them. He had other revolutionary ideas — such as the creation of a Joint Chiefs of Staff. Hoare soon saw himself as interpreter and ardent mouthpiece for the prophet.[19]

[19] Hoare — later 1st Viscount Templewood — soon upset established ideas of decorum for high government officials by flying everywhere to prove flying was not a stunt. He was four times Secretary of State for Air; in 1936 First Lord of the Admiralty, Churchill's Lord Privy Seal at the outbreak of World War II, Ambassador to Spain 1940–44.

On November 25, 1922, Law presided over the full Committee of Imperial Defence and decreed the extermination of the RAF. Balfour, because of his earlier position, demurred and Law hesitated. Lord Salisbury was named to perform yet *another* inquiry, another opening wedge seized upon by the Army and Navy. As 1923 opened there were only 2,500 workers left in the British air industry, the RAF — which could muster only 371 service aeroplanes — for practical purposes had been virtually annihilated anyway, and the Air Estimates were a paltry £12 million. On February 20, Beatty called on the P.M. and issued an ultimatum: unless the government returned to the Royal Navy its own air arm he would resign to carry on the fight in Parliament. Hoare was summoned at once to 10 Downing Street and told to settle with Beatty directly. Hoare recalled that Beatty "pressed his case quite pleasantly but in its extreme form." The Air Minister urged Beatty in vain to postpone his actions, but the bulldog's patience had vanished and he said no. Three days after Beatty's ultimatum, the exasperated Trenchard — who always attacked hard when menaced — boomed "Two can play that game" and he too threatened to resign: "I won't stay a moment longer if the RAF is carved up to suit Beatty." Trenchard, now virtually transported, threw his soul into convincing members of Salisbury's group that air power under any authority other than the Air Ministry would mean the destruction of a single air strategy — and especially that (in his view) air power's diminution in the shadow of naval glory, its subjugation to naval strategy, would render full recognition of its potential impossible. The battle raged. Lord Salisbury could envision a broad role for the RAF in national defense, but Balfour again had to step in to mediate the irreconcilable differences between Air and Admiralty.

Bonar Law was sinking fast with cancer and resigned the premiership

in May 1923. He was replaced by his Tory protégé Stanley Baldwin, a reflective businessman from Worcestershire who assumed Law's government and pledge unchanged — but Baldwin had a romantic streak and found aeroplanes appealing.[20] Balfour had fallen ill with phlebitis and was bedridden at his Norfolk home where the report of his committee reached him. He could agree with the recommendation to uphold the RAF because it "provided a service common to the Army and Navy but in an element strange to them both," but when his committee concluded that the reason for the Admiralty's intransigence was simply *amour-propre*, he refused to endorse their report. There *must* be a deeper reason not yet understood. It seemed the only way to resolve the issue would be to examine joint RAF and RN operations at the working level.

The committee members put to sea aboard two aircraft carriers and observed remarkably trouble-free relations between the working members of ship's company (RN) and flying men (RAF). It was true: the struggle turned on no more complex a hinge than the injured pride of those at the top, and the Balfour findings stood. When the news reached the Admiralty on July 21, Beatty, outraged, stormed that he would quit with his entire Board of Admirals. "Well, let them," Trenchard snorted; "it would be good riddance!" On July 26 Baldwin, speaking in Commons, not only upheld the RAF but announced a plan — based on Lord Salisbury's findings — to add virility: there would begin at once a program to provide fifty-two air squadrons for home defense.[21] And on August 2 the entire Cabinet decided

[20] This led to his approval of modest funding for aviation and eventual elevation of Hoare to Cabinet level — although Hoare's annual salary remained at £3,000, not the £5,000 of other Cabinet ministers!

[21] The pace of this program was slow, however. By 1930 only thirty-seven squadrons had been provided.

in favor of Air.[22] Trenchard, with another trick on his side of the table, was able to find respite from the Admiralty and politicians for the first time in four and a half years, and left for the Highlands.[23]

Billy Mitchell, meanwhile, was not faring so well. He had released his frozen internal report of the bombing tests to the press, where it caused a sensation, and for this sin his chief, General Menoher, sought to have him disciplined. Menoher was told in effect either to bring his own subordinates effectively in line or to take another command. Chastised, weary of the struggles surrounding a controversial discipline he neither understood nor believed in, the doughty old general quit the Air Service on September 17, 1921, and returned with relief to the Infantry. Mitchell, too, submitted a resignation out of protocol, but the public now clamored for his elevation to Air Service chief. This, however, would have been a pill too large for the politicians to swallow. Mitchell was retained as assistant chief and non-flier Colonel Mason M. Patrick, a stalwart

old engineer-soldier skillful in diplomacy, second in his West Point class (1886, same as Pershing) and Mitchell's friend for fifteen years, was raised to major general and installed above him.

Patrick recognized astutely the jealousy his old-line Army colleagues harbored toward what they viewed as his pampered class of young warriors, a little too glamorous and a little too independent of their commanders; but Patrick defended his new command. He was at least loyal to the Air Service if not an exponent of air power — he believed air power should develop before Mitchell's grand revision of defense was implemented — thus his methods were restrained, his support on the controversial issues halfhearted and for the most part unsuccessful. He also had an exasperating habit of interrupting testily with "Yes, I know — I know" and often missed the point being made. With his elevation to Air Service chief, Patrick became a four-toupee general. He owned three of different lengths which he would vary to give the impression of growing hair; the fourth was tousled, to wear when engaged in his flying lessons (he never soloed).

As 1922 opened, Patrick's new command was about to stall out. The Reverend Lester Maitland, then an aide to General Mitchell, recalled the tough times when officers at Bolling Field, D.C., were encouraged *not* to wear uniforms in downtown Washington to avoid reminding people of the military; yet the total Air Service officer corps was smaller than the New York City police force. Matters were so bad that when Mitchell flew from Washington to Dayton along his "model airway" to survey emergency landing fields, he was allotted only $25 for whitewash to mark hazards on the fields! All cross-country flying — even vaunted record flights — were accomplished by means of Rand-McNally road maps. Mitchell's axiom was *per pecuniam ad astra* — technological success would be realized only in direct proportion to the number of

dollars devoted to research and development. He spent long hours before congressional finance committees fighting to pry money loose, and in 1922 received a green light for advanced pursuit development.

Mitchell at once envisioned a grand race with widely publicized speed records, and inspired by his characteristic *élan* several designers took bold, innovative steps. This effort — as we shall see — made possible some of the most important speedplanes built between the wars. U. S. speed classics soon outdistanced similar events in Europe, and by 1924 the United States owned most of the important aviation world records; indeed, Grover Loening has called the years 1920–25 "the golden age of records" in the United States. Yet the French Under-Secretary for Air jeered, "Records, yes, but they are a façade. One cannot fight with records. Back of that there is nothing." Mitchell's spectacular air records failed to bring prosperity to the aviation industry, and Loening could also recall "valleys of depression, mountains of obstructions."

One important result of Mitchell's 1922 effort was to inspire a concerted Army-Navy air rivalry. Admiral Moffett believed emphatically that the key to technological progress, even more crucial perhaps than money, was *competition*, and it must be noted that the aeroplane attained its maximum rate of development in the United States during the 1920s in part because of the intense competition Admiral Moffett fostered. Moffett abhorred, for example, the stifling aspects already apparent in the British system, which even went so far as to combine both civil and military aviation under a single Air Ministry.[24]

To many British, competition among government branches was not only "extravagant" but "dangerous" and the concept of one organization — even a private contractor — handling a project was considered more civilized than the "cut-throat" of several. To Trenchard, service involvement in the competition of air racing was particularly repugnant. "I can see no value in it," he admonished; moreover, the depth of adulation accorded winning pilots frightened him. Despite his prewar brevet Trenchard was by temperament a non-flier himself; already well known was his distaste for the individual glory accorded wartime fighter aces — a distaste so strong he was accused of jealousy. His thesis was that "aerial duels [were] a waste of time and manpower . . . one strategic bomber . . . could do more good in a week [by destroying an enemy's equipment *en masse* at its factory] than all our multi-decorated aces [could] accomplish in a year." Personal glamour, ephemeral and shallow, was alien to his old-school ideals and seemed to him somehow to cheapen the air service, a sin to be avoided at all costs if he was to win his fight for survival. He would also have found it painfully awkward to select from among perhaps hundreds of equally qualified young men the one or two whose names would be bannered

was Major General Sir W. Sefton Brancker, a compact man with a hyperthyroid temperament 180 degrees to that of Trenchard. Indeed, Trenchard was wary of civil aviation and found Brancker's inflammatory and unorthodox oratory not to his liking. Brancker, however, recognized that strong civil airlines effectively knit the Empire, and he built up civil aviation in Great Britain in a remarkable way until 1930 when, on October 4, he boarded the huge airship R-101 for a heralded journey to Egypt and India. In the pre-dawn darkness next morning the dirigible struck a hill at Allone near Beauvais, France, and exploded, killing forty-seven of the fifty-four aboard including G. H. Scott (1919 commander of the transatlantic R-34), C. B. Thomson, and Brancker. The disaster marked the abrupt termination of airship development in Great Britain.

[22] The RAF remained autonomous for nineteen years. The RNAS had existed separately for almost four years before it was absorbed into the RAF in 1918; however, Admiral Beatty's position ultimately prevailed when the RNAS was reestablished as a separate entity on July 1, 1937. Thus, on the eve of World War II, Britain's air organization was similar to that of the United States, which, largely because of Admiral Moffett's perseverance, had remained in effect throughout.

[23] It was a time of political upheaval in Great Britain. Late in 1923 Baldwin dissolved the government he inherited from Law, but Labour under Ramsay MacDonald, who wanted to be the world's peacemaker, won the ensuing general election. Vivid, merry General Christopher B. Thomson, a Sapper officer, replaced Hoare as Air Minister. But Labour collapsed from weakness and internal division within one year and by late 1924 Baldwin and Hoare were back in office, to remain until 1929 — when, once again, Baldwin was ousted by Ramsay MacDonald. Though of different political persuasions, Baldwin and MacDonald were remarkably alike in outlook, temperament, and method.

[24] It was true. The Air Navigation Act of 1919 placed statutory power over all civil flying under the Air Ministry, thus centralizing *all* aviation under one roof — something the Americans resolutely refused to do. Serving directly under the Secretary of State for Air as a counterpart to Trenchard was the Director of Civil Aviation, who from May 10, 1922,

16

in headlines and carved in the plaques of history — or who would perhaps needlessly die. Trenchard was ever resolute in his sense of duty and remained throughout quite prepared to accept for himself — and for those under his command — permanent obscurity. To the end of his tenure he strenuously opposed RAF participation in air racing. On the subject of the Schneider seaplane races Trenchard was particularly adamant, and even years later after the RAF had won the trophy for Great Britain Trenchard felt deeply that government intervention had accorded the contest a character out of keeping with its donor's intentions. Sam Hoare as Air Minister took a more pragmatic view, aware that for all the technical progress made in the half-dozen years following World War I the British aviation industry lacked the prestige of international victories, conspicuously irksome in an increasingly commercial world. Hoare also knew the British public was apt to judge the performance of British aviation as it does any sport, as "when British horses do not win the Derby or British elevens the Test Matches." Failure to win blue ribbons in the air made the public, indiscriminate to the color of pilot uniforms, restless and many unfairly deprecated technical progress which had been achieved more quietly. From this standpoint, as Hoare has written, "government intervention [in air racing] seemed worthwhile."[25]

The United States was now soaring at the height of "the ballyhoo decade," surrounded by the clamor of a public "drunk on stunts." Mitchell and Moffett eagerly pushed their service racers and pilots to ever greater glories. The rationale was not hard to come by, for as Moffett stated, "The Navy Department has adopted the policy that aeroplane racing while not of military value in itself is of great technical

importance in subjecting service material, especially power plants, to conditions of maximum severity." The air races became very popular in the United States during this period, and it appeared at last that the recognition of air power's possibilities was making headway.

General William Lassiter, named head of a board of inquiry into the status of military aviation, submitted his report in March 1923. It noted an "alarming situation" and urged the immediate initiation of a ten-year program requiring $25 million annually as the minimum to ensure an adequate air situation. Lassiter's remarkable report, which in many respects went even further than Mitchell's contentions, remains perhaps the single most important air power document produced between the wars. Secretary of War Weeks initialed it April 24 and sent it to the Joint Army-Navy Board, where it was tabled.

After such frustrations Mitchell determined to take his fight for air power directly to the people. Dozens of articles issued from his office on the second floor of the Munitions Building in downtown Washington — littered with steel bomb fragments, fishing waders draped over a hatrack, a Zeppelin steering wheel and Siamese tiger skull on the wall next to attack formation diagrams, indeed a veritable "museum worth seeing" recalled New York *Times* political cartoonist Oscar Cesare — where Mitchell might be found adorned in golf suit, knickerbockers, and buckskin shoes dictating animatedly to his private secretary Ellen Short. Often referred to as "impassioned" by drama-seeking commentators, Mitchell's written discourses were generally not emotional but remarkably understated, reasoned and reasonable, articulate — and convincing. When taking a break late at night Mitchell could usually be found at an oyster bar spending money, which he liked to carry in wads.

Mitchell launched an active campaign with an address to the National

Aeronautic Association Convention at Dayton October 3, 1924, during the 1924 air races. The gist of his message had a ring that echoed Trenchard: the Army and Navy do everything on precedent, he reminded the audience, but you cannot do that in the air business. You have to look ahead. Within days his superiors bristled and Mitchell's debate soon degenerated into wrangling over the ticklish issue of free speech for military officers. The New York *Times*, in commenting, noted that "Admiral Moffett is diplomatic. General Mitchell freely attacks those who fail to agree with him even though they may be his superiors." The New York *Evening Post* coined the term "Mitchellism." Mitchell was well on his way to becoming the most talked-about celebrity in the United States — why, people even talked of booming him for President. Admiral Moffett recoiled, concerned that Mitchell was bent on gathering unto himself the means to become super-leader of the air — of the military — perhaps even Emperor of America.

Another secret test by battleship advocates served only to revolt Mitchell. The new hull of the USS *Washington*, to be scrapped as part of Washington Conference terms, was used, but the news leaked: Navy aeroplanes had dropped only sand-filled projectiles which did not penetrate the deck; yet depth charges approximating aircraft-size bombs had done devastating underwater damage. Flustered admirals claimed the rended hull during a real battle situation could be plugged with pine wedges! "There isn't a pine tree growing [that could plug a bombed battleship]," croaked Admiral Fullam from his deathbed. Mitchell's comment was more cogent. When President Coolidge, fulfilling his role as the High Priest of Business, continued to uphold the battleship, on which much of the nation's industrial economy depended, Mitchell rebutted with the message the Navy resolutely ignored: "Battleships in the Pacific are an easy target from the air and would be

helpless against an Asiatic enemy." Mitchell made this statement in March 1925, almost seventeen years before the debacle of Pearl Harbor. Henry Ford said simply, "If they spend one billion dollars on ships they'll get 'Mitchelled'!"[26]

During 1924 the nation reeled to the revelations of the dead President Harding's Teapot Dome naval oil reserves scandal, one repercussion of which was the replacement of an embarrassed Edwin Denby by California Chief Justice Dwight Wilbur as Secretary of the Navy. President Coolidge was campaigning for election that November to his first full term, and in the spirit of economy and isolation that marked the times, he had slashed government spending by 50 per cent, personal income taxes by 25 per cent, and would thus be invincible at the polls. On March 26, 1925, a few days after Coolidge's inauguration, Mitchell's four-year term as Air Service assistant chief would be up, and the question of his reappointment was being considered in the upper councils. General Patrick wanted to retain Mitchell as his number two, but Secretary of War Weeks, who deeply resented the brash and popular flier, was "sorely tried" and said no. On March 5, the day following the inauguration, Weeks informed President Coolidge of his plan to drop Mitchell[27] and to announce

---

[25] It was not until 1927, however, that the RAF took over the organization and training of the British Schneider Trophy effort.

[26] Mitchell made two visits to Japan in 1924, and his report of these visits details a dramatized version of both the Pearl Harbor and Philippines air attacks correct to the time of day and formation arrangement. The Japanese respected Mitchell's views highly — and copies of his pigeonholed report were not classified until belatedly when they became germane to his court-martial, making it tempting to believe the Japanese might have perversely used Mitchell's own seventeen-year-old battle plan as their model. Anyway, in the United States no one was then listening, and subsequent events in World War II which fully vindicated Mitchell's bizarre perception make it impossible for us to view Mitchell as he was viewed by inhabitants of a 1924 world.

[27] Who would thus lose his general's star and revert to his permanent rank of colonel.

his downfall the next day at Fort Monroe, Virginia, during a test he had concocted to prove once and for all that the Coast Artillery was a better means of coastal defense than aerial interception. Weeks, Mitchell, a large press contingent, and others were present to watch an Air Service aeroplane trundle slowly by – on a straight, precise course – towing a banner which the shore-based guns tried again and again – and failed – to hit. In the midst of the gunfire the orders relieving Mitchell of his position as Air Service assistant chief arrived. It was obvious that the deeply humiliated Weeks had counted on only one outcome to the test. Mitchell, who already knew his fate was sealed, reacted calmly, observing that "changes in military systems come about only through the pressure of public opinion – or through disaster in war." Lieutenant Colonel James E. Fechet, a Texas cavalryman, was raised to brigadier general and replaced Colonel Mitchell, who was sent to San Antonio, Texas, where, it was thought, his troublesome blasts would be out of hearing range. Even Mitchell might have worried that the burning issues he had raised would now be quenched.

Then, early in September 1925 two black headlines appeared in rapid and startling succession. The first reported Navy Commander John Rodgers was missing in the Pacific, overdue on the first attempted flight from the West Coast to Hawaii, an inadequately prepared flight Mitchell was convinced was staged to gain headlines for the Navy, not to advance the true cause of aviation. Within hours the second headline announced the tragic crash of the proud Navy dirigible *Shenandoah* in violent thunderstorms over Ohio, killing fourteen of the forty-three aboard. The entire nation was shocked. Secretary of the Navy Wilbur in a display of singularly bad taste issued a political sermon literally before the dust had settled in which he intimated that the disasters provided proof at last that "the Atlantic and Pacific [Oceans; i.e.,

their expanse] are still our best defense!" Billy Mitchell was now roused to arms. Indignant, furious, scornful, ready to "deliver himself into the hands of the Philistines," he paced for hours and dictated a scorching 6,080-word statement which was released to the press at 5 A.M. on September 5, forty-eight hours after the *Shenandoah* crash, just as the Labor Day weekend was getting under way. The operative sentence was:

These accidents are the direct result of the incompetency, criminal negligence, and almost treasonable administration of the national defense by the Navy and War Departments.

To this shot across the Navy's bow, Admiral Moffett struck back thunderously, charging Mitchell's statement with "falseness and vindictiveness almost without precedent . . . [it was] absurd in its very extravagance"; and he called Mitchell an "unscrupulous self-seeker . . . [using] the tactics of the demagogue . . . The example of military officers in the employ of the government making a political appeal over the heads of Congress to the people . . . might be the opening wedge for a military dictatorship in the United States . . . The most charitable way to regard these charges is that their author is of unsound mind and is suffering from delusions of grandeur."[28]

In truth, Mitchell's challenge was in places exaggerated, hypothetical, and contained much unsubstantiated assertion. One of his most scathing charges referred to "an arrangement between the Navy and Army that the Navy should take the [air] races one year and the Army should take them the next year, thereby equalizing propaganda, not service." While it might have appeared that the 1923 and 1924 races fell into this pattern, Moffett

asserted "this statement [regarding the so-called race arrangement] is utterly and unqualifiedly false." If careless in details, however, Mitchell had made his broader point to an aroused public. Of this there could be no doubt.[29]

Billy Mitchell almost relished his court-martial. He entered Washington "like a conquering hero," was chaired from his train by a triumphant crowd of hundreds, many shouting, "Put it there, General – tell 'em what's wrong with America!" In fact, Washington was site for a veritable three-ring circus then getting into full swing: in the House Office Building the Morrow Board was hearing witnesses, including Mitchell, in another inquiry into the state of aviation owing its existence in part to Mitchell's earlier sniping; in the Old Navy Building the *Shenandoah* inquiry was under way, where beautiful, young (twenty-three) Margaret Lansdowne, widow of the airship's dead skipper, kept the nation agog with her sensational bombshells alluding to political interference with her husband and attempts at behind-the-scenes evidence fixing; and the Mitchell court-martial which, even though held in a damp, crumbling, abandoned warehouse meant to be totally unappetizing (the Emory Building at First and B Streets), was rampant with pomp. Mitchell, under house arrest at the Anchorage Hotel (a name which must have seemed particularly perverse), was accused of conduct "to the prejudice of good order and military discipline . . . [and] of a nature to bring discredit upon the military service" and tried under the 96th Article of War, known as "the Old Mother Hubbard"

rule; the accuser was President Coolidge himself. The order came down from Secretary of War Davis (who had recently replaced Weeks) that no hint of persecution or martyrdom must exist. The nine generals who sat in judgment all were Mitchell's long-time acquaintances; indeed, one was Doug MacArthur. The court-martial was a military tribunal of unprecedented length, beginning October 28, 1925, and running more than seven weeks until December 17 – the twenty-second anniversary of powered flight. Mitchell's defense was handled ably by his counsel, freshman Illinois congressman Frank R. Reid, forty-six, who had practised law with Clarence Darrow, together with assistant defense counsel Clayton Bissell. Dozens of airmen, many destined to hold high command in World War II, were called to testify in Mitchell's behalf and scored point after smashing point,[30] but the final result could have been predicted even before the festivities began: conviction.

The court refused to rule on the broader concept of whether truth constitutes a defense. Many felt that Mitchell proved the truth of his important charges; in his closing statement he called his trial the culmination of General Staff efforts to deprecate air power and keep it in an "auxiliary position," thus "compromising the whole system of national defense." Mitchell was suspended from rank, command, duty, and ordered to forfeit his $639·33 monthly pay and allowances for five years (the President restored half pay plus full subsistence – yielding $397·67 monthly – on review).

An enterprising Washington reporter who rummaged through the wastepaper basket found one vote for acquittal. It bore the handwriting of

---

[28] It has been reported that Eugene Wilson prepared this statement as a strong countersalvo to Mitchell's blast, but could not get the impatient Admiral Moffett to review it before it was released over his name. In any event, the admiral made no attempt to alter it, so the question of its authorship is moot.

[29] Mrs. Bea Arnold, wife of future general Hap, said of her friend, "Billy felt that unless you went overboard, you could not get the attention of this country . . . he lost his perspective . . . no one could stop him." Her husband, whose own star even then was fast rising, tried to stop him, but Mitchell demurred: "I'm doing it for the good of the air force – for the good of you fellows. I can afford to do it. You can't." Secretly, Mitchell was convinced of victory.

[30] Even prosecution witnesses sided with Mitchell. One was Thurman Bane, who was so resolute the flustered prosecution dismissed him. When later he apologized to Mitchell for earlier criticisms, Mitchell replied lightly, "Forget it. All that's water over the dam. We've got to work together now, and save air power."

Major General Douglas MacArthur, who had sat silent — "his features as cold as carved stone" according to Mitchell — during the entire seven-week trial.

During the same period the Morrow Board findings were released, effectively timed to distract notice from the court-martial. The report concluded that many of Mitchell's chief concerns were unwarranted, and he considered its compromises a disaster. It was a comfortable report designed especially to gratify President Coolidge. It called for some but not much money — "half a loaf" as some said. It did foster the 1926 Air Corps Act and a five-year building program, and put civil aviation in the United States on firmer footing, although leaving it still far weaker than what already existed in Europe. These years (1925 and 1926) were also permeated with the spirit of Locarno[31] and the Kellogg-Briand movements for outlawing war. Mitchell, who had resigned his commission and become a civilian immediately his court-martial was concluded, forecast pessimistically that the "same influences which brought about the former conflict are again at work." Now

unshackled from military restraint, he wrote and spoke even more widely.

In 1928 Mitchell was frequently mentioned as a potential candidate for Vice-President on Al Smith's Democratic ticket, but he declined. He remained the prophet; he dedicated his book *Skyways* to his two children, "who in their lifetime will see aeronautics become the greatest and principal means of national defense and rapid transportation all over the world and possibly beyond our world into interstellar space." This was written in 1930. In 1932 he attended the Democratic National Convention as a delegate from Virginia and strongly supported Franklin D. Roosevelt in his successful bid for the presidency, hoping for high office — perhaps even a Cabinet post as Secretary for Air, his most cherished dream — in a revitalized air department. Roosevelt's earlier promises were sidetracked, however — Mitchell's dream was not to be. He was still forced to defend himself against charges of jingoism. "A jingoist seeks to drive a nation into war," he commented. "No, it is not jingoism I profess, merely self-preservation." Billy Mitchell, the stormy petrel, his dream if not his conviction broken, died in 1936.[32]

Admiral Moffett had already died, tragically drowned April 4, 1933, with seventy-three others near Barnegat Light on the New Jersey coast in the crash of the Navy's huge rigid airship USS *Akron* — one of the foredoomed craft the admiral had hoped to develop into flotillas of flying aircraft carriers.

Across the Atlantic, Trenchard's struggle seemed perpetual. The continuing cry for economy had become "a peg on which the older services would hang a fresh demand for our abolition." Even the ardor of Churchill, still at the Treasury and under mounting pressure, had cooled. But Tren-

chard, wise and wary in the ways of his adversaries, played his trump card and convinced the government that *effective* air disarmament meant *total* disbanding of not only military aviation but civil aviation as well, since civil aeroplanes on short notice were easily adaptable to combat use. The argument was a telling one, and Trenchard survived yet again. In December 1925, the month Mitchell lost his last fight and was convicted by the service he loved so dearly, Trenchard mused, "I've had my toughest fight . . . and gained my finest victory."

Early in 1930, six months after the 1929 general elections in which Labour's MacDonald once again ousted Baldwin's Tories, Trenchard retired after nearly a dozen years as Chief of the Air Staff. The first Air Marshal and his strong disciple Hoare had forged an indomitable partnership. Trenchard was succeeded by the two remarkable Salmond brothers, each in turn. Geoffrey, the elder, died at age fifty-five just after getting the post in 1933, succeeding his brother John, who had been first Air Officer Commanding in the Middle East and who had succeeded Trenchard — and who resumed the top job upon his brother's death.

In 1930 Trenchard, the somber old irregular who had waged such a brilliant campaign and won such a profound victory, put on the uniform of Chief Commissioner, London Metropolitan Police. He took no active part in World War II, during which the RAF he forged proved so decisive. Trenchard died in 1956. He was buried in Westminster Abbey, given a place of honor alongside the great personages of a millennium of Empire.

History must note that, as in nearly all great fights of reform, the forces of reaction draw first blood by finding a fanatic to be shot at the wall, burnt at the stake, or crucified. Mitchell filled that role. Later the quiet reformers — exemplified by Trenchard — if they too be resolute in their determination, live to see their prophecy vindicated.

Conditions elsewhere

Italy too had her air prophet, General Giulio Douhet, who became Mussolini's Commissioner of Aviation. As early as 1905 Douhet postulated an incredible campaign of terror waged from the air — the air which he foresaw even then as the only decisive means in forthcoming twentieth-century wars to gain unconditional surrender, a condition not achieved in World War I, in which the air was only auxiliary. Douhet's black doctrine appeared under the title *Il domino dell'aria (Command of the Air)* in 1921, almost simultaneous with Mitchell's bombing of the *Ostfriesland*, during a crucial year for the recognition of air power. Douhet's outrageous predictions went even further than Mitchell's, for while the American seemed content with sinking battleships, Douhet wrote, "The disintegration of nations . . . will be accomplished directly . . . by aerial forces . . ." and, because such monstrous views contradicted the fundamental tenets of decency seemingly inculcated by Christianity into Western civilization, Douhet was repudiated by many.[33]

Italy needed the stimulus of pride. After World War I she suffered from inflation compounded by staggering taxation to cover war costs, widespread unemployment, and poverty. Nevertheless, nationalism was intense; when the Austro-Hungarian Empire was broken up during 1919–20 Italy regained most of the territories of Trentino, Istria, and Gorizia (Trieste), the *Italia Irredenta* of strong Italian heritage. The red-hot nationalistic embers were soon enflamed by a florid zealot who invoked the authority symbol of ancient Rome, an ax enveloped by rods — the *fasces*. This was Benito Mussolini.

In 1922 Italy was still a monarchy under King Victor Emmanuel III, but that year Mussolini's "March on Rome" overran the capital and soon

---

[31] The Germans came to the calm lake by Locarno, Switzerland, on October 4, 1925, to cement peace pacts with France, Great Britain, Belgium, Italy, Poland, and Czechoslovakia, pacts fat with promises of peace, brotherhood, and disarmament. In September 1926 Germany joined the League of Nations. Yet four years earlier Mitchell had noted "the military spirit in Germany is by no means crushed" in the report of his December 1921–March 1922 European inspection trip conducted together with Alfred Verville and Clayton Bissell. It was true. Even as the Germans sat at Locarno, they were already building up the nucleus of the Luftwaffe at secret training bases in Russia. In addition, German aircraft manufacturers becoming active included Junkers, who made stoves, bathtubs, and plumbing fixtures at Dessau in Germany but put the profits into his love, aviation, at Fili near Moscow; Dornier, visible at the old Zeppelin factory at Friedrichshafen, but who contemplated the transformation of his metal planes into bombers at plants in Switzerland and Italy; Rohrbach in Denmark; and Heinkel at Rostock in Germany itself — the Allied Commission simply closed its eyes.

[32] It was not until 1947 that Mitchell's dream — a single Department of National Defense overseeing co-equal Departments of Army, Navy, and now separate Air Force — became a reality.

[33] The Italian air attaché in the United States, General Guidoni, often spoke of Douhet's views with General Mitchell.

Il Duce — as Mussolini came to be called — declaring he was Italy's savior from communism, assumed absolute power, stridently demanding that the people "believe, fight, obey." Mussolini's strict control extended to all facets of Italian life. It was dispensed from his vast hollow room in Rome's grand Palazzo di Venezia, the only furniture his writing table with a Benvenuto Cellini figure, two or three upright chairs at the far end, two paintings on the otherwise cold, stark walls which somehow shrank in the presence of the thick-necked, brick-faced dictator.

Mussolini also sought military grandeur for his impoverished, predominately agrarian nation; he expanded the armed forces, imposed four-year conscription, launched superpatriotic fascist youth groups. He also espoused the Douhet air doctrine and in 1923 formed the Regia Aeronautica (Army of the Air), which, with the RAF, was the world's only other totally independent air force; indeed, the Regia Aeronautica was in many respects modeled after Trenchard's RAF. It was headed by a fierce, bearded Renaissance *condottiere*, one of four men who with Mussolini had seized the reins of Italian power in 1922, Il Duce's then Minister of Aeronautics, Italo Balbo. Italian aviation soon came to reflect Balbo's dynamism. From turbulent Romagna, Balbo had been one of the first to support poet-aviator D'Annunzio's demand for Italian intervention in World War I; he became a captain in the courageous Alpini, later learned to fly in two weeks, and after the war edited *l'Alpino*, a periodical published in the Udine in which he supported D'Annunzio's *coup* against Fiume.[34] General Balbo, ever the opportunist, was also among

[34] Balbo enjoyed a life fast and loose. During the 1920s he was a convinced Anglophile. He later led two celebrated transatlantic aerial expeditions which enhanced his popularity and made Mussolini jealous. Il Duce sent him to Libya and eventually had him liquidated in Tobruk in 1940.

the first to sense the advantage presented by air racing, in particular the Schneider Trophy competition, and thanks in large part to his influence Italy pursued a vigorous, positive air racing policy.

Douhet's harsh but majestically proportioned philosophy — cited often as "the bible" of early air power advocates — had in turn influenced other nations. This seemed especially apparent in Great Britain to the extent that all aviation, including civil, as Douhet advocated, had been placed under *state* control in a ministry dominated by the independent military air force. Indeed, to have adopted this policy represented a curious reversal from earlier times, highlighted by Britain's seventeenth-century supremacy over France, then achieved by means of private initiative and enterprise, whereas France, guided by the darkly brilliant Colbert, had staked all on government support of the monopolistic trade guilds; but when he asked the industrialists what more he could do to help, they shouted together, *"Laissez nous faire!"*

Yet France was now in the throes of imitating Colbert's earlier design. Certainly France's official aviation policy at that time was exceedingly vigorous and the generous government civil aviation subsidy was pointed to by jealous foreign observers as the model of forward-looking enlightenment. France was in those days the undisputed world leader in the *amount* of aviation and this in turn alleviated the French fear of a German Armageddon reawakening, a specter that haunted the French and gave rise to the pathologic need to accumulate large quantities of aeroplanes — of whatever type — because they provided a feeling of security. French military philosophy had been transformed from the thrusting, attack-oriented *élan* of early World War I to an almost wholly defensive state; under Pétain the apologist, French offensive weapons were almost totally discouraged. High-placed French planners — despite the

fulminations of air prophets Douhet, Trenchard, and Mitchell — were dominated by the Maginot-line mentality of Army thought and regarded the aeroplane in their broad scheme as little more than an auxiliary to be relegated to local defense duties, subordinate and servile; pilots were for the most part considered little more than chauffeurs. The French General Staff stoutly opposed the use of air power for strategic purposes. Nevertheless, the French government during this period swelled their uniformed Air Corps personnel to approximately 300,000 officers and men and in 1921 maintained more than 2,000 front-line aeroplanes. Thus, in terms of personnel, French Air Corps size was ten times that of the RAF; in terms of aeroplanes, the French were five times larger than the RAF, fifteen times larger than the Italian air service at the time the Regia Aeronautica came into being.

Under Raymond Poincaré's coalition government, French economy seemed on the verge of strong recovery. The government aviation policy was guided primarily by M. Laurent-Eynac, former wartime pilot, Under-Secretary of State for Aviation, who headed a huge staff and commanded a high salary.

Thus a curious paradox existed. For on the surface the lavish financial support France poured into her aviation system was obvious to world observers, who also took careful measure of France's numerically superior air fleet, both civil and military; yet underneath there was already at work that strong, impractical element implicit in French nature that often impedes bargaining, thus halts development, inhibits compromise, hinders design, and ultimately restricts progress. Fat government subsidy by itself allowed growing numbers of inefficient flying crates to be operated as paying propositions. Insidiously the government produced an effect opposite to that desired. Since the factor of competition for excellence had been

largely eliminated in French aviation, softness inevitably set in and France let her modernism decline. By not pursuing an energetic R&D policy to sustain her brilliant peak of 1918–22, French power-plant technology in particular fell behind. France also deluded herself with a Russian alliance which later contributed to the French Air Corps becoming progressively infiltrated with communism until, by 1938, her demoralized officer corps was riddled with fifth columnists. Her once proud fleet-in-being had by then decayed into so much ponderous, outdated junk, and France through cruel irony stood the *least* prepared of all Western nations for the terrible onslaught she had hoped to deter.

The paradox was compounded because the French Third Republic — victorious in World War I and during the 1920s considered "the Greatest Power in Europe" — was the regime under which the decline was allowed to accelerate. The heaviest burden of guilt for the undermining of French military-industrial toughness lies with the weak, vengeful, and often stupid men who grasped control of France's affairs during the crucial two decades; the political, economic, and moral atrophy finally — and unbelievably — culminated in Marshal Foch's old *wagon-lit* in the Forest of Compiègne on June 21, 1940, when, after only twenty-two short years, France once again faced Germany across the same wooden table of surrender — but on opposite sides. The French national soul had disintegrated behind a false façade of wit and fashion.

Nowhere was the release of sudden pleasure pent up by the long, toilsome burdens of World War I more manifest than in Paris, the city which since the eighteenth century had befriended so many aviation pioneers. After weary years of difficult wartime renunciation, years of nearby cannon fire and threats to her very existence, Paris now nourished the heady surrealism of a new age expounded by writers and artists swirling in the psychological vortex left by war's tidal wave, a wave which had shifted the very bedrock of Western being. Young expatriates giving semblance to life's uprooted disarray lived a noisy, sparse existence in small Left Bank hotels near Place Saint-Germain-des-Prés. Ernest Hemingway, gruff and virile, might be seen at a back table of the large corner cafe Les Deux Magots; a fragile man with shabby white sneakers but defiant black cap named James Joyce might be seen shuffling from the nondescript bookstore on Rue de l'Odéon which for his fortieth birthday in 1922 altered the world by publishing his manuscript *Ulysses*; Pablo Picasso might be seen after dark, nursing his one small bottle of mineral water at the bistro on Rue Jacob called La Quatrième République — named, according to its owner, in advance because obviously Poincaré's present republic was not long for this world. Even if the bistro owner was all too guilty of Gallic schizophrenia — an unmerciful denunciation of present conditions while at the same time invoking new utopias on which no one could agree — his city was now suffused with fresh sensations: the sounds of accordions singing in the lascivious *boîtes* of Montparnasse where Bohemians danced the java or *le fox* imported from America, sounds which blended into the singing of fat blackbirds heralding luminous new dawns, dawns with colors too vivid for painters on terraces of the Dôme to capture, dawn-bright pastels of narrow stone façades lining the Seine, tall trees blossoming everywhere to grace lazy afternoons under red awnings, exquisite sunsets exuding a delicate ether that somehow thickened the atmosphere with a mellow element impossible to transport. It was said that if the Huns had kept Paris, within fifty years their offspring would be Parisian. Despite the difficulties that occasionally touched one's life, one was swept up deliriously in the flood of realization — how good it was to be alive!

And this new emphasis on aviation, an activity which had particularly aroused new heights of imagination and romance, seemed now to offer even bolder sensations.

Laurent-Eynac, in a gesture seen as remarkably unselfish, had by April 1924 assumed the non-salaried duties of Poincaré's "High Commissioner of Aviation." His first act was to establish huge government prizes for Frenchmen who would recapture the exalted world's aviation records; war was over and man needed new competitive incentives. That year alone he offered 200,000 francs for the world speed record, to be divided 70–30 between airframe and engine manufacturer; 150,000 francs for the world seaplane speed record; and additional amounts for distance, duration, and height records. There were dozens of other offers during these years. Exuberant and intrepid French aviators in exotic aeroplanes flashed from fields skirting their city of light. But alas, Laurent-Eynac himself was already involved in the increasingly bought favoritism, the creeping cynicism that would eventually sap French aeronautical strength. On September 14, 1928, when a separate French Air Ministry was created, Laurent-Eynac would become France's first Air Minister.

With its ancient aviation heritage it was not surprising that Paris had been chosen as site for the world's aviation clearinghouse — the FAI.

The FAI
On the sixth day of 1920 the FAI — Fédération Aéronautique Internationale (International Aeronautical Federation) — ended the six-year hiatus on official world speed record recognition imposed by war.[35] The FAI, supreme arbiter of aviation records, was first established on October 14, 1905, the outgrowth of an effort by l'Aéro-Club

[35] This had important implications because it meant that no maximum-performance flight of 1919, deserving though it may be, could ever get into the record books.

de France to set up a world federation of national aero clubs which, "through the international regulation of aviation sport, [would ensure] the control and comparison of aerial performance throughout the world, thus contributing to progress in aeronautical construction."

Born three years *before* the first true aeroplane flight in Europe in answer to future needs then only dimly comprehended, the FAI became and remains indispensable to aviation. Its founders, who included French aero club vice-president Count Henri de la Vaulx, Belgian aero club president Fernand Jacobs, and Major Mödebeck of the German Airship League, understood clearly that craft which can fly, irrespective of how they might evolve, have no respect for national boundaries on the ground. On June 10, 1905, this visionary band was welcomed at the Olympic Congress in Brussels, which resolved:

This Congress, recognizing the importance of aeronautics, expresses the wish that there be formed in each country an association having the mission of regulating aeronautic sport and that there be formed later a world federation of aeronautics, including all the national associations, with a view to various needs and general regulations for the popularization of aeronautics as a science and sport.

Four months later aero club representatives from Belgium, Germany, Italy, Spain, Switzerland, Great Britain, and the United States were hosted by the French at Paris to endorse the resolution and bring the federation into being. The first president was H.I.H. Roland Bonaparte of France, who held office for twenty years until 1925, and who established many of the traditions still revered and maintained. He was succeeded by Count de la Vaulx, one of the original founders, who presided until 1930.

All rules for sport and records for each type of aerial craft are contained in the FAI Sporting Codes, consisting

of the main code for basic principles and separate codes for each vehicle. For example, the margin by which a new record must exceed a previous one for each type is stipulated. Responsibility for substantiating a record bid with proper evidence beyond dispute rests with the aero club of the country in which the attempt is made. The FAI also very early concerned itself with the issuance of pilot licenses, and on October 28, 1910, framed regulations patterned after those adopted by France in 1901 and 1909. While most national aero clubs then and national governments later issued their own licenses, some nations adopted the Federation rules and still to this day issue FAI licenses, which are thus internationally recognized. The movement of aeroplanes to "foreign" soils was also considered; overcoming customs restrictions and standardizing rules of passage led to the internationally valid Carnet du Passage en Douanes and eventually the system of General Declaration and regulation Flight Plan, used for most international movements today.

Approximately once each year every member of the Federation may send delegates to the General Conference, where the Sporting Codes are reviewed, policy formulated, and matters before the body decided. From the eight aero clubs represented at its founding, by January 1920 membership had grown to eighteen affiliated aero clubs. At the first postwar meeting, held in Paris May 19, 1919, Prince Roland Bonaparte presiding, it was agreed to exclude Germany, Austria, and Hungary until they became League of Nations members, which had the consequence of rendering all performances in these nations unofficial. Only holders of FAI "sporting licenses" can compete for a world record, and only records made to the strict rules of its code and *homologated* (ratified) at the Paris headquarters can be recognized as official. Aviation sporting bodies of the world have agreed: "The FAI is the sole international sporting body qualified to make and enforce rules to encourage and control . . . aviation records" (*FAI Code Sportif* Section 1.2.1). The quiet harmony of the FAI has somehow persisted through the turbulent century, and so it is to this day.

In the nineteenth century early railroad men gunned their locomotives past 30 mph with trepidation — such mighty speed, after all, might be "too fast" for human beings to progress across the surface of their planet. In 1909 when Glenn Curtiss flew almost 48 mph to win the first Gordon Bennett Aviation prize, it was confidently predicted that, with improved materials, the "ultimate speed" of 100 mph would someday be achieved. Even in the early 1920s many creditable individuals still believed there was an *upper limit* to speed; one offered "proof" that no aeroplane would ever exceed 200 mph. By 1925 the "limit" was placed at 500 feet per second (about 340 mph). Yet the aviators, emboldened by their successes, were saying all along that, as fast as they flew, they were not yet approaching their limit of "endurance," although they did experience "strange reactions on making steep turns [at high speeds].[36]

The excitement intensified as aeronautical sorcerers now pushed speed inexorably upward to undreamed-of values, straight into the face of such skepticism.

Among the FAI conditions specified upon the resumption of speed records in 1920 was the 1-kilometer base line which had to be covered in both directions to minimize wind effect, the requirement for straight and level flight $\frac{1}{2}$ kilometer before entering the base line to eliminate undue advantage from diving, and the necessity for at least 4 kmh improvement to establish a new record. Moreover, accuracy in the final average required that the speed for each individual pass be calculated, then these four speeds averaged. Indeed, the FAI rules explicitly endorsed this method. Not infrequently, however, to reduce the mathematical burden, the four times were averaged and one final speed computed from the average time — but this introduces a subtle error because the aeroplane's longer exposure to headwind during the slower passes disproportionately outweighs the shorter times of the downwind passes. On occasion this was inexplicably overlooked by even the august FAI itself, so that many of the official records through the 1920s were arrived at erroneously.[37]

Through these early years the French were still timing speed trials with a hand-held stopwatch, accurate only to the nearest one fifth of a second, which represented a fair percentage of the measured speed, since racers were soon covering 1 kilometer in less than ten seconds. Thus, the recording of speeds to six significant figures was absurd and controversies over decimal fractions are meaningless. Nevertheless, in the Appendix, officially recognized results to three decimal places have been indicated. In the United States, electric timers manually operated by pressing a telegraph key and accurate to about one twentieth of a second were just coming into use, and by 1926 electric chronographs considered accurate to one four hundredth of a second were available to time aeroplane speeds.

Meanwhile the FAI Conference held in Rome October 8–13, 1922, decided to increase the base line length for the world maximum speed record from 1 to 3 kilometers, this new requirement to go into effect April 1, 1923. This move was prompted by the difficulty in measuring speeds over so short a distance as 1 kilometer with the primitive timing methods then in use. England for one welcomed the new proposal since in their estimation — and recognizing as did all nations that the speed record had become linked with national prestige — the new rule would tend to "reduce to a minimum the unsportsmanlike distrust between nations which has existed where speed records are concerned."

[36] The problem that few seemed to understand was simply that the faster an aeroplane traveled the more easily high centrifugal loads could be induced when changing direction, and it was this load factor — not speed itself — that caused the difficulty. Of course, man never reached the cliff edge he dreaded where one increment faster would propel him into helplessness, and such once popular notions were soon pushed into the musty lore occupied by flat-earth myths and the like. Nevertheless, the pessimistic scientists of that day ultimately proved to be not far off in their final prediction of an "upper limit." This was more perhaps by accident than foresight since they did not fully understand compressibility (subtle but profound aerodynamic changes that take place as one approaches the speed of sound) and had only the haziest ideas about jets. But their calculations indicated the attainment of 480 mph would require the ultimate in a flying piston engine: the aeroplane would become a streamlined, projectile-like engine cowl with the smallest possible projecting fins for stability and control. The Grumman F8F — which in 1969, forty-five years after the prediction, achieved almost precisely 480 mph, the current piston speed record which is not likely to be beaten — fits the description exactly!

[37] To explain by means of one example (several are indicated in Appendix I), consider the October 18, 1922, speed record set by General Billy Mitchell, whose record flight passes were timed at 9·17, 10·95, 9·25 and 10·76 seconds. The respective speeds corresponding to each of these passes are 392·585, 328·767, 389·189, and 334·573 kmh; the average of these four *speeds* is 361·279 kmh (the value that should have been homologated). However, the four *times* averaged 10·03 seconds, which in turn translates to a speed of 358·836 kmh, and this was the speed credited — by mistake.

THE GREAT RACES

3

Early Long-Distance Affairs

The immediate postwar period was characterized by premature long-distance races as aeronautical scientists tried abruptly and all too eagerly to fit their craft with seven-league boots. The ambitiousness of the attempted journeys proved beyond the capability of all but a few faltering aeroplanes even though, in 1919, aeroplane makers already could foresee much of their technical destiny. The lack of suitable hardware was a problem in 1919, this being most obviously manifest in the weak state of aero engines then, and many of the great speedplanes to follow were built strictly as beds for new engines. But that year so many surplus wartime products remained that in spite of inferiority they nevertheless dominated aviation. This was quite apparent in one of the earliest postwar long-range air races, the New York–Toronto Derby.

On the occasion of the Canadian National Exhibition which climaxed during late August 1919, this race was conducted as a round trip between Mineola, Long Island, near New York, and Toronto, a total distance of 1,042 miles. The handicap was provided by judging a contestant's time against his own theoretical still-air performance, a method which did not achieve universal favor. The American Flying Club and Aero Club of Canada each put up trophies, and dapper, mustachioed former auto racer

Chance M. Vought headed the organizers. An insight into aviation's anxieties then is apparent in that the event was supposed to "promote the science and sport of aviation in a manner reflecting its safety, reliability, and permanence." It was an interesting affair even if the results virtually refuted these lofty intentions. Of the fifty-two entries, including twenty-two war-weary German Fokker D-VII fighters delivered straight from the Western Front to Canada in accordance with Article 202 of the Versailles Treaty, and several lumbering, U.S.-built de Havilland 4 "Flaming Coffins" — this alarming sobriquet having originated in a warning from General Billy Mitchell — it was not surprising that only twenty-eight finished, and these required several days to complete the distance. Major Billy Barker, V.C., with one hand rendered useless by a war wound, carried a message to President Woodrow Wilson in a D-VII, pumping fuel with his good hand while holding the joystick with his knees. Cold weather and stiff, gusty wind, splashes of rain and hail, and patches of fog hampered the fliers, and were it not for the good graces of bewildered but helpful farmers along the route many would not have gotten through. One pilot made it on a $5 gold piece and dish towel borrowed from a farmer's wife between Buffalo and Syracuse to plug a radiator leak in a plane called *Phoebe*. The S.E.5A of Lieutenant Charles Colt had its wood prop splintered but he feverishly whittled the blades with his penknife until they were balanced to his satisfaction, and finished the race! Several muddy planes turned turtle, more at Albany's ridiculously short, crowned field — the race's "graveyard" — than anyplace else. Some of the aviators involved who will reappear as leading characters in our story were olive-skinned, hot-blooded Bert Acosta, poking along in a Curtiss Oriole; Harold E. Hartney, wartime commander of the 1st Pursuit Group; Curtiss test pilot Roland Rohlfs, son of a Buffalo

mystery novelist; Sergeant Clarence B. Coombs, whose first race win had been between Belmont Park and the Statue of Liberty in 1918 and whose 215-minute one-way performance here in a D.H.9A impressed many people; mail pilot Lloyd W. Bertaud; and Rudolph Schroeder, gangling 6½-footer inevitably called "Shorty" — or "Roddy" by his friends — who was credited as the race's over-all winner in his Vought VE-7. The handicap was so poorly managed, the results so hopelessly scrambled, that "winners" had to settle for wristwatches instead of prize money. The fastest entrant was "The Flying Parson," a Baptist preacher from Clinton, North Carolina, who never flew on Sunday, Lieutenant Belvin W. Maynard. Occasional holder of the world's looping record — 318 loops in 1:07 — a popular if dubious honor in those days, Lieutenant Maynard, accompanied in the cockpit by his rescued German mascot police dog Trixie, won the next long-distance race, an even more zealous aspiration: the Transcontinental.

The exciting idea of a transcontinental air race was first publicized by a small but pompous and rather noisy contingent in the Aero Club of America headed by Henry Woodhouse, editor and publisher of *Aerial Age Weekly*, a magazine notorious for its fatuous and frequently inflated claims concerning Yankee aeronautical prowess. What came to be called "the Woodhouse Gang" included elderly, stout Charles J. Glidden, one of the Aero Club's founders in 1905 who made a name by sponsoring quaint if mulish prewar auto tours, sport and military ballooning, and was U. S. Air Service publicity officer during World War I. In August 1919 the "Glidden Efficiency Trophy" for a coast-to-coast race from New York to San Francisco along the "Woodrow Wilson Airway" was offered through the Aerial League of America, presided over by Rear Admiral Robert E. Peary, North Pole conqueror. Henry Woodhouse was vice-president. First

prize was to be $20,000, with "over $100,000 in prizes" to be made available. This turned out to be so much hot air, and it was left to the rival American Flying Club, composed primarily of World War I military aviators, once again to get the race off the ground. Certain Aero Club of America members sneered at the American Flying Club, barely one year old, calling it a social club "for disused aviators." But, as with the New York–Toronto race, Flying Club organizers proved to be more quiet — and more competent.

The great Transcontinental Reliability and Endurance Test was held between October 8 and 31, 1919, over a route laid out by Billy Mitchell and the boyish Lieutenant Burdette S. Wright. The Air Service had consequential reasons other than publicity and prizes for jointly sponsoring the race. Depleted of personnel, encumbered with piles of obsolescent surplus material, they needed a tough, realistic test of equipment, organization, logistics, communications, and en route facilities. This time there were seventy-four entries of which sixty-three taxied to the starting posts, but on the first day there were five crashes and three deaths. Harold E. Hartney was back, flying a Fokker D-VII (number 11) with a low-compression 160-hp Mercedes engine. Lugging the extra weight of an auxiliary gas tank installed by his young helpers Larry Bell and Don Douglas, Hartney's plane barely struggled clear of the Rockies, and he suffered seven forced landings en route, an ill omen for the future, but he completed the round trip in 77:17 elapsed flying time. Lieutenant Russell Maughan, a tough gritty Mormon from northern Utah who would gain great fame for a one-day ("dawn-to-dusk") transcontinental flight five years later, flew Spad number 195, almost coming to grief when someone mistakenly poured gasoline into his radiator! In all, there were fifty-four accidents, forty-five to D.H.4s (General Mitchell's "Flaming

Coffins"), leaving nine men dead. Bad landings, high-altitude airports like the one at Green River, Wyoming, which was built on a cliff edge — one had to drop clear of the edge to gain flying speed — and the trap baited by poor weather reports all took their toll. Standard drill when landing the nose-heavy D.H.4s at one of the twenty-two required stops had the "observer" push himself out onto the turtledeck and slide back to weight the tail during the landing roll. At least one slipped off to his death. The pilot up front was perhaps even more vulnerable, exposed to being crushed like salami between the gas tank and bulky Liberty engine if the plane pitched over. The over-all record of one death per 180 flying hours led to "modernizing" the D.H.4. The contest had no single winner since it was divided into several categories: elapsed time, best speed, and other handicap factors. But the performance of preacher Belvin Maynard in his D.H.4 number 31 named *Greyhound*, by doing the 5,400-odd-mile round-trip in 69:04 flying time during nine days 4:25:12 elapsed — about equivalent to then current rail schedules, earned kudos as the best overall. Caught in a blinding snowstorm, he narrowly grazed a mountain peak, and when his crankshaft broke at Wahoo, Nebraska, Maynard changed the engine himself. A temperance man, he claimed the crashes were the result of "too much booze."[1] After his journey was done Maynard stepped out of the cockpit and into the pulpit at the Montclair, New Jersey, Baptist church, which promised more safety if hardly more security.

During June 1919 a New York innkeeper whose conviviality with visiting wartime aviators at his Hotel Brevoort kindled an interest in aviation offered $25,000 for a non-stop transatlantic flight to link America and France. Certainly an oceanic air race

[1] When asked how he felt after landing, Tooey Spaatz said, "like a drink of whiskey!"

would be the ultimate, and the handsome prize did in fact stimulate such an aerial tourney, but not for eight long years . . . because the donor was Raymond Orteig, whose prize would not be won until a Minnesota teenager named Charles Lindbergh grew up. Ironically, by the end of June 1919 the most magnificent long-distance race of all already had been won.

Indeed, for sheer guts and stamina, few aeronautical endeavors in history can match the 1919 transatlantic aerial crossings. More than two dozen serious teams actually got plans past the drawing board. Largest was the U. S. Navy, which financed four huge four-engine flying boats, the Navy Curtiss — or NC — numbers 1 through 4, plus a flotilla of forty-five destroyers stationed one every 50 miles to protect the crossing along the southerly route from Newfoundland to England via the Azores and Portugal. One "Nancy" boat was accidentally damaged and subsequently cannibalized. The other three left Rockaway Beach, New York, early on May 8, 1919, and NC-4 with its crew of six commanded by Lieutenant Commander Albert C. "Putty" Read reached Plymouth, England, the last day of the month. The flagship (NC-3) came to grief midway, but skipper Commander John H. Towers managed to taxi her 205 nautical miles across the open sea into Horta in the Azores, most of the way in darkness.

Scoffing at the Americans' "lack of faith in their engines" because of the protective Navy warships strung along their route, Australian Harry George Hawker, Sopwith's chief test pilot and the race's most famous entry, together with his navigator, Lieutenant Commander Kenneth M. Mackenzie-Grieve, left Newfoundland in a single-engine Sopwith and boldly struck out along the lonely and imposing northerly route direct to Ireland, and in the face of poor weather. Hawker made his determined if unwise decision to take off on May 18, just two days after the NC-4's departure from

Newfoundland, because he was unable to let the honor of the first aerial crossing go to the Yanks unchallenged. But Hawker's engine balked when he was slightly more than halfway across, and it was only by monumental luck the two fliers completed their crossing at all, aboard a tramp steamer that rescued them after their splash-down.

Then, less than a month later, on June 14, RAF seven-victory ace John Alcock and American-sired Arthur Whitten Brown trundled aloft in their overladen Vimy bomber, two Rolls-Royce Eagle VIIIs thrashing evenly between yards and yards of drumming wings. Within an hour their electrically heated flying suits failed, their wireless failed, one exhaust stack ripped away loosing gushes of blue flame; shortly thereafter they were enveloped by storm. Severe icing clogged the engines, forcing Brown, chuteless, to clamber out amid the slippery struts despite one leg crippled from a war wound and hack the ice free from the engine intakes, not once but a half-dozen times. Equipped with scarcely more than a primitive carpenter's level for guidance, the Vimy plunged and bucked its way through that immortal night. Finally, 16:27 after take-off, the 1919 ocean-hurdling winners pulled themselves dripping from their crumpled aeroplane upturned in an Irish bog and claimed their barely achieved prizes, the £10,000 ($50,000) *Daily Mail* award for the first non-stop aerial voyage between the North American and European continents "completed with seventy-two hours," and well-deserved knighthoods. Six months later almost to the day, on December 18, 1919, as though a solitary dissonance sounded after the triumphant tumult, twenty-seven-year-old Sir John Alcock, flying over the Seine en route to the seventh Paris Air Show, crashed his new Vickers Viking in fog near Côte d'Évrard, Normandy, and was killed.

The last crew to complete the Atlantic crossing during 1919 did a return trip! This was accomplished in the huge dirigible *R-34*, launched from

the Clyde by Beardmore in March 1919 to fly patrols off the German coast during the Versailles Peace Conference. Major G. H. Scott with a crew of thirty-one, one stowaway, one cat, and two homing pigeons left East Fortune on July 2 and reached Mitchel Field, Long Island, four days later. Within the month the airship returned to Pulham, quitting the Atlantic's resolute sanctity, and transatlantic fever remained a whimsical malady that would not flare up again for several long years.

Other protagonists in our story were in the Atlantic race. Freddie Raynham, displaying that very English quality of quiet tenacity, spent ninety-seven days in Newfoundland, where he tried to take off twice in his scarlet and lemon yellow Martinsyde, and cracked up both times. The race was over before Italian Francesco Brack-Papa in his just completed Fiat could get to the coast. Other hopefuls were in sundry states of preparedness, but none were successful. This did not prevent self-aggrandizing men from offering bloated if impossible prizes. Nor did it discourage other hazardous long-distance flights — notably that made by the brothers Ross and Keith Smith, who flew another Vimy bomber 15,000 miles from London to Adelaide. A certain Thomas H. Ince from Culver City, California, offered $50,000 for the first aerial crossing of the Pacific Ocean, but the terms he imposed assured his money was quite safe. The lesson was abundantly clear that basic research was needed into aero engine reliability and durable aeroplane construction methods. Even though aviation's future seemed to hold bright promise in the field of commerce rather than weaponry, air race competitors returned to the speed course.

In 1919 all such grandiose plans for aviation made sensational news whether or not fliers were successful. Indeed, it was newspapermen that in large measure got things going.

Newspapermen Stimulate Air Races

Despite the frailty and frequently

haphazard temperament displayed by early flying machines, the electric novelty of actually rising off the earth coupled with the dash and sparkle of aeronauts quickly captured the imagination of dreary masses whose indifferent, horse-dominated life tempo had not altered for centuries. Newspapers were quick to exploit this to their advantage. Much in the same manner that early *grand prix* automobile races were originated at the turn of the century, many early aeronautical affairs were prompted by towering journalists eager to associate their names with aviation.

Alfred C. W. Harmsworth, the swaggering, piratical, moonfaced mogul of Fleet Street who later became Lord Northcliffe of the London and Manchester *Daily Mail*, was among the earliest to grasp the impact the aeroplane would have, in both the commercial and dramatic realms. Northcliffe, though repulsively coarse and ill-educated, had the arrogance and insight of the natural journalist; he frothed at his editors scathingly for according the Wright Brothers only four lines: "Don't you realize England is no longer an island?" His opinionated, topical, often superficial style made the *Daily Mail* the first 1-million-circulation newspaper; he founded the London *Daily Mirror*, still the world's largest; he also owned *The Times* from 1908, but later, when he was going insane — perhaps from syphilis — *The Times* posted guards against their proprietor. Northcliffe's brother was thick-necked Lord Rothermere who survived him and ended up with the *Daily Mail* but not *The Times*. Driven by curiosity but ever transient, Northcliffe was energetic in stimulating newsworthy activities. In 1906 he sponsored a meet for aeroplane models at which an eager engineer in his late twenties named Alliott Verdon Roe won £75. But when later the same year Northcliffe offered a staggering £10,000 sum for a flight between London and Manchester, his offer was derided as a cheap publicity gimmick — the money might as well be offered, according to *Punch*, for a return flight to Mars. Nevertheless the magnificent 1910 aeronautical struggle which this prize stimulated and which served as model for the 1965 20th Century-Fox movie *Those Magnificent Men in Their Flying Machines*, spurred Northcliffe in 1913 to post yet another equally huge sum, this time for the vastly more daring transatlantic gamble which of course was won six years later in 1919 by Alcock and Brown.

James Gordon Bennett

Despite the huge if sporadic splashes made by Northcliffe's *Daily Mail* prizes, the true prototype of the successful journalistic race patron, a man whose very name came to perpetuate races among mechanical contrivances, was perhaps the most unlikely of all prospects, James Gordon Bennett. That Gordon Bennett should have acceded to this particular eminence for which he will always be remembered is curious since he personally preferred a coach-and-four, even in the twentieth century, and never once witnessed any of the famous automobile races which bore his name. Gordon Bennett was an elegant, eccentric man, a tall, spare, frosty man who became legendary in his own time. Because of his naval duty in the U.S. Civil War and his penchant for yachting, he was universally known as "The Commodore." He was son of one of the most vigorous and cynical of American journalists, from whom he inherited great wealth, a prominent social position, and in 1872 at the age of thirty-one the most famous newspaper of its day, the New York *Herald*. Within three years of seizing the helm of this remarkable paper, Bennett provided an extravagant indication of the peculiar whims that would color his years of imperious rule when he spent thousands to send one of his foreign correspondents, a man named H. M. Stanley, into the unknown darkness of central Africa seeking a long-lost Scottish missionary. The event

James Gordon Bennett (LC)

has endured mainly because on the occasion of Stanley's success he uttered the immortal phrase that has come to represent the model of British understatement: "Dr. Livingstone, I presume?"

Bennett loved to dazzle and jolt his readers, who were kept wondering what he would do next. His strong temperament kept him from subordinating his own personality to the demands of the paper, and he soon became known as the Newspaper Napoleon. With his gift of uncanny intuition, his highly successful fads, sensational gossip, and bizarre layouts, he soon established the singular reputations of the *Herald*, the New York *Evening Telegram*, and the Paris edition of the *Herald*. Indeed, after a spectacular eruption of youthful chagrin which led to an unsuccessful duel with the brother of his estranged fiancée, Bennett very early in his tenure moved to Paris, where he remained the rest of his life, dividing his time between his residence

at 104 Avenue des Champs-Elysées and his hundred-man yacht, the *Lysistrata*. For decades Bennett would not succumb to marriage, until at the age of seventy-three while stubbornly refusing to evacuate Paris even though World War I raged around him, he married the widow of George Julius de Reuter, founder of the famous news service. Even though living abroad, Bennett retained his dominant position on the New York paper as thousands of words flashed every day over the transatlantic cable for his personal approval. Bennett's notebook of strict rules was a byword among newspapermen of the era — an automobile could not be called an auto, car, or machine — an aeroplane was never a plane — a record was never broken but a new record could be set — and his fines and firings for their infraction were prodigal. He once asked for the names of the most indispensable men on the *Herald's* New York staff. When twelve names proudly arrived by return cable Bennett

summarily fired them all, saying he did not believe in anyone being indispensable.

Bennett personally enjoyed sporting challenges devoid of commercial or industrial expediency, activities such as polo (which he brought to the United States), sailing, hot-air ballooning, even Arctic exploration. Thus it was only natural for Bennett to be caught in the controversy that raged between Dr. Frederick A. Cook and Commander (later Rear Admiral) Robert E. Peary over which man had first reached the North Pole. Bennett for a time took the side of Cook and the *Herald* paid Cook for the exclusive rights to his story after Cook wired Bennett offering the story for $2,500. A messenger handed the cable to Bennett just as he was boarding a train for the Riviera. Glancing at it hastily and stuffing it into his pocket, Bennett turned to his private secretary and said, "Wire Cook the *Herald* will pay twenty-five thousand for his story." The delighted Cook actually received that amount and *Herald* readers were treated to such soaring descriptions as, "We were lifted to the paradise of winners ... the ice under us seemed almost sacred ... At last we step over colored fields of sparkle, climbing walls of purple and gold ... finally under skies of crystal blue with flaming clouds of glory we touch the mark!" For a time the smooth and personable Cook was feted by the great scientific societies of the world, it not being as easy to accord the honor to the astringent and humorless Peary. But, as Peary pointed out to his newspaper, the New York *Times*, Cook had simply "handed the public a gold brick." It was true. After putting on a good show, Cook was discredited, Peary accepted, and Cook, as we shall see, soon was engaged in the creation of other "gold bricks" to hand a gullible public.

In view of Bennett's willful principles and his virtual disdain for mechanical devices, it was altogether paradoxical that he should have become the patron of the earliest contests of man and engine upon which all subsequent motor racing has been based. Even more surprising, despite the inevitable potential publicity, Bennett seldom used the races that bore his name as a means to make headlines in the *Herald*. The first James Gordon Bennett Trophy, offered in July 1899 and first competed for in 1900, was called, at the whim of its donor, the Coupe Internationale – his own name was never linked with his trophies in the *Herald* – and it was for automobile racing in France. The whole thing began on a chance: the French driver Charron selected the Paris *Herald* office to hold a deposit of 20,000 francs as a mark of good faith upon his acceptance of a challenge from Alex Winton of Cleveland, Ohio. Though the Charron-Winton race never took place, the idea for the Coupe Internationale caught on and by 1903 the trophy had acquired a prominence equaled only by the Le Mans twenty-four-hour race. Due to international disagreement over minor points in the rules, the complicated timing procedure, and Bennett's inflexibility, the race died out by 1905. Yet manufacturers had immediately recognized both the commercial and prestige value of racing, and the sport, originally intended by Bennett to be a sort of international exposition of patriotism, a sporting event between auto clubs, became professional very rapidly, with the wealthy amateur clubman giving way almost immediately to the factory tester. The fact that these races, characterized as they were by immense, slow-turning engines, brassy national anthems, dusty roads, and perseverance, died at their very peak in no small way contributed to their spell, and James Gordon Bennett's name became so closely linked with motor racing in general that motorcycle and boat races with which he had absolutely nothing to do have gone down in history under his name.

The competitions which Bennett personally found most satisfying were the great balloon races for the Gordon

Bennett Aeronautical Cup which were run over a period of twenty-three years from 1906 until 1929, the war years being excepted. Exempt from the kind of commercial exploitation which disgusted Bennett, these leisurely floating bags all looked alike except to true lovers of the sport, and the fact that an operator never knew where he would end up provided just the element of chance that Bennett relished.

At first the same aspects of chance and sporting motivation seemed to apply to aeroplanes of the time and the Gordon Bennett Aviation Cup, ultimately far to overshadow the balloon trophy in prestige and influence, was first contested in 1909 near the Champagne city of Rheims, on the Plain of Bétheny where Jeanne d'Arc had camped. The flying meet lasted a week and attracted crowds of 100,000 people per day, and it was here, with his 47·65-mph performance which left the smug Europeans agog, that dour-faced Yankee upstart Glenn Curtiss beat a field of nine to win the first organized aeroplane race in history. It could then be hardly foreseen that from this modest victory and the prestige Curtiss brought back to American shores there would grow an organization unsurpassed in aeronautical competitive effort for the twenty years to follow. At subsequent Gordon Bennett races the fabled Deperdussin monoplanes, earliest pure-speed planes ever built, first gained fame. By 1913 Armand Deperdussin was singlehandedly contributing most of the competing aircraft and prize money since the Commodore had realized quite early that aeroplanes would follow the same path as automobiles – factories would step in, professionals would replace amateurs, successful commercial names would grow in prominence, all of which to Bennett was anathema. Nevertheless, for the rest of the world the 1914 Gordon Bennett promised to be another gala international affair. Scheduled for September at Buc, on the southwest outskirts of Paris, it was canceled

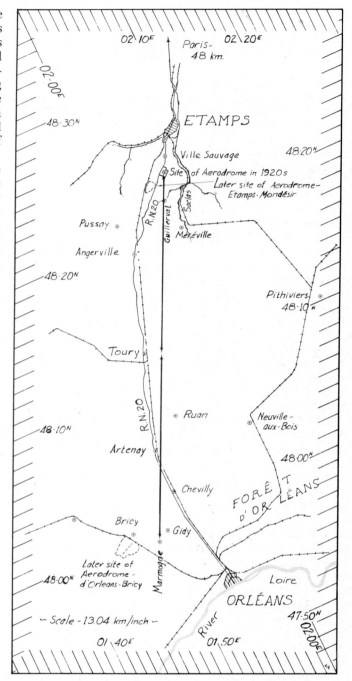

Course for the James Gordon Bennett Aviation Cup race, 1920. This 50-kilometer Étampes–Marmogne course was also used for the 1921 and 1922 Coupes Deutsch de la Meurthe and for subsequent French speed-over-distance record flights through the 1920s.

abruptly a month early by the guns of August. Since France had won two consecutive contests, a third French win under competition rules would retire the race and give France permanent possession of the trophy. James Gordon Bennett did not live to learn the outcome. He died in 1918, leaving a $25-million fortune and a unique legacy in spite of himself as the model journalistic race patron. He could not have ordered posterity better if he had tried.

The 1920 Gordon Bennett was an event of titillating contradictions. The last of an old line, the beginning of a new, it bridged two aeronautical eras. It was the last Gordon Bennett because France secured her third successive win, thus earning permanent possession of the trophy and signaling the close of the elegant, tentative aeroplane races rooted in the effete, proud tower world that died in the Great War; and at the same time it was the first postwar race that excited truly international competition, ushering in bustling, high-powered racers with militaristic and big-business overtones. Imbued with the mystique of its late patron, its character would have diminished had the series continued into the 1920s; still, as in so many races of the 1920s, the glamorous, technically interesting entry list was far more important than the inconclusive race itself.

The French had been anxious to hold the race in 1919 but several months' delay ensued because of the impossibility of organizing an international race before the signing of the Versailles Peace Treaty. The Aéro-Club de France (ACF) presented a prize of 10,000 francs which was supplemented by a like amount from the Aero Club of America (ACA) called the Samuel H. Valentine prize, perpetuating the memory of a former ACA vice-president. The event was finally conducted during the first chill touch of autumn over the historic plains of Beauce in three out-and-back trips that started from Villesauvage

Aerodrome, Étampes, south of Paris between Chartres and Fontainebleau, and proceeded to la Marmogne Farm at Gidy near Orléans before turning back. A race strictly against time, contestants were free to start any time between 7 A.M. and 7 P.M.

More than seven months before Cup day the ACA had already cabled a challenge to the ACF from S. E. J. Cox, flashy Houston oil promoter who decided the Texas Aero Club was big enough to win, and who financed the first postwar Curtiss racers, aptly named Texas Wildcat and Cactus Kitten. The most technically innovative aeroplane at the race was also a private American entry. And the U. S. Army, previewing future militaristic racing ambitions, sent a hastily adapted pursuit design with Shorty Schroeder, its military pilot. Despite the lead time, the U. S. entries were built in a last-minute rush, improperly tested, and unprepared for the demanding race conditions. Extravagant American optimism was dampened by the staggering expense of getting there and lack of success. England was there with a colorful list of bumbling sportsmen. The proud Sopwith firm had folded, depriving the race of Harry Hawker's mount; designer Henry Folland's Goshawk, hung up by red tape, arrived late; this left only Freddie Raynham's Semiquaver to carry the U.K. banner. France fielded five entries from three builders, Borel, Spad, and Nieuport. Elimination day, three days before Cup day when the final French team of three was selected from this stable of hopefuls, proved to be the most interesting day of flying.

An ancient Gordon Bennett tradition was to allow complete liberty to all contestants. Thus simple logic argued that designers should try to outpower each other. But all five French contenders as well as the one British qualifier used almost identical 300-hp Hispano-Suiza engines, which meant careful design and flying finesse — not brute power — determined the successful French team. Sophisticated wind

tunnel models of the French contestants had been tested at St.-Cyr, but poorly understood Reynolds number differences (the scale effect) led to misleading predictions. Still, these tests were indicative of the growing scientific method which would enjoy considerable refinement over the next few years. Biconvex wing profiles were just coming into use, and were credited with extremes for both good and ill. The first serious speed-induced control surface flutter revealed a new problem for technical minds to fathom. Simple expedients such as clipping wings did not produce the expected speed advantage for reasons that would lose their mystery as the scientific base line lengthened. Production cost of the American RB racer seemed enormous by European standards, but this in itself was a harbinger.

The aeroplanes had to be at Étampes not later than 7 A.M. on September 27, the day before Cup day, to allow official "measurement and sealing." This rule was to cause some difficulty for certain hopefuls. The day of the race, September 28, dawned dreary and foggy. A few eager competitors began arriving at 7 A.M. from the Hôtel du Grand Monarque in Étampes, but low clouds dampened spirits and the outlook was discouraging. The French weather report at 10 A.M. said, "A stormy movement comes from the Gulf of Gascony, advancing itself over Brittany. Mist and fog in all regions. At times humid and soft." As the clammy morning wore on, mechanics made small adjustments to the planes, but for the most part competitors and their friends huddled in small groups inside the open hangars. Soon, however, hardy spectators began pouring in by the hundreds, for the Gordon Bennett had enormous prestige. Curious Americans appeared in great throngs and soon seemed to outnumber spectators of all other nationalities combined. Other visitors included Henri Farman, Louis Blériot, René Caudron, Robert Morane, Louis Bréguet, and Marcel Hanriot, the French constructors all

eager for new ideas. Commander H. E. Perrin, tireless secretary of the Royal Aero Club (RAeC), was there with many clubby cohorts. With the weather still poor at noon, Perrin sent a white Rolls-Royce into Étampes to fetch some food, and the large British contingent sat down to an alfresco luncheon outside their hangar. Their guest was Sadi Lecointe, the French pilot who ultimately won the race. It was distinctly a mark of honor for the French favorite to lunch with the representatives of a foreign rival just before the big race, and the good French wine flowed freely.

Soon the wind freshened from the northeast and silver breaks appeared in the overcast. Activity increased, planes were pushed out. The wind picked up — it was directly across the course. In another two hours the air would be boiling. About half-past one the first racer, Kirsch's French Nieuport, took off into the scudding, fleecy white and sunlight. He cruised about for a while, then finally plunged for the starting line, dipped his wing in salute, and was away. The race was on!

Sadi Lecointe's Nieuport — sister ship to Kirsch's — won the race at a speed of less than 170 mph for the 300-kilometer distance. Only one other competitor finished the course, a Spad which had to land midway for repairs. Certainly the engines then were not up to sustained full-throttle demands.

Within hours after the Gordon Bennett the future of high-speed races was being debated. Should speed alone or some other factors of utility be the governing elements of aeroplane tests? Many suggested elimination of the complete liberty which had been a Gordon Bennett hallmark. Limitations on engine power, aeroplane landing speed, and wing loading were proposed. Opponents argued just as strenuously that restrictions were useless, pointing to Gordon Bennett results which clearly indicated that engine power alone was not the key to speed — a myth still being worshiped fifteen years later — but that complete design liberty should nevertheless lead to powerful engines also light and reliable; further, that any correlation between speed and wing loading of the Gordon Bennett aeroplanes was uncertain at best; and that, while fast by 1920 standards, the Gordon Bennett landing speeds were not dangerous. The obvious conclusion was that all-out high speed would remain the most valuable characteristic to be developed in future aeroplanes, but in one major race it would be tempered by limiting landing speed after all. This was the Pulitzer Trophy series.

The Pulitzers

1919 was a year of Pan-Americanism, a desire to further friendly relations between the United States and Latin America. The Argentinian Ambassador, Romulo Naon, passionately appealed for strong Pan-American bonds, "for if we [the nations of the Western Hemisphere] are organized, no combination in the world can upset the peace of the world!" The Second Pan-American Aeronautic Convention reflected the fervor of the day. Following a rather desultory convention two years previously, the postwar meet would last for the entire month of May 1919, in Atlantic City, New Jersey, and offered a huge list of activities that attracted swarms of journalists. By the end of March, a month before opening day, $30,000 had already been posted in prize money for the myriad races planned.

Then, on April 5, the meet received a tremendous boost when the Pulitzer brothers, Ralph, Joseph, Jr., and Herbert, owners of the New York *World* and St. Louis *Post-Dispatch*, established a prize of $5,000 which, following the prevailing vogue, would be given to any aviator covering the greatest distance in a "non-stop cross-country flight" to or from Atlantic City during May. The idea went back three years to May 1916 when the three brothers conceived the prize for a fourfold purpose:

   . . . to quicken American interest in

the science that Americans first developed and gave to mankind; to induce the equipment of military and civilian aviators for national defense; to demonstrate the practical uses of aeroplanes for the transportation of passengers and mail; and to open the first transcontinental aerial highway.

Their original intention was an annual transcontinental race for the trophy, but World War I prevented any competition until 1919. The Pulitzers put no restrictions whatever on the type of aeroplane, and a competitor — civilian or military — could make as many attempts to win as he pleased during the month. It was envisioned that the Pulitzer challenge trophy, to be contested annually, would be retired after any successful competitor won it three times, following the pattern set by James Gordon Bennett.

Despite extravagant endorsements the trophy suffered two temporary setbacks when the War Department refused to let Army aviators fly in the derby, and on April 20 when Assistant Secretary of the Navy Franklin Delano Roosevelt followed suit by declining the Aero Club's invitation for the Navy to compete. Roosevelt's decision no doubt was influenced by the imminent departure of the transatlantic Nancy boats which had been eliminated from eligibility for Lord Northcliffe's prize money. Just days before, the tall Assistant Secretary, preoccupied with the transatlantic effort, had crouched behind the pilot for a bumpy, spray-lashed ride in the NC-2, but the military's attitude toward prizes was decidedly neutral. Nevertheless, the snowball had started to roll. The very next day announcement came that the Boston *Globe*, the Cleveland *Plain-Dealer*, and the Atlanta *Journal*, following the Pulitzer brothers' lead, had all offered air race trophies of their own with total aggregate prizes of $3,500. The list was further swelled by the former Gordon Bennett paper, the New York *Herald*, which added $3,000, and by the Detroit *News*, which

jumped in after it was estimated that 1 million people would witness the Pulitzer contest. These prizes were offered to aviators making the best speed marks between Atlantic City and the home city of the respective newspaper.

The Pulitzers, like James Gordon Bennett, inherited their newspaper tradition from a father world-renowned as a journalist. After emigrating from Hungary and serving in the Union Army while still a teen-ager, Joseph Pulitzer dabbled in Missouri Republican politics, then switched party allegiance and launched his journalistic career by purchasing two St. Louis newspapers. His son Ralph was born in St. Louis in 1879, the same year he united his two papers into the *Post-Dispatch*. Four years later he bought the failing New York *World* and while shaping it into a leading newspaper Joseph, Jr., was born in New York City; he was destined to head the St. Louis paper while Ralph grew up to run the *World*. Herbert was born in 1895, sixteen years junior to Ralph, and was never seen by his famous father, who spent the last twenty-two years of his life totally blind. Joseph Pulitzer died in 1911, aged sixty-four, leaving $2 million to Columbia University, used to establish the famous Pulitzer literary prizes.

Under their father's heavy-handed but sensitive and open-minded influence the sons developed an early interest in aviation. Ralph graduated from Harvard in 1900, and nine years later his New York *World* offered a $10,000 prize for the first aeroplane flight to duplicate Fulton's steamboat route between Albany and New York City in connection with the Hudson-Fulton celebration that year. Glenn Curtiss won the prize, and as the *World* glowingly related, "at times Mr. Curtiss' machine sped 60 mph." Ralph Pulitzer's newspaper pioneered encouragement of aviation during World War I, but in 1918 it was Joseph, Jr., then thirty-three, living in St. Louis with his wife and two children,

who enlisted in the Naval Aviation Corps. Rejected for flying because of poor eyesight, he was made a quartermaster chief petty officer just as the war ended. Shortly after, Ralph was named Chevalier of the Légion d'honneur on the same list as Food Administrator Herbert Hoover while in France, where he wrote commentary on the Versailles Peace Conference.

As the Pan-American Convention opened, total prize money offered exceeded the robust figure of $50,000 and dignitaries chortled expansively amid the hubbub while daredevils plummeted for a dollar a foot in primitive parachutes overhead. Even bicycles and motorcycles with patched-on wings, optimistically called "aviettes" by their promoters, raced excitedly. Ormer Locklear, nerveless wing-walker, exemplified the extreme of exuberance when he changed planes 2,500 feet over the crowded Steel Pier, hanging monkeylike from a rope ladder attached to one Jenny's spreader bar. Locklear was burned to death a year later while performing equally harebrained stunts for the William Fox movie studios.

Then, just three days before the convention's close, Captain Mansell R. James, late of the Royal Air Force, arrived noisily and with great flourish. Originally from Watford, Ontario, the twenty-six-year-old devil-may-care bachelor, who had been a double ace on the French and Italian fronts, had come to the States three weeks earlier with his cousin and wartime comrade Lieutenant Alan Clarke, bringing two surplus Sopwith Camels and planning to pick up some easy prize money at Atlantic City before barnstorming their planes around the countryside. On May 28, with Clarke's Sopwith grounded, James took off alone and in just four hours — despite headwinds and including a forty-minute fuel stop — he covered the 340-mile run from Atlantic City to Boston. Word was flashed that he had won the *Globe*, *Herald*, and Pulitzer prizes, together worth almost $10,000. Everything appeared to be

Mansell R. James, first winner of the Pulitzer Aviation Trophy, at Atlantic City on May 28, 1919, before his disappearance (NA)

coming up roses. All James had to do was return to Atlantic City to claim his money and perhaps beat his own record to boot.

James had landed his Camel at the old Saugus Race Track, sometimes called Atwood Park, 8 miles northwest of Boston.[2] After eating at Jim Conway's Counter Lunch in Cliftondale Square, Saugus, James returned to the track and asked, "Is that the direction [pointing] to Boston where I can find the shoreline tracks of the New York, New Haven, and Hartford railroad?" and someone kidded him about using the "iron compass." He took off but

[2] The Whittemore-Hamm Company of Jamaica Plain, Massachusetts, used the track as a test field for their biplanes. Melvin W. Hodgdon was their test pilot. His earlier performance in the May Pan-American Meet was being challenged by James.

followed a perplexing spur line which led him far to the west of his intended course, deep into the Berkshires. He landed the Camel in Tyringham Meadows, near Lee, Massachusetts, where he spent the night. The next morning he refueled, telegraphed ahead, and pushed on. It was the last time James was ever seen . . . He vanished without any apparent trace.

The disappearance of the popular young hero was among the greater sensations of 1919. An immediate reward was established, search patrols launched, telephone traces conducted along his route, but the frustrating hunt only increased the confusion as it progressed. Aeroplanes had been heard overhead that day, and parts of wrecked aeroplanes were later found all over New England. False hopes appeared and shattered like diabolical bubbles. It seemed as though the ghost of the

Canadian ace, still cavalier, was playfully dropping clues, tantalizing shreds of his fate, now here, now there, toying with the confusion of hapless mortals. In mid-August part of an aeroplane wing that washed ashore in Connecticut excited speculation that James may have crashed in Long Island Sound, but the wing could not be identified. Yet the most mysterious discovery did not occur until 1925, fully six years later, when a hunter temporarily lost deep in the Berkshire woods near Tyringham, his anxiety heightened by a mournful, bitter wind, thrashed with quickened pulse into a gloomy thicket where gossamer tendrils of faded aeroplane fabric hung, and the eerie, moss-encrusted frame of an aeroplane lay. Two days later his news of this find burst like a bombshell. Certainly this must at last be the missing plane of James! Incredibly, three separate searching parties including more than one hundred Pittsfield volunteers and Boy Scouts were unable to relocate the wreckage. Once again the ghost of Mansell James eluded his pursuers. To this day no definite clue as to his fate has been identified.

Certainly the literary prizes are the most famous of all Pulitzer awards. What is not generally realized today is that, despite its ominous beginnings, the Pulitzer Aviation Trophy became the leading American air racing speed classic through the early 1920s. Although that was not at all what Ralph Pulitzer had originally intended, the current volatile aero club situation influenced the terms of his gift.

The aero club situation was aggravated by an impending clash between two groups. The established Aero Club of America with the venerability of fifteen years' existence, membership of 2,800, and forty state affiliates plus the joint Aerial League of America had just elected Colonel Jefferson DeMont Thompson, retired, affluent, former judge of the Vanderbilt auto races, to replace aging Alan R. Hawley, incumbent since 1913, as president.

Its plush headquarters were at 297 Madison Avenue, corner of Forty-first Street, New York City, and its governors included such revered names as Augustus Post and Godfrey Cabot. The ACA officially represented America at the world aeronautic body, the Fédération Aéronautique Internationale in Paris.

On the other hand the budding American Flying Club (AFC), largely amateur but highly active, organizer of the only successful American air races in 1919, was fast displacing the ACA as the actual governing body of American sport flying. This threat was met with bellicose accusations that the AFC was in reality a front for "heavily watered automobile charlatans" who had used aviation to bank an alleged $20 million grafted from unfulfilled wartime contracts, and was trying to capture the ACA to prevent investigation of these claims. The battle's chief villain was Henry Woodhouse, who in fact used his ACA governorship as a means to feed his publications, which, according to the caustic English *Aeroplane* editor Charles G. Grey, were unexcelled for their quantity of "arrant . . . nonsense to the square inch"; Grey also remarked that even if the Woodhouse charges were true, the AFC should still survive as the official American flying body under the theory that the "old poacher makes the best game keeper."

It soon surfaced that Henry Woodhouse's origins involved a two-year prison term in Italy for stabbing a man to death, subsequent immigration to America, and the Americanization of his true name, Enrico Casalegno. A former cook, he concealed a conviction and sentence to Dannemora Prison to obtain his U.S. citizenship, jumped into aviation with both feet in 1911, got into trouble through indiscretions in publishing during the war, but continued to foist on aviation his oppressive brand of promotionalism, which inevitably began to alienate other ACA members. Courtlandt Field Bishop, first ACA president, then in Paris, urged the FAI to recognize the rival AFC. The distasteful battle soon resolved itself; the AFC, led by Albert P. Loening, older brother of famed aeroplane builder Grover C. Loening, "captured" the ACA in a resounding joint vote on August 16, 1920, twelve days after Woodhouse was booted out. The reorganized group, which retained the name Aero Club of America moved to the former AFC headquarters at 11 East Thirty-eighth Street. Casalegno-Woodhouse continued to heckle the club with petty lawsuits and in his magazine *Aerial Age*, which however soon withered and passed from the scene.

Early in August 1920 plans were announced for the new Transcontinental National Air Race for the Pulitzer Trophy between Hazelhurst Field in New York and San Francisco, to be completed between October 18 and November 20 with a $5,000 prize awarded for the "best average flying

The Pulitzer Trophy

time per mile." A few days later, in the midst of the Woodhouse scandal, ACA acting race committee chairman Charles Glidden reported such overwhelming popularity for the proposed coast-to-coast race that a second Pulitzer was being planned between New York and Los Angeles to be completed by March 1921. Before the month was out, however, the reorganized Aero Club's new contest committee postponed the transcontinental race and approached sponsor Ralph Pulitzer with the suggestion his trophy be given for a more practical closed-course speed race of, say, 150 miles over 25-mile laps. Pulitzer, if not overjoyed, was at least receptive to the ACA idea, and on September 3 his written consent was in their hands. The first two speed races were quickly set for November 25, 1920 (Thanksgiving Day), and September 4, 1921. It is difficult to tell if the newspaper publisher, then forty-one, was already growing indifferent to the whole idea of his aviation trophy, especially since his desire for long-range derbies seemed doomed to frustration, or if he became truly enthused by the spectacular aspects associated with a free-for-all speed race which was more easily organized, and from a newsworthy point of view was an equally good headline maker. Pulitzer certainly saw merit in the new race because, departing from Gordon Bennett tradition, he desired that it be perpetual. The journalist had hoped that competition for his trophy would influence the production of practical sport/training aeroplanes within the reach of most affluent sportsmen. But Army and Navy representatives were included in the technical group that drew up the new race rules, and their intent was decidedly different.

The names of Ralph Pulitzer's younger brothers were used far less frequently in connection with the aviation contest. It seems they had little to do with directing it even if still aviation-minded. On October 24, one month before the race, Herbert Pulitzer,

Ralph Pulitzer   *(U)*

while being flown from Paris to London by pilot the Marquis des Champes de Boishebert, crashed 5 miles from Dijon. Pulitzer escaped with bruises but the marquis was pinned under the wreckage and killed. Undismayed, Pulitzer returned to Le Bourget to start for London in another plane that afternoon.

Rules for the 1920 Pulitzer race placed no restrictions on entries other than load factor (6 for monoplanes, 4 for biplanes) and the ability to fly

faster than 100 mph. The famous Pulitzer 75-mph landing speed restriction did not come into effect until 1922 but it could almost be predicted from the negative comments made on fast landing speeds after the 1920 race, certainly reinforced by America's Gordon Bennett disasters two months earlier. The Gordon Bennett Verville had returned just in time to compete in – and win – the Pulitzer. The course was tentatively selected one week after the Gordon Bennett, and the point emphasized that the terrible roughness of Villesauvage Aerodrome was the main factor in America's poor showing in France. Mitchel Field, on the other hand, was a vast, smooth acreage which overlooked large, slumbering fields quilting Long Island's Hempstead Plain. The race was open to all comers but the military crowded the entry list with fleets of war-generated designs including more than a dozen D.H.4 "Flaming Coffins" even though service pilots were still forbidden to receive prizes, public recognition presumably being reward enough. In a gesture meant to be magnanimous, it was announced that mechanics of winning planes would receive cash prizes one fifth the amount awarded to pilots.

Almost 40,000 people saw the huge race, which because of the number of entries had to be run in seven separate flights and which remains today as perhaps the largest closed-course air race in history. Starter Caleb S. Bragg, famous seaplane pilot, raised the red flag for the goggled gentlemen of the race's first flight to start their engines shortly after 11 A.M. Five minutes later, when each mechanic had raised a corresponding red flag indicating his charge was ticking over, Bragg raised the white ten-second warning flag. Chocks were pulled away from wheels. Then . . . both flags dropped and throttles were rammed forward. The racers bounded across Mitchel Field and, wings dancing like drunken puppets, they left a lattice of black, smoky trails as they sped low over the

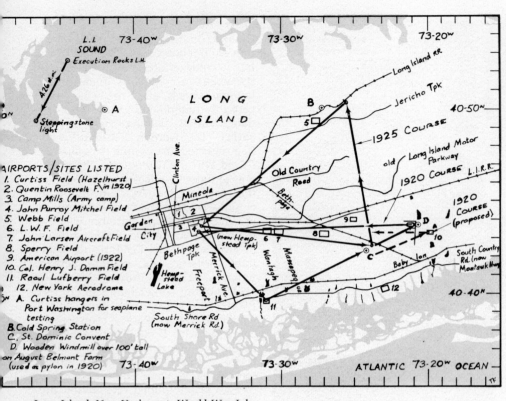

Long Island, New York, post—World War I decade, showing Pulitzer race courses for both the first and last in the classic Pulitzer speed series, the 1920 and 1925 editions; note that the actual 1920 course as flown was shorter than that proposed. The course used for high-speed testing of Curtiss seaplanes over Long Island Sound is seen to the northwest.

trees lining Meadowbrook Country Club and disappeared southward. Race referee was Packard chief engineer Jesse G. Vincent, one of the Liberty engine designers, and the Technical Committee included naval aircraft constructor Jerome C. Hunsaker, Grover Loening, Virginius Clark (of Clark Y airfoil fame), engine greats Charles Manly, Charles Lawrence, and George Mead, young Leroy Grumman, Elmer Sperry, Chance Vought, and Bill Gilmore of Curtiss, who was storing astute ideas for his forthcoming crop of Curtiss racers. It was obvious that, despite short notice, the military placed a premium on pure speed. In all, thirty-eight aeroplanes took off into the chill wind, and the dark gray Verville racer flown by Corliss Moseley, Schroeder's backup pilot in France, won the race with a badly missing engine that could not turn faster than 1,700 rpm. Harold Hartney finished second in a tiny Thomas-Morse with just half the Verville's power, a stunning display that stimulated thinking. Bert Acosta enhanced his growing fame by bringing an Italian Balilla in for third place.

Based on his time of just over eleven minutes per lap the jubilant victor claimed a resounding world's closed-course speed record of 178 mph and this was publicized widely in the press and trade journals of the day. But embarrassment was in store for the winners. The race was planned to have been flown from Mitchel Field to Lufberry Field near Massapequa (7 miles) then to Colonel Henry J. Damm Field north of Babylon (11 miles) and return (15 miles) for what the Contest Committee had computed as a 33-mile triangle, or 132-mile four-lap total. The turning points were to have been marked by war-surplus kite balloons. The Lufberry Field balloon was raised as planned by Lieutenant Commander Carpenter assisted by Lieutenant I. A. Kloor and twenty-five Navy enlisted men from the Rockaway Station who were guests at the South Shore Hotel in Freeport. However, at the eastern end of the triangle the balloon marker did not arrive in time so a suitable alternate marker had to be selected. The most obvious ready-made structure was the imposing wooden windmill northwest of Damm Field on the vast estate of August Belmont, who had achieved fame and fortune raising race horses. The windmill stood just east of the old Belmont Racetrack, which had been called "Belmont Field" since 1918. Old-time Babylon residents remember Belmont's windmill vividly; from Mitchel Field looking east across the broad, flat landscape, it dominated the horizon, and was reportedly wrapped with white bed sheet for the Pulitzer race!

The first indication that something was amiss came from preacher Belvin Maynard, doing welfare work in Brooklyn, who expressed disbelief in the published speeds, pointing out that the D.H.4 results of almost 145 mph were frankly impossible. Brigadier General Billy Mitchell, Air Service assistant chief, ordered an accurate survey of the race circuit as actually flown. The Coast and Geodetic Survey subsequently found it to be precisely 29·0202 miles in length — some *four miles less* than planned! This revelation knocked the pins out from under the initially advertised speeds; after the course survey Moseley's winning speed turned out to be only 156·5 mph with the other contestants' speeds scaled down in proportion.

This mild embarrassment soon passed; in fact, it was almost forgotten, overshadowed by a threat to the Pulitzer's very existence in 1921. Originally scheduled to be conducted at Selfridge Field, north of Detroit, Michigan, during September, the race was summarily canceled July 18 when the military services, hard pressed for funds, withdrew their official entries. For several weeks it seemed as though the Pulitzer was through. Then, at the last minute, it was resurrected and added as an adjunct to the First International Aero Congress, a reunion of World War I fliers to be held in Omaha, Nebraska, during the first week in November.

Credit for bringing the Pulitzer to Omaha belongs to Earl W. Porter, then thirty-two and president of the Omaha Aero Club, and who, as a news staff member on the Omaha *Daily News*, realized the Pulitzer was through unless something was done at once. He planned an air meet to follow immediately on the heels of what promised to be a huge and rousing affair, the Third Annual American Legion Convention in nearby Kansas City the last week in October. Porter was decidedly an optimist, since snow can be a foot deep in Omaha that time of year; notwithstanding, he was confident the American Legion spillover would be substantial and he launched a vigorous campaign for money to stage his "Aero Congress." Omaha was a city dominated by a few old families disinclined to be receptive to the ambitions of a comparative newcomer, and Porter's assurances that the meet would mean worldwide publicity for the city fell largely on deaf ears. Porter himself also recalled "some trouble" with ACA officials and criticized "the manner in which they operated." The new ACA president, elected September 1921, was Benedict Crowell, former Assistant Secretary of War, but despite the events of 1920, widespread discontent existed with the ineffective ACA, too loosely organized and still riddled with dissension which even Crowell could not soothe, and Porter saw to it that his agenda included an event to form yet another national aeronautic group to replace the ACA. Preliminary steps occurred but the issue was not resolved until the following year.

Porter finally wheedled close to $90,000 — about half coming from the Chamber of Commerce at the last minute to avoid disaster — and he tackled the job of preparing an airfield. The only readily suitable spot was a 106-acre dairy farm on the Missouri River flats north of town. Teams of horses and two big tractors driven by volunteer air mail pilots rooted out dozens of cottonwood trees, covered the Minne Lusa sewer, and graded the field to bare dirt — which promptly became mud. Porter persisted. Endorsements were secured and elaborate invitations were sent to 50,000 veteran Air Service personnel. In order to secure racing aeroplanes to compete in the Pulitzer, because of the military embargo, manufacturers had to *borrow* their best racers from the services. Nevertheless, Porter's bright predictions came true and the three-day meet was a "continuous program of hot stuff." "Omaha is air mad," screamed a headline. Because no one had thought to prepare for water rescue, tragedy occurred when parachutist Harry Elbe, twenty-six, dropped by mistake into the river and drifted along in full view, shouting over reporters' questions, until he drowned. But other barnstormers were aloft and there was barely a skip in the beat.

The skies were a cloudless, crystal azure the day of the Pulitzer; the temperature rose to 58 degrees, nice for early November, and a steady northwest breeze rustled the bare autumn trees. Excitement was in the air — the first prize was $3,000! Lloyd Bertaud, remembered by one

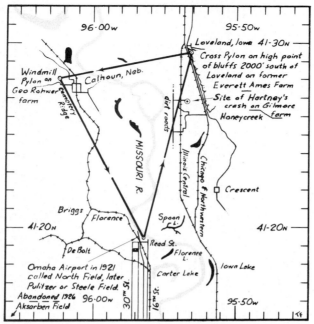

Course for the 1921 Pulitzer, north of Omaha, Nebraska

who knew him as "a big, arrogant chap who always seemed to have a chip on his shoulder," had won first place in the American Legion Air Derby the day before at Kansas City and was on hand hoping for more prize money. The triangular course had been surveyed extremely carefully beforehand this time and determined to be precisely 30·7191 miles in length, but the direction of flight was reversed at the last minute and this caused some grousing. Competitors would now proceed to the first turn at Loveland, Iowa, marked by a huge, whitewashed circle on the ground in which an oil fire to guide the fliers had been intended, but strong wind the morning of race day made the prospect of fire dangerous, so the race was delayed while a huge cross was hastily built on the brow of the bluff. Covered with cheesecloth, it stood no less than 50 feet high and had a spread of some 30 feet! The second turn, near Calhoun, Nebraska,[3] was indicated by a

white, wooden windmill used to water cattle in a shallow valley "40 rods" northwest of the Calhoun cemetery. It was also encircled by a whitewash marker but was hard to see in the dip behind "Cemetery Ridge," so it was topped by a checkered flag. More than a thousand people waited along the high bluffs in Iowa across the river, and bleachers held hundreds more on the field. Admission was $1 plus 10 ¢ "war tax"; "worth twice the price," exclaimed an advertisement. Federal tax collectors scurried after nearby residents who had charged spectators as much as 50 ¢ for using their land.

Six aeroplanes answered Major Howard F. Wehrle's starting flag (he would serve as National Air Race starter for years) and four flashed by the Warner electric timer after finishing the five required laps. One of the non-finishers was Harold Hartney, who was severely

[3] Today Fort Calhoun.

injured trying to crash-land his disabled racer. A new requirement had restricted the race to planes capable of bettering 140 mph, and this effectively eliminated all craft except pursuits and specialized racers, thus establishing the character of subsequent Pulitzers as purely military classics. The Omaha winner, Curtiss test pilot Bert Acosta, was the last civilian to win the race. He looked dashing next to his sleek blue Curtiss biplane with the handsome silver trophy designed by Mario Korbel.

The military services returned to air racing with a flourish the following year. Money for aeronautical development was made available, and thus the 1921 policy of avoiding air racing was resoundingly reversed, confirmed July 26 by letter from Secretary of War John W. Weeks to Sidney Waldon of Detroit which opened the way for the services in 1922 to clash with gusto. The site that had first been selected for 1921 was once again designated: Selfridge Field near Detroit, home of the 1st Pursuit Group. Plans for five principal events plus other minor events were completed, to comprise an elaborate affair lasting the better part of a week and called *National Air Races* (NAR) for the first time. The first main event was the Detroit Aerial Water Derby, in which the staid, old Curtiss Marine Trophy race was transformed into a speed contest of note — as well as the training ground for a galaxy of naval racing stars with a dazzling future in store. General Billy Mitchell perceived great possibilities to be gleaned from speed seeking, and he unabashedly used the Pulitzer race course as justification for a new series of "high-speed pursuits." The Navy also ordered several custom-designed specialized racing aeroplanes; whatever their service colors, even the least of these small projectiles, as individual as knights at a jousting tournament, was capable of piercing the speed marks of just months before, despite the new, formal limitation of a 75-mph limit on landing speed. Young MIT professor Edward Pearson Warner

The Handsome Aviator (from dance program, aviators' ball, Omaha, November 5, 1921, in conjunction with the air races)

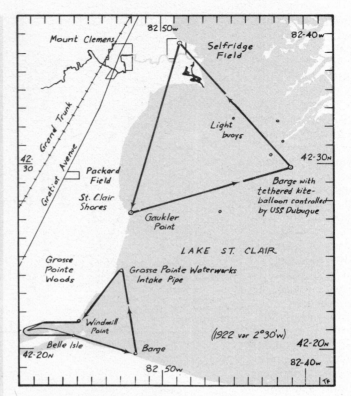

Site of two important 1922 air races, the Pulitzer (originating at Selfridge Field) and the Curtiss Marine Flying Trophy, northeast of Detroit, Michigan

had warned that the "gap between racing aeroplanes and those of direct, practical usefulness would be further widened" without such a limit.[4] Although there was strong disagreement from more liberal quarters — Europeans never did agree with this policy — Warner's advice was heeded.

In 1922 the Pulitzer inspired interservice competition so fierce that fist fights resulted, and this competitive

spirit was also apparent in the air. For the rich and varied abundance of technical ideas manifested among the several novel competing speed planes, the 1922 Pulitzer occupies the zenith of the series. When initially planned, a triangular course was laid out, from Selfridge due west to Troy Corners, back to Packard Field at Roseville on Gratiot Avenue, and return; but concern for safety prompted the change to an over-water course. The final course was an approximately equilateral triangle of exactly 50 kilometers in length; this was the first year a course of metric dimensions was adopted so that any speed records set could be registered with the FAI without complicated mathematical calculations. From Selfridge the racers would fly south to the pylon erected on Gaukler Point;

---

[4] Warner later restated his views in NACA TM-248. He went on to become editor of *Aviation* magazine and a member of the Civil Aeronautics Authority; he also served as Assistant Secretary of the Navy for Aeronautics from 1926–29, and was a member of NACA from 1929 until 1949 when, as International Civil Aviation Organization (ICAO) Council president, he received the Daniel Guggenheim Medal for "... a continuous record for contributions to the art and science of aeronautics."

the next two legs were over Lake St. Clair with the turning point marked by a kite balloon anchored to a moored barge. Edsel B. Ford personally put up $10,000 to guarantee the prizes when a suit brought by Henry Woodhouse threatened suspension. It was not needed. Detroit declared a municipal holiday on October 14, the warm, hazy day of the huge Pulitzer race, which had to be run in three heats.

Thanks to the strong service support, the United States jumped to the front rank of aviation in 1922. Russell Maughan in his shark-nosed R-6 racer set the 100- and 200-kilometer closed-course speed records while winning the Pulitzer, beating the former records held respectively by the Italian Brack-Papa and the Frenchman Kirsch. U. S. journalist William D. Tipton wrote, "Frankly we didn't believe we had it in us!" Later that week General Mitchell himself wrested the world maximum speed record away from France, where it had reposed for more than ten years. It was a proud day for the United States. The British magazine *Flight* lamented, "Isn't it about time we learned a little from our broad-minded cousins across the 'Pond'?"

Meanwhile, the organization of an effective body to govern sporting aviation, sanction air races and speed records, and influence the national aviation policy was still at issue. The leaders were convinced they heard a plea rising from across the country for a non-partisan and truly national air association; it was obvious the marriage of the old AFC and ACA had not worked, and in the words of Harold Hartney, it began "to peter out." The ACA took note of this at its Fourteenth Annual Banquet, held January 9, 1922, at New York's Hotel Commodore, and accused itself of being too local, too centered in New York, leaving affiliated state and city aero clubs to flounder with little effective guidance and no liaison. Moreover, the Yankee temperament would not be entirely satisfied until there existed not a club but a

business. Crowell announced the organization would be "nationalized", and in April 1922 the New York headquarters were closed, to be relocated to 26 Jackson Place, Washington, D.C. A decentralized plan comprising nine districts to coincide with Army corps areas across the nation was drawn up, and early in October, concurrent with the Selfridge Field air races, the new National Aeronautic Association (NAA) was formally established. The birth process took place under the auspices of the Detroit Aviation Society at 4612 Woodward Avenue in the city hailed as an appropriate birthplace, not only because the current races seemed to represent the spirit desired, but because Detroit also represented so much to America in terms of transportation. The most powerful men in motoring were in Detroit, and a hungry aviation industry still looked up to them. The new NAA began life confident of dues from 19,000 members, but the entrenched leaders had not read the pervasive indifference earlier squabbles had caused, and they were hard pressed to get barely 1,000. The first NAA president was Howard Earle Coffin, forty-nine, of Detroit, early internal-combustion engine pioneer, wartime Aircraft Production Board chairman, and current vice-president of Hudson-Frampton Motor Car Company; the first secretary and acting general manager was Harold Hartney. The new charter was flown at once, at the height of race week, to Hartford, where the NAA was incorporated under Connecticut law. In January 1923 the NAA was named sole U.S. representative to the FAI, and it has remained so to this day. But the weaning period was difficult. Coffin, after an extended business trip abroad, returned to find his young charge sick, accused of extravagance, favoritism, petty bickering, and he donated liberally from his personal fortune to prop up the organization.

Exactly one week after the 1922 Pulitzer, St. Louis *Post-Dispatch* publisher Joseph Pulitzer was persuaded by

eager city fathers that St. Louis could obtain the now classic race in 1923. Chicago and Atlanta were also vying for the honor. At Pulitzer's direction a group of twenty business leaders was formed to underwrite the contest and negotiate with the NAA; the group, mentioned in Ralph Pulitzer's New York *World* on November 14, 1922, included ever present St. Louis balloon pioneer Major Albert Bond Lambert and banker Harold Bixby, and became known as the St. Louis Air Board, 511 Locust Street. By February 1923 St. Louis had been assured they would host the race; the city's selection was formalized June 25, at which time a second group — the St. Louis Aeronautic Corporation — was set up, capitalized at $200,000 through public stock sale to fund the race, and headed by Missouri-Pacific Railroad Board chairman Benjamin F. Bush. The NAR had become big business.

The most likely race site seemed to be Scott Field, 35 miles east in Belleville, Illinois, but this was soon rejected as too inaccessible. Instead,

the shrewd businessmen perceived a golden opportunity to build for St. Louis not a short-lived spectacle but the best air terminal in the Midwest, one that would become the veritable "Aerial Cross-Roads of America!" Thus the 183-acre Weldon tract in the nearby Florissant Valley, which Major Lambert had leased for $2,000 per year since 1920, was purchased for $73,200; an additional 316 acres of adjoining farmland was leased for another $19,358. At once the huge job of grading the land was tackled by more than one hundred men, several 10-ton tractors, and no less than seventy-five three-hitch mule teams! A 6-foot hill was removed, a creek diverted, four steel hangars erected, a "huge" 10,000-gallon fuel storage tank sunk (one 747 carries more than four times that amount today), and by August the rich black earth was sown with Italian rye, expected to be thick and sturdy by October 1. Major Lambert personally laid the cornerstone by pitching it from a low-flying aeroplane. Expenses necessary

Home pylon, 1923 National Air Races   (Au)

to prepare the field came to some $173,000 more; for the race a vast grandstand to seat 53,000 was built, including 3,200 six-person boxes. There were bleachers for 12,000 more and a promenade area for yet another 100,000. Space to park more than 20,000 autos was fenced off, judge and press stands built, and a 65-foot-tall yellow-and-black-checkered pylon went up near the grandstand.

The subject of pylons had been a hot issue at a preliminary NAA meeting where Navy Commander Jerome C. Hunsaker told the Contest Committee of recent tests in England which seemed to establish that humans "cannot withstand more than 4 g." It was decided therefore to build *double* pylons at the Pulitzer's three 60-degree turning points to allow wider, less stressful turns.[5] Since pilots would presumably not exceed 4 g, a $7\frac{1}{2}$ g minimum for the racers' structural integrity was considered adequate. The 75-mph landing speed limit was retained, but the minimum top speed was raised to 175 mph. This was reasonable. It was felt the course, as in 1922, should be over water as much as possible, and therefore one leg proceeded almost 6 miles along the wide, muddy Missouri River. The other legs were over sloping, shallow dales and hillocks dotted by woodland.

The endeavor became more grandiose with each passing day. A huge tent housing exhibits worth millions was set up. At night a massive searchlight sent beams visible "100 miles away" piercing through the heavens. Nine major air races with aggregate prizes of $13,300 would be run for which, in late September, 119 entries had been received! These included the Royal Aero Club cable entering Larry Carter and his Gloster I;

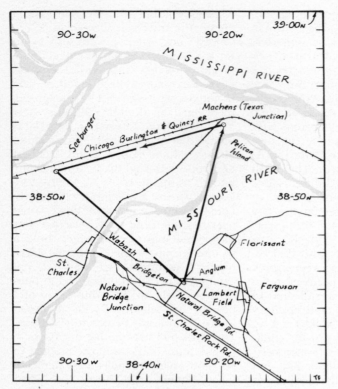

Course for the 1923 Pulitzer northwest of St. Louis, Missouri

"positive assurance" that Sadi Lecointe and his speedy Nieuport would arrive from France; and Brack-Papa and his Fiat, expected from Italy. Unfortunately none of these foreign speedplanes appeared. But 375 aeroplanes did appear to make the 1923 NAR an event which can only be described in superlatives, even by today's standards. These included 230 military ships and an avalanche of kaleidoscopic and tattered Standards, Canucks, and Jennies, bearing all manner of barnstormers and gypsy fliers, which converged on St. Louis and like some helter-skelter quiltwork sat awkwardly staked out in the weeds of little pastures surrounding Lambert Field. Each was anxious to outdo the others in displays of daredevil showmanship, wingwalking, parachute jumping, their pilots eagerly stunting the often woe-

fully inadequate and ancient crates at suicidal altitudes.

The first official event was the "On-to-St. Louis" derby. The "On-to" idea had caught on the year before in Detroit when a young Kansan named Walter H. Beech won it. Curtiss exhibition manager Charles Sherman Jones, better known as "Casey," in an OX-5 Oriole won the St. Louis edition, the first of his many such victories over the next several years. Boyish Lawrence Sperry might have won except for a technicality.

A steady downpour September 30 left the carefully prepared field inundated with puddles and the race managers alarmed. All pylon races had to be postponed three days, upsetting plans. Nevertheless, the event still attracted at least 150,000 people, who streamed to Lambert Field in

endless queues of mud-spattered autos and veritable armies of hikers. A huge attraction, visible for miles, was the silvery sheen reflected from Admiral Moffett's new pet, the gigantic dirigible ZR-1, which hovered over Lambert Field. The ZR-1 was the first U.S.-built rigid airship and the first to use non-flammable helium – 2 million cubic feet (at $175 per thousand cubic feet). It had made its maiden flight at Lakehurst, New Jersey, on September 4, only one month before, and the 2,200-mile round trip to St. Louis so early in its career seemed to confirm Moffett's claim that feasible long-range air transportation in the near term could be only by dirigible. On October 10 at Lakehurst, Mrs. Edwin Denby, wife of the Secretary of the Navy, to whom the ship personified the "Daughter of the Stars," christened it by that name – *Shenandoah*. Few then could have imagined the disaster to occur two years later on September 3, 1925, when the proud vessel broke in a thunderstorm 6,000 feet over Ohio, resulting in great loss of life. The uproar then raised by Billy Mitchell was in part responsible for his celebrated court-martial.

On October 6 the event's highlight, the Pulitzer high-speed race, was run. The entries were not so numerous as in 1922; and if 1922 had belonged to the Army, 1923 was the Navy's year. The Army had spent its meager annual dole on observation planes and bombers, and competed in the Pulitzer with last year's best racers. The Navy, on the other hand, spent freely for high speed in 1923. They had four glossy new Pulitzer racers, and it was evident from the line-up that the true combatants were not the services but Curtiss pitted squarely against Wright. The formidable Navy racing team was gathering strength. Just the week before, a Navy pilot in the 1921 Pulitzer-winning aeroplane scored a smashing victory in the 1923 Schneider seaplane race in England. And now here in St. Louis was Lieutenant

[5] The second pylon at Lambert Field, in an awkward location, was removed and by race time only single pylons stood at all three turning points. By then it was obvious that the English alarms were unfounded.

Commander Marc A. "Pete" Mitscher, already creased and jagged at thirty-six, with his hot landplane platoon in tow. Mitscher, from Hillsboro, Wisconsin, wore a Naval Academy ring dated 1910 and the thirty-third set of gold naval aviator wings. He had been CO of Anacostia naval air station in 1922 when he commanded the contingent of naval pilots at the Detroit Curtiss Marine Trophy race. Shortly thereafter he was assigned to the Bureau of Aeronautics (BuAer) Plans Division, and seized the moment to make the group into the nucleus of the world's first "high-speed flight."

Marc A. "Pete" Mitscher, still plotting destiny twenty years later (NA)

Under the watchful eye of the official FAI observer and NAA Contest Committee chairman Colonel Frank P. Lahm, who as a lieutenant in 1906 won the first Gordon Bennett balloon race, a new Navy Curtiss racer posted a resounding 40-mph speed boost over 1922 in winning the Pulitzer. This was even more than expected and it made a star of Al Williams, the tall, good-looking pilot whose "howling demon" had given the 85,000 paid spectators (at $1·50 each) and 20,000 more along the course "an almost terrifying demonstration of speed." One woman knitting

with a group in the shade of the Machens pylon did not even look up at the earsplitting racers. "They don't excite me," she sighed. But thousands of others were hoarse. Hunsaker tried to put the Navy's triumph in perspective. "This is no Roman holiday," he said. "It is the focus of applied science. We looked for quality instead of quantity and we got it." Ralph Pulitzer personally presented the award to Williams. Orville Wright, amiable and innocuous and constantly accompanied by his sister Katherine, commented wistfully, "I never expected to see such speed." It was, after all, less than twenty years since he had done it first. Glenn Curtiss was there too, to beam with pride over the 260-mph marvel his engineers had wrought — the last U.S.-built design to hold the world maximum speed record before World War II.

The 1923 St. Louis NAR was without doubt the high-water mark in American aviation, and stood as the model to emulate for years. Despite the $320,000 outlay, its promoters realized a handy profit of nearly $14,000, and pride that more than one-third million miles had been flown without a single fatality. One young king of the air road, barely in his twenties, had wandered in from barnstorming through Minnesota and Wisconsin and parked his grimy and slightly drooping Jenny on the outskirts of the massed activity. Soon after he arrived he chanced to spot Harlan "Bud" Gurney, an old chum who was himself a gypsy, having hoboed to the races from Lincoln, Nebraska. Gurney was an open-faced, nerveless lad who would rather fly than eat, but to manage any eating at all he had to do the greater part of his flying somewhere on the outside of the aeroplane rather than in the relative but still dubious safety of its cockpit. Bud's slow-smiling barnstorming pal was "Slim" Lindbergh. Together the two young fliers, like most other spectators, were wide-eyed at the tremendous variety of aeroplanes on the field. They walked

slowly along the lines of shiny new racers and powerful little fighters parked in neat rows by the hangars, peering and assessing from every angle. No doubt about it — these sharp aeroplanes with their drum-tight fabric and glistening engines that purred like sewing machines would thrill any lad's heart. To young Lindbergh they seemed terribly business-like in contrast to the patched and tired old Jenny which had carried him wheezing across the prairies scratching out a meager living and landed him here in the midst of the largest organized air circus the world had ever seen.

During the races Gurney broke his arm in a parachute jump — it was one of the meet's only casualties — and Lindbergh sold his Jenny to a man from Iowa.[6] Slim had decided to remain at Lambert Field and build up his time instructing; there certainly seemed to be a great deal of interest in flying at St. Louis. Eventually he flew the air mail run to Chicago and back, and within four years he would make the aviation spirit of his chosen city a household topic around the world. Before Bud Gurney's retirement from United Air Lines he became a senior flight captain on DC-8 jets, yet the memory of the 1923 NAR was still fresh in his mind.

The NAA was still a poor joke instead of a real force in the development of aviation, on the one hand trying feebly to be a propagandist body for convincing the U. S. population that aviation should be in their future and not just a financial scandal, yet on the other hand refusing to lobby in Congress, remaining "dignified . . . patriotic . . . serving with loyal co-operation" a government that for the most part ignored them. After his year in office, H. E. Coffin was reelected but stood down in favor of Frederick B. Patterson, son of the founder of National Cash Register Company in

Dayton, Ohio, and himself its current chairman. Orville Wright, also from Dayton, was named honorary chairman, and thus it was no surprise New Year's week when Dayton became the Contest Committee's "unanimous" selection as site for the 1924 Pulitzer, although Minneapolis-St. Paul and other cities had made spirited bids to stage the race. Dayton, a prosperous, not too progressive town very much pleased with itself, was worthy of note chiefly for neglecting the Wright Brothers until World War I, when their young business showed signs of expanding the municipal girth. Now, as home for all Air Service experimental work, it seemed a fitting race site; the races would also be a fitting way to dedicate the 5,000 acres generously donated by the local citizenry and added to the aerodrome at Fairfield 8 miles east and named for Dayton's own Wilbur Wright. Patterson called this vast open expanse "an ideal airport" and sailed for Europe in mid-February to solicit European participation in the Pulitzer, first visiting Colonel Frank Lahm at his home in Paris. Soon word returned that Patterson on behalf of the NAA had offered to cover all expenses for visiting foreign entries.[7]

This decidedly generous offer to stake foreign racers certainly reflected a warm, spontaneous side of the Yankee personality, but it raised many discreet hackles in Europe, and exacerbated a basic difference in American and European speed-seeking philosophy. In the United States, the government sponsored the development and construction of speedplanes while in Europe the constructors bore the expenses. Also, in the United States military pilots freely engaged in air racing, but European constructors had their own pilots under retainer fees and these were the men — not

---

[6] Incredibly, it resurfaced after decaying forgotten in a barn loft for decades, and in 1974 was being prepared for museum display by the Long Island Early Fliers Club.

[7] The Patterson portion of the 8,400-acre complex known today as Wright-Patterson AFB was officially named for Lieutenant Frank S. Patterson, who died in a 1918 plane crash.

service pilots — who competed; if the occasional military pilot participated it was while he was on leave, and not entitled to military benefits in case of accident. Indeed, European opinion generally was vehemently opposed to the participation of government services in air racing. There had already been some grumbling that the American speed records of 1922, set with service aeroplanes, should be listed under a category *separate* from civilian-set records in the FAI world record book. Only the French demurred on this point since they also felt the personal equation played such a preponderant part in the setting of a record that it made small difference whether the pilot wore a military uniform or mufti; and that speed for speed's sake — regardless of the "technicalities" — was the important issue. (No separate category of records was ever established.) The United States, defending their practice, cited the precedent of the Cavalry, in which the military had long been identified with improving the breed of the horse. Europeans pointed out this stopped short of military horse racing, however.

Europe had already expressed shock in 1923 when the U. S. Navy "rudely invaded" the previously private domain of the Schneider seaplane race to walk off with the trophy, forgetting the Army might have done the same thing at the 1920 Gordon Bennett. The question was whether a race like the Pulitzer should be an exercise of pure sport or whether its purpose was to help develop aeroplanes applicable to the national defense. Professor Edward P. Warner, lecturing from MIT, was adamant that the Pulitzer was *not* a sporting contest. It was only logical, he said, that if you invite a pilot to take the considerable risk in flying a very fast aeroplane close to the ground, something useful should be learned from the result. Beyond that, Warner criticized air racing in general and echoed a widespread feeling: the air race, even by 1923, had become "too perfect, too mechanical." The racer

that leads at the end of lap one will win, he reasoned, and the one that wins today will win tomorrow, etc., barring accidents or breakdowns. There was no holding back for a final sprint, the whole distance in an air race being covered at top speed which could be measured early, leaving thereafter only a contest of endurance. For spectators it was no spectacle, just a "dreary procession" of identical turns around the home pylon, the planes otherwise being out of sight. No, Warner said emphatically, the only justification for such activity was to improve the machine, and if such machines were applicable to government use, then governments should be involved. If left to private initiative, the speed records might have remained in the class they occupied before World War I, and thus the United States congratulated itself for its sagacity, but to the eyes of Europe it looked as if this policy would halt international air racing. The NAA's own slogan, "Make America First in the Air," had an ominous ring as heard abroad, and what Patterson did not seem to understand was that if U.S. constructors had been left to defend their speed records without government support they would be just as reluctant to compete against potentially limitless government resources as were the European constructors, who now politely but firmly refused his gesture. Had they accepted it would have meant an untenable position: a European win would require them to reciprocate and stake U.S. entries, which they were not prepared to do; a loss would be a double shame demonstrating they could not put up a decent show even if paid for. Europeans were not yet quite ready for air racing between governments, which to them was heavy with many ticklish complications. Patterson came home empty-handed. Even eager French speed king Sadi Lecointe, entered in a Dewoitine racer, had to beg off: his employer was Nieuport-Astra, and with no racer of their own to send which could meet

the Pulitzer's 75-mph landing speed limit, Sadi could not go.

Patterson was further rebuffed in early February when the Navy quit the Pulitzer, pleading insufficient appropriations. Also, they said, in view of their many world records set in 1923 it would be "imprudent" to push further. Nevertheless, from his headquarters at 217 Realty Building, North Main Street, in what was now billed as "The Air City," Patterson could lean back in partial satisfaction, anticipating early October when $43,750 in prize money — more than triple the amount offered in 1923 — would be awarded in twelve events. These included two new low-power events, a recognition of the growing popularity of the light aeroplane. Indeed, Walt Beech was back with his brother Irl to greet old friends with names like Eddie Stinson, Clyde Cessna, Lloyd Stearman, Matty Laird, and naturally there was Casey Jones who won the "star race," the On-to-Dayton derby, in his clipped-wing Oriole. "Hell's Half-Acre" was the corner reserved for parking the more than 120 civilian aeroplanes that attended. One Jenny, indistinguishable, giving no preview of its owner's

Gala procession leaving from McCook Field for Wright Field and the 1924 National Air Races. Note the admonition to aviators painted on the hangar. (Au)

future flamboyance, belonged to young Roscoe Turner, who had flown it in from Corinth, Mississippi, with his new bride. An astounded English visitor remarked, "You Yanks use aeroplanes like Fords . . . leaving them any old place . . . on the other side we would overhaul a plane that sat out in the rain all night!"

Hell's Half-Acre proved to be more interesting than the Pulitzer. The 1924 edition was the series' nadir. On a theoretical basis, extrapolating past trends, the 1924 winning speed should have been on the order of 260 mph, yet when it was all over the 1924 Pulitzer victor was slower than the 1923 sixth place — almost 30 mph off the previous year's pace! Two fatal crashes sounded a glum note for racing as well. The Navy had unloaded one Curtiss Pulitzer racer from 1923 on the Army for a dollar, and Alex Pearson was subsequently killed testing this ship. Then Buck Skeel in Maughan's 1922 R-6 died when the racer disintegrated on his diving start. Neither had the Army built any new specialized racers in 1924; in fact, the only racers the Army dusted off for the race were one 1922 Verville-Sperry

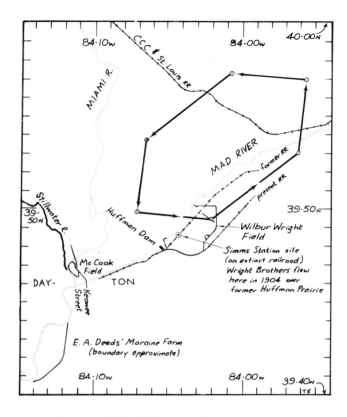

Course for the 1924 Pulitzer northeast of Dayton, Ohio

monoplane and the two 1922 R-6s. A new rule even required contestants to revert back to wood props — Uncle Sam's — and this opened the question regarding Air Service engineering procedure, whether a government engineering laboratory that also manufactures its own products (in this case propellers) is fit to judge impartially the products of other constructors. The prospects of the Pulitzer were so disappointing that a PW-8 pursuit was entered to maintain at least some semblance of competition. Only three competitors finished the "race" and the PW-8 made a good showing. The Verville R-3 won the dismal affair at just over 216 mph.

In contrast to the Pulitzer, the John L. Mitchell race between no less than eleven new Curtiss PW-8 *Hawk* fighters became the true highlight of the NAR.

This was the PW-8's first public display; it was powered by the D-12 engine introduced in the 1922 Pulitzer, and the "symphony of noise" created by the racing squadron was truly an "awe-inspiring spectacle." Buck Steel had put one through dazzling aerobatics, rolling four times in a low fly-by, boring upward in vertical rolls, and certainly, if one purpose of racing is to develop in the atmosphere of sharp competition designs that will prove useful in later service, the operational PW-8 fighters in 1924 were evidence that the lessons learned back in 1921 and 1922 were being applied. Yet the great irony was that the revolutionary technical design features of the Pulitzer's R-3 did not receive widespread recognition for almost two decades.

The Army Air Service had blamed

Congress for its sad state in 1924 but in fact millions of appropriated money remained unspent, proving that military administrators in those days were at least as parsimonious as those they accused. Of the little money spent, a large portion went toward renewed emphasis on long-distance flying. France, England, and the U. S. Army all launched round-the-world expeditions in 1924 (only the U. S. Army was successful). By 1924 the Pulitzer was no longer novel, and effective participation seemed to be too costly for the times. Shorty Schroeder, the new NAA vice-president, even suggested that the Pulitzer be reorganized into an all-civilian competition and that the services go on to develop future pursuits without further recourse to racing. This view seemed to be reinforced by the NAR's disastrous reversal in fortune: the 1924 races lost $70,000. During its convention the 7,000-member NAA dumped Patterson, despite his voting bloc of 500 members, all National Cash Register employees, in a riotous election described as "more fun than an acre of billy-goats," and chose refined Bostonian Godfrey Cabot, sixty-three, to replace him.

The prospect of repeating such financial calamity did not faze the Twin Cities, still eager to stage the Pulitzer. A Minneapolis *Tribune* editorial expressed the conviction that their city's civic spirit would "make it the irresistibly logical choice [of the NAA Contest Committee] for the 1925 contests . . . It will require no great effort to keep the 1925 goal in sight and try for a touchdown . . ." Galveston, Texas, and New York City also wanted the races. The committee, at a meeting on January 30, 1925, could not decide where to hold the 1925 Pulitzer, but set the date — again, early October — and modified the 1924 regulations to allow potential foreign entrants to test their wing models abroad instead of submitting them to the MIT wind tunnel, as previously required. Just one month before, in

December 1924, the French had recaptured the world maximum speed record and the race promoters were more eager than ever for foreign participation. The committee hoped the French would modify their speedplanes to meet the Pulitzer landing speed limit, but this prospect seemed slight. There was also a conflict with the French Coupe Beaumont race, to be run at about the same time as the Pulitzer.

At a May meeting held in St. Joseph, Missouri, the NAA awarded the Pulitzer races to New York. Minneapolis felt quite crushed, but perhaps it was a blessing in disguise. Mitchel Field would for the second time host a Pulitzer race. It had been five years since the first pure speed Pulitzer was held there, and in the interim the field had come close to fulfilling its original objective, to become the center of service aviation in the east. Already 1919 seemed so long ago; that was when the aerodrome — then called Hazelhurst II (adjacent to old Camp Mills) — was purchased for just $450,000, and renamed for brilliant New York City mayor John Purroy Mitchel, who the year before had patriotically enlisted in the Air Service at the age of thirty-nine only to die five months later in Louisiana when he spilled out of his pursuit trainer's open cockpit. Even before that oldtimers could still remember spirited flying that dated back more than fifteen years. One would hop from the train at Mineola's sprawling old wooden railroad station, near the Gold Bug Inn where Glenn Curtiss relaxed and Bert Acosta used to sing "My Wild Irish Rose" while nursing a crème de menthe. Then one would hike a mile or so east along Old Country Road to the Aeronautical Society Field, the glimpse of a plane aloft quickening the pace. There were three hangars on the side toward Clinton Avenue and the field extended nearly 2 miles farther east — the Hempstead Plain was almost completely barren in those days — the row of ramshackle sheds

The flavor of early air meets is captured in this view of Curtiss Field on October 16, 1921, looking east (the hangars adjoin Old Country Road), near Garden City, Long Island, New York. (C)

along Old Country Road being among the few structures apparent. The old elm tree that shaded so many early flying conversations still stood when the field was named Hazelhurst for a fallen aviator. The eastern half was later named Roosevelt Field after Quentin Roosevelt, "T. R.'s" son, killed in air combat. The Curtiss company acquired the western half — Hazelhurst I — along Old Country Road and Clinton Avenue in 1920, renamed it Curtiss Field, and rapidly built it into the flight test center for their immortal line of racers and many other distinctive aeroplanes. Bert Acosta and others would open up the Curtiss racers over the old Long Island Motor Parkway, using telephone poles as distance markers along the same straight stretch used for early Vanderbilt Cup auto races. South of Stewart Avenue, site of Curtiss' new Garden City headquarters, the trio of airfields was completed by Mitchel Field. Its first big event occurred in July 1919 when the triumphant British dirigible *R-34* moored there during its epic round-trip Atlantic crossing, the executive officer para-

chuting stiffly from its gondola in full uniform to direct the landing operations! Then in 1920 the Pulitzer race was held there, now — half a decade later — to be repeated.

In contrast to the more than three dozen Pulitzer competitors that flooded the course in 1920, however, the Army and Navy together fielded only two new racers for the 1925 edition. The fact that these two new Curtiss racers were superb aeroplanes — and even more significant, were closer to the current absolute speed frontier than any subsequent racing aeroplane built in the United States — served but little to provide the real impetus aviation then needed. In fact, the concept of air power in the United States was about to be buried together with Billy Mitchell, whose court-martial began within days of the Pulitzer race.

Thus 1925 marked the Pulitzer's swan song; so perhaps it was fitting after all the last edition should be at the site of the first. 1925 was also the year when the government, for the first time, was threatening to regulate aviation, to establish rules of the road and licensing procedures, to define

infractions and their penalties. It is difficult to imagine today a time when literally anyone could get into anything with wings and fly it anywhere, answering to no one, yet to the hardy, nomadic souls devoted to flying then, it seemed overwhelmingly as if the government was about to give aviation the ax when it most needed the needle. Yet there was still time at the 1925 NAR for droves of barnstormers to congregate and compete among themselves in a last flourish, much as the last authentic cowboys must have congregated at a desperate rodeo the year before the iron horse and other pretenders contaminated the West.

Optimistic plans were drawn up at the 1925 Air Races office, 30 East Forty-second Street, to accommodate the 500,000 spectators expected. Parking space for 50,000 autos was set outside the field, and the use of Meadowbrook Polo Field's 30,000-seat grandstand adjacent to Mitchel Field would certainly help. Among the visitors were World War aces, the first round-the-world fliers, plane builders, foreign dignitaries including Japan's young assistant naval attaché Lieutenant C. Yamamoto, who was an interested and discerning observer of American air power, the visiting British and Italian Schneider team members (the Schneider was held at Baltimore less than a fortnight after the Pulitzer), and brothers Louis and Jacques Bréguet from France, who brought two Bréguet 19s, the NAR's first foreign entries. One went on to beat fourteen other entries in a race for observation planes; the other was piloted by French hero Pelletier d'Oisy fresh from his epic 1924 Paris–Tokyo flight. Ralph Pulitzer motored out from his Manhattan residence at 7 East Seventy-third Street to see the last edition of his race which still had no foreign entries. Dwight F. Davis, the new Secretary of War and donator of the Davis Cup for tennis, who had just instituted court-martial proceedings against Billy Mitchell, was there as were members of the Aircraft Investi-

gating Board, including H. E. Coffin and chairman Dwight W. Morrow, 1895 Amherst classmate of President Coolidge, partner in J. P. Morgan Company, and future father-in-law of Charles Lindbergh. His Board, deep in the throes of drawing up national air policy, would visit the NAR for a look at flying's practical side.

This included more than two hundred civilian aeroplanes, the largest number seen in one place to that time, crowding many of the NAR's ten regular events. The races opened October 8 under a splendid blue sky dusted by fleecy clouds, but tragedy occurred almost at once when Lawrence Burnelli, younger brother of plane builder Vincent, was killed in the crash of Clarence Chamberlin's Bellanca during the Glenn Curtiss Trophy race. Chamberlin escaped serious injury and Basil Rowe won the race in his Thomas-Morse S4E. To the consternation of race promoters, large crowds did not appear; moreover, to those spectators that came, sentries with fixed bayonets seemed to be everywhere. Even Russell Maughan, 1922 Pulitzer winner and Dawn-to-Dusk hero, Admiral Moffett, and various congressmen were brusquely turned away for not having the proper armbands. To the credit of Mitchel Field's CO, Lieutenant Colonel Benjamin D. Foulois,[8] such harsh militarism was deemphasized and the bayonets disappeared before the Pulitzer was run.

To publicize the upcoming Pulitzer, the Army's designated pilot Cy Bettis and his alternate Jimmy Doolittle rolled, looped, and twisted in two pursuits over Manhattan's skyscrapers, Doolittle swooping down Broadway beneath the building tops. At night Gene Barksdale dropped fireworks over the city from his stunting aeroplane, and two huge searchlights played over western Long Island. But October 9 was cold (43 degrees) and misty, and some events were called off. An ominous storm had been brewing over

[8] Air Corps chief less than ten years later.

the middle Atlantic wastes and it now churned around upon itself, slashing up the coast and rolling over New York with all its fury. A fierce 80-mph gale laced with snow swept through the city on October 10, felling trees and power lines, toppling high cornices that threatened to brain struggling, slanting people below. "Horses, wagons and pedestrians were blown violently about," reported the New York *Times* which soberly mentioned that the rollers tumbling down the Hudson were 10 feet tall. Things were less sober at the Hotel Pennsylvania, where grounded race participants, opening bottles of Old Smuggler and Canada Dry on bureau drawer handles, later recalled the real sport was held. "Today an international race [was held], the participants being Italian, American, and Scotch. Of the three the latter was the most potent," wrote one who was there.

Two days later the weather cleared and the Pulitzer race was run, but only 25,000 paid to watch it. Seats in the half-full boxes were down from $6 to $2, and wind still flung stinging pebbles and filled eyes with grit. The wind was blamed in part for the race's "disappointing" speeds of about 250 mph; 270 had been expected. Nevertheless, the speeds achieved — still considered by many as "unholy" — would not be matched in the Thompson Trophy, the unlimited high-speed air race classic of the 1930s, until 1936, *eleven years later*! There was no diving start as in past years. Al Williams was back for the Navy; he spiraled to the northeast, danced in the sky for a few moments, then tore by the home pylon and disappeared. But the "race" was in fact another time trial and Williams, bitterly disappointed, lost to Bettis.

The Pulitzer had a second heat in which four standard service fighters competed. The race was intended to have had three Army planes pitted against three from the Navy, but the Navy had to borrow two Army PW-8s to fill its quota. Both Army

pilots were aces, veterans of Eddie Rickenbacker's famous Hat-in-the-Ring squadron, and a new Curtiss P-1 reserved for one of them led the second heat all the way. Though more of a crowd pleaser that the Bettis-Williams trial had been, the day's real thrills were provided by Jimmy Doolittle, who gave a singularly picturesque display of precision aerobatics in the P-1.

If anything, the 1925 NAR had been less coherent and novel than the 1924 edition. Moreover, NAR steersman, the NAA, had fallen into a comatose state; its chapters were ineffective, its policy violently reactionary, and pundits were beginning to laugh it off as the National Aero-narcotic Association. Only slight impact was provided by a few energetic members like the new secretary, Donald Wills Douglas. But B. Russell Shaw, NAA Contest Committee executive who had managed the later Pulitzer races so ably, quit to join Ford Motor Company, and early in 1926 the NAA decision was announced: there would be no more Pulitzer air race. Subsequent NARs became civilian affairs almost exclusively, accompanied by the hoop-la of barkers barking merry-go-rounds of garage-built aeroplanes in gaudy swarms, hot dawgs and dust stirred up by thrill seekers drunk on stunts, crowds indifferent to the esoterics of finely honed engineering controversies but keen on noise and surprises. Reliability, range, and payload began to dominate the interests of more pragmatic aviation backers; by decade's end moving spirits like H. E. Coffin and Curtiss' C. M. Keys had become czars in the nation's budding airline system. The era of pure speed seeking in the United States had come to an end. After 1926 U.S. military planners considered air racing outdated as a means for frontier R&D, and the world speed record moved abroad.

The English Aerial Derbies
In contrast to American militaristic overtones, the English took their

sportsmanship quite seriously. War's stagnation disappeared in the fresh sporting slipstream that first blew on Whitsun weekend at the ancient Hendon flying grounds (London N.W.9), for years mecca to that insular stock of enthusiast fliers, whether monocled peerage or tweeded gentry. Revival of the Aerial Derby (pronounced *Darby*), the classic air race around London, was scheduled for the year's longest day, which promised lingering June twilight until well past 10 P.M. Shopkeepers normally latched their doors in London at 1 P.M. on Saturdays and thus had ample time to motor out Edgware Road and witness the race start shortly before 4 P.M. Derby pilots contested for both absolute and handicap speed prizes, the handicap being a typically English arrangement that in an air race allowed puddlejumpers to compete against powerful speed planes on an equal basis. Major J. H. Ledeboer and Mr. C. T. Glazebrook of the Royal Aero Club, in that meticulous manner of English clerks, computed a different time allowance for each entry so as to manufacture artificially a speed of 130 mph. The slowest plane, an Avro Baby with a ten-year-old 35-hp engine, had a 1:25 advantage over the scratch entrant which was publicly displaying the 450-hp Napier Lion engine for the first time, yet the handicap worked so well that handicap results of the three fastest planes were within forty seconds of each other — after, in the Baby's case, some two and a half hours' flight! This led, in future, to actually staggering the takeoff times of entrants so that a "race-horse finish" would result.

Derby history went back to 1912 when young Tom Sopwith won the first edition on a Blériot. In those days contestants circled London only once; now two trips around were required. The day was sunny and soft for this, the fourth edition — the "Victory Derby" — and the bookies in the paddocks were frantic and hoarse. Of twenty hopefuls, twelve started, seven finished. John Alcock was entered

to fly a Vimy but was unable to start, indisposed as he was, receiving royal congratulations from King George V at Windsor Castle for his transatlantic epic made just the week before! Harry Hawker also sat out the race — his Sopwith entry was still on the Air Ministry secret list. The five that dropped out en route were all victims of engine trouble.

The race was won by Gerald Gathergood, a test pilot with eighty-seven types to his credit, who flew a plane not unlike the D.H.4s that were soon to struggle across the American continent — hardly a sleek design — except for its sterling new Napier Lion engine. Nevertheless his winning speed was virtually identical to that made six years before by the prewar Gordon Bennett Deperdussin racer, which had only one third the Lion's power, an observation not lost on astute airframe designers.

The whole affair called for that restrained camaraderie that distinguished Royal Aero Club social gatherings in their city retreat on Clifford Street joining the rear of Savile Row, the Victorian red brick corner house (number 3) which housed the bar, their true rallying point — trophies soon gave it the tone of a silver gallery — upstairs lounges, and — for London — superb dining room. This building served as the club's home from 1916 until 1931. The club was formed in 1901, prodded into existence largely by Charlie Rolls of Rolls-Royce fame, who always wanted to go faster than was possible and whose delight in the absurdity of everything about aviation in those days was quite infectious. The club was especially lucky to have the splendid organizing talents of their secretary, ample-waisted, kindly-eyed Harold "The Hearty" Ernest Perrin. And, of course, the fraternity of sportsmen was the mainspring that made it all tick.

Though government policy in England could be considered timid as return to peace deflated the war-engorged aeronautic industry, there

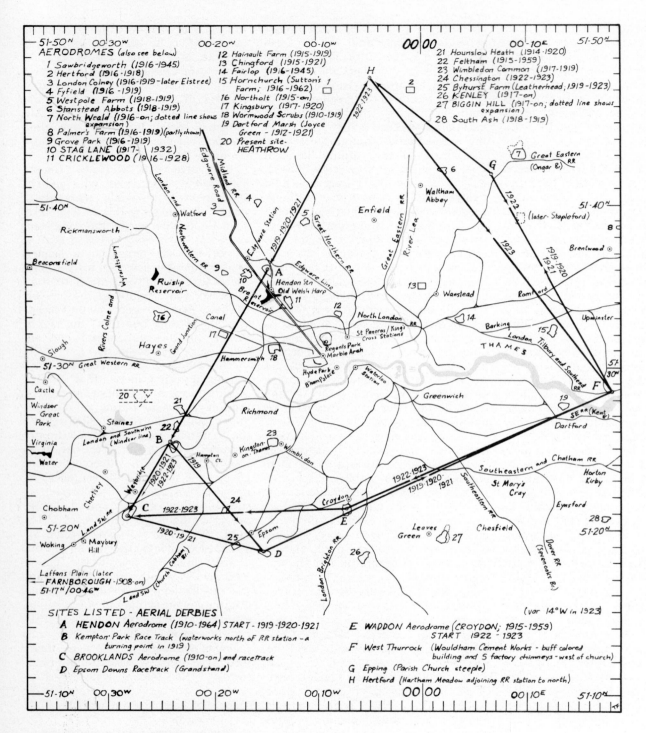

Inside the map (labels and legend):

51-50N 00-30W   00-20W   00-10W   00|00   00-10E 51-50N

AERODROMES (also see below)
1 Sawbridgeworth (1916-1945)
2 Hertford (1916-1918)
3 London Colney (1916-1919-later Elstree)
4 Fyfield (1916-1919)
5 Westpole Farm (1918-1919)
6 Stanstead Abbots (1918-1919)
7 North Weald (1916-on; dotted line shows expansion)
8 Palmer's Farm (1916-1919)(partly shown)
9 Grove Park (1916-1919)
10 STAG LANE (1917-1932)
11 CRICKLEWOOD (1916-1928)

12 Hainault Farm (1915-1919)
13 Chingford (1915-1921)
14 Fairlop (1916-1945)
15 Hornchurch (Sutton's Farm; 1916-1962)
16 Northolt (1915-on)
17 Kingsbury (1917-1920)
18 Wormwood Scrubs (1910-1919)
19 Dartford Marsh (Joyce Green - 1912-1921)
20 Present site- HEATHROW

21 Hounslow Heath (1914-1920)
22 Feltham (1915-1959)
23 Wimbledon Common (1917-1919)
24 Chessington (1922-1923)
25 Byhurst Farm (Leatherhead; 1919-1923)
26 KENLEY (1917-on)
27 BIGGIN HILL (1917-on; dotted line shows expansion)
28 South Ash (1918-1919)

SITES LISTED - AERIAL DERBIES
A HENDON Aerodrome (1910-1964) START - 1919-1920-1921
B Kempton Park Race Track (waterworks north of RR station - a turning point in 1919)
C BROOKLANDS Aerodrome (1910-on) and racetrack
D Epsom Downs Racetrack (Grandstand)
E WADDON Aerodrome (CROYDON; 1915-1959) START 1922 - 1923
F West Thurrock (Wouldham Cement Works - buff colored building and 5 factory chimneys - west of church)
G Epping (Parish Church steeple)
H Hertford (Hartham Meadow adjoining RR station to north)

(var 14°W in 1923)

London aeronautical, post—World War I decade, also showing courses for all postwar Aerial Derbies, 1919–23 – the great air races around London

42

---

was no sign of timidity among the happy, grimy fliers at Hendon, where on July 24, 1920, the next Aerial Derby would once again start and finish, and where the myriad weekend and even occasional Wednesday pylon races in which virtually everybody flew maintained a lively atmosphere. Few Englishmen are happy as spectators; everyone must participate no matter what the sport or how minor his contribution. But the Aerial Derby was no impromptu affair. It was the year's top race and only a select group of pilots would compete. Moreover, the Aerial Derby had become a large social event at which the public might glimpse even royalty. Bookies set up their stands and full race-track rituals held sway.

Of fifteen entries, fourteen started (one French entry failed to arrive) and eight finished, with engine troubles of various sorts plaguing those that retired. The day's first calamity occurred when a de Havilland tangled some telephone lines during its hectic emergency landing, sending one man to the hospital. The first Avro Baby was away shortly after two, fully 1:41 ahead of the scratch Goshawk, but odds-making was difficult since Britain's four fastest planes were entered, all built within the previous year, and their handicap allowances were all grouped within only eight minutes, frustrating the harried bookmakers busy in the enclosures. The Bristol Bullet was flown by Cyril Uwins, the Sopwith 107 by Harry Hawker, the British-Nieuport Goshawk by Leslie Tait-Cox, and the Martinsyde Semi-quaver was to have been flown by Freddie Raynham. The latter two planes and respective pilots had recently taken turns raising the British speed record, the Goshawk being current champion. The race's finish was marred by frustration when the Goshawk retired with engine trouble and an inadvertent rules infraction disqualified Hawker, leaving the Semi-quaver to gallop home the victor at slightly over 150 mph for the 200 miles, piloted by Frank T. Courtney, who had filled in for an injured Raynham at almost the last minute. On landing, Courtney's mount bounded over on its back to the horror of thousands, but when Courtney emerged he required only aspirin. All four speedplanes survived; three came in for intensive grooming in preparation for the decisive international Gordon Bennett race in just two months' time.

France won the Gordon Bennett and English speed seeking suffered a hiatus until the following summer. The 1921 Derby then promised to be the biggest and best of the series; despite the crowd-pleasing RAF Pageant held at Hendon July 2, two weeks earlier, which included military stunts but no speed seeking, the civil Derby was truly the largest affair in the European air-racing world that year. Of twenty entries for the speed event at least seven were serious contenders, and aeroplanes with more than 400 hp were considered in the "super-power" class. Fortified by their Gordon Bennett victory, France posed a threat with their entries, and the list was capped by designer Henry Folland's new Bamel. His year-old Goshawk was still considered an "immensely fast machine" and rumors that British Nieuport was also the builder of his new racer were intense, but slightly off the mark.

Folland, then leading spirit of British speed seeking, was quietly consulting for a little-known firm in Gloucestershire and this is where his new bird was hatched, thus launching Gloster as an aggressive, imaginative producer of speedplanes. With no time to be fledged, the Bamel's work seemed cut out.

Almost before anyone realized it, race preparations were marred by a series of accidents. Two French entries and one speedy Avro were eliminated — then tragedy struck when Harry Hawker was killed in the crash of Folland's Goshawk. Others washed out. The touted Alula-Semiquaver became a non-starter. Yet so many spirited rivals remained that ultimately these eliminations could not altogether dampen the race spirit. It seemed to many almost as if World War I was being refought with so many Camels, Pups, and S.E.5s about; in fact, eight S.E.5s had been divided among teams from Oxford and Cambridge for a spirited intercollegiate race on Derby day. All pilots were university students who had formerly flown in the RAF, and the Cambridge racers, their tail feathers splashed light blue in contrast to the dark blue tails of Oxford's racers, led all the way. Two of these S.E.5s, unaltered, reappeared in the Derby, which might as well have been

Folland's race since this pitted his wartime S.E.5 design with his Nieuhawk and brand-new Bamel. The weather was splendid, the handicapping excellent. The first two finishers across the line were within six seconds of one another. James in the winning Bamel flew wide and Noakes in a Nieuhawk ran out of gas at the last moment, otherwise the first three would have finished inside that! "Catering was good," observed a witness, bookmakers were offering quite reasonable odds, and the large wood-slat notice board, connected by telephone to the far turning points, ran like clockwork. In all it was "a very good show" and in their euphoria people talked of resuming the "pleasant Sunday afternoons" with perhaps a couple of pylon races every weekend such as the late Richard Gates and Bernard Isaac had created at Hendon before World War I.

Jimmie James, Bamel pilot who had won both speed and handicap events at a speed within 7 per cent of Bert Acosta's performance in the 1921 Omaha Pulitzer four months later, walked away with his "brace of pots" and £600 prize money, an amount

equivalent to Acosta's prize. Later, in town at the Royal Aero Club, it was "drinks all 'round, chaps!" at the elegant club bar, a place never seriously short of its characters, most of whom might have stepped straight from the pages of Wodehouse. Then Mr. Frisbee, club chef, had dinner ready; afterward one called for a cigar over billiards or cards in one of the club's many small rooms, or went back to the bar. Indeed, the club had come in for some stiff criticism for seeming to place hotel keeping and the comfort of members ahead of the sport of flying. The much harassed Racing Sub-Committee seemed unable to convince the club's governing body that the club was not a cooperative hotel after the fashion of the famous clubs of Pall Mall, but in fact was a Public Body that sent delegates to the FAI; yet this was largely ignored by individually competent men who, when combined in such an organization, became, as one observed, a "collective congenital idiot." The problem was really one of money. The club's elegant were content for their names to appear on club stationery as a guarantee of club respectability; Lord Dewar might even give

First Oxford-Cambridge air race, 1921, held in conjunction with the Aerial Derby. Number 30 won for Cambridge.   (MA)

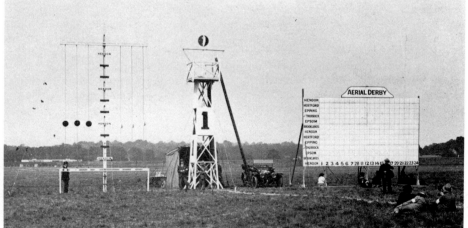

Notice board and home pylon, Hendon, 1921
Aerial Derby   (F)

the occasional £100 as he did toward the Oxford-Cambridge air race, but this was nothing to the vast sums Sir Thomas Lipton and others were then donating to the sport of yachting. The club badly needed another "full pager" — another Northcliffe, who before the war had put up three whopping £10,000 prizes to encourage aviation. A few staid, lofty members thought high-speed events ought not to be encouraged at all. But the technically inclined and visionary club members knew that, just as in automobile racing, the machine must be stressed to its limit for improvement to occur. And the candle must be worth the game. So the continued plea for private benefactors went on.

The deepening economic malaise was even more vividly reflected in the life-style of the typical British factory test pilot, usually a young bachelor living in cheap "digs" run by a certain "Ma" known for her homey and simple fare as well as for her perpetual worry about getting paid; a vaguely genteel, basically comfortable existence if faded, short of space, with the inevitable china washbasin and jug of "hideous rose patterns" and "shilling-in-the-slot" gas fire to ward off winter's wet, dreary, endless chill. Derby prospects for 1922 did little to rid winter's discouragement. The total purse for all positions had shriveled to less than 1921's combined first prizes of £600.

Race site had been changed to Waddon Aerodrome, Croydon, London's terminal for Europe's bustling airlines, in a decision that met with groans from many club members, but Hendon (it was patiently explained), although long the center of sport flying, was neither level nor long enough for the current crop of fast racing planes; moreover, to club governors, Croydon appeared to offer commercial advantages. The air route around London was altered as well. For the first time it was run clockwise with right-hand pylon turns: west to the large Brooklands motor racing track at Weybridge (a large X had

been placed in the oval's center last year); this year the racers would fly direct, skipping Epsom racecourse grandstand; they would also skip the five huge chimneys of the Wouldham Cement Works at West Thurrock on the return to Croydon. Speedplanes were fewer in number — France did not enter — but Bristol's new "hush-hush" Jupiter-powered monoplane seemed a serious rival for the Bamel.

Unfortunately this Bristol was not ready, and the Bamel had little difficulty in posting its second Derby win under a threatening, overcast sky and before a strong, turbulent southwest wind that gave the pilots a rough ride. A few sunny spells cheered the hardy but pitifully few spectators — compared to Hendon, Croydon had proven relatively inaccessible through the jammed maze of streets that carved London's south bulwarks. Club officials were also hampered by poor organization and accommodations. But perhaps the major factor contributing to the Derby's diminished prominence was the establishment in 1922 of the King's Cup race, a new major event with hoped-for universal appeal which had preoccupied scurrying club organizers largely to the exclusion of the speed-oriented Derby. King George V was Patron of the RAeC (Vice-Patron was his dashing young son, the Prince of Wales, later to become King Edward VIII then Duke of Windsor) and the gift by the King of an air-racing cup was indeed timely; it came at a desperate moment for sport aviation, which badly needed a shot in the arm. Literally anyone with any kind of crate could participate in the new event and this no doubt added to the event's appeal, as did its direct association with royalty; distance would be the equalizer so that the winner, according to 1923 victor Frank Courtney, "was more likely than not . . . the pilot whose equipment survived long enough for him to find his way with luck to the finishing point." But all this did little for speed seeking.

The demise was further evident in

1923, year of the last of the fashionable Aerial Derbies. Gloster was still hammering away with Folland's Bamel, now disguised as Gloster I, flown by Larry Carter. The 1923 event had fourteen entries — four more than in 1922 — but prizes were again reduced. The course, still right-hand, now had only three turning points (Epping was eliminated) and despite 1922's attendance plight, it was set for Croydon again although Hendon almost got it back, mainly because the new Underground rail station was almost ready to open there.

August Bank Holiday in 1923, Derby day, enjoyed gloriously fine weather which brought out huge enthusiastic crowds. Via wireless from the turning points to the notice board, and megaphone to the crowd, many of whom held bets with the surfeit of bookies present, the progress of Gloster I in posting her third straight Derby win could be followed. Gloster's racing spirit in putting up the winner year after year was admirable, but to their discouragement little government money was forthcoming as a result of their effort, and by 1923 the updated racer's speed had slipped to 21 per cent behind the current Curtiss racing performance. The paltry Derby prize was awarded by Sir Sefton Brancker, the voluble and popular Director of Civil Aviation, replete with spats, monocle, and clipped Charlie Chaplin moustache. But Brancker's luxuriant demeanor could not hide the aspect of undernourishment.

The year 1924 was disastrous for air racing all over the world. For the first time in six years there was no Schneider, the Pulitzer that year was a joke, and when in July the Aerial Derby, Britain's only speed race and then the world's oldest active air race, was abandoned "because Great Britain had not a single racing machine" ready, it was a signal for Charles Grey Grey to issue a blast from the pages of his Aeroplane magazine. From his high-ceiling office in 175 Piccadilly which overlooked Bond Street all the

way to Oxford Street, there had long issued forth an extraordinary torrent of tart, shrewish comment.[9] Now Grey's reproof reflected even more the strong prejudices and loyalties characteristic of the English spirit, and he reminded his readers that "nothing can be more sporting than air racing!" This was in direct opposition to the views of pragmatic American professor E. P. Warner, but to Grey no sport contained the element of chance to such a degree: the most likely contender might be felled midway by a forced landing or a change in the weather. As for what it might lead to, one need only consider the British Turkoman thoroughbred horse which had made the British Army great and whose bloodlines had improved from constant competition since the time of the Crusades. Moreover, Grey noted, the best people were in horse racing — one need only refer to Burke's Nobility and Gentry to verify that. What then explained the current lack of support for this superb sport of air racing? Grey pondered. The sport of aviation in England is run ("or walked," Grey chided) by the Royal Aero Club, "an entirely amicable institution conducted by amiable gentlemen who — like the House of Lords in Iolanthe — do nothing in particular and do it very well." Lord Edward Grosvenor, Alan Butler, and Dr. Whitehead-Reid were worthy club stewards, said Grey, but of the rest — men of title, officers of high rank — "90 per cent have done nothing." Few subscribed to the Racing Fund, Grey admonished, and their donations were distinctly dérisoire.

In England the RAF did not then compete in open races. The aircraft

[9] Always signed by his familiar initials "C.G.G." In life Grey, tall and charming, was a gentle, urbane, thoroughly likable man. He founded The Aeroplane in 1911 and edited it until 1939; he also edited Jane's All the World's Aircraft 1916–41. Grey died in 1953. Aeroplane readers also enjoyed the lampooning style of "G.D.", Geoffrey Dorman, Grey's assistant; the notes of "W.H.S.", William Higley Sayers, former captain, RAF, technical editor; and the excellent artwork of Leonard Bridgman.

industry — known as "The Trade" — because they were too busy elsewhere or too poor, found it difficult to support races proposed by the RAeC, just as the RAeC found it difficult to adapt race rules to meet Trade wishes. This resulted in the Aerial Derby being abolished altogether and made the King's Cup entirely uninteresting and unsatisfactory, perpetuated only out of loyalty to the Crown. Grey thought the RAeC should be modeled after the Jockey Club, not a social club but a working organization of Gentlemen and Players. Otherwise, he warned, as had happened to the Aero Club of America, the club would "fall to pieces from lack of support." The NAA in the United States, he pointed out, was of a form anathema to Englishmen: it was not a club at all but an unwieldy political organization which like "the President of a Republic ... does what it damn well pleases then blames the people," whereas the Royal Aero Club like "the King in a limited Monarchy . . . does what the people tell it, then blames itself."

Despite Grey's fulminations, the club remained essentially unaltered and its problems persisted. In 1923 they were reduced to organizing competitions among ultra-light, extremely low-powered aeroplanes and the names of Britain's most famous pilots, transferred from the Aerial Derby, can be found on the entry lists. They made a brave show of such activity, citing some convincing rationale and putting the airfield at Lympne (pronounced Limm) on the map. In December 1924 an international Aerial Derby to be held August 1925 was optimistically planned, also to be held at Lympne over a 200-mile course, but this aspiration came to nought. Until the RAF, with great discomfort, briefly entered the Schneider Trophy contest later in the decade, true British speed seeking hibernated.

Industrial Patrons
Henry Deutsch de la Meurthe

A small but potent number of great industrialists joined the newspapermen as patrons of early air racing. The most vigorous and munificent was Henry Deutsch de la Meurthe, born in Paris, heir to the original petroleum fortune in France, who despite his privileged condition proved himself a dedicated engineering student during the early 1860s and graduated from l'École Centrale with a brilliant record. With his brother Émile he then guided the family business — Les Fils de Alexandre Deutsch — to new heights of success. With sage perception he was convinced that the key to unshackle man, to free him from the barn, indeed from the surface of the earth itself, would be found in the technique of refining petroleum thus allowing the embryonic gasoline engine to develop. As Henry Deutsch saw it in the 1880s, success in achieving heavier-than-air flight was hindered not by the inability to build wings but by the inability to provide them with capable motive power — *gasoline engine* power. To be so close to unlocking this power was terribly exciting to the intensely dedicated young man – then in his thirties – who divided his time between laboratory, where he plunged into the problem of refining petroleum into gasoline, and hobbies which included hot-air ballooning. A memorable voyage in a balloon equipped with clumsy and dangerous electric engines convinced him more than ever of the need for an efficient gasoline engine.

At l'Exposition Universelle de 1889, the great Paris fair for which the Eiffel Tower was built, Deutsch exhibited the earliest engine-driven vehicles seen in France. Soon, under his aegis, l'Automobile-Club de France was founded and for his prizes autos were racing each other in great cross-country events. His first aerial prize (100,000 francs) was offered for ballooning before the turn of the century – the popular idol, slouch-hatted Brazilian

Henry Deutsch de la Meurthe (with Roland Garros, 1913) (MA)

Alberto Santos-Dumont, won it in 1901 – and in 1904, barely weeks after the Wright Brothers' first flight, impatient Henry Deutsch established a joint prize of 50,000 francs with Ernest Archdeacon for the first airman to fly a closed circuit of 1 kilometer. This prize was won by Henri Farman in 1908, shortly after Deutsch had created the first true Prix Deutsch de la Meurthe, valued at 70,000 francs, for an air race around Paris. The race was first conducted in 1912 on an annual basis, interrupted by World War I.

Henry Deutsch de la Meurthe continued to donate immense chunks of his rapidly accumulating fortune in philanthropy for the new technology. He created l'Institut Aérotechnique de Saint-Cyr, soon renowned as perhaps the most respected aeronautical school in France, and he endowed numerous chairs of aeronautics at other universities. When he was not giving money away he indulged in big-game hunting

in that grand style that only the prewar opulent could affect, and during 1911 in collaboration with Henri Cain and Camille Erlanger he even composed an opera, aptly entitled *Icare*. During World War I the financial support of Deutsch directly contributed to the leading position of the French aviation industry. Deutsch had three daughters; one married the Nieuport aeroplane-manufacturing firm's general manager, whose access to the Deutsch fortune prevented the firm's collapse in the wake of World War I; the youngest daughter, Suzanne, became namesake for the final Coupe Deutsch air race series, contested annually from 1933 until 1936.

The name Deutsch de la Meurthe, like that of Gordon Bennett, was for decades a powerful spur to auto, balloon, and aeroplane races, but for a totally different reason, for unlike the newspaper baron who was adamant toward preserving nineteenth-century values, Henry Deutsch embraced the burgeoning industrial growth spawned by the gasoline engine, and actively encouraged change. President of l'Aéro-Club de France for many years, Commander in the Légion d'honneur, awards were showered on him by grateful Frenchmen who could not do enough for the man they called the "Maecenas of Aviation." On June 6, 1919, shortly before his classic air race around Paris resumed, and with his rare gift of prescience perhaps anticipating his death some five months later, Henry Deutsch in a true *beau geste* gave the Aéro-Club a whopping 2 million francs with no strings attached. Thus the preeminent elegance of French sporting aviation was assured for the next several years.

Resumption of the air race around Paris was announced in late summer 1919 and irrepressible Sadi Lecointe immediately made a flight around the 200-kilometer prewar course in a Spad racer. But he had jumped the gun. The new postwar rules had not been finalized, so this flight was not recognized. The prewar conditions which

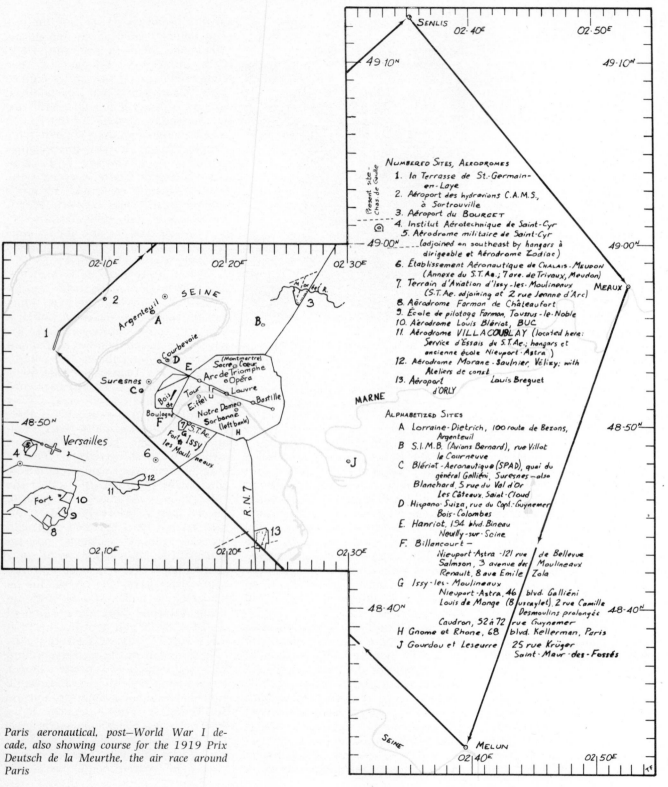

SENLIS
02·40E   02·50E
49·10N   49·10N

NUMBERED SITES, AERODROMES

1. la Terrasse de St.-Germain-
       en-Laye
2. Aéroport des hydravions C.A.M.S.,
       à Sartrouville
3. Aéroport du BOURGET
4. Institut Aérotechnique de Saint-Cyr
5. Aérodrome militaire de Saint-Cyr
49·00N ____ (adjoined on southeast by hangars à
       dirigeable et Aérodrome Zodiac)
6. Établissement Aéronautique de CHALAIS-MEUDON
       (Annexe du S.T.Aé.; Tore de Trivaux, Meudon)
7. Terrain d'Aviation d'Issy-les-Moulineaux
       (S.T.Aé. adjoining at 2 rue Jeanne d'Arc)
8. Aérodrome Farman de Châteaufort
9. École de pilotage Farman, Toussus-le-Noble
10. Aérodrome Louis Blériot, BUC
11. Aérodrome VILLACOUBLAY (located here:
       Service d'Essais du S.T.Aé.; hangars et
       ancienne école Nieuport-Astra)
12. Aérodrome Morane-Saulnier, Vélizy; with
       Ateliers de const.
13. Aéroport   Louis Breguet
         d'ORLY

MARNE

ALPHABETIZED SITES

A Lorraine-Dietrich, 100 route de Bezons,
       Argenteuil
B S.I.M.B. (Avions Bernard), rue Villot
       le Courneuve
C Blériot-Aéronautique (SPAD), quai du
       général Galliéni, Suresnes—also
       Blanchard, 5 rue du Val d'Or
         Les Côteaux, Saint-Cloud
D Hispano-Suiza, rue du Capt.-Guynemer
         Bois-Colombes
E Hanriot, 194 blvd. Bineau
         Neuilly-sur-Seine
F Billancourt —
       Nieuport-Astra -121 rue | de Bellevue
       Salmson, 3 avenue des | Moulineaux
       Renault, 8 ave Emile | Zola
G Issy-les-Moulineaux
       Nieuport-Astra, 46 | blvd. Galliéni
       Louis de Monge (Buscaylet), 2 rue Camille
                              | Desmoulins prolongée
       Caudron, 52 à 72 | rue Guynemer
H Gnome et Rhone, 68 | blvd. Kellerman, Paris
J Gourdou et Leseurre | 25 rue Krüger
         | Saint-Maur-des-Fossés

MEAUX

48·50N   48·50N

48·40N   48·40N

MELUN
02·40E   02·50E

SEINE

Present site - Chas. de Gaulle

02·10E   02·20E   02·30E
SEINE
Argenteuil
2
A
B
3
Marne R.
Courbevoie
(Montmartre)
Sacré Cœur
Arc de Triomphe Opéra
D
E
Louvre
Suresnes
C
Tour
Bois de
Boulogne Eiffel
F
Notre Dame
Sorbonne
(left bank)
Bastille
H
S.T.Aé.
G Issy
les Mouli-ne-aux
48·50N
Versailles
4
6
5
J
12
11
Fort
10
9
R.N.7
8
13
48·40N
02·10E   02·20E   02·30E

*Paris aeronautical, post–World War I de-
cade, also showing course for the 1919 Prix
Deutsch de la Meurthe, the air race around
Paris*

required a competitor to exceed the previous record by 10 per cent in order to win were retained, this being a device contrived by restless Henry Deutsch to compel rapid improvement in aeroplane speed. Eugène Gilbert's 1913 performance of 162 kmh in a Deperdussin meant the postwar performance must exceed 178 kmh to qualify. This would pose no problem, but the succeeding steps would rapidly compound the difficulty, so despite the inauspicious misty weather of opening day three pilots immediately scrambled to establish the first speed mark which should carry a strong measure of security for its owner. Only Leth Jensen in his 180-hp Nieuport monoplane finished the course at a desultory 201 kmh, threading his way around the fog-enshrouded landmarks, but forcing future competitors to better 222 kmh. The postwar course, established early in October, was somewhat shorter than the prewar circuit, and for turning points used prominent spires atop some of the ornate medieval cathedrals surrounding Paris. The contest was opened October 13, 1919, to run with a one-year deadline until the following October 31. Most of the action took place during the first October as competitors fought rough weather, rough engines, and the stiff 10 per cent rule. By January 3, 1920, Sadi Lecointe, on a new Nieuport racer, established the officially recognized final winning speed, earning for himself 20,000 francs and the trophy, and thus closing the first Deutsch de la Meurthe series of races. On November 24, 1919, at Romainville-les-Mureaux, Henry Deutsch died, aged seventy-three; yet within two years the new Coupe Deutsch de la Meurthe air race series had been established by his widow, who early in 1921 presented an international challenge cup for aeroplane speed together with another 200,000 francs. What had gone before was just a springboard for these subsequent events. Sadi Lecointe and his colleagues would waste no time in grasping additional glory.

The first of the new Coupe Deutsch races took place Saturday, October 1, 1921, over the identical course used for the final Gordon Bennett one year before. The selection of Villesauvage Aerodrome, four miles from Étampes, seemed unfortunate to many and caused candid dismay. Certainly, it was argued, Le Bourget Aerodrome, just northeast of Paris, would be far more convenient for spectators to reach. But the Coupe Deutsch was not meant for spectators. It was not in the conventional sense a race at all since pilots could begin any time between sunrise and sunset – and most competitors arranged their departures so as to have the whole sky to themselves! No, the Coupe Deutsch was a series of strenuous time trials which presumably could be appreciated only by the serious constructor; thus crowds were discouraged. In fact, the rules made it quite clear that only constructors – that is, established manufacturers – were permitted to enter. Nevertheless, substantial crowds materialized. Even one speedplane aloft at a time was an exciting event!

The Coupe Deutsch was a speed contest pure and simple. There were no restrictions of any kind, no useful load required over the weight of pilot and fuel, no minimum landing speed as was becoming popular in the American Pulitzer. The French had a long tradition of allowing complete liberty in the races of mechanical contrivances, and now reiterated justification by explaining that the Coupe Deutsch was for the world's fastest aeroplanes: let the designer and the pilot, using their experience and intuition, judge what landing speed or other limitation is sufficiently safe. The personal element made the whole difference; if it had not entered into the equation, restrictive rules would be necessary. But the harsh demands of a totally unlimited speed race between ultrarefined machines in which 1 kmh might determine triumph or defeat are of great importance, for nothing finds weaknesses so quickly, and the

constructor and pilot must go all out to compete effectively. Henry Deutsch would have heartily agreed, and would have been proud that his race was meant to replace the world's first aeroplane race classic, the Gordon Bennett; in fact, the French eliminations were scheduled September 28, first anniversary of the final edition of that revered series.

When it became known that Nieuport-Astra's designer Delage was designing a monoplane for the race, unfounded rumors abounded that Spad too was secretly developing a super monoplane and that Gabriel Borel, a name honored from the earliest days of aeronautics, was updating his 1920 Gordon Bennett challenger as well. Marcel and René Hanriot were actually producing an all-metal monoplane racer with retractable landing gear! And Viscount Louis de Monge, of an old Belgian family and renowned as a propeller specialist, would soup up his biplane racer by clipping the lower wing off completely. Then tragedy struck when Count Bernard de Romanet, popular French speed ace, was killed in the de Monge racer, five days before elimination day. Hanriot withdrew on elimination day, leaving three French entries, as allowed by the rules, and thus no need for eliminations.

The contest was made international by the appearance of the British Bamel racer fresh from her first Aerial Derby triumph six weeks before, and by the giant Fiat speedplane from Italy. Except for the Gloucestershire team, Britons seemed indifferent or discouraged. Their Gordon Bennett entries of 1920 had been financed for the most part by pilots and friends; now here was the Bamel by herself, amid the excitement of the eager French team, up against a powerful French aeronautic industry basking in the generous smile of French bounteousness. Two days before elimination day Sadi Lecointe gave the world a taste of what it was up against by posting the world speed record; no aeroplane in the world could catch the lovely Nieuport-Delage

sesquiplane he flew. All competitors found the technical arrangements excellent, and it was noted that, remarkably, not a single racer had to be built on the morning of the race!

The *objet d'art*, worth 20,000 francs, and 60,000-franc *prix* was carried off by the second sesquiplane; Sadi cracked up during the race. The dearth of numbers in the tabulated results was misleading: in fact the event went a long way toward fulfilling Henry Deutsch's altruistic intentions by bringing into focus the realization that the two French crashes of de Romanet and Sadi Lecointe and the Bamel's withdrawal during the race all stemmed from analogous causes. Stick struts, piano wire, aluminum castings, and plain cotton cover had got man to 100 mph; built-up laminated struts, swaged wires, high-tensile steel plate fittings, and special linen cover had brought him to 200 mph; now designers, suddenly made wary, were given insights into what new methods might be needed to achieve even more speed. Impetus provided by the Coupe Deutsch hastened this realization. Moreover, the 1921 Deutsch signaled the return of the monoplane and the opening salvos of an intensely fought Franco-American speed duel.

The 1922 edition was again held on a Saturday, September 30, governed by the same rules and philosophy. By now there was no question it was the most important international speed race in Europe. Bristol and Gloucestershire racers were entered from England – only the Bamel appeared, however – and the Fiat returned from Italy. The French ranks were filled again; several new racers characterized by wild departures in design were known to be in the works, and among others, tailless racers enjoyed brief but intense popularity in 1922. The tried and proven sesquiplane, cleaned up from the year before and flown by Sadi Lecointe, again set a new world speed record a few days before the race. Sadi never won the Coupe Deutsch, but his personality dominated it. Once again

he cracked up during the race, but his speed for the 100 kilometers he covered was 3 per cent faster than the speed made by the second-place Curtiss R-6 in the 1922 Pulitzer two weeks later, and only 1·5 per cent slower than the winning Pulitzer R-6's best 100 kilometers.

Unfortunately only one competitor finished the course. Three entries were absent; others gave up as parts broke. Two made course mistakes. The Nieuport-Delage biplane that endured finished with a speed slower than the first five 1922 Pulitzer finishers (based on 200 kilometers). Thus, although some of the world's fastest aeroplanes attended, the Coupe Deutsch did not determine which was the fastest, and it was generally lamented as an unsatisfactory affair. In accordance with rules which specified that a competitor (constructor) winning twice in succession would win outright, the *prix* was awarded to Nieuport-Astra and it was confirmed in February 1923 that the Coupe Henry Deutsch de la Meurthe was closed.

The world speed record moved to the United States. But an American in Paris thought he could breathe new life into the idea of a satisfactory Gordon Bennett replacement.

Louis D. Beaumont

In September 1919 the Woodhouse group in the Aero Club of America launched, amid great fanfare, a Round-the-World Derby promising no less than $1 million in prizes! A small commission of club governors was established to circle the globe and lay the groundwork for what was touted to be the greatest aerial extravaganza of all time. Draped in the mantle of conservative respectability, this commission included Charles Glidden and was headed by an elderly *nouveau riche* eager to enhance his name in the halls of aviation posterity, Louis Dudley Beaumont, usually known – as James Gordon Bennett had been – as "Commodore." Curiously, neither his name nor the naval title which he would thus ennoble were strictly merited.

Louis D. Beaumont (U)

He assumed the title Commodore late in life in connection with his indulgence in yachting, and even the name Beaumont had been adapted from his original Teutonic family name Schönberg – "Beaumont" is the French equivalent of "Schönberg," translated "beautiful mountain" – during an extended stay in France. A native of Dayton, Ohio, son of a Mexican War veteran, young Schönberg found himself in Denver during the final blaze of America's Wild West period in the 1880s where he teamed up with David May, who married his sister, to open a general store which soon grew to a prosperous chain – the May department stores, later headquartered in St. Louis. Shortly before World War I Schönberg left active administration

of the firm and moved to Paris, where he changed his name, an act prompted in part, no doubt, by the rabid anti-German feelings then flaming, became enamored with wartime flying aces, and founded a sumptuous Aviation Officers Club on the Champs-Elysées.

Unfortunately, during its travels to promote the 1919 transglobal air derby, Beaumont's commission made up for its almost total misconception of aviation's capability then with self-advertising bombast, even to the extent of bringing American aviation into contempt among many Europeans. After this fiasco, Beaumont ingratiated himself with the prestigious and elegant Aéro-Club de France. The Beaumont *prix* for pure speed was first donated March 9, 1923, at the meeting of the Commission d'Aviation de l'Aéro-Club de France where Colonel Frank P. Lahm represented Commodore Beaumont[10] and agreed the competition should be held at Étampes or Istres.

Beaumont had grasped what seemed then a golden opportunity to thrust his name into posterity as successor to James Gordon Bennett and Henry Deutsch de la Meurthe. He supplied 200,000 francs, to be distributed as 150,000 francs in cash for two annual prizes of 75,000 francs each and two *objets d'art* worth 25,000 francs apiece. He entrusted the organization of his race to the Aéro-Club de France, then headquartered at 35, rue François 1, Paris, with the stipulation that government entries were unacceptable – only the private entries of constructors would be considered, after the current fashion. The club's Comité d'Aviation (Contest Committee) consisted of forty-five members, of which fifteen represented the Chambre Syndicale des

[10] Commodore Beaumont should not be confused with the French naval aviator Commander Jean Louis Camille de Conneau, who used the pseudonym André Beaumont in bringing 1911 honors to France by winning the First European Circuit Air Race – he took off June 18, 1911, in view of 700,000 – and Circuit-of-Britain air race, and who in 1914 founded FBA (Franco-British Aviation). Even *The Times* of London made this error.

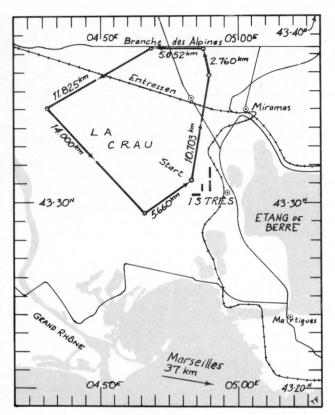

Course laid out in 1923 near Istres, France, for the Coupe Beaumont high-speed air race, competed in 1924 and 1925

Constructeurs d'Avions – what would be termed "The Trade" in England – and this scheme stimulated free discussion of appropriate procedural methods, not only to provide race rules equitable to all but to ensure direct translation of useful race techniques to the construction of new aeroplanes. By choosing the wastes of Istres (Bouches-du-Rhône) as race site, the Comité virtually ensured the race would receive no popular interest – or support. If Folland could be persuaded to send the Bamel so far, it looked as if he and Delage of Nieuport would fight it out. Despite the prize, Folland considered it an unlikely prospect.

The first race was set for mid-October 1923, a date unfortunately in the wakes of the rousing Schneider

race and St. Louis Pulitzer. Nieuport withdrew their three entries when English competition did not materialize, and only one aeroplane appeared. This was a Gourdou-Leseurre which was also withdrawn, thus canceling the race, but which flew one lap of the 50-kilometer closed course to show off its speed with its radial air-cooled Bristol Jupiter engine, a type distinctly novel for high speed in 1923. The first true competition for Beaumont's *prix* occurred in June 1924; indeed, the Beaumont was the only bright spot in the air-racing world that year. Three new French designs, all in the powerful 600-hp class, were prepared by Nieuport, Salmson-Béchéreau, and Bernard. The British Gloster I was withdrawn and others faltered but

Sadi Lecointe in his brutish Nieuport racer flew the 300-kilometer distance to win the *prix*, and did not land until he had covered 500 kilometers for a new closed-course speed record for that distance. Sadi was the only man ever to complete the Beaumont course; he did it a second time on October 18, 1925, when the air-racing world was again preoccupied with the Pulitzer (six days before) and Schneider (eight days later).

Even Commodore Beaumont himself must have lost interest by then. It was obvious that he had hardly succeeded in his endeavor to replace earlier race patrons in stature. On January 14, 1926, at its *séance* the Aéro-Club awarded the second Beaumont *prix* to Nieuport-Astra and declared the contest closed. Beaumont's ardor not only in French aviation but in France itself soon waned, and he returned to New York City, where he died in October 1942 at the age of eighty-five, leaving $15 million of his mercantile fortune to charities restricted exclusively to the United States.

Ironically the French industrialist who was perhaps air racing's greatest patron and whose name became the most widely known was a man who unlike Beaumont had not dreamt of personal veneration. His name was Jacques Schneider.

Jacques Schneider

The first flurries of activity in the 1919 race for the Prix Deutsch de la Meurthe overlapped the 1919 contest for the prestigious Schneider Trophy, held on a September Wednesday at Bournemouth, a popular seaside resort on the south coast of England. The Schneider races were strictly for seaplanes and the 1919 event was also the renewal of a stylish international air race interrupted by World War I. Its terms, borrowed from the pattern set by Gordon Bennett, required three victories within five years to gain permanent possession of the trophy, but on four occasions nations on the verge of conclusive victory were top-pled, thus prolonging the contest until 1931. Because of its longevity and a certain mystique about aeroplanes that fly from the water, the Schneider of all the early speed events evokes a particularly virile nostalgia. As the procession of Schneider races accumulated, the expenditure of national effort to contrive increasingly refined high-speed seaplanes multiplied far beyond what seemed at that time rational plausibility. This was all the more ironic since the race's patron, Jacques P. Schneider — whose identity, alone among the early air race patrons, has almost ceased to exist as a viable part of the competition he sponsored — originally donated the trophy to promote the rather mundane commercial possibilities of seaplanes, independently realized by the huge Clipper flying boats almost a quarter century later. Instead, subordination of the contest's seaworthiness aspects to the glamour of speed over its eighteen years of existence led to the ultra-extreme development of pontoon-equipped sprint planes, few of which possessed discernible commercial utility.

Jacques P. Schneider, whose father was a wealthy metallurgist and owner of the Schneider armament works at Le Creusot, was born near Paris in January 1879, and like Henry Deutsch he grew up to inhabit the elite world of French industrialists. After studying mining engineering at Janson-de-Sailly he descended into the coal mines at Courrières. Shortly afterward he met and became close friends with pioneer aviators Bréguet and Blériot. His father's wealth gave him the means to indulge in the expensive new sport, all the more exhilarating since it provided a means to emerge from the pits, and he earned his pilot license (number 409) in March 1911 at Pau on an Anzani-Blériot. A fortnight later he qualified for his free balloon license (number 181) and in 1913 with Maurice Brenaime, Schneider set the French altitude record of 10,081 meters — well over 30,000 feet! — in his balloon *Icare*.

Fond of vacations at ivory watering spots on the Mediterranean, Schneider developed an enthusiasm for unlimited racing powerboats (*canots automobiles*), but during one race at Monte Carlo on the 1910 circuit the pounding foam crumbled his rudder and flung a piece up which badly shattered his arm. For maintaining control of his boat the Prince of Monaco decorated him, but the wound left him permanently handicapped. Undaunted, Schneider became enamored with the hydrofoil (*l'hydroglisseur*) concepts of Lambert, and even piloted such a machine from Cairo up the Nile, past Khartoum to Abyssinia!

Largely due to the limited use of his arm Schneider gave up active flying but used his prosperity to organize numerous aerial competitions, from Paris to Rome, at Rheims, and at Monaco. He served as French Under-Secretary of State for Aviation and founded the Aerial League of France in 1911 — as well as the fraternal order of Vieilles Tiges (literally, the "Old Twigs") for retired aviators — but his boating activities brought into sharp focus the realization that after a decade of powered flight there had been hardly any attempt to develop seaplanes. This was nonsensical to Schneider's practical mind since 70 per cent of the globe is water, and the vast flat oceans and lakes of the world seemed to offer perfect alighting spots for the fleets of international aerial merchant ships he foresaw. Schneider accompanied Vedrines to Chicago for the Fourth Gordon Bennett aeroplane race and took the occasion of the victory banquet on December 5, 1912, to present his vaunted Coupe d'Aviation Maritime Jacques Schneider. A massive trophy was fashioned — hardly a "coupe" — on a marble base topped with a silver statue of a nude winged female — Zephyr — kissing the Spirit of the Waves. Schneider's personal influence in the competition waned, and his original motivation for its

Jacques Schneider at the wheel of his favorite canot automobile   *(MA)*

creation was hardly realized. Abed with appendicitis, he missed the 1927 contest, and while recuperating at Beaulieu-sur-Mer he died suddenly — and not in reduced means as it has become fashionable to believe — on May 1, 1928, never to know the ultimate outcome of his famous speed trophy.

Even by 1919 the portion of the contest devoted to speed was assuming paramount importance, although the flying boat type of design was still favored by the industry. But expensive and comparatively fragile new speed racers were beginning to appear; unfortunately the Royal Aero Club, hosts of the first postwar contest, had neglected to lay moorings, nor had they made any other arrangements to protect the visiting racers. Only the efforts of an odd motorboat named *Tiddlywinks*, provided by Supermarines, and George Newman, Saunders' works manager, kept the frustrated French and Italians from being totally ignored while RAeC officials floated in splendor aboard the yacht *Ombra*, "an epicurean epithalamium" provided by Claude Grahame-White's brother.

At the appointed race time of two-thirty patches of fog, now thin, now thick, were rolling in to shroud the three marking boats near Bournemouth, Swanage, and Christchurch, and visibility from the beach was down to 400 meters, obscuring even HMS *Barham* lying a few hundred yards from shore. Impatient and bored spectators shuddered in the moist air which stripped one of warmth. By four o'clock the fog had thinned, the sun was dim through dense haze, and The Needles of the Isle of Wight could just be made out, although no one bothered to check conditions at other corners of the triangular course. The French were repairing their leaky floats, damaged on the unprepared, stony beaches, when, with no warning, the race was suddenly declared on! Four of the seven entrants took to the air in confusion, some not awaiting — or not

sure of — their start signal. Presently two returned, reporting they were unable to locate the Swanage mark boat. Misfortune dogged the Supermarine flying boat, which struck submerged wreckage on takeoff and capsized upon alighting at Boscombe Pier, changing at once "from a Supermarine into a submarine!" Its pilot was rescued by *Tiddlywinks*. The lone Italian aeroplane, an underpowered Savoia S.13 piloted by a fair, young non-commissioned warrant officer, Guido Jannello, dutifully plowed around eleven times, confident of victory after all others had dropped out. But when the Swanage boat crew later reported they had never seen him, that he had apparently mistaken his course in the fog, and that his results would not count, the hot Italian temper flared. Jannello affirmed he had seen a boat carrying the red-and-white sign similar to the one at Christchurch. In confusion the British said it must have been a spare boat. Signor D. Lorenzo Santoni, President of SIAI (Società Idrovolanti Alta Italia), who had entered the S.13, issued a stern protest. Twelve days after the race the flustered Royal Aero Club belatedly recommended to the FAI that Jannello be awarded the trophy, but to their great embarrassment the FAI at its October meeting annulled the race. French aeroplane builder M. Mortane struck proud British sensibilities of fair play to the quick when he wrote of the fiasco, "Our English friends have not yet regained their customary skill as organizers — or as sportsmen."

Although there had been no 1919 winner, Jannello's plucky performance prompted selection of Italy to host the 1920 contest. To the commissaires of Aero Club d'Italia, then at 24 Via Tor de'Specchi in Rome, the ideal site for the race would be Venice, the "Pearl of the Adriatic," and a triangular course of 20 nautical miles, to be flown ten times, was drawn in front of the Hotel Excelsior across from the placid Laguna Veneta. At the FAI meeting to draft race conditions the RAeC, no doubt

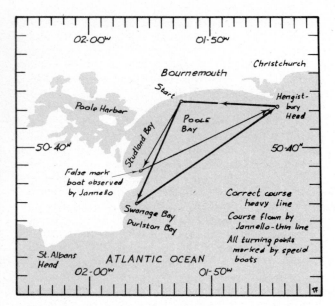

Course for the abortive 1919 Schneider Trophy race near Bournemouth on the south coast of England

considering the advantage that would accrue to their own sturdy, load-carrying flying boats, proposed that each entry be required to haul 300 kilograms "commercial weight" (unusable ballast), and this was adopted. A second proposal that entries be required to remain afloat twelve hours unattended was rejected, but the implied intention to make the contest more than just a speed race would be carried forward to varying degrees in subsequent years. After this furor over the rules the British embarrassed themselves by totally avoiding the contest; this only compounded the conspicuity of their absence noted five months earlier at the more prestigious Monaco seaplane Rallye. Elegant Monaco had been site of the first international contest between *hydroavions* as well as the two prewar Schneider contests, and the patina still graced the first postwar Monaco meet where Spads, Nieuports, and others from France vied with many Italian aeroplanes for some 160,000 francs in prizes. The Fairey seaplane, a 1919

English Schneider participant, had been entered but its pilot, Captain Nicholls, "was called to the United States suddenly," leaving the nation that boasted of its seaplane supremacy totally unrepresented. As it turned out, the 1920 Schneider in Venice was almost a complete fiasco. One Italian alone finished the course. A huge Macchi designed around the 300-kilogram ballast requirement was unable to participate but this mattered little; the aeroplane that finished, an adaptation of a wartime Savoia bomber-reconnaissance flying boat, proved adequate — although hardly a racer. The real speedplanes were then clustered in France where one week later the last Gordon Bennett race was held.

As early as November 29, 1920, at a joint meeting, members of the Society of British Aircraft Constructors (SBAC) — "The Trade" — and RAeC committee members discussed the entry of British flying boats ("among the best in the world") in the 1921 contest, but such considerations

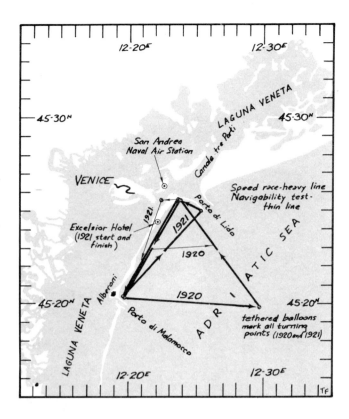

Courses for the 1920 and 1921 Schneider Trophy races, Venice, Italy

degenerated into disagreements with France over race regulations. The requirement to carry 300 kilograms was dropped, but a six-hour "fully loaded" unattended watertightness test was introduced, with the stipulation that any water taken on could not be drained! Despite the haggling these new conditions represented, no one in 1921 was yet convinced the Schneider Trophy was in fact a viable stimulant to the production and operation of financially feasible commercial seaplanes. Indeed, after the talking was done, the actual non-Italian participation — one solitary French entry — reflected the deepening economic retrenchment in England and France. Nevertheless, Italy proceeded to make the 1921 event part of a gala aeronautical occasion lasting more than a week. Venice again was race site. A

slightly smaller triangle was drawn, intended to be 25 kilometers around; sixteen laps would make 400 kilometers, considered to be a suitable distance. The actual triangle flown, however, when the balloons marking the turning points were hoisted, turned out to be some 1·5 per cent shorter.

Squadrons of Italian service seaplanes were nominated for the Schneider eliminations; surprisingly, all Savoia S.13s — similar to 1920's winner — were eliminated. But 1921 was the year of the specialized Savoia S.21, which, at 160 mph, was doubtless the year's fastest flying boat. Jannello, Italy's 1919 Schneider hero, was assigned to fly it but fell ill. His backup, Signor Guarnieri, flew the aeroplane extensively in other events but had engine trouble on Schneider

elimination day. Thus the race was robbed of any real speed interest and again lapsed into a one-man show; two faster planes faltered en route and in an aeronautical version of the tortoise-and-hare fable, an ancient war-horse Macchi M.7 alone chugged across the finish line in what a visiting French pilot termed a "*valk-vaire.*" Except for the 1919 race annulment, Italy would have earned the trophy outright at that moment . . . but history sometimes works in devious, inscrutable ways. Actually the meet enjoyed a far more interesting race, the Gran Premio Venezia, which took place August 9 and 10, requiring two days for two categories: *velocità e trasporte*. Eight of the designated Schneider aeroplanes participated (numbers 2, 4 and 6 through 11). Buonsembiante won the speed event at 198 kmh in an exciting finish after two hours' flying, just beating De Briganti (the Schneider Trophy winner) at 196 kmh and Falaschi at 194 kmh. More air races continued through the following week, including the fairly insignificant and misnamed Grand Prix d'Aviation and various rallies.

The International Sporting Club of Monaco had organized in April 1921 another seaplane meet featuring a long-distance "race" designed to stimulate aerial postal services between France and Corsica. Italy was present in force, the Italian Schneider pilots getting plenty of practice, but as a race meeting the event was a farce and was the last Monaco Rallye.

Despite their seeming monopoly in speedy seaplanes, Italy was not idle in 1922. Giovanni Pegna was hard at work on his highly imaginative speed designs and Savoia, buttressed by the addition of clever Alessandro Marchetti, was turning out entirely new speed designs. The world's fastest seaplane that year was his Savoia S.51, which was expected to reverse the firm's frustrating bad fortune and win for Italy their third and conclusive Schneider victory. After two years of Venetian flavor the race venue was

shifted to Naples on Italy's west coast, where the waters of Golfo di Napoli lapped softly against Castello del'Uovo and a brilliant Neapolitan sun bore down relentlessly, blindingly on the swarthy Italian aviators. As in 1921 the FAI specified a distance of 200 nautical miles but the animated Italians — according to their official race program — again intended a full 400 kilometers (8 per cent longer); the final distance as flown was 200·2 nautical miles, comprising thirteen laps of a triangular course that started at the small gulfside air station, proceeded south along the coast to Capo di Posillipo, then turned to cross the gulf, the pilots keeping the smoky cone of mighty Vesuvius 20 degrees to port, with another sharp turn around the mark balloon at Torre del Greco to return across the gulf to Naples. Savoia's top designer prior to Marchetti's arrival, Raphael Conflenti, had gone to France, where the government increasingly smiled on aviation, but his two CAMS-built flying boats, owing to labor unrest in Italy, were not delivered to Naples. It began to look like a depressing repeat of the previous two years, the Italians being left without competitors.

Spurning any aerodynamic revolution in 1922, the English firm Supermarine resurrected an ancient hull, indeed hardly different from their 1919 Schneider entry. It certainly did not look like a racer. Napier pitched in with an engine as did Shell and Wakefield Oil with their products, for in England Schneider entries were distinctly private affairs, and Supermarine's effort was a decided risk. The Italians unaccountably moved the race date up two weeks, and had it not been for the timely diversion of a steamer already bound for Naples the British challenger would not have arrived in time. It was fortuitous that he did. The resulting race was extremely exciting; in effect the entire future of the Schneider Trophy hung on the ability of the English pilot Henri Biard, who ended up the only

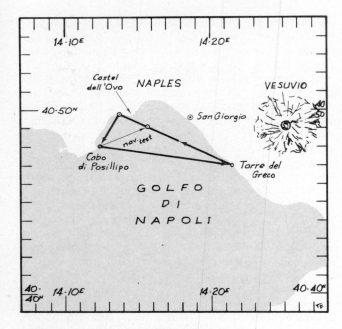

Course for the 1922 Schneider Trophy race,
Naples, Italy

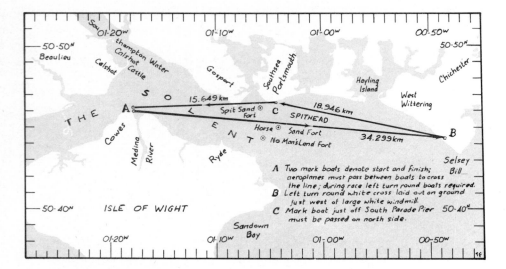

Course for the 1923 Schneider Trophy race
adjacent to the south coast of England near
Southampton

non-Italian entry and thus must win. Moreover, for the first time all three Italian entries finished the course, even exerting an irksome team effort against the Englishman, who had to use all his tactical cunning and flying skill to succeed – and just barely. The vaunted S.51, suffering from a faulty propeller which forced it to throttle back, finished just two minutes off Biard's pace – after almost two hours' flying. It later set a decisive world seaplane speed record. But Biard's performance, which incidentally opened the FAI record book on class C *bis* (seaplanes), had ended the Italian phase of Schneider history.

The next phase belonged entirely to the U.S. which in 1923 came to Europe and with a flourish took the Schneider Trophy away. Jerome C. Hunsaker,[11] famed designer of the

[11] In 1924 Hunsaker would be assistant naval attaché at the U. S. Embassy in London; during the 1930s he became president of the Goodyear-Zeppelin Company. His name is inseparably linked with the Massachusetts Institute of Technology (MIT).

Navy's 1919 transatlantic NC flying boats, now reiterated the philosophy expressed by fellow academician Edward P. Warner that the air race had become a legitimate means to stimulate high-speed fighter design and development, and he urged the Navy to become directly involved in the Schneider as indeed they had already become involved in the Pulitzer. The Navy in 1923 owned superlative Curtiss racers, with which they pushed the world speed record to almost 270 mph that year, direct design outgrowths of the intense Army-Navy Pulitzer rivalry of 1922; certainly, the military-industrial pattern having been established, it seemed only logical to apply the same approach to the Schneider.

Thus the pattern was set; the United States had purchased their aeroplanes before the race. France was giving financial assistance to the manufacturers of competitors completing the course; they would appear in 1923 with a first string of two sleek "fair weather" flying boats and a second

string of two slower, twin-engine "foul weather" boats which might fly the course unopposed if the weather turned bad. The best England could do was a paltry Air Ministry offer to purchase the *winning* airframe, if entirely British-designed, -owned, and -built, and not a previous winner – minus engine – for £3,000. Race conditions had now consolidated into the familiar navigability test, water-tightness test, and speed test. The former required contestants to taxi two distances of ½ nautical mile at better than 12 knots; the aeroplane would be immediately moored to a buoy and left unattended for six hours to complete the second requirement. The only adjustment allowed before the next day's speed test was a propeller change, and in 1923 the world-famous Reed prop became the first metal prop used in air racing. Initially *Flight* magazine of London suggested a course across the English Channel touching both France and England; *l'Auto* of Paris concurred in what seemed a clever means to enhance the

race's international character. But the site finally chosen was the Solent, the strip of water between England's south coast at Portsmouth and Southampton and the Isle of Wight. Later, when the apparently rough-water-sensitive Curtiss racers appeared, some wished they had stuck to the Channel idea. The course length had to be within 10 per cent of 200 nautical miles; the final distance was 186 nautical miles, flown in five laps.

The U. S. Navy was on hand a month early to practice, their aeroplanes housed in the sheds of S. E. Saunders at Cowes in a self-confident, remarkably open manner quite unlike the spirit Sam Saunders recalled from the "prewar Monte Carlo days when everybody was suspicious of the other." C. G. Grey wrote, "The American organization was beautiful . . ." The imposing USS *Pittsburgh* soon appeared to lend inspiration. The only English entry to get airborne for the race, Biard, did 12 mph better in his souped-up 1922 winner, but he "could not get out and push," and "hopelessly outclassed," he was far too slow for the U. S. Navy.

Their win was a sensation which took the stunned English completely by surprise. The extent of English complacency was indicated by the graph on page 572 of the September 27 issue of *Flight*, designed for the spectator's thumbnail use in computing lap speeds — but the graph extended only to 170 mph! Both American CR-3s were well off the scale for every lap except the first, which involved taking off opposite to the course direction; indeed, they flew fully 30 mph faster than Biard. What the British did not comprehend was that even as they had for years smugly nurtured their scorn for America's paltry aeronautical war contribution — virtually nil compared to the great quantities of fighting planes poured by England into combat — this very factor, the relative vacuum in American technology at war's end, forced originality in U. S. postwar racers. The United States now brought to Europe convincing evidence of superior technology: the low frontal area wetsleeve monobloc engine — "astonishing" wrote W. H. Sayers, technical editor of *The Aeroplane* — the metal propeller, the wing radiator, the successful twin pontoon design, the perfection of detail not only in aeroplanes but in teamwork organization that must henceforth be copied by those serious about winning.

The inevitable impact of this rude American intrusion must have been sensed even by many of those tradition-bound Englishmen who found the U. S. *modus operandi* repugnant. *The Times* of London editorialized haughtily, "British habits do not support the idea of entering a team organized by the state for a sporting event." This, however, seemed curiously contradictory to the blame heaped upon their own government just weeks before for the absence of significant state support for their own emaciated team. Beyond that, it was folly to expect a frontier of technology, which the Schneider was rapidly coming to represent, to be

pushed outward without the corresponding means to build organization, to muster and coalesce the best from an ever broadening industrial base, a process which could only come about from expenditure of resources far greater than private investors could afford no matter how noble or altruistic their pure sporting objectives might be. Each new advance in the technology uncovered problems increasingly complex. Eight days after the Schneider a Navy racer won the 1923 Pulitzer at almost 250 mph.

As for mounting a Schneider challenge in 1924, even *The Times* predicted it would take a whopping £25,000 just to send a British expedition to the States. Where was this money to come from? The glum and apparently inevitable prospects were that no "sportsmen" would step forward with private money.

It was also somewhat silly to begrudge the U. S. Navy efforts in 1923. The D-12 engine resulted from the tenuous success of C. M. Keys's tenacious and bold policy at a time when U. S. government support was distinctly — and painfully — scant. The winning plane was of 1921 vintage, not 1923; indeed, it had been taken from storage and refurbished to race. Under the impetus of air prophet Billy Mitchell the U. S. government was persuaded to promote competition in 1922 and during that year alone U. S. industry built more racers than England had built in her whole history. It was only natural to put the best of this technology to an international test. The time was gone when the Schneider Trophy race was simply a rich man's game. It was rightly a crucible, a laboratory for progress, for proving and improving, and W. H. Sayers, recognizing as did many that the entire nature of the race had been irreversibly altered, urged after the U. S. victory in 1923 that the "precedent of the U. S. government should be followed by other governments . . . [for the] good of international relations and technology."

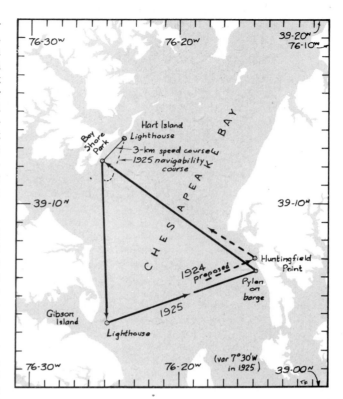

Course for the 1925 Schneider Trophy race southeast of Baltimore, Maryland; course proposed for the 1924 race (later canceled) is also shown.

Dissenting English voices quickly took on the decidedly unpleasant taste of sour grapes.

To many Royal Aero Club members, however, the loss of the Schneider Trophy from the club foyer was particularly tiresome since it had become the club hatrack for members on their way to the bar![12]

Elated by their victory, the United States began laying immediate plans to host the 1924 race. An early and

likely site was Long Island Sound, but during February 1924 the NAA Contest Committee, 1623 H Street NW, Washington, responding to the energetic persuasiveness of Baltimore Flying Club president R. W. Alexander, awarded the race to nearby Baltimore. More specifically, the race site would be Bay Shore Park, an amusement park and beach 14 miles southeast of the city, owned by the United Railways & Electric Company, a streetcar line. It was famous for its long causeway, a giant pier which could accommodate 10,000 people. The Flying Club would provide canvas hangars, wooden slipways, electricity, and tools for the visiting race teams, and the streetcar line in what was certainly a shared arrangement would charge a modest

---

[12] The Americans also noticed that the rounded *derrière* of the statue's nude winged female had taken on a brilliant silver sheen decidedly in contrast to the tarnished dark surface of the rest of the statue. It seems that bar-bound members would lovingly pat their trophy in the most inviting place in addition to hanging their hats on it!

admission from the thousands who would line the beach. Since only one dead-end road ran to the park there would be little advantage to those in cars seeking a free view in what early aviators called "hedge tickets." The racers would fly over an almost equilateral triangle, first proceeding south across the estuary of the Patapsco River along Lake Shore Beach to a lighthouse a mile off the south tip of Gibson Island, then turning left and crossing Chesapeake Bay to Huntingfield Point, then crossing back again to the judge's stand at Bay Shore Park. All confusion with nautical miles was dropped by the Americans, who, as they had done for the Pulitzer, adopted exact metric dimensions: the triangle was surveyed to be exactly 50 kilometers around and seven laps would yield 350 kilometers, well within the 10 per cent of 200 nautical miles stipulated earlier — and so it would be for *all* remaining Schneider Trophy races.

Italy, who after their early postwar successes had curiously avoided the 1923 race, was almost frantic in renewed preparations for 1924. They had purchased examples of 1923's best aero engines from England and the United States and four aeroplane manufacturers were at work. Conflenti had returned from France. Pegna was active. Macchi and Savoia, the renowned firms, were producing new designs. General A. Guidoni, director of aircraft construction, even had his own personal design built (it failed). In England the RAeC had started a charity drive, "it being quite obvious we cannot expect any help from the Air Ministry." But the Air Ministry surprised them and ordered two seaplanes, one each from Supermarine and Gloster. Only the Gloster had reached the flight test stage by late September, little more than a month before race day. The U. S. Navy team was in serious training, even to the extent of avoiding the Pulitzer that year — all eggs went into the Schneider basket. Dave Rittenhouse, sporting a flamboy-

ant new moustache and eager for win number two, slammed over the Long Island Sound speed course in the 1923 Pulitzer winner, now on floats, at almost 230 mph — unheard of for a seaplane.

Then the Italians faltered and the lone Briton crashed. Suddenly there was no competition for the United States and it looked as if they would achieve their second leg on the trophy with a walkover. The United States was indeed ready to race despite the costly loss of one of their own team racers, the Navy-Wright. But with exceedingly rare magnanimity the Baltimore Flying Club early in October, in a gesture that without doubt must rank as the most generous in Schneider history, canceled the race. The RAeC immediately cabled "warmest appreciation for this sporting action."

In 1925 the British mounted a massive effort. Once again the Air Ministry ordered two aeroplanes, one each from Supermarine and Gloster, paid for out of the experimental fund "for technical development." The Schneider Trophy committee formed in the RAeC at once adopted an attitude of almost comic secrecy. It was true that the new aeroplanes, built to Air Ministry order as experimental types, then *loaned* to the constructing firms, were still subject to the Official Secrets Act, a fine turn of bureaucracy; yet what began as a perfectly innocuous and rational situation was soon being overoperated by the inevitable overzealous time-clock punchers. Commander Jack Towers was still the shrewd American air attaché in London, however, guaranteeing that the United States, according to the popular euphemism, was "perfectly instructed." *The Aeroplane* magazine made a couple of good guesses about technical matters which threw the Air Ministry into a small fit. Preoccupied with the tactics of preserving this vacuous security, the English allowed a major strategic blunder to occur: apparently because the Air Ministry had ordered only two aeroplanes, only

two entries were filed for the race! Later, when the British team sent four aeroplanes to the States, normally comprising a full team of three plus one reserve, only two would be allowed to race. R. J. Mitchell of Supermarine and H. P. Folland of Gloster, designers respectively of the sleek new S.4 monoplane — literally Britain's white hope — and Gloster racers, accompanied the team to America. The S.4 was a definite design departure in Schneider annals and its pilot, Henri Biard, who had already flown it to the world speed record for seaplanes, was expected to post his second Schneider victory.

In a turnabout, Macchi *privately* supported the brave Italian effort of 1925. The 1924 Italian fiasco made the Italian government wary of participation in 1925 although they did loan Macchi the well-tested U. S. engines bought previously. Mario Castoldi, like Mitchell in England, produced a cantilever monoplane but retained the flying boat form. The *Minnewaska* from England and *Conte Verde* from Italy, each carrying their respective national entries, sailed for America the same day, September 26, one month before the race.

In the United States 1925 was the year of the Curtiss R3C, a joint Army-Navy project. Two participated in the last Pulitzer race which preceded the Schneider by just one and a half weeks, but their failure to exceed 250 mph around the pylons as landplanes left the United States deeply disturbed, even though the aeroplane had done 285 mph in sprints as a landplane unofficially. The Army's R3C won the Pulitzer piloted by Cy Bettis; it would now be up to his backup pilot, a short, husky man named Jimmy Doolittle, who would race the plane in the Schneider after it was hurriedly put on floats (an *Army* aeroplane on *floats*!).

The race was held over Chesapeake Bay at Bay Shore Park, the same site selected for the canceled 1924 contest; the turning points had been altered slightly, but not the distance. But

a year had not seen any noticeable improvement in accommodations. The aeroplanes were housed in flimsy tents, leaky and cold, and when the weather turned foul so did British tempers. This was certainly nothing to compare with the superb Saunders facilities at Cowes which had generously seen to every need of the Americans on their 1923 visit to England. C. M. Keys of Curtiss had to agree. He called conditions "execrable." The American racers arrived just days before the event, but the Europeans had been on hand putting up with the misery for three weeks. Despite the forced and frustrating inactivity the British decided not to uncrate their reserve planes and this later proved to be a tactical mistake. Then the almost continual storms climaxed with stiff easterly gales which caused considerable damage and delayed the race two days. The distraught Britons saw their high hopes crumble; in fact they had come essentially unprepared since neither Biard — who crashed in his lovely S.4 before the race — nor Broad, the Gloster pilot, had sufficient opportunity to become familiar with their high-strung racers. Moreover, the British were to a large extent using inferior equipment: sheet-type Reed props, whereas the U. S. racers were equipped with the improved forged type; Lamblin radiators, whereas the United States was already three years ahead with their skin radiators; external fittings, whereas Curtiss used internal fittings throughout. Bert Hinkler, the second Gloster pilot, cracked up in his belated attempt to qualify the first reserve. The waters of Bay Shore Park became the waters of Babylon for Britain. The two flying boats of Italy, too, were obviously outclassed, but their pilots remained brave and high-spirited.

Doolittle's flying was immaculate and he won the race decisively. The two Navy R3C entrants fell by the wayside with failed propulsion components. Only De Briganti crossed the start line for Italy in his Macchi, to finish a poor third behind Broad's mediocre second. For his triumph in what was then considered the "most interesting air race" in the United States, Doolittle was elevated to the status of national hero. Yet, in spite of their ill fortune, the foreign monoplanes were a portent: Doolittle's R3C was the last biplane to win the Schneider Trophy. By now all of the great land-plane races of the world had terminated. If the United States could sustain their momentum they would terminate the Schneider race as well.

English reaction was stated by Sir Samuel Hoare, who said, "We are all sorry we had such bad luck in the race, but we shall not give up trying, and I intend at once to take up the question of next year's entry with the British constructors, whom I hope will see the way to enter on their own resources." He urged private enterprise to take the gauntlet, but conceded that if "there is no other way of securing a British entry for next year's race, I shall be prepared to consider again the loan of Air Ministry machines under the same conditions as this year." C. G. Grey echoed the call, seeing the challenge in far broader terms: "Now is the time for the British aircraft industry to make its great effort to capture the world's aviation as in the past we captured the world's sea traffic in the shipbuilding trade . . . The mass mind of humanity is moving toward aviation and now is our opportunity to make use of that psychological momentum." Clearly the Schneider Trophy had come to represent the most visible single mark of aeronautical omnipotence to a proud seafaring nation like Great Britain.

However, in America, a virtual aviation depression had deepened between the years 1923 and 1925. An increasing amount of publicity was being given to the impending crisis in the federal aviation program, a program which C. M. Keys of Curtiss more accurately described as "non-existent." Billy Mitchell had gone further: he called it "criminally negligent" and for this he would pay. His more

politically suave opponent, Admiral Moffett, had adroitly outmaneuvered him, but Mitchell, martyred on the pillar of air power, tried his cause at his celebrated court-martial in the fall of 1925. The boulder he heaved into the stagnating pool of aviation caused waves that washed over even the feet of remote President Coolidge, the same frugal Coolidge who once revealed his impatience with the heady new phenomenon when he uttered, "Why can't we have just one aeroplane and let the aviators take turns flying it?" but who now grudgingly accepted the need for a government policy that would both sustain and stabilize the industry. On September 12, 1925, one month before Mitchell went on trial, Coolidge announced the appointment of an investigating board under the chairmanship of his old friend Dwight Morrow. Many members of this board received their first aeroplane ride when flown to Mitchel Field to witness the Pulitzer race in 1925, a year when the total Air Service budget was $65 million. The Morrow Board recommended three separate five-year production programs to nurture the prodigious infant. The first had to do with civil aviation and resulted in the Air Commerce Act of May 1926; the second, directed to the Navy, was recommended to begin in June 1926; and one month later the third, for the Army. Billy Mitchell resigned January 27, 1926, into waning years of vociferous impotency, his vision of a Department of Defense overseeing separate heads of Army, Navy, and Air to recede, awaiting a later day. The sixty-ninth Congress authorized $164 million for defense in 1926 as a result of the Morrow Board recommendations.

Nevertheless this new appropriation contained no provisions to continue Schneider Trophy efforts. Thus it was not surprising that the Navy attitude toward the trophy had undergone a distinct transformation. Far from the magnanimity that characterized their generous cancellation in 1924 when no competition materialized, the Navy

now realized that had they claimed the trophy with a fly-over, permissible by the rules, America's 1925 victory would have been decisive, retiring the trophy forever. Now the Navy, its policy guided by tough-minded Assistant Secretary Edward P. Warner, determined to make the 1926 competition the last come what may. Curtiss, too, was deriving little measurable business from the Schneider effort. Their R3C represented the culmination of their racer development, and was thus a perfectly logical point to end the series.

Meanwhile, England could not bring herself to forgive the United States for causing such acute embarrassment in 1923 with the D-12 engine even as her best engineers frantically used it as the basis for improved engines of their own. But such development work would take time. Air Vice-Marshal W. Geoffrey H. Salmond, Air Member for Supply and Research, suggested the RAF take over responsibility for the next Schneider team, but the Chief of Staff, Trenchard, demurred, restating on December 29, 1925, that service machines and pilots should *not* be entered for "private" races. Samuel Hoare, Secretary of State for Air, believed the Schneider was a "special case," and that for the RAF to order "experimental" aeroplanes would be justifiable support for the English effort. But all this was based on a *1927* race. It was considered hopeless to mount a challenge in 1926. When the U.S. NAA on December 12, 1925, announced the 1926 Schneider race would be held October 24 at the huge naval base at Norfolk, Virginia, Geoffrey Salmond snapped, "It is almost impossible to imagine an international trophy of this nature being competed for by one nation alone in the absence of other entries." [13]

[13] He might have tempered his words had he foreseen 1931, when his own country did just that to post their third and conclusive win despite Italian challengers already in the works — and which later proved faster. But that is beyond the scope of our story.

Vestiges of the past, misgivings, and nostalgia variously provoked European delegates to the FAI conference that opened January 11, 1926; shrill voices were raised denouncing the new direction the Schneider was taking, leading to the production of nothing more than "racing freaks," seen by some as impractical, good for nothing but a sprint of dangerously high speed, failing to recognize that even if this were so, the *engines* built to power such freaks could just as easily be installed in far different aircraft types. In a sense it was true that the evolving racing seaplane was no longer able to negotiate Jacques Schneider's *plein mer* in the manner originally envisioned; by 1926 *plein mer* meant any sheltered bay with water a little too salt to drink. To counter this design trend, Italy, supported by France, suggested imposing a ballast requirement of 250 kilograms on contestants and increasing the distance to 500 kilometers. But America saw this as an ill-disguised attempt to disqualify the Curtiss racers and objected vigorously. Great Britain, though they had no racing planes afoot that year, and though they might have been sympathetic to efforts designed to render America — two legs up — impotent in 1926, misread the American resolve to end the series that year and so joined the United States in rejecting the idea since their own racing designs were on the lines of the light Supermarine S.4. Thus, through their smug self-confidence, they left themselves wide open. The race would be run as before.

The English were supremely confident the Americans would *postpone* the race until 1927; after all, who would go through the "farce" of a fly-over? But on this point, too, the U. S. delegate, Jerome Hunsaker, was adamant. There would be absolutely no postponement. The event would be run and done with, period. The English were dumbfounded. The Royal Aero Club went through a formality of officially informing the United States they would be unable to compete, hoping this would somehow "shame" the Americans into a postponement, but the Americans were totally unmoved by the nuances of such useless protocol. America's persistence in her plans to stage the contest brought English cries of bad sportsmanship which, in view of the recent 1924 gesture, seemed especially bad manners. Director of English Civil Aviation Sir Sefton Brancker then made a personal pilgrimage to American shores to bring his obdurate powers of persuasion to bear on the United States for a postponement. Meanwhile, in England Sammy Saunders and Colonel Whiston A. Bristow, earnest and patriotic, each offered a considerable private investment together with a racer design. This vastly relieved Trenchard because the emergence of private efforts meant the RAF could wash its hands of the affair. But the Air Ministry, supported by the SBAC at a Royal Aero Club meeting March 19, to the consternation and bewilderment of Saunders and Bristow, adopted a harsh attitude quite opposite to the encouragement they expected. It was rather forcefully pointed out by Marshal Salmond himself that theirs were futile efforts, and England's only hope, with America so close to total victory, was somehow to buy time for Supermarine and Gloster to prepare. Thus there could be no hint of a challenge now because a challenge would definitely mean a race.

Imagine then the shock and consternation that erupted in the tranquil club lounges like a bomb bursting when Brancker returned not only empty-handed but with the news that the Americans *had* received a challenge — from Italy! This gave the Americans the green light to stage more than a fly-over. The Italians had been deeply wounded by some derogatory remarks regarding their 1925 effort at Baltimore, and it was understandable they wanted to go another round. But how could the Italians hope to compete with the Curtiss racers? Their aeroplanes in 1925 had been powered with aging, hand-me-down Curtiss-built

engines and were fully 60 mph slower than what was predicted necessary to win in 1926. Not one factory in Italy was then doing airframe or engine work that could remotely be adapted to successful Schneider racers, and the race was only nine months away! The disconsolate Royal Aero Club began laying plans to capture the world speed record with their racers, which should be ready in 1927, in order to mitigate the obvious prestige America would gain from winning the trophy permanently. What they did not realize was that another government was entering the fray full blast: Benito Mussolini had given the order that the Schneider Trophy must be won by Italy *at all costs*.

Macchi and Fiat launched a concerted campaign estimated to have cost the Italian treasury the equivalent of almost $1 million in order to produce an entirely new Schneider Trophy racer. The Macchi M.39 which resulted, powered by its new Fiat engine, a veritable Italian *macchina nervosa*, could not have been produced so fast without the aerodynamic and propulsion base line already consolidated by the year 1925, and in a sense it represents the culmination of those efforts. The feverish work took place under the new director of aircraft construction, General Verduzio of SVA fame; General Guidoni had been posted to England as air attaché. The new Macchis had teething troubles and the United States generously set the race back three weeks to allow the barely completed Italian team time to establish themselves in Norfolk. This short delay was also welcomed by the Americans. Lieutenant Commander Homer Wick, as in 1925, had been named team leader but soon found himself presiding over disaster. Two of the Navy's three first-string pilots were killed in air crashes just weeks prior to the race. Admiral Moffett stepped in and pilot reassignments continued up until the very moment of the race itself.

Bad weather caused another two-

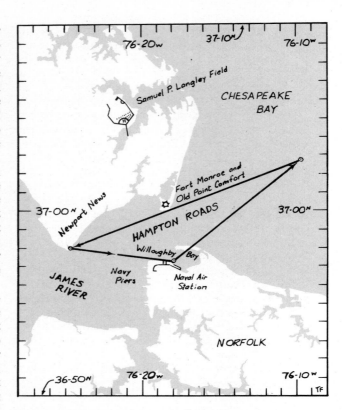

Course for the 1926 Schneider Trophy race near Norfolk, Virginia

day postponement. Both sides suffered mishaps in the navigability trials, those to the United States being of more serious consequence: they lost one entry and had a second seriously damaged. Finally race day itself dawned; the brilliant weather was all one could hope for and tens of thousands lined the beaches at Norfolk, Newport News, and Old Point Comfort hoping for a glimpse of the blazing red and blue aerial scimitars as they slashed around the pylons. An ancient HS2L "fire ship" flying boat patrolled the course over congested Hampton Roads. Odis A. Porter of Indianapolis was on hand with his "extremely delicate" electric chronograph, good to one four hundredth of a second, and Monroe calculator to time the most hotly contested and thrill-packed Schneider race in the long series. He

also would mark some new speed records along the way. The United States, not expecting so formidable a challenge, had made for themselves a "race within a race" by equipping their three R3Cs with different engines and props. Unhappily the results were inconclusive since only one R3C finished the entire Schneider distance — Doolittle's largely unaltered 1925 winning aeroplane, which posted a strong second place. An M.39 won for Italy and glasses were raised in rousing tribute at Norfolk's Hotel Montecello that night.

The Schneider Trophy went back to Europe to stay forever. The scientific and industrial methods man needed to achieve his best pre–World War II performance were now at hand, needing only refinement, and an era of speed seeking had passed into history.

AN ERA OF TECHNOLOGICAL INNOVATION

4

PROPULSION – THE HEART OF THE AEROPLANE

The engine

As Henry Deutsch de la Meurthe had envisioned in the nineteenth century, progress in man's flight would parallel his ability to provoke, control, and quench huge fires at will. Thus at the very heart of every aeroplane is its engine, a device so fundamental that the histories of aviation progress and engine power-to-weight bear a virtual one-to-one relationship. The phenomenal spurt in man's speed frontier that occurred during the first half of the 1920s can be related directly to the vast growth in this power-to-weight ratio; by 1925 man had with prodigious effort reached a high plateau on which his aero engines for the first time produced one full horsepower for every pound of weight. It was at essentially this level that man remained – with few short-term exceptions – for more than fifteen years, and history demonstrates that subsequent significant performance improvements awaited the gas turbine, the power source that relatively recently broke the sustained 1-hp-per-pound barrier.

Evaporated gasoline together with oxygen is a mixture normally to be avoided; even inside a closed chamber its shattering qualities demand caution, and so it was with the cylinders of early internal-combustion engines. These were made from heavy, stiff cast iron, and had the valves necessary to admit and expel the explosive mixture side-mounted to avoid its hardest blasts. This arrangement prevented sufficient squeeze of the mixture, however, leading some obscure but highly courageous engineer to place the valves directly on top. The first commercial internal-combustion engine was produced in 1860 by Jean Joseph Étienne Lenoir, a Belgian living in Paris. Soon the growing popularity of automobiles provided the impetus for further internal-combustion engine development, with the emphasis more on improving the engine's mechanical durability than reducing its weight, and the cumbersome engines that for years took early aeroplanes aloft were little more than transplanted automobile engines. Some efforts had been made to use lighter metal for the cylinders. Aluminum was tried — it was one of the lightest metals known — but unreinforced, it proved too weak. Instead, steel cylinder barrels had come into use, bolted individually onto the traditional rigid, heavy, cast-iron crankcase. Surrounding each cylinder, welded into place, was its own steel jacket in which the cooling water circulated. This fairly dependable arrangement worked well enough and to many it became apparent that the auto engines of this style perhaps best adapted to aeronautical use were produced in Germany by Mercedes. The outstanding features then — a line of individual steel cylinders in one vertical row or two rows forming a V, well cooled by water, and equipped with totally exposed overhead valves, characterized the Mercedes and its many imitators, which included the Rolls-Royce and famous American Liberty engines.

Other profound but far more obscure improvements added to the aero engine's early evolution; among the most important and yet most frequently overlooked are the *hemispherical combustion chamber*; the associated *inclined overhead valves*; and the *spur gear train* (and *double* overhead camshafts) to drive them. These innovations, so

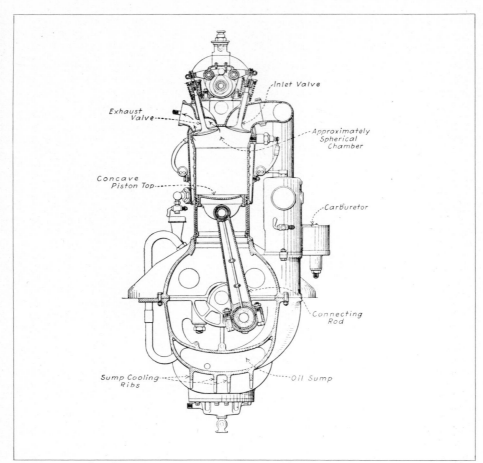

Pre–World War I Mercedes aero engine, ancestor to many important wartime and postwar types

advanced that their widespread use would be delayed for years, did not originate with Mercedes as is widely believed, but were in fact pioneered in France, appearing first on pre–World War I Peugeot engines, which could still pass for *grand prix* auto racing engines of 1970! The very human story behind these quietly momentous evolutionary steps, which has baffled and frustrated automotive historians for years, involves four men — "three mechanics and a draftsman" — all considered "imposters" by the smug diploma engineers of their time. The

"three mechanics" were Frenchmen Georges Boillot and Jules Goux, and Italian Paolo Zuccarelli, famous prewar auto racing drivers; the "draftsman" was the controversial Ernest Henry, a Swiss engineer born January 2, 1885, in Geneva, educated at École Technicum there, an intense, very reserved, delicate, almost frail man with a mass of dark hair, a man of old-school severity too honest to be successful, who died in bitterness and poverty on December 12, 1950. After his schooling, Henry worked for Picker-Moccand et Cie., at Chêne-

Bougeries near Geneva; interestingly, Lucien Picker produced a type of cylinder head and combustion chamber for which Harry Ricardo was later credited. Henry moved to Paris in 1909 to work for a Picker branch office under M. Jatte after the parent company folded.

Meanwhile, Marc Birkigt, also from Geneva, had founded Hispano-Suiza in Barcelona in 1904. When later political instability made him briefly consider moving his firm to Italy, he sent a trusted aide, Louis Pilleverdier, to Milan on a survey; Pilleverdier returned with a shaggy, puppy-eager but incisively intelligent mechanic, Zuccarelli, who became fascinated by Birkigt's technical ideas, and who soon distinguished himself as a *voiturette* racing driver. In a four-cylinder (typical long-stroke T-head) Hispano-Suiza he won the Grand Prix des Voiturettes at Boulogne-sur-Mer in 1910, beating two Peugeots driven by Goux and Boillot. At this point Birkigt decided to deemphasize racing and move his factory instead to Paris. Thus, in 1911, Zuccarelli left Birkigt to join Peugeot, a giant firm then indulging lavishly in prestige racers unlike Birkigt's dwarf firm (and in a neat switch, the Italian convinced Pilleverdier to come over with him!). The three inspired, audacious drivers became fast friends — all were twenty-six — and inevitably became convinced that they, with practical driving experience and mechanical expertise learned on the track, could design and build a true *grand prix* auto superior to anything the formal engineers, heavy with congealed theory and prejudice, could produce. They undoubtedly had avant-garde mechanical ideas but were unable to translate them in a valid physical manner. It would take the meticulous and imaginative Henry, who by coincidence joined Peugeot at the same time as Zuccarelli, to render the resulting mix into a practical mechanical entity. From their collaboration an engine emerged that has been hailed as

Image labels: Inlet Valve / Exhaust Valve / Approximately Spherical Chamber / Concave Piston Top / Carburetor / Connecting Rod / Sump Cooling Ribs / Oil Sump

phenomenal — the classic racing engine.[1] How much of the final product was contributed by each of the participants? No one will ever know.

Robert Peugeot first had to be sold on the plan of his independents. He agreed — but hedged his risk by staging a contest among many designers for a car worthy of the Grand Prix de l'Automobile-Club de France to be held at Dieppe, 1912. He also demanded that all calculations of his independents be checked by his Engineering Center at Sochaux, a proud group who came to resent bitterly *les Charlatans* — "Oh, how they hunger to find errors in my work," lamented Henry from his bedroom where his drawings were made. Their 7·6-liter car at 185 kmh beat one designed by Ettore Bugatti (whose style Peugeot preferred) to win Peugeot's contest for patronage, and it went on decisively to win the Dieppe Grand Prix, beating a 15-liter Fiat and providing a milestone in racing history. Similar Peugeots employing the remarkably advanced *Charlatan* features went on to score international successes, including their second consecutive *grand prix* in 1913 and the 1913 Indianapolis 500, thus causing a veritable revolution in American racing engine design still apparent in, among others, the Miller-Offenhauser engines of a half century later. Curiously, perhaps because of their working methods, Peugeot did not capitalize on or try to protect the *Charlatan* features, freely selling his racing cars to anyone.

Zuccarelli's untimely death in 1913 *grand prix* practice coupled with the advent of war disbanded the team. Pilleverdier became director of Peugeot's aero engine factory where Ernest Henry designed a *Charlatan* V-8 aero engine, a truly advanced but unsung affair. Beginning in 1915, four hundred

were produced to power Voisin fighters, but the military soon standardized on Birkigt's simple single overhead cam Hispano-Suiza (Peugeot built 8,060 under license) and Henry's engine disappeared. The *Charlatan* V-8 was perniciously labeled "a failure" and Henry, ostracized by the entrenched engineers, left Peugeot. He worked briefly with Société Barriquand et Marre on a sixteen-cylinder Bugatti aero engine that was a "colossal failure,"[2] then joined Ernest Ballot to build spirited cars that would be challengers in some of the world's great auto races. Louis Coatalen of Sunbeam-Talbot — Darracq earned Henry's lifelong bitterness for adopting some of his ideas on Sunbeam aero engines, so successfully that many believe Henry worked for Sunbeam. He never did. His fellow engineer Marc Birkigt, a friend despite their different social levels, provided sanctuary for Henry during World War II, his first and only direct contact with Hispano-Suiza. Marc Birkigt, who so overshadowed Henry, lived until 1953.

The common synonym for excellence in quality was for decades the name Rolls-Royce, a name which carried an eminence originally achieved not by brilliant inventiveness but through the infinitely painstaking handcraftsmanship of Frederick Henry Royce. Born a miller's son in south Rutlandshire, young Royce grew up as poor as any Dickens urchin and tramped for jobs through the ugly industrialism that sprawled across nineteenth-century England. Until she died his aunt financed his short apprenticeship to a locomotive works; other dreary jobs followed, and when just of age he set up a business as an electrician with Ernest A. Claremont in a shed on Cook Street, Manchester. His arc lamps, electric cranes, and dynamos for cotton mills and ships for a while were selling briskly, but an economic slump coupled

with his refusal to cheapen his product forced him to look elsewhere for business. Spare-time tinkering to improve his secondhand French Decauville automobile soon led to his construction of three experimental cars. Enter the Honorable Charles Stewart Rolls, son of Lord Llangattock, born to leisure and wealth, schooled at Eton and Cambridge, but devoted to progressivism and speed. Rolls advanced from undergraduate cycle racing to motor and balloon racing — he was a lively twenty-four (fourteen years younger than Royce) when he helped found the Royal Aero Club in 1901, and held pilot certificate number 2. He also held, together with fatherly Claude Johnson, a fellow organizer of the Royal Automobile Club, the franchises to sell several established makes of cars in London.

In need of wheels one evening, Rolls borrowed the little Royce car. He was amazed at its wonders and with characteristic zest routed Johnson from midnight slumber to demonstrate the marvelous machine. At once he gave up all other makes to acquire exclusive selling rights — and the firm of Rolls-Royce was born. The cars that followed set the fashion: rugged, quiet, complicated with many intricate parts but always beautifully running.

Royce's austere appearance resembling the academician belied his lifelong suspicion of scholarly qualifications. His life existed entirely on the shop floor, where he was an intolerant perfectionist but able to extract the fullest measure of that intense loyalty peculiar to the British spirit. Yet Royce was not creative in the original sense. The most important facet of his work was his ability to improve details where others had left off. Years later, when being lionized for his engines at the height of the Schneider Trophy air races, he firmly declared, "I invent nothing; inventors go broke." Forgetful of meals, of the clock itself, Royce severely and repeatedly overtaxed himself, suffered an operation which left him semi-invalided, and though he

Frederick Henry Royce (F)

kept his house near the sea at West Wittering, Chichester, he spent his winters at Le Canadel on the French Riviera. The memory of young Charlie Rolls was dimming; Rolls had crashed to an untimely death on his modified Wright Flyer at Bournemouth in mid-July 1910, only one month after

---

[1] Henry provided four valves per cylinder, not for the esoteric engineering rationale of optimized valve area and minimum inertia reciprocating machinery later ascribed to him, but for the more prosaic reason of simply providing a backup in case one valve failed!

[2] A type, however, later adopted and built by Peugeot in 1923!

making the first round-trip aerial crossing of the English Channel. Royce survived to be knighted in 1930 and lived until 1933.

When World War I started the Admiralty prodded Rolls-Royce to produce "official" Royal Aircraft Factory Renault-originated rotary air-cooled engines in quantity, but Royce balked, severely critical of their cast-iron cylinders and generally poor design. Just three weeks before the first guns sounded, the top three spots of Europe's largest 1914 *grand prix* auto race had been won on a circuit near Lyon by three German Mercedes cars, all of which were powered by adaptations of the latest German water-cooled aero engines; the fact that they had Junkers fuel-injection pumps instead of carburetors had been a well-kept German secret. One racing car had been sent to a London showroom by the smug Germans for a window display, but had to be hastily hidden in a cellar when hostilities suddenly erupted. A stern search by the Royal Navy eventually located the car; it was dispatched at once to the Rolls-Royce factory at Derby, where its engine was carefully tested, torn apart, and every piece studied. Thus it transpired that the earliest Rolls-Royce aero engine — the Hawk — was modeled directly from the Mercedes. To Royce's credit, he improved the basic features of the Mercedes engine, yet the Rolls-Royce Falcon which powered hundreds of Bristol "Brisfit" fighters, and Eagle engines which powered the transatlantic Vimy of Alcock and Brown, like most wartime and early postwar water-cooled aero engines, were little more than updated Mercedes types.

In the United States the situation in the main was worse as automotive interests grasped aviation by the throat in what almost became a death grip. First to feel the clutch was Orville Wright's factory, sold together with his patent rights to a syndicate in 1914 after he was left stranded by his brother's death two years earlier.

Rolls-Royce Eagle IX engine, typical of Mercedes-influenced designs of the early 1920s
(F)

In 1916 the Wright factory was merged with Glenn L. Martin to form Wright-Martin Aircraft Company; the same syndicate also owned the Simplex auto factory, hence the auto connection. Next in line was America's second-oldest aircraft factory, Curtiss, a substantial piece of which was acquired by auto baron John North Willys. But the most grave threat was posed by Dayton-Wright Aeroplane Company (which had no connection with Wright-Martin although Orville Wright acted as consultant), organized in 1916 as a subsidiary of General Motors expressly to win big wartime orders. Two groups controlled it. The first was known to insiders by the misleading sobriquet "Ohio hicks," and was led by National Cash Register Company (the "Cash" to all Daytonians) general manager Edward Andrew Deeds, from Granville, Ohio, a Cornell-trained electrical draftsman, owner of Moraine Farm near Dayton. His group included GM's Charles F. Kettering and Harold E. Talbot, Sr., a Dayton banker and builder, and Jr. Deeds and Kettering

were already millionaires from Dayton Engineering Laboratories Corporation — Delco — which they had formed. The second group, the "Detroit gang," was headed by Hudson Motors' H. E. Coffin, and included Packard's chief engineer Jesse G. Vincent and vice-president Sidney D. Waldon. Coffin, spark plug of the budding Society of Automotive Engineers, had infiltrated the War Department (for $1 per year) and made the Washington connection. In 1917 he was named chairman of the powerful wartime Aircraft Production Board and appointed Deeds to head the Board's Equipment Division. When Deeds became a "swivel-chair colonel" firms in which he owned stock began to receive fat cost-plus contracts. Dayton-Wright was ordered to build thousands of aeroplanes; although the concept of an aeroplane using heavy battery ignition was ludicrous, all must use Delco ignition, as stipulated in blatant government contracts written by Deeds. Kettering's annual salary alone from these enterprises rose to $110,000.

Together this group of sometimes ruthless opportunists thoroughly exploited Washington's lack of confidence in the nation's raw and untried aviation manufacturers. It was a bald attempt on the part of the auto men to secure a total monopoly in aviation production, and the hard-pressed, inexperienced military managers then were unable to see the disastrous flaws in bloated guarantees that tens of thousands of combat aeroplanes would soon "blacken the sky." Hundreds of millions of dollars were appropriated, huge factories were presumptuously built on the "expectation" of obtaining large aviation production orders, factories which later proved useful for postwar auto production, and the situation smelled very badly of at the least favoritism if not outright scandal. It all might have gone well for the shrewd manipulators had not unforeseen technical problems compounded, leading to delay in engine deliveries, panic, and excuses. What resulted was a monumental debacle; for the government's vast aviation investment, only a pitifully few mediocre-quality products ever dribbled to the war zone. John D. Ryan of Anaconda Copper, named head of the Bureau of Aircraft Production when the Air Division was removed from the Signal Corps, replaced Deeds and reorganized production by giving contracts to aeroplane men like Glenn Martin, Grover Loening, and Chance Vought. Some decent planes began to appear. But too late — the war was over. A Senate investigation (the Thomas Committee) dredged up buckets of testimony, and accusations of criminal conspiracy were inevitable. Jurist Charles Evans Hughes,[3] a Republican bent on discrediting the Wilson administration, wanted to have Deeds and Vincent court-martialed, but Secretary of War Newton D. Baker applied

[3] Later Chief Justice, United States Supreme Court.

liberal amounts of whitewash and said no.[4]

It was the same Jesse Vincent who as legend has it was locked *incommunicado* for six days in a room of Washington's Willard Hotel with Elbert J. Hall, not allowed to leave until they had designed the aero engine with which America was expected to win the war — the Liberty. What they came up with was in fact a 285-hp V-8, a hodgepodge of ideas filched from Packard and Hall-Scott (Hall's contribution was mainly a decent rocker arm) which needed extensive revision to make it into a more practical, mass-producible, decent-sized 400-hp V-12. Even so, more than three thousand new tools, jigs, and dies were required to build it. The first completed Liberty — which embodied Mercedes principles almost entirely — was set up in July 1917. Some 22,500 were ordered even before it passed a fifty-hour test, but by April 1918, one year after the United States had entered the war, only four had been shipped overseas.[5] By the end of 1918, after the war was over, 17,935 Liberties had been produced. Major George E. A. Hallett, who headed

[4] Indeed, Warren G. Harding, President of the United States 1921–23, was an "Ohio hick." During the year prior to his inauguration, when he was an Ohio senator, Deeds had returned to the Aircraft Production Board, again in charge of production!

[5] Roland Rohlfs made probably the first flights ever powered by a Liberty engine, which was first installed in an ungainly Curtiss biplane operating from the Niagara River. On one occasion, after making an uneventful landing and approaching the dock, he cut the switch, expecting to coast to a normal stop. But six of the twelve cylinders, because of pre-ignition, kept firing. "Helpless to turn, I yelled at the men on the pier to ward off the wings," Rohlfs recalled. "The upper wing was about four feet above the pier and as the steadily approaching craft drew near, the men leaned forward to grasp the wing and ease the shock. However, it never reached their outstretched hands. The long pontoon, sticking out in front, struck the dock and bounced back. The overbalanced rescuers in one long line took a dive into the water. Colonel Hall, the co-designer of the Liberty engine, witnessed this hilarious performance."

Marc Birkigt   *(MA)*

the Army Engine Section for a time and nursemaided the Liberty, remembered it "cracked spark plugs like popcorn"; it had no exhaust-valve cooling, gears split, heads warped, but the Liberty — simply because it was there — went on later to power the first transatlantic and round-the-world voyages by aeroplane, the transcontinental U. S. Air Mail, rumrunners during Prohibition; and 6,500 built in Britain powered World War II tanks!

Meanwhile, in France — where, during World War I, anyone who could run an aero engine twenty-five hours without overhaul received from the builder a case of champagne — work

was progressing on a remarkable engine which from 1919 would dominate aviation's speed frontier for three years. Forged in the crucible of war, it represented for its time the ultimate in aero engine evolution, and perfection of its technical merits can be traced to the focal dissimilarity in the working methods of the two cardinal engineering personalities of the period, F. H. Royce and Marc Birkigt.

Birkigt, born in Geneva, Switzerland, in 1878, had been a designer of intricate mining machinery in the late 1890s when he left his homeland to work with a Spanish mining company near Barcelona. Whether harsh politics repulsed him or some warm romance

beckoned him is indefinite; in any event he undertook to design an auto which would give reliable performance on the rough Spanish roads, and formed Hispano-Suiza (which means "Spanish-Swiss") to build it in Barcelona. When exhibited in the 1906 Paris auto salon it excited such interest that Charles Faroux urged Birkigt to build the car in France, and in due course a second factory was opened in an abandoned streetcar shed in the Paris suburb of Levallois. Racing versions were built to earn prestige, and by 1913 Hispano-Suiza had consolidated its long and brilliant reputation for excellence. Birkigt's famous automobiles established themselves auspiciously among the *grand marque* of luxury cars during the Edwardian and Vintage periods of motor history. The Hispano-Suiza factory in Paris was soon producing beautiful engines for these cars, but in "bloc" form — that is, instead of bolting individual cylinders onto a crankcase, hollows for all cylinders were simply bored out from a single chunk of cast iron.

At war's outbreak Hispano-Suiza like Rolls-Royce received the bureaucrats' request to build rotary engines under license, and likewise refused. Instead, Birkigt's Paris factory was turned over to the French Gnôme company and he returned to Barcelona. It was there, in September 1914, that his creative genius as an inventor shone: not content merely to modify existing concepts as Royce had been, Birkigt conceived in a brilliant flash of ingenuity how to marry aluminum and steel to make the engine far lighter, yet improve its rigidity and retain the heat-resistant properties of steel cylinders. He fashioned the first "monobloc" aero engine — but now the block was cast aluminum, properly bored out, into which he screwed forged steel barrels (or liners) with exceedingly thin walls *threaded along their entire length*. The cooling water flowed through ports hollowed in the block, but never touched the steel cylinder liners directly, leading to the term "dry liner." Two such blocks containing four cylinders each and mounted at right angles comprised one V-8 engine; a light crankcase was hung underneath the blocks, and the vertical overhead valves and their single overhead camshaft — of which Birkigt was a keen exponent since it eliminated pushrods and rockers — were enclosed and protected inside oil-tight covers. Birkigt's radical departure from traditional aero engine development was an engineering tour de force.

The V-8 Hispano-Suiza when it appeared for its first tests in 1915 ran with such remarkable efficiency, a decided rarity in those days, that even Joffre was persuaded to overcome his strong prejudice against non-French war material, and the Hispano-Suiza aero engine was adopted officially by France that December, reaching the Somme Front early in 1916. Several variants were produced, but in the main the engine had 719 cubic inches displacement (cid) and produced 150 hp (valve modifications later allowed 180 and finally gearing allowed up to 220 hp) for a weight of slightly more than 400 pounds, as compared to the 160-hp Mercedes which had 901 cid and was 200 pounds heavier. More significantly, casting was quicker than welding, and the trim Hispano-Suiza comprised only four hundred parts to the Mercedes' more than nine hundred! The Hispano-Suiza soon became the most important Allied engine on the Western Front and was extensively mass-produced, 150 per day being disgorged by fourteen firms in France and seven elsewhere: in the United States (Wright-Martin, later Wright Aeronautical), England (who called it the Wolseley Viper), and Italy. In Europe, however, careful handiwork by patient, skilled craftsmen was a way of life that did not always mix with impatient Yankee machine-tool, mass-production methods, and it soon became distressingly apparent that Birkigt's original engines were superior not because of simplicity but because of fanatic precision in maintaining their

Hispano-Suiza modèle 42, as seen from rear; carburetors were mounted vertically in V formed by cylinder blocks; cylinders were fed by pipes from carburetors, then exhausted outboard. (MA)

exceedingly close tolerances. Although more than 50,000 wartime Hispano-Suizas were built, its reproduction proved to be fairly difficult. It took the Americans fully thirteen months to reproduce a satisfactory Hispano-Suiza, and although several thousand were eventually built, no American-produced example was used in combat.

By 1917 the 180-hp Hispano-Suiza was no longer powerful enough, so Birkigt set to work on a 300-hp V-8 (he enlarged the bore and stroke each 20 mm); the new engine displaced 1,127 cid, weighed a compact 605 pounds, and was known by Hispano-Suiza as the modèle 42. Although the Armistice prevented extensive combat use, it became important as powerplant for all important French and some key English speedplanes through 1922. Despite its flawless aluminum blocks enameled under pressure and threaded cylinder liners of hardened "nitralloy" steel, it never worked quite as well as its little brother since dry liner

cooling became more critical with the enlarged bore. It could not tolerate overheating, and raising compression markedly lowered reliability. Nevertheless its secure grip on the world speed record for three years eventually lulled France into allowing postwar development to languish. The next major step in aero engine technology was taken in the United States.

A clever engineer named Charles B. Kirkham had built motorcycle engines with his brother at the turn of the century at Bath, New York, a few miles south of Glenn Curtiss' home town, Hammondsport, and fashioned aero engines in 1910 before becoming chief engineer of the Aeromarine Plane & Motor Company. Lured in spite of meager and infrequent pay, Kirkham transferred to take charge of engine development at Curtiss, his imagination fired by the new monobloc idea. Interpreting Wright's sudden production of the Hispano-Suiza design in the United

Charles B. Kirkham (S)

States as a dare to build something better, he began at once. His new engine would be in V-12 form, which in itself was then considered unorthodox because prevailing opinion held that a fighter engine should be short to allow a close-coupled, maneuverable aeroplane. But Kirkham already saw in 1916 the beginning of the trend toward pure speed and he desired to couple high volume to low frontal area. So urgently did he undertake his work that he became almost obsessed with the notion that all mechanical and metallurgical problems would somehow vanish before his resolve.

Kirkham made two important modifications to the Hispano-Suiza monobloc idea: (1) he greatly reduced the size of the aluminum blocks so that only the very tops of the steel cylinder barrels (now called sleeves) were threaded and screwed into the blocks; and (2) by mounting below the blocks a massive, hollow aluminum casting which contained the water passages and crankcase in one unit, he allowed the cooling water to come into direct contact with virtually the entire length of the steel cylinder sleeves. This accomplishment in an aluminum monobloc engine was truly a master stroke of engineering, and wetsleeve construction became a milestone. His marvel was called, appropriately, the K (for Kirkham)-12.

The K-12 also employed, somewhat after the *Charlatan* design, double overhead camshafts – one each for inlet and exhaust valves – which allowed the exhaust valves (two per cylinder) to be on the outside for unimpeded escape of the burned mixture, resulting in the long row of exhaust stubs which became a trademark of Curtiss-powered aeroplanes. The prototype was tested Christmas, 1917, and first flew July 5, 1918, in the 18-T Curtiss Triplane which had been especially designed around the engine – also by Kirkham, lest his engine be wasted on some unsuitable aeroplane! The twelve cylinders of the K-12 displaced 1,145 cid – only 1·5 per cent more volume than the eight cylinders of the Hispano-Suiza *modèle 42* – but for almost identical swept volume it was capable of well over 400 hp wide open, and weighed under 700 pounds.

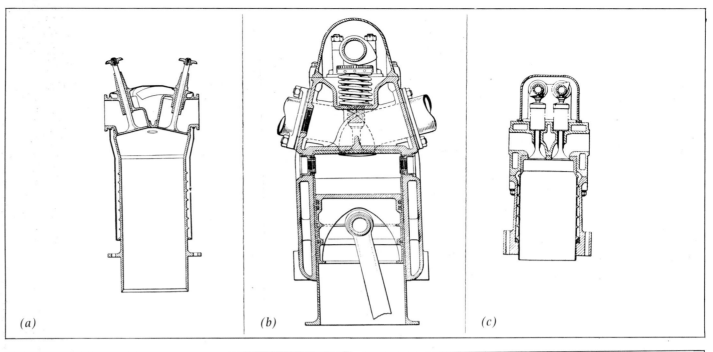

(a)   (b)   (c)

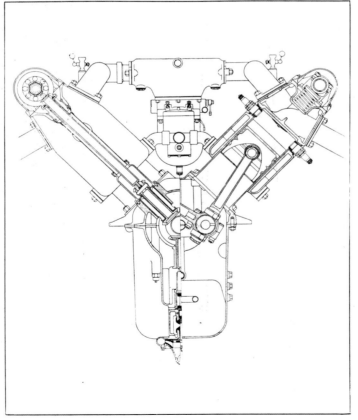

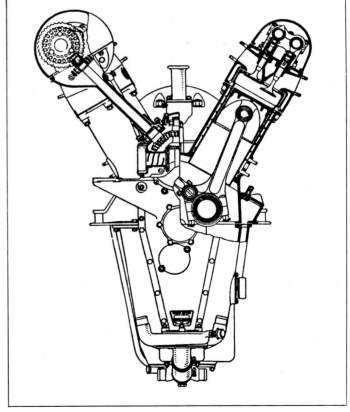

(Top) *Evolution of the aero engine cylinder through the 1920s: (a) shows the Liberty engine cylinder, bearing strong similarity to the early Mercedes; (b) shows the revolutionary Hispano-Suiza cylinder in which the thin steel barrel (or sleeve) is screwed into the aluminum block along its entire length; water passages in the block do not permit water to contact the sleeve; (c) shows the evolutionary Curtiss wetsleeve construction in which only the top of the sleeve is screwed into the block; the bulk of the sleeve below is thus available for direct contact with the cooling water. Note the overhead cams in the Hispano and Curtiss cylinders.*

(Bottom left) *Cross-section view of complete Hispano-Suiza aero engine*

(Bottom right) *Cross-section view of Kirkham's milestone, the Curtiss K-12*

The potential superiority of the aluminum monobloc engine was ignored in the United States in 1918 and its developers were unable to divert any of the millions then being poured into the safe, traditionally designed Liberty engine. After the close of "the war to end all war" military interest in experimental projects dropped sharply, but Kirkham was not ready to quit development of his K-12. He was up against the opposition of Curtiss boss John N. Willys, however, who felt unable to justify the money required since no production contracts were then likely. Their bitter disagreement caused both Kirkham and his assistant chief engineer Thomas S. Kemble to leave Curtiss in April 1919, and Kirkham's name was subsequently abolished from Curtiss products. Kirkham formed his own company on Long Island, not far from his former employer, and continued to design and consult on a host of aeroplanes and engines for years.

Meanwhile, Clement M. Keys, in 1919 a Curtiss vice-president, while on a European survey witnessed some spirited French attacks on the world speed record with the 300-hp Hispano-Suiza *modèle 42*. He was convinced the K-12 was inherently better and upon his return he advised strongly that its development not be suspended.

Despite its success the K-12 had three problems. The huge aluminum crankcase casting did not lend itself to disassembly for maintenance; it was also somewhat complicated to manufacture and subject to problems with porosity and warping which resulted in far too many misruns at the Buffalo foundry of Alcoa (Aluminum Company of America) where it was produced. The four-bearing statically balanced crankshaft was unreliable and broke often. And the reduction gears — then considered a necessary evil because the wooden clubs used for propellers in those days could not turn very fast — were constantly breaking or seizing.

The next step was called C-12

Curtiss C-12, 1920 — the Gordon Bennett engine. Note cooling fins on oil sump at bottom of engine. Prop shaft in raised position because of gearing. (S)

(Curtiss-12), designed under Finlay Robertson Porter, Kirkham's successor. The single large casting was eliminated by making the wetsleeve mounting and crankcase separate and bolting the two pieces together, but the castings were still large and prone to porosity; a running engine would often drip hot water which had oozed through the porous metal! A new crankshaft with no counterweights and seven bearings was adopted, but engine length remained the same, thus each bearing surface was smaller. New twelve-cylinder magnetos were provided, replacing the older "double-6s," so that if a magneto failed all cylinders would still retain one functioning spark plug instead of one complete bank of cylinders being lost as before. The troublesome reduction gears remained since there seemed no way then to eliminate them, and they would all too often lose their teeth.

The C-12 was tested during the spring of 1920, produced 427 hp at 2,250 rpm, and proved itself durable — but there was no market. Willys and

Porter both quit Curtiss to enter the burgeoning automobile business, leaving Clement Keys to take over the reins, and his enthusiasm saved the C-12. It was installed in the two Curtiss-built Gordon Bennett racers but the treachery of the aeroplanes prevented the C-12 from showing what it might truly do. And the Hispano-Suiza remained supreme for speedplanes.

Arthur Nutt, a serious apprentice who had joined Curtiss five years before to help test engines, now at the age of twenty-six, suddenly found himself chief motor engineer with the heavy responsibility to prepare an engine capable of meeting current military specifications so that Curtiss might begin to enjoy some sales. Nutt's first cautious step was to derate the high-strung C-12 and throw away the troublesome reduction gears; this resulted in the CD-12 (Curtiss-Direct-drive-12), which was ready for testing early in 1921. Derating paid off: the new CD-12 became the first Curtiss engine to pass the stringent fifty-hour

Direct-drive Curtiss CD-12, 1921 (S)

test; moreover, with a compression of 6·1 (quite high for those days) it achieved 405 hp at only 2,000 rpm. The two 1921 Curtiss Navy racers were ordered as beds for these engines and Curtiss pinned their hopes on military sales since the civilian market was glutted with cheap, surplus Liberties.

Although the military was interested in the CD-12, it too had weaknesses. By far the most serious was that Porter's seven-bearing crankshaft, though superior dynamically, had given far more trouble than Kirkham's four-bearing design because the bearings were too narrow. Young Arthur Nutt now had two alternatives: (1) adopt a K-12 four-bearing crankshaft, which would be the quickest and cheapest way to deliver an adequate 375-hp engine, the military's request; or (2) retain the preferred seven-bearing arrangement and redesign a longer crankshaft to provide enlarged bearing

Arthur Nutt (Au)

surfaces – but this would also require a complete redesign of the cylinder block as well since the cylinders must be farther apart. It was a tough spot to be in. Nutt was well aware of Curtiss' plight, their urgent need to come up with a salable engine fast. But he also had a feeling of what the engine could be . . . After some hard and searching wrestling with himself the young engineer made the difficult but vastly more redeeming choice. Desks were cleared, fresh paper taped to boards, and feverish shop work launched by the Curtiss gang, whose dedication earned Nutt's unlimited praise. Within weeks Nutt's brand-new lengthened seven-journal crankshaft was drop-forged at the Wyman-Gordon Company in Worcester, Massachusetts, and twelve weeks after the first line went on paper, the gleaming new engine was ready. Because it somehow seemed apt, it was called simply D-12.

Suddenly the formula was right. Curtiss was quickly inundated with military orders; the D-12 triumphed at the 1922 Pulitzer race, its first public appearance, and was soon hailed as the speed champion of its day. Its cardinal achievement came in 1923 at the Schneider Trophy race, where it turned the smug condescensions of many Europeans upside down. The sun had set forever on the pioneering Mercedes and Hispano-Suiza engines and the Curtiss wetsleeve aluminum monobloc now represented a true technical watershed, an engine form which would have profound influence on future aviation progress, even until the advent of jet propulsion. When the D-12 first bulled a Curtiss R-6 racer steeply into the sky, all the basic engine components had been devised. The final steps remaining to be taken in order to define the World War II liquid-cooled aero engine were merely ancillary: improvement in reduction gearing to allow higher engine rpm; addition of a durable supercharger to provide higher cylinder pressure; development of better fuels to allow higher cylinder pressure to be used; perfection

Curtiss D-12, 1922. Frontal area has been reduced virtually to the minimum. (S)

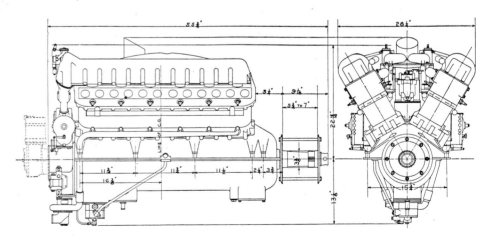

Curtiss D-12 engine, section views

of high-temperature coolants to reduce radiator size; and perfection of salt-cooled valves. These developments were hastened by speed seeking, in large measure by the later Schneider Trophy machines which were descended directly from the Curtiss racer/D-12 combination. The clear superiority of the basic D-12 formula, power-to-weight (only 1·1 pounds per horsepower as early as 1925) and, even more important for speed, power-to-frontal area, forced Great Britain to return to the liquid-cooled engine for their Hurricanes and Spitfires of World War II: the first operational liquid-cooled fighters in their inventory — with one insignificant exception — since the S.E.5!

As the Hispano-Suiza and then Curtiss engines matured in sequence, hastened by air racing and speed seeking, corollary developments contributed. Much of the engine's success depended on the wondrous device which vaporizes the liquid fuel and mixes it with air in just the right amount, then delivers it evenly to the cylinders — called *carburetor*. Differences in temperature, humidity, fuel quality, and with aero engines altitude, vastly complicated the carburetor's task, and as engine speed increased there came a point where it simply gave up. The commonly used carburetors such as those built by Henri Claudel or the large Zenith firm would begin to protest above 2,300 rpm, whereas the remarkable new Stromberg carburetors designed by Frank C. Mock[6] were still behaving

[6] Mock in fact initiated the first double-barrel, double-float-chamber Stromberg carburetor for the D-12 engine at the Curtiss plant on Nutt's own drawing board! The Curtiss foundry made the castings, which Mock took back to Stromberg in his suitcase for machining. Mock's colleague, Leonard S. "Luke" Hobbs, who is sometimes credited erroneously with the carburetor design, no doubt worked on it. He left Stromberg, however, to become engineering manager of Pratt & Whitney in 1936 where he later led development of the R-1830 Twin Wasp and J-57 jet engine, for which he received the 1953 Collier Trophy.

decently at 2,600 rpm and more — which, because of prop tip-speed limits was far above a feasible maximum flight rpm — but such bench tests heartened designers because certainly they hinted that a suitable margin of rpm existed, and held the hope that the engine would be ready to turn faster when propeller improvements allowed it.[7]

This was very important during an era when other means to increase power output still seemed far in the future. The most severe limitation in those days was imposed by the poor quality of fuel available. The most widely used, termed D.A.G. (Domestic Aviation Gasoline), had an equivalent octane rating of no more than 55, although the word "octane" itself would remain unknown for years. Compressing a fuel-air mixture containing this gasoline to 18 per cent of its original volume, corresponding to a compression ratio of only 5·5, caused serious detonation, referred to then by the euphemisms "kerosene knock" or "pinking." To open the throttle wide often made the engine pound so hard the porcelain in the spark plugs would fracture or worse, the pistons would begin to cave in! To boost the compression ratio to values of 6 or more (only half that of many of today's ordinary automobiles) required "doping" the fuel; picric acid or similar substances were occasionally used, or good "varnish removers" which ranged from aniline to xyloline. These tended to take out detonation's peak hammer blows, lower the burning pressure inside the cylinder, and sustain it longer. Alcohol was tried as a fuel with moderate success; it has only half the intrinsic heat content of

[7] The pressure carburetor — an engineering jewel containing a fuel pump and vacuum in its own sealed atmosphere — did not appear until 1938, when Malcolm Philip Ferguson, then general manager of Bendix Products Division, is credited with perfecting it. Ferguson became Bendix president in 1946, just after World War II, during which his marvelous carburetor was credited with saving countless lives.

gasoline, thus resulting in higher fuel consumption, but its high latent heat of evaporation meant that engines could handle richer mixtures without exceeding temperature limits, and this tended to make alcohol attractive for racing engines. It was not plentiful or cheap enough to be feasible for widespread use. The most popular fuel additive to thwart detonation during the early 1920s was a plentiful, cheap, aromatic compound called benzole (or, in the United States, benzol), a by-product from the coking of coal, a process required in steel production. The source of benzole's punch was suggested by its contents: about 75 per cent benzene with 25 per cent xylene and toluene, the latter important in the manufacture of the explosive TNT. A fuel blend containing D.A.G. with at least 20 per cent benzole was necessary to run compression ratios near 6, the percentage of benzole required going up as compression went up. Some racers in the mid-twenties when compression ratios began to exceed 7 burned pure benzole, but its abrasive emory powder-like carbon residue was intolerably high and engine life ridiculously short. Moreover, instant evaporation promoted rapid and severe carburetor icing. As early as 1919, laboratory tests of an alcohol-benzole mixture allowed knock-free compression ratios of up to 8·2, seeming to offer strong encouragement for the future, but this represented a plateau until the introduction of the most remarkable fuel additive of all, tetraethyl lead, later in the 1920s. Meanwhile, in the United States, the important Cooperative Fuel Research (CFR) program between 1921 and 1926 involved every major oil producer and many universities, which set up laboratories devoted to fuel improvement. This contributed mightily if indirectly to speed seeking.

Since fuel quality limited engine compression, there was little immediate incentive to apply to speed seeking the engine's most promising accessory: the

supercharger. Nevertheless its development proceeded rapidly during this period. Since air density diminishes with height, the aero engine's power output falls off dramatically as altitude is gained — maximum output is reduced to half at 18,000 feet — and the supercharger was at first seen as only a device to maintain sea level pressure at high altitudes. It is interesting to consider the odd theory then prevalent that low compression ratios were better suited to low-altitude flying of all forms — including racing — and since it was thought that Army planes flew high while Navy planes flew low, the Hispano-Suiza engines used in early air races such as the 1920 Gordon Bennett were naval "type Marine" versions with compression of only 4·7. Although these Hispanos had high-lift cams (*grande levée de soupapes*) for better breathing, especially at higher revs, the idea that low compression was somehow suited to air racing was soon demolished. By decade's end, when fuel quality permitted it, racing engines were supercharged to pressures far in excess of sea level pressure for vastly higher power output at sea level.

How best to increase the pressure inside the cylinder? An *impeller* rotating inside a shrouded casing would squeeze the fresh intake air before packing it into the engine. How best to turn the impeller? It might be done directly from the engine by means of gears. But engineers knew that much unused energy was expelled from the engine exhaust pipes, and to one or two astute observers it appeared this energy could somehow be harnessed for the job, seemingly in the manner of lifting oneself up by the bootstraps. Why not place a *turbine* (nothing more than a windmill) in the exhaust stream and let this turbine in turn drive the impeller? Such a device would add to complexity and weight. Would the advantage to engine performance justify it? Dr. Auguste Rateau of the French Académie des Sciences thought so, and during early World War I he tested his first exhaust-driven turbine, designed to whirl at no less than 30,000 rpm, the maximum allowed by the then available steels. Since in air combat the combatant with superior height generally commands the situation, Rateau's fervent hope was to have a "surprise in store for the Germans," even though he was aware that independent work along similar lines was being carried out in other nations.

Shortly after the United States entered the war in 1917, Dr. W. F. Durand, then chairman of the National Advisory Committee for Aeronautics (NACA), engaged E. H. Sherbondy of Fergus Motors Company, Newark, New Jersey, and bearded Dr. Sanford A. Moss of General Electric Company, Lynn, Massachusetts, working completely independently, each to design a supercharger for the Liberty engine. Sherbondy had gained broad experience with marine turbine design at De Laval Steam Turbine Company, Trenton, New Jersey, while Moss's employer, GE, had done its first work on centrifugal compressors (impellers) in 1903 and by 1920 was making $1·5 million annually from the sale of both single- and multi-stage compressors. Confidence in Rateau's then highly advanced work influenced both designers to proceed with turbo-supercharger development, as it came to be known. Moss worked exclusively with the turbo scheme, employing a centrifugal impeller designed to deliver pressure equivalent to two atmospheres, and in which the critical need for proper cooling was recognized, even at the expense of engine changes. Sherbondy, on the other hand, preferred not to tamper with the basic engine and proceeded on two fronts: a turbo system plus a gear-driven design. B. F. Sturtevant Airplane Company in Boston also favored gears and had built a gear train whose output was ten times engine crankshaft speed, but the enormous stresses on gear teeth and terrible difficulties with bearings forced both Sherbondy and Sturtevant to abandon geared superchargers. They

would not be made trouble-free until the 1930s.

Meanwhile, extensive ground testing of the turbo-supercharger, including a trip by Moss's group to the 14,000-foot summit of Pikes Peak, Colorado, during September and October 1918, gradually cured many persistent mechanical ills, and although the device might have been ready for combat in 1919, none were delivered before the Armistice. The pace of work then slowed. Development of Moss's system, which now was the survivor, had proceeded under the military cognizance of Jesse Vincent, Thurman H. Bane, and Rudolph W. Schroeder, who made the earliest supercharged high-altitude test flights beginning late in 1918.

The amount of charge to the engine was indirectly regulated by a "waste gate" in the engine exhaust manifold which could be opened to spill part of the exhaust overboard rather than direct it against the turbine; as altitude increased, the waste gate was gradually closed. In the early systems the turbine was mounted between two bearings and located directly on the nose, its diameter facing into the wind. It still ran cherry red, far too hot. Development was turned over to E. T. Jones at McCook Field, who removed one bearing and remounted the now overhanging turbine edgewise, flush with the side of the aeroplane where the wind could flow past it. This mounting worked so well it was common twenty years later on the heavy bombers of World War II. Jones's bearing was now good to 34,000 rpm, and the turbine typically turned at 20,000. The compressed air heated by the impeller still tended to cause detonation, sometimes cracking spark plugs, a difficulty which led to the development of mica plugs. John Macready made the first high-altitude flights of Jones's updated system in a modified French LePère aeroplane at McCook Field, and became involved in a Franco-American duel for the world altitude record. Macready was still

testing superchargers in 1925 (notably on the second production Curtiss PW-8 during March when he operated easily at almost 31,000 feet).

Meanwhile, on the other side, in a move that augured importantly for the future, James E. Ellor came to Rolls-Royce from the Royal Aircraft Establishment in 1921 to work on superchargers at the recommendation of A. J. Rowledge. Thanks to Ellor's excellent work the later Rolls-Royce Buzzard and Kestrel engines were able to make the first use of supercharging in Britain. At the same time, the United States Air Service ordered from GE in Schenectady, New York, seventy type T single-stage turbo-superchargers which could maintain sea level pressure at 20,000 feet, followed by an order for fifteen more in 1924 rated to 35,000 feet. By 1926 practically all operational Air Service engines had superchargers. Although used for pure speed seeking by decade's end, this important device — perfected in the speed seekers' era — would persist primarily for high-altitude flying, to find its most extensive use on air-cooled engines. More importantly, perfection of the supercharger's turbine and compressor had profound influence on the later development of the turbojet engine.

At the same time the wetsleeve monobloc water-cooled engines were being perfected, equally diligent efforts were being invested in what many others saw as the white hope for aviation's future: the air-cooled engine. Indeed, a new breed of vehement and enterprising engine entrepreneurs scoffed at water-cooled aero engines, regarding the growing bitter controversy between water cooling and air cooling as symptomatic of a deeper rivalry between government monopoly and private enterprise. The polemics involved philosophical basics. Air-cooled proponents were characterized — largely by themselves — as those who would "let nature take its course," while water-cooled proponents were

Twin-row rotary engine in 1913 Deperdussin racer   (MA)

viewed as an arrant and reactionary group who would divert nature's course, somehow corrupting it. In the United States the Navy's Admiral William Moffett championed the former while the Army's General Billy Mitchell became associated with the latter. Many factors influenced this situation.

The earliest widely used air-cooled aero engines were *rotary*: even though their cylinders sprouted like daisy petals around a central shaft to face the wind head on, reasonable cooling was not effected unless the entire package was rotated rapidly, hence the propeller was bolted directly to the cylinders. In the United States an obscure nineteenth-century engineer named F. O. Farwell is sometimes credited with the rotary idea, but the first useful models were conceived in 1907 by the Frenchmen Laurent Seguin and his brother, who for *grand prix* auto racing chose the lightweight rotary simply because the engine was its own flywheel and the crankshaft could be built short and extremely rigid with no "torsional whip." It also eliminated the radiator's often balky plumbing. The first Seguin rotary was completed in 1908; it produced 34 hp and weighed only 112 pounds even though built of steel, and appropriately was nicknamed the Gnôme. Before World War I versions with two rows of cylinders powered swift Deperdussin racing aeroplanes and single-row Gnômes were adopted widely for wartime aeroplanes. Although sweet-running, rotaries could be irksome. Two throttles, one each for air and fuel, required a great deal of fiddling to get just right, and it became easier to leave the throttles wide open and simply turn the ignition on and off in order to regulate power output — especially during approach and landing! Moreover, rotaries were typically lubricated with castor oil, which they consumed with wild abandon, their hapless pilots bravely facing the liberal doses slung at them, half-blinded and choking — and presumably suffering other unfortunate effects — but aside from the disadvantages of poor lubrication and limited revs, the gyroscopic forces set up by rotaries were fierce and often made rotary-powered aeroplanes dangerous to fly. Fixed air-cooled engines — called *radial* engines if built with the same daisy-like cylinder geometry — capable of even moderate power still awaited development. They would always retain the disadvantage of presenting a large diameter to the wind, a severe hindrance to streamlining.

Actually fixed radial aero engines had an astonishing and distinguished if largely forgotten predecessor. Charles M. Manly, assistant to Smithsonian secretary Samuel Pierpont Langley, had taken over a small rotary designed by Stephen M. Balzer, and after considerable improvement he altered it into a fixed radial and produced for Langley's ill-fated 1903 Aerodrome a five-cylinder engineering jewel which delivered 52·4 hp at 950 rpm and weighed only 147 pounds! Manly

made first use of the drum cam, standard on virtually all radials a half century later, and his power-to-weight ratio would not be equaled for fifteen years! Nine days after Langley's spectacular failure to fly — through no fault of his engine — the Wright Brothers first flew using a primitive home-built engine that weighed 179 pounds but produced little more than 12 hp, and was unable to hold together longer than six minutes. Italian Alessandro Anzani built both single and two-row radials, but like so many of the type they were prone to overheating. A fortuitous rain shower cooled Blériot's Anzani, enabling him to complete his momentous 1909 cross-Channel flight.

Sam Heron (S)

The problem of adequately cooling a highly stressed cylinder with air was more difficult than it first appeared, and was tackled tenaciously by two Englishmen, Roy Fedden at Fishponds, Bristol, who went on to build a series of important air-cooled engines, and Sam D. Heron (most assuredly, *not* Samuel!). Serious and opinionated, Heron was not one to encourage personal closeness; his brief marriage remained a secret even to working associates. With his fiercely independent eyes penetrating like nails from

a sharp, bony face, Sam Heron had always been indifferent to the fickle whims of notoriety ever since 1910 when as a single-minded nineteen-year-old he began his aviation career. By 1915 he had gained the praise of Professor H. A. Gibson, whom he assisted at the Royal Aircraft Factory, Farnborough, and with whom that year he laid down the cardinal rules of air-cooled cylinder construction which remain valid to this day. In 1916 with Major Fred M. Green, whom he followed to Siddeley-Deasy where they transformed the twin — row RAF8 into the Jaguar, Heron patented a clutch for a gear-driven supercharger which awaited the 1927 Wasp engine for its first use. A true

technician, the dour[8] Heron became increasingly impatient with what he viewed as the sometimes Byzantine absurdity of British politics blindly stifling valid technological progress, and was soon ripe for a change in atmosphere. Whether or not there is any truth to the story that a freewheeling, highly placed U.S. military official enticed Heron by offering a generous salary supplement from his own personal funds, by 1921 Heron

[8] Heron is variously remembered for his risque good humor and generous martinis which he mixed — 5 gallons at a time — and served to close friends; his dourness may have been exacerbated by the constant pain from a tubercular hip that rendered one leg virtually useless.

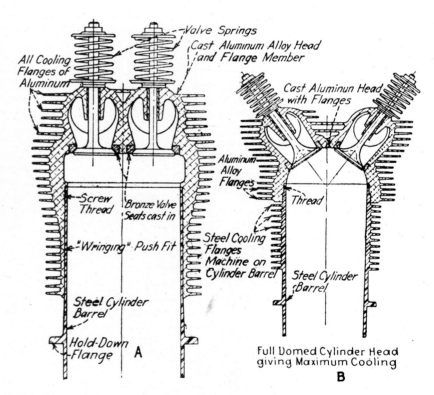

Air-cooled cylinder construction, 1920s: (a) shows steel barrel screwed into cylinder head of aluminum alloy which has extra cast cooling flanges extending down to cover the barrel; (b) shows steel barrel with its own cooling flanges, short aluminum alloy head screwed to it; this was superior.

with some acrimony had left England and was working at McCook Field, determined to design an air-cooled cylinder that would work. The task proved monumental. On his experimental single-cylinder engines, valves would warp and stick. Pistons would scuff. In one year Heron designed eight different cylinders; his novel model K was the best, although he modestly credited his concepts in cylinder construction to the 1913 work of Italian S. M. Viale, who, during the war, was in charge of Gwynne-built Clergêt rotaries and later took over Siddeley Jaguar development from F. M. Green. By 1923 Heron had built a remarkably advanced air-cooled radial under Army auspices. He had discarded the then popular Alemite valve fittings and force-lubricated his valve gear, and his cylinders worked quite well, but the Army did not cultivate the momentous crop he spawned in their own McCook laboratories. In 1926 Ed T. Jones and Heron, who was again feeling stifled under a bureaucratic yoke, both left McCook to join private industry at Wright Aeronautical, where Heron soon replaced the open-valve cylinders of Charles L. Lawrence's pop-bottle J-4 radial with his model K cylinders, and thus gave the world the J-5 Whirlwind, an engine that changed history in 1927 when one took Lindbergh on his epic flight from New York to Paris.

Thus it came to pass that before 1925 all antagonists were in place on the engineering chessboard. The Army had their knight-champion of centralized air power, Billy Mitchell, their giant, arsenal-like Engineering Division at McCook ("The Field"), and their highly developed Curtiss water-cooled pets. The Navy fielded their wily, resourceful Admiral Moffett intent on preserving the autonomy of naval aviation, their drive to stimulate excellence by dependence on R&D from competing private manufacturers, and their brave hope — the radial.

The rules of the game were slightly different from what had governed before. With aviation houses now struggling desperately to stay solvent, the wartime manufacturing philosophy of mass production was forgotten. The U.S. automotive industry, charged with unbridled greed by blame-shifting politicians, had in fact during their wartime debacle lost approximately $1 billion — about half their net worth. They had learned bitterly that there was more to building a complicated aero engine than just modifying auto equipment, and licking their wounds, many had no heart to continue an emsaculated R&D role in aviation. Only those auto firms obsessed with zeal for aviation stuck it out.[9] Nevertheless, Bruce G. Leighton, head of the Navy BuAer (Bureau of Aeronautics) Engine Section from 1921 until 1924, and his successor, Commander Eugene E. Wilson, both stood staunchly by the struggling private development of the air-cooled engine during a difficult time when well-entrenched Curtiss had no intention of letting a "radial rock crusher" replace their D-12. Indeed, as the maturing Wright air-cooled engine threatened D-12 supremacy, Curtiss moved inexorably toward merger — and control.[10]

At the height of this struggle, a new knight appeared on the chessboard. Young, brash Princeton-educated (class of 1909) Frederick Brant Rentschler, Wright Aeronautical's first president and one of the most ambitious of the "Ohio hicks," recognized their urgent need to plow profits back into R&D,

[9] Packard alone in the United States remained. The same was happening to the auto industry elsewhere: in England, only Rolls-Royce, Napier, and Sunbeam remained in aviation; in France only Hispano-Suiza and Renault; and only Isotta-Fraschini and Fiat in Italy, where SPA and Ansaldo-San Giorgio had abandoned aero engine construction by 1921 and 1924 respectively.

[10] In August 1929 Curtiss finally absorbed Wright to form a giant controlling twenty-nine subdivisions affiliated with eighteen other aviation companies.

Frederick B. Rentschler with Edward A. Deeds   (U)

but his outspokenness led to bitter disagreement with Wright chairman Richard F. "Dick" Hoyt, who favored using the money for stock dividends.[11]

[11] Hoyt was primarily a financier; as an executive of Haydn, Stone & Company he had been a member of the syndicate that bought Orville Wright's factory and patent rights in 1914. This syndicate — which included Thomas Chadbourne and Harvey Gibson of Manufacturers' Trust and Albert Wiggen of the Chase National Bank — bought out Wright and Martin separately; they also controlled Simplex Auto and acquired the license to build the French Hispano-Suiza in the United States. George J. Mead and Andrew Wilgoos were important in implementing this endeavor. The Army engine inspector at Wright-Martin was young Captain F. B. Rentschler. In 1919 Wright-Martin liquidated but Rentschler, having impressed the financial experts, was given $3 million to reorganize Wright Aeronautical, which he did, keeping Mead and Wilgoos.

Rentschler also bridled at Wright's 1923 acquisition of ambitious Charles Lawrence together with his air-cooled radial J-1 engine design. Before long Rentschler had had enough; although he briefly considered returning to Hooven, Owens & Rentschler in Hamilton, Ohio, the firm of his father, who had no faith in aviation, the break in truth was the excuse he needed to hatch his own Big Plan — which included control of his own company. By 1925 it looked as if Wright's line of air-cooled radials might, because of technical reasons, be limited indefinitely to no more than 250 hp, virtually useless to the military, but George Mead had become convinced he could build an air-cooled radial capable of twice this power. His ideas had been strengthened by design work done by associate Andy Wilgoos in his home garage, converted to a drafting room, at Montclair, New Jersey, where the new engine was born. They, along with Donald Brown and others, were ready to quit Wright with Rentschler, who had decided the future lay in playing ball with the Navy and going whole-hog on the air-cooled radial.

The suggestion that Rentschler should look in the direction of Hartford, Connecticut, for ready space and hard cash almost certainly came from E. A. Deeds, then fifty-one and a director of Niles-Bement-Pond Tool Company there. Rentschler, thirty-eight, was glib, polished, and confident, and soon had Niles's commitment for a heavy investment and their approval for him to take over the excess vacant loft space under their control. Currently rented for tobacco warehousing, it had been formerly used by an almost forgotten Hartford machine tool firm founded more than sixty years earlier by two long-dead gunsmiths in the Colt pistol factory, men who would have been astounded to know their names would earn lasting world renown for inventions they never heard of: Francis Pratt and Amos Whitney.

Wright suffered a body blow when so many of their old team, working day and night, in scant months built a rival engine. This new air-cooled radial used a cleverly designed forged crankcase (not cast as on Wright engines), a two-piece crankshaft allowing a solid master rod (not split as in Wright's); it also used nine of Sam Heron's new model M cylinders, except with the rocker box an integral part of the cylinder casting instead of the compensating type Heron favored. On Christmas Eve, 1925, Pratt & Whitney's first engine was finished. It had 1,344 cid and produced 425 hp – more than the Liberty – yet it weighed little more than half as much. And it would run ten times as long between overhauls. They called it the Wasp.

On May 5, 1926, the Wasp first

The first Cyclone: Wright's P-2, representative of the significant break away from water cooling for high-power engines that began after 1925   (Au)

flew, powering an Apache aeroplane built, ironically, by Wright and flown by Navy Lieutenant C. C. Champion. That year, under Moffett's fatherly smile, the Navy specified the use of air-cooled radials on all future aircraft, and the destiny of the type was secure. Niles' revitalized subsidiary flourished; in just three years shipment value rose 278 times, and Rentschler's personal 1925 investment of $253 in P&W stock mushroomed in value within four years to $35 million; salary and bonuses alone had already made him a millionaire.[12] And the

[12] Rentschler went on to become America's first great airline chief when P&W became part of United Aircraft & Transport Corporation, parent of United Air Lines. With William E. Boeing, Rentschler snatched National Air Transport away from rivals H. E. Coffin and C. M. Keys in a fight reminiscent of the early robber-baron railroad days.

wily Deeds, now fully recovered from his wartime embarrassment, thus ended up with big pieces of both Wright and P&W; quite content to sit unobtrusively in the background, he could neatly play his companies off against each other, pocketing rich profits from both.

In England and France as well, air-cooled engines were becoming increasingly popular in both civil and military roles. The later development of Fred E. Weick's NACA ring cowl (a special shell to streamline the radial's cylinder heads) together with "positive-pressure cooling" (a system of baffles in the cowl to direct the airflow) and twin-row design to increase the power-to-frontal-area ratio (pioneered in a production engine by the English with the Armstrong-Siddeley Jaguar), consolidated the air-cooled radial's grip. Pratt & Whitney's 985-cid Wasp Jr. would be in continuous production for the next forty years!

Nevertheless, the water-cooled engine still delivered greater power for identical cylinder capacity, and with its closely spaced cylinders it was a lighter unit even if the total installed propulsion system (including the water) was often heavier. And for speed seeking, power-to-frontal area still ruled. Indeed, no air-cooled radial would push an aeroplane past 300 mph until after 1932. The simple fact is, liquid-cooled aeroplanes held the world maximum speed record (piston engine) for a full half century, and until 1969, no fixed air-cooled engine ever held the speed record!

Installed in the U. S. Navy Schneider racers, the Curtiss D-12 changed the course of history one fine September day in 1923 when, to the undisguised astonishment of European observers, it outshone their best. One enormously impressed race witness was Charles Richard Fairey, a towering, forceful man of broad understanding. In his capacity as Chairman, Society of British Aircraft Constructors (SBAC), he was looked upon as titular head of

the British aircraft-manufacturing industry;[13] his manufacturing plant, founded in 1915, is still prominent in Hayes, Middlesex, despite the growth of bustling London-Heathrow Airport nearby which threatens finally to overwhelm it. At a Royal Aero Club House Dinner in November 1925 Fairey put his case in a nutshell. "The fundamental law of resistance in a fluid is our old friend KSV^2," he pointed out. "K" was the term then used relating to cleanness – the cleaner the shape the lower the value of K – and "S" the frontal area; reduction of either or both lowered drag. The trim D-12 had allowed a vastly reduced frontal area to win the Schneider race. At least two persons attending the dinner frankly took issue with Fairey's explanation; earlier the same evening at the Royal Aeronautical Society across town, Roy Fedden had spoken on the installation of air-cooled radial engines and their apparent enhancement to speed in commercial types. But to Fairey there was no question. Behind the Curtiss racer design "new brains had been at work. The reason for the American superiority was that American designers recognized the fundamental law of KSV^2 whilst European designers had not, or failed to heed it."

Immediately after the 1923 Schneider, Fairey visited Curtiss in the United States and by February 1924 he was on his way back to England aboard the *Leviathan*, hardly able to restrain himself, bursting with anticipation and pride over the Curtiss license in his pocket and an almost uncontrollable urge to show someone – anyone – the glistening new D-12 engine locked securely in his stateroom!

Fairey had a plan for his new engine, which he renamed Felix "because it keeps on walking," after the euphemism of the day. Fairey was frustrated with his Fawn, the current RAF two-

[13] Fairey was awarded the Wakefield Gold Medal by the Royal Aeronautical Society for the invention of the wing flap.

seat day bomber on which he had been forced to load so much useless external equipment that it hardly made 90 mph with its Napier Lion, the robust engine enjoying a *de facto* monopoly in England then.[14] Fairey knew that with a free hand he could produce a dramatically superior new bomber around the D-12, and in complete defiance of all existing specifications he designed an aeroplane called Fox, gracefully streamlining the D-12 engine into its pencil-thin nose. The Fox, which first flew January 3, 1925, with the Fawn's identical load could hit almost 160 mph and fly the pants off the best RAF fighters! On July 28 Boom Trenchard first saw the plane and ordered a complete squadron of thirty on the spot! The embarrassment to the bureaucrats was intense; Fairey's nose-thumb at the rules, to be sure, was highly irregular and he found his energy suddenly stunted by British chauvinism as much as by stringent government economy. He began to lose potentially lucrative orders and would never be entirely forgiven. In Parliament on November 18 the Secretary of State for Air, Sir Samuel Hoare, when asked why Fairey had to install an American-built D-12 engine into his brilliant new bomber, replied: "There was no other engine available." Nevertheless, vicious attempts to belittle publicly the American D-12 began. The parochial policy "Buy British" was invoked. The severity of American engine tests was questioned — but this was not entirely cricket because Fairey's license stipulated the D-12 must pass British tests as well. These required ten periods of ten hours' continuous running at 90 per cent throttle with five minutes at full throttle at the end of each period. Not many engines had passed this test, British or otherwise. A stock

D-12 did. In 1926 the few Foxes built went operational with No. 12 Bombing Squadron, and as late as the August 1928 RAF Pageant they were still escaping fighter interception with ease.

Meanwhile, before November 1925 two D-12s — not Fairey's but ones quietly secured by the Air Ministry — had been tested by the government and greatly admired. Lieutenant Colonel L. F. Rudston Fell, D.S.O., assistant director of engine research and design, realized at once, national pride aside, that a new engine with D-12 qualities was needed. Fairey would not be asked to build it, ostensibly because the market was too lean to bring in new engine manufacturers, although of course that was only part of the reason. Napier, content with the Lion and preoccupied with the 1,000-hp Cub, wanted no part of a new project, especially one involving large aluminum castings which had proven troublesome to them.

Rolls-Royce had languished after the war. The Eagle engine, unparalleled for soundness, solidity, and reliability even if outmoded, had been exported to nearly every civilized country in the world and every epic British long-distance flight had been Rolls-Royce-powered, but F. H. Royce was now retired in the south of France, his firm's active management oriented more toward finance than engineering and bewildered by the deepening economic chasm. Then Ernest Hives took over control, ready to carry new technical ideas forward. An additional shot in the arm occurred when Arthur Rowledge came over from Napier in 1921 because he did not like working under Harry Vane, whom he considered just another non-engineering accountant. But it was the solid American Schneider Trophy triumph in 1923 that now led to the full reawakening of Rolls-Royce, and thus it came to pass that for the second time in ten years the firm would build a phenomenal career on the cornerstone of a foreign engine. The Air Ministry with understandable

stealth loaned a D-12 to the Derby factory with orders to do it one better.

Work started in July 1925, the same month Trenchard ordered his squadron of Foxes. The project proceeded under Rowledge and Ellor, who had the new Rolls engine — a wetsleeve monobloc like the D-12, with a 5-inch bore and 1,210 cid — ready in March 1926. At first they called it Falcon-X, but since it bore no recognizable similarity to the World War I Falcon, its name was modified to just F-X. Indeed, *Flight* commented "one could not recognize the engine as a Rolls-Royce!"

In fairness, the F-X updated the D-12. Only the oil pump was copied directly. The blocks were of hiduminium, a new aluminum alloy, with cylinder heads and inlet and exhaust passages integrally cast, unlike the D-12 and just opposite to the old K-12, in which the block had been integral with the crankcase. The F-X used sleeves open on top as opposed to the D-12's closed sleeves, but similar to the new Curtiss V-1400. Meanwhile Tom Sopwith's Hawker firm, not Fairey, worked with Rolls to produce the new RAF day bomber, called Hart. Fairey had built the excellent D-12–powered Firefly fighter to complement his Fox, but the Air Ministry adamantly opted for air-cooled radials in new fighters, forcing Fairey to build his aeroplanes in Belgium, where for years he enjoyed a measure of success.

Until 1927 there was no significant advance beyond the D-12's specific power of 30 hp per liter of swept volume nor beyond the limits of 140 pounds per square inch mean effective cylinder pressure, compression ratios of 6 to 7, and rpm of 2,500. By then fully unleashed, Rolls's water-cooled engine development proceeded at an accelerating pace. Fuels capable of tolerating increased cylinder pressure began to appear, and metallurgy caught up with engine design. Tougher, more durable reduction gears were brought back into use and Ellor's super-

charger was fitted, two items which in those days could be used to best effectiveness only on liquid-cooled engines, and by 1929 the Rolls F-XI delivered 620 hp at 2,700 rpm, a rate that even the Reed metal prop could hardly cope with. In 1931 the engine was named Kestrel. Other developments followed. Sam Heron, who had returned to McCook Field in 1928, had used Kettering's mercury-cooled valves as a basis to develop his revolutionary sodium-cooled valves, introduced operationally on the Kestrel in 1933.[15] Heron also perfected the technique of applying Stellite to valves. Soon thereafter he wrote the specifications for high-octane fuels used through and beyond World War II.

In France, too, the importance of engine development was belatedly recognized. The French Under-Secretary of State for Aviation Laurent-Eynac announced that no less than 1 million francs in cash prizes would be awarded in an engine competition held in 1924 lasting into 1925, part of an updated pursuit program begun in 1923. New twelve-cylinder Hispano-Suizas, a new Lorraine, and the water-cooled radial Salmson resulted, but for the most part these engines were built to formulas already obsolescent.

The scene of real water-cooled engine progress had now shifted to Derby, where, at the same time they were developing the Kestrel, Rolls engineers expanded their technology to build an even more powerful engine with an enlarged 6-inch bore — the 36·7 liter, 825-hp Buzzard or H engine, developed over the objection of Managing Director Basil Johnson (brother of Claude Johnson who had brought Rolls and Royce together) who wanted to concentrate on cars. He was overruled by Henry Royce and Hives. Although this engine was not conspicuously successful, its follow-on was the brilliant

[14] The Lion's already large frontal area was worsened by Air Ministry "experts" who insisted on locating carburetors *outside* the engine instead of in the Vs. The long inlet pipes also made carburetion problems more difficult.

[15] The technique was perfected by Thompson Products, Cleveland, Ohio, who filled hollow tungsten valves with a mixture of sodium nitrate and potassium nitrate, which absorbed and carried away the heat.

Rolls-Royce R (for racing) engine. Geared and supercharged, the R produced 1,900 hp in 1929 and 2,300 hp in 1931 to win the last two Schneider Trophy races, and prompted Hives to remark, "it's no use putting the speed record up to 399·99 mph. The next step is 400 and over." Thus, using exotic fuel,[16] its water coolant acting like a buffer to prevent destructive overheating from the punishing power burst, the engine produced an incredible 2,650 hp to capture the 1931 world speed record, boosting the Supermarine S.6B floatplane to over 400 mph. For those few brutal minutes the R engine produced a fantastic 72·2 horsepower/liter!

By the eve of World War II, Rolls had come full circle and reverted to Charles Kirkham's original K-12 pattern, a single large casting containing the coolant passages and crankcase, to build the first Merlin engine, a V-12 of 1,647 cid.[17] Two years before the Merlin appeared, N. H. Gilman in the United States began the design of a 1,710-cid V-12 almost identical in size to the Merlin in order to tackle the problems of high-temperature cooling in the aluminum monobloc. This engine was built by an Indianapolis firm already famous for producing reduction gears and which bore the

name of an early mechanic at the Indy 500 auto races – James A. Allison. General Motors took over Allison in 1930 and the V-1710 engine powered airships before being put into the shark-nosed snouts of Curtiss P-40 Hawks. Allisons and Merlins went on to power the great Allied fighters of World War II. The Merlin's swept volume almost exactly equaled that of the World War I Liberty, yet by 1945 a Merlin – one of more than 150,000 built – produced 2,640 hp, virtually duplicating the specific power output of the 1931 R sprint engine. Such evolution and success tended to prove convincingly that in the long run gradual but definite improvement in details – at which Royce had always been such a genius – was just as important as the invention of new ideas.[18]

Thus the evolution of the aero engine progressed – an accumulation of human ambition and logic – combinations of ideas, new but more often old ideas in new applications. The naked heart of an aeroplane was a thrilling, glistening thing, its myriad polished metal pieces whirring in perfect synchronization immersed in a torrent of sound loud and satisfying; it sometimes represented the semblance of man's thought, sometimes the essence. Such marvelous engines overtook the aeroplane itself to become the repository for the speed seekers' deepest efforts. Aerodynamic technology was not greatly altered in the fifteen years after 1924, but during those years engines continued to become vastly more powerful, and although the blueprints of the final Schneider racers could be overlaid almost directly on those of the 1925 monoplanes, their engines, compared to the earliest

Schneider engines, produced three times the horsepower-to-weight (for brief periods the water-cooled R engine could deliver 1·68 hp for each pound of weight); four times the horsepower-to-volume, and five times the horsepower-to-frontal area.

Yet there were othey key technological innovations of the early 1920s that put the speed seeker on his high plateau by mid-decade. In the realm of propulsion technology, it is important to consider the propeller and the radiator.

The prop grows up

The device that translates engine power into aeroplane performance is the propeller, and propeller efficiency is a direct measure of how much engine output is usefully transmitted in moving the aeroplane. The essential principles of the modern propeller – called "airscrew" by the English – were discovered by the Englishman Rankine and first published in 1865. Yet, more than fifty years later, at the end of World War I, the best available propellers performed at less than 65 per cent efficiency when engines were straining in climb and at best seldom delivered more than 75 per cent maximum efficiency. The single most limiting constraint was that pitch – the slant of the blades – had to be built for only one flight condition. If the designer wanted high speed the blades were slanted steeply, but the aeroplane then suffered on takeoff when the blades could not screw their way through the air cleanly, or on occasion even stalled. The need for a prop whose pitch could be varied in flight to match changing flight conditions was recognized early, but developments to achieve practical variable-pitch (VP) props were well in the future.

A Canadian named Turnbull built a VP prop at Peterborough during World War I but centrifugal force flung the blades free; yet a novel VP prop was tested successfully at 1,100 rpm in 1917 on an S.E.5 at RAE Farnborough, but its extra weight and control

complexity precluded development. Similarly, a certain eager Seth Hart, who even had in mind reversible – in pitch, not direction! – props, with his companion Eustis of San Diego tested a VP prop on a Hisso-Jenny at McCook Field in 1919, but the backlash and vibration were intolerable. On September 5, 1920, the Air Service conducted a successful experiment with a VP prop, stopping the test plane "within 75 feet" of where its wheels first touched the ground, but inconclusive aspects halted development. In France, Pierre Levasseur exhibited a wood-blade VP prop at the 1921 Paris Air Show. Despite French government tests (a ten-hour run up to 1,800 rpm) no one was buying. Some time later Spencer Heath of the Paragon Propeller Company demonstrated his reversible-pitch prop at Bolling Field, D.C., but interest in reversible props generated in 1921 suddenly ceased in 1922 with the widespread introduction of wheel brakes!

Such experiments, though numerous, were curiosities. Almost all early props were fixed pitch devices carved from solid chunks of mahogany, birch, white oak, or black walnut. Perfectly grained single blocks of uniform density were not only prone to warping but were difficult to obtain, factors which hastened the adoption of props laminated from several thin layers of wood. The popular deGrandeville lamination method became the basis for methods used even today.[19] Later wood props were sheathed or tipped with metal (copper was common) or even pigskin.

Among the most successful wood props in Europe were those designed by Viscount Louis P. de Monge de Franeau and produced by Établissement Lumière. Scion of an elite Belgian family whose roots could be traced to the eleventh century, a cousin of

[16] Concocted by "fuel wizard" Air Commodore F. R. "Rod" Banks who in 1929 buffered pure benzole by using a fuel mixture consisting of 53·5 per cent gasoline, 23·0 per cent ethyl alcohol, 22·0 per cent benzole, and 1·5 per cent tetra-ethyl lead. This was used as a "reference fuel", modified in 1931 to reduce supercharger temperature by adding methanol, recovering 100 brake hp on charge cooling alone. The "cocktail" for the 1931 world speed record had no gasoline in it, being a mixture of benzole, methanol, and acetone which would vigorously remove the paint from the aeroplane! The supercharger gear ratio was raised and they got 2,800 bhp, but the cylinder head bolts began to pull out, so they went back to the original gear ratio and got 2,650, sufficient for the job. Engine life was pegged at seven hours.

[17] History seems to repeat itself incessantly; Rolls to some extent repeated Curtiss' development cycle and built the Merlin II like the F-X and Kestrel.

[18] After decades during which the name Rolls-Royce was regarded as part of the language synonymous with unimpeachable integrity, the world was shocked in February 1971 to learn the firm had gone bankrupt after overextending themselves in turbofan aero engine development.

[19] A method in which smaller and thinner wood strips are placed in a step-like series from the hub, economical because imperfect long pieces of wood can be cut down and used.

the eminently successful French Nieuport brothers, de Monge asserted his mechanical inventiveness before World War I and soon came to Paris — the "center of aviation" as he termed it — seeking an Anzani engine for an aeroplane he was building. He remained to do laboratory tests in the Eiffel wind tunnel on bi-convex airfoils and became convinced of their superiority. In 1916, unavoidably drafted into the Belgian Army, de Monge was sent to the trenches as an artillery observer, a frustrating existence for the young engineer now burning with ideas. Using the door from a bombed, gutted farmhouse as a drawing board, he designed his first propeller — its blade cross section was bi-convex — intended for the 300-hp Renault engine powering the Voisin bomber, and sent the drawings to a Parisian cabinetmaker. This prototype propeller so dramatically improved the Voisin's performance that within weeks orders came to replace all outstanding brands with the de Monge design. To produce the numbers required, de Monge expanded a small firm already set up under his guidance, then building wing ribs, and operated by the widow of Lumière, a prewar friend of de Monge's and one of the first French pilots killed in the war. With the sudden advent of props Madame Lumière saw her situation improve rapidly. The firm soon won a stiff competition to produce props for Hispano-Suiza *modèle 42* 300-hp engines and in less than one year some 40,000 Lumière-de Monge props were ordered! To his mounting dismay, and that of the French as well, de Monge was still restricted to the trenches by the Belgian authorities and had to consult *in absentia* with users of his props. He derived a clever transformation of the classical expression of torque which enabled him to telegraph from the Front coded figures for blade width, diameter, and pitch, all a prop builder needs to know to achieve the proper torque.

Despite such novel innovations wood props had several drawbacks. Wood's low mechanical resistance imposed definite centrifugal force limits restricting rotational velocity, and the blades had to be made unduly thick to ensure necessary strength. Micarta (canvas laminated with bakelite) had been used as a wood substitute as early as 1920. But there were also aerodynamic problems: engine builders found that turning their engines at higher rpm pushed blunt prop blades toward tip speeds where drag soared and efficiency fell off drastically (geared engines had not been widely developed, nor were they about to be). The immediate and most promising answer seemed to be thin-blade, all-metal props which would allow higher revolution rates.

During 1917 in England Dr. H. C. Watts, who later became one of the famous partners of Alec Ogilvie, together with Henry Leitner, started the development of steel props using hollow blades of laminated steel sheet, pressed into shape and welded together at the edges. In 1919 these two formed the Metal Airscrew Company Ltd. to market their product, which by then included provisions to set blade pitch on the ground before takeoff. Such props were imported to France, where they were used on the 1922 French world duration record flight of Bossoutrot and Drouhin, and much larger versions propelled many of Britain's huge dirigibles. Finding extensive use in Japan in 1921, they were, at that time, the only type of metal prop in production anywhere in the world.

In the United States Thomas Dicks also experimented with hollow steel blades for the Army in 1918, and soon after joined the small Standard Steel Propeller Company, organized in 1919 and then located in a drab former cap pistol factory in Homestead, Pennsylvania, across the Monongahela River from Pittsburgh. Dicks then began the development of solid duralumin, drop-forged blades. A three-blade version incorporating his ideas, with pitch adjustable by means of a screw-and-wedge device, was used on the Navy-Wright mystery racers of 1923–24. The adjustable prop was placed on the market in 1925 and used extensively by Western Air Express Douglas mailplanes. In France during 1924, Nieuport-Astra produced a somewhat similar ground adjustable metal prop fabricated from steel tube slit, opened, and partially flattened. It did not enjoy wide success, although the French were anxious to exploit another major advantage of metal props — in a crash they would not splinter but merely bend.

Tip speeds in excess of sound, although approached, were not studied until 1918. The British Advisory Committee on Aeronautics in March 1919 concluded that thrust diminished unacceptably as flow over the blade became sonic, a view corroborated and supported by the Air Service Engineering Division at McCook Field. Indeed, because of tests with artillery shells, there already existed a strong set of beliefs concerning the problems that arose when an object approached the speed of sound. Yet if some way could be found to increase prop tip speed, engines could be turned faster and a great reservoir of unused power tapped. The key was developed in the workshop of Sylvanus Albert Reed, Ph.D., a retired engineer interested in acoustics. While engaged in 1915 in private research having to do with high-frequency sounds, Dr. Reed employed an apparatus carrying radiating arms of sharp-edged thin metal which he rotated at 36,000 rpm. Intrigued that his small paddles were analogous to aeroplane propellers, Reed shifted the emphasis of his investigation, demonstrating an open-minded, properly scientific attitude by rejecting the current dire pessimism regarding sonic speed. Reed considered prop tip speed a special area not systematically explored, and harboring a strong hunch that the difficulties encountered might well depend on subtle differences in an object's shape, he began a long series of experiments with a 10-hp electric motor turning small, 20-inch–diameter metal props up to 19,000 rpm which gave tip speeds of 1,600 feet per second (fps); Mach 1, the sonic velocity, is about 1,100 fps at sea level. Dr. Reed triumphantly observed — a bit prematurely — that ominously predicted physical limits at Mach 1 were "non-existent."

Late in 1920 Dr. Reed approached Curtiss to secure better experimental facilities and made a case sufficient to convince chief engineer William Gilmore to place a laboratory at his disposal. Together with then director of research Mike Thurston, Reed continued his tests using a 100-hp engine turning a 4-foot metal prop called the Z-1 which had exceedingly thin tips with razor-sharp edges. In light of today's knowledge — namely, that for a given "solidity," the prop that avoids sonic tips will be more

S. A. Reed by an early metal propeller of his design (mounted on a Curtiss Jenny for test) (USAF)

efficient — the inevitable conclusion is that Dr. Reed in fact contributed little of value to propeller theory. Reed's thin tips simply resulted in lower drag than props of similar diameter which, until then, all were much thicker; they also allowed higher rpm, making the Reed metal prop the ideal mate for the new direct-drive Curtiss wetsleeve monobloc racing engines, which seemed eager to turn at several hundred rpm in excess of 2,000. Without knowing it, Reed did anticipate what aero engineers would rediscover a generation later when full-size wings, thin and sharp-edged, were devised to attack Mach 1, in the 1940s still termed "the sound barrier." In April 1921 Reed's Z-1 prop achieved a tip speed of 1,508 fps (Mach 1·36 under the laboratory atmospheric conditions) with what was then unheard-of efficiency.

The first full-size Reed props were made from a single forged duralumin plate $1\frac{1}{2}$ inches thick, properly thinned and tapered by machining, then bent into the proper pitch angle. Slightly heavier than the wood props they replaced, they nevertheless depended on centrifugal force for rigidity.[20] Flight testing, which began August 30, 1921, at Curtiss Field, Long Island, was continued through December at McCook Field, Ohio, and Dr. Reed's plots of tip speed against thrust yielded virtually continuous lines. Reed was ready to try his prop on the D-12—powered R-6 racer of 1922 and carried one to Detroit as hand baggage, but under the race rules it was disallowed. Testing continued through 1922, and in 1923, the year Dr. Reed was formally retained by Curtiss, the Reed prop made its racing debut with an impact even more shattering than its earsplitting howl: both the Pulitzer and Schneider races were decisively won by Navy racers equipped with Reed props said to be capable of some

[20] This lack of static rigidity contributed to the delay of full Air Service acceptance of Reed metal props until after 1924.

84 per cent efficiency. The Reed prop was suddenly the rage. Soon in mass production the world over (foreign licensees included, in England, Fairey/Reed; in France, Levasseur/Reed; in Italy, Caproni/Reed; in Germany, Aeron/Reed; in Japan, Mitsubishi/Reed), it earned millions for both Dr. Reed and Curtiss. Curtiss president C. M. Keys exulted, "The Reed prop will not break in rain, hail, or high grass!"

In France de Monge considered the Reed "a poor design" and when offered the French license he turned it down, letting it pass to rival Levasseur, a decision no doubt based on conscientious engineering but certainly unwise commercial judgment. Although the abrupt halt in orders caused by the Armistice had dealt his Lumière concern a tremendous wallop, leaving him reeling and with warehouses filled with more wood props than the cutback air force could use in years, de Monge persisted in building custom props and equipped all important French speed record aeroplanes through 1922, the year he successfully tested and demonstrated at the Paris Air Show a prototype VP prop. De Monge, too, recognized the need for metal props, and spurning the Reed, he turned to the significantly different Leitner-Watts VP metal props, redesigning the flat-bottom metal blades to have a bi-convex airfoil which, as he explained, used a shape based on "a logarithmic spiral, not the circular arcs used by V. E. Clark and others." After the tragic September 1921 crash of his high-speed racer in which Count de Romanet was killed, de Monge's hopes — and finances — were dashed.

The Reed prop in France, as elsewhere in the world, from 1923 onward dominated every major speed record and air race (except the 1924 Pulitzer) until almost the decade's end. Simple and inexpensive construction was in fact the Reed prop's prime advantage, enabling it to be adapted for more widespread use. In 1925, fifty of the eighty-five planes in the

American National Air Races used Reed props, the U. S. Air Mail was using them almost exclusively, and Dr. Reed received the 1925 Collier Trophy for his pioneering work. This was also the year Dr. Reed largely solved the outstanding difficulties in producing forged blades. An improved, drop-forged model R version of his prop appeared in which the thin forged blades extended in a smooth, true helix along the entire blade length for greater efficiency. The model R prop on the 280-mph Curtiss R3C in 1925 was credited with an efficiency of 89 per cent at nearly 3,000 rpm with a tip speed of Mach 1·091 — approximately 1,200 fps.

Standard Steel's metal props were also popular, and the company was destined to become part of the second — and ultimately largest — major U.S. prop manufacturer. In reality this firm owed its origins to Thomas Hamilton, a Seattle native steeped in the guile of the Pacific Northwest. Hamilton had wanted badly to make aeroplanes but was urged by the War Department to go to Milwaukee, a Wisconsin furniture center, where he set up his Aero Company along the Northwestern railroad right of way to manufacture wood props.[21] He supplied metal-tipped laminated wood props for the Curtiss NC transatlantic flying boats of 1919 and Douglas World Cruisers of 1924. Despite deep personal differences, Tom Hamilton and Standard Steel's Harry Kraeling and Frank W. Caldwell (the latter lured away from the Army) were all convinced that Reed's one-piece props were inferior to the multi-piece designs they favored. Caldwell recalled well a 1921 Army test at McCook Field in which he gave C. Fayette Taylor a one-piece metal prop to test on a 300-hp Hispano-Suiza. After a few minutes'

[21] Hamilton later fulfilled his dream briefly; he set up a company which produced high-wing, single-engine metal transports that antedated Ford's tin geese and were used mostly in the Canadian bush and Panama.

running at rated power a blade broke, slashed through the control board between the heads of two operators, climbed a wooden staircase, and burst through the roof. "The men became a little nervous after that," Caldwell recalled. "We had to construct bomb shelters to test our props." Both small firms — Hamilton's and Standard Steel — knew full well, however, that Reed had the formidable power of Curtiss behind him.

When Fred Rentschler's United Aircraft later acquired Hamilton Aero, Standard Steel, afraid of being edged out, moved quickly and made a deal with Curtiss: they would pay royalties on the Reed patents (even though they considered the patents invalid) in return for which Curtiss would sue all "infringers" — including Hamilton. Rentschler, anxious to avoid a court fight with Curtiss, extended himself to buy Standard Steel as well, a move calculated to quench the patent fight and potentially to establish a propeller dynasty — if he could stifle antagonism among the respective personalities. Astute and competent Eugene E. Wilson was persuaded by Rentschler (together with apparently a lavish promise of Deeds-supplied money) to leave the Navy and become a neutral manager of Hamilton-Standard, married under the United umbrella in 1929. Tom Hamilton later went to Europe, where for several years he served as United Aircraft's elegant and polished emissary. Wilson was destined to lead United Aircraft through World War II. And Hamilton-Standard became the world's most renowned maker of aeroplane propellers.

In England the VP prop was still trying to make an entry. Dr. Hele-Shaw and T. E. Beacham of London, through the early 1920s, were developing a hydraulically operated VP prop in a small mews shop in Victoria. Frustrated repeatedly by intolerable bulk, weight, and the complicated procedures of operation, they persisted and in 1925 attracted the attention of Hugh Burroughes of the Gloster Aircraft Company. GAC acquired the rights to the H-S-B prop in August 1926, excited by Beacham's novel solution to the earlier problems: the prop would turn at a *constant speed*, which meant the pilot did not have continuously to regulate pitch. Instead, a governor automatically maintained the engine rpm at the setting chosen by the pilot, and the prop pitch would change by itself, adapting to any changes in aeroplane speed. The first constant-speed prop was flight-tested on a Gloster Grebe (a fighter based on the Gloster racers) in 1927. GAC tried hard to push the idea with apathetic RAF brass but it was not until 1929 that even moderate interest in the concept was aroused. Burroughes recalled with a bitter note of acrimony the visit paid by Tom Hamilton, who witnessed a working model of the GAC prop and "rushed back to America to patent his two-position [controllable in flight] prop." Burroughes was thoroughly frustrated by his own government's indifference and angered by what seemed to be bald American appropriation of essential elements of the GAC device. Hamilton-Standard's prop went into production in 1933; in 1934 de Havilland—again minus British government support—in a queer turnabout, acquired the license to produce the *American* prop in England! By 1935 constant-speed props began to come into wide use, later becoming the world standard. The final step, full-feathering (to align the blades dead into oncoming airflow for minimum resistance in case of engine failure), came in 1938.

Meanwhile, fixed-pitch metal props, tough and simple with "high solidity" blades (i.e., a large percentage of the swept disc area was in fact solid blade), persisted for speed records and racing well into the 1930s, mainly because the longer takeoff distances available to Schneider seaplanes together with increasingly powerful engines tended to deemphasize the need for high prop efficiency at low speeds.

The ultimate versions of these props, used on the final racing seaplanes, almost dangerously sacrificed takeoff performance to secure the maximum benefit at high speed. Disc loading rose from 17·4 hp per square foot of swept disc area on the 1926 Macchi M.39 — which, with a blade angle at 3/4 radius of 33·5 degrees and tip speed of Mach 0·891, had an efficiency of 81 per cent — to a staggering 37·5 hp per square foot of disc on the 1931 Supermarine S.6B, the final Schneider winner — which achieved a prop efficiency of 84 per cent with a tip speed of Mach 1·037 using an extremely coarse blade angle of 44·5 degrees! These racing props were directly descended from Dr. Reed's thin blade metal prop which, despite its shortcomings, remains one of the most potent advances made by the speed seekers.

Flying radiators

The Navy's Bruce Leighton once remarked that "water-cooling an aeroplane engine makes about as much sense as air-cooling a submarine!" but early designers of high-power engines were stuck with water cooling. Because of poor fuels, primitive metallurgy, and the slow-turning engines of that day, large piston volume was essential to achieve adequate power. The only engine geometry suitable to combine sufficiently large volume with the small frontal area necessary for streamlining was to line the cylinders in rows. Hence water cooling to maintain constant, even cylinder head temperatures. Water cooling, however, meant radiators. And there was the rub.

The only suitable cooling fluid, moreover, was water. But as every schoolboy knows, water boils at 212°F.; thus the water in the cooling system had to be kept cooler than this to prevent boiling away. This in turn dictated the need for huge surface areas to radiate enough heat and maintain low water temperatures. Early aeroplanes were forced to lug huge, cumbersome radiators, and aside

from added weight and drag, their rigid mountings often caused the bulky units to vibrate and leak, adding to the mechanical headaches. As engines became more powerful they produced more BTUs, meaning one thing: radiators had to become even larger as well.

The dilemma was particularly acute when designing a powerful speedplane, where minimum air resistance is imperative. The typical early honeycomb radiator most readily available, bearing strong resemblance to a mattress turned on edge, was mounted traditionally in the nose, facing dead into the oncoming airflow in the same fashion used for almost a century by automobiles. Speedplanes, however, suffered intolerable drag using this arrangement. Side-mounted radiators were tried by some builders in order to leave the nose uncluttered, and the Germans during World War I tried radiators shaped to conform to the wing center-section, but cost and complexity more than offset the slight

aerodynamic advantage. It was left for a French designer, A. Lamblin, working at Neuilly-sur-Seine early in 1918, to devise a novel, new form for the radiator. The shape of Lamblin's streamlined radiator resulted in a nickname: *casier à homards* ("lobster pot"). It consisted of several radially mounted copper fins inside which the water was circulated and between which the air had free passage, and tests in the Eiffel laboratory indicated the Lamblin radiator had twice the radiating effectiveness of standard honeycomb radiators with the same capacity. Lamblin himself scornfully dubbed the nose radiator an "abomination" and the side-mounted radiators "nearly equally obnoxious," saying it was scarcely worthwhile to fair a fuselage blunted by a honeycomb radiator. The Nieuport 29V speed record racers of 1920 gained 25 kmh when converted from nose radiators to Lamblins which were nestled in the landing gear struts. Mounted with four bolts, the Lamblin could be replaced in just ten minutes.

Lamblin lobster-pot radiators   (MA)

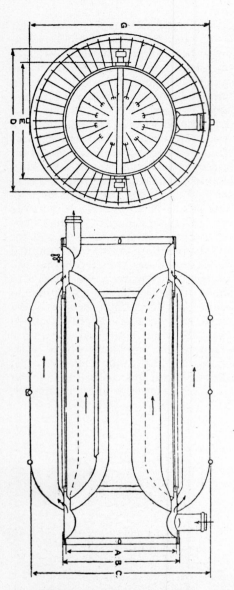

Lamblin lobster-pot radiator, section views. (Dimensions A through G varied; several sizes were built.)

Lamblins were produced in several sizes ranging in empty weight from 17 to 50 kilograms and in radiating surface from 7 to 19 square meters with water capacity 4·5 to 17·7 liters respectively; especially impressive was the ratio of radiating surface to projected frontal area, which was on

Lamblin's ad attests to the wide popularity — and success — of his radiators.

the order of 100:1. Lamblins almost immediately became universal in France and by 1921 had been exported to Holland, Japan, and the United States. Over 30,000 were built, and even automobiles were equipped with them, running indefinitely with no water pumps or cooling fans — the pumps could be eliminated because of the siphon effect the radiator exerted. It was said that, because his radiators kept the Nieuport's engine cool even as other engines overheated and faltered, it was really M. Lamblin who won the 1920 Gordon Bennett race.

The Curtiss 1920 Gordon Bennett racers were equipped with flat plate radiators which hung on the sides

like huge growths and which pierced the air with a screeching howl audible ten miles away. What was not known in France then was that Curtiss had decided to postpone the use of an even more novel radiator arrangement than the Lamblin.

The ultimate design goal, of course, would be to devise a cooling system that permitted a completely clean aerodynamic body and thus cost no extra drag at all. Curtiss, striving for this in 1920 for their ultra-fast Gordon Bennett racers, conceived the *skin radiator*. The concept was to use the aeroplane's skin itself as the radiating surface and devise some way to bring the cooling water into proximity with

Early Curtiss experimental wing radiators mounted on Curtiss Oriole for flight tests, 1922; Casey Jones, pilot (C)

the skin. By race time in the autumn of 1920 the idea had not been implemented, but during 1921 two skin radiators were fabricated by Curtiss under the direction of Mike Thurston and tested on the wings of a C-6–powered Oriole flown by Charles S. "Casey" Jones, Curtiss exhibition organizer. Two thin, corrugated brass sheets were joined along the edges and shaped to conform to the wing curvature; the water would pass between the corrugations in narrow streams and the airflow around the wing would carry off the heat. With 84 square feet of cooling surface they weighed ·88 pounds per square foot (psf) and carried 4 gallons of water which weighed 32 pounds — or ·38 psf of radiator surface. Due to faulty construction and inadequate surface area they both failed and were discarded.

Three new Curtiss wing radiators with 50 per cent more cooling surface were made early in 1922. As in 1921, the first employed soldered headers, (the collection spaces from which the water was distributed on its journey to the wing surface and back to the engine), weighed ·794 psf, and carried relatively less water: ·27 psf. The second represented a new design in which each radiating strip was built and tested separately; it weighed ·77 psf with water weight down to ·23 psf. The third was improved over this, weighing only ·682 psf with water weight now down to ·203 psf. The second and third were tested on a C-6A Oriole between January 24 and June 16, 1922, under ambient conditions ranging between 2°F. and 80°F. During this period Casey Jones made a remarkable 1,500-mile flight in the Oriole from New York to Kansas City, and wing radiators were proudly shown off publicly for the first time at the 1922 Omaha spring flying meet.

These early radiators had both water inlet and outlet tubes inside the wing, requiring the use of forceps in a difficult, delicate procedure to install the plumbing. It also proved difficult to remove all air from the cooling system when filling, and air trapped in the thin brass sheet water jackets would form steam pockets which occasionally – and dramatically – exploded. To avoid this consequence, the version being installed at that moment to replace the old Lamblins on a 1921 Curtiss Navy racer had a very large spring safety valve installed in the header. The two Army R-6s, then in design, adopted skin radiators from the outset – they were the first racers to do so – and the devices were credited with adding at least 20 mph to the racers' top speed. Curtiss ultimately achieved a radiator weight of ·5 psf with water weight of ·2 psf. Mike Thurston and Bill Wait of Curtiss held two patents on wing radiators covering their method of manufacture and use. The Curtiss radiators, as Wait explained, were "not too delicate! The brass sheet used was quite tough." Proof of their strength occurred in 1926 when the R3C-4 radiators were badly distorted after disastrous engine detonation but were pounded back into shape and reused. The climax of early skin radiator development came at the 1922 Pulitzer where the first four finishers, all Curtiss racers, used the devices.

In France the Société Moreux late in 1922 fabricated a "laminar type" wing radiator which in many ways was built on the lines of the Curtiss, the most successful example being used on the Nieuport-Delage sesquiplane which set the world speed record in February 1923. Yet it was Lamblin – not Curtiss – who filed suit against Moreux for infringement of patent and in the fall of 1923 won a judgment of 20,000 francs, 10,000 to

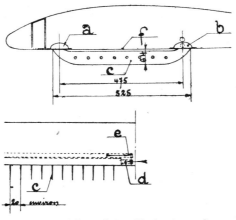

Beginning of the end: Lamblin's wing radiators (here is the 1924 version used on the world speed record Bernard, dimensions in millimeters) were technically inferior to the flush, streamlined Curtiss type.

be paid each by Moreux and Bréguet, who had also used the radiator. The Bernard world speed record aeroplane of 1924 then used Lamblin wing radiators, but these, mounted on the wing bottom surface, consisted of copper, finlike cooling elements precisely like those used in the lobster pots, only set on a pair of header strips just as if one of the lobster pots had been cut, then unrolled until flat. This caused the fins to stick out vertically from the wing about 5 or 6 inches, an arrangement certainly inferior to the Curtiss scheme. If these protruding fins had been mounted on the top wing surface they no doubt would have caused unacceptable aerodynamic problems. A similar Lamblin arrangement was used on the otherwise sleek Supermarine S.4 monoplane of 1925, and while not entirely satisfactory they were an improvement over the flat, box radiators that sprouted grotesquely from the lower wings of the contemporary Gloster IIIs. The first Lamblins ever used in England had been lobster pots attached to the Bamel when it was sent to France for the 1921 Coupe Deutsch; wing skin radiators similar to the Curtiss models were not used until after 1925, when they were fitted to the Gloster III-B.

Of course, racer designers were optimizing only ground-level performance with little regard for the potential differences a skin-radiator–equipped pursuit plane at the atmospheric pressure and temperature of 20,000 feet might encounter. The Curtiss PW-8 Hawk with wing radiators entered squadron operations in 1924, but the delicate devices proved unsuitable for continuous, rugged, high-altitude service, and repeated exposure to maneuvering loads led to cracks and seepage. Their most severe drawback on potential combat aeroplanes was their vulnerability to bullet holes. Skin radiators remained exclusive for low-level, high-speed sprint planes, and freed from all but the minimum reliability constraints, they were further

developed in the following years, reaching their peak with the final Schneider-inspired racers. Almost every square inch of available area on the Supermarine S.6B and Macchi-Castoldi M.C.72 world speed record seaplanes became radiating surface; the S.6B wing cooling surface was smooth while the incredible 440-mph M.C.72 of 1934 employed corrugated skin radiators on the top and bottom of each wing, all four pontoon-mounting struts, two on the fuselage, and six on the pontoons! M.C.72 maximum radiating capacity was some 600 calories/minute/square meter while its tandem engines were imparting to the water 10 calories/minute/hp, or enough heat to require 40 square meters of radiator surface for equilibrium. Its actual radiating surface was less than this, which meant its engines would begin to overheat seriously after just a few minutes of high-power operation. (Skin radiator effectiveness depended on not only the extent of surface but the surface finish, speed and temperature of the airflow, and flow rate of the water inside.)

It was apparent that as long as man was restricted to water as a cooling medium he was severely limited – the Italians had already miscalculated and built a twin-engine racer in 1929, the Savoia-Marchetti S.65 "Flying Egg" hampered by its radiator surface which was adequate to run only one engine at a time! Obviously a breakthrough had to be made: man needed a new fluid suitable for high-temperature operation without boiling away, enabling the fluid to work at temperatures closer to actual engine temperatures. Then radiator size could be drastically reduced since there would be no need to keep the fluid below 212° F. A search for such a fluid began seriously in 1923 but persisted for years without success until, late in the 1920s, a remarkable substance with the necessary heat-transfer properties was developed. Called ethylene glycol (somewhat similar to Prestone commercially), its high boiling point

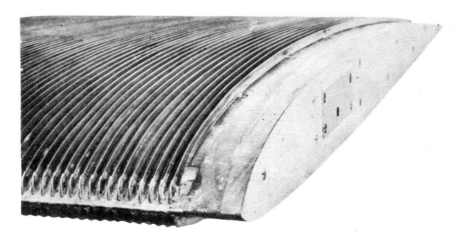

Evolution of radiators for water cooling led to this advanced form of wing radiator, in use for high-speed flying by the late 1920s. (N)

enabled it to run hotter than 212° F and still cool the engine. Optimistic early tests were conducted at fluid temperatures above 300° F., but it was later determined that 265° F. was near the optimum. The use of glycol led to the term "liquid-cooled" — as opposed to "water-cooled" — and certainly the most dramatic early exhibition of glycol cooling occurred at the 1929 NAR when, to Jimmy Doolittle's surprise, the new, small radiator on his P-1 allowed so much speed to build up during an outside loop that the wings shed and Doolittle had to take to his parachute!

The first planes to use glycol cooling operationally were the Curtiss P-6As delivered in 1930, whose new radiators were 70 per cent smaller than the water radiators they replaced. In Europe glycol cooling was not yet available; thus the Italian Macchi-Castoldi M.C.72 racer even in 1934 was forced to fly with water and accommodate the massive skin radiators this entailed. Although these had become anachronisms in an age of increasing emphasis on air-cooled engines, skin radiators allowed the speed seekers almost complete freedom in the art of streamlining, and skin-radiator-equipped racers held the world speed record for seventeen years. Yet, paradoxically, development of glycol cooling helped abolish the seaplane as a high-speed vehicle because, while Schneider racers were suitable as beds for increasingly highly stressed engines, their pontoons, as devices on which to mount the no-longer-needed immense skin radiators, became liabilities. Such aeroplanes, moreover, were never very good on rough water. Liquid cooling receded through the 1930s until the need for high power and maximum streamlining compelled its return for the landplane fighters of World War II.

AIRFRAME: TRANSFORMING THE AEROPLANE

Rebirth of the monoplane

In terms of aerodynamic design another major evolutionary step taken by the speed seekers during the 1920s was to reestablish the invincibility of the monoplane. Anyone asked today would agree the monoplane is the fundamentally correct form for high-speed aeroplanes, but it was not always so. In 1914 all international speed records were held by monoplanes, but from 1914 until the end of 1924 — a period of more than ten years — no speed record was made and no great race was won by a monoplane. The biplane's invincibility went virtually undisputed, leading to the question: why should opinion as to the merits of biplanes versus monoplanes have wavered to such an extent?

In 1906 Trajan Vuia flew the first powered monoplane almost — but not quite — 80 feet with a carbonic acid engine good for just three minutes! Despite this inauspicious beginning, and in the face of the withering influence of such biplane proponents as the Wright Brothers, the prewar monoplane grew rapidly in popularity and stature and became by far the favorite for speed. The "magnificent men" are almost reverently remembered for their Antoinettes, Demoiselles, and Blériots, while less well-known monoplanes also previewed future trends. Robert Esnault-Pelterie's R.E.P. no. 2*bis* of 1910 employed a monoplane wing quite thick for those days, built of composite spars of wood, aluminum, and steel. The single main wheel was mounted on an oleo-equipped steel tube fork (two small outrigger wheels were fitted at the wingtips) and the whole thing was pulled along by a four-blade metal prop, foot-throttle–operated! But this R.E.P. pointed out the root of the controversy. Although a cleaner design than a biplane — even in 1910 — the biplane permitted the use of a considerably lighter wing structure.

Louis Blériot's landmark flight across the English Channel in 1909 in a monoplane of his own design nevertheless seemed to fix this design form securely in the orbit of aviation, and indeed, monoplanes soon outnumbered biplanes. Early doubts regarding the monoplane occurred in Britain, where scientists at the prestigious Royal Aircraft Establishment, Farnborough, were becoming obsessed with stability in a period when stability was regarded elsewhere as unimportant or even objectionable because it operates at cross-purposes to control and maneuverability. Pitch stability considerations were based on "center of pressure travel," which, for a given area, would be less for the shorter chord of a biplane than for the longer chord of an equivalent monoplane.[22] Thus the

[22] The ability of an airfoil to act on an airstream depends on the airfoil's curvature (called camber), its thickness (the line connecting the airfoil's leading and trailing edges is the chord line; thickness is usually given as a percentage of chord length), and the airfoil's attitude in the airstream (the angle its chord makes with the airstream, called angle of attack; curiously, the British call this the angle of incidence, whereas in the United States — and in this book — angle of incidence refers instead to the angle at which the wing is fixed to the aeroplane, that is, the angle the chord makes with the aeroplane's longitudinal axis). It is convenient to consider all forces generated by the airstream on the airfoil as though concentrated at one point, called the center of pressure, c.p., a point much like the fulcrum of a seesaw — but a fulcrum that *moves along the seesaw* as the seesaw (wing chord) angle changes in the airstream! For example, when an airfoil shaped like the segment of an arc is at an angle of attack of 90 degrees (as might occur in a wind tunnel test), the c.p. is obviously at the mid-point, that is, at 50 per cent of the chord. As the angle of attack is reduced the c.p. moves forward along the chord until the angle of attack is approximately 15 degrees; but with further reduction of angle of attack the c.p. reverses and moves aft until at an angle of attack of 0 degrees it may be off the trailing edge! Thus the c.p. is said to be stable at angles of attack down to 15 degrees but unstable below that. By varying airfoil shape (camber and thickness) the stability of the c.p. can be controlled somewhat; that is, the angle of attack at which the onset of rearward c.p. movement occurs can be reduced to perhaps 2 degrees, typical

balancing arm to the tail could be shorter for the biplane and the final design dynamically more effective.

The doubts were fueled because relatively weak engines of that day demanded abundant lifting surface, and the subdivision of such large areas into two units seemed only logical. This in turn allowed a natural bridge-like structure, lightweight but strong, in which biplane wing spars formed beams which could be readily trussed together by vertical struts and diagonal wires, and since the large surface could be arranged in a very compact, short span manner, it had the added advantage of possessing very low damping (resistance) to roll. This enabled biplanes to remain handy and quick to maneuver in close-turn aerial combats throughout World War I. In fact, the philosophy was extended and Germany's Red Baron, Manfred von Richthofen, flew a triplane, a form which enjoyed brief but intense popularity and was still important in air racing during the early 1920s. To achieve similar maneuverability, a monoplane had to be tapered, resulting in slow, costly construction and difficult repairs for those days.

The gravest doubts of all arose during 1912 when a series of unfortunate fatal accidents involving monoplanes occurred owing to structural collapse during flight, in one instance due to a main spar buckling *downward*, and this especially seemed to confirm that not enough was known about the distribution of aerodynamic loads on monoplanes.

This growing set of doubts was not

of actual flight angles of attack, and this effort is what so preoccupied the speed seekers. But it was not until the later introduction of the mathematical concept of defining the airfoil's aerodynamic center (a.c.) — the point or fulcrum that does not move and around which the resultant moment from lift and drag forces acting through their lever arms does not vary with angle of attack (even though the forces themselves may vary) — that designers could begin to predict and manage their aeroplane characteristics in the design stage prior to flight.

pleasing to the rigidly organized academic minds characteristic of the ruling faction in aviation then. Whenever a monoplane crashed the doubts multiplied and soon a religious fervor permeated the spreading impression that the monoplane as a type was somehow dangerous. After five pilots had been killed in France because of structural failure, all monoplanes were prohibited from flying in France until they had been beefed up in accordance with modifications developed by Louis Blériot. Circumstances were worse in England. By late summer 1912, despite repeated indications of the monoplane's superior high-speed potential, the British War Office, following France's lead, banned the monoplane from military use! The ban was absolute. (The British Admiralty, avoiding panic, imposed no ban, but with one exception all RNAS monoplanes were French-built and had been beefed up.)

At this very time, as luck would have it, Tom Sopwith demonstrated to a startled aeronautical world a biplane which, power for power, was as fast as current monoplanes. This was the remarkable Sopwith Tabloid and it shattered any hopes for immediate monoplane resurgence. Though the French monoplane restriction was reasonable and the British ban temporary – a report issued early in February 1913 acquitted the monoplane as a type from blame, the ban subsequently being lifted when certain monoplanes had been beefed up – psychologically the damage had been done. The ban had an enormous impact far beyond its surface effect. The all-powerful RAE at Farnborough had become, as described by one who was there at the time, the "Vatican of British prejudice" against the monoplane from which a single-minded, understated but tenacious passion served to suppress the type and effectively distort the orderly development of aeroplane design for almost twenty years. Men with a poverty of imagination could exist and even flourish in this atmposhere; fortunately there were a few icono-

clastic individuals elsewhere in the industry whose imaginations soared above such pettiness – and almost made up the difference. More typical, however, were men like George Handasyde, prewar champion of monoplanes, who to his disgust was ordered to design biplanes (the Martinsydes) for wartime combat duty, and it is fully to his credit that he designed probably the fastest operational aeroplane built during World War I, the Martinsyde F.4 Buzzard, which did something just over 140 mph. After his one notable biplane racer in 1920 (which was ironically converted in 1921 into a weird monoplane called the Alula with which he had nothing to do), Handasyde simply gave up and retired to Surrey, thoroughly discouraged. England's solitary wartime monoplane was the lean 1916 Bristol, whose frugal lines reflected the Scottish ancestry of its designer, Captain Frank Barnwell, and though it did a creditable 127 mph with just a 110-hp LeRhone, it was relegated to obscure service in the Middle East; only one survived to grace air race circuits until 1923.

In Germany the situation was somewhat different. Tony Fokker was interested in monoplanes – he began the war with the E-I Eindecker and ended it with the razorback D-VIII – yet virtually all these early monoplanes were to some extent externally braced. Hugo Junkers' celebrated use of metal was only incidental to his vastly more ambitious goal, namely to build an internally braced *cantilever* monoplane wing, and his early wartime designs embodied a definite if crude beginning toward the successful application of this principle.

Following the generally sterile marktime of warplane design in terms of speed, resurgence of postwar air racing promised resumption of a solid technical march. The availability of more powerful engines meant the aeroplane could take off with heavier wing loadings – or, in the case of a maximum performance racer with no load requirement other than pilot and fuel, with

wings of reduced area. As required area comes down so does the biplane's weight advantage because the monoplane wing forms a smaller proportion of the aeroplane's total weight. But of course landing speed goes up. In 1920 the process of design was purely empirical, and landing speeds were limited only by the pilot's courage. Yet the 1920 Gordon Bennett, as the first major influence, spawned two monoplane designs. The first became notorious as the Texas Wildcat but it was plagued with wicked flutter and terrifying landing speeds; quickly changed to a biplane before the race and later even a triplane, it was fast but never entirely successful. The second was perhaps the most visionary single design of the immediate postwar era, the Dayton-Wright RB, a remarkable cantilever monoplane which employed a "variable camber" wing that made this modest racer, astonishing for its time, the pioneer of a technique widely used today. Although a striking experiment, its momentous ideas inevitably received a setback when the plane became a race dropout. Too much too soon, the RB was swimming upstream: consider that of eight entries in the 1913 Gordon Bennett, seven were monoplanes (one biplane failed to start); by contrast, among the fourteen entries filed for the 1920 Gordon Bennett seven years later – after the supposed impetus of World War I – the RB was the *only* monoplane at the starting line! Although there would be no rational blame on its ideas, its failure tended to squelch additional "radical" breakaways from traditional types, and the externally braced thin-wing biplane – enhanced by improved streamlining of struts and bracing wires which considerably reduced monoplane advantage – would dominate aeroplane design through the rest of the decade.

Similar ideas often seem to blossom simultaneously. During 1920 the French firm Gastambide & Levavasseur also produced a variable surface wing in which both the leading and trailing

edges slid on projecting rails. Although ostensibly a logical concept which should enable clipped-wing speed-planes to enjoy moderate landing speeds, wing "disassembly" in flight was primitive and impractical in those days. Orville Wright himself patented the "split flap" in 1923 (the type used on the Douglas DC-3); Handley Page and Lachmann in Europe and Harlan Fowler in the United States continued to pursue such trends. Yet high lift devices were almost totally avoided on racers. Only R. J. Mitchell of the early speed seekers equipped a racer with flaps. But the drag of unsealed gaps together with structural problems with his Supermarine S.4 cantilever monoplane in 1925 caused him to renounce their use on subsequent speedplanes, and in Europe high landing speeds became accepted as a penalty of air racing.

In postwar France monoplane popularity was unhampered. Nieuport-Delage championed the form in beauteous racers beginning in 1921 and developed it almost ostentatiously through the early 1920s while rival Adolphe Bernard, with less public visibility, built cantilever monoplane racers which strongly influenced subsequent high-speed design thinking. The well-known British Supermarine Schneider monoplanes after 1925 undoubtedly owe their origins in large measure to the 280-mph French Bernard monoplane of 1924, although after 1925 all successful Schneider-oriented monoplanes were externally braced.

Even within the growing monoplane camp, controversy existed in the increasing preoccupation over differences between thick and thin wings. Designers took for granted that internally braced wings also meant very thick wings in order to provide for sufficiently strong spars. The momentous idea of internal bracing was at first opposed because it was assumed, on inadequate scientific basis, that a thick cantilever wing would necessarily have more drag at high speed than an externally braced thin wing of equivalent area, a belief that deepened the monoplane's early stigma. The bulky, lavishly bearded mechanical wizard Léon Levavasseur had built the first thick cantilever wing monoplane — called Monobloc — for a 1911 military competition; although lovely, it proved too heavy to fly. Hugo Junkers had used thick, symmetrical "tadpole" airfoils, poor performers. William Stout, a whimsical but cunning American engineer called "Detroit's Da Vinci" who became father of Ford's thick, cantilever-wing "Tin Goose" Tri-Motor transport, originally provided wing depth not by thicker airfoils but by longer chords (e.g., the Bat Wing of 1921). The efficiency given up was somewhat compensated because the wing did not have to lift so much per square foot of area. Yet this approach, too, was inadequate. Thick airfoil shapes were researched by Prandtl and his colleagues at Göttingen and in 1921 by NACA in the United States. These tests proved that thick wings had been sadly misjudged. Tiny wind tunnel models proved to be quite misleading when compared to full-size wings, and engineers were only beginning to learn about such factors as Reynolds number — or scale effect. It was soon discovered in meaningful tests that full-size airfoils three times the thickness of the venerable RAF-15, if properly designed, could achieve equivalent ratios of lift to drag. Imperfect information was being rectified and systematic development of low-drag, stable airfoils suitable for use on internally braced monoplane wings was undertaken. (The speed seekers' ideal wing — a feasible thin cantilever — was still more than twenty-five years in the future).

As early as April 1921, *Flight* editorialized the "return of the monoplane" — it seemed the world was on the verge of a "new era." The development of retractable-gear, cantilever-wing racing monoplanes was optimistically predicted in May. Indeed, in France, several monoplanes were

at that moment under construction for the autumn Coupe Deutsch race, and one, René Hanriot's HD.22, was a full-fledged version of this very concept! Barely completed and untried by race time, it withdrew, but its Nieuport-Delage competitor, essentially a monoplane, although externally braced with a fixed gear and built of wood, on September 26, 1921, became the first aeroplane officially to exceed 200 mph.

Junkers in 1915 demonstrated how to make cantilever monoplane wings statically safe from collapse by implementing his conviction that the wing structure could only be practical if built with metal, even though the authorities thought his iron and steel contraptions too heavy. Verville, when he designed the R-3 racer of 1922, employed a fully cantilever wing built of wood. Both designers mounted their wings low, Junkers primarily to provide crew protection in a crash, Verville to provide convenient storage space for his then novel retractable landing gear, allowing the gear legs to be short, thus light. Again, the idea was not exclusive to Verville. Booth and Thurston, working in Hammondsport, New York, scene of Glenn Curtiss' earliest triumphs, developed the same formula at precisely the same time, and built the two Bee-Line racers for the Navy's 1922 Pulitzer team. Though smaller than the R-3 (200 pounds lighter, over 2 feet less span), and powered by the same model engine, the ill-chosen, thick airfoil plagued their maximum performance; Verville had used a new NACA airfoil of similar thickness but which produced comparatively far less drag.

Although the relatively thick wings on cantilever monoplanes at the 1922 Pulitzer provided a glimpse of the future — they were the first genuine American examples of this type — the Curtiss R-6 triumph seemed a definite victory for the thin-wing biplane and assured its further development. Many concluded that monoplanes were unsuitable for high speed after their

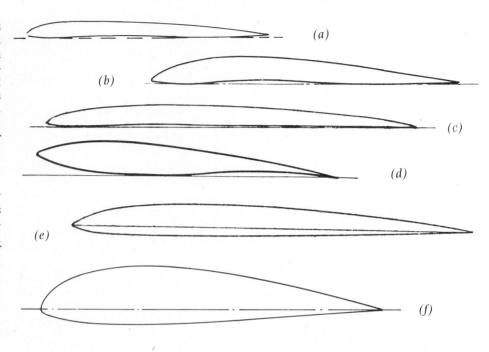

Typical speed airfoils used during the early 1920s: (a) the widely used RAF-15 reflecting World War I technology; (b) the U. S. Navy M-80, 1921; (c) thin Sloan airfoil used on Curtiss racers, 1921; (d) under-cambered airfoil used on the world speed record Nieuport-Delage sesquiplane, 1922; (e) Curtiss C-62 airfoil, 1923; (f) airfoil used on world speed record Bernard, 1924, reflecting the trend toward thick-wing cantilever monoplanes

mediocre 1922 showing, but made the mistake of equating the thick airfoils of 1922 with the monoplane principle. Designers of cantilever wings in 1922 had little precedent to go by compared to two decades of continuous development of the thin-wing biplane. The sun was setting on thin-wing speed biplanes even then, of course; just five years later the practical limit of true speed biplanes was achieved with virtually the last of the species, the Gloster IV-B, which did 295 mph at the 1927 Schneider — not even 60 mph faster than the Curtiss R-6. On the other hand, that the speed seekers had discovered many of the

answers with their pioneering monoplanes in 1921–22 can be appreciated by comparing their racers with Britain's immortal Battle-of-Britain Hawker Hurricane monoplane fighter, which first appeared in 1934. Even then, twelve years after the R-3, the Hurricane's cantilever wing was built entirely of wood and had a root airfoil fully 19½ per cent thick.

The move from wood to metal
Efforts to surmount difficulties imposed by higher speeds with totally new construction methods resulted in some of the most significant yet least appreciated contributions made by

the speed seekers of the early 1920s. In this regard they contrived early solutions to some fundamental problems, the successful examples of which would be repeated in later years, often to be cited as novel in their turn. When dealing with less glamorous and often not well-understood aeronautical considerations, it has been convenient frequently to overlook building blocks first assiduously laid during the 1920s.

For over sixty years the most important structural element of any currently modern aerospace vehicle has been the *thin-walled shell*. This is as true today as it was when first extensively used by the early speed seekers; that this basic form of construction should remain essentially the same for so long a time span, particularly when virtually all other aspects of the maximum performance aerospace vehicle — its shape, its density, its size — have undergone radical changes, is remarkable. Although credit for devising the first aeronautically adapted thin-shell structure is variously accorded to Frederick Handley Page for a plane exhibited at the 1911 Olympia Aero Show or to the Frenchman Ruchonnet, the first practical streamlined fuselage which made use of a load-carrying skin appeared on a Deperdussin racer designed by Louis Béchéreau in France in 1912. Three thin (approximately 1·5 mm) layers of tulipwood veneer were glued together around a cigar-shaped mold, and the finished form — which had no internal bracing — was nicknamed *monocoque* (single eggshell), a word which upsets language purists since it is formed from the Greek *monos* and the Latin *coccum*; i.e., the fuselage structure provided rigidity in the same manner as a stiff eggshell with no internal skeleton.

Despite its hybrid origins the nickname stuck, and Béchéreau's monumental example of genius was widely copied. Gabriel Borel and Louis Blériot built wood monocoques in 1912, and in a remarkable glimpse of the future, Morane-Saulnier in 1915 built a primitive steel shell, reinforced internally with steel rings braced with steel wires. During World War I many beautiful wood monocoque fighters appeared over the Western Front, notably the German Albatros (which used a three-ply covering, always superbly made), Roland, and Pfalz fighters, and after the war the wood monocoque was developed to a high degree for speedplanes. Lieutenant Alexander Klemin continued the development of stressed wood veneer construction at McCook Field in 1918. Thin plywood — sometimes thinner than $1/16$-inch — was used for wing and fuselage skin. One-sixteenth-inch three-ply required $1/48$-inch veneer; poplar veneer as thin as $1/60$-inch was available then but only in widths up to 24 inches, therefore the planking of large structures was done with narrow strips. Mahogany and spruce veneers were also used as well as other low-density woods such as redwood which occasionally were employed as the core ply between high-density birch or maple face plies. Grain deviation between plies proved critical; 90 degrees is best for strength, although a deviation of only 10 degrees often caused serious warping. In addition, poor glue quality often contributed to warping as well as unexpected failures in wood structures. Most frequently used were blood albumin glues which generally required hot pressing with steam-heated plates to achieve maximum strength. The Army and Navy for years early in the 1920s considered Jeffery's Patent Waterproof Liquid Glue the standard; in the meantime a strenuous effort lasting years was urged to perfect improved strong waterproof cold-press glues.

Thin-wall wood racers which soon appeared included the Verville VCP-R, built in halves and then joined along the center line, which competed in the 1920 Gordon Bennett with similar wood-shell Nieuports and Spad-Herbemonts. The French, spurred by the earlier Deperdussin success, were eager experimenters in wood monocoques, using strips that varied from $3/4$ inch to 2 inches wide; the Nieuport racers were built of as many as six layers of strips, each as thin as 0·9 mm. Curtiss in the United States continued to exploit this form of construction with "Curtiss-ply," a spruce plywood $3/32$ inch thick in 2-inch-wide strips which was used to plank their entire line of superlative racers through 1925. Not only were thin-wood monocoque shells efficient, light, rigid structures, they could be polished to a glassy smooth flawless finish.

Naturally, early designers attempted to maintain the rigidity of their structures; no wrinkling of the skin could be tolerated, especially with wood that would warp, crack, splinter, or even worse. Thus, despite the popularity of thin veneers, the wall thickness had to be kept reasonably large compared to the shell's radius of curvature, and extensive internal bulkheading was generally used. Wood is also notoriously non-homogeneous and uncertain in its strength-to-weight; moreover, it becomes weak in the cold temperatures at high altitudes and can deflect excessively under load, allowing wings easily to get out of true. It also loses strength when wet. A sodden machine in the tropics may have only half the strength of the same machine when tested in a dry workshop at home, and this factor was important in France's early trend toward metal construction since wood aeroplanes fared badly in France's widespread equatorial colonies. A severe wartime spruce famine, hastened by blind policies which early in the war caused great quantities of superior, prefabricated spruce spars to be discarded for often ridiculously minor defects, forced Britain to consider metal construction. Had the war lasted a year longer it is doubtful that even inferior, artificially seasoned spruce would have held out. Near war's end, in the words of Boulton & Paul's J. D. North, "Metal construction blossomed in the sun of official approval, watered by the gentle dew of financial assistance." Nevertheless, significant metal aeroplane development in England awaited the early 1920s. Metal was attractive because of its unlimited variety in shapes, forms, and dimensions; the comparative reliability and accuracy in establishing its strength; its imperviousness to climate; its adaptability to mass production; and, certainly of prime importance, the fact that it is fireproof.

When metal aeroplanes were first built, however, the metal was *not* adapted to thin-shell structures and in a sense this was a regression. Instead, for the most part, only "vital members" — spars, struts, longerons, wires — were fabricated in metal, but such simple substitution of metal girders where formerly wood had been used was terribly inefficient from both the standpoint of excessive weight and not making full use of the structural advantages metal afforded.

In addition, the first metal used in aeroplane construction was steel. The French designer Louis Bréguet in 1910 used a steel-tube structure sheathed in metal skin called the "coffeepot," and Major A. R. Low, RAF, designed the first all-steel wing in England, which was built by Vickers in 1912; both were junked because of enormous weight. In 1919 Boulton & Paul at Norwich first formed ribs, spars, and other forms of wood replacement from high-tensile, narrow (5 inches wide) steel strip, usually ·35 per cent carbon steel from the Sheffield district, cold-rolled and "blued" (tempered at 400° C.). Use of steel proved difficult and costly, and in addition the metal was too heavy, but early steel strip spars were particularly good at resisting buckling when compressed (squeezed toward the middle). An influential exponent of steel construction was Major Fred M. Green, formerly chief engineer on the Siddeley-Deasy Jaguar engine who, because he found it difficult to work under John Siddeley, became chief engineer of Armstrong-Whitworth in 1921, noted for steel construction.

J. D. North in 1920 patented (160107) the processes of "sheradizing" and "cosletizing" (zinc-coating) steel strips, and alloying steel with chromium. He also scrapped his woodworking plant, convinced metal aeroplanes were here to stay.

During these early days, when alterations to new aeroplanes were frequent and sometimes extensive and when high-speed racers were generally one of a kind, the use of specially designed metal parts which required costly tools was generally inexpedient. Moreover, metal must be distributed efficiently to maximize strength and minimize weight, and designers had yet to learn how to use metal reliably in the slender forms required. Highly developed forms of wood construction for aeroplanes were thus perpetuated. Early development of huge, rigid, lighter-than-air ships at Germany's Zeppelin works provided an exception. Since wood was obviously unsuitable for such giants, Zeppelin success depended on very light metal structures, and Zeppelin designers naturally turned to aluminum, specifically the new wrought alloy developed by Alfred Wilm, a tough, copper-rich metal called *duralumin*, since pure aluminum was too soft. In England, Vickers, Ltd., made early use of one such alloy, a typical duralumin containing 95·5 per cent aluminum and 3·0 per cent copper together with 1·0 per cent manganese and 0·5 per cent magnesium, to build the huge *R-80* dirigible at war's end. Airship success inspired a young Zeppelin engineer, Claudius Dornier, to embark in 1914 on the construction of metal flying boats. By 1918 he had designed a twin-engine eight-passenger monoplane flying boat with steel spars and duralumin box ribs which led to the remarkable Dornier Wal, first built in 1922 and still being produced in 1936. In England, however, because steel had seemed apt in aeroplane structures, the Air Ministry inveigled persuasively against a growing proclivity for aluminum alloys, citing the pride of

England's steel industry and forgetting that London itself was built on aluminum-bearing clay. Oswald Short in 1920 demolished this narrow prejudice by building the first all-aluminum monocoque structure in England, the fuselage of the Short Silver Streak. Short had tested steel and aluminum in Medway tides; he selected paper-thin aluminum for his wrap-around skin, and his structure was remarkably advanced, but his outspokenness hardened reactionary resistance from the RAE. Short was unable for months to obtain a copy of the test report which proved the great strength of his structure. In November 1921 he finally secured a patent (185992) but the delay worked against him. Nothing further was heard from the British on aluminum structures in a speed-seeking sense until 1927.

Another early objection to the use of duralumin was its high wartime cost when it was so scarce as to be virtually precious. By October 1919, however, Vickers' prices were down to 2/11d (about 75¢) per pound for extruded sections, and duralumin became plentiful in the early 1920s. A far more serious prejudice against the alloy grew up over the fear of corrosion which appeared occasionally, largely the result of ignorance over its properties with and without heat treatment. It was said that duralumin "properly varnished" would not corrode, but in fact the metal had to be worked hot then allowed to harden to full strength, a process which could take several days. In the United States, despite European airship success, aluminum was so mistrusted that the Navy issued the infamous specification 100-A which prohibited its use! The stereotype of the too rigid edict based on what *appeared* to have worked best in the past, it was soon overruled under the weight of forward-looking designs. The Alcoa firm was already developing a wide family of alloys for aircraft use with copper content that varied from 2·5 to 4·5 per cent. Traces of magnesium and/or manganese were

generally added, and up to 1·0 per cent silicon when the alloy was to be used in forgings. All such Alcoa alloys – the widely used 17ST, for example – could be called "duralumin," a word which by then had become a generic term applied to all wrought aluminum alloys. Before 1930 Alcoa had also developed Alclad, a thin sheet in sandwich form, using a core of 17ST dural, heat-treated at 950° F. for twenty minutes and aged at room temperature for six days, with surface layers of pure aluminum. Combining the strength of duralumin with the corrosion-resistant properties of the pure metal, it was used extensively as aircraft skin for the next twenty years.

Another very early metal aeroplane was built in 1912 by Professor Hans Reissner at Aachen, Germany, and flown by Swiss pilot Robert Gsell, but its distinctive feature was a wing covered by *corrugated* skin to increase the chordwise bending rigidity, the corrugations running parallel to the wind so as to avoid unacceptable drag. This principle of stiffness by means of corrugation was further refined by Hugo Junkers, famous before the war as a maker of household heating apparatus and later professor of thermodynamics at Aachen, who had patented his cantilever monoplane wing in 1910 but did not render it in metal until December 1915 when he built the Junkers J.1. Despite efforts by his government to suppress his designs, a series of similar corrugated Junkers monoplanes extended through the J.10 of 1918 – some ground-strafer versions carried an incredible barrage of sixteen guns pointing through the bottom to rake the ground below – and beyond to the J.L.6, irreverently remembered by old timers as the "Tin Donkey," which was exported to the United States and flown by Bert Acosta in 1920. In December 1921 a similar Junkers with a German BMW (Bavarian Motor Works) engine set a world duration record of almost twenty-seven hours at Roosevelt Field piloted by Eddie Stinson and Lloyd

Bertaud.[23] William B. Stout adapted the Junkers-style corrugated skin into a series of huge, cumbersome aeroplanes in the United States beginning with a twin-engine tanklike torpedo carrier in 1922 and resulting by decade's end in the redoubtable Ford "Tin Goose." Stout was assisted by George Henry Prudden, sometimes credited as designer (in 1910) of the first all-metal plane built in the United States, who was Stout's stress engineer from 1920–22 and chief engineer from 1923–25. Corrugations were also used extensively in the walls of internal box spars and to provide stiffness in metal bulkheads, uses which made more sense and which persisted long after the mid-1930s when corrugated outer skins were discontinued.

At the 1921 Paris Air Show observers were amazed at the vastly increased use of metal in French designs, which extended from several large transports to the all-metal, smooth-skin Hanriot HD.22 racer. These aeroplanes, despite their generally inefficient forms of construction, were noteworthy because of the increased and bold use of duralumin. But the aeroplane designers who ventured to use it were still preoccupied with correct girder design, taking comfort that their spars and struts were only two thirds the weight of the wood members they replaced. Little emphasis was placed on the efficient use of metal skin. Indeed, thin metal structures were highly suspect because, according to Dr. Albert P. Thurston, F.R.Ae.S., a brilliant and prophetic engineer who in 1919 boldly predicted all-metal transports weighing several hundred thousand pounds, "Local failures due to local flexure [in thin metal] can occur

[23] After that, the Junkers were ignored in the United States because of lingering distaste for things German. Elsewhere they helped forge airline success, notably with Scadta (later Avianca), serving along Colombia's rugged Magdalena River.

Typical of early 1920s metal aeroplane technology was the Gallaudet DB.1 two-place monoplane bomber. Like most of its brave contemporaries, it was overweight. (Au)

Another example of all-metal aero technology in 1922. Seated in the cockpit of his twin-Packard ST-1 duralumin torpedo bomber is pungent, persuasive, philosophical William Bushnell Stout, forty-two, called "Detroit's da Vinci." When this aeroplane was built many called him crackpot. His lifelong doctrine was "simplicate and add lightness." Stout sold Henry Ford on his all-metal ideas and fathered the Ford Tri-Motor transports. He lived until 1956. (Au)

before the full strength of the material has been developed." In those days engineers had concluded that shell radius should be *less* than twenty times wall thickness!

Despite these fears the next major step was the use of smooth, very thin metal skin to cover a structure built of light, mutually perpendicular frames. At first designers proceeded cautiously because, unlike the Deperdussin's wood skin, the skin on most of these early thin-wall metal planes served merely as a covering and carried none of the main load. Indeed, on the 1921 Hanriot racer the skin was attached to the structure with simple snaps! But one year later another French racer used all-metal, thin-skin construction — it was the Bernard C.1 — and it proved to be the *pièce de résistance* of the 1922 Paris Air Show. With the Bernard there was an important difference: the skin itself was planned to take some 20 per cent of the stresses.

To appreciate how this difference was the harbinger of a breakthrough one must understand that later development of lightweight metal aeroplane construction still awaited the discovery that a thin-wall structure could safely carry loads even if the skin was wrinkled. This was a momentous discovery which was first exploited systematically by the German firm of Adolf K. Rohrbach in two obscure all-metal transports (the Roland and Romar) which did not appear until several years after the Bernard. Rohrbach had designed smooth metal skin wings in 1919; the incredible four-engine, all-metal Zeppelin-Staaken 19,000-pound monoplane in 1921, destroyed by the Disarmament Commission; coined the term "stressed skin" in 1924; and Rohrbach engineer Herbert A. Wagner, who developed the analysis methods for the buckled shell (the tension diagonal field theory), first lectured on these revolutionary ideas at Aachen in 1929. The two later Rohrbach transports were forgotten but the ideas they embodied, later reflected in the Wagner beam — strong edge flanges connected by an extremely thin web which wrinkled under any applied load — became textbook classics.

The skin of the Bernard C.1 racer even though load-bearing had been designed *not* to wrinkle since in 1922 wrinkling was still considered unsafe. The basis for most work involving thin shells early in the 1920s was Love's theory of shells and Bryan's theory of stability, both dating to the 1890s. With its ring bulkheads, sturdy stringers, and tough skin the Bernard had an unnecessarily high load factor of 18, indicating imperfection in the theories. The true significance of the Bernard was that its designers used stressed metal skin in a smooth, thin-wall monocoque and thus turned the course of metal construction away from inept designs represented by its contemporary, the inefficient, structurally deficient, corrugated Thomas-Morse R-5 racer built the same year. It would not be until 1933 that the nineteenth-century theories were successfully submerged and Wagner's methods, supplemented in 1931 by Theodore von Karman, generally adopted. Subsequent metal thin-shell aeroplanes of the 1930s often wrinkled even under 1 g — but such "semi-monocoque" structures proved to be optimum for high-performance aeroplanes until World War II.

Not surprisingly, the Bernard C.1 was strongly criticized in 1922. The need to fabricate complicated metal parts on a piecemeal basis and assemble them largely by hand made its manufacturing costs tremendous. Construction techniques were painstaking and difficult, early dural alloys were not always of uniform quality, and criticism of impracticability from the industry's more entrenched and conservative quarters at that time all combined to stifle the design. Thus its incipient promise would remain unfulfilled for a decade and its sisters of two years later, the sleek and widely copied Bernard racers of 1924, one of which set the world speed record of almost 280 mph, were built of wood!

Interestingly enough a casual observer would notice few obvious differences in viewing the structure of a modern jet transport today placed next to the Bernard C.1 of 1922. The skin of the transport – like that of the early racer – does not wrinkle, even under limit loads, but today this is because the drag of wrinkled skin would become intolerable at near sonic speeds. Metal skins used today are thicker and often integrally stiffened, with the internal reinforcing members a part of the skin panel itself. (Newer non-metallic skin materials are often of sandwich construction or "filament-wound"). Metal structures today have been designed to accommodate requirements not relevant in 1922: aero-elasticity (today's transports are not nearly so rigid as the Bernard; engineers have learned how properly to build them flexible so as not to be brittle in gusts); creep fatigue (high temperatures aggravate this in supersonic flight); acoustic fatigue, which demands high local rigidity; and other forms of deterioration affecting a transport's service life, which must extend twenty years – certainly longer than the racing season! – and strength-to-density relationships because of differences in the modern aeroplane's complexity, shape, and inertia. Shell structure frames are now made of multiple pieces to limit crack growth and guarantee "fail safe" redundancy. After decades of experience using aviation alloys since the pioneering Bernard, it is particularly noteworthy that modern aluminum alloys are again copper-rich,[24] following a period

[24] For example, hyduminium RR.58, main structural material of the Concorde supersonic transport, is a sandwich sheet the core of which consists of a somewhat dural-like alloy: 93·5 per cent aluminum, 2·5 per cent copper, 1·5 per cent magnesium, 1·2 per cent nickel, 1·0 per cent iron, 0·2 per cent silicon, and 0·1 per cent titanium, clad with aluminum outer layers containing 1·0 per cent zirconium. Metallurgists have developed such "messy" compositions to meet a variety of modern-day needs, but the basis of virtually all such alloys is essentially the duralumin used by the speed seekers in the 1920s.

during the 1940s–50s when stronger but more brittle (fatigue-susceptible) zinc-rich recipes were used. Today's alloys, moreover, are carefully limited to steady loads no more than 25 per cent their ultimate tensile capability. Extruded stringers today are often spot-welded to skins, eliminating hard-to-get-at rivets. During the 1920s rivets were suspect because the rivet which does not fill up its hole may cause danger under vibration, yet in those days riveting was the only feasible method for joining metal parts. The Bernard's pioneering use of flush rivets was marveled at in 1922 although not copied extensively until after World War II!

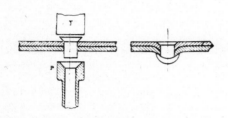

Bernard's revolutionary attempt at flush-riveting metal skins – in 1922! (contemporary drawing)

Wing skins today are integral panels machined by tape-controlled machine tools from pre-stretched planks, reflecting today's vastly increased use of machined components which allow more exact correlation of shapes and thicknesses to the stresses which modern calculation methods can now precisely define. Finished pieces often weigh as little as one twelfth the original rough blank, but manufacturers argue that cost savings from ease of assembly offset the greater raw material cost. Yet finished aerodynamic surfaces (tails, fins, etc.) today are multi-cell torsion boxes patterned very much like those on the pioneering racers built by the speed seekers of the 1920s.

The bite of flutter

As designers struggled with novel construction methods they gradually became aware of a treacherous gremlin lurking in the darkness of ignorance, a gremlin that would rise up like some Loch Ness monster and strike its quick but powerful blow before being clearly perceived.

Listen to test pilot Roland Rohlfs describing the first flight of the Curtiss-Cox Texas Wildcat, America's 200-mph racer of 1920:

"I started a right turn over Mitchel Field when almost immediately the control stick all but flew from my hands and began thrashing violently from left to right and back again. Startled, I looked at the ailerons. What I saw was not reassuring. They were moving up and down at such a rate that I wondered how much bending action they were inducing in the wings holding me aloft. Throttling the engine as a last resort caused the speed to fall off and gradually stopped the ailerons' wild dance."

In this instance Rohlfs landed safely, hobbled from the cockpit on black-and-blue knees, and the ailerons were re-rigged.

Listen to pilot Henri Biard in 1925 telling of a pre-race test flight in the Supermarine S.4, the plane on which Britain that year pinned her Schneider Trophy hopes:

"As the wind caught the wings with colossal pressure on the turn, the flutter which I had noticed so faintly before that it only seemed fancy began with a vengeance. I worked feverishly at my controls – got the machine almost round – tried to relieve that awful pressure that was making the wings flutter almost like a moth's wings – felt the air tearing at them like a living, malicious thing superhumanly bent on smashing and twisting and wrenching this mechanical intruder and hurling it to destruction – spinning down like a leaf before a gale – and then with an effort which tore at every muscle in my body, I got her righted again and

on an even keel, only to find that we had lost flying speed and it was too late . . ."

The S.4 was demolished upon impact with the bay, and Biard, coughing and spitting Chesapeake mud, just managed to survive.

Listen to Viscount Louis de Monge describe a maximum speed trial of the de Monge 5.1, a French racer in 1921:

"The pilot [had] reported aileron vibrations which caused the stick to shake. Inspection of the aileron linkage showed an excess of play in some bearings. This was indeed unfortunate because after these bearings had been readjusted the aeroplane, in a subsequent flight, was found free from aileron vibration. Taking the bearing play as the cause of the vibration was therefore a natural conclusion . . . [On its next test flight] the plane came as expected [on its speed run] following the highway at low altitude and passed close to us, then made a sharp left turn heading toward the airfield, but that turn ended in a spin nose down to the ground in front of us."

In this case catastrophe was complete. The plane was destroyed and Count Bernard de Romanet, the pilot, was killed.

In all three cases the culprit was flutter.

Flutter was insidious. It came and went with apparently no pattern, even affecting individual planes of a given type while neglecting others seemingly identical. It would sneak up, its onset barely perceptible, or in a different mood pounce in a furious onslaught with no warning. The three incidents described involved aileron flutter, but rudders, elevators, whole tails, even wings were also subject to the menace.

A few factors were beginning to be understood. All aeroplanes are to some extent elastic; high-speed airflow beating over wings or tail can stretch or bend these surfaces, depending also on their inertia, but this distortion can in turn drastically change the airflow's effect; when this mutual interaction becomes unstable, flutter results — a wild vibration like venetian blinds in a gust. Sometimes, instead of vibration, there is simply a divergence . . . and structural collapse. An early victim was Samuel Pierpont Langley, Smithsonian secretary, when his aeroplane suffered wing torsional divergence in view of 50,000 spectators on December 8, 1903 — nine days before the Wright Brothers (with far fewer witnesses) pulled off the trick he had been trying to accomplish. Through the 1920s, as aeroplane speeds increased, there was no equivalent increase in the formal requirements for aeroplane stiffness. In fact, the perpetuation of biplane superiority was influenced in no small measure by the absence of rational torsional stiffness criteria for monoplanes.

In France two important monoplane crashes in 1921 — the de Monge racer and Sadi Lecointe's Nieuport-Delage sesquiplane during the Coupe Deutsch — although publicly blamed on other causes, were both privately deemed by insiders to have resulted from aileron flutter. Yet thin, relatively flimsy wing panels which should have been more prone to flutter often remained flutter-free, apparently since ample external wire bracing provided sufficient torsional stiffness. During this time, before pilots and designers were fully aware that the mysterious, disturbing vibrations they were occasionally encountering represented entirely new aerodynamic-*cum*-structural problems, they usually supposed some mechanic had merely fumbled when rigging their planes. Many wings commonly buzzed if improperly rigged, especially pylon-braced monoplanes with bracing wires at flat angles. The problem was somewhat compounded by the lack of information transfer; seldom did an isolated experience seem sufficiently important to be brought to the attention of builders of similar aeroplanes elsewhere.

Cantilever wings were made thick for rigidity but curiously enough more often encountered serious flutter problems. Even in 1925 the Italian Macchi M.33 monoplane alarmed its pilot with ominous "wing vibrations" and he flew the Schneider race that year throttled well back. The cause was inexperience in predicting the dynamics of internally braced structures. Thick wings had first been endowed with an aura of respectability by the immortal Fokker D-VII fighter of World War I, on which their use then represented a significant departure in design practice. D-VII wings were essentially cantilevered, but their legendary N-struts, considered unnecessary even by the builders, were in fact effective anti-flutter devices. The next Fokker fighter, called E-V, was a parasol monoplane with thick, plywood-covered, cantilever outer wing panels whose torsional stiffness was determined by the same formulae which had worked for the D-VII. Shortly after its appearance at the Front in early August 1918, however, three almost immediate wing failures made it notorious and threatened to decimate the ranks of Germany's top squadron. The puzzling aspect was that the wing had apparently met all static strength standards. Tony Fokker personally reran sandbag tests. "I discovered that with increasing load," he commented later, "the angle of incidence at the wingtips increased perceptibly. It suddenly dawned on me that this increasing angle was the cause of the wing's collapse." [25]

[25] The sandbag tests may or may not have taken place in this manner. Tony Fokker indulged in a great deal of guesswork, and was notorious for his technical ignorance, neglect of detail, and brash arrogance — he also would not allow his designers to attend official strength tests or technical conferences with German Army authorities! He always stood ready to belittle staid aerodynamicists and would be eager to shift the blame away from his factory's workmanship onto them. The E-Vs, however, had been made hurriedly at Perinza Pianoforte works at Aldershof, and evidenced workmanship careless and inferior to a shocking degree.

Wreckage of cantilever plywood wing of Niedermeyer's Fokker pursuit which broke to pieces because of flutter, 1922   (USAF)

The E-V wings were condemned and sturdier wings, using members 2 millimeters thicker to accommodate slipshod manufacturing errors, were built; fighters with these wings were redesignated D-VIII, and about one

Several Aldershof wings when tested collapsed under less than 80 per cent of the normal design load! This — not flutter alone — was no doubt the primary cause of the crashes, because a wing built strictly to the specifications of his then unknown designer, Reinhold Platz, a former welder who designed Fokker aeroplanes until 1934, took a static load 191 per cent its design value (equivalent to 9·5 g) when tested in September 1918, and twisted less than 2 degrees. In 1922 Dr. W. Hoff, the director of the German aeronautical research establishment in charge of airworthiness, published the devastating E-V wing test findings, contradicting Fokker's personal and oversimplified version. In 1918 Hoff had threatened Fokker with criminal charges for what the iron-disciplined Prussian high command considered a breach of trust to send such shoddily built aeroplanes to the Front, the sin compounded by Fokker's own breezy denials of any culpability on his part. It is virtually certain that Fokker himself never fully understood the esoterics of flutter, and it was not until more powerful versions of the parasol fighter (e.g., the D-VIIIg) appeared, capable of higher speed, that pilots noticed wings ominously "began to vibrate during steep turns." In Europe the Fokker D-X parasol fighter suffered complete wing failure in flight due to wing flutter in 1924.

hundred reached the Front in time for the last three weeks of the war (almost four hundred of both types were built altogether). After the war several D-VIIIs went to the Allies. England and France ignored the D-VIII on the basis of its reputation for fragility, but the Dutch kept them operational until 1923, Italy until 1925. Two went to the United States for test work at McCook Field and were numbered P-165 and P-169; the former survived until March 1927. Lieutenant Leigh Wade wrote a test report on the D-VIII in May 1921, describing it as "maneuverable" and "easy to fly" — his only criticism being the inconvenient engine controls, with "throttle for gas on the left side of the fuselage; throttle for air on the left side of the control stick." However, other test pilots noted occasional vicious wing flutter, and Fred Verville, a witness, personally described how the D-VIII wing would "wave and shake." Verville also witnessed the tragic death of Frederick W. Niedermeyer on March 13, 1922, when the flapping right wing of "Niedy's" Fokker PW-5 — a pursuit with a parasol wing almost identical to that of the D-VIII — collapsed upward, taking away the aileron.

Verville's own R-3 racer later that year, with a thick, cantilever wood wing, exhibited serious flutter and its bewildered builders were feverishly adding plywood in a last-ditch attempt to change the airfoil hours before the Pulitzer race. Even so, its pilots fought alarming control reversals at high speeds and one test culminated when the engine cowl was shaken off. Then, six days after the Pulitzer race, in crisp fall weather Lieutenant John Macready in a Thomas-Morse MB-3 took on the Loening monoplane pursuit flown by USAS chief test pilot Lieutenant Harold R. Harris in a mock dogfight over Dayton, Ohio. Harris, who before takeoff had considered leaving behind his too tight parachute, suddenly felt his diving aeroplane wrench and watched in horror as the "wobbling" wing peeled off amid a rip of wood and canvas. Harris took to his chute and floated into a grape arbor at 337 Troy Street, the first American flier whose life was recognized as saved by parachute.[26] Colonel Carl Green was then head of the McCook Field Structures Branch, and these incidents prompted him to become probably the first man in the United States and among the first in the world to study systematically and describe the phenomenon of wing-aileron flutter.

The heavy, plywood-covered ailerons, with their center of gravity well behind the hinge line, coupled to a fairly elastic control circuit, induced the flutter. The weight moment of the ailerons — not lack of strength — was the source of trouble but, of course, the early, struggling, largely shop-trained designers could not easily fathom that. One cut-and-dry solution to come out of Harris' and the D-VIII

[26] Harris, later an executive of Pan American World Airways, president of Northwest Airlines, and World War II Air Transport Command chief of staff, thus became the first member of the McCook Field Lifesavers Club, soon to become world-famous as the Caterpillar Club, named after the insect whose silk was used in making parachutes.

experiences and endorsed by Green, a solution which gained notice slowly at first but with gathering respect, was to add weights to the aileron ahead of its hinge line, a technique called *mass balancing*. Professor Leonard Bairstow in England had confirmed the 1923 work of Baumhamer in Amsterdam that the aileron center of gravity must lie coincident with its hinge axis. This was effective in *damping* or muffling the ailerons' tendency to buzz. Despite these findings, several designers still resisted; for example, Reinhold Platz of Fokker, his view colored by an early antipathy to any protruding, hornlike devices, which he rejected to preserve streamlining. Undismayed, Fokker persisted with cantilever, all-wood wings on his ever larger transports almost until 1940, when massive, four-engine versions were still flying, years after a 1931 crash, fatal to Notre Dame football great Knute Rockne, had clinched Fokker's demise in the United States. This Fokker was victim of what rival metal Tri-Motor builder Bill Stout called "Veneer-eal disease." Thus, flutter-preventive techniques took years to gain acceptance. Meanwhile, the flutter often experienced tended to discourage enthusiasm for cantilever monoplanes for years except among the most progressive speed seekers.

The first racing monoplanes in effect stimulated the beginning of serious research into what later became the formal discipline of aeroelasticity. The speed seekers were working hard to define the true basis for rational stiffness criteria. After the Supermarine S.4 crash in 1925 it was expedient for designers to revert to the use of externally braced wings (even for the 440-mph M.C.72 in 1934) until means to predict and ensure equivalent stiffness for internally braced wings were perfected. Hans Reissner in 1926 postulated a comprehensive theory of wing load distribution but it and similar subsequent theories were not specifically applied in aeroplane design until 1935! Such esoteric

theories were not well understood in the 1920s, when even the finest aeroplane construction methods were largely empirical. Many designers in those days remained suspicious and reluctant to trust mathematicians to compute the sizes of their wing spars.

In 1931 a Supermarine S.6B racer was forced to land after experiencing rudder flutter so severe its fuselage was damaged. Its Italian racing contemporary, the M.C.72, also experienced similar problems. Indeed, the earliest insights into the nature of flutter came about because of tail flutter, more common when biplanes, which were not generally prone to wing flutter, were numerous. A classic case was the British D.H.9, which had independently mounted elevators, each with a separate set of cables to the joystick. The two elevators, however, tended to vibrate out of phase with each other, a circumstance easily induced when the "soft" fuselage would slowly swivel back and forth in a twisting motion. These two effects unfortunately reinforced each other — a phenomenon called *coupling*. The solution: put the elevators on one common torque tube. Yet, because of the unmodified fuselage, high-powered racing D.H.9s still exhibited vestiges of tail flutter in 1919. The tail broke off the Bristol 77 in the 1923 Grosvenor Cup race, killing Leslie Foot, although engine vibration certainly contributed; and pure tail flutter caused the crash of the Gloster II Bluebird on a speed record run in 1925, resulting in the death of Larry Carter. And it still existed on racers six years later.

Gloster, during the mid-1920s when the success their earlier racers forged was threatened, was forced to launch perhaps the first systematic flight tests designed expressly to investigate flutter. These took place at Brockworth Aerodrome using Gamecock and Gorcock fighters, designs based on earlier racers, but the fighters, relatively heavy aeroplanes, used a redesigned long top wing which overhung the interplane struts, and it was this overhang that

was prone to vicious flutter. Test pilot Frank Courtney, who participated in the tests, recalled vividly the "terminal velocity" power dives, letting the wing flutter build up little by little each time, using raw judgment as to when to begin the pullout. This was made more colorful by the absence of a parachute. The tests finally resulted in the death of Flight Lieutenant Junor, RAF, emboldened by his new parachute, when his wings fluttered to pieces in a shrieking terminal dive too low for successful bailout. The flutter was eventually checked with extra struts and redesigned ailerons, and the fixes proven in a daring dive by Flight Lieutenant D'Arcy Grieg, but dealing with this vexatious problem in fact set Gloster back probably five years and certainly spoiled the firm's ascendancy in the fighter field.

When metal racers became prevalent, high speeds would cause a lower-frequency oscillation in high-tensile members, more like a ponderous shake than a flutter. But true flutter alleviation and means of predictive prevention did not come until the research occasioned by World War II provided understanding of its elusive causes. Means of accommodating the aeroplane's natural frequencies during design, sophisticated control surface balancing, gap (between fixed and movable surface) design, hinge friction, proper fairing, the adoption of irreversible controls, and other means of natural and artificial damping were developed and applied. Prandtl, von Karman, and Junkers all contributed to progress in this field, in large measure because the Germans in the early days tended to adapt aerodynamic requirements to their preferred heavy, solid structures, while the British and French adapted light, often wire-braced structures to their dominant ideas of low-drag, high-efficiency aerodynamics. The monster was eventually quieted, less apt perhaps to emerge, but he still lurks, and effort and vigilance are demanded in order to avoid his bite.

Hiding the landing gear

It might be said the first "gearless" aeroplane was the 1903 Wright Flyer since its catapult apparatus allowed launching without wheels! Apparently the first rectractable gear was fitted in 1911 to the German Wiencziers monoplane, on which each gear strut was equipped with a hinge to allow the wheels to come up and rearward and lie flush alongside the fuselage, but this primitive application was not pursued, not even by the first man who perhaps fully appreciated the importance of drag reduction, Édouard de Nieport, who with his brother Charles made the name Nieuport immortal and synonymous with speed. Despite the leanings of Nieuport and Esnault-Pelterie (who in 1908 first used an oil-filled gear strut to dampen rebound, that is, the first *oleo strut*), development of the retractable gear awaited the years following World War I.

Certainly by 1918 several designers had suggested the gear be "stowed away" during flight. Walter Brierley of the British Varioplane Company patented a rectractable-gear scheme in December 1914, and in 1917 a young man then at Princeton, in a fit of patriotic zeal — tempered with definite commercial overtones — drew plans for a pursuit with a "collapsible gear" in which the wheels moved upward and to the rear as the rear strut articulated along a sliding tube. This was the Grant Fast Fighter and the student was Charles Hampson Grant, son of a wealthy banker. Since 1901 young Grant had summered in Peru, Vermont, where he had flown highly successful model aeroplanes and even hang-gliders since his early teens, gaily leaping from barntops and hilltops, and forming many ideas about aeroplane construction. Though Grant's imaginative design elicited favorable comments no one wanted to buy it or produce it. World War I aero engineers had already estimated that, of an aeroplane's total drag, the landing gear typically caused over 15 per cent — certainly obvious to young Grant —

but this drag penalty was less than the time, weight, cost, and reliability penalties that would be incurred to build and operate retractable gear on the desperately needed, mass-produced warplanes then.

In 1918 there appeared a mini-biplane sporting wheels that could actually be tucked away in flight, built by James V. Martin of Elyria, Ohio, schooled at the University of Virginia and Harvard, where he organized the Harvard Aeronautical Society. He had learned to fly at the Herring-Curtiss Company in 1909 and even instructed at the Grahame-White School, Hendon, in 1911. Martin mixed his aeronautical enthusiasm with a love for the sea — he had sailed Alaskan waters extensively — and must have heard Tony Fokker's admonition to aircraft designers that boat designers had the distinct benefit of "seeing the spray, thus seeing whether their boat was clean or not. If we could see the spray most aeroplane designers would be ashamed of themselves." Certainly, in these terms, the Martin K-III Scout with its retractable gear made a great deal of sense.

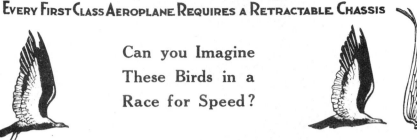

EVERY FIRST CLASS AEROPLANE REQUIRES A RETRACTABLE CHASSIS

Can you Imagine
These Birds in a
Race for Speed?

Portion of full-page advertisement placed by J. V. Martin in January 1920 in which he stated a design axiom that would take almost two decades to gain wide acceptance!

Impractical for combat, Martin's venture was unsuccessfully promoted during the hostile postwar slump. Powered with a 45-hp ABC Gnat engine, it was buoyantly touted to get 22 miles/gallon (it had a 9-gallon capacity) and cost just $2,000. Weighing barely 350 pounds of which 17 pounds was landing gear and retracting mechanism, its Ackerman spring

Martin K-III Scout with retractable landing gear, 1918   (USAF)

wheels, sized 2 × 20, could be drawn up and aft by hand-operated worm gear into circular wing-root receptacles and a safety factor of 20 for this arrangement was advertised. In 1919 Martin made a trip to Europe and upon his return, in a letter to the Aero Club of America, he offered his patents to manufacturers but was totally ignored. Despite the eccentricity variously ascribed to Martin at this time he had early recognized the formula for success. In January 1920 one of his ads stated unequivocally: "Strength and weight of retractable chassis should equal that of fixed; it should *not* require an enlarged fuselage to house it; it should close the housing recesses automatically so skin forms a flush surface; the tread should be independent of fuselage width; and it should have free-fall safety features." Martin placed many full-page ads in trade journals emblazoned with the motto "Every first-class plane requires a retractable chassis." Sadly, few took him seriously, although he was highly original. He never made any money on his ideas, and after World War I he waged a kind of *guerilla* on anyone connected with government contracts, but with resignation. He merely claimed a $51 million loss and was hoping for the best! By the end of 1924 Martin joined engine wizard Kirkham and aeroplane designers Booth and Thurston at Kirkham's small plant on Long Island, but he eventually returned to Harvard to become a professor of astronomy and later served as captain of a troop transport in the Pacific during World War II. He then operated an aeroplane-development laboratory of sorts at New Rochelle Park, New Jersey, and died at his home in nearby Paramus on February 28, 1956. By a stroke of foresight his 1918 K-III Scout exists today in the Smithsonian Institution.

The next aeroplane with retractable gear was the lovely gull-wing Louis Clément–Moineau racer exhibited at the 1919 Paris Air Show, but there is no record that it ever flew. The first entirely practical and fully retracting gear appeared in 1920 on the advanced and prophetic Dayton-Wright RB racer taken to the Gordon Bennett. C. H. Grant, his Fast Fighter not forgotten, exerted a strong and not widely appreciated influence on the RB design. After enlisting in 1917 but being rejected for combat duty, Grant was assigned to McCook Field in Dayton as an engineer and there befriended Howard Rinehart, who soon caught his contagious enthusiasm for unorthodox ideas; some, including the retractable gear, were incorporated directly into the RB which Rinehart would fly in the Gordon Bennett. Unfortunately the RB did not complete the race and in 1921 Grant returned to Vermont to become increasingly involved with aeroplane modeling and youth programs.

The retractable gear next appeared on racers built in 1922. In America Fred Verville built the first gear which retracted inboard into wing receptacles in his three handsome R-3 racers, as did Booth and Thurston in their two Bee-Lines, making five aeroplanes thus equipped in the 1922 Pulitzer, the first public display in the United States of retractable gear. Advancing on a common front, European designers were also experimenting with such radical concepts. Han-

riot's unsuccessful racer of 1921, planned to have retractable gear but built with fixed, was forgotten, but in England Bristol built a retractable-gear monoplane racer, the type 72, for the 1922 Aerial Derby. It was powered by a huge, air-cooled Bristol Jupiter of 450 hp, "streamlined" inside a stubby, barrel-like fuselage whose diameter could accommodate a standing man, thus pre-dating America's surprisingly similar, folk-hero — but fixed-gear — Gee-Bees by almost a decade. The Bristol's splayed-out, tubular gear when lowered resembled the inadequate undercarriage of an obese duck, but it worked. A labor strike halted its development and it never raced — certainly an ignominious fate for the one and only retractable-gear plane built in England before well into the 1930s! In 1923, one year later, the French firm of Gourdou-Leseurre built a novel, parasol-wing, retractable-gear racer for the 1923 Coupe Beaumont. Called the CT no. 1, powered by the same Jupiter engine, and built entirely of metal, it sportingly withdrew from competition when no others appeared at the starting line, but overflew 50 kilometers of the prescribed course in a test and averaged more than 200 mph, putting it in a class with the fastest planes of that era. Its slim wheels were housed on narrow-tread, stiff-legged forks that became part of the plane's surprisingly slim belly when they were screwed up by the pilot.

In the United States after 1924 the last R-3 was retired and with it the concept of the retractable gear for many years, much to the bitterness of its designer, Verville, who harbored lifelong resentment toward Air Service conservatism for excessive delay in its development. Meanwhile, racing aeroplanes went to sea. The demise of land racing events, the growing prestige of the Schneider Trophy, the simple factor of unlimited landing distances on water all contributed. Brute power alone enabled Schneider seaplanes —

despite huge pontoons which, ironically, could be streamlined better than unretracted wheels — to gain the world maximum speed record, raising it eventually to more than 100 mph in excess of the fastest landplane, and retaining the record from 1927 until 1939.

Even as these seaplanes were flashing over speed courses a decade after the R-3, Boeings, Lockheeds, Severskys, Northrops, and others were using highly elaborate pantaloons to enable that awful obstruction — the ordinary wheel — to be pushed through the air with less effort. It was not until 1931 that a version of the low-wing Boeing Monomail appeared with retractable gear and set the trend on its inevitable course. The Navy's 1932 Grumman FF-1 and 1933 Curtiss F11C-3 were early retractable-gear fighters, but each grew pregnant bellies to house their wheels, violating one of the basic tenets laid down by the seafarer J. V. Martin thirteen years before.

Part Two

France

SPEEDY SPADS 5

The Spad-Herbemont Racers

The story has its improbable beginning in 1909 with a middle-aged silk merchant originally from Lyon who had come to Paris from a Brussels silk firm at the turn of the century and in the intervening years, with great persuasiveness and charm, amassed a fortune. Success only made him audacious and he expanded his interests into other enterprises, always on the lookout for novel promotional innovations. It occurred to him that to exhibit an aeroplane – in those days a distinct curiosity – at the Bon Marché store might help draw large crowds to his display. But how to get hold of one? He visited engineer Louis Bêchéreau, then twenty-nine, at his small firm only recently co-founded with Clement

Ader's nephew, bearing the name Société de Construction d'Appareils Aériens. For Bêchéreau the visit of the flamboyant merchant, named Armand Deperdussin, brought a gust of heady excitement; it had been Deperdussin who, fourteen years before when the brothers Lumière presented the first public cinematograph, stationed himself outside to lure the public into the room! His urgent request now took some doing, but duly installed among the Christmas toys that winter perched the first of Deperdussin's fabulous flying machines.

Bêchéreau, who had acquired a lifelong interest in speed and had a few novel ideas of his own, found the unlimited financial backing of Deperdussin a godsend. Their next plane

91

Louis Bêchéreau (MA)

Typical Deperdussin racer, circa 1913 — the world's fastest prewar aeroplane (MA)

was built at Bétheny, near Rheims, where the firm had been reorganized in 1910 as Société pour les Appareils Deperdussin — or, simply, SPAD. In 1912, at about the time Bêchéreau was perfecting the technically giant monocoque form of construction, a young engineering graduate named André Armand-Marie Herbemont was engaged by the firm as chief carpenter.

M. Deperdussin, meanwhile, had purchased the aerodromes at Étampes, Villacoublay, and Rheims, and was busy as benefactor to the classic Gordon Bennett aeroplane races. It was for these prewar races that Bêchéreau, together with the Dutch designer Fritz Koolhoven, fashioned a series of speedplanes destined to stand as the most important prewar types. The man who translated Bêchéreau's ideas into beautiful hardware was Spad's long-time unsung shop foreman, a man named M. Papa.

A Deperdussin racer produced by this team won handily in 1912 and M. Deperdussin was awarded the Légion d'honneur. The following year Bêchéreau assigned young Herbemont his first major task, to design smaller wings for the 1913 Deperdussin racer, but the wings turned out so small that Bêchéreau decided against using them. On the brisk, clear September morning of race day young Herbemont timed Émile Vedrines' swift trials in the rival Ponnier monoplane, which seemed faster than the Deperdussin was expected to go. Suddenly alarmed, he hurriedly fitted the small wings to the Deperdussin racer F.1 on his own initiative. The result was Prevost's impressive victory, marking the first time in history that man exceeded 2 miles per minute. In addition, this climaxed a series of ten consecutive world speed records (from 90·14 to 126·59 mph) set by Deperdussins.

The flavor of triumph, however, had a sour tinge. A few days previously, M. Deperdussin had been arrested on the shattering revelation of swindles involving 28 million francs (at that time over $6 million!) The great Deperdussin racers, like the first great Curtiss racers a decade later, were

Armand Deperdussin (on left) and friends during his heyday before World War I (MA)

bought with stolen money, and *le bon patron* received his Gordon Bennett victory congratulations in prison. Deperdussin was convicted in 1917 and given a five-year suspended sentence but it ruined him completely.

His company rapidly went into liquidation, his fortune turned to ashes, and on June 11, 1924, in a dingy hotel on the rue St. Lazare in Paris, Armand Deperdussin shot himself.

When Deperdussin's company foundered in 1913, Louis Charles-Joseph Blériot (of cross-Channel fame) acquired it for virtually nothing. The firm's name was changed to Société Anonyme pour l'Aviation et ses dérives, thus loosely retaining the acronym "Spad," but it was also variously known as Blériot Aéronautique, and there is a story that Alfred Leblanc, who was

Louis Blériot in flying gear (circa 1909) (MA)

Blériot's close associate, and who was then enthusiastic about a new international language called Volapük (a kind of Esperanto), independently suggested the name "Spad" – which is, one has it, Volapük for "speed." Whether this was actually significant or not is uncertain, but in any event the meaning would certainly fit.

During World War I Bêchéreau designed the immortal Spad fighters which made so many aces famous, the firm flourished, and Blériot made a fortune. In July 1914 Herbemont was detailed by Bêchéreau to visit London to assist in the demonstration of a new two-seat fighter whose front cockpit he would occupy as "machine gunner," but on an early practice flight in France the plane crashed. Herbemont survived but was permanently injured and thereafter always walked with a cane. Rendered unable to qualify for active military service, he continued as engineer and ultimately designed the Spad S.20 pursuit, remarkable for its nimbleness and dash.

Wartime Spad, shown here as S.14 Canon *equipped with floats for a seaplane race, Monaco, 1920* (F)

The wartime Spad fighters brought fame to Marc Birkigt's Hispano-Suiza engines, the first water-cooled aero engine to challenge successfully the supremacy of the air-cooled rotary type for high-speed application. Because of its good breathing and short stroke the Hispano-Suiza ran sweetly at rpm higher by several hundred than the rotaries, and in fact early Hispanos had reduction gears. These proved too delicate for hard use and most pilots preferred direct-drive engine types. The basic Hispano engine itself, built in the fine Swiss watch tradition, was also delicate and it took months to indoctrinate mechanics, who soon found that it ran either well or not at all. Its one major shortcoming soon became obvious – the inability of the dry liner to withstand even the slightest degree of overheating, which caused the valves to suffer at once. But the demand for ever greater amounts of power was insistent, so Birkigt designed a larger V-8 (bore and stroke equal at 140 mm) to deliver 300 hp *with* a reduction gear. This project seemed to be biting off too much, even to Birkigt, and was dropped, to be almost immediately superseded by a direct-drive design with slightly longer (150 mm) stroke: the *modèle 42,* with a 300-hp rating at 1,800 rpm. In a sense this engine was a regression because its cooling difficulties were more acute than those of earlier Hispanos; in fact, Birkigt had an extremely difficult time with dry liners as he went to bigger bores. But the *modèle 42* at that time, for its power, was by far the most compact unit built anywhere in the world and thus was the only aero engine then really suitable for racing. The first aeroplane to be equipped with it was Herbemont's S.20, which was thus virtually guaranteed success on the speed course. Yet, through the years 1920–21 the engine's racing power output rarely exceeded 320 hp at 1,900 rpm and as its compression was boosted, aggravating its cooling problems, it became unreliable. Variants used in S.20 types frequently did not reach their rated power. (A Zenith Carburetor Company report of 1924 included power curves – presumably from a well-tuned engine – which indicated only 295 hp at 1,800 rpm, 5 hp less than rated, and 304 hp at 1,900 rpm full throttle.) Nevertheless, until the Curtiss D-12 appeared on the scene a few years later, all post-World War I world speed records were set with the Hispano-Suiza *modèle 42.*

In February 1919, just three months after the Armistice, Louis Bêchéreau left Spad; it is difficult to understand why. Perhaps there existed some growing conflict with Herbemont, who in his own right had consolidated his position as one of France's most highly respected designers; perhaps some lure across the fence appeared greener. But this is only speculation. In any case, Bêchéreau teamed up with Birkigt and Adolphe Bernard to found Société des Aériens Bernard, known familiarly as the "Society of the three Bs." Bêchéreau did not remain in this fairly tenuous association very long, for within a couple of years he was allied with Salmson, the engine builder, where we shall meet him again briefly. Later his name was associated with Jacques Kellner, son of the famous coach builder who built bodies for the elegant Hispano-Kellner automobiles. Bêchéreau's last speedplane was the ill-fated Kellner-Bêchéreau racer (powered with a Louis Delage 370-hp engine) intended for the 1933 Coupe Suzanne Deutsch de la Meurthe race. It seemed somehow as if the energy of years had been infused all at once into the single dazzling brilliance cast by his masterpiece, the monocoque fuselage, and what remained could only fuel occasional candles, dim by comparison, through the subsequent years. Bêchéreau lived quietly in Paris until his death in 1970, when he was almost ninety-one.

When Bêchéreau left Spad, his protégé Herbemont became *directeur technique,* a post he would occupy for several years. By 1921 Herbemont enjoyed a preeminence among French designers shared by few. Using the S.20 as the root from which most of his designs grew over the next few years, he quickly fashioned aeroplanes for *la vitesse pure,* but Herbemont had an unparalleled ability to translate truths won on the race course directly into practical, money-making aeroplanes as well. A contemporary commented with rare perspicacity that Herbemont was not the type "to be led astray by captivating schemes unless he sees a practical solution for them." Herbemont produced several additional Spad types over the years; in 1940 he designed the Marcel Bloch type 700 fighter. Marcel Bloch later became Marcel Dassault, builder of the supersonic Mirage, providing some appreciation as to where it all led. Herbemont lived until April 13, 1966.

The S.20 was originally designed to avoid the pitfalls of earlier combat planes: the rearward vulnerability of single-seaters and the sluggish performance of two-seaters. Herbemont

93

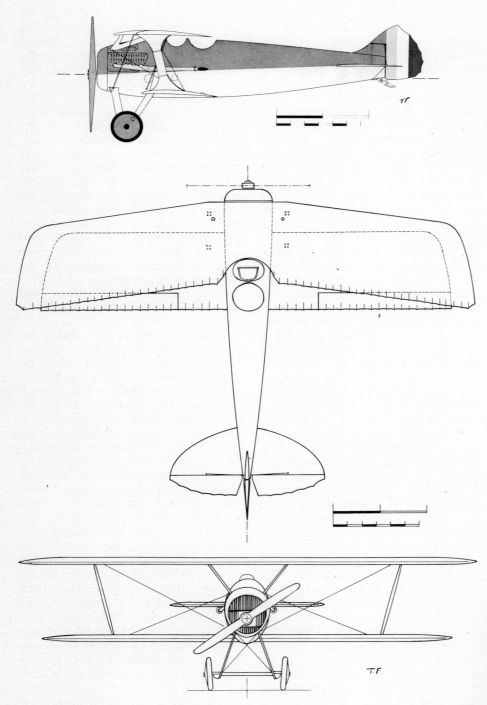

succeeded admirably well. His sleek fighter was heavily armored forward in the style of single-seaters but employed a gunner who faced aft, crouching back-to-back with the pilot to protect the rear. The S.20 had a single-piece upper wing, the first Spad wing to be swept back, a step taken to locate the top center-section forward to enhance visibility yet keep the interplane struts at a reasonable angle. It had four machined I-section spruce spars and a thin (2·5 mm) plywood leading edge to maintain the then popular sharp airfoil section. Wingtips were curved from poplar and strut attachments were recessed. The fuselage was wrapped on a mold using three plies of tulipwood, each 1·5 mm thick, in strips 40 mm wide, then linen-covered and varnished. The landing gear consisted of two built-up plywood vees, fabric-covered, bolted to the fuselage shell with large steel fittings, united by horizontal steel tubes and cross-braced, the axle pivoted in the center. A two-piece tailskid

was used, the upper piece of hardwood to which the lower was bungee-mounted. Herbemont's Spads all had the same flowing, elegant lines set off smartly by the piscatorial-shaped fin and scalloped rudder.

The S.20 was built at the Blériot factory, Suresnes (Seine), and first flew August 7, 1918, from their private flying ground at Buc, 3 miles from Villacoublay on the southwest outskirts of Paris. At once its superior performance was evident. Despite the war's end, the design was so successful that it spawned no less than eighteen variants. Some — such as the S.27 and S.33 — had the streaked oil wiped from their barrel-like interiors, the raw wood bulkheads dressed by whitewash, sets of staggered blue velvet seats anchored into place, ornate mahogany fitted to adorn their hatches, and thus outfitted they established the Paris–London airline service, harbingers of a line of single-engine Spad transports that would be in production for ten years. Others were built for upcoming

*Spad S.20*bis *warming up for the 1919 Prix Deutsch air race around Paris* (MA)

*Spad S.20*bis, *1918–20; representative:* bis$_1$, bis$_2$, bis$_3$, bis$_4$; *1919 Prix Deutsch participant, world speed record February 1920*

94

*Spad S.20*bis *aloft in the 1919 Prix Deutsch race*   *(MA)*

speed competitions and secured twenty-four speed and altitude records within two postwar years. For the most part, racing versions were designated S.20-*bis*, with sub-marks from *bis*$_1$ through *bis*$_6$, all powered with variants of the Hispano-Suiza *modèle 42* engine.

Resumption of the classic air race around Paris, the Prix Henry Deutsch de la Meurthe, originated in 1912 and interrupted by war, provided the first peacetime French speed contest of importance. It had been originally established as a running contest in which a competitor, to win, had to better the current speed by 10 per cent, and not be beaten in turn for a year. When plans to renew the race were announced in late summer 1919, irrepressible Sadi Lecointe, then flying for Spad, immediately made a competition flight in an S.20*bis*$_1$, a large-wing production type which had made its first flight September 1, 1919, the day before Sadi's trip around the

200-kilometer prewar course. But Sadi had jumped the gun. Neither the new postwar rules — nor course — had been finalized, so this attempt was not officially recognized.

The new course, established early in October, was some 10 kilometers shorter and the one-year contest was officially opened October 13, 1919, with a deadline of October 31, 1920. The stiff requirement that a successful winner must better the standing mark by 10 per cent was a spur to three hasty pilots who charged aloft to establish the speed reference on a foggy opening day. Only Leth Jensen finished the course, but his performance meant a future winner must better 222 kmh. The Spad, this time an S.20*bis*$_2$ with smaller wings (which had made its first flight September 25, 1919), made two takeoffs in the misty weather but retired both times, the second at Juvisy with a rough-running engine.

Two days later, however, Sadi again posted two competition flights in the Spad. On his morning circuit, although fast enough to qualify, he was not recognized by the observer at Meaux, so this flight did not count. At half-past three, fortified by a hearty *déjeuner*, he sped away again, hurtling off into the lowering, early dusk of an autumn afternoon, chasing Paris' lengthening shadows at over 240 kmh and thus becoming tentative holder of the Prix. Five days later on October 20, with an S.20*bis*$_3$, the third racing variant completed in 1919 fitted with even smaller wings and which had first flown September 10, Sadi improved his own record, completing the course at more than 250 kmh with Jean Bernard, his ancient, faithful "grease monkey," riding the rear seat. This performance meant that future competitors to wrest the Prix from Sadi must do at least 273 kmh, in those days a severe task for such a distance. The S.20*bis*$_3$ was later unofficially credited with a speed of 265·745 kmh, but over a much shorter distance.

Sadi remained as pilot for Spad until the end of 1919, when he quit to join Nieuport. On January 3, 1920, he again raised his own Prix Deutsch record, doing the course at just over 266 kmh on virtually his first flight in the first Nieuport 29V. This put the Prix effectively out of reach and thus established the officially recognized final performance, earning Sadi 20,000 francs, the trophy, and closing the first Deutsch de la Meurthe aeroplane speed competitions.

The first flurries of activity in the 1919 Prix Deutsch overlapped the 1919 Schneider race held September 10 at Bournemouth, also the renewal of an earlier series interrupted by war. While French contest officials were hammering out the Prix Deutsch rules, Spad entered Sadi Lecointe in the maritime race with an S.20*bis* converted into a seaplane which had only made its first flight with pontoons on August 28, 1919. Sadi was in England

with this racer, accompanied by Herbemont, less than a week after his first Deutsch circuit.

In those days there was considerable controversy raging over which was the most suitable form a water-borne aeroplane should take. One school stuck solidly to the flying boat type while the opposition were equally avid proponents of perching the aeroplane on separate pontoons. Each configuration, of course, would ultimately mature and prove feasible — but for separate applications. The irony was that Jacques Schneider's original intention — to stimulate the commercial possibilities of seaplanes — was subverted; instead, his race over eighteen years led to super-speed, pontoon-equipped sprint planes, in themselves virtually devoid of any redeeming commercial value.

In the early days when the pontoon type was just beginning to prove its superiority as a speed racer, there were two factions in the ranks of pontoon proponents. One faction believed a system of very short main floats assisted by a third, stabilizing tail float — the small *flotteur de queue* — was better than two long main floats. Even the slightest waves often caused types equipped with two long floats to porpoise badly, and poor step and chine shapes severely hindered takeoff performance. Nevertheless, the two-float type was enjoying a rapidly emerging popularity. Thus, early in 1919, Robert Duhamel began the study of pontoon design for the 1919 Schneider Spad. His efforts resulted in a long pontoon of circular cross section, its torpedo-like shape derived from the fluid-dynamic formulae devised by Italian dirigible designer Forlanini. These pontoons had no step; instead, two sets of stabilizing fins resembling small hydroskis (and called "hydrovanes") were attached underneath. Construction of Forlanini floats was begun but they were not completed in time for the race, so the Spad entry was equipped with the flat veneer floats originally employed on an earlier

Spad S.20bis entry in the 1919 Schneider Trophy race, in sheds at Cowes before wings were clipped (Au)

Spad S.20bis entry in the 1919 Schneider Trophy race. Note upper wingtips, clipped by Sadi Lecointe. Also note starboard float sinking. (MA)

Spad, the S.14 Canon (which also appeared at the 1920 Monaco seaplane meeting). The Forlanini-style pontoons were finally completed during spring 1920 but turned in a dismal performance during tests; moreover, their hydrovanes would scoop up great masses of clinging, slimy seaweeds, which destroyed all efficiency.

Perched on its aging floats, the Spad arrived by sea in England for the 1919 Schneider. Sadi took it on a short flight test, reportedly a race "preview" in which it did a respectable 245·25 kmh, but Herbemont was dissatisfied; he then succumbed to a mythical belief then common among French speed seekers, that top wing span of a biplane should be shorter than the bottom. In Saunders' shed the Spad had a generous 75 centimeters (over 2 feet) hacksawed from each upper wingtip, making the upper wing span 1·35 meters less than the lower, and a rough patch-and-dope job was applied to heal the ragged edges. The next noontime, with the dope barely dry, Sadi flew it to Bournemouth, confident of victory. But all was for nought: the starboard float sprang leaks and the aeroplane was disqualified. Herbemont, irritable from being up late the night before doctoring the wing, exploded in vain annoyance.

This Schneider Spad, after some slight modifications and presumably after the Forlanini float trials, was redesignated S.26, reequipped with a set of conventional floats, and entered in the Monaco Rallye; the racer made its first flight as S.26 in March 1920. The Monaco meet, conducted between April 19 and May 2, included both aviation and powerboat events. The Grand Prix de Monaco and 50,000 francs would be awarded for a flight to Tunis and back, and in addition there was the Prix Guynemer for speed and the Prix Roland Garros for altitude. Postponed by a railway strike (most entries were shipped to Monaco by rail), the aviation activities got under way April 20 just after the famed Sunbeam-Despujols III won the "Championship of the Sea" powerboat race. It was the soft Monegasque season of calm seas and blue skies.

Two Spads were in fact prepared for the 1920 Monaco competitions, the S.26 plus a slightly different model called S.31 which first flew April 10. But the Blériot factory sent only one seaplane, the S.26, south to Monaco. However, it had a double set of wings, pilots – and race numbers. A small, new set of wings was provided for the speed races and a larger set for the altitude competitions (with which it became S.26bis).

The speed wings, in characteristic fashion, included an upper wing of considerably shorter span than the lower, and had a distinctly narrow gap. The altitude conversion added 40 kilograms to the aeroplane's weight

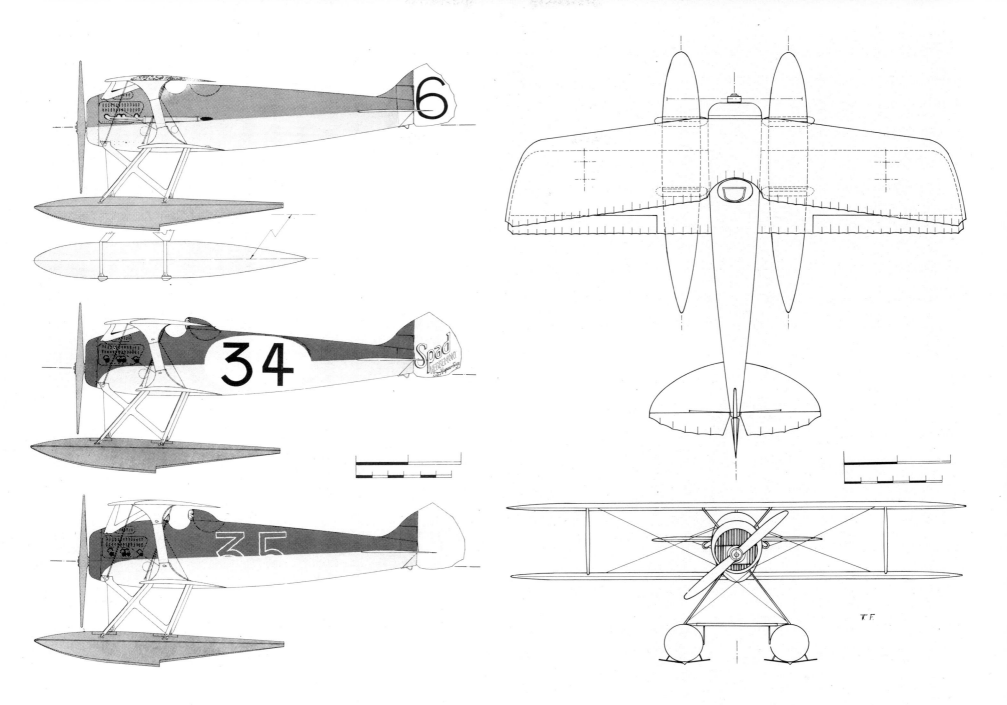

Spad S.20bis seaplane, 1919–20. Side views, reading down: as entered in the 1919 Schneider Trophy race (experimental Forlanini pontoons are shown below standard pontoons, and in plan and front views); S.26, winner 1920 Prix Guynemer at Monaco; S.26bis, winner 1920 Prix Garros at Monaco.

Spad S.26 taking off at Monaco, 1920 (F)

but the altitude wings provided half again as much area and sported large, protruding ailerons (all S.20 types carried ailerons on the lower wing only). Four separate wing changes were accomplished during the contest. The aeroplane's original Hispano "type Marine" 275-hp *modèle 42* engine, with its novel Letombe compressed-air self-starter, chugged merrily away through the meet without missing a beat.

The two pilots who accompanied the Spad to Monaco were the Count de Romanet and Jean Casale, slated for speed and altitude contests respectively. Le Marquis Bernard de Romanet was one of the most skillful pilots in France and personally one of the most popular, combining the charm and manner of the old French *noblesse* with the dash of a modern young sportsman. He was born at Mâcon on January 28, 1894, the scion of a very old French family which in pre-Revolution days was technically included in the "untitled nobility." The de Romanets belonged to the Midi as did the

André Herbemont and Count Bernard de Romanet, 1920 (F)

de Havillands, a fact that always particularly interested the pilot. When war broke out de Romanet distinguished himself as a young cavalry sergeant but soon transferred to aviation. One evening in 1916, while a non-commissioned pilot in Escadrille C.51, he returned from a Somme patrol to his field at Sacy-le-Grand with a brilliant idea, and at once set about installing the first angled aerial camera on his Caudron G.4. After serving with Escadrille 37 he took command of Escadrille 167 in the fabled *groupe des Cigognes* ("the Stork group"), where he became a battlefield comrade of Fonck, France's highest-scoring ace. De Romanet scored eighteen kills himself, seventeen planes and one *Drache*, and finished the war holding the Légion d'honneur and Croix de guerre with ten palms. Retained by Spad to fly the latest experimental aircraft, his cheerful greeting and merry modesty soon became familiar at speed circuits all over Europe.

Jean Hyacinthe Casale, Marquis de Montferrato, was born Christmas Eve, 1893, in Olmeto, Corsica. He earned his pilot certificate in May 1915 as a private, then served in Escadrilles N.3, N.67 and N.23, scoring twelve victories for which he won the Légion d'honneur, Croix de guerre with several palms, and other decorations. After the war he joined Herbemont and flew the Paris-London airline in Spad Berlines. He also specialized in both speed and a long string of altitude records with various combinations of passengers and payload. Casale, who was unmarried, took great delight in the romantic power his darkly exotic, Mediterranean good looks together with the almost mystical appeal of his profession exerted over women. Of his current women, the one most frequently by his side was Basque actress Loulou Egaburu, then the toast of Paris for her performance in *No, No, Nanette*. While de Romanet dreamed of being the world's fastest man, Casale's dream was to climb the highest.

Jean Casale (MA)

Casale made the first flight of the meet and began his altitude trials. Even with its heavy fuel load for the long, grinding climb, the S.26*bis* took off easily, its long, V-bottom pontoons with their pronounced upward slope from stem to stern proving stable and causing very little spray. Side number 35 was assigned for the altitude competition, but for the first few days the number was merely chalked onto the Spad's flanks. Sticky barographs and one day of stormy weather interrupted the trials, but on April 23 Casale took off into a light southeast breeze and in just one hour climbed 6,350 meters. After he landed, de Romanet put on an exhibition flight to show off the beautiful Spad "in a series of *virages* and *glissades*."

One day was taken to bolt the speed wings in place and change the race number to 34, set off by a huge white oval. During the afternoon of

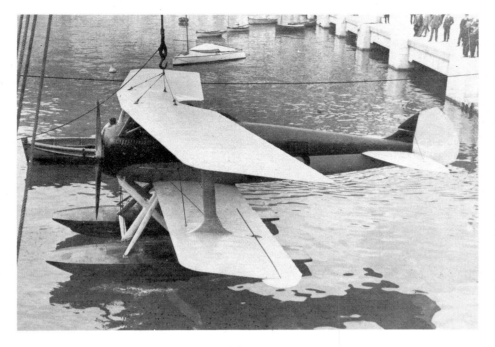

Spad S.26bis at Monaco, 1920   *(F)*

The altitude wings were reassembled, the number 35 painted in, and for the next five days through May 1 Casale made altitude flights, establishing on April 27 a world altitude record for seaplanes of 6,500 meters and winning the Prix Garros. (This compares to the altitude performance of 8,155 meters made by Sadi Lecointe May 9, 1919, with an S.20C.1 landplane.) The Spad team worked all night May 1 to re-rig the speed wings once more for the second of the two speed contests. The Italian pilot Arturo Zanetti on the faster Nieuport-Macchi M.17 won the race the next day, but flipped over on landing. Nevertheless, in fifteen flights totaling 14:30, the S.26 had posted two seaplane records. It was subsequently considered for the 1920 Schneider race to be held in Venice, but labor problems, doubts over the then difficult transportation situation in Italy, and the impending Gordon Bennett race which required Herbemont's staff to remain in France, forced them to withdraw. Moreover, the S.26 was barely capable of carrying the mandatory 300 kilograms "commercial weight" load required in the Schneider race that year.

Casale and de Romanet, to some extent, had been exchanging roles at Monaco since at that time Casale was in fact the world's supreme speed merchant. Two months earlier, on February 28, at Villacoublay, Casale made four officially timed passes over the measured kilometer to establish a world maximum speed record of 283·464 kmh. He thus exceeded by almost 8 kmh the world record Sadi Lecointe had established exactly three weeks before on the 1919 Prix Deutsch competition Nieuport. The specific Spad Casale used was almost certainly the S.20bis$_4$, a variant that first flew January 2, 1920, with wings clipped to virtually half the area of the standard military S.20. Casale's brilliant record, the first world speed record set by a Spad, would stand for seven months.

Another classic race series interrupted by war was going to be resumed in late September 1920, the oldest aeroplane race of all, the contest for the Gordon Bennett Aviation Cup. The prewar French Deperdussins had won the previous two races, so France only needed its third consecutive victory to win the cup outright, but stiff competition was expected from several other nations. Triumph in the Gordon Bennett would drape the victor in a mantle of singular glory, and the best French aviators all wanted the honor of representing France on the Gordon Bennett team, limited to three. The eliminations were held at Villesauvage Aerodrome, Étampes, on September 25, three days before Cup day, and required one out-and-back trip over the course chosen for the race, with participants given three chances to start. The three with the fastest times would constitute the team.

Herbemont was there with his star pilots Casale and de Romanet, who were to fly two new highly polished

April 25 the Prix Guynemer would be contested over the sparkling blue Mediterranean in a round-trip circuit to Cape Martin near Mentone, back over a marking boat near the Tir aux Pigeons at Monaco, then to disappear from view behind Fort Antoine en route to the Garoupe Lighthouse past Nice, near Cannes, the course's far turning point. The determined Italian race pilot, Jannello, who had been the vortex of controversy over the annulled Schneider race seven months before, was there with his nimble Savoia S.17 flying boat. But de Romanet sped over the course, roaring low over the sun-washed sea with a feeling of supreme joy, looking up at the Corniche Road, at white and yellow villas that speckled the coast, bright dabs on the broad green brush strokes of mountains and valleys beyond. His speed was 211·395 kmh, sufficient to beat Jannello by one minute, capture the prize, and establish a world speed record for seaplanes.

Spad S.26 approaching mark boat in Prix Guynemer speed race   *(F)*

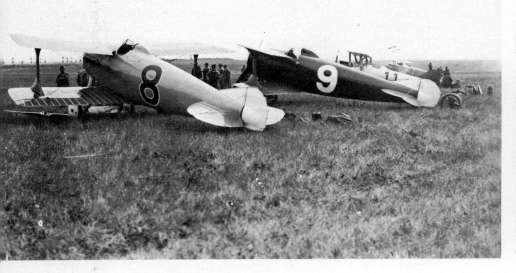

The two Gordon Bennett Spad S.20bis₅ racers at Étampes, 1920 (MA)

Jean Casale aboard his Spad S.20bis₅, 1920 (MA)

and rakish racing Spads. Besides shaving surface dimensions to squeeze more speed from these jobs, M. Herbemont decided to implement another theory originated by the late José Weiss and then somewhat in favor with many European speed seekers, especially in Germany. This was the idea that a fuselage made to fill the entire gap between top and bottom wings would be the fastest. Even Fritz Koolhoven, former associate of Bêchéreau's, subscribed to the concept. Herbemont's basic S.20 fuselage had been retained, but virtually at the last minute special wings were fitted. These had a double-cambered, nearly symmetrical airfoil and the upper wing roots had been dropped 20 centimeters below the standard dimension and attached directly to the fuselage. A new, exceptionally small fin and rudder had been fitted to each racer as well. Their Hispano engines could produce 320 hp at 2,000 rpm and turned Lumière props. These planes made their first flights on September 22 and 23, just two days before elimination day. They were issued race numbers 8 and 9 and designated S.20bis₅.

The Spads still used flat-face honeycomb radiators and appeared bulky next to their thin-line Nieuport rivals. A small spinner was tried briefly on number 8 and seemed to help. M. Herbemont, already beginning to doubt the efficacy of the Weiss speed theory and disturbed by the poor flying qualities his racers exhibited on their initial flights, said before the race that his design was not *au point*. Indeed, the racers soon proved to have a wicked lateral-directional instability caused by insufficient fin area.

The two Nieuports scored one-two in the eliminations and the Borel racer could have scored third but for a technicality. Instead, Bernard de Romanet in Spad number 8 qualified as the team's third member at 257·819 kmh, almost 22 kmh behind Sadi Lecointe. There is no doubt the Spad was capable of much higher speed performance-wise, but control-wise it was yawing violently, flying like a worm at 160 mph. To French observers it appeared to be a "nervous mustang." Jean Casale, still world speed champion, finished fourth at 251·228 kmh in number 9, but he made a slight course

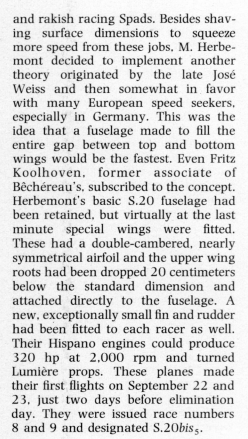

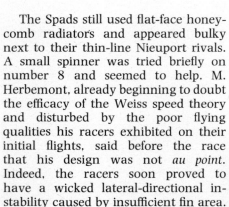

Spad S.20bis₅, 1920 (MA)

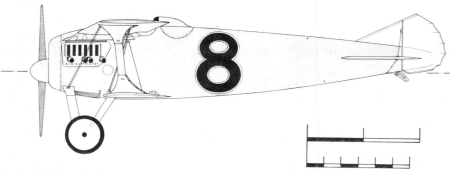

Spad S.20bis₅ Gordon Bennett competitors, 1920

error which would have disqualified him anyway. His ship also flew wildly but when he realized he would not make the team he put on a daring stunt show with his big, dark Spad.

In order to reduce the directional control problems and enable his racer perhaps to realize its full speed potential, Herbemont, during the three days between the eliminations and Cup day, made hurried — but apparently insignificant — alterations to the vertical

"Papa" Blériot briefs de Romanet for the 1920 Gordon Bennett. (MA)

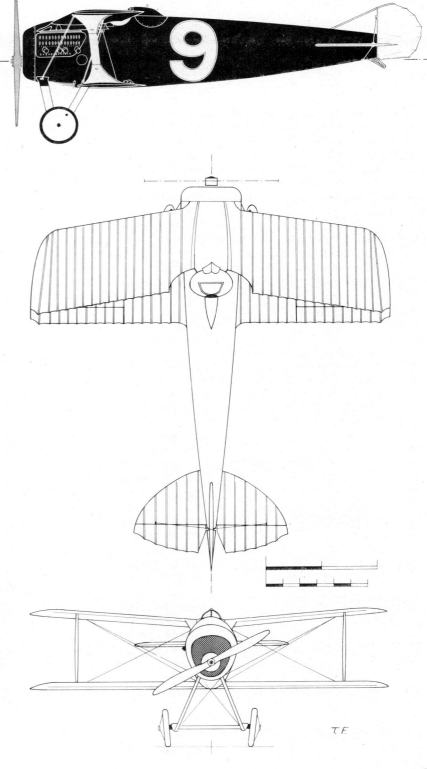

tail of number 8. Cup day dawned foggy which forced de Romanet to wait impatiently all morning for the weather to improve; it was not until almost quarter to two that he finally climbed aboard, took off, and headed south on his first long lap. Twice he roared overhead, clicking off the laps, the plane not behaving so badly as it had done during tests, and his speed slightly better than it had been in the eliminations.

Spectators at Étampes became suddenly aware of the rasping bark of a short-stack Hispano at low power accompanied by the shrill wind song of bracing wires. Squinting into the white afternoon haze, alarmed mechanics saw the big Spad racer slide steeply down a shaft of sunlight, sink sharply into the wheel-thick grass, careen slightly, and trundle toward them. Their hearts were in their mouths — de Romanet could not be out of the race? But here he was, with a lap still to go, cutting the engine and clambering out of his cockpit.

Just twenty minutes before, Kirsch, first of the French team to take off, had retired with oiled-up spark plugs. Now de Romanet was down. Sadi

de Romanet aloft during the 1920 Gordon Bennett race   (MA)

Lecointe in his white Nieuport speedster had just knifed overhead with two laps to go. If he should falter . . . The twelve cannon-like cylinders of the American Verville's huge Packard engine resounded with authority as it prepared to take off. The Americans were taking things very seriously and the Gordon Bennett marked the beginning of active competition flying by their armed services. The British, too, had their hottest racer, the Semiquaver, poised in reserve awaiting the coolness of late afternoon to start. The odds were stacking up against the French.

De Romanet, who personally had been eager to snatch as much glory away from rival Nieuport as possible, was bitterly disappointed. The running battle between Spad and Nieuport for the world speed record was heating up, and now a Nieuport was aloft and de Romanet's Spad was down with lubrication problems. But the rules allowed "replenishments," never mind the odds — they were just as likely to shift — so with plucky grit the Spad mechanics unbuttoned the cowl and went to work. Time seemed to drag for the pacing pilot. The Nieuport whizzed by again right on time to begin its last lap. The awkward American racer overheated and retired — at least he was no longer a threat. Finally, ten minutes before the Nieuport was due back, the mechanics were done. De Romanet leapt aboard, fired up, bent the throttle forward, and racked the tricky Spad toward its last lap. His first lap speed had been almost 160 mph and he should at least equal that.

De Romanet's troubles were not over yet. Just as he pounded around the final pylon with 30 miles to go, his oil pressure gauge suddenly burst and a fierce stream of scalding oil speared straight at his face. Half-blinded, shocked, and gasping for breath, de Romanet squirmed in his straps, plunged his face into the slipstream's cool bite, but could not avoid the needle-like spew of oil. When he thought he must quit the aerodrome appeared through

his smeared goggles and he dove for its near edge, landing downwind at almost full speed, cutting the switch as soon as he was able, running hundreds of yards, digging the tailskid in to slow the brute down. He stumbled out of the cockpit looking as if someone had dumped a bucket of black paint over him — but not a wire was broken on the Spad.

Although he finished last, his average speed of less than 110 mph — which included the one-half-hour stop — turned out to be good enough for second place behind Sadi's winning Nieuport!

Just a week after the international Gordon Bennett racing teams had sailed home, the ebullient French organized a three-day aeronautic meeting of their own. It was conducted at Spad's home field, Buc, and the nation's best planes and pilots came. The list of visiting aces was headed by Fonck and Nungesser. Herbemont's sleek new Spad S.33 was there for a race between transport planes. The fast Nieuport racers were there also, and Spad wanted to keep them from wresting the world speed record.

For the Buc meeting Herbemont abandoned the Weiss theory of upper-wing location as quickly as he had

embraced it, and artisans scurried in the few remaining days to prepare one Spad racer by installing a one-piece upper wing, raised above the fuselage on new, streamlined cabane struts. This wing was built around two spars, each a box structure formed by enclosing a machined I-section spruce beam with two vertical three-ply webs; these spars ran parallel, spaced 70 centimeters apart. The treacherous vertical fin was again enlarged to improve stability. Recognizing that their radiator's drag put them at a disadvantage, Herbemont's artisans fashioned a fat propeller hub of gigantic proportions to streamline the nose, mounted by means of a ball bearing so as not to revolve with the prop. Herbemont realized he had one additional disadvantage about which he could do nothing — his new speedster weighed fully 200 kilograms more than the Nieuport racers, but he was not discouraged. Designated S.20bis_6, the converted Spad made its first flight October 6, just two days before the Buc meeting opened, and was rolled out for the meeting still bearing its large Gordon Bennett race number 8.

Listed in the long string of events at 10:30 A.M. October 9 were competition trials for the world speed record!

Spad S.20bis$_6$ world speed record aeroplane with spinner that failed; pilot, Bernard de Romanet   (Au)

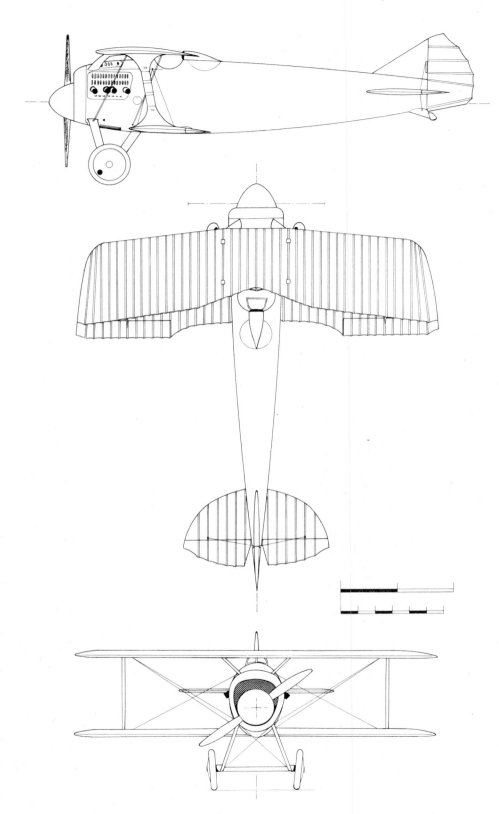

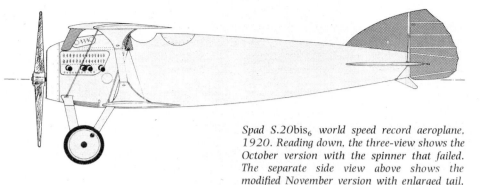

Now this was a race! Jean Casale's February record still stood. His compatriot Bernard de Romanet now mounted the modified Spad and streaked over the measured kilometer four times to average 292·682 kmh — a new world record. De Romanet had won the supreme prize in full view of thousands. Sadi Lecointe's first try in the Gordon Bennett Nieuport was 288 kmh; later that day he actually made 293·877 kmh. Since this speed did not exceed de Romanet's by 4 kmh it did not qualify as a new record. Nevertheless, de Romanet was not comfortable with his thin margin. The trials were timed by a hand-held stop watch, and a mere one-fifth second either way could make the difference.

De Romanet made one more try to better his own mark that afternoon. As the Spad came blazing over the course at nearly 200 mph, the massive pot on its nose suddenly let go. The flailing prop shattered, showering the racer with an explosion of splinters. Boiling water from the pierced radiator doused de Romanet as the screeching aeroplane went almost out of control. Already past the aerodrome, de Romanet aimed his plunging Spad for the nearest clearing, hurtled underneath a telephone line, skimmed across a road, and crunched to a stop — barely intact — in plowed furrows.

Out of service during the meet's closing events, de Romanet had to watch helplessly the next day as Sadi Lecointe indeed surpassed his record almost precisely by the minimum required 4 kmh. But again the Spad team displayed their admirable pluck, and within a month they were ready to try again. On October 20 Sadi had shoved the mark past 300 kmh, which added to their task.

The Spad's cockpit was modified slightly by lowering the pilot's seat, removing the headrest, and lowering the windscreen. From his buried position de Romanet could only see laterally, the top of his head no higher than the fuselage line. A new engine, with compression boosted from 4·7 to 5·3 in hopes of realizing 350 hp, was installed under a new, more rounded cowl, and the huge spinner was not replaced. The vertical tail was replaced with new surfaces of much greater chordwise dimensions. Herbemont's main aerodynamic thrust was then in airfoil design as he sought to use the new double-cambered profiles and at the same time find ways to improve longitudinal stability. The wing was modified again, its area reduced slightly. The S.20bis$_6$ in this form was described as "blue and white." This aeroplane, for its day, truly represented a considerable advance in the art. It was a racer that could have been made into an effective fighter, and thus strongly impressed Charles G. Grey, acerbic editor of

Jane's All the World's Aircraft; not often given to praising non-British products, Grey wrote of this Spad two decades later in 1941, "It influenced the evolution of combat aeroplanes."

The chill morning of November 4, 1920, was dismal and foggy. About 600 yards from the hangar at Buc, Herbemont, Casale, and other freezing spectators stamped their feet as the balloons were raised to mark the 1-kilometer course. De Romanet was impatient; he had tasted the sweetness of his lifelong ambition, to be world speed champion, but only for a tantalizingly brief period in October. Now his new opportunity had arrived. He gunned the nimble Spad and it was swallowed up by the fog. Only its engine could be heard. Suddenly the engine whined, there was a blue-gray blur barely ten feet high, and de Romanet vanished again into the soup. One pass was made in 11·2 seconds for the kilometer — over 320 kmh. The official average was 309·012 kmh, a new world record! Upon landing, as de Romanet cut the switch (he had no brakes), the red-hot engine dieseled and de Romanet had to turn on the ignition and haul back barely to clear the hangars. Once aloft he cut the fuel, stopping the engine, and glided in for a dead-stick landing.

Casale commented, "I've never seen such a sight in my life . . ."

One month later Sadi's Nieuport edged by again, adding another 4 kmh to the mark in this true battle royal for speed. De Romanet's November flight had established the third — and last — official world maximum speed record to be held by a Spad. It was also de Romanet's last record. Less than a year later the handsome young count lay dead in the wreckage of a new speedplane built for the 1921 Coupe Deutsch.

The year 1921 saw Spad turn away from pure speed seeking; their hopes for a comeback in the speed duel were effectively dashed with the Nieuport sesquiplane's arrival. Rumors that Herbemont was developing a new "supermonoplane" — to be called S.44 — for the 1921 Coupe Deutsch proved unfounded. He now concentrated on larger aeroplanes, more functional in a commercial world. Many French designers were already beginning to show signs of the trends that led to aeroplanes so eccentric they achieved nothing, but Herbemont was not led astray by such artistic freakishness. Two updated Berlines (aerial limousines) first flew during the year, and the twenty-passenger S.45 was also brought out in 1921. It had four

engines totaling 1,200 hp mounted in tandem pairs — Herbemont, ever prescient, also used tandem main landing gear wheels — and like all Spads, beneath the lavish paint and polish, its construction was beautifully neat in detail.

One company that profited handsomely from the early commercial expansion was Société Lorraine des Anciens Établissements de Dietrich et Cie de Lunéville, of Argenteuil, Seine-et-Oise, formerly a distinguished automobile works but as a result of the war the maker of exceptionally successful aero engines. Hundreds of popular Lorraine-Dietrich V-12 engines were then in use all over the world. Herbemont especially liked them for his commercial Spads and his encouragement prompted the company in 1921 to renew the development of a twelve-cylinder, broad-arrow engine design which had lain dormant since the Armistice.

Lorraine-Dietrich modèle 14 (12E) *engine, circa 1922*   (Au)

This was the Lorraine *modèle 14*. The prototype had been first conceived in 1917, the year in which the popularity of the broad-arrow or W form was first consolidated. The new *modèle 14*, designated 12E by the STAé, the French government aviation technical bureau, had cylinders short and compact (120mm × 170mm), water-jacketed in pairs; the valves operated via

tappets and rockers from two camshafts located in the angles formed by the two Vs. Shortly after its first flight in 1918 the only prototype was wrecked and Lorraine then dropped its development altogether, concentrating on increased production of their earlier, successful 370-hp V-12 engine, the *modèle 13* (STAé designation 12Da). The efficiency of Lorraine-Dietrich engines soon became world-recognized; Japan began construction of Lorraines under license in 1921. The same degree of unanimity concerning the Lorraines' reliability does not exist, however. On one hand they have been lavishly praised as among the most faithful of engines, while at the same time they have been disparaged with equal vociferousness as not very dependable. It must be concluded that such extreme positions in all likelihood were generated more from limited personal experience rather than from an appreciation of the overview. That Lorraine engines were for the most part successful is suggested by the firm resurrecting development of the *modèle 14* in 1921. Another compelling reason for bringing back the W-12 was simply that for its weight of 365 kilograms this four-year-old design was still the lightest 400-hp engine available in Europe (it had delivered 422 hp at 1,800 rpm during bench testing).

Construction details virtually identical to the wartime prototype were retained, but the stroke was now lengthened to 180 mm, giving an increase of some 7 per cent in swept volume.[1] Despite this major dimension change the engine was still called *modèle 14* by Lorraine (probably 14² although company records that would positively verify this were destroyed during World War II) and 12E by the French government. The first of the

[1] Lorraine had also designed a wartime *modèle 15* W-12 (120mm × 175mm) which developed 435 hp at 1,800 rpm in tests, but it almost certainly never flew. It was developed alongside the *modèle 14*, and one of these designs was to have powered Bréguet 14 bombers, but the Armistice intervened.

Spad S.20bis₆ after modifications, ready for its second world speed record performance
(MA)

new 180-mm stroke *modèle 14* engines was tested in 1922 and then *loaned* to Blériot for use in the S.58 Coupe Deutsch racer.

The Gordon Bennett fiasco two years earlier had proven how extraordinarily delicate the high-power engines of that day were when any sustained effort was demanded of them. Use of the updated *modèle 14* aboard the S.58 in the most important international full-bore speed race in Europe was now expected to confirm its durability under stress and to enhance Lorraine prestige. The Lorraine used in the new Spad had a cautiously low compression ratio of 5·0, yet was expected to deliver an honest 450 hp, but like the Napier Lion the design was somewhat criticized for high-speed racing because of its handicap of excessive frontal area.

Strictly speaking, the new Spad itself was not a racer but a standard military fighter, type S.41, from which the inevitable Hispano-Suiza *modèle 42* engine had been removed when the new W-12 Lorraine was substituted. With the new engine, and minus all military equipment, it was designated S.58, named Louis Blériot after the firm's chief, and in deference to its pilot often called Type Casale or Blériot Casale as in the official announcement of race entries. The original S.41 fighter did not emphasize top speed but rather speed-spread. Herbemont wanted to combine acceptable high-speed performance with low-speed, short takeoff and landing capability, and in one test the S.58 took off after a run of 63 meters and landed at less than 40 mph, rolling to a stop in only 60 meters! Its top speed, though respectable, was perhaps 25 per cent less than the world's fastest racers in late 1922. Its remarkable low-speed performance was due to exceptionally light weight, which Herbemont achieved by the almost 100 per cent use of duralumin in its construction. Externally, the S.58 had the characteristic I-strut, swept-back upper wing, scalloped rudder, and tulipwood monocoque fuselage of earlier Spad racers. But the structure of both wings (except for the fabric covering), the struts, the landing gear members, and most internal structural members of the fuselage were all-metal. Ingenious pin-joints devised for the landing gear struts as well as special steel fittings throughout were designed to flex and thus avoid the then little-understood bugaboo of metal fatigue. Herbemont estimated the S.58 was 20 per cent lighter and 50 per cent stronger than if wood-constructed. To reduce drag the admittedly inferior honeycomb radiators of earlier Spads had been replaced by the popular Lamblin lobster pots nestled in the landing gear struts. On the S.58 these radiators were not mounted parallel to the aeroplane's axis but in line with the local airflow.

The S.58 first flew July 17, 1922, at Buc. Its performance in the Coupe Deutsch race a few weeks later unfortunately was not remarkable and neither added to nor detracted from the already well-established prestige of Lorraine-Dietrich aero engines. Taking off into a perfectly marvelous, crisp, clear fall morning shortly after 10 A.M., the S.58 was the first competitor away and literally sparkled as it rose from the turf, undoubtedly one of the most beautiful aeroplanes ever to grace a race course. Casale was adorned with his white helmet and the checkered scarf that had become his trademark. Just as he began the second lap one of the Lamblin radiators sprang a leak and Casale was forced to return to Étampes. He pulled up in a sizzling cloud of steam accompanied by the unpleasant odor of burning paint. The

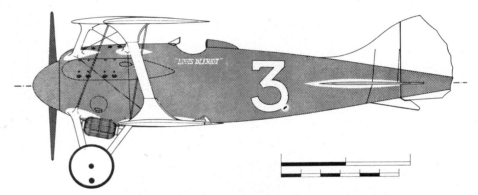

Spad S.58, 1922 Coupe Deutsch de la Meurthe

Spad S.58 Louis Blériot *at Étampes for the Coupe Deutsch race, 1922*   (F)

Spad S.58 taking off in 1922 Coupe Deutsch race   (F)

entire affair was unsatisfactory as a race, proving again it was the entry list that counted during the 1920s. The S.58 was the last racing Spad, and for Casale it was the last race.

Just three weeks before the 1920 Gordon Bennett race, Casale had made the first forty-minute test flight of the new four-engine Blériot Mammoth, the largest transport of its day. On June 23, 1923, less than one year after competing in the S.58, he piloted a similar Mammoth to shuttle dignitaries from Paris to Touquet for an "Aerial Weekend." He had just delivered the government minister P. E. Flandin together with Louis Blériot, and was returning to Buc with his mechanic Boulet for another group. While cruising at 1,500 feet abeam Daméraucourt, 6 miles north of Granvilliers, the huge aeroplane veered. A control cable had jammed and though Casale struggled desperately he was unable to free it. He jazzed the engines asymmetrically —

nothing worked. Casale ordered Boulet to the rear as the Mammoth skidded earthward and crumpled into the trees out of control. Boulet was only shaken. Casale, however, was found dead in his seat, crushed by a tree. He was only twenty-nine.

Casale's death, following de Romanet's by two years, was a grievous blow to Herbemont. It seemed in some ways incongruous that the slightly dissipated, semi-crippled designer would persist through four additional productive decades beyond the cruel moment when the life of his robust, virile young test pilot was snuffed out. So many lessons remained unlearned, so many experiments unfinished . . . The very next year, in 1924, Herbemont brought out three new Spad fighters, the S.51, S.61, and S.81, which were all equipped with the very first elevator trim tabs. Herbemont had decided a stabilizer not rigidly fixed to a fighter's fuselage was a

structural hazard, and not really practical either since non-fixed stabilizers commonly in use in those days were ground-adjustable only. So Herbemont anchored the stabilizer solidly and devised the small, pilot-operated supplementary surfaces — later called trim tabs — to relieve forces in the control stick. His racing and speed record experience also made him impatient with fixed-pitch props which were inefficient across a large speed range, and Herbemont became one of the first to employ VP props. Those used on his 1924 fighters were all-wood, each blade clamped into a socket which could be rotated on its axis by a pilot-operated cable! As with so many insights and innovations pioneered by the speed seekers, such ideas often languished for several crucial years.

Meanwhile, Spad's great rival in the realm of speed had forged ahead to reach new heights. Their continuing quest for *vitesse — la vitesse pure —* was conducted with ever increasing flamboyance by the rash designer and star pilot who represented the house of Nieuport.

André Herbemont and Jean Casale, 1922 (F)

QUEST FOR VITESSE

The Nieuport Biplane Racers

The noise is *presto vivace con brio* — a joyous bass rising from the throng of people, a lilting treble melody from the little white biplane dancing overhead. The plane lands and its pilot is hoisted upon the shoulders of the crowd with a cheer. He is short, fat, smiling broadly, and teetering there amid the jostle he seems like Humpty Dumpty with goggles. But he is the champion Sadi-Joseph Lecointe, winner of the Gordon Bennett prize. And, *mon ami*, what a race he has flown! His flashy style was truly *casse-cou* — breakneck. For pure communion with stick and rudder Sadi had no equal, nor is he ever likely to have one. The churning Chauvière prop on the snout of his racer laid a flat swath in the grass of every pasture between Villesauvage Aerodrome and La Marmogne Farm, six time in all. Sadi plunged straight for the pylons, "flung the machine over sideways," as an observer wrote, "then pulled it around abruptly as one pulls a horse on its haunches!" On one pylon turn he was officially timed at a phenomenal three seconds between crossing the line inbound and outbound! Sadi never rose above 100 feet, spent most of his time below 30. And now the victory cup was his.

To have met Sadi Lecointe, who was almost reverently called *l'homme-oiseau*, would have been misleading: having the appearance of a prosperous businessman, Sadi was the *père tranquille*, one of the most placid souls in aviation. But his life was built on speed and he was always getting involved in some sort of race. Once late in 1920 Sadi even pitted his six-cylinder touring car against a race horse. These were the days when men still debated on which was faster, a horse at full gallop or an automobile! The horse in question was owned by the determined English journalist Gordon D. Knox, Paris correspondent for the London *Morning Post*, who challenged. So confident was Sadi that he generously offered to give Knox a "flying start." A huge crowd came to the Bois de Boulogne to witness the great event and the betting was fairly even. The distance chosen was $1/2$ kilometer but Knox was a heavy man and used a couple of hundred extra yards to get his nag up to speed. As he thundered by the white car Sadi flung in the clutch and dug out. At 350 meters Sadi's mechanic, gripping the seat beside him, threw off his cap — car and horse were even! Knox spurred his horse faster but Sadi roared over the finish line in a cloud of gravel, 50 meters ahead! The horse — and the nineteenth-century life it represented — were, for better or worse, in their inevitable twilight glimmer, while Sadi and his thrashing car represented man's new mechanical progress, the twentieth century. That year Sadi Lecointe became famous, after all, as the fastest man on the planet — because of an aeroplane.

Sadi Lecointe came from St.-Germain-sur-Bresles (Somme), where he was born July 11, 1891. When only nineteen he became a pilot, taking his license on a Blériot (French Aero Club brevet number 431 awarded March 3, 1911). Mobilized for war, after eighteen months at the Front he came to Avord in 1916 and earned the Croix de guerre testing warplanes and instructing some 1,500 students. His skill was apparent and after the Armistice he continued as test pilot for Établissements Blériot-Spad, working closely with André Herbemont; in fact, Sadi was godfather to Herbemont's first son. He also became *gonflé à bloc*,

Sadi Lecointe on left, standing with his favorite navigator, the fated François Coli (F)

and it was written of him in England that "the fatter he gets the faster he goes!" But Sadi impatiently took journalists to task for calling him fat. (Engineering weight schedules for his custom racers invariably listed, under *poids utile, pilote — 86 kg*).

It was on the afternoon of October 14, 1919, during the Prix Henry Deutsch de la Meurthe, that a small, sleek biplane enshrouded in glossy black, its flowing lines seemingly smoothed by the wind's own caress, appeared suddenly on the scene. Eight Hispano cylinders spoke with sharp

authority when its pilot, the Count de Romanet, opened the throttle. This was the Nieuport 29 Vitesse, and though it failed to complete the course that day there was no doubt that the kiss of victory had touched this plane. A few days later de Romanet sallied forth once again in the enchanting black Nieuport and streaked over the route at nearly 270 kmh. Sadi knew then that he must have her, measure her ultimate response. Late in 1919 he left Spad to join Nieuport (Jean Casale at the same time transferred from Nieuport to Spad) and within three months, on January 3, 1920, Sadi drove the 29V around Paris in less than forty-three minutes, winning the first Prix Deutsch de la Meurthe and beginning a star-struck affair that would last for over twenty years.

The 29V racer had a distinguished lineage. Its earliest ancestor was built by a devout believer in the concept that speed was aviation's primary *raison d'être*. This was Édouard de Nieport, born at Blida, Northern Algeria, who came to France where in 1908, when he was thirty-three, he built a startling monoplane, both beautiful and practical, whose fuselage framework had been streamlined with cloth covering. (This, incidentally, was an important influence in changing the name of an

de Romanet's black Nieuport 29 Vitesse, Prix Deutsch race, 1919 (MA)

aeroplane's main body from *carlingue* to *fuselage*, a word with strong connection to the verb *fuseler* – or even the noun *fusée*, if you will.) De Nieport also designed and built his own engine, magneto, spark plugs, and propeller! The *u* was added to his name as his fame grew, in order to avoid embarrassment to his family, to whom, in those days, being associated with an aviator was a distinct humiliation. After setting several speed records, M. Nieuport was accidentally killed at Charny on September 6, 1911; his brother Charles met a similar fate two years later. Henry Deutsch de la Meurthe took over Nieuport's affairs and transformed them into a limited company – Société Anonyme des Établissement Nieuport, at Issy-les-Moulineaux (Seine), a Paris suburb. During World War I, of course, Nieuports were used by almost every Allied nation.

There were spin-off companies organized in Britain and Italy, occasioned by the war. Upon the death of M. Deutsch de la Meurthe in 1919 his son-in-law, M. Gradis, became the firm's managing director. In August 1921 a merger was announced which resulted in a new firm titled Nieuport-Astra, with combined assets of some 38 million francs. One of the most powerful cartels in France, their product line extended to motorboats and airships. All aeroplanes produced after this merger took the name Nieuport-Delage, which celebrated the name of the firm's distinguished chief engineer and which was also intended to eliminate confusion with the aircraft built by "British Nieuport," some of which were still in use.

The name Delage has long meant superior quality in some of France's loveliest mechanical contrivances, but, surprisingly, this name that simultaneously achieved preeminence in two fields – automobiles and aviation – originated not with one but with two *entirely separate* sources. Perhaps the most famous Delage was Louis, the ostentatious one-eyed builder of fine automobiles at Courbevoie-sur-Seine. The man whose name was painted on France's most successful racing aeroplanes was Paul-Aristide Gustave Delage. Although they were in no way related – indeed, there is no definite record they ever met (though that seems somewhat unlikely) – they were remarkably similar in outlook, temperament, and method. Both believed implicitly in the value of racing and both became invincible on the *grand prix* circuits in their respective fields. And both were willing to take unorthodox and unproven ideas into battle publicly on the race course.

Louis Delage, born in the Cognac region in 1874, built his first car at Lavellois in 1906, determined to be the finest and fastest in France. He spent money lavishly when he had it, even indulging himself by purchasing Château du Pecq at St.-Germain, and in the mid-twenties his jewel-like race cars won the undisputed championship of Europe, while his saloon cars inspired a favorite saying which became a virtual cliché: "One drives an Alfa, one is driven in a Rolls, but to one's favorite mistress one gives only a Delage." Coincidentally, a 10·5-liter V-12 Delage driven by René Thomas at Arpajon on July 6, 1924, set the world's land speed record (143·24 mph) at the very time when a Delage aeroplane held important air speed records. The mechanical genius behind the Delage cars was engine builder Albert Lory, who had come from building aero engines at Salmson and who in 1933 built the sixteen-cylinder engine that powered the Kellner-Béchéreau Coupe Deutsch racing aeroplane. Manifesting another parallel with his aviation namesake, Louis Delage was egocentric, even somewhat arrogant. By 1935, having completely alienated his Board of Directors, he saw his company fail. The assets were absorbed by Delahaye, who paid him a pension but made it clear he was to stay away; Louis Delage was eventually forced to sell his possessions one by one until he died, destitute, in 1947.

Gustave Delage   (MA)

Gustave Delage was born at Limoges on March 8, 1883, schooled in Brest, and then attended l'École Navale, becoming a naval officer just after the turn of the century. He became interested in aviation and began experiments with gliders which soon led to his training as an aviator (French Aero Club brevet number 219, September 19, 1910). The next month he set a non-stop record. During large-scale 1911 military maneuvers, Delage commanded the first squadron of Nieuport aeroplanes, one pilot under his command being Édouard Nieuport himself, and was made Chevalier of the Légion d'honneur. He continued technical studies at Vincennes, where seaplanes captured his attention, and he was variously credited with designing the first water-going monoplane, certainly a form adaptable to floats. He was promoted to *lieutenant de vaisseau* in 1913 but when the second Nieuport brother was killed, Delage happened to be "at the right place at the right time," as Nieuport's cousin Viscount Louis de Monge recalled, and Delage at once left the Navy to become the Nieuport firm's chief engineer under Henry Deutsch de la Meurthe in January 1914. That summer he presented the design of an armored aeroplane which might have influenced the war's early course, but it was ignored. Delage was recalled to active duty as a naval aviator, serving in the Mediterranean, Adriatic, and Port Said, but by spring 1915 he was back at the helm of Nieuport's engineering office. Almost at once his "Bébé" scout appeared, a diminutive fighter which made several aces famous. By 1919, when his staff numbered three thousand, Delage had personally given up flying and was working full-time to produce new designs. In 1920 variations of his model 29 won the Prix Deutsch and Gordon Bennett Aviation Cup plus the world altitude and speed records. Remarkably, those achievements were entirely free of fatal accidents, continuing the wartime record when more than seven thousand Nieuports were delivered without one fatality!

Delage's original Nieuport 29 was a single-seat biplane designed for combat. It had large, two-bay wings, and its engine was the Hispano-Suiza *modèle 42* cowled snugly into a wood-shell fuselage of exceptionally small cross section. The fuselage frame had four plywood ring bulkheads joined by sixteen spruce longerons, this being covered by a shell made from tulipwood strips (4 mm thick forward tapering to 2 mm thick aft), wound spirally around a mold in cross-grain fashion, glued up and fabric-covered. The bulkheads at cabane and landing gear attachment points were reinforced. Wing ribs were plywood with spruce stiffeners fitted around box

109

spars, the whole strengthened by steel tube compression members and braced with sturdy *cordes à piano*. Two Lamblin lobster-pot radiators nestled in the landing gear struts, which were built up from layers of poplar, the streamlined cross-member being duralumin. The potential of this craft encouraged its creators to remove the two hooded 11-mm Vickers machine guns and prepare it for speed. During the summer of 1919, test pilots Casale and Henri Mallard set up impressive performances in climbing, height, and speed.

The initiation of the Nieuport 29 to racing was abortive. Two were prepared for the 1919 Schneider; the first followed conservative design practice, credited variously to M. Chassraux, an assistant of Delage's, using the long-span wings with elephant-ear ailerons of the standard military 29 together with alighting gear based on prewar experience, consisting of two broad, short, dual-stepped floats with a duralumin *flotteur de queue* under the tail. The second was a more daring design employing a clipped, one-bay wing arrangement and the new, long, single-stepped floats. This plane would be flown by Jean Casale, who hoped to hit 150 mph with it. Both planes, however, were damaged in test flights from the Seine; Casale's was a write-off while Mallard, returning from a late-afternoon flight, misjudged his distance in the dusk and plowed into a pillar of the bridge at Argenteuil. Two racers were finally readied and Casale took off in his from Paris, after lunch on Sunday, September 7, three days before the race. In two and a half hours he had crossed the Channel and arrived at Cowes, via Brighton, but again gathering dusk laid a trap. The disturbing look of Cowes Roads's rough surface caused Casale to set up his approach to the Medina River's sheltered estuary. He touched down neatly but just when he thought he had it made there was a horrible crunch. The racer had struck a buoy and Casale felt himself being rudely up-

ended. The engine submerged with a sharp hiss and with sinking heart Casale knew the floats and wings were badly damaged. He was rescued and the aeroplane towed ashore but it seemed impossible to have it ready in two days without any French repair facilities.

Henri Mallard left Paris in the second Nieuport the next day. No word was received but a rumor that he was down in Le Havre with engine trouble gained strength. Meanwhile, Sam Saunders and his men, guided by works manager George Newman, that morning had taken Casale's Nieuport into their shed, stripped the wings, built new float struts, and repaired the fuselage and tail. A new engine and floats were sent from France and the plane was essentially rebuilt. By race-day morning, after forty-eight hours of virtual non-stop work, the racer was ready. Saunders, when the job was done, remarked somewhat defensively, in light of the abominable welcome the RAeC race committee had provided, that his men's work stood "in defiance of all modern labor notions . . . and demonstrating conclusively that, whatever the British workman may be, he is at heart a sportsman."

By noon, however, something was terribly wrong: Mallard still had not arrived. The Air Ministry soon determined that he had indeed left Paris and was definitely not in Le Havre, and a search was hastily organized. In some ways Mallard had been lucky. When he was discovered in mid-Channel he had been favored with twenty-four hours of perfect weather which enabled him to cling that long to floating pieces of his Nieuport!

Casale was the last competitor to arrive for the race proper at Bournemouth, even as the afternoon fog thickened. In the rough, unprepared conditions, beset by utter confusion and swarms of people speaking a strange language, Casale's floats were again damaged. It did not matter, of course, since fog ruined the race.

After that floats were temporarily

Long-float Nieuport 29 at the 1919 Schneider Trophy race   (MA)

abandoned and the design had more than half its original wing area clipped away. The 29V, with fuel for only one hour, became a pure speed seeker. The starboard Lamblin radiator was replaced by a small honeycomb radiator, less than 1 foot square, in the nose just behind the Lumière prop swung by its *modèle 42* Hispano-Suiza; this is the 29V Count de Romanet brought to the 1919 Prix Deutsch. On December 17, 1919, it was unofficially timed at 307 kmh in sprints with Sadi Lecointe at the controls, and in one blistering downwind pass an overexuberant timekeeper, trying to look ahead three years, registered a speed of 364 kmh!

On opening day of the gala Paris Air Show in January 1920, the Nieuport stand sported three trim biplanes, two military 29C.1s and the 29V. During the night, however, the racer disappeared from its stand. Sadi Lecointe had removed it to the Nieuport aerodrome at Villacoublay, just southeast of Versailles. He was impatient for more records.

On February 1, 1920, Sadi succeeded in averaging 273 kmh, which bettered his Prix Deutsch mark of a month earlier. Then, six days later on February 7, he flew the 29V to set the first officially homologated postwar world maximum speed record, 275·862 kmh. The honor was his for just three weeks, for on February 28 Jean Casale on a Spad-Herbemont raised the record by almost 8 kmh. Down at Mirafiori Aerodrome near Turin, Italy, Francesco Brack-Papa was doing some fast flying as well. The record was like a balloon, being stretched in three directions. Casale, however, retained the record until October. In the meantime, the Nieuport 29 made its appearance in three more races.

Striped sun and shadows of ancient columns along the Condamine framed the blue of Monaco harbor, the dapple of sunlight, and quiet sailboats gliding by, with the mottled green summit of "Tête de Chien" pushing into shaggy cloud behind. Colorful seaplanes bobbed in the gentle swells, adorning the North Quay. The peaceful warm azure

Nieuport 29G at Monaco, 1920. Note flotteur de queue. (MA)

during the 1920 Olympiade in early September. Later that month, a few miles south of Paris, the Nieuport 29 enjoyed the climax of its racing career at the 1920 Gordon Bennett. Two 29Vs were prepared for what was anticipated to be the best aeroplane race ever held; certainly the long entry list was a compendium of the fastest planes and finest pilots from two continents.

September 25 was the day appointed for the eliminations when the French team of three would be determined from the five hopefuls. Sadi Lecointe arrived about ten days early and both he and his *protégé* Georges Kirsch, who would fly the second racer, flew time and again over the course to memorize landmarks. This would be Kirsch's air racing debut though his flying experience went back to 1910 when he first went aloft at Mourmelon, an eager young passenger of Hubert Latham's. Renouncing at once all other ambitions, he continued as Latham's mechanic on the *Antoinette* until 1911 when he transferred his allegiance to the speedier Nieuports, thereafter flying often with prewar racing pilot Charles T. Weymann. During World War I, after a short stint

Nieuport 29G, 1920 (F)

of a Monegasque April backdropped the 1920 Monaco seaplane meeting which lasted for two uneventful weeks. Casale and de Romanet with their Spads ruled the speed and altitude trials, such as they were. Sadi Lecointe won the 50,000-franc *prix* offered for a round-trip flight to Tunis, even though his clumsy flying boat broke down en route — he was the only competitor! A lovely Nieuport 29G had also been sent, fitted with the conservative (three-float) arrangement used on Mallard's 1919 Schneider entry, but the short, fat pontoons porpoised badly in choppy water. Two sets of wings were provided, standard two-bay wings used for

the altitude trials and unequal span racing wings with a short top panel which could be substituted for the speed events. Sadi was in daily competition with Casale's Spad for the Prix Garros, in which both reached 6,400 meters in a hour's climbing, the edge determined largely by luck. But on the day of the big speed race to Cannes and back for the Prix Guynemer, Sadi was grounded at Bizerte — and he was Nieuport's only pilot! In a word, both logistics and preparation were inadequate. But it *was* a lovely holiday.

A Nieuport 29 (F-ABAV in the French civil register) flown by Sadi Lecointe won a speed test at Antwerp

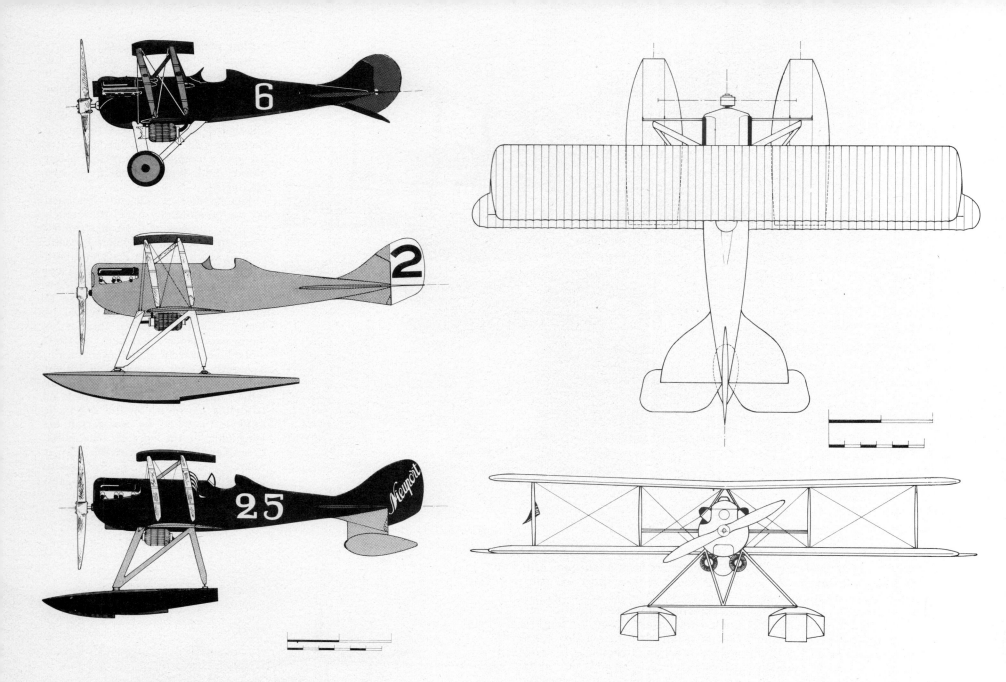

*Side views, reading down: Nieuport 29
Vitesse (13·2 m²), winner Prix Deutsch,
January 1920, and world speed record,
February 1920; Nieuport 29 seaplane racer
entered in the 1919 Schneider Trophy race;
Nieuport 29G as flown in the 1920 Monaco
seaplane Rallye (note* flotteur de queue); *
plan and front views are of long-wing Nieuport
29 with* flotteur de queue.*

The two Gordon Bennett Nieuport racers, 1920   (MA)

The Gordon Bennett victor taking off, 1920
                                          (Au)

in Voisin bombers, Kirsch switched to pursuits and put in many dawn patrols until he was shot down disastrously, grievously wounded in the belly, knee, and foot. This put him in the hospital for a year but he emerged undaunted and became a test pilot. He survived several more years of flying to retire in Paris, where he died in 1970.

Kirsch's race mount was a 29V with equal-span wings tied by single lift wires, whereas Sadi's had a clipped top wing and double lift wires. Both aeroplanes had *modèle 42* type Marine engines with compression ratio of only 4·7, a type which in fact could deliver little more than 260 hp despite trade journal specifications. Even the *modèle 42* with 4·9 compression ratio did not attain quite 300 hp, a performance which required the 5·3 pistons.

The French elimination trials required one trip out and back over the 50-kilometer course — the race itself required three — and were strictly against the clock. Sadi took off in the morning and gave a preview of his quixotic style, but he suffered a vapor lock near Toury and force-landed.

Nieuport pilot Georges Kirsch   (MA)

When he was not spotted after a few minutes, he stamped out a long line in the ground to make himself more visible to the frantic searchers, who were by then out in force. Two planes took off to retrace the route and famous race driver de Courcelles hustled Sadi's mechanic Jean Bernard into his Bignan auto and in a cloud of dust roared southward at 70 mph. Sadi was discovered calmly smoking a cigarette and leaning against his plane, which was sitting in view of Toury's sugar factory.

"— Eh bien?"

"La panne, mon petit vieux, ne t'en fais pas, 'ça' va repartir. Mais c'est à s'arracher les cheveux: le 'lion' volait si bien . . ."

Bernard soon had the engine running and Sadi took off easily, skimming the hedgerow and wheeling in the direction of Villesauvage, where Gustave Delage, assisted by engineer M. Mary, awaited. The punctured right wheel was changed and after lunch Sadi roared off for a second try — three were allowed — completing the 100 kilometers in 21:28 for a world's closed-course speed record! Kirsch's first lap time in the race three days

later (21:29) was the race record and led race observers, unaware of the elimination performances, to comment that Sadi's clipped upper wing actually hindered his speed. Yet during the race, Sadi added the 200-kilometer and 300-kilometer closed-course records to his list and the evidence seems to indicate that the wing arrangement did not affect his speed significantly one way or the other. It is true that Sadi had tested an even smaller (11 m² area) set of wings and found, to his great surprise, the aeroplane was 30 kmh slower. The reason was induced drag, caused by stronger pressure losses around the wingtips on the shorter span.

On Cup day the wet bite of fall swelled the air but after midday the misty early morning scud broke into great, white clefts of cloud and Kirsch took off. The first contestant airborne, he dipped his wing in salute and plunged across the starting line, roaring out and back two times, but when beginning his third and final lap his straining Hispano oiled her spark plugs. This fairly common malady occurred when overheated, frothy oil worked past the piston rings into the

113

Lecointe and Count de Romanet over the measured kilometer resumed in earnest at the huge Buc aeronautic meeting. On October 10 de Romanet set a new record in his Spad-Herbemont S.20bis₆ but the very next day, as thousands watched, Sadi pushed the record to 296·694 kmh, and nine days later, in the clipped wing 29V at Villacoublay, he raised the mark to 302·529 kmh. This was a round, satisfying number and it established Sadi as the first man to better 300 kmh for the record book, a feat which had long been one of his cherished ambitions. His next goal was to be the first officially to exceed 200 mph.

The flying count was not beaten yet. On the foggy morning of November 4 he flew his modified Spad to over 309 kmh. Sadi's little white Nieuport must be capable of beating that mark. Seemingly every detail of streamlining had been considered; its glistening surface had been polished until it resembled glass. But one trick so far had not been tried. The drag of the gaping hole that was the open cockpit, with its blunt windscreen, obviously

cost several kilometers. Herbemont had considered it in the Spad, but Delage went one better. During November Kirsch's Gordon Bennett number 11 was hauled into the sheds at Villacoublay, where artisans removed the windscreen and devised a clever sliding hatch to close completely over the hole after the pilot was in place. Two small windows resembling fish-eyes provided limited lateral vision. On December 12 Sadi Lecointe enclosed himself inside this tiny capsule and in a wild flight barely 4 meters high, made all the more spectacular by the hazard of the blind cockpit, he squeezed by de Romanet's speed mark, boosting the official world speed record to 313·043 kmh. For having won the Prix Deutsch, Grand Prix de Monaco, Gordon Bennett Aviation Cup, and world speed record four times — all in 1920 — Sadi was presented with the Gold Medal of l'Aéro-Club de France.

This speed-record Nieuport seemed the ultimate biplane, and plans were made to exploit its prowess the following summer. It was duly entered in the British Aerial Derby to be held July

Sadi Lecointe (holding goggles) and Gustave Delage (in checkered cap) beaming over their 1920 Gordon Bennett victory (MA)

The world speed record Nieuport 29V after modifications to cockpit, 1920. Note Sadi Lecointe peeking through "fish-eye" window. (Au)

cylinder head. Then the law of gravity took over. Kirsch landed and clumped to his hangar, completely disgusted.

Sadi, on the other hand, continually delighted in showing off the stunning aerobatic qualities of his racer with never a fear of engine trouble. Roland Rohlfs recalled Sadi asking him, "Do you want to see me fly?" Without awaiting an answer Sadi climbed

aboard his white 29V parked in the shade of a tree near the hangars, and proceeded to "beat up" the aerodrome in a superb display of flying virtuosity. Even as he departed for the race he "warmed up" with a few stunts then flashed away in the performance that stands as a hallmark in air race history.

Two weeks after the Gordon Bennett, the speed duel between Sadi

16, 1921, and during early spring it resumed flight tests, but on one landing a wheel collapsed and the plane was thrown over onto its back. Both landing gear and wings were wiped off and the mishap prevented the plane's participation in any further racing. Sadi was lucky to escape with no more than a broken arm.

Another Nieuport racer, a seaplane, was dispatched to Venice for the 1921 Schneider Trophy race held the first week in August. Subsidized by the French government, it was that year's only non-Italian contestant. Today, after more than half a century, the surviving records concerning this lone French contender are vague and incomplete; from what remains the conclusion most likely if indefinite is that it was apparently the long-float (*flotteur en catamaran*) Nieuport fitted with short-span wings similar to Casale's entry in the 1919 Schneider. This tentative conclusion is based on incomplete but revealing references to the aeroplane in original Italian records pertaining to the contest — and logic. The *flotteur de queue*-equipped aeroplane was larger (two-bay wings), heavier, slower, and not as likely to have its float chassis broken very easily. Nevertheless, the French had sent *flotteur de queue* versions to the 1919 Schneider and 1920 Monaco; they were known to be still somewhat suspicious of the *flotteur en catamaran* and cautious in their attitude toward dispatching entries that might be likely to cause them embarrassment. Despite this, on Sadi's first landing for his navigability trials on August 6, the spreader bar between the floats broke, the floats folded upward, and the wings slumped. Sadi was not hurt but for the second — and last — time, a Nieuport 29 had suffered elimination from the Schneider.

On September 4, 1921, with the remaining Gordon Bennett 29V (the clipped-wing version), Sadi Lecointe won the Gran Premio d'Italia d'Aviazione, an aeroplane race held in connection with the Italian *grand prix*

for motorcars at Brescia, Italy. The event resulted in a double French victory: Jules Goux in the 255-kilometer auto race and Sadi Lecointe in the 280-kilometer air circuit. Sadi's time was 1:13:09, almost 42 kmh slower than his Gordon Bennett speed, but sufficient to beat Brack-Papa, who finished second in 1:18:58. The other ten entries trailed behind.

Meanwhile, with the blessing of Madame Deutsch de la Meurthe and M. André Michelin, President of l'Aéro-Club de France, the first race in the new Coupe Deutsch de la Meurthe series was set for the first day of October 1921, over the 1920 Gordon Bennett course. This was a speed race pure and simple and entries were completely unrestricted. The same Gordon Bennett 29V was entered and despite a long list of exotic competition, it actually finished second, one of only two racers to complete the distance. Although overshadowed by the brilliant new Nieuport-Delage sesquiplane which won the race, the 29V managed a respectable performance, 21 kmh off the winner's pace, with Fernand Lasne at the controls.

Nieuport pilot Fernand Lasne (MA)

Fernand Lasne preparing to take off in the 1921 Coupe Deutsch (MA)

Lasne, a new star in Nieuport's firmament, was born during November 1894 at La Ferté-St.-Aubin (Loiret), a pastoral village several miles south of Paris. He was mechanically inclined, meticulous, and determined. He saw Louis Blériot land at Arthenay near his home in 1908 and the event so excited him that he vowed to make aviation his life. Lasne was called to arms on September 1, 1914, together with millions of his generation, but he begged to be posted to the aviation contingent, the warriors elite; he got his posting — as a lorry driver in Escadrille M.S.38 in 1915! But that was only temporary. Lasne went for flight training at Avord in 1916, where his instructor was Sadi Lecointe, and he qualified in March 1917 (French Aero Club brevet number 5870). He then flew with Escadrille N.93 in the Vosges from May 1917 until August 1918 when he was posted to the flight test escadrille at Villacoublay. Lasne joined Nieuport as test pilot on April 1, 1920. More than fifty years later, with his flying exploits piquant memories, M. Lasne was living contentedly — in La Ferté-St.-Aubin.

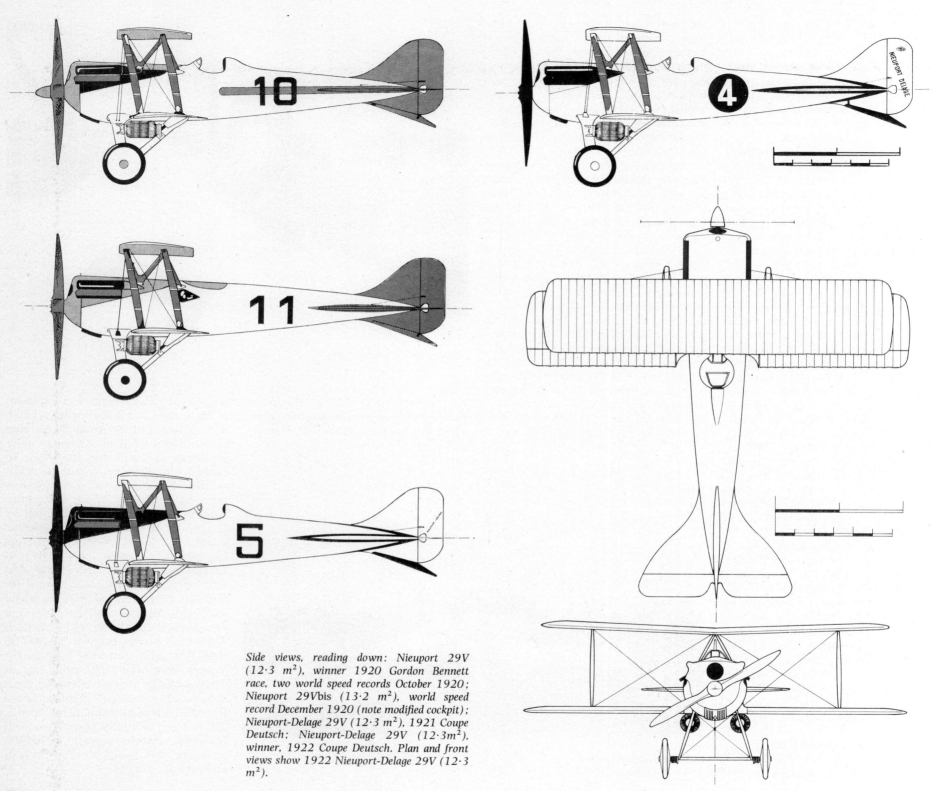

Side views, reading down: Nieuport 29V
(12·3 m²), winner 1920 Gordon Bennett
race, two world speed records October 1920;
Nieuport 29Vbis (13·2 m²), world speed
record December 1920 (note modified cockpit);
Nieuport-Delage 29V (12·3 m²), 1921 Coupe
Deutsch; Nieuport-Delage 29V (12·3m²),
winner, 1922 Coupe Deutsch. Plan and front
views show 1922 Nieuport-Delage 29V (12·3
m²).

The lovely Nieuport 29V of Lasne, winner, 1922 Coupe Deutsch   *(MA)*

The aging Gordon Bennett 29V, piloted by Lasne, ended its racing career in a blaze of glory by winning the 1922 Coupe Deutsch de la Meurthe, held over the same course and to the same rules as the 1921 contest. The 29V not only won the "race," but as it had done so often in the past, it displayed its singular attribute of endurance once again and was the only plane to finish the distance! Powered with a newer, high-compression *modèle 42* Hispano-Suiza engine whose output was reputedly boosted to 350 hp, the 29V set a closed-course record for the 300 kilometers, finishing with a speed some 18 kmh faster than its Gordon Bennett performance two years previously. Lasne had fought a splendidly played-out duel around the pylons with Brack-Papa, who raced virtually neck-and-neck with the 29V for 300 kilometers, not realizing he had been disqualified for an improper start! After Brack-Papa's forced landing on his second start, Lasne took off in a Bréguet to fly to the Italian's aid. He soon returned to Villesauvage, where the clear sky was glorious, victory was glorious, and after he landed Lasne sat down to a glorious *pique-nique sur l'herbe* and the good French wine flowed freely. The Coupe Deutsch was awarded to Nieuport-Astra and the contest was closed.

The basic Nieuport 29 had demonstrated fine altitude performance as well, so in 1923 a new Nieuport biplane was built, based somewhat on the 29 but using updated construction features to make it more efficient for attacks on the altitude record, then held by Macready and now almost two years old. The resulting aeroplane, designated Nieuport-Delage 40, used a tulipwood shell fuselage adapted from the standard military version — updated in the meantime from the 29 and now called type 40C.1 — to which monstrous wings spanning 14 meters with a total area of 34 square meters and aspect ratio of 11 were fitted. It was powered with a high-compression Hispano-Suiza *modèle 42* swinging a special Régy prop at 2,000 rpm. Incredibly, no supercharger was used. The fuel was pure benzole up to 5,000 meters altitude and gasoline above. Cooling was, of course, by Lamblin lobster pot but special thin-wall versions were used. Sadi Lecointe began training for his bouts with high altitude in mid-July. He would sit for up to seventy-five minutes in an evacuated *caisson* made of glass and while curious doctors peered through the walls, the pressure inside was lowered until Sadi huddled, breathing oxygen, at the equivalent of 12,000 meters altitude. This was his goal, a height he considered unbeatable. When he emerged from what was perhaps aviation's first low-pressure chamber, he was still shivering in his heavy fur coat while the conditions outside were sweltering. Journalists wrote that Sadi was undoubtedly "the only cool man in Paris."

Nieuport-Delage type 40 high-altitude biplane at Villacoublay, 1923   *(MA)*

Gas cartridge Odier starter attached to Lasne's Nieuport, 1922   *(MA)*

Nieuport-Delage 40 which set the world altitude record, 11,145 meters (36,564 feet), October 30, 1923. The last Nieuport-Delage world record biplane.

On August 1, 1923, Sadi rose from Villacoublay in his first altitude trial aboard the 40 and climbed 10,127 meters in 1:20 when an oxygen bottle broke and his thermometer congealed at −40° C. This was just 391 meters less than the current world record, set by Macready in September 1921 on a LePère at Dayton, Ohio. One week later, on August 8, Sadi equalled Macready's mark. He tried again on August 14 but did no better. Finally,

on September 8, Sadi reached 10,722 meters (35,178 feet) and thus, to its speed marks, the Nieuport-Delage biplane added the altitude record. Still not satisfied, Sadi improved on this in late October; in addition to his other aspirations he hoped to be the first man to top 11,000 meters. On October 30 he made it! From the Nieuport-Astra factory field at Issy-les-Moulineaux Sadi mounted to 11,145 meters (36,564 feet), a world record and

certainly one of the greatest heights reached in a piston-powered aeroplane without supercharger.[1]

This was perhaps the last major record set by a Nieuport-Delage biplane. Standard 29s, of course, saw years of military service in great numbers, both in France and elsewhere. In Japan during 1924 between twelve and twenty-five N.29s per month were being produced by Nakajima at Ota, and Billy Mitchell, observing this, called the N.29 "the best pursuit plane of the high-speed diving type with which any nation is now equipped." During early 1923, promoters from Nieuport-Astra were well represented at the Concours International de Madrid, a huge Spanish military display were two sample 29s, both flown by Captain Jaille, were most impressive. As late as July 1936 the Republican government could still field two dozen 29s for service in the bloody Spanish Civil War.

The Nieuport-Delage 29V was extraordinarily reliable, with speed to match its beauty, and it was no surprise that the aeroplane that replaced it as the world's fastest was its direct descendant — the Nieuport-Delage *sesquiplane*.

Nieuport-Delage type 40 taking off to set the world altitude record (some 36,000 feet), 1923 (MA)

[1] Sadi's record stood for more than one year. Macready assaulted it repeatedly through the winter and spring of 1923–24 using the old LePère (P-53) fitted with a turbo-supercharger developed by Dr. Sanford A. Moss of the General Electric Company, but each time he faltered, once just 404 meters shy of the goal. Meanwhile Sadi put the Nieuport-Delage 40 on floats at Meulan and set the world altitude record for seaplanes (8,980 meters, March 11, 1924). Then, on October 10, 1924, in an all-metal Gourdou-Leseurre equipped with a *modèle 42* boosted by a new Rateau supercharger, Jean Marie Callizo climbed to 12,066 meters (39,587 feet), and as Sadi had predicted, this height put the record out of reach for some time.

QUEST FOR VITESSE

7

The Nieuport-Delage Sesquiplane Racers

Just what is a sesquiplane? This was a question that puzzled aviation aficionados in 1921 before Gustave Delage rolled out his promised new racer. The French, retorting to a rash of English sarcasm, pointed out with grave seriousness that the word did not imply the concoction of some mysterious new designer named Monsieur Sesqui, nor was it an adaptation of such frivolous remarks as "*C'est ce qui plane!*" The prefix "sesqui-" simply means "more than one but less than two," and the term "sesquiplane" was usually applied to a one-and-a-half–winged aeroplane. Delage's new racer was more on the order of one-and-one-tenth–winged, so the name, strictly speaking, was a misnomer. (The French good-naturedly parried the English chiding by saying that Delage had wanted to give his new racer a zoological name, but that the names of all animals – past, present, and future – had been reserved by the British!)

Delage's racing sesquiplane was certainly a refreshing change from the pedestrian designs of World War I. Its altogether pleasing lines reminded one of the great prewar Deperdussins, of past glory. Its fuselage was a beautiful stretched teardrop with rounded nose, almost a perfect streamline, a tulipwood *coque* with the same external dimensions as the shell of the 29V. The wing had two box spars made of spruce and fabric-covered to prevent splitting, wing ribs built up from 1·5-mm

Nieuport-Delage sesquiplane at 1921 Paris Air Show (F)

Sadi Lecointe, ace of speed, 1921 (MA)

mahogany plywood webs, steel tube and steel strap cross members, the whole plywood then fabric-covered, and attached shoulder-high. In 1921 the wing was practically flat-bottomed with a constant chord and perfectly rounded tips. The "inferior" wing — in fact, nothing more than a built-up axle fairing — provided depth for the rigid, single-strut external bracing. The finished racer was quite clean; even with two Lamblin lobster pots its equivalent flat plate area was only ·176 m². Its relatively high wing loading was considered daring in those days but of course the French placed no restrictions on landing speeds as was done in the United States. Two sesquiplanes were built, powered by the inevitable Hispano-Suiza *modèle 42*, both sparkling white. One had light

blue trim, the other's was fire-engine red.

The world's maximum speed record had stood resolute all year at 313·043 kmh, the mark posted by Sadi Lecointe the previous December in the highly modified Nieuport-Delage biplane. During semi-secret pre-race trials at Villesauvage beginning September 25, 1921, three days before the abortive Coupe Deutsch de la Meurthe race eliminations (all but the Nieuport-Astra team of three withdrew), Sadi drove the red-tailed sesquiplane (race number 6) many times over the measured kilometer. On September 25 he was clocked unofficially at a remarkable 10·2 seconds (about 350 kmh) for the kilometer; the next day, in four official passes, he attained 330·275 kmh for a new world speed record.

Although Sadi knew the racer had more in hand, this warmup enabled him to realize a deep ambition — Sadi and his sesquiplane became the first officially to crack 200 mph!

This record actually stood for one year. In November 1921 Bert Acosta tried unsuccessfully to surpass it in the Curtiss Navy racer with which he triumphed at the Omaha Pulitzer.

Then, in August 1922, at Mirafiori Aerodrome, Turin, Brack-Papa and his massive Fiat racer actually exceeded Sadi's record, but the Italian mark was never officially recorded.

Aside from Sadi's record there was a great deal of excitement surrounding preliminaries to the 1921 Coupe Deutsch with its packed entry list. On race day Sadi took off shortly

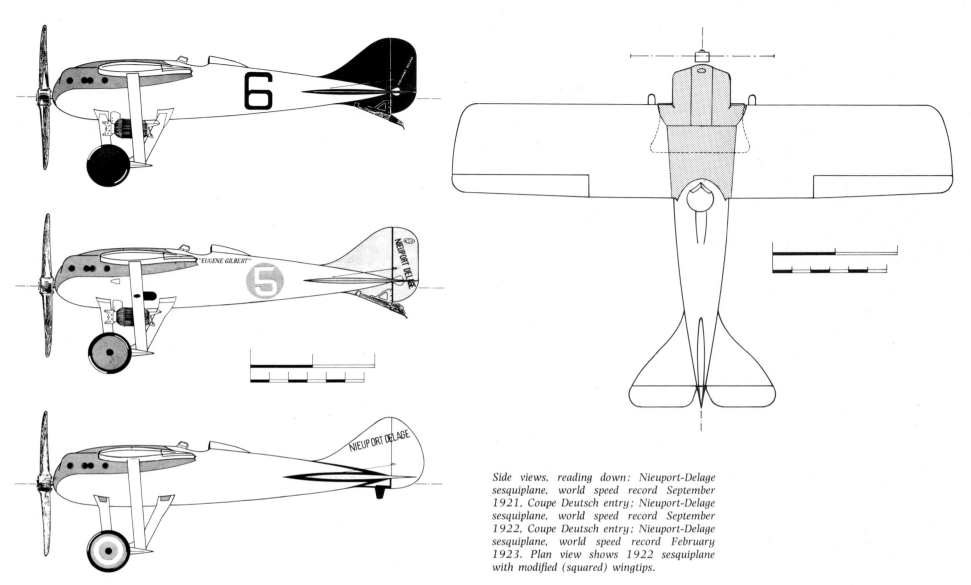

Side views, reading down: Nieuport-Delage sesquiplane, world speed record September 1921, Coupe Deutsch entry; Nieuport-Delage sesquiplane, world speed record September 1922, Coupe Deutsch entry; Nieuport-Delage sesquiplane, world speed record February 1923. Plan view shows 1922 sesquiplane with modified (squared) wingtips.

before 10 A.M., the easy favorite in his speed record sesquiplane, and roared toward the first pylon, shaving almost 15 per cent off the time he posted for the same distance in the victorious Gordon Bennett biplane one year before. Sadi was flying his plane "as never before, even on his wonder flights." His small white charger flashed over the rim of an auburn hill, the country road just below turned slightly, and Sadi, peering into the blinding wind, bent over in a sharp bank. With radiators screeching the racer

wheeled on a nimble wing, its bright red tail glinting briefly in the sun. Sadi exulted; never had he felt such sweetness. Even cinched deep in his pit, he experienced an uncommon freedom in slipping past the enchanting French grape arbors, now basking after harvest. And he knew, amid the loud song of his engine, that no one could touch his time.

Then all hell broke loose. The sparse wood shell in which he huddled seemed to shatter around him. With frantic suddenness his eyes gulped for a

clearing; but with hardly time to react, he was rudely dashed to the ground. His ears rang. In a moment he realized it was only the strange sensation of silence.

Sadi was down in a field of beetroot at Cernonville, near Toury. He had landed heavily, stopping in hardly more than 10 meters. Fragments from the shattered windshield had cut his cheek, his right eye was injured (the eyebrow cracked), he had a broken left wrist and bad sprains. (Though his eye was threatened, it

recovered and Sadi's only permanent souvenirs were two small scars.) The prop had also shattered — Sadi had ducked instinctively as pieces shot back like machine gun bullets, some just missing his head, others leaving gaping holes in his wings. The butt of the broken prop was found underneath his seat.

What caused Sadi's crash? The preponderance of opinion at the time acknowledged that a bird must have struck Sadi's whirling prop disc, exploding the wooden prop into tooth-

Nieuport-Delage sesquiplane flown by Kirsch to win the 1921 Coupe Deutsch (MA)

picks. Indeed, the bird strike theory seemed quite plausible; great flocks of partridge had been observed in profusion along the route, and the wings of Kirsch's twin sesquiplane — which won the race — were reported "splashed with blood" where birds had struck. Lasne, who took Sadi to the Toury hospital, later recalled the accident, saying it was "probably" caused by a bird strike. But another theory has been voiced, citing a reason with which designers of 1921 had hardly come to grips, a reason more terrifying simply because it was not then understood, a reason termed "flutter." This theory has been put forward with great conviction by Viscount Louis de Monge, and some might read ulterior motives into his opinion since it was his own Lumière firm that produced the sesquiplane's propeller. But de Monge had also built his own racing aeroplane for the 1921 Coupe Deutsch, a rakish monoplane which crashed just eight days before, killing Count de Romanet,

and though this tragedy was publicly laid to another cause, de Monge himself insisted with no false guile that he too had been victim of flutter. His conviction gained strength in later years after the physical nature of flutter was explored and became better understood.

With Sadi out of the race, it would be up to Georges Kirsch, assigned to fly the blue-tailed twin sesquiplane numbered 7. Kirsch studied with redoubled determination the factors affecting his chance. Patiently he waited through the heat of the day, outlasting his rivals. Finally, at nine minutes to five, after all other competitors had made their try (and all, save one, failed to complete the distance), Kirsch took off. Lacking skill in the sleek racer, Kirsch's cornering was careful and he kept a bit of throttle in reserve, making sure to finish. As the red sun threw its last feeble glimmer onto the gray, thickening shapes of barnlike hangars, Kirsch roared in at

90 mph, ballooned, gunned the throttle but killed the engine, porpoised across the downhill slope, careening badly — a lucky rut bounced the plane level and saved a wingtip — then slewed around and stopped backward! None the worse, Kirsch was hoisted to a welcome which included 60,000 francs cold cash and a permanent niche in air racing history. Kirsch's winning speed — about 173 mph — set the world's 200-kilometer closed-course record. One month later it was surpassed by Bert Acosta winning the Omaha Pulitzer by a speed increase of less than 4 mph. Kirsch was suitably chaired on the shoulders of well-wishers after his victory. When asked if the pressure to finish gave him cold feet, he answered, "No, they were hot — in fact, they were both blistered by the intense heat from the engine!"

As 1922 opened it was apparent to European speed seekers that the Nieuport-Delage sesquiplane would be the one to beat. During July that year hearsay was rife that Delage was designing a new sesquiplane with the then unheard-of wing loading of 105 kg/m^2 (15 per cent more than the 1921 sesquiplane) and fitted with a Sunbeam-Coatalen engine boosted to 500 hp; the "Matabele" engine was

then in vogue for land speed records. But this entrancing vignette turned out to be rumor only.

Yet, through mid-1922, Gustave Delage *was* closeted with plans for a new sesquiplane racer, a very hush-hush type with many novel features. The designer, in seeking a layout for a new high-altitude fighter, perched the pilot almost directly above the engine, a position from which he would unquestionably have an outstanding view, but such an arrangement prevented reasonable streamlining or efficient weight distribution. Nevertheless, one racer version was built to preview the form; designated Nieuport-Delage 37 (type *course*), it was to be flown by Sadi Lecointe in the Coupe Deutsch that autumn. Sadi's cockpit sat high atop a bulbous fuselage, so far forward that the rudder bar was squeezed directly between the cylinder blocks of the buried V-8 engine. One huge Lamblin radiator was slung beneath, fitted with a four-leaf shutter to regulate airflow through the center core. The cantilever monoplane wing, which was bolted to the fuselage at eight points, employed four full-span spars and was completely plywood-covered, indicating that Delage had anticipated the flutter problems being

Kirsch being chaired after his 1921 Coupe Deutsch victory (MA)

Nieuport-Delage 37 type course *built for the 1922 Coupe Deutsch race*   *(USAF)*

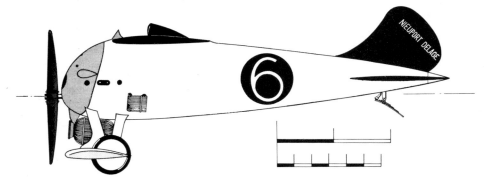

Nieuport-Delage 37 type course, *built for 1922 Coupe Deutsch*

were soon building a superior, more powerful, and essentially new engine, the Wright model H ("H" was a coincidence; it did not stand for Hispano). As early as 1919 the Americans had urged 376 hp at 2,240 rpm from their engine, using a compression ratio of 5·32. While high-compression (in those days anything more than 5·3) *modèle 42*s in France were increasingly unreliable, George Mead in the United States already had versions of the Wright H running well with powers approaching 400 hp. The H-2 engine in 1920 when well tuned gave 380 hp with compression of 5·5, and the H-3 engine in 1921, using a compression of 6·0, gave the honest 400 hp that Delage needed. The only problem was that a 90-degree V-8 cylinder arrangement, because of its inherent dynamics, tends to aggravate any disharmonious explosion pressures. When such an engine begins to misfire or detonate, it can easily wrench itself loose from its bearers, and this made speed seekers doubly cautious when it came to boosting compression, especially hampered as they were by poor fuels in those days. The problem was not a limited one then; many contemporary engine designers had not adequately anticipated vibration problems and built aero engines doomed

to failure: the Sunbeam Arab, the Liberty 8 – a 45-degree V-8 which is one of the worst – the ABC Dragonfly, and others.

The first three Wright H-3 engines designated for air racing went to Thomas-Morse for the MB-6 in 1921, but the first examples to gain wide notice went into 1922 Pulitzer racers. At the same time an H-3 was shipped to France where, in a bench test at Chalais-Meudon, it produced 407 hp (its compression was 6·0 and the liberal use of benzole in the fuel certainly contributed). It was *this* American-built engine that was installed in the Nieuport-Delage 37. When the bizarre racer was rolled out it was painted in stunning red and white racing trim, but even more stunning, it could not be coaxed off the ground! It seems the carburetor, in its buried location – not to mention directly beneath the soles of the pilot's shoes – caught fire, certainly a condition to deflate Sadi's enthusiasm rapidly!

The French have an extraordinary way of dissimulating their failures. The one-of-a-kind 37 racer faded almost completely from memory, and meager, vague references to it have been easily confused with the other, more successful sesquiplane types. At the 1922 Paris Air Show, held

experienced at that very moment in the United States and England with cantilever monoplane racers. The "inferior" wing – grown large and ungainly (thus making this a true sesquiplane) – partially enclosed the wheels, and was mounted well forward, hopefully to correct aerodynamic faults. The plywood *coque*, especially where the empennage was faired in, was truly a three-dimensional woodworking masterpiece. Belleville expandable washers were fitted to the tailskid for shock absorption. For his model 37 fighter version (type *chasse*) Delage planned to

employ a Rateau turbo-supercharger and Levasseur VP propeller.

Delage needed an engine that produced an honest 400 hp at 2,000 rpm for his 37 racer. Above 2,000 rpm excessive prop tipspeeds caused difficulties, but the Hispano-Suiza *modèle 42*, essentially unimproved since its inception, was incapable of delivering the necessary power at just 2,000 rpm. Meanwhile American engineers, having begun when Wright-Martin was the wartime U.S. Hispano licensee, had put a great deal of effort into detail improvements, to the extent that they

Nieuport-Delage 37 type chasse *at the 1922 Paris Air Show*   *(MA)*

Warming up the Eugène Gilbert *before the 1922 Coupe Deutsch* (USAF)

Sadi Lecointe preparing to take off in the 1922 Coupe Deutsch race (MA)

during December, the only 37 ever seen in public was exhibited. It was quite different from the racer: instead of thin, tapered, cantilever wings, the 37C.1 *avion de chasse* bulged ominously with thick, strut-braced wings spanning 11·6 meters and curved back at an odd angle near the fuselage to accommodate the grotesquely upholstered cockpit.

During 1922 the one remaining 1921 racing sesquiplane was modified. A new main wing with square tips and tapered trailing edge was fitted, although span and surface area dimensions were not altered. A new airfoil, the bi-convex Göttingen 416, was adopted and the wing was plywood-covered back to the false spar (the aileron hinge line). A Zenith carburetor and Régy prop were installed and it was quickly rushed to Villesauvage to prepare for the upcoming Coupe Deutsch and make fresh speed trials. On September 10, 1922, Sadi flew 100 kilometers at 325·491 kmh and did 1 kilometer at 358 kmh although unofficially, but a few days later, on September 21, nine days before the race, Sadi took the freshly painted

The Nieuport-Delage sesquiplane Eugène Gilbert *aloft, 1922. Note squared wingtips. (MA)*

sesquiplane aloft and officially achieved 341·239 kmh for the world record book. Its *modèle 42* engine was reputedly burning a benzole-alcohol mixture, producing perhaps more than 350 hp, but running terribly hot. The question was how long it would stand up under such a strain in the 300-kilometer race.

Sadi was the real artist of the French team, and on race day at quarter to four he soared off in this beautiful sesquiplane, now number 5 and named for prewar Deperdussin racing hero Eugène Gilbert, who had been killed during the war.[1] In less than twenty minutes Sadi finished the first 100 kilometers, ripped around the home pylon in a maneuver resembling an

---

[1] Eugène Gilbert set various prewar speed and duration records. He finished in third place in the 1913 Gordon Bennett, flying a Deperdussin. On the outbreak of war he joined the French Army air service. During a raid on the Zeppelin works at Friedrichshafen on June 27, 1915, he was forced down in Switzerland and interned. He made three attempts to escape — once disguised as a woman, once as an aged and infirm peasant — the latter successful. He was killed at Villacoublay on May 16, 1918, while serving as a test pilot.

Immelmann, and engine screaming was soon lost to view. Suddenly, on a sick note, he returned. The hot fuel had blasted a spark plug out of its cylinder with such force that it pierced the cowl. Sadi was soon forced to shut down the protesting engine. He whistled low over the grass of the airfield, bumped on, but hit a wicked rut while still running fast. The plane swerved, then tossed abruptly onto its back. Groans of "Sadi! Ah, Sadi!" could be heard from hundreds of horrified spectators, and soldiers with fixed bayonets fell aside under the surge of people. The first to arrive panting at the scene saw Sadi wedging himself free, entirely without a scratch.

Sadi's speed for 100 kilometers, about 202 mph, set a closed-course world record. It was short-lived, however. In a repeat of history, two weeks later the new Curtiss racer (this year an Army R-6 flown by Lieutenant Russ Maughan) pelted around the Detroit Pulitzer course at almost 206 mph to wrest this record away from France. Lasne, who won the Coupe Deutsch in his aging Nieuport biplane, briefly held the record for 200 kilometers. His time for this distance, however,

Sadi's crash, 1922 Coupe Deutsch (MA)

was bested by the first five Pulitzer finishers. Since the Pulitzer covered only 250 kilometers, the French retained the 300-kilometer closed-course mark.

The Coupe Deutsch was now closed and would remain so until its final resurrection, as the Coupe Suzanne Deutsch de la Meurthe, in 1933, which ran for four annual editions. Meanwhile, until a new European race was instituted, aeronautical speed merchants had to take their incentive from attempts on the world record. They wasted no time in continuing this quest. On October 3 and 4, 1922, Jimmie James, who briefly remained in France after the race, made four valiant attempts in the Bamel. He added just 0·2 kmh, thus not enough for a new record, but it did tend to prove that the English racer had performance equivalent to the sesquiplane, although the French mildly rebuked the English for their excessive diving on the course, pointing out (from barograph traces) that Sadi had flown the sesquiplane level on his record flight. This soon became irrelevant, because in the United States the new R-6 and its incomparable D-12 engine in a blinding display quickly made aeronautical headlines, climaxed on October 18 when it chalked up a world speed record that added a solid 18 kmh to the best European mark. Certainly this was the more remarkable, being done by General Billy Mitchell himself on his first R-6 flight!

The end of the monopoly on speed held by the Hispano-Suiza *modèle 42* was at hand. Despite the handicap to high speed imposed in the United States by the Pulitzer 75-mph landing speed limit (French racers generally had cut down wings and landed much hotter), the D-12 now made the speed record an international prize.

The French set to work at once to recapture the golden mark. During the next two months Sadi's sesquiplane *Eugène Gilbert* was rebuilt and cleaned up under the direction of Delage's assistant, *l'ingénieur* Mary. It still sported Lamblin radiators but a new

Nieuport-Delage speed record sesquiplane Eugène Gilbert, 1923. Note wing radiators. (MA)

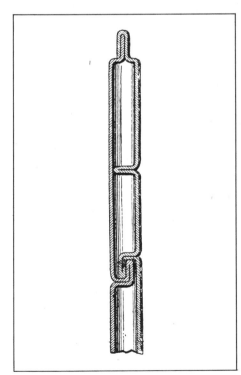

Cross section of Moreux wing radiator used on the world speed record Nieuport-Delage sesquiplane, February 1923

Régy prop was bolted on and it was shipped to Marseille. The desolate wastes surrounding the nearby French military flight test center at Istres (Bouches-du-Rhône) would be the site for new speed attempts, partly because the sesquiplane's landing speed was now an alarming 112 mph. Late in December Sadi Lecointe began his flight trials, eager to get the record back during 1922. On New Year's Eve he put the sesquiplane over the measured kilometer four times and averaged 348·028 kmh, but this was more than 10 kmh slow. He tried again on January 2 but could do no better.

The racer was then hauled into the sheds, where the Lamblin pots were stripped off and thin brass-sheet skin radiators, developed by G. Moreux, were installed on the bottom surfaces of the main wing. The almost knife-sharp leading edge became the return header; the feed header was a flattened spanwise tube just ahead of the aileron. These radiators were similar to Curtiss' pace-setting skin radiators introduced just weeks before except in the ingenious way in which their edges were

sealed. Obviously the French had been developing the skin radiator concept simultaneously with the Americans, reaching a state of maturity which allowed them to use the device on a world speed record aeroplane, although Lasne criticized the Moreux radiators for having capacity sufficient only for the speed record sprints, not for a 300-kilometer race.

In addition, while it cannot be definitely confirmed, it seems almost certain that the American-built Wright H-3 engine was removed from the now abandoned 37 racer and installed in the sesquiplane *Eugène Gilbert*. The engine used was not referred to in the trade press as a Wright but as a "Hispano built under license," perhaps forgivable, but as we have seen, by early 1923 simply no longer true. On February 15, 1923, a delighted Sadi Lecointe cinched himself deep in the pit of the modified sesquiplane. The bursts of acrid exhaust from the new engine's fistlike stacks carried the smell of success. Quickly aloft, he wasted no time attacking the measured course, and averaged an impressive 375·000 kmh, a new world record. On February 17 Sadi returned to Paris, where he was met and feted with exuberant acclaim.

If indeed the Wright engine was used, as seems likely, the significance of Wright having whipped Curtiss, even for one round, was never used for propaganda. Certainly the circumstances were unique; perhaps Wright in the United States did not realize that, in a French plane, they had temporarily obtained supremacy over their leading rival. Just one month later, however, on March 29, 1923, at a U. S. Army "Field Day," the R-6 again edged by Sadi's record when it topped 380 kmh. This, moreover, was the final speed record recognized over a 1-kilometer course. On April 1, 1923, the distance was amended to 3 kilometers in recognition of the timing difficulties.

The rather pained French attitude toward this brash American display was expressed by M. Laurent-Eynac,

Under-Secretary of State for Air, when he exhorted, "It is absolutely necessary that our constructors should attack the records. The record is the publicity of a country." The French had been frankly astonished to find "a young and energetic general who himself flies over 300 kmh" spearheading the vigorous American assault on the records. "There is no red tape [in America]," the French lamented. "The people simply *fly*!" The sudden and virtually complete loss of all records in FAI class C (powered aeroplanes) during 1923 produced the effect of a "thunderstroke" in France.

In July 1923 Laurent-Eynac, growing anxious, announced two staggering grants of 50,000 francs each for constructors of French planes that would recapture the speed and altitude records. Sadi was successful in capturing the altitude mark flying the Nieuport-Delage 40.

It was obvious by 1923 that further use of the Hispano-Suiza *modèle 42* for serious speed seeking was through. Engines capable of 450 hp were already being produced by Lorraine, Renault, Gnôme-Rhône, and others in France, but power with compactness was necessary to serve Laurent-Eynac's bid. The French industry instinctively turned to Marc Birkigt, Hispano-Suiza's brilliant chief engineer, who in the meantime had established the production of excellent Hispano-Suiza automobiles at Bois-Colombes-sur-Seine. (In fact, during 1923, Nieuport-Astra applied their aviation expertise in manufacturing the exquisite tulipwood body for the famous 8-liter Hispano-Suiza auto owned by French wine king André Dubonnet.) Birkigt went back to his well-worn drawing board in September 1923; however, he still believed so abundantly in the merits of his *modèle 42* that he simply adapted three of its cylinder blocks, unmodified, to fashion a new broad-arrow W-12. Within three months the prototype engine, designated *modèle 50* in-house, 12Ga by the government, had been built and passed its official

Hispano-Suiza modèle 51 *(12H) engine, circa 1923*   *(Au)*

tests, achieving 497 hp at 1,800 rpm with compression of 5·3. At the rear of each block was mounted one Zenith carburetor from which a straight, thin induction pipe extended to four cylinders; the shaft-driven overhead cam, operating two vertical valves per cylinder, sat above. The engine was of decently light weight although its frontal area seemed slightly indecent, but by having the same length precisely as the *modèle 42*, it lent itself to compact installations.

During early 1924 Birkigt built a second new design, the *modèle 51* (militarily 12Ha), but this engine, while it employed cylinders identical to those of the *modèle 42*, consisted of two blocks containing six cylinders each, resulting in a V-12, longer but with less frontal area. Its inlet ports were on the inside of the V (as in the *modèle 42*) but *six* carburetors were mounted on the outside, three per block, with their throttles in line,

fixed to a common shaft on each side. Air was taken in through the cast aluminum oil cooler bolted to the bottom of the crankcase and was distributed to the carburetors, each of which alimented only two cylinders by means of pipes passing through the block. The exhaust stubs, of course, were on the outside. The *modèle 51* had the same rating (450 hp at 1,800 rpm) as the *modèle 50*, but its first bench run in February proved it could easily top 500 hp. During its fifty-hour government type test it produced 505 hp at 1,800 rpm, 545 hp at 2,000 rpm, and with high-compression (6·2) pistons, both engines were said to deliver between 570 and 600 hp at 2,000 rpm, and were redesignated 12Gb and 12Hb respectively. Although the external carburetor arrangement of the more powerful *modele 51* had certain advantages for maintenance, it is easy to speculate that the long curved manifolds degraded

engine performance during dynamic, high-speed flight conditions.

These new Hispano-Suiza engines were built specifically to power two new speedplanes; the *modèle 50* W-12 was planned for the Bernard V.2 and the *modèle 51* V-12 for Gustave Delage's new Nieuport sesquiplane, and side by side, the engines were highly acclaimed, central features of the 1924 Paris Air Show.

The last of the fashionable racing sesquiplanes, the Nieuport-Delage 42, was larger than its predecessors, straightforward and rugged, a true harbinger of the next generation's fighters. Its lines were well-proportioned and uncluttered, taking advantage of skin radiators which covered nearly all the main wing surface. The duralumin "inferior" wing was virtually an afterthought, again providing little more than structural support for the beech-and-tulipwood landing gear legs and girder support for the wing struts. The wings themselves employed sturdy dual box spars built in II form, plywood ribs, spruce stringers, this framework then ply- and fabric-covered. Internal drag bracing was provided by dural tubes in the wing's supported section and by steel wires in the overhang portion. Ailerons, hinged to a false spruce spar, were operated by torque-tube while tail controls were cable-operated. Fuel tanks were carried in the wings, and in the military version they could be jettisoned by the pilot. A so-called "bi-valve" *coque* was employed; that is, it was built in two halves similar to plastic model aeroplanes; except joined along a horizontal line, internally stiffened by a number of trapeze-shaped longitudinal stringers molded together with the skin, and by ring-shaped ply bulkheads notched to accept the stringers. Outer planking consisted of the famous Nieuport tulipwood in several cross-grain layers (six forward varying to three at the stern), each strip shaved to a mere 0·9-mm thinness. A long, husky duralumin backbone bearing metal

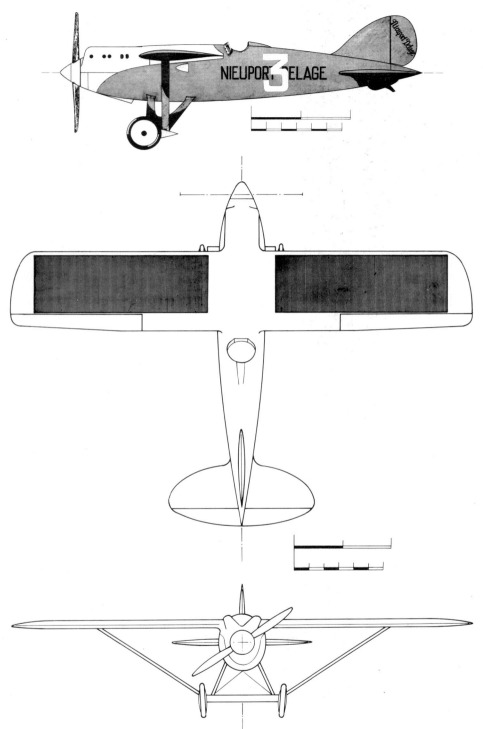

Nieuport-Delage type 42 racer built for the Coupe Beaumont and world speed record attempts (MA)

Nieuport-Delage 42 type course, winner Coupe Beaumont races 1924 and 1925; side view shows 1924 version.

bulkheads carried the pilot's seat, wing, and landing gear, and had dural engine cradles to support the V-12 Hispano's heavy bulk.

The Nieuport-Delage 42 had been built for one purpose: to regain the world speed record. Beginning June 12 at Istres, Sadi Lecointe repeatedly attacked the record, which, thanks to the Curtiss R2C, stood firm at almost 270 mph. Late in 1923, when he held simultaneously nineteen European and three world titles, Sadi himself had expressed rare pessimism during a discussion on racing aeroplanes as then constructed, by voicing the opinion that the "utmost speed ever to be developed" would be "about 500 kmh" (that is, about 300 mph). Independently, Sadi's intuition had been stated unequivocally a few months before, by Dr. E. Everling (NACA TM203), who stated that 500 kmh was indeed man's *theoretical speed limit*! Sadi's trials through the hot summer, all unsuccessful, continued until July 7. On June 23, at the height of these speed trials, the 1924 Coupe Beaumont was held at Istres.

The rich Beaumont prize had been established in 1923 upon the demise of the Coupe Deutsch, but was not awarded that year because of a lack of starters. The absence of foreign competition prompted Nieuport's withdrawal and other French constructors withdrew in domino fashion. An exciting contest seemed assured in 1924 since a half-dozen racers of two nationalities were being groomed in European speed labs, but in a depressing repeat of history all other competition withdrew, allowing Sadi Lecointe in the Nieuport-Delage 42 to "walk over" the hexagonal Beaumont course and garner the 75,000 francs *prix*. After completing the required 300 kilometers at 311·239 kmh, Sadi did not land but continued until he had done 500 kilometers. His speed for this closed-course distance, 306·696 kmh, was 36 kmh above the current world record set March 29, 1923, by an American Army R-3 at the Dayton "Field Day." Slowly the records were returning to the Old World.

Three quite different variations of Nieuport-Delage 42-inspired sesqui-planes were also being built for French military use: an all-wood single-seat

127

Nieuport-Delage type 42 racer about to begin the 1924 Coupe Beaumont race (Au)

fighter, type 42C.1, with wing area almost double that of the racer; an all-metal version of this fighter; and the 42C.2, the wood fighter with larger inferior wing and gunner's seat added. Strut radiators looking like great moustaches and a bewildering array of Vickers and Darne guns bristled on these ships. Their thick wing section, seen from the side, resembled a fat tadpole swimming through the air.

Sadi Lecointe was now more than France's star pilot, he was held in the virtual esteem of French national hero. His status in the Légion d'honneur was raised from Chevalier to Officer in 1924 and each new record brought gushes of adoration. Trying to capitalize on this fame he sought election to the Chamber of Deputies that year on the Radical Socialist ticket, a party with a large, generally bourgeois constituency who were not radical and hardly socialist. Sadi lost. The message was clear: his public wanted him to forego politics and stick to aviation, where he was certainly better off. When asked of his reaction to the rash of round-the-world flight attempts that year, Sadi's reply was more characteristic of his approach to aviation if not politics: "A trip of that kind is merely a matter of organization . . .. if one day I announce I am going to fly to the pole, I will fly to the pole. I think it might tickle me considerably to do so. I quite believe it can be done, but there must be no false starts."

In 1925 the French sent several pilots to the shereefian empire of Morocco in North Africa where they would help combat wily Abd-el-Krim, fiery escaped seditionist who sought independence for the Riff, a rugged mountainous territory on Spanish Morocco's eastern fringe. The rebels' strength had thrived through the use of terror and a growing zeal, almost a religious fervor, in their cause and leader; they handed the Spanish a colossal defeat at Melilla in 1921 to gain autonomy, but seeking a better frontier, they dared to bite out a piece of French Morocco as well. French power in the area was embodied by *le Maréchal* Louis Lyautey, then seventy-one, whose thirteen-year rule had been beneficent but absolute. The French decided to snuff out the bothersome Arab. In July 1925 Pétain of Verdun, still lean and youthful-looking at sixty-nine and who outranked Lyautey, came to command the forces in the field. Sadi Lecointe, volunteer *capitaine de réserve*, was given leave of absence by Nieuport-Astra to command the Sherifian Escadrille, a squadron of Bréguet and Hanriot bombers which in September 1925 began blasting Riff strongholds to smithereens. Many of the pilots under Sadi's command were American volunteers (Colonel Charles Sweeney, Lieutenant Colonel Kerwood, Majors Pollock and Parker, and Captains Rockwell, Weller, and Buffum, one of whom with unwarranted but accurate foresight said, "The occasion may arise when the United States will need pilots with knowledge of fighting an invisible enemy"). Pétain's campaign was brilliant and even served as a model for later students of African warfare. Loyalties to the Riff state once harbored so intensely by petty Arab chieftains soon waned, and one by one they surrendered to France. When the October rains came, Sadi returned to France — the one stipulation in his leave was that he would be in Istres to fly in the 1925 Coupe Beaumont. In 1926 Abd-el-Krim, the "soldier of Islam," was captured and the campaign came to an end.

On October 18, 1925, the Nieuport-Delage 42 racer again "walked over" the final Coupe Beaumont. Sadi Lecointe covered the 300-kilometer course at 312·464 kmh after his only competition withdrew. Prior to this, Fernand Lasne had already taken over reins of the 42, ordered to attack every conceivable speed-over-distance-with-useful-load record which the 42 could garner. Starting in August 1925 and proceeding into the summer of 1926, M. Lasne dutifully bored back and forth over the old Coupe Deutsch course hour after droning hour. French aviation, under M. Laurent-Eynac, put record breaking on a production-line basis.

Nevertheless, the brutish 42 racer never did achieve its one true purpose, to capture the world maximum speed record. To avoid adverse publicity over failure, the French practice was to publish nothing concerning record attempts until they achieved success. Perhaps we shall never know how many times the 42 tried for the supreme prize or how close it came.

As for Sadi Lecointe, he thereafter dropped out of aviation's limelight although he flew almost daily for another fifteen years as Nieuport-Astra's chief test pilot. His flights ceased to make headlines, but as late as 1939 he was forced to bale out of a burning prototype, only to test another of the same type the next day. The flood of fame that swept over Lindbergh and other long-distance fliers after 1927 washed away the public's memory of Sadi Lecointe as a wave washes sand castles smooth. Sadi also lost perhaps his favorite flying companion in 1927, the vibrant and droll one-eyed navigator François Coli, who disappeared in May that year with Nungesser aboard *L'Oiseau Blanc* en route to New York. Mention of Coli was almost certain to make the reticent Sadi open up. He once recalled animatedly his trans-Mediterranean flight and breakdown with Coli at the 1920 Monaco seaplane meeting: "With Coli all I had to do was fly, and that's not much!"

Sadi later became inspector general of civil aviation in the prewar Popular Front government. He was also active in the intensely fraternal Freemasons, powerful, well-structured, and for insiders politically expedient; probably three out of every four important French political figures were Freemasons through the 1920s and early 1930s despite the group's mysterious origins and secret methods. Because of their atheism, the Freemasons were later driven almost underground by the onslaughts of strong religious factions. When World War II broke out, Sadi Lecointe returned to North Africa to become base commander of French air forces there. After France fell in 1940 many French people fled to North Africa, causing the Vichy government to attempt to maintain some semblance of *status quo*, and many French retained their previous posts. But Sadi stood with de Gaulle, earning Vichy condemnation in January 1941 when his duties were stripped under a decree "banning Freemasons from command in the Vichy armed forces." Sadi Lecointe died in Paris on July 17, 1944, aged fifty-three. Through it all the charming ace of speed never once lost his *sang froid*.

Sadi's great Nieuport-Delage racers roared across the years wearing the garland of speed taken from Spad until a rapidly evolving family of Curtiss racers captured the prize for America. There it remained until 1924 when another French star cast its triumphal light on the golden laurel — the star of Bernard.

BERNARD & THE UNSUNG BREAKTHROUGHS

Observers were startled at the 1922 Paris Air Show by a sleek, silver monoplane jauntily perched in a way to catch the eye – which was virtually assured in any event simply because such racy lines were so out of place among its conventional neighbors. This was the C.1, built by the small but enterprising firm of Adolphe Bernard, and the plane's glitter reflected the man's life-style, one of extravagant bonhomie and careless presumption; Bernard was a heavy-lidded epicurean but tall and grandly handsome at forty-two. He had come to Paris from Asnières and seized the opportunity to cash in on aviation's huge expansion during the height of World War I when he entered into an agreement with Louis Bêchéreau and Marc Birkigt, a curiously loose alliance occasionally called Société Trois B. But the "three Bs" also embraced Louis Blériot and thus in fact were four, three of whom had already established a formidable record of aviation design, engineering, and production.

In the spring of 1917, through the grace of Blériot, a Spad assembly plant at La Courneuve near Paris was taken under supervision by Bernard, but in March one year later an accidental ammunition explosion resulted in a fire and destruction. Nevertheless, new facilities arose from the ashes and by the Armistice large-scale warplane production had been restored. Meanwhile, the new young association, now more formally Société Avions Bernard.

129

had set out to design their own single-seat pursuit, powered by Birkigt's Hispano-Suiza *modèle 42*, and called SAB, the initials of the firm. Five were built at the Levasseur factory before the Armistice closed down production, and one survivor, quite neat with an annular radiator and plywood wings, was exhibited on the Levasseur stand at the 1919 Paris Air Show. Also featured was an ambitious Bernard twin-engine two-seater (the A.B.3). But peace also brought near financial collapse to Bernard.

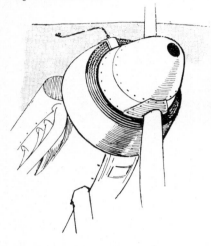

Pierre Levasseur circular radiator, used by Bernard on the SAB pursuit, 1919; adapted by Verville for use on the VCP pursuit, 1920 (see Chapter 11) (contemporary drawing)

After more than two years of inactivity, a reorganization of Bernard's assets during 1922 resulted in a new firm: Société Industrielle des Métaux et du Bois (SIMB), still located at La Courneuve in the earlier works. It was often informally referred to as "Bernard" or "Ferbois," the latter a handy trade name derived from the words *fer* (iron) and *bois* (wood), but this was something of a misnomer since Bernard's first new aeroplane, the C.1, did not use either substance! Instead, the new speedplane was built entirely of duralumin. Its designer was Jean Hubert, who had joined as SIMB's first *directeur technique* in 1922, assisted

Jean Hubert (MA)

then by André Vautier. Hubert was born a doctor's son at St.-Vaast-la-Hougue and trained to be an electrical engineer. He joined Compagnie de Navigation Aérienne, which was set up to exploit the designs of the Wright Brothers. In 1911, when he was twenty-five, he became associated with Robert Esnault-Pelterie and the young but growing firm of Louis Bréguet.

At the Grand Palais in 1921, site of the Paris Air Show, many examples of duralumin metalwork had been exhibited. It is fair to surmise that designers would not have made such extensive use of duralumin, but France did not produce thin sheet steel in those days, and French steel tubing had not progressed beyond the degree of that used on Esnault-Pelterie's monoplane in 1910. The cost of fabricating dural in so many weird and exotically impractical ways must have been colossal. Dural basket-weave fuselage frames were shown, built up from short lengths of channel

Adolphe Bernard (MA)

130

section girders which met at six-way junctions where they were riveted to small discs with single 2-mm rivets, then sheathed with 20-gauge skin! Also dural bulkheads with latticed, box-section sides and countless rivets, used on wire-braced fuselages! One aeroplane was skinned with ·003-inch dural sheet which had been folded in on itself every 1½ inches to form "bulbed fins" in lieu of separate stringers (which nobody seems to have thought of). Although tightened by hundreds of rivets, the application of a finger would result in excellent stage thunder!

It was against this almost burlesque background that Jean Hubert perceived how to proceed and carry metal aeroplane construction almost to its logical final form. The idea was really beautifully simple. The thin wall shell form of structure, Bêchéreau's monumental accomplishment, would now, for the first time, be rendered in metal. Hubert recognized at once the fundamental mistakes of other designers in generally trying to make metal conform to the lines of the wood structures they replaced. He, on the other hand, would use the thinnest possible metal sheet throughout and make every element — including the skin itself — contribute to the aeroplane's strength. The internal framework would be vastly simplified; there would be no conventional truss assemblies, spars, or ribs! Certainly, in 1922, this was a distinctly original undertaking which required bold courage. But Hubert's plan, if it worked, also would have excellent advantages: it allowed the lightest weight and the highest degree of streamlining. His speed objective was 315 kmh, about 200 mph, using a Hispano-Suiza 300-hp *modèle 42* and a thick cantilever wing.

The C.1 fuselage was built in three sections bolted together; engine, wing, landing gear, and pilot were carried by the main section; there were also mid and tail sections. That Hubert's pioneering masterwork inevitably fell short was evidenced by his insistence on

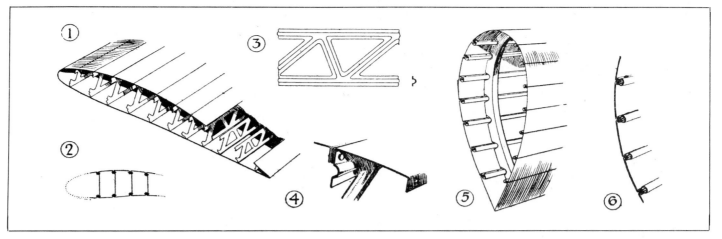

Construction details of the Bernard C.1, 1922: (1) wing structure; (2) wing cross section showing channel strips riveted together and to the spanwise webs; (3) elevation of a wing spar web; (4) details of attachment of wing skin to spar; (5) and (6), details of fuselage construction (contemporary drawings)

orienting his rivets parallel to the skin they fastened (not through the skin as is done today), but this forced him to use lengthwise strips of dural sheet, 0·5 mm thick and not very wide, called *bandes* (literally, "stringers") to form the fuselage *coque*. Their edges were flanged (bent 90 degrees) and butted against one another tightly, reinforced by "omega" strips (that is, Ω-shaped pieces which would be called stringers today) and riveted internally. This meant the outside surface was not perfectly smooth, there being unavoidable hairline grooves where the adjacent strips of skin were butted. The *coque* was built in two halves and joined, but how the last strip was got at for riveting remains a mystery!

The central framework consisted of two longitudinal and seven transverse plates of sheet dural, latticed and flanged for lightness and strength. The longitudinal plates, 5 mm thick, served as both engine bearers and supports for the fuel tank and pilot seat. The transverse plates formed the lower V of the fuselage where it

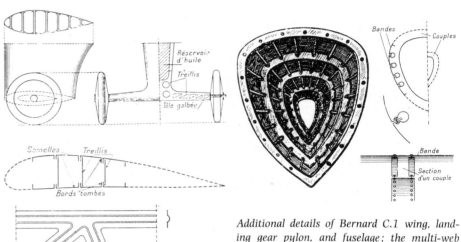

Additional details of Bernard C.1 wing, landing gear pylon, and fuselage; the multi-web lightweight framework was decidedly novel in 1922. Bernard's method of outer skin attachment needed revision; otherwise, he had anticipated decades of development (contemporary drawings).

blended into the landing gear structure, the sides comprising the wing roots. The similarly constructed landing gear framework, using skin 1 mm thick, was bolted on. In 1922 builders in the United States and England were working at that very moment to solve the practical problems of retractable gear with the Bee-Line, Verville R-3, and Bristol 72 racers; yet, despite not having retractable

gear, and though the accolade "revolutionary" applied to it was too strong, the C.1 gear with its clean, single strut was an elegant attempt to reduce drag. The short axle housings were wing-shaped and articulated to accommodate the bungee cord shock absorbers.

The wing skin was similar to the fuselage *coque* in that it consisted of spanwise dural sheet strips, in this case called *semelles* (flanges), whose edges were bent 90 degrees to be butted and riveted internally. Several thin spanwise webs replaced conventional spars; called *treillis*, each was stamped from a single, flat sheet together with triangular lightening holes, resulting in a Warren-truss pattern, and fluted (given one corrugation) for stiffness. They were located not between adjacent skin flanges but alongside, thus allowing the maximum stress to be taken by the flanges. In addition this enabled minimum surface grooves. Whereas the fuselage flanges tapered toward the stern, the wing flanges were straight but with heavier-gauge skin near the root (2 mm thick), thinner toward the tip (0·5 mm thick), based on Hubert's attempt to tailor skin thickness in relation to local stress magnitude. In effect, the wing was a series of boxlike cells, quite deep (over a foot thick at the root) and incredibly strong. On static tests the wings were loaded to the equivalent of 18 g, which deflected the tips only 160 mm! There was no permanent set.

During the year Hubert attempted to patent his wing in France, but he was informed that to avoid a legal fight he would have to change the number of webs. A multi-cell wing (although all wood) with coincidentally the same number of webs had been registered in the United States. In those days, when aviation was still strange to most people, the features most obvious to a patent lawyer — such as the number of webs he could count — became contestable elements rather than the general concept of a multi-cell, torsion-resistant, all-metal structure. It took Hubert three months to remove one web and relocate the remainder.

Chordwise webs were used instead of wing ribs, spaced to fit between the openings of the spanwise webs, and designed to take compression, working together with the skin. The ailerons were all metal, torque-tube operated. The wings were detachable, and where

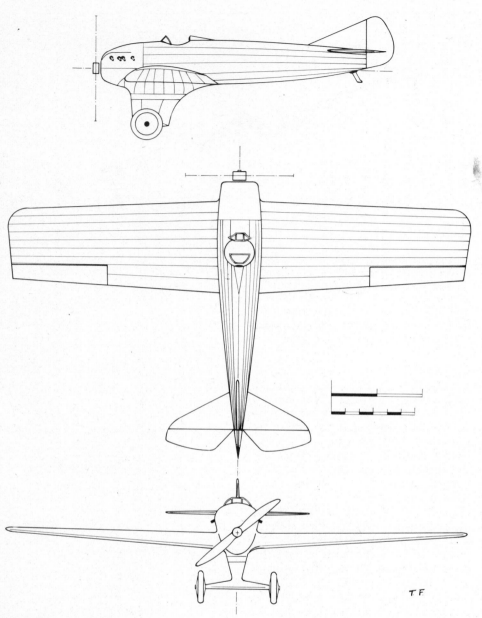

The all-metal Bernard C.1, 1922

the carry-through structure was cut out to accommodate engine and pilot, compression loading was taken by an arched piece of dural 4 mm thick extending between the two wing roots and bolted to the engine crankcase. Tail surfaces were full cantilever, built like the wing except the stamped web thickness varied from 0·8 mm to 0·5 mm, strengthened by omega stringers. These surfaces in static tests withstood loads of up to 400 kg/m² (about 80 psf) without serious distortion. The stabilizer was ground-adjustable by means of bolts, and control leads (all cable-operated) were internal.

When first publicly displayed between December 15, 1922, and January 2, 1923, at the VIII Salon Aéronautique (the eighth Paris Air Show), no radiators were mounted and the aeroplane appeared very clean. American observers commented on its "wonderfully all-inclusive streamlining." Two Lamblin lobster pots, one on either side of the central pylon, were planned but never used. Later a bulky, finned box-shaped radiator was mounted ahead of the landing gear center pylon, virtually destroying the aeroplane's clean lines. A self-sealing fuel tank was located beneath the wing directly at the c.g., avoiding balance changes as fuel was consumed, and the oil tank was inside the landing gear center pylon.

Hubert was stung by the scathing criticism his C.1 received in 1923 because of "prohibitive" construction costs. During the eighteen months following the Paris Air Show, Hubert attempted to "industrialize" his speedplane, to transform it into a fighter suitable for quantity production, paying special attention to providing methods of quick disassembly for maintenance in the field, and means for easy repairs to the skin. Dimensions and weight increased, and its top speed capability shrank correspondingly, to 245 kmh. It thus became the 10C.1, and its first flights in this form took place in August 1924 at Étampes.

After these flights, further development of the C.1 itself ceased, but engineers Jean Galtier and Marcel Gianoli used it as forerunner to the 420-hp Jupiter-powered Bernard 12C.1, a more traditional design which first flew in May 1926. The original C.1 structural concepts receded until the moment for their application arrived fifteen years later as the world's next great cataclysm loomed.

At the height of C.1 construction in 1922 a young Polish engineer was hired by SIMB as chief of the drafting office. This was S. G. Bruner, then twenty-six, who had been sent to

Bernard C.1, 1922 Paris Air Show (MA)

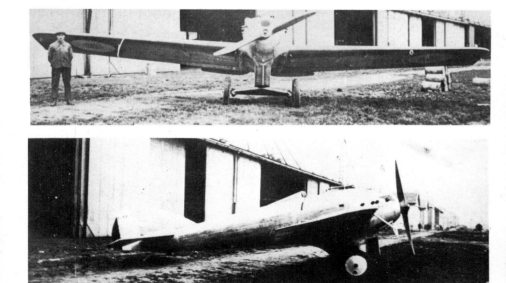

*Two views of Bernard C.1 after modifications,
1924* (Au)

S. Georges Bruner (Au)

France by the Polytechnic Institute in Warsaw to work with René Hanriot for six months. But when the time came to return, Bruner balked. There was virtually a complete absence of aviation in Poland in those days and Bruner was unwilling to renounce an endeavor so exciting. He began at once a concerted search for permanent French employment. As he recalled years later, the search was at first discouraging, then desperate. "There must have been thirty-two aeroplane factories in France then, and I visited every one. Finally I was down to the thirty-second and resigned to return to Poland . . . and it was there I got a job!" He recalled the day of his employment interview, the nervous wait outside Hubert's office together with a young military pilot, Florentin Bonnet. Both suitably impressed Hubert. And although there is no definite record that the C.1 flew in 1922, Bruner recalled that Bonnet in fact made "several flights" in the C.1 before the Paris Air Show, but with two extra vertical struts temporarily inserted for added landing gear support.

Bruner was small and lively with eyes that fairly sparkled when the talk turned to the technical. He had made his own start in aviation in 1911 when, at the age of fifteen, he built a successful hang-glider lofted by 4 boypower — at a full run. During World War II he collaborated with Alexander Kartveli, famous as designer of the P-47 Thunderbolt fighter. Georges Bruner dropped active use of his first name (Sigismond) since he absolutely hated it; when almost sixty years later he retired from active engineering duties at Bréguet, where he had spearheaded the design of the world-famous 941 STOL (Short Take Off and Landing) transport, he was known as "His Majesty" — behind his back perhaps, but with sincere reverence. In the 1970s Bruner, still as enthusiastic as a pink-cheeked graduate, wrote extensively and was consulted on the designs of VTOLs (Vertical Take Off and Landing aeroplanes) and

133

SSTs (Supersonic Transports) being launched in an era scarcely imagined in 1922.

As Hubert and Bruner struggled through 1923 and into 1924, it became increasingly obvious that what then seemed excessive cost and complexity of all-duralumin structures had soured French officials, who increasingly turned to the German and Dutch techniques using welded steel tubes. Hubert, whose personality tended to impetuosity and impatience, was crushed when he accepted the inevitable. His thin-shell duralumin structure was discontinued much as England at the same time dropped the idea of retractable landing gear; neither feature, after all, was then considered necessary for commercial viability. Hubert's next racer would be fashioned entirely of wood, and over the next several years, increasingly complex Bernard racers were built of wood, some with more than a dozen wing webs!

Attempts by SIMB to secure large production orders were further frustrated by Adolphe Bernard himself, who was playing the stock market with SIMB money. The government's attitude was stern: until a more substantial guarantee was forthcoming that the company's affairs would be conducted seriously, no sizeable orders would be. SIMB fortunes roller-coastered but the workers, intrigued with turning out Hubert's elegant designs to a level of perfection worthy of their pride, seemed hardly to notice. Bernard decided his company's chances for the big time hinged on earning capital — and prestige — that could not be ignored. He would enter the new Coupe Beaumont with its huge cash prize, of course. But, even more convincing, his Beaumont racer would then set the world speed record — which, incidentally, would also earn one of Laurent-Eynac's whopping incentive prizes. The racer's designation was easy: type V — for *vitesse*.

There is no positive indication that either Hubert or his assistants, Bruner

and Gianoli, ever heard of an obscure Russian named Woyewodski. Yet their new V.1 bore remarkable resemblance to a "bodyless" speedplane on which, as reported in mid-1921, the Russian had filed patents.[1] The term "bodyless" referred to a form in which the cantilever monoplane wing's central section was swelled out to absorb the fuselage in such a way that the entire structure had a smooth contour with no abrupt change of form. The idea was that a decently shaped — if wide — fuselage interposed in this manner would not spoil wing efficiency; on the contrary, it should be enhanced.

Design of the two Bernard type V racers began in August 1923, each with slightly different dimensions and

[1] The novel "bodyless" ideas had been discovered by the British on a wartime mission to Russia to set up D.H.4 production factories abroad; it had shocked them, making all too clearly evident that the extent of their wartime progress had been essentially to upgrade methods of structural, stability, and control engineering from ones of empirical guesswork to ones based on more rational, mathematical procedures — but they were still building aeroplanes conceptually tied to prewar notions. Harold Bolas at Parnalls in 1919, too late for a wartime contract, did the first design study based on the bluntly rounded monoplane idea, sleek as a sting ray. Unfortunately, his wind tunnel revealed L/D values no better than typical World War I biplane fighters, confirming for some the biplane's God-given superiority. Nevertheless, the Russian idea (now spelled variously Woyavodsky) was pursued, ostensibly because thick airfoils suitable for internal bracing were thought to spin easily, and the new form might alleviate this lethal tendency. More model experiments were conducted, and the International Steel Wing Aircraft Syndicate in Kingsway took out a patent (193980) but did not implement the idea. It was left for elderly but vigorous Robert Bruce of Westlands to pursue the idea in his Lion-powered, eight-passenger Dreadnought (J.6986), which represented probably the most inspired level of construction — its metal wing had six spars — and aerodynamics in England when it was rolled out early in 1924. Pilot Stuart Keep attempted its first flight at Yeovil on May 9 that year, but the aeroplane stalled and ended in a heap, which cost Keep both his legs. More significantly, this largely unheralded crackup quietly reinforced even more convincingly the biplane trend in England, and thus had enormous effect.

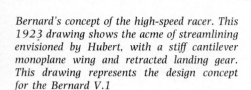

Bernard's concept of the high-speed racer. This 1923 drawing shows the acme of streamlining envisioned by Hubert, with a stiff cantilever monoplane wing and retracted landing gear. This drawing represents the design concept for the Bernard V.1

structure, and each to be powered by a different engine. The V.1 would use a 500-hp Lorraine-Dietrich driving a slender wood prop while the V.2 would have the new 600-hp Hispano-Suiza *modèle 50*, companion design to the *modèle 51* that was installed in the contemporary Nieuport-Delage 42 sesquiplane, driving a Levasseur/Reed sheet metal prop similar to the Curtiss-Reed of 1923. Both choices were W-12 — when Hubert needed power he preferred the W-12 form over the V-12 — but short and broad, these engines bulged his fuselages almost into the

"bodyless" style. Of the two racers, the V.2 had a somewhat slimmer fuselage. Wings were placed well forward, almost to an extreme degree on the V.1, which had a calculated top speed of 420 kmh — which would then make it the fastest aeroplane in the world.

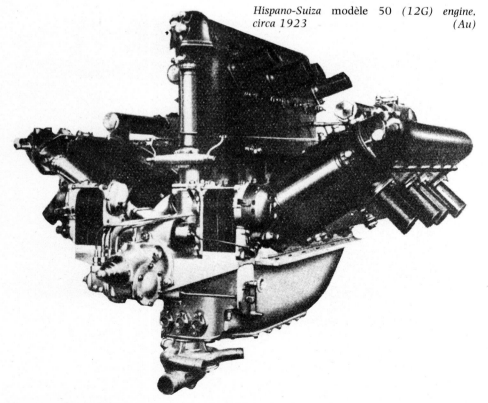

Hispano-Suiza modèle 50 *(12G) engine, circa 1923* (Au)

Despite the disappointing and inconclusive race results of the first 180-mm-stroke Lorraine *modèle 14 W-12* engine – now more commonly called 12E, its government designation – in the 1922 Coupe Deutsch, the engine's development continued. It was type-tested in 1923 and performed so well that 12Es were used well into the 1930s. In 1925 the 12Eb appeared and became the first French engine to pass the demanding fifty-hour test at a 450-hp rating; reduction gear was also introduced in 1925, resulting in the 12Ed, one of which later powered the modified Levasseur torpedo plane *L'Oiseau Blanc*, which took off in May 1927 with Nungesser and Coli. The first production series of twenty-five type 12E engines was begun in mid-1923; the second engine of this series was *poussé* or boosted to over 500 hp by raising compression first to 5·3, later to 6·0, and given to Bernard for an attempt on the world speed record in the V.1 racer.

Both new racers had four-longeron plywood-covered monocoque fuselages, all wood even to the Warren-truss engine bearers, three-spar plywood-covered tailplane, and three-ply covered cantilever wings; in both racers the skin would take 20 per cent of the stress. The wings were designed by Hubert and Bruner, who selected for the V.1 a slightly undercambered airfoil, whereas the V.2 was designed from the outset with a bi-convex airfoil. V.1 wings used four narrow box spars while the V.2 wing was built around a single box spar formed by two widely separated one-piece spar webs and closed on top and bottom by flanges of spruce which extended across some 75 per cent of the span, tapered in thickness toward the tips. Heavy, capstripped plywood ribs with vertical and diagonal stiffeners were used within the box spar area, but outboard of the spar box the ribs were of much lighter plywood. One day as Bruner drove to work, his mind filled with details of the cantilever wing design

that had everyone preoccupied, the front fender of his small Citroën came loose and began slapping against the wheel. He quickly anchored it with some well-placed baling wire and continued to Rue Villot, parking at the factory absent-mindedly, not noticing his car was in conspicuous isolation. Just then Adolphe Bernard drove up and Bruner was startled out of his reverie by a sharp rebuke from the boss. "Get that contraption repaired properly, Bruner! We'll have no cable-braced structures around here!" Bruner had to go to the shop at once and modify his fender to a cantilever form.

To reduce drag further, Hubert considered retractable gear, the wheels when raised to be stowed in the fuselage adjacent to the cockpit. Bruner was put in charge of perfecting the gear and had already worked out an ingenious scheme whereby the wheels would be raised and lowered by an engine-driven mechanism! In personal recollection, Bruner indicated that he was unaware of retractable-gear developments abroad when U. S. racers in 1922 were fitted with wide-track gear built to fold inward into wing recesses. Such an arrangement was out of the question in Bruner's case because the shoulder-mounted wings would have meant intolerably long landing gear struts, but Bruner also realized his aft-folding scheme meant a dangerously narrow track, although careful piloting technique was expected to overcome this disadvantage. A full-scale, detailed, wood "equipment mockup" was built on which the gear could be actuated and adjusted and various internal components relocated for balance. Unavoidable structural problems finally squelched the idea: the fuselage cutouts necessary to house the raised wheels were too large. A conventional gear with rigidly mounted plywood legs braced by two diagonal streamline wires and one thin vertical wire, carrying a rubber-cord-sprung divided axle, was fitted to both racers and the drag penalty accepted.

The two type V racers incorporated several noteworthy details. Their distinctive vertical tail profile was developed by Bruner; its elegant line was a simple method both to provide a sweeping streamline and to put more area at the rear where, with longer leverage, it would be more effective. This was based on the results of earlier tailspin trials, Bruner said. Tail surfaces and wing root junctions were faired neatly with duralumin sheet. Wing-mounted radiators were used but were not nearly as clean as the Curtiss or Moreux skin types. Instead, Lamblin lobster-pot fins protruded vertically from the wing's lower surface, undoubtedly adding unnecessary drag.

The V.1 – or Bernard-Hubert as it was sometimes called – was completed in May 1924, nine months after its design commenced and one month before the Coupe Beaumont. The V.2 was not yet complete. The pilot of all early Bernard racers, Florentin Bonnet.

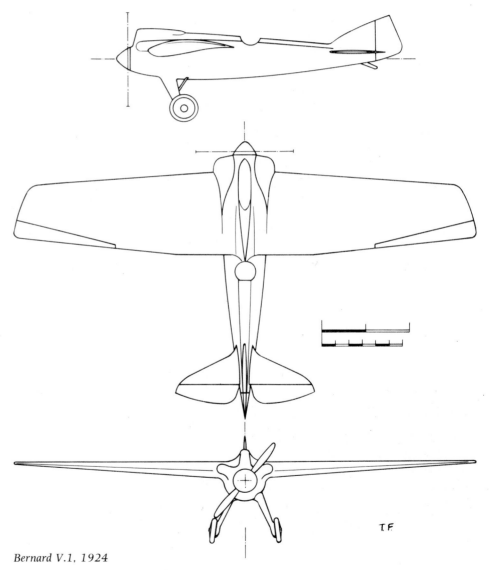

Bernard V.1, 1924

had returned to his military duties in 1923 as adjutant pilot with the 38th Aviation Regiment stationed at Thionville and further distinguished himself that year with his victory in the Coupe Lamblin, a long-distance military race. Flying a Nieuport 29, Bonnet covered the Paris–Strasbourg–Lyon–Paris course in 6:09:13 (194·962 kmh); he also placed second in a similar race, the 1923 Coupe Zenith, at 162 kmh. These accomplishments did not go unnoticed by Hubert, and Bonnet soon had military leave to test-fly the new type V racers.

The V.1 was erected at Istres, finally ready for its first flight short weeks before the Coupe Beaumont. Bonnet took off well but it was soon apparent he was in trouble. The plane was oscillating badly in pitch and Bonnet had somehow circled around to set up a long, straight-in landing approach. He descended but was unable to control the plane's bucking as he got lower and tried to reduce speed. The V.1 contacted the ground nose down, its landing gear crumpled, and it skidded several yards on its nose, decelerating until almost leisurely it lofted, tottered, and crunched to a halt upside down. Deathly afraid of fire, Bonnet from his inverted position was digging furiously in the rocky soil with shredded fingernails, and managed to squirm free before the ambulance arrived! The V.1 was wrecked beyond repair.

This was a serious setback to Hubert's racing team. In pre-race haste no wind-tunnel tests had been run on the V.1 design, and its horizontal tail area (some 13 per cent of total wing area) had been empirically determined from biplane experience. As Bruner said, "We didn't know much about high-speed monoplane design in those days," and while speedplane designers must keep drag-producing surfaces small, they had gone too far with the V.1. M. Chabonnat, head of the Eiffel wind tunnel facility, came to Hubert's aid, and Bruner, assigned to do the dirty work, soon found himself deeply involved in conducting pitch stability tests with a model of the V.2. Pivoting the model at its wingtips, Bruner mounted a small paddle similar to a horizontal windvane and by varying its size to balance the model's tendency to pitch, he determined the best size for the V.2 horizontal tail — some 22 per cent of the wing area. Previous ambitions to win the Coupe Beaumont had been deemphasized, and the V.2 was now completed for only one purpose: to establish the world maximum speed record and earn Laurent-Eynac's rich prize (200,000 francs, divided into 140,000 francs for the successful aeroplane builder and 60,000 francs for the engine builder). The V.2 was sleeked with sandpaper by dedicated workers, who attended it slowly, deliberately; painted eggshell blue like the V.1, it

Autographed photo of Bonnet (marked by X) and the world speed record Bernard V.2, 1924 *(Au)*

was rubbed until not one blister marred its streamline, and was then shipped to Istres in late September 1924.

Hubert was there to nursemaid his new baby. Bonnet had been granted four months' leave from his regiment, and on October 2 he made the first of sixteen flights (totaling 2:10) that were completed by October 7. Several Reed props, each with a slightly different pitch, were tested to determine the best compromise between high speed and takeoff performance. The plane at first seemed dangerous to Bonnet at high speed, and several minor mishaps occurred at low speed: the nose-heavy V.2 seemed eager to somersault, and there were several heart-stopping landings; one axle was bent; and the prop continually blew stones against the fuselage and wings, in some cases splintering the carefully smoothed plywood skin. Center cylinder bank exhaust stacks projecting from the top cowl made both vision and breathing difficult for Bonnet. Nevertheless, after repairs, he took off on November 8 to try for the world

record despite a stiff 30-mph mistral. The V.2 slithered over the course, slashing by the timers as low as 10 feet — *click* went the stop watches — but the speed was only 393·340 kmh, good enough for a new French record (it beat Sadi Lecointe's 375 kmh achieved in the 1923 sesquiplane *Eugène Gilbert*), but 36 kmh short of Al Williams' world mark, made in the Curtiss R2C.

The V.2 was then extensively modified. Hubert supervised the reduction of its wing surface by 7 per cent, almost a full square meter; 20 centimeters were clipped from both root and tip of each wing, reducing the span by ·8 meter (the area amputated from the tips also excessively pared the ailerons, making low-speed handling qualities perilous), and the wings were remounted with a slight negative angle of incidence. The offending exhaust stacks were relocated away from atop the central cowl, the slope of which was increased together with more tapered lateral cowlings in an attempt to reduce high-speed buffeting,

Crash of the Bernard V.1, 1924 *(Au)*

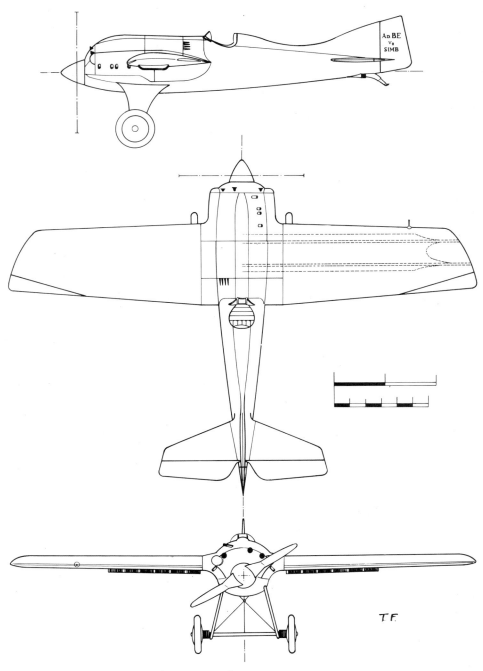

The world speed record Bernard V.2, 278 mph, December 1924

considerably cleaned-up V.2 was ready on December 8. After three days of additional delay the V.2 reappeared on the flight line at 9 A.M. fully ready again to challenge the world speed record.

At almost precisely the same time in Paris, several hundred miles to the north, the IX Salon Aéronautique opened, to run from December 5—21, the first Paris Air Show held in two years. The SIMB stand featured a V.2 airframe seemingly so finished in detail that ever since, the surprisingly strong belief has been perpetuated that two V.2s existed. One sharp-eyed correspondent at the show, upon taking a closer look at the exhibit, wrote of the puzzling method by which the under-wing radiator elements were attached — with obviously un-airworthy brass wood screws! But it seems never to have dawned on anybody that this elaborate V.2 exhibit was not an actual aeroplane at all but in fact the *equipment mockup*. After its use by the designers to locate and balance the racer's internal equipment, it was completed with false wings, tail, and landing gear, according to

Bruner who supervised its installation at the show. Indeed, there was *no engine* under its cowl nor could its propeller turn!

At 10:26 A.M. on December 11, 1924, Bonnet lifted the only real V.2 from the airfield at Istres and with a roar he attacked the measured 3-kilometer course six times. Unlike the day of his previous attempt, the breeze was light. Flying never higher than 50 feet, using about two minutes to swing wide and reverse direction after each pass, the lighter weight of his aeroplane (from burning fuel at the rate of 260 pounds per hour) adding about 3 kmh to each pass, he achieved Bernard's cherished goal. His new world speed record of 448·171 kmh (just shy of 280 mph) capped the efforts of postwar speed seekers by demonstrating that man had *doubled* the best speeds achieved at the close of World War I, little more than half a decade before. Bonnet made an "impeccable" landing at 10:46 to the wild excitement of Bernard's staff. The champagne was uncorked — Hubert particularly was always especially fond of good wine —

Bernard V.2 mockup at the 1924 Paris Air Show   *(Au)*

thought to be induced by propeller-cowl interference. The three bell-mouth carburetor air intakes were made shorter and much larger and the

external Lamblin oil radiator was removed. Aluminum sheathed wheels replaced the fabric-faired versions, all blemishes were repaired, and the

The world speed record Bernard V.2, December 1924 (MA)

and slowly, with the warm glow of the wine, the feeling seeped in that they had really done something momentous. Adolphe Bernard relished the huge government prize, Hubert was at once elected to the Légion d'honneur, Bonnet was promoted to *sous-lieutenant*, and Bruner remembered receiving a one-month salary bonus — "the only one I ever got in my life!" It had been only one year since Marc Birkigt decided to produce the twelve-cylinder Hispano-Suiza aero engines. Now the *modèle 50* held the world speed record and the *modèle 51* had won the Coupe Beaumont, the obscure race whose existence stimulated creation of the aeroplane that established a watershed of speed in the 1920s. Its record stood absolute for almost three years, untouched by another landplane for eight years.

Bonnet, responding to the now intense rivalry between SIMB and Nieuport-Astra, loudly predicted early in 1925 that he would soon raise the world speed record to 500 kmh — Hispano was said to be looking for 750 hp in a supercharged engine to be used in conjunction with "retractable radiators" and a landing gear jettisoned after takeoff (the plane to land on skis). Such a speedplane — which would have been illegal for the world speed record in any event — was never built.

Nor was the V.3 built; it was to have been a V.2 with a supercharged Lorraine engine and retractable landing

Florentin Bonnet, world speed recordman, 1924 (MA)

gear. It made no difference. Sadi Lecointe never did officially beat the record set by the V.2.

On October 31, 1927, not three years after the V.2 triumph, Jean Hubert, riding in a car driven by his brother, was critically injured in a collision at Formigny between Caen and Cherbourg. He died two days later, two days before his forty-second birthday. Bonnet remained to fly later Bernard racers, the gorgeous HV (Haute Vitesse) seaplanes designed for the Schneider Trophy by Bruner, who succeeded Hubert, and Roger Robert, who joined Bernard in 1928, shortly after Ing. Gianoli's departure for René Couzinet, builder of transports with flowing lines not unlike the early Bernard racers. Bonnet, star of the French 1929 Schneider team, was assigned to test the new Bernard HV racers from the lakeside base at Hourtin, in the Gironde. On August 6, departing Bordeaux after a visit, he opened the throttle in his hack Nieuport 62 to take off, but tried to pull the plane into a loop as his wheels left the ground. He got over the top but never pulled out. There was a terrific crash and Bonnet was dead.

None of the Bernard HV seaplanes ever appeared at the starting line of a Schneider race, generally for reasons having nothing to do with their design which was superb and which would have almost certainly assured them a place in the final standings. The last landplane racer was the V.4, converted from the HV.120 number 02 after the final Schneider race, in hopes of winning a new state prize of 500,000 francs offered for the French design which would set a new world speed record before the end of 1933, but because of ineffective controls it never took off. Georges Bruner remained with Bernard for thirteen years in charge of research until 1935, when the firm was absorbed by Schreck FBA at Argenteuil. The resplendent Adolphe Bernard eventually left aviation; he died in December 1955 after a long illness, aged seventy-four.

Despite the more widely publicized misfortune that befell his later Schneider efforts, Bernard made the cantilever monoplane work. His victorious V.2 was never bothered with flutter and carried its pilot to the very limits for which it had been built. Although it never flew again after its record,[2] it stands as godfather to the subsequent racers and World War II fighters of importance. One year after its record flight, George Handasyde, designer of great prewar English monoplanes, in a letter referring to Britain's poor showing in the 1925 Schneider race, took note that much blame had been heaped at the feet of engine builders for "too much frontal area," but no complaints had been made about the "poor attempts made by aircraft constructors to get decent lines in their machines." The letter went on,

No doubt the various bits in themselves were very fine things in streamlines. But when lumped together collectively to form a machine they produced a surface of semi-detached fairings with a remarkable likeness to the contour of the Downs. The French "Bernard" aeroplane was far and away better in lines than anything we sent to America. And when it is remembered that its engine gave considerably less than 600 hp [sic] and that its frontal area does not differ much from that of the Napier, its remarkable speed must have been got from somewhere, even allowing that the landing speed was higher — it is, however, doubtful whether it was.

Other designers got the message, and Bernard's unsung breakthroughs defined the plateau from which all speedplanes took off until the jet engine allowed man to push past the speed of sound, the next rung toward the stars.

---

[2] According to Bruner, its clipped ailerons made it difficult to fly and it was almost certainly scrapped and burned.

FRENCH FREAKS & OTHER FASTBACKS

9

The Louis Clément-Moineau Racer

At the Paris Air Show which opened in December 1919 and lasted until early 1920 there appeared a remarkable aeroplane, not the less so because it was almost totally ignored. It had trim lines, its distinctive gull-wing was quite pretty, and significantly it was the first racer in aviation history to use retractable landing gear, pre-dating the next type to use this feature by almost a full year.

In the fashion of French aeroplane designation at that time, the racer bore the names of its manufacturer and designer. It was built at the small Ateliers Louis Clément, where novel aeroplanes, some the precursors of metal construction, had been built in previous years. Its designer was M.

R. Moineau, who had earned prewar fame as a pilot for Bréguet, from whom he acquired a fondness for tubular construction. Moineau turned to manufacturing in 1915, joining Salmson, with whom, in 1916, he was responsible for the Salmson-Moineau, a disjointed biplane powered by a ponderous Salmson-Canton-Unné engine mounted sideways, its shaft projecting athwartship to drive a prop on either side. After this unsuccessful design Moineau's aerodynamic ideas became distinctly avant-garde and the form of his postwar racer was a decided improvement.

Its power was low by contemporary racing standards: only 180 hp, provided by the wartime Hispano-Suiza *modèle 34* V-8, but the engine was

139

neatly cowled, its cooling provided by a small, belly-mounted radiator behind the engine which could be retracted for high-speed flight. Its wings were particularly interesting with roots mounted low from where they extended sharply upward to bends level with the top longeron from where two husky, horizontal steel tubes on each side provided rigid bracing. The fairly thick wings were fabric-covered but used all-duralumin spars, each built up from a vertical sheet web of about 10-gauge thickness, the flanges formed by four angle-section strips riveted in place at top and bottom. The spars were built in single pieces, carefully curved into the gull shape; the front spar was about 7 inches deep at its maximum point.

The aeroplane's main feature, its retractable landing gear, consisted of two simple Vs built from steel tube of half-circular "streamline" cross section, each V carrying a disc wheel; no shock absorbing whatever was employed. The rear tube of each V extended 6 inches into the fuselage where a horizontal telescopic strut connected these ends to prevent the gear from spreading outward on landing, but when mechanically unlocked allowed the legs to be rotated outward for retraction. As the gear swung out, pivoted on the lower longeron, the wheels traveled through an arc of some 120 degrees to lodge in cutouts in the gull portion of the wing. The insubstantial telescopic strut, as well as the flimsy fabric edges around the wheel cutouts in the wings, led to serious criticism. Another drawback was the racer's lack of apparent directional stability, since it was equipped with only a tiny rudder and no fin whatever, although the rear portion of the

Louis Clément-Moineau racer with wheels retracted, 1919 Paris Air Show   (MA)

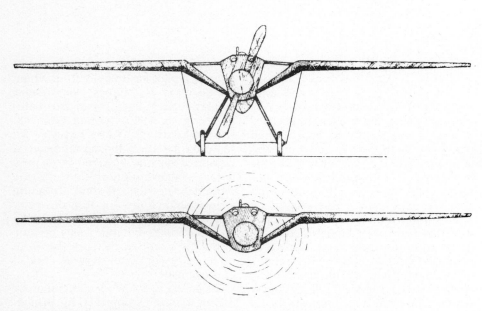

Clément-Moineau monoplane, 1919 (contemporary drawing)

Clément-Moineau monoplane showing details of retractable landing gear, 1919 (contemporary drawing)

140

fuselage was hinged to move slightly from side to side with the rudder.

It is not clear in what race the Clément-Moineau was intended to compete. There are no definite records of any flights and it seems its only appearance was under the roof of the Grand Palais. Within a year Louis Clément had left the aeroplane-building business, devoting his later energies to the production of metal aircraft accessories, but his legacy was one of innovation and progressive ideas. It would be carried on.

The Borel-Boccaccio Racer

The name of Gabriel Borel was an honored one in French aeronautics; his achievements had earned renown long before World War I. His designer was slim Paul Boccaccio, who near war's end had produced a military two-seater with very fine lines, and this was adapted into the Borel-Boccaccio racer intended for the 1920 Gordon Bennett race. Its most distinctive feature was the use of extremely narrow chord wings, a novelty which generated heated controversy over the use of high aspect ratio in the

design of a speedplane.[1] Many considered unadvisable and excessive the Borel's aspect ratio of 8 (the mean for racers of that vintage was about 5); in fact, clipping the wings — a practice which reduces aspect ratio — was then by far the preferred vogue for speed, but Boccaccio had noticed astutely that this practice sometimes — seemingly unaccountably — hindered speed. Boccaccio with great anticipation took a carefully detailed model of his racer to be tested in the wind tunnel of the St.-Cyr Aerotechnical Institute, but to his dismay the results were anything but promising. The wind tunnel results, even after double-checking, showed enormous drag.

[1] Aspect ratio refers to the comparison of span to chord. If wing span is increased (or chord reduced) aspect ratio goes up; so does flight efficiency (hence sailplanes have enormously high aspect ratios); but maneuverability suffers. High aspect ratio means relatively less induced drag but relatively more parasite drag; moreover, wing construction problems multiply. Hence the controversy among the speed seekers. (For any wing, aspect ratio is equivalent to span squared divided by wing area: b^2/S.)

Borel racer, 1920   *(MA)*

To Boccaccio's great relief if bewilderment, later flight tests of the finished racer proved the actual drag of its struts and rigging was only one fifth the value predicted from the model tests. Inadvertent neglect of the then poorly understood scale

factor (Reynolds number) had badly misled the designer. Indeed, his racer was one of the cleanest aeroplanes built anywhere in 1920, and undoubtedly one of the fastest.

The Borel's builders had paid great attention to detail. Its fuselage was

Barault in cockpit of Borel racer, 1920 (MA)

Borel-Boccaccio Gordon Bennett racer, 1920. Note offset cockpit.   (MA)

adapted with little change from the military Borel, built around four longerons of ash with spruce cross members, piano-wire-braced. Aluminum sheet was used liberally from the cockpit forward, including the neat cowl around its Hispano-Suiza *modèle 42* engine. The empennage was all wood, fabric-covered, Boccaccio claiming his small vertical tail (curiously, of low aspect ratio) permitted a gain in speed. In fact, the rudder was far too small and this had repercussions. The horizontal stabilizer was adjustable and the hardwood tailskid steerable. Its long, thin wings were supplemented by a small, wing-shaped axle fairing.

On September 25, 1920, at the elimination contest to determine France's Gordon Bennett team of three, the Borel-Boccaccio racer on its first circuit, piloted by Barault, covered the 100-kilometer distance at 269 kmh, its time only five seconds off the pace set by Kirsch's Nieuport 29V, and almost a full minute ahead of de Romanet's Spad. Thus the Borel had apparently earned with ease a solid position as France's third qualifier — but Barault had misunderstood the

starting line and failed to pass between the correct pylons. His first circuit (of three allowed) was thus disqualified. Unfortunately he was prevented from a second chance when he cracked up on landing, in part because the abbreviated tail proved to be simply too small to offset the twisting pull from the souped-up engine. Many high-powered planes of that vintage could be landed successfully only if wheeled on at fairly high speed dead into the wind, and even under this condition such planes completely lost rudder effectiveness as the tail settled to the ground, blanketed by the wings. One blast of engine or one gust of wind and a ground-loop was a likely possibility. One rut hidden in the grass if encountered while running fast, tail up — with the heavy mass of engine up front — and the aeroplane would toss over headfirst. This is what happened to Barault. Time was insufficient to get the Borel back into the air on elimination day. After the race Boccaccio continued flight tests for a time to investigate the effects of high aspect ratio on speed.

In 1922 an updated Borel racer,

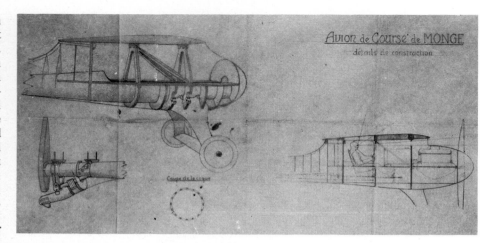

Sketches by Louis de Monge showing his novel ideas of high-speed racer construction, 1921 (MA)

presumably to be powered with the ubiquitous Hispano-Suiza *modèle 42* and intended for the Coupe Deutsch race, was rumored to be in the works, but it never appeared and nothing more was heard of it.

The Lumière-de Monge Racer
During 1921 Viscount Louis Pierre de Monge de Franeau, owner, general manager, and *directeur technique* of Établissements Lumière, the highly successful wartime propeller firm he had founded, decided to enter that season's major European air races with a new speedplane that would incorporate some of his novel aerodynamic ideas. The origins of the firm went back to 1909 when de Monge had engaged pioneer aviator Georges Lumière to fly his "dynamically stable" aeroplane; when Lumière was killed at Dunkirk early in the war, de Monge and the flier's widow began the famous propeller firm bearing the fallen aviator's name. By 1921, however, with warehouses full of surplus props and production orders almost non-existent, it was apparent that war's harsh economic aftermath had dealt the propeller business a crippling blow. Energetic and doggedly persistent, his

eyes flashing with vitality, the tall, slender engineer brimming with ideas about aerodynamic efficiency, wing design, engine cooling, and more, was eager to expand into the production of aeroplanes. He designed a sleek, high-wing monoplane shaped like a graceful teardrop, confident it would hit at least 220 mph, making it the world's fastest aeroplane.

To make initial flight testing easier, de Monge added a removable lower wing, one third the size of the main trapezoidal panel. This temporary appendage would make handling qualities docile as early flight experience was gained, but wind tunnel tests indicated its removal would add at least 20 kmh to the top speed for racing, after the fashion already employed by Curtiss in their Gordon Bennett racers of 1920. And, like Curtiss, de Monge also used the daring new thin, bi-convex, symmetrical airfoils. His *avion de course*, designated 5.1, employed additional innovative features such as differential-travel ailerons torque-tube—operated (the only non-rigid control linkages were the rudder cables). The main wing, whose low aspect ratio was in conspicuous contrast to the theories of Borel, was braced with

Borel-Boccaccio racer after its accident in the 1920 Gordon Bennett eliminations (MA)

de Monge 5·1 racer in its original configuration; note small fin and rudder (F)

carried. Naturally, the Hispano-Suiza *modèle 42* engine swung a Lumière prop, streamlined by a marvelous, huge plywood spinner. The completed 5.1 was said to have had the least drag of all 1921 Coupe Deutsch racers tested.

The 5.1 was first flown as a biplane from the then tiny Orly airfield just south of Paris by de Monge's close friend Comte Bernard de Romanet, who, eager to regain the crown of world's fastest man, sought de Monge and negotiated to fly his racer. On virtually the first flight de Romanet's airspeed indicated a dazzling 340 kmh, well in excess of the then current world speed record, and this was exciting tonic for both pilot and designer. De Monge hoped to capture the English Aerial Derby speed prize in mid-July with what the English had come to call the Blanc Mange (a slight misnomer: the 5.1, according to de Monge's personal recollection, had light brown wings and dark brown fuselage). The English press had credited the racer with "198 mph as a biplane" and it was entered in the Derby as what promised to be an even faster monoplane, handicapped even with the Bamel, but upon landing after a test flight (still as a biplane) the plane began to totter from side to side on the rough field. The racer crunched to a lopsided halt when a wingtip dug in and broke; the tailskid had also been splintered. Insufficient time remained to complete repairs, forcing the 5.1 to sit out its first race. A couple of other

only a single mahogany strut on each side. Its main spar, built in two pieces, ran parallel to the wing leading edge while a one-piece rear spar perpendicular to the aeroplane center-line extended from tip to tip. Where the main struts joined the wing under-surface, large fairings doubled as fuel tanks.

Fuselage construction was quite novel. The main structural member was a hollow, all-wood tube which ran lengthwise inside the body like a kind of backbone; to it were attached the light plywood frames which gave the fabric-covered body its outer shape. Gracefully rounded in front, the aft fuselage tapered dramatically in a concave curve to the very dimensions of the internal backbone tube. Small but tough, this tube was built up of long, narrow planks whose edges, which met together, were carefully grooved to accommodate thin hardwood strips which, when inserted, firmly joined them. The cockpit was entirely enclosed, having a side door for entrance, side windows, and narrow, slotlike cutout ahead for limited forward view. One large Lamblin radiator with its water tank was fitted above the main wing. A Letombe compressed-air self-starter was also

Count Bernard de Romanet and Viscount Louis de Monge, 1921 (MA)

Two views of de Monge 5·1 racer as a biplane at Orly Aerodrome, 1921 (MA)

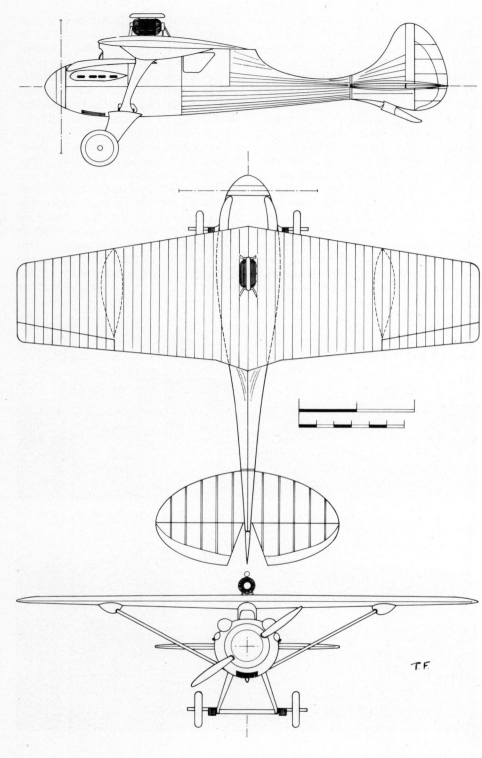

planes were mentioned as last-minute mounts for de Romanet (the BAT Crow, the Alula-Semiquaver) but these attempts did not work and he watched the 1921 Derby from the sidelines.

In mid-September, the racer was taken to Villesauvage Aerodrome 4 miles south of Étampes, site of the upcoming Coupe Deutsch de la Meurthe race, held two and a half months after the Aerial Derby. The relatively large dimensions of Villesauvage now permitted de Monge to remove the lower wing and prepare the racer for its first flight as a monoplane. During the lengthy repairs which stretched through August, shock absorbers were added (none had been installed before), the cowl streamlined, the vertical tail enlarged, and the aileron linkage tightened as the result of de Romanet's complaints about peculiar control vibrations.

The gods of fortune seemed to be smiling on de Monge at that heady moment. He was already at work on the design of a tailless flying wing, a type whose popularity was suddenly burgeoning. And only a few months before he had purchased drawings to produce the Fiat BR single-engine bomber after consultations with its designer Rosatelli. These plans cost de Monge 40,000 francs but he had

been encouraged by the STAé and soon expected to begin large-scale production. By military edict de Monge replaced all steel parts with duralumin, and during structural tests of the first completed airframe he escorted Air Minister Paul Painleve through the workshops. When Painleve expressed curiosity about the complicated test rig, de Monge, in the course of conversation, casually mentioned that the plane they were viewing should break. Just at that instant as though on command there was a tremendous crack and a wing splintered. Painleve, who had never seen an aeroplane strength test before, stared in astonishment at de Monge as though he were some sort of sorcerer, shook his head, and slowly muttered, *"Formidable!"* De Monge completed the prototype, which was flight-tested, but then for reasons having nothing to do with its merits, it was rolled into a hangar and the doors closed upon it forever. With a trace of rancor de Monge recalled that almost a decade later the BR was "still the best bomber in Europe" but the tastes of business had gone sour for him.

The turning point came with brutal suddenness on September 23, 1921, just a week prior to the Coupe Deutsch race. De Romanet, who had briefly

Cockpit of de Monge 5·1 racer, 1921   (MA)

T.F.

De Monge 5.1 racer, 1921

held the world speed record twice during 1920 only to have it snatched away by Sadi Lecointe both times, was determined to grasp the record, his lifelong ambition, once again. The lovely de Monge, looking uncluttered and elegantly sleek as a monoplane, seemed to offer conclusive promise for the job. As he fastened his helmet and squeezed into the cockpit, de Romanet outlined his plan to de Monge. He would fly north to Étampes checking out the monoplane's handling qualities, then reverse course and make a full-speed run heading south, away from town, along the highway which bordered the airfield. A small bank to either side would signal that all was OK. De Monge stood back as the racer fired up, flattening the tall grass with the sudden wind from its prop. It trundled a few yards, swung its flashing nose into the northeast breeze. De Romanet opened the throttle and the racer fairly leapt forward, bounding into the sky on a note of urgent insistence. The small group on the ground watched it recede rapidly out of sight, then walked across to the hedgerow and narrow highway to await its return.

The high-pitched sound reached them first. Then the racer appeared, some 200 feet high, rushing at them,

chewing the distance in enormous gulps. It roared close by, de Monge tingled with elation awaiting the wing-waggle that was sure to come, when suddenly — all too suddenly to comprehend — the plane reefed over in a sharp left bank (his bank seems too steep for a wing-waggle, he should right it, why doesn't he right it?). The plane's top view presented itself in a bizarre picture, a fleeting view of something streaming from the left wing, but now the plane was desperately trying to point itself toward the field, it was horribly nose down, the scene froze in startling clarity for one suspended instant as de Monge, with the shock of disbelief, suffered that irretrievable realization, even with his aeroplane whole before his eyes, that a mortal wound had been inflicted. The scene abruptly restarted — indeed, it had never stopped — and there came the inevitable moment of crash bringing its violent, jarring sound which, even more than the sight, especially sears itself on the brain. The final tableaux was horrifying. There lay de Romanet, at the end of his *carrière si belle et si courte*, the blood and oil spoiling his suit, the top of his skull sliced off at the forehead and peeled back, his brains spilled over the splintered cockpit.

Witnesses had seen the fabric rip

underneath the left wing and stream away, and *l'Auto* reported with a hint of scorn that the fabric had been stitched at 12-centimeter intervals, "not the usual 2-centimeter," but *The Aeroplane* pointed out with perhaps more sympathy that the fabric was in fact secured by exactly the same method as that universally used on wartime Spads, which had never been known to rip except "when shot to pieces." They concluded some "shock" had burst the fabric — but what? Initial speculation was not at all kind, and mostly ill-informed. The answer was not fully pieced together for years, but in the midst of his grief de Monge almost immediately got inklings, especially when Sadi Lecointe crashed during the race (de Monge later pointed out that Sadi landed straight ahead to save his life whereas de Romanet had tried to make the airport to save the plane) and other similar accidents occurred in Spain and Germany. The problem was flutter. When the racer's lower wing disappeared so did the added factor of stiffening it provided, leaving the broad upper wing free to flutter, and the ominous aileron vibrations experienced earlier — even with the girder support of the lower wing in place — now were able to reinforce themselves and make their true nature apparent.

Initially, the problem was confused by James's withdrawal from the race when the wing fabric on his Bamel racer lifted; the apparent similarity to the de Monge accident convinced many that speeds by 1921 had resulted in forces "incalculable" by the then available data, and there was much hushed clucking among the heads bent together over the rickety tables at Foyer des Soldats, the fliers' amiable watering spot in Étampes. De Romanet's death had thrown a tangible pall of gloom over the 1921 Coupe Deutsch. More than that, it almost broke de Monge. The crash marked the end of his Lumière firm. Yet, somehow, with firmly gritted determination the tall Fleming prevailed. He raised money

from his family to build the all-metal 5.2, *avion de chasse* companion to his ill-fated racer. Exhibited at the 1922 Paris Air Show, it elicited glowing comments: ". . . here is a plane which instead of being hidden in a corner, deserves to be placed on a pedestal in the middle of the Grand Palais," one correspondent gushed; ". . . its lines are beautiful . . . it is certainly the best-looking plane to date." De Monge hoped to receive his long-sought-after production order, but politics intervened. Already the seeds of corruption that would drain away the Third Republic's cream had taken root, and de Monge explained the truth behind Laurent-Eynac's complaint that he had not been properly "connected" by the builder. Instead, during 1922, the officially favored firm of Dewoitine was founded to build all-metal aeroplanes. Laurent-Eynac had also decided that prototype orders should go only to firms with demonstrated mass-production capability. De Monge then united with Buscaylet, a furniture maker who knew little of aviation but who had large production facilities at Issy-les-Moulineaux, but the large orders never came. Forced to submit crippling low bids in order to get token contracts, the production of fewer than a couple of dozen aeroplanes inevitably led to financial disaster. Buscaylet-de Monge lasted only a few short years.

Among the last planes built by this highly creative designer was the Buscaylet-de Monge 7.4, first flown in September 1923, and the follow-on 7.5 flown in 1925, embodying de Monge's flying wing concepts for efficiency. The 7.5 was flown by Deschamps, Boussoutrot, and Nungesser, who enthusiastically urged that the concept be developed for the Paris–New York attempt. This dream never materialized. The 7.5 was powered by two engines built in the shops of the compulsive Ettore Bugatti, who had met de Monge in Paris during the early days of World War I and with whom de Monge teamed in 1937. This was

Crash of de Monge racer in which de Romanet died, 1921 (MA)

145

after a return of several years to his native Belgium to serve as chief research engineer of Imperia Excelsior, the huge auto concern where he perfected a torsion-bar suspension system as early as 1927 as well as automatic transmissions, variable-compression engines, and induction-cooling methods. But drawn back to aviation in the 1930s, he and Bugatti set out to design a twin-engine, contra-prop racer of plywood-balsa sandwich construction to top the world speed record, then 440 mph. Once again de Monge tasted defeat when the Nazi invasion put a sudden, brutal halt to these plans. In March 1946 he came to the United States, eventually becoming a U. S. citizen, and from his vantage in the 1970s he still recalled with vivid feeling the days when he stood tall in the company of speed seekers.

The Hanriot Racer

The novel Hanriot HD.22 racer, built for the 1921 Coupe Deutsch, was product of the famous father-son firm of René and Marcel Hanriot. The father, René, charter member of the Vieilles Tiges and renowned *grand champion de l'automobile*, was in his mid-forties when he earned his pilot brevet (Aéro-Club de France number 368, February 3, 1911) after his early interest in aeroplanes had been sparked at the gala 1909 Rheims meeting. Perhaps he was further spurred by his precocious son Marcel, who was born at the ancient family home in Champlitte (Haute-Saône) four days before his father's twenty-seventh birthday, but who beat the older man aloft, earning his brevet (number 95) in May 1910 when only fifteen years old! Young Marcel had his *brevet militaire* at the age of seventeen and studied at the college of Châlons-sur-Marne. In the meantime beautifully built Hanriot aeroplanes began to appear and win a basketful of prewar aviation prizes. Besides competing in France, a pioneer Hanriot fondly dubbed "Henrietta," whose colorful aerial antics made Brooklands unsafe in the

early days of flying, became well known in England, and by 1913 René Hanriot, his luxuriant black mustachios emphasizing the electricity of his eyes, which always seemed to be lit with that singular passion to fly, had been named Chevalier in the Légion d'honneur. It was on a Hanriot HD.1 fighter shortly after war's outbreak that Belgian ace Willy Coppens secured thirty-seven kills in six months. The formula of René Hanriot, who was fifty-four at the time of the 1921 Coupe Deutsch, was brief: *il fut simple, juste, et bon*, and it served as the standard at the factory which he and Marcel operated at 192 Boulevard Bineau, Neuilly-sur-Seine.

For the upcoming race the Hanriot chief designer, M. R. Pouit,[2] obsessed with achieving high lift from small wings, had fashioned plans for a monoplane racer especially noteworthy, not only because it was to be all-metal, but because it was to employ both cantilever wings and landing gear retractable into wells in the fuselage. Wind tunnel tests of a model (minus radiators and landing gear — as though the gear were retracted) led the exuberant designer to forecast the unheard-of speed of 400 kmh for his racer. The fuselage frame was built from steel tube, acetylene-welded, a practice considered common in the construction of small aeroplanes today but distinctly novel — especially by French standards — in 1921. The fuselage frame employed only three main longerons in a triangular form. The engine mount consisted of husky steel strips riveted into box-section members, and the ubiquitous Hispano-Suiza *modèle 42* was neatly cowled in, the camshaft casings housed in duralumin troughs formed directly into the cowl. Plywood bulkheads were attached to the tubular frame, and to these the dural skin — which had been beaten into its

[2] Author of the classic text *Aérodynamique* (Dunod, Paris, 1947).

Hanriot HD.22 metal racer, 1921 (MA)

compound-curved shape by hand-wielded ball-peen hammers — was attached. The skin was thick to the extent that hard pushing against it by hand produced no deflection, which rendered the over-all structure sadly inefficient since this heavy skin took no loads. In fact, the skin covering the vertical fin was held in place by simple turn buttons, dangerously weak attachments even though supplemented by two or three canopy clips and a single 1·5-mm brass bolt. On the bottom an adjustable fin could be set before takeoff to counteract yaw from the engine. Wing ribs for the under-cambered, constant-chord wings were built up from trough-section duralumin, N-braced between flanges, and fitted over two metal-box spars which slipped into thick, rectangular metal receptacles welded to the top longerons. Only the torque-tube—operated ailerons were dural-sheet—covered; the main wing surface was fabric. Two fuel tanks were mounted in the cockpit by the pilot's knees on either side, the faucets on the dashboard. When rolled out, the HD.22 had a conventional fixed landing gear, said to be "temporary," but in fact the racer was never fitted with the retractable gear which had been so loudly promised. Its stubby outline was

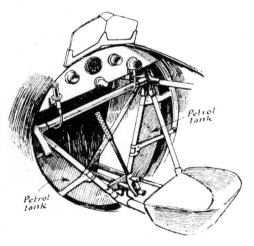

View inside cockpit of metal Hanriot racer, 1921; note mounting of fuel tanks (contemporary drawing).

additionally spoiled by the two boxy radiators in front of the cockpit, their tops leaning together.

The pilot picked for the HD.22 was Maurice Rost, but he never had a chance to show his mettle. The HD.22, at Étampes for runups preparatory to flight, was seen next to its rival, the new Nieuport-Delage sesquiplane, which looked slender, graceful, almost

146

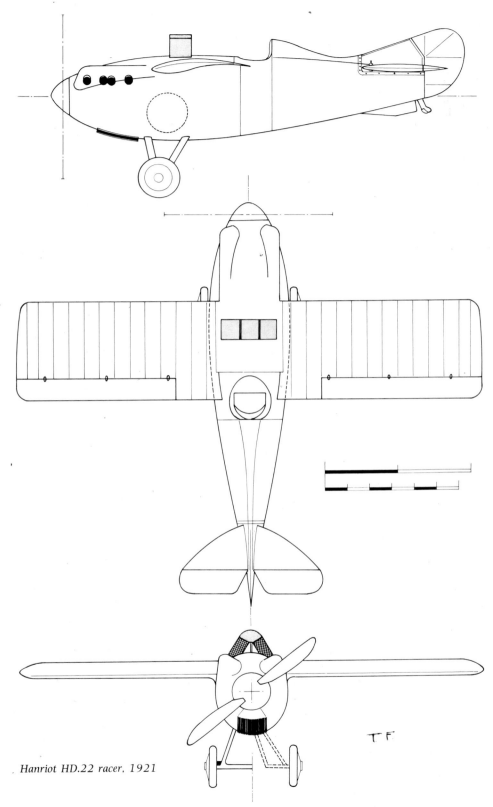

Hanriot HD.22 racer, 1921

feminine in contrast to the Hanriot's look of bulky, muscular strength giving the impression of a *terrible bolide*. Despite overtime work, slow delivery of final parts prevented flight test. At 7 P.M. Sunday, September 25, with the race less than a week off and after Sadi Lecointe landed from some lively speed trials in his sesquiplane, thoroughly disgusted René Hanriot threatened to withdraw if he could not get the impatient Rost airborne soon. On Wednesday, September 28, the day of the French team eliminations, with his aeroplane still grounded but at last ready to fly, Hanriot was attempting to secure insurance for Rost. The unsettled prospects caused the insurance company to decline, and this was the last straw. Hanriot threw in the towel, leaving only three competitors and thus rendering the eliminations unnecessary. Two pilots — wartime ace Madon and English test pilot Tait-Cox — were both mentioned as ready to conduct speed trials with the HD.22 after the 1922 Paris Air Show where it was exhibited. Apparently neither did. René Hanriot died at Neuilly in November 1925, aged fifty-eight, leaving his son Marcel to carry on the firm which had produced an almost forgotten metal monoplane milestone in the search for speed.

The Tailless Racers of 1922

Speed seekers had long recognized the apparent advantage that could be secured by eliminating from their racers the enormous drag of conventional fuselage and empennage, and reducing the speedplane to the minimum essentials required for flight and control. Many experts shook their heads at what seemed a futile task: to build a wing that did not require supplementary stabilizing or controlling surfaces, either ahead or astern — after all, even birds have tail feathers — but the younger, bolder generation saw at the end of the struggle an aerodynamic Holy Grail. To understand their struggle better, some background is in order.

Richard Harte first detailed the idea of the tailless aeroplane, even specifying dual-function, flaplike control surfaces ("controllers" he called them) that would operate simultaneously in the same sense as elevators and in the opposite sense as ailerons, these to be hinged to a cantilever wing. But such prodigious ideas were so advanced they had no real effect when Harte patented them in 1870! The same year Alphonse Penaud declared the apparent need for a separate tailplane mounted on an arm which would locate it away from the wing. This category — to which all modern conventional aeroplanes belong — came to be called the "Penaud type." In 1876 this incredibly visionary Frenchman had already foreseen stressed skin, contra-rotating metal full-feathering props which could be oversped then brought to proper pitch to help the takeoff, retractable landing gear with oleopneumatic shock absorbers, and blind flying made possible by instruments such as the artificial horizon, barometric and mechanical altimeters, airspeed indicator — and autopilot! His ideas, like those of Harte, were hardly comprehensible in an age of horses and were doomed to languish; frustrated, Penaud committed suicide in 1880. Before his death, however, he had also foreseen that a wing with a reflexed trailing edge would tend to provide inherent stability in a tailless configuration, and this idea was further pursued beginning in 1890 by José Weiss, the French artist naturalized in Britain. Weiss's spirited studies of birds led to a crescent-shaped, twisted "parabolic" wing design, an attempt to achieve an elliptical distribution of lift across the span, mathematically the most efficient. It was clumsily copied years later by the Dutchman Holle in his Alula. Meanwhile, in 1908 Weiss built a precursor to the modern trim tab, a device first realized successfully some twenty years later on the Spads of Herbemont, many of whose ideas were strongly influenced by the artist.

Although certain aspects of tailless

147

aircraft had been considered by these pioneers, it was not until German naturalists noticed the exceptional soaring qualities of the seed leaf *Zanonia macrocarpa*, a fibrous oval about 3″ × 7″ produced by a cucumber plant peculiar to Java, that hope was seriously entertained that a successful flying wing could be built. The Moravian father and son team of Ignaz and Igo Etrich in 1906 copied the *Zanonia* leaf and built the first inherently stable man-carrying flying wing, but its poor performance was disappointing. The addition of a Penaud tail resulted in the famous Taube (Dove), manufactured by the hundreds early in World War I. In 1914 a Taube left unattended with ungated throttle took off, flew until it ran out of gas, and landed without the slightest damage!

The first *practical* tailless plane was built by Lieutenant J. W. Dunne, RN, who rejected the *Zanonia* leaf design and with it, to some extent, the idea of inherent stability since he saw the need to preserve a measure of controllability. Although brilliantly visionary, Dunne was patiently methodical, a quiet man whose plodding studies brought him to such a thorough understanding of esoteric aerodynamic principles that his papers contain much of what World War II designers decades later took for granted they had originated. Dunne's trademark was sharp sweepback (an idea first suggested by Mouillard); about 30 degrees with substantial washout (leading edge twisted down) at the tips, the latter feature not for stability but to enhance speed by allowing a significant c.g. shift. At a time when flexible, warpable wings were in vogue Dunne disdained the concept because of their proneness to what he called "oscillations"; he was also aware of the benefits of spanwise flow over his swept wings and as early as 1909 he anticipated the modern delta wing as well as streamlined wing-root fairings! Dunne's planes did not have true rudders, just vertical "curtains" at the wingtips. Charles R. Fairey

oversaw the construction of Dunne tailless aeroplanes at Eastchurch between 1910 and 1913 where an early version was flown by a one-armed pilot! The pesky British monoplane ban coupled with Dunne's chronic ill-health forced him in 1914 to relinquish his rights which were acquired by Astra in France, W. Starling Burgess in the United States, and Armstrong-Whitworth in England. In the United States Burgess won the 1915 Collier Trophy for his efforts with Dunne's designs, which he built and supplied to the U. S. Navy for years. In the meantime the restless Dunne had recovered sufficiently to pioneer a two-control system whose form was theoretically proven years later to be the optimum.

Much less dramatic than Dunne's was the work begun by René Arnoux in 1909. A man of modest output, Arnoux served quietly and competently for years as Technical Committee vice-president of l'Aéro-Club de France. His first tailless monoplane in 1912 used full-span trailing edge controllers after Harte, but these were equipped with stops to limit their downward travel. This prevented the reflex-cambered wing from being transformed inadvertently into one with simple camber and corresponding unstable c.p. travel, anathema for a tailless design. The following year Arnoux produced a low-wing, tailless pusher monoplane called Stablavion which for unexplained reasons was totally ignored. Arnoux nevertheless stands out for being the originator and only designer for years to promote what has come to be called the "flying plank" — a plain wing with no sweepback, dihedral, twisted wingtips, or other supplementary devices. He invented a clever composite instrument which he called *girouette de l'aviation* to show the pilot of his craft angle of attack, deck angle, airspeed, and rate of climb all at once! Arnoux also realized early that the thrust vector was all-important to the success of his tailless craft, and the throttle, as he

carefully pointed out, became the key to control. When war broke out he was diligently developing a system by which variations in wing lift would somehow govern engine output (perhaps control surface position could be linked to the throttle, he theorized, to make thrust roughly inversely proportional to lift) with pilot option to override. The results of tests made at Issy-les-Moulineaux are unknown but they must have been at least partly successful because in 1919, after the war, Arnoux resumed his efforts.

At this time Arnoux acquired the services of pilot Georges Félix Madon, a thin, short, pallid man who became thirty near the end of July 1922. Madon had come from his native Bizerte in Tunisia to Paris for schooling before the war and earned his brevet (number 595) on a Blériot at Étampes in 1911 when he was nineteen years old. From that moment aviation dominated his life. He flew night bombers early in the war, was interned in Switzerland during 1915, but returned to the front to become CO of Escadrille

Georges Madon, 1922   (MA)

148

N.38 and score forty-one confirmed kills, making him one of France's top aces. After the war this dour ace who had thrived in a peculiar way on combat found himself at loose ends and vaguely dissatisfied. Wan and solemn, he tried several unrewarding *affaires d'aviation*. Meeting Arnoux seemed to him a godsend, and his name soon became so thoroughly associated with Arnoux's tailless aeroplanes that they have often been mistakenly referred to under the name of Madon alone.

Madon's first assignment was to test-fly a tailless biplane built from surplus parts and powered by a 130-hp rotary engine, the machine that marked the resumption of Arnoux's postwar labor. Madon demonstrated it before STAé officials in 1922 with such success that Arnoux was encouraged to establish a company for further research and hopefully lucrative production work. The name chosen was intended to reveal his design philosophy to even the least initiated: Société des Avions Simplex. But shortly thereafter his biplane was destroyed

in a crash, severely injuring Fetu, another pilot who had mindlessly removed the control stops, rendering the plane unstable.

Arnoux's next tailless design was his company's first product, the Simplex-Arnoux racer built for the 1922 Coupe Deutsch. It was a design that truly deserved its contemporary description: *far too courageous*. Ing. Carmier, chief engineer of Schwarts and Léon See, assisted to a great extent in the detail design. The light robust racer was certainly one of the earliest full-size aeroplanes to use a fully symmetrical airfoil, a type which although handicapped by low values of maximum lift has the advantage of neutral stability at the median angle of attack. The slightly tapered, otherwise plain wing was covered with thin mahogany veneer in four layers near the root tapering to three layers midway out, and two layers at the tip. The two box spars were of spruce, and poplar ribs — each designed to take compression loads — were spaced at 25-centimeter intervals. The monocoque fuselage was built like a boat and

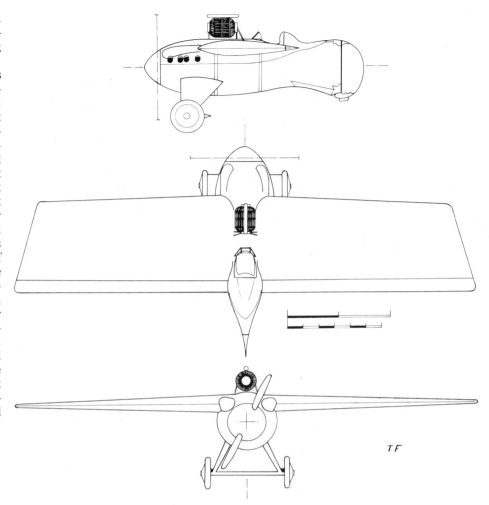

Simplex-Arnoux tailless racer, 1922

Simplex-Arnoux tailless racer, 1922 Coupe Deutsch (MA)

covered with two layers of mahogany veneer enclosing a core of basswood, a species good in compression. All landing gear members were of tough gray poplar (*grisard*; not white poplar more frequently used elsewhere). Full span "controllers" which served as both ailerons and elevators were operated by rigid tubes connected to the short control stick which was rooted in a complicated gear train under the pilot's seat. Cables ran from the rudder bar aft to the tailskid, which was fixed to the rudder surface and equipped with a spring-leaf shock absorber. The racer's predicted speed.

if achieved, would have made it the world's fastest aeroplane in 1922.

Again, the stops restricting the controllers' downward movement were removed, this time on the insistence of Madon which no doubt drowned out the intense but quiet objections of Arnoux. Certain disadvantages had been apparent to Madon even before he started the engine: the cockpit was far back, his view hampered by the broad wing and Lamblin radiator perched directly in his view. On September 24, 1922, just a few days before the race while apparently trying to land the sensitive racer, Madon lost

Simplex-Arnoux racer　　　　(MA)

shaped tailless racer for the 1922 Coupe Deutsch in one of the Hanriot workshops. This curious aeroplane, powered by a ferocious 700-hp 57-liter Fiat A-14 engine, was to be flown by France's great wartime ace Charles Nungesser.

The wings of Nungesser's racer were swept forward some 30 degrees and had pronounced washin, i.e., a greater angle of incidence, at the tips — a scheme theoretically providing just as much longitudinal stability as Dunne's sweptback wings with washed-out tips. The swept-forward system allows separation of controls; Landwerlin and Berreur took out a British patent in 1922 (203654) claiming a stable swept-forward system controlled laterally by ailerons placed even with or ahead of the c.g., thus locating them outboard on the wing where their moment arm is greatest; and in pitch by separate elevators aft of the c.g., thus, inboard on the wing. The builders claimed either set of control surfaces could serve a dual control function. The Landwerlin-Berreur racer was a cantilever high-aspect-ratio monoplane with the engine mounted in front. The constant-chord wings had no dihedral and used the bi-convex, symmetrical Göttingen 410 airfoil which had been designed by Alexander Lippisch in 1918. Behind the closed cockpit the stubby fuselage terminated in a large fin and rudder. Wind tunnel tests indicated the racer had good stability up to the angle of attack for stall (about 10 degrees), and a top speed of

control near the ground and turned over after a wheel was wrenched off. The racer was demolished and Madon was lucky to emerge with only minor injuries, but the reaction was immediate and severe with strong implications of rebuke for Arnoux. Madon, it was said, should not risk his life again in such a "freak" design. This second unnecessary accident sealed the immediate fate of Arnoux's tailless schemes, and thoroughly discouraged, he disbanded Simplex. The scorn heaped upon this unfortunate man, who had been widely misunderstood and frequently misinterpreted, was unwarranted insult after injury. Actually, the design of his racer — certainly the simplest tailless configuration possible to devise — was structurally superior to any other known tailless arrangement, and except for particular care necessary to position its c.g. and its sensitivity to any c.g. change, the design is entirely satisfactory aerodynamically. Among the speed seekers, patient, unsung René Arnoux deserves more credit that he has received.

About 1926 Charles Fauvel began experimenting with tailless designs characterized by an absence of sweep, dihedral, or twist, in fact continuing the work of Arnoux. Initially Fauvel mistakenly assumed that his predecessors had sought a stationary c.p.; but Arnoux, who eventually teamed with Fauvel (their names appear together on the 1930 patent of a flying wing), pointed out that his Coupe Deutsch racer had used a wing on which the c.p. did travel, but in a stable manner. The importance of precise c.g. location was reemphasized by Fauvel, and his experiments provided additional steppingstones for later developments. Meanwhile, Madon had returned to Tunisia to become a farmer after leaving the Bapt round-the-world expedition when the untimely death of Picard brought it to an abrupt conclusion. Madon failed at farming too. In July 1923 he rejoined the Army, but on November 11, 1924, an air show accident at Bizerte terminated his short, cheerless life.

At the same time the Simplex-Arnoux racer was being built, two other French designers, Georges-Marie Landwerlin and Georges André Berreur, were building a huge, egg-

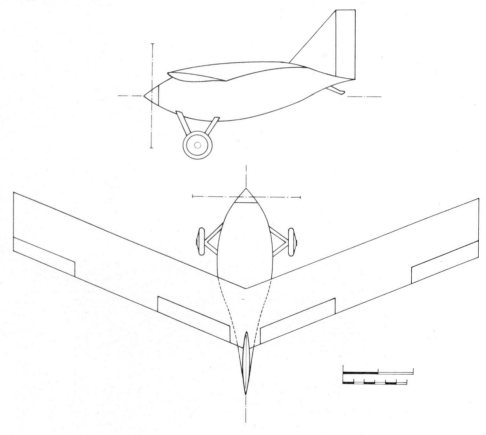

Landwerlin-Berreur tailless racer, 1922; drawing adapted from original patent application

450 kmh, in those days a staggering figure, was optimistically forecast. The design was undoubtedly one of 1922's most daring experiments, unfortunately not finished in time for the race, and it is doubtful if it ever flew. If it did, it must have had bugs because the concept was dropped, not to be resurrected until the Cornelius monoplane of 1943 employed almost precisely the identical form.

This brief treatise would not be complete without a recount of how the tailless racers of 1922 interfered with subsequent developments. Setbacks were inevitable to the builders of tailless aircraft in 1922, who were hamstrung by an almost non-existent base of research data. Despite this there were great efforts to persist, especially in England, under the pressure of solving one of the most troublesome problems in aviation: the lethal inadvertent stall which was then killing an average of one English aviator per week. Frederick Handley Page's novel wing slots which delayed the stall were gaining popularity, but to Geoffrey Hill, brother of 1912 pioneer Roderick Hill, the slots did not seem to provide the total solution to the problem — which, he thought, should be to *eliminate* the stall. Hill began by building a tailless glider, working rather uncertainly for a year, but gaining confidence. He adopted many of Dunne's ideas: his monoplane wing employed 31-degree sweep and 6-degree washout; rudders which could double as air brakes hung underneath the tips; tips whose extensions were "controllers" (later "elevons") that floated to remain faired with the airstream. The trailing edge was slightly reflexed and variable gearing was employed in the control circuits. In December 1924, despite awful weather and the absence of any pilot enclosure, Hill flew his glider over the South Downs, achieving a glide ratio of 11. The success earned him a Cherub engine granted by the Air Ministry, and in 1925 the design reappeared as the Pterodactyl light plane whose

enclosed cabin achieved weight saving through use of a then almost unknown substance, balsa wood. Flown early in November 1925, the tailless plane was very sensitive in pitch but stable about all axes. Most important to Hill, it could not be stalled, maintaining controlled flight even at an angle of attack of 45 degrees — although the control stick in these circumstances seemed topped by a lead block. Geoffrey Hill commented that "normal design [moves] through the bog of convention [while my new] ideas form an avenue of escape." He continued his efforts at Westlands, where in 1927 Laurence Openshaw flew his three-seat Pterodactyl but because of inadequate control crashed in a wing-down manner depressingly similar to the stall-spin accidents Hill was struggling to eliminate. Hill persisted — the model IC was the ultimate Pterodactyl, flown in 1927 at Weyhill, Andover, by Louis Paget, Westland's exuberant test pilot, more or less successfully but hampered by failings that were purely mechanical. Although dropped thereafter and never intended for racing, the Pterodactyl is probably the best-remembered of the 1920s' tailless designs.

The Arnoux flying plank idea was not seriously revived until after Max Munk perfected the NACA M-series of airfoils having reflexed camber, longitudinally stable with neither sweep nor twist, and the remarkable steadiness of flying planks built two and three decades later fully vindicated Arnoux's earlier work. The German Alexander Lippisch in 1930 carried the idea even further: he married the sweepback of Dunne to the flying plank of Arnoux, forming a triangular shape which today we call the delta wing. Lippisch, one of the great promoters of the flying wing, had been a young soaring enthusiast when he spent one bitter winter alone doing esoteric experiments with models above the cloudy Wasserkuppe in the Rhön Mountains, discovering and rediscovering much about powered tailless and tail-first aeroplanes. He did

not strive for inherent stability — his later sailplanes could perform a full bag of aerobatics — but rather wanted to establish the technical baseline from which a large transport flying wing could be built. Lippisch also claimed credit for the "inverted arrow" (swept-foward wing), presumably unaware that he had been preempted by Landwerlin and Berreur in 1922. To help overcome torsional difficulties, Lippisch varied his airfoil along the span, again claiming credit, forgetting (or unaware) that Dunne had already described his own use of this technique in 1911! Nevertheless, Lippisch built several entirely successful small deltas and flying wings, broadly expanding the body of knowledge furnished by the pioneers before his time; but no practical application resulted from his experiments until John Northrop in the United States built large flying wings which more than proved the feasibility of the type for use in the manner Lippisch had envisioned. Despite their intrinsic advantages and quite acceptable flying qualities, such craft have proven to be too unorthodox even for the progressive field of aviation, and all efforts to promote them died out. The tailless racers of 1922 are recalled in the 1970s only dimly by modern delta-wing aircraft which have come to take such complex forms as the Concorde supersonic transport; but such modern craft truly represent an effective reminder of the audacious originality applied by earlier speed seekers.

The Gourdou-Leseurre Racer
Jean Adolphe Leseurre, only twenty-five and afflicted with a congenital malformation which severely restricted his activity, was an unlikely aspirant to the role of aeroplane impresario at the height of France's 1917 war effort. Born in Beaugency, he first met Charles Édouard Pierre Gourdou, a young man from Castres, at l'École Centrale in Orléans during 1904 when both were teen-agers. Gourdou, who was six years older, at first took pity on the

physically unfortunate young Leseurre, but soon came to develop a high regard for his considerable technical talents. Later Gourdou was recalled from infantry duty with the Seventeenth Army to work on radio at Chalais-Meudon, but soon rejoined his former schoolmate to construct a handsome fighter plane externally similar to the popular Morane parasols. Its impact was slight since it could not effectively compete with the masses of Spads then flooding the Front, but the pair were encouraged to continue. They established their factory at 25 rue Krüger, St.-Maur-des-Fossés (Seine), and the day was saved by a contract for Bréguet 14s which their own modifications transformed into one of the strongest aeroplanes built. By mid-decade production orders for their own designs mounted to the several hundreds.

The lure of speed beckoned, however, and when the 1923 Coupe Beaumont race was announced Gourdou and Leseurre set at once to producing a high-speed design adapted from their successful parasol fighter. Experience gained in building an intricate metal two-seater in 1922 encouraged them to make their racer largely from metal. Called the CT no. 1, it was a braced parasol monoplane with striking appearance. Its wings violated the builders' earlier practice of draping their designs with extreme quantities of sail and in fact were trimmed to little more than half the wing area used on the military fighter later spawned from the racer. Built with two dural box spars, plywood ribs, and fabric-covered, braced by a central steel tube cabane and dural struts, the CT wing was characterized by a swept leading edge and very narrow ailerons. The fuselage was of narrow oval cross section with a framework not of built-up sheet dural members but of dural tubing, fabric-covered. Perhaps the Hanriot racer's novel tubular frame had served as precedent; in any event, the use of tubing was gaining popularity but

Gourdou-Leseurre CT racer built for the 1923 Coupe Beaumont   (Au)

Gourdou and Leseurre did not weld their structure after the new fashion, preferring to brace it in the classical manner with steel fittings and piano-wire cross ties. Five longerons were used, three upper and two lower, which with the mid-upper formed a triangular section that withstood torsion.

The aeroplane's distinctive look was enhanced by the nine dural helmets that individually shielded the nine protruding cylinders of its Jupiter air-cooled engine. Radial air-cooled engines were having a hard fight to gain recognition, especially for high speed, in 1923. Aside from severe difficulties in making overboosted air-cooled cylinders work, moderate weight savings over water-cooled types were offset by increased drag. The several handmade pots that streamlined the CT engine tended to obviate this, and while such a scheme would be impractical for mass-produced aeroplanes

Gourdou-Leseurre racer, 1923. Standing alongside is pilot Adjutant Devillers.   (Au)

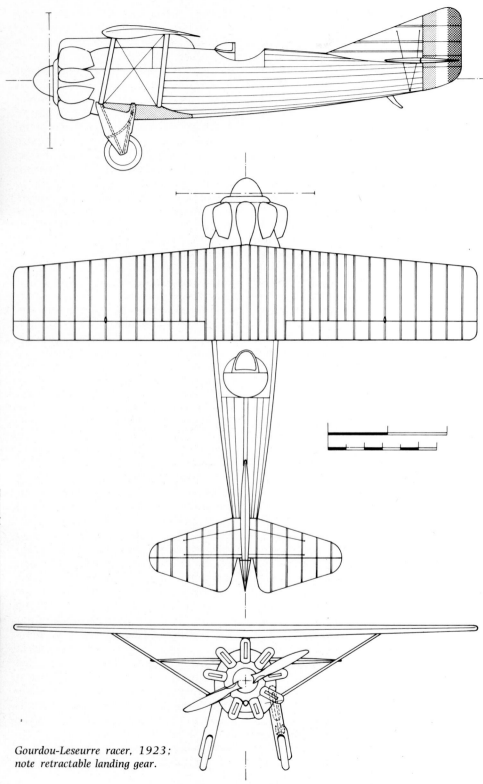

Gourdou-Leseurre racer, 1923; note retractable landing gear.

152

it was hoped suitable results would justify its use on the racer. The hope was in large measure realized; the CT with essentially equivalent power virtually equaled the year-old performance of the Curtiss R-6, current official world record holder, and this indeed was a tremendous accomplishment in an era dominated by water-cooled engines. Just days before the CT debut its American contemporary, the new Curtiss R2C, won the 1923 Pulitzer at a speed 10 per cent faster over a closed course, a definite but not considerable increment. Gourdou and Leseurre, disenchanted with the aging Hispano-Suiza, continued to push the use of air-cooled radials for fighters in France, with conviction in their simplicity and maneuverability afforded by low longitudinal moment of inertia.

Certain French sources refer to the racer's engine as a Jupiter IV built under license by Gnôme-Rhône, but in fact it was a Bristol-built Jupiter I–Mark III, indeed the very engine (s/n 855) which had been used in the bulbous Bristol type 72 racer and brought to France after the Bristol racer was dismantled.

The CT had another feature in common with the Bristol racer: its retractable landing gear. The short, stiff legs retracted aft into fuselage recesses in the manner envisioned by Bruner for his Bernard racers. Each wheel was carried on a steel V, the forward struts of which were hinged to the lower longerons, the rear struts secured at their upper ends to guides within the wheel recesses. As a part of each leg, fixed to each forward strut, was a circular quadrant with teeth meshed to a worm gear on a shaft which the pilot could twist, thus raising the legs. When extended the narrow landing gear did not appear too strong against side loads, but there was general resignation that drift upon landing would topple the top-heavy racer anyway, so no special design precautions were taken. The burden to avoid such calamity was squarely in the cockpit!

The CT was shipped to Marseille for the race, to be held October 14, 1923, at Istres (Bouches-du-Rhône). As events transpired it was the only racer to appear at the starting line! It could have made a fly-over to garner the 75,000-franc *prix*, but Gourdou and Leseurre sportingly withdrew it. Its assigned pilot, Warrant Officer Devillers from the French Aéronautique Militaire, did fly it once around the five-cornered 50-kilometer circuit and achieved a remarkable 223·7 mph. The engine and landing gear worked perfectly. But the CT was never seen again after that one performance, either on a speed course or at an air race.

In August 1924 a stiff competition between six French manufacturers was under way, the prize being a fat production order for single-seat military fighters. Gourdou-Leseurre entered the Jupiter-powered, large-winged type 13, evolved from the CT racer. An intermediate Gourdou-Leseurre was used by Jean Callizo for his world altitude record flight which reached 12,066 meters. These later planes had fixed landing gear; retractable gear developed for high-speed racing was not yet judged sufficiently mature to be carried over to rugged service types, which Gourdou-Leseurre continued to manufacture during the halcyon years.

The Salmson-Bêchéreau Racer
A more persistent Beaumont racer than the Gourdou-Leseurre was that designed by prewar Deperdussin pioneer Louis Bêchéreau who in 1923 was ensconced as Avions L. Bêchéreau, 85 Ave. de la Muette, Paris, and built by Société Anonyme des Moteurs Salmson. The impetus was provided by Salmson's eagerness to employ for racing a huge eighteen-cylinder engine they had developed. This was the CM.18, a massive radial affair with two rows each sprouting nine cylinders, *water-cooled*! Near war's end Salmson had developed an eighteen-cylinder two-row version of the popular 260-hp nine-cylinder Z.9; the Z.18 (as it was

then called) was huge, displacing an imposing 2,293 cubic inches, and was rated at 500 hp at 1,600 rpm. The design appeared too late for use during the war and remained dormant until 1922 when both it and its predecessor were updated into the CM.9 and CM.18, the latter now rated at 520 hp. With its compression boosted to 6·5 it was credited with almost 700 hp, then considered a highly respectable performance even for a bulky engine weighing well over half a ton (some 1,100 pounds, compared to the 680 pounds of the contemporary Curtiss D-12). Bêchéreau, his reputation firmly consolidated by his Deperdussin masterpieces and wartime Spad designs, was engaged by Salmson late in 1922 to design a racer around the CM.18 for competition in the first scheduled Coupe Beaumont, the 1923 edition. Bêchéreau began by designing a scaled-down version of the racer he envisioned, a "school machine" (*école d'course*) or trainer for race pilots as it were, powered by an air-cooled 120-hp Salmson AC.9.

In one sense Bêchéreau had an easy commission, working with what was undoubtedly one of the world's most powerful aero engines, but its radial configuration coupled with cumbersome water-cooling problems made it decidedly awkward to fit into a streamlined speedplane. Bêchéreau set the engine well back in the fuselage where

it was buried completely, sheathed in a steel case, and attached a sturdy shaft 60 centimeters long with an elastic coupling to drive the prop at the business end of the long, gracefully tapered nose. The four-blade prop had been devised by mating two standard two-blade wood props in tandem, their blades perpendicular to each other. The racer had rather good-looking lines – Bêchéreau was certainly no newcomer – but it was so large as to be almost ungainly.

The rather plain wing (conventional structure with two wood spars) was not cantilever, being braced from below by large struts emanating from the landing gear. In 1924 this configuration was modified by substituting a system of cables anchored above and below to replace the struts. Radiators were carried in the wing leading edge. Other features included Bêchéreau's oleopneumatic shock-absorbing landing gear and the long dorsal spine leading to the vertical fin. Not completed in time for the 1923 race, which was called off anyway, the racer was pulled back into the shops and modified at leisure for the 1924 contest. Initial concern over its flying qualities was assuaged by enlarging the wing area 2 square meters, more than 10 per cent, resulting in almost twice the amount of sail carried by contemporary racers; very neat wing-root fairings were also installed. Special Lamblin

Salmson-Bêchéreau Coupe Beaumont racer, 1925 (MA)

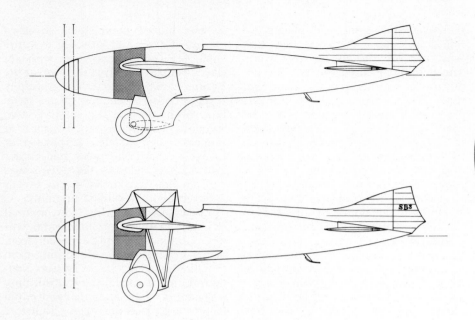

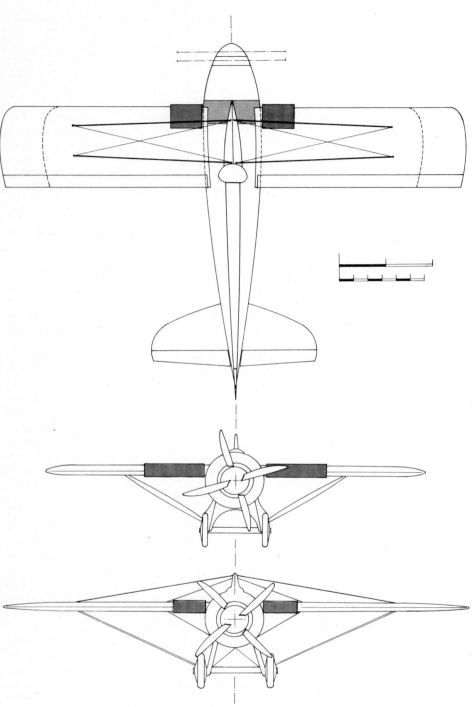

radiators were attached to the bottom wing surface inboard, but serious cooling problems developed almost immediately, and in the "race" at Istres, Lieutenant G. Ferigoule, the pilot, was forced out on the first lap.

The racer, sometimes erroneously called the Ferigoule-Salmson, was again entered in the Coupe Beaumont, where in 1925 it was the only competitor for Sadi Lecointe and his Nieuport-Delage 42 sesquiplane, but another radiator malfunction resulted in serious over-heating and detonation and forced Ferigoule to drop out, a depressing repeat of earlier bad luck. Salmson had spent a veritable fortune to perfect and promote his aero engines, but he was left with pitifully little to show for his venture into big-time air racing. The Coupe Beaumont died and the Salmson-Bêchéreau racer was never seen again. Rumors of a Salmson-Bêchéreau fighter with the same large engine appear to be unfounded. The CM.18 engine, however, was produced until nearly 1930, demon-strating a surprisingly tenacious grip in the rapidly developing aero engine market, increasingly dominated by radial engines, true, but ones which

were otherwise exclusively air-cooled.[3] Bêchéreau left aviation to work in an auto factory making shock absorbers, a far cry from earlier aeronautical suc-cess. His last brief and inconclusive return to aviation did not occur until after 1930.

French Flying Boat Racers
During the early 1920s French builders made concerted but insufficient efforts to capture the Schneider Trophy, these efforts reflecting a decidedly more tra-ditional design approach than that exhibited in French landplane racers. After the promising 1919 float con-versions of Spad and Nieuport racers, the French avoided the Schneider contests for three years until 1922 when a new high-speed flying boat built on classical lines appeared. The guiding spirit behind its launching was that of Signor Raphael Conflenti, who as chief engineer of Savoia had designed the impressive Italian Schnei-der Trophy Savoias of 1919–21. Conflenti came to France to join D.

[3] Liquid-cooled radials were briefly considered for the B-36 during its design years later. They were not used.

Salmson-Bêchéreau Coupe Beaumont racer: side and front views, reading down: as designed in 1923; modified version that raced in 1925; note longer wing, added bracing.

CAMS 36 racer, 1922. Note Conflenti's in-verted hull bottom. (MA)

Lorenzo Santoni, his former mentor at Savoia who left Italy to become *administrateur délégué* of a new firm established late in 1920 at St.-Denis; this was Chantiers Aéro-Maritimes de la Seine (CAMS). Construction of CAMS flying boats began during 1921, and soon the clean, smart boats were seen undergoing flight tests at Le Pecq near St.-Germain and at the St.-Raphaël air station on the Mediter-ranean.

Conflenti's first French racing design was the CAMS 36, adapted directly from work he had been doing at Savoia and in fact built under license from the Italian firm. Powered by the Hispano-Suiza *modèle 42*, two were entered in the 1922 Schneider race at Naples. Conflenti was working hard to perfect a concave-shaped hull bottom, a definite design departure from the more widely accepted V-bottom style. His new hull pushed up a mountainous bow wave but eliminated the bother-some spray other hull types threw outward and aft; instead the bow wave was pushed ahead. A British observer noticed that "in a bit of a lop [the concave hulls] would bore by the head," and great broken fragments

of sea would stream right across the bow; this would last until the hull reached "hump speed" when it seemed to climb neatly atop the hill of water and rise gracefully away. If it did not get away cleanly the first time it fell back with a jarring thud, but this was rare with the high-power racers, and other builders began to favor Con-flenti's concave hull, notably Oswald Short. The CAMS racer hull had a cross section that was roughly rec-tangular forward, the top domed, very smooth, the pilot seated well aft behind the wings where visibility was restrict-ed, the fixed empennage just behind the cockpit formed as an integral part of the hull. Conflenti's practice was to plank the hull bottom with three-ply, reinforcing the single step with plank-ing strips over the plywood. The single-bay biplane wings were simple and crisp, the lower wing sporting a small chord, the engine nacelle built into the upper center-section, the engine mount forming the upper wing central support (unlike many other flying boat racers of that vintage), a large spinner streamlining the tractor prop. The racers were barely finished and flight tests had only begun when

they had to be crated and shipped, but owing to an Italian rail strike they could not be delivered in Naples in time to race. The names of Lieutenant de vaisseau de Corv. Teste and Poiré appear in the official race program, but Vroman was to have replaced the latter in the cockpit of the second racer. In flight tests the CAMS 36 showed a nice turn of speed, achieving 250 kmh. Unfortunately, it was irrelevant.

The following year, for the momen-tous 1923 Schneider race over the English Solent at Cowes, Conflenti updated his design, producing one CAMS 36*bis* (it is unclear if this was one of the 1922 racers modified or an entirely new hull; its registry mark F-ESFC was next in sequence after those of the two 1922 racers, F-ESFA and F-ESFB). The designer admitted

freely in 1923 that the design was not fast enough, but the pilot picked to fly it was expected to race it to its best advantage: this was Lieutenant de vaisseau Georges E. M. C. Pelletier d'Oisy, who one year later was des-tined to carve a lasting niche in the annals of French aviation heroes for his remarkable Paris–Tokyo flight in the Bréguet 19 *Jacqueline*.[4] This high adventure still awaited d'Oisy as he

---

[4] Leaving April 24, 1924, d'Oisy made Paris–Karachi in one fantastic week; not satisfied with this speed he left Karachi May 3 and in ten days reached the placid, tree-lined city of Hanoi in French Indo-China, where he changed engines; between May 18 and June 9, when he reached Tokyo, he suffered several mishaps flying through China, touching Canton, Shang-hai, and Peking.

CAMS 36 details, 1922. Note the superb hand-carved propeller, Lamblin radiator. (MA)

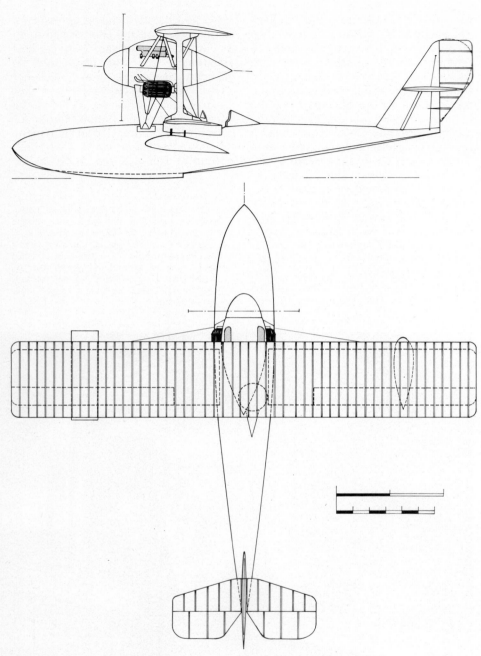

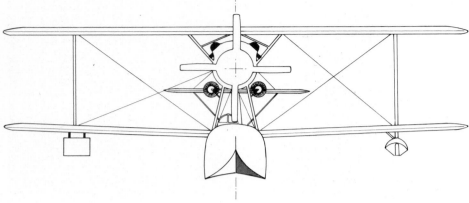

prepared to race the CAMS 36*bis* in the 1923 Schneider.

Conflenti was dissatisfied with his tractor design and for 1923 laid out a new flying boat racer, the CAMS 38, in which he placed the Hispano-Suiza engine backward to become a pusher, and located the pilot forward near the bow for better visibility. The same concave hull shape was used, and as before the wings were straightforward with spruce spars and poplar plywood structure. The configuration change was worth an added 10 mph at top speed, enhanced no doubt by the new streamlined Lamblin radiators fitted to the front engine nacelle struts. The CAMS 38 was flown by Maurice Hurel.

The French had decided to take the 1923 Schneider seriously, and if the two CAMS racers were suitable only for relatively calm weather, which was the general consensus, then French strategists felt they should have entries which need not be fast but which could complete the course in the roughest foreseeable weather; indeed, with such a boat on the team it was almost hoped the weather would be foul since it was

CAMS 36 (1922) and 36bis (1923). Side view shows original version (1923 tail denoted by dotted line); plan and front views show differences in pontoons and rigging with 1922 version on observer's left and 1923 on right. Note Conflenti-designed inverse hull bottom, following Italian Savoia practice.

CAMS 36bis of Pelletier d'Oisy being prepared for the 1923 Schneider Trophy race (Au)

CAMS 38 at the 1923 Schneider Trophy race; "fair weather" ship (F)

Latham No. 1, prototype twin-engine (push-pull) racer built for the 1923 Schneider Trophy race; "foul weather" ship (MA)

likely none of the other entries, speedier but more delicate, could finish. Thus, a young cousin of famous prewar pioneer Hubert Latham produced two husky flying boats for the race at his new firm, Société Industrielle de Caudebec-en-Caux (SICC–Latham & Company). The Latham racers (numbers 1 and 2) each used *two* Lorraine-Dietrich *modèle 13* V-12 engines, a venerable design which had been uprated in 1922 by over 30 hp (STAé designation 12Db). These delivered a total of more than 800 hp. They were placed back to back in push-pull fashion; thus their props were turning in opposite directions with respect to each other, which gave a bonus to directional stability. The British seemed mildly surprised that the two props were of equal diameter as opposed to their own preference for different-diameter props

on their tandem engine installations. Two new Lamblin radiators, each with 7 square meters radiating surface, were mounted in the cabane. Another noteworthy feature was the use of Latham's patented laminated streamline wires for all external bracing. Although workers struggled day and night, the Lathams were not ready to travel across to England until thirty-six hours before the navigability trials were due to begin. The Latham pilots were Lieutenant de vaisseau Benoist and SICC test pilot Alphonse Duhamel.

Two other French flying boat racers were entered in the Schneider race during March 1923; these were the Blanchard-Blériot C.1 Jupiter-powered monoplanes built by Société Aéronautique Blanchard, a small firm located at Les Coteaux-de-St.-Cloud. A compromise racing design adapted from a doubtful fighter-scout and attributable to no one designer, the Blanchard truly seemed to fulfill the cliché that a horse designed by committee becomes a camel! De Corv. Teste was selected as test pilot, but his disappointing speed of 220 kmh achieved during early tests was obviously too slow, so the French-built, direct-drive Jupiter in the second racer was boosted to deliver 550 hp, which resulted in a more hopeful 280 kmh, but this second aircraft suffered a decisive collision before it could be registered and dispatched to the race.

Two French naval vessels were to have carried the CAMS and Latham aeroplanes across to England. When the vessel assigned to CAMS broke down, the other ship was assigned to them — and the sturdier Lathams were designated to fly across. It was September 25, a day on which the Channel boiled and frothed under mounting southwesterly gales which at times gusted to 60 mph. This was the kind of weather Duhamel and Benoist wanted on race day, not now when it threatened their transit! In mist and spray which sliced their faces with tremendous force and cut visibility to a few gray yards, Duhamel

boats intended for the race, was the only one to cross the starting line! Shortly before noon, from his forward vantage, the roar of his spitting engine muffled by sleek, glistening cowl behind, gritting against the hard spank of sparkling water, he poured on the coal for takeoff. There was one bone-thudding collision with the sea just before lift-off – unknown to Hurel this had damaged the starboard stabilizer and breached a longeron – but Hurel soon had other, even more serious problems. His engine began acting up – perhaps the rough takeoff had affected it as well. He should have done one lap in fifteen minutes but to French embarrassment and dismay he took almost twenty. On the second circuit his prop hub worked loose and the engine crankshaft seized near Selsey Bill. The chagrined Hurel, France's last

hope, was out of the race too and watched helplessly as the American Curtiss racers won their resounding victory. It was the last Schneider race attempt made by a French flying boat.

Early in 1924 Hurel took the CAMS 36bis to 6,200 meters to set a world altitude record for seaplanes. A half-hearted design attempt for a new flying boat racer was launched about the same time; this was designated CAMS 45, to be powered by the new Hispano-Suiza *modèle 50* W-12 engine, but it was discontinued in May 1924 and Hurel left air racing for good. Conflenti went back to Italy, where he resumed his design work at Savoia.

Thus ends the chronicle of French curiosities. Amid great successes the dim but no less worthy torches borne by lesser-known speed seekers lit byways along the formidable path to

Blanchard racer built for the 1923 Schneider Trophy race (MA)

made a magnificent flight, somehow finding Cowes and landing safely on the Medina, well past the Saunders sheds, even above the floating bridge. Benoist was not so lucky. He had just passed Littlehampton when one of his push-pull engines began to run rough, and with mounting anxiety he surveyed through the streaks of mist what little he could of the confusing and in-hospitable British coastline. He made his decision quickly and turned back to Littlehampton, where he managed to land in the shallow harbor. A large, helpful crowd of people materialized but they were disorganized and in-experienced and soon began to pull large pieces off the racer as it pounded helplessly in the surf. It was disabled for the race.

On race day, after negotiating the seaworthiness trials in fine style, one of Duhamel's engines was ailing –

and after all its rugged tribulations, the remaining Latham was rendered *hors de combat* by a balky magneto!

The two CAMS racers came across from France to England aboard the French destroyer *Verdun*, a lavish display of government support second only to the vast American Navy effort, all being noted ruefully by British constructors, who were bitterly critical of their own government's parsi-monious attitude. After performing their seaworthiness trials in workman-like fashion, they prepared for the speed race. Then tragicomic disaster struck. Pelletier d'Oisy, while taxiing out to take off, perhaps unable to see clearly from his aft cockpit, collided with a moored yacht. "Damage was slight," it was reported, "especially to the yacht." But d'Oisy was unable to continue. Thus Hurel, on the CAMS 38, of the six original French flying

Latham racer on hoist before 1923 Schneider (Au)

CAMS 38 of Hurel aloft during the 1923 Schneider Trophy race. Note starboard stabilizer, damaged in heavy sea before takeoff, pilot unaware. *(F)*

speed. The great voyage extended across borders, across oceans; the speed frontier first defined and assaulted so sharply in France was breached in the New World — by the speed seekers of America.

United States

A STRANGER IN THEIR MIDST

10

The Dayton-Wright Racer

The edge on January's wintry chill in 1920 was markedly softened by the prospect of grand-scale air races resuming during the coming summer. That month telegrams soliciting American entries for the Gordon Bennett International Aviation Cup race to be held in France later in the year went out from the Aero Club of America to its affiliates as soon as the new postwar regulations were drawn up. The news was received with interest in Dayton, Ohio, birthplace of the Wright Brothers and site of the Dayton-Wright Airplane Company, whose three plants had been opened during World War I when awarded large (and controversial) orders for the mass production of warplanes, mainly D.H.4s. Patriarch

Orville Wright still influenced Dayton-Wright operations as chief consulting engineer and his concept for the future had been revealed back in May 1917, even as hostilities raged, when he wrote Glenn L. Martin, "The [Dayton-Wright] company was organized by Messrs. Deeds and Kettering and H. E. Talbott, Senior and Junior . . . [who] are going to carry out some of my ideas in creating a sport in aeronautics."

A return wire from Dayton-Wright chief pilot Howard Rinehart was received by Aero Club officials during February, within a month of the invitation, announcing Dayton-Wright's intention to build a competitor. This delighted the club because, as the second definite U.S. entry, it looked as if a full American team of three might yet sail for foreign shores.

Original Dayton-Wright RB with strut-braced wings   *(Au)*

Dayton-Wright RB; original, strut-braced prototype, 1920. Note wing flaps on both leading and trailing edges.   *(Au)*

The conceptual origins of the remarkable racer that resulted are obscure although its designation – simply 'RB' – is the initials of Howard Max Rinehart and Milton C. Baumann, purported to be its two principal designers. They worked under the cognizance of Orville Wright although just how much he personally had to do with the design is uncertain. One of the unsung contributors to the RB design was a long-time friend of Rinehart's, model enthusiast Charles Hampson Grant, who had been approached by Rinehart for new ideas in wing construction. Rinehart knew that Grant had already made a deep study of airfoil behavior under the influence of movable leading and trailing edge devices, and being convinced that his racer's chances of success would be enhanced if the RB wing curve could be varied while airborne to adjust to both fast and slow

speed flight, he and Grant applied results of Grant's experiments to the new design. Indeed, the true importance of the RB wing is that it embodied the first practical application of wing flaps, flaps which in fact were quite sophisticated. Grant's wing was composed of three main pieces which allowed *both* leading and trailing edges to pivot from the center-piece so that both could be drooped simultaneously.

Grant was born in Elizabeth, New Jersey; in 1908 when he was fourteen he visited an aviation show in New York City that intrigued the dreamer in him. The next year, eager to partake of the thrilling new adventure of flight, he built a hang-glider, a wing fixed by pole to bicycle handlebar and seat. His conservative father would not "contribute to fooling around with contraptions of the Devil," but his mother, Gertrude Grant, a moderately

Charles Hampson Grant   *(S)*

162

well-known landscape painter, patiently sewed the muslin cover for the glider's wings. With this and similar machines which he rebuilt often after crackups, Grant slowly learned his aerodynamic lessons — many the hard way. He said later, "Everyone thought I was nuts and usually approached me with an air of toleration and often sympathy."

But by 1913, when he was nineteen, he had made flights of over 400 feet at altitudes of up to 30 feet, landing at 10 mph, good running speed. He reported, "The thrill of such flights cannot be described. [You get] a sensation that one does not get while riding in an engine-driven aeroplane . . . you must control [a hang-glider] by your own actions . . . swinging one's body and legs forward for nosing down or backward for climbing." Meanwhile he was winning model aeroplane contests with superb, A-frame rubber-powered designs of exceptional stability which could make straight-line flights of half a mile. One young assistant was his brother Duncan, later killed in a 1918 mid-air collision while flying Sopwith Camels with the 135th Aero Squadron. Grant went to Princeton (civil engineering, class of 1917), then worked in the assembly shop of the B. F. Sturtevant Airplane Company in Boston for $8 per week; his boss was Sturtevant's chief engineer, Grover Loening. It was during his military service while stationed at Dayton that he met Rinehart.

After his brief association with the RB, Grant returned to his beloved Vermont. A humanist, he came away from World War I dedicated to improving the state of aviation through youth, and this led him into a life devoted to teaching youth aviation by means of modeling. In 1932 he became associated with the three-year-old Bernarr MacFadden magazine *Model Airplane News* and as its editor for the next eleven years until 1943 led it to new heights; he also formed nationwide model clubs, founded the prestigious Academy of Model Aeronautics, and thus in turn inspired the next genera-

tion of aero engineers, mechanics, and pilots.

Other personalities apparently involved with the RB design during the early stages were W. N. Conover and E. F. Longchamps. George Montague Williams, a thirty-year-old Canadian who had gravitated to Dayton via the Great Lakes and the H. E. Talbott Company, was general manager of Dayton-Wright and a very able aeroplane constructor. Harold E. Talbott, Jr., thirty-two, Yale-educated and later to become Secretary of the Air Force, was then president of Dayton-Wright. Certainly these men contributed to the new racer's progress.

Howard Rinehart began his flying career in 1914 at Simms Station near Dayton (his birthplace was Eaton) on a Wright model "B" boxkite, graduated to exhibition flying and even flew Wright planes in Mexico during the dispute with Pancho Villa where his hair-raising escapades got him shot at by both sides. His Aero Club pilot certificate was number 266. Long associated with Wright, he became chief instructor at Mineola for Wright-Martin when the two firms amalgamated. In 1916 Edward A. Deeds and Charles F. "Ket" Kettering started their aviation enterprise near downtown Dayton on the site later known as McCook Field, and when they had forged it into the Dayton-Wright Company that year Rinehart came back home to become the backbone of its flight staff.

Ket Kettering, when only five years out of Ohio State, had invented an automobile starting, lighting, and ignition system and organized the Dayton Engineering Laboratories to produce it under the trade name Delco. This invention catapulted him rapidly into the president's chair of the General Motors Research Corporation, a director's chair of GM, and the position of president of the Society of Automotive Engineers. His ignition equipment was used on wartime Liberty engines, and his fertile mechanical genius also devised a practical mercury-cooled

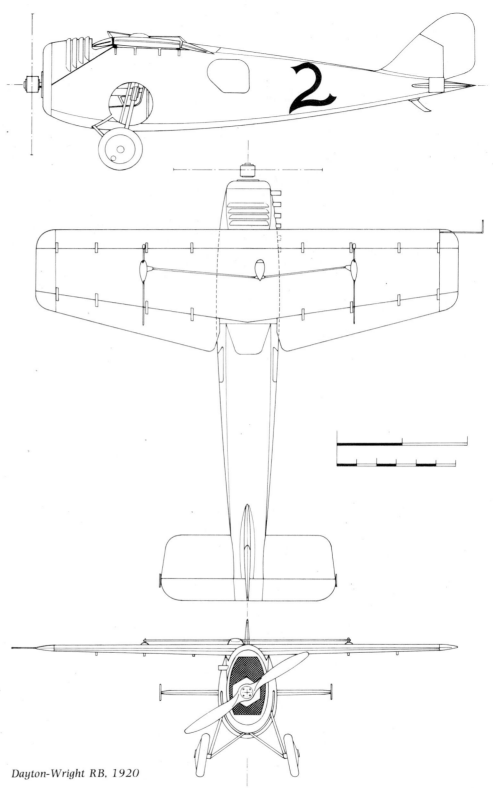

Dayton-Wright RB, 1920

*Dayton-Wright RB as dispatched to the 1920
Gordon Bennett race*   *(USAF)*

*Cockpit of Dayton-Wright RB, 1920. Note the
single crank for actuating the landing gear and
wing flaps.*   *(S)*

exhaust valve which in the 1920s inspired Sam Heron's monumental step to sodium-cooled valves, which in turn made high-power piston engines practicable. The Dayton-Wright aeroplane concern became a division of GM, and Kettering, with his high-pitched, almost whining voice, was its intensely enthusiastic vice-president who used any excuse to travel by air. Rinehart flew Kettering back and forth extensively for business engagements in what amounted to their private D.H.4B, with Kettering keen to the aeroplane's vast practical possibilities even while his pragmatic mind was quick to see obvious design weaknesses in the war relics then commonly in use, such as the fixed wheels and forests of wires and struts.

The Gordon Bennett design that rapidly took form reflected both common sense and great daring. In some ways its features seemed almost too obvious: make the landing gear stowable and provide the variable camber wing to allow reasonable landing speeds and yet achieve the 200 mph predicted necessary to win. But in 1920 these ideas, both implemented largely by Grant, were decidedly revolutionary. A streamline body for minimum resistance was sketched which would completely encapsulate the pilot, making him blind ahead, above, and below. Rinehart, whose easygoing, casual demeanor belied his enterprising resolve, was willing. Entrance would be through a sliding trap door on top or alternatively through one of the large cutouts on the side which accommodated celluloid windows which, once in place, Rinehart could bulge outward with his head to provide some visibility. The fuselage would be built by binding thin strips of wood tightly with strips of fabric laid in glue, the strips crisscrossing the underlayer each time a layer of wood was applied. The final finish was superb, glassy smooth and flawless.

As the design progressed a feeling of gut-clenching anticipation rose like mercury in a thermometer. Mentally the excited builders could already picture their sleek plane standing out among the rows of unwieldy flying cathedrals. Rinehart, more discerning than most, sagely said the RB was "frankly an experiment," and never promised to win, only put up a "damn good show." The prototype was first assembled with oversize, constant-chord, strut-braced wings which allowed slow takeoff and landing speeds in order to test landing gear feasibility. Each big wheel was mounted on a steel tube V, hinged at its points of contact with the fuselage. Another thick tube extended inside, passing through a phosphor-bronze casting on which was wrapped the shock absorber cords and which itself was threaded to travel along a threaded shaft mounted vertically inside the fuselage; this in turn could be rotated by the pilot's crank through an arrangement of bevel gears. As the pilot turned the crank, which took between twelve and twenty seconds, the wheels were pulled flush into large, porthole-like recesses in the fuselage sides. The effect of this on witnesses could be quite emotional, many confessing to becoming frankly uncomfortable as they watched the aeroplane's wheels drawn "out of sight." The whole scheme was amazingly simple — most importantly, it *worked*. Indeed, the absence of the typical cross axle allowed the RB to operate easily from fields with high grass. Though Rinehart did not know it yet, this would come in handy in France.

Success gave birth to resolve. Remove the bulky flight-test wing and its struts. Fit the sleek, cantilever racing wing. The new wing had a pleasing, efficient layout, tapered in both plan and thickness. In the interest of combining lightness with rigidity it was built from solid chunks of balsa

Wing of Lockheed F-104 supersonic fighter in landing configuration; note similarity to RB wing design developed some forty years before.   *(Lockheed)*

wood, a substance which curious Europeans would find as exotic as the aeroplane's design. These were covered with a three-ply veneer skin which was then painted silver and polished. Startled observers would occasionally glance up to see one or two men crouching on the racer's wingtip with no apparent effect on its strength or surface. The operating mechanism for its

movable leading and trailing edge flaps was simple: a large shaft which extended spanwise to bellcranks, one on each side, to move the flaps was connected internally by bevel gears to the same pilot's crank that operated the landing gear — thus the gear and flaps always worked together. But to keep it simple the push-pull shafts were all mounted externally in the

Dayton-Wright RB showing original wing flap actuating mechanism   *(Au)*

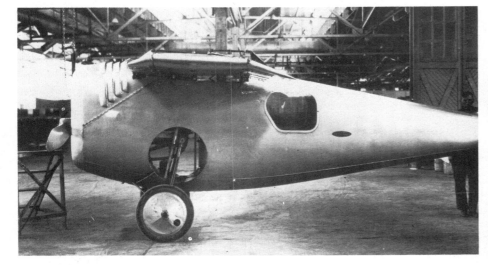

Sequence of views showing simultaneous landing gear and wing flap extension, Dayton-Wright RB, 1920   *(Au)*

165

wind above the wing. This undoubtedly caused tremendous drag, which must have virtually canceled most of the benefit provided by having a flattened wing for high speed.

Many Europeans remained skeptical about variable camber practicability. Some recalled experiments in 1916 at the Eiffel laboratory in which a "similar" three-piece variable camber wing was tested. The results of those experiments showed that a variable camber wing was equivalent to a rigid wing "with a camber of 3 per cent" but of course the experimental conditions could have had a lot to do with such negligible results, said the defensive Americans. The variable camber wing did accommodate a strong belief that existed in 1920 that low landing speeds resulted from concavity in the wing's undersurface. In any event, its production cost, in the European view, was enormous.[1]

The aeroplane's performance was further limited by the choice of engine, the Hall-Scott L-6a, a tall, cumbersome affair often called the "Liberty six," a reference to its resemblance to half the Liberty V-12 engine. Indeed, the rugged, heavy Liberty, in those days

[1] The true significance of Grant's wing would not be appreciated for many years; the RB wing was forerunner of vastly more sophisticated flap systems developed by Grant in later years when he became convinced that the pendulum had swung too far, that safety was being sacrificed for speed. Any air traveler who has peered through his window at the awesome sight of a huge Boeing 747 wing disassembling itself for landing can see the direct tie – through Grant's unceasing efforts in wing design – to the RB racer. Grant continued to work on advanced wing design and after much struggle managed to secure patents on all manner of exotic variable camber, leading and trailing edge flaps, and tailless delta-shaped wing designs. Some of these later became the subjects of extended litigation – against Martin (who eventually settled) for use of Grant's segmented flaps on the 202/404 airliners, against Convair for use of the delta shape on the B-58 supersonic bomber, etc. But Grant never received the measure of credit he felt he deserved or the financial recognition he craved. He eventually gave up these long, bitter, and unproductive fights and retired to Vermont, his inventive mind remaining active into the 1970s.

Dayton-Wright RB in France with Lumière propeller and added tail fins, the latter fitted to improve directional stability (MA)

still the darling of the U. S. military, owed its crash wartime design in large part to sometime Lieutenant Colonel E. J. Hall of Hall-Scott Automobile Company, West Berkeley, California, who built his first aeroplane engine in 1908 and whose company had manufactured vertical six-cylinder engines since 1914. The RB's engine, a Liberty spin-off, was still tied to the prewar Mercedes with its individual steel-jacketed cylinders. Its shape accounted in part for the racer's deep fuselage, and the large, flat radiator out front contributed to drag. Even when wound up at top rpm the L-6a produced only 250 hp, well below the snorting powerplants of its competitors. Of course, the designers were attempting to achieve high speed through aerodynamic finesse, in which case brute power would be unnecessary.

The deep fuselage, by lodging almost as much vertical surface area ahead of the aeroplane's c.g. as the small tail provided behind, also made the aeroplane's directional stability poor. It wallowed like a whale; thus, shortly after arrival in France, Rinehart screwed two extra fins onto the tailplane. These helped matters somewhat even though the racer still tended to

"wander" through the sky. Nevertheless, on September 25, during the French team eliminations three days before Cup day, Rinehart gave a very impressive demonstration by flying one lap of the 100-kilometer course, throttled back, at 165 mph. Certainly the RB was capable of higher performance, but it is also reasonable to speculate that Rinehart's directional stability deteriorated at higher speeds, and despite its extra tail fins the racer weaved and hunted alarmingly, forcing Rinehart to keep it throttled down. Also strongly criticized was the racer's absence of forward visibility, which

Howard M. Rinehart, 1920 (MA)

Dayton-Wright RB, 1920. On wing, from left: Howard Rinehart, pilot; Jim Jacobs; J. P. Henry; Harvey Geyer; Ben Whelan (later Sikorsky vice-president); Wallace Whittaker; Thomas Midgley (who later developed ethyl fuel); Al Timmer; Milton Baumann, designer; Harold Talbott, Jr., (later secretary of the Air Force); G. M. Williams (president, Russell Manufacturing Company); and Charles Kettering of General Motors. (Au)

may have been its major design fault, forcing Rinehart to fly a zigzag course. Before the race the American prop on the RB was replaced by a French Lumière.

On Cup day Rinehart was the first American aloft. He took off at quarter past two, cranked up the gear, and crossed the line headed south. An observer commented on the plane's strong resemblance to a "huge, flying mackerel." After only twenty minutes, however, Rinehart reappeared with his gear down and landed. A cable had failed, jamming his leading edge flap, preventing it from fully retracting.[2] Rinehart reckoned he had no chance, unaware that other mishaps would

put so many competitors out of the race that had he continued he would surely have come in second. A French spectator was heard to remark, "Personally, I wish he had won." What would destiny have held for this design had Rinehart won the race? When he

[2] Some references say it was the "port rudder cable" that failed.

167

climbed out of his cockpit his earnest expression was creased with tears.

In a sanguine full-page advertisement, placed two weeks after the race, Dayton-Wright stated auspiciously that the RB monoplane "represents some recent departures in aeroplane construction which will be developed in building planes for commercial purposes. Chief among these are the Retractable Landing Chassis and Variable Camber Wings." Dayton-Wright had two objectives in building the RB. The first was to bring the Gordon Bennett Cup back to America and in this endeavor it failed, but it did "offer the aviation world something new in aeroplane construction and performance." Its momentous ideas, even if somewhat crudely implemented, were not immediately followed up. Even though Dayton-Wright was dissolved by GM in 1923 one can only speculate on what curious twists of engineering indifference or prejudice caused the aerodynamic concepts pioneered by the RB to languish for some twenty years.

A corollary development taking place at this time which involved Dayton-Wright protagonists had to do with fuels. The "knock" or detonation in engines was becoming a bothersome problem to Delco because Kettering's battery ignition system was being widely blamed — quite mistakenly — for knock. The phenomenon was already being investigated at Cambridge by Professor Bertram Hopkinson and his assistant Harry Ricardo, who first associated knock not with ignition but with fuel grade, and by A. H. Gibson at Farnborough. In Dayton Kettering launched his young assistant Thomas A. Midgley on his own investigation of detonation, motivated as much by a desire to protect Delco's reputation as by scientific altruism. Midgley worked for months over his single-cylinder engine and famous "bouncing pin" which was devised to measure differences in detonation pressures, and he soon determined that detonation depended on both fuel grade and engine compression ratio. Thinking at first that fuel color influenced knock, Midgley added iodine to his fuel, theorizing a dark-colored fuel would absorb more heat energy and vaporize more quickly. When the knock diminished he smelled success, but it did not come in the form he suspected. Further experiments forced him to discard the fuel color idea but led in turn to a long, frustrating line of trial anti-knock additives. GM, parent company of Delco, encouraged Midgley and his assistant T. A. Boyd, who in a vigorous program, individually tested more than 30,000 compounds, and their discouragement mounted with the list. On December 9, 1921, a chilly Friday, Midgley and Boyd were anticipating the weekend's respite from their series of relentless, routine tests when suddenly the engine was not behaving the same at all. Jolted into disbelief, Midgley had quite literally stumbled onto the remarkable anti-knock properties of an obscure substance called tetraethyl lead. This proved to be without doubt the greatest single discovery in the development of aviation fuels; not only did this additive make higher power possible, it enabled the aeroplane to fly farther on a given amount of fuel — it gave the aeroplane *range* — and in turn enabled the successful engines that dominated aviation until the advent of gas turbines.

Midgley and Kettering, who must have been no more than incidentally involved in the genesis of the RB racer, nevertheless filed out to be duly photographed standing bravely on the racer's wings shortly before its hopeful trip to France for the Gordon Bennett race; characteristically, Kettering ventured all the way to the wingtip! This, of course, was a year and a half before Midgley's important fuel discovery, and fully seven years before fuels were first rated by octane number. In 1967 the remarkable Mr. Midgley was still active as president of the American Chemical Society.

Howard Rinehart eventually left aviation; he died in Mississippi in 1949, aged sixty-four. His little RB racer for one brief moment had been truly a forward-looking stranger in the midst of aeroplanes whose designs were lodged in contemporary junctures. It never raced again, and its demise lent false comfort to many cramped minds who found thereby sufficient reason to avoid breaking away from traditional design practice even though no blame for the RB's failure could be placed directly on its original design concepts. Today one can see the RB, polished like a silver dollar, at the Ford Museum near Detroit.

THE ARMY'S BLOCKBUSTER

11

The Verville VCP Racer

America's earliest entry for the Gordon Bennett was, significantly, a military plane, and the Army team that took this plane to France, thus opening U. S. military interest in air racing, was the only military team at the race. The aeroplane's origin, ironically, can be traced directly back to France.

In 1918 Alfred Victor "Fred" Verville, a young, highly capable yet sternly devout engineer who was fascinated by electricity – his education included an International Correspondence Course in electrical engineering – and who made his hobby flying kites, had been loaned by his employer, Fisher Body Company of Detroit, to the Air Service Engineering Division at McCook Field in order to spark originality into America's wartime aeroplane designs. Verville came highly recommended. In 1914, when aged twenty-four, he witnessed a daredevil flying exhibition and immediately left a secure job at Hudson Motor Car Company to plunge straight into aviation, joining Curtiss at Hammondsport and doing valuable design work on many early Curtiss planes, notably the Jenny. He soon returned to his home in Detroit, branching out and building seaplanes under his own name. Now in 1918, not yet thirty, he was placed by the director of the Bureau of Aircraft Production on the Lockhart Mission, which was sent straightaway on a survey trip to France to study Allied pursuit programs and designs.

Quiet and intense, Verville was

Designer Alfred V. Verville (in center) between,
from left, Benjamin D. Thomas (see Chapter
18), Dr. A. F. Zahm (see Chapter 12),
C. Witmer, and E. Kelly (Au)

deeply impressed by French designer Louis Bêchéreau. Verville himself was a staunch Catholic of French-Canadian origin who spoke fluent French and found himself warmly received in France. Bêchéreau's immortal Spad fighters had enjoyed spectacular success on the Western Front and his protégé André Herbemont had updated the design into a beautiful wood monocoque, swept-wing configuration with smoothly flowing lines. Verville remarked years later that he got his first inkling of what pursuit planes should be from his French visit, but his fertile mind was already conjuring changes. Upon his return to McCook he was deep into the design of a new American fighter, the Verville Chasse Plane (VCP), to be built around the ubiquitous Hispano 300-hp engine.[1] Despite the

[1] It has also been stated that the letters VCP were an abbreviation for Verville-Clark-Packard. Packard was the engine later substituted. Clark would have been Virginius "Ginny" Evans Clark, thirty-four in 1920, Naval Academy and MIT graduate who transferred to the Aviation Section, Army Signal Corps, in 1913, became Army chief aero engineer in 1916, helped to organize McCook Field, later became Engineering Division chief until 1921 when he went to Dayton-Wright as chief engineer, then became vice-president of Consolidated

intervention of the Armistice design work continued. Verville's tapered wings and faired lower wing attachment represented distinct design innovations, but his airfoil was the elderly RAF-15 which had long predominated. Verville, however, defended it: "a damn good section." The top wing was continuous (no center-section) with tapered spars built from two spruce channel sections placed back to back with three-ply webs in between and covering the sides. The leading edge had three-ply covering back to the front spar. Heavily balanced ailerons were fitted to the bottom wing. The tail surfaces were cantilever, all control masts concealed.

Wind tunnel results issued April 25, 1919, indicated an uncommonly high L/D of 9·9 for the VCP and predicted good stability with low stick forces. The fuselage with its smooth plywood monocoque was given credit for the low drag, but its four layers of

Aircraft Company. Clark is best known for his simple masterpiece, the world's most popular airfoil – the Clark Y. That VCP stood for these names is plausible but erroneous. Etienne Dormoy is also credited with having participated in the VCP design.

ply made it extremely heavy. The final lines were distinctly Spad-like.

By June 1919 one airframe had been destroyed in static loading tests to verify the plane's strength, but it was not until one year later that the only flying example of the VCP rolled out of the Army's engineering sheds where it had been built, ready to be test-flown. At this point the Army had invested $141,371·88 in its new pursuit. It should be emphasized that Verville, a civilian on government retainer, received no royalties or fees for his design contribution. Indeed, Verville's particular personal belief in the special nature of man's duty prevented him from ever applying for patents on his many inventions.

J. M. Johnson, the test pilot, expressed concern about the undersized tailskid; the rear fuselage was so heavy it required a special leather girth with handholds for use on the ground to give two or three men enough purchase to lift it. Ballast was added forward before the first flight, which took place June 11, 1920. Verville's annular radiator, looking like a horse collar,

gave the plane's nose an odd appearance, but the shroud was supposed to direct cooling air smoothly over the radiator. It was an idea brought back from France; developed by Bêchéreau and employed on the Bernard SAB fighter earlier that year, it was one of many attempts made in those days to minimize the resistance of radiators which water-cooled engines had to lug around, and to hide the "awful protrusions" of large V engines, but this particular annular form proved unsuitable for the widely used Liberty engines and the money for its development stopped.

A few weeks earlier, during May, that great firebrand and air power prophet General Billy Mitchell, who was then Assistant Chief of the Air Service and continually on the lookout for no-nonsense exploits with solid PR impact to boom the cause of air power, burst into Verville's McCook office with a flourish and broached the idea of grooming the VCP for the Gordon Bennett race. Verville quickly got hold of Ginny Clark and together they decided yes, it could be done, but

Verville VCP-1 pursuit (original configuration)
equipped with 300-hp Hispano-Suiza engine
and annular radiator patterned after French
SAB fighter, 1920 (USAF)

Jesse G. Vincent (U)

Verville VCP-R racer with 600-hp Packard engine, 1920 (USAF)

engineer of Packard, where he had remained ever since except for the period between August 1917 and November 1918, when he took time out to wear colonel's eagles and contribute to the war effort. He became CO of McCook experimental station in February 1918, Air Service Chief of Engineering in September, and he achieved lasting fame together with E. J. Hall, credited with the design of the Liberty engine. Vincent brought to the Liberty a background in aircraft engines dating to early 1915, and he took from his Liberty experience many new ideas when he returned to his vice-president's office at Packard — as well as a presidential pardon from Woodrow Wilson after Justice Charles Evans Hughes declared him to be guilty of conflict of interest. His new 1A-2025 engine was quite traditional in form, a water-cooled affair which had not broken the 2 pounds per horsepower barrier, employing Mercedes-style individually jacketed steel cylinders. Its only novel feature was the rather questionable placement of a single, gravity-fed carburetor of double-venturi design to feed that vast engine volume, mounted outside and below the crankcase, a feature which Vincent, however, insisted would "entirely eliminate" any fire hazard; the engine was "absolutely fireproof." The engine first ran May 19, 1920.

As it turned out Vincent was not blessed with particular powers of clairvoyance, but he made up for it by the baldness of the high-pressure selling job with which he inundated the trade press. Aside from his optimistic and premature guarantee regarding his engine's fireproof characteristics, he was quoted at the time of its tests as saying, "The greatest value of this engine, of course, will be in the commercial field . . . This is not and never has been a military nation and we can be quite certain that Congress will never provide for the military air services the money which would permit the proper development of aeronautics . . . Efficient and economic

the plane would need twice the power. With his heart beginning to pound Verville scratched out some quick calculations which convinced them the VCP could accommodate the new 500-hp Packard 1A-2025 engine, a huge V-12 with 2,025 cid, which only then was undergoing its bench tests. This was all the general wanted to know. By the end of May Mitchell had secured an appropriation and the Army was in the air race business. The plane was redesignated VCP-R (R for "Racer") and suddenly the pace of work accelerated.

The new Packard engine was the brain child of thirty-nine-year-old Jesse Gurney Vincent, like Kettering, one-time president of the SAE, an engineer from Arkansas whom Verville had known since his prewar Hudson Motor days. In 1912 Vincent moved from Hudson up to vice-president and chief

Captain Rudolf "Shorty" Schroeder with his wife, 1920 (MA)

engines like this, which will make commercial aeronautics profitable, are therefore important . . ." Packard's famous motto was "Ask the Man Who Owns One." Unfortunately, when it came to the 1A-2025 engine, which was used in many racing aeroplanes of this era, the answers would have been decidedly unflattering. In 1924 Packard went back to twin carburetors placed inside the V and adopted the monobloc wetsleeve method of construction — but embarked on other questionable innovations (e.g., oil-cooled valves).

None of this was yet known, of course, by the budding Army race team who, on July 15, 1920, were ready to launch the VCP-R on its first test flight as a racer. The shiny Packard which now bulged in the plane's nose thundered reassuringly. The sunken chin and drooping lip of tail, lanky Captain Rudolph William "Shorty" Schroeder could be clearly discerned in the racer's cockpit.

Schroeder would pilot the VCP-R in the Gordon Bennett. A Chicagoan of thirty-five who was first bitten by the flying bug in 1910 when the Gordon Bennett aeroplane race was held in his

171

home town, Schroeder got his start as grease monkey for Otto Brodie, teenager Katherine Stinson, and other bamboo-and-linen pioneers. Handicap winner of the 1919 New York–Toronto derby, he had been Air Service chief test pilot since 1918, earning world renown for his daring high-altitude flights to test the Moss turbo-supercharger. The previous February 27, puzzled by what appeared to be a 200-mph wind pushing him backwards, his oxygen suddenly exhausted, his LePère biplane leaving a contrail which in those days was mistaken for a comet, his eyes blinded by frostbite from the −67° F. windblast in his open cockpit, his gas tanks crushed by pressure, a "terrible explosion within his head," and numb despite his electric flying suit lined with fur from Chinese Nuchwang dogs, Schroeder fell 6 miles unconscious and out of control from over 33,000 feet before recovering, barely able to land. But his peak height on this flight surpassed that of Rohlfs and Casale, and Schroeder now held the world's altitude record. Then, in July, the very month of his

VCP flight tests, Schroeder received word he was being reduced in rank from major to captain as part of a broad Air Service peacetime cutback. Infuriated, he submitted his resignation in disgust and refused to fly in France wearing captain's bars after having achieved such fame as a major. Concerted pressure from the McCook team finally persuaded Schroeder to relent. Nevertheless, as soon as the race was done, and while still in France, Schroeder did quit the service. In 1924 he was vice president of the National Aeronautic Association, in 1926 the test pilot of Ford Tri-Motors and remembered by old-time Ford employees for his accordion playing. In the 1930s Schroeder, who held Commercial Pilot license number 7, became chief airline inspector with the U. S. Department of Commerce. He joined United Air Lines in 1936, retiring from the post of Vice-President for Safety in 1941 owing to ill health. He died four days after Christmas, 1952.

Schroeder's first flight in the VCP-R was inauspicious — the engine quit on takeoff. He was able to force-land

Crash of VCP-R after collision with car on Wright Field, August 1920 (Au)

without doing more than blowing a tire and bending an axle. This flight had been made with large wings which had ample area for flight test. To evaluate the clipped racing wings they would have to move to the much larger expanse of Wilbur Wright Field northeast of Dayton. There four more long-wing flights with happier endings were made, so on August 2 they decided to try the smaller wings for the first time, and an official car carrying special apparatus for timing speed runs was sent out to monitor the flight. Reports that this car measured the racer's speed at 190 mph are mistaken; no valid speed measurements were made, but 190 mph was estimated by "very approximate mathematical computations." More importantly, this car failed to judge the speed of the VCP at the critical moment. Even though the landing plane and rushing car were the only two objects on the entire expanse of Wright Field, they crashed together! It was truly a scene worthy of a Keystone Kops

slapstick. One wing was crumpled and the landing gear demolished. Rebuilding the racer took over a week of round-the-clock effort, but by August 11 repairs had been completed, a new 638-hp high-compression Packard installed, and the top wing raised 10 inches — for a better forward view! Then it was time to leave for France. There would be no further flight testing. The expedition, under Captain Walter G. Kilner, sailed from Hoboken for Antwerp on August 20, arrived at Étampes, and set about assembling the VCP-R.

The similarity of the VCP lines to the Spad racers was immediately noted by the French, who also thought the thick leather girth fitted to the tail was the plane's "most interesting" feature. The Europeans also noted, rather uncharitably, that the eagle painted on the racer's fuselage was making a bad landing! The fuel system was changed from a pressure feed of 4·5 psi and a new carburetor installed. Then the troubles began in earnest.

Verville VCP-R racer with large flight-test wings, 1920 (USAF)

Verville VCP-R racer in France for the 1920 Gordon Bennett race. Note the eagle, which to the French appeared to be making a bad landing! (MA)

Lugging the blockbuster to the Gordon Bennett start line, 1920. Note men lifting the heavy tail with leather girth; this amused the French. (F)

At first teams of men would be reduced to a frazzle hauling on the 9-foot prop just trying to get the brute to pop off. Once started the malicious engine sent torches of fire scorching back along the fuselage. Mechanics found they could quell the more spectacular aspects of this by covering the carburetor air scoops when starting, then removing the covers, but in spite of this Sadi Lecointe, the French favorite, watched one turnup with squads of fire extinguishers standing by and remarked to his friends, "I'll make sure not to be up at the same time as this fellow; he'll use up all the air!" Incredibly the VCP made no preliminary flight trials before the race.

On Cup day almost thirty minutes were needed to get the engine started. The huge Packard had cylinders like cannons and once it rumbled into life one spectator thought it sounded "like a can of nails"; another remarked, "No, more like a boiler full of rocks." Schroeder finally took off amid loud cheers from the large contingent of American spectators. This was the first time more than a few dozen people had ever seen the VCP-R, which up until then had been very closely guarded. Nevertheless, almost anyone could get odds on how many laps the smoking engine would last. Ricketts, a highly regarded chauffeur in the British contingent, offered to bet anybody anything the engine would not last two laps. In fact it did not last one.

Schroeder almost at once noticed a disturbing tendency for the engine to pour out quantities of flame when he opened the throttle, and in retrospect, aisde from the carburetion problems, there is compelling reason to believe that the fuel supplied to the Americans was not suited to the engine's high compression (half again as much as the French Hispano engines) and contributed greatly to its pre-ignition. Schroeder had not flown 10 miles when his water temperature hit 97° C., and clouds of steam, gushing from the small boxlike radiator carried between the landing gear struts, soon enveloped the entire plane. He climbed from 300 feet to over 1,000 and throttled back to cool the engine but the water temperature kept right on climbing. On the rather hurried landing the shock on the small tailskid cracked the fuselage open like an eggshell. The sting of this ignominity was sharpened by the British, who took great delight in accusing the Yanks of giving way "to a lust for high power" and rather smugly pointing out that European racers with only half the power of the VCP could equal its top performance.

Back in crates the VCP was shipped to the Curtiss plant in Garden City to be made ready for the 1920 Pulitzer Trophy race set for Thanksgiving Day just two months away. Because Schroeder had departed, his Gordon Bennett backup pilot, First Lieutenant Corliss Champion Moseley, twenty-six, would take over flying duties. Moseley, a ruggedly handsome pilot from Boise, Idaho, had played halfback at USC, ventured to France in the fall of 1917 where he trained at Tours and Issoudun, flew with the 27th Aero Squadron, 1st Pursuit Group, and officially shot down one German plane (a two-seater). After acting as test pilot at the 1st Air Depot he returned to the United States in August 1919. He did not have much opportunity to become familiar with the VCP before race day, but he approached his task with great determination.

The gray racer was the last to depart in the wild melee that was the

Lieutenant Corliss C. Moseley, 1920 (Au)

173

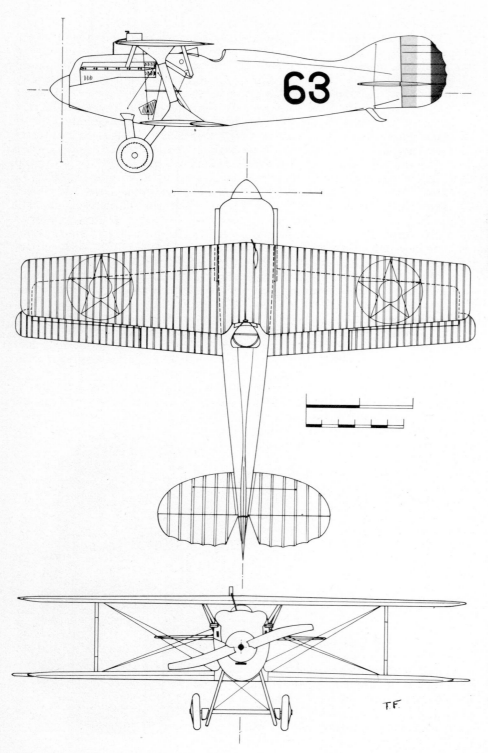

Verville VCP-R, winner 1920 Pulitzer

Verville VCP-R preparing to start in the 1920 Pulitzer race; Moseley in cockpit adjusting his goggles   *(Au)*

1920 Pulitzer, a race in which over three dozen swirling planes were flagged off from Long Island's muddy Mitchel Field. Disappearing in the haze as he circled the field, Moseley was soon seen pounding across the starting-line in a blur under lowering gray snow clouds, leaving a stream of dark smoke "several hundred feet in length." Then, in Moseley's words, "During the first three laps I managed to get the motor to run wide open for about thirty seconds each time on the second leg of the triangle and the air-speed indicator immediately ran up to over 200 miles an hour, but the violent missing would commence again and I would have to throttle down . . . With my head placed back against the headrest the blast of air produced a sort of pounding effect on my head which was very uncomfortable and the combined noises of the wires and rush of air [was] almost deafening. My own personal opinion as to the cause of the 'miss' is in the location of the carburetor . . . [which] is placed on the bottom of the motor with the air intake opening downward. I believe that at high speed the air rushing by the opening of the intake . . . makes a vacuum which causes an overrich mixture. To bear out this theory bursts of black smoke were thrown out when the motor missed. I flew the entire race at an altitude of 400 feet and although my airspeed indicator registered around 180 mph most of the time I could not quite realize I was going that fast except for the terrific windblast."

Despite his troubles; Moseley won the race. In second place, nipping at his heels, was a Thomas-Morse which once again had just half the power of the VCP. Moseley's speed was heralded as a phenomenal 178 mph — easily a world's closed-course speed record if true — and General Mitchell, smiling broadly, reached the cockpit to clasp Moseley's hand as soon as he had landed. Before others could congratulate him he was briefly glimpsed, still in flying togs, disappearing in a car with two pretty girls. A few days later a resurvey of the race course ordered by General Mitchell revealed Moseley's actual winning speed had been a disappointing 156·5 mph, and earlier inflated claims had to be downgraded.

On November 27, the Saturday

following the race, and just two weeks after Gordon Bennett competitor de Romanet had raised the world speed record to 193 mph, a series of speed flights was held at Mitchel Field and several planes took part. The VCP valiantly tried to wrest the world's speed record from France but the carburetion problems that still plagued the racer made this hopeless. Moseley was back aboard for these tests and had made six separate flights over the measured course, laid between two adjacent fields near Mitchel. The big Packard engine turned up 1,950 rpm on the ground but after takeoff, as the speed was increased, the rpm dropped off to only 1,750. Jesse Vincent himself was present but his eager ground staff, who tried every possible adjustment between flights, was unable to help. Verville later remarked, "We had more trouble with the Packard than anyone cares to admit." The top speed achieved was 186 mph, a bit short of a record. The plane was then shipped to McCook, where it was planned to put the offending carburetor in a wind tunnel and work out a redesign. Costs to this point included another $86,138·78 for converting the VCP to VCP-R and $2,541·39 to repair it for the Pulitzer race; the

Army's total investment now came to $233,802·64.

There was no military interest in the Pulitzer race during 1921, but in 1922 the tremendous resurgence in military air racing interest more than made up for the one-year hiatus. On April 16, 1922, the chief of the Air Service requested McCook Field to restore the VCP-R to top condition for participation in the 1922 Pulitzer, to be held that year at Detroit's Selfridge Field. Moseley would again fly the racer. A new Packard engine, propeller, Lamblin radiators, and smaller wheels were fitted. As flight tests progressed Moseley also asked for a new windscreen. Reconditioning work was completed June 20, 1922, and the plane redesignated R-1 (Army Racer number one). On July 14 the rejuvenated racer made a first test hop of thirty-seven minutes with Moseley flying. Its second test, a flight of 1:11, took place August 9, after which Moseley departed for over a month, thus grounding the plane until September 21 when he flew it twice. The next day its coat of new, glossy white enamel was applied and on September 25, during two hops, Moseley clocked 172·5 mph despite an overheated engine turning only 1,940 rpm. On

Verville R-1 racer, 1922, after being repainted glossy white for the Pulitzer race (USAF)

Verville R-1 racer, 1922 (USAF)

Corliss Moseley by his 1920 winning mount before their second Pulitzer try, 1922 (Au)

*Mechanic pulling propeller through on Verville
R-1 racer, Selfridge Field, 1922*   *(Au)*

September 26 he flew twelve speed runs in three flights and was electrically timed at 176 mph, hand-timed at 179. The racer was then crated and trucked from Dayton to Detroit for the race. In view of Moseley's speed of 178·9 mph for the 250-kilometer race course, which required fifty-two minutes full-throttle running and garnered sixth place, as well as surpassing his 1920 winning speed by almost 13 mph, the pre-race speed trial results seem somewhat low.

In any event the day of the R-1 was waning. Five days after the 1922 race it was reassembled at McCook Field but officially retired from service, eventually being pushed into a dusty corner of the McCook Museum warehouse. The $10,893·37 cost of revamping it for the 1922 race brought the total Army investment up to $244,696·01. Moseley too left air racing; in 1925 he organized Western Air Express, becoming vice-president and director. Twenty years later he was president of Aircraft Industries Corporation, a west coast firm. He later ran a flying school in southern California, retiring there.

Many people in those days considered a quarter of a million dollars for one racer — which only won one race — extravagant if not completely foolish. But the VCP proved to be an invaluable flying laboratory for many technical innovations. More than that, it showed for the first time how valuable such a flying laboratory could be. It also convinced the speed seekers that if they were to realize the full potential offered by their charges there was much work to be done.

WILDCAT & KITTEN

12

The most ambitious American entries for the Gordon Bennett were financed by a brazen Texas oil promoter, Seymour Ernest Jacobson Cox, who strode noisily onto the scene in yellow cowboy boots, armed with an outlandish gold-encrusted cane and topped with an umbrageous black sombrero. Nothing would have tickled Cox more than to bring the prestigious Gordon Bennett Trophy to the Lone Star State.

In the summer of 1919, before any other plans had been made to have America represented in the Gordon Bennett, the Aero Club of Texas, in true bigger-than-life Texan style, decided they alone were big enough to succeed where nations had failed. An appeal was made to Cox, president of

the General Oil Company and Prudential Securities Company, and already well known in Houston for the three aeroplanes he used daily to oversee his more than 200 miles of oil properties, and he boomed, "Let's get started. Go ahead with your plans and I'll foot all the bills." In February 1920 Cox, together with C. Anderson Wright, the Aero Club of Texas president, came to New York to meet with Henry Woodhouse, then on the Aero Club of America Contest Committee, and Augustus Post, club secretary, who had just returned from Europe and warned them that it would take no less than 200 mph to win.

Requests for a suitable design were

S. E. J. and Nellie Cox   (UPI)

Curtiss chief engineer William Gilmore with test pilot Roland Rohlfs and Curtiss manager Frank Russell   (Au)

From left, Charles D. Case, Arthur L. "Mike" Thurston, T. J. Johnston (Mrs. Nellie Cox's "personal engineer"), and Bill Irwin, the Curtiss team for the 1920 Gordon Bennett race   (MA)

sent to every U. S. manufacturer, and the news that Cox was in the market for the world's fastest plane brought forty-nine proposals. Some were unique (one designer proposed a plane without wings) and some were fantastic (another promised 1,000 mph!). At a luncheon given by Cox at the Engineers' Club in Dayton during March the list was narrowed down to twelve, and a fanciful story of the time has it that the design selected was "based on the ideas of" Cox's imperious wife Nellie, who had already made headlines as the first woman in the United States to own a personal plane. On April 13, 1920, Clement Melville Keys, president of the Curtiss Aeroplane Company at Garden City, Long Island, contracted with Mrs. Nellie Edith Cox to build one Gordon Bennett racer for her. Two months later on June 19, even though only rough layouts had so far been sketched, a second plane was ordered,

this time by Mr. Cox, whose Texas-sized bankroll of $100,000 (for starters) guaranteed that money was no object. All details were to be kept secret — these would be authentic aerial "dark horses." Such an extravagant order looked like a bonanza for Curtiss, whose seven plants had so recently and in less than two years disgorged 5,811 aeroplanes and more than 5,000 engines, almost 40 per cent of the nation's wartime aeronautic production, but who were already feeling the severe peacetime pinch. Thus they welcomed Cox's order even though in 1920 hardly any data existed upon which to base a design of 150 mph let alone the "stupendous" speed of 200.

The Texas spirit soon swept through the Curtiss engineering staff headed by William L. "Bill" Gilmore and his assistant Arthur L. "Mike" Thurston, who supervised the detail design, well aware he had less than two months

Two Texas Wildcat aeroplanes under construction, 1920 (C)

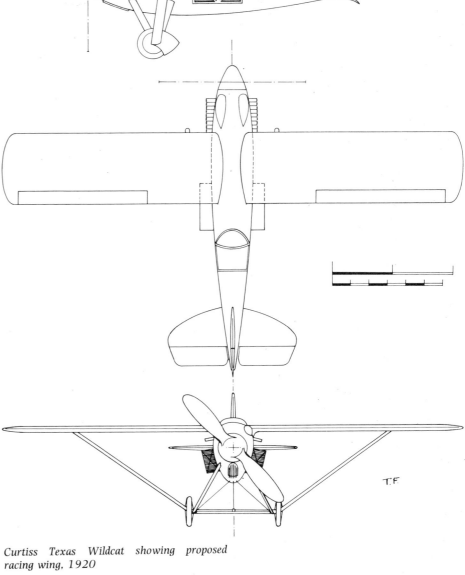

Curtiss Texas Wildcat showing proposed racing wing, 1920

before the finished racers had to be ready for shipment to France. Mrs. Cox also had her own "personal engineer," a certain T. J. Johnson who stood Texas-tall (6 feet 4 inches) but who, despite press reports, had very little to do with the design.

Frightened by the expected competition, the designers sacrificed everything in order to achieve pure speed. The fuselage would be wood, planked with stressed-skin veneer, and the pilot would sit in a virtually blind cockpit back by the tail. The wing was covered with two layers of veneer, but these were merely cover, not load-bearing. Wood was used because, as Gilmore stated, they were afraid of fabric blowing off at 200 mph. Its engine was the brand-new Curtiss C-12, a geared design capable of 430 hp which had just completed its initial bench tests in April with great

success. Wing skin radiators were considered but they were still in their infancy so boxy plate radiators were attached to the sides of the fuselage. Built of flattened tubes of brass some 8 inches wide and almost 3 feet long, placed about 1 inch apart, and trussed together by wood cross bracing, these were slung to the plane's sides like the loads of a burro, but when they cut the wind one could hear the plane "more than 10 miles away, long before seeing it," according to a witness, and it acquired the nickname "Whistling Bill." Anyone unlucky enough to be standing underneath when the plane did a slashing, full-bore pylon turn readily recalls the monumental, even terrifying screech made by these radiators.

Certainly the most profound design decision taken during the racer's conception was to build a rigid

landing gear — no shock absorbers were used — and even the tires were brick-hard. This was based on the theory that all landing fields in France were "like billiard tables" with unlimited dimensions. Unfortunately no one had

bothered to check the theory. The top speed was optimistically predicted to be 214 mph, a value considered beyond human capability by many serious scientists in those days.

A fat, high-lift wing with elephant

Texas Wildcat under construction, showing original convertible biplane configuration (C)

To my friend
Tom Foxworth
Roland Rohlfs

Curtiss Texas Wildcat with pilot Roland Rohlfs, 1920. Note fat flight-test wings, "elephant ear" ailerons susceptible to flutter.
(Au)

ear ailerons was constructed for test flights. A much smaller wing with a new and daring thin double-cambered (bi-convex) airfoil designed by Professor A. F. Zahm was planned for the race. Its use would result in a landing speed of something near 100 mph but with large, smooth fields this would not matter . . . However, just in case, both racers were designed from the very outset to accommodate a second wing so they could be converted directly into biplanes.

On July 25 the first completed craft with its large, fat wing was rolled out to await flight tests. Roland Rohlfs, twenty-eight, was to be the pilot. Rohlfs was the son of a Buffalo furniture designer; his mother was famous for writing mystery novels under the name Anna Katherine Green. He had developed an early passion for speed as a motorcycle mechanic at the Velodrome in Buffalo. The aviation bug bit him in 1914, and he started with Curtiss as a shop apprentice, eventually learned how to fly, and arrived at the chief test pilot's job through dead men's shoes. On July 30, at a ceremony held to christen the first racer, Nellie Cox, surrounded by beaming Curtiss officials, swung a bottle of vintage New York champagne

(from Glenn Curtiss' home in Hammondsport) against the racer's nose. The name chosen was indeed appropriate: Texas Wildcat. Since one radiator was not ready Rohlfs's first flight was delayed until August 2, the same day Schroeder's VCP crashed at Wright Field. Both pilots should have stayed in bed! Rohlfs, however, was up at 4 A.M. in the pre-dawn stillness to fly the Texas Wildcat from Roosevelt Field just after sunrise. The thick grass was wet and the narrow wheels cut deeply into the turf as men pushed the racer to its takeoff position, facing the burnished sun. Everybody had his fingers crossed as Rohlfs opened the throttle. The thrashing mahogany prop did not bite the air when the racer was moving at low speed and it took the entire length of Roosevelt Field to take off. Then, as he circled Mitchel Field just gaining confidence, the ailerons rippled ominously and suddenly the stick wrenched from his hand and began savagely to beat the insides of his legs. Rohlfs quickly terminated the first flight. Puzzled engineers raised the ailerons about an inch to put them in higher-energy airflow, away from a suspected "dead spot," and Rohlfs was persuaded to try more flights although at first the prospect was not too

Curtiss Texas Wildcat in racing configuration planned for the 1920 Gordon Bennett; never flown before reaching France (Au)

reassuring. For another week he flew the Wildcat with increasing success but he never did test the aeroplane with its smaller racing wing. There simply was not enough room at Roosevelt Field.

The Wildcat's sister ship, dubbed Cactus Kitten – also a suitable name; one suspects Cox was paying tribute to his wife's thorny personality – was completed but never test-flown at all – there simply was not enough time.

This frenzied activity paralleled events which increasingly preoccupied Curtiss executives. In June 1920, concerned by an unchecked invasion of penny-on-the-dollar British war surplus stock which threatened, in Keys's words, to "crush and practically annihilate" American aviation, Curtiss considered halting aeroplane production altogether. This reflected the concern of John Willys, whose Willys Overland Corporation controlled Curtiss and whose misgivings about aviation were mounting. But in mid-July, in a seeming reversal of policy, Curtiss purchased Hazelhurst Field, the 135-acre former Army field adjacent to Roosevelt

Field, bounded by Stewart and Clinton avenues, and site of Curtiss executive offices. On September 26, just two days prior to the Gordon Bennett, company undercurrents crested when control of Curtiss was sold by Willys (at a discount price) to its vice-president C. M. Keys, who now became president. Despite Curtiss' 1919 record (sales $11·806 million, profit before taxes $1·94 million), Willys had had enough of aviation. The new president was forty-four, a former Canadian from Chatsworth, Ontario, whose demeanor could be as hard and frosty as his native clime. Keys taught history after receiving his degree from the University of Toronto, but soon began a meteoric financial career as railroad editor for the *Wall Street Journal* (1903–6) and financial editor of Walter Hines Page's *World's Work*. In 1911, after becoming a U. S. citizen, he opened a successful New York brokerage house, and in 1916 was offered by Willys the post of Curtiss vice-president to market its securities and oversee the wartime expansion that overnight swelled the tiny concern to huge proportions.

From right to left, S. E. J. Cox with pilots Roland Rohlfs and Clarence Coombs, August 1920 (Au)

Keys had a brother, Conrad Roy Keys, younger by seventeen years, who in 1915 started as clerk to the production manager of the Curtiss Canada plant in Toronto, but now suddenly found himself, by virtue of his sibling status, elevated to the executive offices as assistant to the president. In 1921 Roy Keys, still in his twenties, returned to Buffalo as vice-president to manage Curtiss' plant there and to preside over the Curtiss Exhibition Company, a leftover from pre-World War I days. He managed the job quite adequately.

To his credit C. M. Keys held the iron-firm conviction that aviation had a bright future and he steered his new company adroitly through the frequent buffeting of financial storm clouds. Keys, who said "aviation is 90 per cent on the ground," was an empire builder with imperial dreams. He would not falter now; Curtiss would be the cornerstone for the vast, sprawling aviation edifice he envisioned. He built Curtiss into the GM of aeroplane

builders in the United States, and later branched out into airlines as well: in 1929 as president of TAT and later chairman of the Board when it became TWA. But Key's fortunes changed; in 1946 he was in Peru, where he was still pursuing his fading dream of world airline control. He returned to the United States, where in later years he headed a small firm producing engine components.

S. E. J. Cox needed a pilot for his Cactus Kitten. His wife had received a great deal of publicity in October 1919 when she brought her nine-year-old son from Houston to a New York boarding school by air – "the longest flight ever made by a woman" – piloted by Harold C. Block in a Curtiss K-6 Oriole. But Block was hopeless as a race pilot. Bill Wait, a young designer on the Wildcat project, recalled how, in order to give Block practice in fast landings, they stripped the fabric off an Oriole's lower wing, leaving it supported by its upper wing alone. Block cracked it up "two or three times

Clement M. Keys (C)

and never could fly it." Cox then picked ex-Sergeant Clarence B. Coombs, who was then chief test pilot with the Ordnance Engineering Company ("Orenco") and had made various obscure climbing records carrying passengers. The short, almost tiny pilot got along famously with the swarthy, loquacious Cox; as Rohlfs put it, "Birds of a feather flock together." Coombs's aviation career began in Alameda, California, in 1909 but was interrupted when he took up engine testing and auto racing for various firms including Fiat and Stutz. After enlisting, his Army flight instructors at Mineola included Reynal C. Bolling and Bert Acosta. In 1917 Coombs was a sergeant pilot with the 15th Aero Squadron; in October 1918, participating at the Belmont Air Carnival he won a widely acclaimed "race around the Statue of Liberty," flashing low over the center of Belmont Racetrack just seconds ahead of number two; and in 1919 he became a test pilot and master signal electrician at McCook

Field, having also flown in the New York–Toronto race that year.

Cox initially appointed Coombs to fly the Texas Wildcat in the Gordon Bennett race but this infuriated Rohlfs, who had taken all the risk in testing the plane yet now would apparently be deprived from having a chance at the glory. He cajoled Cox into signing an agreement that he – Rohlfs – would fly the Texas Wildcat; Coombs was reassigned to the untried Cactus Kitten. But neither plane was labeled and only Rohlfs could prove which of the two now crated planes was which. He also began to realize his paper, which had not been witnessed, might not stand up. So, when no one was looking, Rohlfs took some black paint and with a dribbling 1-inch brush he block-lettered "TEXAS WILDCAT" over the glassy red fuselage of his plane.

That Cox personally intended to send a full team of three planes to the Gordon Bennett is clearly indicated in two letters dated August 13, 1920, from Augustus Post to the Aero Club

of France affirming the "three racers" met all race requirements. The incomplete third plane provided some spare parts but they were lucky to get two completed in time. Unaccountably, the large, fat monoplane wing was not included in the 100 tons of freight Cox sent to France. Just before the expedition embarked Cox asserted loudly that his racer had attained 223 mph "in a secret test flight" but this was certainly stretching the truth.

Together with fifteen men the expedition sailed September 5 on *La Lorraine* for Le Havre. Two days later Cox and his wife followed aboard the *Imperator* with a party of five and, legend has it, a live Texas coyote – presumably the "Texas Wildcat" in person! – after a gala sendoff dinner at New York's Vanderbilt Hotel attended by Glenn Curtiss, who had entrusted to Rohlfs the American flag he carried when he won the first Gordon Bennett race back in 1909. Upon arrival in France, instead of proceeding to Étampes, site of the race, Cox had his team located at Villacoublay, airport of Morane-Saulnier, near Versailles far to the north. This was to give Cox better access to Paris. Their first hang-up came with a jolt at the first railroad tunnel: the crates carrying the planes were too wide to pass through! Rerouting cost valuable time. The second shock came when they saw the flying field. Smaller than the Long Island fields, badly rutted, and covered with grass in some places 18 inches high, it sent their morale plunging.

Meanwhile Cox had arrived in "Yew-rope" swaggering as cocksurely as a general presiding over the entire campaign, and certain of victory. Here was a species of "critter" few Europeans had ever before encountered, and Cox unwittingly added to the show by taking himself deadly seriously. The Europeans tolerated him with indulgent bemusement as they might tolerate a jam-faced kid who blundered into a drawing room. After one day most people had Cox pretty well sized up and the favorite sport, aside from the

air race, soon came to be talking to Cox merely for the sake of pulling his leg.

Back at Villacoublay more weighty matters confronted Cox's technicians. Without the large, fat flight test wing there was nothing to do but assemble the Wildcat with its untried racing wings in biplane form for maximum area and hope for the best. Rohlfs climbed aboard for the first flight but when he opened the throttle nothing happened. Flushed, he signaled animatedly again to have the chocks pulled, but they had been! The racing prop with its extreme pitch, designed for 200 mph, simply did not bite at all. So here they were with a racer which needed to be pushed to get started, even at full throttle! It took all of Villacoublay plus an adjacent farm field to lift off. The rest of the flight Rohlfs described as a "nightmare." The wing design made the plane violently unstable in pitch and it began to gallop through the air so viciously that all the inspection doors, retained by stiff springs, were torn out. Rohlfs was just able to cut the switch and deadstick back into Villacoublay, again using up both fields to land and stop. The situation was desperate. It seemed impossible that in the time remaining they could salvage their chances. Here they were 3,000 miles from home and yet the plane needed to be completely rebuilt. Impossible perhaps . . . but they must try.

Mike Thurston was awake all night feverishly laying out a new set of wings and tail section. They could use the same spars but would need all new ribs. Thurston picked the trustworthy RAF-15 airfoil; obviously they still had a lot to learn about thin, double cambered speed foils. The next day they hauled the racer into the Morane-Saulnier factory and in four more days with spirited help from the French had completely built a brand-new set of biplane wings, changed the tail, and even the prop. But time was terribly short. The plane had to be down at Étampes by 7 A.M. the

Glenn H. Curtiss at the wheel of the first aeroplane to win a race, 1909 (MA)

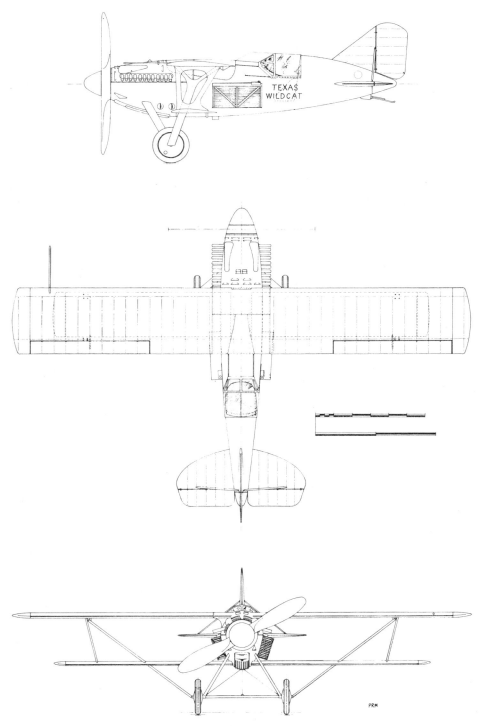

Curtiss Texas Wildcat as biplane, 1920 Gordon Bennett race

Curtiss Texas Wildcat in Morane sheds after hasty modification to biplane form for 1920 Gordon Bennett   (Au)

twenty-seventh to qualify, and it was late the afternoon of the twenty-sixth before they were applying the final coat of dope. Rohlfs's first test of the rebuilt Wildcat would have to be its 30-mile ferry flight to Étampes as well. Rohlfs put just enough fuel in "for 50 miles," then started. He gunned the racer over Villacoublay in the gathering dusk but just at the moment of liftoff his wheels struck a rut hidden in the grass. There was a sharp jolt and the racer bounded into the air, clawing for altitude. Rohlfs rejoiced over the great improvement in flying qualities, completely unaware that the shock on takeoff had collapsed all the spokes in his wheels. Rohlfs later explained that on the original American wheels the spokes had been attached tangent to the inside rim which gave them fair purchase; after a few landings had stretched these spokes a couple of turns of the nipples tightened them up and they were ready again. Nevertheless Thurston thought it would be safer to mount new wheels, so they put on a set of British Palmers, failing to notice the spokes now converged straight into a tiny piece of the rim, but this arrangement was not strong enough to withstand the takeoff jolt.

Taking a bearing from the Eiffel Tower, Rohlfs reached Étampes and set up his approach at 100 mph, slightly crosswind and "diagonal to the slope of the ground" but in the direction parallel to a line of men he could see, who he thought were standing alongside the desired landing path. Just as he made his final turn toward the field the last drop of fuel was used. No matter . . . the plane contacted the ground — and that's the last Rohlfs remembered!

The broken wheels had crumpled and the points of the rigid undercarriage dug in. The Wildcat was flipped on its back and split in two with a sickening crunch. Coming to, Rohlfs felt a stabbing pain in his shoulder, which had dislocated, at the same time thinking he'd been blinded; his goggles had filled with blood from a wound in his head. Unknown to him his life had been saved by his parachute, which absorbed the thrust of a splintered longeron which otherwise would have impaled him. Having consumed all the fuel was also fortunate — there was no fire. The French were the first at the wreckage and revived Rohlfs, according to the local custom, with *soins énergiques* which included copious draughts of brandy.

183

Texas Wildcat after crash at Étampes, 1920.
Note Palmer wheels, TEXAS WILDCAT *lettered*
on side. (Au)

Curtiss S-3 scout (C)

Glenn Curtiss and Roland Rohlfs, circa 1920
(Au)

The aerodrome, Villesauvage, in terms of its "medical, sanitary, and catering arrangements," according to the British, "thoroughly deserves its name." Rohlfs was rather painfully carted to the local hospital, such as it was, but was able to reappear and witness the race on the twenty-eighth. Remains of the Wildcat were brought into the sheds, minus the tail. Then Rohlfs took the next ship home to tell Glenn Curtiss "what a lovely guy Cox was."

The Cactus Kitten had never been uncrated. Upon its return to the States, in view of the design's failures as both monoplane and biplane, the Curtiss staff decided to try it as a triplane. It was Bill Wait's idea to use wings built for the S-3 aeroplane on the Kitten. Designed as a fighting scout near the end of World War I at that time when the blossoming of triplanes reached its culmination, only four S-3s (all 100-hp OXX-2–powered) had been built. Eddie Stinson had tested the prototype, taking off but needing full up elevator to manage the treacherous, nose-heavy plane. Although later corrections did not solve all S-3

problems, its triplane wings used a promising, thin, high-speed airfoil, the Sloan, and adapting these wings for the Cactus Kitten alleviated the dual problems of improving its flying qualities and limiting the expense of modification. It should be noted that among Curtiss staff neither racer was commonly called "Wildcat" or "Kitten"; rather, they were referred to as the "Gordon Bennetts." The new triplane became "the pet" of Glenn Curtiss, according to Wait. Bert Acosta test-flew the gaudy racer on October 21, 1921, its fire-engine–red fuselage and silver wings flashing in the sun as he streaked 193 mph over Curtiss Field. The plane was still extremely tricky, a real brute to fly, and after landing Bert swore "never again."

Wildcat and Kitten owner S. E. J. Cox still considered his racers useful as part of his grandiose scheme to stage a big air race in Texas. Deprived of his plan for the greatest oil-promotion deal of all time, the 1921 Gordon Bennett air race in Houston, Cox — while still in France — expansively offered the Cox Aeroplane Trophy with a first prize of $10,000, hoping to

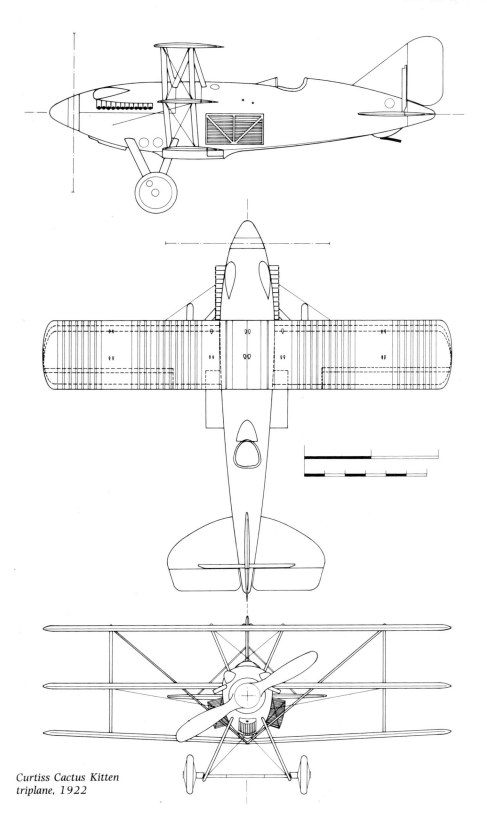

Curtiss Cactus Kitten
triplane, 1922

replace the Gordon Bennett. Nobody took him seriously and his idea aborted. Therefore, he reasoned, he must go after the 1921 Pulitzer. He was the first to deposit entry fees and with his two planes he journeyed to Omaha, Nebraska, at the end of October, the Pulitzer Trophy a gleam in his eye. There is no question that a Texas Wildcat was at Omaha. Was it the original Texas Wildcat rebuilt, despite the oft-stated general assumption that its career ended abruptly with Rohlfs's crackup in France, or perhaps the third airframe, begun in 1920 and completed in the meantime? It appeared in racing monoplane form and was to be piloted in the 1921 Pulitzer by skywriter and air mail pilot Charles B. D. Collyer. Though the Pulitzer's famous landing speed limit of 75 mph did not become official until 1922, the Texas Wildcat was ruled out in 1921 because of "excessive landing speed" (about 95 mph), but it remained on exhibition during the event. Omaha resident Louis Cutler, who as an awe-struck boy of sixteen witnessed the race and had hung around the bustling flying field for days beforehand, vividly recalled the "bright red-orange" Wildcat monoplane years later. Young

Collyer, who did not get to race, earned later fame in July 1928 with Broadway and Hollywood theatrical producer John Henry Mears when they circled the globe in twenty-three and a half days "racing the moon" in a Fairchild monoplane, *The City of New York*. They became the first Americans to fly across Siberia under the Soviet regime. On October 24 that year Collyer with California oil and auto baron Harry J. Tucker made a notable 24:51 non-stop record flight from New York to Los Angeles in Tucker's Lockheed Vega *Yankee Doodle*, beating Mac-ready's 1923 record of 26:50; on November 5 the pair departed Mines Field (today Los Angeles International), attempting the return. But fate lurked. In a blinding rainstorm Collyer slammed into the wall of Crook Canyon in the Bradshaw Mountains near Prescott, Arizona, and both were killed.

Clarence Coombs was again named to pilot the Cactus Kitten. On November 1 he surveyed the race course from an Oriole, saw only two spots suitable for emergency landing, and muttered, "The boys better keep movin'." The next day he commented, "Just a little more sun and the field will be the best I ever landed on," but the days of work

Curtiss Cactus Kitten, 1921   *(C)*

to ready the field, situated on the Missouri River flats north of town, had left areas of mud up to 6 inches deep in some spots. Bonfires burned all night did not firm up the soft spots. Ten thousand people flooded to the tiny field the next day to witness a continuous program of "hot stuff" — parachute jumping, wing-walking, and the Pulitzer air race. Coombs was the crowd's favorite and they cheered when his vivid red triplane vaulted into the air, swept around the field in a wide circle, and thundered by the starting pole at full speed, traveling "faster than anything most of the beholders had ever seen before unless it was a full-grown Nebraska tornado." Coombs flew "wild and wide," saying later, "The boat was wild and I let it have its head." The triplane was actually faster than Acosta's winning CR on the straightaways but lost time in sweeping left-hand pylon turns. A local reporter noted, "The thrill the triplane gave the crowd when Coombs — one of the smallest pilots entered, when in the plane he was hardly visible — essayed a landing at 70 mph was [even] wilder . . . [just as the pilot] took his dive for the ground his elevator mechanism stuck [sic] and the Cactus Kitten became an animated rubber ball. For 100 yards the ship galloped across the landing field, a perfect imitation of a bucking bronco from its native state." Rohlfs, witnessing the race from the sidelines, called Coombs's landing "a terrible exhibition." Coombs bounced almost 40 feet into the air — the Cactus Kitten, during its conversion, had been fitted with very effective shock absorbers, thus eliminating the design flaw that proved so disastrous to its sister ship at the Gordon Bennett. In all fairness, however, this was Coombs's first flight in the Kitten — and his last as well. Exhausted as he struggled from the cockpit after the race, he seemed bitter. "Sure I could have won the race if I had flown a course of right-hand turns" — the course direction had been changed to left-hand at the last moment over

Coombs's protest although his reason for this was not made clear — and he added he "wore himself out fighting the ship around the pylons."

Nevertheless Coombs's second place was worth $2,000, and if he seemed bitter Cox was the opposite, jovially hosting dinner for twenty-five pilots and race officials that night at Omaha's Fontenelle Hotel. The racers were brought back to New York and presumably placed in storage. In later years Clarence Coombs became manager of local service airlines and airports in upstate New York. He died in 1944, aged fifty-six.

Despite Acosta's vow never to fly the Kitten again, it was rolled out to highlight the National Flying Meet held at Curtiss Field April 30 which opened the 1922 flying season. The crowd gaped at the blurred red streak which streamed across the peaked-roof row of wooden hangars three times; Acosta is said to have done 208 mph, which would have made the Kitten the world's fastest aeroplane, but his speed was unofficial.

At this point Cox dropped rather suddenly out of the picture. Nellie Cox, while in France for the Gordon Bennett, had stridently boasted that her husband spent $250,000 to enter the event. Certainly by 1921 Cox had committed himself for at least this much and no doubt was facing the unpleasant conclusion that the return on this investment had been painfully disappointing. When the enormity of Cox's financial commitment became apparent late in 1920, General Oil Company was put into the hands of a receiver and Cox enjoined from acting as president. Had Curtiss taken this action as a clue to look deeper into Cox's background they would have discovered that Cox had already answered federal charges of fraudulent advertising in 1919. But their first clue that all was not well came in March 1922 when the bottom fell out. Cox, in New York with his wife, was arrested and charged with using the mails to defraud in connection with

stock sales in three of his companies. Then in July Cox was sued for the two Curtiss racing planes by the General Oil Company trustees, who claimed he had illegally used General Oil funds to pay for their construction. The suit, which claimed both planes had been returned to the Curtiss Long Island plant, was brought for $625,000, which Cox was accused of having retained for his own use, and of which "at least" $200,000 was used to pay for the racers.

For a time Cox's world began to crumble. The Federal Trade Commission ordered Cox and his wife to stop "fake representations" but Cox, still blasé in spite of it all, remarked only that he might have been "a little too optimistic in some of the things I said." Taken to Houston in custody, he was indicted before a federal grand jury which heard a parade of government witnesses tell how faith in Cox's literature led them to invest in worthless stocks. Cox's flamboyant brochures had promised his shareholders "a lake of gold" and indicated the value of land acreage held in west Texas was some $5,000 per acre. But the owner stepped up and said he'd "sell it all for a good cigar." General Oil stock which Cox peddled for $14 per share was in fact worth no more than 8 ¢. Nevertheless the jury returned deadlocked and Cox was freed. The legend of "Lucky Cox" had begun.

The oil business was big and rowdy in those days and it reached all the way to the White House; the scandal involving the Naval Oil Reserve at Teapot Dome, Wyoming, was filling headlines simultaneously with Cox's machinations in Texas. Lucky Cox managed for a time to steer clear of his adversaries. Curtiss apparently never got paid in full for their racers and hung on to them, even feeling free to make extensive new air race plans for the triplane Kitten.

Yet by January 1923 Cox was embroiled in an intrigue of greed gigantic even by Texas standards. Dr. Frederick A. Cook of Polar notoriety,

who by then had found richer game than his tame Eskimos Ahwelch and Etukisuk to hand a gold brick, was embarked on a "reloading scheme" so profitable that Cox, on Cook's staff as publicity manager, was drawing $2,000 per week. Cook's scheme was deceptively simple. He merely consolidated two hundred defunct oil companies into a single holding company and promised mutual solidarity on the theory that "a combination of nothing equals something." Credulous stockholders would merely exchange their worthless stock for shares in the new holding company, but with the sly kicker that they had to ante up another 25 per cent in cash. So successful was the scheme that stockholders in over fifty solvent oil companies were also bombarded by Cox under forged letterheads urging the same plan for them. Cox blitzed Houston and its environs in his personal planes to advertise while Cook raked in literally millions. Such a blatant plot was possible in 1923 because of loose Texas statutes which allowed promoters to operate unsupervised as common law trusts. When the federal government began to crack down most fraudulent operators soon folded, but Cook and Cox showed enough sheer effrontery to face it out and stay "in business."

Cox in the meantime found that a very successful method for selling oil stock was as old as the Middle Ages. His advertising now brazenly listed on his staff an "oil witch" whose forked peach-tree limb was irresistibly attracted to oil deposits. The faithful and opportunistic flocked to buy stock in the company that had exclusive claim to this wizard, and with more than a dozen firms between which to juggle his funds Cox was staying one step ahead of the government. In reality the only salable assets these companies owned were their "sucker lists."

Finally the long arm caught up with Cox as it raked in scores of fast-talking, freewheeling, wildcat oil promoters. On November 21, 1923, both Cook and Cox were sentenced to federal

Al Williams with the "U. S. Navy Triplane" (the Cactus Kitten), proposed 1922 Pulitzer entry (C)

Al Williams in cockpit of the Cactus Kitten, still hopeful to be a 1922 Pulitzer entry (Au)

penitentiary, Cook swearing he had only "altruistic aims" in his ventures; what he really wanted was an oil field that would "remain a monument to my name and memory." Roland Rohlfs recalled that years before, his father had taken him to see Dr. Cook at Buffalo's Saturn Club just after Cook's Polar exploits. The elder Rohlfs told his son, "This man Cook is either the world's greatest adventurer or the world's greatest crook; either way I want you to shake his hand!"

Cox went to Leavenworth Federal Penitentiary in February 1924 and Cook arrived to be his cellmate in April 1925. Together they edited the prison publication but Cook had lost his taste for the orotund discourses New York *Herald* readers had been subjected to during his days of Polar publicity. Cox was in and out of Leavenworth twice over the next sixteen years, spending almost ten years behind bars, but he left behind at Curtiss a crack aeronautic team that

would not have been put together without his stimulus. This team became the nucleus of a vigorous young company that now found itself irrevocably attuned to speed and racing.

The Kitten's story ended in 1922 but not until it had been briefly considered for the Pulitzer race that year, designated Curtiss TR (not to be confused with the Curtiss-built Navy TS/TR), and in mid-September slated to be flown by the Navy's Al Williams. With Cox gone, Curtiss funded the racer's preparations; they may have been aided by the Navy since the words "U. S. Navy triplane" were applied, but this is unconfirmed and the Kitten never received a Navy serial number. Another possibility is that Curtiss was courting Navy favor in hopes of eliciting Navy support. Al Williams did test-fly the Kitten. Eugene E. Wilson, then attached to the Navy's aero engine department, witnessed the flight and reported that Williams admitted afterward he had

been "taken for a ride"; "He sure looked it when he got out of the ship," recalled Wilson. Shortly after October 1 Williams was reassigned to the second and recently modified CR racer. Neither the Texas Wildcat nor the Cactus Kitten triplane ever flew again.[1]

The Cactus Kitten was by no means the only Curtiss triplane racer. An earlier triplane appeared even before the end of World War I and indeed even outlasted the Kitten in active air

racing. This was the Curtiss model 18, originally designed by Charles Kirkham in 1917, the last great year of triplanes, as a bed for his remarkable K-12 engine.

Charles B. Kirkham was born in the pleasant, lush vineyard region of New York at Thurston on a serene November day in 1881, son of John Kirkham, an ambitious carpenter who soon moved his family to Taggart's, a small road junction between Bath and Hammondsport, where he set up first a planing mill and later a machine shop. Before he was twenty, Charles, eager to obtain experience away from home, took a job at Seneca Falls in a plant making printing presses, but he caught diphtheria and had to return home, where, to occupy his five-month bedridden convalescence, he enrolled in an International Correspondence Schools engineering course. In 1901, before Charles had returned home sick, an enterprising young bicycle dealer living nearby, who had secured from

---

[1] S. E. J. Cox had nothing to do with the Cox-Klemin Aircraft Company, producers of several types of military planes, and also in financial straits at this time. Its organizers were Captain L. George Cox, a nine-victory ace of the RAF, and Professor Alexander Klemin, World War I head of the McCook Field Structures Branch, who by 1922 had left aircraft manufacturing to return to teaching as associate professor of aeronautical engineering at NYU.

Curtiss-Kirkham 18-B, 1918, Kirkham's battleplane design as a bed for his remarkable new K-12 engine, after later modification to biplane (C)

Buffalo a set of mail-order castings for a small engine with which to equip his bicycle, came to John Kirkham to have the parts machined. Charles Kirkham later took up serious competitive cycling, and thus met the would-be motorcycle dealer – Glenn Curtiss. Curtiss' contraption intrigued Charlie Kirkham, who in 1902 designed and built a twin-cylinder motorcycle engine which he was soon producing for Curtiss to enhance his burgeoning motorcycle sales. Charlie Kirkham soon had assistants under his tutelage, his younger brothers Clarence and Percy. They outgrew their first small facilities and moved to Bath, where the business grew until October 1905 when Curtiss formed his own company in Hammondsport, and began to produce his own engines. Having looked beyond the loss of Curtiss' business, Kirkham had in 1904 built two four-cylinder automobile engines, the earliest to have adjustable tappets, high-tension distributor using a single coil, and cone clutch. These were followed by a six-cylinder version, undoubtedly the first auto engine of

this type in the United States. By 1906 Kirkham's company had begun a four-year production run of six-cylinder engines for the Pullman Car Company of Harrisburg, Pennsylvania. Charlie, who always loved speed, became a fairly expert driver and occasional auto racer.

When his old friend Glenn Curtiss began pioneering aviation experiments a few miles away in 1907 with Alexander Graham Bell's Aerial Experiment Association, Kirkham became intrigued. Presently, he was approached about producing specially lightened versions of his auto engines for use in the flying machines, and during 1909 two aeroplanes built by AEA members at Baddeck, Nova Scotia, Bell's home, used Kirkham six-cylinder 35-hp engines. Late that year he also supplied a four-cylinder 22-hp engine to William T. Thomas, a Curtiss employee at Hammondsport who was busy building an aeroplane in a barn there. Thomas completed his plane and began flying it in the spring of 1910, an activity which previewed his own company (see Chapter 18). Kirkham's novel

feature was an odd concentric valve arrangement in which both intake and exhaust valves were assembled coaxially with the intake valve in the center so that the intake gas would cool the troublesome exhaust valve. Kirkham used this feature successfully for years.

Activities blossomed. Kirkham and a local mechanic named Fred Eells, who learned to fly in a Kirkham-powered plane, formed an aeroplane company at Bath which lasted a year. Then Kirkham moved to Savona and devoted himself full time to aviation, coming out with three new aeroplane engines – four-cylinder 35 hp, six-cylinder 70 hp, and even a V-12 of 120 hp. By 1912 Kirkham's aero engines were established nationwide. However, in 1913 competitive engines began appearing in numbers, the inevitable slump of public interest in exhibition flying occurred, and Kirkham's business declined; the last ads of his company at Savona appeared significantly in the magazines of August 1914. Unknown to the despondent engineer events in Europe that month would ensure a continuing need for his talent. He worked briefly as Aeromarine chief engineer at Avondale, New Jersey, but early in 1915 his old associate Curtiss, in desperation, implored Kirkham to return to upstate New York after the British stopped all deliveries of Curtiss' OX engine because it did not produce the advertised horsepower. Curtiss was appalled at Kirkham's brutal full-throttle tests of the OX, but Charlie has written that "you do not have to baby properly designed engines."

Within two weeks Kirkham had completely redesigned the intake manifold, altered the cam followers and bearings, changed the carburetor, and installed aluminum pistons using three narrow rings instead of two wide ones, and thus transformed an engine unable to exceed 75 hp at 1,400 rpm – 90 had been promised – into one which could deliver over 100 hp "for more than four hours steady," as Charlie

boasted. Deliveries of the OX, now the -2, resumed in 1916, and the design soon evolved into the world-famous OX-5. Curtiss, who disliked the growing humdrum of production problems, was at heart a Yankee tinkerer and longed for a hideaway for pure experimenting in his expanding empire. His heart lured him back to Garden City, site of early flying, and in 1917 he took a select staff there to install them in such a department. Included was that irascible man, in so many curious ways Curtiss' own shadow, Charlie Kirkham with his extraordinary and already legendary ability to see through the nuts and bolts and perceive remarkable evolutions, using hard judgment both sound and visionary. He became chief engineer.

It was to counter the challenge of Wright-Martin's mammoth Hispano engine production that Curtiss endorsed Kirkham's bold plan for an all-new advanced military engine. Kirkham's first prototype, the AB, which was ready in April 1917, displeased the master because of its weight. He enlarged the bore and stroke each $\frac{1}{2}$ inch and lightened the structure, and thus produced the momentous K-12 engine which, Kirkham insisted, deserved its own special aeroplane.

Under Gilmore's approval, Kirkham worked on the model 18 as his own project. The K-12 embodied bold new concepts in engine construction and Kirkham wanted a similarly inspired battleplane of great firepower (two forward-pointing Marlin guns, two rearward-pointing Lewis guns) yet possessing superior performance, which the light (136 pounds less than the Liberty) but powerful (also 400 hp) K-12 should provide. Referred to variously as the Kirkham fighter or Curtiss Wasp, its construction embodied the first use by Curtiss of three-ply monocoque on a landplane; its wing employed seven spanwise beams very close together with no ribs, only chordwise cap strips; and its tail surfaces were covered with sweet-smelling cedar.

Curtiss-Kirkham 18-T-2 with straight wings, 1918   *(C)*

Curtiss-Kirkham 18-T-2 at Rockaway, 1919   *(C)*

On March 30, 1918, the Navy ordered two triplanes under contract 37372 — their first American-designed fighters — and just three months later on July 5, under the accelerated pace of war, Roland Rohlfs made the first test flight. As he buckled in, Rohlfs cast a glance toward Kirkham, who was talking to a group of men, his back turned; impressed by this show of confidence in the untried triplane, Rohlfs took off. The three large wings provided phenomenal powers of climb, something over 2,000 feet per minute and the aeroplane's success prompted Mike Thurston to comment, "Now we know how to balance an aeroplane before it flies." He spoke prematurely; the wings had to be subsequently swept back 5 degrees to accommodate a c.g. which had been too far aft with the prototype straight wings. The side-mounted plate radiators cooled too much but at 1,900 rpm the K-12 behaved perfectly. The triplane was also speedy. On August 19, 1918, Rohlfs in A-3325, the first of the Navy's two, was credited unofficially with reaching 163 mph, faster than any World War I combat plane; he later commented "it didn't seem very fast to me but in 1918 that was it [i.e., probably the world's fastest]." If the Gordon Bennett racer was "Whistling Bill," the triplane became "Whistling Rufus."

Despite such promising results the Navy was reluctant to order more. Interest was waning in triplanes, which because of their structure were generally poor gun platforms and were also plagued with poor visibility. The Army especially wanted a biplane after borrowing the Navy triplane for testing in September and experiencing disappointing results. Curtiss responded by putting biplane wings on the 18 fuselage which led to the new designations 18-B (biplane) and 18-T (triplane). The Army ordered two of each (order CS-152); their two triplanes were issued serial numbers 40065 and 40066, but only the former was delivered, arriving at McCook Field in February 1919 for static strength tests. The first of two 18-Bs arrived in June but a crash soon after ended the Army's interest in that type. Only the Navy's two 18-Ts and one which went to Bolivia remained active.

Rohlfs vividly demonstrated the aeroplane's climbing powers beginning in March 1919. During the first six test flights he burnt out three of the unsupercharged K-12 engines because, according to Rohlfs, a "faulty oiling system would not work at the steep climb angle." On one of the test hops Rohlfs from his mighty altitude was "admiring the fleecy grandeur of a giant cumulus cloud [which] suddenly turned over in the sky, or so it appeared. The sky turned gray, and thinking perhaps another cloud was blocking the light, I turned to look at the sun, and all went black. The next thing I remembered was a high-pitched screech and I could see nothing. Then the world opened up before me as the Wasp emerged from a cloud in a headlong plunge. I barely regained control before landing on the field underneath." The oxygen supply had frozen in the dispensing apparatus and he had passed out. The barograph trace revealed a vertical drop of 10,000 feet! On July 25, 1919, Rohlfs climbed 30,100 feet and a few weeks later, on September 19, he struggled up to an unofficial world's altitude record of 34,610 feet. During the flight Rohlfs recalled that he "could see nearly 200 miles away . . . yet to my surprise there was no apparent curvature to the horizon. I marveled at this seemingly straight line, the immensity of the circle, the mass it enclosed, the weight. Could it be possible — I wondered — does all this float in space? With a feeling akin to awe I turned from the surrounding void and started my descent to Mother Earth."

Glenn Curtiss, who was tied up that day in a board meeting, left the conference room to welcome Rohlfs down. Rohlfs's mount was A-3325 with large area wings spanning almost 41 feet and having two bays, thus resulting in the designation 18-T-2; interchangeable, short-span, single-bay wings could be fitted for speed, resulting in an 18-T-1.

Bolivia, a nation long eager for its own air force but checked by the high, thin altitudes of its Andean fields – no aeroplane had yet succeeded in taking off from El Alto, the 13,500-foot airport at La Paz – ordered an 18-T-2 after hearing of Rohlfs's impressive altitude record. One was sent late in 1919 – it was probably the undelivered Army 40066 – together with demonstration pilot Donald Hudson, who took off from El Alto with such ease the Bolivians became ecstatic and formed their own air force on the spot, naming Hudson chief pilot! On May 19, 1920, Hudson made a magnificent flight over the high (21,185 feet), majestic peak of Mount Illimani, crossing the Andes at more than 30,000 feet, a South American altitude record. A crash one year later in May 1921 which demolished the triplane (Hudson was unhurt) ended the air force and cooled U. S.-Bolivian relations considerably.

Curtiss had put A-3325 on floats

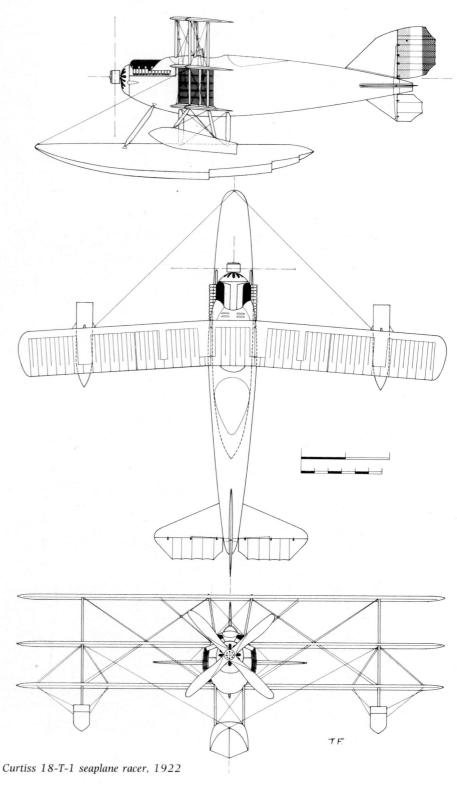

(the type used on N-9 trainers) and in April 1920 at Rockaway Beach on Long Island's south shore Rohlfs flew it to 138 mph. However, both U. S. Navy triplanes were entered in the 1920 Pulitzer to race as 18-T-1 landplanes. A-3325 was flown by Lieutenant Commander Willis Bradley Haviland, thirty, a Lafayette Escadrille veteran from St. Paul, Minnesota. Haviland had scored one victory during his eleven-month Lafayette tenure, then transferred to naval aviation. Marine Second Lieutenant W. D. Culbertson flew A-3326, taking off in the race's last heat, and flashed around the course for the fastest first lap in the race, but unfortunately neither pilot had a chance to distinguish himself. Both were forced to retire with engine malfunctions before finishing the distance. In 1920 Haviland was Director of Schools for American Airways; he also represented a national distillery. In World War II, after South Pacific service, he became CO of NAS Whidbey Island, Washington, but died in November 1944.

The 18-T triplane had been designed strictly to get maximum advantage from the K-12 engine, but after the

Curtiss 18-T-1 as flown in the 1920 Pulitzer race; pilot, Lafayette Escadrille alumnus Willis B. Haviland (USAF)

Curtiss 18-T-1 seaplane racer, 1922

Armistice J. N. Willys was unsure how to proceed with K-12 development. Charles Kirkham had left on a sour note to be succeeded by Finlay R. Porter, who took the brilliant K-12 principles and updated them into the geared C-12, tested in January 1920, displayed on the Curtiss Eagle-2 at the New York Aero Show in March, and fitted to the Wildcat and Kitten in July. These were all civil planes but there was no civil market in 1920. Willys and Porter both began to question the future for high-powered engines no one seemed to want, and both soon quit Curtiss. Clement M. Keys then took over with his intuitive, gut feeling that engineering-wise they were on the right track and to hell with the civil market, so he temporarily submerged the emphasis on civil aspects and concentrated on seeking speed. The C-12 had performed beautifully in the Wildcat and Kitten; the treachery of the aeroplanes it powered prevented it from showing what its formula was

really worth for pure speed. An updated C-12, called CD-12 (D for "direct drive"), had appeared in 1921, and during the summer of 1922 the Navy decided to use two of these new engines to stage a comeback for the 18-T triplane. After their K-12 engine breakdowns suffered during the 1920 Pulitzer, the two triplanes had been placed in storage in Philadelphia. Now, a year and a half later, they were fitted with three pontoons – a large central pontoon supplemented by two small wingtip floats; these necessitated an auxiliary rudder beneath the fuselage – and entered in the 1922 Curtiss Marine Trophy race. The first CD-12 built, which had been the first Curtiss engine to pass the grueling fifty-hour endurance test, was installed in A-3325 turning a four-blade Charavay prop; this plane was to be flown by Rutledge Irvine, and a maximum speed of 131 mph was confidently predicted.

The Curtiss Marine Trophy was a huge silver statue sponsored by Glenn

Curtiss 18-T-1 racer in flight, 1922 Curtiss Marine Trophy race   *(USAF)*

Curtiss 18-T-1 racer "hydroplaning" during the 1922 Curtiss Marine Trophy race (USAF)

Curtiss, who had been intrigued with the possibilities of seaplanes ever since his pioneering hydro-aeroplane experiments of 1911, and determined to promote them with a competition. Never properly organized, the trophy in previous years before and during World War I had drifted between unknown aviators for obscure feats of endurance. But in 1922 in a move that was to augur propitiously for the future, the competition's objective was changed from distance to speed, and this new emphasis provided the perfect opportunity for the spirited group of Navy pilots that comprised Lieutenant Commander Marc A. "Pete" Mitscher's Test Board at Anacostia – a sort of rudimentary high-speed flight – to gain air racing experience. The significance and reverberations were profound. The 1922 Curtiss Marine Trophy was the initiation for later, more important air races, both land and sea, which would be overwhelmed by many of these Navy pilots.

For no-holds-barred rivalry the 1922 Curtiss Marine Trophy has to rank as one of the most aggressively flown air races of the 1920s. After being delayed one day by driving rain and gales, it was flown in blustery, wind-whipped chop and contested over eight laps of a triangle set on the Detroit River literally in downtown Detroit, the real thrills coming in the fifth lap when contestants had to dive for the water and negotiate a hairpin turn while taxiing. Again, the Curtiss triplanes proved to be the speediest entries. Rutledge Irvine, flying A-3325, dove his big triplane onto the river, hardly slowing down and seemingly unmindful of the stiff crosswind blowing him steadily toward a barge on which the race judges were becoming decidedly nervous. He bounced several times until he could kill his speed and slithered steeply around the control in a plume of spray. The rough landing wrenched the left wing pontoon loose, however, and on his next flying lap Irvine

Curtiss 18-T-1 in the 1923 Liberty Engine Builders' Trophy race, before its crash (USAF)

found the throbbing aeroplane almost impossible to fly. Grimly he forged on, but when roaring just above the Edison plant's six belching smokestacks the plane was tossed out of control. Irvine forced it into a steep slip toward a small cove, but realizing he would overshoot he deliberately aimed for a mountain of coal piled nearby. The ungainly machine crumpled around Irvine, who rolled out unhurt and picked himself up, black with coal dust but smiling wanly, at the bottom 40 feet below.

Flying A-3326 was Marine Lawson H. Sanderson, who, porpoising badly while shooting the hairpin at almost flying speed, had narrowly averted a collision with Patterson's Gallaudet, which conked out at the control barge. Now, turning into the last lap he was in the lead by some 12 mph after brilliantly cutting out his competition on wing-to-wing pylon turns. Suddenly his engine faltered — and Sanderson, with victory literally in sight, was helplessly reduced to the ignominity of having to be towed to shore — out of gas! The race winner was Lieutenant A. W. "Jake" Gorton, who thus earned

a sure spot on the Navy's historic 1923 Schneider team, then forming. Harold Brow, whose engine boiled over in the race, recalled that the pilots — all close friends — split the prize, each coming away with "about $200."

In 1923 the Curtiss triplane story comes to a close when the last remaining 18-T triplane, A-3326, painted a deep orange and still CD-12—equipped, was entered in the 1923 Liberty Engine Builders' Trophy race, one of the many races at the NAR that year. Its pilot was Ensign D. C. Allen, who had been picked to win hands down. The plane "screamed like a typhoon" as it neared the end of its first lap. Suddenly, approaching the edge of Lambert Field, which was packed with people and popcorn, the engine crankshaft broke. Allen was at 500 feet, high enough to turn away from the clusters of booths and crowds and land in a muddy field. He and his mechanic, Chief Machinist's Mate T. G. Hughes, aboard in the rear seat, ducked as the plane bounced along 50 feet then flipped over onto its back. They emerged shaken but unhurt, but the triplane was demolished. Curtiss,

after this incident, seemed especially anxious to make clear that the engine had been an overboosted CD-12, raced against their wishes, in which the offending crankshaft — running 400 rpm too fast — was not a Curtiss drop-forged model but an experimental slab-forging without proper grain flow.

Kirkham had left Curtiss in the summer of 1919 and opened an office in New York City as an aviation consultant. In 1920 he went to Germany where he was engineer in charge of construction of twenty all-metal Junkers J.L.6 monoplanes to be exported to the United States; he always particularly valued this experience with early metal aeroplanes. Upon his return he founded the Kirkham Products Corporation in the old James V. Martin factory in Garden City, to undertake special projects, subcontracts, and difficult parts machining jobs. The officers of his firm included besides himself as president speedplane designers Harry T. Booth as vice-president and Mike Thurston as secretary-treasurer. Through the 1920s this team produced a unique and often visionary collection of aeroplanes and engines for customers who included Harold S. Vanderbilt, pioneer aviator Leonard W. Bonney, and speed king Al Williams. By the early 1930s the firm had moved to Farmingdale, Long Island, first occupying part of the Fairchild plant there, later in 1934 moving to the site formerly occupied by Fulton Motor Company. In 1938 Kirkham reorganized his firm with pioneer aviator Robert Simon to become the Liberty Aircraft Products Corporation, but left soon after in 1940. Thereafter he engaged in part-time consulting and lived in Montgomery, New York, until his death on New Year's Eve, 1969, at the age of 88.

Roland Rohlfs left Curtiss in 1921 to become operations manager of Aeromarine Airways, later sales manager of Claude Neon Lights. He originated the first aerial advertising by aeroplane, flying at night with neon messages fixed below the wings, and

became vice-president of Aerial Advertising. This effort faltered in the Depression, and during the early 1930s Rohlfs could be found shuttling Ford Tri-Motors between the three New York airports, North Beach (later La Guardia), Floyd Bennett, and Newark. He joined the Civil Aeronautics Administration in 1938 and became chief of the technical section. He retired in 1953 after nearly four decades in aviation, but remained vital and active until well into the 1970s.

So ended the triplane racers which for a time had been among the fastest in the world. Curtiss applied important lessons gleaned from these curious machines as steppingstones toward the vastly improved racers to follow.

THE GOLDEN THOROUGHBREDS

13

The Curtiss CR Racers

The lessons of 1920 had been difficult to take but definite. Inadequate preparation on top of allowing themselves to be misled into sacrificing everything for speed cost the Americans dearly. The 1920 Gordon Bennett, to their great surprise, was won by a Nieuport 29V, a fairly standard biplane incapable of the exotic speed Curtiss had sought. This, then, called for a total about-face in their racer design philosophy, and the Curtiss racers of 1921, designed for the U. S. Navy, were conventional biplanes with docile landing speeds and gentle flying qualities — planes that pilots had confidence in riding out to their limits of speed.

The 1921 racers were built around the latest version of Curtiss' maturing V-12 aero engine. The departure of F. R. Porter, although not regretted since he had proven to be almost totally disorganized and had no regard for quality control, nevertheless put the future of the C-12 in jeopardy, but a young engineering graduate from Massachusetts, who had joined Curtiss in July 1916 fresh from Worcester Tech, now, at the age of twenty-six, succeeded Porter as chief motor engineer. His name was Arthur Nutt and he took over just when Curtiss needed to arrest their costly development and start selling. The single biggest hang-up with the C-12 was its irksome reduction gearing, so this was thrown out. By adopting direct drive — which meant reduction of engine rpm, so as not to whirl too fast the wooden clubs then generally used as propellers – durability was dramatically improved. The spark plugs were relocated to the inside of the V, although less accessible, to improve combustion.[1] Otherwise the new engine – called CD-12 – was identical to the C-12, including at first, for bench testing, the use of temperamental, impractical, and even hazardous Claudel-Hobson double-inverted carburetors. Zenith carburetors were soon fitted and used for all flying.

The first CD-12 was shipped from Curtiss to McCook Field for testing February 25, 1921, amid Army and Navy bickering over the test duration. The Navy wanted sixty hours while the Army said fifty was enough. An Army telegram of March 9 stated that if fifty hours was not agreed upon they would relinquish the CD-12 to the Navy and pursue geared C-12 development, which makes it appear Curtiss still foresaw a future for the C-12. Finally a fifty-hour test was agreed upon in five-hour segments, preceded by a ten-hour preliminary test to satisfy the Navy. On the preliminary run, made during April with CD-12 number 1 (USN bureau number 9673), the engine produced 368 hp at 2,100 rpm, some 65 hp less than the geared C-12 for the same propeller speed, but since it came through in such good condition it was decided to run the fifty-hour test at 2,000 rpm instead of 1,800 as originally planned. To regain some lost power the compression was boldly raised from 5·23 to 5·65 but had to be lowered to 5·37 after piston trouble began to develop. The test was completed on June 24 to the jubilation of young Arthur Nutt, for this was the first Curtiss wetsleeve monobloc engine to complete the fifty-hour run successfully. His CD-12 had given an average power of 367 hp at 1,976 rpm, with a peak of 393 hp at 2,090

rpm. News of CD-12 success reached even to England, where Bristol chief engineer Captain Frank Barnwell in March 1921 suggested substituting a shark-nosed CD-12 for the daisy-like air-cooled radial mounted flat to the wind in one of his F-scouts. This idea was not carried through then but, coming from England, proved to be prophetic.

Meanwhile the Navy had ordered two CD-12s (contract 53933) and plans were already afoot to use them for racing. Even in its derated form this engine seemed unbeatable. They found they could coax 405 hp from it at 2,000 rpm by using racing pistons of 6·1 compression and 50 per cent benzole fuel. This was about the same power produced by its grandfather, the K-12 – but on 500 less rpm, which reveals the benefit of lessons learned in mixing fuels and boosting cylinder pressures over the intervening three years. Only four CD-12s were built, however, all eventually going to the Navy. The second and fourth were installed in the 1921 racers during July 1921 after changing over to intake manifolds and Ball & Ball carburetors like those of the K-12. The third and fourth CD-12s were later used to power a prototype twin-engine Curtiss torpedo bomber, the CT A-5890, delivered January 1922, but orders for more were canceled. The first CD-12, which had passed the fifty-hour test so beautifully, powered the 18-T triplane A-3325 in 1922 and today is preserved in the Smithsonian.

The new racer design was designated CR for "Curtiss Racer" (S. E. J. Cox's 1920 racers, although Curtiss-built, were always called by insiders the Gordon Bennetts). Harry T. Booth and Mike Thurston were the CR project engineers in charge, reporting to Curtiss chief engineer William L. Gilmore. Their target completion date would have the racer ready for entry in the Pulitzer race scheduled for early September in Detroit. Still smarting from the Texas Wildcat fiasco, the designers were more than happy to

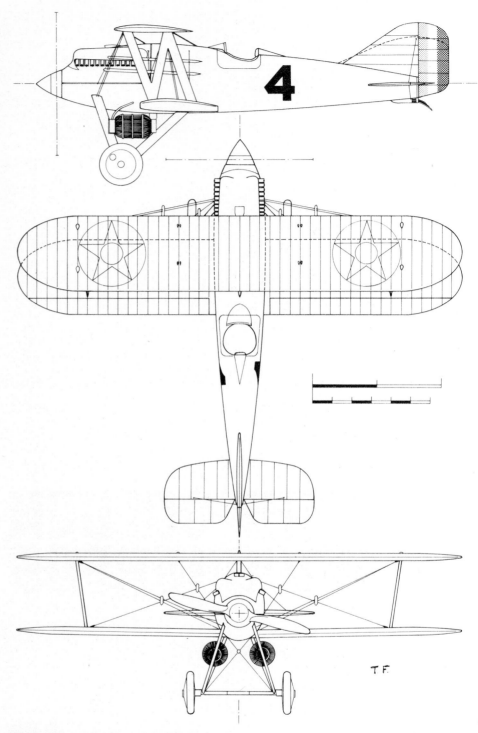

Curtiss CR-1, winner 1921 Pulitzer; note Lamblin radiators and original, low-profile tail denoted by dotted line.

[1] Despite some reports, the move had nothing to do with the oil fouling that had occasionally plagued the C-12's outboard plugs.

accommodate Navy wishes that landing speeds be limited to something near 75 mph, which of course was later invoked as a Pulitzer requirement. This involved the use of "lots of sail" together with a sturdy undercarriage; yet the surface exposed head on to the wind had to be kept to a minimum. Kirkham's genius had forseen as early as 1916 that the correct formula for speed was high power (large engine volume) coupled with low frontal area. This philosophy, carried down to the CD-12, now paid off handsomely. Two years later, when the CRs reached Europe with such stunning success, the Italians coined a new word when referring to CR frontal area: they called it *piccolissimo*. Grover Loening called it simply "aerodynamic penetration."

The new racer's layout was conceived "about the first of June," according to Bill Wait, who headed the design team's drafting department then. Young William Wait was rapidly acquiring responsibility in the Curtiss experimental projects office. He had shared patents on wing radiators with Mike Thurston and was destined to become responsible for the designs of future Curtiss racers. As a boy in Kinderhook, New York, in those days a town still well known as the birthplace of Martin Van Buren, his life came under the weighty juridical shadow cast by his renowned grandfather which had always pointed toward a law career for him. In 1910 he was running a neighbor's garage when Glenn Curtiss flew in, preparing for his Albany–New York *Scientific American* flight. Wait went to see Curtiss' contraption in its tent at Albany and there confronted the dark, scraggly pilot whose hypnotic hazel eyes glowed with a single-minded intensity. After proving his mettle by assisting the repair of a missing cylinder he "stayed three days chewing the rag" with Curtiss. Thoroughly bitten, he tried to build his own aeroplane around a Cameron auto engine, but cracked it up towing it behind a car. Years passed until, in

the spring of 1917, while visiting the Sperry factory on Long Island, he suddenly found himself face to face with Curtiss. Those hazel eyes were still as intense and they bored right into him. "Come on over to Garden City for lunch . . ." Then, all at once, "Nels [Dawson, shop foreman] — put this man to work." That was it.

Wait's drawings passed to the shop, where construction was straightforward with very close attention to detail. The fuselage was a wood monocoque covered with 2-inch–wide strips of Curtiss-ply — a two-ply spruce veneer 3/32 inch thick — which was casein-glued and tacked in three layers diagonal to the bulkheads but crosswise to each other. When building the shell, copper tacks were driven through the ply into the hardwood form underneath, then clinched over inside when the form was removed. The engine mount was wood. Wings were all-wood multi-cellular structures employing several solid spruce spanwise webs, also planked with Curtiss-ply, but unlike the high-speed wing of 1920, this year the wing skin was load-bearing. The wood construction was easy to fabricate, strong and rigid, and lent itself to an exquisite, glossy surface finish. Once again, the Sloan airfoil was adopted. The CR upper wing was built in one complete piece, the lower in two panels, with ailerons on the lower wings only. Small duralumin root fillets were used to fair the lower wing attachments. CR control surfaces were steel frame, linen-covered, and the empennage was externally braced. The tailskid was made from an auto leaf spring. A rather long-legged V-chassis was used for the landing gear, shock absorption provided by rubber cords. A single-strut chassis had been proposed to the Navy but turned down. For the Lamblin lobster-pot radiators carried in this chassis, streamlined "bullet" fairings were fabricated and frequently put into place on the ground for looks, but they restricted cooling too severely to be used in flight.

Curtiss CR, August 1921, showing original fin; also note Lamblin radiators　　(C)

On August 1, nine weeks exactly after the Navy's order, A-6080, the first CR, rolled out with the "round cowl" (referring to the attachment line for its removable dural cowl panel); on August 8 A-6081 was pushed into the sunlight. It had the "square cowl" and a trial fin and rudder of very low height.

Even though government support

for the Pulitzer race had withered abruptly when the new fiscal year began July 1, CR flight testing proceeded with Bert Acosta aboard for the first flight at Roosevelt Field. The plane flew delightfully but Acosta was rudely shocked on landing when the fuselage cracked in two around the cockpit. The fuselage had been built up in halves on right- and left-hand hardwood

Bert Acosta and the Curtiss Navy racer, 1921　　(C)

molds, and according to Wait they "forgot to reinforce the cockpit" when the halves were joined together. This deficiency was rectified and throughout August, September, and early October both planes were flown repeatedly by Acosta and Marine Lieutenant Benjamin G. Bradley, another veteran of the 1920 Pulitzer race.

As these tests progressed the Pulitzer was resurrected as a purely civilian venture and added to the agenda of a fliers' reunion at Omaha. Curtiss arranged without too much difficulty to "borrow" one of their new CR racers from the Navy (it was A-6081). Since Navy pilots were forbidden to fly, hot-blooded Bert Acosta went to Omaha to pilot the CR-1.

As a boy in southern California Acosta had been unruly, an irrepressible outdoors type, fond of fast ponies and nights in the mountains near his home. When just fourteen, in 1909, he built his first aeroplane. It was not much, fashioned mostly of balloon silk, haywire, and a fearsome two-cycle Eldbridge engine, but when it supported him aloft, even for a few precious seconds, he felt a magic communion with the soaring duck hawks of the mountains, the sleek, strongly masculine birds that fascinated him in hours of youthful fantasy. Even then, hanging onto the bamboo control, his shock of thick black hair flattened by the wind, it was apparent he had the inborn sixth sense that later marked him as perhaps the world's finest natural flier. Glenn Curtiss opened camp on the barren, jackrabbit flats of nearby North Island January 17, 1911, to experiment with hydro-aeroplanes. Within weeks young Acosta was working as a Curtiss grease monkey for 50¢ a day plus ferryboat fare, but it did not take him long to become a flight instructor. War broke out and Acosta, still a teen-ager, suddenly found himself in charge of training hundreds of men to fly in an atmosphere of war hysteria and fervid patriotism. It was then he established two more lifelong repu-

tations. In his leisure hours the young aviator with his sleek hair center-parted under a tweed cap, dark olive skin, and low, musical voice — and lionized as only aviators of that era were — found it no difficulty to dazzle women with his virile charm. At the same time he developed a strong proclivity for alcohol. His flying experience and reputation as the pilot "with the finest touch" mounted, and when Roland Rohlfs left Curtiss for Aeromarine, Acosta became chief test pilot.

Acosta had splashed into the tabloids in 1920 when a team of three German Junkers-built J.L.6s piloted by Harold Hartney, Samuel Eaton, and himself set out July 29 to fly both ways across the United States. More than a hundred letters were ceremoniously carried in what was ballyhooed by the planes' American promoter, John M. Larsen, as the "first transcontinental aerial mail." Famous wartime ace Eddie Rickenbacker was along for the ride, eager to determine the feasibility of long airline routes (he would later head Eastern Air Lines), as well as William B. Stout, later famous as chimerical father of the Ford Tri-Motor. Not all the aeroplanes made it: attempting an overloaded takeoff from Omaha on a boiling August day with Rickenbacker aboard as passenger, Hartney rolled straight into a house well past the field boundary. Fortunately the residents were outside gaping at the flying machines, and the only injury was a "severely fractured straw hat," as Rickenbacker later put it.

For Acosta, twenty-five, carefree and reckless, the flight was a pure joy ride. With his powerful Latin charm, Bert's experience was that anything the female population along the entire route could offer was his for the taking; he later recalled he did not sleep for four nights in Reno. His co-pilot, a German lad named Buhl, had come to the American West with trepidation, expecting wild Indians and frontier ruffians. Buhl, however, adapted readily.

Curtiss CR Navy racer (A-6081), winner of the 1921 Pulitzer; this is the only known photograph of the CR in Omaha bearing its Pulitzer race number 4.   (Au)

Little more than a month earlier, on June 27, Bert had flown a similar J.L.6 from Omaha almost 1,200 miles non-stop to a potato patch 20 miles east of Lancaster, Pennsylvania . . . and completed the trip to New York the next day when the weather lifted. This was a phenomenal flight for 1920 and people idolized the young pilot. Bert, who seldom took his flying seriously, was nevertheless the picaresque pilot who said, "Give me a kitchen table with a motor on it and I'll fly it," who gave matchless performances of flying virtuosity, but who was disarmingly forthright about his one flying weakness — which was also his weakness in life — when he said, "I'm strictly a fair-weather boy." Bert was the archetype of the leather-cloaked, silk-scarfed flying heroes during the madcap 1920s, and his life remained a mind-boggling sequence of sensual pleasures for only as long as aviation could produce the spellbinders.

He had flown an Italian-built Balilla in the 1920 Pulitzer, garnering third place after chattering around the course seven and a half minutes slower than the winner. Now in 1921 he was out to do better.

In Omaha by November 1 he exulted, "It looks great: the field, the weather, and the planes." A battle supreme was predicted between Acosta's CD-12–powered biplane and Coombs's C-12–powered Cactus Kitten triplane. Lloyd Bertaud, in an aging K-12–powered Balilla, merely commented, "All I want is to be in the money." He was not. Moreover, this race was the swan song for Kirkham's original K-12 engine.

Starting positions were assigned by lot which Acosta won. The start was delayed from 1 P.M. to shortly after two-thirty to await stragglers flying up from the American Legion Convention flying derbies at Kansas City. Acosta was cinched in his open cockpit, the engine ticking over. The red-and-white flag dropped, he rammed the throttle open, and in a blur of blue he slanted steeply into the sky, bending the lovely CR on one wing, careening around the field. Then, in a rush of wind and thunder he ripped straight over the starting line and tore quickly out of sight. A witness reported, "It seemed scarcely the drawing of a breath before a tiny speck appeared over the Florence bluffs in the direction

Bert Acosta and the Pulitzer Trophy, photographed in front of the Curtiss plant at Garden City, New York, 1921   (C)

of the Calhoun windmill pylon and the whisper of the motor in an instant became a terrifying torrent of sound as Acosta swung close around the white field posts" and departed on his second lap.

On his first turn at Calhoun, two of Acosta's flying wires snapped and the wings started to wobble and buzz. He said later that the thought of one of his girl friends and her tender pleas to leave the danger of flying came to mind at that moment. But with characteristic fatalism and reckless aplomb he pounded on with wide-open throttle. On the third lap, as he hauled the CR-1 into a vertical turn, swaying the whitewashed phone poles marking the home pylon, the judge reckoned he came "within 30 feet of disqualifying." He roared on in equal fashion for the final two laps. After landing Acosta was limp and had to be helped from the cockpit; his left arm and leg were "practically paralyzed" from the cramped squeeze. "It was a grand race," he said. The broken wires made the "riding rough," forcing him into wider pylon turns. "I could have clipped three or four

minutes from my time otherwise. My motor was perfect and the visibility fine." Acosta had more reason to grin. He was $3,000 richer and, even with the snapped flying wires, he had set an unofficial closed-course world speed record of 176·75 mph. Standing with his silver prize and sleek aeroplane, Acosta, smiling coolly, looked like an airborne d'Artagnan in his favorite three-quarter–length black leather coat (Abercrombie & Fitch, $50).

The next morning Arthur Nutt, eager to talk technical matters, went to Bert's hotel room, knocked on the door, was invited in. To the young New Englander's consternation there was the hero, grinning from his bed, "with two females, one lying on each side." Omaha was quickly learning what fliers already knew : Bert's prowess in bed was even more admired than his ability aloft.

Three weeks after the race, on November 22, 1921, Acosta made eight officially timed flat-out speed passes over Curtiss Field's measured kilometer in the CR-1 in the first officially observed American world

Curtiss CR-1 taking off, 1921   (Au)

maximum speed record trials since World War I. Caleb Bragg of the Aero Club of America, representing the FAI, was there, and the speed to beat was 205 mph, set in September by the French Nieuport-Delage sesquiplane. Acosta's speed averaged 184·8 mph with his fastest pass timed at 197·8 mph. No world mark, but an official American one; and it showed that the speed penalty for adopting good flying qualities was not excessive.

A large group of naval officials gathered at Curtiss Field for the CR-1 racer's official demonstration. Spectators clustered along the roads, for this test promised to be a rare display of Acosta's superb flying virtuosity. He did not let them down. As his wheels left the earth on takeoff he smoothly kept the plane's sharp snout coming up and over in a loop. A dizzy series of rolls and whipstalls followed. He rocketed the tiny plane to 7,000 feet, where, as a tiny sun-flashed speck, he pushed over in a shrieking power dive, grazing the ground on his heart-stopping pullout. He closed the demonstration by rolling the CR-1 upside down and thundering over the tarmac just 30 feet above the shattered authorities. Curtiss officials soundly criticized Acosta for endangering congested Long Island communities, but with a wink in one eye. For the fabulous CR was successful beyond their wildest hopes. Rutledge Irvine also later commented on what pure joy it was to aerobat the CR.

More hot water awaited Acosta after his landing. One of his part-time flying students – an attractive married woman – rushed from the crowd and announced to nearby reporters that she and Acosta were soon to be married. Acosta in fact was recently divorced and it can be safely assumed that he was strongly anti-marriage. But the next day's headlines screamed "Peck's Bad Boy of the Air" was stealing a millionaire's wife! It may have been so, but the style was definitely not Acosta's, and for once he arranged to meet the husband involved.

At a Long Island speakeasy the husband told Acosta the woman was bored and publicity-hungry. "What's one more publicity gag to a guy like you?" It could only have happened during the wild and wacky twenties. The millionaire and Acosta got very drunk together that night. And presumably the flying matron got what she wanted . . .

Acosta's later career peaked in 1927 when he became involved in that year's transatlantic race. First allied with Clarence D. Chamberlin and the single-engine Wright-Bellanca *Columbia* – they set the world's endurance record of 51:11:25 on April 12–14 – he left during a squabble that involved his former Pulitzer competitor Lloyd Bertaud (who was later lost on a transatlantic attempt when his Fokker *Old Glory* crashed) to become one of the pilots of Richard E. Byrd's Fokker tri-motor *America* after Byrd's first pilot, Floyd Bennett, had been injured. One month after Lindbergh's historic solo flight from New York to Paris, and two weeks after Chamberlin flew the *Columbia* to Germany, Acosta on June 29, 1927, took off and in forty-two chilling hours with Byrd, Bernt Balchen, and George Noville flew the Fokker to the coast of France, joining that small company of transatlantic heroes. Nonchalant Bert managed to enjoy the glamour to the fullest. On their way to board the *Leviathan* for the return trip home, the fliers stopped at a small casino near Deauville where the Prince of Wales, then thirty-two, slim, and handsome, was dining with friends. He asked the *America* crew to join his party, and Bert at once eyed the prince's companion, a beautiful Hungarian dancer with a frosty demeanor. Quantities of wine soon had Bert glowing. "Say, boy, can I dance with your girl?" he said, slapping the prince on the shoulder. There was a shocked silence, but irrepressible Bert squeezed a five-franc piece into his eye, rudely mimicking an appalled and monocled general. Graciously the prince put everyone at ease and said,

"Go ahead, old chap." That was the last he saw of either that evening. The next morning Balchen, beginning to get impatient, finally found a bellhop who for a fee took him to the room where Bert had slept with the prince's not-so-frosty dancer.

After the ticker tape had settled and the balloons had burst, Acosta's life went rapidly downhill. He and Curtiss had parted ways after the 1925 National Air Races when his stunts became too bizarre for Curtiss' taste. He became a frequent tenant in jail, for drunkenness, for non-payment of alimony, even for stealing aeroplanes. An attempt to start an aeroplane-manufacturing company under his name and build planes in the old Mercer Automobile factory near Trenton collapsed in the 1929 stock market crash. Unable to adjust to aviation's increasing pragmatism, Acosta was grounded for five staggering years and quickly hit skid row. In 1936 he recovered long enough to become a mercenary pilot during the Civil War in Spain where he flew on the Loyalist side for one month, but the whole adventure was a black scene; details of his bald sky exploits have become obscured in a mixture of fact and myth. He returned to the United States where he dropped out of sight for years, but in reality was living in despair. He tried several times to make a comeback but never was able to, and in 1954 he died of tuberculosis in Spivak, Colorado, aged fifty-nine.

Both CR racers were readied for the 1922 Pulitzer and indeed underwent some face-lifting. The 1921 winner, A-6081, had been equipped with the new brass sheet wing skin radiators during the summer of 1922. This racer also received a new D-12 engine and was redesignated CR-2. Flight tests showed a remarkable gain in speed of some 16–17 mph! The CR-2 was now truly a 200-mph aeroplane. Other changes were made as well. Because of

Curtiss CR-2 aloft on early wing radiator test, September 1922   (C)

The two Curtiss Navy racers undergoing modification, 1922   (C)

the greater load on the upper wing the rear center-section flying wires were replaced by struts on A-6081 (forward struts appeared on A-6080); an oil-cooling duct was fitted ahead of the wing pylon, which now was extended 4 inches beyond the wing trailing edge; the wheels were covered with sheet aluminum discs to build them into elliptical shape, then linen-covered and doped, which resulted in a saving of "37 per cent in wheel drag" according to Curtiss; finally, control surface gaps were sealed by gluing strips of rubber sheet in place, and happily, controllability was also reported improved.

The Navy had taken over their racers with gusto, for in 1922 the Pulitzer became a spirited military duel. The first Navy pilot selected was Lieutenant Frank C. Fechteler, twenty-five, from San Rafael, California, son of distinguished Rear Admiral Augustus C. Fechteler. A Naval Academy graduate (1917) and naval aviator since 1920, young Fechteler reported to Selfridge Field from the USS *Langley*, where he was "in charge of the ship's planes." But on September 18, while flying a Spad on his first survey trip over the intended race course, the exuberant pilot hauled back too steeply, stalled, spun in from only 150 feet, and was killed instantly.[2]

Harold "Hap" Brow was assigned to replace Fechteler. Also in his mid-twenties, Brow's first love had been ham radio during the long winter nights of his youth in Fall River, Massachusetts, and later Providence, Rhode Island. He strung Ford coils and galena together and could receive Morse code at twenty-five words/minute. When war threatened he joined the Rhode Island Naval Militia "to avoid the draft", and recalled a fateful encounter with Richard E. Byrd, not then the famous explorer

[2] Two Navy destroyers later bore his name.

Harold J. Brow and Curtiss CR-2 at the 1922 Pulitzer race (C)

Curtiss CR-2 taking off in 1922 Pulitzer race (USAF)

he was destined to become, who advised the young sailor to forget radio and go into aviation. Brow's one brief encounter with things aeronautical had been a model "made from an umbrella frame and rubber bands which flew only by virtue of being launched from a third-story window!" But he decided to try out Byrd's advice. He won his wings of gold and in his first year piled up 560 hours in every type of World War I peashooter. He then served in the Atlantic Fleet Torpedo Plane Squadron from July 1920 until December 1921, recalling one of his "proudest flights" occurred March 18, 1921, when General Billy Mitchell rode his extra cockpit as passenger during the fateful 1921 battleship bombing tests. Brow got on Pete Mitscher's Test Board and roomed with Al Williams in the old Army-Navy Club on Central Park South when he came to New York to check out in the Curtiss racer. His first flight was in A-6080 on August 30, 1922, and lasted fifteen minutes. On September 14 he was aloft for his second ride, this time in A-6081, on a "wing radiator

test." That the early race pilots did not have much rehearsal time is revealed by Brow's logbook: the Pulitzer race was his sixth and last CR

Servicing Curtiss CR-2 before 1922 Pulitzer race (NA)

flight. He finished third in the race at over 190 mph, ahead of more than a dozen of the military's hottest racers. He remembered vividly flashing low

over Lake St. Clair, the sun-silvered streak of mottled ripples on the lake racing to stay ahead of him, when one of the sheet rubber gap fairings on his elevator blew off. Without warning the racer "shot for the sky." Startled, he shoved the stick forward and soon collected his wits. "Lucky it didn't go the other way." He walked away from the race with 2:55 CR time in 1,130 total hours.

His roommate Al Williams began the 1922 racing season thinking he would fly the Navy-X (see Chapter 17), then switched to the Cactus Kitten triplane, which apparently was too high-spirited, even for him. So, with less than a month to go before the race, A-6080 was pulled back into the factory and given the same face lifting as A-6081, emerging just days before the race sporting new wing radiators and a new D-12 engine; Williams was now assigned to fly it. Tall, taciturn, with a commanding, almost intimidating bearing, Williams had come from the Bronx, gone to school at P. S. 8 and finished Fordham in 1915, then pitched the next two seasons of

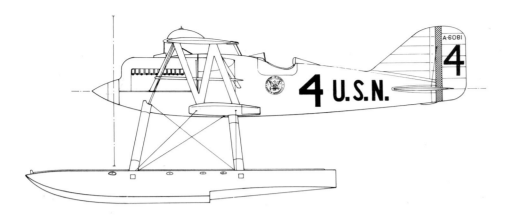

baseball with the New York Giants, who farmed him out to Tennessee to gain experience. By then war was impending and Giant manager John McGraw bewailed losing a baseball ace when Williams left to join naval aviation.

After instructing at Pensacola he went to Hampton Roads as a test pilot, which in view of his single-directed style of few words but forceful action was almost inevitable. He received an LL.B. from Georgetown in 1925 and a peacetime D.F.C. in 1929 for experiments in inverted tactical flying. Williams eventually turned in complete flight characteristics reports on eighty types of aircraft. In the 1922 Pulitzer he finished fourth in spite of a cockpit fire extinguisher that exploded virtually into his face on the second lap. Pieces of the shattered bottle took his goggles and part of his helmet as they left the cockpit, and the fumes made him "violently sick." Williams had his "hands full for a couple of seconds," but it was characteristic that he carried on and made an excellent showing. Indeed, he beat Acosta's 1921 speed by 11 mph.

The CR-2 racers, already considered obsolescent, were placed in storage, and it would have floored anyone then to have foreseen a glimpse of the historic destiny that still awaited them. This was to occur at the momentous 1923 Schneider Trophy race, where the CRs would be the catalysts in the

transformation of the Schneider formula from one composed of staid, ladylike flying boats doing minuets of navigability into a brew smoking with demons and banshees in a fire dance of speed. They would also become the center of a raging controversy which is still virulent even today, because the CRs were for the first time in Schneider history the tools not of a private sporting group but of a national government. This factor also occasioned an important transformation in the race's character because the convincing victory of the Curtiss racers made potential competitors realize that only the lavish resources of governments could in the future buy the technology needed to recapture this holy grail of air racing.

In February 1923 the U. S. Navy arranged to enter the race and began to prepare their racers. The twin pontoons attached to the CRs were built directly onto the undercarriage struts; that is, these struts extended into the pontoon and were made integral with the pontoon structure before covering. The pontoons were almost as long as the basic aeroplane, broad with shallow V-bottoms, a single step nearly underneath the c.g., planked with Curtiss-ply and each containing an 8-gallon auxiliary fuel tank. The English scoffed at their design, convinced they would porpoise unacceptably in any kind of sea. They did porpoise – slightly – but it did not

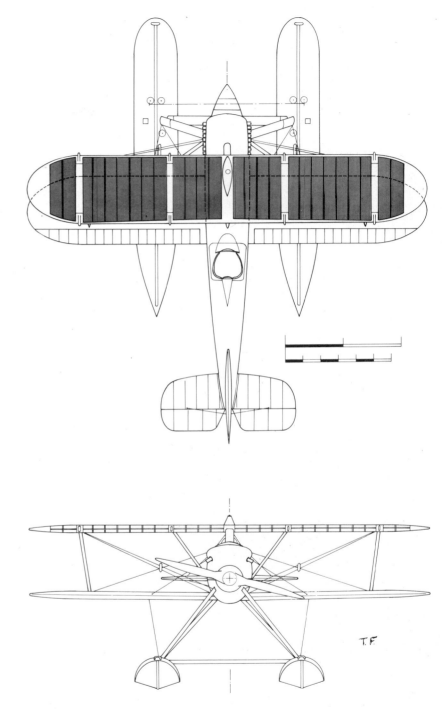

Curtiss CR-3, winner 1923 Schneider Trophy race; note wing radiators.

matter. The D-12 engines fitted could deliver 485 hp and swung the new Reed metal props, made from a single sheet of dural twisted and machined to shape. The engine cowlings were more rounded with additional fairing panels extending aft to blend the increased width into the fuselage contours. Because of the directionally destabilizing pontoons the vertical fin height was increased 6 inches. The wing radiators were extended and struts now replaced both sets of center-section bracing wires, the rear strut extending sharply aft. Cabane pylon extensions were shortened, ending at the wing trailing edge. The aeroplanes were prepared with a painstaking, almost frantic attention to detail. Ailerons were recessed into the lower wing "so that one could not put a piece of thin paper into the gap," as one astounded English engineer observed; after the pontoon tanks were filled and filler caps replaced, these slight recesses were covered neatly by square patches of doped-on fabric and varnished to give an unblemished surface! Both planes now received the designation CR-3.

The pilots picked to fly the CR-3s were Lieutenants David Rittenhouse and Rutledge Irvine. Rittenhouse, twenty-nine, was born in St. Paul, Minnesota, in 1894 and entered the University of Minnesota (class of 1918) but left before graduation to join the Norton Harjes Ambulance Corps in France, enlisting in Paris in March 1917. He spent six months at the Front with the 21st Division of the French Army, then returned to the United States before winter 1917 and attended the Dunwoody Institute, Minneapolis, preparing for a ground job in naval aviation; but by May 1918 he was on his way to Key West for flight training. Two months before the Armistice he had his wings and ensign's commission, and decided to remain in the service, flying spotting planes in the Pacific Fleet from 1919

Curtiss CR-3 and freshly numbered TR-3A in Saunders' sheds, Cowes, 1923   (MA)

until 1922. He came to the Schneider team with 1,400 hours. In a later war Rittenhouse gained wide recognition as the production manager at Grumman Aircraft Corporation; it was he who saw to it that thousands of Hellcat fighters and other Grumman aeroplanes were delivered to the war zones on time. He died shortly thereafter.

Irvine, twenty-seven, was born in Brooklyn in 1896 and attended Cornell. He became a naval aviator in August 1918 and flew with long-range patrol squadrons. In April 1919 he set an endurance record of over twenty hours aloft in an F5L; he then went to the Test Board and, like Rittenhouse, was weaned on air racing in the 1922 Curtiss Marine Trophy.

The CR-3s were ready for testing in mid-July. The entire USN Schneider team, headed by Lieutenant Frank W. "Spig" Wead, who was later immortalized by John Wayne in the 1957 M-G-M movie Wings of Eagles, had put in many hours of difficult practice flying twin-pontoon seaplanes from Anacostia, D.C., on the Potomac in the roughest conditions they could find. Now Rittenhouse and Irvine would try the CR-3s on Long Island Sound flying from Port Washington and for speed runs timing themselves over the 4·26 statute miles between Stepping Stone Light and Execution Rock near Throgs Neck. Curtiss vice-president Frank H. Russell and chief engineer Bill Gilmore witnessed many of these tests, including the one made July 30 by Irvine which the press reported as having set a new world seaplane speed record of 175·3 mph. In reality his hotted-up CR-3 was capable of 197 mph at full bore and he recalled that Rittenhouse's plane "was about 4 mph faster ..." No matter, the English thought claims of 175 outlandish enough to be labelled "Yank Swank." Too many people still remembered S. E. J. Cox and American braggadocio was a standing joke in

Curtiss CR-3 under tow during preliminaries to the 1923 Schneider Trophy race   (F)

England. Besides, the 1922 winner, Biard in his Supermarine flying boat, had done 146 mph at Naples and that was really moving.

The Americans embarked on the *Leviathan*, arriving in England August 25, more than a month before the race. The team organization was superb. The crew included Wright employees George Mead and Eddie Mulligan, the civilian "tech reps," plus seven Navy mechanics, the youngest of whom was W. H. "Joe" Bush, a *Langley* "plank-owner" who would later leave the Navy in 1926 to work as a globe-trotting tech rep himself with Wright until 1969. The Navy came completely organized, "even to the steerable loading trolleys and the waders which the men wore," observed the British journal *Aeroplane*.

The navigability and watertightness tests took place September 27. These required three takeoffs and landings, taxiing a total of 1 nautical mile at 12 knots, followed by unattended mooring out for six hours. The weeks of CR-3 warmups were causing deepening concern in all but the most complacent Europeans; in vain they looked for the predicted porpoising difficulties on the water. It seemed their only chance: "All England is praying for a wind, a lop, and an extra strong tide race up The Solent." A severe storm on the twenty-fifth even had the Americans worried, but it had blown out by the twenty-seventh, when The Solent reminded one of a "millpond," and the Curtiss racers, in very business-like fashion, passed their trials handily. Irvine had to repeat part of his trials because of a rules misunderstanding but this he did with no difficulty.

On the morning of the twenty-eighth, race day, the neatly edged Hampshire fields rising from the sea shimmered a vivid green, and white houses eight miles away stood out clearly. The castle-like building of the Royal Yacht Squadron was in full bloom with its gay bunting fluttering on the esplanade. The bristling profile of America's cruiser USS *Pittsburgh* darkened the

west approach to The Solent after its stately pass by Portsmouth, where it exchanged formal salutes with the Royal Navy, whose own embarrassing sea-going absence could not be ignored; finally, almost in consternation, a RN "P-boat" made a lame showing. Even the French seaplanes had been delivered by destroyer. The *Pittsburgh* came, according to Commander John H. Towers, then naval air attaché in London, only "to see fair play." Her presence was imposing. In fact, the Navy called her "the ugliest ship afloat" but few at Cowes were inclined to offer any aesthetic criticism, especially as she later supplied a celebration at the Royal Marine Hotel, Cowes, that packed broadsides still remembered forty-five years later. "A great party . . ." commented the normally caustic C. G. Grey, *Aeroplane* editor whose monocle was frequently misfocused on Americans; aside from the saxophone band, Grey was amazed a dry ship from a dry country could supply "so much wetness!"

A west wind freshened prior to the start, and since the rules required that contestants cross the starting line between two mark barges while taxiing on the water, planes would have to take off to the west, then make a 180-degree turn onto the course's first leg. Thousands of spectators jammed beaches and creaking piers for miles, yachts littered The Solent — then, four minutes before the start, the two CR-3s could be seen maneuvering into position about a mile from the line. The one-minute black cone was hoisted on Mr. Withers' steam yacht, the "start barge" and the CR-3s, side by side, gathered speed, creaming The Solent with bow waves "as big as a destroyer," the crescendo from their engines blending in unison as they now rushed ahead, hard by when the cone dropped for the start, roaring between the mark boats in their peculiar, rocked-back, skidding fashion before breaking free, Irvine first, the insistent jarring becoming velvet smooth. Then on prearranged signal Rittenhouse

Curtiss CR-3 of Rittenhouse taking off in the 1923 Schneider Trophy race (F)

banked steeply left directly over the Royal London Yacht Club of Cowes and Irvine banked right, and they roared low onto the course, east past Spithead with over 18 miles to run, directly over Horse Sand Fort, Rittenhouse's speed advantage apparent as he slowly crept away from Irvine, the rolling green texture of Selsey growing from the haze ahead, the white windmill spiking into view, then the cross laid out on the hillside. Wing down, feel the CR-3 carry beyond the cross, wind's sliding it wide as well, stick back, feel the g's pile on, wing up — put the haze of Portsmouth on the nose, the South Parade Pier of Southsea the target — engines humming a high sweet melody of perfection — flashing by the pier, hundreds of waving people, and there is the unmistakable mountainous shape of the *Pittsburgh* to aim for on the last lap, good old rustbucket, when roaring by to start the next lap catch a glimpse of decks loaded with cheering sailors. The CR-3s came in one-two, Rittenhouse in the lead, Irvine a close second. No

one else came close. It was a resounding triumph.

The victory was a sensation and the CR-3 was hailed as "the most perfect example of a racing plane ever seen

Rutledge Irvine and David Rittenhouse after the U. S. Navy Schneider triumph, 1923 (MA)

Curtiss CR-3 at the Baltimore seaplane meet, 1924 (USN)

in Europe." The throne of power had passed from Napier and Hispano to Curtiss, the reign of speed to American shores. *La Gazzetta dell'Aviazione* of Milan noted, "The clean-cut American victory caused a great impression, particularly in certain circles which are prone to believe that on the other side of the Atlantic Ocean everything is exaggerated. Rittenhouse and Irvine have given them a telling answer." After the last huzzahs the jubilant team departed October 9, again aboard the *Leviathan*, which had its majestic social hall graced by the Schneider Trophy, a novel center of attraction for passengers during the five-day crossing.

The CR-3s finished their flying career in Baltimore at the 1924 meet that should have been the Schneider Trophy race that year — but was not. A-6081 was groomed as America's third team plane, A-6080 the team alternate. The fuselages of both had been reinforced by screwing on two longitudinal duralumin strips some 1½ inches wide. Pilots were to be

Curtiss CR-3 aloft during Baltimore seaplane meet, 1924 (Au)

George T. Cuddihy and Ralph A. Ofstie respectively. On September 4, during pre-race warmups made before the race itself was canceled, Cuddihy flew A-6081 — which had won the 1923 race — to 197·6 mph at the Naval Aircraft Factory facilities on the Delaware River, and Ofstie hit 190 mph in the other ship. To substitute for the

canceled race, on Saturday, October 25, the two CR-3s staged speed trials in public view at Bay Shore Park, Maryland, 14 miles southeast of Baltimore. Over the 3-kilometer course Cuddihy took the faster of the two racers in four officially timed passes and established a new world maximum speed record for seaplanes at just over 188 mph. Ofstie drove A-6080 around the planned Schneider triangle not seven but ten times to set official speed records for the officially recognized closed-course distances of 100 kilometers, 200 kilometers, both at approximately 177 mph, and 500 kilometers at just over 161 mph. After making the 200-kilometer mark he throttled back to conserve both his engine and his fuel, finishing the last 300 kilometers at 150 mph, but making sure to get the 500-kilometer record on the books.

The CR-3 racers were then scientifically destroyed in structural tests at the Naval Aircraft Factory in Philadelphia. Their offspring had already taken the garland.

Remnants of CR-3 after structures tests at Naval Aircraft Factory. Note longitudinal strips which had been added for fuselage stiffening. (S)

THE GOLDEN THOROUGHBREDS

14

The Curtiss R-6 Racers

CR designers Booth and Thurston left Curtiss during late 1921 or early 1922, whereupon young Bill Wait found himself, under Gilmore's guidance, virtually in charge of Curtiss' 1922 experimental racer design, called in house the L-19-1. Wait's layout, first sketched during a burst of inspiration on the proverbial "back of an envelope," as Wait recalled with a twinkle in his eye, was a vastly cleaned-up version of the 1921 CR, and it was also smaller: almost 4 feet less span, 30 square feet less wing area, 215 pounds lighter; its cross section, barely enough to fair engine and pilot, was 25 per cent smaller; it used the famous "I" interplane struts instead of the N-type; a single landing gear strut replaced the earlier V-chassis; the tail surfaces became cantilever with all control actuators buried.

At first Curtiss had no success promoting their design. The Navy was approached but expressed reluctance to acquire competition for their successful 1921-model racers, especially from the same manufacturer. Private interests were sought but with equally negative results. Meanwhile the Pulitzer Trophy race, which had been a purely civilian affair in 1921, now enjoyed a sudden resurgence of military enthusiasm. This was whipped to life by General Billy Mitchell, who viewed the race as a practical laboratory for the development of high-speed pursuits – the fastest current service pursuits did only 160 mph at that time – and with this motivation the Army suddenly discovered an immediate need for two of the new Curtiss biplanes. They were ordered on contract 552, dated May 27, 1922, would be designated R-6, and must be delivered in only three months!

The R-6 was designed around the brand-new Curtiss D-12 engine, one of the few truly great aero engines of all time, and this alone would make it a benchmark of progress. The D-12 resulted when engine designer Arthur Nutt made his important transformation of the CD-12 by lengthening the engine slightly to accommodate a new, redesigned seven-bearing crankshaft with increased bearing surface. On the basis of McCook Field tests of the CD-12, two other improvements were adopted in the D-12: a dry-sump oil system with separate oil reservoir, allowing the new crankcase to be made considerably smaller, reducing frontal area, and stiffer; and new carburetors were fitted. In 1922 two Zenith U.S. 54-millimeter carburetors

were employed but they limited maximum power output. In 1923 remarkable new Stromberg NA-Y5 carburetors incorporating altitude compensation and other novel features were fitted, and the D-12 could wind up to nearly 2,600 rpm on the test bench. This magnificent new engine weighed 40 pounds less than the CD-12, and passed the fifty-hour test May 27, 1922, the same day the R-6 was ordered. The Navy ordered twelve D-12s immediately — two of these went to the Army — and by July 1922 another fifty-seven were on order. Subsequent orders cascaded. After years of doubts and trials the D-12 would finally achieve Keys's dream of vast sales and expanding Curtiss prestige.

Ironically the Navy at first did not look upon D-12s as powerplants for speedplanes but simply as Liberty replacements, and early deliveries were duly installed in lumbering torpedo and observation squirrel cages. Even though the Navy had provided the bulk

Curtiss R-6 fuselage under construction. Note spirally wound strips of "Curtiss-ply" used to form coque. *(C)*

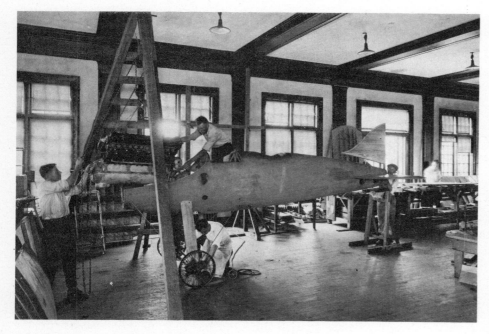

Fitting revolutionary new Curtiss D-12 engine into R-6 racer, August 1922 (C)

of engine-development sponsorship and encouragement it was the Army who became turned on to the D-12's fantastic potential, and they abruptly ordered the two R-6 racers in 1922 as beds for their first two D-12s.

The R-6 was also the first racer to make use of the skin radiator from the inception of its design. Indeed, its D-12 engine and skin radiator were acclaimed by many observers to be the two outstanding aeronautical achievements of 1922. The R-6 also employed a variety of noteworthy propellers, from the initial blueprints on which it sported a four-blade prop (never built) to its final prop in 1924 which became the central issue in a raging controversy and which marked the last time wooden propellers were required on high-speed aeroplanes. The 1922 tests of S. A. Reed's new metal prop, just days before the Pulitzer race, were so encouraging that Curtiss officials carried an experimental ver-

sion for the R-6 as hand baggage to the 1922 Detroit races. It was not acceptable under the Pulitzer's strict rules nor was it needed to win. All Curtiss racers would make decisive use of the Reed prop later, in 1923.

The R-6 airframe itself was sturdily built and excellent in detail. The fuselage shell, which weighed just 127 pounds complete, incorporated minor design refinements over those of 1921 but like its predecessors was a Curtiss-ply-skinned wood monocoque. Using the thin new C-27 airfoil — a vast improvement over the Sloan — developed in Curtiss' own 7-foot wind tunnel, the wings were multi-cellular units composed of five spars, not solid as in 1921 but routed to save weight, and plywood ribs supporting Curtiss-ply covering over which the corrugated brass sheet radiators were laid, the radiator header becoming the wing's sharp leading edge. The wing was required by contract to withstand a

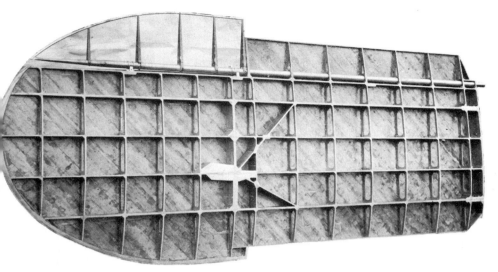

Wing structure of Curtiss R-6 (C)

than ninety days, a remarkable feat even in 1922. The government paid $71,000 plus $5,000 for spare parts; a penalty clause to deduct $2,500 for each 1 mph of maximum speed attained less than 190 proved to be unnecessary. During that hectic summer of 1922 there were still some misgivings over the gamble of using in such a diminutive machine an untried engine coupled to the untried wing radiator units, especially with so much prestige at stake. But the R-6 blended with the sky as though she owned it. Only minor adjustments were necessary during flight test.

Landing gear, Curtiss R-6, 1922 (C)

Building fuselage for second Curtiss R-6, August 1922 (C)

Rudder construction, Curtiss R-6 (C)

load factor of 8·5 positive and 3·5 negative; during static testing an upper wing did not fail until the load exceeded 10·0 while an I-strut held up to 12·0. Fuselage design anticipated a load of 7·0 and one of the two finished fuselages was tested to 4·0 with no significant effects. Tail surfaces were now cantilever, and all movable control surfaces now were built of duralumin frames, linen-covered and doped.

Lighter than the steel frames used on the 1921 racers, they weighed only ·7 pounds per square foot yet supported an actual load of 15 pounds per square foot, about half their design capability, in sandbag tests during the second weekend in August. At this time a maximum stick force of 25 pounds and rudder pedal force of 4·5 pounds were measured, under static conditions.

The two racers were built in less

Proof test of horizontal tail surfaces (15 pounds per square foot), Curtiss R-6, August 1922 (C)

Final engine test, Curtiss R-6, September 1922   (C)

racers and shipped them to Detroit where they were assembled October 9 and flown in pre-race warmups by the two happy fliers. Hangar gossip already named Russ Maughan the sure winner.

Of the Army fliers selected to pilot the profusion of custom-built Pulitzer racers that year, Maitland and Maughan were excellent choices for the favored R-6s. First Lieutenant Lester J. Maitland, born in 1899 in Milwaukee, Wisconsin, received his commission in the Aviation Section shortly after his twentieth birthday. Following six weeks' duty with the Test School at Taliaferro Field, Texas, he was sent to Hawaii for two years and thus began a lifelong love affair with the enchanted land of pineapples and poi. By 1922 he already had over 1,000 hours, 150 in pursuits, and later recalled the over-all impression they left with him: one of "pure joy". Long before any flying regulations had been framed, when no one was

watching except incredulous land-lubbers, these carefree knights of the air skimmed between trees and over barntops "at a height of 75 feet for mile after mile," drinking in the exhilaration like some heady wine. Maitland had sixteen forced landings during his first fifteen hours of cross-country, which added to the adventure. And now he was handpicked from stuffy duties at Bolling Field to strap himself to the R-6, a nimble jewel in which to close one's watering eyes in the propblast and let the wind song of the wires strum a canon to speed.

Maitland would achieve later fame for his 1927 non-stop transpacific flight to Hawaii in the Fokker tri-motor *Bird of Paradise* which overlapped by a few hours Richard Byrd's flight to France with Bert Acosta in a similar ship. Maitland had been General Mitchell's aide, flying wing on Mitchell for many exciting hours, and praised his former mentor: "Mitchell was always the best in whatever he would

In fact, when exuberant Lester Maitland took the R-6 aloft on her very first flight he poured on full power and blistered Curtiss Field at 223 mph! This was the more remarkable because the official world speed record then stood at 205 mph and Maitland's average from six sizzling passes, carefully timed but unofficial, beat that by 6 mph. A few days later Russ Maughan bettered this performance on the second R-6's initial flight when he reached 233 mph. His average of 220 obliterated the official speed record. Clearly the little R-6s were the world's fastest aeroplanes, and this thoroughly delighted C. M. Keys, who had wanted a decisive speed record on the R-6's very first flight to enhance company prestige and stimulate the dwindling price of Curtiss stock. Keys had taken a river boat gamble to forge ahead on experimental development to the exclusion of business effort, in the midst of a hostile, surplus-glutted market, and he needed vindication for

his decision. This was of course before he had sold large numbers of D-12s or aeroplanes to the military and while Curtiss was in desperate financial straits. It was said half facetiously, half critically, "There's a lot of money in aviation because Keys put a lot of it there."

Just twelve days before the big race Maughan jockeyed his steed aloft on its first four flights. Both R-6s were pure pleasure to fly with comfortable cockpits and beautiful handling qualities, "similar to the Fokker D-VII," Maitland recalled. "The aeroplane flew beautifully," he went on, "the rudder was sensitive but I felt confident after just a few minutes that I could take it over a speed course at low altitude." Controls were taut, precise and steep turns were made "with the greatest of ease." Maitland's engine experienced a short rash of "cutting out at intervals," and changes were made to the engine cowl and air scoop. Overjoyed, Curtiss personnel immediately crated the

Lester D. Maitland, 1922   (Au)

Russell Maughan, winner of the 1922 Pulitzer race, and his mount (S)

tackle." Maitland's later career included a harrowing escape from Bataan. CO of Clark Field in the Philippines when the Japanese attacked, Maitland moved his three thousand troops and before Manila fell he hid a Philippines Air Transport twin-Beech in a cemetery from which he later managed to take off, dodging gravestones. He was sent at once to Europe, where he commanded a B-26 group bombing Germany. After this distinguished service and his retirement as a brigadier general, Maitland began a second career when, two days before Christmas 1956, he was ordained minister in the Episcopal Church. His home, naturally, was then in Hawaii. Later he became rector of the Church of the Good Shepherd of the Hills in Arizona, but he never forgot how to fly. His commercial license bore number 88 and was still active in 1972 — one-half century after his sensational R-6 flights.

First Lieutenant Russell Maughan was a gritty rancher from northern Utah who came into the world with the last snows of 1893, a grandson of Mormon Peter Maughan, who had been sent to colonize the Cache Valley by Brigham Young. As a boy Maughan delivered newspapers from horseback while his father ran an orchard in River Heights and homesteaded 160 acres a few miles north in Idaho. Maughan graduated from Utah State Agricultural College just as America entered World War I, so he "temporarily" forewent his plans of farming to join the Army, first the Infantry, but a quick transfer put him in the Air Service. After training in California and France he was commissioned in November 1917 and posted to the 139th Pursuit Squadron. He shot down four Germans, two of them on one cold autumn day hardly two weeks before the Armistice to save the life of a buddy under attack and win the D.S.C. At the time of the Pulitzer Maughan had 800 hours and was on temporary duty from Mather Field, Mills, California.

Like Maitland, Maughan was a born flier. His natural skill and split-second judgment combined with a sturdy, supreme self-confidence to produce that extra touch, a distinct flying style that was brash but not reckless, and a joy to watch. He was remembered by Bill Wait as "a tough bimbo who never took second," and by many as positive, even opinionated to the point of irritation. But his impatience with vacillation was not idle, and his endurance was demonstrated two years later in 1924 when on his third valiant try he blazed the single-day ocean-to-ocean air trail with his famous "Dawn-to-Dusk" flight, made in a D-12–powered PW-8, the standard Army fighter inspired by the R-6 racer. Maughan turned down a 1930 offer to head up the maintenance department of then fledgling Western Air Lines and remained in the service, spending five years in the Philippines, first with the 8th Pursuit Group, then as chief aviation technical adviser to Governor General Parker. Once, on a survey flight over the island of Mindanao, they discovered an uncharted volcano topped by a large lake within the cone, features appearing on maps today as Mount Parker and Maughan Lake. Maughan later distinguished himself in 1939 when sent on a highly secret mission to the west coast of Greenland, where he spent three months in whaleboats and dog sleds selecting emergency landing sites for the large wartime aerial convoys soon to come. Hundreds of fliers came to know the fields Maughan picked — the famous Bluey West 1, 2, etc. — as safe haven, and far above the Arctic Circle Sonderstrom AFB was built on one of his sites. He spent his second war as a colonel in troop carrier and bombardment wings, retired in 1947, remarried, got a trailer, and moved with the seasons until 1958, when, undergoing a heart operation at Lackland AFB, he died.

The 1922 Pulitzer race was flagged off in three heats and thousands strained to see as the second heat prepared for departure. This heat introduced the world to that special bass staccato that only the D-12 engine ever produced, and not one but a quartet of Curtiss racers — the two R-6s and two CR-2s — were lined up wing to wing with D-12s tuning up to race, all singing their prelude fortissimo. When Maughan and Maitland were flagged off both leaped into the air and shot up almost vertically, causing one Curtiss official to comment to the press, only half in jest, that Curtiss soon expected to exhibit a plane "capable of vertical flight!" Their smoky trails merging into thick afternoon haze, and their small-diameter wood props turning at more than 2,200 rpm, the screaming D-12s were belching almost 460 hp. In less than eight minutes sharp-eyed but disbelieving spectators already saw

Curtiss R-6 racer flown by Russell Maughan winning the 1922 Pulitzer, pulling some 7 g on the pylon turns and lapping in excess of 200 mph! (USAF)

specks far out over Lake St. Clair, growing rapidly in size. Maughan had made up his mind to win and engineers had told him to stay as low as possible. In fact he was so low during the first lap that Wait swore his passage knocked the paddle from the hands of a man in a canoe! A quarter mile from the pylon he neatly placed the R-6 on its side as it hurtled ahead on momentum and fuselage lift, then at the pylon he heaved back on the stick. Practicing this a few days before in a 100-foot pass over the field, presumably intending "only to turn", he rolled the R-6, to the horror of the ground staff. Wait gave him hell, but now his practice was paying off in spectacular fashion. And right behind him, their props almost chewing his rudder, flashed Maitland then the two Navy CRs. *This* was an air race!

Already Maughan was coming around again. "Here he comes, look out for your hats!" blurted a judge atop the home pylon to his companions as a blur of black and copper flashed by. Maughan flattened out just above the hangar roofs and dipped into ground effect for his next dust-spewing dash across Selfridge Field.

Maughan won, a correspondent wrote, "at a speed so terrific he was unconscious at times." None of the 75,000 spectators budged until the last plane in the go-for-broke holiday race landed just before dark. Maughan was exhausted as he leaned against his plane, and worried about his pregnant wife — until he was informed excitedly that she had just given birth to a healthy son even as he was winning the race![1]

"On one of the laps I'm certain I made 220 mph," Maughan said. "On the Gaukler Point turn on the fourth

[1] The child was Maughan's third, his second son, Weston F. Maughan, who grew up to graduate from West Point in 1943 with his older brother, become a pilot, and fly combat missions in Asia. After the war he entered business and raised his family in California, keeping the propeller hub from his father's winning Pulitzer racer as a treasured office memento.

This 1922 etching shows Russell Maughan's R-6 infuriating Father Time as it annihilates distance at the then unheard-of rate of 206 mph!

lap . . . I was whirled into unconsciousness for three or four seconds. When I regained my senses I was almost skimming the waves of Lake St. Clair . . . At times during the race I was thinking about a telegram I had been expecting announcing the birth of a child to Mrs. Maughan. I got lost four times in the haze . . . [and] was stunned more or less at each of the fifteen turns. My worst moments, however, were at the turn at Gaukler Point. I lost confidence, which a good aviator ought not to do, and then became unconscious. On the straightaway I came to." No wonder: Maughan had pulled up to 7 g on his violent, 80-degree — banked pylon turns and had simply blacked out! In those days this was a little-understood phenomenon. "Another trouble I had was with my feet going to sleep." Maughan's winning speed was 206 mph and he held the new 100- and 200-kilometer closed-course world speed marks. After the victory, Major General Mason

Patrick, Chief of the Air Service, was so excited he patted Maughan on the head instead of shaking his hand!

Maitland finished second, almost duplicating Maughan's striking performance, even though his engine was missing, forcing him to bend over and vigorously work his fuel wobble pump with his right hand after the first lap in order to finish the race. (Later inspection revealed lead clogging the gasoline.) Army had trounced Navy and Curtiss had trounced Wright. This was tonic for Keys because Wright, at that time, was the largest purveyor of fighter engines in the United States with their venerable but now outclassed H-3, a descendant of the original Hispano.

The time was now long overdue to recapture the most glamorous record of all for America: *maximum speed.* In those days 300 mph was still "impossible" and 200 mph was "annihilating distance." Yet Maughan had done more than 220 mph on his first

flight in the R-6 over an electrically timed kilometer in a 10-mile straightaway. Now, two days after its Pulitzer triumph and only fourteen days after its first flight, the R-6 was going to attack the world speed record under official observation. A 1-kilometer course was carefully measured in the center of Selfridge Field, oriented NW-SE. The Indianapolis Motor Speedway electric timer, which had been used for the Pulitzer race, was set up to be operable by hand-operated telegraph key from both sets of timers' sights at either end of the course. The official chronometer was calibrated by the Bureau of Standards. The National Aeronautic Association did not exist then, though its turbulent birth was imminent, so the Aero Club of America represented the FAI. Maughan had conducted preliminary speed flights on October 16, 1922, a day of official government contract trials of all planes that participated in the air races, and he averaged 232·22 mph for four passes, 229 for eight, and hit 248·5 mph on his fastest downwind pass. But these trials were not carried out in a single flight of four passes, two in each direction, as the rules required, and for this reason Maughan's performance could not be officially recognized.

Nevertheless Maughan did prove the R-6 could sustain high speed, and his flight made it "virtually certain" a Curtiss biplane would be selected as the standard Army pursuit, a rumor certain to tickle C. M. Keys. More importantly, the superb R-6 performance caused many aero engineers for the first time to digest the startling realization that there might be no upper limit to speed. After his timed speed runs Maughan astonished observers by making one last pass on his side, hurtling low across Selfridge Field, more than a mile, in a beautiful "knife-edge."

Maughan took leave to be with his wife and new baby, and Billy Mitchell, who was certainly no armchair general, took over. Indeed, the speed

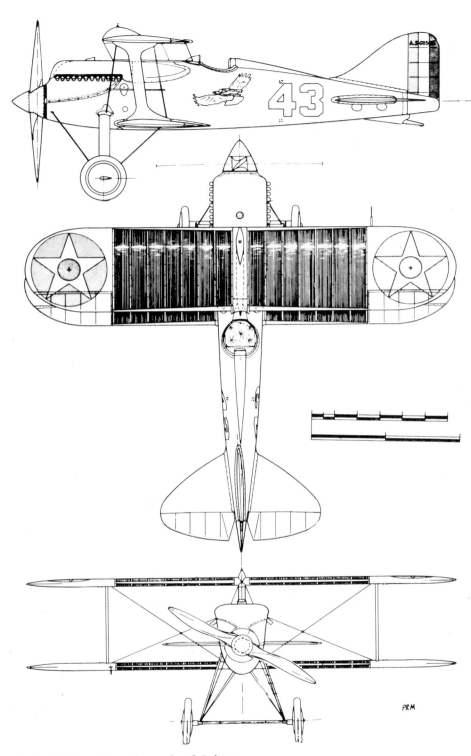

Curtiss R-6, world speed record and Pulitzer race winner, 1922

record would be a real feather in the cap of air power's fighting crusader, especially in view of the conviction held by his groundling boss General Patrick that there was an upper speed limit. Besides, General Mitchell never expected a subordinate to do anything he was not fully prepared to do himself — including setting the world speed record!

October 18 was cold (45° F.) and blustery. A stiff 18-mph NNW wind blew across Selfridge Field. The little black racers looked like lumps of chilled steel as they were prepared for their next speed onslaughts. Blue bursts of exhaust were whipped by the propblast past the flying general cinched in his cockpit, his jaw set, his face etched with determination. Mitchell looked upon the speed record not as a feat of personal heroics, which is how the press treated it somewhat to his irritation, but as just one of many weapons he was forging to wage the grand fight for air power. In fact, as he impatiently saw it, it was perfectly reasonable and damn well about time for aeroplanes to do some 4 miles per minute. Just months before, his predictions of such speeds were made amid a raucous din of skepticism, but Mitchell only wished each of his second lieutenants had such planes. He firmly believed, even then, that aeroplanes would fly "300 mph in five years and that the eventual speed man could reach would not be known for years to come — and might never be known." But this sort of heresy usually met with utter disbelief in 1922.

The trials were conducted between 3:30 and 4:30 P.M. and General Mitchell flew both R-6s — this was his first flight in the R-6, incidentally — making two methodical sets of four passes in each. Of the four attempts the fastest was achieved in Maughan's racer number 43. Landing from his record flight, his headgear slit by the wind, General Mitchell dryly commented with his customary penchant for prophecy that fighter planes of the future would have enclosed cockpits.

The speed officially homologated was 358·836 kmh (222·97 mph), but Mitchell was deprived by the subtle mathematical error of averaging times instead of speeds. He should have been credited with 361·279 kmh (224·499 mph). After General Mitchell's speed record was made official the Air Service publication commented that he had "further endeared himself to the flyers of the Army by being willing to lead in any contest in which the Air Service takes part." According to Maitland, the Army pilots as a group concurred that Mitchell should have the well-deserved acclaim for his efforts in making the race possible. But another side to the story exists. Maughan had done 248 unofficially; Mitchell's slower rate of 223 was officially recognized, and to many it looked like a bit of rank-pulling. Several newspapers cried foul. DISSENSION BUZZES IN RANKS OF ARMY headlined the Detroit *Free Press*. Mitchell at once began arrangements for a new speed record attempt for Maughan and never again attempted a record himself.

In December 1922 a study was made to determine if the R-6 design could be modified to meet military operational requirements but necessary design changes appeared too extensive to undertake. At that time both racers were at McCook Field, where they had been shipped during November and assigned numbers P-278 (the world record aeroplane) and P-279. The original engine had been removed from Maitland's R-6 P-279 and replaced. Maughan's engine was overhauled and reinstalled, and repair work performed on the wings, radiators, hoses and tanks, wheels, and elevator fabric. The new Stromberg carburetors were installed together with extra strainers between the fuel tanks and pumps.

Two months later in February 1923, at the zenith of the toughly fought Franco-American speed battle, the updated French Nieuport-Delage sesquiplane again raised the world speed record to 375 kmh, but on April 1 the officially recognized course length was to be increased to 3 kilometers. As March approached the two R-6s were engaged in an all-out effort to recapture the record over 3,280·8 feet — 1 kilometer — for all time. Just days remained to beat the deadline.

The Stromberg-equipped D-12s, capable of nearly 300 more rpm, turned efficient new Reed metal propellers which could absorb the higher speed. These remarkable props made a significant difference in R-6 performance, and even a verbal recollection of the terrible, mouth-opening shriek of the Reed prop as the tips went supersonic, howling above the shattering bark of twenty-four sawed-off exhaust stacks, raises hackles on the back. During the lengthy trials the 1922 wood racing prop and new Air Service Engineering Division birch props were used in addition to the Reed, because, it was cautioned, any Reed prop not precisely balanced would tend to vibrate.

Beginning March 21 at Wright Field both Maughan and Maitland repeated attempts on the record. The new NAA, formed late in 1922, now represented the FAI, and their chief observer was Orville Wright himself. On March 26, with the electric timers in place, Maughan took off first and made two tries of six passes each, still with the 1922 wood prop. His averages were 233·877 mph and 219·530 mph from the fastest four passes of each set. Maitland was next and made 209·460 mph and 218·942 mph. Maughan's first attempt actually beat the standing French record but not by the necessary 4 kmh, thus it could not be counted and, in any event, the electric timing mark was blurred on the first pass. But it was tantalizingly close to victory.

As early dawn broke three days later on March 29, an Army "Field Day" on which many records were assaulted, all was again in readiness. Maitland was off at first light, climbed to 7,000 feet in just over a minute, and pushed over for the first of thirty straining, flat-out passes over the kilometer; his fastest four yielded 386·174 kmh (239·961 mph), while one downwind pass was marked at a fantastic 281·4 mph. Unquestionably this seemed fast enough to qualify, and the achievement of "4 miles per minute" was heralded widely in the press. In fact, NAA statement B-1090 of April 12 obliquely credited Maitland with the record, but did not strictly homologate it. After the flight Maitland said, "Well, I guess there is nothing to it except which one is the biggest fool and takes the highest dive. That's where I got most of my speed." As quickly as Maitland's performance was praised it was disqualified because he "did not maintain horizontal flight throughout the trials." In its letter of regret to Maitland the NAA said: "Believe us it is with sincere regret we are forced to eliminate your trials. You have shown yourself to be one of the greatest high-speed pilots in the world, and regardless of our inability to homologate your flight, it will always be felt that you have traveled faster than any human being on earth." One thing Maitland did notice during these trials was a disturbing, ominous nibble in pitch as the R-6 gathered speed on its high, steep dive.

Maughan, following his colleague aloft the same morning, made twenty-four passes over the kilometer. He apparently also dove "several thousand feet . . . flattening out at 60 feet" — but he maintained level flight for the required distance prior to and over the course. And he established a new world record: 380·751 kmh (236·598 mph), the speed officially homologated April 10. Again, curiously, this figure was computed erroneously by averaging the times for each pair of south-north passes, and the mistaken result was accepted by the FAI! If the four individual speeds had been averaged correctly, Maughan's performance — the final 1-kilometer record — would be in fact 386·240 kmh (240·010 mph), proving the R-6 was indeed the first "4-mile-per-minute" aeroplane.

After the successful speed record flights inspection revealed several components loosened or torn off the aeroplanes. The aluminum carburetor air intake scoops were practically demolished, so new ones were made of steel. Where they had cracked, the cowls were repaired, and the exhaust stacks were cut down to the point where they were exposed only 1/8 inch. All open gaps (cowl-fuselage, etc.) were faired with doped-on cloth patches. Aeroplane P-279 was ready to continue speed trials April 7 in the hopes that to its laurels of being the final 1-kilometer record holder it would add the honor of making the first record over the new 3-kilometer distance. Lester Maitland was again aboard his earlier mount for these trials at Wright Field, still trying to get his name in the official record book, and accredited FAI observers were in attendance.

After a day of choppy air April 9 dawned clear and smooth. The R-6 was warmed up at 6:30 A.M., but after taxiing only 100 feet Maitland's left wheel struck a rut and the racer pitched up vertically on its nose. The damage was fairly extensive, requiring wing repairs, new struts, and one rebuilt fuselage bulkhead. Repairs were completed April 18, but when tests were resumed one week later, no new record was set. On April 26 Maitland ground-looped on takeoff, damaging the left wing and wheel. Obviously the chances of squeezing out enough for a new record were slim, so the tests were postponed indefinitely and both R-6s disassembled and hauled back to McCook for "inspection and reinforcing." New brass fuel tanks and all-steel torque-tube controls were installed and a new cowl for P-279 was made. Maitland's flight of April 25 was his last of thirteen R-6 flights, for a total time of approximately six hours.

R-6 after Maitland's takeoff accident, April 1923 (Au)

212

Curtiss R-6 with pilots Walter Miller, Lucas "Vic" Beau (not positively identified), and Johnny Corkille, 1923 (Au)

On May 3 the work, which had now slipped to low priority, stopped altogether.

Early in July the R-6 effort was rejuvenated in preparation for the 1923 Pulitzer race. Late in August P-278 was shipped to Wright Field for two weeks of final pre-race flight tests. Maughan and Maitland were not allowed to race again so that other pilots might "have a chance." The new pilot of Maughan's record-holding R-6, appointed August 20 by General Patrick, was First Lieutenant John D. Corkille from Brooks Field, one of the best-known instructors in the Air Service. To the several classes of flying cadets that required his final test upon completion of training he had become an institution; fledgling aviators agreed, "You don't know whether you can fly until you have passed Johnny Corkille." A Chicagoan, he had been a high school teacher before entering the Air Service in 1917. He was destined to become a highly regarded B-17 test pilot with Boeing as America girded for World War II.

Unfortunately during Corkille's first takeoff in the R-6 on September 4 he ground-looped, causing light damage to the left wingtip. After repairs he made two successful flights; then on September 10 his alternate, First Lieutenant Harry H. Mills, flew the ship. On landing Mills struck a rock and the left wingtip was again damaged! No doubt benefiting from their rapidly accumulating experience the ground crew again patched the wing and fuselage. The plane was then flown daily by Corkille, Mills, and the other two R-6 pilots assigned to the 1923 race team, First Lieutenant Walter Miller, a Bostonian on temporary duty from Crissy Field in San Francisco, prime pilot for R-6 P-279, and his backup, First Lieutenant Lucas V. "Vic" Beau, Jr., from Bolling Field, D.C. Son of the operator of one of the pioneer flying fields at Mineola, Long Island, young Vic would trolley daily to the flying field from his Larchmont home; he attended Mamaroneck High School, Syracuse and Cornell Universities before joining the Air Service. During World War II he flew heavy bombers and later, in 1947, became first commanding general of the Civil Air Patrol, serving eight years.

Decked out with their black fuselages, gold wings, and even one gold-painted Reed prop, the racers were shipped to St. Louis September 18, 1923. While P-278 was serving as a race trainer for the four handpicked pilots, still equipped with the original engine with which it won the 1922 race, the other R-6 was being fitted with a new D-12A engine in which horsepower had been boosted to over 500 (at 2,400 rpm) by boring out the cylinder sleeves. Miller's large-bore engine swung the Reed prop, Corkille's standard D-12 swung a newly designed wood prop. In truth, the Air Service had badly neglected air racing in 1923, devoting most of its meager funds that year to observation craft and the new Martin and Barling bombers. Nevertheless the Navy's devastating triumph in the 1923 Pulitzer should not completely overshadow the improvement gained from cleaning up both R-6s. Even though fifth and sixth in the final race standings, and some 25 mph off the winner's pace, their 219 mph and 216·5 mph closed-course performances were almost 10 per cent faster than in 1922.

On race day Corkille took off in the first heat following Sanderson's blood-red Navy F2W aloft while 85,000 spectators watched. With the whining sound of a high-explosive shell followed by an ear-numbing bark decrescendoing in the distance, Corkille dove from 3,000 feet and cut the pylon so tightly his start at first appeared illegal. He was slightly off course streaking in from the first lap because vibration had shaken the glass loose in his goggles. "The earth seemed to be quivering in front of me, and as I neared the pylons the only way I could see them was out of the corner of my eye. On the second lap I could not see the railroad and was again thrown off my course. Finally on the third lap I succeeded in getting my hand to my goggles for a second to readjust them, and was more comfortable for the remainder of the race." The top of Corkille's helmet was stripped off by the wind.

Miller's R-6 flew in the third heat behind one of the Navy R2Cs, which

Johnny Corkille in cockpit of Curtiss R-6, awaiting start of 1923 Pulitzer race (USAF)

was burning up the race course 40 mph faster than the previous year's winning speed, but in its transition to higher power the overbored R-6 had developed some hairy characteristics. As Miller popped into sight above the Missouri River approaching the pylon at Machens, he disappeared briefly behind a tall sycamore being used by the cluster of spectators there as a mark to spot the oncoming racers. Then he appeared again, "pitching and yawing," sending the spectators scurrying for cover. The group of officials atop the fragile, 100-foot pylon tower gulped and flattened as Miller's unsteady wingtip just missed clipping their flag. "Look out for number 49!" was the call passed along by those on the ground.

"My engine cut out on me at intervals from the very start of the race and I knew I was in for a tough job," Miller stated later. "I could not get the speed out of it although I did my best. It seems to me the motor is too fast for the plane. It seemed to be heavy in the nose and I had . . . difficulty on that account. I had no other trouble and I know the ship will do better because I have taken her over faster sprints in trial flights." Nevertheless, Miller pushed his mount hard enough to beat his comrade and average almost 220 mph.

After the race both R-6s were shipped back to McCook Field and placed in storage October 18, 1923 — anniversary of the first R-6 world speed record.

In the back-and-forth Army-Navy Pulitzer seesaw, the Army would now administer the 1924 event exclusively while the Navy attended to Schneider Trophy preparations, but the number, condition, and performance of Pulitzer participants all indicated a serious decline. The two R-6s made up half the entry list. Early in March 1924 it was proposed to modify both R-6s with Packard engines and differential controls such as those used on the successful Navy R2C racers, but a tight budget dictated less ambitious

plans. P-278 still retained its original D-12 and was slated for training. If it "survived" it would be equipped with a new, high-power D-12A for the race.

Both remodeled R-6s were bright silver when they emerged for their 1924 duties. On July 1 Alex Pearson, another Army Pulitzer pilot, test-flew P-279 and recommended a change to differential controls, so this originally canceled suggestion was resurrected and the installation completed on both aeroplanes. Pearson was killed in a test two months later when a hollowed-out interplane strut on his R-8 racer suddenly collapsed, so new wing struts having solid laminations were quickly fitted to both R-6s.

Several R-6 test flights were accomplished during August, mostly to test different props and engine modifications. Captain Burt E. "Buck" Skeel, because he had won the 1923 Mitchell Trophy race, was already slated as one of the Pulitzer pilots and he flew his mount, P-278, from McCook to Wright Field August 25. The other R-6, delivered by truck, would be raced by First Lieutenant Wendell H. Brookley, a McCook Field test pilot. Both racers now had D-12A engines but the Air Service imposed another decree which would soon generate scathing criticism. They decided that no possibility existed of exceeding the Navy's 1923 speeds with their three restored racers, but professed an intention to provide "an interesting race" between "evenly matched" aeroplanes. Therefore, since three metal props were "unavailable," wood props (design X-45101) would be used on all racers.

The new prop, manufactured of birch at McCook Field, was "especially designed for the high-power D-12A" and given the "customary 50 per cent overload whirl tests." However, two props of similar design (X-44059) failed in whirl tests because some of the glue joints between laminations were open, being "starved joints" where the glue had been pressed out during manufacture. One of the failed

Curtiss R-6 at Wright Field, 1924, fitted with controversial Air Service wood prop   (USAF)

props had a starved joint between laminations 3 and 4 over a 20-inch length from the tip. Moreover, the shear strength of these glue joints tested consistently inferior to that of solid wood. According to McCook Field engineering data, several starved joints were found to exist in USAS wood props.

During a pre-race flight in P-278 by Skeel the plane ground-looped on landing, damaging the lower wing. It was "replaced by another wing in good condition" and the tendency to ground-loop was reduced by realigning the tailskid with the aeroplane's axis. The total flying time on each R-6 prior to the 1924 Pulitzer was certainly less than fifty hours, probably less than twenty-five; P-278 had 8:28 since overhaul at race time, its engine 4:50 since new. Both planes had been put in "the best possible condition."

Buck Skeel was a determined pilot with 826 hours to his credit. After a wartime tour with the 14th Division (Infantry) and six months' dreary service during 1919–20 as American

delegate to the Inter-Allied Waterways Commission in Germany, he opted for Air Service glamour in August 1920, trained at Carlstrom Field, Arcadia, Florida, and reached the 1st Pursuit Group one year later, August 29, 1921. He lived at Selfridge Field with his wife and two small children, and before the Pulitzer he remarked to his friends, "I'm going to win this race or else . . ."

During a pre-race conference it was stated that the length of the starting dive was "entirely up to the pilot's judgment." During test flights Brookley had also noticed the disturbing tendency for the R-6 to oscillate longitudinally in long, steep dives, and he intended to limit his dive, beginning no higher than 1,000 feet and recovering by 350 feet, which he would then maintain around the course. The silver R-6s took off in tandem at 2:45 P.M. before 50,000 spectators and drilled skyward into a sharp, southwest wind. Over Huffman Dam they disappeared into a lumpy overcast through which the sun was trying to break, and an electricity of anticipation crackled through the

Burt E. Skeel and his Curtiss R-6, 1924 Pulitzer *(USAF)*

Wendell Brookley at the 1924 Pulitzer *(USAF)*

crowd, all eyes squinting skyward, searching for the first glimpse of the racers to reappear in their downward streak toward the starting line.

Brookley followed Skeel into the clouds, losing sight of him as he rose through the billowy mist, bursting into a clean, blue sunlit world above a mantle of blinding white and seeing the other R-6 again. With the cold knife of wind slicing at his cheek Brookley leveled at 4,000 feet, watching the silver flash of Skeel's R-6 diminish far above him. Then he saw Skeel's tiny racer peel off and hurtle steeply down. Throttling his engine, Brookley sank into the soft white floor, wires humming. As purple-gray details of the ground began to form, he eased on power and pushed over, catching sight of Skeel already below. Suddenly Brookley's R-6 began a violent oscillation which interrupted his engine. He grabbed the stick with both hands to hold it in neutral, gradually damp the oscillation, and flatten his dive.

As the sun grew bright through a break in the clouds, directly into

thousands of upturned eyes, the first R-6 appeared in edge-on view, diving at an angle of some 60 degrees. Suddenly sunlight flared on what "appeared to be a bursting shell." A moment of quiet perplexity passed before one realized with horrifying abruptness that Skeel's R-6 had disintegrated and was plummeting vertically into the ground. Bits of wreckage floated down after the ship buried itself 10 feet deep in the muck of a creek bank 1 mile from the grandstand.

Brookley continued undaunted around the hexagonal race course and finished in second place, just edged out by Harry Mills in the Verville-Sperry R-3. Both ships averaged within a mile of 215 mph even though Brookley reported "at several times during the race my motor sputtered on hitting heavy bumps." As a tribute to his dead comrade, and a mark of confidence in his racer, Brookley stunted briefly before landing.

Within forty-five minutes a hastily convened four-member board of inquiry headed by Major Clinton W. Howard was already at the crash site and

Remnants of Skeel's R-6 after fatal crash, 1924 Pulitzer *(USAF)*

Brookley's R-6 rounding home pylon, 1924 Pulitzer. Note dummy city used for air attack demonstration. (USAF)

1,500 feet and the flying wires then in turn pulled off the upper wing as they tore loose. They stated flatly that the failures found in the R-6 wings "could not have been caused by a failure in any other part of the aeroplane," and also pointed out that post-race inspection of P-279 disclosed evidence of structural deterioration in some wing ribs and spars. When P-279 was later destroyed in sand static tests it held up surprisingly well.

The Board's recommendations included eliminating diving race starts, neglecting to see that in one sense this was ostrich-like because diving was necessary for combat fighters, which these racers were supposed to foster; and significantly, excluding wood props from future high-speed racing. Indeed, this only made sense since Dr. Reed's metal props enabled newer Curtiss racers to achieve more brilliant performances.

End of last R-6's career as subject for structural loading tests (S)

beginning to realize that the unanswered question would be simply: did the wings peel off or did the prop split? The racer's fuselage had gone in steeply and they found most of it buried 10 feet deep with parts of the lower wing deeply imbedded, still attached to the fuselage. The wing panels, virtually intact, had fluttered down to land hundreds of feet away. They also found the prop hub and one intact bank of cylinders — "not even scored" — in the water adjacent to the crater. The other bank of cylinders was recovered, badly crushed, with a broken crankshaft and twisted connecting rods, about 100 yards from the crash site. The prop laminations were noted to have parted cleanly. If indeed the prop laminations had split apart when the engine wound up during the dive, the flailing, unbalanced club would have yanked the engine apart like a wishbone, torn out the center cabane, and allowed the wings to fold. Escaping coolant water would form a bomb-burst in the sky. English aviation journalist C. G. Grey, who

was a witness, wrote, "Later it was proved fairly conclusively that the airscrew burst . . ." and, in his opinion, it was "singularly imbecile to fit a wooden airscrew to an engine of such power designed for such speed." This severe indictment was widely echoed in unofficial circles. D-12 engine designer Arthur Nutt, who was present to witness the tragedy, agreed wholeheartedly.

Certainly, having ordered the use of wood props, the Air Service would understandably be reluctant to admit one might have caused the accident. The Board of Inquiry took a contrary view that the engine had been intact until impact, although they could not explain why it split apart so curiously. Interrogation of several witnesses by the Board revealed disagreement over the sequence of the aeroplane's breakup since it occurred so suddenly; however, most observers thought the top wing came off first. Yet the Board concluded, from certain structural evidence, that the left lower wing had failed first in horizontal shear at an altitude below

216

THE GOLDEN THOROUGHBREDS

15

The Curtiss R2C Racers

At Curtiss' annual meeting in February 1923 Board Chairman C. M. Keys had a lot to crow about. True, 1922 profits were low ($16,000, down from $101,000 in 1921), but order backlog stood at almost $4 million, more than double the previous year, and the Buffalo plant, closed by the Armistice, would be reopened to produce engines. But what Keys really wanted to talk about was the results of his audacious policy of "development and invention": the brilliantly successful D-12 engine; the equally successful wing radiator ("a new method of cooling engines," Keys reported); and Curtiss domination of the nation's premier speed classic and world maximum speed

record. Keys did not know it then but Curtiss was about to enjoy another successful year, indeed a momentous one. In 1923 Curtiss racers would win both Pulitzer and Schneider trophies and set a commanding new world speed record; the practicability of Dr. Reed's metal propeller would be demonstrated; C. R. Fairey would buy rights to produce the D-12 in England, to be called Felix abroad; and PW-8 fighter production would begin, the PW-8 becoming the standard Army type. But there was one 1923 Curtiss product that would stand out above all others: the R2C Navy racer.

In 1922 Curtiss finances had become considerably complicated, and although the firm was solvent, Keys,

First Curtiss R2C-1, September 1923; note wood propeller. (C)

Curtiss R2C-1; note wing radiators. (C)

the largest single stockholder, was struggling to liquidate excess capitalization and reduce long-term debt so that the company might begin to pay some dividends. In a confusing financial reorganization that took place March 1923 the manufacturing division emerged under the title Curtiss Aeroplane & Motor Company. Their military business was picking up nicely. After the Army's stunning success in 1922 with the R-6, the Navy now determined to make a comeback and invested in the development of updated racers. The new design can be largely attributed to Bill Wait, who was now racing aeroplane project engineer, still answering to Gilmore. Arthur Nutt was, of course, largely responsible for the new D-12A engine. The two new racers were direct descendants of the R-6 but with some important differences.

The Navy was spending large sums of money to develop two new types of service engines: a bomber/torpedoplane engine of 700 hp (the Wright T-series) and a fighter engine of 500 hp (an improved D-12). The Navy's 1923 racers would be flying test-beds for the

new engines, with promised orders for one hundred engines of each type. To boost the standard 465-hp D-12 power output by almost 50 hp, Curtiss enlarged the cylinder bore by 1/8 inch and increased the compression ratio to 5·8. The new engine produced 507 hp at 2,300 rpm on a dynamometer run using fuel "doped" with 50 per cent benzole, and the racing D-12A engine to go into the new racers could boast a weight-power ratio of 1·3 pounds per horsepower together with one of the highest power-frontal area ratios achieved to that time. A wood propeller was originally fitted to the first R2C but when replaced with a Reed twisted duralumin prop a speed increase of more than 10 mph was realized. The second R2C had the metal prop from its inception.

The R2C design employed refinements of high-speed techniques begun in 1922, but Gilmore later commented that eight separate configurations were "laid out before the final design was chosen": one triplane, two sesquiplanes (one with retractable gear), one monoplane, and four bi-

Landing wheel hub of Curtiss R2C-1 showing internal shock absorber (C)

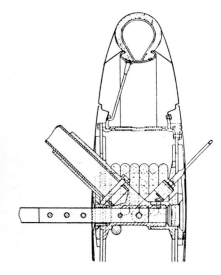

Cross section of Curtiss internally sprung wheel used on the R2C-1

planes. Metal wings were also considered. Even though Curtiss was aware of such advances they were too deeply involved with their own special brand of fixed-gear, thin-wing biplane to abandon it.

The R2C wing area was increased over the R-6's by 10 square feet and the upper wing lowered to the fuselage summit to eliminate cabane drag but not, assuredly, from any residual regard for Koolhoven's outdated

Rudder pedal assembly, Curtiss R2C; note the gearing and the elliptical-shaped cable pulleys. (C)

The dearly obtained hickory tailskid, capped with steel runner, Curtiss R2C-1 (C)

Harold Brow with the first Curtiss R2C-1, September 1923 (C)

Al Williams with the second R2C-1, September 1923; note Reed metal prop. This team set the world speed record two months later — 266 mph. (C)

eye of Harold J. Brow, already chosen by the Navy as one of its 1923 racing team.

On September 9, 1923, less than a month before the Pulitzer race, Lieutenant Brow took R2C A-6691 aloft on its first ten-minute test flight at Mitchel Field, and on a test four days later he recorded a level speed of 244·15 mph with the wood prop. A day-to-day running battle was being waged with the Wright F2W, built to carry the larger 700-hp T-3 engine, which was being flight-tested at the same field. The second R2C, A-6692, was soon

1919 theory. The R2C wings were now of unequal span and chord and used a further updated speed airfoil, the Curtiss C-62. Wing construction was further improved over the R-6's; it was discovered that by changing the grain of the plywood planking wing torsional strength could be improved considerably, allowing a very light internal structure of thin webs and capstrips. Only two beams were solid spruce. The wing radiators were fabricated of ·004-inch corrugated brass sheet, with the entire water supply circulated through the engine and radiator five times per minute. The main lift wires were attached to the undercarriage in a steep angle that made a very rigid brace. The R2C used a cross-axle single-strut rigid chassis with the shock absorbers cleverly contained inside special wheels which were faired with aluminum shields and fabric-covered. Fuselage construction was

virtually identical to the R-6's with high-tensile steel tube now used forward of the firewall, the engine mount designed to be readily detachable. The rudder and elevator used differentially geared controls so that normal control movements would produce very small surface deflections, making the plane less sensitive at high speed, but large control inputs would still result in large deflections. This made the aeroplane "very easy to fly" compared to earlier racers, according to Gilmore. The tailskid, which had to be small but tough, presented a unique problem because the best wood known for the job was second-growth hickory and this Wait wanted to use. 'We had a hell of a time finding it," Wait recalled. The search took days but they were finally rewarded by "an old wagonmaker in upstate New York who had some." The racers were built at Garden City under the watchful

Line-up of Navy racers, 1923 Pulitzer   (S)

Starting the winning racer, 1923 Pulitzer; note men with linked wrists preparing to swing the propeller.   (USN)

Harold Brow and his R2C-1 at the 1923 Pulitzer   (USN)

finished and undergoing flight tests by its pilot, Lieutenant (jg) Al Williams.

The three-day 1923 St. Louis air meet was, for its time and even for years afterwards, the largest and most successful flying meet the world had seen. The highlight, of course, was the unlimited free-for-all Pulitzer race, which in 1923 covered only 200 kilometers, an officially recognized closed-course distance — the Navy expected to break some records! The exuberant pilots and ground crews poured into town, most of them staying at the Chase Hotel, where an unbridled holiday atmosphere prevailed. Brow was provided the means for some memorable expeditions during his leisure hours when he was given the use of a Packard touring car, one of those magnificent glistening chariots with an ostentatious, fuel-guzzling V-12 engine. He naturally tried siphoning the Navy's blended aviation fuel into the car but this resulted in "horrible vapor lock inside of a mile." Finally he was forced to buy regular gas. "It cost me 20¢ a day!" he laughed.

An exploding bomb signaled the Pulitzer race and the sky filled with screaming, charging racers. The careful attention to racer development gave the Navy a Roman holiday, the four Navy planes capturing the first four places. Since the Army had spent virtually nothing toward racing in 1923 the real battle that evolved was between Curtiss and Wright, but even with their high-powered Tornado engines the Wright racers were no match for the sleek R2Cs and they finished more than 10 mph off the pace. Al Williams was wearing his one and only greasy, tattered good-luck shirt and his little blue-and-gold R2C beat the world speed record for 100 and 200 kilometers by over 37 mph. Prior to the race Williams and Brow had practiced high-g turns around the course until they knew the landmarks perfectly, Williams even covering part of the windshield in his practice plane to simulate the almost blind $2'' \times 6''$ panels of the R2C windshield. The immaculate flying job by both pilots included 7-g pylon turns during the race. "Spad" belts, which included one of the earliest shoulder harness arrangements, were provided in the R2C and gave a solid, secure feeling to the ride. Nevertheless, during the violent pylon turns Williams blacked out, causing the "speed king of the world" to comment after the race, "It feels funny and you can say for me that I felt funny when it was all happening. I knew I was making great speed, but I did not know just what it was. I crossed the starting line with my indicator showing 280 mph. I kept her wide open but my speed dropped some, and somewhere in the

Al Williams taking off to win the 1923 Pulitzer   *(USN)*

third lap I went woozy. I felt just like I was asleep. It was those turns that did it. I couldn't see so I jerked off my goggles but that didn't help any, it seemed. I was all mixed up and lost track of the laps. Sure was woozy. I knew things were mixed up so I went around again to make sure." As in 1922 the puzzling phenomenon of blackout left pilots discomforted and confused. After he landed, the victorious Williams was greeted by Admiral Moffett, flushed with excitement, who slammed his

gold-encrusted hat onto Williams' head and shouted for someone to "give the boy a drink!"[1]

Williams averaged almost 244 mph to win, an astonishing performance — his average, including the turns, was faster than the official world speed record. Brow posted a close second in

[1] A fanciful article entitled "How I Won the Pulitzer" over Al Williams' name appeared in *Aeronautical Digest* but was disavowed by the pilot in a November 21 letter to *Aviation* magazine, published in the December 10, 1923, issue.

A-6691 with a speed not even 2 mph less than his compatriot despite a serious overheat that developed during the third lap. As he later described it, one connection came unsoldered at the water header tank located in the top wing with connections soldered to tubes going to the radiators on each wing panel. "It looked something like a turtle with eight legs," Brow explained. When one leg came loose, water seeped out at a rapid rate, and soon his water temperature gauge hit

the peg at 212° F. Shortly thereafter, on the last lap, the engine rpm dropped from 2,300 to 2,250, but Brow kept the throttle "two-blocked" and thundered by the last pylon, After he landed and cut the switch the steaming engine continued to diesel for almost a full minute.

On October 7, the day following the race, Al Williams was to make speed trials over a measured 3-kilometer course at St. Louis with A-6692, but the difficulty in mustering observers, and inability to lay out a proper measured course, compounded by a stiff, gusty northeast wind, caused NAA officials to recommend the trials be postponed. Rear Admiral Moffett concurred. Instead, for the hundreds still on the scene, Williams put on a thrilling demonstration of the racer's amazing aerobatic qualities.

The R2Cs were then shipped back to the Curtiss plant on Long Island. There, a month after the Pulitzer race, both were ready for official attempts on Maughan's already obsolete world speed record. The real question was which R2C would perform the trick. Williams and Brow were back to fly in what was probably the most thrilling high-speed duel in aviation history. The course was measured between the southeast corner of Mitchel Field in Mineola and the northwest corner of Curtiss Field in Garden City. The average of the speeds — not times, to avoid mistakes made before — of the best four consecutive passes was to be taken, and the planes were restricted to 50 meters (164 feet) altitude. The duel started on November 2, 1923, with hundreds of curious spectators clogging the roads adjoining the airfields. Brow and Williams would take turns batting the record back and forth in a good-natured but competitive Alphonse and Gaston style.

On November 2, Brow in A-6691 was first aloft and for thirty minutes he zipped back and forth past the markers, his best four-pass average on this flight being just over 257 mph. Then Al Williams shot skyward in

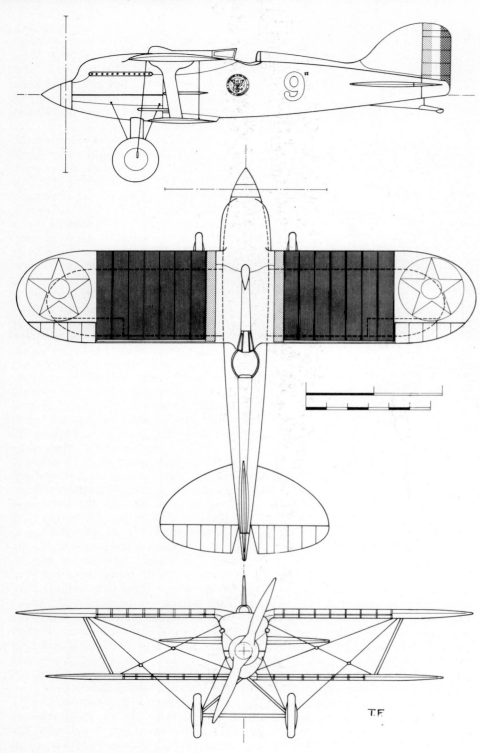

The 266-mph Curtiss R2C-1, world speed record and Pulitzer race winner, 1923

222

A-6692 and raised the speed mark to almost 259 mph. It was Brow's turn again, and on his forty-minute flight, displaying beautiful control and a true finesse between the markers he eked out enough extra to average 417·590 kmh, which was officially homologated as a world maximum speed record – not quite 260 mph, but it stands as the first record in excess of 400 kmh. Brow's golden-bordered *diplôme de record* became historical just two days later, however. The winds had been strong on November 3, which gave the ground staff a good excuse to give both racers a thorough going-over and tune-up. Both pilots were back at Curtiss Field early on November 4, sniffing the wind, which happily had slackened enough to resume festivities. Since Brow was record holder, Williams had first honors and in the best consecutive four out of twelve passes he averaged 263·3 mph, establishing a solid, definite margin, well over 260 mph. Williams considered his flying duties finished for the day and changed his sweater for an overcoat, preparing to leave. But Brow was already aloft, and Williams decided to wait and watch his trial. Brow pushed A-6691 to 265·69 mph in four straight passes, with his best pass being a blistering 274·2 mph downwind.

Williams heard the results, quickly traded outer garments again, and stalked to his aeroplane, making a good-natured crack to the grinning Brow, who had just taxied up. Three mechanics gripped arms and swung the D-12A into action, its staccato exhaust barking out sharply. Williams was quickly off and climbing urgently, his tiny ship almost disappearing at its peak altitude of 9,000 feet. Then he came shrieking down in a breakneck dive, waiting until the last possible moment to flatten out and hurtle across the course at barely 30 feet altitude. Even grizzled Curtiss veterans held their breath at Williams' heedless display. Panels on the ground arranged in plus or minus signs signaled his

results after each pass. Pulling up after his sixth and last pass at almost 270 mph he streaked straight through the middle of a ponderous flight of Martin bombers as they were approaching for landings at Mitchel Field, unaware of the speed contest, and a spectacular collision was avoided by mere chance. This display worried the base commanding officer, who wanted the speed duel called off before something nasty happened. Indeed, in their supreme battle the two R2Cs had broken the world speed record three times in less than two hours!

Williams' average of 429·025 kmh (266·59 mph) was officially recognized as a world maximum speed record and stood for over thirteen months until December 1924 when Warrant Officer Bonnet, in the Bernard V.2, beat it by less than 12 mph. On November 5 both Secretary of the Navy Denby and Rear Admiral Moffett telegraphed congratulations to the fliers, Moffett adding in his wire, "Discontinue speed tests but permit both pilots to fly planes for Army Relief Benefit."

Al Williams in a month had flown the R2C to a Pulitzer win and a world speed record, and after a rousing (20,000) parade at Van Cortlandt Park for the big ex-pitcher he was back at Mitchel Field on Election Day, November 6, for an "Air Carnival" to benefit the Army Relief Society. In spite of threatening weather more than 100 planes showed up and nearly 12,000 people paid admission to get in while 10,000 more lined the roads skirting the field. Most expected another speed duel, and the atmosphere tightened when Williams and Brow fired up their racers. Every plane in the sky was ordered to land to make way for the day's big attraction. But additional speed trials had been expressly forbidden so a display of beautiful aerobatics was put on by the snappy R2Cs, and Williams made a spectacular climb to 5,000 feet in less than one minute from a low pass. The French war ace Charles Nungesser, who was attending with his new bride, remarked, "If I had a plane like that with two guns I could drive down anything."

Brow's twenty-minute exhibition flight that day was his ninth and last R2C flight, all in A-6691; his total R2C time was just 4:25, logged in two months, but in that scant amount was included a first test flight in type, a second in the world's premier speed classic, and a world speed record! On November 10 the Mitchel Field Air Carnival was repeated and Rear Admiral Moffett gave Army Lieutenant Edward E. Johnson permission to give an exhibition in R2C A-6692. In its last known flight as a landplane the racer was put through daring aerobatics at up to 250 mph for the crowd.

After November 1923 the great Navy team of Brow and Williams never raced together again although Williams went on to fly the Curtiss R3C and other racers including two abortive Schneider Trophy challengers. When in 1930 he was finally, unavoidably ordered to sea duty Williams promptly resigned

from the Navy and joined Gulf Oil Corporation, becoming Aviation Manager from 1933 until 1951. While with Gulf his flamboyance gave everlasting fame to a series of orange, blue, and white sunburst aeroplanes called the Gulfhawks, the most famous being a Grumman biplane which was a fixture at air meets during the 1930s. The "speed king's" last Gulfhawk was a Grumman F8F, fittingly the same type that in 1969 proved itself officially as the fastest piston-powered aeroplane ever to be built. Williams served in the Marine Corps Reserve between 1935 and 1940 as a major, and wrote an iconoclastic column for the Scripps-Howard newspaper chain. He shot well from the hip, seldom bothering to shoot from the shoulder, and was eventually forced to leave the Marines when he "spoke out on some tender subjects," as Brow put it. The subject was air power. Williams, like Lindbergh, toured Germany in 1938; they both test-flew the amazing Messerschmitt Me.109. Williams called it a

The fatal interplane strut. Its collapse caused the crash in which Alex Pearson was killed, September 1924   (USAF)

Curtiss R-8 (ex-R2C), sold to the Army for $1, 1924   (USAF)

"perfect fighter" but no one back home wanted to listen – then. Still the rugged individualist, he served as a technical consultant during World War II but accepted no pay. Despite his thirteen years' Navy service Williams made his only carrier landings in 1934 with his old speed antagonist Hap Brow while riding the observer's seat of a torpedo plane from VT-2, the squadron Brow then commanded. They were flying from the old Saratoga and Williams was in the back seat describing a naval review on a short-wave hookup for NBC. Williams eventually retired to his farm retreat Eyrie near Elizabeth City, North Carolina. Brow recalled he "had a bad back." Al Williams died in 1958, aged sixty-four.

The R2Cs were placed in storage over the winter of 1923–24. On April 14, 1924, A-6691 was transferred to the Army in a sale made official by the Navy, which collected the sum of one dollar. The aeroplane

reached McCook on May 12, where it was numbered P-354 and given Air Service serial 23-1235. In June it was designated R-8, given a silver paint job and otherwise groomed for the 1924 Pulitzer race at Dayton, with First Lieutenant Alex Pearson selected to fly it. A "Lazy Tong" mechanical starter was installed to do away with punishing and dangerous hand starts. On August 2 Pearson hopped the refurbished racer over to Wright Field, where during the next month he built up 4:51 running speed trials and other tests.

On September 2 three Army Pulitzer pilots, Skeel, Brookley, and Pearson, were on trial runs in the two R-6s and R-8. Pearson, perched high over the flat green countryside in his silver craft, pointed its shark nose down, noting the texture of Wright Field's grass expanse forming through the prop arc, the 3-kilometer course a mile ahead. At 300 feet he pulled back

223

to flatten out – suddenly there was a report like a howitzer, the cockpit side felt heavy, the horizon went crazily awry like a windmill gone wild. Pearson was strong – he struggled . . . Witnesses saw the left wing fold down and the racer suddenly roll violently several times. Pearson had cut the gun, and "appeared" to be outside the cockpit holding onto or being held by something. He jumped clear in desperation or fell, landing about 75 yards from the aeroplane's impact point. Rescuers who rushed to the scene found him dead on the spot.

The crash has been attributed to the failure of the left I-type laminated wood interplane strut from which the inner layers of laminate were cut to save weight, making the strut hollow and subject to high-speed flutter. Pearson had been an especially resourceful pilot, first distinguishing himself in the Army's 1919 transcontinental derby. On a later transconti-nental flight attempt he was forced down in Mexico, where he was given up for lost, but several days later he reappeared astride a burro. He had been forced out of the 1923 Pulitzer while flying a Verville-Sperry R-3 in the same heat with Al Williams, which led a pundit to say, "No sooner were the racers away/than the Navy's Williams began to sink the Army gray!" Now Pearson, who hoped to turn the tables by racing the very type that beat him, would never have the chance. Ironically, the same R-3 that let him down in 1923 won the 1924 race a few weeks later.

The services called a joint conference after Pearson's accident. The Navy had suddenly become concerned lest their planned use of the R2C in the upcoming Schneider be jeopardized, and recalled uneasily the stress both planes had undergone in their November speed trials. But the problem seemed clearly to be the hollow strut.

Curtiss R2C-2 at Port Washington, Long Island, for high-speed testing, 1924   (NA)

Curtiss R2C-2 built for the 1924 Schneider Trophy race   (NA)

Solid struts were substituted, and as a final thought, it was recommended that race pilots wear parachutes.

Early in 1924 the Navy detailed Curtiss to redesign their remaining R2C as a seaplane for the upcoming defense of the Schneider Trophy, to be piloted by the 1923 Schneider winner David Rittenhouse. A-6692 was taken from storage and its engineering data thoroughly overhauled. The 500-hp Curtiss D-12A engine was retained with fuel capacity increased by placing tanks in the pontoons; wings and fuselage remained unaltered although wind tunnel tests led to the adoption of larger control surfaces. The 1924 Schneider was canceled when foreign competition withdrew, but plans were made for the R2C-2, as the seaplane version was designated, to fly the intended fifty-kilometer course ten times to attack every seaplane speed record up to that distance. Then a later decision was made to "save" the R2C-2 for the 1925 contest, and its only flights in 1924 were contractor trials.

On September 27, 1924, Rittenhouse took the plane from the hangars of the Curtiss Metropolitan Airplane Company (formerly the American Trans-Oceanic Company) at Port Washington, Long Island, where it had been assembled as a seaplane, and on its first flight, lasting thirty minutes, he averaged 227·5 mph in several passes over the 4·26 miles between Execution Light and Stepping Stone Light. The pontoons had cut only 40 mph from the racer's top speed! On one downwind pass he clocked himself with a hand-held stopwatch at 242 mph. This average beat his own record, set in a CR-3 during the 1923 Schneider race, by more than 30 mph, but the R2C speeds were unofficial, being merely a part of contractor guarantees.

In 1925 the advent of the R3C racers overshadowed the R2C-2, but the first American entry list for the 1925 Schneider — before the Army got into the act — listed, besides the Navy's two R3C-2s, the R2C-2 which Lieutenant Frank H. "Hersey" Conant II, USN, had been detailed to fly. When the Army later arranged to enter its R3C, the R2C-2 was dropped back to alternate status and missed its chance to race.

In 1926 the R2C-2 was assigned as a training aeroplane for the U. S. Navy Schneider pilots selected to defend the trophy against Italy. Lieutenant George T. Cuddihy flew it from the Naval Aircraft Factory at Philadelphia, where it had been overhauled, to Anacostia NAS in Washington in just thirty-two minutes to set a new record between those points. The original three Schneider pilots were Cuddihy, Conant, and First Lieutenant Harmon J. Norton, USMC. On September 13, 1926, Norton was out in the R2C-2 practicing low-level speed runs over the Potomac River near Anacostia. After finishing a speed trial over the measured course he pulled up behind two Army planes which were droning lazily at 2,000 feet toward Bolling, which borders Anacostia. Just as Norton was sliding into a neat parade formation, too intent on his position even to be aware of the horizon, the racer's rakish Eversharp nose was seen suddenly to pop down into a perpendicular dive. Norton had stalled, and now the massive pontoons were wrenching the racer into a violent spin. The pilot fought desperately to avoid his impending inverted crash by trying to roll over just before striking the water but he was unsuccessful. The R2C-2 plummeted into 6 feet of water just south of Haines Point and Norton was killed instantly. This was a severe blow to the American Schneider team. Norton had been one of the Marines' crack pilots, having flown in the 1925 Pulitzer, and his death was the first of a series of tragedies that decimated the American hopes for its third and conclusive Schneider win.

Thus ended abruptly the memoir of the remarkable R2C, a racer which began its existence with promise for a long career but which participated in only one race. Its outstanding performance presaged the final Curtiss racer design: the R3C.

THE GOLDEN THOROUGHBREDS

The Curtiss R3C Racers

Arthur Nutt, under the continued influence of Navy encouragement, started the design of a new engine in 1924 to be ready for the 1925 races. As he had done in the D-12A Nutt increased engine volume by enlarging the bore, this time by $\frac{1}{4}$ inch; he also lengthened the stroke the same amount, giving a swept volume of 1,400 cubic inches, but significantly he departed from D-12 practice by adopting open-ended cylinder liners similar to those of the Wright T-series engines. This was the only major design difference from the original wetsleeve monobloc methods that dated back to Kirkham. Confidence in construction techniques gained from accumulating D-12 experience enabled Nutt to pack this

increased volume into virtually the same outside dimensions, and even build a lighter unit by 30 pounds.

Designated V-1400, the new engine smoothly passed its Army fifty-hour test in February 1925, in less than seven days, but because on one bench test run at 2,525 rpm the test engine produced 619 hp, a figure quickly promoted in the press and recopied ever since, the myth of a 619-hp engine has somehow been transformed after a half century into fact. Actually the one 619-hp engine was considered a "freak." The others fell short of this figure and no doubt the freak did too after its bench run. Among the engine's teething troubles was a propensity to consume great quantities of oil; the "freak" engine was also

Curtiss V-1400 engine, 1925 (S)

termed "oil-less" for using less than 1 quart per hour during its test.[1] The military services were somewhat disappointed with the V-1400 and only twelve were built, five going to Curtiss P-2 fighters. But three were reserved for the 1925 air races.

Under C. M. Keys's vigorous leadership during the recent lean years which he characterized as "curiously uncertain for aviation," Curtiss had actually grown financially much stronger. As 1924 closed most major liabilities had been eliminated, Curtiss Field and the Garden City plant had been cleared of debt, the working capital position was healthy, net earnings had crept up to $156,000, but most significantly from Keys's standpoint, Curtiss was paying $6 dividend per

---

[1] At about this time Nutt was actively making the switch to tapered piston rings — that is, rings which would scrape down along the cylinder walls but not up; he personally credited the tapered ring with the greatest contribution to reducing oil consumption. It is possible the freak engine happened to have an early set of such rings, although Nutt cannot recall specifically and no documents have survived to confirm it. There seems to be no other rational explanation, however, for the disparity.

---

share of preferred stock. A major portion of earnings came from the growing commercial business, a field which Curtiss was now reentering with a vengeance. Dr. Reed's spectacularly successful metal propeller was proving to be a bonanza, especially in foreign markets, and Curtiss was expanding her exports. Indeed, the Italians has decreed that all 1924 Schneider designs were to be powered by Curtiss D-12 engines and a number had been shipped abroad, adding to those already sent to England in response to C. R. Fairey's enthusiasm. On the other hand, the capital advanced into experimental activities at Curtiss itself began to dwindle. It was time to begin translating techniques already perfected on the race course into improved products which could be sold in order to generate long overdue profits. Moreover, dependence on racing as a means to determine flying performance was growing less important as designers refined and perfected analytical skills. The improvement of experimental facilities and the accumulation of data from past racing programs hastened a gradual but

definite shift away from the expedience of the race course toward the deliberation of the laboratory, and by 1925 racer performance could be predicted quite accurately even before the aeroplane flew. The blue ribbon air race was taking on the aspect of an excruciating verification of hardware, glamorous to be sure, but an increasingly unnecessary luxury as cheaper and more repeatable means for this function were matured. Finally, Curtiss was beginning to find intolerable the financial drain involved in privately sustaining the highly skilled team of men who had to be painstakingly organized yet whose output at best was a small number of technically complex super-speed racers. The V-1400 owed its development in part to a long gap between military D-12 deliveries, which dried up in June 1924, not to resume for six months, prompting Curtiss privately to undertake the new engine in order to keep workers on the payroll during the interim. A firm policy of

ongoing government support for such frontier R&D appeared to be years away. Indeed, the total government expenditure for the 1925 racers came to only $500,000, a paltry sum to pay for what was purported to be frontier technology.

In order to acquire the new racers — the last American service racers built during the decade — without depleting limited funds, the services in a particularly noteworthy cooperative action joined forces in their procurement. In April 1925 the go-ahead was given unofficially by the Army and Navy jointly for a September delivery. Apparently the funding for one racer to be partially built and used for static strength tests to destruction was shared, whereas three flying versions were funded by the Navy (contract 63396) and designated R3C. They also were briefly labeled F3C-1, the standard fighter designation, and although one can speculate that this was simply a sop to justify funding, it cannot be

Curtiss R3C test airframe before undergoing landing gear drop test (2-foot drop), July 1925 (C)

227

confirmed. There was no special Army designation, and occasional references to "Curtiss R-9" are in error. The services agreed that the first of the three flying R3Cs would be tested by pilots of both services. Then, for the 1925 Pulitzer, the second would go to the Navy, the third to the Army. At this point the first would be put on pontoons for Navy use in Schneider Trophy preparations.

Bill Wait's 1923 racing design, the R2C, was used as the basis for the new plane and most dimensions remained unchanged. A new star was rising within the Curtiss galaxy and the name of T. P. Wright assumed prominence in the engineering organization.[2] Chief structures engineer was now Frank Hubbard. Under Gilmore the design effort became quite sophisticated for there were many detail improvements to be considered, aside from mounting the more powerful engine, and his staff was organized into aerodynamic, design, structure, weight, and propeller sections. The slim new C-80 airfoil, with a thickness only 6 per cent of its chord dimension, was chosen from a family of airfoils developed jointly by Curtiss and MIT. Curtiss perfected a machine which in just six hours could carve to specification any desired airfoil shape accurate to ·002 inch for wind tunnel test, and from these experiments the R3C was provided a wing whose peak lift-to-drag occurred at the angle for least drag — desirable to enable the racer to fly at this angle of minimum resistance while at the same time using the smallest wing surface possible. A set of even smaller wings for world speed record trials was contemplated but not built.

Design load factor was 12·5, yet to retain a light structure a detailed weight schedule — or weight "bogey"

[2] Theodore Paul Wright, educated at Lombard (Knox) College and MIT, had learned to fly with Curtiss at Mineola in 1917, became Navy Inspector at the Buffalo plant in 1920, Chief Engineer when Gilmore departed, and eventually rose to be Curtiss President.

as it came to be known — was prepared and posted prominently in the engineering department. Drawings could not be released to the shop unless the bogey weight was met or bettered, and on this point Gilmore was adamant. Overweight meant automatic redesign. If doubt existed over the strength of any part an example was built and tested to destruction. In this manner Curtiss perfected special bronze fittings for the R3C with 105,000-psi tensile strength; ordinary bronze was capable of only 60,000 psi. A one-twelfth-scale wind tunnel model of the finished plane was hand-carved from mahogany and tested in Curtiss' 7-foot tunnel, then one of the world's largest. Liberal use was made of modeling clay to develop the nose contours, for beyond the cold design formulae Gilmore strongly believed a successful design synthesis involved something more, some intangible factor warm and living. "If it looks well it will fly well . . ." he said. "An experienced designer is able to give to a racing aeroplane a certain touch of *something* that undoubtedly adds several miles to the top speed."

The final aeroplane was only some 100 pounds heavier than the R2C and was constructed using methods almost identical to those perfected in

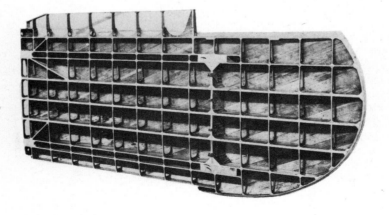

Curtiss R3C wing assembly   *(C)*

1923, which enabled a significant cost-saving. Cockpit visibility was improved by cutting out a portion of the top wing near the fuselage; window panels were triplex glass. The water expansion tank was mounted atop the fuselage as fairing for the windshield. Navy R3Cs were also built with the hinged metal cockpit panels called "breakaways." After Alex Pearson's death in 1924 provisions were made for racing pilots to wear parachutes, and the Navy moreover wanted a means for quick egress. The breakaways preserved a small cockpit opening until the pilot activated a dashboard mounted release connected to spring-loaded tripwires which pulled the breakaways free, enlarging the cockpit opening. A low-altitude, high-speed bailout was not practical, but in the event of engine failure the pilot could soar perhaps 1,000 feet on momentum alone, an altitude where an entirely feasible bailout could be made. The Army, however, felt breakaways were unnecessary and their R3C was built from the beginning without them. The tailskid of the Navy plane was built integrally with the fuselage and left in place after its later conversion to pontoons, while the Army's tailskid was later traded in for a bumper. The R3Cs were built

over the summer at Garden City and although of excellent construction they were not fashioned with the same fanatic care applied to earlier polished Curtiss racers; Wait himself called the finished R3C "rough." And it was, but it was smooth enough to exceed its contract speed guarantee by 10 mph.

The first R3C built (Navy A-6978) was equipped with the "freak oil-less" engine previously discussed, and in its own right became known as the "dogship" from the then popular euphemism "trying it on the dog." On the business end of its V-1400 was bolted the new Reed model "R" propeller whose dural blades were drop-forged, not twisted as earlier Reed props had been. The blade extended in a true helix to the hub and was variously credited with an efficiency as high as 89 per cent. This vastly improved prop had allowed engine designers to turn direct-drive engines at much higher rpm, a far cry from Nutt's power-derating exercise with the CD-12 back in 1921. An improved oil cooler in which the oil surrounded tubes through which the engine cooling water was routed was fitted to the R3C.

The first racer was rolled out September 11, 1925, with the Army's James H. "Jimmy" Doolittle and the Navy's Al Williams on hand to conduct test flights. A coin flip was won by Williams and he had the first go. Later, when the next two V-1400s reached Garden City for installation in the next two R3Cs — which would be the two Pulitzer competitors — Williams won his second coin flip, this time with Army Pulitzer pilot Cy Bettis, for first choice of engine. The services had also hoped to enter a number of service pursuits equipped with V-1400s in the Pulitzer for comparison with standard models under the stress of a throttle-bending race, but this plan fell through.

On Al Williams' first flight in the dogship one of the aluminum wheel streamlines cracked and the other blew off. As soon as mechanics

Curtiss R3C-1 cockpit, 1925. Throttle, fuel (mixture), and spark advance controls mounted on left; adjacent large lever (just below airspeed dial) is fuel wobble pump. Instruments on dashboard are all related to engine operation. Note pipes leading from wing radiators: protruding from fuselage above (for upper wing) and forward of control stick (inverted Y, routed to lower wing). (C)

repaired these shields Doolittle took a turn at the controls and on his first flight he made a 200-foot dive on the measured course and shot past the observers at nearly 300 mph. Suddenly the R3C became wing-heavy. Doolittle glanced out to see the left upper wingtip beginning to fail. He quickly throttled back and landed the racer for more extensive repairs. On the eighteenth Doolittle flew two laps of the 1925 Pulitzer course, which included sharp turns, and Gilmore personally timed him at 254 mph to the delight of all. Later the same day Al Williams made some high-speed dashes over a measured course and on one downwind pass he tore past at 302 mph. The wind was light – about 10 mph – but Williams was diving as he had done in his 1923 R2C world speed record flights and this no doubt contributed to his speed. Nevertheless, five miles per minute . . . This was far too sensational for the press to ignore! Williams is said to have done 268 mph upwind and averaged 285 mph, a speed that exceeded the 1924 French world mark, but unofficially.

Man was now truly on the verge of 300 mph and despite its drawbacks the V-1400 was performing flawlessly. The V-1400 power-to-weight was an incredible 1·12 pounds per horsepower, equal to the World War II Merlin, and its specific power of 26 hp per liter represented a watershed for the basic wetsleeve monobloc engine. Indeed, this figure did not increase until 1927, when geared engines were reintroduced successfully together with superchargers and better fuels, ancillary developments which allowed cylinder pressure and rpm to increase. There is no doubt that with its smaller frontal area when compared to the Hispano W-12 that powered the world record Bernard, the V-1400 could easily have bulled a specially designed plane to well over 300 mph. But such a plane almost assuredly would have a high landing speed, as did the French Bernard, and aside from the absence of money

for such a venture the Americans saw no practicality in it. Memories of the Texas Wildcat fiasco still hurt.

On September 22 Cy Bettis was aloft practicing for the Pulitzer race when half the nose spinner broke loose. The prop kicked it back where it slashed open two wing radiator sections, hit the interplane strut, and flung itself mangled into the stabilizer. Bettis managed to land in one piece and the aeroplane was pulled back into the shop for repairs. It was also put onto pontoons, emerging a week later. On September 29 it was photographed with its pilots at Port Washington, Long Island, and it is here that the oft-published photograph was snapped showing Doolittle standing on the pontoon of the dogship – *not* the plane he later flew to victory in the Schneider Trophy race.

Not only were the initial flight tests quite promising but considerable work had gone into refining race techniques as well. The young Army pilot who now held the reins of this latest Curtiss thoroughbred was particularly well suited to carry out the task of optimizing race performance. Jimmy Doolittle, more than most, was aware that air racing was no longer the slapdash affair it had been in Bert Acosta's day at Omaha, but was becoming a highly specialized type of flying subject to the rules of keen analysis like any other complex discipline. Doolittle, born in Alameda, California, in 1896, raised for part of his childhood in Alaska, did three years' work at the University of California School of Mining and learned at an early age, because of his small stature, to take care of himself, becoming Pacific Coast bantamweight boxing champion during his college days. From the School of Military Aeronautics at Berkeley in November 1917 he went to Rockwell Field, San Diego, for flight training, receiving his commission in March 1918 with an assignment to Dallas as an instructor, where he served until 1919, frustrated from being deprived of combat duty. He

The famous photograph of Jimmy Doolittle standing on the R3C pontoon in 1925; this was not his plane. (C)

to Doolittle the ideal turn should be entered and left smoothly, the radius centered to allow the aeroplane's path to slice by the pylon as closely as possible, and be of constant altitude and bank angle, the bank angle — and hence the turn radius — determined by the limit of g that did not kill speed unduly. Bill Wait also studied pylon turn tactics and came to the same conclusions with one modification that seemed necessary for the R3C. At high speed the racer proved to be very slightly out of trim, requiring forward pressure on the stick to hold level flight. But this deflected the elevator somewhat, which in turn retarded speed. Wait therefore suggested to both Bettis and Williams — as well as Doolittle — that they let the aeroplane rise slightly on the straightaway with stick neutral (faired elevator for least resistance), then dive 50 feet or so during the turn, which had the added

advantage of picking up speed at the pylon. Bettis agreed but Wait recalled that Al Williams "would have none of it," adding with a slight note of contempt for Williams' hauteur, "Al flew it his way but Cy won the race!" Doolittle also adopted Wait's suggestion in the Schneider race and applied one further modification to his technique by flying the upwind legs at the lowest possible altitude but the downwind legs at about 300 feet. This was done to take advantage of wind gradients near the ground which commonly exceed 10 mph in 100 feet (meaning the wind at a height of 200 feet would be blowing 20 mph faster than the wind at the surface); in fact, vertical "windshears" sometimes can reach 30 mph in 100 feet! Doolittle's experience was that the 300-foot height difference usually produced a gain of about 6–8 mph in achieved speed. Interestingly, the subject of

then put in two years of duty on the Mexican border. Doolittle was always noticeably modest, unassuming, and patient; in fact, he possessed these qualities to such a degree that he endeared himself to almost everyone with whom he came in contact and generated deep loyalty in those who worked with him. In September 1922 he made an exceptional one-stop transcontinental trip in a rickety D.H.4, taking off from the sand of Pablo Beach, Florida, and after 22:35 flying time arriving at Rockwell Field, California. This proved to be an important milestone in his career by setting him apart as an especially resourceful, competent pilot. Doolittle then attended MIT and earned an Sc.D. in aeronautics in two years, an incredible feat unequalled before or since. His next assignment was naturally to McCook Field as test pilot, and there his flying prowess increased daily, as well as his flying time. During 1924 Doolittle had several 100-hour months and in August he piled up 150:22 in test that involved virtually every type

of Army plane and took him to all parts of the country. Probably because of his compact size his tolerance to load factor was high and he was known to have tested a plane to destruction and then bailed out. He taught himself to withstand 4 g for long periods and it was largely through his effort that the phenomenon of blackout, so bewildering in 1922, was now in 1925 fully understood. Doolittle had equipped himself with an accelerometer and practiced the most violent aerobatics, deliberately subjecting himself to blackout, expanding the frontier of knowledge, and thereby indirectly of speed.

Now the knowledge was to be applied to the technique of pylon turns. The problem was that steeply banked, high-g turns, while of short radius, killed too much speed. Full-throttle, shallow banked turns — such as the Navy employed — cost time in flying the extra distance. Then there was the technique often used by the Italians of climbing on the turn and diving into the straightaway. Logically it seemed

Curtiss R3C Pulitzer racers with Curtiss race team at Mitchel Field, 1925. Kneeling in foreground, Army pilot Cy Bettis and Curtiss designer Bill Wait. Among those standing are from left: 2nd, Stanley Vaughan, Experimental Shop Foreman; 3rd, Al Blashill; 5th, Bill Irwin; 7th, George Wurtz. (C)

pylon tactics received a great deal more study over the years after 1925, but following all this study the 1931 conclusions of the RAF High Speed Flight, Schneider Trophy winners that year with the 400-mph S.6B, still agreed with Doolittle. The optimum pylon turn, said the RAF, is a constant altitude, constant banked turn of 4 g.

First Lieutenant Cyrus K. Bettis, the Army Pulitzer pilot, had earned his assignment by winning the 1924 Mitchell Trophy race. Doolittle was Bettis' alternate for the Pulitzer; their roles were reversed at the Schneider two weeks later. Bettis was born in Carsonville, Michigan, in 1893 and like Doolittle he served with the Mexican border patrol, then went to the Philippines for two years before reporting to the 1st Pursuit Group. Although an aggressive pilot with 1,800 hours in the air, Bettis was quiet and retiring on the ground, a bachelor subject to fits of lonesomeness. He lived in a guest room at Bill Wait's house during his stay on Long Island for the Pulitzer race and Wait recalled one evening he, his wife, and Bettis were sitting at Jones Beach in a languorous mood, a new moon high in the sky, the water softly lapping a few yards away. Bettis was contemplative, absently sifting the sand, talking about his chances in the race. Wait suggested he "toss some sand over his shoulder toward the east for luck." Bettis scooped a handful, then halted, examining something, cleaning it off. "What is it?" asked Wait. It was a gold antique earring of exquisite beauty. Almost at once the presence of the delicate lost bauble seemed to probe with a deep, unspoken meaning and touch in Bettis some wellspring of feeling. Bettis had it cleaned by a jeweler, who put it on a pin, and the pilot had it pinned to his helmet during his winning performance in the race. Ten months later Bettis was back on duty with the 1st Pursuit Group. Together with two squadron mates he had flown from Selfridge Field to Philadelphia, and on August 23, 1926,

Army and Navy huddle before the 1925 Pulitzer. Cy Bettis on left — note gold earring pinned to his helmet — and Al Williams. (Au)

in the lead, flying the Army's second P-1A (26-277), Bettis and his companions were returning to Detroit. Fifteen miles north of Lewistown, Pennsylvania, in the Seven Mountain region, the weather soured. Seeking a pass, Bettis was suddenly swallowed by cloud but refrained from maneuvering sharply to avoid confusing his wingmen, who were pulling away. Just then Bettis struck the south face of Bald Mountain (or Jack Mountain) near Milroy. He awoke ninety minutes later to find his leg snapped, his face crushed, shivers of bone awry. He remained at the crash site in agony for twenty-seven hours but finally — over another twenty-four desperate hours — dragged himself 2 miles along the rocky slope seeking help. He was found and flown by Ira Eaker to Walter Reed Hospital. Bettis improved rapidly at first but contracted spinal meningitis and died September 4 — less than a year after his Pulitzer triumph.

Shortly after, Wait was talking to one of his squadron mates and asked the whereabouts of the pin. The answer left him shaken. "Oh, that? The day before Cy cracked up he lost that pin." Cy Bettis shared with Doolittle the Clarence Mackay Trophy in 1926 for their 1925 racing achievements and Bettis Field in Pittsburgh was later named for him.

The Pulitzer drew near. On October 6 Bettis and Doolittle, to advertise the aerial extravaganza, stunted two pursuits over Manhattan, diving directly over Broadway below rooftop level, pulling up into graceful chandelles, and racing to the Statue of Liberty to settle a personal bet. The next afternoon R3C A-6979 made its first flight, only just having been finished. French war ace René Fonck was at Mitchel Field enviously observing the tests, remarking he had "never seen such beautiful ships." A newspaper reporter was moved to write, "The life of a high-speed racing pilot is not a merry one while in action."

Al Williams in cockpit of Curtiss R3C-1, preparing to start in the 1925 Pulitzer (Au)

Curtiss racers warming up for the 1925 Pulitzer (Au)

Al Williams, 1925 (S)

A huge storm lashed the city on what was to have been race day, with 80-mph gales sweeping across the Long Island plain. Someone asked Al Williams if he could race in such weather. "Getting off would be all right," he opined, "and once in the air the racers would be easy to handle, but in landing we would have trouble. And I don't want to crack up *this* baby," he added, tapping his chest. The Pulitzer race, obviously, was postponed, and race participants contemplated other current news — the Pirates and Senators had just opened the World Series; Mussolini was grasping for supreme power in Italy; the carrier USS *Lexington* had just been launched at Quincy, Massachusetts, taking some of the sting out of Billy Mitchell's shocking charges. His celebrated court-martial began October 13.

On October 12 the storm was spent although low, gray clouds still scudded in a bitter sky, a stiff wind blew across the course, and a thick haze hung in the air. Shortly after 3 P.M. the V-1400s were cranked into action and with bursts of flame visible from his exhaust stacks Williams took off and circled the field until the engine was performing to his satisfaction. Two minutes later Bettis was in the air in the Army's black-and-gold R3C when suddenly Williams shot past the

starting pylon like a blue-and-gold bullet, so fast a fabric wheel streamline blew away. Instead of chasing Williams, Bettis held back a few minutes before starting around the course, disappointing the 25,000 paid spectators, who had expected a close race instead of such obvious time trials. Since no dive was allowed neither pilot got above 300 feet. It was also observed that both aeroplanes were noticeably quieter than earlier Curtiss racers. This was largely attributed to the new R prop, although the Army R3C had a decidedly higher pitch than its competitor, this curious difference first being pointed out by a woman spectator who knew nothing of flying but who was an accomplished singer. The Army racer gained with each lap while Williams progressively lost, his last lap being a dismal 234 mph. Later the blame was partially laid on Williams' earlier full-power flight tests, where Bettis on the other hand had been content to break in his engine more slowly. Bettis' winning speed was just short of 250 when close to 270 had been expected, and Williams' performance was poorer than his R2C time in winning the 1923 Pulitzer. As he climbed out of his R3C in the old, soiled white shirt and blue trousers he always wore for racing, he was disconsolate and refused to talk about

the race. In fact, he refused to shake Bettis' hand until friends made him apologize like a churlish schoolboy. His sister Frances tried to console him, saying he had flown a beautiful race and it was time he left the Navy anyway to start practicing law; Williams would be admitted to the New York State Bar the following year, but had many more Navy flying exploits still to look forward to. Williams, it seems, was used to glamour; he strutted and swaggered, he occasionally blustered, especially to non-fliers, often giving a petulant, immature impression, and certainly that of a poor loser. There was no doubting his skill and tenacity, however, and he mellowed considerably during the 1930s, but ever remained caustic and somewhat patronizing.

Bettis taxied up grinning broadly and stood in his cockpit jostled by the crowd surging around him. His first words were, "Where's Al?" Later he commented, "The ship did better than I thought it would. The turns are important but to win you have to have a

combination of everything in your favor." He was asked about the pin on his helmet — Wait rode the R3C's tail as it was pulled back to the hangar and called reporters' attention to the pin — and Bettis laughed, simply saying it won the race for him.

The Navy, putting its Pulitzer disappointment aside, had now to concentrate on winning the Schneider. Both England and Italy had sent formidable teams, the English arriving October 4 with smug expressions to go with their spectacularly beautiful Supermarine S.4 monoplane which was already the world seaplane speed record holder, and their pilots came to New York to witness the Pulitzer race. Suddenly the Schneider opposition seemed overwhelming to the increasingly nervous Americans. They would arrive in Baltimore in a high state of anxiety, with all three R3Cs converted to pontoons.

The pontoons used in 1925 followed the Curtiss philosophy of ruggedness at some cost in high speed, first espoused so successfully on the CR-3

Judges atop home pylon hail the 1925 Pulitzer victor. (Au)

George D. Cuddihy, 1925 (C)

of 1923. The one significant design difference between the new pontoon of 1925 and that of 1923 was apparent in the angle of the bottom V. As Gilmore explained it, earlier aeroplanes which had limited power available for takeoff needed pontoons with an included angle of about 155 degrees in the V, but these were rather poor shock absorbers on alighting. As engines improved and available horsepower increased, and as landing speeds increased correspondingly, the angle was deepened to 120 degrees with good results. Special care was given to these pontoons, whose plywood skin, if not scrupulously smooth, could be peeled away with dramatic results by a hard, fast landing.

The American Navy pilots were George Cuddihy and Ralph A. Ofstie. Cuddihy, born in Alto, Michigan, in 1896, graduated from the Naval Academy in 1917, then served on the battleship USS *Mississippi* until June 1921, when he began flight training. Six months later he reported to VF-1 (Fighting Squadron 1) in the Pacific Fleet and promptly became high-score gunnery champion for two consecutive years, which brought him to the attention of Mitscher. In June 1924

233

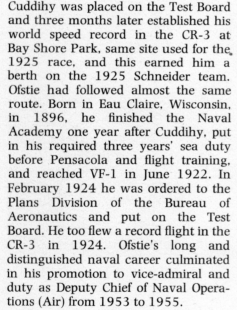

Cuddihy preparing to take off in the 1925 Schneider Trophy race   (NA)

Doolittle whips overhead on his way to victory in the 1925 Schneider Trophy race. (UPI)

Cuddihy was placed on the Test Board and three months later established his world speed record in the CR-3 at Bay Shore Park, same site used for the 1925 race, and this earned him a berth on the 1925 Schneider team. Ofstie had followed almost the same route. Born in Eau Claire, Wisconsin, in 1896, he finished the Naval Academy one year after Cuddihy, put in his required three years' sea duty before Pensacola and flight training, and reached VF-1 in June 1922. In February 1924 he was ordered to the Plans Division of the Bureau of Aeronautics and put on the Test Board. He too flew a record flight in the CR-3 in 1924. Ofstie's long and distinguished naval career culminated in his promotion to vice-admiral and duty as Deputy Chief of Naval Operations (Air) from 1953 to 1955.

The Army pilot was of course Doolittle, flying the same R3C in which Bettis had scored the Army victory in the Pulitzer. But how did the Army get into the seaplane business? A plausible story popular at the time related how the Army solemnly warned the Navy that their two R3Cs could not possibly finish the Schneider's 350 kilometers distance because of insufficient fuel

and oil supply (Pulitzer rules required fuel sufficient for only 1.33 times its 200-kilometer distance), thus, to "uphold U.S. honor," the Army R3C would be fitted with pontoons and entered in the race. This was announced on October 13; pontoons were ready — obviously the Army had planned this move beforehand — and the conversion of their racer was completed less than a week after the Pulitzer race. The Army entry displaced Hersey Conant's R2C-2 from the first team, limited to three aeroplanes.

Thoroughly business-like before the race, Bettis unselfishly acting as a "virtual mechanic" to him, Doolittle had already earned great respect even before he flew. In competition, no other pilot was up to his dazzling performance. His navigability trials on October 23 went off beautifully, especially his landings, which were better than the Navy's. On October 26, race day, at precisely two-thirty the black-and-gold Army R3C taxied out onto the ruffled surface of Chesapeake Bay, maneuvered into position, and soon thundered aloft. Doolittle then put his knowledge and experience to the test as he flashed around the Schneider course in what was described

as "the most perfect exhibition of flying yet seen." His first lap was 223 mph from a standing start (the Supermarine S.4, wrecked during its navigability trials, had achieved only 226 mph on its current world record) and his "cornering" caused a sensation, the officials on the judges' stand actually getting the wind from his propeller. Cuddihy and Ofstie were averaging about 10 mph slower, making much wider pylon turns, no match for Doolittle's deadly precision. Ofstie was flying the dogship in which Al Williams had hit 302 mph before the Pulitzer, but the freak engine was not up to its earlier performance. Halfway around the sixth lap a magneto shaft broke and Ofstie was out, alighting 5 miles west of Hunting-field Point. Cuddihy's oil-temperature gauge was climbing ominously, but he doggedly hung on, hoping to finish his laps before the tortured engine destroyed itself. He almost made it. His smoking racer was roaring around the seventh and last lap when suddenly fire spurted from the engine. Cuddihy chopped the gun even as he wrenched the small cockpit fire extinguisher free to douse the blaze. Rescue launches charged up to find the fire out and

Cuddihy safe but very glum. When Doolittle's R3C streaked across the finish line clearly the winner, it mounted up the vault of resplendent blue in a victory climb, the sun laughing from its shiny radiators.

Second place was taken by Hubert Broad in the Gloster III. Obviously, if the seaplane business had been left to the American Navy the British would have won the trophy. But, as English journalist C. G. Grey disconsolately pointed out, history long ago proved that "soldiers [not sailors] had always been the more dependable organizers of victory at sea!"

Some looked on the race as a Curtiss versus Napier competition. Broad's Napier Lion ran beautifully throughout in contrast to the troubles of the Navy's V-1400s. The Lion VII, like the American engine, was capable of just about 1 horsepower per pound of weight, but was hampered by its larger frontal area, although British designer R. J. Mitchell, who had also used the Lion in his S.4, was convinced it could have won the trophy if the British aeroplanes had been more thoroughly debugged. It was a moot question.

The next day, October 27, Ofstie

Smiles reflect Army pride on occasion of their 1925 Schneider triumph. From left, Army pilot "Admiral" Jimmy Doolittle, his wife, and Army Air Service chief General Mason M. Patrick. *(Au)*

and Conant flew the repaired Navy R3Cs to the Naval Aircraft Factory at Philadelphia for storage where they would await the next Schneider contest. But Doolittle was not in such a hurry to depart. That day he laid S.4 claims permanently to rest when he set a new world maximum seaplane speed record at an astounding 246 mph! As they had done for so many years in the past, Odis A. Porter and B. Russell Shaw acted as official timers for the speed trials, measuring

Doolittle's eight passes, made in a brisk wind and conditions so gusty that Doolittle reported "the tachometer hand would not stand still." He took advantage of the 1,300-foot dive allowed, leveling out $\frac{1}{2}$ kilometer prior to entry over the measured 3 kilometers. On his best pass he exceeded 248 mph.

After the 1925 Schneider Curtiss used Doolittle many times to demonstrate their products, which he always did to advantage. He was sent to Chile

on one memorable occasion in hopes of securing a large order for Hawk fighters. Clowning at a high-spirited get-together the night before his demonstration, Doolittle fell two stories from a balcony on which he was handstanding and broke both ankles. The next day, his legs in casts, he took off as planned, determined not to default, and outfought a German competing for the same order. Days later, still in casts, he took the Hawk across the Andes — and thus it can be said he

accomplished the mission left unfinished by Donald Hudson's Curtiss triplane years earlier. Doolittle's career somewhat paralleled Al Williams' between the wars, but if anything was even more colorful. After a series of Air Service scientific projects (the first outside loop in 1927, the first completely blind landing in 1929) he left the military to join Shell Oil Company in 1930 and promptly made a name for himself in the razzle-dazzle Cleveland Air Races, winning the first Bendix Trophy in 1931 flying a Laird Super Solution biplane and a year later the Thompson Trophy flying one of the "flying silos," the infamous Gee-Bees built by Zantford "Granny" Granville and his four brothers in an abandoned dance pavilion. Doolittle also piloted a Gee-Bee in 1932 to the first new landplane speed record since 1924, beating the French Bernard by just 18 mph after a lapse of eight years — but, by then, over 100 mph slower than the current world maximum speed record! When World War II started Doolittle was called from Shell back into the service and promptly given the rank of major general. On April 18, 1942, he led the immortal hit-and-run "thirty seconds" raid on Tokyo, leading a squadron of B-25 bombers from the rain-lashed deck of the carrier *Hornet*, an audacious venture which boosted American morale after the Pearl Harbor debacle four months earlier and perpetuated the accolade "national hero" Doolittle had first earned for himself in 1925 at Baltimore with the Curtiss R3C. Doolittle rose to become commanding general of the Twelfth Air Force in North Africa and the Eighth Air Force in England with its massive bombardment capacity, then returned to Shell Oil in 1946; a quarter century after that "General Jim" was still an active consultant on implementing the exotic space systems of the 1970s.

The Navy had decreed that the next Schneider would be flown in October 1926 regardless of the pressure for postponement since competition, for

235

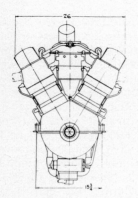
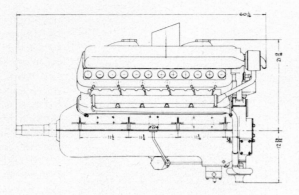

Curtiss V-1550 engine, 1926

many weeks, had appeared in doubt. Just hours before the March 31 entry deadline a challenge was received by radiogram from the Italians, who were considered valiant certainly but technically not much of a threat. The Americans, confident of victory, would use the race as a competition between their own engines. Each of the three Curtiss racers would be equipped with a different engine, since this was to be the Americans' last high-speed service-sponsored air race and as much useful engineering data as possible should be accumulated.

Curtiss once again augmented the volume of their monobloc design. The 1926 engine cylinder bore was enlarged another ¼ inch but to hold frontal area dimensions in check the stroke was not altered; in fact, the engine was made narrower, yet fit standard D-12 mountings. In 1926 the engine was called V-1550; later the designation was changed to V-1570 when the engine was named Conqueror, and in this guise its development lasted until 1933.[3] The V-1550 was originally laid down as a geared engine but misgivings over gearing and confidence in the Reed R prop prompted the design change to direct drive for racing. It had a larger crankshaft (diameter 3½ inches versus

[3] For more on this designation discrepancy, see Appendix 4.

3 inches in the D-12). Its design rating in this form was 600 hp. An early V-1550 was bench-tested on faulty, poor-grade fuel and nearly wrecked, but on a later bench test with a compression ratio of 7·5 and running on 100 per cent benzole, the V-1550 produced 736 hp (normal compression was 5·8 using 20 per cent benzole). Arthur Nutt expected 685–700 hp at 2,600 rpm with the high-compression pistons during the upcoming race, which meant the engine weighed only 1·07 pounds per horsepower!

Immediately after the embarrassment of the 1922 Pulitzer when his brutish Packard 2,025-cid engines finished last, it became quite obvious to Jesse Vincent that unless he developed something more refined, especially in view of the amazing evolutionary progress exhibited by the Curtiss wetsleeve monobloc, the 1922 race would be his last. Packard had been one of the many firms to go from auto production into aviation during World War I. Virtually all had dropped aviation like a hot potato after the Armistice – high-quality precision demanded in aviation was incompatible with the low-cost volume production of autos. But aviation was in Vincent's blood and he hung on. His experimental engineer was Lionel M. Woolson, who later lost his life in the crash of a diesel-powered aeroplane he test flew himself.

Thus in December 1922 Packard, with the strong encouragement of the Navy, launched a huge effort into engine design and especially into the problems of gearing. The Curtiss D-12 had resulted from efforts inspired by Navy competition and finally proved so good it now had a virtual strangle hold on the industry. Jesse Vincent, still highly regarded, was tapped by the Navy as one of the most likely to break this monopoly as they sought to launch new competition. In 1923 Vincent built ten examples of a new 450 hp engine entirely financed by the Navy and which made all earlier Packards obsolete. In 1924 the Army ordered an enlarged version; compared to the D-12 it challenged, this larger version had considerably more swept volume (by 30 per cent) with a much larger bore and slightly shorter stroke. It was called A-1500, rated at 510 hp at 2,100 rpm, and offered in three versions: one was geared (called 1A-1500, gear ratio 2:1); and two were direct drive, in both upright and inverted forms. The geared model powered the famous PN-9 of Commander John Rodgers' epic but incomplete Hawaiian flight in 1925, while examples of the inverted version inevitably found their way into various Loening aeroplanes.

In 1925 an updated design – the geared 2A-1500 – was developed. It was first tested at Packard's Detroit factory in January 1926 and ran wide open non-stop for twenty-eight hours during its successful fifty-hour test. The 2A-1500, for which seventy-four units rated at 600 hp at 2,500 rpm were contracted, could be wound up to 650 hp at 2,700 rpm during high-speed tests, and in its racing form, with a compression of 7·6, it is said to have produced 700 hp at 2,800 rpm, turning its propeller at a speed of 1,421 rpm. Experience gained with both upright and inverted engines led eventually to a twenty-four-cylinder marriage of the two, called X-2775, which powered the abortive Kirkham racers later built beginning in 1927

for Al Williams, but with atrociously narrow bearings this would prove to be a distinctly unsuccessful engine. Moreover, Packard never made exhaust valve cooling adequate, and they never solved the problem of excessive oil consumption which Arthur Nutt at Curtiss was tackling with tapered piston rings. Packard did bring to bear outstanding workmanship in machining its parts. Nutt particularly remembers Packard's mirror-like conrod bearings and other internal components, and praised Packard's machining as being "far superior to anyone else – even the English."

The geared Packard 2A-1500 was especially suited to the R3C; when fitted into the racer its raised prop shaft allowed a perfectly symmetrical, beautifully streamlined nose, but the geared prop, a two-piece affair especially built by Standard Steel Propeller Company, now turned clockwise, opposite to the conventional American direction. The Schneider was already shaping up into a contest between the geared and direct-drive engine, as well as the one-piece dural (Curtiss) and two-piece steel (Standard) propeller.

The month after its 1925 triumph, enthusiastic but unfounded reports were published of a conversion of the R3C into a monoplane! The only airframe change to take place, however, was the fitting of new pontoons designed by the Navy in 1926, built by Curtiss, and distinguished by their distinctly rounded bows and curved shape on top (the 1925 pontoons had been straight on top with pointed bows). The new pontoons carried fuel tanks equipped with a hand-operated wobble pump to raise this fuel through copper lines in the rear struts into the fuselage tanks, from where it was fed to the engine.

Doolittle's 1925 winning R3C-2, now in the Navy inventory as A-7054, except for the new pontoons, remained unaltered and retained its V-1400 engine. Certainly attempts were made to upgrade the engine through the use

Christian F. Schilt, Marine (MA)

of higher compression, doped fuels, and other detail improvements, but how much additional power was extracted is open to doubt, although a figure of 665 hp has been reported. It was to have been flown by Harmon Norton, but Norton was killed in September while testing the R2C-2. This berth on the team, reserved for a Marine, was then reassigned to First Lieutenant Christian Frank Schilt.

Schilt, born in Richland County, Illinois, in 1895, spent two years at Rose Polytechnic in Terre Haute, Indiana, after which he enlisted in the Marines and served as a private until 1919. He then went to flight training and soon after acquired a reputation as an ace aerial photographer. His racing debut was made at the joystick of a lumbering DT-4 in a minor event at the 1925 NAR. Schilt's greatest adventure was to come fourteen months after the 1926 Schneider, in January 1928, near the tiny settlement of Quilali, Nicaragua, where a 200-man patrol of the 2nd Marine Brigade had been savagely ambushed in a bloody skirmish with rebel bandit Augusto

Sandino. Cornered on three sides by thick, steaming jungle and on the fourth by a sheer cliff, surrounded by the bandits, the desperate Marines had to use axes dropped by air to hack out an airstrip. Working under fire, doused by torrential rains, they managed to clear barely 100 meters. Then Schilt, in a Vought Corsair biplane stripped of all excess weight — including his own parachute, a fact he kept to himself — and fitted with oversize wheels from a D.H.4, early on the morning of January 6, made his approach over the treacherous, drafty cliff edge and careened to a halt inches before slamming into the tangled jungle wall. Flying out one wounded at a time, later two (to hell with the weight), Schilt over the next three days, in history's first air evacuation, transported eighteen seriously wounded men to Ocotal and safety. For this

action Schilt was awarded the Congressional Medal of Honor. Later, from 1955 to 1957, Lieutenant General Schilt served as Director, Marine Corps Aviation.

The dogship of 1925, A-6978, was sent to the Naval Aircraft Factory for conversion to the geared Packard 2A-1500 engine, new pontoons, and removal of its cockpit breakaways. It emerged as the R3C-3, to be piloted by George T. Cuddihy. There is some question as to how much preliminary flight-testing the R3C-3 received although Admiral Moffett later reported to the press it had done "258 mph over 1,400 yards." The Naval Aircraft Factory came in for a certain amount of criticism for its management of the R3C-3 program. There may have been teething troubles and certainly unpredictable delays, but it is a shame a more thorough flight program was not

Curtiss R3C-3 with geared Packard engine after conversion at the Naval Aircraft Factory, Philadelphia, 1926 (fuselage still bears 1925 race number) (NA)

accomplished. With its clean new outline and higher power the R3C-3 was no doubt in the 260-mph class and as a landplane it should have been capable of 300 mph, a speed sufficient to return world speed record honors to the United States. One thing is certain, however: the R3C-3 was not easy to fly. The reverse-direction prop, aside from being confusing to pilots, made the starboard pontoon virtually bury itself during taxiing. It can be presumed the aeroplane's directional stability was poor, making it very prone to yaw (swerve) with little tendency to return to its intended path; there was only one possibility for improvement, to keep the rudder fixed in place during high-speed flight by applying rigid pressure with both feet on the rudder pedals. The slightest yaw would upset the balance of lift across the wing span and thus cause the aeroplane to roll, requiring prompt and precise lateral correction with the stick, but because the ailerons were not balanced, heavy forces were produced in the pilot's control stick when he moved it to counter the roll; hence the long stick, necessary for leverage. These factors added up to an altogether nasty combination, and far from being corrected in later years the final Schneider racers were plagued with the same ills in aggravated form. The short pontoons made the R3C-3 difficult to manage on takeoff or landing, exhibiting to a greater extent now, three years later, the tendency toward bad porpoising expected by the British in 1923. Despite these stiff demands Cuddihy, with his natural skill and long experience with Curtiss racers, could handle the R3C-3 quite well and he was odds-on favorite with most to win the race.

Curtiss got the job of updating the third R3C, the one Cuddihy had flown in 1925 (A-6979), into the R3C-4 under the direction of Bill Wait. Gilmore had left Curtiss, allegedly on not the most amicable of terms; in fact, he left aviation altogether to make a comfortable fortune with

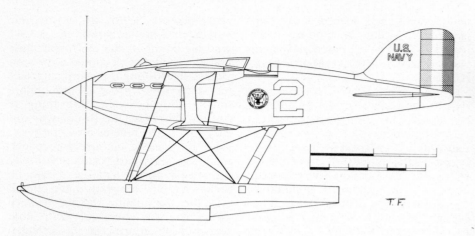

Curtiss R3C-3 with geared Packard engine, 1926

R3C-4 with skin radiators on the forward pontoon struts, 1926. These proved unnecessary for racing. (Au)

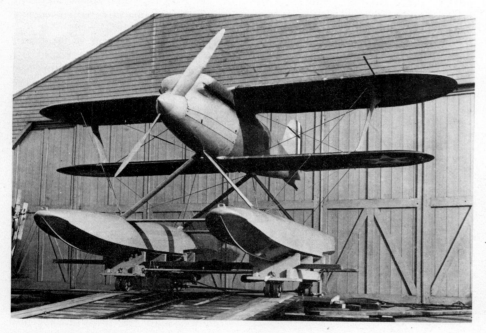

Curtiss R3C-4 with Curtiss V-1550 engine, 1926 (C)

Towne Manufacturing Company in Maryland from patents he held in connection with the Talon zipper. Ted Wright recalled Gilmore as a man "who probably did not even finish high school but who had lots of wonderful ideas." Curtiss hand Hallock

Ketchum recalled the old air-cooled Franklin car which Gilmore, "a wonderful mechanic," took apart and put together innumerable times. Wright sensed that Gilmore felt "behind the times," unable to compete with more formally educated engineers then ris-

ing. Gilmore presumably was not too personally inhibited by any such drawbacks; he often appeared at fashionable watering spots in later years on a magnificent teakwood yacht.

The R3C-4 received a new V-1550 engine and new pontoons. A tendency for the V-1400 to overheat in 1925 prompted the construction of extra skin radiators for the forward pontoon struts, providing more cooling capacity for the V-1550. Similar strut radiators were also fashioned for the R3C-3, but no tendency to overheat manifested itself in either racer, thus the strut radiators were not used in the race. The R3C-4 also sprouted a second, larger snout on its top cowl to take in more carburetor air. It was assigned to Hersey Conant, a Navy brat born at and later graduated from the Naval Academy, one of the Navy's first twenty-five carrier pilots, and looking forward with assurance to a brilliant Navy career. When conversion was complete the updated racer was taken to Port Washington, Long Island, where it was copiously photographed by Curtiss photographer William Tomer and thoroughly tested

over the same 4·26-mile course in Long Island Sound used by all Curtiss seaplane racers since 1923. A request from the Italian team for a short race postponement to enable them to set up their barely completed aeroplanes was granted, putting the race back from October 24 (the Italians had only arrived in the United States October 23) to November 11, a delay welcomed by the R3C-4 team, as they were now provided more time to wring out their racer. Conant was staying in Mineola on Willis Avenue, where Wait would pick him up to drive back and forth to Port Washington every day. On October 26 and 27 Conant made some extended high-speed dashes over the sound after which the top speed figure given to the press was 251·5 mph, although Wait later said the R3C-4 actually achieved speeds "20–30 mph faster than the Macchi made in the race." While this can never be confirmed it is reasonable to assume the R3C-4 speed was somewhat faster than the figure given out and that the Curtiss tactic of disguising the true speed, used with such success in 1923, was being applied once again.

On Friday evening, October 29, the

Frank H. Conant with Curtiss R3C-4 shortly before his death, 1926   *(Au)*

Savannah, Georgia, and like Conant was a 1920 Naval Academy graduate who had followed almost the identical route to his position on the racing team: three years in the fleet, flight training, and VF-1 (1,000 flying hours). Four months earlier he had made the first flight powered by a P&W Wasp air-cooled radial engine and shortly thereafter achieved some prominence at the 1926 NAR by setting an altitude mark with the engine in a Wright Apache.

Throughout its testing at Port Washington contemporary accounts indicate that the R3C-4 burned 100 per cent benzole to avoid detonation in its — for those days — "super-compressed" engine.[4] Wait had arrived in Norfolk to supervise assembly of the R3Cs, and then Champion appeared for his first flight, objecting to the use of pure benzole, demanding the use of a mixed fuel reportedly with 40 per cent gasoline, 60 per cent benzole. Wait tried to answer his objections by explaining the peculiarities of the

V-1550 but Champion, stubborn, arrogant, and a self-styled fuels expert, was insistent. When Wait said "nothing doing" to the use of anything but the pure benzole, Champion *ordered* him to fuel the plane as desired, but civilian Wait was unused to taking such orders; the ground crew, however, were Navy enlisted men whom Champion now brusquely ordered to fuel the plane, bypassing Wait. Bill Irwin of Curtiss, serving as crew chief, also tried to stop the adamant pilot, to whom the situation had now become a test of wills, a principle of authority. Arthur Nutt, telephoned in Buffalo, blurted, "Oh my god, he'll ruin the engine!" At that point Wait, quietly furious, made a sage decision: he told Irwin not to fuel the racer without a written order from Champion.

Even as the V-1550 ticked over on the slipway the detonation was terrible. Champion taxied into Little Bay amid a raucous clatter that scraped Irwin's sensitive ears with foreboding; already the engine was dangerously over-

---

[4] Dr. Nutt refused to confirm this — based solely on memory — because, as he pointed out, the pervasive fear of carburetor icing when using pure benzole. Nevertheless, contemporary evidence suggests pure benzole was the intended fuel.

group gathered for a cocktail party. Exhilarated by the test flying, Conant, a charming, lively bachelor, coined a popular phrase. The gin had just been lifted steaming from the stove, gravely poured with orange juice and ice, and handed to Hersey, who held his glass high, paused . . . and said, "Let it age a second!" Then, laughing, he downed the mixture. The next day, after lunch, Wait drove him to Port Washington one last time where he would depart by air for Norfolk and the race in a standard service seaplane while the R3C-4, now in crates, was shipped. Wait drove home whistling, elated, eager to pack his own bag. He would go to Norfolk to oversee the R3C operations at Navy request. That evening his phone clamored shrilly. Wait heard Curtiss vice-president Frank Russell's voice with sudden foreboding. The news was bad: Hersey Conant was dead.

Conant was on the last leg of his cross-country, flying low, elated himself as he skimmed the shoreline

pointing toward Cape Charles. He could almost see Norfolk on the horizon and should be over Breezy Point in fifteen minutes. The wind felt cool and good, the sensation delicious as the bay rushed at him in blurred gulps of blue. He forced the plane even lower, enjoying the challenge of running the pontoons close to the surface, as close as he dared without touching. Suddenly a jolt, hard, wrenching, tremendous clangor, upended horizon . . . The plane plowed in, disintegrating, slow-motion pieces flying ahead end over end, and when the foam subsided a still, sad heap floated just offshore at Winter Harbor, near Mathews, Virginia. Did Conant hit an unseen fish stake projecting from the water or merely "stub his toe" as some said? No one would know. And now two thirds of the original race team were dead. America's 1926 Schneider effort had been dealt a crippling blow.

Conant's alternate, Lieutenant Carleton C. Champion, was assigned to the R3C-4. Champion was from

Attaching lines to Curtiss R3C, 1926   *(Au)*

heated but Champion persisted, pointing the racer dead into wind, and then he opened the throttle. The R3C-4 lurched like a wounded animal. There was a long, agonizing sound of metal grating and even from the beach men could see the clouds of smoke and steam geysering skyward.

When they hauled the aeroplane ashore Champion seemed chastened but Wait was aghast. Both leading and trailing edge radiator headers were bulged out and several radiator sections had been ballooned by steam pressure. The engine pistons were "burned through by detonation" and the propeller "could be free-wheeled," recalled Wait. Frank Russell was flown down from Garden City by Casey Jones. Arthur Nutt "never forgot" his emergency sixteen-hour all-night drive from Buffalo. Admiral Moffett arrived from Washington and personally took charge of the team, relieving Lieutenant Commander Homer C. Wick. Moffett held a summary hearing behind closed doors to find out just what went wrong. Champion, still cocky and opinionated, denied Wait's story, but when Wait produced the written order — which Irwin had carefully saved — Admiral Moffett's knuckles hardened, his craggy face froze iceberg-cold, and there was a red speck in his eye when he glared at the sagging pilot.

An urgent call to Buffalo had a spare V-1550 on an overnight truck bound for Norfolk. Wait recalled it gave "40–50 hp less," since it almost certainly did not have high-compression racing pistons. Since no spare wings were available there was nothing to do but pound the bent wing radiators back into shape, hoping not to open cracks. The tough ·005-inch brass sheet, the same type used in ammunition shells (it came from the U. S. Cartridge Company in Lowell, Massachusetts), withstood the hammering well and to their relief they were able to put the wing into reasonably good condition though not quite so smooth as new. The R3C-4 was not ready to fly until November 8 as last-minute

repairs seemed to follow a preordained, years-old pattern of pushing the deadline. Cuddihy took it aloft that day and clocked 256 mph over a short distance. Both Americans and Italians were being very secretive during trial flights lest they betray their top performance. But now it seemed as if the R3C-4 was not only back in the running but probably the best racer the Americans could field. The new V-1550 turned up 2,600 rpm and seemed so robust a spare prop with 3 inches greater diameter was bolted on. Cuddihy had only one complaint: the pontoon fuel wobble pump seemed sticky. It was replaced.

Inclement weather then put the contest back another two days. On November 11, the first day of two allotted for navigability trials, Cuddihy was back in his originally assigned racer, the R3C-3, hoping to complete the qualifying tasks before dark. Had he done so he would have been required to fly the R3C-3 for the speed race. But navigability trials became impossible in the fast-fading light, especially with other planes still on the course, two of them catching the last beams of sunlight like jewels before the leaden sky, one being Schilt's bright blue R3C-2 in spectacular contrast to Bacula's blood-red Macchi. Cuddihy still had time for a short hop to test his prop, recently straightened after having been bent by spray. Some lubrication problems appeared during the test and the ground crew hoped to have them repaired so that all would be in readiness for the navigability trials the next morning, when both the R3C-3 and R3C-4 would have to qualify.

The team was now faced with a dilemma. Cuddihy's originally assigned racer, the R3C-3 with its difficult flying qualities, certainly required a proficient pilot. On the other hand the R3C-4, which now seemed to have the edge needed to win, should be flown by the most experienced pilot — Cuddihy again, although Cuddihy himself was not so confident in the R3C-4.

The Navy had kept its dirty linen well closeted; all the press knew was that Champion had suddenly "felt unwell" and while this abrupt *mal de mer* smacked not of physiology but of a tactical illness, the reason was not divulged, and hardly surmised. Furthermore, Admiral Moffett kept everyone in the dark as to his batting order. The next pilot on deck was Lieutenant William G. "Red" Tomlinson, a newcomer to the racing team. But it would not be known which of the two racers he would fly until Admiral Moffett personally announced his decision the next morning.

The next morning, November 12, two Navy pilots walked toward two waiting Curtiss racers, both perched on dollies. Onlookers identified Cuddihy instantly; the other was obviously the new man, Tomlinson. Cuddihy then turned and walked to the R3C-4 — and Tomlinson clambered aboard the sleek, mean-looking R3C-3. Obviously Cuddihy's misgivings had been over-

ruled by the admiral. Cuddihy took off smoothly and undertook his navigability trials in competent fashion. Then Tomlinson was let down the slipway, the Packard engine beating out an even bark of power. He pointed into the east wind what was probably the most beautiful — and perhaps fastest — Curtiss racer ever built, and opened the throttle. This was his first flight in the ship and immediately it became apparent he was having difficulty with the opposite-turning prop and short, low-buoyancy pontoons. Spectators gasped for breath when at one point his right wing dipped steeply toward the waves. The racer bucked badly, tending to jump out too soon, but Tomlinson finally hauled it aloft safely. Once airborne he flew the racer well enough, remaining overhead thirty-eight minutes to feel it out. He then began his approach for the first required landing in the navigability trials, but a CS seaplane from the Naval Air Station, which should have

Launching the R3C-3 in which William G. Tomlinson made his disastrous 1926 Schneider attempt (USN)

Remains of the Curtiss R3C-3   (USN)

(it had been feigned — he wanted to tail Cuddihy and measure the R3C-4 performance). Ferrarin's strategy worked fine until the third lap when engine trouble forced him to retire. Then de Bernardi in the Italians' fastest Macchi opened up and his convincing lap speeds marked him the sure winner if he finished the distance. Finish he did, and this put Cuddihy in contention for second place, which he appeared to have clinched. But Cuddihy was having his own problems. On the third lap, concerned to see his main fuel capacity down to 25 gallons, he began to work the recently installed hand pump which should raise the pontoon fuel. Funny, it did not seem to be raising fuel very fast . . . Cuddihy pumped harder, concentrating with one hand on bending his aeroplane around the race pylons, his teeth clenched, flying aggressively, much tighter than the Italians, and lapping on most circuits well over 240 mph. By the last lap Cuddihy was pumping so fiercely his hand was raw and blistered, but to no avail. Even as he saw the home pylon ahead the main tank ran dry and his engine sputtered and quit. The pontoon tanks were still full — not one drop had been lifted. For the second year in a row Cuddihy had to be towed in from the homestretch. It was the end of his racing career. Three years later George Cuddihy was killed flight-testing a new Navy aeroplane at Anacostia, D.C.

Schilt's R3C-2, despite turning up 45 rpm low compared to its last pre-race test, performed nicely until a bracing wire between the wing and pontoon broke, carrying away at the bottom end, its whipping forcing the ailerons into an annoying flutter, banging the stick back and forth, but in a masterful performance Schilt brought the racer home in second place at over 231 mph, just 1 mph less than Doolittle's winning speed with the same plane one year before.

So ended the 1926 Schneider and the saga of the immortal Curtiss racers, the last of the great factory-built racers to appear in America. In 1923 the revolutionary CR-3 had appeared at Cowes with a frontal area

been grounded during the race, started a wallowing takeoff right across Tomlinson's path, forcing him, when he saw it at the last moment, to stab the throttle open and veer aloft to go around. On his second approach the bay was clear. Tomlinson brought the racer in a nice glide down toward the water, killing speed, rounding out — too high. The R3C-3 paid out and dropped to the surface, slapping on in a huge splash. The impact stripped the starboard pontoon open and the right wing dropped, Tomlinson shoved on left stick to counteract, but with 60-mph headway this was enough to flip the racer over in a left cartwheel. Tomlinson found himself upside down in an icy, bilious, and very wet green world, but struggled to the surface where, crouched on the bottom of an upturned pontoon 300 yards offshore, he greeted "Pappy" Byrne's rescue HS2L flying boat. To show his spirit, Tomlinson flew a standard Hawk fighter in the race, 100 mph too slow to match the others, but a certainty to finish — just in case everyone else had equally foul luck!

The next day 30,000 were on hand, clustered at Breezy Point and along Willoughby Spit to see the race action at the home pylon, 100 yards offshore, while many thousands more lined the beaches at Newport News and Old Point Comfort along the backstretch. Nothing like the three scarlet Italian monoplanes had ever been seen by the crowd and the tempo quickened when Bacula roared aloft. Unknown to the crowd Bacula was purposely flying slowly to conserve his engine, so when his first lap speeds were announced the Americans looked like winners. Arturo Ferrarin was scheduled to launch before Cuddihy but seemed to be having engine difficulty, so Cuddihy, impatient to be off, roared across the bay and shot into the sky. Ferrarin's trouble suddenly disappeared

Extension of Curtiss biplane racer design philosophy: the Kirkham Vespa of Al Williams with Packard X-24 engine, 1927 (landplane version); it was unable to recapture past glory.
(Au)

less than 60 per cent that of the Supermarine Sea Lion, at that time the finest British flying boat (·686 square meter to 1·22 square meter); the R3C at ·52 square meter was almost as clean as the Supermarine S.6B at ·47 square meter which would not appear until 1931. Their drag coefficients were remarkably alike: ·039 for the 1925 R3C, ·036 for the 1931 S.6B.[5] Thus the greatest gains made over the six years following the R3C were in the field of horsepower – the S.6B had four times the R3C's power packed within the same frontal area, and the final Schneider races were won primarily on brute force. Of course, the biplane would not persist as a racer. But many aerodynamic improvements, beginning with the philosophy of design which pointed everyone in the correct direction, and which included propellers, wing radiators, fuselage design, airfoil research, handling qualities, and control requirements, were all elements in the aerodynamic formula which, apparent not only from the R3C but its competitors in its final races, had been realized by 1925.

Only one Curtiss racer survives today, the R3C-2 (A-7054), which reposes in the Air Force Museum at Dayton, Ohio, repainted in the Army color scheme used when Doolittle flew it to victory in 1925, the last biplane to win the Schneider Trophy. Bill Wait retired to a home on Long Island's north shore, overlooking the Sound which one echoed with his racers' special screech. Dr. Arthur Nutt continued a distinguished engineering career, being honored with the Society of Automotive Engineers presidency in 1940, but in a turnabout of sorts, from October 1944 serving as Packard's Director of Aircraft Engineering at Toledo, Ohio, where he supervised Packard production of the famous wartime Rolls-Royce Merlin engine, the grandson of his own D-12. Three decades later, still active in retirement, he could look back on a remarkable age.

It was a golden age of aviation, an age of flowering technical innovations, and the Curtiss racers truly represented the thoroughbred strain – golden thoroughbreds, all.

[5] The drag coefficient is a number which, if multiplied by the dynamic pressure of the airstream together with a known surface area of the aerodynamic body in question, yields the total air resistance force – drag – of that body. The use of such "coefficients" (lift, drag, etc.) provides a convenient means for comparison of different aerodynamic bodies.

THE MYSTERY RACERS

17

The Navy-Wright Racers

The mystery racers were four obscure speedplanes concocted as beds for the Wright Tornado (T-series) engines, at that time among the world's most powerful, and they appeared as both landplanes and seaplanes; all were used strictly as racing craft even though the last two were touted as thinly disguised fighters since Wright was trying to capture some military business, then going mainly to Curtiss. They earned the name "mystery" because Wright successfully kept their preliminary trials secret and created a state of suspense as to their predicted performance, but the name fits equally well today since so little has been told of their brief career. All four crashed and the Wright company eventually reverted to building aero engines exclusively, enjoying later and prolonged success after discontinuing, again at Navy insistence, the water-cooled models in favor of air-cooled Whirlwinds and Cyclones.

In June 1921 the original Wright T-2 engine design was laid down, intended for use in the Curtiss CS torpedo plane. The T-2, a huge V-12, was planned to fill the expected need for an engine essentially the same size as the Liberty — indeed, its bearing pedestals were identical so as to fit the same engine bearing timbers — but which would produce 500 hp on straight, "undoped" gasoline.

Wright, with experience gained from

producing the Hispano aluminum monobloc engine under license, modified this remarkable form of construction for the T-2. To avoid problems common with large aluminum castings, each bank of six cylinders was made of two blocks of three cylinders each. The well-proven wetsleeve arrangement was adopted and there were no welded water jackets. Probably the engine's most noteworthy feature was the use of steel cylinder sleeves open at the top which acted only as bearing surfaces for the pistons and did not take tension loads as in most of the eight-cylinder Wright engines. The open sleeve had first been used by J. D. Siddeley on the Puma engine when he tried to outdo Hispano, but its first truly successful application was on the T-2. Shrunk-fit, aluminum-bronze valve seats were mounted directly into the aluminum cylinder blocks, and each cylinder was equipped with four overhead "silichrome" tulip valves of new design. The crankshaft was held in the upper case by seven forged aluminum alloy bearing caps (babbitt-lined bearings were not used) rather than in the upper and lower halves together as was the common practice; the bottom half of the T-2 was merely a pan carrying the sump and oil and water pumps. Oil was fed to all parts of the engine under 75 psi. The intake manifold was made integral with a truss-type box which carried camshafts and rocker arms, allowing the two carburetors to be mounted either below the crankcase, as in the original T-2X, or in the center of the V, as in the model T-2P and all racing versions of the engine. At 360-hp output the low-compression T-2 consumed 26 gallons per hour.

The first T-2 was tested in May 1922 and the second T-2 was completed three months later during August. The May bench tests had been so successful that, over the summer, the Navy decided to put the T-2 to the full-throttle rigors of the Pulitzer race. No suitable "flying laboratory" existed, so a requirement for the construction of two

Commander Jerome Hunsaker, Navy aircraft designer, 1922 (U)

planes of new design was put forth, the plans to be drawn up under the direction of Commander Jerome Clarke Hunsaker, then head of Navy Bureau of Aeronautics Design Section. Hunsaker had come from Iowa to the Naval Academy (class of 1908) and went on to MIT to get an advanced degree in naval architecture in 1912, in the meantime making a thorough study of Eiffel's work in aerodynamics and translating much of it from French into English. Later he was on the design team of the Navy's 1919 transatlantic NC boats, and shortly thereafter received an appointment by President Harding to serve on the NACA (National Advisory Committee for Aeronautics), where he succeeded retiring Rear Admiral David W. Taylor, formerly Navy Chief Constructor. Hunsaker had also been awarded the Navy Cross for his pioneering work in the R&D aspects of naval aircraft. A highly prestigious Chair of Aeronautical

Engineering was named for him at MIT, where he was still active into the 1970s.

This was to be Hunsaker's first experience in directing the design of a racer, and with his background primarily in large aircraft and dirigibles he naturally looked around to see what sort of planes had recently been most successful in the realm of speed. Aside from Curtiss and Thomas-Morse racers, the year 1921 had produced little original in the United States, and even the vaunted Pulitzer race had been run as an afterthought to a fliers' reunion in Omaha. But over in France Gustave Delage had built the extraordinarily pleasing Nieuport sesquiplane racer, which won the wealthy new Coupe Deutsch de la Meurthe speed race and on only 300 hp had even pushed above 200 mph, then an almost unheard-of speed. With the great regard for French work in aerodynamics he had acquired through his study of Eiffel, it was only instinctive for Hunsaker to turn in that

direction for the inspiration with which to pattern his new plane. The basic lines of the Navy mystery racer were thus preordained in 1921 in the house of Nieuport. The racer, called by the press "Navy-X," was officially designated NW (Navy-Wright).

Wright officials organized an Aeroplane Department on July 5, 1922, just three months prior to the race, to build the two NW planes. Space at the Long Island City plant of Chance M. Vought Company was rented — in fact, the rented building was the same one originally used by the earlier Wright-Martin Company to produce Wright Hispano engines during World War I — and many extra technicians were hired by Wright to work hand in hand with the Navy to develop the racer "around" the T-2. One of these was an ex-USN lieutenant, Fred Given, who had amassed 2,300 pilot hours during his Navy tour, and who now became Superintendent of Construction. Down on the shop floor C. G. "Pete" Peterson was the engineer who

Wind tunnel model, Navy-X Mystery, 1922 (Au)

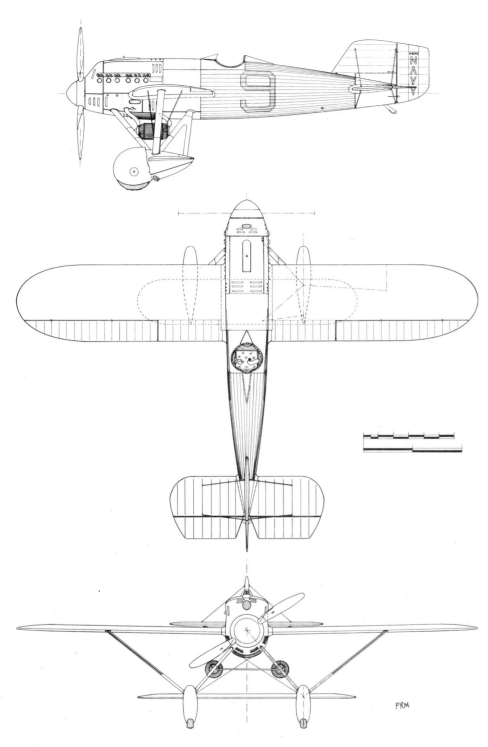

Navy-Wright NW-1 Mystery racer, 1922
Pulitzer entry

seemed to be everywhere at once, directing construction details, building fires under people. His frequent companion was the firm's President, a bright, young (thirty-four) Princeton-educated engineer named Fred B. Rentschler.

The product of this combined effort would be by far the largest aeroplane in the race. Like the French Nieuport it had a sesquiplane (one-and-a-half-wing) configuration, design intentions being to avoid the biplane's drag yet retain its structural advantages, plus preserve enough wing area to use a relatively thin airfoil. The result gave some the impression of "a dubious monoplane or halfhearted biplane" — they could not decide which! The upper wing, plywood-covered back to the rear spar, sprouted from the fuselage center-line while the lower half-wing was completely plywood-covered and utilized the landing gear axle as part of its bracing. To enable this an ingenious shock absorber was devised.

The wheel was supported inside a metal, streamline housing and worked on link motion with rubber shock cords at the rear end of a steel rocker arm, concealed in the housing and reaching very close to the ground. The fuselage structure was welded steel tube braced with wire diagonals, the empennage was steel frame, fabric-covered, and the massive prop spinner had a diameter of more than 2 feet.

The engine used in the NW-1 was the second T-2 built and its availability just two months before the race necessitated three shifts of artisans and engineers, working twenty-four hours around the clock, to complete the first plane, bureau number A-6543. Due to the lack of an additional engine and time it was impossible to complete the second NW; A-6544, for the Pulitzer. Yet A-6544 went on to become a mystery racer in its own right.

In early September 1922 it was announced that both Ensign Al Williams and Lieutenant Rutledge Irvine

Sandy Sanderson in the cockpit of his Navy-Wright Mystery racer, 1922   *(Au)*

Navy-Wright NW-1 warming up for test flight at Selfridge Field, 1922; note Lamblin radiators between wings, absence of top engine cowl. (USAF)

unfinished from Long Island to Selfridge Field, where Wright technicians worked feverishly to assemble it. Even though some components were incomplete, one being the upper engine cowling, the plane was readied for a much-needed test flight on October 11, just three days before the race. Sanderson recalled that just as he was strapping into the cockpit Mitscher came over to him and said laughingly, "You know, they call this the mystery racer. You know why? . . . Because it will be a mystery if it flies!"

Sanderson proved otherwise. On its thirty-minute first flight the NW-1 unofficially reached 209 mph over the measured course even without its cowl, and Sanderson commented that with a little "working in" the "gob's choice" for the race should demonstrate even greater speed. This was the plane's only flight before the race and with so many last-minute details to preoccupy the technicians an oil temperature of 160° F., not particularly alarming, tended to be overlooked.

The NW-1 test was made just three days after Sanderson was prevented from finishing the Curtiss Marine Trophy race in the Curtiss 18-T, an omen of discouragement to come.

Actually, Sanderson was quite pleased with the NW-1. This was . by far the hottest plane he had flown and it showed itself extraordinarily free from vibration and very easy to fly. It was a thoroughly "honest" aeroplane and not overly sensitive. The absence of the traditional biplane top wing over his head made visibility seem superb, and Sanderson commented as well on how easy the big mystery racer was to land. But as Commander Hunsaker told reporters covering the Detroit event, the aeroplane was "literally off the drawing board and into the race."

Three days later the big moment arrived. The NW-1 with racing number 9 decorating its silver fuselage was rolled from its shed and soon took the air in the second heat of the premier speed classic, the official wishes of the Navy Department riding with it. It was

had been entered in the Pulitzer as pilots of the two Navy-X racers, but the pilot finally picked by Navy Test Board chief Lieutenant Commander Pete Mitscher to fly the one completed aeroplane was Second Lieutenant Lawson H. "Sandy" Sanderson, a sturdy Marine of twenty-seven from Shelton, Washington, who had distinguished himself as a football star at the University of Montana. Sanderson had already made history in February 1919, early in his flying career, when his unit, the 1st Marine Air Squadron, 2nd Marine Brigade, was sent to San Pedro on the island of Hispaniola to help put down uprisings by the *cacos* rebels in the area. During a tough battle Marine ground forces were pinned down by native jungle fighters, and the only available land-based help was a ten-days-march away. Young Lieutenant Sanderson strapped an empty gun barrel to his Jenny directly ahead of the windshield, put a bomb

into a burlap gunny-sack sling beneath the lower wing, and took off carrying an observer in the rear cockpit. By prearrangement, signal banners on the ground pointed to where he should bomb. Chugging almost leisurely overhead, Sandy spotted a likely-looking target and pushed the Jenny's nose down into a creaking dive. When he sighted the target through the gun barrel he yanked the lanyard. The gunny sack split open to spill the bomb, which plummeted down to score a near bull's-eye. During the rest of the day Sandy and his fellow pilots plastered the rebels, marking the first time in aviation history that true dive bombing was employed, using a bombsight, steep dive, and all.

After being picked to fly the NW racer, Sanderson was at the factory almost every day to follow the aeroplane through most of its construction stages. But time was so short the aeroplane had to be crated and shipped

Navy-Wright NW-1 kicks up grass taking off in 1922 Pulitzer race. (USAF)

through mud, but when he popped to the surface his customary chew of Beech-Nut tobacco was still lodged firmly in his cheek.

Though it had occurred to some witnesses that the "durn fool aviator" had been under water "a bit long," many wide-eyed spectators were seeing aeroplanes for literally the first time in their lives, and unsure of just what to expect no one had made a move to save Sanderson. He vividly recalled an old man drawling laconically to him as he waded ashore, "I thought it was about time you came up, son." The old man thought the whole display had been staged!

Sanderson later described his handling of the Navy-X during the race as "cautious," but it was masterful enough to elicit a great deal of favorable comment from race observers. He racked the huge racer into extremely steep banks and in turns of up to 5 g he shaved the pylons with uncanny accuracy, demonstrating a nimble maneuverability unexpected from the sesquiplane.

On December 22, 1922, the second racer, A-6544, was finally completed and designated NW-2 (second Navy-Wright). Certain changes had been incorporated, most notably a different engine cowl arrangement exposing more of the engine in deference to cooling requirements. Between January 19 and 26, 1923, it underwent its first and only test flights as a sesquiplane at Mitchel Field, Long Island, with Lieutenant Sanderson again at the controls. Describing these flights, Sanderson wrote,

Six or seven separate flights were made, and by chance the wind at each time was in such a direction that it was necessary to taxi twice across the full width of Mitchel Field. The ground was frozen hard with snow at times, there was ice

Navy-Wright NW-1 slashes overhead during 1922 Pulitzer race. (USAF)

flagged off with the four Curtiss racers which finished the race in the first four places. Sanderson averaged 186 mph for the first 150 kilometers and had a sure fifth place in sight, but his oil temperature had been steadily climbing since takeoff. The oil radiator, a fin type set into the fuselage bottom above the lower wing, was too small and with the new cowl installed the oil was overheating due to inadequate radiation. On the third lap the oil thermometer hit the peg but Sanderson hid the offending dial by stuffing his handkerchief over it.

On the fourth lap his trouble began. There was a sinister odor and a stream of thick, white smoke appeared. Sanderson glanced over his shoulder to see a trail of dense smoke streaming out in a wavering ribbon behind him, merging rapidly into the milky haze. He was approaching the second turn in the course which was marked by a balloon moored to a barge near the center of Lake St. Clair. Sanderson turned back, heading for the nearest shore, Gaukler Point, a wooded peninsula jutting into the lake behind him. Site of the first pylon as well as the huge Dodge estate, the point was jammed with spectators, leaving no suitable place on the beach to set the racer down. Just then the red-hot engine seized tight, so Sanderson had no choice but to cut the switch and glide toward shallow water close to shore. Spectators saw the silver racer, humming like a cello, grow huge as it lined up to land. It skimmed across the surface for a considerable distance, losing speed, but all at once somersaulted onto its back and settled inverted in some 4 feet of water. Sanderson had literally to dig himself out of the submerged cockpit

Remains of Sanderson's NW-1 after its crash in the 1922 Pulitzer race (USAF)

Second NW-1 at Mitchel Field, January 1923; note modified engine cowl and landing gear fairings. (S)

on the puddles, and all the ruts and hillets were as hard as rock. This, of course, was a severe strain on the landing gear of the original design, but everything functioned well on this landing gear except when the plane went through the ice on the puddles and the ice caught in the shock-absorber fairing; also, another time when one of the shock-absorber cords let go. Needless to say, this long taxiing from an exceedingly hard field was a severe strain on the landing gear. A tailskid with a knife-edge was used, but no indication of the desire to ground-loop was noticed, even though the ground was frozen so hard that the knife-edge on the tailskid hardly made a mark on the ground.

We tried to give a thorough test of the powerplant; the same size and design of oil radiator was used as on the NW-1. It was found that even in cold weather the oil temperature hovered from 160°F. to 165°F. If the flying had been done in warmer weather undoubtedly the oil temperature would have risen beyond the safe limit. It is of interest to note that not even a single spark plug

was changed during this long, grilling [sic] test, although the compression on the engine was six and a half to one. No particular trouble was found in starting the engine, although it was considered desirable to heat the oil and water.

From a flying standpoint it was interesting to note how the plane seemed to float through the air at low throttle. Throttling down to 1,700 rpm, the plane was still making 186½ mph, and a further throttling to 1,500 rpm gave 148 mph over the measured course. A little trouble was experienced with one of the fins of one of the Lamblin radiators leaking, but fortunately Mr. Given, in charge of the Wright working party, had had experience abroad with servicing hundreds of Lamblin radiators in fighting service, so it was no difficult task for him to cut out the leaking fin and solder up the connection. This was the only trouble experienced with the Lamblin radiators, although, as a precaution, a small quantity of alcohol was inserted in them each night. The weather conditions were so severe during these flight tests

that very little flying was being done on the field.

The object of the test was to give a thorough demonstration of the dependability of this type of plane and the powerplant. It is doubtful if any extremely fast plane has ever been given as hard or grilling a test as this went through, flying, as it did, for over five and a half hours, during which time the engine was absolutely full-out for considerably more than four hours at a speed of more than 200 mph.

These welcome test results, which demonstrated the design's soundness, gratified both Wright and the Navy. The engine used, which was almost certainly the first production T-2 (s/n 6140) especially fitted with high-compression (6.5) pistons, was removed, torn down, and discovered to be in excellent condition. It had previously passed its fifty-hour continuous run — of which eight hours had been at full throttle — at the

Paterson, New Jersey, factory as required by Navy specification E4C. After its flights in the NW-2 it was reassembled with low-compression (5.3) pistons and installed in a DT-4 seaplane to make daily flights beginning June 14, 1923, between Washington and Norfolk to determine its suitability for operational use. At the end of 285 hours the engine was still in good condition.

After its flights as a sesquiplane A-6544 was taken back to the Wright factory at Paterson for conversion to a seaplane with the intention of entering it in the 1923 Schneider Trophy race eight months later. The Navy assigned Lieutenant Edward W. "Eddie" Rounds as Navy project engineer but this time Wright engineers had virtually a free hand in its modification in contrast to its original construction to the officially concocted Navy designs. When it once again emerged A-6544 was almost a brand-new aeroplane. Its wing configuration had been completely altered by fitting a standard biplane arrangement. The new wings

Navy-Wright NW-2 at the Naval Aircraft Factory, 1923; note two-blade wood prop. (USN)

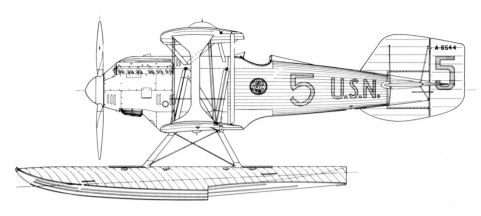

were multi-cellular, plywood-covered with deeply corrugated, easily removable wing radiators fitted on all wing surfaces. Twin pontoons with V-bottoms and semicircular tops as developed by the Navy were installed and the strutting was changed fairly extensively. The fuel capacity was almost double that of the original sesquiplane version. A new T-2 engine (s/n 6200) with high-compression pistons was installed, and with this powerplant A-6544 claimed honors as the highest-powered seaplane in the world. The oil tank had been located under the engine together with a new temperature regulator that worked in conjunction with the engine-cooling water so that the temperature of one fluid could regulate the other. When the engine was first started the water heated quickly and could be used to bring the cold oil up to its proper temperature. Then the flow of heat reversed to prevent the oil from becoming hotter than the engine-cooling water. This system was simple and worked quite well.

In June 1923 Mitscher selected the Navy's Schneider pilots, giving first choice to Lieutenant Adolphus Worthington "Jake" Gorton, twenty-six, as reward for his victory in the 1922 Curtiss Marine Trophy. From Pawtucket, Rhode Island, Gorton spent one year at Dartmouth before enlisting in the French ambulance corps, where he saw five months' duty on the Western Front. He returned home for

flight training, was designated a naval aviator in October 1918, and at the time of his selection in 1923 had 1,200 hours. Wright engineers told Mitscher the NW-2 would undoubtedly be the fastest seaplane in the world, so he suggested Gorton should choose to fly it. Gorton was easily persuaded, and piloted A-6544 on all its flights as a seaplane, making the first test July 23, 1923, during which he found the NW-2 slightly tail-heavy, requiring him at times to brace his arm against his chest to hold the stick forward. The plane also tended to throw up an inordinate amount of spray on the initial takeoff run before rising on the step. All testing was done from the Delaware River at the Naval Aircraft Factory, Philadelphia, Pennsylvania, where the racer had been shipped after its conversion. At the same time the two Curtiss Schneider CR-3 racers were undergoing their first tests quietly at Port Washington, Long Island. The press unexpectedly announced that on July 30 Rutledge Irvine, flying a CR-3, had established a new world seaplane speed record of 175·3 mph.

For its first tests the NW-2 was fitted with a two-blade wood prop but a special three-blade metal prop with reduced diameter to secure maximum clearance from water spray had been devised for the Schneider race. The first specimen, brought to the Naval Aircraft Factory by a representative of the Hamilton Propeller Company, had three very thin blades of

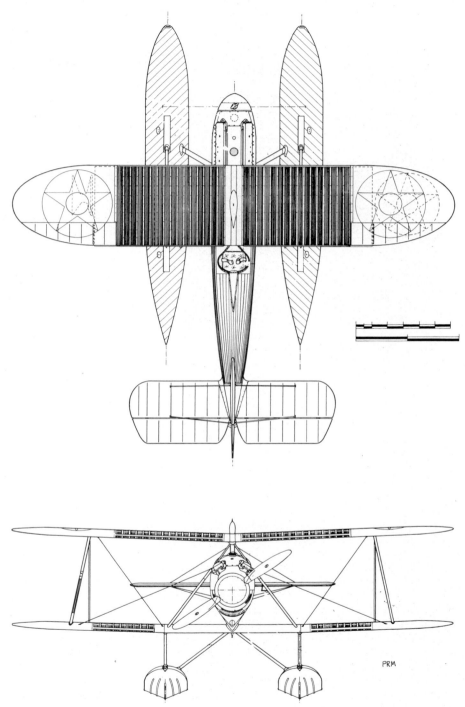

Navy-Wright NW-2 Mystery racer, 1923 Schneider entry

Navy-Wright NW-2 at Cowes, ready for the 1923 Schneider Trophy race; note three-blade metal prop. (F)

Navy pilot A. W. "Jake" Gorton, pleased with his flight speeds (U)

forged duralumin locked by a screw-and-wedge adjustment to a forged steel propeller hub, covered by an aluminum spinner; blade pitch could be adjusted only on the ground. In these heady "by guess and by gosh" days of aviation even the Hamilton man freely admitted to Gorton that he could not guarantee the prop would hold together under the maximum stress of full throttle. With a stentorian edge to his voice's gravelly sonority, Gorton boomed, "Hell, don't tell *me* that! I'm the test pilot!" Such dire possibilities did not long upset the tall, rangy aviator for with this prop he set two successive seaplane speed records in one day, eclipsing the published mark of the CR-3: during the morning of August 9 he flew 177·5 mph, and just before sundown he was clocked at 180·8 mph. On this last flight, during which he remained below 700 feet, his takeoff was timed at just seventeen seconds after leaving the slip, and his

spectacular speed passes were all made below 50 feet.

After the first tests the engine was removed and installed in a DT-4, flown to St. Louis where it participated in the 1923 National Air Races, and after logging fifty-two hours it was finally attached to the Naval Base, Hampton Roads, for service flying. A new T-2 was installed in A-6544 for the Schneider.

On August 18 planes and pilots sailed for England aboard the liner *Leviathan*, the expedition filling one fifth the ship's immense hold. On the way over Dave Rittenhouse got Jake Gorton aside and queried him about the accuracy of press reports he had seen concerning the NW-2's speed record of over 180 mph. When Jake proudly admitted that in fact he had achieved that speed Dave laughed and said, "Hell, we've got you whipped. Irvine is doing 197 and I'm doing 201!" Jake blanched; only then did he realize the true speeds made by the

CR-3s had been kept secret to avoid publicity. And he was chagrined for having been misled into choosing the slower plane. So Gorton and team leader Lieutenant Frank "Spig" Wead, over a bottle of scotch, decided the only

thing to do to put Gorton back in the running was reset the pitch of the metal propeller allowing the T-2 to wind up to 2,250 rpm, and Wead wired Wright to put a T-2 on the test block and run it at the higher rpm to see what would happen. Upon arrival at Southampton the U.S. Navy team was taken to Cowes, Isle of Wight, and installed in the works of "Sammy" E. Saunders, Ltd.

The aura of "mystery racer" that had surrounded the unique NW design since its conception still remained. The English and French had heard vague but disturbing stories as to its prowess and the incredible speeds attributed to it. When the big race number 5 was boldly affixed to its wide flanks and broad rudder, and with its almost ludicrously huge engine, it bore a certain regal mien of authority. Its warmup flights were watched with keen interest and most witnesses considered it the dark horse of the race. In fact, eager to see what results the new blade setting would produce, Gorton flew an unofficial speed trial over the measured course at Calshot and made 204 mph. The results of this brief test, however, were kept secret even from the other USN Schneider team members. In the meantime Wright had wired back that the test T-2 ran at the high rpm for five hours, and then, in the words of Gorton, "it blew higher than a kite!" So, over a second bottle of scotch, Gorton and Wead decided to stick with the plan to run the race at high rpm. Since the race should take no more than 1:45 they should be all right if they "saved" the engine until race time. Gorton set out to do his course familiarization work on a standard service seaplane, but then Wead further decided that Gorton should make at least one run over the intended Schneider course in the huge, blind aeroplane he was going to race.

And so, on September 24, just four days prior to the race, Gorton went aloft in the mighty NW-2, but while headed west on the leg from Selsey Bill to Southsea Pier, about twenty minutes after takeoff and long before the five-hour limit they expected, the screaming engine virtually exploded. Pieces ripped into different parts of the plane — Gorton vividly remembered a rocker-box cover sailing at him and ducking as other bits of metal went slashing by the cockpit — and since he was piloting at very low altitude with a stiff, 20-knot east wind on his tail, the crash came almost instantaneously. The NW-2 plowed into the water at what "must have been 220 mph," catapulting Gorton completely out. He surfaced thoroughly waterlogged but totally uninjured! After clinging to wreckage for a short time a British

Wreckage of NW-2 after its engine exploded over Spithead, 1923   *(Au)*

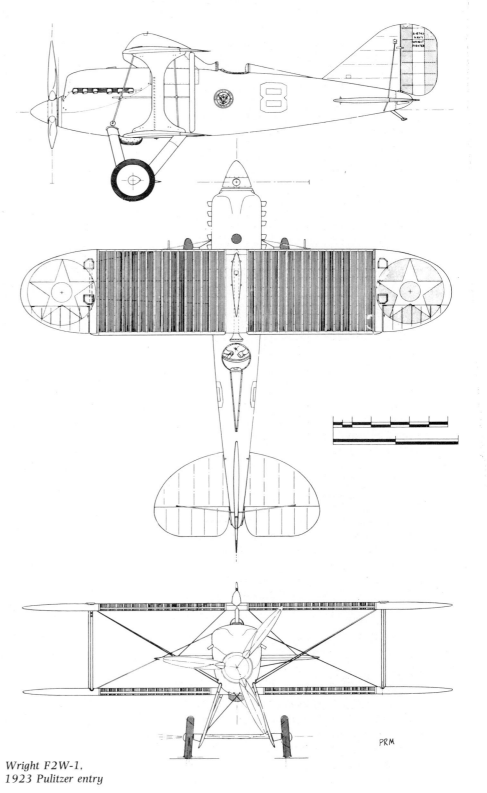

Wright F2W-1, 1923 Pulitzer entry

fishing boat reached him and returned him to Cowes, where he was given "restoratives." First reports indicated a prop blade had let go and they stuck to that story, but it was the T-2 that had destroyed itself under the brutal strain. The NW-2 wreckage was later towed up to Southsea, where it rested upside down, its nose submerged, a total loss. The English and French breathed a sigh of relief for their own chances after this accident, but their relief was premature. Just as in the Pulitzer race the previous autumn, the Curtiss racers walked away with the show.

The two NW racers were only the forerunners of a more modern racing design built to challenge the well-established Curtiss racing lead in the autumn of 1923, and hopefully to capture some production business for service fighters. In fact, to point out the applicability of their product for standard service work Wright designated the new aeroplanes F2W (fighter prefix) rather than R2W (racer prefix), and billed the design from the outset as a fighter prototype. Indeed, Wright boldly announced in March 1923 they were embarking on the serious construction of aeroplanes in addition to their well-established engine line, thus making their embryo Aeroplane Department a going concern. As with the NW, their new showpiece racer was built around an engine.

That same March a remarkable engine test at NAS Anacostia demonstrated the durability of T-2 construction techniques. In this test a Wright E-4 became the first engine to make a three-hundred-hour full-throttle endurance run during which no parts had to be changed. This was at a time when the Liberty engine, still considered the standard of durability, would provide only seventy-two hours between overhauls. The E-4 cylinder blocks, which used the new techniques developed for the T-2, were built into a 718-cubic-inch V-8 engine producing 215 hp and weighing 480 pounds which in size was almost identical to the earlier, Wright-produced

model A Hispano-Suiza engine. But there the resemblance stopped. The E-4's outstanding success led to the conclusion that the new methods of construction would increase service overhaul times sixfold.

Yet the development of T-series engines did not stop. T-2 engines had gone into production and their durability for service was unexcelled. At the same time work was progressing on the new T-3 engine, a development project undertaken completely at Wright's expense. During the late spring of 1923 the first T-3 was completed, carrying both a heavy-duty rating with low compression and high-speed rating with high compression.[1] Built to be more durable and rugged than the T-2, it could safely turn many more revs; at its maximum racing output, nearly 780 hp at 2,300 rpm, the weight-power ratio was on the order of 1·5 pounds/horsepower. It was 1 inch shorter and 1 inch narrower than the T-2. In construction it differed from the T-2 in detail only, having identical bore, stroke, and swept volume, but achieving greater power by means of an improved intake system, and greater durability by means of certain changes in material and by increasing the size of the forged aluminum alloy bearings. To secure even smoother running than that of the exceptionally vibration-free T-2, the crankshaft diameter was increased from 3 to 3¼ inches and the crankcase made more rigid. The T-3 used one single, large port for both exhaust valves of each cylinder, whereas in the T-2 separate ports had been fitted to each exhaust valve, a feature that allows easy recognition of the respective engines. Wright claimed a power-to-frontal-area ratio 10 per

[1] The T-3 was also developed into a marine powerplant called the Typhoon and saw wide service in many military and civilian applications, not the least notable of which was high-speed rum-running. In its marine configuration it weighed 1,800 pounds and had a specially constructed crankcase to include the necessary gearing.

cent more for the Tornado than any other engine flying at that time. In fact, with its frontal area of 5·49 square feet, the T-3 delivered 100 hp per square foot of fuselage frontal area after being cowled into the F2W racer. This is all the more remarkable when one considers that less than two decades earlier the namesakes of the Wright company had to build their own engine, a cumbersome, wheezing 12-hp affair weighing over 5 pounds/horsepower in order to make the first powered flight.

After passing a fifty-hour endurance test to USN specification E4D which was issued April 28, 1923, as well as overload duration tests including runs up to almost 800 hp, it was decided to put two of these engines to the practical test of the 1923 Pulitzer Trophy race.

Early in 1923 the Wright Company secured the services of the two designers Harry T. Booth and Arthur L. "Mike" Thurston, who had most recently been Chief Engineer and

President respectively of Aerial Service Corporation, Hammondsport, New York, and who had produced the two novel, retractable-gear, cantilever-wing BR monoplane racers for the 1922 Pulitzer. Mike Thurston, it will be remembered, went to France with S. E. J. Cox's 1920 Gordon Bennett team and rebuilt the Texas Wildcat while abroad. In 1921 both men were intimately involved in the preliminary design of the Curtiss CR racers. Once with Wright they immediately began working on the initial layout of a new, powerful racer to be built around the T-3 engine. During the summer, while the testing of the NW-2 seaplane was under way, Booth, Thurston, and other Wright engineers and technicians were working rapidly to have their new landplane, known then simply as the TX (Tornado-Experimental), ready for the Pulitzer deadline. Conditions had improved over 1922, and in 1923 both aeroplanes were completed in time for the race.

Each year since 1920 had witnessed

Wright F2W-1, 1923; note wood prop, flight test airspeed probe on upper wing. (S)

a considerable jump in racing performance and Wright officials knew this. The late entry of the Wright hat into the racing ring put them at a decided disadvantage, especially against the formidable Curtiss giant. This is one reason why Booth and Thurston had been retained, and the influence of their earlier days at Curtiss was apparent in their Wright TX design. Working against time they adopted lines quite like the popular R-6 of 1922. Construction techniques were similar as well. The entire fuselage was wood monocoque, built up of four spruce longerons and covered with a two-ply spruce shell, with plywood bulkheads placed close together for rigidity. Even the engine mount below the engine bearing timbers was of similar wood construction with the only metal components aside from the top engine cowl being a single steel tube strut on each side running diagonally down from the firewall to brace the engine bearers from above. Neither TX had transparent windshields but both were fitted with half-conical windbreak/crash-pads in front of the cockpit. The wings used the W-1 (Wright-one) airfoil and were built of spruce beams covered with two-ply spruce planking in three complete panels, two lower panels and one full-span upper panel. The I-struts were laminated spruce while the center cabane was built up of four welded steel tubes with wood fairing. A novel construction feature was the ingenious way the ends of the swaged bracing wires were carried by steel fittings buried inside the wing, allowing the wires to pass through the wings so that their ends were easily accessible for adjustment although entirely out of the airflow. The F2Ws could be readily distinguished by the thick aileron tie-rod behind the interplane strut on each side.

Each wing-mounted skin radiator element could be easily removed and replaced and consisted of two sheets of thin brass sweated together, the lower sheet being slightly corrugated while the upper sheet was more deeply corrugated to direct the water in very thin streams. An engine-driven pump provided a water flow rate of 70 gallons per minute, yet total water capacity was just under 8 gallons, which meant that at full power the entire cooling supply of water circulated through the tortuous passages of the engine cooling jacket and out through the wing radiators once every seven and a half seconds! Spanwise headers extended along the leading and trailing edges of both wings with an expansion tank located at midspan above the top wing.

The fin and stabilizer were built up of spruce webs with mahogany plywood covering while the rudder and elevators had steel frames with linen cover; however, the empennage was externally braced, a feature which undoubtedly cost a few mph of top speed. The horizontal stabilizer was ground-adjustable for trim and this in itself represented a small breakthrough since contemporary aeroplanes could, for the most part, have their pitch trim set only at the factory.

The landing gear was conventional, built up of steel with wood fairing, used elastic cord shock absorbers, and had an airfoil-shaped spreader bar. But design techniques such as using a landing gear V-chassis and mounting the top wing above the fuselage were features Curtiss had already discarded as obsolete in their racers by 1923. And although the TX was an exceptionally clean design, especially by 1923 standards, it did not match the remarkable attention to detail achieved by the Curtiss R2C. Despite having some 200 hp less than the Wright and being very nearly the same size, the Curtiss racer enjoyed a significant speed advantage.

When initially conceived the TX was, strictly speaking, a "sprint plane" designed expressly for a race of some thirty minutes' duration (200 kilometers or 120 miles at 240 mph). Beyond that its usefulness was severely restricted. Coolant water temperature rise was carefully considered so that

Wright T-3 engine pulling hard in pre-race warm-up, 1923 Pulitzer   (USAF)

the cooling capacity for the powerful engine was just adequate for the race duration but marginal – even critical – soon thereafter; moreover, from lessons learned through past experience with the 1922 NW aeroplanes, designers were better able to predict oil temperature rise in the TX and keep it within safe limits at full-power operation, but for little more than one half hour. In line with this design philosophy, and in order to keep the weight down, the first TX had just enough fuel capacity to fly the race, some 31·7 gallons, based on a predicted consumption of 1 gallon per minute at maximum racing output.

Reason suggested that to build an aeroplane with design limits so close to the operating requirements, leaving insufficient margin for contingency, was not a wise procedure, and this was later dramatically borne out by Sanderson's experience during the race. Moreover, the aircraft ostensibly did have a double purpose, being touted not only as racers but also as fighter prototypes. And a fighter plane with only one half-hour endurance was not too useful. So the second TX, which in fact led to the designation F2W-1, had a larger fuel tank of 60·1 gallons capacity installed. The resulting 7 per cent weight increase had no discernible effect on the high-speed performance, which was remarkably identical for both racers. Based on a full 750 hp the power loading for the entire aeroplane at maximum weight was a fantastic 3·81 pounds/horsepower which gave it a theoretical service ceiling of 36,300 feet and a phenomenal rate of climb rivaling the best World War II fighters!

The T-3 engines used in the two racers (s/n 6372 and 6373) were equipped with high-compression pistons and otherwise outfitted for racing. Engine 6373 had made a five-hour continuous run at 2,200 rpm producing 750 hp on the test stand before being installed in the first aeroplane, A-6743, flown on all its flights by Sandy Sanderson. Engine 6372 was installed in the second aeroplane, A-6744, flown as a landplane by Navy Lieutenant Steven W. Calloway.

A little more than a week after his compatriots had departed for England and the Schneider competition with the NW-2 aboard the *Leviathan*, Sanderson, on August 27, 1923, took the first of

Pilots Sanderson and Calloway confer before the 1923 Pulitzer race; note wing radiators.
(Au)

the two TX racers (A-6743) aloft on its first flight at Curtiss Field, Long Island. Two weeks later, on September 10, during the week in which the Curtiss R2C made its first flight at the same field, Sanderson averaged 238 mph in several passes over the 2-mile measured course at Mitchel Field. Three days later Harold Brow did 244·15 mph over the same course in the first R2C; then, on September 16, during a thirty-six-minute test flight "wide open" Sanderson hit 247·7 mph with the TX and thus continued in even greater ferocity the brief but intense racing rivalry between Curtiss and Wright, reviving again memories of earlier struggles between these two honored names for the supremacy of the air.

In reporting these test flights to the Navy Test Board Sanderson wrote of his aeroplane, "Lands fast but no trouble experienced after getting plane on the ground," and "Answers all controls excellently and very quickly."

On September 18 the second racer, A-6744, was test-flown by Steven Calloway, recently handpicked by Mitscher to join the 1923 Navy racing team. Calloway was twenty-eight, a naval aviator from Bismarck, North Dakota, who had started his aviation career by building his own pusher aeroplane in 1910 at the age of fifteen. He made no general comments about his first flight in the new racer but reported temperature increases during his thirty-minute ride: water from 165°F. to 180°F. and oil outlet from 155°F. to 180°F., which fell close to the predicted values. Calloway bettered 230 mph on the hop.

The first TX initially appeared in a light blue hue with a two-blade wood prop, a long flight-test Pitot tube on the upper starboard wing, and the huge word WRIGHT on the port side of the vertical fin. All of Sanderson's tests at Curtiss and Mitchel fields were flown in this configuration. The second aircraft was rolled out with the fire-engine-red fuselage and blazing white wings and tail color scheme and three-blade Hamilton forged duralumin, ground-adjustable prop *à la* NW-2 with which it raced. This propeller was retained for all its flying, both as a landplane and a seaplane, and gave remarkably trouble-free service. A-6743 subsequently acquired the bright red-and-white paint job and a similar three-blade metal prop for the race. Just before the planes were shipped to St. Louis the words NAVY WRIGHT FIGHTER were hopefully emblazoned across each side of the rudder. A story popular at the time had it that the F2W engine cowlings were held in place by eighteen Corbin locks, each with a different key, and that no single Wright mechanic who attended the St. Louis race had all eighteen keys! One real problem facing them at St. Louis was trying to keep the mobs of people from using their boxes of tools and spare parts as seats. One cunning mechanic strung an unobtrusive copper wire along the crates and hooked it to a set of booster magnetos. A few hefty cranks on the mags would quickly clear the mob!

Race day greeted the thousands of spectators with perfect weather. There was also a charged air of expectancy, for while past Curtiss race successes had been hailed for years, many were anxious to see what the new, powerful, unknown Wright challengers — as much mystery racers as their forebears had been — could do. Sanderson was first aloft in his beautiful racer, its red and white colors electric against the blue sky and the large race number 8 bold in the sun. He circled up to 4,000 feet, swung into the sun, then pushed over in a steep dive straight for the brightly checkered pylon, flashing by the timers at 2:31 P.M., and leaving a smoky trail he streaked out of sight over the northeast horizon. Sanderson's first lap was his fastest. He turned a blistering 240·3 mph (just 3 mph off the winner's average) and in just over half an hour the sleek F2W-1 had gobbled up the course four times. Sanderson pounded over the finish line in third place, hauled back on the stick, and hurtled up to 2,000 feet. As he then circled lazily away from the field to avoid the next heat of racers his crimson plane began to plummet straight for the ground. Startled onlookers saw it disappear behind a railroad embankment; women gasped and men ran toward the spot in disbelief. In a few minutes Sanderson appeared on the embankment waving his arms to signal he was all right. His fuel had been completely exhausted at 1,500 feet (his was the first racer with the small

The two F2W racers shortly before the 1923 Pulitzer
(Au)

Wright F2W kicking up dust as it roars ahead to begin the 1923 Pulitzer race (Au)

Remains of Sanderson's F2W after his crash, 1923 Pulitzer race (Au)

tank), and seeing no suitable field within gliding range, he pointed his ship straight at a fat haystack hoping it would absorb the shock of impact. The crash came and when Sanderson woke up his first instinct was to get out of the wreck. He felt for his belt and began to unbuckle it, not comprehending that he had been tossed far from the broken aeroplane but that his seat and belt were still attached to him as well as part of the padded ring around the cockpit opening which had detached itself from the fuselage and ended up around his neck like a horse collar! Panting men raced up to the scene to find Sanderson tugging at his new "collar," trying to get out. "Help me get out!" he shouted. "But you are out! There's no plane here!" Sanderson shook his head and his vision cleared. His sole injury, aside from minor bruises, was a sprained ankle. But – just as in 1922 – his Pulitzer racer was a complete washout.

Steve Calloway in the second F2W-1 was the first off in the third and last heat. But like Sanderson he could not match the pace set by Al Williams and Hap Brow, who were driving the ferocious little Curtiss R2Cs. Calloway roared over the finish line at an even 230 mph for fourth place. When he clambered from his cockpit after landing safely his wife was the first to greet him and shout his speed into his ringing ears.

The surviving racer was returned to the Wright company at Paterson, where, like its cousin the NW of the previous year, it was converted into a twin-pontoon seaplane for competition in the Schneider Trophy race. The conversion took place during mid-1924 and the aeroplane was redesignated F2W-2. Its original engine, s/n 6372, was removed and subsequently installed in a Wright-built Douglas SDW-1 for heavy-duty operations. After a trip from Washington to

Florida and back it had 110 faultless hours and was still in immaculate condition. A new T-3 engine was installed for the Schneider race.

During its conversion the entire F2W design was overhauled and entirely new wings were fabricated. Early in 1924 three airfoils in the new Navy (or "N") family had been tested at the Washington Navy Yard, the N-9, N-10, and N-11, all thinner modifications of the Göttingen 398 which had unusually low drag but was too thick for efficient spans on small aeroplanes. Data showed the N-9 to be the best airfoil so far tested at the Navy Yard and it was immediately adapted to the F2W wings; it was still being used years later on early Vought fighters. The upper wing was lowered to eliminate cabane interference drag, and despite the decided hump caused by the larger water expansion tank the aeroplane had a much sleeker appearance. Dimensions were altered

and the wing skin radiators were slightly redesigned, with fewer individual cooling elements provided per wing panel. Though the wings were still of wood, the new interplane struts were built of metal; smaller ailerons were fitted and the thick aileron tie-rods were eliminated. As in 1922 Lieutenant Eddie Rounds was Navy project engineer for the Wright racer and Lieutenant Spig Wead was Schneider team leader.

Lieutenant A. W. "Jake" Gorton was once again selected by Lieutenant Commander Mitscher to pilot the Wright Schneider entry. The completed racer was shipped to the Naval Aircraft Factory where, just three weeks before the scheduled race date, the new craft began its trials on the Delaware River. The engineers confidently expected a high speed of 235 mph, and Rounds also briefed Gorton to take off and land at 110 mph – the calculated stall speed was over 90!

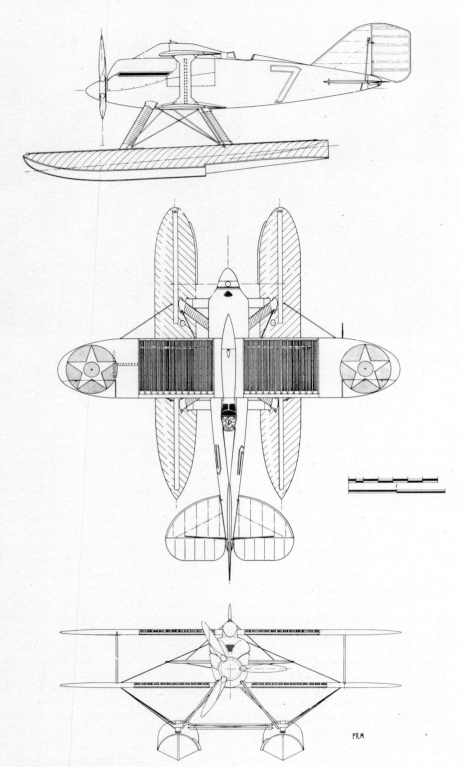

Wright F2W-2, proposed 1924 Schneider entry

Wright F2W-2 with small rudder on Delaware River, 1924. Pilot Jake Gorton atop fuselage.
(Au)

On this first attempt at flight in the F2W-2 Gorton lined himself up in the river and opened the throttle. The engine bellowed mightily and the plane plowed ahead. "These early seaplane racers plowed a lot until they could be rocked up on the step," Gorton later explained. "The big twin floats would suck on with the aeroplane in a nose-down attitude. It took back pressure [on the control stick] to make them break suction and grab air." The prop was throwing a blinding spray and Gorton had the stick full back and "full rudder against the gas tank." But the rudder was ineffective against the twisting power of the huge engine and the racer, still plowing, swerved in a sliding, rocking circle to the left. Gorton could not get it going fast enough to ride up on the step and still maintain directional control. Spray caused the engine to miss badly as well. After several more tries Gorton returned to the slip and told Wead and Rounds in disgust

that "there was not enough vertical surface to keep it going straight." The engineers rechecked their figures but Gorton was adamant. "I was leery of that plane from the very beginning," he admitted. "I never did like the looks of it." He tried for three days but never once got it on the step. Every time the story was the same — the plane plowed heavily through the water, the engine fouled and missed, and she turned badly to the left against full opposite rudder.

After the third unsuccessful day Gorton told Wead to have Washington send another pilot to fly the racer because he "couldn't and refused to make any more futile attempts." Wead, though not as experienced as Gorton, had a go at the F2W-2 on Gorton's insistence and had the same poor luck. So Gorton and Wead finally persuaded Rounds to have the engineering figures subjected to another complete check. After this evaluation it was decided to fit a slightly larger rudder, providing a 10 per cent increase in vertical surface area. The new rudder was quickly fabricated and the racer presented to Gorton once again. With the same misgivings Gorton hauled himself aboard for his first try in the modified plane during the afternoon of October 10, 1924.

"I was mad," he recounted. "I was still leery, and the engine was still missing badly from the spray. It was turning an average of only 1,500 rpm, but the rudder seemed to be holding against this power and suddenly the plane eased up on the step beautifully." It was late in the afternoon, so Gorton taxied the racer back to its slip and told the ground handlers, "Clean it up. I'll take it out tomorrow."

The next morning Gorton was back in the pit of the F2W-2 and taxiing toward the center of the river. He checked the river clear ahead, turned to line up, and slowly eased the throttle open. At 1,200 rpm the racer was picking up speed and throwing a little spray. Keeping the throttle well back Gorton was able to keep the ship straight, and soon it was going fast enough for him gently to rock it up on the step. This was the moment! The racer was now surging ahead, even on part throttle, its floats skimming the surface in white pencil streams. After one last glance ahead Gorton ducked into the blind cockpit, noted the airspeed needle flicking nervously at 100 mph, and shoved the throttle open. As he felt the sudden press of power he eased back on the stick. The racer shot into the sky.

Gorton then recalled, "She went straight up. I threw full rudder and stick into it but the next thing I knew I was 5,000 feet over New Jersey! The throttle had crept back, I remember 1,495 rpm, and I was excited. My only thought was 'I'm hooked. This plane has got me.' I added throttle but she torque-rolled right over on her back. So I cut the gun, rolled it off, and decided to land right then. I wasn't going to make a turn, change the power, or do anything. I was mad at myself for even being up in the thing because I had known from the beginning that the son-of-a-bitch was no damn good."

Gorton glided westward toward the river, facing Hog Island, the old shipyard. He was indicating 130 mph, a good 20 mph above the 110-mph landing speed, and carrying just enough power to check his rate of descent. "She was tail-heavy, just like the NW-2 of the year before. I knew that was wrong. There were many other things wrong with her too, but just then I wasn't in any mind to find out what they were. I did a great job of judging the distance. Out of the corner of my eye I saw a tug coming downriver but I knew I had him beat. I was going to touch down just off-shore on the Jersey side."

But bad luck was dogging him. By mistake someone had installed the vent on the overwing surge tank backward, facing the pilot. As Gorton closed the throttle to touch down the direct-drive water pumps changed speed and surges of scalding water filled the tank. "Suddenly, just as I'm leveling off, she lets go with a couple of healthy blasts of hot steam right in my face." In sudden consternation Gorton jerked the stick and the racer spanked into the water at nearly 140 mph. It ricocheted smartly into the air and hurtled drunkenly back toward the water. "At a time like that you work automatically, you don't think. I slapped the throttle open to take it around but the power rolled her perfectly over on her back. There was Hog Island facing me upside down. All I could do was duck my head, chop the gun, level the wings, and let her in on the top wing. The impact didn't knock me out but a toe clip on the rudder bar jammed my ankle. When you think you're going to drown you can exert superhuman strength. I ripped the entire rudder bar from the floor of the cockpit and got my only injury – a bruised ankle."

When Gorton reached the surface he was faced with a head-on view of the tugboat furiously backing down. As it neared in a great swell and wash one of the deck hands threw him a ring-buoy and he was hauled aboard. The deck hand expressed great curiosity about the odd devices "on top of the plane." Gorton, in a state of shock, boomed, "Top, hell! Those are the floats! I landed upside down. Do you have a drink on here?" They calmed him down with a pint of whiskey and got him ashore. Still dripping from his ordeal, he stalked immediately over to the startled Eddie Rounds, raised him roughly by the collar to meet his own impressive height face to face, and blared, "You S.O.B.! If you're an aeronautical engineer then I'm a——" Captain G. C. "Scrappy" Westervelt, Naval Aircraft Factory Commanding Officer, slapped a pudgy hand across Gorton's mouth, and turning to the battalion of reporters there to cover the racer's first flight, said soothingly, "Disregard this officer, gentlemen. He's obviously suffering from shock." "Shock, hell!" Gorton retorted, recalling his recent rescue, "I'm —— drunk!"

The 1924 Schneider race was subsequently called off in a generous display of American good sportsmanship since no international competition was forthcoming. One of the Navy's other souped-up seaplanes could easily have staged a fly-over to establish the second consecutive American victory in the classic — but did not. So ended the feats of the four Wright mystery racers. The F2W-2 had gone the way of its three sister ships and thus the two highly acclaimed 1923 Pulitzer Navy landplane racers, the F2W-1 and R2C-1, both refitted for the great international seaplane race, would never compete. In fact, after their conversion, neither was ever seen in public exhibition. And with Gorton's second crash the Wright effort in producing racing aeroplanes ended. Unable to outclass Curtiss, their efforts to develop high-performance aluminum monobloc engines also came to an end and they changed course drastically. Charles Lawrence, designer of the important J-1 air-cooled radial engine, and whose firm merged with Wright in March 1923, would succeed to the presidency of Wright within two years, thus the future was secure.

Wright F2W-2 at the Naval Aircraft Factory before its crash, 1924; note enlarged rudder, vent for water surge tank on top (installed correctly), start crank for engine. (NA)

THE THOMAS-MORSE RACERS

18

Benjamin Douglas Thomas was a man intrigued by the unconventional. Although no relation to the founding Thomas Brothers he was the driving force behind the Thomas-Morse Aircraft Company at Ithaca on the shores of Lake Cayuga in upstate New York. He let his questing mind range far and wide over the myriad ideas for flight that blossomed during the twenties and many found form in the sometimes odd aeroplanes that bore the Thomas flying-bird signature.

B. D. Thomas was English; as a teen-ager during the first decade of the twentieth century he apprenticed with Vickers' Sons and Maxim, aeroplane builders in Erith, where he trained in design for four years. He graduated from King's College, London, and in 1912 at age twenty-one he became Assistant Chief Engineer at Sopwith's Kingston facility. It was there he first met Glenn Curtiss, an already legendary pioneer of flight. Thomas later described the incident:

I was too shy to talk to Curtiss, but I tagged along as one of the party of engineers who were to greet him and answer his questions about tractor aeroplanes. We were with him half a day. I seldom went to London but that night I did. It started to rain and I ducked into a shop on the Strand. A chap who was reading a newspaper looked up and I saw it was Curtiss. He was en route to Russia where he was to attempt to open an aircraft factory on the strength of an order to build one plane for the government. I was surprised he remembered my face when he spoke.

Curtiss wanted to learn more about the tractor biplane design already begun by Thomas, and he offered to pay Thomas' fare to Paris so that they might continue the conversation. While crossing the English Channel the basic idea that eventually became the Jenny was conceived, and Curtiss commissioned Thomas to design an aeroplane that would be designated the model J — Curtiss' first tractor aeroplane. During the cold 1913–14 winter Thomas toiled at his task in a tent in his family's yard, pedaling 20 miles on his bicycle to have blueprints made which he then mailed to Curtiss in the United States. In April 1914 Curtiss cabled him casually, "Come on over." Thomas arrived May 2 and lived in the United States ever after. His model J first flew from Lake Keuka as a float seaplane. Thomas found his aeroplane and a sister, Curtiss' own model N (which had mid-wing ailerons to avoid the Wright patent), at about equivalent stages of development, and working together with a young newcomer named Alfred Verville, he combined the best features of each into an aeroplane called the JN, soon affectionately dubbed "Jenny." But the organized, pragmatic Thomas did not understand — or get along with — an intuitive experimenter like Curtiss, and soon sought new horizons. With his bright, piercing eyes and pink cheeks together with a coolly distant, somewhat expectant bearing, B. D. Thomas could be almost intimidating, seldom softening his austere English reserve. He almost certainly knew William Thomas Thomas during his early Curtiss days, and might well have known him earlier since W. T. Thomas had also been educated in England.

Born in Rosario, Argentina, when his father was on foreign duty, W. T. Thomas journeyed to England to attend Dulwich and the Central Technical College, graduating in 1908 and coming straight to America, where he became a draftsman with the Herring-Curtiss Company. His own strong streak of originality asserted itself and

he began aerial experiments in 1909. With his brother Oliver W. Thomas, who soon came from England to join him, he founded the Thomas Brothers Company at nearby Bath, New York, and by 1913, the year he married a cousin, his mother's namesake, his firm had already built several planes including a flying boat with a thirty-gauge galvanized iron-covered hull!

In 1914 the firm was invited by the Ithaca "Board of Trade" to relocate in the larger town. They occupied the vacant E. G. Wyckoff plant on Brindley Street. A British order for 24 aeroplanes was coupled with the suggestion that Thomas Brothers take on English designer B. D. Thomas. It was done. A swampy lakeside peach orchard became their flying field (site of Ithaca's municipal airport today.) As the malignant European war spread, the rapidly expanding need for vast, well-financed aeroplane-manufacturing facilities became apparent. Frank L. Morse, a roughhewn native of Ithaca, who had been in business for himself there since he was sixteen, owned the Morse Chain Company and was financially well set. His rustic savvy became intrigued by the aeronauts, and he provided the money to expand the fledgling Thomas aviation activities which by now also included the Thomas Aeromotor Corporation, formed in 1915 and made conspicuous by George Able and Harold N. Bliss,[1] and the Thomas Brothers School of Aviation. W. T. Thomas was not yet thirty; Morse was a shrewd fifty-three and became President of the new concern, the Thomas-Morse Aircraft Company, incorporated in January 1917, while his Morse Chain Company continued to exist separately. Young W. T. Thomas became Vice-President; by that time O. W. Thomas had ceased to be active in the company.

B. D. Thomas had worked with the

[1] Bliss had come from B. F. Sturtevant Company, where he had designed engines with Nobel Foss, son of the Massachusetts governor; he would go on to make Bliss aero engines famous.

concern before they moved to Ithaca from Bath. His immediate assistant was young Randolph F. Hall, who had joined the Thomas Brothers in the spring of 1915 and who later described his English mentor both as "absolutely reliable" in his commitments and "highly original with a warm heart . . . once you got to know him." Hall himself added a strong measure of originality, designing the famous S-4 "Tommy Scout," several of which survived more than half a century. Karl White, then a young man of about twenty who had quit the University of Kansas to enlist, only to be refused on physical grounds, came to Thomas-Morse as a "war worker" and spent his days punching eyelets in metal fittings with a hand-held punching press. He recalled that Hall lived upstairs in the same rooming house and he often heard the great man tramping up and down the stairs outside his door but he was too shy himself to approach him; Hall was "Mr. Aeroplane" to young White, who years later designed the

Curtiss-Wright Junior. B. D. Thomas in turn seemed like Mr. Aeroplane to Hall, who recalled his boss occasionally took him to musical vaudeville at Ithaca's Lyceum Theatre and was not altogether terrifying.

At their wartime peak Thomas-Morse employed 1,200, and produced some 800 aeroplanes worth $4,177,000. They moved much of their production effort to South Hill, where the impetus that launched the company to the ranks of the leading aircraft-manufacturing houses of the day was generated by the successful development of some fairly straight-forward scout planes. The most important was an undistinguished-looking biplane, bulky in its lines, with a two-bay wing arrangement, rather awkward for a ship so small. This was the MB-3, conceived during hostilities as a single-seat fighter to be built around the Wright-built Hisso based on the ever popular Hispano-Suiza 300-hp engine; its H-2 model, when coaxed, could belch out 340 horses

Prototype Thomas-Morse MB-3, 1919   (Au)

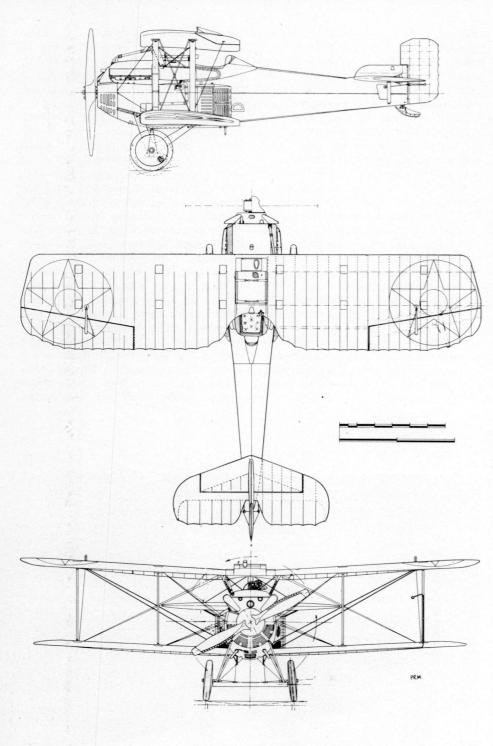

Thomas-Morse MB-3, 1919–23

on 1,900 revs, and its wired-up wings were an adaptation of the "Spad truss," a contemporary means to avoid unduly heavy wing spars. The first MB-3 was fashioned immediately after the Armistice, and despite its plain appearance it managed to demonstrate the Thomas ingenuity, if only in detail. The coolant radiator was carried on the wing to allow a cleaner nose; in later Boeing-built production versions radiators were mounted on the fuselage sides. Ailerons were fitted to the top wing only, yet despite their curiously lopped-off appearance, the large, angular control surfaces provided ample maneuverability. MB-3 standard armament was two synchronized ·30-caliber Browning machine guns with 1,500 rounds of ammunition.

Despite its ungraceful lines the MB-3 had plenty of sauce. This was demonstrated by pilot Frank H. Burnside on its first flight February 21, 1919, at Ithaca. On subsequent tests he climbed the ship to 1,000 feet in just twenty seconds, to 10,000 feet in eight seconds under five minutes, and later, during January 1920, he made a high speed of 163·68 mph, thus proving the MB-3 could easily have outperformed the best 1918 German fighters. The little MB-3 in 1919 thus represented the pinnacle of development of the speedy biplane in the United States.

Test pilot Frank Burnside was another early figure at Thomas-Morse, having made the initial flights in all Thomas designs until the MB-4. He came originally from Oneonta, New York, to be one of the early students at the Thomas Brothers School of Aviation when the brothers were building bamboo exhibition planes powered with Kirkham engines. Burnside gradually took over from Walter Johnson and flew extensively in the western United States and the Caribbean. He was very cautious and never trusted any early designs until after making a few low-level hops within the field boundary to test controllability and basic sturdiness. His fellow test pilot, Ithacan Paul D. Wilson, holder of transport

license number 87, recalled, "With B. D. Thomas' designs this was a must if you wanted to live long." Burnside's wife long prevailed on him to quit, and the unsuccessful MB-4 twin-boom mailplane was apparently the deciding factor. He obtained a Maxwell auto franchise in Geneva, New York, but his timing was unfortunate and he lost most of his life's savings. He then became an airmail inspector at Chicago's Maywood Field but could not be kept grounded, eventually flying the Chicago–Cleveland airmail run for four years in Boeing biplanes until his wife again forced him to resign. He moved back to Bath, her home, but in 1936 he became ill during a bad flood and died as the result of a doctor's blunder.

Burnside's remarkable demonstrations were in MB-3 prototypes built to Army contract 126, dated November 4, 1918, just one week before the Armistice, for five experimental models; these aeroplanes (S.C. 40091–40095 of which only the latter three were flying articles) were taken to McCook Field for further testing. The war's conclusion, which prevented use of the MB-3 at the Front, also stopped its procurement at these five until almost two years had gone by. But General Mitchell flew a prototype MB-3 at McCook, and although not everyone there was happy with it, to him the larger problem was that the Army, still flying foreign-built war relics, badly needed a standard fighter of its own. Thus, on June 19, 1920, the Army contracted for fifty MB-3s, each "built around a 300-hp Hispano-Suiza engine." They would cost $13,200 each, and with spares the contract (number 265) was worth $720,435·75 to Thomas-Morse. Interestingly enough, the Army contracting officer was Captain Reuben H. Fleet, who later formed the Consolidated Aircraft Company which eventually absorbed Thomas-Morse.

Since neither the MB-3 nor its derivations ever got the chance to fight, their principal achievements were made in the field of air racing. Early success was gained at the 1920 Pulitzer, where two MB-3s were included in the entries and despite the course-length mix-up one finished the race in rather spectacular fashion. Its pilot was a short, taciturn Canadian of thirty-two with a bland face but whose bulldog spirit was indicated by his clipped "misplaced eyebrow" fighter pilot's moustache. His name was Captain Harold Evans Hartney, USAS, and he drove his mount to second place, managing almost to match the time made by the sleek Verville VCP-R although his bus had just half the Verville's power. This was all the more remarkable since his MB-3 had in no way been modified or souped up for racing. Indeed, it was already showing marked evidence of flight weariness since it was actually the second prototype of the original experimental batch of five.

The unexpected MB-3 performance in the Pulitzer came as no surprise to those who knew Harold Hartney. Described as a "polished gentleman" by Paul Wilson, this determined pilot had been a lawyer in the United States but went back to his native Canada to enlist in 1915. Hartney then served in the trenches with the British, got assigned to the Royal Flying Corps and fought in the air over Italy and France. When America entered the war he transferred to the U.S. Air Service and was rapidly promoted to the temporary ranks of major and lieutenant colonel. He commanded the 1st Pursuit Group in action, instituted some of the earliest night fighter operations, got six official kills during the bloody Meuse-Argonne and St.-Mihiel offensives, won virtually every decoration three grateful nations could bestow, and worked closely with General Mitchell planning tactics during the closing months of the war. In 1919 he headed the Civil Affairs Division of the Air Service, the true grandfather of today's FAA, and he flew a captured German Fokker D-VII coast to coast and back in the 1919 transcontinental air derby.

He created a great stir among the throngs of onlookers at the Pulitzer since he was the first contestant airborne for the race. His MB-3 number 41 roared into the brisk fall sky at eleven-twenty followed closely by the other six planes of the race's first "flight." Hartney was also competing for the Aero Club of America's Invitation Class Prize, open to planes of the first flight, and his time garnered that prize easily. The other MB-3 in the race was also an original prototype; it carried race number 43 and was flown by Second Lieutenant Leigh Wade, destined to achieve fame as one of the round-the-world pioneers four years later. After doing the first lap some forty-five seconds slower than Hartney, a wing bracing wire let go on the second lap, forcing him to return to Mitchel Field.

The significance of Hartney's second place was not lost on the public relations people at Thomas-Morse, and after the race many advertisements ballyhooed the MB-3's superb performance. This paid dividends because the simple fact that a standard pursuit — and a tired prototype at that — could keep up with their best racer made a profound impact on the Air Service and Thomas-Morse suddenly found itself established as the purveyor of racing aeroplanes, a decidedly lucky occurrence because it came just as the company was entering difficult times.

In an ironic and bitter surprise, Thomas-Morse found on February 21, 1921, that they had lost out on a bid to build two hundred more of their own MB-3s. Such a large quantity was indeed a coveted morsel at a table otherwise lean and impoverished, and tenders were requested in four lots of fifty so the business could be spread around. But of fourteen firms submitting bids, nine put in for all two hundred, one being the young, aggressive Boeing Company in the north woods lumbering town of Seattle, Washington, whose phenomenally low bid of $1,448,845·97 — almost a half million less than the average bid and so low it seemed almost frivolous, requiring the Secretary of War's personal approval — was too good for the Air Service to pass up. This caused consternation among several eager companies then already at a standstill who soon thereafter would go bankrupt. The contract signed with Boeing (number 365 of April 8, 1921, for two-hundred MB-3As) was the largest peacetime order for aeroplanes placed by the Air Service until well into the 1930s, and it established Boeing as a

Harold E. Hartney, 1921   *(USAF)*

Boeing-built MB-3A, 1922   *(Boeing)*

dominant force in the manufacture of aeroplanes.

Thomas-Morse was temporarily saved by the racing contracts which were not long in coming. On May 24, 1921, contract 370 was signed with Thomas-Morse calling for three racing biplanes for the Army to be called MB-6 and intended as Army entries in the 1921 Pulitzer. They were to be delivered to McCook Field before August 23, which gave Thomas-Morse just three months for design and construction. The Army paid $48,000 for these planes and furnished engines, props, and instruments, to be installed at the Ithaca factory. Although the MB-6 was to be capable of taking an engine that would deliver 400 hp at 2,000 rpm, the same type Wright Hispano H-2s that the 1920 MB-3s used were provided. Contract terms

Thomas-Morse MB-6 built for the 1921 Pulitzer race   *(Au)*

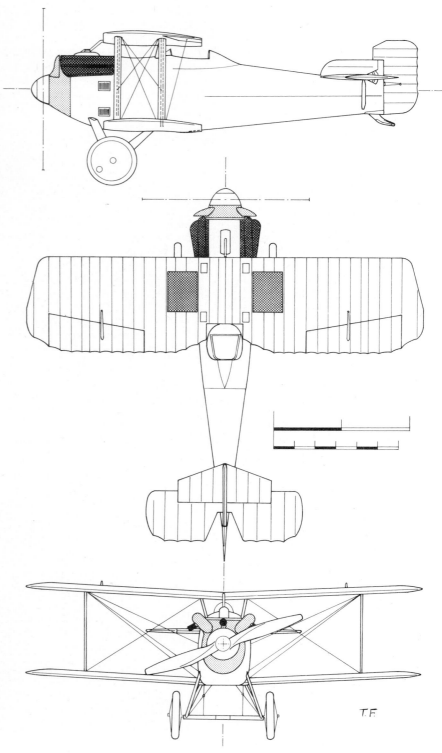

Thomas-Morse MB-6 (the R-2), 1921

required performance exceeding 175 mph high speed and 75 mph or less landing speed; one MB-6 would be used for static strength tests and had to demonstrate a minimum capability of 4 g while the other two would be used for racing and flight test. It was further stated in the contract that the top dope coat would be aluminum but this was later changed to white on one of the racers.

With so little time to engineer and build the three MB-6 racers, and spurred by the success of the standard MB-3 the previous autumn, B. D. Thomas decided simply to soup up his basic pursuit. The plane that resulted was essentially a clipped-wing MB-3 with a single-bay wing configuration. Seven feet were cut from the MB-3 wing, making the span a minuscule 19 feet, and the fuselage was shortened 1½ feet from the pursuit. One radiator was mounted on the left side of the fuselage between the wings. The gross weight was trimmed by some 500 pounds — since the MB-6 was a pure racer there were no provisions for military equipment. Air Service serials 68537 through 68539 were issued.

Despite the fact they were merely cleaning up the MB-3, the work went

Remains of MB-6 after Moseley's crash at McCook Field, Ohio, October 1921   (USAF)

slowly and two extensions on the contract deadline had to be granted. On September 20 the three MB-6s, never having been flown in Ithaca, arrived crated and untried at McCook Field. Number 68538 was immediately set up for sandbag structural tests and as soon as it was determined that the plane met the specified strength requirements number 68537 was placed in flying condition. First Lieutenant John A. Macready, a wiry man with an easy grin and kind blue eyes peering out from a seamed, rugged face older than its years, was picked as the test pilot.

On the morning of October 21, just two weeks before the Pulitzer race, Macready took the MB-6 aloft on its first fifteen-minute flight and came back very impressed. He had opened the throttle bit by bit in several passes over the McCook Field measured course, and on his last pass the airspeed indicator showed 182 mph. The MB-6 had a breath-taking rate of sink with power off, yet Macready intimated that although the ship's flying qualities were "tricky [they were] not dangerous." The MB-6 proved to be skittery on the ground as well with its narrow tread making it hard to land, especially on

the often rough pastures then used as airfields.

Captain Corliss C. Moseley, 1920 Pulitzer victor, was also assigned to the MB-6. On October 23 he made his first flight in 68537, and two days later, on his second flight in this plane, everything went well until he was on final approach, when the plane began to sink. He was indicating 105 mph (well above stall) but the little racer was settling much too fast. Moseley came on with a sharp blast of power but it was too late and the plane sank dramatically into the ground, pancaked hard, and somersaulted one and a half times, coming to rest upside down 40 yards from its first point of impact. The MB-6 was crumpled beyond recognition both ahead and aft of the cockpit and drenched with fuel from the burst tank but no fire ensued and Moseley escaped virtually uninjured. But this left only one MB-6 intact in the Army inventory. Still crated and never flown, it was shipped to Omaha for the Pulitzer race where Macready, who had taken leave from his military duties at McCook Field, would be the pilot. The MB-6 was apparently entered privately by Thomas-Morse since the military had canceled all sponsorship of the race at the beginning of the fiscal year in July; in fact, Thomas-Morse had arranged to borrow back their racers to enter in the Pulitzer much as auto manufacturers often race their cars under company flags. Thomas-Morse had secured the loan of the remaining MB-6 (68539) from the Army and the one completed MB-7 (64373) from the Navy.

Macready could already boast previous experience as test pilot of Thomas-Morse aircraft, although one earlier episode should have killed him. On March 30, 1921, almost seven months before, Macready had fallen some 9,000 feet in the third production MB-3 while on a test flight over Ithaca. Shortly after starting a dive at 10,000 feet he heard a sudden, sharp report and to his horror saw shards of fabric

peeling back in the wind from the leading edge of the upper wing, which had entirely failed. Despite Macready's every desperate effort the plane would not respond to the controls and plummeted out of the sky in a sickening, shrieking spiral to crash upside down with terrific force in the center of the Thomas-Morse field. When the wreckage was cleared Macready was found hanging in the straps of his seat bruised but otherwise uninjured.

That night a dinner organized by Hall with the Aero Club of Ithaca was scheduled at the Ithaca Hotel's Dutch Kitchen. The reluctant speaker was Charles C. Cresswell, the first military aircraft inspector, veteran of several years in the Royal Navy, who agreed to go on only if properly primed, a task easily accomplished with a full half-pint of "white mule" straight from the Thomas-Morse shop foreman's cellar still. Hall recalled Cresswell "darn near swallowed the mule in one gulp," gagged loudly, and spluttered in his brisk British accent, "What the bloody hell was that?" Needless to say, the entertainment was a huge success and Macready quickly forgot his crackup.

Shortly after Macready's crash a supplement to the Thomas-Morse contract (265-S dated May 11, 1921) called for reinforcement to the wings of the remaining forty-nine MB-3s produced by Thomas-Morse and this cost the Air Service another $26,396·21, but a few things were being learned about B. D. Thomas' designs: while highly progressive in many ways, they were notoriously lightweight and structurally weak. After these changes Macready went on to complete, in thoroughly professional style, a complete performance analysis of the production MB-3 (Performance Test Report Number 71 dated September 16, 1921). On September 28, just five weeks before the race, Macready reached an altitude of 34,507 feet in an open-cockpit LePère C.11 biplane equipped with one of Dr. Sanford A. Moss's earliest turbo-superchargers. This flight established an official world

263

John A. Macready in his high-altitude LePère (USAF)

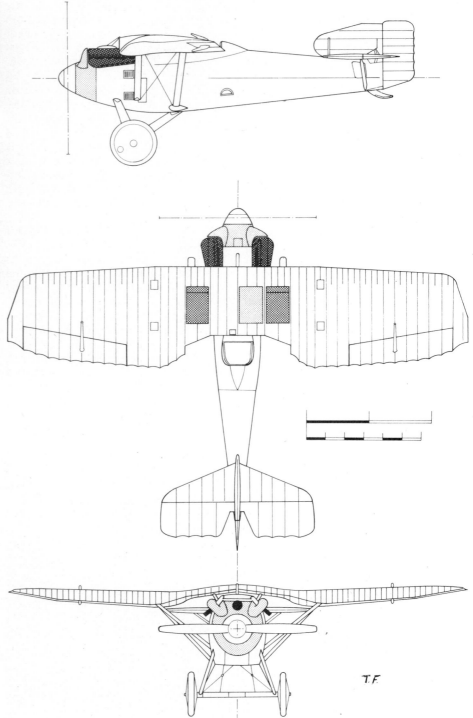

Thomas-Morse MB-7, 1921–22

altitude record and was only one of many such flights Macready made, carrying on high-altitude exploration where Shorty Schroeder had left off. In fact, Macready's research earned him the sobriquet "Altitude King" until the fame he achieved with Oakley G. Kelly for their 1923 non-stop transcontinental flight in the Fokker T-2 eclipsed his former achievements.

Five days after the first supplement to Thomas-Morse's MB-3 contract, the second supplement (265-S-1 dated May 16) was finalized, specifying twelve additional MB-3s, each to be built around a Wright 300-hp engine, constructed to the same updated specifications as earlier Thomas-Morse MB-3s, and similarly priced at $13,200 each; with spares the new contract totaled $174,733·25. The Army had

"plant cognizance" over Thomas-Morse, hence all contracts with the firm were let by the Army, and the new batch of MB-3s were duly issued Army serials (64373–64384) but in fact these twelve fighters were ordered at the Navy's request (requisition CR80 Bu21) for their exclusive use in "Marine Corps expeditionary work and also shipboard plane work." Thus the Navy issued their own numbers (A-6060 to A-6071); indeed, this joint aspect was a rare example of military technical and administrative cooperation at a time of bitter policy dispute. The contract explicitly specified "Time is of the essence," and deliveries were to be completed by November.

The first inkling that a new round of Thomas-Morse racers was in the offing appeared in a dispatch dated July 5, 1921, from Marine Headquarters which apparently indicated that the Navy was considering modifying two of the twelve MB-3s; the "proposed modification," however, would mean the "loss to the Marine Corps of two Thomas-Morse planes . . . [with] no assurance Marine Corps pilots will fly the modified planes." Nevertheless, on July 15 the Navy Bureau of Construction & Repair asked the Air Service further to amend contract 265 so that two Navy MB-3s could be modified for racing (at an additional cost of $2,000 each) into a type designated MB-7. The next day the Chief of the Air Service directed that two MB-7s be built, even before the contract was amended, giving the go-ahead to Thomas-Morse to start work.[2] This was welcomed by B. D. Thomas, who was anxious to finish at least one MB-7 in the short time remaining before the 1921 Pulitzer since it would embody his latest unconventional idea. Thomas had become intrigued with the curious Alula monoplane wing then being developed in England and fitted to the Martinsyde Semiquaver racer (see Chapter 21).

For the monoplane MB-7 Thomas modified the Alula design to use a thicker airfoil (a slightly altered USA-27) in the interest of spar depth for greater strength; he did away with the sharply tapered tip in the interest of more effective ailerons; and rather than a gradually changing washout of the airfoil, he built a decided "crank" into his wing at the outer lift strut attachment. It is highly unlikely that Thomas gave any credence to Holle's outlandish "velocity-cubed" lift claims for the Alula wing, but he might have

Thomas-Morse MB-7 under construction (foreground) in Ithaca factory, 1921 (Au)

suspected that Holle's promise of reduced tip losses had merit. For whatever reasons, Thomas persisted and his studies resulted in a humped, flared wing, ugly and yet curiously beautiful; but aesthetic and performance questions aside, Randy Hall had to prove it was also sufficiently strong. Hall did much of the MB-7

detail design and stress analysis, and recalled that its two wing panels were butted at the center-line, which gave him misgivings about the complicated fittings required. He analyzed them, in classical bridgebuilder's fashion for "both the fixed and pinned cases," specifying members based on the more severe condition, and was

The first Thomas-Morse MB-7 at Ithaca factory, October 1921 (Au)

relieved during his supervision of static testing when proof loading to a factor of 4 produced "only moderate deflection" (they were designed for 9 g). With the exception of this wing the MB-7 was almost identical to the MB-6. The vertical fin had been enlarged but the fuselage was very similar to the biplane racer and it was fitted with the same engine, the Wright H-2. Test pilot Paul Wilson managed only to taxi the MB-7 before Harold Hartney, recently resigned from the Army and installed as executive secretary of the Aero Club of America, arrived at Ithaca to flight-test the aeroplane he had been retained to race. Like the MB-6, the MB-7 was barely finished in time. Hartney took it up for its first flight on October 24. A week later it had been shipped from Ithaca to Omaha as one of the two Thomas-Morse race entries.

Wilson, who had also traveled to the Midwest under the Thomas-Morse banner, was awarded a prize for winning an altitude competition for single-seaters at the Kansas City meet. He climbed an MB-3 to 22,400 feet, which was just about its limit (company literature quoted a 23,000-foot service ceiling). The weather for this meet and the follow-on Omaha meet was ideal, and Wilson traveled up to Omaha to help nursemaid the Thomas-Morse racers into the air.

At Omaha Hartney's MB-7 and Macready's MB-6 were the favorites of bettors "in the know"; even though the two Curtiss jobs looked a good deal faster than the chunky Thomas-Morse ships, most aviation folks considered the rugged Wright Hissos more able to withstand the grueling pace than the finely tuned Curtiss engines. But they were wrong. With Bert Acosta in the lead, the two Curtiss racers finished one-two. Actually the day had started off quite glumly in the Thomas-Morse camp. Early in the morning both racers had been warmed up and both quit suddenly while at full throttle. Both were burning a 60 per cent benzole

[2] The highly involved interservice paper work and subsequent scattering of records have resulted in great confusion to many historians, especially those interested in tracking down the later history of the MB-3s in Marine service. In the Army serial block the first two numbers were allotted to the two planned MB-7s (64373 and 64374) but the Navy at this point only reserved its first number (A-6060) for the first MB-7, the only one then undertaken. After its completion just the Army number 64373 appeared on it.

*The first MB-7 at Omaha for the 1921
Pulitzer race* (Au)

mixture, but it appeared to be fuel
pump trouble in both cases. Paul
Wilson recalled how he worked together with Eddie Mulligan and Harold
T. "Doc" Kincade, Wright representatives, and after many trials and pump
adjustments succeeded in correcting
the trouble on the MB-6.

Starter Howard Wehrle gave
Macready the red-and-white flag
minutes after the first two racers were
away and the MB-6 roared aloft.
The ten thousand spectators on the
muddy field and the thousands more
that lined the course would hear the
Hisso's insistent buzz crescendo into a
deep, staccato shriek, see the plane
appear, slash vertically in a wing-
straining turn, a flash-bulb impression
of sun-glinted silver literally brushing
the pylon, then recede rapidly out of
sight leaving a smoky trail to the
horizon. Time after time with beautiful precision, Macready turned the
laps. It was hard to imagine the
variance that guides a human hand
during his fifteen mechanically perfect
turns in a performance hailed as

probably the prettiest, most consistently
flown race of the day. Later Macready
admitted that "for some reason" he
had found the Calhoun turn somewhat
difficult, and his engine had overheated
but not seriously; he was able to keep
the throttle wide open for all five laps.

The MB-6 proved more tricky to
fly at full throttle than was apparent to
spectators or Macready himself on his
earlier test flights. He found a strong
tendency for the little racer to "hunt
longitudinally" at high speed, a characteristic common to other types of
small, overpowered, close-coupled biplane racing craft of this era. As
Macready zoomed the MB-6 to 1,000
feet after his last lap the worst fears of
his ground crew were realized: the
rasping drone of his engine stopped
with startling suddenness. He popped
the nose down to prevent stalling,
and thinking all too clearly of the
MB-6's fiendish sink rate, started a
shallow turn to attempt a downwind
landing, the most advantageous possibility from his position. But then,
as suddenly as it had quit, the engine

roared to life again. Macready quickly
reefed the ship around, made a normal
downwind leg, and landed nicely into
the wind.

In the case of Hartney's MB-7, a
copper spring was found broken in his
fuel pump, which meant the pump had
to be removed for repairs. Wilson recalled how he had to withdraw the
pump through a small inspection door,
a process which produced lacerated
wrists; cracks were found in the pump
"sylphons" as well, and these were
soldered. By four-thirty the hurriedly
reassembled pump was reinstalled in
the racer and Wilson, doubtful about
the repairs, urged Hartney "to keep
plenty of extra altitude." His fears
seemed borne out even before Hartney's
departure because the engine was still
balky. Hartney's wife pleaded with him
not to go in the cranky plane but this
only put a firmer edge on his resolve.
He felt sure the MB-7 could be a
winner and in addition he had strong
feelings against defaulting to Acosta,
who had taken third to his second in
the previous year's Pulitzer. The Contest
Committee had already granted one
twenty-minute extension but even this

deadline was fast approaching and
Hartney was impatient to be off. Under
the rules winning planes must finish
before nightfall, which would come in
another hour, and Hartney had over
150 miles to cover. With a last, frantic
wave from his wife he charged into the
air and hurtled across the starting
line with just two minutes to spare.
As the MB-7 plunged by many
thought it seemed much faster than
the other racers but ten minutes went
by, then fifteen, and still Hartney had
not reappeared. There were several
more minutes of increasingly anxious
concern and search planes began
taking off; finally a farmer telephoned
with definite news.

Ed Campbell, a tenant on the Gilmore
Farm near Honey Creek, Iowa, just
south of Loveland, was shucking corn
with his brother-in-law Arthur Kady
that day but neither was getting much
done as they watched the racing aeroplanes passing almost directly overhead. Campbell's wife was with her
small son at a windmill to the southeast and it was with some relief that
she thought the race was finally over
because no planes had passed for some

*John Macready and his Thomas-Morse MB-6
at Omaha before the 1921 Pulitzer race* (Au)

time. All day she had been "afraid a plane would fall on the farmstead." Then she heard the small silver monoplane boring over the trees to the south. Hartney, disregarding Wilson's advice, was flying close to the ground and doing over 180 mph when his fuel pump failed and the engine quit cold. He soared the racer several hundred feet while hurriedly searching for a place to land. There should have been enough fuel in the gravity tank located in the wing to bring him in, and some reports say Hartney was unable to use it because of a jammed valve, but Wilson later pointed out the valves used had cork seats and "never stuck"; it is more likely that Hartney was simply too busy, startled, or both to shift — or did shift only to have the engine remain dead. He tried to set up an approach to the pasture south of the Gilmore farmhouse, the only decent place available. Despite the alarmingly fast speed necessary to maintain control Hartney was able to handle the MB-7 fairly well without power, but it became apparent almost at once that he could not reach the pasture, so he maneuvered to land into the wind on a small, triangular plowed field just north of the farmhouse.

He touched down fast and the landing gear ripped away, the plane veered to the left, slid on its belly for a few

Remains of Hartney's MB-7 after its crash in the 1921 Pulitzer race (Au)

yards leaving an 18-inch-deep furrow, then suddenly lurched off like a torpedo and hit on its nose in a brush-covered gully 60 feet farther on. Hartney was catapulted from the cockpit and hit the ground with such tremendous force that his hip and one thigh were shattered and even his forehead was skinned when his helmet was flung off. Mrs. Campbell had seen the MB-7 getting "lower and lower, then it turned and crashed." She did not see the impact, however. Neither did Campbell or Kady, but Campbell almost fifty years later, living in the same farmhouse, could vividly recall the distinct crunch of wood and metal. With Kady he raced to the slough where both plane and Hartney lay in a heap, and as they bent over the injured flier he told them, "Telephone my wife and tell her I've only sprained my ankle." They carried him the few yards to the farmhouse and tried to make him comfortable with blankets and towels.

People soon clustered at the accident site and souvenir hunters hastily stripped the demolished MB-7 of everything portable from pieces of its engine to bits of cable. About an hour after the crash, through the carelessness of one Fred Offertag who was smoking a cigar near the wreck and fuel-soaked ground, the remains of MB-7 64373 were burned to ashes. Hartney, on Campbell's cot, wept when he learned the plane was in flames and could not be saved. He told the *World-Herald* correspondent that the MB-7 was the "prettiest and most graceful plane I ever handled. If I could have stayed in the air I would have beat Acosta by two minutes." He was admitted to Omaha's Methodist Hospital and although discharged two weeks later for transfer, he spent the next two months in bed. Hartney was destined to have a lifelong limp as the result of this crash, and was ever after known to his friends as "Gimpy."

After the race Macready's MB-6 was disassembled and shipped back to McCook Field, where it picked up the

designation R-2. It was reassembled but no records can be found indicating it was ever flown again. It remained there in storage until October 31, 1924, when it was removed and used for crash tests.

Twenty-seven days after the first MB-7 was lost the Army finally concluded the MB-7 contract with Thomas-Morse (supplement number 265-S-3 dated November 30, 1921; 265-S-2 of October 21 had specified additional wing reinforcements costing $70,000 to thirty-six unaccepted MB-3s). The new contract supplement contained the first specific mention of the MB-7 and provided that only the first of the twelve additional MB-3s called for in 265-S-1 be redesigned and built as a "special single-seater pursuit monoplane type MB-7"; it also contained the detail MB-7 specifications first outlined in the Navy's Memorandum of Alteration dated the previous July 13. The Navy was presumably satisfied at this point to receive only one MB-7, the second of

the two intended, but they decided Thomas-Morse should still deliver twelve aeroplanes, that is, replace the MB-7 that crashed, but with an MB-3, which would increase the number of Navy MB-3s to eleven. The lost MB-7 and the eleventh MB-3 were considered one aircraft for payment purposes — the Navy did not feel obligated to pay for the lost MB-7 since it had been operated privately by Thomas-Morse during its one week of existence and was crashed by a civilian pilot — and the new MB-3 would be reissued both Army number 64373 and Navy number A-6060, the serials originally assigned to the lost MB-7. The second MB-7, still 64374 in the Army numbers, for record purposes, was allotted Navy number A-6071, *last* number in the Navy block of twelve, although, again, just the Army number appeared on the aeroplane.

On December 2, 1921, supplement 265-S-4 called for the eleven Navy MB-3s to be updated to the same

Army MB-3As in flight (Au)

Francis P. Mulcahy standing by the second Thomas-Morse MB-7 which he flew in 1922 (NA)

standards as the Army MB-3 design for a cost of $9,143·22, and their delivery date slipped to late February 1922, six months late, after having been requested with such urgency. The cost for all sixty-one MB-3s produced by Thomas-Morse under contract 265 was $1,000,705·43 ($16,405 @), almost exorbitant when compared to the final cost of the two-hundred Boeing-built MB-3As, which was $1,593,741·12 ($7,969 @).

The eleven MB-3s arrived at Reid, Virginia, the Marine Flying Field, Marine Barracks (Brown Field, later Quantico), where they were in fact the first true Marine Corps fighters. By February 25, 1922, ten had been shipped and by March 6 the eleventh too had left the South Hill Plant at Ithaca for Quantico, where in piecemeal fashion, usually three at a time, they operated with Flight F, 3rd Air Squadron, which, though in existence since December 1920, thus in 1922 became the first operational Marine fighter unit. Curiously, the word "Marine" did not appear in its title

until 1927. Despite the structural beefing up specified by the numerous contract changes, tough Marines were somewhat disappointed in the generally flimsy MB-3s; their inner wing struts often bowed disturbingly and such features as B. D. Thomas' light plywood engine mount, attached by aluminum rivets which quickly shook free, did not instill confidence. Even after being steel-bolted in place the mountings were still easily loosened by vibration from the H-2 engine. Captain Fred O. "Tex" Rogers, later a Marine general, said the MB-3s were "fast, tricky, but tiring as hell to fly." By July 1922 all eleven were withdrawn from operational service by the major general commandant, John A. Lejeune, and held in reserve for "experimental purposes only"; later in 1923 they were transferred to the Army at Langley Field.

By late January 1922 the second MB-7 was completed and shipped to Mitchel Field, where, after five days in transit, it arrived January 30. Identical in structure to Hartney's 1921 model,

its Wright H-3 with high-compression pistons, reinforced cylinder heads, and a new "T-manifold" made it more powerful than its predecessor. The originally assigned pilot, Navy Lieutenant Fleer, was replaced by First Lieutenant Francis "Pat" Mulcahy, USMC, although the MB-7 itself was never assigned to the Marines. Mulcahy was a leatherneck who had graduated from Notre Dame in 1914, flown rickety bombers over France in 1918, and served with the Marine contingent in Haiti; after a distinguished career he retired as a general to live in San Diego. The MB-7, under Navy project 307, was at Mitchel Field awaiting favorable weather for testing. Further delay was incurred by the wait for a new Hartzell propeller and the completion of a new measured speed course then being surveyed between Garden City and Westbury, in those days communities small enough to be termed "two neighboring villages." Eddie Mulligan and Paul Wilson were at Mitchel for the tests while Lieutenant Donald Royce (a later admiral) supervised the timing of all Navy speedplanes tested in 1922 at Garden City. The MB-7 mechanic was George Dupré.

Finally on April 14 Mulcahy made his first MB-7 flight, which lasted eleven minutes. Later in the day he made another flight, this one for fourteen minutes, but landed hurriedly with engine trouble, pointing out later, "The MB-7 was continually a source of trouble due to insufficient cooling of the engine at high power settings." With some foresight the Navy had anticipated these problems and specified contractually a water outlet temperature of no more than 170°F. on an 80°F. day at full throttle, but obviously the small radiator fitted was not up to the task, even on brisk April days. According to Wilson, B. D. Thomas never provided ample cooling in any of his designs. The contract also required specifically water and oil thermometers, oil pressure gauge, and tachometer, but allowed the use of an airspeed indicator only

temporarily, during speed trials, saying "no navigating or flying instruments shall be permanently installed."

Mulcahy's first speed trials were made April 19, 1922, when he averaged 175 mph in nine runs while on his four best (two east, two west) he managed a respectable 180·75 mph. A week later on the twenty-sixth he made another eight runs but averaged only 174 mph. Still not satisfied, he tried once again on the thirtieth but after a flight of only ten minutes he had to make an immediate landing "with the cockpit enveloped in white smoke from the crippled engine. Fortunately I was close to Mitchel Field with ample room for landing, but had to slip and fishtail the aircraft to get enough forward visibility to get it safely on the ground. My logbook notation says, 'piston in number 2 cylinder crumbled – have to change motor.' " His last speed trial, after the engine change, was run July 25 and all concerned felt reasonably ready for the upcoming Pulitzer race. General Mulcahy remembered the MB-7 was "comparatively stable and behaved well in the air. Forward visibility was poor, especially on landing, due to wing placement."

In the meantime B. D. Thomas' imagination was as active as ever. He had boldly and earnestly begun to plumb the mysteries of all-metal construction and set up an Experimental Metal Department, such as it was, housed in a loft reached by three flights of rickety wooden stairs where four workers, including young Karl White, headed by a foreman named McComb worked diligently to fabricate pieces from blueprints drawn for the most part by Hall. In the winter this loft would get so cold water dripping from a faucet froze into icicles, but despite such a meager and inauspicious setting this small, restricted shop was doing serious work in all-metal aeroplane structures before any other major builder in America. The first two metal aeroplanes to emerge from the Thomas-Morse factory were monoplanes, both prototypes: the MB-9

Thomas-Morse all-metal MB-9 with test pilot Frank Burnside, 1922 (Au)

Thomas-Morse all-metal MB-10 with test pilot Paul D. Wilson, 1922 (Au)

single-seat pursuit and the MB-10 two-seat trainer, essentially identical in structure except for the forward fuselage and engine mounts, the idea being to devise a means for quick conversion from trainer to pursuit. Both aeroplanes had humped wings, almost grotesque, with the large center-section only faintly reminiscent of the Alula principle, which otherwise had been completely abandoned. These aeroplanes further contributed to a technical evolvement in which each new model broke new ground, having little to do with former designs, and this distinguished Thomas-Morse as virtually unique among current American manufacturers.

Paul Wilson, who in those days was a compact 150 pounds, test-flew both aeroplanes, but even he complained about the undersized cockpits. He also found a great deal more to criticize. The MB-10, completed first, was originally intended to accommodate a 200-hp Lawrence air-cooled engine, but finally mounted a 110-hp LeRhône

rotary. Wilson, who spent many hours in the drenching oilbath of a rotary slipstream, maintained it was "unfortunate B. D. Thomas did not realize much sooner the rotary was obsolete — the cost of lubrication alone, even in those days, ran to 8 to 10 dollars an hour!" Wilson had six crankshaft failures and one prop come off flying early Thomas-Morse planes. Beyond that, the MB-10 flew sluggishly with control forces that varied alarmingly with changes in airspeed, requiring heavy left rudder and even left aileron in right-hand turns; it "never would have recovered from a spin," explained Wilson. Perhaps luckily, it suffered its demise during preliminary testing. The MB-9 on the other hand had the Wright H-3 engine, and while it handled slightly better than the MB-10, the heavy vibration from its engine caused structural problems which led to early abandonment of the program. Wilson remembered once taxiing across the field to take off in the MB-9 "when suddenly a wing strut fell off." B. D.

Thomas — for once — accepted his test pilot's advice and the MB-9 was not taken to McCook Field. These drawbacks might be excused since these weird metal contraptions were pioneering new construction methods, but Wilson also attributed their existence partly to Thomas' stubbornness and cunning, saying he was "about the only person who ever pulled the wool over Frank Morse's eyes." There were other factors that distracted attention away from the troubles experienced by the two metal prototypes. Thomas had a wife dying from a lingering three-year bout with tuberculosis and two small, unruly sons. Then there were his two new all-metal racers.

Thomas had hardly stopped racer development with the MB-7. As part of the renewed Air Service racing program Thomas-Morse early in 1922 received contract 551, which called for two new racers to be designated R-5, and as with all the 1922 contracts, a penalty clause for failure to achieve 190-mph high speed was included.

Total price was placed at $81,000 and Army serials 68561 and 68562 were assigned. Two of the latest versions of Jesse Vincent's 1920 Packard, the 1A-2025 model V-12 engines each capable of over 600 hp, were furnished by the Army. The two R-5s, called TM-22 by Thomas-Morse, would suffer aesthetically from the primitive metal construction techniques employed. Tubing slit open and formed into rings formed the aft fuselage structure to which ·018-inch — thick corrugated duralumin sheet skin was riveted. The covering from the cockpit forward was smooth sheet aluminum over steel-tube structure. A modified USA-27 airfoil was used, as on the MB-7, with a thickened center-section — which housed almost 220 pounds of fuel — set at a pronounced incidence angle, while intermediate, swept-back wing panels were twisted fully 5 degrees along their short spans, and outer wing panels were attached at a negative angle — theoretically the angle for minimum drag — but provided

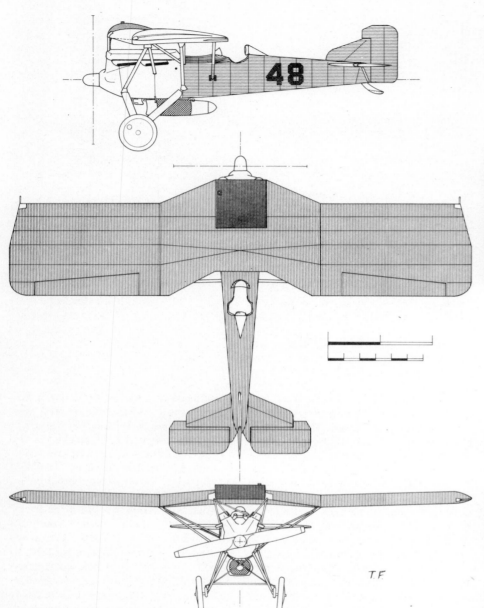

Thomas-Morse R-5, 1922

Thomas-Morse R-5 racer flown in the 1922 Pulitzer (USAF)

Designer Benjamin Douglas Thomas confers with pilot Frank O'D. "Monk" Hunter, seated in short-wing R-5 before the 1922 Pulitzer race. (USAF)

negligible lift in normal flight attitudes; almost all support thus came from the fat center-section. Four main wing spars were employed, each formed from corrugated dural web trusses and aluminum extrusions, but Thomas used no wing ribs since he felt the ·020-inch-thick corrugated dural sheet skin by itself provided adequate stiffness. The center-section was mounted atop a peculiar truss which was devised to distribute the flight loads widely, and in another example of his notoriously ingenious but sparse aircraft structures, B. D. Thomas even made use of the engine crankcase as a load-bearing member in the R-5. An underslung, bomblike affair with an open "fish-mouth" forward housed both the extruded-copper-tube 11-inch-long water radiator and air-cooled oil tank behind it. The radiator was built up by "nestling" the tubes together, then dipping them in solder, so that when mounted the air passages were some 15 degrees to the center-line, and air outlets were on the outside of the "bomb." The wheels were independently sprung, using rubber-cord shock absorbers affixed to a complicated arrangement of hinged linkages, but all but the most severe shocks were absorbed by wheel deflection alone, making shock damping marginal.

Both racers were ready for delivery four months from the contract date. The first R-5 (68561), with a wing span 4 feet greater than its sister's, was shipped to Selfridge Field by rail and made its first flight September 29, 1922,

Clayton Bissell standing by the R-5 he flew in the 1922 Pulitzer race (USAF)

with Captain Frank O'Driscoll "Monk" Hunter at the controls. Considered one of the hottest pilots in the service, Hunter, twenty-eight, was a veteran of Eddie Rickenbacker's Hat-in-the-Ring squadron who had bagged nine "Huns" and won no less than five D.S.C.s while doing it. Hunter was destined to become Commanding General of the Eighth Air Force Fighter Command in 1942 and later CG of the First Air Force. His flamboyant trademarks were his flashing black eyes and rakish, spiked moustache, and Wilson recalled wistfully he had a similarly black-eyed, unmarried sister who was "just about the most beautiful thing you ever laid eyes on." Hunter's first flight in the R-5 was cut short by cooling problems which developed almost immediately; moreover, the ship was difficult — even dangerous — to fly. After the flight larger radiators and a new set of

clipped wings, as used on the other R-5, were ordered. After the new radiator was installed Hunter made his second flight in the racer for eleven minutes on October 5 but there was insufficient time to construct a new set of short wings. They would not have helped much. Paul Wilson declared all the Thomas-Morse metal planes with oversized center-sections were "problem aeroplanes. One could tell [the R-5s] handled badly just by watching them."

The second R-5 (68562) arrived at Selfridge and was assigned to First Lieutenant Clayton L. Bissell, twenty-six, a suave Pennsylvanian who, as General Mitchell's closest aide for several years, remained unobtrusive yet efficient, utterly dependable, always exercising impeccable protocol. A seven victory ace in World War I, he would later be Commanding General of the Air Forces in China, Burma, and India during World War II. He had only just returned from a survey of aviation in Europe where he accompanied Alfred Verville and General Mitchell.

Hectic last-minute finishing touches characterized the R-5 effort. Hall and Leon "Jake" Swirbul, destined to become President of Grumman Aircraft Engineering Corporation, made a hurried dash from Ithaca in an old Essex auto with a new, high-pitch prop for one R-5 lashed to the top. From Buffalo they took a lake steamer across Lake Erie to Detroit, and despite his rugged physique Swirbul became uncomfortably seasick during the choppy crossing. Hall, who loved to munch chocolate bars, merrily recalled how Swirbul's discomfiture increased at the sight.

The 1st Pursuit Group meanwhile had arrived to be stationed at Selfridge during June 1922, having been relocated from Ellington Field, Texas. Soon after the transfer their glistening new Boeing MB-3As started arriving in boxcars from Seattle; Boeing delivered all two hundred in the five months between July 29 and December 27, 1922. The four tactical squadrons in

the 1st Pursuit Group at that time were the 17th, 27th, 94th, and 95th; there were also a Headquarters Squadron and a Service Squadron. All were thrilled with the breezy little fighters, which made their first squadron flights some three months before the races. Detroit residents soon became used to seeing Vs of the boxy little pursuits flitting almost furiously among the summer clouds and sunlight.

Compared to the new super racers that were beginning to arrive at the field to make short, tentative test flights, the MB-3A was certainly outclassed. Although the Army initially entered six MB-3As in the Pulitzer they were withdrawn when it was shown on a test hop that the fighter did not have the fuel capacity to complete the Pulitzer distance at full throttle. But they were not out of competition. On almost the spur of the moment a special race was originated that these pursuits would have all to themselves, and interestingly enough, as a pure "horse race," it soon came far to exceed in spectator interest the more sophisticated Pulitzer. The new race was to be a competition between the various squadrons of the 1st Pursuit Group and would outlive the Pulitzer series by a full ten years.

This new race was called the John L. Mitchell Trophy race and its benefactor was the picturesque, dynamic flying general, Billy Mitchell, who was at the peak of his energy and influence during these years. Fresh from his historic victory in the celebrated bombing tests ("We do not sink battleships — we loop them!") he had more recently done an exhaustive survey of aviation in Europe, where he had become regarded as the world's leading master of aerial strategy, especially by Germany, whose military planners had come to take his views quite seriously. He returned in the spring of 1922 and within weeks was courting his future bride, whom he met at a horse show — he was also a master equestrian and published authority on horse jumping. This exuberant

General Billy Mitchell in his personal MB-3 named Hawk, *1922* (NA)

John Lendrum Mitchell, Jr., killed May 1918 (Mrs. Harriet Mitchell Fladoes)

thirteen years Billy's junior in age. After graduating from the University of Wisconsin where he had studied engineering, John took up aviation under the influence of his brother's career and became, during August 1917, one of the first ten flying cadets to come to the battle zone. But on May 26, 1918, while the general was having luncheon at the Café Bosquet in Toul, his aide, Captain Kelleher, arrived with a grave expression and the tragic news that John had just been killed. The youth was attempting a landing at Colombey-les-Belles when the rear of the fuselage "apparently broke" and he was killed instantly. There had been

an especially tender bond between Billy and his "kid brother" and he felt a painful sense of responsibility for John's death. He always thought John's eyes were not what they should have been and the tragedy made him resolve to rely more heavily in the future on the objective judgment of doctors regarding a man's fitness for flight.

Billy could still remember well the time when little John, then only thirteen, paid a visit to his company when he was a captain at Fort Leavenworth. The young officer allowed his little brother to march on maneuvers with the men to Fort Riley, and even wear a special private's uniform fashioned

man was enjoying life immensely and the ways he promoted the Air Service were legion, including organizing air races. A reporter who described Mitchell at the time wrote, "General Mitchell has speed written all over him. He talks, thinks, and practices speed . . . Looking about ten years younger than his actual forty-two, the most competent and intrepid pilot in America is as fit and trim as a college halfback . . . And the most remarkable thing is that pilot Mitchell, with the safe and easy rank of general, does a second lieutenant's work . . . He was quite cockily gabardined and Sam Browne-belted, silver wings embroidered across his heart, with row on row of campaign ribbons . . ."

Yet organizing the race was more than just a public relations gesture for the Air Service; it also reflected a solemn side of his nature. For the handsome trophy he donated was in memory of his only brother, John Lendrum Mitchell, Jr., namesake of their United States senator father and

General Billy Mitchell and his wife at gravesite of Mitchell's brother, John L. Mitchell (LC)

for him by the company tailor. The boy then played the part of a soldier in the field for five days much to his mother's dismay. Years later in France, John, who was still full of deviltry, once took his brother's custom Mercedes and personal driver and had a fling in Paris. The carefree young lieutenant cut a dashing hero's figure in the general's car. And then, suddenly, he was dead.

On the day of his brother's funeral General Mitchell made a flying inspection of the Western Front; few of the men around him realized how deeply affected he was by his brother's death. Writing to their sister Harriet he said, ". . . John was so much younger that he was like a son . . . It hit me . . . harder than anything ever has . . ." John was buried in Sevastopol Cemetery near Thiaucourt. Billy put a wreath of Lorraine thistles on the grave, which "is near a pretty wood . . . the quietest spot around . . . I sometimes fly low over this place to see how it is getting along

The John L. Mitchell race trophy   (S)

. . ." Throughout his life the event remained fresh in his mind but he seldom spoke of it. The donation of the race trophy was only a small token of his deep regard for the fallen young aviator. Part of the terms of its donation was that it would be restricted to pilots and planes of the 1st Pursuit Group. The first contest was held at the Detroit races in 1922, and the six MB-3As that had been withdrawn from the Pulitzer became the first six contenders for the John L. Mitchell Trophy.

The two races were contested over the same course, the Pulitzer requiring five laps, the Mitchell four. The winner of the first Mitchell race was Second Lieutenant Donald F. Stace, who at twenty-two was by three years the youngest pilot competing. He had finished West Point in two years, went to pilot training from the Coast Artillery Corps, and had only received his wings June 30, 1922, not four months before the race. Assigned as Assistant Group Engineering Officer under Ennis Whitehead upon arrival at the 1st Pursuit Group, Stace worked in the Service Squadron. There was great incentive for the Service Squadron to win the Mitchell race against the tactical units, so Stace's men cleaned the MB-3A he had been assigned to race until it literally shone. Since the eager young lieutenant was in charge of engine overhaul he had his H-3 engine removed and carefully balanced. All appurtenances were removed from his aeroplane, even to the radiator shutters and compass on the top wing; struts were faired, the fuselage foot-step was patched over, and the entire aeroplane varnished the night before the race! Meanwhile Stace was checking out the course. That afternoon, which happened to be Friday the thirteenth, he flew his Spad — number 13, with his personal black cat insignia — around the course at increasingly lower altitudes to memorize landmarks. When he strapped into his MB-3A number 54 the next day he had less than 100 hours total pilot

Line-up of MB-3A aeroplanes for the first John L. Mitchell race — the "Thomas-Morse race" – 1922   (Au)

time but made up for his lack of experience with a strong measure of determination.

The day of the two big races, October 14, dawned bright; a steady, light wind blew and it was an ideal day for air racing with the exception of a slowly thickening milky haze. By 11:35 A.M. the six Mitchell contestants were sitting helmeted in their cockpits, their faces hidden behind expressionless goggles and their little fighters ticking over in readiness for the takeoff. Soon the first pilot taxied slowly away from the rest, turned into the wind, and opened the throttle. The large white numerals 54 were clearly visible as the fighter went jouncing across the grass and slanted into the sky. One by one the others quickly followed, and once aloft they maneuvered for the start, the slightly out-of-synch drone of the six H-3 engines sounding like a cluster of angry bees. A sudden sharp dive and the race was on! The six MBs ripped by the starting pylon — number 54 was still in the lead, the others right on his tail — and all streaked out of sight to the south. Within minutes the aviators were bending their coursers sharply around the pylon at Gaukler Point and heading northeast over the lake toward the moored barge some 10 miles away.

Although Stace's efforts had paid off and he had a swifter mount, and Captain H. M. Elmendorf's number 53 appeared somewhat sluggish, for the most part the planes were evenly matched so it became essentially a contest of flying skill and cool nerve. The man who could best judge his distances on the turns and cut the pylons the tightest would win. The little planes seemed almost to jostle each other for position on the straight-aways, then come screaming straight for a pylon, rack up on their sides, and flip around as though on a wire. Around and around the triangle they flew, Stace gaining about a minute per lap and Elmendorf losing roughly the same, and on the third lap Lieutenant James D. Summers returning his number 56 to Selfridge with minor troubles. This left five to continue the fight in a true battle royal, sometimes flying so low they had to pull up to clear trees lining the south side of Selfridge Field, and leaving rooster tails with their prop-wash on the lake.

General Stace later recalled that the MB-3A was a "nice flying aeroplane . . . The only trouble was the engine, which ran very rough." Actually, the extreme vibration of the Wright H-series engines almost eliminated the MB-3 as an effective service fighter. The cockpit

Donald F. Stace by his winning MB-3A; note helmet, slit by the wind. (USAF)

Pat Mulcahy made a short flight in the MB-7 to test an additional small water radiator which had been "jury-rigged" below the bottom engine cowl in the prop slipstream. It was hoped this would provide sufficient cooling to complete the race at full throttle. It did not, and Mulcahy had to land with overheat problems on the second lap only thirty minutes after takeoff, after averaging a slow 145 mph on the first lap. This was the last flight of the MB-7, which after the race went into storage at the Naval Aircraft Factory, Philadelphia, where it remained until it was stricken from the Navy inventory — as A-6071 — on May 7, 1925. General Mulcahy's pilot logbook indicated no Navy bureau number for any of his seventeen flights in the MB-7, which, over the six-month period April 14–October 14, 1922, added up to 5:41 total MB-7 flight time.

The two R-5s, resembling flying humpbacked washboards with their dull, corrugated duralumin skin, finished the Pulitzer in tenth and eleventh spots, slowest of the specialized racers despite their huge Packard engines. Hunter's speed in the race classic was under 150 mph but this was due both to a rough-running engine early in the race and to becoming disoriented in the haze for several valuable minutes, giving him a first lap average of only 113 mph. His best lap was 165 mph, which helped to raise his over-all average. The clipped-wing R-5 flown by Bissell finished the race at just over 155 mph, more than 50 mph less than the pace posted by Maughan's winning Curtiss R-6.

After the race the R-5 still had to complete speed runs for contract fulfillment. Monk Hunter took over the clipped-wing R-5 for these tests but he was able to achieve only 181·1 mph in his speed runs. Lieutenant Gene Barksdale then tried to better this mark but without success; however,

was too cramped, the narrow gear gave it a built-in ground-loop, and pitch trim would change abruptly when the radiator shutters were opened or closed. In fact, aerodynamic analysis revealed the aeroplane was almost neutrally stable in pitch and pilots learned quickly that it gave little spin warning. Despite these ills the exhilarating little fighter was exceptionally maneuverable, making it in Stace's words "a pleasure to fly." On the ground it could be an exasperating maintenance headache. During the summer, three months before the race, twenty MB-3s had been tested extensively at Ellington Field, Texas, and nineteen were unserviceable after only ten hours of flying, mostly with warped wing struts. Simultaneously the first Boeing-built H-3-powered MB-3As were being tested at Camp Lewis, Washington, and they proved much more rugged. Later, during the winter of 1923–24, some MB-3As were shipped to Hawaii, where Lieutenant Stace and Captain Elmendorf both flew them.

The Mitchell race's intense excitement served to whet the crowd's appetite for the Pulitzer race which immediately followed it, but the swarming battle of MBs had been a huge success on its own merit and was afterwards always remembered as "the Thomas-Morse race" — in something of a misnomer since the racers were all Boeing-built. General Mitchell, of course, was greatly pleased, as was Don Stace, who three months later received the not inconsiderable sum of $400 from the Dodge Brothers concern toward a shiny new Dodge auto! Later Lieutenant Lester Schulze, pilot of a Loening R-4 in the Pulitzer, was killed in Stace's MB-3A number 54 while on a routine gunnery mission.

In contrast to the Mitchell race success, the results of B. D. Thomas' racers in the Pulitzer were discouraging. A last-ditch attempt to get MB-3s into the big race fell through, and two which had been hastily modified and numbered 61 and 62 were withdrawn.

During the morning of race day

Bissell taking off in his R-5, 1922 Pulitzer race (USAF)

on October 30 Lieutenant Ennis Whitehead averaged 187·74 mph in six passes over the measured course. Finally, on November 8, 1922, Thomas-Morse received a check for $75,998·40 from the Air Service, the odd sum reflecting a deduction of $1·60 for parts and $5,000 penalty for the 2 mph under the specified 190 mark.

The two R-5s were shipped to McCook Field, where 68561 was placed in storage. On December 13, 1922, number P-268 was given to the one assembled R-5 (68562), which was released for test-flying January 17, 1923. A few flights – probably fewer than twenty – were made between January and June 1923. On August 15 it was returned to storage with its sister where they both remained until February 6, 1924, when they were removed to finish their service by being loaded to destruction with sandbags to determine the strength of their all-metal structures.

None of this, however, diminished General Mitchell's eagerness to continue the success of the race named after his brother. By early August the Mitchell race was not included in the list of scheduled events nor was mention made of it in any of the handbills or advertising for the 1923 NAR, but the flying general soon saw to it this oversight was corrected. Six weeks before the scheduled NAR opening, the Mitchell Trophy was inserted as event 8a with five planes from the 1st Pursuit Group listed as contestants, and by August 20 General Patrick, Air Service Chief, announced the pilots and alternates selected to participate in the race events. As in 1922 the Mitchell contestants were to fly four laps of the Pulitzer course for a total of 200 kilometers. To make the competition even keener a choice incentive was provided: the winning Mitchell pilot would be named to fly the Army's hottest custom racer in the following year's Pulitzer classic.

The Mitchell race was the second event on October 4, and mechanics were grasping wrists to swing the clublike props by twelve forty-five. The engines coughed to life and helmet straps fluttered in the slipstream as the pilots, with stabbing bursts of throttle against unresponsive rudders, sought to taxi to the take-off line with mechanics gripping the tails to lunge them around against the clumsy tailskids and others hanging onto wingtips. All pilots were flying identical ships so the race promised to be a fight of skill right down to the finish line.

At precisely one o'clock Thomas W. Blackburn gunned his MB into the air followed at half-minute intervals by Thomas K. Matthews, George P. Tourtellot, Vincent B. Dixon, the Reverend J. Thad Johnson, and Burt E. "Buck" Skeel, twenty-nine, acting O-in-C of the group race detachment. The six MB-3As climbed steeply to 1,000 feet as they circled to the southwest when suddenly Blackburn peeled off and screamed straight for the brightly checkered starting pylon. The others were right behind him in hot pursuit, and conforming to race rules all turned the starting pylon in the order of takeoff. Almost before the spectators realized what was happening the race was on! Skeel made his dive with full throttle, a maneuver that would cost him his life in the Pulitzer race a year later, and the stubby fighters disappeared to the north, strung out at a distance of about 3 miles. But by the third pylon, Skeel had already passed Johnson and was driving hard for Dixon. Soon Blackburn was seen churning in from the hazy northwestern sky, engine all out, about 100 feet off the deck. He bent his MB steeply around the pylon and was off on lap two. Skeel overtook Dixon on the second lap and Blackburn, Tourtellot, Matthews, and Skeel whipped by the starter's pylon in that order to start lap three. Soon Skeel slid by Matthews and coming down the stretch of the third lap he was pressing Tourtellot. Here Matthews had trouble with his gasoline feed and after his pylon turn completing the third lap he landed, leaving his five colleagues to fight it out. As the three leaders entered the last 5 miles of the final lap Skeel was straining hard but could not quite make it past Blackburn and Tourtellot. Dixon and Johnson appeared not far behind, maneuvering furiously for last place. Suddenly Tourtellot seemed to be in trouble; his engine sputtered for a split second – then quit! He had run completely out of fuel but was valiantly keeping his plane aloft in a flat glide. The pilots in the timers' stand were shouting "Hold 'er! Hold 'er!" at the top of their lungs but Tourtellot's speed was bleeding off too fast. So he deliberately nosed the fighter down, pancaked hard on the graded earth, and the resulting bounce carried him across the finish line in full flight! In the stirring finish the first three MBs plunged by the pylon in a blur, one on a completely dead stick, and seconds later the other two roared by. The final results, based on elapsed time, established Skeel the resounding winner at over 146 mph.

But that marked the end of formal air race competition by Thomas-Morse. W. T. Thomas died in 1966; his brother O. W. had died years earlier. B. D. Thomas, always so proper and lacking in spontaneity, the designer who once told Randy Hall "History is written from the end of the book onward," worked with Convair in San Diego, and eventually retired to nearby La Jolla, California. Hall left Thomas-Morse in 1928 after thirteen years and with Paul Wilson and W. R. R. Winans, who left with him, formed the Cunningham-Hall Aircraft Company in Rochester, New York, where he remained until 1941 when he joined Bell Aircraft in Buffalo, later to become chief project engineer on the P-59 fighter, America's first jet-propelled aeroplane. He retired in

Burt E. "Buck" Skeel standing by his MB-3A after winning the 1923 John L. Mitchell race (USAF)

Thomas-Morse's last racer, the all-metal TM-23, built in 1924 and flown by Paul Wilson at Ithaca. It was dangerously nose heavy, and on its first flight it disappeared over the fields of Newfield. Jerome A. Fried, Thomas-Morse general superintendent, chased afterward in his car. He returned to find the TM-23 overturned on the airfield and Wilson aloft in another plane lest he lose his nerve. The TM-23 never raced. (Au)

The final Thomas-Morse to race, an S4E named Space Eater, raced by Basil Rowe, 1924–26. Rowe was a noted barnstormer and exhibition pilot who also operated the famous Rowe Fliers from 1919 until 1927, the year he went to the West Indies to avoid the impending federal aviation laws. After a year of flying a nightly "sugar cane patrol" he was offered a better job by a young Yale graduate named Juan T. Trippe; decades later Rowe retired as the senior captain of Trippe's Pan American World Airways. (Au)

1959 and moved to Connecticut where he died in 1974, aged 78; his brother, Theodore P. Hall, during World War II was chief design engineer at Consolidated, the firm that absorbed Thomas-Morse. Wilson later retired to Florida, where he indulged his lifelong love of quality automobiles, continuing a string that stretched half a century from his early Chrysler 80 roadster, in which he often transported B. D. Thomas, to a fast Porsche which "kept him awake" well into his eighties.

PORTRAIT OF THE FUTURE

19

The Verville R-3 Racers

In early 1918 Captain Frederick M. Green, RAF, in a paper before the Royal Aeronautical Society, astonished his listeners with some singularly daring predictions about aeroplane performance. Green first postulated several prospective improvements, each in itself reasonably attainable – an improved engine of 430 hp weighing only 2 pounds per horsepower; improved propeller efficiency of 85 per cent; the elimination of drag caused by engine cooling requirements (later approximated with the skin radiator); by unnecessary structure and wires (approximated with the cantilever monoplane); even by the landing gear itself which would be stowed in flight —yet, after sensible combination, his final calculations were to say the least quite startling. Green reasoned that an aeroplane that incorporated all his improvements should be capable of 240 mph at 10,000 feet! This seemed utterly fantastic in 1918 when aeroplanes were miserably slow structures, noisy, cold, and drafty. Yet five years later it was a technical accomplishment. The aeroplane in Green's crystal ball, although he did not know it then, was the Verville R-3.

The R-3 in 1922, like Green's imaginative dream plane in 1918, embodied a combination of many novel technical notions, none of which individually were entirely original in concept or even in hardware at that time, but which were, for the first time, put together with an intrinsic cohesion non-existent in any of its radical contemporaries. Placed next to almost any other flying machine of its era the R-3 is handsomely modern; that it did not presage a fleet of brilliant aeroplanes blazing the skies with innovations a decade ahead of their time represents a delinquency tangled with strands tied to the technical, the politic, and blind human inertia.

The R-3's origins can be traced back to 1921 at a time when ironically the *Navy* was facing its most crucial political challenge in history. The Washington Conference on the Limitation of Armaments, devoting itself mainly to scrapping capital ships at a time when entrenched battleship proponents were being squeezed by the forces of pacifism on one side and Billy Mitchell, champion of air power, on the other, was due to convene and friends and foes alike were anxious to get Mitchell out of the way. It seemed as if suddenly there was an acute need to study aviation in Europe, a job

Alfred V. Verville   (Au)

278

Mitchell would be particularly suited to undertake. The mission he headed, which also included First Lieutenant Clayton Bissell and civilian aeronautical engineer Fred Verville, sailed early in December 1921 just when the aircraft committee of the Armaments Conference was about to hold its opening meeting.

Verville, far removed from these steamy upper councils politics, found the technical harvest of this, his second survey trip abroad in three years, bountiful. His boss, Thurman Bane, did not want to relinquish Verville for the four-month survey, but Mitchell overruled him; and the impressions brought back by the designer were invaluable. No longer were Spad-like blockbusters the most potent aèroplanes flying. The mission covered France, Italy, Germany, Holland, and England; France, "in abject terror of a future military Germany," demonstrated their intense interest in metal construction and high-altitude planes made possible by the Rateau supercharger. Italy's mechanical ingenuity seemed impressive. In Germany, "resourcefulness of design [combined] with the practical ability to create excellent aircraft." Moreover, Mitchell noted that in Germany "we found a greater confidence in aeronautics probably than in any other country." He dined with Winston Churchill March 9, 1922, and after more than three months abroad, during which the Washington Conference scrapped sixty-eight capital ships but placed no limitation on aircraft, the mission sailed home on the *Aquitania.*

Mitchell, as always, was impatient. His anathema was the status quo whether in ideas, attitudes, or the shapes aeroplanes took, and both he and Fred Verville had gained in Europe some definite impressions as to the course America's air service should take. With great zest Mitchell immediately threw himself into organizing the 1922 Pulitzer air race, in his view an arsenal for high-speed aeroplanes which, with the simple addition of armament and "self-sealing gas tanks," he envisioned could be converted into "super-speed alert types." Calling Verville into his office, he fixed his steely gaze steadily upon the intent young eyes of the engineer.

"Verveel, I want tomorrow's aeroplane today," he ordered, "and I don't want any squirrel cage." Characteristically, he gave Verville "until tomorrow morning" to come up with a rendering.

Verville went back to Washington's Occidental Hotel and pored all night over his sketches. If Mitchell wanted a radical new idea by God Verville would give it to him, but it must be mechanically practical. Logically, the fastest aeroplane, the one with the least frontal area, would be an internally braced monoplane; furthermore, one must "hide" the landing gear. The only previous aeroplane using both these ideas had been the Dayton-Wright RB, which had impressed Verville greatly at the 1920 Gordon Bennett, but the shape beginning to grow in his sketches had a low wing from which a short-legged, wide-track landing gear was mounted to fold inboard for stowage in the wing roots, a far lighter, stronger, and cleaner arrangement than the RB had used. The wing would have to be thick. Should it be built of metal or wood? In 1922 metal construction was still considered unproven, heavy, and costly. Verville's wing, which would be almost $1\frac{1}{2}$ feet thick at the root, therefore would be of wood. But Verville personally had reservations about this choice, recalling later the best example of a thick plywood-covered wing he had seen in the United States had been the Fokker D-VIII sent after World War I for evaluation, and the distinct impression this left with him was not reassuring; for a lingering time this notorious wing made many designers "leery of unbraced monoplanes." In his briefcase he had the latest NACA report detailing the new NACA 81 airfoil, double-cambered with only moderate drag and a stable center of

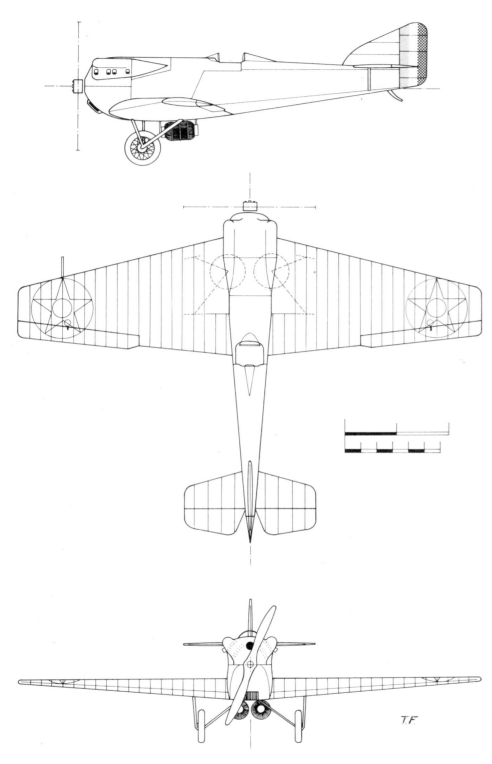

Verville-Sperry R-3, original version, 1922

pressure, thick enough both for strong spars and to enclose the wheels, and this was his choice. For speed he reduced the thickness dimensions about the profile median line by 25 per cent and McCook Field structural engineers later assured him the wing would be strong enough statically, but dynamics and flutter remained exotic mysteries.

For Verville, disregarding the night's passing hours, his sketches growing more detailed, the only engine suitable would be the remarkable new Curtiss D-12. He had no engine data in his hotel room but the D-12 had earlier impressed him as so compact, especially for its astonishing performance, that he recalled the dimensions vividly and neatly drew them in. The D-12's nearest rival in 1922 was the Wright H-3, long notorious for vibration of which Verville was all too aware, having used its predecessor in his earlier VCP, and the prospect of wing flutter was real enough without the additional factor of an engine that wobbled.

The next day Verville showed his sketches to General Mitchell, who sat back and whistled. "Now that's what I call a modern aeroplane!" Mitchell then looked up and asked the designer to suggest a builder. Caught off guard, Verville — who just as in 1920 was still receiving his government payroll check every other week and had no financial or business connection with any aeroplane manufacturer — stammered the first names that came to mind, Curtiss, Thomas-Morse, Grover Loening. As it turned out, each of these was already building new racers. The Lawrence Sperry Aircraft Company of Farmingdale, Long Island, New York, who bid on the project, received the contract (number 7388 of May 23, 1922) to build three racers capable of 190 mph high speed and 75 mph landing speed, priced at $25,000 each, less engine which was to be provided by the Air Service. Verville's plans to use the D-12 were frustrated; as he recalled, "I was *ordered* to use the Wright H engine against my wishes." Neither could he obtain the use of Curtiss' new skin radiators, which would appear only on the four Curtiss racers and one new Navy BR racer built independently by Mike Thurston, who held patents on the device. Verville on the other hand must use Lamblin "lobster pot" radiators. He also wanted to use a Curtiss/Reed metal prop, but of course in 1922 this was still too new for use by anyone. Verville indicated rather bitterly that Curtiss themselves had a lot to do with initially restricting the use of their propulsion equipment (engines, radiators, and props), realizing early that it would do Curtiss prestige no good to have their innovations used on the R-3 and possibly outdo their own racers. Thus Curtiss, who set out to win the race with all-Curtiss equipment, gain worldwide notice, and strengthen their unassailable position in the industry, brought great pressure to bear on McCook Field to restrict the use of Curtiss components owned by the Air Service. Though certainly not unreasonable for Curtiss to move decisively to protect their proprietary interest, the process of internal politicking rubbed against Verville's broad puritan keel and made him "sick."

High-compression H-3 engines costing $750 each to modify were to be used for the race and afterward returned to Wright for "un-modification" to normal compression for service use. On August 18 four new birch propellers were ordered from the Hartzell Walnut Propeller Company of Piqua, Ohio (two with 99-inch diameter, 100-inch pitch, and two with 96-inch diameter, 104·5-inch pitch) to be whirl-tested and trimmed as necessary until 2,000 rpm was achieved. These designs seemed the best alternatives to the unobtainable Reed propeller, but on September 12, three days before the Hartzell props arrived, the Air Service notified Sperry that McCook Field had also built four different types of wood prop, and it must be from the McCook Field props that the type used on the R-3 would be chosen. The Hartzell

First R-3 under construction in Sperry's Long Island factory, 1922 (Au)

Verville-designed R-3 at Selfridge Field, October 1922 (USAF)

Installing Wright H-3 engine in first R-3, 1922 (Au)

props proved quite successful but they were replaced at Detroit, two days before the race, and this government heavy-handedness further soured Verville's frame of mind. He was beginning to feel strongly that any chance for a

significant impact by his racer's progressive design was eroding under an avalanche of shortsighted military decisions and mediocre propulsion equipment.

The racers were built at Sperry's

Long Island factory over the summer of 1922. The monoplane wing was built around a swept-back box spar which ran through the fuselage and was spliced at the wheel fitting, and a rear spar perpendicular to the fuselage center-line. Originally plywood cover was used only from the root out to the wheel fitting (about one-third span) and for the outboard 2 feet at the tip, the remainder of the wing being fabric-covered. Sand static tests were conducted to a load factor of 4·8 on both fuselage and wings, which seemed sufficient, but on its first flight the R-3 passed 50 feet over the anxious spectators and the vibrating wing was alarmingly apparent. Verville later exclaimed, "Jesus, the wing flutter that could be induced by high speed on a monoplane cantilever wing!" He knew at once he was in trouble. His suspicions included engine, prop, ailerons, and airfoil, but he had scant time to trouble-shoot. In an attempt to prevent the H-3 from transmitting vibration to the frame and exciting wing flutter Verville had incorporated into the design what was probably the first practical use of shock absorbing

engine mounts — indeed, he is often credited with their invention — by imbedding his engine mounting bolts ingeniously into rubber spools.[1] Yet the flutter he feared was all too obviously present.

A quick decision to cover the entire wing with plywood to improve its torsional rigidity was made before the second flight. After this modification the R-3 flew much better, making four successful hops on October 4, the day before being shipped to Selfridge Field for the race, and wing flutter by itself never again occurred to such a serious degree. Verville, heartened by this dramatic improvement, passed on a warning to the Loening R-4 team, already at Selfridge, who took his advice and covered their buzz-prone wings with plywood.

The R-3's entire landing gear and retracting assembly weighed just 130 per cent of the lightest equivalent

[1] It would be a fair bet that Verville did not see NACA TN-148 by the German Adlershof, who had tried "flexible engine mounting" in 1918 but concluded his engine "vibrates more when freely suspended than when rigidly mounted!"

280

R-3 landing gear in retracted position, 1922 (Au)

"orthodox" gear in 1922. It employed no wires or pulleys, thereby eliminating the need for adjustments; rather, a hand-crank on a shaft to beveled gears with a two-thread screw was used for raising the wheels. Wheel hubs were Laddon type with internally sprung rubber-cord shock absorbers, the axles imbedded in rubber. Unfortunately the R-3's open wheel wells

The Verville/Sperry team with R-3 racer before the 1922 Pulitzer. From left to right: Fonda B. Johnson, Eugene H. Barksdale, and St. Clair Streett, pilots; Alfred V. Verville, Charles B. Kirkham, Bernie W. Sheahan, R. E. Van Horn, Roscoe Markey, and J. Culver. (Au)

caused drag virtually equivalent to fixed gear on clean wings and this factor seriously impeded acceptance of the concept. Nevertheless the very sight of the new "gadget" caused "waves of emotion" to sweep over dumbfounded spectators.

The finished R-3 represented three thousand man-hours of labor, just 10 per cent of that ultimately invested

in Verville's 1920 Gordon Bennett racer, and was now called "Verville-Sperry," which implies an association that did not in fact exist. Indeed, in later years, Verville was emphatic in pointing out that he had "letters of apology" from Lawrence Sperry regretting the use of his name with the R-3, although even Verville must have realized that it was in no way unusual for the actual builder's name to be attached to an aeroplane's designation. Its first flight was made at Mitchel Field in the early morning of September 24, 1922 just three weeks before the race, by First Lieutenant Eugene Hay Barksdale. The takeoff run was very long, the high-compression engine ran rough despite the use of 70 per cent benzole, and Barksdale did not retract the gear or make speed runs. The additional promised high-compression engines had not arrived at the factory, so on September 28 standard H-3 engines were installed in all three racers. Plans were changed to have the three high-compression engines shipped directly to Selfridge, where, if time remained for pre-race testing, they would be substituted. At Detroit Charles Kirkham, Rudy Funk, and Bob Simons, Sperry's industrious shop superintendent, would continue the anxious debugging process. The race pilots, chosen by the Air Service, were Lieutenants Barksdale and Fonda B. Johnson and Captain St. Clair Streett.

Barksdale, twenty-seven, was born at Goshen Springs, Mississippi, graduated from Mississippi A. & M., and became Assistant State Chemist. Enlisting in 1917, he learned to fly at Oxford, England, and was assigned to 41 Squadron, RAF, where he flew four months and shot down three enemy aircraft before transferring to the 25th U. S. Aero Squadron. By race time 1922 he had logged 1,100 hours. Four years later on August 11, 1926, Barksdale would be killed testing an observation plane near Dayton. An air base near Shreveport, Louisiana, was named for him in 1929.

St. Clair "Wingbone" Streett, twenty-

nine, was from Washington, D.C., where he enlisted in 1916, completing aviation training in September 1917 at Wilbur Wright Field followed by more than a year in French combat zones – his 1,500 hours included 500 combat hours in Spads and Nieuports – and achieving command of the 31st Aero Squadron. He also commanded the notable New York–Nome, Alaska, flying expedition during July–August 1920, and had previous air race experience, having finished fourth in the 1920 Pulitzer.

Fonda Johnson, at thirty-one, was the oldest of the R-3 pilots, born at Clyde, New York; a graduate of Colgate University, he remained there to teach chemistry. He never reached combat after his enlistment but managed to accumulate 1,200 exciting hours. Flying as an escort during the 1921 bombing tests, Johnson's Thomas-Morse pursuit one day ran out of fuel while returning to Langley Field. He glided down to a beach 35 miles from Langley, touching down near a Martin bomber which had just been force-landed offshore by Lieutenant Dunlap. Johnson swam out to the wrecked bomber, wrenched a gas tank from its wing, refueled his fighter, and flew home! He was on duty at Kelly Field, Texas, serving as an instructor when selected to fly the R-3.

Johnson made his first test flight in 22-328 just two days before the race, using the standard H-3 fueled with a 50 per cent benzole mixture, turning the McCook Field prop which had replaced the Hartzell. The engine still wrenched with detonation and mis-firing, vibrating so severely that only three instruments were functioning. But beyond that the control difficulties at high speed were horrible. The aeroplane flew reasonably well up to an indicated airspeed of 185 mph, but above that just to fly straight demanded both feet on the right rudder. On his first attempt at a steep left bank the racer rolled one and a quarter times! Johnson nursemaided the R-3 back to

The three R-3 pilots with their 1922 Pulitzer race mounts: Eugene H. Barksdale;

and Fonda B. Johnson (USAF)

St. Clair Streett;

Selfridge, where later that night (October 12) he and his crew swapped engines, installing a high-compression (6·0 pistons) H-3. None of the pilots thought the R-3s would last through the race if they were subjected to such sustained pounding from the H-3s.

The following morning on Johnson's next test flight the vibration was no better. His tachometer quit and suddenly the top cowling from the firewall back to the cockpit tore free, sailed by Johnson to carom into the horizontal stabilizer, and drifted down into Lake St. Clair. In Johnson's words the aeroplane then "began to camel" so he cut the gun and glided into Selfridge for a landing. Early the next morning (race day) Johnson made his third flight in the R-3, which had had its cowl replaced, new instruments installed, and its prop balanced and tracked. The vibration was still awful and Johnson was alarmed to find the left-hand pylon turns required forward stick and heavy top rudder, but it was now or never. Barksdale and Streett reported their racers responded in essentially the same manner and agreed that visibility was poor "due to the broad-backed fuselage." The R-3s were fueled with a 35 per cent benzole mixture and the three pilots awaited the race with deep misgivings.

Barksdale and Johnson were flagged off together with the BR Bee-Line and Thomas-Morse MB-7. These takeoffs presented a truly remarkable sight because it was the first public display of retractable gear in America and not one but three planes in the heat cranked up their wheels! A witness remarked how strange it was "to watch snarling planes shorn of their wheels!"

Neither R-3 had oil or water outlet thermometers but as Johnson ripped across the starting line he could already smell his engine beginning to cook, even at only 2,100 rpm; his water inlet temperature climbed ominously to 70° C. and the rpm fell to 2,000. Johnson was jockeying mixture and throttle — he got the water inlet temperature to drop 5 degrees momentarily and the engine smoothed out, "better than on any previous flight" — but bad pre-ignition began on the second lap, so bad in fact that Johnson chopped his throttle preparing to ditch. He then found, quite by accident, that by jazzing the throttle he could almost kill the pre-ignition. This relief lasted only until the final lap when Johnson was flying on half throttle with sparks streaming like Roman candles from the engine exhaust. The engine seized solid on the landing roll. Nevertheless his performance was good enough for seventh place at an average speed of 178 mph.

Barksdale garnered fifth place at 181·2 mph but Streett was forced out with a broken oil line on the last lap and his average of 165 mph was 40 mph

off the winning Curtiss R-6's pace. On his forced landing he trundled into a tree and hedge, putting two deep slices in the racer's left wing. It was altogether a discouraging show by "tomorrow's aeroplanes today." When the ground crew removed the cowl from Johnson's racer they discovered a water line had broken from vibration, the engine mounts were loose, the cowl cracked with many hold-down bolts sheared off, and many internal fuselage bracing wires had snapped. Johnson had been lucky to land alive.

Two days after the race the speed trials required by Army contract began. Barksdale, back in 22-326, made 190 mph on his runs and the next day achieved 191 mph in several flat-out passes over a 1-kilometer course to fulfill the contract requirements. The day after that General Mitchell himself rocketed to his world speed record in the Curtiss R-6, beating the best R-3 speed by 32 mph, and leading to the inescapable conclusion that even if the R-3 had been fitted with the D-12 engine and skin radiators in 1922 it might not have equaled this performance which, like those of other fast biplanes in previous years – the S.E.4, the Sopwith Tabloid – had momentous didactic consequences. Long after the Curtiss success of 1922

which lent strong persuasion to further development of thin-wing biplanes there seemed no viable reason for designers to pursue other forms. Many frankly concluded that cantilever wings were unsuitable for high speed after the R-3's mediocre showing, while the few that still believed in it did so on shaken intuition and a strong measure of faith.

Then, as if to feed what Verville called the "prejudice" of R-3 skeptics, after Johnson's next flight, intended for speed runs, he came down – but with his wheels up! On October 16 he had taken off in his freshly repaired 22-328 just after Barksdale landed. Sadly, the mechanics had not yet gotten to the root of its ills and the engine vibration was so violent that an oil line broke. Johnson, thoroughly disgusted, cut the switch when he saw he could make Selfridge Field, but to his amazement the windmilling engine dieseled at 1,400 rpm from pre-ignition and this provided enough speed to carry his racer rapidly across the field. Now alarmed, and "too busy" to lower the gear, he pancaked the R-3 hard on the extreme edge of Selfridge, skidded 75 yards, and lurched to a halt almost – but not quite – on his nose. This sort of embarrassment was adding insult to injury.

It was more than a month before

the R-3s were trucked to McCook Field, arriving December 4; 22-326 was numbered P-269 and put into flying condition for airfoil and engine research, the other two placed in storage. At this time NACA at Langley Field attempted to secure an R-3. They were eager to review the design on the basis of pure technical merit and Verville's solid contention was that if given the chance they "probably could have straightened out the R-3 within a year and the military could have had monoplane fighters ten years before the P-26." Unfortunately NACA was summarily denied access to an R-3, probably more as the result of military red tape coupled with the Army's feeling that the McCook flight test program would produce as much useful data as an analytical program by NACA than from any ulterior motive, although Verville himself firmly believed the Army program was insufficient. In his view, perfection of the R-3 would have upset traditions then being established by powerful and favored contractors.

On February 3, 1923, P-269 was released for its first test flight since the 1922 speed runs, with First Lieutenant Alex Pearson now assigned as pilot. During February and March Pearson, who took great pleasure in wringing out the R-3, performed many tests; on March 5 he climbed to 22,900 feet and over the speed course he averaged 185·4 mph gear up, 161·8 mph gear down, indicating the retractable gear was worth almost 25 mph to R-3 top speed. On March 29 the Army held a "Field Day" where the R-3 was slated to attack the world speed record over a closed course of 500 kilometers.

For this task, since the 40-gallon fuel capacity was insufficient, Verville proposed a new 50-gallon tank but Pearson objected, "Hell, that'll take too long to fit. Why can't you just install a second smaller tank behind the main one and put a petcock on it so I can turn it on when I need to?"

"That will throw the plane out of balance," Verville contended.

"No, it won't, not if we rig it so I can use the smaller tank first."

"She'll still be tail-heavy on takeoff. Besides, we don't have time to put an extra small tank in."

"I can control her," Pearson insisted. And in fact, a small tank was really all they did have time for.

Verville fashioned the smaller second tank but the limited room available restricted it to 9 gallons. Figuring the H-3 consumed some 24 gallons per hour they should just make the distance. Pearson had to fly ten times around a 50-kilometer triangle measured between McCook Field, Wright Field, and New Carlisle, Ohio. On his departure for the record flight he barreled across the field, zoomed up, and found himself being slung around a neat, unintentional roll. He had disregarded what Verville called "the tail-heavy whip," but he managed to avoid a repeat during the remainder of the flight, which took just under two hours. Pearson's record speed for the 500 kilometers was 167·8 mph (270·060 kmh). At the same Field Day the Curtiss R-6 once again raised the world maximum speed record over 1 kilometer.[2]

The Army soon thereafter made plans to equip two R-3s for entry in the 1923 Pulitzer, which was scheduled for early in October. Earlier restrictions had eased and the planes would get D-12 engines and wing radiators. Sperry's estimate was $30,541.04 to recondition two racers but the Air Service balked at such extravagance and only one R-3 (22-328) was shipped to Sperry's Long Island factory for updating. The other R-3, 22-327, which had been the most extensively damaged at the 1922 race, was then tested to destruction. Some parts held

R-3 after its gear-up landing, 1922 (USAF)

[2] On March 31, two days later, the NAA received a cable from France indicating that Lieutenant Batelier, flying the old Etampes-Marmogne circuit on March 30, had apparently set a new 500-kilometer closed-course record at 114·461 mph, unaware he had been preempted by twenty-four hours – and 53 mph!

load factors of 8·5 for six minutes before failure.

During the remodeling, which took ten days, most major R-3 dimensions grew: span and length by almost a foot and weight by over 100 pounds. The Lamblin radiators were replaced by Curtiss wing radiators reducing the aeroplane's effective flat-plate area some 20 per cent. The new radiators were built in four main sections, the upper and lower on each side being independent units composed of two thin corrugated sheets of brass sweated together, each supported on the wing surface by $\frac{1}{16}$-inch steel wires spaced 9 inches apart, threaded over the radiator's surface and through strip metal loops screwed to the wing covering and extending through eyelets soldered in the radiator panel. Spanwise headers ran along the leading and trailing edges with the radiator units held in place at the header tanks by $\frac{1}{8}$-inch hinge pins. The entire wing had first been covered with $\frac{3}{32}$-inch plywood, then the radiators laid on; this increased structural rigidity which in turn eliminated uneven span deflection caused by changing aerodynamic loads. It also increased weight.

Engine oil was cooled by water leaving the radiator, which allowed a more nearly constant oil temperature. A 9-inch cartridge core regulator was used with a bypass to prevent cold oil from clogging the outlet line when starting.

Work was completed by Labor Day. Lieutenant Pearson arrived at Mitchel Field, and on the morning of September 9 the R-3 team was ready to fly. Ironically the D-12 engine now installed in the R-3 had been removed from its nemesis of 1922, the Curtiss R-6. It was still swinging a wood prop, however, which at full throttle turned only 2,100 rpm static, 2,340 rpm in flight, which was considered too low by both Verville and Pearson even though the racer could now reach a very respectable 220 mph. At this point a Reed prop was ordered from Curtiss.

With the smooth-running D-12 the R-3 was no longer plagued with vibration but there were other difficulties. Pearson experienced aileron reversal in steep turns with the rebuilt wings. This phenomenon, quite prevalent decades later among sailplanes and even jet fighters, occurs when the wingtip is so flexible that force from the deflected aileron actually twists it, changing its angle to the oncoming air, and produces a roll in the opposite sense to that commanded — and expected — by the pilot! The R-3 also had a severe tendency to roll left, which took both hands on the stick to control. Completely in the dark, the builders tried three sets of increasingly smaller ailerons to eliminate the reversal, and four lengths of $\frac{3}{8}$-inch shock-absorber cord were strung between the stick and cockpit wall to relieve the 12 pounds of lateral control pressure needed to maintain level flight. The pre-race "crash program" was again in effect.

With the jimmied stick Pearson clocked 219 mph on his fourth test at Mitchel but this was slower than the 1923-model biplanes were doing. Verville, who was at the Sperry factory, was again under great pressure to work out the bugs and prove his R-3 design concept practical "with eighteen hours and a slide rule." When the work gang broke for meals Verville was sketching, deep in thought, ignoring the sly remarks being made. The R-3 was to be crated and shipped to St. Louis the next day. Bob Simons had a crew work all night to glue plywood on the left wing upper surface from the leading edge back to the quarter chord along 4 feet of span, changing the airfoil, adding lift. The right wing bottom surface was reworked similarly to decrease lift. It was all a guess. The plane was shipped on schedule.

The first test flight at St. Louis was made September 21 and to Verville's relief the reworked wings worked perfectly, allowing the control stick to be un-jimmied. To eliminate excessive drag caused by the open wheel

Alex Pearson standing by the R-3 he flew in the 1923 Pulitzer. The racer had been refitted with a Curtiss D-12 engine and wing radiators.
(Au)

receptacles, covers had been carefully built to close flush over these openings when the wheels retracted, and they were now attached. On October 1, at long last, the R-3's Reed metal prop arrived; Pearson made a 218-mph speed run with the wood prop, landed, and had the metal prop immediately installed. He then took off and plunged over the course in a slate-colored blur at 233 mph, a remarkable performance that came within 10 mph of the current world maximum speed record. However, after five minutes at full throttle

the prop spinner broke free, causing the engine to vibrate and cutting short Pearson's speed test.

After this brief but significant flight the infuriating equipment controversy of 1922 was renewed with a last-minute decree that prohibited the R-3 from racing with the metal prop. Verville was adamant in his contention that the application of Curtiss pressure, virtually on the eve of the race, was behind this order, although Curtiss must have realized the R-3, even if equipped with a metal prop, presented

R-3 taking off in the 1923 Pulitzer race
(USAF)

no serious threat unless both new R2C biplanes faltered. Verville also stoutly maintained that the order came too late for General Mitchell, at his Milwaukee farm recuperating from a spill off his horse, to intervene. The disruption and hasty substitution of a suitable wood prop postponed fashioning a new spinner until just one hour remained before race time.

With his R-3 bearing race number 48, Pearson was flagged off in the race's second heat together with Al Williams in the Curtiss R2C biplane. Pearson made a 4,000-foot dive on the starting line but had hardly crossed the field when spectators saw the R-3 "start to weave." The cockpit seemed more like the business end of a pneumatic drill: vibration was 6 to 8 inches in amplitude, shuddering at five cycles per second, making the R-3 almost impossible to fly. Pearson, thinking his problem might be wing flutter, aborted the race and landed at once. Although the preliminary report lamely listed the cause as "undetermined," the replacement wood prop and new spinner proved to be badly out of balance. Curtiss, of course, easily dominated the race. Al Williams won at an average speed of almost 244 mph.

General Mitchell, married five days after the 1923 Pulitzer race to socialite Elizabeth Trumbull Miller, sailed with his new bride before the end of October to Hawaii and the Far East on a voyage that took nine months, during which he made a detailed survey of aviation in the Pacific basin and formed the strong convictions behind his startlingly accurate prediction of the Pearl Harbor debacle seventeen years before it occurred. Returning to Washington in July 1924 he immediately set Verville to work preparing design studies for a 1924 world speed record attempt, not fully appreciating the extent to which the astringent and contrary Coolidge administration would dry up Air Service funds. During his absence General Patrick had struggled in vain to pull weak aviation programs out of bureaucratic

morass; moreover it was no secret that in the three-cornered 1924 presidential race then being waged Mitchell privately favored Wisconsin Progressive Senator Robert M. La Follette, which did not endear him to Coolidge forces. In 1924 nothing was as dead as the issue of national defense; jazz, bootlegging, and business-as-usual were the preoccupations of people who saw aviation only in terms of stunts, but a new world speed record attempt, Mitchell thought, might have enough popular appeal to survive. Excited by the prospect, generally remote from prosaic political battles, and ever immersed in formulae, Verville began his preliminary design using as a basis R-3 philosophy. In order to cram the most power into the least frontal area Verville placed two engines in tandem, effectively making a V-24, turning a single prop through an Allison gear box. Based on MIT wind tunnel tests the predicted high speed was 290 mph, but inevitably the project had to be deferred and finally dropped. Verville derived spiteful satisfaction ten years later when the Italians applied almost precisely the identical formula to their tandem-engine racer, the Macchi-Castoldi M.C.72 — which boasted a phenomenal 477·5 hp per square foot of frontal area — to achieve a world speed record of 440·41 mph which for its class (piston-powered seaplane) stands to this day, almost certainly never to be beaten.

After its disappointing performance in the 1923 Pulitzer the R-3 was shipped to McCook Field, where the remainder of the year was spent testing wood and metal props. A tragic incident indirectly related to the R-3 occurred late in the year on December 13, 1923, when Lawrence B. Sperry, young (twenty-nine), handsome, and vital President of Sperry Aircraft Company, the R-3 manufacturer, was killed while attempting to cross the English Channel in his favorite Messenger, a minuscule "flying flivver" also designed by Verville, which Sperry

Lawrence B. Sperry   *(U)*

had made famous. Sperry was seen at Pett, 5 miles from Rye, flying seaward at 500 feet when 3 miles offshore his 60-hp Lawrence three-cylinder "pop-bottle" engine faltered, forcing him to ditch. His body washed ashore one month later. The untimely death was a great shock to Sperry's illustrious father, Elmer A. Sperry, then sixty-two, developer of the gyroscope, gyrocompass, automatic pilot in 1914, "aerial torpedo," and Collier Trophy winner in 1918. It was also a shock from which the Sperry Aircraft Company as an aeroplane-manufacturing entity never recovered.

On January 1, 1924, project P-269 was considered complete and both R-3s joined each other in storage. Soon thereafter, on February 19, 1924, 22-326 was scrapped. Six months later, on August 31, 22-328, now two years old and the only remaining R-3, was removed, assigned number P-362, and reconditioned for the 1924 Pulitzer race, scheduled at Wright Field, Dayton, Ohio. First Lieutenant Harry H. Mills, a quiet pilot whose resourcefulness,

according to Verville, was largely unappreciated, was named pilot. He had been Alex Pearson's alternate for the Curtiss R-8, but Pearson was killed and the R-8 demolished in a flight test accident on September 2.

The R-3 was entered as race number 70 in 1924. Mills flew it on its first test September 13, 1924, and almost daily until the race.[3] One week prior to race day a new Curtiss D-12A 500-hp high-compression engine was installed and with this engine the R-3 at last won the Pulitzer race, but at just 215·72 mph, a discouraging speed in view of prior Pulitzer performances. Indeed, the Air Service had merely dusted off and rejuvenated three racers from their 1922 stable — the two R-6s and one remaining R-3 — for the 1924 Pulitzer. But at last the R-3's ills were cured. It "handled well and the engine functioned perfectly," Mills reported, finally achieving a strong measure of vindication for Verville's faith and perseverance in the concept.

As Harry Mills taxied the surviving R-3 to the line after its 1924 victory, the climax of its effort, it showed ominous signs of disintegration — joints beginning to open out, dope and fabric stripped in places — and obviously its days were over. Had the R-3 beat the R-6 two years previously, however, aviation history might have been vastly different. But in 1924 a race performance of less than 220 mph attracted scant recognition. The height of irony occurred when the Army was indicted as "ineffectual in designing new types" by *Aviation* magazine in a scathing editorial after the 1924 fiasco.

The one resurrected R-3 had been the only retractable-gear aeroplane seriously operated in the United States

[3] It has been reported that Jimmy Doolittle once flew the R-3 after having a false undercarriage mounted on top and false cockpit painted below. He flew over Dayton with the normal landing gear retracted, giving the appearance of being upside down; but it was the dummy hanging from the false cockpit that sent Daytonites scurrying!

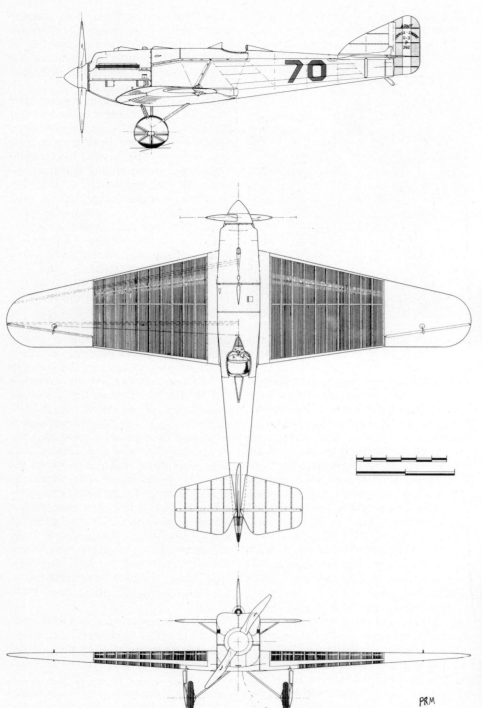

R-3 circling home pylon to win the 1924 Pulitzer race   *(Au)*

Harry H. Mills, winner, 1924 Pulitzer race   *(USAF)*

Verville-Sperry R-3, winner, 1924 Pulitzer race

in 1924. Even two years after its introduction spectators still found it "uncomfortable" to watch a plane fold up its wheels "like a card table." A witness to the R-3's 1924 Pulitzer triumph described the racer as it "cleaved the air . . . sliding on its fuselage . . . a vision of the dim future." Just how dim the future would be was forewarned in an inconspicuous little book issued April 1924 which Verville was personally convinced had disastrous, long-lasting consequences. Entitled *Simple Aerodynamics and the Airplane*, it was prepared by First Lieutenant Charles N. "Monty" Monteith, USAS, Chief, Airplane Section, Engineering Division, McCook Field, and member of the NACA subcommittee on aerodynamics, destined to become Boeing chief engineer, where his reputation as a super-cautious engineer suspicious of progressive ideas would continue to grow. His momen-

R-3 making speed dash, 1924 — a portrait of the future (Au)

tous little book was published under the direction of the Chief, Air Service, to provide "official information and guidance" to the Air Service. It included an important article, "The Retractable Chassis," in which the last paragraph concluded, ". . . the retractable landing gear has not been regarded favorably by the Air Service. The race for the supremacy of the air may eventually make it necessary to incorporate such a device to improve performance, but it is felt that such a development is in the distant future." Thus the fate of retractable landing gear development in the United States was effectively sealed for the remainder of the 1920s.

Thick cantilever wings were not sufficiently developed for high speed although in 1924, despite the faster French Bernard V.2, the R-3 was certainly one of the most important examples of the form. Other monoplane racers of this era, though somewhat

similar in appearance to the casual observer, were for the most part quite dissimilar dimensionally, structurally, and aerodynamically. The monoplane languished, according to Verville, because of "prejudice, negative speed performance, and wing vibration [flutter] . . . plus the lack of effort for its development [in America] after General Mitchell was gone." Verville for one was, to put it mildly, "disappointed" by its lack of acceptance, regretting as needlessly lost the eight years that elapsed until it drew "favorable attention."

Yet all retractable-gear, monoplane racers of the 1920s generally failed to win air races simply because their builders did not provide time for preparation. This remained a human lesson largely unheeded even as complex technical solutions were positively identified. Despite being hamstrung by its inadequate pre-race "crash programs," the R-3 can be summed up as a classic 1920s example of synergism — a machine in which truly the whole was greater than the sum of its parts. For its day its design features were not only daring but so skillfully integrated that together they lit the way on the stumbling road of technical progress with a light brighter than that cast by each of its design advances individually. The R-3 was a tour de force which deserved considerably more success; its disappointing performance was insufficient to crack the mossback barrier and left authorities unconvinced of its merit, but this failure concealed experience not appreciated until the moment for its application arrived. Ten years later, in 1934, Sydney Camm employed its visionary concepts directly into the immortal Hawker Hurricane.

On November 25, 1924, only six weeks after the Pulitzer race, the last R-3 was shipped as "salvage" to the McCook Field Museum. It eventually ended up on a bonfire heap. Pilot Harry Mills, the least flamboyant of the Pulitzer winners, died of tuberculosis in 1937. Verville, disgusted with what he

called "military back-biting policies and favorite sons jazz," resigned from the Air Service Engineering Division in February 1925 after six years as Chief, Pursuit and Racing Planes Projects, and organized the Buhl-Verville Aircraft Company at Detroit, Michigan. The era of commercial aviation was then just dawning, and in 1924 it seemed the only bright spot on the aeronautical horizon. Verville remained active in aviation until his death in 1970.

OTHER AMERICAN EFFORTS 20

Loening

"Don't be downhearted. You learned something, didn't you?"

Thus General Billy Mitchell consoled Grover Loening after the deplorable showing made by the two Loening R-4 racers in the 1922 Pulitzer. Indeed, in his own words, Loening had learned "quite a lot." Aside from the technical lessons, the stringy, sanguine thirty-four-year-old plane builder never again forgot the difference between specialized racers and aeroplanes with more immediate practicality — and salability.

Loening was born in the American consulate in Bremen, Germany, where his father served as consul general. He was educated at Lawrenceville and Columbia, receiving the first master's degree in aeronautics awarded in the United States. He then worked as Orville Wright's assistant at Dayton shortly before war broke out in Europe, served briefly as Chief Engineer, United States Army Air Service, and managed the B. F. Sturtevant Company in Boston where he used steel construction in aeroplanes as early as 1916. At that point Loening, just twenty-eight, founded his own aeroplane-manufacturing company to capitalize on the massive wartime aeroplane orders he knew were coming, setting up his factory in a dingy fifth floor loft at 351 West Fifty-second Street in the heart of New York City. Loening was indignant by what he

Loening M-8 pursuit, 1918   *(Au)*

felt to be the unjustified portion of aeroplane business grasped by the heavy hand of the automotive industry. But building aeroplanes proved to be very different from building cars and his resentment was vindicated when scandalous delivery delays resulted. Finally, after almost a year, General Motors' venal, avaricious Colonel E. A. Deeds, military Equipment Division Chief, was replaced by William C. Potter, a tough, no-nonsense mining executive who served directly under John D. Ryan, the new head of the Bureau of Aircraft Production, and who doled out sensible orders to the aviation industry. Loening's assignment was to produce a two-seat fighter. The prototype first flew at Mineola on August 4, 1918.

Loening's fighter was a striking-looking monoplane powered by a 300-hp Wright-Martin (Simplex)-built Hispano-Suiza, capable of taking off from a dead start in four seconds, hitting 146 mph, and climbing with two men, four machine guns, and two thousand rounds of ammunition to 24,600 feet. Its fuselage had slab sides which boxed a series of spruce veneer bulkheads and tapered to a knife-edge aft. The sturdy wing fastened directly to the top longerons with pin joints, its two spars carried

right through the fuselage with the pilot seated between them. This feature plus enormous, lifting struts of steel tube and wood gave the wing great torsional rigidity and allowed Loening to cut weight elsewhere. The finished aeroplane Loening claimed was built with only 10 per cent the number of parts required for an "ordinary European design"; moreover, with but 70 more available horsepower than the Bristol fighter (Wright Hisso H versus Rolls-Royce Falcon III) the Loening carried 100 pounds more military load, vastly exceeded its performance, yet weighed some 400 pounds less. Lord Semphill of the RAF, in a report to his government, praised the Loening in great detail as one of the "most advanced and original designs" of the war.

The war ended and with it plans to mass-produce the remarkable fighter which had earned Grover Loening wide respect. On January 18, 1919, Shorty Schroeder with two passengers climbed one to almost 20,000 feet, setting an unofficial altitude record, and this so impressed the Navy that they placed the first peacetime order with Loening for six planes, designated M-8 (Monoplane-8 cylinders). Wright-Martin had also bought a few to serve as beds for test engines. On September

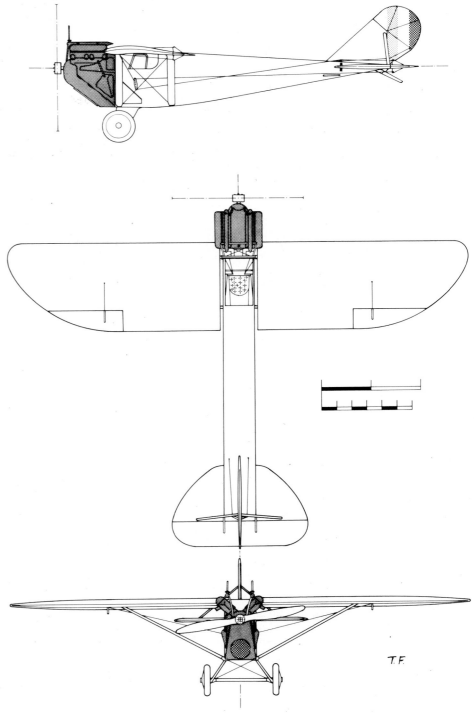

Loening M-81S racer, 1920 Pulitzer entry

Loening Special racer — the best American monoplane of 1919 — seen here as it was flown in the 1920 Pulitzer race (USN)

29 the Navy almost duplicated the altitude feat, reaching 18,500 feet — with a Loening on floats! In 1920 the Navy entered three Loenings in the Pulitzer race; two were standard two-seaters but one was extensively modified. Called the "Loening Special," or M-81S, it had been cut down to a single-seater, the cockpit completely enclosed under considerably smaller, entirely new wings with rakish elliptical tips. There were no large, lifting struts; indeed, the Special had been generally redesigned and cleaned up throughout. Exposed engine cylinder blocks together with two adjacent water expansion tanks were unfortunate excrescences although the radiator was slung below and somewhat streamlined, air reaching it through an oval opening in the cowl. Marine pilot Benjamin G. Bradley was assigned to race the Loening Special, which could hit almost 170 mph, and this, with a bit of luck, was certainly fast enough to win.

Bradley was airborne right behind Harold Hartney, whom he was confident of passing, but his engine was turning 150 rpm low and he had to struggle along, content to hold position. On the third lap an aluminum water connection cracked, releasing a jet of steam, but Bradley thundered into the fourth and final lap. Streaking westward on the homestretch, low over the Bethpage Turnpike with the Long Island Railroad tracks snaking alongside to his right, Bradley, with desperation growing as rapidly as his water temperature, could just make out Mitchel Field, the finish line, and despite his balky engine an easy third place dead ahead. Suddenly the red-hot engine wrenched violently and almost jumped from its mount. It had seized solid and within seconds Bradley found himself crunching to a safe if splintery stop on a golf fairway, 1 mile short. Neither of the other Loenings had any better luck. One was involved in a tragicomedy collision while taxiing to the starting line; its pilot was unhurt but the other pilot, Oakley Kelly, who

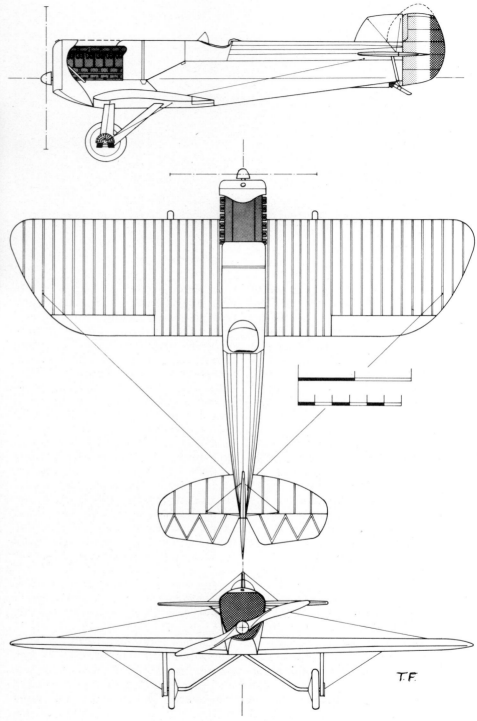

Loening R-4, 1922; note added fin; original tail denoted by dotted line.

achieved non-stop transcontinental fame three years later, had three teeth knocked out for his trouble.

In spite of its singular lack of success at the 1920 Pulitzer, the Navy ordered eighty-three Loenings, and to oversee the burgeoning business finances Grover appointed his brother Albert Palmer Loening, older by two years, as vice-president–treasurer. The midtown fifth-floor loft was hardly the place to produce so many important government aeroplanes, so fifty were constructed at the Naval Aircraft Factory under the direction of a young Cornell graduate, Navy Lieutenant Leroy Randle Grumman, who did such a good job that Loening persuaded him to leave the service and become his shop manager, a post he held for the next ten years — until he followed the boss's example, and went into business for himself.

Loening's reputation as a reliable builder of solid aeroplanes was now well established, and thus in 1922 he received a new plum: an Air Service contract for two high-speed racing aeroplanes to compete in the 1922 Pulitzer. The contract (number 550)

would be worth $76,000 if his racers, designated R-4, could do 190 mph, but — as in all the 1922 racer contracts — a penalty clause provided that Loening would be docked $2,500 for every mile under this speed, with no payment if the planes did not achieve 175 mph. Packard engines (600-hp model 1A-2025) and wood propellers would be furnished by the Air Service; sandbag static tests were to be conducted at the factory, now an expanded area in Long Island City. Little did Loening know then, but this juicy plum would turn into a sour grape.

With the monster Packard engines for power, and with only three months to engineer his speedplanes, Loening — whose talent was always an ability to slice through superfluous layers and expose the essential kernel of a problem — proposed quite simply a flying engine, "the simplest flying engine ever built." The R-4 was touted to have the lightest weight per horsepower of any aeroplane built, a fantastic 4 pounds per horsepower, and if judged on this basis alone it should have performance exceeding any other racer at the contest. The layout was

Ennis C. Whitehead in cockpit of his R-4, 1922 Pulitzer   *(USAF)*

Loening R-4 with Packard 600-hp engine, built for the 1922 Pulitzer race; Grover Loening on right   *(USAF)*

uncluttered and strong, a monoplane with heavy, continuous wing spars that doubled as the engine bed; indeed, the engine, which alone weighed almost triple the entire airframe, comprised over one quarter of the fuselage length, actually reaching back almost to the rear spar! The R-4 design deserves credit as one of the earliest attempts to build a thick-wing monoplane capable of penetrating to 200 mph, especially against its background of a virtually non-existent technical base line. Working largely in the dark, Loening made an unfortunate airfoil choice, heavily undercambered, which proved to have enormous drag at higher speed — plus the tendency toward other, more dangerous effects. On its original drawings the R-4's empennage is quite different from what evolved on the finished racer. The drawings also called for strut-braced wings and a streamline covered landing gear, but when rolled out the finished R-4 had cantilever wings and bare wheels, void

of any covering, although the struts were faired and the shock absorber cords were neatly arranged in an edgewise manner. The racer had no vertical fin, only a small rudder hinged to the fuselage sternpost. The pilot was sandwiched between the engine and a large fuel tank but this was excused because it allowed the cockpit to be placed forward for better visibility. All control surface hinge gaps were closed with soft metal, fabric-covered.

The first R-4 was soon completed and publicly displayed to the press on September 18, 1922, on Long Island amid optimistic ballyhoo. Then both racers were shipped to Selfridge Field, where they were issued race numbers 45 and 46 and assigned to Lieutenants Ennis C. Whitehead and Lester D. Schulze respectively. Schulze, whose brooding, intense eyes gleamed under a dark shock of hair, was a resourceful pilot from Los Angeles who had attended Stanford and was in the auto business at war's outbreak. Sent first to

Italy, then to Issoudun, France, as a test pilot, he left the service in February 1919 but rejoined on a permanent basis in the summer of 1920. Ennis Clement Whitehead, twenty-seven, entered the Air Service from Westphalia, Kansas, also became a test pilot at Issoudun, and like Schulze left the service in 1919. Whitehead then finished college (University of Kansas, 1920) but immediately reentered the Air Service and was soon assigned to the 1st Pursuit Group. By race time he had logged 1,311 hours. As late as 1940 Whitehead was only a major, working in Air Intelligence; but by 1943 he had rocketed in rank to major general. It was he who saw to it that Charles A. Lindbergh, a civilian, was allowed to fly combat missions in the P-38s and F4Us under his command in New Guinea in 1944. Whitehead, regarded by Lindbergh as one of the nation's finest officers, became Commanding General of the wartime Fifth Air Force.

Whitehead took off on the R-4's first flight at 10:15 A.M., October 1, 1922. On his half-hour test he hit 170 mph but the report he turned in spelled trouble. Whitehead found the cockpit too windy, the instrumentation, visibility, and control positions poor; he was disturbed when the wings "flexed" and when the ship responded weakly to the ailerons — or sometimes not at all! In his estimation the R-4 did not handle well enough to stunt or even stall, and went "out of control" in any maneuver attempted. It was particularly prone to a frightening yawing oscillation.

At 2:50 P.M. the same day, Lieutenant Schulze took off in the second R-4 but was back on the ground eighteen minutes later. His report was also negative, only more so. His R-4 was tail-heavy, he was unable to open the throttle on speed runs without losing control, and if anything his wings vibrated more dangerously than Whitehead's. This situation was aggravated

Plywood skin added to R-4 wing in vain attempt to alleviate flutter (USAF)

Loening R-4 racer, 1922; note wire bracing between wing and tail, an attempt to alleviate flutter; also note absence of vertical fin. (USAF)

in both racers since the engine's vibrations were transmitted directly to the wings through the spar on which it rested, reinforcing the wing's natural tendency to flutter. That night a huge vertical stabilizer was added to each R-4 and at ten-thirty the next morning Whitehead was again aloft in his ship for fifteen minutes. After landing yet another change was made to the vertical fin and rudder, and he took off again for a seven-minute test . . . but the yawing was still present. After this flight the landing gear struts were unfaired in hopes this would dampen the yaw. So far no one had any good ideas regarding the wing flutter.

By October 5, less than ten days before the big race, it was common knowledge that Grover Loening was in deep trouble with his "flying engine" R-4s. Gathering his harried pilots and long-suffering staff together, he called upon them earnestly to maintain the utmost secrecy regarding changes made to the R-4s. In retrospect, Loening seemingly had little to gain by this move unless perhaps he wanted to steal a march on his competitors by preventing any successful fixes he devised from falling into their hands,

but considering the terrible problems he was individually up against, this would have been a decidedly egotistical and unwarranted rationale for secrecy. Actually, Loening needed badly to learn from his more successful competitors. Perhaps he wanted secrecy as protection from the dozens of suggestions which now were inundating him, offered by those who were well-meaning but just as confused as he. Some of the suggestions he adopted, such as adding "anti-drift" wires which extended from the wings near the tips to the horizontal stabilizer, fitted in hopes of bracing the wings and damping flutter. Large windshields were mounted to cut down draft in the cockpit, and even these were wire-braced to prevent deflection in the slipstream! Here was a team of bewildered speed seekers trying desperately to dig themselves out of a very deep hole.

The crippling blow came when Lieutenant R. S. Worthington, the tall, stern Chief Engineer of Selfridge Field, requested he be allowed to inspect the R-4s. On both aeroplanes he found two ominous cracks developing in identical spots in the main wing spar supporting the engine. He then

Lester D. Schulze with the R-4 he flew in the 1922 Pulitzer; note vertical fin and king post wing bracing added at last minute before the race. (Au)

had the fabric ripped off the wing of number 45 and this revealed that "all parts" of the wing structure were "loose and distorted"; most metal fittings, which appeared too light, were pulling through the wood; moreover, the main spar was "knotty and sappy." The work to be done amounted to virtually complete overhauls for both racers, and time was running out.

It is not entirely clear if Worthington's inspection was occasioned by a telegram sent by Alfred Verville to Selfridge Field. Verville was experiencing baffling wing flutter problems with his R-3 in flight tests over Long Island and the news of Loening's trouble had filtered even as far afield as that. Verville immediately telegraphed a warning, urging Loening to cover his wings not with fabric but with stiff plywood as he had done. Metal patches were placed over the cracks and flying wires were added, extending from each axle to the spars. Then the wings were recovered, as Verville had suggested, with veneer back to the rear spar. In view of its more severe flutter problems, number 46 was additionally fitted with a husky king-post wing brace. The fixes were all hit or miss — and were all too painfully in plain view for anyone to see.

Obviously, Loening lamented, much remained to be learned about the dynamic interrelationships of aerodynamics, load, and structure. After the race Ennis Whitehead put his arm around Verville, gave him a cheek kiss in the French noble tradition, and said, "Thanks for saving my life." Loening too had high regard for Verville, later claiming that if Verville's R-3 had been equipped with the same propulsion equipment as the R-6 in 1922 it would have outperformed it.

The changes made added approximately 700 pounds to the R-4s, but even more exasperating, the changes did not entirely eliminate the wing flutter! By race day it appeared as if all efforts had been in vain. The R-4s rolled to the starting line with many additional wires and braces, and were forced to race without cowls to keep their engines cool. Actually, viewed from a different perspective, the R-4 was an impressive aeroplane and Loening's concept of design simplicity might have worked had he had more time for research. Both R-4s finished the race. Whitehead came in eighth, 35 mph slower than the winning R-6, and Schulze ninth, 8 mph slower than his compatriot. Schulze was later killed while flying a standard pursuit.

The R-4 still had to meet its contract obligations. On October 16, in ship 45, Whitehead made the required four speed runs (his slowest was 173·41 mph upwind, his fastest 200·62 mph downwind); he averaged 187 mph, 3 mph under 190, and this cost Loening $7,500. A further deduction of $562·97 was charged for parts furnished during the hectic repairs made at Selfridge, yielding the sum of $67,937·03, which Loening received by check on October 19. The Air Service then crated the two R-4s and shipped them to McCook Field, where on December 1 ship 46 was placed in storage and 45 was readied for flight. The number P-267 was painted on her rudder (the race number removed) and on December 15 she made three short flights piloted by Lieutenants Boyd, Brookley, and Pearson. Meanwhile the Air Service was considering fitting the R-4s with guns or bomb racks. On January 11 and 17, 1923, Lieutenant Pearson again flew the R-4 but both times he reported it to be "dangerous, . . . unsatisfactory," and urged that it be retired. Work on it continued, however; in early February the engine and fuel tank from the sister ship were installed. It flew once more on February 17 but was still considered too dangerous to be useful. So in early March it was retired to the McCook Field Museum, one of the dimmer beacons lighting a byway on the road of aeronautical progress. It was surveyed in January 1926. The other R-4 never flew again.

During that summer of 1922 Grover Loening was already deeply involved in marketing an "air yacht", the first of a long and successful series of Loening seaplanes and amphibians. In the tough civil market that existed then Loening's shrewd idea was to make a few high-priced sales to the wealthy in order to establish a foothold in general aviation. The Social Register became his mailing list, and his pilots were setting records between Palm Beach, Port Washington, and Newport. The impressive performances they made did result in sales

of air yachts to Vincent Astor, Harold S. Vanderbilt, Ross Jackson of Detroit (compensation for Loening's dismal performance in the Detroit Pulitzer), and others. The air yacht cost $19,500 — or almost $5 per pound, quite dear in 1922 dollars. In the midst of his Pulitzer worries, Loening managed to get General Mitchell aloft in one over the Detroit races and this later resulted in an Air Service order for eight, worth a tidy $133,000, proving far more lucrative than the R-4. It was for this impetus to general aviation that Loening received the 1921 Collier Trophy. He remained head of his company for many years; during World War II he was consultant to the War Production Board and to NACA; he received the Wright Memorial Trophy in 1950, the Guggenheim Medal in 1960, and in the 1970s, a half century after the Pulitzers, Grover Loening was again in the race pits, eagerly crewing for his son Mike Loening, who piloted a clipped-wing P-51 in those splashy races of regenerated World War II fighters at Reno.

Wind tunnel model of the Air Service Engineering Division–designed R-7, a proposed Pulitzer racing biplane with retractable landing gear, 1922. Preliminary work began on the actual aeroplane, and pilots were assigned — Lieutenants Barksdale, Macready, Batter, and Hitchison — but shortly afterward the project was canceled. (USAF)

The Bee-Line Racers

Trees far to the southwest shimmered in a milky haze, aureole of the hot white orb which now pierced uncomfortably, penetrating beneath the stinging, sticky leather in concert with heat waves rising from the engine. Steve Calloway squirmed to make his legs comfortable in the packing-box cockpit, the unfamiliar shoulder straps checking him with an abrupt bite on the collarbone. Nearby he could see other glistening racers coming to life with snorts of blue smoke, waggling rudders, grass flattening in waves of wind. He knew they eyed him too, and with even greater wonder, since in 1922 nothing like his plane — which bore the intriguing name Bee-Line — had ever raced before.

Down to business. He had to rehearse the drills just one more time. Next to the fire extinguisher on his right were two strange, new devices: the one called retracting safety lever he had first to reset to "up" — this unlocked the landing gear mechanism — and above it, protected by leather padding, was the retracting crank behind which dimly hid bicycle chains and sprockets. All very complicated, to be sure, but a few twists on this hand-crank and his wheels would actually withdraw from the airstream! Really quite amazing. On the floor by his left knee Calloway fingered the gasoline wobble pump, and above it the throttle and altitude adjustment. Cockpit workload, increased by new levers for the wheels, was somewhat compensated by elimination of the engine spark adjustment. Directly in front, the ignition switch protruded like a big disjointed nose from the center of the otherwise barren dashboard. Buried in the shadows diagonally in front of his left knee was a miniature board from which peeped a tachometer surrounded by four small gauges, oil and fuel pressure, oil and water temperature. Except for old friends, joystick and rudder bar, that was the cockpit.

Other quivers of mistrust trembled into Calloway as the engine rumbled.

No cabane wires tangled with his view, and the white sky above looked splendidly, distressingly vacant with no sturdy wing to blot it out. This plane's single wing was mounted low, and it looked awfully small from Calloway's vantage. Muted sunlight bounced in comb-teeth rows from the shiny skin radiators, another of this plane's newfangled gimmicks. Calloway scrutinized their edges skeptically for telltale bubbles or wisps of steam, and slowly shook his head. To clean up an aeroplane any more they would have to chop off the tail! (Little did he know that in France that very month they had done precisely that!) The Bee-Line was nothing at all like the sturdy, agreeable ship he had flown in the Curtiss Marine Trophy race six days previously.

Of course, his Bee-Line had been designed, they said, to hit 216 mph, and it actually had hit 213 — faster than the official world speed record — in a test hop two weeks before, flown by the current Pulitzer champion, Bert Acosta. But then Bert had forgotten his cockpit drill and landed with the wheels up! Mustn't forget that drill.

Two Bee-Lines, designated BR (for "Booth Racer"), were produced by the Aerial Engineering Corporation, a new firm formed that summer by two of the Curtiss company's hottest protégés, President Arthur L. "Mike" Thurston and Chief Engineer Harry T. Booth, the very men who had designed Curtiss' blazing CR racer of 1921. Both were known to be aggressively innovative, brimming with new ideas in speedplane design. To have a free hand they left Curtiss and early in 1922 launched their own company. Ironically, the site they chose — Hammondsport, New York — had been the scene of Glenn Curtiss' earliest triumphs. But now to put theory to the test. With barely four months until race time the Navy ordered two racers. They would be low-wing cantilever monoplanes with retractable gear. Thurston, moreover, held patent rights on the skin radiators developed at Curtiss

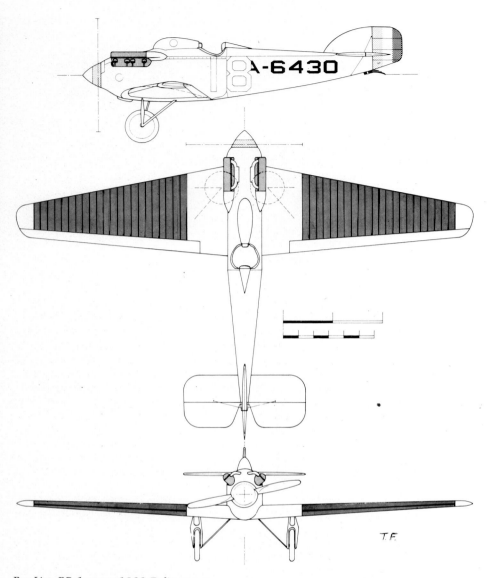

Bee-Line BR-1 racer, 1922 Pulitzer entry

under his direction, and he expected to reap at least 15 mph more from their use.

Used to Curtiss' meticulous design methods, Booth and Thurston were not surprised when their finished racer's empty weight was within 4 ounces of that predicted. Power was supplied by the high-compression Wright H-3, prone to vibration but capable of 400 hp, and mounted

directly on the front wing beam stub. A Lamblin oil radiator and engine-driven fuel pump which delivered the gasoline under a pressure of 3 psi were fitted. The fuselage, reinforced veneer, was of rectangular cross section forward of the cockpit blending to a triangular cross section aft. Internal bulkheading resulted in exceptional rigidity despite a complete absence of wire stays and turnbuckles. Wing construction was in many ways very advanced. The BR introduced a novel method of stub beam wing attachment, a feature which would contribute to the success ten years later of the earliest Northrop and Douglas transports. Furthermore, although they had never heard the word "aeroelasticity," Booth and Thurston knew that wing strength could be greatly augmented by building non-rigid structures. In a sandbag test equivalent to 6·33 g their wing was deflected $17\frac{1}{2}$ inches at the tip, a distance more than 10 per cent the panel length, yet returned to normal with no permanent set. This remarkable wing was built around a rectangular, tapered, three-ply veneer multi-cell torsion box buttressed by solid, tapered spruce spars. Ribs external to the box, providing the airfoil shape, and in turn covered by the outer skin, were attached to ribs inside the box by pieces passing through holes carefully cut in the veneer, which was thus held to its support but was permitted flexibility under load. The wing's major design flaw was not structural but aerodynamic: the airfoil chosen

(Göttingen 387) unduly hindered speed.

Screwed to the ribs at $5\frac{1}{2}$-inch intervals were Thurston's daring skin radiators, which, except for those of his Curtiss competition, were the first ever to be thrust into the racing arena. Formed from thin sheets of corrugated brass sweated together, Thurston's radiators had headers embossed on the inner sheet to which external copper connecting pipes were soldered. Two steel pipes, inlet and outlet, extended along the front spar, carefully tapered to control the flow rate. Water flowed aft through radiators on the wing top surface, forward through those on the bottom. Only one BR was finished with wing radiators. Either time or caution — or both — prompted Booth and Thurston to equip the other racer with the tried and true Lamblin lobster pots.

Presumably Booth and Thurston were unaware that in a Washington hotel room Fred Verville had dreamed up the almost identical formula for high speed, using the low mounted wing as receptacle for the retracted landing gear. In some ways the Bee-Line's gear

Bee-Line racer being prepared for the 1922 Pulitzer race; note Lamblin radiators. (Au)

was superior. Each wheel was mounted in a double fork, the front flexibly connected by rubber shock absorbers to a fore-and-aft steel tube mounted in bronze fittings, the rear rigidly attached with universal hinges to the same tube. Rods to the axles pulled the wheels inboard when actuated by a sprocket-cable and pulley system from the cockpit, requiring only eight seconds for retraction. Doors of veneer and aluminum closed over the wheel wells for streamlining.

Probably because Bert Acosta had flown their 1921 design to a Pulitzer victory, Booth and Thurston approached their hot-blooded former test pilot to take the Bee-Line into battle. Navy drawbacks seemed forestalled inasmuch as Acosta had been gazetted a lieutenant, USNR, by the Secretary of the Navy on August 8, 1922, as reward for his 1921 victory in the borrowed Navy racer.[1] But six weeks earlier Acosta had experienced a shattering turning point in his life. He was aloft in an untried Sperry Messenger, a tiny biplane, late in the

afternoon of June 28. As usual with Bert the flight was half serious, half clowning. He pointed the craft in a humming steep glide, dropping below the hedgerow bordering Mitchel Field. There was a sharp note of power and the plane started to roll abruptly, but when it was on its back, no more than 50 feet high, the gravity-fed engine misfired once and quit. With consummate skill Bert completed the roll, but the engine failed to catch. Dirt exploded as the Messenger plowed into the turf. It took ten minutes for shocked men, panting for breath, to work Bert free. The fuselage had split lengthwise and the engine was on Bert's feet, the heels torn from his shoes. Though no bones were broken, Bert was unconscious. The cowl was dented where his head had rammed into it. Bert spent the next several weeks in the hospital, in and out of delirium.

Bert Acosta always enjoyed the dizzy glamour, the pungent gaiety, the faceless people who idolized him, especially the women who in large numbers sensed an irresistible magnetic aura of male predator exuded by this darkly dashing libertine, ornamented in

Bee-Line racer, entry in the 1922 Pulitzer; note wing radiators. (Au)

[1] Acosta held this rank until 1926.

his musky leather garb and debonair moustache. He relished the fleeting adoration summoned by his disdain for prudence, his skill and irresponsibility. But with the crash in 1922 there came a subtle turning point. Acosta's courage never faltered; but after the crash there was an underlying note of depression, a loneliness, a dimension of stoicism. His sense of mortality had been touched. Acosta's equally well-known reputation as a prodigious drinker then threatened to get out of hand, and his antics became bizarre — the excessive kind that are laughed off uneasily. Incapable of adjusting as the improvements perfected by engineers like Booth and Thurston gradually transformed aviation from a raw and reckless game to a mundane enterprise in which he had no heart, Acosta remained ever ready to grasp the momentary thrill. His first flight tests in the Bee-Line were almost defiant. Within minutes he had complete confidence in the little silver-gray and yellow racer, and on the afternoon of October 1 he thrilled several thousand spectators with a slashing speed demonstration. The trade press, which called the Bee-Lines the race's "most promising designs," further commented, "if [the Bee-Lines] sustain the strain of the race it is believed that they will affect the future design of all military and naval aircraft."

It might be construed that Acosta's speed flight was indeed the first public display of retractable gear in the United States. Cold mention of this fact does little to describe the "waves of emotion" the new "gadget" caused to sweep over dumbfounded witnesses who recalled it was "strange to watch snarling planes shorn of their wheels." Certainly it was the first public display of a gear-up landing. Bert hit the turf at 60 mph, startled at the unexpected reaction and the wrenching skid to an abrupt halt. He declined any comment, regretted the broken prop and slight damage. It might have been this incident which caused the Navy suddenly to bar his participation four days before the race. The public reason was that his presence would tend to reflect unfavorably on the ability of regular Navy pilots. Two such pilots who had competed in the Curtiss Marine Trophy race were hurriedly picked to fly the two Bee-Lines; they were Steve Calloway and David Rittenhouse. It proved to be a mistake for Booth and Thurston. Rittenhouse, unable to get in even one test flight on such short notice, declined to race the unorthodox craft, withdrawing at virtually the last minute. Rittenhouse thus would have to wait one year to show his prowess on the race circuit.

Calloway, in his cockpit, now saw the time was near. Cinching his straps, he gunned the engine, watching the starter's flag. Now! Whap open the throttle, feel the sudden wind lace the exhaust smell away, see the leafy treetops fall away. He cranked up the wheels, unaware of the wonder this caused below. His engine was running well with that reassuring if slightly uncomfortable drumming H-3s were known for when suddenly he smelled the hot oil. By his left knee he could see with dismay that the line to the oil pressure gauge had parted, allowing oil to squirt away. In minutes it would be gone. With his engine in otherwise perfect condition he landed, out of the race. Two days later on October 16, the first day of Army speed trials, Calloway took the Bee-Line over the measured course. His average speed was 177 mph. Booth and Thurston, discouraged after their brave but futile attempt, one of the pioneering attempts to build a 200-mph thick-wing monoplane, and unable to keep their business going, closed the doors in Hammondsport and joined Curtiss' great rival, Wright.

The Navy TS and TR

Navy development of the TS/TR aeroplanes deserves mention because it was the earliest manifestation of the Navy's significant breakaway from traditional water-cooled engines to air-cooled radials — and it launched the racing careers of some of the Navy's star speed pilots. The TS-1, the Navy's first postwar fighter, was designed under Commander Jerry Hunsaker, and as their first custom fighter the naval designers furnished it with features then foreseen as essential: ease of disassembly and erection; a single fuel tank on the lower wing center-section which the pilot could jettison in case of fire; interchangeable wheels and pontoons. The first TS, A-6248, was completed at the Naval Aircraft Factory in early July 1922; the second was built by Curtiss, who eventually built more than thirty; a total of forty-three was procured. The TS was powered by a promising new engine which was the Navy's great white hope — the Lawrence J-1.

Charles Lanier Lawrence, a sturdy, block-faced engineer with kindly, mellow eyes, was well-connected: from Lenox, Massachusetts, he had gone to Groton, Yale (class of 1905), and l'École des Beaux Arts before beginning his engineering career with B. L. M. Motor Car Company, then S. S. Pierce Aeroplane Company. While still a student in Paris, he had become fascinated by the three-cylinder, 60-hp Clerget air-cooled radial (Y-style) engine, and this fascination would alter aviation history. Convinced that a feasible air-cooled engine of much greater power could be built, Lawrence combined three Y-style engines together into a daisy-like nine-cylinder affair only 44 inches in diameter but capable of 200 hp. It was built by the De la Verne Machine Company under his guidance. Lawrence had no pretensions; he was of the "run 'em, bust 'em, fix 'em, run 'em again" school and his "coffee grinder" J-1 soon developed into a quite creditable powerplant — and at that time the only air-cooled radial aero engine available anywhere in the United States. Lawrence, who did so much for the air-cooled radial, was always self-deprecating, still remembered years

Steven Calloway in cockpit of Bee-Line racer before his takeoff in the 1922 Pulitzer race
(USAF)

Curtiss-built Navy TS-1 with Lawrence J-1 engine, 1922 (C)

Charles L. Lawrence (S)

later for the remark he made when the real importance of what he did was linked with contributions of more famous pioneers, "Who remembers the name of Paul Revere's horse?"

The Navy, meanwhile, spurred by Admiral W. A. Moffett and his Engine Section chief, boyish Bruce G. Leighton, were anxious to stimulate air-cooled-engine manufacture. Bulky engines which had to lug circulating water were poor contraptions on board ship where you "kept 'em small or left 'em off"; or, in the phrase coined by Moffett which had become the watchword of his Bureau of Aeronautics, he needed a new breed of aeroplanes which could ride "on the backs of the fleet." Moffett was also unimpressed with current statistics on engine failure, more than one third attributed to plumbing faults. As he saw it, liquid-cooled engines were being perpetuated not by technical merit but strictly by politics — none of the entrenched manufacturers were anxious to obsolete their designs. Thus the Lawrence J-1 soon became the Navy's pride and joy — and its hope and fear. Early naval aviators who flew behind the brave little pop-bottles often tended

to premature grayness; as a matter of course they soon learned to carry a "quiverful" of spare pushrods to replace those invariably sprayed along the route! The J-1 was also prone to piston scuffing, and salt spray did its accessories no good since all were mounted on the front!

Throughout July the TS fighters underwent their flight tests on pontoons at Anacostia, and two (A-6300, A-6301) were quickly dispatched that month to a new observation squadron (VO-1) formed to equip four-pipe destroyers with their own means of scouting. One of the next planes in line, A-6303, was reserved for the upcoming Curtiss Marine Trophy race. In fact, as the race, a little more than two months away, approached, four new TS fighters were earmarked for entry. This gave the Navy a rare opportunity to pit water-cooled engines against the new J-1. Thus two TS fighters were reequipped with water-cooled engines (an Aeromarine U-873 which had just passed the Navy 300-hour test and a Wright E-3); in addition, two were reequipped with thinner "racing" wings, leading to the designation TR. This meant that the stock TS would

TR-3 as it appeared in the 1922 Curtiss Marine Trophy race (Au)

297

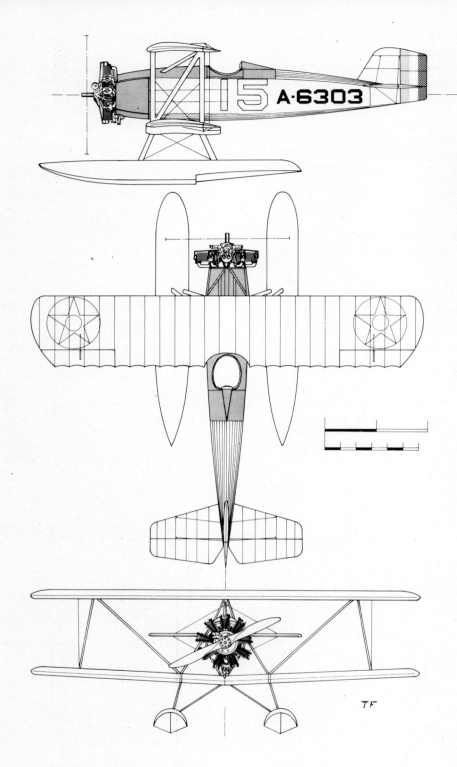

U. S. Navy TR-1 (modified TS), winner, 1922
Curtiss Marine Flying Trophy

*Jake Gorton with his Navy TR-1, victorious
in the 1922 Curtiss Marine Trophy race*

(NA)

race with both air- and water-cooled engines, likewise the TR conversions, resulting somewhat confusingly in designations TS-1, TR-1, TS-2, and TR-3, but all airframes were identical. Their pilots were Steve Calloway, Jake Gorton, Hap Brow, and Dave Rittenhouse respectively, a gallery destined for stardom.

The race itself was a wild and woolly affair, competed under low hanging cloud and in the teeth of a nasty wind. Starting from a barge in front of Detroit's Memorial Park facing Belle Isle, in view of 200,000 chattering but spellbound onlookers, the contestants had to complete eight 20-mile laps, landing and taxiing 400 yards on three laps including a hairpin turn around the starting barge. This was guaranteed to produce blood-tingling risks entirely absent from the Schneider competitions, in which seaworthiness trials took place at the contestant's leisure, entirely separate from the speed race. Indeed, the Curtiss Marine Trophy of

1922 was an aerial Keystone Kops, the wobbly planes chasing each other on and off the water in harrowing, wind-whipped close calls. Brow had to quit on the fourth lap minus all his radiator water, bearing out Moffett's contempt for water-cooled reliability. On the same lap Rittenhouse's prop worked loose, setting up a wild vibration, and he sideslipped in near the Edison "gas house," deleting most of one wing. Calloway's J-1 started to come apart under the strain and he was out. Only Gorton of the TS/TR pilots finished the race. Even though he had slid from first to fourth place in six laps he managed to win since all his serious competition dropped out. Sanderson, who should have won after a magnificent, aggressive race in the Curtiss triplane, ran out of gas on the last lap! Gorton's winning speed was not even 120 mph, which reflected the speed lost during the taxi requirements, but Moffett was ecstatic, saying, "The pilots who participated in the race told me more practicable suggestions for improvement of naval fighting aircraft than BuAer would have discovered in a year of lab experiments."

Even more significant, a J-1 had survived the race rigors to win and this added fuel to the fire Moffett was kindling under the air-cooled radial engine. The Old Man could proudly testify before Congress, "The only air-cooled engines of U.S. design or manufacture which by 1922 have been developed and successfully flown have been initiated by the Navy, developed under Navy control, with Navy funds, and first flown in Navy aircraft." In June 1923 Lawrence's small company was merged into Wright Aero at Paterson, New Jersey, to mass-produce air-cooled engines for the growing squadrons of stubby Navy carrier-based aeroplanes, and C. L. Lawrence became

a Wright Vice-President. Now the J-series would renew Wright's air-cooled development[2] and be further improved under remorseless chief engineer George J. Mead, solid, open-faced with bushy eyebrows, and his assistant Andy Wilgoos. These engines soon achieved world renown as the Wright Whirlwind; it was a J-5 model which in 1927 powered Charles A. Lindbergh's *Spirit of St. Louis*.

Still, it was a water-cooled engine which in 1923 was fitted to Rittenhouse's rebuilt TR racer (A-6447) to prepare it as the Navy's Schneider team alternate. Extensive modifications were

[2] Wright back in 1920 had won an Army design competition for a 300-hp air-cooled radial engine and built three experimental engines called R-1 — the first large air-cooled aviation engines built in the United States — but this project had long since been dropped.

TR-3A as it appeared for shipment to England for the 1923 Schneider Trophy race; note wing radiators.   (NA)

undertaken at the Naval Aircraft Factory. Its new engine was a "super-compressed" Wright E-4, a type which had done remarkably well in bench tests that year, neatly streamlined in a tight cowl and fitted with wing radiators which replaced the bulky box radiator of 1922. The upper wing was lowered to the fuselage; the completed racer was designated TR-3A and taken to Cowes. After the NW-2 crash race number 5 was painted on the TR-3A and team leader Spig Wead made ready to fly it. A backfire on start sheared its inertial engine starting mechanism and it did not race.

Float-equipped TS fighters in the fleet, meanwhile, were adorned with the diving bird insignia of Fighting One (VF-1), later famous as the Tophatters after their bird, too much like the Ghirardelli Chocolate logo, was dropped. In March 1925 they were assigned to eleven battleships on which, more often than not, they disgruntled salty bo'suns since the grease from their turret-mounted catapults spoiled laboriously holystoned teakwood decks. In 1926 less than twenty were still in the inventory, the VF-1 aeroplanes by then refitted with wheels and tailhooks, but by 1927, their duty finished, all had been retired.

Gallaudet

Edson Fessenden Gallaudet, a man of bold ingenuity, had devised a warp-wing lateral control several years before the Wright Brothers employed and received great credit for this method, but these early ambitious experiments were terminated by Yale, where Gallaudet was a physics instructor, because aviation activities did not then fit standards of university dignity. He left Yale, formed his own company in January 1908 at Norwich, Connecticut, and began an unceasing search for ever improved engine/propeller arrangements, bringing to bear an originality which certainly ranks him high in the company of speed seekers. On July 24, 1912, his

own active flying career was terminated by injuries received at Hempstead Plain, Long Island, in the crash of his pusher *Bullet* aeroplane which was credited with the then astonishing speed of 130 mph!

In 1914 he conceived the "Gallaudet Drive" (patent 1,262,660), a scheme which, by mounting the propeller *amidships*, would allow the "center of thrust and resistance [to be] coincident." It promised the added feature that, by eliminating the propeller's low-thrust/high-drag portion near the hub, only the most efficient propeller working area would be exposed. Moreover, his arrangement permitted a clean nose (in those days a distinct novelty) and superb pilot visibility. Gallaudet tackled the formidable mechanical challenge by mounting his prop blades on a large ring connected to a hollow hub which ran on ball-bearing races surrounding a fixed longitudinal steel drum that supported the aft fuselage and tail. He sold the Navy on his idea but incurred months of frustration and enormous financial loss getting his prototype aeroplane to work. Called 59A (the Navy's fifty-ninth aeroplane) and completed during the summer of 1916, it was overweight; test pilot incompetence resulted in frequent costly and time-consuming mishaps; and its two Duesenberg engines, coupled to the single propeller, gave headaches.

The propeller idea itself, however, always worked splendidly; in fact, it can be concluded that Gallaudet put so much attention into making the engine/prop coupling work that all else by comparison suffered from neglect. The final appearance of Gallaudet's brave design occurred during 1922, when Gallaudet had been reduced to manufacturing textile accessories and duralumin auto parts at East Greenwich, Rhode Island. Entered in the important 1922 Curtiss Marine Trophy race was the second of his two D-4s, each having been powered by a single Liberty engine. (The D-designs, which meant Gallaudet Drive aeroplane, were

Gallaudet D-4 in 1918; note novel propeller mounting details. The unmounted prop sits in foreground. (Au)

Gallaudet D-4; note clean nose and Liberty engine detail. (Au)

proposed through D-14 but only seven examples were built; none past the D-4 was completed.) The first D-4 had crashed on July 19, 1918, the result of control failure, killing pilot Lieutenant (j.g.) Arthur F. Souther. The second aeroplane, intended not as a racer but as a two-place seaplane coastal defense fighter, first flew October 1918 and was accepted by the Navy in April 1919.

Thus, by 1922, it was already an aging relic despite its still novel engine/prop arrangement. For the race its forward cockpit was faired over. Its unfortunate failure to finish the race, simply because after five laps the prop, in its vulnerable position, was broken by debris thrown up in the spray, put the *coup de grâce* to the efforts of Edson Gallaudet.

Dare

Offsetting an otherwise complete reversion to total military dominance from the all-civilian 1921 Pulitzer, the only civilian entry in the great 1922 Pulitzer air race was the Dare Variable Camber monoplane, designed and built in Detroit by Melvin E. Dare and a Mr. Carns. It was perhaps the first aeroplane to make use of an idea which

today is called direct lift control (DLC); that is, the pilot's fore-and-aft movement of the control stick, which normally changes the aeroplane's angle to the oncoming airstream (and thus can exert indirect influence on its height), would instead directly change the lift of the wing itself, causing the aeroplane to rise or descend with no change in fuselage attitude. In Dare's

Gallaudet D-4 entry in 1922 Curtiss Marine Trophy race; note propeller amidships. (Au)

aeroplane this was done by changing the wing camber through a system of flaps. In addition, side-to-side stick movement would change the camber asymmetrically to provide lateral control, but conventional control surfaces were also fitted as a safety precaution. As originally built the camber controls were in the rear cockpit, the standard controls in front! The aeroplane was metal-covered steel frame and was advanced in that it even used stressed skin over small areas, a feature which might have been influenced by Dare's mechanic Ed Jakobi, who had just left all-metal pioneer William Stout to work for Dare after the crash of the highly vaunted Stout torpedo bomber.

The Dare was first flown by a pilot named Mills at Selfridge Field in the spring of 1921, fitted with a 140-hp German four-cylinder Benz. Terribly underpowered, it staggered for 1 mile, barely clearing the field boundary, and came to grief in a pasture with washed-out landing gear. Gar Wood, a stockholder in Dare's company, rescued the

hapless experimenters by giving them the Liberty engine from his boat. It had accumulated 500 hours and badly needed an overhaul but this was overruled by Dare, who was more concerned with the dwindling nature of his finances. In the meantime Selfridge had been reactivated as the home of the 1st Pursuit Group. When the reengined plane was rolled out a couple of soldiers offered to swing the prop and in the time-honored procedure locked wrists and heaved, lunging flat on their faces in the mud — the engine had no compression! This plus the use of the original Benz fuel line limited the wheezing Liberty to only 1,000 rpm. Dare relented and the engine got new piston rings and fuel line. The nearby Packard company, after a test, assured Dare it produced 402 hp on the dynamometer, but this seems optimistic.

To enhance his status, Dare obtained well-known test pilot Eddie A. Stinson, Jr., twenty-eight, member of a celebrated aviation family raised in Missis-

Gallaudet D-4 during race with Detroit skyline close at hand, just prior to retiring with prop damage (USAF)

Dare variable camber aeroplane at Selfridge Field, Detroit, 1922. (John Underwood)

301

sippi and Arkansas which boasted his two heroine aviatrix sisters, Katherine (Kate) Stinson, three years older, who began flying in 1913, and Marjorie (Madge) Stinson, one year younger, for whom he had been mechanic during their pre-war exhibition flying days. The girls had refused to teach Eddie to fly, for even at twenty-one he was known as irresponsible and a freewheeling drinker. The Stinsons relocated to San Antonio in 1915, and when Eddie did learn to fly he earned accolades as a "natural born" aviator. He was named by the nation's 1st Aero Squadron CO, Captain Ben Foulois, as a civil instructor for Army pilots in 1916, and was variously credited with having discovered in 1917 the secret of tailspin recovery (or, in those days, the "corkscrew twist," a mysterious dive to be avoided at all costs.) The popular story had it that Stinson entered the spin inadvertently, and at the last moment shoved the stick forward to hasten the inevitable — and recovered! But the truth is that he probably knew just what he was doing from having listened to accounts of earlier spin experiences of others. He was the first pilot in the United States to teach spin recovery to others. He also held the looping record (157 in 1917) and he could never resist looping any aeroplane he flew. He once did a series of power-off aileron rolls to a

Eddie Stinson on left, with Lloyd Bertaud; photographed December 30, 1921, upon completion of their world's duration record of 26:19:35, set at Roosevelt Field, New York, in a Junkers-Larsen J.L.6 (MA)

landing with a Jenny, crossing the fence inverted, rolling out so low his wings brushed the grass. With uncanny accuracy he could break a row of light bulbs in the grass with his wingtip at 70 mph; more than once he won $100 bets by breaking a bulb atop a pole, a more demanding variant on the theme. The Stinson siblings were one quarter Cherokee and prey to lung diseases, but despite his constant cough, Eddie, with a measure of Indian stoicism, chain-smoked constantly. Kate waged a six year battle with TB which forced her to give up flying forever in 1918.

After the war Eddie barnstormed continuously. In May, 1919, he flew cameramen at the Second Pan American aviation meet, Atlantic City. He was employed briefly during 1921 as test pilot for the Aero Import Company of New York, the American agency for Ansaldo aircraft (see Chapter 27); later in 1921 he did some testing of Junkers all-metal monoplanes, imported by promoter John Larsen and called J.L.6 to convey the impression they were of American manufacture in deference to strong anti-German feeling still lingering from the war. On December 29, 1921, in a J.L.6 Stinson and Lloyd Bertaud took off in a blinding snowstorm and, remaining no higher than one hundred feet, droned through the night. When the oil began to congeal in the bitter cold, Stinson had to hand feed it to the engine, getting three frost-bitten fingers in the process. Their only sustenance during the 26:19:35 world endurance record flight had been coffee fortified copiously with whiskey.

Eddie Stinson flew the Dare aeroplane once with Jakobi in the back seat to work the camber, but this form of control was too cumbersome for Stinson. After the camber controls were relocated to the pilot's cockpit Stinson made several flights. The lateral control remained poor; witnesses recalled Stinson skidding around the field in flat turns. He called the Dare "the penguin" because "it wasn't much of a flier." Optimistically entered in the

Pulitzer race, it was disqualified when Dare was unable to provide the contest officials with its specifications. No doubt Stinson would have refused to race it in a pylon event anyway. All efforts to sell stock failed and Dare's bold venture ended in bankruptcy.

Eddie Stinson became involved almost simultaneously in flight testing William Stout's huge ST-1 all-metal twin-engine torpedo bomber, a truly remarkable aeroplane hardly remembered today. Stinson flew it eleven times, but on its thirteenth flight Stout's $165,000 gamble cracked up, a total loss after a Marine pilot misjudged his landing. Stinson remained in Detroit. In 1925 he began his own aircraft manufacturing company in an old warehouse at 439 West Congress Street where he built a cabin plane called the Stinson Detroiter, hailed for its inherent stability, unprecedented comfort, self-starter, and daring wheel brakes. It soon figured prominently in the Ford Reliability tours, long distance competitions based on the Charles Glidden formula used years before to popularize the automobile. (Two of Stinson's backers had been associated with Glidden.) A series of long-distance Stinsons followed, earning renown in the plethora of trans-oceanic efforts that followed in Lindbergh's wake. In late 1931, as the Depression deepened, Stinson came out with his model R, a stubby design influenced by Bob Ayer who had helped design the Gee-Bee "flying silo" racers of the early 1930s, and Eddie, by then the "Dean of American airmen" with some 15,000 hours, had to take the new model R on a desperately needed sales demonstration tour. On the morning of January 25, 1932, he left Detroit. That evening, in Chicago, on the last of the day's many demonstration flights, he ran out of gas and crashed in Jackson Park. Eddie Stinson died the next morning, aged thirty seven. Jimmy Doolittle paid tribute in a farewell flight over the funeral. Stinson's firm was eventually absorbed in 1940 by Vultee, later Convair (General Dynamics); it lasted as a corporate entity, producing a series of light planes, until 1949.

Great Britain

EARLY BRITISH SPORTING EFFORTS

21

The Bantams

The first organized aeroplane race in England in more than five years occurred shortly after May 1, 1919, when civil flying resumed; it took place on Whitsun weekend, and naturally such a heroic effort to restore sporting aviation could only be accomplished by the Grahame-White Company at Hendon. Darkly handsome, cigarette-smoking and dashing, wealthy and supremely confident, fond of escorting his showpiece wife Ethel Levey, former wife of George M. Cohan, Claude Grahame-White was holder of RAeC aviator certificate number 6, still youthful in 1919 at age forty, and had literally fathered air racing in Great Britain. Born in Bursledon, Hants, a second son, he worked with his uncle in a

Yorkshire woolen factory, acquiring an early interest in the application of technology; he made the profound change from horses to motor lorries at the factory. He was briefly steward of a 10,000-acre Sussex estate, then gravitated to South Africa and almost into a stage career when on the voyage an agent tried to sign him up after hearing him sing French chansons in a sweet, pure voice. Returning to England, Grahame-White became a Renault auto salesman in London, took up ballooning as an interesting diversion, and went to Rheims for the 1909 flying meet. There, after meeting the most famous men in aviation face to face, his imagination was fired and he purchased a Blériot monoplane on the spot; in fact, this plane caught fire

total darkness of night, with no instruments of course, scarcely five months after learning how to fly – and on the occasion presented aviation with a classic one-liner: "There's hardly a difference between day and night time flying," he said, "only at night you can't see." His stature was firmly established when he won the 1910 Gordon Bennett at Belmont Park, Long Island, and upon returning to England he acquired Hendon, a tract of 350 acres, and established weekly aeroplane pylon races. Grahame-White won thousands in prizes during these years, and received tidy fees as well from the scores of famous English aviation pioneers who learned to fly at his school. He started the Aerial Derby in 1912, won that year by a youngster named Tommy Sopwith; his displays were attended by royalty; and during 1913 he held no fewer than fifty-one air races! During World War I he put Hendon at government disposal and was appointed a flight commander in the RNAS. On February 12, 1915, while participating in the first raid to bomb German bases on the Belgian coast his engine conked out in a snowstorm, forcing him to ditch in the sea 4 miles off Nieuport. His luck held and he was rescued, half frozen, by a French mine sweeper. Before the war was out he returned to Hendon to supervise the output of his own factory – having started with twenty in the halcyon days, by August 1915 he employed more than a thousand – but Grahame-White, used to the view from his prewar pinnacle as the number-one personality in British aviation, already had become a source of irritation in high places by stubbornly refusing to bend to the often inexpedient dictates of officialdom.

His chief designer was H. J. Hedderwick in 1917, the year the Grahame-White Bantam idea had its origins, although the design has been variously credited to an obscure designer named Boudot. "Bantam" was a name then fairly commonly applied to any small, speedy aeroplane. Grahame-White's were powered by the 80 hp LeRhône rotary, cowled neatly in an aluminum ring and looking very sporty. Captain P. R. T. Chamberlayne's in the 1919 Victory Derby had a bright yellow

Seen with his wife is Claude Grahame-White (cracking his knuckles); the man on the right is Harry Hawker; circa 1913. (F)

Grahame-White Bantam at the 1919 Aerial Derby (F)

during the first Gordon Bennett aeroplane race, almost costing Louis Blériot his life. Blériot built a replacement and Grahame-White got his pilot's certificate at Issy-les-Moulineaux in December 1909, becoming one of the first ten men to remain aloft longer than one hour in an aeroplane.

Grahame-White competed for Northcliffe's £10,000 *Daily Mail* London–Manchester race prize in 1910; indeed, Grahame-White made two gallant attempts and although he finished second to Paulhan he gained wide fame. During the flight he also became the first aviator to fly in the

F. K. "Kully" Koolhoven; man in helmet is Charles Nungesser. (F)

unrepentant critic of officialdom, even after being spurned by the Air Ministry. He had been forced to sell Hendon to the government in 1916 after a bitter and acrimonious fight, regaining part of it for a short period after the war; he finally sold it all at the end of 1925 for a reported $2·5 million. He later became a real estate dealer and lived in California. Grahame-White died in Nice on his eightieth birthday in 1959.

The other early racing Bantams were the products of the British Aerial Transport Company, Ltd., BAT for short, a firm founded by Sir Samuel Waring in 1917 together with Major J. C. "Jack" Savage, later of skywriting fame, when they took over as an experimental works the Joucques Aviation Company of Willesden. Their chief engineer was Fritz "Kully" Koolhoven, the huge Dutch designer who stood 6 feet 6 inches tall and weighed some 230 pounds, a domineering man with a mind as large as his body. He had learned to fly on Farmans in 1910,

joined Louis Bêchéreau to collaborate on the design of the immortal Deperdussin, then went to England before 1912 to serve as works manager of the British Deperdussin Company under D. Lorenzo Santoni. Kully came in for a lot of kidding from his new colleagues, who delighted in reminding him he was popularly known as Fritz before he became a naturalized Englishman and began calling himself Frederick. His wife was a pretty Belgian only half his height. Following the arrest of Armand Deperdussin and the acquisition of his interests by Blériot, Koolhoven joined Sir W. G. Armstrong-Whitworth & Company, Ltd., as works manager in an old skating rink at Newcastle, responsible for B.E.2 production. His first design, the F.K.1 built August 1914, was similar to a plane designed by John North for the Grahame-White Company as their entry in the Circuit-of-Britain race, although Koolhoven's employed floating elevators, an inverted balanced rudder, and other novelties. The F.K.3, "Little Ack," was

BAT Bantam; note the aeroplane's nose which represented a Koolhoven scheme to streamline the radial engine; also note the hole in the upper wing — the only means for entrance and egress for the pilot. (F)

fuselage with blue wings. Major Reggie Carr flew a similar aeroplane, but neither pilot finished the course. A few days later on July 5, the prewar Hendon pylon course was used for the first time in five years at an air meet to celebrate the Versailles Peace Treaty. Chamberlayne won the six-lap race in Bantam K-150, Carr in K-153 in his wake. By 1920 the small, underpowered Grahame-White Bantams were obsolete for racing, although their clean lines certainly provided inspiration for many speedplanes to follow. Grahame-White himself remained a sharp and particularly

Koolhoven's redesigned B.E.2c, and the F.K.10 was a heavily staggered quadriplane (four wings), doing the then popular triplane one better! Despite such revealed imagination Koolhoven was racked by doubts about his designs; he would often make enormous design changes on the slightest whim and it became increasingly difficult to persuade him into the air, especially in his own planes!

Koolhoven was coaxed away from Armstrong-Whitworth in 1917 by the lure of the top technical job at the new BAT firm, where his able assistant was a youngster and fellow Dutchman named R. B. C. "Bob" Noorduijn (later famous in North America as Noorduyn). Koolhoven immediately began work on his BAT Bantam, designated F.K.23, designed in 1917 as a single-seat fighter adaptable for immediate mass production by the major Allied powers. It was a diminutive two-bay biplane powered by an ABC 170 hp Wasp seven-cylinder air-cooled radial. To guarantee good landings Koolhoven provided it with an exceptionally wide-track landing gear, the legs extensions of the rugged inner bay wing struts, the wheels sprung with generous amounts of rubber cord. It had fine performance, the best of its contemporaries – indeed, Chris Draper

called it "the most perfect single-seat aeroplane for stunting I flew" – but it was never adopted by the Air Board.

Large sheets of three-ply birch fixed to oval-section formers supported by four ash longitudinals comprised the monocoque fuselage, which contained only four metal fittings. Koolhoven claimed an "ordinary joiner" could build it directly with no special instructions. The front end was capped by a duralumin plate to which the engine was bolted, and reflecting a Koolhoven theory on high speed, the fuselage filled the entire gap between the wings; indeed, the pilot's head protruded Kilroy-fashion above the top wing between the center-section spars. The tailplane was of wood construction, the fin three-ply and integral with the fuselage shell, the movable surfaces fabric-covered steel frames mounted and sealed so that no gap existed at the hinge lines. No cast or machined parts were used; simplicity was the keynote. As originally conceived the Bantam would carry two Vickers guns mounted internally on either side of the pilot, firing through the prop, and a thousand rounds of ammunition, but such equipment had been discarded by Aerial Derby time.

Seven of the nine Bantams produced were registered for sporting purposes

BAT Bantam flown by Christopher Draper in the 1919 Aerial Derby; called "Skinned Bat" because of its severely clipped lower wing (F)

Flying at Hendon, 1919; BAT Bantam in foreground   (Au)

between 1919 and 1921; no Certificate of Airworthiness was issued since this was not obligatory for single-seaters then. Koolhoven was also responsible for two other BAT 1919 Aerial Derby entries. Construction of one F.K.27, a two-seat side-by-side sporting biplane based on the Bantam, was undertaken but it had to be withdrawn when it remained unfinished by Derby time. Its 200-hp Wasp II eventually made it capable of 142 mph. The five-seater F.K.26 which made its first flight at Hendon in April 1919 was the first British aircraft conceived and built as a transport. The cockpit was located well astern in accordance with Koolhoven's intent to ensure pilot survival on the theory that he would be the only occupant able to give an intelligent account of any accident! Four were eventually built; the first, intended for the race, had to be withdrawn when it was damaged on the Saturday morning prior to race day, depriving pilot C. Turner of his chance to fly in the Derby. Later, on a six-week visit to Holland, Koolhoven's countryman Tony Fokker had a good look at these

BAT aeroplanes and was deeply impressed. One F.K.26 still existed in Holland in 1937! Previously, on Saturday, June 7, 1919, Turner had raced a BAT Bantam numbered 5 in a 100-mile handicap between Hendon and Bittacy Hill but did not finish in the money, although the next day with the same plane he won a 40-mile handicap for the Pratt Trophy, a racing prize put up by the Anglo-American Oil Company, purveyors of widely used Pratt Motor Spirit.

Koolhoven took on a "demobbed" wartime pilot, Christopher Draper, twenty-seven, as BAT chief test pilot after Peter Legh was killed on May 3, 1919, when Legh's BAT Basilisk caught fire and crashed in the Holy Trinity vicarage garden, East Finchley. Draper as a youngster had weathered stiff setbacks during the decline of his once well-to-do family in Bebington, Cheshire. He was taught to fly by Marcus Manton, an early Grahame-White instructor, received RAeC ticket number 646 on October 6, 1913, and went on to serve in the RNAS during the war. He tried to sell used cars on

The Skinned Bat rounding the Hendon pylon, 1919 Aerial Derby (F)

Clifford Street a few doors down from the Royal Aero Club after the big show packed up, but was possessed of rather cavalier tendencies which did not presage an easy peacetime passage for him. "Give me my moments, you can have your years," was the free-wheeling credo of his life. Of three BAT Bantams entered in the 1919 Derby two participated, Draper flying the first, which sported a specially clipped lower wing and was called the "Skinned Bat." He finished second in the handicap at just under 120 mph.

The other, white with red trim and a long lower wing, was flown by Clifford B. Prodger, the only American in the race. Transplanted from Alexandria, Minnesota, Prodger had come to England in 1915 to help train pilots and remained as Handley Page test pilot, later becoming a free-lance test pilot, forming the Prodger-Isaacs Syndicate with Bernard Isaacs, prewar Hendon manager for Grahame-White. Mentioned as a hopeful in the epic 1919 transatlantic race won by Alcock

and Brown, Prodger was thoroughly Anglicized to the extent that his English colleagues were "tempted to forget he's American." Engine trouble forced him out of the Derby. He was killed in August 1920 while testing Bristol aeroplanes in the United States.

Bravely Draper promoted the BAT aeroplanes with great intensity. The first great postwar international aviation exhibition was convened by the Dutch at Amsterdam in August 1919, and the British, miffed at being preempted, were cool toward supporting hopeful exhibitors; nevertheless, Koolhoven took his F.K.26 transport and a sporting Bantam, eager to promote both in his homeland. Tony Fokker was present, digging into his pockets for chocolates which he munched incessantly as usual, and admired the Bantam, but a British witness darkly remarked, "The future of the BAT Company lies in international commercial aeronautics, for the British Technical Department will never forgive Fritz Koolhoven for being a

genius while the best men which the Department could produce were merely journeyman designers — so the firm need never expect government orders."

On March 23, 1920, Draper almost got his. Flying with a bad case of flu, he fainted at 3,000 feet and fell into a vicious tailspin; Frank Courtney said it was the first "flat spin" he'd ever seen and there and then resolved to avoid the maneuver! The Bantam was crushed and Draper lay in a coma for a week. But he lived to collect his £400 insurance money with a light heart and by 1921 had entered another Bantam for that year's Derby. The plan to race fell through. It had been more than a year since any new BAT planes were built, a slump which forced Waring to sell the few remaining to C. P. B. Ogilvie of Willesden and close down BAT. Kully Koolhoven had long since returned to Holland, where he began producing planes that first appeared there in 1924, later teaming with Marcel Desoutter in 1929; by 1935 he was credited with having designed more than fifty types. Koolhoven died July 1, 1946.

After the demise of BAT, Chris Draper began a dozen years "on the boards," earning vaudeville fame in a year-long revue at the Hippodrome, but in 1931 he briefly returned to aviation to pull off a wild publicity stunt by flying a light plane down the Thames, *underneath* London's low-slung bridges! After that he was always known as "the Mad Major." The saucy little BAT Bantams, which like their Grahame-White namesakes had helped provide the means for the earliest post-war English air racing, remained but dim memories.

Avro

Alliott Verdon Roe, fondly known as "A.V.," was son of a frock-coated Manchester general practitioner who launched him at age six in 1883 on a "penny-farthing" cycle, beginning a lifelong love for a sport in which he won several racing prizes. Feckless and footloose and bitten by the wanderlust

Alliott Verdon "A.V." Roe, circa 1913 (F)

at the age of fifteen, the youngster had gone to British Columbia ostensibly to learn surveying, but found himself planting fruit trees and painting church roofs instead. He soon returned to England, hired by a locomotive works, but that was not satisfactory for very long so he entered King's College, next planning to join the Navy as an engineer. Somehow that did not sit right either, and after listlessly flunking the irrelevant (i.e., non-engineering) subjects he embarked on a world tour which stretched two years and during which, gazing at the sea birds, his interest in flying was aroused. Like the meanderings of his trip, his life had no direction until, at the age of twenty-nine, he gained recognition at a model aeroplane contest. Single-handedly and with growing frustration he began trying unsuccessfully to shake the stolid British indifference to the new reality of flight. At the coach house of his brother S. Verdon Roe in Putney he built a man-carrying version of his model, but pioneers were not wanted and he was kicked out of Brooklands, undiscouraged by strong press disapproval. Official agencies were obdurate in withholding permission to use areas such as Laffan's Plain, and commons were forbidden, but Roe finally found a humble cave under the railway arches in Lea Marshes and there continued on his quest of flight, facing as difficult a proposition as ever human ingenuity and perseverance conquered. His first Avro triplane was called "The Yellow Peril" for the color of her cotton-oiled packing-paper wings; with it he earned his Royal Aero Club pilot certificate (number 18) in 1910, the year that with his brother Humphrey Verdon Roe he launched the firm Avro at Bromsfield Mills (later at Newton Heath), Manchester. Thereafter, success smiled on A.V. Ronald Kemp and Fred Raynham in 1911 made several good flights in Avros, and in 1913 there appeared the Avro 504, which became one of the half-dozen great — and longest-lived — trainers of all time, carrying the name Avro to the ends of the earth.

During World War I Avro's fortune increased and an active experimental works was built at Hamble, near Southampton. There, in August 1919, the model 539 racer was completed, built expressly for that year's Schneider Trophy race, and called "Puma" after its engine, or "Avro Schneider Cup." Since it was the first — and only — plane with this model number, its correct Avro designation was 539/1. Unlike the long, graceful 504 which had by then come to characterize the expected Avro pattern, the 539 was short and stumpy. Conventional in construction (wire-braced wood

girder, fabric-covered), the 539 mounted twin wooden pontoons, each with two small steps well aft. The racer — like the 504 — was designed by Roy Chadwick, just twenty-six in 1919, a highly artistic, neat, and skillful draftsman whose designs were more the result of intuition than science. Chadwick became Avro chief draftsman during World War I, was later elevated to chief designer, and was still hard at work decades later when he designed the Avro Anson and four-engine Lancaster heavy bomber, both of which served in World War II. In 1948 Chadwick, as enthusiastic and energetic as ever, was tragically killed in the crash of an Avro Tudor because of crossed control wires.

The Puma engine Chadwick selected for his Schneider racer in 1919 was certainly not much of a racing engine and is noteworthy only because it was part of the aluminum monobloc revolution. In 1915 a young RFC officer named Frank B. Halford enlarged the 120-hp Beardmore-Austro-Daimler six-cylinder engine into the larger 160-hp Beardmore; that autumn he went to France as an engine expert to witness tests of the new Hispano-Suiza. Like many other engineers his imagination was ignited by the completely novel aluminum monobloc idea, and he returned to England to plead for an even larger six-cylinder Beardmore built along the ingenious Hispano lines. Beardmore management backed him and the new engine — made at Arrol-Johnston Ltd. of Dumfries and known as the BHP (for Beardmore-Halford-Pullinger) prototype — was ready in June 1916, capable of 200 hp, and tested on the prototype D.H.4. The large aluminum castings, so susceptible to cracking and warping, baited for Beardmore a then common manufacturing mousetrap from which the Ministry of Munitions asked Siddeley-Deasy Motor Car Company of Coventry to extricate them — indeed, two thousand were ordered — but Siddeley did not have much better luck with the BHP. Nevertheless, from March 1917

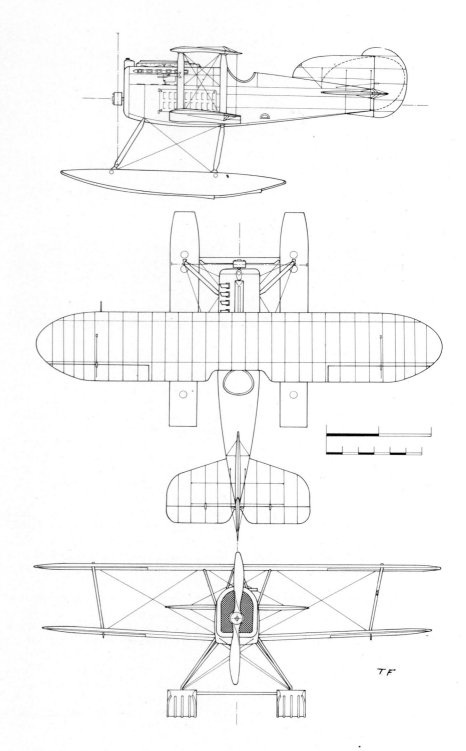

Avro 539/1 Schneider, 1919 Schneider Trophy race entry; original small round tail denoted by dotted line

310

wound up to 1,700 rpm with luck, giving 290 hp in short bursts; it had the odd three-valve cylinder arrangement (two small intake, one large exhaust). Used to power wartime D.H.9s mostly, it never came up to expectations, engine trouble on D.H.9s becoming the rule. Presumably its use by Avro on a racer was simply due to expedience, since hundreds of idle Pumas lay about after the war.

First flight of the Puma-powered 539, registered G-EALG, was made August 29, 1919, by Captain H. A. Hamersley, who on a test five days later hit floating debris which damaged a pontoon. Apparently the racer also had directional instability, because when it emerged after being repaired it sported entirely new vertical tail surfaces: its original, graceful round tail had been replaced by an elongated fin and balanced rudder. The Avro racer was the fourth British contender built for the Schneider contest, in which only three by the rules could compete, and it was soon apparent that it must better the Supermarine Sea Lion for the

Sir John Siddeley on left with Supermarine's Hubert Scott-Paine, circa 1923 (F)

until the Armistice Siddeley delivered 625 slightly improved versions of the engine, now called Puma. John D. Siddeley personally had seen to it that the BHP's cast-iron cylinder heads were replaced by aluminum heads into which the steel cylinder liners were screwed on short threads instead of being threaded over their entire length as was Hispano practice, and that aluminum water jackets replaced the original BHP sheet-steel jackets. Moreover, Siddeley for the first time used cylinder liners open at the top, also unlike the Hispano; interestingly, this form of construction was later used most effectively in the Wright T-2 and Curtiss V-1400 engines and ultimately in the Rolls-Royce racing engine line developed by Arthur Rowledge after 1925 which powered the final Supermarine Schneider racers. The Puma was an 18·8-liter engine rated at 240 hp but which could be

Avro 539/1 afloat in the Solent awaiting the 1919 Schneider Trophy race (Au)

team's third spot. Although the Lion produced almost twice the Puma's power, performance differences between the two aeroplanes were hardly

Avro 539/1 during modifications for the 1919 Schneider Trophy race; note enlarged vertical tail. (F)

noticeable. For the elimination contest on September 8, involving a flight from Cowes to Bournemouth Pier and return, with landings and takeoffs, the Sea Lion had been fitted with an improved propeller and just managed to edge out the Avro, relegating it to team reserve. It hardly mattered because the race was ruined by fog, but the 539 appeared at Southampton to make a pretty demonstration flight at the race meeting.

Hamersley had won the Aerial Derby sealed handicap first prize of £100 and a nice Shell Oil Company trophy earlier in 1919, flying another Chadwick-designed Avro, the model 543 Baby, a diminutive biplane powered by a vertical four-cylinder in-line, water-cooled Green engine developing only 35 hp! Designed after the Armistice for sport and touring, a total of eight Babies was built at Hamble and at least one, often more, flew in every postwar Aerial Derby held.

The Avro Baby's most famous pilot was Herbert John Louis Hinkler, a Queenslander from the great sheep district of Bundaberg where he was born in 1892. Hinkler, who did his

Avro Baby in the 1919 Aerial Derby   (F)

Hinkler's Avro Baby The Old Hen   (F)

H. J. L. "Bert" Hinkler   (F)

best to forget his Christian names and was always called "Bert," began his aviation career as a wartime mechanic on the Tyne, advancing to gunlayer petty officer with No. 3 Naval Wing, RFC, at Luxeuil; he soon learned to fly and served in France and Italy before casting his postwar lot with Avro, where he developed a life-long love for light planes. On May 31, 1920, with typical Australian contempt for danger, he departed Croydon on an incredibly ambitious air voyage between England and Australia using his recently purchased Baby (G-EACQ), the 1919 Aerial Derby participant which indeed was equipped with the original Green engine that had powered the Avro triplane in 1910! On his first leg Hinkler flew the flimsy Baby from London straight across the Alps to Turin *non-stop*, taking nine and a half hours but using only 20 gallons of fuel for the 650 miles! This feat earned Hinkler the coveted Britannia Trophy, presented to the RAeC by Horatio Barber and given for the "most meritorious performance in the air during the preceding year." However, to Hinkler's disappointment, the continuing flight to Australia was thwarted by refusal to overfly Meso-

potamia (later Iraq), and he landed back in England on June 9. He won the 1920 Aerial Derby handicap the very next month, his venerable Green engine humming merrily. Hamersley placed second in that year's handicap in another Baby.

Later that year Hinkler went to Australia (by boat), taking his Baby. With the same ancient engine he flew it, on April 11, 1921, 800 miles non-stop from Sydney to Bundaberg in under nine hours. On the twenty-eighth he tried to fly it from Brisbane back to Sydney to appear at a banquet in his honor at the Hotel Australia which he had twice postponed and about which he felt guilty. Taking off in heavy rain he pushed southward, several times sure he was "out for six." When 70 miles north of Sydney the rain came down in full fury, "absolutely walloping down," in Hinkler's words. Unable to proceed, he landed safely on the beach to wait, but shortly a gust flipped the "poor old Baby" onto her back. Despite forbidding scrub brush stretching desolately inland Hinkler trudged bedraggled several miles until he stumbled upon a lone house, refuge from the storm. The Baby was later saved by a team of men

and horses. A few weeks later Hinkler sailed for England, arriving in June, in time for the 1921 Aerial Derby. The Baby was brought back with him and re-registered G-EAUM, to be flown in the three remaining Aerial Derbies. In 1923, still being raced by Hinkler, it was fondly called "the old hen," and was apparently still flying actively thirteen years after that!

A single-seat "racing Baby" (G-EAXL) with wings clipped by 5 feet was flown by Hinkler in the 1921 Aerial Derby but he was unable to finish, force-landing at Sidcup. In early September 1922, just after his takeoff in this aeroplane from the Avro airport at Hamble, magneto trouble caused the engine to quit suddenly. Hinkler began a sharp turn back toward the beach but being too low he crashed in Southampton Water on the turn. He received some nasty cuts about the face and a cold dunking, and the racing Baby was a total write-off.

Hinkler's restless urge to accomplish ever greater feats was paradoxically counterbalanced by retreat from any public adulation. Hinkler had no conceit; indeed, being physically small, he required constant reassurance from friends as to his personal qualities. Typical Australian wit salted his banter and his grin "could light a room." He won the 1924 Grosvenor Cup and participated in numerous light-plane races but was unlucky more often than not. His next major racing effort was as participant in England's 1925 Schneider Trophy effort. He also flew acceptance tests on the Short Crusader seaplane racer in 1927. That year he also flew a light plane, the Avro Avian, from London to Riga and won a Latvian medal, which greatly pleased him, and the next year he flew the Avian 11,000 miles all the way to Port Darwin, Australia, in sixteen days, fulfilling a cherished ambition and winning his second Britannia Trophy. He was made a squadron leader in the RAAF but never bought the uniform. Instead his ambitions now expanded across oceans. In 1931, between October 20 and December 7, Hinkler flew his D.H.80A Puss Moth *Karohi* (CF-APK) with a single Gipsy III 120-hp engine from Toronto all the way to Hamble, the route taking him in stages that included a flight from North Beach Airport (later La Guardia) in New York non-stop to Jamaica, then to Brazil, non-stop across the South Atlantic to Gambia, and northward to England; this earned him the 1931 Britannia Trophy, his third. In 1933, using the same Puss Moth, he attempted to set up a new record for the flight to Australia, then eight days twenty hours, held by Charles W. A. Scott, who later won the great 1934 Mac-Robertson England–Australia air race. Hinkler departed Feltham in Middlesex at 3:10 A.M. on January 7 for his first leg to Rome, but never arrived. Nine feet of snow fell in some regions along his route during the next three weeks; Captain W. L. Hope (twice King's Cup winner), searching for his colleague in the Bernese Oberland, was forced down by carburetor ice in treacherous weather and surmised the same fate might have befallen the gritty little Australian. Finally, on April 28, 1933, after nearly four months, Hinkler's mutilated remains were discovered 300 yards from his wrecked plane on a mountain slope in the Apennines near Florence. The Italians accorded him full honors. He was later buried in Australia.

The Avro Schneider, meanwhile,

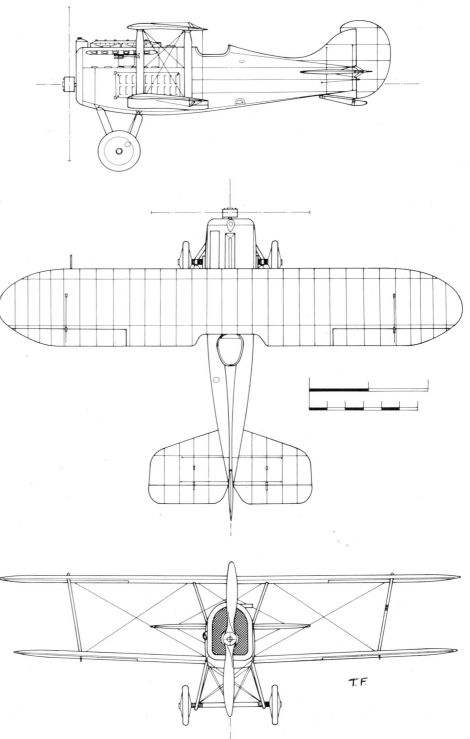

Avro 539A/1, 1920 Aerial Derby entry

Avro 539A/1 as flown in the 1920 Aerial Derby (F)

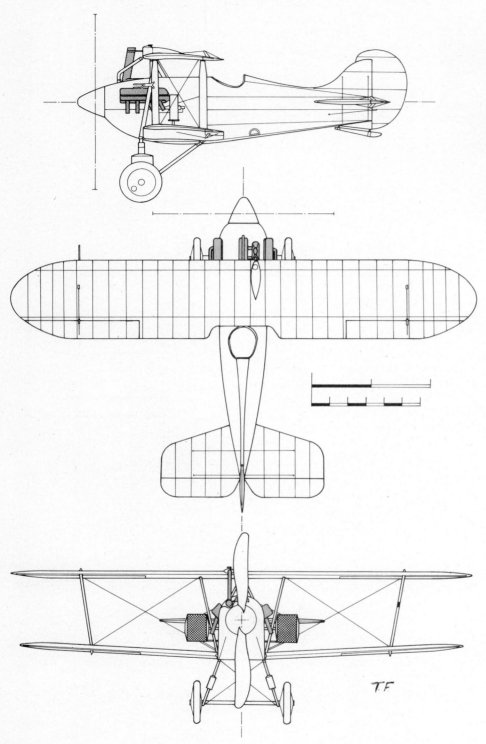

Avro 539B/1 Lion, 1921 Aerial Derby entry

Avro 539B/1 Lion as modified for the 1921 Aerial Derby; note side-mounted radiators. (F)

had been converted into a landplane for entry in the 1920 Aerial Derby, making it the 539A/1. The only noticeable changes were the rear turtledecking which now incorporated a headrest and a revised fin. Its original Puma engine was retained, totally cowled in, even its exhaust pipes enclosed in an aluminum streamline fairing on the port side. Its pilot was Captain Denis G. Westgarth-Heslam, who landed at Abridge near Epping when a fuel line broke, spraying him with gasoline.

In 1921 the aeroplane appeared as the 539B/1, re-registered G-EAXM and renamed "Lion" for her new engine, a Napier Lion which doubled the power of the discarded Puma. Its thrust line was markedly higher than the Puma's had been, the side banks exhausting downward while the center bank exhausted up and over the top wing. Unfortunate boxlike radiators, braced to the fuselage sides, spoiled her otherwise clean if slightly potbellied lines. Other changes included an improved landing gear with a telescopic front leg of large travel, and the whole of the rear fuselage, now semi-monocoque and entirely plywood-covered. The plane was to be flown once again by Westgarth-Heslam, now a major, who had had an unlucky

crash at Ipswich the previous autumn. Indeed, he had not yet fully recovered and ought not to have been allowed to fly for another three months, but with characteristic if unwise British aplomb he mounted the souped-up Lion for flight tests, eager to see if her performance was superior – as he suspected – to the new Bamel. Its hot landing speed was certainly a surprise to him. He overshot his first try badly, and at full tilt burrowed into an abandoned railway cutting bordering the field, part of a suspended RAF assembly park left over from the war. Heslam rebroke his previously broken leg and was otherwise severely "knocked about." The Avro Lion was totally demolished.

Of the four Avros entered in the 1921 Aerial Derby, only one, an unpretentious 504 reengined with a Wolseley Viper, a British-built 180-hp Hispano-Suiza, and flown by Leslie Tait-Cox, finished the race, undistinguished in fifth place. After the Lion's demise Avro's subsequent interest in pure speed seeking tapered off although Babies and 504s continued to participate actively in the typically English handicap events. A. V. Roe, the man who always spoke with such infectious quickness, later tried the auto business (Crossley bodies) during the

314

mid-twenties, and in 1928 sold his shares in Avro to John Siddeley (later Lord Kenilworth). He then purchased an interest in the business of Sammy Saunders at Cowes to form Saunders-Roe, Ltd., and there pursued his interest in large flying boats. In later years he embarked on curious, unproductive projects, becoming regarded by acquaintances as "intractable," somewhat of a "crank," sympathetic to the Germans when that was becoming unpopular, but he remained inventive until his death in 1958.

The Martinsyde Semiquaver

Among the most beautiful vintage aeroplanes raced by the speed seekers were those built at Maybury Hill, Woking, Surrey, by a firm whose name was the contraction of the names of its two founders, Helmuth Paul Martin and George Harris Handasyde; C. G. Grey wrote in 1911 an article about a recent "Martinsyde (full name takes up too much space)." The name was registered officially in 1915.

Martin, who was educated at London's Central Technical College and became a talented mechanical engineer, was only seventeen in 1900 when he built an engine and mounted it on the handle bars of his pedal-bike, with a belt drive to the front wheel, and toured Germany on the contraption! He worked in a Glasgow locomotive works and spent three years in Uruguay before forming in England the firm Trier & Martin to produce carburetors. Martin was always inquisitive, scientifically minded. Handasyde, six years older, was on the other hand possessed of a strong Celtic disdain for Saxon dogmatism. As a boy he flew kites by the hour in Queen's Park, Edinburgh, where he was trained, becoming a marine engineer with Ramage & Ferguson before coming to London as an auto mechanic. Handasyde has received mountains of praise for his tough, expedient approach to mechanics; for brilliance with his hands and cleverness with

George Handasyde, circa 1920 (F)

details of finish; for his great gift of natural empiricism, his instinctive *feel* for the rightness of his designs, which needed little substantiation by mathematical analysis. He chanced to take a new carburetor to Trier & Martin one day, and struck an instant rapport with young Martin. In 1908 the pair built their first aeroplane in the ballroom of the Old Welsh Harp, a pub only 1 mile from a choice clearing which later became Hendon Aerodrome. Handasyde believed fiercely in the superior efficiency of the monoplane, hence it was no surprise that his first design was similar to the French Antoinette. Martin-Handasyde were the first to settle at Brooklands, and while there prior to World War I they

produced a series of stunningly elegant monoplanes, but their early days were beset by disappointments, puzzling crashes, and untimely tragedies. Despite it all, Handasyde never lost his faith in the monoplane; and despite these setbacks coupled with personal reticence to a fault — they sought no publicity, did no advertising — Martinsyde, on technical merit alone, prospered.

Under the pressure of war, Handasyde was persuaded to design biplanes, and to these he applied the same degree of skill and patience with finer points. The design that stood to achieve overwhelming renown was the F.4 Buzzard, first test-flown in June 1918, the fastest combat aeroplane built during World War I. Hundreds were ordered (Curtiss, in the United States, was tooling up to build 1,500) but production was abruptly halted by the Armistice after fewer than two hundred had been built. Only four F.4s received civil

registrations; in a strong attempt to perpetuate the breed, one was taken to Spain on a sales tour in October 1919 by pilot Fred Raynham, where his performances deeply impressed observers. He then flew to Portugal, and became the first aviator to fly into that country, where the British in Lisbon donated the F.4 in a presentation by Sir Lancelot Carnegie, British ambassador. The gift paid off. Several F.4s were ordered, and six were still in service in Barcelona when the Spanish Civil War broke out in 1936! Other F.4s were sold in Finland, where one was still in existence until at least 1968, the longest-surviving Martinsyde. A two-seat version, called F.4A, evolved and there were at least three versions of this. A Rolls-Royce Falcon-powered single-seat F.4 flew in the 1919 Aerial Derby, and the first two-seater, powered by the ubiquitous 300-hp Hispano-Suiza, flew in the 1920 edition. F.4 variants flew in several later Derbies.

Martinsyde F.4 Buzzard, probably World War I's fastest combat aeroplane, being photographed during the 1921 Aerial Derby (Au)

Frederick P. Raynham (F)

One such variant was the F.6, virtually an F.4 with a short-span center-section, modified wing bracing and landing gear, designed for use as either a two-seat reconnaissance plane or one-seat fighter. Only three were built. The third and last, which was also the last of all Martinsyde aircraft, was bought in 1922 by Fred Raynham for only £15 (its originally quoted price was two hundred times that amount); he painted it a gaudy, vivid yellow, earning it the sobriquet "Mustardsyde." He then flew it in the 1922 Aerial Derby as a one-seater and 1922 and 1923 King's Cup races with two seats. One of Handasyde's inspired 1914 recruits was young Sydney Camm, who would achieve lasting fame years later as the leading design genius at Hawker; in the 1922 King's Cup affair Camm rode Raynham's front cockpit as a mechanic and earned his passage in an hour's time when he repaired a broken pipe during a stop in Birmingham.

Frederick Phillip "Freddie" Raynham had been trained by A. V. Roe when still a teen-ager, earning RAeC pilot certificate number 85, and had done much test-flying of Avro aeroplanes before World War I. He is sometimes credited with being the first pilot successfully to recover from a tailspin. During the war he became chief test pilot for Martinsyde, and became involved in the firm's endeavor to win Northcliffe's prize for crossing the Atlantic as soon as peace returned. Before March 1919 a huge two-seater called the *Atlantic*, similar to a scaled-up F.4 and powered by a 275-hp Rolls-Royce Falcon III, had been designed, built, and test-flown. Together with Captain C. W. F. Morgan, ex-RNAS, his navigator, Raynham did two preparatory non-stop ground runs strapped in the aeroplane of ten and twenty-four hours before going to Quidi Vidi, Newfoundland, a small field leased privately by Morgan in January. The plane was

renamed *Raymor* after its crew, and Raynham attempted his epic takeoff on May 18 barely one hour after Harry Hawker's departure, only to crash in a stiff crosswind, injuring Morgan severely on his face and head. The plane was rebuilt in two months, remarkable considering the poor facilities, and despite the success of Alcock and Brown in the meantime, Raynham chose a new navigator, Lieutenant C. H. Biddlecombe, renamed his plane *Chimera*, and tried again to take off on July 17. There was another crash and that was the end of Martinsyde's transatlantic effort. That autumn Raynham made his flying visit to Portugal, and he remained the Martinsyde star pilot until their aeroplane line ceased. On October 17, 1922, at Firle Beacon, Raynham remained aloft soaring for almost two hours in a glider designed jointly by Handasyde, Sydney Camm, and himself. It was a duration record that earned him a £1,000 *Daily Mail* prize and the 1922 Britannia Trophy. During the summer of 1925 he sailed to the Far East with Ronald Kemp to do air survey work in north Borneo. Raynham remained abroad with Kemp's Air Survey Company Ltd. for several years, doing considerable flying in India. He died in 1954, aged sixty-two.

A few months after the 1919 Atlantic fiasco Handasyde designed a new speedplane, in some ways a scaled-down F.4; it had the fin-and-rudder profile which had been his trademark since before the war. Powered by the 300-hp Hispano-Suiza, it was an extremely sturdy aeroplane. I-section wing spars were built up from three laminates, the center thin, the front and back thicker and spindled out. The interplane struts rested on "packing pieces" of duralumin while metal straps for interplane bracing wire attachment were wrapped around

Martinsyde Semiquaver on display at the 1920 Olympia Aero Show (F)

316

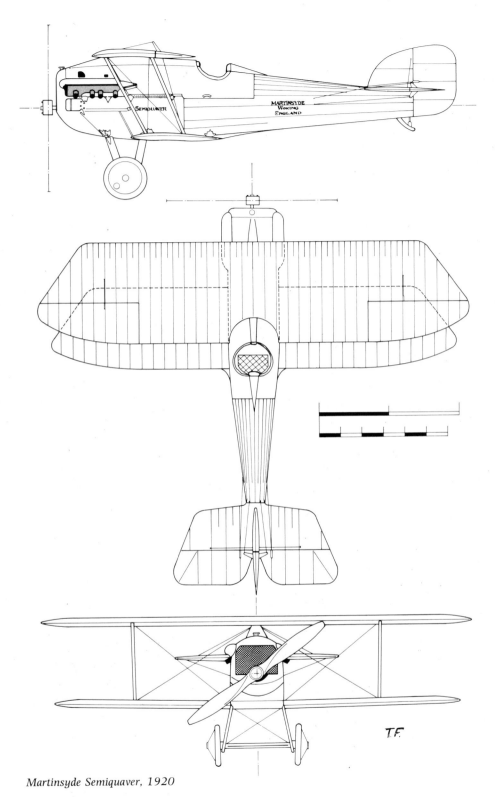

Martinsyde Semiquaver, 1920

the spars, with each spar pierced on its neutral axis to accommodate horizontal attachment bolts. The forward fuselage was three-ply-covered, but perhaps the most important feature of strength was the built-up fuselage hump to which the one-piece upper wing — which had no center-section — was anchored directly, totally eliminating cabane struts. *Flight* magazine said of the racer that it was "of the most beautiful outline imaginable"; spectators who saw it fly called it the "little red devil." At Martlesham Heath on March 21, 1920, Raynham flew the brand-new racer to an official British speed record of slightly more than 161 mph in four measured 1-kilometer passes, virtually on her first flight! Remarkable though it was, this flight left her 13 mph shy of achieving the world record, and her British speed mark lasted less than three months until Folland's L.S.3 Goshawk racer broke it by 5 mph. During June, when the downfall of the Martinsyde firm was already inevitable, the new racer highlighted a courageous display of three Martinsyde planes at the Olympia Aero Show.

The racer achieved wide fame as the Semiquaver, but source of this name is uncertain. The word "semiquaver" in musical terminology is proper English for a sixteenth note (♪). No other Martinsyde had any musically connected or inclined names and one is unable to discover to what extent Martin or Handasyde — or perhaps one of the shopworkers — was a music aficionado. Anyway, somebody soon realized the new crimson speedplane was a "fast note" — and "semiquaver" fit that description perfectly.

Raynham was entered in the upcoming Aerial Derby, but late on the eve of the race he telephoned his close friend, test pilot Frank Courtney, to say he had wrenched his knee in a minor mishap while flying another plane that day, and to ask if Courtney would care to race the Semiquaver. Despite its British speed record, Semiquaver flight tests had not been com-

pleted and Raynham urged Courtney to take a one-hour familiarization flight before the race. The aeroplane had recently been disassembled at the Olympia exhibition hall and was only then being erected at Hendon, but Courtney made an odd decision: presuming he would inevitably find fault with the racer, and forgetting that a familiarization flight, even with faults, would be prudent preparation, he decided to "go for broke" and make the race his first flight.

Courtney took off, swung low around the central pylon, and pointed toward Brooklands, 20 miles to the south. He immediately perceived the prop pitch was too high, overloading the engine, cutting down rpm, and raising temperature. Scalding water was being thrown into the open cockpit from an overflow pipe on the undersized radiator. Courtney recalled that he had a "three-handed job" with throttle, joystick, and maps, mostly throttle, trying to keep maximum power consistent with a water temperature 2–3 degrees below boiling. While rounding the Hendon pylon to finish lap one Courtney blacked out, an entirely new, totally unexpected, and frightening experience for him. Thinking something might be wrong with him, he kept the experience secret for months for fear the licensing medical authorities would lift his license.

As he approached the finish line after his second circuit of London, Courtney decided "to hell with the temperature" and shoved the throttle open. Clouds of steam chugged and spit as the Semiquaver shot by the home pylon, the winner. Courtney could not imagine how any water could possibly remain, and headed at once for a short landing. Unknown to him the landing gear shock absorber cords had been pulled up tight so the racer could sit rigidly on its Olympia exhibition stand, and in the hectic rush before takeoff no one had thought to slack them off. When the Semiquaver hit a little ridge hidden in high grass it bolted stiffly into the air

Frank T. Courtney, circa 1920 (MA)

intensity, this extremely persuasive and articulate young man steered an unswerving course to the pinnacle of his chosen field. He did this, moreover, in the face of considerable handicap: rejected for military flight training in 1914 because he wore glasses — even though he had learned to fly earlier as a civilian with Grahame-White — he enlisted as a mechanic. It soon transpired that no one in those days *without* glasses could fly any better, and Courtney, always quite sure of himself, promptly got a job as pilot. While flying a Morane parasol with No. 3 Squadron, Courtney was wounded in the Battle of Loos, catching some Archie in his back and three bullets in his leg. He left the hospital with a commission and a job as test pilot at the Royal Aircraft Factory, Farnborough. In 1917 he did a "tough period" in No. 45 Squadron, flying the peculiar, quivering-winged Sopwith 1½-Strutter, and after the war, as a highly regarded free-lance test pilot who enjoyed a sustained demand for his talents, Courtney spent years testing every sort of crate in existence, flying from the Arctic Circle to the Balkan tropics doing engine tests, blind flying experiments, at night, at high altitude, in terminal velocity dives in the earliest tests for flutter, in tests on the original slotted wings, on autogiros, on flying boats large and small. Lean and lanky, with a dry, sophisticated sense of humor, Courtney made an improbable-looking test pilot with his helmet crushed down onto his tight, black hair and his glasses jutting imperiously out front on his beaklike nose. He won the glamorous 1923 King's Cup race in the new Siskin fighter. In 1928 he tried to span the North Atlantic but 680 miles from Newfoundland his flying boat caught fire when a gasoline line broke, and he had a lucky escape, being rescued by a passing liner after being adrift for two days. The following year he was in the United States as aviation adviser to Haydn, Stone & Company, stockbrokers, and remained, becoming

a naturalized U.S. citizen, and spending several years at Convair before retiring in San Diego. In 1971 Courtney was still writing prolifically and lecturing widely, the sharp edges of his definitely stated views still retaining a strong British bias, not in the least blunted by time. Courtney once said the only place he had not flown was Haiti — they would not guarantee cracked ice for his rum punch so he refused the job!

During the two months following the Aerial Derby, the Semiquaver was put back into top form, having its wing area reduced "slightly" — although just how much is uncertain — and it was entered in the Gordon Bennett.

The British were smug and blasé as this classic air race approached — perhaps too blasé. Raynham had put the Semiquaver tailskid on the back of his car, and accompanied by his good friend McGeagh Hurst, he towed the aeroplane all the way from Brooklands to Étampes, taking the Southampton–Le Havre ferry. Its only damage from the trip was a chafed shock cord and one puncture, but it flew the race with the same tires. As soon as he arrived in Étampes, Raynham gave the Semiquaver a twenty-minute "airing" — his term for a trial flight — but on Cup day he was in no hurry to take off, leaving the racer in its shed until late

Two views of Martinsyde Semiquaver at Étampes for the 1920 Gordon Bennett race
(MA)

only to stagger in on its left wingtip. With a crunch it came to rest upside down, becoming the *semi*-Semiquaver, and St. John's Ambulance Corps stretcher-bearers raced to the scene. They arrived breathless to find that Courtney had been saved from serious injury by the solid fuselage hump and stout rudder post, both still intact, which gave him enough room not only to avoid bashing in his head but to squirm free.

Courtney was no stranger to aviation's zanier aspects. As a bored pre-war bank clerk in Paris, he decided early to get into aviation, joined the Boulton & Paul drawing office, and with single-minded drive rare for its

afternoon, even after spectators were going home. He was waiting for the sun to sink, partly to take the bumps out of the air, but mostly to cool it, since the plane's radiator capacity had not been increased. Despite its "old engine," the French favorite Sadi Lecointe considered the Semiquaver his most dangerous competition, yet when Raynham arrived in Étampes, friendless and rather forlorn, Sadi Lecointe went out of his way to befriend the Englishman, lending him tools and mechanics and engaging him in voluble conversations. Raynham's special fuel, ordered in advance, had not arrived, so Colonel Bristow of Ogilvie & Partners, then in Paris, sent a lorry to Rouen to obtain the proper *essence*. The fuel finally delivered to Raynham had a specific gravity of ·68 while his carburetor was tuned for ·70. The improper fuel would heat the engine unduly unless his carburetor was readjusted – a ticklish job which Raynham did not want to risk.

At 4:30 P.M. Raynham had the Semiquaver wheeled to the starting line. With no fuss he took off, using less than half the distance of anyone else, hurtled by the pylon straight into the setting sun, and left a gaggle of anxious British spectators to await his return, stopwatches in hand. The anxiety increased, especially when Raynham had not returned in twenty-five minutes. Then he appeared, his engine misfiring badly, and landed. A joint in an oil pipe had blown out its packing and the Semiquaver was deluged with black, dripping oil. If Raynham could have kept up his initial pace he would have won by three minutes, but he did not, and with his landing all British hopes expired. In his completely unostentatious way he calmly hitched the Semiquaver to his car and trundled back to England again.

The postwar economic lapse had reduced Martinsyde to a struggling producer of motorcycles, and Handasyde, who had been the dynamo running the wartime business, resigned toward the end of 1920, as did Hamilton Fulton and Fred Raynham. Martinsyde officially folded November 2, 1920. The three then formed the Handasyde Aircraft Company Ltd., Carlton House, 11D Regent Street, and Handasyde went back to his first love, the design of supremely handsome monoplanes. His new business did not last long in the hostile economic climate prevalent then; its end came early in 1924. Discouraged, Handasyde retired to the solitude of a Surrey cottage.

Ironically, Handasyde's comely Semiquaver finished her career as a monoplane, though one with which he had nothing to do. Early in 1921 Frank Courtney had been engaged as test pilot by a highly egotistical Dutch designer called A. A. Holle, known for his unsuccessful parasol Varioplane of World War I, and who had convinced himself that he had perfected the formula for a new wing which would produce lift in proportion to the cube of its velocity (V^3, instead of the long-proven factor V^2); this was roughly equivalent to bragging he had found a magnet of brass. Nevertheless, Holle had started a company with the imposing name Commercial Airplane Wing Syndicate, Ltd., 34 Gresham Street, E.C.2, capitalized at £30,000 in part by Robert Blackburn. Holle's freak, new wing, on which he had taken patent 167086, was a thin, unbraced device mounted on the clumsy frame of a D.H.6 at Sherburn-in-Elmet, Yorkshire, near Leeds, and it recalled somewhat the early José Weiss "bird-wing" and Etrich Taube aeroplane. Holle called it the "Alula" wing; in nature, the alula is an auxiliary digit on the leading edge of a gull's wing which can be extended to form a slot and delay premature leading edge stall during slow flight. No such sophistication was apparent in Holle's wing, however, which had a straight trailing edge and swept leading edge tapering to a sharp point at the tip. Large incidence gradually changed to a zero-lift, negative incidence at the tip, claimed to eliminate spanwise flow and consequent tip losses, but in fact the flimsy tip, prone to aeroelastic twist, rendered conventional ailerons "perfectly useless." After his first test pilot almost killed himself, Holle provided two hinged slats in the leading edge for lateral control, but these on the other hand proved far too sensitive,

although presumably they provided the origin of the name Alula. Actually, with a bit more luck Holle might have invented the Handley Page slot by mistake. But refusing to face the truth, Holle maintained stoutly that his wing was being inhibited by the cumbersome D.H.6, whereas (he said) if mounted on the clean fuselage of a

Two views of Martinsyde Semiquaver with Alula wing, 1921   (F)

racer it would perform with glorious efficiency. Holle thus induced Handasyde to sell the Semiquaver for an undetermined sum, the money in all likelihood provided by Captain Vertholen, another stiff, Prussian-style Dutchman who had already sunk a lot of guilders into Holle's misguided dreams.

Although Holle's early claims were for his wing's load-carrying ability — Robert Blackburn was then interested in promoting a proposed 4-ton "aerial lorry" named Pelican — Holle began construction of an Alula wing adapted for racing. His "stress analysis" was obviously done by guesswork, since the wing had no spars, only thin spanwise and chordwise formers, with its skin being mere 1/8-inch single-ply mahogany veneer! The first such wing completed, sent to Farnborough on June 11, 1921, was too flexible and had a load factor of only 1·75 (which meant it would have collapsed in a banked turn of only some 50 degrees!) These results delayed completion of the second, which in July was sent to the French Institut Aérotechnique St.-Cyr. Either the third or fourth was to be mounted on the Semiquaver after her original biplane wings were discarded. The "Handalula" (a misnomer unfair to George Handasyde conceived by the press) or "Semi-Alula-Quaver" was assembled at Addlestone and towed to Northolt, where Courtney was to test it in preparation of flying it in the 1921 Aerial Derby virtually the very next day. After a few taxi runs, noting it was excessively top-heavy on its original, narrow landing gear, and also noting that the wing still "wobbled in all directions," Courtney declined to fly it. Holle was disgusted with his test pilot and with indignation was forced to look elsewhere for a pilot to race his creation. French speed ace Count Bernard de Romanet, then in London and looking for a race mount, was tempted to Northolt only a couple of hours before the race, but after one look at the aeroplane he told Holle that Courtney's

assessment was sound enough for him. Christopher Draper also turned Holle down, and the plane did not race.

Three months later Holle set up a demonstration for almost a dozen of British aviation's top dignitaries, to take place at Northolt on the afternoon of October 12. It is not clear if Holle used this interim to beef up his wing. The ailerons were again on the trailing edge, located at mid-span, and a new, sturdy landing gear with much wider tread had been fitted. Holle had solicited the services of noted pilot Reginald W. Kenworthy, whom Courtney described as "a fine fellow but not known for his technical judgment or reasonable caution." Kenworthy, who had an apartment in Leeds, was financially well fixed and did not need the fees; he was also "deaf," which meant he could not hear what he did not want to hear. He usually did want to "try anything once." He made an unconvincing demonstration flight for the brass and press on the appointed afternoon. It is fairly unlikely this was his first flight in the Martinsyde-Alula monoplane; it is highly probable he first flew the plane as early as only five days after the Derby in July, a flight which Courtney, a witness, recalled as harrowing. It is also impossible to determine how many flights Kenworthy made in it. Leslie Foot is also reported to have flown the plane. One thing is clear: the weird monoplane failed to live up to its promise, and even the insouciant Reggie had had enough.

Curiously, despite its problems, B. D. Thomas, designer of the Thomas-Morse racers in the United States, became enamored with some of the claims made for the Alula wing, and its strange shape influenced his subsequent racers. But the once lovely Semiquaver was abandoned at Northolt, left to rot.

AirCo and de Havilland
The 1919 Aerial Derby was won by an AirCo D.H.4R powered by the first publicly displayed Napier Lion. Both aeroplane and engine were conceived

Geoffrey de Havilland as a young man　　(F)

during the war, the airframe being designed by Geoffrey de Havilland, fondly known as "D.H.," the son of the rector of a remote country parish near Newbury on the Hampshire Downs. His grandfather, a Victorian farmer-squire living near Oxford, had started him off with £1,000; toughened by months of disappointment and frugality, D.H. finally succeeded in flying in 1910 when he was twenty-eight, and soon thereafter found himself working as designer at the Royal Aircraft Establishment, Farnborough. His shyness could be mistaken for aloofness, but he never gave orders, just discussed problems, and what needed doing got done. In this way he collected the most loyal band of

workers in British aviation and always turned out aeroplanes that were exceptionally rugged and practical. Shortly after the outbreak of war he became Technical Director of the Aircraft Manufacturing Company (AirCo) of Hendon, which in 1916 brought out a remarkable warplane called the D.H.4; indeed, to many who did not know the regard D.H. had already earned, it seemed odd that the plane bore the initials of its designer rather than its manufacturer.

Quickly in action over the Western Front, the design was adopted for mass production in the United States, and in late 1917, powered by the Liberty engine, it began coming off U.S. production lines at a rate that soon

De Havilland D.H.4 in U.S. military service, early 1920s. The D.H.4 was widely used in the United States throughout the decade; almost all were powered by Liberty engines. (S)

D.H.4 in U.S. Air Mail service, early 1920s (S)

grew to 260 per week until some 4,846 were built in America alone.[1] The D.H.4, called optimistically the "Liberty plane," was the first U.S.-built aeroplane to go into squadron service; more importantly, over three thousand of these remained in the United States after the war, and between 1919 and 1926 they formed the backbone of both the U. S. Air Service and the U. S. Air Mail. The entry lists of the air derbies and races held in the United States during 1919 and 1920 will attest to their domination of that sphere of aviation as well. Assembly of hundreds of war-produced but uncrated D.H.4s and conversion to D.H.4M (for "Modernized") created work for struggling aeroplane builders when there was little new business. Fewer than a hundred American D.H.4s flew more than 1,000 hours although they remained in active service until 1932! Other D.H.4s built in Europe were flying in Spain until as late as 1940.

In England the AirCo D.H.4R (R for "Racer") had been specially modified for the Aerial Derby, the job given to Frank Hearle, who was urged to produce

[1] Major Reynal C. Bolling, a flier and former United States Steel lawyer, led the important Bolling Mission that largely influenced the U.S. decision to build only one European type — the D.H.4 — a decision which outraged Billy Mitchell, who had opted for a French pursuit plane but was ignored. Mitchell remained suspicious that "inside work" on the part of the English manufacturers had a lot to do with America's production of what he frankly considered a "worthless" aeroplane. Bolling became well known for the complex system of air support he managed at the Front until killed in March 1918, defending himself with a pistol until the end.

Gathergood's AirCo D.H.4R with Napier Lion engine, winner of the 1919 Aerial Derby (Au)

321

an aeroplane appropriate for a gala sporting event yet accomplish the job with minimum expenditure of funds. A contemporary recorded of Hearle's effort, "Joking about workshop engineers who stepped boldly in where aerodynamics angels feared to tread, he clipped the lower wings of a D.H.4, fitted oblique struts to the upper planes, and somewhat crudely installed a 450-hp Napier Lion. It gave more than 150 mph. Despite a rather inadequate radiator, this lash-up, effected in a matter of ten days . . . won the Derby . . . a surprise for the mathematicians!" The new Lion engine turned a four-blade prop. The winning pilot was AirCo chief pilot Gerald Gathergood, who had seen wartime service with the RFC in France in 1915 and later participated in the night air defense of London. He won the Derby handily as all odds-makers had predicted. After the success of the jury-rigged D.H.4R, a second, carefully built AirCo racer, the Lion-equipped D.H.9R (G-EAHT) with single-bay, equal-span wings, was produced during the summer and with it Gathergood won a

September race in Amsterdam, averaging 145 mph to beat no less than thirty-four others over a 220-kilometer closed course. Yet this aeroplane was slower than the older D.H.4R! Nevertheless, shortly after that triumph, Gathergood used the D.H.9R to set twenty-three minor British speed records, eighteen in one flight, on November, 15, 1919, at Hendon. Despite these successes Gathergood eventually gave up active flying in late 1921, a year after his early employer, AirCo, was forced to fold in the economic blight of 1920.

As ever undaunted, Geoffrey de Havilland built his own company from the ashes of AirCo, officially opening his new works at Stag Lane, Edgware, Middlesex, on September 25, 1920, inadequately financed and facing on the one hand a very thin civil aircraft market and on the other an Air Ministry both indifferent and inexperienced, trying to maintain more than a dozen firms virtually on prototype business alone. Despite these inauspicious prospects, several men who had worked with D.H. at AirCo

came into his new firm, notably Charles C. Walker, his chief engineer. D.H. secured early stability by building the world-famous Moth and a series of eminently successful commercial transports with which he almost monopolized British airline orders. He also operated the de Havilland Hire Service, a successful air taxi firm whose chief pilot was young Alan Cobham.

De Havilland's struggling new firm was in fact virtually saved from financial disaster in October 1921 by Alan Samuel Butler, whose purchase of a custom-built three-seat touring aeroplane (the one-of-a-kind D.H.37) led him to make a substantial investment; this in turn enabled Butler to become a director, later chairman of the firm until 1950. Meanwhile Butler frequently used his new touring aeroplane, which he had named *Sylvia* after his sister, for handicap racing. Having finished fourth in the 1921 Aerial Derby flying a Bristol Tourer, Butler was anxious to improve his performance in the 1922 race with the D.H.37, but was forced by magneto trouble to retire, although he flew it to fifth place in both the 1922 and 1923 King's Cup races. It was painted bilious black with gold wings and white lettering, and had Arthur Hagg differential ailerons — Hagg had come with D.H. from AirCo and was chief of his drawing office staff, and his perfection of ailerons with unequal up/down travel to reduce spanwise imbalance in drag that opposed turns (patent 184317) was one of those quiet but enormous gains made during this era. Major Harold Hemming flew the D.H.37 in the 1923 Aerial Derby but again it did not finish, although it was third in the King's Cup races of both 1924 and 1925, being renamed *Lois* for Butler's wife after his marriage in 1925. Modified in 1926 with Major F. B. Halford's redesigned 340-hp Puma, it became the *Nimbus*, but on June 4, 1927, at the Bournemouth Whitsun meeting Hemming stalled and crashed the D.H.37. It was

destroyed, his passenger was killed, and he lost an eye.

AirCo had also produced several wartime D.H.9s, a D.H.4 conversion — the pilot's cockpit had been moved back adjacent to the observer among other modifications — and a few found their way into various handicap air racing events. Frank Courtney flew one in the 1923 Aerial Derby, others appeared in King's Cup races. But in general, after the first tentative forays, D.H. avoided pure speed seeking. His transport line culminated in the Comet, the world's first operational jet transport, but when its mysterious structural failures brought his firm to its knees in 1953, D.H. calmly went to work and saw to it that the Comet was reestablished as a successful transport like the many which had gone before. In his private hours D.H., who was intrigued with photography of wild animals and butterfly collecting, lived with the grief of having lost two sons in flying accidents. After his death in 1965 his ashes were scattered over Beacon Hill at Seven Barrows, where he had first flown almost six decades before.

Although many of those involved in the early postwar British sporting efforts did not pursue the path toward pure speed, they worked side by side with other men who would take this avenue. From the early, often ill-adapted racers several successful high-speed British aeroplanes were developed by these men. The first man we shall meet began as the early colleague of de Havilland at Farnborough. His name was H. P. Folland.

Gerald Gathergood (holding maps), 1919 (F)

FOLLAND'S FLYING FASTBACKS 22

The "British Nieuport" and Gloucestershire Racers

It was hard to tell whether his pipe acted as a tractor for Folland, or Folland acted as a pusher for the pipe. There was no doubt, however, that concentration brought a series of puffs from Folland's pipe as furious as the exhaust from his many autocratic speedplanes. Henry Phillip Folland, as an assistant designer in Mervyn O'Gorman's brilliant staff at the British government's own Royal Aircraft Factory at Farnborough during World War I, first gained fame when he fashioned the immortal S.E.5, one of history's most distinguished fighters.

Mervyn O'Gorman had been appointed from his successful London firm of consulting engineers (O'Gorman and Cozens-Hardy) to be superintendent of the balloon factory at Farnborough in 1909. He took with him his junior technical assistant, young "H.B." – Hugh Burroughes. In 1912 young Henry Folland, then twenty-three, limped into O'Gorman's office (Folland's lifelong limp was the result of childhood polio) and was soon a hard-working member of the staff. In March 1914 George Holt-Thomas, son of the London *Daily Graphic* founder, persuaded Burroughes to become manager of the Aircraft Manufacturing Company – AirCo – at Hendon, and H.B. in turn got young Geoff de Havilland appointed chief designer three months later. Meanwhile young Folland flourished in the strait-laced climate of the Royal Air-

Henry P. Folland with his ever present fixtures, pipe and slide rule, circa 1921 (F)

turning a prop with a large spinner open in front to accommodate fan blades for cooling. It also had an enclosed cockpit canopy but no pilot would use it! Folland also used I-struts between the wings, a feature which would distinguish his later racer designs, and full-span ailerons that drooped to double as flaps for landing. After a wheel collapsed in August 1914 – the opening month of war – the S.E.4, considered "too fast", was dropped.

The use of so many novel techniques provides insight into Folland's imagination, for in later years novelty was considered somewhat out of character for Folland, who would always loftily refuse to acknowledge many aspects of technological change. Certainly Folland, among the major designers, was the last emphatic holdout for the biplane. He designed several of the greatest biplanes to fly, and it was natural that he should be responsible for the fastest big-bore racing biplane,

the last of the species (the Gloster IV-B), and the most successful among the very last service biplane fighters (the Gloster Gladiator).

Folland's heyday, which began during World War I, peaked in the immediate postwar period in spite of the economic slump that hit England hard.

In the beginning, as World War I intensified and the need for literally thousands of aeroplanes was foreseen, the hard-pressed British aviation industry turned for help to many outside concerns possessing expertise in almost any field remotely related to aeroplane construction. Two such firms were H. H. Martyn & Company Ltd., and Waring & Gillow, both long noted for craftsmanship in architectural woodworking and cabinet making. Samuel Waring was leading spirit in the latter firm. In 1915, at a wartime businessmen's luncheon organized to recruit woodworking firms into aviation, hosted by W. J. Mallinson and attended by Hugh Burroughes,

craft Factory, which seemed particularly suited to his temperament. The upper echelon of designers there tended to be academic and were decidedly cautious – to wit, the monoplane ban – which accounted in large measure for the lack of flair in their World War I designs; Folland too was not by nature a bold innovator except in flashes. Yet Folland was not reticent except in a critical atmosphere, but then he could easily justify the observation of a friend who described him as "soundly conservative." Throughout most of his career he remained strongly anti-monoplane, anti-metal structure, anti-VP prop, since almost any horse from another stable Folland perceived as a threat to his own position. Nevertheless, enough of his bright ideas burst forth that he will always stand out as one of the leading and most gifted creators of speedplanes during these classic vintage years.

The first appeared in June 1914

when as a lowly section leader of twenty-five Folland designed the S.E.4 and this – indeed, his first major design task – proved to be virtually as fast as the French Deperdussin, then the world's fastest aeroplane. His plane's performance reinforced Folland's conviction that designers could get better performance from biplanes than from monoplanes in those days. The S.E.4 was authorized by Lieutenant Colonel J. E. B. Seely, then Secretary of State for War, to make a speed record on behalf of the Royal Aircraft Factory, and was flown to 135 mph by J. M. Salmond, its smooth and daring thin-shell monocoque structure no doubt enhancing this amazing albeit unofficial performance. Brigadier General Sir David Henderson, Director of Military Aeronautics, exulted "If anyone wants to know which country has the fastest aeroplane in the world, it is Great Britain!" The S.E.4 engine was a twin-row fourteen-cylinder 160-hp Gnôme rotary entirely cowled in,

Folland's earliest fastback, the S.E.4 (*U.K. Ministry of Defence*)

Waring's interest in the new science was aroused. Burroughes recalled that Waring "was the type to climb on the band wagon and collar the baton." Thus on November 16, 1916, Waring established business connections with the French Nieuport firm in order to produce the French designs on English soil. He named this offshoot firm Nieuport & General Aircraft Company Ltd. It rapidly came to be called – quite unofficially – "British Nieuport," and used factory space on Langton Road between Temple Road and the railroad tracks in Cricklewood just 4 miles northwest of Marble Arch. Waring had no mission in aviation beyond making money, hence when he later received a baronetcy for his loudly self-proclaimed "services to aviation" it was sneered at unmercifully, especially in scathing commentary by C. G. Grey in his weekly paper *The Aeroplane*. This presumably bothered Waring not in the least.

In 1917 parliamentary agitation against nationalized aviation led to the notorious Bailhache Judicial Committee allegations which in turn induced the unraveling of the Royal Aircraft Factory, scattering many of the great designers to the winds. Major S. Heckstall-Smith, who had been Assistant Superintendent, together with Folland and his leading draftsman and "stress henchman" Howard E. "Joe" Preston, went to Nieuport & General, where Heckstall-Smith became general manager and Folland chief designer. Folland, now known universally as "HPF", always considered this move into private industry "the turning point in my life." Thus fortified, "British Nieuport" embarked on designs of their own. Folland's first product there was the B.N.1, built to rival the Sopwith Snipe. It looked rather like his spectacularly successful S.E.5 and used Camel parts which the factory had in abundance, their most

recent job being the construction of two hundred subcontracted Camels, but its two-bay wings sported daring I-struts. One was built, but on March 10, 1918, at Sutton's Farm during comparative trials with the Snipe, the B.N.1 caught fire and was demolished. The Snipe got the production order and Folland went back to the drawing board.

At this point the Air Board became enthralled with the claims made for a new fixed radial engine designed by Granville Bradshaw of the Walton Motor Company, Walton-on-Thames, Hersham, Surrey. So promising did it seem that the RAF was totally committed to it – all the eggs went into one basket – and no less than 11,050 were ordered from thirteen subcontractors. However, only 1,147 were made and a major disaster was luckily averted by the Armistice – for this was the infamous ABC Dragonfly. The use of Professor A. H. Gibson's and Sam D. Heron's novel new air-cooled cylinders temporarily disguised in optimism its basic flaw: the engine was out of balance dynamically and indeed had been accidentally designed to run precisely on its prime critical vibration frequency!

The Dragonfly followed earlier ABC air-cooled Gnat and Wasp designs. Copper coating on the steel cooling fins of its nine cylinders was its outstanding novel feature. Its predicted rated power was 320 hp and maximum expected output 350 hp, but when built it produced only 295 hp. The finished engine was also 50 pounds overweight, its power loading not even competitive with some contemporary water-cooled designs. The Dragonfly had a diameter just 2 inches less than the Bristol Jupiter. Like the Jupiter it used Hispano-like closed-end steel barrels for cylinders, but employed no true cylinder head at all, just exposed lifters for the two small exhaust valves which opened directly, using no exhaust manifold, and one large inlet valve atop each cylinder. The engine was normally fitted with two belching, fire-prone

H.C.8 carburetors. But its greatest fault by far was the alarming synchronous torsional vibration which compounded upon itself, invariably causing the power to expire within two hours of overhaul! Needless to say, the Dragonfly earned early notoriety as an unreliable, even dangerous engine. What is not well appreciated is that the Dragonfly's problem was not well understood until later, and builders of other radial engines had escaped the same difficulty by sheer good luck!

Folland's next design was the Nighthawk fighter to RAF specification 1/18, planned around the then unbuilt Dragonfly. The design's tie aesthetically to the S.E.4 and S.E.5 was readily discernible; moreover, for economy, it was expressly designed to use numerous S.E.5 components which existed in profusion. It also reflected Folland's determination to surpass technically the ever popular Sopwiths, which were then flourishing in part because of the fast-growing power of shrewd and wealthy Tom Sopwith inside Air Ministry halls, an influence that would later fix his Hawker firm's unassailable preeminence among British aircraft constructors. Folland's diligence seemingly paid off: the Nighthawk was chosen for mass production on the basis of proof tests only! However, it was too late for combat, just beginning to appear at war's end. The vast contracts were summarily canceled (Nieuport & General built only forty-one) and the Dragonfly's failure seemed to nail the coffin shut on the Nighthawk.

Remarkably, the design survived. The Nighthawks completed enjoyed popular success, being strong, simple, and pure delight to fly, unquestionably one of the all-time greats for aerobatics. But the many modifications to the basic design were what secured its place in history.

Nieuport & General realized after the war that they must race their aeroplanes to maintain prestige. They adopted a gaudy blue-and-

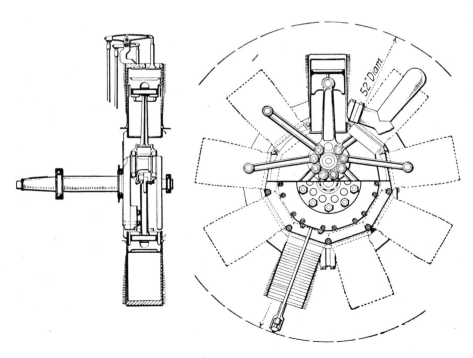

The ill-fated ABC Dragonfly, one of the earliest fixed air-cooled radial engines put into large-scale production

52" Diam.

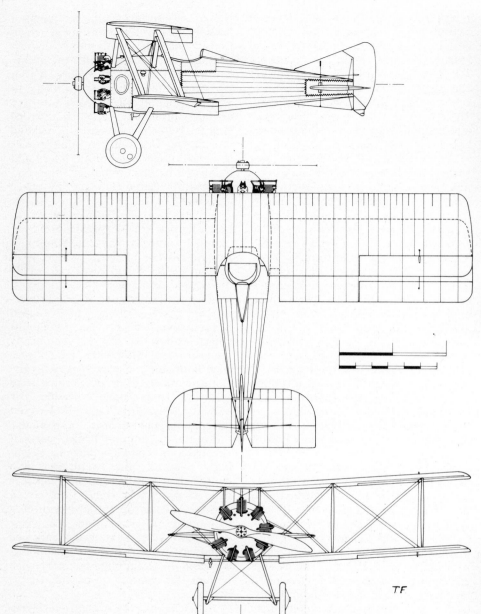

Nieuport General Nighthawk, 1919.

Leslie R. Tait-Cox, 1919   (F)

He received RAeC certificate number 315 in October 1912, barnstormed Wales in a prewar Caudron with his brother, and instructed at Hendon (Ruffy Baumann school) in 1915. Tait-Cox combined the first Nighthawk "long distance" test with the first delivery of newspapers by air under "commercial conditions" when, at 6:25 A.M. on March 14, 1919, he left Acton Aerodrome and in fifty minutes reached Bournemouth, where he deposited copies of the *Daily Mail* with the sleepy-eyed mayor – still in his pyjamas – "forty-five minutes before any other London papers reached the town." HPF with his wife and two young sons then lived at Dollis Hill near Willesden Green in what was open country then, driving to work in an ABC twin-cylinder air-cooled two-seater "dickey car" painted the same blue as the checkerboard blue used on his racing planes, its engine presumably more reliable.

Nieuport & General L.C.1 Nieuhawk number 1, 1919 Aerial Derby   (Au)

yellow checkerboard racing scheme that dressed their entire racing stable. Their aerial jockeys, who had joined the firm after the war, were level-headed Leslie R. Tait-Cox and his number two, a brash young Welshman, James Herbert James. Both had been test pilots at Farnborough under Frank Gooden during the war, beginning a close association in 1916. Before that, James had learned to fly at the Ewen School, Hendon, from winning a scholarship offered by the International Correspondence Schools.

The L.C.1 number 1, marked as in the 1919 Aerial Derby, but modified to include a second cockpit   (F)

Nieuport & General L.C.1 Nieuhawk number 2, 1921 Aerial Derby   (F)

The Nighthawk design was converted slightly for civil use to capitalize on its potential. The first civil version built adopted the designation "Land Commercial type one" (L.C.1), number 1. The pilot's cockpit was moved slightly aft from its military position. It was registered K-151 in the civil K-series in use before adoption of the G-alphabetical series and entered in the 1919 Aerial Derby as number 11, flown by Tait-Cox. The Dragonfly, true to form, forced it down at West Thurrock on the second lap, although up until then it had almost matched the winner's speed and would have finished an easy second. Two weeks later, on July 7, 1919, it received its Certificate of Airworthiness and became G-EAEQ. A second cockpit was installed, the passenger placed in front of the pilot. It then went to India with Captain Reggie S. Carroll, accompanied by Jimmie James, in an attempt to promote aeroplane sales in Britain's largest colony. On December 15, 1919, the day after its arrival in crates, it flew in the Bombay peace demonstration from the Willingdon Club grounds, and a

week later hauled a stack of newspapers from Bombay to Poona. In May 1920 it went to Penang — Carroll became the company's managing director in Bombay — and was demonstrated by him to an enthusiastic crowd at the

Nieuport & General L.S.3 Goshawk racer, 1920   (F)

Penang race course. Later, in September, it was sold in India.

The L.C.1 number 2 was a single-seater Nighthawk with clipped wings, registered G-EAJY, which made its first flight September 3, 1919, and

participated in two Aerial Derbies. James returned from India in time to fly it in the 1920 race, numbered 10, finishing second at nearly 133 mph, its Dragonfly lasting the distance. In 1921 it was cleaned up with a larger spinner and flown as number 12 by Flight Lieutenant J. Noakes, often called "the crazy flier" for his nerveless antics; he did one lap at almost 143 mph but force-landed due to fuel starvation on the second lap.[1] Later in 1921 it was sold to C. P. B. Ogilvie of 437 High Road, Willesden.

Both L.C.1 racers were named "Nieuhawk" to distinguish them from the military Nighthawk. These were the only two aeroplanes known to be named Nieuhawk, even though a few two-seater Nighthawks, similar to the first Nieuhawk, were built in 1920.

[1] Noakes had been awarded a commission in the Field in 1917. He was a test pilot from 1920–22 and after a period of overseas service he was again appointed to the RAF Experimental Station at Martlesham Heath, where he served until 1928, when he had a very serious accident. By 1930 he was a Squadron Leader, still remembered as the originator of Crazy Flying.

The basic design revealed Folland's foresight inasmuch as it served as an intermediate stage between the rotary-powered "quick" (to maneuver) fighters of World War I and the later, larger radial-powered and V-engine-powered aeroplanes faster in speed but slower in control response. It had visionary features, such as a stabilizer adjustable in flight to maintain trim across its broader speed range — in those days a distinct novelty — but others surprising for their unavailing complexity, such as dihedral built into the center-section outboard of the cabane struts.

Folland's next design was a pure racer, a sturdy, barrel-shaped affair built early in 1920 which retained from the Nighthawk only the distinctive tail with its steerable tailskid and the Dragonfly engine, employing the 340-hp model Ia, a version updated in the futile attempts to cure the engine's ills. The racer was designated L.S.3, an abbreviation for "Land Sporting," and nicknamed Goshawk. The term L.S. never came into general use, and it can only be surmised that what would have been the L.S.1 and L.S.2 were two small designs, never built, both to have had the Bristol Lucifer engine, one a side-by-side two-seater, the other a single-seater. The Goshawk had small, unstaggered wings connected by I-struts (streamlined spruce shafts to which horizontal walnut ends were scarfed and held by narrow aluminum plates secured by hollow rivets, vertically bolted to the wing), and single flying wires. The wing planform for the first time exhibited Folland's racer trademark with the upper wing having round tips while the lower wing was square-tipped. The rationale made sense: the rounded upper wing, with no ailerons, was thus *thin*-tipped, while the squared-off lower wing permitted broad, ample ailerons.

The Goshawk first gained notice on June 17, 1920, when Leslie Tait-Cox put it over the measured kilometer at Martlesham Heath near Ipswich, Suffolk, looking for the world maximum speed record, then 176·03 mph, held

by a French Spad. Failing the supreme prize, he made what the British press exalted as the "British speed record" under FAI class C.4B, achieving officially 166·4 mph, an entirely creditable performance for the radial-engined racer. One month later Tait-Cox flew it in the 1920 Aerial Derby as number 16. Taking off just before 4 P.M., scratch in the handicap, he landed at Brooklands on the first lap with Dragonfly trouble.

Never mind, the prestigious Gordon Bennett classic was coming up in just a couple of months, and the Goshawk could really show its smoke. As Cup day, September 28, approached Tait-Cox fell ill, so his assistant James was substituted. First the racer had to be transported to the race site at Étampes, 30 miles south of Paris, but its owner, an increasingly indifferent Sir Samuel Waring, was too frugal to finance surface transportation, so on Saturday, September 25, James leaped off in the Goshawk from the ancient field at Hendon bound for France by air. He disappeared into a solid, murky overcast, climbing to 6,000 feet at one point, but was gradually forced back down below 400 feet to maintain visual contact with the ground. At this point a flying wire broke, the buzzing wings began to shrivel, and James was forced to make a skidding 180 back to Hendon. The plane was repaired, but race rules required its presence by 7 A.M. the twenty-seventh for "measurement and sealing," making time now critical.

As the twenty-sixth dawned, all southeast England was cloaked in a pea-soup fog. After lunch when at last it seemed to be burning off James again departed. He found Lympne on the Kentish coast where he landed at 4 P.M. to obtain customs clearance, but was then forced to cool his heels for two hours until the proper officer appeared! When the red tape was duly dispensed with it was six-twenty and too dark to fly across to France, so James spent the night at Lympne. The next morning, when in fact he was due

The L.S.3 at Étampes for the 1920 Gordon Bennett — already disqualified; note left tire pulled off rim. And while Jimmie James looks glum, the French mascot offers his own comment on the whole silly business! (Au)

at Etampes to qualify, James finally left England. Unsure of the way, he made nine landings in small French pastures en route to ask directions! Apparently James himself did not understand the rules' finer points because after reaching Le Bourget in one piece he decided to spend the night in Paris. The next morning, Cup day, no doubt still thinking he was in plenty of time, James flew to Étampes, requiring two or three more landings to negotiate the last 30 miles, and pulling a tire off its rim on the last one, but as he rolled to a stop in front of the sheds his smile of greeting was erased by Folland's bitter disappointment that they would not be allowed to compete. For once the temperamental Dragonfly had not skipped a beat. A bit of comic relief was provided by the French journalists, who went wild when someone told them the checkerboard racer was the representative

from Czechoslovakia — and it was thereafter called "the Czech Nieuport!" C. G. Grey likened the fiasco to "spoiling the ship for a ha'p'orth of tar" and Waring's penny-pinching probably cost him the race and several thousand pounds' worth of prize and prestige.

The L.S.3 was entered in the 1921 Aerial Derby, Harry Hawker having been asked to fly it by Waring. But on July 12, four days before the race, an accident occurred in which the racer was demolished and Hawker killed (see Chapter 23). The Goshawk was the last plane built by Nieuport & General, and its demise marked the end of their activity.

The second prewar woodworking firm mentioned earlier, H. H. Martyn, Sunningend Works, Cheltenham, Gloucestershire, had a well-established reputation for excellent carpentry, having long decorated theater and luxury ship interiors and produced memorial statuary. Their first aviation contract, generated by war's voracious appetite, was the production of wooden propellers for Short seaplanes, soon followed by a large order for fuselages from AirCo of Hendon, predecessors of de Havilland, who in December 1914 found themselves short of production space. Expansion of Martyn's aviation work over the next two years was so great that on June 5, 1917, the Gloucestershire Aircraft Company Ltd. was formed separately, capitalized at £10,000 and guided by three men.

David Longden started as an architect from Glasgow but prospered in aviation as a successful opportunist with a lively imagination, enticed to join the firm by A. W. Martyn, who in turn left in September 1927; tied too closely to woodworking origins, he considered later changes to metal aeroplanes premature. The third was Hugh Burroughes, who still sat on the Board fifty years later! (H.B. retired in 1968.) Before war's end GAC had produced 150 de Havilland D.H.6 "Sky Hooks" and 435 complete, Sunbeam Arab-powered Bristol fighters at the not inconsiderable rate of 80 per month. They also landed a huge production order for Nieuport Nighthawks.

The suddenness with which the Armistice converted the feast into famine was stunning. Managing director Longden's change of pace was drastic, clearing the factory, wondering what to do until Martyn's prewar trade could be reestablished, but his wily business acumen prompted him to purchase from the Air Ministry all the Nighthawk bits and pieces which were then stacked in the Cheltenham Winter Gardens in Imperial Square. It was a wise move. In 1920 GAC, a dwarf among giants and still virtually unknown, stubbornly decided to make it purely in aviation, despite the struggle.

A Dragonfly Nighthawk flew at the RAF Pageant, Hendon, July 5, 1920, and while the RAF had lost interest, the Japanese observers were fascinated.

Soon GAC had its first firm order for fifty fighters plus forty spares sold to the Imperial Japanese Navy. These would be Nighthawks made from the parts in storage, but Bentley B.R.2 rotaries replaced the Dragonfly engines. They were named Sparrowhawk I, II, and III depending on minor modifications – and at the same time, confusingly, Mars II, III, and IV respectively in GAC typing – and they started a close association between GAC and Japan that lasted the better part of a decade.

In the United States Billy Mitchell was dismayed by Britain's sale of their fighters and aviation technology to Japan. Apart from the "yellow peril" scare campaign that William Randolph Hearst had started in his tabloids, Mitchell had soberly assessed the ominous prospects of a wide-ranging, air power-dominated war over the Pacific basin; indeed, this preoccupation was the cornerstone of his clarion call for air power improvement in the West. He wrote Major Melvin Hall, U. S. Air Attaché in London, protesting the sale. Colonel the Master of Semphill led the British technical and training team of thirty to Japan as civilians "to avoid making a bad impression on the United States." C. G. Grey shared Mitchell's fears; he was firmly convinced that war between Japan and the Western world must occur and did not mind informing the world of these iconoclastic views in the acerb pages of *The Aeroplane*, beginning as early as 1921 and increasing in tempo and furore.[2]

[2] Grey's predictions included the Germans, whose resourcefulness he greatly admired, fighting side by side with the British and Americans. To the proud Grey it was "the white race" versus "the yellow race" and he made frequent and pointed allusions to white race supremacy. Interestingly, Mitchell considered the yellow races biologically superior to any other in the world, and worked hard to convince skeptics and bigots back home that Japanese *could* learn to fly as well as Anglo-Saxons. During the late 1930s Grey, maintaining his views, was not averse to allowing himself to be feted in Hitler's Germany, and to some he became regarded as a "crank."

Meanwhile, Henry Folland was becoming disenchanted at Nieuport & General, which had lain dormant since August 1920, the Cricklewood factory long since closed down. He was contracted to them for only three days per week to clear up unfinished business, his other time occupied as consulting engineer to GAC, where he was supervising the conversion of his Nighthawk design to Bentley rotary engines for the Japanese. Early in 1921 he was encouraged to begin the design of a new racer. Still working as a consultant, with barely weeks before the 1921 Aerial Derby, Folland started a new speedplane which, as the first wholly GAC aeroplane, was named Mars I and was designed and built in one month's time! This was in part made possible by using Nighthawk components from those in storage (the fuselage and tail were left over from the Japanese contract) and wings larger – but similar – to the Goshawk's. But Folland also used a brilliant new engine which was everything the hated Dragonfly was not in terms of reliability. This was the Napier Lion.

Messrs. D. Napier & Son Ltd. of Acton, London, W.3, was established in 1808 as builders of machinery for printing, coining, and weighing bullion, gaining lasting fame for manufacturing accuracy – and for always being close to where the money was! They built guns for the Crimean War and minting presses used well into the twentieth century. Family scion Montagu Stanley Napier in Victorian days rode a high bicycle (the "old ordinary") along Birmingham Road from Coventry at astonishing speeds, even besting the racing "safeties." In 1899 he allied with S. F. Edge and H. T. Vane of Dunlop Tyre Company to build the first Napier automobile, which proceeded to collect racing trophies with monotonous regularity. During the early days of the twentieth century, when Folland was serving a four-years' apprenticeship as draftsman with Lanchester Motor Company and Daimler's at Coventry,

Montagu S. Napier (F)

Napier's great cars remained unsurpassed in the number of trophies they won. Napier built the first successful six-cylinder car and a Napier was the first to exceed 60 mph for twenty-four hours on end.

Napier has been variously credited with pioneering the idea of the cast monobloc engine. Certainly one of the earliest such engines was indeed built by Napier for the 1901 Gordon Bennett race (the Coupe Internationale). It was a 700-pound brute with four cavernous cylinders (6·5″ × 7·5″ bore/stroke) whose water jackets, crank chamber, and cylinders were all cast in aluminum, the cylinders fitted with cast-iron liners. Too heavy and powerful for the 1901 auto, the idea was abandoned until 1904 when a four-cylinder racing Napier was built especially for Mayhew, again

329

Arthur J. Rowledge, circa 1922 (F)

with a cast aluminum block and cast iron cylinder liners (6·5″ × 6·0″ bore/stroke) which had to be inserted under hydraulic pressure. In 1905 a detachable cylinder head was adopted but in 1906 the whole development was dropped with a thud. Neither Napier nor anyone else could get these early block engines to work well. It was almost ten years until Birkigt's Hispano-Suiza monobloc appeared with the one characteristic that distinguished it from its predecessors: it *worked*; thus it became the standard to be emulated, copied, and modified.

When World War I opened Napier was subcontracted to build aero equipment designed by the Royal Aircraft Factory. Vane soon decided they should do something on their own, so in 1916 when the government issued a specification for a "high-power altitude engine," the Lion, Napier's first aero engine, was conceived. It was designed by Arthur John Rowledge, who had designed a number of beautiful Napier autos. His engine would be water-cooled, a compact high-compression unit. Reliability was paramount; the engine could not be high-

strung. In view of its task, frontal area was of minor importance, so the twelve cylinders were arranged in broad arrow-fashion, allowing rigid construction and a short, stiff crankshaft. Though not the best for streamlining, the Lion could be close-cowled and fitted with a large spinner. The press of war forced designs that could be built without special tools, yet under Rowledge's meticulous guidance the Lion's cylinder head was made to attach metal to metal (no gaskets!).

Rowledge did not insist on innovation, and while he adopted the brilliant Hispano-Suiza style of aluminum monobloc castings for his cylinder groups, he applied it to the heads only, leaving the steel cylinder barrels separately fixed to the cast aluminum crankcase for rigidity, each having its own steel cooling water jacket Mercedes-style. Two overhead camshafts per block actuated four valves per cylinder. There was concern whether the W-12 was even a feasible arrangement since secondary forces are unbalanced, both in a group of four in-line cylinders and in a three-row arrangement. Moreover, Napier's four-throw crankshaft required a complex arrangement of three connecting rods per single crank-pin. Rowledge used for the center-row pistons an I-section master rod with lugs to which articulated, tubular rods from the outer-row pistons were attached, unequalizing the stroke. But the Lion's dynamic balance proved superb, and it purred like a kitten in velvet. The carburetor intakes appeared as pipes low down on the side, placed so as to eliminate any fire hazard from backfires. Two intake pipes fed a Claudel-Hobson N.S.2 for the center and left banks, and one pipe on the other side went to an N.S.1 for the right bank only. Water jackets surrounded the throttle barrels to keep them from freezing at high altitude.

Reduction gear was included from the engine's inception and gave surprisingly carefree service, especially at a time when reduction gears were

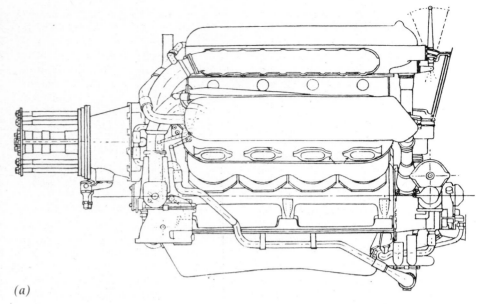

(a)

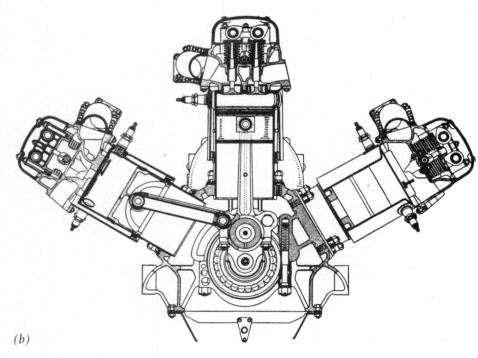

(b)

The Napier Lion engine, one of the most important types throughout the 1920s: (a) side; (b) cross section through end showing the W or "broad-arrow" configuration.

particularly onerous. The first Lion was produced well before war's end, but its first public appearance was not until January 2, 1919. On that day an AirCo D.H.9 (C.6078) piloted by Captain Andrew Lang, RAF, with Lieutenant A. W. Blowes, nineteen, took off from Martlesham Heath shortly before noon in a stiff gale and in 1:07 reached an indicated 30,500 feet (corrected to 27,350 feet) 25 miles at sea off Yarmouth, an unofficial altitude record. Blowes collapsed from hypoxia and both men suffered frozen hands and feet[3] and insult was added to

[3] Two objectives of the test were to evaluate the Lion's induction system under conditions of extreme cold, as well as the fliers' new clothing, called "Sidcots" after their innovator, Flight Lieutenant Sidney Cotton, who determined that heated mechanics' overalls, while not photogenic, were more practical than the long leather jackets then in vogue.

injury when the excited Lang was placed under open arrest for making a "public disclosure" of the feat after landing! Shortly thereafter the 1919 Aerial Derby was won at 130 mph by an AirCo D.H.4R fitted with the race's only Lion as thousands watched. At the 1919 Schneider, Lions in the Fairey and Supermarine flying boats were producing approximately 500 hp and the version Folland used in his 1921 Mars I racer (the Lion II) delivered 531 hp on the dynamometer in a government test, burning a mixture of 30 per cent benzole at 32 gallons per hour.

After the war Montagu Napier, old and ill and like Henry Royce living in the south of France, closed down Napier's entire auto production, pinning his complete faith on the aero engine industry in which he was then top dog. H. T. Vane was Board chairman, and by 1923 the Lion was

probably the best all-around European aero engine, plying the early civil airline routes by the hundreds. One Lion flew 1,700 hours in cross-Channel passenger service, getting 200 hours between overhauls, in those days truly astounding. But designer Rowledge had resigned in 1921 to join Rolls-Royce, where he remained until 1945; ironically, his signature was engraved in the Kestrel and Merlin engines, the Lion's later rivals. The Lion came under the responsibility of George Shakespeare Wilkinson, but Napier's 1921 profit was £79,098 — Lions sold for £2,400, a surfeit of orders had caused a six-month delivery delay — and coasting on the wave of success, taking for granted their fat dividends, Napier neglected the persevering R&D program needed for an eventual replacement.

The Lion itself grew: by the end of 1924 the tidal wave caused by the Curtiss D-12 splash had washed over engine blueprints around the world and the Lion was modified to have its carburetors relocated to the rear, its magnetos to the front, and its propeller gearing eliminated. The first direct-drive version, called Lion VI, appeared

in military trim, while the direct-drive racing Lion VII was built to capture the Schneider Trophy in 1925. In 1927 the Lion VII-A could deliver 875 hp for a full three hours, and the Lion's most revered moment of glory came when a geared VII-B — equipped Supermarine brought the "hat rack" back to the Royal Aero Club that year after all the Italian engines blew up, proving reliability was a key factor. Charles Fairey had said years before the Lion was "excellent except for that one fundamental law of frontal area," so the VII-B had been cleaned up, having 34 per cent less frontal area than the first Lions. The Lion delivered the highest thermal efficiency ever recorded by Ricardo: a specific fuel consumption of ·32 lb./bhp./hr., a tribute to its high mechanical efficiency — it ran on ball and roller bearings and used no supercharger which diminishes mechanical efficiency. In 1929, after a supercharger was added, the Lion VII-D was pushed to an incredible 1,320 hp, but problems arose and the supercharged Lion in the 1929 Gloster VI racer was dubbed a "catastrophe" by Air Commodore Rod Banks. The Lion's demise

Napier Lions under construction, circa 1923, when the Lion ruled European air lanes   (F)

Brand-new Bamel at Hendon for the 1921 Aerial Derby   (F)

came around 1930 when Napier backed away from the evolutionary monobloc idea, troubled by cracks in the overstressed aluminum castings. Then, with sales disappearing and desperate, their next engines were more audacious than the monobloc had ever been. Nevertheless, Lions were powering PT boats in World War II, and in its final achievement of note, as though some return to the automobile were predestined, a Lion powered John Cobb's Railton Mobil Special in 1947 to push the world land speed record above 400 mph!

In 1921, to squeeze the Lion II into his racer's small dimensions, Folland maintained balance but sacrificed visibility by mounting the fuel tank behind a finned water header tank, both inside a humplike cabane compartment supporting the upper wing. Double bracing wires — called "Rafwires" — anchored the rear spar since the center of pressure placed a greater load on the rear truss at high speeds. The I-struts, built of spruce and attached to a mortice joint which had walnut feet spreading fore and aft to meet the ash main spars, were still considered risky by some. Multi-ply bulkheads supported ash engine bearers, braced by a diagonal steel-tube framework. The prop with its integral spinner was designed especially by H. C. Watts of Ogilvie Partners. The spruce V-chassis was straight Nighthawk except for aluminum casings over the shock cords. Despite its blocky planform the racer turned out "quite fetching" at a time when the pretty aeroplanes mostly came from France.

Two stories purport to relate how the racer got her name — Bamel. In one version Folland was lunching with some journalists some six weeks before the Derby when the racer was still on paper. The group recalled nostalgically the imaginary hybrid animals so faddish among servicemen during the war. With its cabane hump and sturdy lines, the racer appeared "a cross between a bear and camel" — hence the Bamel. This account seems most likely and was even reported in *The Aeroplane*, but a second version has Folland and Hugh Burroughes at the factory to inspect the racer, then under construction. With her hump completed but rear fuselage as yet uncovered, Burroughes is said to have remarked how she was "half bare, half camel!" In any event Leonard Bridgman later painted the insignia — Jimmie James riding the hybrid animal — on her flanks.[4] But there was insufficient time before the 1921 Aerial Derby. Bamel was barely completed.

Just four weeks after her design began, the completed Bamel was trucked from Sunningend to Hucclecote — the crew making the regulation stop at Oddfellow's Inn, Shurdington, halfway — and she made her first flight June 20, 1921, from the famous flying field which was bisected by the parish line between Hucclecote and Brockworth where GAC had already rented number 2 shed. Bamel's testing was among the earliest flying at this location (the duality of township explains the later discrepancy between Gloster's Hucclecote postal address and references to Brockworth Aerodrome). Just four days before the Derby the racer suffered bad damage to the rear fuselage, tailskid, and rudder after Jimmie James, her pilot, made a hard landing. Repairs were not completed until the afternoon before race day.

Bamel became scratch in the Derby handicap upon withdrawal of France's Nieuport 29V. Hendon's rough surface was baked hard as a brick by the hot July sun. In the sheds both Bamel and Nieuhawk were dismantled, Noakes on his motorcycle whizzing between Hendon and de Havilland's facilities at Stag Lane trying to fix a locknut for his propeller boss. Bamel's aluminum carburetor intake pipes had cracked on her ferry flight to Hendon that morning. Working to hasty scribblings by Folland, de Havilland technicians made new pipes of steel with neatly welded flanges, and they too were rushed by motorcycle from Stag Lane with only ten minutes to spare prior to her starting time! She took off to race a few seconds after 4:43 P.M. — "James's outfit rather resembled a howitzer shell," said a witness. For the first lap bookies offered 2:1 against but quickly realized they were giving money away and changed the odds. James finished the two laps in record time even though throttled back because the hand-wound, retractable box radiator was too small to cool the Lion at full throttle. He won £600, first prizes for both speed and handicap. Noakes's Nieuhawk, which had the handicap prize in the bag, ran out of gas within sight of the finish line! Bamel's double triumph was a great boost to Folland's prestige. He was hailed as "king of the racing aircraft designers" by the press, and overnight the surprise, last-minute Bamel catapulted GAC into the big time.

After the race Folland severed connections with the now defunct Nieuport & General concern, took his first holiday since before the war, and in August 1921 was installed as chief engineer at GAC. His able number two, Joe Preston, as well as the brothers G. and T. E. Gibson, followed him into the new firm. Aviators Tait-Cox and James had left Nieuport & General in February 1921 to form a partnership for free-lance test-flying. This did not fare so Tait-Cox joined Jack Savage's Sky-Writing outfit, later moving to British Oil & Turpentine Company, and James alone came to GAC as the firm's first chief test pilot shortly thereafter. His first big job was Bamel.

At this point in time Folland was

Jimmie James in the Bamel's cockpit; note Leonard Bridgman's rendition of the hybrid bear-camel — the "Bamel" — painted on the fuselage. (MA)

[4] Records dating to 1911, a year when Folland's interest in aviation was flowering, indicate a particularly fond regard he had for a Reverend Bammel, but no survivors today can attest to the significance of this person to his life. On the other hand, the Manchester *Guardian* of July 12, 1921, suggested the racer be called "Flying Pig" because of its snub nose.

From left to right: A. W. Martyn, managing director, GAC; James H. James, pilot; David Longden, managing director, GAC; H. P. Folland, chief engineer, GAC; 1921

(Henri Beaubois)

engaged in one of the few innovative achievements of his career, the perfection of new biplane airfoils to enhance speed. He combined a thick, high-lift section for the upper wing with a medium-lift, convex (Philips entry) lower wing whose drag should "virtually disappear" in cruise flight, the object being to enjoy biplane advantages for short takeoffs and landings but approximate monoplane efficiency at high speed. The design was refined by tapering the thickness of the top wing over the outboard 20 per cent of the span and in the center, in the region of prop slipstream. The aileron chord also increased toward the tips to enhance control. Another advantage claimed was that of small net c.p. travel so that very short fuselages could be fitted allowing nimble maneuverability, as on the Grebe fighter of 1924. Folland's scheme was eventually patented (225257)

and named the HLB (High Lift Biplane) wing; the earliest precursors of the final form first appeared on the Bamel at her subsequent races. On March 31, 1922, Folland read a momentous paper on aeroplane design to the Institute of Aeronautical Engineers (later incorporated into the Royal Aeronautical Society) which was one of the first academic attempts to formalize the entire aeroplane design process; to organize the aeroplane's requirements, to use statistically based design data, a visionary idea in a day when the fund of experience was meager, and to accord to detail design its often unappreciated importance. This paper was remembered long afterward as a "lamp lighting the way," a precursor of methods used today.

A few weeks later Folland's Mars III "Sprawk" G-EAYN was flown by Tait-Cox in the 1922 Aerial Derby as

number 7. This was really a two-seater Nighthawk equipped with a Bentley B.R.2 rotary and S.E.5 tail, and did the first lap at 103 mph before retiring. It later gained importance as the Grouse I fighter in 1923, fitted with Folland's latest HLB.1 (upper) and HLB.2 (lower) airfoils, before being sold in Sweden. Folland by then was already experimenting with wing sections similar to those used on the 260-mph Curtiss R2C racers that caused such a stir at St. Louis in 1923. Even though his later Gloster Schneider racers benefited from this research, Folland refrained from other advances even as the world turned, relying on essentially World War I construction practices. He did not believe in welding; the bits of press-plate metal in his structures were joined by tubular, unthreaded rivets and dip-brazing. Yet by 1924 when GAC began transferring completely to Brockworth Aerodrome they were considered in the first rank of British fighter constructors. And three years of success by one racer — the Bamel — had a lot to do with it.

The Bamel was the only British racer ever to compete for the Coupe Deutsch. In 1921, less than three months after the Derby, she went to

France "by post to avoid the Goshawk problems." Her new wings with 20 square feet lopped off made the originals "look like a touring set." By Friday, one day before the race, they were rigged and James was aloft to wring her out, noting a 10-mph speed gain. Late that night her box radiator was exchanged for Lamblin lobster pots — two new ones, sized for the Renault 300-hp engine. Two fitted in England had leaked so had been left behind. Her full-throttle runup was spectacular with the huge prop disc glistening in the back-lit darkness and blue exhaust fire streaming along the fuselage. Wide open her water temperature was now a comfortable 63° Centigrade. C. F. Woodgate was crew boss; Percy Turner and W. Trenhaile (GAC) and Reggie Smith of Napier were there.

Next morning as French racers scurried James was in no hurry. After lunch he made ready and at three-forty took off to begin the three required laps, but just as he reached the Gidy pylon on the first circuit he was shocked to see the fabric on the underside of the left upper wing bulging downward from one rib. Fascinated, he forgot to turn until he crossed the rail-

Bamel in her shed at Étampes being readied for the 1921 Coupe Deutsch de la Meurthe race

(Au)

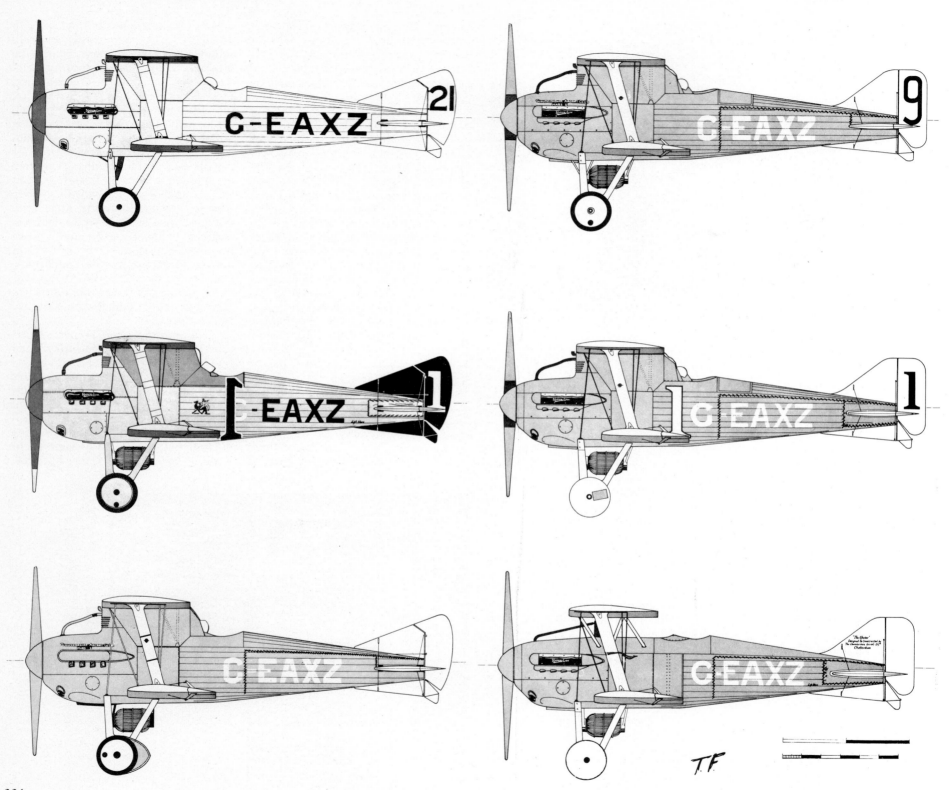

334

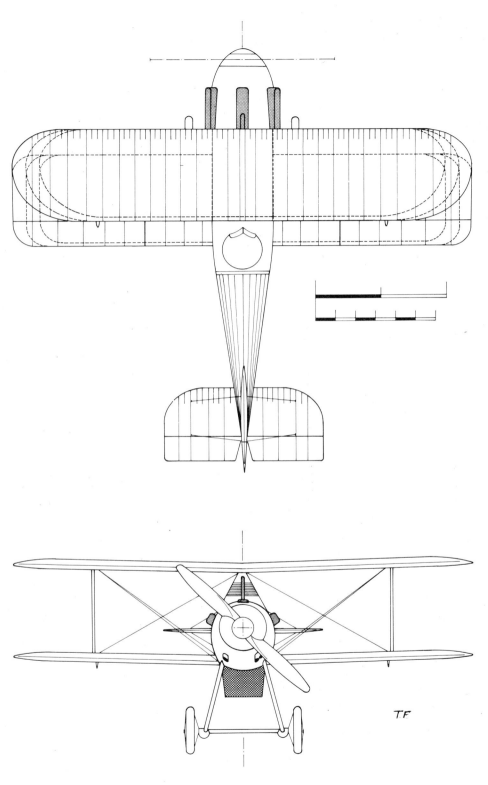

road 2 miles southwest, thus losing a minute on lap one. But he continued, banking vertically to start lap two, "the Lion pulling splendidly." Halfway to Gidy in four and a half minutes he noticed the fabric now bulging from one rib on the right side and to his horror four on the left — and his overactive imagination conjured an alarming picture of the unseen wing upper surface. Still fresh in his mind were accounts of shed fabric on the Coupe Deutsch racer in which Count de Romanet was killed just days before. James gave up at once and cautiously returned to land.

Back in the shed the taut fabric gave no hint of weakness but Folland, in his inevitable Homburg, wing collar, and spats, clumped over and jabbed a penknife between fabric and ribs confirming that something had indeed burst the stitching, luckily on just the ribs James observed. Folland, who probably had only the haziest ideas of the true nature of wing flutter, expressed the view that the cause was "pulsating suction" from the huge prop. The new Titanine dope was credited with keeping the fabric intact, being superior to the Emaillite silver "scheme X" used originally.[5] Even so, the failure was a blow to the GAC pride — and a preview of unsolved flutter problems that would recur in later GAC aeroplanes.

[5] Acetyl-cellulose dope covered by transparent oil varnish.

Gloucestershire Mars 1 Bamel and variants. Side views, reading down: original version, winner 1921 Aerial Derby (July); entry, 1921 Coupe Deutsch (October); holder, British speed record (December 1921); winner, 1922 Aerial Derby (August); entry, 1922 Coupe Deutsch (September) and winner RAeC Certificate of Performance (November 1922); winner, 1923 Aerial Derby as the Gloster I (after extensive modification). Plan and front views show Bamel, 1921–22; original wings (solid line); dotted lines show progressive reductions in wing size.

The Bamel was brought back to Cheltenham and with no immediate deadlines, carefully cleaned up. She had been, in Folland's words, "a very rough job" before. New wings were fitted, again 20 square feet smaller, with 2½-inch shorter chord, still retaining the round upper tip/square lower tip planform. At this point, to prevent a recurrence of the Coupe Deutsch embarrassment, Folland developed the GAC method, later patented, of first wrapping the wing ribs with fabric to which the outer fabric covering was then sewed directly. By early December she was put on view at Cricklewood (the old Nieuport & General works), where her new sheet metal fairings — on I-strut corners, over the cylinder heads, and behind the tires with only a ¼-inch gap — were marveled at, then on December 12 she flew to Martlesham Heath to seek the world speed record and vindicate the soundness of her construction.

On Monday morning, December 19, over the official RAF measured course and into a bitter 8-knot WSW wind James rocketed the Bamel four times. His average was electrically timed at 196·6 mph (the world's record then was 205·22 mph, held by the French twin to the recent Coupe Deutsch winner) but James's fastest pass of 212 mph led the press to comment that for the first time in history "Britain had built the world's fastest aeroplane." This was close to the truth, but lacking FAI homologation it was at best another "British speed record." In February 1922 Bamel was displayed at Croydon's famous Waddon Aerodrome, still with her Nighthawk tail.

Croydon was the site for the 1922 Aerial Derby on August Bank Holiday. Bamel had been further modified, adopting a new tail reminiscent of the S.E.5. James was back to post Bamel's second decisive win, doing Hertford–West Thurrock once under threatening skies at 246 mph before a stiff northwest wind. There was a tense moment after the race when he made a hot landing — he said later his "fastest

Bamel taking off to win the 1922 Aerial Derby
(F)

ever" – floated, bumped on, and skittered toward the crowds lining Plough Lane. Wrenching the Bamel into a violent ground-loop he avoided the crowds and was lucky only to burst the left tire. The Derby success led to an all-out effort for the Coupe Deutsch two months later.

She was fitted with yet another set of wings said to be the smallest of her career although the exact area is unknown. Presumably slightly less than the 165 square feet of the Derby wings, no reliable GAC records exist – GAC veterans recall 160 square feet – but the French, who examined all Coupe Deutsch entries, reported the area to be 15·14 square meters, which equates to 163 square feet. Such confusion is typical in many aspects of specific detail and is why only the most intrepid would dare report half-century–old details as incontrovertible. Often racing planes were altered within hours – even minutes – of race time, modified by eye, especially when under the care of a superb designer such as Folland who had an intuitive communion with his racers; no drawings were needed and no records survive.

Slick and glossy, her Lion snorting evenly at the top of its voice, the Bamel arrived on the French starting line under glorious skies. Then occurred probably the most incredible bungle of air racing history. James had his map glued to a piece of plywood board which hung on a string around his neck. But on the first lap this board suddenly blew out of the open cockpit! With a jerk on his neck James found himself being strangled by the wire-like string. Luckily he had a penknife and was able to cut the map free, but there he was, in one of the fastest and most expensive racers in Europe, snarling aimlessly over the country-side, too lost even to return to Étampes and quit!

It was just too humiliating for Folland, who still remembered all too well his impetuous Welsh pilot's fiasco two years before in the "Czech Nieu-port." The maddening part was that all other competitors save one were rendered *hors de combat* and the Bamel could have walked over, an easy winner. The next day, in a lame attempt to exculpate himself, James flew one lap of the course at a rate faster than any other racer there. But it was a moot performance and pointless: the Coupe Henry Deutsch had been won by Nieuport and retired forever. Even as James charged over

Bamel at Étampes for the 1922 Coupe Deutsch race   *(F)*

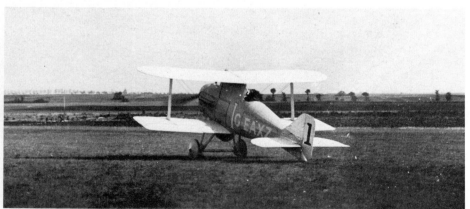

Jimmie James taxiing the Bamel across Ville-sauvage Aerodrome to start his comic-opera performance in the 1922 Coupe Deutsch race
(F)

Bamel at Étampes, October 1922   *(F)*

the course Folland was thinking how to make the Bamel faster. He became convinced then that they should get rid of the hump.

On October 3, still trying to salvage something, James made three unsuccessful attempts on the world speed record. On October 4 he made yet another and actually exceeded the standing record, then 341·239 kmh, set only thirteen days before by the French. James's four runs were timed at 10·8, 9·8, 11·4, and 10·2 seconds for the kilometer, which the FAI, by erroneously averaging the times in pairs, translated to 341·423 kmh. Had they averaged the four individual speeds (the mathematically correct method), James's performance would have been 342·352 kmh — after making the rather charitable assumption, of course, that hand-held watches were accurate enough to record speeds to three decimal places! Even if corrected, his speed exceeded the standing record by only slightly more than 1 kmh, not enough under the rules, which required 4 kmh

difference to be homologated. But it was another British speed record which stood until 1925; and in any event, two weeks later the Curtiss R-6 shattered all European records by a good margin.

After the 1922 Coupe Deutsch James went to Salonika, Greece, to test a large batch of Mars VI fighters which were simply Nighthawks equipped with another notorious air-cooled radial, the complex and fire-prone 325-hp Siddeley Jaguar II. Twenty-five were delivered to the Greek Air Force as the result of the second large foreign sale (in addition to the Japanese) that sustained GAC; the Greek fighters were built from the old bits and pieces in storage and delivered in less than three months. A few Mars VIs, some with the far better Bristol Jupiter I-Mark III engine, also went to RAF No. 1 Squadron serving in Mesopotamia (later Iraq) in 1923. The old Nighthawk was rapidly approaching obsolescence but GAC still sold it aggressively. The last version was the Mars X, called Nightjar; twenty-two with out-

dated Bentley rotaries went to the Royal Navy for carrier duty and saw service in the 1923 Chanak crisis with fleet squadrons 203 and 401.

James's flamboyant but careless brand of flying had frustrated Folland quite enough. He was fired, his contract terminated April 1, 1923, and was replaced by a man remembered as "lacking a certain flair," but certainly this was more suitable to Folland's stable nature. This new chief test pilot was Larry L. Carter, schooled on the Western Front, 1922 Aerial Derby handicap winner in a Bristol monoplane, and otherwise airline pilot on Handley Page W.8s. The Grouse with HLB wings had generated such enthusiasm that a whopping 129 more were ordered for the RAF, a tremendous shot in the arm for GAC, and one of Carter's first jobs was to show off the new birds, called Grebe. He flew a civil demonstrator G-EBHA (385-hp Jaguar III-A) as scratch in the 794-mile King's Cup race in mid-July 1923, and despite the stiff handicap he was in second place approaching Manchester. Then a landing wire parted, forcing him out.

As for James, in November 1923 he joined Smith Aero Instruments, then located at Cricklewood in the old

Nieuport & General works, and famous for pioneering black dials with white numerals, standard throughout the world today. Although James later had to give up flying, becoming medically unfit for the commercial B license, he returned to active duty in 1941 as an RAF Link Trainer instructor, but early in 1944, when only forty-nine, little Jimmie James suddenly died.

In November 1922 the Bamel — or Mars I officially — was back at Martlesham Heath for more performance tests with her slightly larger (Aerial Derby) wings refitted. She was flown by Flight Lieutenant Rollo de Haga Haig and received a Royal Aero Club Certificate of Performance for some fabulous climbs, thundering uphill initially at something approaching 3,500 feet per minute. Rate of climb at 5,000 feet was an impressive 2,390 fpm, and at 19,500 feet it was still 854 fpm.

During spring 1923 Folland prepared the Bamel for her third Aerial Derby, scheduled again for Bank Holiday. Incentive was provided by an Air Ministry offer made in May to purchase the Derby winner, less engine, for £3,000, despite a haggle over the price. The Bamel was stripped right

Gloster I taking off from Croydon to win the 1923 Aerial Derby   *(F)*

Larry L. Carter standing by Gloster I after
winning the 1923 Aerial Derby   (F)

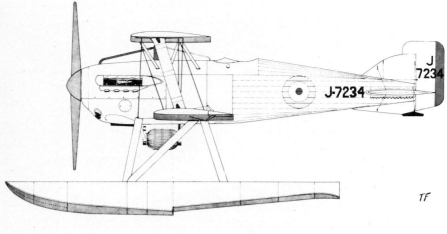

Gloster I seaplane after transfer to the RAF in
December 1923 for Schneider Trophy race
practice and test; served as second reserve on
British Schneider team, 1925.

down and thoroughly rebuilt. Folland
installed a newer, souped-up Lion
of well over 500 hp and did in fact
remove her distinctive hump, placing
the fuel tank inside the fuselage. Her
wings were essentially those of the
1922 Coupe Deutsch but with all new
ribs using updated Folland airfoils.
The racer would now be called Gloster I.
Carter called her "Bamel-I-beg-your-
pardon-Gloster" and Folland himself
was "a bit puzzled" as to where Bamel
left off and Gloster began.

Summer had been cruel to Gloucestershire County, where a volcanic
epidemic of smallpox raged, so when
Carter flew the Gloster I down to
Croydon for the August race she
streamed a red ribbon from her strut,
the west country's mark signifying
exposure. In just over an hour's flying
she won her third consecutive Aerial
Derby, gleaning the meager prize of
£100. Upon landing Carter was drenched with oil from a leaking pipe but
the faithful Lion had come through
beautifully. The following July, because

of insufficient prize money and lack
of competition for Gloster I, the Aerial
Derby was canceled. It was never run
again.

The RAF assigned the number
J.7234 to the aging hot rod, which
by then was 50 mph slower than the
latest U.S. Curtiss racers. Back at
Martlesham Rollo de Haga Haig put
her through more climbing trials and
in one he reached 20,000 feet in
just :12:24. After the Aerial Derby was
abandoned in 1924 there was a flurry
of effort to get Gloster I to the 1924
Coupe Beaumont in France. Plans
included fitting a new 600-hp Lion
engine and wing radiators, but she
had to be withdrawn when Folland's
radiators developed the same growing
pains Curtiss had experienced two
years before. After this, Gloster I was
put to work testing floats for Schneider
racers, operating from Harwich Harbor,
Felixstowe. After he stole a hop in her,
A. H. Orlebar remarked, "She's a
nice little thing but a bit fierce!"

Based on the Bamel's splendid

Gloster II which sank in September 1924 on
its first flight   (Au)

success GAC was invited by the Air
Ministry by means of Specification
37/23 to build two speedplanes for
the Schneider Trophy and world speed
record trials. These were the ill-starred

Gloster II racers, the seaplane J.7504
and later the landplane J.7505 (G-
EBJZ) Bluebird, each to be powered
by a Lion V, versions of which were
exceeding 600 hp on bench tests,

turning a fairey Reed sheet metal propeller, and each costing the Air Ministry £3,000. On September 12, 1924, the first Gloster II was trucked from Cheltenham to Felixstowe to be hurriedly groomed for the Schneider race, scheduled for October in Baltimore. One week later, on Friday evening, September 19, Hubert Stanford Broad, test pilot loaned to Folland by de Havilland, climbed aboard to make the first flight. All went well until his landing in Harwich Harbor when the racer suddenly porpoised and sank. The fault was laid to the breaking of a fitting at the top of the forward port float strut due to a "flaw in the metal." Broad credited his quick escape to *not* having worn a seat belt! It was too late to prepare a replacement so the Americans sportingly postponed the race.

The second Gloster II was made into a landplane to test metal props, wing radiators, and hopefully to compete in the 1925 Pulitzer; but first it would attack the world speed record. Then tragedy struck. On June 11, 1925, as Larry Carter was making his fourth flight in the Bluebird, plunging over the measured course at Cranwell, Lincs, 633-hp Lion screeching all out, doing over 250 mph no more than 40 feet high, the tail flutter started. Carter chopped the gun but the violently pitching plane plowed

into the ground at something over 200 mph, leaving an eruption of dust and exploding pieces for 150 yards. The metal prop, having contacted the ground vertically, bent backward and acted as a slide, preventing the aeroplane from overturning. Carter was gently lifted from the demolished racer and rushed to the RAF hospital with a fractured skull, broken leg, and other injuries. At first he made good progress although Folland could not bear to speak of aviation with him, but then he contracted meningitis and on September 27, 1926, at age twenty-eight, Larry Carter died.

The postponed Schneider was rescheduled in October 1925 with the same venue. Seven months before the race the Air Ministry placed orders for new seaplane racers with Supermarine and GAC, on the same basis as the orders of 1924, namely, the planes would be loaned to the constructors for racing provided a specified minimum performance was achieved; all flying was to be done at Air Ministry risk. This last stipulation caused an almost comic shroud of exaggerated secrecy to descend around the racers. GAC built two Gloster III aeroplanes which cost the Air Ministry a total of £16,000, from funds originally allocated for experimental RAF purposes.

While R. J. Mitchell of Supermarine abandoned the biplane form forever in

Gloster III with original tail, 1925   (F)

1925, Folland, stung by the failures of his Gloster II racers, was deeply immersed in making the biplane form even more robust and suitable for the rigors of high-speed maritime flying. Indeed, after the Gloster II failures no one realized more than Folland that British aircraftsmen had a lot to learn about high-speed flight, but he chose to improve traditional forms rather than try to tame the radical. The new Gloster IIIs would be the smallest planes for their power built in England until that time, and for Folland that was radical enough. Each had a sturdy wood monocoque fuselage with three-ply skin over light ash formers. Wood wings with fabric covering applied in the manner of the GAC patent were used. Folland now built his airfoils exceedingly thin with impunity, not only because the biplane bracing made the whole structure strong, but to accommodate skin radiators which were still under development. Again construction problems delayed their readiness. Folland's reaction was decisive — and typical. There was no time to muddle about with wing radiators, he ordered. They had only got the first one right a fortnight before. The bulky rectangular

Lamblins — now attached to the lower wing leading edge — were good and reliable, and they would remain even if a blemish on the plane's appearance — and performance. When the Gloster III first appeared it had the S.E.5-style fin and rudder as used on Glosters I and II, its tailplane braced with two round wires on each side!

Gloster I, still fondly called Bamel, was relegated to training duties. Bert Hinkler, the compact Australian loaned by A. V. Roe to the team as reserve pilot, had his first real taste of high-powered flight on September 13, 1925, in the Bamel to determine his g tolerance, and Hubert Broad, again loaned by de Havilland, did much testing of Gloster III pontoons with her, beginning in May. A contributing factor in his previous year's mishap on Gloster II had been the poorly designed May, Harden, & May[6] pontoons on which the step was too far aft, so for Gloster III Short Brothers fashioned improved pontoons from duralumin; each pair weighed just 368 pounds. First tested on the Bamel, one pontoon was merely bent in a mishap which would have stove in wood; Felixstowe records

[6] A de Havilland subsidiary.

Remains of Gloster II Bluebird after its crash, July 1925   (Au)

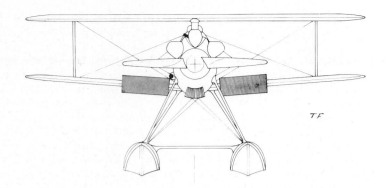

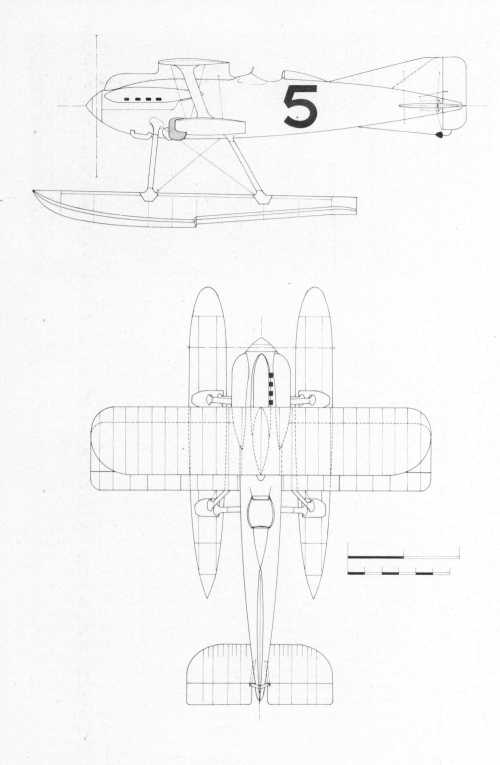

Gloster III-A, 1925 (original Gloster III tail denoted by dotted line).

also indicate the metal pontoons added 3 mph to the Bamel's speed compared with wood. The older she got the faster she went, and by 1925 she was jogging along at a steady 200 mph.

Gloster III taxi trials began at Felixstowe on August 16, 1925, in spite of inclement weather, and took twelve days to complete. Then on August 29 Hubert Broad made the first flight in N.194. To his dismay the racer's directional stability was poor and upon landing Broad's urgent recommendation was to increase the dihedral of both upper and lower wings. But there was insufficient time to undertake such a major structural change; instead both racers were quickly fitted with new ventral and dorsal fins vastly increased in area. With the new fins installed both racers became Gloster III-A. By mid-September the Air Ministry was satisfied with their performance even if the test pilot still had misgivings. Unfortunately the bad weather had persisted, keeping Hinkler grounded and limiting Broad to only four flights amounting to less than two hours total time. Indeed, Broad had managed to open the throttle wide for just five minutes!

Amid the confusing claims and guesses generated by the often fatuous secrecy imposed by the RAeC Schneider Trophy Committee, the Gloster III-A was finally displayed publicly for the first time on Friday, September 18. Members of the press gathered at London's Liverpool Street Station ("Loop 'ole Street" to the cabbies then) with Dave Longden, Harry Vane, and Hugh Burroughes for an hour's train ride to Ipswich, and from there by bus to Felixstowe, passing within 3 miles of Martlesham Heath. At the Seaplane Experimental Station metal sheds they were met by Folland and Hinkler. Inside, the first Gloster III-A was already dismantled for packing, but on the seaward side there stood the second racer on its dolly, glistening blue and white in the sun, being prepared for a test flight that afternoon. The first impression was one of incredibly small size, especially alongside the Bamel; fuselage narrowness was particularly evident. Before shipment both racers received new Mark VII Lions capable of 700 hp.

By a curious — indeed, appalling — mistake the RAeC had only entered two racers, one Gloster III-A and the one Supermarine S.4, presumably because these two types represented the original Air Ministry order. Therefore, even though both Gloster III-As would go to the United States together with the S.4, making a complete team of three, plus the Bamel as reserve, only two planes could race! On September 26, under Captain Charles B. Wilson, who had replaced Lord Edward Grosvenor as leader, the British team sailed aboard SS *Minnewaska*, dubbed "many whiskey", an allusion America was able to absorb without prejudice, being — for the record — officially dry! During the voyage Folland relieved the anxiety by dressing up as a sailor for a ship's dance. His costume was

Hubert Broad's Gloster III-A, second in the 1925 Schneider Trophy race (Au)

Hubert S. Broad (F)

so convincing that he was hauled by the chief steward before the captain, who, to Folland's glee, bawled him out for being found in the passengers' quarters! On arrival at Bay Shore Park, near Baltimore, Maryland, the crated racers were housed in tent hangars of such dubious and leaky construction that despite over two weeks of virtual inactivity before race day the alternate machines were never assembled. This proved to be a grave tactical error.

Hubert Broad, small and youthful, was anxious to fledge his race mount more fully. It would not be his first flying in the United States. He had "taken his ticket" in 1915, joined the RNAS at Dunkirk, and later flew Sopwith Camels in No. 46 Squadron, RAF, scoring six kills, and being wounded over Cambrai. He flew a year for Avro, then flew briefly as a stunt pilot in the United States with Welsh Aviation Company, a barnstorming group. After his return to England, Broad in 1920 joined de Havilland as a test pilot, where he remained. His first flight at Baltimore in the Gloster III-A was a fifteen-minute test on October 13, but the mediocre weather and facilities coupled with British attempts at secrecy prevented him from adding to his meager full-throttle experience.

Schneider preliminary trials began October 23. Broad's white Gloster with its rakish fin and large blue 5 took off at 9:32 A.M., fifteen minutes ahead of Biard's S.4. When Biard crashed, Broad, having just completed his navigability trials, was first to reach him. The crash, however, meant that the second Gloster III-A had to be rushed into service. According to the rules its navigability test had to be completed that day — but the plane had not yet been unpacked! Nevertheless, after an incredible flurry of activity, Hinkler by 5 P.M. was taxiing out in it, thrilled to be in the race. With less than one half hour logged in his high-strung charger, he took off nicely, but a hastily rigged wing bracing wire broke, forcing

him to return. Repairs were soon completed but the late October dusk was already gathering rapidly. Hinkler was ready to try again but team leader Wilson ordered the attempt stopped.

Bert Hinkler, who flew the reserve Gloster III-A in the 1925 Schneider Trophy preliminaries (F)

Just when it seemed to Hinkler that he was out of the race a sporting request to waive the rules and allow his navigability trial the next morning (race day) was signed by the competing American and Italian pilots and approved by Mr. Ericson, the race referee. Thus, at daybreak on October 24 Hinkler was again taxiing out, but this time he was forced to give up in a rough, nasty chop when less than $\frac{1}{2}$ mile from the slipway. Disconsolate, his reprieve apparently wasted, he was towed in only to wait with his colleagues as the easterly wind crescendoed, later in the day reaching 65 mph gale force, swooping over Baltimore, lathering Chesapeake Bay, and playing havoc with the flimsy tent hangars. The Schneider race was postponed for two days.

Thus, at daybreak on October 26, the new race day, Hinkler was on the slipway once again. During the two-day wait the Italians had second

Hinkler's Gloster III-A at the 1925 Schneider Trophy race, renumbered after the Super-marine S.4 crash   (Au)

Gloster III-A taking off to compete in the 1925 Schneider Trophy race   (UPI)

thoughts about Hinkler's delayed trial, fearing what the precedent of allowing a fresh challenger to begin three days late might mean in future races. But the harried contest officials who had arisen at 3 A.M. were not to be put off at this point and allowed Hinkler to continue. Time was critical: Hinkler had to fly the 50-kilometer course twice, land and taxi $\frac{1}{2}$ nautical mile at a speed no less than 12 knots twice; his plane then must complete a six-hour unattended mooring to prove watertightness, all before 2:30 P.M. Hinkler taxied away shortly after 7 A.M., but the turbulent bay was still upset in the storm's aftermath. With mounting alarm he observed the mark boats rolling heavily in 3-foot waves, but it was now or never. The gritty Australian gunned his Napier to taxi across the starting line, as the rules provided, and begin his trial. Suddenly his racer lurched. The pounding seas had collapsed two float struts, the Gloster tilted, a foaming wave washed over a wingtip. All at once, with the sound of a jackhammer, the prop was

slicing into a pontoon. That was it. Hinkler was ignominiously towed in by a gig from USS *Shawmut*. Bill Wait, the Curtiss project engineer, watching from the sidelines, recalled the scene years later. He had befriended Broad and showed the Englishman Doolittle's magnificent R3C. When he was allowed to inspect the Gloster III-A in return his first impression was that it "was built like a canoe. It was way too light . . . it 'duck-walked' on the water, and when [Hinkler's] wingtip dug in that was it. He never did get airborne."

After Hinkler's accident there was simply no time to prepare the Bamel, thus preventing the venerable racer her chance to fly in the Schneider. That afternoon Broad was second off in the main event. At full speed the Gloster III-A was still directionally unstable. To Broad its slithering felt "like the back wheels of a car on an icy road." Broad had to take the pylons wide, and during the race he was convinced he was losing up to 20 mph. Although lapping the course at some 200 mph, faster than the winner in

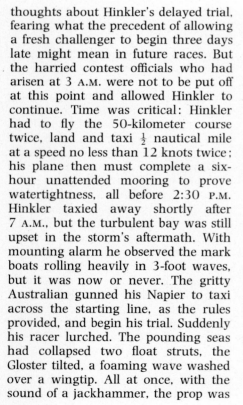

Gloster III-A rounding a pylon during the 1925 Schneider Trophy race

(Hubert Broad)

342

any previous Schneider race, and putting GAC closer to a Schneider victory then than ever before or since, Broad was far slower than Doolittle and had to settle for second place. His Lion ran perfectly, his lap times were remarkably consistent, and he set the British 100-kilometer record.

After the 1925 Schneider there were further modifications to the vertical tails on both Gloster III racers. N.195 alone then received skin radiators on all four wings, which allowed a speed increase from 225 to 252 mph, a large expansion tank on its upper wing, an enlarged windscreen, a fully cantilever tail from which all external control horns had been removed, a rounded fin leading edge, and streamline bracing wires, as opposed to the round wires on N.194. With these changes N.195 became the only Gloster III-B. She is also reported to have been assigned the civil registry G-EBLJ. Following modifications at

Brockworth, N.194 reached Felixstowe in June 1926 followed by N.195 that November to serve as trainers for the RAF High Speed Flight, the group of hand-picked military aviators who would compete for Great Britain in the 1927 Schneider Trophy race. N.194, equipped with a Lion VII (s/n 62015), was used to test propellers with high tip speeds. On December 2, 1926, O. E. Worseley began the tests with experimental props having adjustable blades. Fairey/Reed and GAC props of several diameters (6·75 feet to 7·75 feet) were flight-tested through the following April.

As for the Bamel, she was cleared for 2,950 pounds, which all but eliminated pontoon freeboard, and put to work testing wing skin radiators. For this work Folland retained test pilot Frank T. Courtney. Because the cramped cockpit restricted movement, Courtney would memorize flight data, land to scribble a few notes on his pad, then

take off again. He recalled that on March 29, 1926, after his final landing and while awaiting a tow, the fast outgoing tide came from behind as he headed upwind — torque from the huge prop made downwind turns impossible. When the port float began to submerge Courtney thought it was just a passing swell, but the float stayed under and began to drag the racer over. Then the left wing dipped and Courtney extricated himself just as the launch arrived and threw him a line. He just managed to make it fast around the fuselage ahead of the tail before the plane sank completely. It took one and a quarter hours to tow the Bamel ashore and another three hours before she was hoisted out. Salt-water action on magnesium in the custom-lightened Lion produced some vivid chemical fireworks, but the pontoon, thought to be punctured, proved to be dry. Experiments later proved a small external vane would

prevent the original problem. In addition, later pontoon designs generally provided more buoyancy at the stern.

Early in 1926 Folland started the design of the Gloster IV, in which he approached a degree of sleekness hardly matched during the decade — head resistance was cut by 40 per cent over the Gloster III — even though the new racer was once again a biplane. Three were built at a cost of £8,250 each (the direct-drive Gloster IV and IV-B and the geared Gloster IV-A), all intended for participation in the 1927 Schneider since they were not ready in 1926. Only the Gloster IV-B ever raced, but prop shaft failure forced it out of the 1927 contest after it had averaged 272·53 mph for five laps.

On November 11, 1926, shortly after the firm's name was officially changed from Gloucestershire to Gloster, primarily for the benefit of foreign buyers who found the former spelling both difficult and unpro-

Folland's later fastbacks: the last of the true high-speed biplane racers, the Gloster IV, 1927; and . . .   (UK Ministry of Defence)

the Gloster VI Golden Arrow, 1929   (Au)

nounceable, Folland's Gloster V racer was begun. It was also to be a biplane, but balance problems caused by the 300-pound supercharger attached to its Lion VII-D forced the upper wing main spar too far forward where it interfered with the center bank of cylinders. Folland rigidly refused to substitute a Rolls-Royce engine when given the chance, persisting in his fierce loyalty to Napier. But unable to resolve the design conflict, Folland for the first time was forced to design a monoplane. His rigidity in engine choice thus paradoxically led to a remarkable freedom in aeroplane layout — the almost supple lines of his new racer seemed more appropriate to the inspired brush strokes of a painting than to an engineering blueprint. The resulting Gloster VI *Golden Arrow* emerged to open that extraordinary decade when the world speed record was dominated by seaplanes, hurtling 336·22 mph on September 10, 1929, under the hand of George H. Stainforth.

In fact, GAC preoccupation with pure Schneider racing craft through the last half of the 1920s seriously undermined the firm's over-all corporate effectiveness. Hugh Burroughes has pointed out that from the Board's viewpoint air racing was relatively unimportant as a "breadwinning" activity; it was originally undertaken in order to keep GAC in the picture against the leading government purveyors such as giants Bristol and Hawker. Yet beyond ensuring the RAF was kept adequate as a police force in the Middle East the British government was then apathetic — occasionally seemingly hostile — to aviation. Early GAC racing success gained notice, but like a drug led Folland to increasingly ambitious pure speed seeking with insufficient emphasis on its practical application. GAC soon lost her hold on the single-seater fighter business and became easy prey for a takeover by Hawker in February 1934 — so Tom Sopwith prevailed after all. During the Battle of Britain

Hawker's Gloster division turned out a Hurricane every four hours night and day. The fighter started Monday entered combat by week's end.

After Tom Sopwith's take-over of GAC, Folland did not remain long. Fearing if not intimidation at least subsidence under the more brightly rising star of Hawker's Sydney Camm, Folland left in December 1935, formed his own company, small but successful, at Hamble near Southampton in 1937, and remained at its helm until 1951. He received no further design recognition but prospered as a subcontractor. He attempted only one more major design, to specification F.5/34, a monoplane fighter contemporary with the Hurricane and Spitfire, but air-cooled using the Bristol Mercury engine. It was aesthetically beautiful but bucked the trend back to liquid-cooled fighters then and was unsuccessful.

In spite of the secure place he earned in British aviation history, Folland's career was rather sad. In truth he often was fairly bursting with innovative ideas but for so long had been suppressed by dreary caution during his early days that caution became a habit. Although an enormously striving man, defiant in the face of setback, Folland almost agonized over each step taken toward the next clearly logical development. He remained vaguely frustrated and outwardly conservative although always enormously kind and humble. Never having realized his highest personal ambitions, Folland died in Nottingham in 1954, aged sixty-five. His ashes were scattered over Laffan's Plain, where the romance of flight had first enchanted him so many eventful years before.

HARRY HAWKER & THE SOPWITH RACER

23

Bright blue-and-yellow checkerboard gaily decorated Henry Folland's snorting Goshawk racer, complementing its frolic in the sky. With characteristic dash the pilot bent it over, intent on speed. Suddenly it faltered, rolling onto its back, and to horrified gasps of witnesses below, began a sickening dive, the wind's scream crescendoing in its wires. Some say there was a flicker of fire after it was righted and before the thudding impact. The pilot, thrown clear, was dead within minutes. He was thirty-one years old and his name was Harry Hawker.

Entered in the 1921 Aerial Derby, Hawker was testing his borrowed mount at 6:20 P.M. on a warm July 12 over Hendon. At nearby Stag Lane Aerodrome Geoffrey de Havilland was strolling with his chief engineer, Charles Walker; both saw the racer rise above the trees. Then they saw flames lick backward momentarily from its engine as it plunged toward a field of dry grass at Burnt Oak, less than 2 miles from Hendon. Amid burning grass, with both legs broken, "the man who won't be killed" expired in the arms of a doctor. After the crash the Air Ministry became convinced the float chamber covering Hawker's carburetor, located in front of the cylinders, came loose in flight, allowing gasoline to be thrown back into the hot exhaust, causing fire to begin. This verdict seemed to be supported by Hawker's charred feet and by the fact that his petrol valve was found "off".

345

This spirited career started in Australia, where Harry George Hawker, born in 1889, personified the Wild Colonial Boy. A school drop-out at age twelve, by fifteen he was one of the hottest auto drivers in the state of Victoria. (He was also one of the only auto drivers then!) Seven years later in 1911 he had accumulated enough money to buy passage to England. Reduced to taking a factory job at 7 pence per hour, Hawker briefly suffered perhaps the only period of discouragement in his otherwise exuberant life. For Hawker lived in that final heroic age when the path from abject poverty to gilt-edged pinnacle could be straight and quick for those who would take it.

Through a friend the youth, down to his last coppers, secured a job at Brooklands as grease monkey for the flying operations of wealthy, enthusiastic Thomas Octave Murdoch (T.O.M.) Sopwith — who himself was only twenty-four — and tall, hard, intensely practical Frederick Sigrist, thirty-two, who had been first employed as engine mechanic on the splendid motor cruiser owned by Sopwith and his friend Bill Eyre.

Sopwith was son of a wealthy civil engineer and had begun his aviation career as an early ballooning devotee, earning RAeC certificate number 31. Throughout the years of spectacular success that followed he always

Harry George Hawker (F)

Thomas O. M. Sopwith, circa 1920 (F)

But Hawker suffered from incurable spinal tuberculosis, and in the only official report issued upon his death the coroner, a Dr. Gardiner (or Garner) of Weybridge indicated compelling evidence that a sudden, massive spinal hemorrhage had occurred before impact, causing Hawker's legs to become paralyzed at the controls. It was entirely characteristic for Hawker — who had known of his terminal condition for eighteen months — to incur this mortal sentence where he loved to be most, at the controls of a speedplane. The controversy over the cause of his death, which exists even to this day, serves to add an extra measure of romance to a short but intense career which has cast his name in the sort of reverence bestowed on few men.

346

shunned publicity, remaining in the background, the unseen but potent presence, content to let others represent his firm's image to the public. It was inevitable that Hawker would receive the lion's share of adulation. Unfailingly cheery and stubbornly persistent, a lifelong teetotaler and non-smoker, Hawker loved doing things worthwhile – which in aviation's headstrong early days meant taking risks – just for the sake of doing them. Four days after his first flying lesson he went solo and "took his ticket" (number 297) on September 17, 1912. The very next month, on October 24, with a 40-hp Sopwith-built copy of a Wright Brothers biplane, he captured the British Empire Michelin Cup and £500 prize by staying aloft for the incredible time of 8:23. Unsophisticated public adoration deluged the heady twenty-three-year-old overnight, for in those days aviators were looked upon as supermen. Hawker soon took a bride, vivacious Muriel Peaty, sister of an amusing RAF captain (L. F. Peaty, later on the firm's Board of Directors), and they settled in at Ennadale, Hook Road, Surbiton, Surrey. Fifty years later Muriel Hawker observed the anniversary of her husband's death at the Farnborough Air Show.

Flying at Brooklands had been tonic for Hawker. Boom Trenchard, the great architect of the RAF, was one of Hawker's pupils. During 1913, between May 31 and July 27, the restless upstart set four altitude records in the first aircraft entirely designed by Sopwith, a three-seater "tractor biplane." On June 16 he broke a record of pioneer Geoff de Havilland. Within a month, on July 13, he won the Mortimer Singer Prize of £500 put up by the son of the sewing machine magnate for "out-and-back" flights, using Sopwith's 100-hp Bat Boat, first British-produced flying boat which incorporated "collapsible undercarriage" making it amphibian. Then he tried for the London *Daily Mail* £5,000 round-England prize put up by Lord Northcliffe (1,550 miles within seventy-two consecutive

hours). He did not finish; in fact, he crashed near Dublin, two thirds of the way around, when his valve springs gave out, "a piece of ghastly bad luck." Inasmuch as he was the only competitor, the *Daily Mail* awarded him £1,000 consolation money. The story of the failure, splashed in banners across the paper, was worth far more to Northcliffe.

The crowning achievement of 1913, however, was the appearance of a clean, side-by-side biplane which Hawker first flew on November 29 at

Fred Sigrist, circa 1920   (F)

The Sopwith Tabloid, seen here as winner of the 1914 Schneider Trophy race, was a design that had profound influence on the evolution of aeroplanes.   (MA)

Hendon. Arranging a trip to Australia to see his parents, Hawker swayed Sopwith with the idea for a sales tour "down under," and this in turn inspired plans for the compact two-seater. At once the outline was drawn full-scale on the floor of a local skating rink. Sopwith personally regarded the design as "rather a family affair . . . everybody had a crack at it," and thus would it continue to be with virtually every Sopwith aeroplane; it was said that Sopwith judged if it looked right, Sigrist if it was built right, and Hawker if it flew right. Sopwith's intuition and Sigrist's unequaled shopwork always guaranteed an efficient, lightweight structure in a period when mediocrity was characterized by overweight.

The new biplane first acquired fame in the battle with Messrs. Burroughs and Wellcome, medical pill producers, over its nickname "Tabloid." Adjectives that appeared in contemporary trade journals include "extraordinary," "astounding"; the Tabloid's speed

capability of 36–92 mph on 80 hp left spectators "agape." With uncharacteristic zeal, British military authorities suddenly became convinced by the Tabloid of biplane superiority. A Tabloid was ordered for Winston Churchill in 1913, and C. Howard Pixton won the 1914 Schneider Trophy race at Monaco in one at 87 mph. Hawker took one to Australia for several months in 1914 – his sales tour – returning to England in June, two months before the "big uproar" started. The Tabloid then became the first fighter, with steel deflector plates on its prop. Only about forty were built, powered by thrashing Gnôme rotary engines, and the first few even used wing warping for lateral control. Yet the Tabloid caused a bump in the curve of aviation development that still could be felt in biplane fighter squadrons a quarter century later. While looping a Tabloid at an early exhibition, Hawker stalled off the top and spun into trees bordering the airfield. The impact was known at the time to have bruised his spine.

During World War I Harry Hawker flew virtually every individual Sopwith aeroplane put together in his capacity as test pilot. He was up daily in the endless parade of Pups, Camels, Snipes, Dolphins, 1½-Strutters, and he received £25 ($125) for each flight. Inasmuch as he could test up to twelve planes per day this was no mean achievement financially. In fact, for the last three years of the war Hawker, not yet thirty, received fees in excess of $100,000 equivalent per year (and these were 1917 dollars), making him certainly the highest-paid airman in the world at that time and probably for all time, especially when one considers subsequent inflation. The irony was that he should receive so much for flying warplanes in time of war, for he was never once exposed to combat.

In the meantime his aerobatic prowess was exhibited far and wide. The Sopwith Bee, a virtual two-thirds-scale Pup, was built to his order in the mid-war year 1916, and the 110-hp Clerget-powered Swallow of 1919 was another one-of-a-kind Sopwith aerobatic bus built just for Hawker, who delighted in showing it off at Hendon throughout 1920.

The next Sopwith creation built specifically for Hawker was the Transport — later the Atlantic — of 1919. A huge two-seater spanning 46 feet, it was powered with a single 375-hp Rolls-Royce Eagle VIII engine. Its bulky 3 tons included 330 gallons of fuel, good for twenty-two hours, and at an advertised 118-mph cruising speed this was more than enough to brave even the imposing North Atlantic itself! The three-ply fuselage turtleback was detachable, doubling as a lifeboat, and the landing gear could be jettisoned which added 7 mph. Indeed, released from war and spurred by Lord Northcliffe's mammoth *Daily Mail* prize of £10,000 for the first non-stop transatlantic crossing completed within seventy-two hours, eager hopefuls sprouted literally by the dozens. Hawk-

er's navigator was phlegmatic, thirty-nine year-old Lieutenant Commander Kenneth M. Mackenzie-Grieve, RN. They were at St. John's, Newfoundland, by late March together with several others, each awaiting favorable weather and working up to a frenzy trying to outguess their rivals' plans.

Tests worried Hawker that his radiator pipes would clog with rust and bits of solder from the cooling jacket, so he devised a makeshift filter of gauze and inserted this in his cooling system, hoping to prevent such misfortune. A new threat was introduced by the Americans with their ungainly NC flying boats; though they were ineligible for the prize (they would stop at the Azores) the British could not bear to let the *honor* of the first aerial crossing go to the Yanks unchallenged. In the afternoon of May 18, two days after the NC-4 departure and despite unfavorable weather predictions, Hawker and Mackenzie-Grieve said *au revoir*, sent to nearby competitor Fred Raynham hopes of seeing him again at Brooklands, and shoved off from Newfoundland.

They should have reached Ireland twenty hours later. Twice that time went by with no word. The entire nation sat vigil, but resignation slowly crept in and the perfunctory search was finally abandoned. Hawker was mourned for lost, obituaries appeared, and even the King sent condolences to Hawker's wife and two small daughters. All this had been virtually forgotten by the sleepy lighthouse keeper who, a week later, idly watched an old Danish tramp plod by his post at Lloyd's Telegraph Station on the Butt of Lewis in the Outer Hebrides. He raised a disinterested eyebrow as the ship began hoisting signal flags. The first couple, curiously, seemed the code for "Saved Hands." Then, one by one, in electrifying procession, the individual letters slowly fluttered up: "Sop Aeroplane." Incredulous, the keeper signaled back, "Is it Hawker?" The answer came: "YES!"

Hawker had truly returned from the dead. In a celebration wilder than even Armistice night six months earlier, he was joyously welcomed back. His train to London was stopped again and again by throngs gone mad, and two hundred delirious, bush-hatted Australians tried to roll his carriage bodily through London's King's Cross Station.

The fliers' ordeal over the Atlantic stands as a hallmark of adventure — and incredible luck. Flying into the brittle night, beset by worsening weather, Hawker's greatest concern was realized when the water temperature rose ominously from 168°F. to 176°F., despite wide-open radiator shutters and the outside air temperature, which was "getting on for zero," in Hawker's words. Straining to reach the bitter cold of altitude, the climb instead demanded too much of the engine, heating it dangerously. Finally on top of solid cloud at 12,000 feet, Mackenzie-Grieve was able to take a latitude from Polaris and found that a northerly gale had blown them 200 miles south of their intended track, the fiftieth parallel. Worse, this put them far from any shipping lanes. Hawker had to throttle back, diving to cool the boiling engine. In the pre-dawn gloom they could perceive a massif of cloud ahead rearing like a fantastic mountain range; Hawker "had a shot" at going over some lower clouds, but each time furious boiling set in. It was "no good going on with that scheme." By now steam was shooting in a geyser from the radiator relief pipe "quite merrily."

Hawker was forced to admit that Ireland was "out of the range of practical politics," but he remained absurdly optimistic as he glided down, tacking northward toward the shipping lanes. On one occasion, after gliding below 1,000 feet, feeling for the cloud base, the engine did not catch and the two fliers braced for the landing — which promised to be "a crash of sorts." As he flared 10 feet high in the spume of a wave, Hawker jabbed the throttle

in vicious frustration — and the engine barked to life! He gave her "a good mouthful of throttle" as they began to zigzag, now frantically searching for a ship, their engine's steam blending with the gray morning mist. Almost three desperate hours later, their cooling water completely boiled away, and just as a greasy, black storm loomed, they spotted the Danish tramp *Mary*. Shooting their very pistol they "pushed off a couple of miles on her course," and Hawker made "a cushy landing" in waves so mountainous the intrepid Danes at times lost sight of them.

In fourteen and a half hours they had come 1,130 miles, which left 750 remaining. The *Mary* had no wireless, hence the lack of news of their recovery. Incredibly, the American freighter *Lake Charlotteville* came upon the abandoned, floating wreckage some time later and brought the remains, together with its valuable mail pouch, into Falmouth. It seems Hawker's own precautionary gauze filter had come loose — and it had clogged the radiator! Three weeks later Alcock and Brown won the *Dail Mail* prize. After this no aeroplane would profane the Atlantic's resolute sanctity for five years; Lindbergh would not cross for eight.

Just one month after his harrowing sea rescue, irrepressible Harry Hawker, now an O.B.E., A.F.C., was entered in the Aerial Derby, the great air race around London resurrected after the Armistice. Tom Sopwith himself had won the very first Aerial Derby in 1912 in a 70-hp Blériot monoplane at less than 60 mph. Amid the chaos of closing down war production, and with scant time to prepare new racers, designers scurried to adapt the most up-to-date planes on hand. Hawker was first detailed to fly a Sopwith monoplane with a 130-hp Clerget rotary, bearing race number 17. At the last minute a Dragonfly-powered Sopwith Snapper retaining the same race number was substituted. But this aeroplane, a sure winner, was withdrawn, censored by the Air Ministry,

348

Construction detail of the Sopwith Schneider showing the first Jupiter engine, 1919 (F)

and Hawker had to sit out the "Victory Derby's" ebullience.

Three months later Hawker was entered in the resurrected race for the prestigious Schneider Trophy, for which Tom Sopwith had decided to construct a specialized racer. It was designed principally by Wilfred G. Carter and combined a strong mixture of Snapper and earlier ingredients, employing the usual wood girder-braced, fabric-covered construction. Work commenced over the summer in hopes of finishing the racer in time for the race scheduled at Bournemouth in early September. It was designated Sopwith model 107, registered G-EAKI, appropriately named Sopwith Schneider, and boasted as powerplant the very first of Roy Fedden's new Cosmos Jupiter engines. The round shape of its huge nine-cylinder air-cooled radial was merged smoothly into flat sides of the rear fuselage by stringers, although the engine cylinders protruded through the aluminum cowl. Its twin-pontoon configuration was novel compared to general contemporary British seaplane design, although the rudder's lower portion was very thick, fairing the fuselage and serving as tail float. Tom Sopwith's new racer was destined to be always the bridesmaid of the vintage racers, never the bride.

At the appointed race time thick haze merged sky and water where muted sparkles from an indistinct sun played on the quiet surface. Delay in starting ensued and soon thick fog rolled in. Nevertheless, four of the seven entrants took to the air, the Sopwith Schneider with Harry Hawker at the controls among them, certainly the race's fastest entry. Presently he returned, landed, began to heel, and ran his racer onto the stony beach to save it, but ruined the pontoons. He had been unable to locate the Swanage marking boat. The race, of course, was later annulled in great embarrassment.

The Sopwith racer's next appearance occurred during July 1920 in the popular Aerial Derby. It had been re-named Sopwith Rainbow, its ruined pontoons replaced by fixed landing

Adjusting the Jupiter engine on the Sopwith Schneider, 1919 (F)

Sopwith Schneider taking off at Bournemouth, 1919 (F)

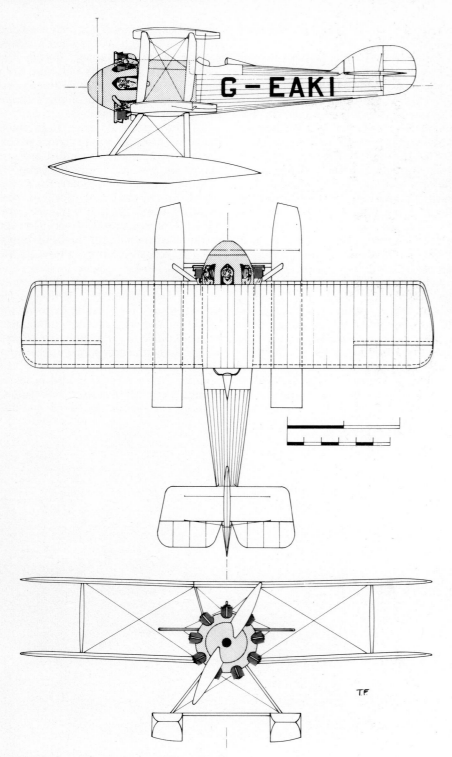

Sopwith 107 racer 1919–23; 1919 Schneider entry shown

Sopwith racer, renamed Rainbow for the 1920 Aerial Derby, reequipped with wheels, smaller wings, and Dragonfly engine   (H-S)

wheels. The prototype Jupiter engine used in 1919 was unavailable, so with misgivings Sigrist substituted an ABC Dragonfly, similar in size. Owing to the lighter weight realized upon removal of the pontoons and the slightly heavier (60 pounds) Jupiter engine, Sigrist clipped 3 feet from the racer's wings. The fact that all control cables passed inside to housed-in crank levers caused favorable comment on the plane's neat appearance in 1920. Harry Hawker, strapped in the Rainbow's pit, had drawn race number 13, issued in order of start, and was due to take off nine minutes ahead of the scratch racer, Folland's checkerboard Goshawk, flown in 1920 by L. R. Tait-Cox.

Hawker gunned his Dragonfly engine, the sharp spurts of exhaust smoke merging into a blue haze riven by prop-wash. The nine steel cannons arranged around the plane's nose thundered in unison, sending cascades of shudders through its tiny frame under their blast. Hawker roared away and did his two laps in excellent time, but 13 was his unlucky number. Upon return to Hendon completing the second lap, a half circuit of the aerodrome was required. To everyone's surprise Hawker flew straight past the number one pylon, but not across the proper finish line, and this unfortunately disqualified his time, which otherwise would have garnered second in speed, third in handicap. The winner averaged only 10 mph faster with seven racers finishing slower and five others not finishing at all.

Never mind, the classic Gordon Bennett race was coming up in just two months. Hawker would show in France what the Rainbow could really do. The Sopwith team needed luck, and it looked as if they got it in the form of a new Jupiter engine for the Gordon Bennett race.

But the once great Sopwith firm was in deep financial trouble. As early as

Harry Hawker taking off from Hendon in the 1920 Aerial Derby; 13 was his unlucky number. (F)

withdrawn from the Gordon Bennett, not even becoming a bridesmaid. Harry Hawker drove down to the race from Paris with his wife in a beautiful six-cylinder Sunbeam. He had already taken up motorcar racing again at Brooklands during the aviation slump.

To their everlasting credit, Sopwith, Sigrist, and Hawker, instead of retiring on their individual fortunes, soon organized a new company. They called it the H. G. Hawker Engineering Company, Ltd., and reopened the old Sopwith factory on Canbury Park Road, Kingston-on-Thames. Reconditioning weary D.H.9s and Snipes started them off. Upon reorganization, Captain B. Thomson became chief designer and Fred Sigrist was promoted from works manager to managing director. Harry Hawker, just thirty-one, was now a top executive, albeit of a firm on quite precarious footing in those days.

Less than one year later the spunky, intense young Australian was tragically dead, killed in the borrowed Goshawk. Out of loyalty to his memory, Tom Sopwith refused all attempts to reinstitute the original name "Sopwith" which had earned his earlier firm priceless good will during the years of World War I. "Hawker" it now was, and "Hawker" it would be.

Understandably, Tom Sopwith's interest in racing planes was at a low ebb for the next couple of years. But Sopwith's own early prosperity had been rooted in racing; as a youth he had successfully raced cars and boats himself before taking up aviation, and the deep fervor soon stirred within him. His own racing aeroplane was dusted off, duly entered in the 1923 Aerial Derby, and installation of its Jupiter engine was completed. It rapidly became the Derby dark horse, expected to do great things in the race

December 1918 Tom Sopwith, looking ahead, announced to the press ambitious plans to convert his factory's vast wartime production over to "one hundred ABC motorcycles per day." He began to lay reorganization plans with Captain Ronald Charteris, ABC's managing director. When Sopwith's extensive government contracts suddenly ceased along with hostilities, the proud firm struggled, but even with motorcycles they were unable to continue and still pay the enormous excess-profits duty owed the government. After absorbing a vast loss of war-acquired machinery stock, Sopwith paid his creditors a full 20 shillings on the pound and on September 11, 1920, quietly folded.

This occurred just two weeks before the Gordon Bennett race. Work on the Rainbow racer halted when liquidators of the Sopwith firm refused to loan or even rent the aeroplane for the race unless indemnified for loss. A small group of sportsmen in the Royal Aero Club managed to buy the racer — which in fact was had for the price of

scrap metal and firewood! Then the liquidators prohibited the purchasers' mechanics from using the empty floor of the Sopwith factory to erect the aeroplane. This obstacle was hurdled when a nearby garage owner in Kingston graciously offered the use of his garage floor. But Bristol had already been informed on September 10 by the liquidators that the engine reserved would not be required, and when on September 20 the engine was urgently requested by the sportsmen, it was found to be hard at work in Bristol's experimental shop. It was impossible to make this engine airworthy in time. Valiant efforts were made to locate another engine; a military engine could not be had without an Air Council meeting and hopeless red tape. Bristol reported an engine sent to a "customer firm" but the firm in question had no engine, leading to the unavoidable but bewildering conclusion that a good Jupiter engine was wandering about the countryside with no owner. Meanwhile the Rainbow, with no engine, had to be reluctantly

Jupiter engine in renamed Sopwith Hawker sings in readiness for the 1923 Aerial Derby. (F)

Walter H. Longton, circa 1923 (F)

Sopwith Hawker at Croydon for the final Aerial Derby, 1923. This was the only time the two celebrated names Sopwith and Hawker were ever officially coupled together. (F)

scheduled for Bank Holiday in August. Lieutenant Walter H. "Scruffie" Longton D.F.C., A.F.C., who had flown a privately owned Snipe in the 1920 Derby, as well as various Sopwiths in King's Cup races, was picked to fly the refurbished racer. Longton had been a pioneer motorcyclist and prewar engine tester with Sunbeam Motor Company, and "Longton's opinion" came to be highly valued. His new racing mount had been renamed once more, in 1923 being called, appropriately, the Sopwith Hawker. Already the Hawker legend was beginning to cast its overpowering spell. Incidentally, this was the only known time when these two great names of aviation were officially coupled together.

On Derby day Longton made a nice takeoff shortly after 3 P.M., seven minutes ahead of the scratch racer (Gloster I) in a field of thirteen, skimmed over the heads of spectators in the enclosures, and rapidly disappeared. The racer's speed was fully 20 mph faster than it had achieved in 1920, and it proved stable in flight despite its small size and disproportionately large engine. Upon returning from his two circuits of London, Longton made a perfect three-point landing and rolled to a stop. But the Sopwith Hawker had only finished second, again a bridesmaid.

The racer was entered in the upcoming Schneider Trophy race to be held at Cowes, and plans were completed to mount it on twin pontoons again, as in 1919. A large spinner was fitted to streamline the Jupiter engine, but during the week of September 2, on its last flight before the pontoons were to be fitted, the spinner blew off and wedged itself in the wing bracing wires. On its forced landing in a small field near Brooklands — "an unsuitable spot," according to Longton — it turned over and was demolished, and Longton was lucky to emerge uninjured. Thus G-EAKI lost forever its chance to become a bride among the racers. Walter Longton was later killed in 1927 during an air race of light planes at Bournemouth when he had a midair collision with Westland test pilot L. P. Openshaw at the final pylon.

The small firm bearing Harry Hawker's name continued to flourish, primarily through the good foresight and financial wizardry of Tom Sopwith. He took on Sydney Camm, who later designed the Hawker Hurricane and was praised as "the man who saved Great Britain," and he began to absorb other aeroplane manufacturers — Armstrong-Whitworth, Gloster, A. V. Roe among them — so that two decades after World War I the Hawker combine was the giant of British aeronautics, with Sir Thomas Chairman of the Board. Sopwith saw to it that the Hawker company always secured the most lucrative government contracts, occasionally to the strong consterna-

tion of his rivals. His standing with the Air Ministry was always more than impeccable; his wealth and influence increased bountifully; he was an excellent host; Trenchard owed his earliest flying knowledge to Sopwith — and these were all useful attributes which he exploited most skillfully. Sigrist, now an M.B.E., rose to be joint managing director of the combine; it was he who perfected the famous and unique Hawker system of tubular metal structures using flitch plates and square ends on the tubes. During the days of the original Sopwith company, Sigrist, like Hawker, had been given a handsome bonus for every aeroplane produced during the war, and with this money he purchased land in Bermuda, eventually retiring there owing to ill health. His land developed making him, at the time of his death in 1957, an extremely wealthy ex-mechanic. Sopwith's only prominent public exposure came during the 1930s when he built two J-class yachts to contest the America's Cup; in this venture he was unsuccessful. Hale and hearty, he received the plaudits of his early colleagues in 1969 and marvelled that the Hawker company, capitalized in 1920 at £20,000, had in a half-century grown into the Hawker-Siddeley combine with a net worth of £53.6 million.

The memory of Harry Hawker, who had so much to do with starting it all, has been long since overshadowed by decades of subsequent events. Yet Harry Hawker's indomitable spirit still lives, manifest in any adventurer who accomplishes that which he considers worthwhile, in spite of risk.

THE BRISTOL RACERS

24

Two influential men, both brilliant, incisive, imbued with purpose, and yet both curiously quiet-spoken, each ready to criticize his own work and each largely devoid of the politician's instinct, made their considerable contributions to speed seeking while working at Bristol, 110 miles west of London. One was Frank Sowter Barnwell, Scottish flying pioneer whose first tentative aeroplanes were harbinger to a host of later designs which helped change the world. The other was Alfred Hubert Roy Fedden, whose genius and perseverance gave birth to a host of aero engines which, if anything, were even more historically remarkable; these engines powered many of Barnwell's craft.

Barnwell was thirty-one on Christ-mas day, 1911, when he first became associated with the already celebrated British & Colonial Airplane Company, founded in February 1910 by Sir George Stanley White, baronet, avuncular and Victorian with opulent mutton-chop whiskers, who had made himself electric "Tramway King" of the British Isles during a sleepy age of clopping hooves and ships under sail. Still vigorous and visionary at fifty-six, Sir George, with rare acumen, already foresaw that flying machines would inevitably be part of the world's transportation system and he meant to manage the lot. The new aeroplane company was installed in Filton House, Bristol, an eighteenth-century mansion splashed with dahlias and twists of ivy. Barnwell was lodged behind

Sir George White (BAC)

Frank Barnwell, circa 1917 (BAC)

354

the frosted-glass, Edwardian façade at 4 Fairlawn Avenue which promptly became the firm's famous X-Department. It was here in 1912 that he designed the first Bristol Scout, a biplane which proved to be one of the fastest in the air at the outbreak of World War I when the embryonic RFC had only the haziest ideas about air fighting. Barnwell's background included Clydeside shipbuilding and automobile engineering — he and his elder brother, Richard Harold Barnwell, had begun the Grampian Motor Company — but ever since 1900 when together they built a 5 hp monoplane which failed to fly, both had been obsessed with aviation. Harold became chief test pilot for Vickers but was killed in a 1917 crash. Frank came to Bristol, where his own urge to fly became notorious, mainly because his great talents always remained firmly on the ground.

Barnwell held a commission in the RFC, becoming a captain in 1915 when he was officially assigned to the design branch of British & Colonial as a serving officer. The progression of Barnwell's successful designs through the war paid testimony to his superb ability to balance hard necessity with the visionary. Although Barnwell helped develop steel strip construction, his most famous wartime product was a huge wood-and-fabric fighter with pilot and gunner sitting back to back, working as a team. Slow but strong, it entered service during "bloody April" 1917 and achieved immortality as the F.2B "Biff," "Brisfit," or simply "Bristol fighter." Despite its resounding success — more than 4,500 were built and Brisfits were hailed by RAF air crews who flew them actively well into the 1930s — Barnwell never got over his propensity to ponder interminably and discuss his designs and ideas as though he was a beginner just trying to pick up a few tips.

Barnwell, who was always called the "old man," even in his thirties, toured France in 1917 in an F.2B to gain firsthand information on fighting

Barnwell's Bristol M.1, one of England's few wartime monoplanes (BAC)

conditions. He was a popular visitor to the combat units, and in his amiable fashion he offered to give a delighted officer a lift to another squadron. The poor chap had no way of knowing the famous designer was such a terrible pilot; in the ensuing crash Barnwell broke both his ankles. Barnwell was always intensely aware of his modest capabilities as a pilot and occasionally got into trouble through overcaution. In thirty years he logged only a few hundred hours, probably less than 300. In 1919 he flew his metal-structured M.R.1 fighter into a tree, wrecking it without hurting himself, and afterward remarked to a friend in his soft Scots burr, "Silly of me, wasn't it, old boy, but do you know, I just wasn't looking."

Although the war was largely an affair of biplanes, Barnwell in 1915 designed a shoulder-wing monoplane fighter around the 110-hp LeRhône rotary engine, his idea being to use the largest practical engine with the smallest possible aeroplane behind it. The distinctly novel wartime idea of building a monoplane might have

had its origins in the popular Prier and Coanda monoplanes built at Bristol before the war. Barnwell's fighter was designated M.1 (Bristol type 20) and was given to Freddie Dunn to fly in its crucial demonstration to RAF brass including tall, austere Boom Trenchard, Chief of the Air Staff. Dunn had been Frank Courtney's prewar roommate at Hendon, where both learned to fly, but sadly Dunn made a mess of the landing, badly damaging the little Bristol, and in embarrassment he tried to cover up to Trenchard by blaming the plane's "high landing speed." Others who flew the M.1 — which had delightful flying qualities and a 130-mph capability — called Dunn's condemnation "rubbish," but Trenchard, despite his towering, almost mystical vision with regard to air power, was then under the strong Farnborough anti-monoplane influence and was even accused of being "technically stupid" by no less a luminary than Hugh Dowding, then a young major, destined to lead RAF Fighter Command in the Battle of Britain. Trenchard accepted Dunn's

Bristol 77 racer, 1922   *(BAC)*

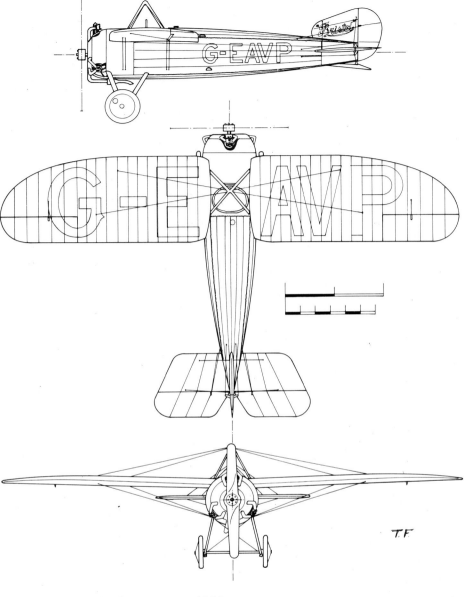

Bristol 77 racer, handicap winner, 1922 Aerial Derby

criticism and the RAF was thus deprived of a fine fighter which it badly needed at the time. Nevertheless, strong Bristol persistence resulted in the production of 130 M.1Cs but none served on the Western Front, most going to Palestine to perform obscure duties against the Turks during 1916–17. The only British monoplanes built during the war, they had in common with their F.2B cousins the intense loyalty of their pilots; indeed, the pilot of any wartime Bristol, irrespective of type, will tell you his was the finest plane built.

The M.1C made history in South America in 1919 shortly after the war when a Captain Godoy of the Chilean Air Force flew one from Santiago to Mendoza in a daring adventure through the Uspallata Pass to make the first aerial crossing of the Andes; a student pilot named Lieutenant Cortinez, presumably inspired by this feat, duplicated it in a similar M.1C, departing Santiago by night! Cortinez was given up for lost but telephoned the next morning from Mendoza for instructions. He was told gruffly to return at once, which he did — again by air! — in an

exploit which earned him instead of punishment early promotion. Other versions of this doughty monoplane, dressed for civil duties, appeared shortly after the Armistice. One M.1C, still equipped with its LeRhône rotary and the wing cutouts for downward visibility, was flown by Major C. H. Chichester-Smith, D.S.O., in the ebullient 1919 Victory Aerial Derby, the first important postwar British air race. It was the only monoplane entered and did the first circuit of London at just under 100 mph, but returned to Hendon on the second lap with engine trouble. The following spring the design was updated and one completely civil version was prepared. This was the M.1D (Bristol type 77); compared to its predecessor it was cleaned up, painted with blazing "Cellon red" color scheme, and rapidly became popular as Bristol's standard-bearer, registered G-EAVP. It also sported a new, fixed radial, three-cylinder air-cooled 100-hp Cosmos Lucifer engine in place of the now obsolete rotary.

The Lucifer was one of several engines being developed by young Roy Fedden then, deeply involved in the

perfection of the air-cooled cylinder, and on the track of techniques that marked him as one of the world's leading proponents and designers of fixed air-cooled engines. Fedden's father was the head of an old established Bristol West Indies sugar importing company, and founder of the National Nautical School for Boys at Portishead, where his son received a disciplined beginning. Yet young Roy renounced Sandhurst for a career in mechanical engineering and first became involved with engine design in 1906 when he was a high-strung, intensely demanding twenty-one, shortly after he entered

A. H. Roy Fedden   (F)

den began aero engine development, and when war began, partly due to his insistence, Brazil-Straker started aero engine work for the RNAS, at first overhauling OX-5s and later building 2,500 complete Rolls-Royce Hawks and Falcons (Fedden received a 1919 M.B.E. for supervising this construction). They also built several 80-hp air-cooled Renaults — static, not rotary — which may have started Fedden thinking seriously about air-cooled fixed radials. Early in 1917 Fedden persuaded Brazil-Straker to enter a naval engine competition to build a

300-hp air-cooled engine weighing less than 600 pounds. Both Brazil-Straker and Siddeley received production contracts but war's end precluded deliveries and neither firm showed a profit. Fedden's engine, named Mercury, was a remarkable affair with fourteen steel cylinders in two rows of seven. Of medium bore (4 3/8 inches), each was topped with his patented aluminum cylinder head. Long tappet rods to rocking levers supported on the head activated the three valves (one inlet, two exhaust); the engine, which first flew in April 1918, weighed

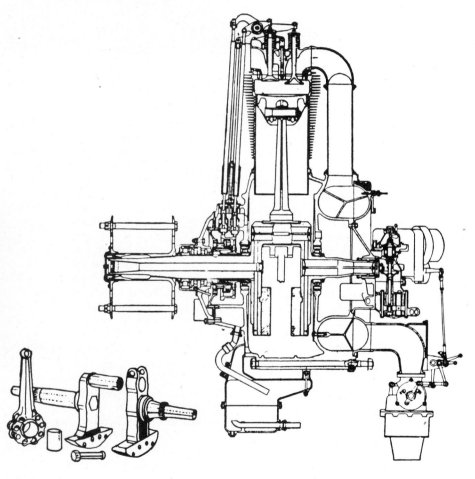

Cross-section view of Fedden's remarkable Jupiter air-cooled radial engine. Detail shows the two-piece (single-throw, counterbalanced) crankshaft and the one-piece master rod.

the Brazil-Straker engineering works at Fishponds, Bristol. He was apprenticed to a wise old mechanic who told him "you must never dash off when the whistle blows," an admonition he never forgot. Fedden soon designed an automobile and persuaded J. P. Brazil, the managing director, to

build it. Ready in 1907, it proved to be a great success and launched a flourishing auto business. Fedden then did a great deal of competition driving in Straker-Squire cars. Shortly before the outbreak of World War I, impressed with the Anzani and Robert Esnault-Pelterie R.E.P. air-cooled engines, Fed-

587 pounds and produced 315 hp at 1,800 rpm, more than meeting the specification.

Fedden spent considerable time and energy endeavoring to improve the air-cooled cylinder in his laboratory, where he experimented incessantly with at least eight different types of individual large-bore cylinders. The best proved to be a closed steel cylinder cast at 40 tons pressure in a single piece together with its short, hence light, cooling fins from a solid billet of K.1 carbon steel; to this was bolted a two-piece cylinder head split vertically, cast of copper-rich aluminum alloy suitably annealed then machined, accommodating tungsten steel exhaust valves capable of withstanding 1,260° F. His air-cooled cylinder seemed to run best at 350° F., far hotter than water-cooled cylinders, which had to be limited to roughly 175° F. to avoid undue water evaporation. One such cylinder of 5·75-inch bore and 7·5-inch stroke, giving 194·75 cid, at a mean effective pressure of 114·5 psi (compression ratio 5), could produce 50 hp at 1,600 rpm, maintaining even temperature in a 75-mph wind. Fedden became convinced early that bores larger than 4·65 inches required more than two valves to supply the charge evenly, but the cylinder head and valve control caused him untold hours of frustration. Aside from cooling problems valve play bothered him greatly; cams were not always exact and often produced high stresses, but the most pernicious problem occurred when heated cylinder heads expanded and lifted the rocker supports almost 1/10 inch, rupturing the valve springs! Within a few years Fedden turned away from poppet valves and worked even more doggedly to perfect the sleeve valve.

Despite these problems Fedden was a devout apostle of air-cooling and he was already deep into the construction of the Mercury's follow-on. This was an engine called Jupiter, a single-row radial sprouting nine big-bore cylinders, each with four valves and equivalent in size to those used in his lab tests, giving a total of 1,753 cid. To Fedden this form of engine was only logical; the air-cooled engine provided excellent mechanical efficiency in its weight distribution, using a very short, very rigid crankshaft, a definite improvement over the long shafts of V-12 engines which often wobbled or "twanged" like guitar strings. These features were enhanced in the Jupiter by the use of sliding bob-weights on Fedden's ingenious master connecting rod which gave the engine perfect balance; moreover, Fedden's rigid shafts eliminated most gear failures.[1] The ungeared Jupiter weighed less than 700 pounds, demonstrating that air-cooled engines were lighter and simpler, since neither radiator nor water plumbing was required, and had fewer total parts, only 370 in the Jupiter, some 20 per cent fewer than a typical water-cooled

[1] A curious twist in designation has perpetuated the common myth that *geared* Jupiters were widely used before 1926. They were not, and the mistake came about through some sleight of hand on paper. When Fedden first designed the Jupiter he drew up plans for three versions: Jupiter I, a direct-drive engine designed to achieve 400 hp at 1,650 rpm; Jupiter II, a geared version turning the propeller at 1,200 rpm to 1,850 rpm for the crankshaft, and designed to achieve 450 hp; and Jupiter III, a geared version with even greater reduction ratio. Of the two geared proposals, only Jupiter II was built, and that only in prototype form. This sole geared version was exhibited at the 1920 Olympia Aero Show, but gears — even Fedden's ingenious epicyc ic variety — gave more problems than they were worth, and were quickly and quietly discarded. Nevertheless, Bristol was stuck with the early designations, so when the next *direct-drive* version appeared the problem was faced by calling it Jupiter I-Mark II; similarly, the next update (still direct-drive) was called Jupiter I-Mark III; for subsequent versions, since things were becoming too confusing, they reverted to straight series numbers, i.e., Jupiter IV, Jupiter V, etc., and carried on in that fashion, common among other builders. The mistaken belief that geared Jupiters were employed when in fact they were not come about by the understandable but careless use of terms such as Jupiter II — instead of the proper but awkward Jupiter I-Mark II. The first *geared* Jupiter which saw wide service was in fact the French-built model 9Ak of 1926; the English did not follow suit until 1928 with the Jupiter VIII.

engine of equivalent power. The Jupiter also featured a large circular flange which doubled as mounting support and induction manifold, inside of which a three-way aluminum spiral directed the output from three separate carburetors, each of which fed three cylinders independently at high mixture velocity.

The Jupiter design received Air Ministry acceptance in July 1918 and the prototype made its first bench run in mid-October, just days before the Armistice and too late for hostilities. After the war the aero engine business of Brazil-Straker was organized as the Cosmos Company, a new group, still located at Fishponds, but it was not until June 18, 1919, twelve days after Fedden's thirty-third birthday, that the first Cosmos Jupiter made its first flight in the second model of a Bristol fighter improbably named Badger. It was flown by Bristol chief test pilot Cyril Frank Uwins with Frank Barnwell occupying the observer's seat. In September this same engine was fitted to the Sopwith 107 for the 1919 Schneider race and seemed destined to vindicate Fedden's enthusiasm of March 1919 when he exulted, "The air-cooled fixed radial will prove to be the key to all future development of faster aircraft for the next twenty to thirty years, and powerplants of several thousand horsepower in one unit will enable vast improvement in the design of commercial aircraft." As if to hurry this prophecy singlehandedly, Fedden even then was optimistically developing an incredible 5,000-cid air-cooled engine with two rows of nine huge cylinders designed to produce 1,000 hp at 1,750 rpm, a Hercules planned "to revolutionize the design of aircraft intended for flights of great duration."

The hard economic facts of life soon checked this development. Government interest in the Jupiter did not include financial support or even the promise of a contract, forcing Cosmos to fund engine development themselves. As a result they went broke early in 1920.

In July 1920 Stanley White, who had become managing director in 1916 upon his father's death, and who remained active well into the 1960s, took a river-boat gamble by acquiring for Bristol the Cosmos assets — a book value of £60,000 for which he paid £15,000 — acquiring in the process Roy Fedden and five of his Jupiters, one of which had started a successful but incomplete government type test. Bristol, it seemed, would now be able to build for their planes their own aero engines, which portended a happy marriage, and Fedden was able to continue his efforts to perfect Jupiter with hardly a break. Working with unflagging drive through the summer of 1921, he devised an ingenious valve gear that compensated for the expansion of heated cylinders; this cylinder head was dubbed the "poultice head," and was fitted to the Jupiter I-Mark II which passed the stringent Air Ministry fifty-hour test in September. During its fifty-four-hour run the engine's average output was 348 hp at 1,575 rpm, but it made extended runs up to 462 hp at 1,840 rpm and operated one hour producing 193 hp on only six cylinders with hardly any vibration; when the three dead cylinders were cut in the engine picked up a full load at once. It demonstrated slam accelerations from under 400 rpm to full power in less than five seconds. This was more than a good test, it was spectacular. The Jupiter was only the third engine to pass the Air Ministry test. And it was the first air-cooled engine to do so.

However, fifteen months of intensive work and the expenditure of £200,000 by Bristol had resulted in the construction and sale of only eleven Jupiters, which had returned just £25,000; of these only two had been delivered. Thus it was no big surprise when, within a month of his engine's triumphant test, Fedden was told his aero engine department would be shut down at the end of 1921 unless financial matters improved drastically. Prospects of this seemed depressingly slim to the man who found himself father of a highly complex and expensive engine born into the cold famine of postwar economics. Anxious, almost despairing, Fedden took a Jupiter to the Continent in November, at virtually the last minute, for the 1921 Paris Air Show. He delivered a historic paper on air-cooled engines[2] at the Premier Congrès International de la Navigation Aérienne but was forlorn for their immediate future – and his.

Then it happened. Gnôme-Rhône, whose rotary-engine business had fizzled, took a very expensive license to build Jupiters in France, and this saved the engine from extinction. During 1921 strong government encouragement enabled the French aeronautic industry to produce on a scale far in excess of the British, building scores of planes to the British twos and threes. This resulted in such a success for the Jupiter that eventually firms in thirteen other nations acquired licenses (including Siemens in Germany and E. W. Bliss of Brooklyn, New York, in the United States), and in two years' time the Jupiter had gained world renown. The final Jupiter development, called Pegasus, was giving 1,000 hp twenty years later in World War II.

During 1919, when Fedden's Jupiter was still brand-new, he persuaded Frank Barnwell to build a brand-new aeroplane to show it off. Lucid and persuasive, Fedden was himself always an ardent flier, and was always urging Bristol test pilot Cyril Frank Uwins to race his engines, to pour it on. Thus they evolved the type 32 racer, built like the earlier Badger, only smaller. It bore a name that had achieved prestige in the war – Bristol Bullet – and was exceptionally strong, employing double spars in wing and tail; although some critics called it unnecessarily heavy its top speed of nearly 160 mph was close to the world record in those days. The Bullet racer,

Bristol 32 Bullet, original configuration, 1920 (BAC)

Cyril F. Uwins, circa 1922 (F)

registered G-EATS, made its first appearance at the 1919 Paris Air Show, from where it went on to spawn the great Bristol golden-age fighters. C. F. Uwins was mounted in the Bullet for the 1920 Aerial Derby the following July. Bookies gave it excellent odds, basing Uwins' prospects solely on the power of his huge Jupiter, not realizing the Bullet's size in relation to the tiny Martinsyde and British Nieuport racers. Starter George Reynolds dropped the flag precisely on time "ack-Emma" and the churning Jupiter – whose sound was described as "tinny" by some – hauled the graceful biplane steeply aloft, but its slow first lap was disappointing. This did not discourage Uwins, who rocketed around the second 100-mile circuit, shaving nearly five minutes off his first lap time, but having to settle for third place.

Cyril Uwins was already Bristol chief test pilot, a post he held for twenty-seven years through the end of World War II, during which tenure he tested fifty-four prototypes and set several records, notably the world's altitude record on September 16,

1932, when he climbed to 43,976 feet, a performance that earned him the Britannia Trophy. He had first come to Filton after recovering from an accident in 1916 when, as a young RFC officer, he broke his neck; he soon was recovered and ferrying three

Bristol Bullet after clipped wings and experimental spinner were fitted, the configuration planned for the 1921 Aerial Derby (BAC)

F.2Bs per week from the Filton acceptance park to the Western Front. Almost fifty years later Uwins, tall, solid, quiet, seemingly everlasting, was still active on the Board of Directors. One of his earliest flight test jobs had been the Bullet, and with the sleek, crimson

[2] Produced in the United States as NACA TM-185.

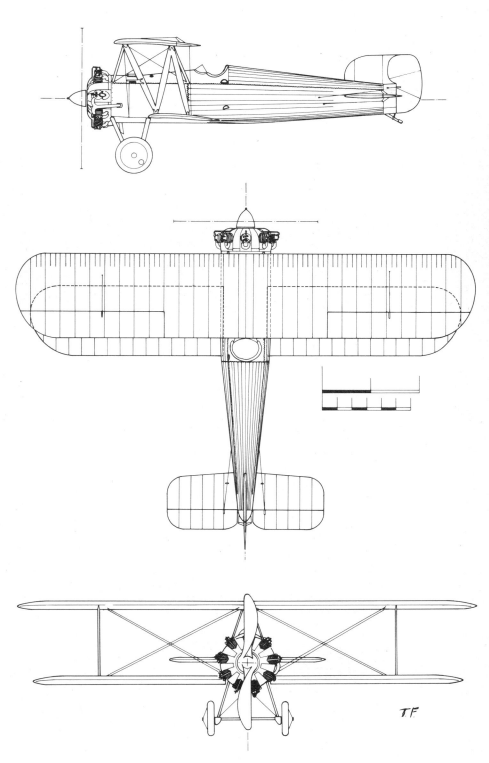

Bristol 32 Bullet racer, original version, 1919–20

Preparing the Bullet for the 1921 Aerial Derby. The spinner has already been removed.
(F)

biplane Uwins was back for the 1921 Aerial Derby, for which it had been virtually rebuilt. The most noticeable change was evident in her wings, which were minuscule compared to the ungainly sails of 1920. A new cowling used scoops behind the cylinders instead of 1920's fairings.

The Bullet's pre-race trials evoked a great deal of conjecture on the worth of spinners. Several aluminum spinners were tried in attempts to streamline the nose, a tall order in view of the Jupiter's fearful (52½-inch) diameter, but centrifugal force at the spinner edge caused bad vibration, and the large, bulbous spinner planned for the race developed a crack and had to be removed before the plane reached the starting line. The spare had a defect in the same spot. The spinner's absence cost "about 7 mph" in the race and also caused a draft in the cockpit which, Uwins said, "very nearly lifted me out of the seat!" Even so, there was only one racer on the long entry list that posed a threat to Uwins: the brand-new Bamel built just weeks before the Derby. The tens of thousands of Londoners who turned out to view the classic race saw the Bullet exceed her 1920 mark by more than 12 mph, even without a spinner, but she finished second to the Bamel. After the race some said that just a flat disc attached behind the prop to cover the cowl opening would have added to its speed during the race. Thus, during September and October 1921 a series of flight tests was conducted using different nose configurations; as she flew in the race the Bullet managed 140 mph; fitted with the spinner her speed was 157 mph; and with a flat, three-ply disc fixed behind the prop she made 156 mph, which would have given the Bamel a run for the money. It should be noted

359

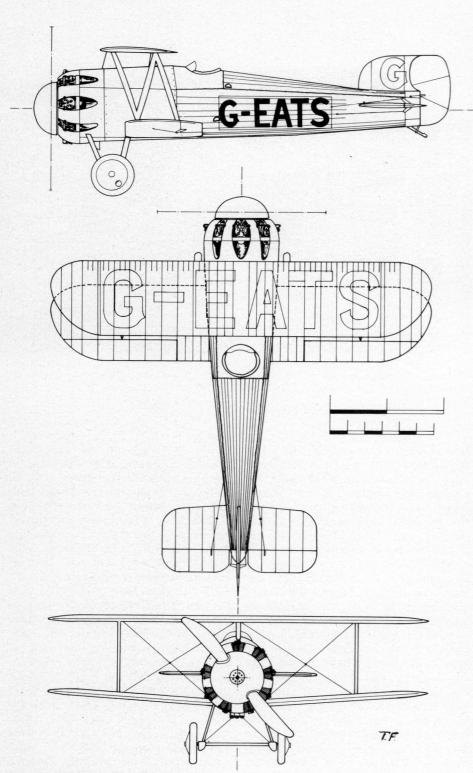

Bristol 32 Bullet racer, 1921–22

Bristol Bullet aloft in the 1921 Aerial Derby
(F)

Bristol 32 Bullet, 1921   (BAC)

that Fedden, too, was at the same time trying a weird variety of cowling schemes to improve cooling and reduce the enormous drag of air-cooled radials, but the best scheme, the famed ring cowl together with its intricate cylinder baffling, was still years away, awaiting the efforts of NACA in the United States.

"Roll-o" A. de Haga Haig, 1922   (F)

Rollo Amyatt de Haga Haig, an RAF test pilot at Martlesham Heath experimental station and a "wild colonial broth of a boy" if ever there was one, flew the Bullet essentially unchanged in the 1922 Aerial Derby. A gray morning and nippy southwest wind greeted Derby spectators but the sun started breaking through after lunch. Blasting off shortly before 3 P.M., "Roll-o" slashed over the haze-draped, sun-speckled hedgerows at 150 mph, but over West Thurrock on his second lap his oil pressure faltered. De Haga Haig throttled back

Bristol Bullet at Croydon for the 1922 Aerial Derby with its Jupiter engine covered by a plywood face which replaced the balky spinner
(F)

to 1,000 rpm and managed to finish the race at 145 mph, salvaging two second places (speed and handicap), again in the dust of the Bamel. This proved to be the Bullet's last race.

Barnwell's response was loss of heart. There seemed to be no viable aviation future in England just then, and in frustration he was ready to trade in his mufti for a uniform. He agreed to serve in the Royal Australian Air Force for two years, mainly because he had ambitions of establishing an aircraft industry down under. On May 18, 1921, the Australian Air Board recommended that he be offered a temporary commission as Squadron-Leader Technical, and after his appointment at the Office of the Australian High Commissioner in London on October 3, 1921, and a few weeks' liaison duty, he with his wife and two children enjoyed free first-class passage to Sydney. Barnwell arrived at the First Experimental Air Station in Australia,

headed by Leonard J. Wackett, in February 1922, but he felt cold-shouldered, and his ulterior hopes for expanding aviation there soon withered. He resigned his commission on July 31, 1923, and returned unheralded to Bristol to resume his duties as chief designer in October. His two-year absence left a gap at Bristol during which his assistant, Wilfred T. Reid, filled in as temporary chief designer, but Reid was anxious to emigrate to Canada.

When Barnwell departed in 1921, Reid set to work immediately on the design of a new super racer which became the Bristol type 72, conceived specifically to win the 1922 Aerial Derby. Expected to benefit from hundreds of hours in Bristol's wind tunnel, it would be in many ways the most advanced aeroplane produced in England, employing two important features

Bristol 72 under construction; note bicycle chain drive for retracting the landing gear.
(BAC)

Fitting the fuselage coque into position, Bristol 72 racer, 1922; compare wing construction here with the 1922 Curtiss R-6 (see Chapter 14). (BAC)

at that time decidedly unique in British aviation: thin-walled shell fuselage structure and retractable landing gear. Indeed, up until this time it can be safely said that fewer than a half-dozen aeroplanes with retractable gear had been built in the world, and the Bristol 72 was preceded by only two other racers using this feature. The flimsy, curved tubes supporting the racer's huge bulk gave the racer a peculiar top-heavy, splayed-out appearance, but in fact the tubular legs were shaped to fit neatly into the fat fuselage which had been built round enough to enclose the huge Jupiter engine.

The direct-drive Jupiter I-Mark III (s/n 855) built for the new racer turned 490 hp at 1,875 rpm in bench tests, making G-EBDR the most powerful dark horse entry in the Aerial Derby and qualifying it for the handicap scratch position in the race scheduled for Bank Holiday in early August.

The racer was ready to fly in July with Cyril Uwins assigned as pilot. On its first flight the full-span ailerons proved far too powerful, causing the cantilever wings to twist dangerously, upsetting the racer's flying qualities, and Uwins was lucky to bring the aeroplane back to the field for a landing unscathed. External bracing wires were added to give the wings torsional stiffness but the second test flight was also cut short when the curious spinner burst just after takeoff. Aileron trouble dogged the next two test flights, made without a spinner, but the racer had to be withdrawn from the Derby when an engineers' labor strike prevented the completion of the intricate spinner, resembling a partially covered bicycle wheel, a distinct departure from the Bullet's spinners of 1921, and without which the racer's performance was severely hampered.

The strike was symptomatic of the

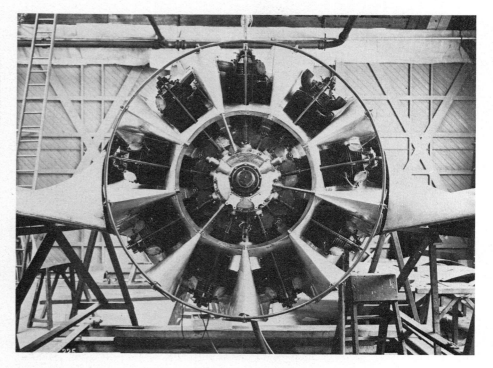

Bristol Jupiter engine on the type 72 racer; note cooling baffles to direct airflow between cylinders. (BAC)

Empennage for the Bristol 72 racer, 1922 (BAC)

362

Bristol 72 racer, 1922; note spinner with "bicycle wheel" attachment to prop boss which allowed an open duct for admission of cooling air to engine. (BAC)

Uwins in cockpit of Bristol 72, entered in the 1922 Aerial Derby (BAC)

growing disgruntlement then prevalent in the middle-class English working-man's life. English workmen for the most part were indifferent but deliberate at their jobs, frequently capable of turning out beautiful quality and precise detail yet equally capable of incredibly slow output; workmen whose volition was somehow becoming constricted in parallel with their national economy and their helplessly declining Empire, even as these factors more firmly entrenched their loyalties. The Bristol plant at Filton was a perfect stereotype of the English aeroplane factory, its featureless brick buildings

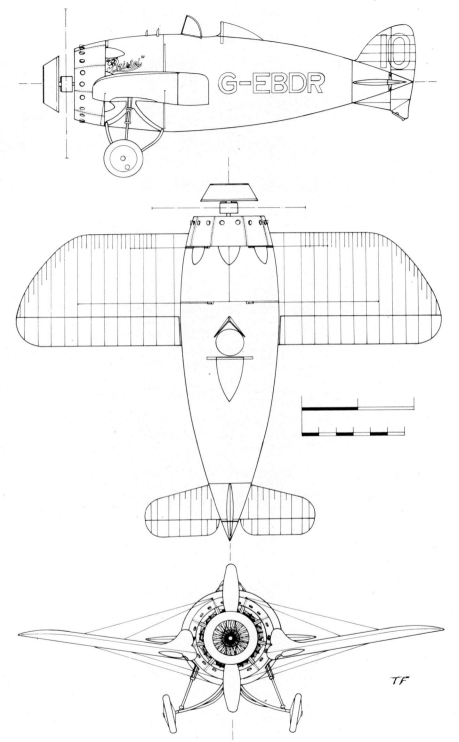

Bristol 72 racer, 1922

Engine runs without spinner, Bristol 72, 1922
(BAC)

The size of the Bristol 72 fuselage is apparent.
(BAC)

more mediocre test flights, making a total of seven flights, proud Bristol officials were far from convinced the 72 could make a suitable showing, and once again it was withdrawn. The 72's final demise came shortly after, when its huge fuselage was cut in two to provide playhouses for the children of the Experimental Shop manager.

Its engine was removed, shipped to France (current price was then £2,300), and fitted to the Gourdou-Leseurre racer entered in the 1923 Coupe Beaumont. The 72's designer, W. T. Reid, later formed a company in Canada which was ultimately absorbed by Curtiss-Wright. He later built the Curtiss-Reid Rambler which flew out of a grassy field that today is Montreal's huge Dorval Airport.

In May 1922 the little 100-hp Lucifer engine passed its Air Ministry type test. Its design, which placed ease of production and low cost ahead of performance, could be essentially called a three-cylinder, short-stroke Jupiter

with an aluminum crankcase, but the Lucifer was in reality a makeshift engine for the Air Ministry light plane program. First built by Cosmos in 1919 and displayed at the 1919 Paris Air Show on a Boulton & Paul P.10, it weighed 220 pounds complete and had its starting crank in the cockpit! The three cylinders, like cannons arranged in a Y, caused what has been described firsthand as "god-awful vibration, making it painful to fly behind." One was fitted to the charming type 77 racer in time for Cyril Uwins to win the 1922 Croydon Whitsun Handicap. Larry L. Carter next flew the 77 in the 1922 Aerial Derby, finishing fourth in speed and earning another first in handicap.

One month later, on September 8, 1922, the first King's Cup race began. Presented to the Royal Aero Club by King George V to encourage sporting aviation development, the glamorous King's Cup race has been contested regularly ever since, even to the

Preparing the Bristol 77, sporting its Cellon-red racing trim, for the 1922 Aerial Derby
(BAC)

in an ugly bunch on one side of the flying field, typical of industrial England at its worst, and the workers to fill them spilling from their tight, carbon-copy row houses which crowded the landing area, trudging through depressing mornings under darkly lowering clouds, gray misty rain falling lightly, with the thick smell of coal smoke in the air. It is not hard to reconcile the occasional outcroppings of bluff and vanity rising from granite foundations of fierce prejudice that

characterized their defensiveness and their reaction to the competitive results of their product.

Eager to vindicate the ignominity of not participating in the Derby, the workers hastened to enter their novel racer in the 1922 Coupe Deutsch to be held seven weeks later in France. Aileron size was reduced some 60 per cent, a modified spinner was devised, and the French were agog at the prospect of a "220-mph racer" invading their contest, but after three

present day. The 1922 race, a two-day circuit around Britain which tested endurance even more than speed, covered 810 miles. The Bristol 77 was entered with Rollo de Haga Haig at the controls, but its string of luck snapped and it was forced to retire at Aylesbury on the first day with engine trouble.

During 1923 the new Jupiter IV appeared and one was fitted to the Bullet racer in hopes for better luck after its string of seconds. Remarkably reliable, one Jupiter IV ran 50 hours non-stop at 90 per cent full throttle during a 150-hour endurance test, an incredible performance for 1923, but improvements in power came slowly due to the difficulty in cooling steel cylinders under heavier loads. Moreover, the Jupiter IV employed a variable timing gear allowing the pilot to control the closing of the inlet valves from 20 degrees late to delay compression at low altitude, to 9 degrees early at a predetermined altitude for maximum power, but this odd innovation proved troublesome and unpopular with pilots. Before the reengined Bullet could race in the 1923 Aerial Derby, however, its pilot, Major E. L. "Leslie" Foot, M.C., often fondly called "Feet," was killed. The Bullet was withdrawn and never raced again.

On June 23, 1923, this final episode took place on the occasion of the first Grosvenor Challenge Cup race, presented by Lord Edward Grosvenor (RAeC certificate number 607), a 404-mile point-to-point handicap for British planes of not over 150 hp. The exhilaration of the 1923 season's first air race was shattered when Leslie Foot crashed into Stonehill Road between Chertsey and Chobham shortly before 3 P.M., after leaving Bristol on his homeward leg. Foot was flying the Bristol 77, the race's scratch entry; during his required stop at Bristol shortly before the mishap he complained of a leaky fuel tank and seemed affected by the petrol fumes. But this apparently had nothing to do with his accident, which was variously

E. L. "Leslie" Foot, killed 1923   (F)

attributed to his racer's tail — or possibly a wing flying wire — breaking, apparently under the Lucifer's terrible vibration. Foot lost his life and the Bristol racer burned to ashes. His new bride Loraine was anticipating his gala return and an evening on the town together with Mr. and Mrs. Frank Courtney, who were waiting at the aerodrome with her when the terrible news arrived.

Fedden even more than Barnwell placed high value on air racing, especially when it came to consolidating the superiority of his Jupiter engine, and he persuaded Barnwell to design a new racer in March 1924, but the project was turned down by the financially nervous directors. Again in November 1924 Fedden proposed a smaller racer, to cost some £10,000 and intended for the 1925/26 racing seasons, but the idea was again rejected. However, by bringing some of his famous indomitable perseverance to bear, Fedden was at last successful in enabling Barnwell to produce an attractive small fast aeroplane called Badminton, built to achieve 180 mph using the

Bristol Badminton, 1926   (BAC)

510-hp Orion (Jupiter VI) engine. Engine cowling studies soon resulted in individually helmeted cylinders, quite reminiscent of the helmets that enclosed the Jupiter engine cylinders on the 1923 French Gourdou-Leseurre racer. About this time Colonel W. A. Bristow's offer to participate in building an air-cooled Schneider Trophy racer using a short-life Jupiter intrigued Fedden. Barnwell was much cooler toward this project, being of the in-line engine school for high-speed racing. However, thin, intense, resolute Oswald Short came forward to provide additional backing, and Bristow's designer, Wilfred G. Carter, who had recently left Hawker, laid out a semi-cantilever monoplane. After early pitfalls — strut changes and engine cooling problems which led to a helmeted Jupiter much like the Badminton — the Air Ministry contracted to buy one. This of course was the ill-fated Short Crusader of 1927[3]. That also was the year the

<hr />

[3] The Short Crusader (N.226) was designed for a speed range of 90–265 mph to answer criticisms of air-cooled engines for racing. Its acceptance trials were flown by Bert Hinkler in May, 1927. It was shipped to Venice for the Schneider race but on September 11, 1927, it flipped over and was destroyed on take-off because the aileron cables had been reversed by mistake. Miraculously the pilot, Flight Lieutenant H. M. Schofield, emerged alive.

pretty Badminton crashed with disastrous results. It had first flown on May 5, 1926, piloted by Cyril Uwins, and participated in that year's King's Cup piloted by Franklin L. Barnard, Imperial Airways pilot and former commodore of the Instone Air Lines. Barnard made the first airline flight in Instone's converted 11-passenger Vickers Vimy March 21, 1921, and had gained additional fame as the first ever winner of the King's Cup in 1922, winning a second time in 1925. In 1926 he started in the Badminton as the favorite, but was forced to retire en route with engine failure, caused by a fuel supply problem. Invited to fly the Badminton again in 1927, Barnard on July 28 took off on a short pre-race test flight to try a new propeller. At an altitude of some 200 feet, pointed toward Winterbourne near Filton, its souped-up 525-hp Jupiter seized due to insufficient clearance between the cylinder skirts and crankshaft balance weights. Barnard turned toward a field nearby, but the Badminton stalled and spun in from about 80 feet. Barnard was killed instantly. The Badminton was the last Bristol aeroplane ever intended specifically for racing.

In the meantime Frank Barnwell had recommended designing full speed ahead at Bristol; in 1927 he produced the famed Bristol Bulldog, which became a standard RAF fighter. In 1935 he designed a compact twin-engine metal transport called *Britain First* for Harold S. Harmsworth, first Viscount Rothermere, who had been Air Minister during World War I. The new trim aeroplane could outfly the best fighters of its day, but Barnwell did not live to see its wartime success as the Blenheim, for on August 2, 1938, while testing a 25-hp monoplane, Barnwell stalled and crashed to his death. His three sons were all killed in World War II, and by cruel irony two were flying Blenheims.

It was not until 1927 that Roy Fedden again brought to bear his quiet, intense persuasiveness to urge the government into a contract for a high-power version of his newest design, named Mercury, but nothing at all like the 1917 Mercury. The prototype was completed in August 1926 with an entirely new cylinder construction patterned after the successful American Pratt & Whitney Wasp, using open-ended steel cylinders and forged aluminum heads containing the combustion chamber and four valves. But Fedden was already embarked on the development of the large, air-cooled sleeve valve cylinder for mass production, a prodigious effort which required more than a decade and which more than once made him consider giving up the quest as hopeless. Like his earlier Jupiter, Fedden's sleeve valve Centaurus was a tribute to his ability to make the impossible work. Yet in 1937, even as his sleeve valve engines were on the verge of widespread success, Fedden with his uncanny mechanical insight predicted that piston engines would reach no more than 3,500 hp and that higher powers must come from gas turbines! This proved to be absolutely correct. Fedden was knighted in 1942 after the outbreak of World War II when 52 per cent of the RAF engines in service were of Bristol manufacture; Bristol built 116,200 more engines during the war. Honored and feted,

Sir Roy retired to Bwlch, Breconshire, where he died November 21, 1973, aged eighty-seven.

Despite never having won a race, the elegant Bristol racers stand out not only for their remarkable features but for the remarkable speed seekers who brought them into being.

BOATS, FLOATS, BRITANNIA 25

The Supermarine and Blackburn Racers

England is, after all, an island, and in spite of her lovely landplane racers the strong maritime imperative intrinsic in the British soul inspired equally lovely seaplanes. Indeed, in England as in Italy, the highest form of the art became embodied not in landplanes but in seaplanes; this transfer from land to sea first occurred in 1925 when the landplane's form reached the stage of 300 mph, to be adopted directly into the seaplane's role. The name in England universally revered for putting aeroplane racing to sea is Supermarine.

The Pemberton Billing Company Limited was founded at Woolston (Southampton) in 1912 by raw-boned, sharp-tongued Noel Pemberton Billing — motorist, yachtsman, devotee of golfing — whose young assistant, then twenty-one, was ruddy Hubert Scott-Paine, who became known as "Red-Hot" Scott after the flaming color of his hair — and his manner. The firm's cable address was registered "Supermarine" and early fame was consolidated by means of a hull design associated with Major Linton-Hope. This was built on a framework of very light and flexible circular rings of elm, light longitudinal members, and planked with strips of polished mahogany veneer to form a tubular body stiff against bending and torsion yet not rigid, the elm rings capable of being distorted into ovals undamaged as protection against hard landing shocks. External steps attached to the sides

367

as separate units made the hull seaworthy. Hulls built to this formula were so successful the British government took over and extended the plant for wartime construction, but despite several prototypes there was little production. Billing soon departed to enter Parliament as M.P. for East Hertfordshire,[1] and control of the firm passed to Scott-Paine, whose corpulence belied his iron-sinewed tenacity. He was joined by Squadron Commander James Bird in 1919; their motto was "not an aeroplane that will float but a seaworthy boat hull that will fly." Through years of extraordinary difficulty after the war, when the flying boat came into disfavor, their motto was always kept as an ideal, and after more than a decade of flying boat development the original Linton-Hope hull construction was still retained.

Powerful industrial currents which included the landplane orientation of the RAF; the studious neglect of flying boats by the carrier-oriented RN, who actually feared flying boats as a means for the land-based RAF to usurp their traditional function of home defense; the premature state of civil aviation as yet unready for far-flung commercial flying boat routes, all threatened to founder Scott-Paine, but he remained doggedly devoted to his beloved flying boat. In 1917 he had taken on a personal assistant four years his junior, a tall, blond, very serious young man named Reginald Joseph Mitchell, born a printer's son in Stoke-on-Trent twenty-two years before and who, like so many of his aviation contemporaries, served his

Reginald J. Mitchell (F)

[1] Billing served one term as an M.P. during which he coined the term "Fokker-fodder" referring to English boys whom he insisted were being sent to "sheer murder" at the Front. His policies were controversial, but the long-term results momentous. He pressed establishment of the Air Enquiry Board, which examined operations and efficiency of the RFC; out of this body evolved the Air Board, later made into the Air Ministry, and the Independent RAF. Billing died November 11, 1948, at his home in Burnham, aged sixty-eight.

apprenticeship in a locomotive works, beginning at age sixteen. Mitchell was entirely self-taught in matters aeronautical, but his great talent assured him of early notice and his apprenticeship at Supermarine was brief but dazzling: he became chief designer in 1919 upon the departure of J. Hargreaves, and chief engineer in 1920 at the age of twenty-five. Between the Armistice and the end of 1923 Supermarine built twelve new types of experimental flying boats, eight at their

Supermarine Sea King I prototype, 1919 (Au)

own expense, an incredible number of new designs. Most were fashioned by Mitchell. Outwardly retiring and seemingly shy, Mitchell had a wonderful sense of humor and with his close friends was the "life of the party." He played snooker, golf, and tennis, and learned to fly at the nearby Hampshire Flying Club. As a designer, Mitchell had what Henry Royce considered to be that rare and marvelous combination of being "slow to decide — but quick to act." No one had more intense powers of concentration or impatience at interruption when hard at work than Reginald Mitchell.

Attaching line to Sea Lion I, 1919 (Au)

Supermarine Sea Lion I, entry, 1919 Schneider Trophy race. Pilot Basil Hobbs on bow. (F)

Mitchell had assisted on the design of a single-seater scout flying boat in 1918 to meet Air Board specification N.1B, a measure to neutralize the threat of German Brandenburg seaplane fighters on North Sea patrols. Called the Baby, it was halted by the Armistice and only two were built. After the war Scott-Paine launched a campaign to promote an improved amphibian version for the private sportsman called the Sea King I, but it was expensive and impractical and there were no takers. Undaunted, Scott-Paine entered the 1919 Schneider Trophy race, to be conducted virtually on Supermarine's doorstep, and Mitchell reengined the Sea King with a Napier Lion engine, which tripled the aeroplane's power and resulted in a new name: Sea Lion I. The combination looked like a sure thing.

The pilot was colorless but competent Squadron Leader Basil D. Hobbs, who was met by James Bird at Bournemouth shortly after noon on a race day marred by wet gray fog. When slight improvement in the local visibility prompted the decision to start the race shortly after 4 P.M. Bird strongly protested, telling the committee the fog would surely not lift in Swanage Bay, site of a boat marking the first turn, but his concern was haughtily dismissed. Hobbs with misgivings began his takeoff, narrowly averting collision with rowboats, which no one stopped from wandering at will among the aeroplanes! Bird had been right. The fog in Swanage Bay was so thick that Hobbs, after another narrow miss with the blundering Fairey racer, landed to locate the mark boat on the surface. He taxied back and forth peering into the gloom without success, decided to hell with it, and opened the throttle to take off. Just then he felt a severe bump — he had struck a submerged object — but seconds later he soared above the ground-clutching layer of mist and saw friendly, familiar hilltops rising from the woolly blanket to the west. His plan was to carry on as though he had been observed, and he came in for his first required landing east of Boscombe Pier, but only then did the degree of damage rudely make itself known. Water gushed in, the Supermarine began to capsize, and Hobbs had to be rescued by a motor launch. The Linton-Hope hull was "salved" during the night and returned to Woolston the next day; it was later presented to the Imperial College of Science at South Kensington and loaned for exhibition to the Science Museum in 1921.

In 1920 Supermarine won an impressive £8,000 in an Air Ministry commercial amphibian competition for the durability of their hulls. A Supermarine was purposely stalled and dropped in from 30 feet, sustaining no damage! But sales remained stagnant although a military Sea King version appeared the following year, a single-seat fighting scout amphibian designed to be catapulted from capital-ship gun turret platforms. The first deck landing flying boat also appeared in 1921, and exports, modest in number if widespread, of the larger, passenger-carrying Channel and similar flying boats sustained Supermarine (to Norway for the first civil air mail route in that country, New Zealand, Sweden, Trinidad, Spain to fight the Riffs in Morocco, Bermuda, Fiji, Chile, Japan where some sported machine guns, and even the Orinoco delta for photo mapping). Supermarine also expanded their product line to include motor-boats, and King George V used a Supermarine motorboat built in 1921.

In 1919 Supermarine began operating passenger-carrying flying boats between Southampton and Guernsey in the Channel Islands on an occasional basis, briefly extending the service to Le Havre on September 28 during a massive coal and rail strike. Southampton-Guernsey passenger service prospered to the credit of Scott-Paine even as prospects for civil flying boat sales remained dim.

Plying the air route to the Channel Islands was a slight, extremely taciturn pilot named Henri C. Biard who had taken up flying at the Grahame-White School, Hendon, in 1912, at the age of twenty-two and served in the RNAS during World War I. Biard was the *doyen* of postwar British civilian pilots, having flown from an earlier date than almost any other, and in his capacity as Supermarine test pilot since 1920 he had flown multifarious types of flying boats. Taking time out from his passenger joy rides Biard flew the Sea King II, powered with a 300-hp Hispano-Suiza, to an astonishing 163 mph in March 1922 and proved it capable of rolls, loops, and spins.

In June 1922 Supermarine decided to build a new challenger for the Schneider Trophy. In contrast to French and Italian builders, who enjoyed government financial aid, Supermarine's was a private venture — "We did ours ourselves, you know," Scott-Paine later remarked. Design and shopwork was carried on in utmost secrecy, and a covert subterfuge was mounted to encourage the Italians into thinking they would win easily. Napier lent a new Lion at no cost to replace the Hispano-Suiza, Shell supplied free fuel, Wakefield free oil, etc. Of the two Sea Kings built in 1919, the second had become the military Sea King II version; it was now further modified into the Sea Lion II racer. The amphibian gear was removed, the bow modified, and tough wooden steps divided into watertight compartments, fabric-covered and given a Cellon "tropical doping scheme" over their plywood planking, were fitted to the hull. The Lion, turning a four-blade wood prop, was contained in a nacelle with the oil tank, Serck radiator of ample capacity, and shutters. The original mainplane structure was retained, the upper wing supported by four vertical struts entirely separate from the structure supporting the powerplant; the complete wing structure could be removed by withdrawing eight bolts. Wing area was reduced by using wings of reduced chord although the span was unchanged. To offset the greater slipstream twist from the Lion the fin area above the tail-

Supermarine Sea Lion II before shipment to Naples, 1922; note Lion engine, Sea King tail before enlarging fin. (F)

Supermarine Sea Lion II, winner, 1922 Schneider Trophy race (F)

plane was enlarged, and as with all small flying boats of this vintage using top-mounted engines, the tailplane was built with a generous negative camber to counteract the nose-down pitch from thrust. Biard's cockpit, in true maritime tradition, was provided with anchor and cable, bilge pump, towing fairleads, make-fast cleats and boat hook!

Scott-Paine's decision to mount a singlehanded challenge was bold and quite likely to result in undignified failure, especially since his entry seemed a doleful repeat of the three-year-out-of-date 1919 design. She certainly did not look like the typical racer. On her first takeoff her Lion quit cold 200 feet over Southampton docks, but Biard threaded his way between funnels and cranes into a clear area to plunk down. Repairs were not completed until sunset next day, but then Biard proved Scott-Paine's order to Mitchell had been carried out — the order was to build a flying boat that could sustain an honest 160 mph.

To the consternation of the British the race was advanced two weeks, and

after all their work it appeared they would miss it, allowing the Italians to secure their third and conclusive victory unchallenged. The French would not reach Naples due to an Italian rail strike. The generosity of the General Steam Navigation Company was hastily invoked and the SS *Philomel*, en route to Naples, was diverted to call at Southampton and fetch the Sea Lion II; otherwise there was no way she could have arrived in time. Biard, his white pallor and rather delicate physique in sharp contrast to the swarthy, sun-baked Italians, found the August Neapolitan sun "unbearably hot," even to the extent of fearing sunstroke. Perhaps the Italians deduced weakness from Biard's demeanor; certainly they were lulled by his clumsy practice laps flown at 140 mph, causing the betting odds to skyrocket in their favor. They should have perceived the sham from the incredibly smooth way Biard's Sea Lion smelled its way to its moorings after landing, finding the slipway without fuss, its light pneumatic-wheeled undercarriage slipped un-

erringly into special sockets by a grimy ensemble working in unison to a bosun's whistle without one shouted order.

The espionage was quite overt — every time Biard flew a practice run a group of stopwatch-equipped Italians was obvious; the Italian trade journals soon classified the Sea Lion as a 150-mph aeroplane. Their own S.51 was an honest 15 mph faster than that. On one flight Biard had a look down into nearby Vesuvius — and was flung upward several hundred feet by heat from the crater! On race day he mounted his open cockpit in gray flannels and shirt sleeves even though the start had been put off until late afternoon. He was the first to take off, the Italians' white hope, the S.51, last, but to the Italians' shocked chagrin Biard's stubby Supermarine acquired a measure of grace as it ripped across Golfo di Napoli toward Torre del Greco at nearly 160 mph. Virtually at the foot of the towering volcano Biard rounded the white balloon pylon with wide-open throttle, determined to build up what lead he could while he assessed

the Italians; he would nurse his engine later if his lead was sufficient. But he also knew that as the only foreign representative, with the only hope of keeping the trophy alive, he *must* finish. The Italians had started at carefully timed intervals and after a couple of laps had bunched together in a knot to impede his progress, neatly cutting him out at the corners. If he went outside he would lose time — just what the Italians wanted; inside would inevitably lead to a cut pylon and disqualification. He would somehow have to climb over the slow Macchis and hope to outpace them in a dive. Rocking in their wake turbulence he slowly closed on their tails and was able to dart above, where he found himself looking down clearly into their upturned goggled faces. Then he was diving for all he was worth toward the white sphere a mile away. He hauled around the pylon in a percussed groaning turn, leaving the nonplused Italians in his wake!

For seven laps Biard flew flat out but his sixth lap, corresponding to the S.51's fourth, was only six seconds

The Schneider Trophy in the entrance hall of the Royal Aero Club (3 Clifford Street), 1922. On the left is Harry T. Vane, C.B.E., of Napier; Hubert Scott-Paine of Supermarine is on the right. (F)

Supermarine Sea Lion taxiing in Southampton Water during modifications, 1923 (Au)

Henri Biard in the cockpit of Sea Lion III before the 1923 Schneider Trophy race (F)

better. Nevertheless he eased off a bit, allowing himself to be paced by the S.51, which was faltering with a vibrating prop, matching its speed almost exactly. The Italian gained slightly on the last few laps but Biard won the race handily by more than two minutes, and flew two extra "insurance" laps. After his upset victory he exuberantly made what was for him a major statement: "Jolly good!" The Sea Lion II had set the world's first officially recognized flying boat records, for closed-course speed over 100 and 200 kilometers, duration, and distance. Biard received a silver salver

at an October banquet hosted by the euphoric Royal Aero Club.

Purchased by the Air Ministry after her 1922 victory, the Sea Lion II was loaned to Supermarine by an increasingly parsimonious government to defend the Schneider Trophy in 1923. She was cleaned up, fitted with new, smaller two-bay wings, a new vertical tail with somewhat cleaner outline but larger area, her hull increased in length by almost 3 feet, and her bottom replaned. The bow was again modified, the marked "ram" of Sea Lion II reduced by bringing the chines in more gradually, making her cleaner

in the air if not the water; bow hydrovanes were added as well as fairing pieces behind the sides of the main step, and wingtip floats of elliptical

cross section were suspended from the outer-bay struts. A new Lion of 550 hp was fitted, equipped with a radiator of the "long tube" type, neatly cowled in a

Sea Lion III taxiing out for takeoff in the 1923 Schneider Trophy race; Blackburn Pellet in background   (F)

Sea Lion III, 1923 Schneider Trophy race
                                    (Real)

duralumin nacelle. Thus modified, she became Sea Lion III. In 1923 it was suddenly fashionable to call flying boats "single-float seaplanes," especially when Great Britain was invaded by the spectacular American twin-float Curtiss CR-3 racers. To a certain extent lulled by their 1922 victory, and reluctant to give credence to what seemed wildly extravagant American claims, the British approached the 1923 Schneider Trophy race with unwarranted complacency.

On race day Biard was not pleased by the "millpond" aspect of The Solent – he preferred a bit of chop. It also seemed to the British that the smooth conditions unduly favored the Americans, who took off first. Fifteen minutes later Biard gunned his bulky racer, leaving a fine curl of foam, and headed for the starting line, but at that very instant a sharp howl was heard overhead and a sun-glint flashed from Rittenhouse's CR-3, slicing vertically over the mark boat as it completed the first lap in unbelievable time. Biard may have been distracted by this totally unexpected event; it seems certain the judges were because when the Sea Lion III suddenly jumped

skyward after its extremely short takeoff run they were not sure if Biard had crossed the line on the water as the rules required. In any event they scrupulously avoided any taint of favoritism by promptly disqualifying Biard. While Biard did not know he had been disqualified he did know that even at full throttle he was hopelessly slower than the Curtiss racers. Meanwhile Commander James Bird was going through paroxysms as he desperately tried to get the disqualification reversed. A written report was soon passed to the judges' barge from the start-line observers confirming Biard had touched the water as he crossed the line, and the uncertain judges just as hastily reinstated their countryman, generating a controversy that would last for weeks. Biard's only hope was a Curtiss breakdown. This did not occur, and though Biard's speed was 12 mph better than his 1922 winning performance in the same aeroplane, he finished a poor third. As he thundered by the mark boat he put the Sea Lion stern end-on to the spectators and sustained a steep climb until almost out of sight. On December 4, two months after the

race, the valiant Sea Lion III was transferred to the RAF, receiving serial N.170.

One thing became abundantly clear to R. J. Mitchell, who had been almost awe-struck by the Curtiss racers: he could no longer be satisfied with last year's model. Nor even last year's concept.

The message was also made all too painfully clear to the makers of the Blackburn Pellet, another British seaplane racer. Robert Blackburn, then thirty-eight, a modest, generous but resolute aeroplane builder from Olympia, Leeds, had built his first aeroplane in 1909 and remained head of his company for four full decades. His seaplane base was at Brough, near Hull, where through the early 1920s he specialized in torpedo planes built to the designs of Major Frank Arnold Bumpus, a charming, cultivated designer one year junior to him. But construction had also begun at the Leeds factory in mid-1918 on a seaplane scout designed by Bumpus to Air Board specification N.1B, the same specification to which the Sea Lion could be traced. In all, eight N.1Bs had been planned: three each from

Blackburn (N.56–N.58) and Supermarine (N.59–N.61) and two from Westland (N.16–N.17). Blackburn's concept was a refined sesquiplane, and the hand of Harris Booth was apparent in its curvaceous lines but too small rudders. Like the Supermarine, its hull was a monocoque Linton-Hope structure designed in 1917, with external side fins extending aft to a main step amidships and a small auxiliary step farther aft toward the stern. The bow was pointed and the tail sharply upswept. In 1918 the Blackburn N.1B was to be powered with a 200-hp Hispano-Suiza driving a two-blade pusher prop, and blueprints showed a biplane tail with twin rudders. The American elmwood to be used in the hull was late in arriving, so other woods were substituted, and the hull when finished needed external stiffening. The project was halted by the Armistice, the wings and tail were never built, and the only hull completed (N.56) was put in storage at Brough, where it would lie for almost five years.

Early in 1923 Blackburn with his firm's other directors, after vigorous discussion, decided to forgo a cash

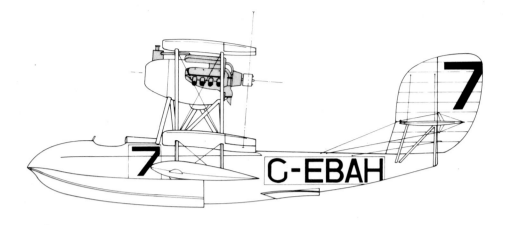

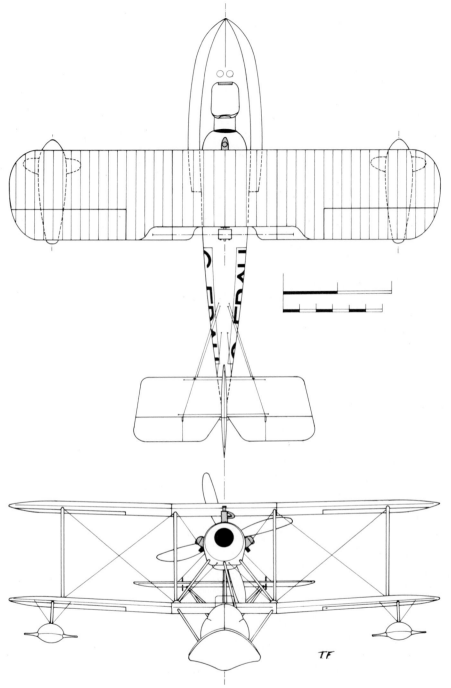

dividend in order to enter the Schneider race, which was being held in England for the first time in four years, making the potential prestige too much to pass up. Besides, with mounting anticipation, Blackburn was convinced he had the ideal hull to win then lying in storage. In March the racer's preparation was announced, making it the first certain British entry that year. The design of new wings and tail was begun. A Napier Lion driving a tractor prop would be mounted on top instead of between the wings, although the Lion finally secured was then installed in the Gloster I, which won the 1923 Aerial Derby in early August. The engine's late availability delayed the racer's readiness until September, only three weeks before the race. The refurbished aeroplane, named Pellet, sported a new single fin and rudder and new wings separated by V-struts with an extremely narrow gap, the lower wing much shorter and less than half the size of the upper in virtual sesquiplane fashion. With test pilot Reggie Kenworthy mounted, the Pellet was launched in a stiff crosswind and tide in the Humber. Almost at once its starboard wingtip float dug in, tipping it over — and it promptly sank.

Blackburn was now grim-lipped but even more obstinate that his plane should race. The five-year-old hull had proven to be defective in strength and tricky to handle on the

water with its narrow beam and high c.g., and under the twisting influence of the huge Lion, which produced more than twice the power for which the N.1B had been designed. Improvisation, it turned out, had handed Blackburn a "precious poor chance." Nevertheless the Pellet was stripped and repaired and larger wingtip floats fitted. The engine was overhauled. As for the press, the accident was blamed on a submerged object. It was September 23, less than a week before the race, when the racer was again airworthy, and untried it was shipped by rail to Southampton to be assembled in Fairey's Hamble works. On September 26, the day before the official navigability trials, Kenworthy was aboard for his second launching. The Pellet bucked alarmingly on takeoff, its wood prop was damaged by spray, and in the air it proved to be nose-heavy. Then, when hardly across the Solent the coolant water began to boil. Kenworthy force-landed by the RAF station at Calshot but drifted for an hour before a Saunders motorboat appeared to tow him 4 miles to Cowes. Working all night, Saunders mechanics bypassed the inadequate tubular radiators, which were recessed into the top wing lower surface, and fitted a single large Lamblin borrowed from Folland below the engine. They also replaced the wood prop with a borrowed Leitner-Watts prop made of

Supermarine Sea Lion Schneider racer; the version shown is Sea Lion III of 1923.

Two views of the Blackburn Pellet, illustrating how the aeroplane bucked and plowed just before capsizing, 1923; note relative position of Mr. Withers' steam yacht, the official start boat, in background. (Au, F)

Pulling Pellet pilot Kenworthy into Lord Montagu of Beaulieu's rescue boat; an agitated Mrs. Kenworthy is apparent. (Au)

steel. Her fin chines were also reinforced with Saunders Consuta, copper-sewn plywood, but the work was not completed until 11:30 A.M. on September 27.

Under great pressure, Kenworthy, inexperienced in seaplane handling and flying an untried entry, clambered aboard and the Pellet was launched immediately to start navigability trials designed to tax the world's finest seaplanes. Taxiing out the Medina, her bows rose considerably; instead of porpoising with a pitching motion the Pellet lifted and sank bodily, slapping the sea resoundingly with her whole length. Kenworthy had the throttle partly open when a small rowboat bothered him and he jabbed the throttle wide. This made the Pellet buck spectacularly and claw free of the water twice in a stalled attitude, plunging back heavily, slowly sideslipping right until the right float plowed in, and the inevitable happened: the Pellet dived vertically under the surface. Kenworthy soon realized he was twisted wrong way around in the inverted, rapidly flooding cockpit, his head toward the floor and his feet outside the cockpit opening, with a bubble of trapped air providing a momentary breathing space as icy daggers of cold sliced through his body. With frenzied, breaking fingernails he somehow freed the choking seatbelt and fought free. When he bobbed gasping to the surface the official race timer reckoned he had been submerged for sixty-one seconds! The motor launch *Vivid*, belonging to Lord Montagu of Beaulieu, arrived moments later to fetch Kenworthy, who promptly fainted and had to be given artificial respiration by his frantic wife. The Pellet was brought ashore during the night by Mr. Newman, Saunders works manager, but her brief racing career was finished for good.

Just days after the race Henri Biard was reestablished in regular passenger flights — indeed, daily service from the

Reginald W. Kenworthy, Blackburn pilot, 1923 (F)

Woolston terminal on the river Itchen had begun only three days before the race. In November Hubert Scott-Paine had what C. G. Grey later called a "tremendous row" with James Bird. Bird wanted to get rid of Scott-Paine and was willing to pay almost anything to have him go. Scott-Paine reportedly demanded a staggering £200,000, whereupon Bird slapped the table and said, "Done with you." Scott-Paine, after thus haughtily and handsomely severing his connection with Supermarine, devoted his full attention to the burgeoning British Marine Air Navigation Company Ltd., an organization he had formed the previous March involving Supermarine flying boats and the Southern Railway; travel time to the bucolic Channel Islands took only one and a half hours by air as opposed to overnight by boat, hence the air route's growing popularity. Huge, new six-passenger Sea Eagle amphibians were put into service, each powered by a 360-hp Rolls-Royce Eagle IX engine.

So promising did they seem that one was entered in the 1923 King's Cup race around England, piloted by Biard

and carrying four passengers. During one control stop heat burst a tire so Biard gamely deflated the other and continued on the rims (he had discarded the spare to save weight). When later he was forced to acquire new tires from "outside" he was disqualified. In the 1924 King's Cup race Biard found himself over Newcastle at 1,200 feet in another Supermarine when suddenly a reduction gear failure allowed the prop to run away with a terrific scream. It smashed the radiator just inches behind his head as it flung itself free, one blade grazing the startled pilot then burying itself in the hull. Biard force-landed in the Blaydon race course on the city outskirts.

On March 31, 1924, British Marine Air Navigation became one of four airlines which joined to form the new Imperial Airways, Ltd., incorporated as the "chosen instrument" of the British government to develop commercial air transport. Scott-Paine became a director of the new company, which sixteen years later on April 1, 1940, was renamed British Overseas Airways Corporation — BOAC. In 1934 Scott-Paine founded the British Powerboat Company at Hythe, designers and producers both in England and the United States of World War II PT boats. After the war he lived in the United States until his death in 1954.

At Supermarine 1924 was a year of profound transition. R. J. Mitchell was a designer brought up strictly to design for practical utility, and despite his abundant imagination and independent tendencies, he was possessed of the British temperament which regards all things novel with indifference if not actual suspicion. Thus did most British designers regard the twin-pontoon Curtiss racers which swept up the Schneider Trophy in their maelstrom. A complicating factor was that just when England's beloved flying boats were overnight rendered obsolete for racing by Curtiss, they were catching on for commercial purposes. In 1924 Mitchell was hard at work designing a new flying boat racer to be called

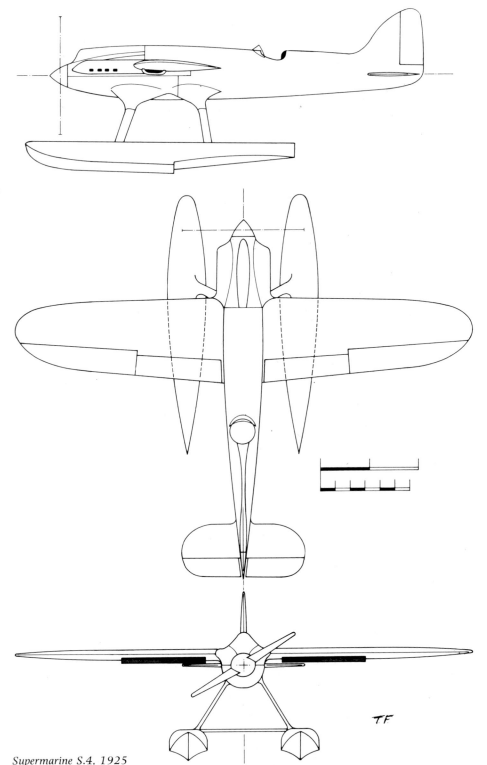

Supermarine S.4, 1925

Sea Urchin, powered with a Rolls-Royce Condor VIII 800-hp engine mounted inside the hull with a geared drive to the propeller. Yet the more he pored over the Sea Urchin blueprints the more the bulky, disjointed lines nagged him. After the sleek Curtiss racers his new plane just did not look right.

Mitchell discarded the Sea Urchin and with it the flying boat idea altogether. Letting his mind soar he began sketching a bold shape, one that would trace a sweeping curl of sky, an aeroplane that should render the Curtiss racers obsolete in their turn. This would be the Supermarine S.4. It would be powered by the Napier Lion, which at that time, Mitchell was convinced, was the best engine available for racing. That very year in France, Bernard produced the graceful all-wood V.2 racer which set the world speed record of nearly 280 mph, powered by a Hispano-Suiza engine of broad-arrow form similar to the Lion, with its outer cylinder blocks enclosed in cowls that blended — indeed, almost melted — into the shoulder-mounted monoplane wing. It seems quite clear that Mitchell was just as deeply influenced by the Bernard monoplane design as he was by the twin-pontoons of the Curtiss racers. Certainly, in taking his point of design departure, his twin-pontoon, shoulder-wing, all-wood monoplane embodied virtually identical features; in addition, Mitchell, who previously had been inclined to underestimate the aerodynamic importance of detail design in the drag of the complete racer, took an important lesson from both Curtiss and Bernard and did not repeat the mistake of his flying boats on which pipes, cleats, and all manner of odds and ends sprouted in hapless confusion. If anything his S.4 set a new standard in streamlining which, unfortunately, proved to be slightly ahead of its time. Nevertheless he had made the giant leap. Often slow to adopt new trends, the British somehow seem to have a precious few geniuses waiting

in the wings to step forward once a new trend has passed muster and push themselves to the world's front rank almost as though the new trend were their exclusive province. And so it was with R. J. Mitchell and the twin-pontoon monoplane racer, the form with which he achieved his highest aspiration.

Naturally Mitchell was concerned over the drag of thick, cantilever monoplane wings which had injured the popularity of the monoplane racers that had already appeared beginning in 1922. Mitchell worked in close collaboration with the Royal Aeronautical Establishment at Farnborough, where his new symmetrical airfoil and over-all wing design took form. In addition, a one-eighth-scale S.4 model was tested in the Duplex wind tunnel of the National Physical Laboratory at Teddington. Mitchell was quite concerned by the dreadful effect from the special Lamblin radiators; on the full-size S.4, 226 vertical plates would protrude from the bottom of each wing, the only excrescences on the entire aeroplane. The model tests indicated these would not only kill some 2 per cent of the potential lift but they also caused tremendous drag. The S.4 over-all drag coefficient was ·049, quite high when compared to that of the Curtiss R3C-2 (·039), and Mitchell's own estimate was that 38 per cent of the racer's total drag was caused by the radiators. The S.4 wing was built in one carry-through piece composed of two spars built up from plywood webs and spruce flanges, several spanwise stringers, and ribs built in a form similar to the spars. The skin was plywood sheet decreasing in thickness from root to tip, and no fabric was used. The bottom surface included a trough to carry the water-coolant pipe to the engine. Wing flaps were provided, interconnected to the ailerons, which could act independently or in conjunction with the flaps, although significantly, Mitchell did not use wing flaps on any of his later racers. A complete wing was

Brand-new Supermarine S.4 in Southampton Water, 1925   (Au)

built and tested to destruction at Farnborough, its apparent strength encouraging the audacious builders, who were resolved to make the cantilever monoplane work.

The S.4 was officially built to specification 2/25, and the go-ahead to begin construction was given by the Air Ministry to both Supermarine and Gloucestershire (for the Gloster III) on March 18, 1925. Construction began one week later. Just five months later, on August 25, three days after the Gloster III first flight, Henri Biard lifted the S.4 from the waters near Woolston for the first time. There had never been an aeroplane built in England like the S.4, which rose like some smooth, silvery scimitar amid the keening of seagulls and the hushed awe of Woolston longshoremen, who stopped to turn and watch entranced as it lanced low behind the maze of masts. In his tiny, cuplike cockpit Biard sat behind two husky, steel-tube, sloping A-frames which formed the S.4's backbone and to which the four

high-tensile steel tube float struts were welded. These were streamlined simply by aluminum casings, a daring experiment in an engineering era of cross-wire—braced girders, and the vibration of these struts during lashed-down runups made skeptics of many old-time Supermarine artisans. The wing passed between the two A-frames with the engine mount attached directly to the forward frame to carry the new, direct-drive Lion VII driving its Fairey/Reed metal prop. This was started ingeniously by a boat-mounted Bristol gas engine with a hose pipe to the S.4 engine manifold. Mitchell defended the large S.4 cross section, which was necessary not just to accommodate the W-12 Lion engine but to allow sufficient anchor for cantilever wings and chassis.

The fuselage was an all-wood shell in three tightly fitting pieces: engine, center, and rear, which carried the one-piece tail unit. Fuel was carried in several tanks since there was insufficient room internally for one large

The lovely Supermarine S.4, world's fastest seaplane, September 1925; note complete absence of any external wire bracing. (Au)

The synthesis of aesthetics with aerodynamic cleanliness, the result of design effort already consolidated by 1925 (F)

The firmest of all belonged to Henri Biard, who for the first time in his life felt spooked by an aeroplane. The S.4 was nothing at all like the staid, sturdy old girls in which he had been plying to the Channel Islands. Visibility from the aft-mounted cockpit was "perfectly dreadful" with wings in the way and even the long snout during nose-high takeoffs and landings. The new one-piece wing especially frightened him; it seemed to "shiver." On two occasions he experienced the disturbing sensation of being followed by a "ghost" aeroplane, neither shadow nor reflection, and yet no other aeroplane

Supermarine S.4 shortly before its shipment to the United States for the 1925 Schneider Trophy race. From left to right: G. H. Brown, rigger; H. Grimes, launchman; A. Powell, in charge of erection; C. Coe, chief mechanic; R. J. Mitchell, designer; C. B. Wilson, 1925 Schneider team leader; Commander J. Bird, Supermarine managing director; H. C. Biard, pilot; W. Lind-Jackson, in charge of running engine; H. B. Pickett, in charge of engine.
(Au)

tank. Each pontoon was built with an all-wood fore-and-aft keel which with port and starboard chines formed a pronounced concave V-shaped underside. Double watertight bulkheads were used but the whole pontoon assembly had to be flexible enough to absorb the impact of 120-mph landings, especially since on landing impact the struts were cement-pole rigid. Mitchell's serious and studied mien lent such authority to the pioneering strides he was taking that he captivated his co-workers and the S.4's construction took place in an atmosphere of pride bordering on a crusade. It seemed a bit unfair if understandable when a British trade journal commented with tactless sincerity, "One cannot help feeling a certain amount of surprise that a British designer has had sufficient imagination to produce such a machine." This, naturally, only served to tighten Supermarine upper lips even more firmly.

in all England could match the S.4's speed. Mitchell was rabid on the subject of Biard's well-being. He followed each test flight in a motor launch, dressed in a bathing suit after promising, "If anything happens I'll dive into the water and get you out." On September 13 Biard took the S.4 four times over a 3-kilometer measured course near Calshot — one wonders with how much trepidation — and managed to set the world maximum speed record for seaplanes of 226·752 mph, flying one pass at 231·406 mph. This beat by 38 mph the official mark of 188·118 mph made in 1924 by Cuddihy in the Curtiss CR-3 which had won the 1923 Schneider Trophy race, although Rittenhouse exactly one year before had flown the R2C-2 to 227·5 mph over Long Island Sound, 1 mph faster, in an unofficial speed test. Still, it was the first time in history that Great Britain had ever held a world maximum speed record. It was short-lived: Doolittle in the Curtiss R3C-2, the last biplane to win the Schneider Trophy, beat it by almost 20 mph just six weeks later. Yet at the time of Biard's record, con-

sidering his limited S.4 experience of less than two hours flying time, it seemed an especially good omen. Managing director James Bird remained cautious regarding the upcoming race: it would be "no walk-over."

Four days after its speed record flight the S.4 was unveiled publicly to the press. Mitchell's "hush-hush" racer was officially on the Air Ministry secret list despite its flight tests, which had been photographed copiously from nearby beaches by foreign attachés carrying cameras in their picnic baskets. The inordinate secrecy had been carried so far that it was mockingly suggested in *The Aeroplane* prior to the "unveiling" that pressmen appear at Waterloo Station for the journey to Southampton dressed "in the uniform of the Ku Klux Klan!"

Aboard the *Minnewaska* a few days later, en route to the United States, Biard slipped while playing deck tennis and cracked a bone in his wrist. It looked as if he might be sidelined but in fact he was indispensable to the S.4 effort. On October 16 he made two short flights from Chesapeake Bay and his wrist seemed strong enough. But

The S.4 taking off from Chesapeake Bay   (Au)

Turning up the Lion engine in the Supermarine S.4 at Bay Shore Park, Maryland, 1925   (F)

then he caught a severe case of flu, which felled him for several more days.

Mitchell was appalled at the flimsy, sodden canvas tent in which his prize beauty was hangared. Makeshift, unfinished wood floors and workbench with bare electric light were provided, which might have been barely suitable in the best of weather, but a baleful storm swooped down upon the hapless entrants. The British team waited in Baltimore's Southern Hotel, frustrated, unable to practice, as rain seeped through their hangars and frigid gales tore at the canvas. A tent pole ripped free and caromed into the S.4 tail, causing moderate damage. It had to be repaired under miserable conditions.

At 9:45 A.M. on October 23 Biard, still weak from his bout with flu, mounted the S.4 to begin the navigability trials. He took off, hoping to get a bit of much needed practice before beginning the official task, and flew over the pier and row of canvas T-hangars, "making steep banks on the turns." He flew out to the judges'

cutter when Mitchell, watching as usual from a motor launch and shivering in his bathing suit, saw Biard turn back toward the pier-head at a height of about 800 feet. The S.4 was then seen to enter a series of almost vertical banks, first to one side then the other. At first it looked like mild aerobatics but it was soon apparent Biard was in trouble. Hunched in his cockpit, Biard was once again overcome by the powerful impression of the "ghost aeroplane" following him. The S.4, rocking from side to side, rapidly lost height, seemed to enter a sharp sideslip, fell 100 feet, and pancaked flat into the bay in a tremendous plume of spray. A witness recalled the S.4 flaps "were hard down . . . [and when it hit it made] a huge hole in the sea."

Agitated almost to the point of apoplexy, especially when his launch broke down, Mitchell was frantic but helpless. Biard found himself 30 feet under still, icy sea water, upside down, pinned in glue-like mud, reflexively struggling to untangle himself in the

The S.4 after its crash in Chesapeake Bay, 1925   *(Au)*

R. J. Mitchell's subsequent racing efforts: the metal, wire-braced S.5 of 1927; and . . .

strangling darkness. At last, somehow, his lungs exploding, he reached the surface and dimly made out Hubert Broad's Gloster III through his smeared goggles. Broad, who had landed and taxied to the scene, first spotted the goggles amid the floating debris, not realizing at once that the goggles were still attached to Biard! Soon Mitchell arrived and he too then realized with tremendous relief that Biard was alive — his major injury being a rebroken wrist. There was a detached moment as he met Biard's eyes with a smile forming on his lips, and asked, "Is it warm?"

A controversy soon evolved over the cause of the accident. The Italians accused the wing of not being strong enough to withstand 45-degree banks, calling this "criminal." But the roots of blame lay deeper and were more tangled than that. The *official* cause was stated by Major J. S. Buchanan, O.B.E., of the Air Ministry Technical Department in a paper delivered at the Royal Aeronautical Society on January 21, 1926, in which he flatly stated Biard had stalled during a steep turn and lost control at a height insufficient to recover. But Biard himself was convinced there had been severe wing flutter.[2] Significantly, Mitchell completely abandoned the cantilever wing for all his later racers.[3]

[2] Biard's description of the accident, quoted in Chapter 4, appeared in *Wings* (Hurst & Blackett, London, 1934). Proponents of the stall theory say this was "surely ghosted" and thus "suspect." As in almost every air disaster, however, the cause is a compendium of several factors. Biard was too experienced a pilot to stall without some serious factor contributing to his obviously severe control difficulty. Aileron flutter could have adversely affected his lateral control, leading to unintentional overbank — and perhaps stall. Thus the argument is moot.

[3] No doubt the fear of flutter was a factor in this decision, but Mitchell also contended that, flutter problems aside, the wire bracing allowed lighter main structure and much thinner wings — hence a theoretical 5 mph speed gain.

the similar, high-speed Rolls-Royce–powered S.6 series of 1929 and 1931   *(Au, Au)*

Indeed, the Supermarine racers to follow were in many ways not as radical in their departure from aeronautical tradition as the S.4 had been. The S.5, also Lion-powered, was built to specification 6/26 for the 1926 Schneider. The wing was dropped from mid to low, its span 5 feet shorter than the S.4's, and plenty of stiff, external wire bracing was added; moreover, Mitchell adopted all-metal structure. The cockpit was moved forward to improve visibility. Unable to compete in 1926, the S.5 was delayed until 1927 awaiting the completion of the geared, 800-hp Lion VII-B. The follow-on S.6 and S.6B (which won the contest respectively in 1929 and 1931, retiring the trophy for all time in favor of the British), aside from their vastly more powerful Rolls-Royce engines and exotic blended fuels, were aerodynamically in all respects quite in accordance with the formula which had already been painstakingly distilled and adopted back in 1924.

The name of Reginald J. Mitchell will always be remembered primarily for his design of the immortal Spitfire. Aerodynamically the Spitfire was not nearly so close to the later S.6B racer as the popular legend, still perpetuated, would have one believe. If anything, it was more a return to the S.4 racer and was fashioned by Mitchell in characteristic maverick style, outside the strict requirements of Air Ministry specifications, because it was the fighter "he thought the RAF would need." Mitchell had become the victim of tuberculosis[4] and underwent a major lung operation in 1933 on the Continent at the very time the Spitfire idea was germinating in his brain.[5] The operation did not help; he deteriorated rapidly and was pronounced incurable in March 1937, one year after the prototype Spitfire first flew, piloted by Vickers-Armstrong test pilot "Mutt" Summers. (Vickers-Armstrong had acquired the entire share capital of Supermarine in 1928.) Sadly, Mitchell did not live to see even the first production Spitfire in the air. He died on June 11, 1937, at the age of forty-two. His beloved Supermarine factory at Woolston, Hants, was bombed to smithereens on September 26, 1940, during the Battle of Britain, which his Spitfire helped so gallantly to win.

---

[4] It has also been reported as cancer.

[5] It has been suggested rather convincingly that in fact the Spitfire was essentially a 5/7 version of the German Heinkel He.70 fast mailplane of the 1930s — even to such details as landing gear trunnions, etc. Mitchell had spent time on the Continent during his illness, thus affording him the opportunity to become familiar with Germany's by then acknowledged aeronautical progress. The author does not pretend to judge the merits of this issue — nor indeed that of the He.70's true design influence itself — since both are beyond the scope of this book, but only offers this as an intriguing observation for other aero historians to ponder.

Italy

THE FEROCIOUS FIAT OF BRACK-PAPA

26

The Ansaldo and Fiat Racers

Sheets of sunlight reflected from glass grillwork in the huge, arched window-walls of the hangars at Mirafiori Aerodrome near Turin (Torino), ringed on the north by the snow-capped Alpine massifs of France and Switzerland, situated less than 70 miles from Mont Blanc, with the lower, verdant ridges nearby now shimmering under a hot Italian sun. It was August 26, 1922. The giant Fiat racer of Francesco Brack-Papa had been trundled out and mechanics now struggled to budge its massive 172-pound propeller against the compression of 3,490 cubic inches, more than twice what the World War II Mustang's Merlin would have. The racer's designer, Celestino Rosatelli, was there, his pudgy face glistening with heat in contrast to the set of Brack-Papa's thin, sharp features. There was a sudden hiss of compressed air, a cough, and the Fiat rumbled to life.

The Italians were eager. They had been infuriated by the whimsical *cavilli*, the "capricious arguments" of the French the year before when Brack-Papa, brave in Italian eyes even to fly such a monster, had "pulverized" the competition in the 1921 Coupe Deutsch — at least for the first 100 kilometers. Deprived of victory, their record unsanctioned, Rosatelli and Fiat "could not tolerate" the affair. So today they would vindicate themselves by setting the world maximum speed record.

The record to beat was 330·275

Mechanics struggling against the compression of 57 liters in the ferocious Fiat, 1922   (F)

example — met with poor success but on the whole he developed the basis for a vast body of aeronautical engineering. He was also keenly interested in perfecting an engineering model of the combustion process inside a cylinder, and he developed new techniques applied to radiators. In 1930 Rosatelli spent months in deep but largely fruitless research into the increasingly baffling mystery of aeroelasticity in cantilever monoplanes, a mystery revealed by the important work he and other speed seekers had done almost ten years earlier.

Possessed of a *grande cuore*, a big heart, Rosatelli was from ancient Milan but found himself a young student of civil engineering in Rome in 1910, specializing in aeronautics under Professor R. Verduzio. Five

years later, still teamed with Verduzio, then a colonel, and Colonel Umberto Savoia, who were then technical officers of the Direzione Tecnica dell'Aeronautica Militare (DTAM) in Turin, Rosatelli was instrumental in the design of a warplane for the holocaust then flaming. The design (initially called S.V. for Savoia and Verduzio) was one of the finest of World War I and was taken to a large manufacturer to be mass-produced. Società Gio Ansaldo was a vast engineering and shipbuilding firm in Genoa then owned by the brothers Pio and Mario Perrone, both in their early forties and progressive, who had inherited the firm from their father, Commander F. M. Perrone, thus perpetuating the custom of strict family ownership common among the largest Italian industrial concerns.

Basil Rowe with his SVA-9 used for barnstorming the United States, circa 1922; note aeroplane's relatively large size, Warren-truss interplane wing bracing.   (Au)

kmh (205 mph) set September 26, 1921, by Sadi Lecointe in France, which had to be bested by at least 4 kmh. Bert Acosta tried to surpass it in the Curtiss Navy racer with which he won the Omaha Pulitzer, but failed. Now, after standing for almost a year, the record was challenged again. And the Italian challenge was splendid. The Fiat's smoky trail crisscrossed the measured kilometer amid terrifying sound and growing excitement as Brack-Papa hurtled up after each of his passes. Hand-held chronometers showed times of 10·9, 10·3, 11·3, and 10·4 seconds. At first the four *times* were averaged, yielding 335·664 kmh, the speed publicized in the press; but even later, after the four *speeds* were averaged correctly, yielding 336·132 kmh (209 mph), this Italian mark never found its way into the hallowed FAI record book. The reason, though seemingly unlikely, is quite simple and entirely consistent with their feelings: their honor satisfied, the

Italians, still fuming over 1921, would not submit their performance to French scrutiny. The achievement — not the formality — was what mattered. They were content to read about their performance in French trade journals, and Brack-Papa himself recalled that the troublesome official paper work was simply never completed!

Rosatelli's intrinsic good-natured congeniality remained intact even though the speed mark was not recorded. Records were ephemeral; Rosatelli was interested more in pure scientific virtue and did more than perhaps any other contemporary designer to evolve the engineering approach toward solving the problems confronting aeroplane builders then, making the important progression from empirical estimation to a systematic means for prediction of foreseeable aerodynamic and structural characteristics. The practical application of some of his theories — the rigid biplane for high speed for

When DTAM made the S.V. biplane a government project of wide scope Ansaldo became the builder and added its initial to the designation – hence SVA. In the ensuing industrial expansion the Ansaldo firm established under its control five *cantieri* (factories): Borzoli, begun in November 1916 and completed eight months later; Bolzaneto; Turin, the former Società Italiana Transarea (SIT) works taken over in September 1917 which formerly held the Blériot and Voisin licenses in Italy; La Spezia, or Cadmian, where fifty SVA seaplanes were built, equipped with two cylindrical, hydro-vane-equipped floats designed by a then little-known but fast-rising star, Dott. Ing. Guidoni; and the O. Pomilio factory in Turin, made into a repair depot early in 1918. Ansaldo also incorporated a factory at San Giorgio near Naples for the manufacture of engines. They built a new tube mill to produce their own steel tube as well as a silk-weaving plant to make aircraft fabric. Soon SVA-5, -9, and -10 models were under construction simultaneously. The fighters were powered by SPA (Società Piemontese Automobili) engines made in Turin, or Isotta-Fraschini engines made in Milan.

The SVA first flew March 3, 1917, over Grosseto, piloted by Flight Sergeant M. Stoppani, and went into production that autumn; 1,248 were eventually built. It had a structure characterized by Vs, Ws, and rigid triangles typical of Rosatelli's early designs, reflecting his classical civil engineering education. The SVA's distinctive feature was its Warren-truss interplane wing bracing, a W-arrangement of steel tubes eliminating standard flying and landing wires although each sloping strut bay was wire-braced within itself. The wings themselves were so thin their tips flattened out at high speed! The SVA's lines, though angular, nevertheless showed off the marvelous flair of Italian woodcraftsmen.

SVA aeroplanes (both SVA-5 single- and SVA-9 two-seaters) were quite large, with endurance unappreciated by early fighter pilots. Gabriele D'Annunzio, brilliant, fiery author of passionate novels, plays, and poetry that streamed from his smoking pen for almost four decades, as a fifty-five-year-old major in the *Serenissima* (Lion of St. Mark) *87° Squadriglia*, together with Lieutenants Locatelli and Ferrarin, on May 21, 1918, left Ghedi near Brescia, crossed the Alps, flew beyond Lake Constance, and photographed Friedrichshafen behind the Rhine, returning safely after four hours over enemy territory! Less than three months later, on August 9, the poet made perhaps his most famous flight, certainly one of the war's most remarkable, when he accompanied a flight of seven Primo scouts, as SVAs became popularly known, on a daring flight from the Italian Front to bombard the "inviolable" Austro-Hungarian capital Vienna with propaganda leaflets. The mission was accomplished after a 6:40 harrowing flight that took them nearly 700 miles over enemy territory. Yet, even with its range capability, the Isotta-Fraschini—powered SVA-5 could outclimb the Fokker D-VII. Postwar adaptations with up to six seats were built to capitalize on commercial possibilities and several came to the United States, advertised for $6,000 (SVA-5), in 1920; the asking price was still $5,950 (SVA-9) as late as September 1921.

A much smaller version with the same distinctive lines, the Ansaldo 1, called "Balilla" — named after a boy hero — was also built to appease the fighter squadrons who did not want or need a large, long-distance aeroplane. The Balilla's smaller wing span enabled conventional wire-braced structure, so Rosatelli's Warren-truss was not used. Its fuselage, like the SVA's, was of inverted triangular cross section aft, covered with thin mahogany veneer, and sheet-aluminum—covered forward. It had a fuel tank which could be jettisoned by a pilot-operated cable, a wartime precaution. The primitive look of its unpainted fuselage and trans-

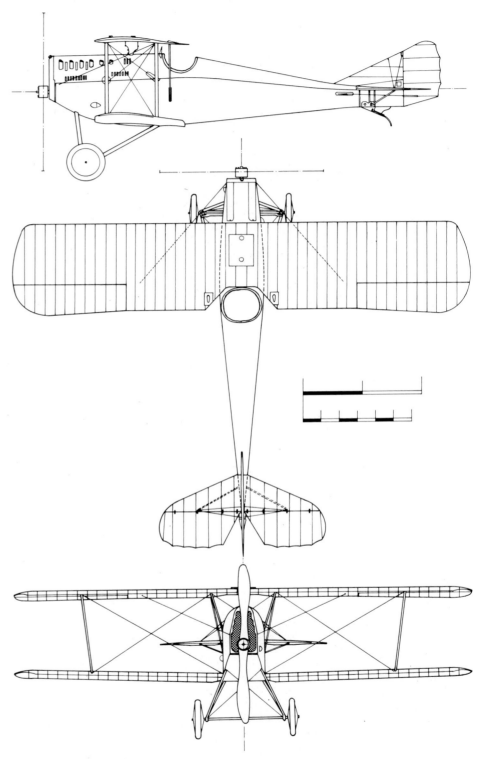

Ansaldo A.1 Balilla, 1919–21

Bert Acosta with his Ansaldo Balilla, 1920
Pulitzer race; note aeroplane's small size,
conventional wing bracing.   (Au)

Lloyd Bertaud's K-12–powered Balilla, 1921
Pulitzer race   (USAF)

386

parent, varnished wings belied its exceptional performance, and Balillas scored well in early U.S. Pulitzer races. Bert Acosta flew one to 135 mph for third place in 1920, and sometime air mail pilot Lloyd Bertaud, who in 1921 flew under retainer for Ansaldo to promote their exports to the United States, flew a Curtiss K-12–powered Balilla to fourth place in 1921.[1] Other Balillas and SVA-9s were entered by several U.S. Ansaldo distributors in both races. In fact, three of the five U.S. distributors indicated their intentions to race in 1921, planning to use the only civilian Pulitzer as a means to push their Italian-built products, especially in the Midwest. Only two Ansaldos answered the starter's flag, and by December, little more than a month later, the deepening economic blight brought the brave import effort to a crashing stop. The Aero Import Company, which could no longer pay for New York storage on its inventory of Ansaldo aeroplanes, went out of business.

The most remarkable of SVA flights occurred early in 1920. The poet-aviator D'Annunzio had planned an ambitious Rome–Tokyo flight to take place in October 1919 involving four Capronis (his son Ugo was then in the United States as Caproni distributor) and seven SVAs. Although nearly sixty at the time, D'Annunzio himself would "pilot an SVA" on the 11,000-mile journey. In July, one month after turning down the proffered post of Italian civil aviation director-general, he announced his singularly aspiring flight plan, which called for his entire fleet to continue beyond Tokyo and span the Pacific, reaching the United States! In the meantime he became embroiled in political adventurism. Violently opposed to the Nitti government, D'Annunzio in late 1919 led an

armed band which captured Fiume, a small seaport on the Adriatic whose control was in dispute between Italy and the newly organized Yugoslav state; there he set up independent rule and remained in power for two years, saying, "My aim is the reestablishment of the worship of man." [2] Thus preoccupied, he renounced participation in the flight, which was postponed; nevertheless, two SVA-9s completed the epic journey to Japan in May 1920.

The only pilot of the eleven starters to finish the entire distance was dashingly handsome, resourceful Arturo Ferrarin, then twenty-five. Together with his equally clever mechanic, Gino Cappannini, Ferrarin from February 20, 1920, made the well-padded cockpit of his SVA (N11849) home for three and a half months. It was rather stark quarters: fuel petcocks on both sides, and on the right a fuel tank pressure pump resembling a bicycle tire pump mounted horizontally, just behind the starting magneto. A large star-shaped handle which operated the water pump greaser occupied the center of the forward panel. Mounted outside forward of the windshield was a horizontal mariner's compass. There was no airspeed indicator. After 109 flying hours across uncharted deserts and jungles in this cockpit, visits to fabled cities of the East, and countless adventures en route, Ferrarin — soon joined by his fellow pilot Guido Masiero, who did the last leg by rail — finally reached Tokyo on May 31. To the Italians his flight has always been *Il Grande Viaggio*. Ferrarin, born in Thiene (Vicenza), was breveted a military fighter pilot in 1917. His

[1] Bertaud took off from Old Orchard Beach, Maine, on September 6, 1927, in the Fokker F-VII *Old Glory* bound for Rome. He was never seen again.

[2] D'Annunzio was later located on Lake Garda where the Italian Government had "exiled" him, giving him a magnificent villa and converted motor torpedo boat fitted out as a yacht. In later years he often entertained the Italian high speed flight for dinner, giving each of the officers a bottle of chianti and a box of cheroots when they left; visiting Britishers got a bottle of whiskey and 500 Wild Woodbine cigarettes from the patriot poet.

name remains near the top of Italy's aeronautical honor roll despite his death in a crash near Rome on July 12, 1941. Thirty years later Alitalia proudly launched a Boeing 747 superjet bearing his name.

Colonel Verduzio assumed the post of *direzione tecnica dell'aviazione di Torino* and Rosatelli, still his associate, found himself designing at the wartime Cantiere number 3 (the ex-SIT works) there. Rosatelli was coming into his own, and his next design, a bomber, took his own name: Bombardamento Rosatelli or model BR. It too had the Warren-truss wing bracing and was a huge aeroplane, spanning almost 52 feet and weighing over 7,000 pounds.

The largest industrial concern in Turin was a boldly managed automobile works founded in 1898. It was first called Fabbrica Italiana Automobili Torino, but one decade later the production of aero engines began, and two decades later the name was reduced to simply "Fiat" since by then they built everything from aeroplanes to tramways. In 1919 Fiat doubled its capital to 200 million lire, adding efficiency to rolling mills and steelworks to lower their auto prices, a remarkable move in the otherwise bleak postwar economic climate. But Fiat has survived because they never put all their eggs into one basket, always following whatever they considered to be the best design of the day. Fiat initially supplied the aero engine for Rosatelli's BR, and like Ansaldo, under the press of war, undertook the mass production of the aeroplanes themselves. Rosatelli joined Fiat, who built his wartime aeroplanes and their follow-ons for years.

The origins of Fiat aero engines can be traced back to 1904 when they were already following the lead established by the undisputed Mercedes automobile. Ten years later the Fiat 100-hp A-10 (six cylinders with bore/stroke of 120mm/140mm) was almost precisely like the Mercedes D-I; the six-cylinder (160mm/180mm) A-12

followed, almost identical to the Mercedes D-IVa of 260 hp. Mass-produced Fiat engines were freely exported, probably because those of their competitor, Isotta-Fraschini, designed by brilliant Giustino Cattaneo, and which were for the most part hand-made, were superior and jealously retained for exclusive Italian use. It was then generally well known that individually Italian-built engines were excellent but mass-produced types often did not live up to their advertised horsepower ratings.

The early success of the Mercedes type inspired Allied designers to build even larger versions, whereas its German originators demurred. Fiat's next model, the A-14, was a blockbuster of an engine, the largest Mercedes type ever built and one of the largest aero engines of all time. Disregarding the empirical, unwritten rule that 150-millimeter bore (about 6 inches) was the limit for steel cylinders in order to avoid cooling problems, Fiat engineers built their twelve-cylinder A-14 with a bore of 170 millimeters and a stroke of 210 millimeters, giving a swept volume of $57\frac{1}{4}$ *liters*! The engine was rated at 600 hp at 1,500 rpm, a very slow-turning affair, and its compression of only 4·5 shows how difficult big bangers were. The A-14 had many teething troubles during its development near the end of World War I, but it was constantly in the care of mechanics who treated it like a newborn baby. Ing. Tranquillo Zerbi, long famous as the designer of Fiat engines, did not design the A-14. Born in Saronno in 1891, Zerbi studied in Italy, Switzerland, and Germany, where he was employed at the Sulzer works at Ludwigshafen on the Rhine before joining Fiat as special projects manager in August 1919. One of his first major projects was to debug the recalcitrant A-14 engine.

The cylinders of the monster A-14 were arranged in a 60-degree V and were built of steel, each with a separate steel water jacket welded on. The

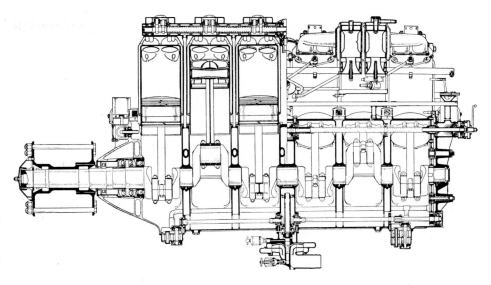

Cross-section view of the monstrous Fiat A-14 (57 liters) racing engine

crankcase and pistons were of aluminum. An overhead cam was used to operate the four valves in each cylinder (each valve was nearly 3 inches in diameter!) by means of a complicated, offset spring affair. Built-up, welded, individual cylinders and the valve arrangement were distinctly Mercedes in origin; only the placement and drive of auxiliaries distinguished the basic design.

Each cylinder had four separate spark plugs, and four water-jacketed carburetors nestled within the V. Total water capacity was close to 8 gallons. The engine, installed, weighed almost 1 ton. Rosatelli had designed the BR around the A-14 before war's end. The massive engine's early teething troubles prevented the BR's total success, but the aeroplane's speed tempted the Italians to use it for records.

Francesco Brack-Papa was ably suited for this quest. When almost forty years after his high-speed exploits Brack-Papa still served as a VIP guide at the Fiat aviation offices, his name by then meant little to most visitors and for them this quietly

distinctive gentleman in gray remained merely a guide. But Brack-Papa was regarded by the insiders as *un cavaliere alato* and had enjoyed one of the most remarkable piloting careers in aviation history. Tall, straight, and spare, with the forbidding, slightly disconcerting reserve characteristic of the Piedmontese, Brack-Papa was born in the rugged northwest Italian town of Corio in 1891, went to France when just twenty to learn to fly on Farmans, and had his license in 1912, becoming the first Italian military pilot. In 1913 he set an Italian altitude record of 3,050 meters, raising it to 4,000 meters two years later in an 80-hp Farman. By 1917 he had reached 6,750 meters with Ing. Mario Fossati along for the ride. Brack-Papa got into combat early in World War I but his skill led him into flight-test work and he soon found himself connected with Fiat's Turin factory. This connection, incidentally, would last more than half a century.

From the earliest days Brack-Papa was the especially trusted test pilot of Rosatelli. Even though Rosatelli beginning with the SVA pioneered in the

Celestino Rosatelli, Fiat designer, with his trusted test pilot Francesco Brack-Papa, 1922 (MA)

with three passengers, he climbed to 7,250 meters in forty minutes and later climbed to 5,516 meters in a BR with a 1,500-kilogram load; on May 28, with Mario Fossati, he set up a speed record of 270 kmh, but unofficially since the FAI did not resume recognition of world records in Italy until January 6, 1920. On June 27, 1919, the BR showed its tail feathers at 255 kmh with Brack-Papa and two passengers, and the next day it beat that speed by 6 kmh. During July, with Fossati and sometime Lieutenant Bonaccini, Brack-Papa took the BR on a tour of European capitals: Rome-Paris-London-Amsterdam-Brussels. On July 14 he snapped the first widely-published aerial photo of Mont Blanc on the Rome-Paris leg.

To add to Rosatelli's prestige, in August 1919 an SVA-5 flew across the South American continent coast to coast from Santiago to Buenos Aires, becoming the first aeroplane to fly across the Cordillera of the Andes, piloted by Lieutenant Locatelli, D'Annunzio's wartime squadron mate. Several SVAs went to South America and Africa as well as the United States, and the U.S. air attaché in Rome used his own SVA in 1922.

The potentially more lucrative commercial possibilities of his large planes were not lost on Rosatelli. Early in 1919 he fashioned a huge biplane with a combination conventional/Warren-truss arrangement to brace its almost 54-foot wings. With a gross weight of nearly 11,000 pounds it too was built around the A-14 engine and was designated ARF: Atlantico-Rosatelli-Fiat. Claiming a speed of 160 mph and an endurance of twenty hours, it had been designed for the 1919 transatlantic competition, which Brack-Papa was to have flown with Captain Guido. After Alcock and Brown won the *Daily Mail* prize, the ARF was not put to the oceanic test. It received plaudits as one of the most beautifully built aeroplanes exhibited at the 1919 Paris Air Show.

Brack-Papa flew the ARF with four

passengers to 260·83 kmh on February 26, 1920, at Mirafiori. On March 3 with one passenger he did 273 kmh and the next day with two passengers he flew the 388 miles from Turin to Rome in 2:15, averaging 276·888 kmh. One of his passengers on that trip was Gabriele D'Annunzio.

In 1921 Rosatelli decided to soup up the A-14 and build around it an aeroplane suited specifically for racing, especially the Coupe Deutsch, the new upcoming French speed classic. His racer, called simply R.700 (Rosatelli-700 hp), was necessarily large to fit around Zerbi's new racing A-14S, but despite its size it was undoubtedly one of the fastest four or five aeroplanes in the world at that time. Once again Rosatelli abandoned the Warren-truss in favor of conventional two-bay wing bracing, but even the critical French were highly impressed by its "impeccable" construction and its thin bi-convex airfoil. Even though adapted from their own St.-Cyr wind tunnel results, the airfoil was of especial interest to them since their own new bi-convex speed foils had plagued them with troublesome problems. The wing leading edge was formed of plywood and was covered with linen, which extended to the trailing edge, its weave 45 degrees to the airflow, and was stitched individually to each rib. The A-14S exhaust pipes were enclosed within streamline casings giving the appearance of short wings — in fact, their incidence angle had been carefully considered! Typical of the beautiful detail work were the faired aluminum casings that enclosed the wing strut attachments and the "park bench" mass balances on the ailerons, although these added drag. The radiators were enclosed in streamline casings near the lower wing roots. All 1921 Coupe Deutsch racers — except Fiat — used Lamblin-produced radiators. On the day before the race M. Lamblin personally sent an "official of justice" to Brack-Papa to "take due note" that in his estimation the Fiat's radiators were Lamblin copies! Presumably this

scientific techniques of predicting an aeroplane's behavior before it was built, there was not much science to the art of test-flying actually to confirm that behavior in those days, and Brack-Papa with his uncanny sensitivity in the air became a precious companion to the designer. Like some sorcerer he divined the subtleties of

Rosatelli's aeroplanes from 1916 until well into the 1930s. Indeed, rarely has such a long line of aeroplanes been imprinted with the particular stamp of one designer as were the Fiats of Rosatelli, nor a test pilot endowed with such success as Brack-Papa.

Brack-Papa soon distinguished himself in the Fiat BR. On May 21, 1919,

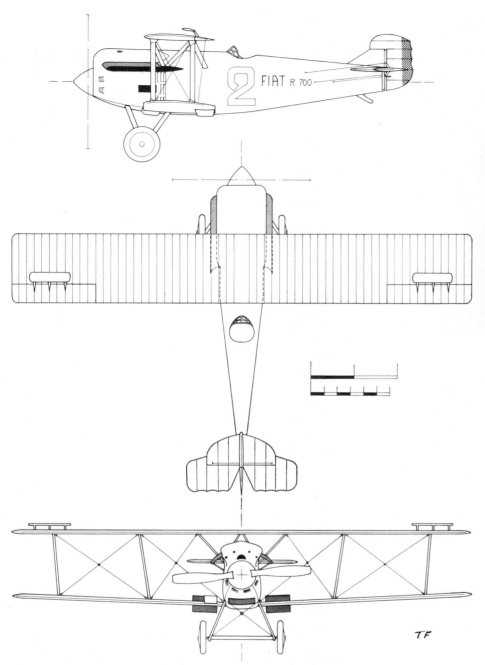

The ferocious Fiat R.700, 1921–22

Fiat R.700 at Étampes for the 1922 Coupe Deutsch race; note compressed air bottle alongside with fitting to aeroplane, used for starting engine (MA)

accusation was enough to set off the sensitive, hot Italian temper.

The list of entrants for the 1921 Coupe Deutsch was large but Brack-Papa was confident his big Fiat, emblazoned with race number 2, was a winner. Shortly before ten-thirty amid storms of dust and grass the Fiat roared away and completed the first 100-kilometer lap at over 185 mph, a fantastic time, easily good enough for a world record for the distance! (It was almost 10 mph faster than Acosta's closed-course time in the Omaha Pulitzer a month later.) The ungainly effect the Fiat produced in the air certainly belied its speed. But 16 kilometers north of the La Marmogne pylon on the second lap the thrashing engine lost fuel pressure and Brack-Papa was forced to land near Ruan. Georges Kirsch in the winning Nieuport-Delage sesquiplane was 16 kmh slower for 100 kilometers, over 20 kmh slower for the race!

If the Italians had their dissatisfactions at the hands of the French, even to the extent of not bothering to claim their world speed record properly a few months later, they returned confidently once again for the 1922 Coupe Deutsch, flown September 30 over the same course. Again, as he had done a year earlier, Brack-Papa took off just before ten-thirty and flew a very nice race at the remarkable speed of 179 mph. But the crowning frustration came when his time was disallowed because he had passed behind the timekeepers on the start! Luck seemed almost diabolically against the Italians.

Brack-Papa was allowed a second start since his first technically did not exist. He was off again in his charging Fiat monster shortly after two-thirty and did one lap which was almost 10 mph off his 1921 pace, but then a blockage occurred in his fuel pump. Brack-Papa force-landed in a beet field near La Marmogne. Colonel Piccio, Italian air attaché, rushed to his aid in a fast car and reported back that only his pride was injured. Lasne, in the aging 1920 Gordon Bennett Nieuport, won by virtue of being the only competitor to finish, beating the Fiat's time (during its disallowed attempt) by only 15·4 seconds. It was noted that Brack-Papa's wider pylon turns took an average of seventeen

*Two views of Fiat R.700 at Étampes for the
1922 Coupe Deutsch race   (MA)*

July 4, 1928, Brack-Papa accompanied General Italo Balbo on a huge twelve-plane "raid" (long and complicated itineraries were called "raids" throughout the 1920s). They flew Rome-London-Paris-Rome, covering over 4,000 kilometers, and Brack-Papa always remembered this flight with particular pride.

There had been other, little-heralded air races in Italy. Brack-Papa, accompanied by Fossati in a BR, had won the Baracca Cup, named after Italy's leading wartime ace, thirty-six-victory Francesco Baracca, who achieved most of his victories in the SVA Primo scout. This competition took place on June 19, 1921, and was a military trial over 1,000 kilometers in which the Fiat beat the second plane by two hours. Gabriele D'Annunzio offered a cup valued at 20,000 lire and 100,000 lire cash for a September 1921 contest at Lake Garda near the Lombardy city of Brescia, 50 miles east of Milan. Planned for "speed seaplanes, Monaco type" and "weight-carrying seaplanes, Schneider type," nothing important came of it. Then, in February 1922 the Italian Minister of War approved a plan of the Comando Superiore di Aeronautica for several big international air races

to be held that September "to increase the creation of new planes." The Grand Prize of Italy and the Grand Prize of the Tyrrhenian Sea would carry bloated prizes of several hundred thousand lire. But the rules were too ambitious. Because of such requirements as an 80-kmh (less than 50 mph) landing speed limit, mandatory night landings, and load requirements the plan came to nothing.

In 1923 Brack-Papa cabled the St. Louis, Missouri, Air Board saying he would come to that year's National Air Races with Mario Fossati to bring two planes, the R.700 racer for the Pulitzer race and a BR for other events. The expedition never materialized, and perhaps just as well. The ferocious Fiat had had its day. The year 1923 saw Rosatelli at work on the first of his fabled CR military fighter series; simultaneously the Regia Aeronautica (Army of the Air) began its existence. Brack-Papa would later muse over that glorious moment when he and his Fiat racer won the world speed record — but never received credit. Italy, bounded almost totally by the sea, would henceforth look to sea-planes for future exploits in the search for absolute speed.

seconds for the 180 degrees (that is, to cross the mark line inbound and outbound) as compared to Lasne's slightly more than eight, the difference costing the Italian forty-five aggregate seconds for the race right there.

Yet the updated British and French racers of 1922 were doing better than 320 kmh. Sadi Lecointe easily beat Brack-Papa's 1921 100-kilometer speed before he was forced out. Despite the performance of the R.700, the big Fiat A-14 was never a true racing engine. It had lots of power but slim Nieuports with less than half the power were going faster. Mercedes-based Fiat engines were in demise; by 1922 Zerbi was already experimenting with monobloc construction, deciding

a combination of Curtiss D-12 techniques together with cylinders patterned after those of the Napier Lion would prove best. Other new Italian engine construction methods were based on French Salmson radials; the Fiat blockbuster would soon be obsolete.

On April 1, 1922, Brack-Papa in a Fiat BR bested Sadi Lecointe in a Nieuport-Delage 29 at the speed race of the International Aviation Reunion held in Nice. The times were :09:42·6 to :09:50, yielding about 180 mph, the victory determined by seconds. This for the Italian was an especially sweet victory, certainly one of the most satisfying of the sixteen thousand flights he had logged by then.

Years later, between June 28 and

*Francesco Brack-Papa, Italian ace of speed,
1922   (MA)*

ITALY GOES TO SEA

27

The Savoia and Macchi Racers — and Others

Today the dark silver statue of a nude winged female kissing a face that appears to be struggling from the foaming crest of a wave stands quietly in the hushed surroundings of an obscure London town house. The sculpture itself is almost ugly; it was the work of a forgotten Frenchman, E. Gabard, and on its artistic merit alone the statue too would soon be forgotten. But Gabard's nude female during the years of her youth exerted a rare and powerful attraction. She became known as the "flying flirt" because of her many love affairs, allowing herself to be possessed briefly by strong men of various nationalities in turn. Her suitors whose ardor was most intense — and despair when she left them forever most grievous — were the hotly passionate Italians, and to them her statue became known, in a curious case of mistaken identity, as a *cup*: the "Coppa Schneider."

The siren-like lure of the blue Mediterranean that laps softly along the long edge of their land, this sea on which they had floated some of history's greatest expeditions and carried on centuries of commerce, led the Italians to apply unparalleled energy and imagination toward seducing the Coppa Schneider. Their serious courtship began shortly after wartime guns were silenced. Britain would host the 1919 Schneider at Bournemouth Bay and the Italians meant to win the

The "Coppa Schneider" reposing in the Aero-Club d'Italia, 1921   *(M)*

Jannello's S.13 in English waters for the 1919 Schneider Trophy race; note short-span racing wings.   *(MA)*

Standard Savoia S.13, 1920; note two-bay wing arrangement.   *(F)*

race with a highly modified type originally used for wartime reconnaissance. It had been built by Società Idrovolanti Alta Italia (SIAI) at their factory on the outskirts of Milan which had been opened in 1913 by founder and president D. Lorenzo Santoni, a man who knew the British well; he had been an early pioneer in British aviation himself as founder of the British Deperdussin Syndicate at Highgate in 1911. Santoni also founded the Savoia firm, as well as half a dozen thriving satellites; SIAI was a twin-firm to Savoia, both of which were set up to build French warplanes for the Italian government under license. Under the guidance of Umberto Savoia SIAI began producing their own types, and SIAI products would later come to be known by Savoia's name. The aeroplane chosen for the race was the S.13, normally a two-seater, but in just two weeks one was converted to a single-seat racer with its dimensions pruned substantially. Equipped with a sweet-running hand-made Isotta-Fraschini engine, it was crated and shipped by rail to England.

Storage and servicing facilities were established at Cowes on the Isle of Wight, several miles east of Bournemouth. At twelve-twenty on race day, after morning fog at the race site had dissipated somewhat, tall, blond Guido Jannello, the Italian pilot, roaring evenly with wide-open throttle alongside Sadi Lecointe's Spad, flew from Cowes to Bournemouth, where the S.13 was dragged up onto the beach. The Italians found themselves at once overrun by hordes of curious swimmers and sight-seers, an occurrence the Royal Aero Club, in the complete confusion that marked their lack of organization, had failed to consider. While 170 club members dined in unconcerned splendor aboard the club yacht *Ombra* the Italians gratefully munched sandwiches scavenged by Sam Saunders, who also appropriated rough planks for a makeshift slipway. The bay was filled with small boats and swimmers but Old Harry Rocks were barely visible in the wet haze. The distinctive red-and-white boats marking the race turning points were already anchored, with an extra standing by in Studland Bay a few miles north of Swanage. The race was set for two-thirty but the thick September fog, which had made the morning so gray and somber, had rolled in again, forcing a postponement. Club officials set the new takeoff time at 6 P.M. while local seafarers shook their heads pessimistically. A slight thinning at 4 P.M. set the *Ombra* into a turmoil and amid agitated arguments the race was suddenly declared on! James Bird's protests that Swanage Bay would undoubtedly still be fogbound were ignored, but before Jannello had completed his first lap, which required landings and taxiing as a seaworthiness test, two British competitors had already retired. Nicholl came back white-faced to tell his boss Dick Fairey it was "far too dangerous" after a terrifying close call when he just missed ramming a mast in the fog that indeed buried Swanage Bay.

Soon everyone had quit but Jannello, who unaccountably was lapping the course with apparent ease. Tom Sopwith, sitting thoughtfully on the beach, was one of the puzzled observers who watched the S.13 thunder by every few minutes with maddening regularity, doing, he judged, about 120 mph. On the next lap Sopwith noted his second hand and it suddenly occurred to him that if Jannello was doing the full distance he would have to be making 140 mph. Jannello finished his eleventh lap, to use the last ten, uninterrupted by landings, for the speed record, but Santoni, by now worried as well, ordered him to fly around the course one more time as insurance he was covering the full distance. Jannello cocked a doubtful eye at his dwindling fuel level and the gathering darkness but took off — and disappeared. Santoni was waiting with stopwatch, but twenty minutes passed — then thirty, and to his growing agitation, forty. The patrol

boats had already departed and the *Ombra*, a scene of ruffled disorder, was also under way, hoping to beat the fog to Cowes. George Newman appeared with a launch to take the Italians to HMS *Malaya* to request help. While the officers were attempting to secure permission from their flagship, a motorboat appeared with the Savoia in tow. She was beached at Bournemouth and, in the fading light, the Italians sped to Cowes. There a telephone call from Bournemouth's Branksome Towers Hotel awaited. It was the Swanage marking boat crew reporting they had never seen Jannello!

When the Italian pilot, finally rescued, heard this news he was outraged. He had rounded an official mark boat at low altitude on every lap. Where? A map was produced and Jannello without hesitating pointed — to Studland Bay! The voluble Italians put the blame squarely on the poor organization of the British and in fact many Royal Aero Club members were sympathetic to Jannello and recommended he be accorded a victory. But the FAI in Brussels on October 24 declared Jannello's performance void on the basis that to declare him victor would be unfair to those pilots who had *tried* the correct course. England was then mildly admonished when the FAI asked Italy — not England — to organize the 1920 Schneider contest.

The next important seaplane races took place during the popular Monaco spring meeting near the end of April 1920. Jannello arrived aboard an S.13 on Saturday, April 24; as a correspondent wrote, "He hates traveling by train and made the trip in the most natural way — by air." On Sunday the meet's first speed race began at 3 P.M., an 80·5-kilometer affair to Cannes and Menton. Jannello's racer, a Savoia S.17 numbered 30 which had been trucked to Monaco, had only one competitor, Count Bernard de Romanet on a Spad. Rock outcroppings for miles along the brilliant blue shore were covered with people, who saw Jannello, in the fastest aeroplane

Savoia designer Raphael Conflenti, Savoia founder D. Lorenzo Santoni, and Savoia star pilot Guido Jannello, circa 1920   (F)

Macchi M.17 at the 1920 Monaco seaplane Rallye, at which it crashed. This was the first of two M.17s.   (MCT)

Macchi M.19 with the huge Fiat A-14 engine, built especially to meet the 1920 Schneider ballast requirement; seen here in the 1921 Schneider Trophy race — which it did not complete (M)

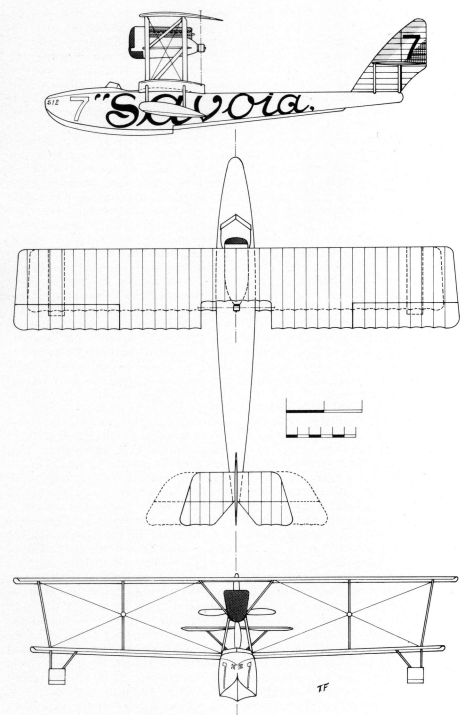

Savoia S.12bis, winner 1920 Schneider Trophy race; original S.12 horizontal tail denoted by dotted line; basic S.12 also had longer-span wings.

(capable of nearly 160 mph), get off to a late start and lose the race. Two additional Savoias, the slightly larger and exceptionally seaworthy S.12 and S.12*bis* with 480-hp Ansaldo San Giorgio engines, were slated to arrive later in the week from the SIAI works at Sesto Calende on Lake Maggiore, piloted by Jannello and Umberto Maddalena. It was noted that all the Savoias had a concave hull bottom forward of the step instead of the flat-sided V-bottom more commonly seen, and although at low speeds they piled up a lot of water, this diminished rapidly into practically no wake at all during their very pretty takeoffs. On Sunday, May 2, the meet's closing day, only two Macchi flying boats, piloted by Riccardo Morselli and Arturo Zanetti, challenged de Romanet for the Grand Prix. Zanetti won the Prix in his pretty new M.17 at 247 kmh but capsized on

landing, destroying his racer and injuring himself slightly.

The M.17 was one of three new flying boat types developed for the upcoming Schneider at Venice by Società Anonima Nieuport-Macchi (SANM) at Varese, an old coach-building firm converted in 1912 by Ing. Giulio Macchi to build French Nieuport designs in Italy under license; the Nieuport name would soon be dropped. Other Macchi competitors were the M.12 and M.19; the M.19 in particular was designed especially to meet a stiff new rule which required all Schneider contestants to carry a 300-kilogram deadweight load as "commercial weight" during the race. This of course favored the Italians, who specialized in large flying boats, as opposed to smaller, pontoon-equipped designs. The M.19 was a huge two-seater powered by Fiat's

394

Macchi M.12, 1920 (M)

blockbuster A-14 engine, and evidence indicates that construction of two M.19s was planned, although only one was built. Zanetti took it aloft on its first flight in August 1920 but its fuselage was too short, resulting in insufficient leverage to offset the reaction from the powerful engine, and Zanetti landed almost exhausted from his struggle to keep the rudder at full travel. The aeroplane would have to be lengthened and the rudder balanced, but not enough time for such repairs remained before the race, and the M.19 was withdrawn.

Like the M.19, the M.17 was derived from the standard M.7 military flying boat. Only one M.17 (of two) was completed in 1920 – the one Zanetti wrecked at Monaco – but in any event, with only one third the M.19's power, it would not have fared well under the 300-kilogram payload requirement. The remaining Macchi was the odd, wide-hulled, twin-boom pusher M.12, which dated back to 1918 and was to be flown by H. Giovanni "Nanni" De Briganti, but it too was withdrawn.

The race was won by the Savoia S.12*bis* pusher flown by Comandante Luigi Bologna. Originally scheduled for late August, one month before the Gordon Bennett race, the Schneider was progressively set back until almost

a month had elapsed, and this conflict with the classic French race discouraged foreign competition. Finally, on September 19, in terrible weather Bologna undertook the navigability trials, the only competitor to attempt the task, and his sturdy Savoia came through unscathed. He tried to fly the speed task the next day but again squally weather put him off; he finally completed the fly-over on September 21. Jannello was to have flown an S.19 but even he withdrew because of the dreadful weather.

The only other Italian designer on the scene in 1920 was in fact the most aggressively imaginative of all, Giovanni Pegna, who then owned and edited the trade journal *L'Aeronautica*. Pegna had participated in early ballistic studies, and wryly recalled years later they taught him "sharp noses reduce drag," a lesson he never forgot; in 1916 he moved to hydrodynamic research in the Froude Tank of La Spezia, and in 1917 was designing remarkably effective hydrofoils. The idea to throw away a seaplane's hideously bulky pontoons and mount hydrofoils instead seemed to Pegna as obvious as looking, and he was well on his way to solving the lateral stability problem that arises when sturdy, widely spaced pontoons disappear; his thin foils, tapered away from the fuselage like raked-down shark fins, would be equipped with ailerons to operate underwater simultaneously with the aerodynamic ailerons on the wing! In May 1920 Pegna wrote in his journal of his conviction that man's highest speed would be attained with a seaplane. Pegna was becoming increasingly disturbed by what he considered to be the trend toward simply increasing horsepower without an allied originality applied to reducing aerodynamic drag, and his fertile brain was already formulating the first of his radical seaplanes. Over the next decade he proposed seven of the most novel and daring answers to the siren call of the flying flirt.

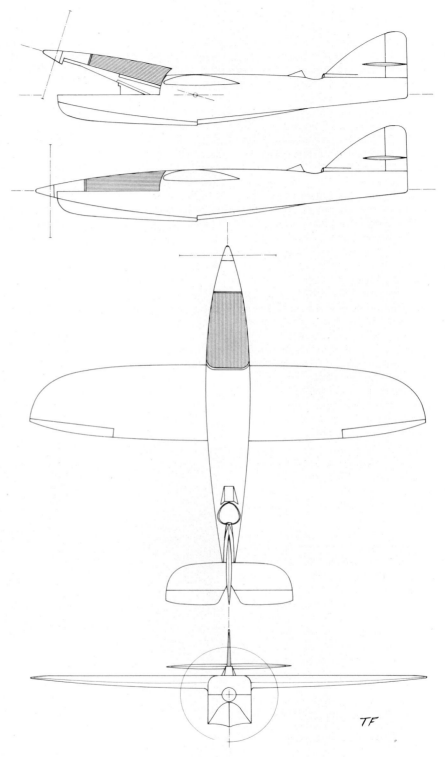

Pegna P.c.1 Schneider racer proposal, 1921

In 1921, for the time being, Pegna deferred the use of hydrofoils, yet his new flying boat design – called P.c.1 (for *Pegna corsa*) – was anything but conventional. A gracefully tapered cantilever monoplane wing sprouted from a clean, exceedingly narrow fuselage-hull with cross section just large enough to contain engine and pilot, and which would sit shoulder-deep in the water, a situation permitted by Pegna's most ingenious proposal: to *raise the propeller* by pivoting its shaft well back and pointing its axis upward until the aeroplane had lifted clear![1] The farseeing Pegna was confident that the structure of such a plane required only a minimal state-of-the-art stretch, even in 1921; on the other hand, the mechanical, thermodynamic, and aerodynamic difficulties could be "grave." His means for lifting the prop clear of the water included the requirement for offsetting the changing aerodynamic forces as the prop axis moved during flight, and it was perfectly evident to Pegna that this subtle compensation must be provided by an automatic, movable tail. He designed one; it was later used on the Piaggio P.2 fighter, which employed the same wing as the P.c.1, and Pierre Levasseur, after witnessing the scheme, patented an almost identical device in France, but Pegna always stoutly maintained the idea had originated with him.

The P.c.1 hull was designed by Signor Arrigoni and construction began in Rome at Società Bastianelli. Untenable economics soon halted the project even as Pegna continued to ridicule the awkward flying boats that did reach the race course. Indeed, his mind leapt ahead to the concept of eliminating the fuselage altogether in favor of providing simply a wing that would "house" the pilot, an idea that

seems to have blossomed simultaneously to free-thinking designers in France and elsewhere. His next design was governed by immediately practical considerations and he returned to the more conventional twin-float configuration, but even this was noticeably influenced by his theories. In fact, he reasoned that twin floats in conjunction with a low-drag fuselage together formed a very strong three-cell entity, rigidly braced; the floats thus allowed the conventional fuselage to be much smaller and lighter than would otherwise be required. To Pegna these were strong advantages over the landplane.

The 1921 seaplane meeting at Monaco, held in conjunction with the thirteenth Monaco meeting, was – as in 1920 – virtually a washout. To begin with, the April weather was poor. Slim, dark, dashingly handsome Umberto Maddalena flew in aboard a Savoia S.12 and a young English woman present gushed, "He is mad to try flying in such weather, but arrived

Savoia S.12 taking off from Monaco harbor during the 1921 seaplane Rallye (MA)

Dashing Umberto Maddalena standing by his Savoia racer, 1921 Monaco seaplane Rallye (MA)

Savoia S.12 detail (Maddalena on bow), 1921 (MA)

safely although he made my heart sink ... it is only the Italians who dare to fly like that!" His Savoia was one of three entered for the speed race (S.12, S.21, S.22), but only two had

set out from Italy for Monaco. The bad weather prevented Jannello's arrival with the S.22. Then Bologna punctured the S.12 hull while taking off for the San Remo–Cannes "Petite

[1] Pegna did not know until 1928 that a Mr. Burney had patented the same idea in England in 1912! His own patent in England – number 318858 issued in May 1930 – was not challenged.

Savoia S.17 racer leaving a smoky trail as it streaks toward the finish line, Monaco, 1921
(F)

Croisière" race; it was hoisted out and did most of its air time dangling from a crane. Meanwhile Maddalena, who had secured a new Savoia, roared in from Ventimiglia on April 19, the day before the *grand prix* speed race, but to finish his 400-kilometer nonstop flight with *éclat*, he landed outside the breakwater forming the harbor and his hull was promptly cracked by heavy seas. Wet and fuming, he was met by a very formal customs official demanding to examine his sodden valise! Except for restraining hands the official would have gotten the valise over his skull.

The 300-kilogram payload stipulation was dropped for the 1921 Schneider but more demanding seaworthiness requirements were added to the rules. In addition, to discourage indifferent entries a 5,000-franc deposit, returnable upon crossing the starting line, was imposed as a

guarantee of non-withdrawal, and this succeeded so well in discouraging prospective foreign entries that only Sadi Lecointe appeared. British flying boats, often heralded as the world's best, were visibly missing. Although Savoia entered two beautiful new flying boats, one without doubt then the world's fastest (S.21), the other a large, eight-passenger, twin-engine type (S.22), the race itself was finally contested by three Macchis.

The S.21, powered by a 330-hp Ansaldo San Giorgio engine (sometimes called Fiat San Giorgio since Fiat absorbed the Ansaldo company in a take-over during 1921), was a single-seater of unusual dimensions, its upper wing considerably shorter in span than the lower, with Warren-truss interplane bracing. Jannello flew its test flights, on which he exceeded 160 mph, a speed within 20 mph of the world's fastest landplane racers in

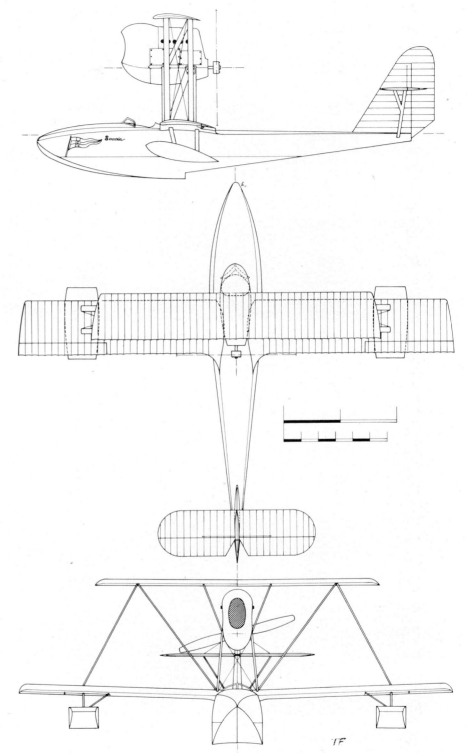

Savoia S.21 racer, 1921

Savoia S.21 high-speed (160 mph) flying boat built for the 1921 Schneider Trophy race (MCT)

The twin-engine, eight-seat Savoia S.22 used briefly for racing, demolished before the 1921 Schneider Trophy race (MCT)

1921. When Jannello fell ill Signor Guarnieri was assigned to the S.21 but engine trouble on elimination day prevented his trials. The S.21 was obviously the fastest aeroplane present and fervent appeals were made — it surely *could* have qualified (why, just the day before it had been aloft) — but rules were rules. Guarnieri put on wonderful speed displays with it, but they were futile performances.

The large S.22, capable of nearly 140 mph, was originally designed for the 1920 Monaco meeting and fitted with two Isotta-Fraschini V-6 engines enclosed by a single nacelle in push-pull! fashion, but these were to be replaced by two 300-hp Fiat A-12 engines for the Schneider. Assigned to Maddalena for the race, it crashed on a pre-race test and was demolished.

The huge, Fiat-powered M.19 had been refurbished in the meantime and upon the S.21 withdrawal it became the race's favorite. It was flown to an easy first in the Italian eliminations by Zanetti together with his mechanic Pedetti, the only instance of a two-man crew in Schneider race history. Surprisingly, not one from a fleet of Savoia S.13s survived the eliminations, leaving as Zanetti's teammates two outdated M.7s. The race itself started in front of the ornate Excelsior Palace Hotel on the Lido near Venice, the course running southwest over a sheltered bit of the Adriatic to a balloon tethered at Porto di Malamocco, then passing northeastward to two more balloons at Porto di Lido, remaining close to shore throughout, not extending nearly so far out to sea as the 1920 course had done. With Sadi's Nieuport out of the race, it became merely a contest to see which Italian would have his name carved on the Coppa Schneider. Zanetti's lap times were consistent at just over seven minutes in contrast to the almost eight-minute laps required by the aging M.7s. Suddenly, on lap twelve, the crankshaft in his huge Fiat engine broke with a terrifying, metallic grinding sound. Fire erupted and Zanetti plunked the M.19 onto the water at once. The two crewmen escaped uninjured but the M.19 was gutted. Of the two remaining M.7s the faster dropped out on the final lap, having run out of gas with only 2 kilometers to go, leaving De Briganti in the slowest

Macchi M.7, circa 1918 (MCT)

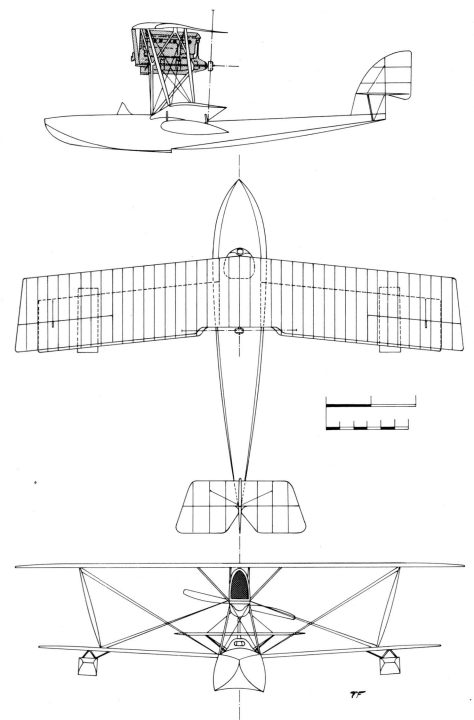

The ubiquitous Macchi M.7, 1918–22; basic version shown; drawing adapted from original Macchi blueprint. In later years, wings were clipped for racing.

Macchi M.17bis — the second of two M.17s — seen in Naples harbor preparing for the 1922 Schneider Trophy race (M)

Macchi M.7, 1922 Schneider Trophy race (Real)

aeroplane to lumber across the finish line unopposed. The fiasco led the press to sneer derisively at the Schneider — "this great speed race!" But the lesson was clear: old tried and true often came through. More importantly, to the Italians' ill-concealed delight, they were two legs up and needed only one more win to possess the "flirt" for all time.

For 1922 the venue was moved to Naples on Italy's west coast. According to Macchi company records supplemented by the personal recollections

of Muzio Macchi, son of the firm's founder, Aeronautica Macchi did not actively participate in the 1922 race; nevertheless, there was a modified M.17 entered, properly referred to as M.17*bis*, especially renovated after the M.19 mishap of 1921, to be flown by Arturo Zanetti. Most available evidence suggests that the construction of two M.17s was started in 1920. The first crashed at the 1920 Monaco meet and although it cannot be positively stated that the remains of this accident were not rebuilt it is highly unlikely that

399

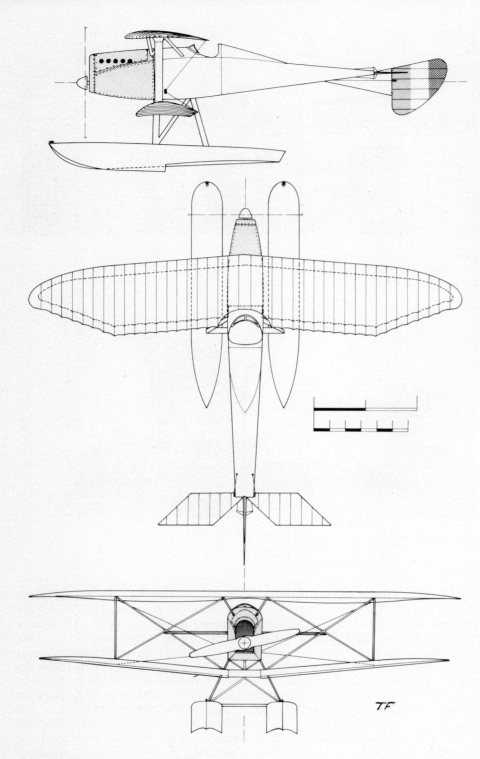

Marchetti's refurbished wartime MVT – the
Savoia S.50 of 1922

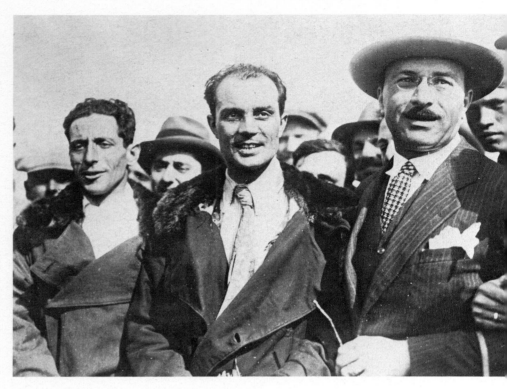

SIAI (Savoia) designer Alessandro Marchetti
on right, with pilot Arturo Ferrarin, circa
1926   (U)

they were. Thus is seems almost
conclusive that the *second* M.17 was
modified for the 1922 Schneider,
although why it had not been entered
in 1921 is uncertain. The other Macchi
entry in 1922 was one of the ubiquitous M.7 boats. Both Macchis finished
the race but were well off the pace
set by the faster racers.

Two new Italian racers were built by
Savoia for the 1922 contest, both to
the designs of Alessandro Marchetti,
an engineer whose star was rapidly
rising. Indeed, it was fervently hoped
in Sesto Calende that Ing. Marchetti,
who joined Savoia in 1922, would
bring the firm a change of luck after
three years of infuriating misfortune.
Jannello's regrettable invalidation of
1919, the S.19's failure to start in
1920, a balky engine preventing the
S.21 from racing in 1921 (and it was

40 mph faster than the winning
Macchi), as well as the S.22's crash
that year, all added up to total adversity
for Savoia. Marchetti's first proposal
for 1922 was designated S.50 but in
fact this was a resurrected project
whose origins went back to 1918
when he had been an engineer at the
La Spezia works of Vickers (Terni), a
large shipbuilding firm partially converted over to wartime aeroplane production. Completed then and powered
by an SPA 6-2A engine, the rather
flimsy biplane was designated MVT
(Marchetti-Vickers-Terni, the names
of its designer, builder, and place of
production respectively), but did not
make its first flight until 1919. It seems
that at least four were eventually
built. The design lay dormant until
Marchetti dusted it off for the 1922
Schneider race. One was put on

floats, had a more powerful engine installed, and began flight tests, but Savoia's bad luck persisted. After qualifying for the final team but prior to the race the S.50 MVT crashed, killing its pilot — presumably Signor Guarnieri, who was assigned to race it.[2]

Marchetti's second design for the 1922 Schneider was the S.51, a large sesquiplane flying boat in which the upper wing span was more than double the lower. Despite the disparity in wing dimensions it was a trim aeroplane with exquisite lines, highly original in detail, and certainly the fastest entered. It seemed a foregone conclusion that Italy would secure her third and decisive Schneider victory with almost

[2] In 1923 when the Regia Aeronautica, Italy's independent air force, was established, a new system of serial numbering was begun, each number preceded by the letters MM, for *Matricola Militare*. Numbers 1–999 were reserved for prototypes and experimental craft, and of these, numbers MM11, 12, and 13 were assigned to MVT aeroplanes. This would indicate that at least three MVTs still existed in 1923, but whether they were actually constructed by Vickers (Terni) or Savoia is uncertain. In addition numbers MM3 and 4 were assigned to the two 300-hp Hispano-Suiza–powered S.52 fighters, ostensibly outgrowths of the MVT design.

absurd ease. The S.51 pilot was Alessandro Passaleva, who was to have raced a promising Macchi M.18 in 1921 but failed to complete the eliminations. This year Passaleva could almost taste the victory cup as his impatience and anticipation mounted. He was grateful to have the wait cut short when the race date was advanced two weeks. Although entirely out of order, the date change was not protested — a possible oversight which seems strange since it came close to eliminating Britain completely — and it was only through concerted effort that they got their one competitor to Naples in time. With an ambivalent mixture of apprehension and self-assurance, Passaleva considered this lone foreign rival, Biard's stubby, gruff Sea Lion II, looking a little too sure of itself. He studied it thoughtfully. There was something a bit too contrived about the bungling way Biard flew his practice laps.

His own S.51 almost came to grief during the navigability trials when, during the unattended six-hour mooring out, she capsized. Her crew righted her — a breach of rules which *specifically required disqualification* — but Hubert Scott-Paine, in a magnani-

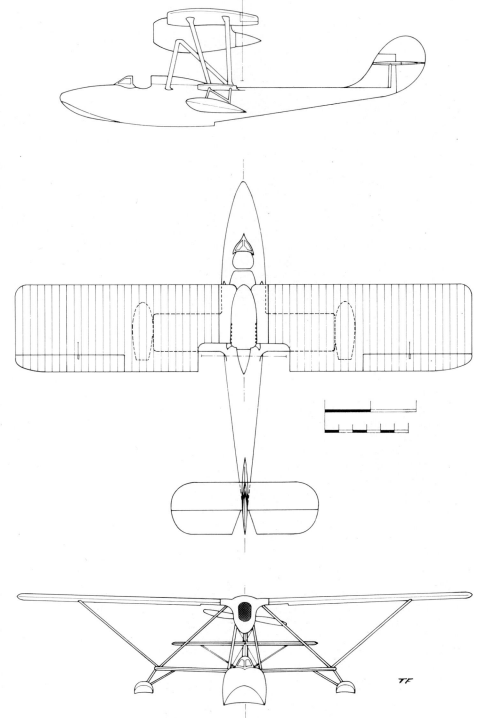

Savoia S.51, 1922

Alessandro Passaleva in the Savoia S.51 cockpit, ready to take off in the 1922 Schneider Trophy race (MA)

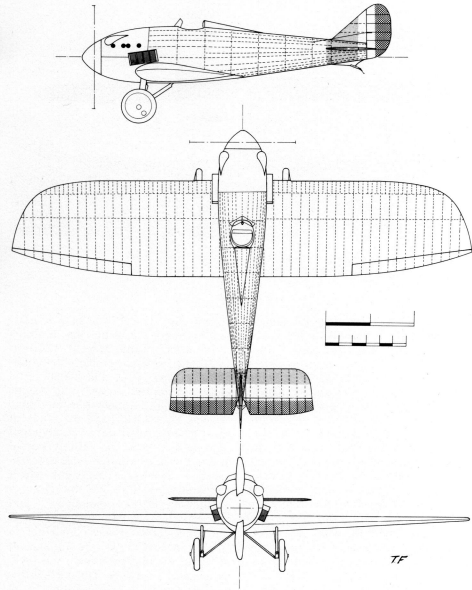

Pegna-designed Piaggio P.2 cantilever monoplane, 1922

mous, risky gesture, again refrained from filing a protest. He had in fact underestimated the S.51. "After all," he said with a trace of unwarranted but characteristic smugness, "we did not want to beat the fastest of the Italians on a disqualification."

Passaleva took off for the speed race just after Biard completed his first lap. Now was his moment! The warm wind tore at the edges of his helmet and he squinted against the ruffled span of brilliant sunlight chasing across Golfo di Napoli. But something was wrong. His aeroplane began to shake dangerously. Passaleva muttered a fierce curse — his prop laminations, from having been soaked when the racer capsized, were now coming unglued. With helpless exasperation he throttled back until the vibration was just at a tolerable threshold. Losing a few seconds each lap, Passaleva finished two minutes behind Biard and once again Savoia had to swallow a bitter pill of misfortune and defeat. Little did

Britain know how close they had come to kissing the flirt goodbye forever, or that their victory hinged on the almost ludicrous circumstance of a soggy prop. Four months later, on December 28, 1922, with a new prop, Passaleva put the S.51 over the measured kilometer and set the world seaplane speed record, averaging more than 174 mph, salvaging some prestige and proving unequivocally the S.51 had performance far superior to the Sea Lion II. Italy's only chance to win the Coppa Schneider outright was now based on the three wins within five years rule but the odds had shifted considerably.

In 1922, for the first time, Signor Pegna had officially entered a racer in the Schneider. Barely three months before the race, in May 1922, the firm of Pegna-Bonmartini-Cerroni was founded in Rome to translate some of Pegna's ideas into flying hardware. Construction of Pegna's second design began. It was an all-wood monoplane powered by an

Itala 300-hp engine, Itala being the name given to Hispano-Suiza engines built under license in Italy. Pegna's aeroplane was not completed in time to race in 1922; in fact, its construction was eventually taken over on August 8, 1923, by Società Anonima Piaggio of 2 Via Petrarca, Genoa, after Signor

Pegna joined Piaggio as technical manager. Piaggio was an old shipbuilding firm which had first entered aviation by producing World War I Capronis; five years later their second start in aviation came when they took over Pegna's aero works, to be called Piaggio-Pegna. Two P.2 prototypes,

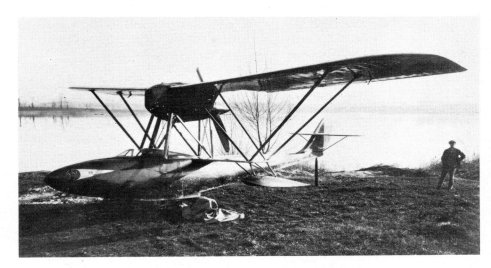

Savoia-Marchetti S.51, world's fastest seaplane, 1922   (MCT)

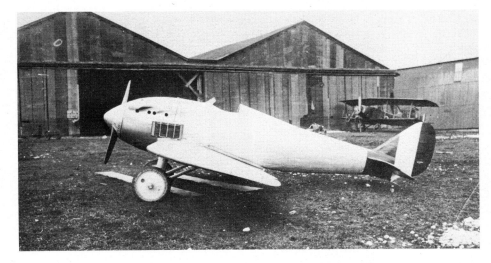

Piaggio-built, Pegna-designed high-speed cantilever monoplane, the P.2, 1923   (Au)

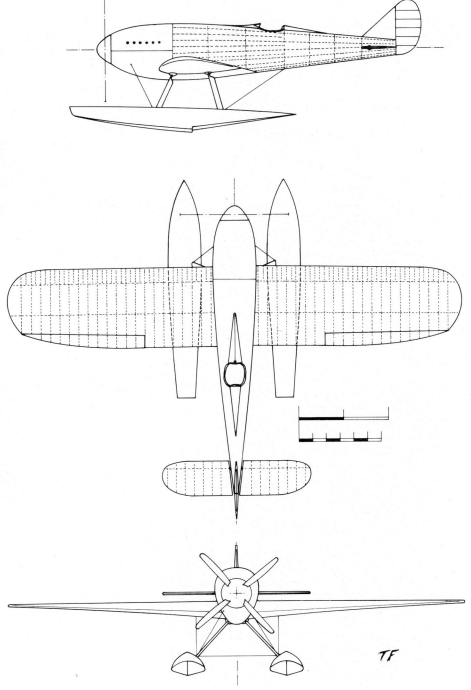

The first Piaggio P.4 (Pegna's P.c.2) of 1923; was 1924 Schneider entry

as they were designated, were completed in 1923 and assigned *Matricola Militare* military prototype numbers MM26 and 27. They were particularly noteworthy since they were among the world's earliest low-wing cantilever monoplane racers; indeed, the one-piece, ply-covered wing could be removed by undoing some simple bolts. In service trim one achieved 180 mph during flight tests and Pegna estimated that if equipped with a Curtiss D-12 engine, a racing version could reach 218 mph. Pegna had also seriously considered retractable landing gear but he discarded the idea for the time being, not so much because of its then radical nature but because he had carefully and quite dispassionately assessed the weight of added mecha-

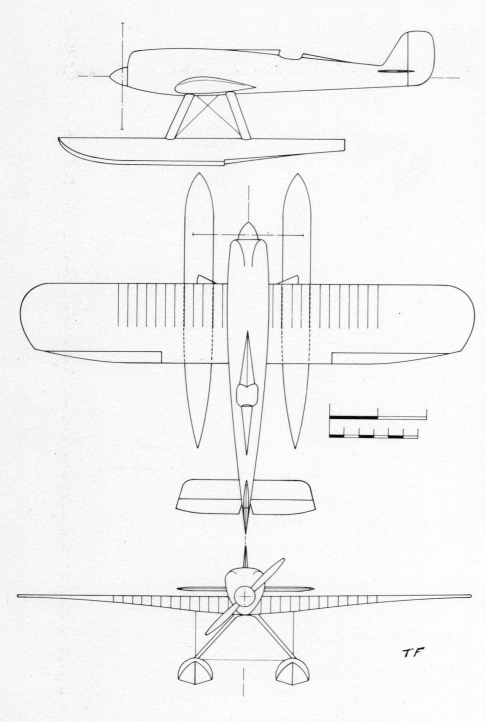

The second Piaggio P.4 (Pegna's P.c.3); was proposed 1924 Schneider entry

nism against the drag of small, fixed gear and decided—for 1922—there was not yet much advantage to retracting. It can be safely assumed that Pegna carried on his work with no recourse to substantive conclusions from similar efforts being made simultaneously by Verville, Booth, and Thurston in the United States, Reid in England, and Hanriot in France.

P.2 flight characteristics with Botali and Clement radiators had been very accurately predicted by wind tunnel tests, which also indicated that the P.2 without radiators should have exceptionally low drag. Thus in 1923 when Piaggio directors asked Pegna to design a new racer, the clean P.2 shape was adopted with great confidence as the basis for his P.c.2, which was also the Piaggio P.4 (military prototype numbers MM32 and 33). Modifications to the racer design led directly to the next in Pegna's series of racing seaplanes, the P.c.3 — still called P.4 by Piaggio — in which the main fuselage cross section was reduced and the shape and volume of the floats changed. The projected lift-drag relationship of the remarkable P.c.3 equaled that of the highly vaunted Supermarine S.5 and S.6 racers, still a half decade in the future, which suggests that Pegna in 1923 had already devised in detail the aerodynamic shape that would almost ten years later prove invincible. His later personal assessment was that

engine progress after 1923 — and not aerodynamic refinement — resulted in the high speeds achieved by the end of the Schneider series, and with understandable righteousness he asked his readers in 1932 to assure him the "satisfaction" of having originated the aerodynamic formula on which the great Macchi and Supermarine designs were based![3]

---

[3] Pegna's own designs became even more exotic after 1927. He built his own wind tunnel at Finalmarina and designed a two-engine push-pull racer (the P.c.5; Savoia-Marchetti built a similar design in 1929); retractable and enlargeable pontoons; a racer employing a winged, retractable pontoon (the P.c.6) — but he eventually decided the floatless P.c.1 of 1921, now covered by British patent 318858, remained after all the best solution, worthy of updating. He abandoned the idea of tilting the prop axis and said later he was sorry he did so; instead he would clutch the engine to a marine prop under the tail to propel the aeroplane fast enough to rise out of the water on hydrofoils, then when the nose was clear, declutch the marine prop and engage the air prop! Pegna studied General Crocco's V-shaped "hydro-wings" (alette), Forlanini and Guidoni ladder-like hydrofoils, and his own tapered hydrofoils which he considered superior, and which would be retractable in flight. The engine clutches were tested in motorboats. This remarkable plane, the P.c.7, undoubtedly the cleanest racing seaplane ever devised, was actually built, but the marine prop clutch — which had done so well in tests — repeatedly filled with oil and skidded, and the P.c.7 never flew. Pegna's dreaded mechanical problems were still too grave. It was his last racer.

Pegna's final racer design, the ingenious P.c.7 of 1929; note hydrofoils, hydrodynamic propeller at rear. (Au)

In 1923, because of Italy's clear need to mount an all-out effort, it was announced that Macchi and Savoia entries financed by the government would participate. This was indeed an announcement of profound import since until that moment no government had seriously proposed the idea of interjecting state resources into what had always been considered a sporting affair between private national clubs. It is especially interesting that the idea apparently occurred to the Italians precisely at the same moment U.S. planners decided active government support would be necessary to ensure victory. Macchi engineers had concluded that the earlier M.17 and M.19 designs were unsuitable as a basis for improvement, and although the government had apparently set aside 15,000 lire to subsidize race entries, neither this money nor any other outside finances to launch an entirely new design were forthcoming. Growing political problems (Benito Mussolini had assumed power in 1922) coupled with urgent business required by the Ministero dell'Aeronautica to strengthen the just-formed independent air force prevented Macchi's private participation in a race to be held several hundred miles away. Savoia, despite owning the world's fastest flying boat as 1923 opened, found themselves faced with the same circumstances.

In Italy's view, the tenor of the race changed in many ways during 1923. The United States, which actually introduced for the first time an entirely government-backed team, captured the fickle flirt and took her far across the sea, and they did it with aeroplanes that threatened to seal the doom of the traditional flying boat. The beautiful CR-3s embodied many features of streamlining and refinement Pegna himself had championed. Most depressing of all was that, on top of virtually losing their chance for a decisive victory, Italy's difficulties in mounting an effective challenge against the United States were increased manifold in 1924.

A more important factor in the American victory — even than the aerodynamic finesse that so impressed Pegna — and a factor that is often overlooked, is that the 1923 Schneider was the cardinal achievement of the Curtiss D-12 engine, reflecting the Americans' tremendous progress in propulsion technology. The Italians were quick to recognise its vast implications, and the Commissariato dell'Aeronautica seized the initiative by purchasing two 1923 model D-12s for close scrutiny in Italian laboratories. Both Fiat and Isotta-Fraschini had begun design work on new engines patterned in certain ways after the D-12, but these would not be ready in 1924. As an alternative the 1924 racers were designed around the updated D-12A itself, and a later buy of several D-12As was made by the Italian government. Fiat was also forging ahead on the development of superchargers and tested one with moderate success in 1924. Whereas most designers looked upon the budding supercharger as strictly a means to improve altitude performance, speed seekers began seriously to consider supercharging for boosting the power in low volume, highly streamlined engines operating down on the deck where speed records were set and races won.

The "reconstruction" of Italy's aircraft industry under Mussolini was just getting under way in 1924, with new design contracts being awarded to many constructors. Government director of aircraft manufacturing was General Guidoni, but as in 1923 — as Muzio Macchi recalled — efforts to persuade the Air Ministry to provide significant financial help for Schneider racers, despite America's strong precedent, proved largely futile. Just then government money for aviation, a staggering 400 million lire in 1924–25, twice the amount appropriated the previous year,[4] was reserved to buttress

the growing *fascisti* air force — the world's second independent air force — and the extent of government participation in 1924 Schneider efforts, aside from allowing the use of wind tunnel facilities, was merely to endorse a competition for Schneider designs. There were apparently no fewer than six suitable designs that at one time or another during the year existed in various stages of development.

In January 1924 a new Savoia being designed by Alessandro Marchetti was mentioned but nothing more was heard of it. Macchi, as might be expected, had a new flying boat on the drawing board. Macchi design chief Ing. Mario Castoldi was asked by his company to begin serious detail design in the autumn of 1924 on his new racer, which had sleek and daring lines with a rakishly tapered cantilever monoplane wing sprouting from a central flying boat hull, the engine mounted above on a pylon, but construction was not begun in time to have it ready for the 1924 race. A twin-float monoplane was proposed by the progressive German firm of Claudius Dornier, who had to some extent avoided the Versailles limitations by establishing manufacturing activity in Italy at Pisa. A wind tunnel model of Dornier's lovely S.4 racer — predating the British Supermarine S.4 which closely resembled it by a full year — was tested but no full-size racer was built. Ing. Conflenti, who had been formerly chief engineer at Savoia, later doing a brief stint with the French CAMS firm, designed a new biplane flying boat to be built under his direction by Cantieri Navali di Monfalcone, the famous naval construction firm which entered the aircraft industry late in 1923 at the naval shipbuilding factory near Trieste with 80,000 square feet of floor space and five hundred workmen to build commercial flying boats for Trieste–Turin passenger service. The racer construction was interrupted and none were built. The Piaggio P.4

(Pegna's P.c.3) was by now almost completed, but its construction was halted for what Pegna later called "administrative reasons." Neither it nor the follow-on P.c.4, both progressive cantilever monoplanes years ahead of their time, was completed. Finally, it has been intimated that General Guidoni himself designed a new racer and with it won the Ministry design competition! This new design — whatever its source — was contracted to CRDA (Cantieri Riuniti dell'Adriatico) — which, indeed, was the name given to the aircraft branch of Cantieri Monfalcone — for construction. One prototype was completed, powered with a tractor-mounted Curtiss D-12, and designated D.G.C.3. Unfortunately its test pilot, Frederico Guazzetti, sank it twice during initial trials and it never got airborne.

The final result of so much inconclusive activity was Italy's complete withdrawal from the race, which was subsequently postponed one year by the United States, who, with rare magnanimity, refused in 1924 to claim a fly-over.

After abandoning the 1924 race, Mussolini apparently considered another design competition, but the entire job of mounting the 1925 challenge eventually passed to Aeronautica Macchi, and contrary to wide belief, as Muzio Macchi has emphasized, the entire cost of Italian participation that year — even to the shipping expense of the expedition to Baltimore — was borne privately by his firm. The eventual extent of government support was the temporary loan to Macchi of two Curtiss-built D-12A engines, part of the lot purchased by the Italian Air Ministry at General Guidoni's insistence and which by March 1924 had been thoroughly run out under great stress in tests by Fiat, thus severely reducing their power output to something near 400 hp.

Mario Castoldi was now beginning to consolidate his renown as the most successful of Italian speed seekers. A more unlikely performer to fill this

4 In 1924 the official exchange rate although twenty lire to one U.S. dollar, did not reflect the strong purchasing power of the lira within Italy.

Mario Castoldi, circa 1924   (MCT)

paring inaccurate drawings and planting them where he suspected (often quite rightly) they would be stolen by his competitors, and he once was on the verge of apoplexy when he thought an important fitting inadvertently had been made to one of the fake drawings! Yet he often refused to take his own staff into his confidence because of a morbid need to shield his own unique ideas. Despite these idiosyncrasies Castoldi's enormous talent, when applied to speed seeking, was incisive and enterprising. Born near Milan in 1888, he did only slightly better than average at Milan Polytechnic, and like Rosatelli became an engineer at the Direzione Tecnica dell'Aeronautica Militare in Turin during the closing days of World War I, after employment at the Pomilio works in 1916. Castoldi came to Macchi in

Macchi M.33, Castoldi's cantilever monoplane flying boat, under construction, 1925
(Au)

Macchi M.33, 1925; note design of original rudder.   (MCT)

role could not be conceived. Castoldi was ruddy and corpulent, unhurried with a sense of ponderous indolence, a confirmed misogynist, fond of good wine, and his unlikely hobby was rice cultivation. It stretched credibility to reconcile his lethargic bulk with the zealous, crusade-like desire he harbored to achieve pure speed in the air.

His intense, almost compulsive thirst for the excitement of speed somehow synchronized with several neurotic fears; for example, it is said that Castoldi, who lashed his test pilots beyond the very limits of contingency, only flew *once* himself! He was distrustful, endlessly concerned about sabotage, even to the extent of pre-

1922 as technical manager. His stature rapidly increased and he was personally responsible for every Macchi design until 1944.

Castoldi in 1924 personally tested a series of hulls with an especially adapted motorboat, and from these tests he developed a hull with excellent wave-riding capability for his new racer. The design initiated in 1924 was developed for the 1925 race and called M.33. Like Reginald Mitchell in England the same year, Castoldi had committed himself to the cantilever monoplane wing, but after considering alternate configurations he retained the flying boat form. His new wing, built in three all-wood sections (a center-section fixed to the hull with outer sections attached to the stub ends), was long and set low, its tips clearing the water by less than 2 feet. He used a bi-convex symmetrical airfoil, thick in order to be cantilever. Three racers were built: two flying versions (MM48 and 49) and one for static strength tests. The completed M.33 could be represented by a flat

surface whose area, if facing the oncoming air, would produce equivalent air resistance; this "flat plate area" was identical to that of the CR-3 of 1923, but only 57 per cent that of the 1922 Sea Lion, yet even this low value was of doubtful utility in 1925. Although the R3C-2 had a higher drag coefficient than the M.33, meaning it was relatively less clean, it was smaller and had half again as much power. The M.33s were tested over a 50-kilometer circuit on Lake Maggiore for distances up to 300 kilometers, flown by company test pilots Nanni De Briganti, Schneider race winner in 1921 hoping for his second victory, and Riccardo Morselli. Although they were clocking 320 kmh with the M.33s neither pilot particularly liked the aeroplane. The run-out engines gave rise to serious misgivings and the cantilever wings were ominously prone to flutter.

There is various evidence that Macchi considered a second racing design in 1925, designated M.27, reputed to be a sesquiplane with a

Aged Curtiss engine in M.33 churns out power as racer prepares for flight, 1925; note external plate radiators. (Au)

Riccardo Morselli and Nanni De Briganti, the M.33 pilots, 1925 Schneider Trophy race (Au)

large upper wing braced by a diagonal rigid strut on each side and a central cabane to which the engine was mounted, supplemented by a thick lower wing of short span built into the lower part of the flying boat hull so as to double as a balancing float for taxiing. It was designed to accommodate either the Fiat 450-hp A-20 or Curtiss D-12A engine (to weigh 2,980 pounds gross with the Fiat, 400 pounds less with the D-12A), with a wing area of 179 square feet and an estimated top speed of 204 mph. But it was realized conservatively that 230 mph would be necessary to win in 1925 and the M.27 was never built.

General Guidoni's major disappointment was the Italian engine industry's failure to perfect their own high-power racing engines in time for the 1925 contest. America's brilliant success in 1923 had completely altered engine design and despite Guidoni's encour-

agement Italy had not yet caught up. Both Fiat and Isotta-Fraschini had been addressing the problem and pushing ever closer toward surmounting that so far formidable barrier: 1 horsepower per pound of weight. Pursuing their own line of development, the Italian engine designers, Tranquillo Zerbi in particular, were not adopting the Curtiss monobloc pattern *in toto*. The Italians often become high-pitched when confronted with something novel, but their initial enthusiasm, just as often, soon fades. Zerbi's first new engine to appear after 1923, the Fiat A-20, had cylinder dimensions of 115mm × 150mm, almost identical to the D-12's, and it developed a more than coincidental 410 hp at 2,000 rpm, but he elected to retain steel cylinders with welded-on steel water jackets, not unlike the Napier Lion. Parallel development led to the A-24 of much larger volume

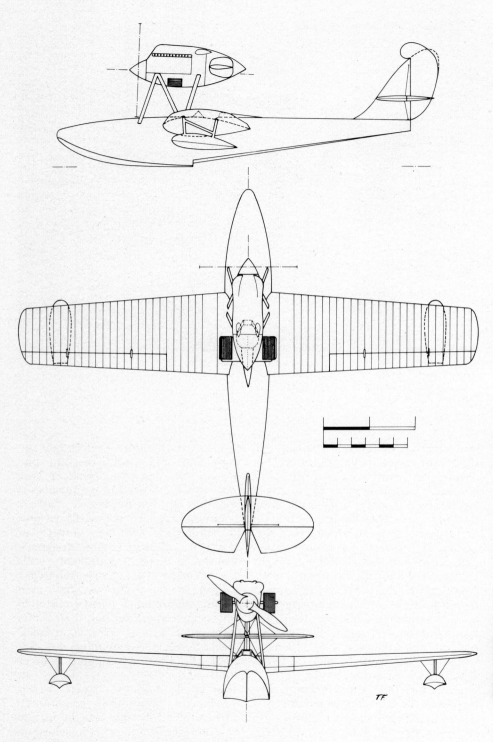

Last of the racing flying boats, the Macchi M.33, 1925. (Original tail denoted by dotted line.)

(1,970 cubic inches). Though still being bench-tested in 1925 its performance portended great success just over the horizon. In the meantime the tired, well-tested D-12As had to be used in the M.33 racers together with external plate radiators. Certainly this was no way to compete for the flying flirt's fickle hand.

The Italian team left Genoa aboard the *Conte Verdi* on September 26, 1925, bound for the New World. Race day was scheduled in slightly less than a month. Upon arrival the Italians, like the British, were dismayed at the makeshift accommodations, flimsy canvas hangars, and appalling weather which caused a two-day race postponement. Castoldi, in a black mood, found nothing to compliment except his gracious interpreter, Commander John Lansing Callan, USN. During the navigability trials the aging engine in De Briganti's M.33 conked out and he

made a pretty deadstick landing in Chesapeake Bay. After repairs he started the trials a second time but the event had been a bad omen. On race day a balky ignition system on Morselli's engine refused to function. Regulations forbade repairs at that point and Morselli, so dejected he wept, returned to the hangar, out of the race.

De Briganti's takeoff to begin the race was long — there was a catch of breath when a wingtip dipped to within a fraction of digging in — but De Briganti had excellent control of his racer and lifted it cleanly, rose above the sparkling water, and smoothly wheeled to join the course. For sheer artistry his steeply banked pylon turns were comparable to Jimmy Doolittle's, but his tactic of climbing sharply at the pylon then diving toward the straightaway was not paying off. On the second lap he blundered, mistaking the far turning point, and flew a few

De Briganti leaves the slipway in his M.33 for the 1925 Schneider Trophy race; note how deep the aeroplane sits in the water; also note final rudder design with added balance area.   (F)

Macchi M.33 at Bay Shore Park, Maryland, 1925   *(M)*

miles out of his way, yet his over-all performance shattered all records for flying boats; nevertheless, De Briganti only finished third behind the American and British twin-float racers. After completing the required seven laps De Briganti flew out over the course intending to land alongside Ofstie's downed R3C-2 and give the American a hand, but he ran out of gas and eventually needed to be towed ashore himself.

The true significance of the 1925 Schneider — as far as Castoldi was concerned — was the superior Curtiss propulsion equipment . . . and that sleek British S.4 monoplane on twin floats which had cracked up. Obviously, in order to compete with the United States on their own terms, against the background of growing technical complexity, the Italian government would have to do far more than merely pay lip service to the Italian expeditions. Macchi could simply not afford another diversion of effort comparable to that of 1925. And now the tables had turned: the United States was two legs up — one more win and she would forever possess the flirt. Would Italy rise to the challenge?

As 1925 drew to a close it seemed impossible that any nation could unloose the potent embrace on the flirt then held by Curtiss. To surpass their formidable technical achievements, time was essential, time for research and development, yet no designer was willing to begin drafting next year's racer since the FAI, in their infinite and unpredictable wisdom, could and occasionally did alter the race in subtle but far-reaching rules modifications at their annual meeting, which was not held until early in the year. The 1926 meeting was convened January 11, and the Italians had planned a stratagem of their own. If they could reinstate the idea of "commercial weight" ballast (discontinued after 1920) it would effectively render the Curtiss racers unsuitable. Their professed rationale was that unless new and necessarily government-funded research led to marketable aeroplanes that could carry profitable loads, the government could not justify its subsidy. Their proposal was not accepted; the British as well as the Americans were opposed to it. The rules for 1926 would be essentially identical to those of 1925. Yet the British, whose demon-

strated level of aeronautical technology far surpassed Italy's in 1925, decided that preparation of a challenge in the few months remaining would be impossible.

There was another, more intangible factor. The Italians, their sensitive pride bruised by callously chauvinistic U.S. press reports, had to swallow hard after 1925. Mussolini, whose fiery breath had by now warmed virtually every facet of Italian society, suddenly decided the Coppa Schneider meant more than a flirtation, and he issued a stern charge to his aviation industry: *"The race must be won at all costs."* All non-essential aviation work would stop. All customers would be put off in a massive disruption of Italy's aviation industry. Macchi was ordered to build five aeroplanes (two trainers, three racers) and the minimum speed acceptable would be 380 kmh.

This was a tall order but there was no choice because with the British out of the race only Italy could stop the United States. Meanwhile, before Italy formalized her challenge, the British spent strenuous months in an odd, quasi-diplomatic barrage of suggestive statements and self-righteous resolutions designed to embarrass the Americans into postponing the race one year; these efforts vividly reflected a curious quirk in the British temper which convinces an Englishman that he has the ability to shame his adversary into reversing a decision illogically. In this case the British completely misread the Americans, who remained resolute if bewildered, with no sense of embarrassment or shame whatsoever, persisting in their plans to conduct the formalities (even if they resulted in a fly-over) that year — exactly as the British themselves would do five years later in 1931, revealing an inconsistency at the opposite pole of the same axis.

The Italians had to be pragmatic and were unable to indulge in the luxury of such fruitless tactics — they could see from afar that the Americans would not be swayed from their resolve to

have done with the Schneider as soon as possible. The brutal truth was that the Italians had neither aeroplane nor engine and the race was barely ten months away. This vacuum was recognized even before the glasses were raised at America's 1925 victory banquet, and as early as December 1925, animated by a moment of alarm, Italy asked an American engine firm to build the engines for the 1926 Italian racers! On January 6, 1926, the request was formally and flatly refused.

Mario Castoldi was bedridden when he received Il Duce's command, but he arose and set to work at once despite his illness. Signor Filipa, the Air Ministry's top draftsman, was dispatched to Varese to aid Castoldi. They were soon swept up in a mad race to build the world's fastest aeroplanes, a wearing, grinding race between tempers and terms, tensions and trials that would ultimately demand far more of them than the Schneider itself. The first drawings for the new racer, issued in January, reached the experimental shop on February 10, 1926.

Castoldi's new aeroplane was designated M.39, its number, a multiple of 13, being chosen in deference to one of the great designer's superstitions. It had an uncluttered outline with graceful curves born of Castoldi's intuition and artistic flair. For him to abandon the flying boat was only logical: as power increased and wing span was cut down the wingtip floats, necessary for balance while taxiing, would grow intolerably large, hence the twin-float configuration was inevitable. No theoretician, Castoldi had a rare genius: an ability to use the world's fastest aeroplanes as stepping-stones, picking their preeminent features and combining them into a durable combination. The M.39, the first "modern" Italian contender, was the logical outgrowth of recent racers; Castoldi was able to tap at once the innovations already pioneered by the Curtiss racers and Supermarine S.4. He at once eliminated two main S.4

The beautiful Macchi M.39 being readied for the 1926 Schneider Trophy race; with this design the final successful Schneider aerodynamic formula achieved consolidation.
(M)

features, the cantilever mid-wing and the external radiators, but by adopting an externally braced wing – as R. J. Mitchell himself would do for all his subsequent racers – Castoldi was able to use a very thin, sharp-edged wing, light in structure yet torsionally rigid; the trick of building flutter-free thin cantilever wings still awaited discovery. The floats, as Pegna had foreseen earlier, became an indistinguishable part of the fuselage, for without them other supplementary structure would have been required. They contained the fuel and this allowed a smaller main fuselage. The fuel tanks were made from steel sheet; to feed the engine, compressed air forced the fuel from the floats up into a small feeder tank in the fuselage. The feeder tank was necessary because during pylon turns high g prevented fuel transfer from the floats. Eventually, in later Schneider types, the floats also carried much of the skin radiator surface, a scheme advantageous on takeoff, when the cool ocean water washed over the radiators at the very

time the engine was working its hardest.

The M.39's over-all drag coefficient (·035) was identical to that of the Supermarine S.6B built five years later, and was 29 per cent less than that of the previous year's S.4. Castoldi's most serious problems lay in the area of stability and control. Despite the use of unbalanced elevators, stick forces in pitch were extremely light and even reversed during maneuvers because of the aft c.g., just opposite to what the piloting task – a low altitude, very precise track – demanded. A disharmony existed because the unbalanced ailerons caused quite heavy stick forces in roll, but this was felt to be a minor disadvantage since the only roll requirements were constant-banked pylon turns. The large floats were destabilizing, forcing the designer to make a difficult compromise because the demands of seaworthiness – large floats – were inimical to flying qualities at high speed. Like the Curtiss engineers before him, Castoldi adopted a geared rudder and M.39 pilots soon learned

to hold the rudder rigidly fixed at high speed (the M.39 was actually directionally unstable up to yaw angles of about 5 degrees) which further complicated the piloting task. On the water the reaction torque from the engine tended to roll the aeroplane and push one float under, causing a lopsided drag which made directional control difficult, especially during the first phase of takeoff. This in turn led to floats with abundant (and later asymmetric) buoyancy reserve but the large size imposed a drag penalty at high speed. The M.39 floats were the result of extensive wind tunnel and water tank tests, and they retained the sharply concave bottoms characteristic of earlier Italian flying boats.

In the meantime Tranquillo Zerbi began a fierce, continuous effort to build a new racing engine. Cooling, mechanical reliability, and combustion efficiency assumed primary importance

as design guidelines. The engine must run wide open for an hour without a breakdown, a demand which differentiates the racer from the short-duration speed record aeroplane. Also, cooling water must do its job steadily aboard the racer, and not be allowed to evaporate – which may be desirable in a short-duration maximum effort – in fact, engine cooling assumes controlling design importance, which is precisely why Italian float-equipped aeroplanes, the floats serving as radiator mounts, became the world's fastest machines until improved liquid cooling methods were developed and applied later in the 1930s. On the M.39 wings Zerbi used elegant inlaid brass skin radiators copied directly from Curtiss.

By February 4, Zerbi, taking the Fiat A-24 as his starting point, began work on a new V-12 racing engine. Construction started eleven days later. Zerbi's objective was 800 hp using a

Macchi M.39 taking off on early secret test flight, 1926
(MCT)

Macchi M.39 with cowl removed exposing its Fiat engine, 1926   (NA)

compression ratio of 6 and rpm of 2,500, limited by prop efficiency. Gearing was not used. Zerbi also made wide use of what the Italians called *electron* — magnesium alloy — especially in the pistons, and the prototype engine, designated A.S.2, was tested at up to 882 hp on the bench. In service it produced some 30 hp per liter of swept volume. Reed metal props were essential to the M.39 success. Muzio Macchi emphasized their contribution and recalled that they were delivered punctually. Their pitch could be fairly easily modified and this enabled the Italians to devise a rather sophisticated strategy for the race itself.

By March 25 the final detail drawings were under way. Fuselage construction began April 15 and by July 1 the first M.39, a training version with wingspan 1 meter longer than the racing version and derated 600-hp engine, was completed. The M.39 static test article withstood the equivalent of 17 g! The cockpit was almost bare, containing (besides controls) airspeed indicator, tachometer, water temperature and oil pressure gauges, and manual lap counter. Nothing more.

Macchi chief test pilot Romeo Sartori climbed aboard to make the M.39 first flight on July 6, 1926, at the Schiranna Air Station on Lake Varese, less than five months after the first blueprints were prepared! Sartori's lack of floatplane experience put him at a disadvantage, and his heavy landing buckled the float struts, which set the schedule back. He excused the bad landing by reporting that "wing twist" worried and preoccupied him. The first members of the hand-picked racing team were arriving to take over flying duties. Team leader was a distinctive and polished young nobleman, Comandante the Marchese Vittorio Centurione, twenty-six. The other assigned pilots were Major Mario de Bernardi, thirty-three, who had learned to fly in 1913 and served as a wartime fighter pilot; Captain Arturo Ferrarin, thirty-one, whose fame was well established as hero of the Rome–Tokyo epic SVA flight and whose selection was in part influenced by certain persuasion applied on the Air Ministry by Fiat; and Lieutenant Adriano Bacula, thirty-two, as reserve pilot. Captain G. Guasconi, another alternate, was assigned from seaplane duty, as was Lieutenant Guazzetti, who had flown the ill-fated D.G.C.3 in 1924. Major de Bernardi was soon flying the M.39 trainer. In early August a flight demonstration was made for the new director of aircraft manufacturing, General Verduzio (of SVA fame), who had replaced General Guidoni, sent to Britain as air attaché.

The first short-span, high-power racing version was moved to Schiranna on August 6, just three months prior to race date. Time was lost conducting seaworthiness tests and testing the new engine, which was plagued by carburetion problems. Finally, after three frustrating weeks of preparation, Romeo Sartori on August 30 took the racer aloft on its first flight. The performance envelope was rapidly expanded and on September 17 de Bernardi put the M.39 to the acid test, its first maximum speed run over 3 kilometers. The result augured well — the racer averaged 414 kmh. This was far in excess of the current seaplane world speed record, but the M.39 trials were shrouded in the utmost secrecy. Press reports that new Italian hopefuls had achieved 243 mph (about 15 mph low) were allowed to leak out. Even the serial numbers (MM72–76) were not divulged.

Four days later, on September 21, Centurione climbed aboard one of the trainers for his first M.39 flight. He moved smartly across the lake, gathering confidence together with speed. The M.39, no doubt the hottest aeroplane Centurione had ever handled, seemed to shoot abruptly into the air. The pilot rolled it sharply into a steep turn but then disaster struck. The sharp-nosed airfoil abruptly stalled and the M.39 snap-rolled over the top out of control, to crash in a geyser of foam. Centurione was killed instantly.[5]

[5] Almost exactly one year later Lt. Borra was killed in an identical accident in the other M.39 trainer.

Grief opened a crack in their spirit and the fatigue accumulated over weeks of day and night effort flooded in. The downcast pilots did not fly for six days after their team leader's death. To Castoldi, Zerbi, and Ettore Ferretti, the Fiat representative who was in charge of the ground crew, it now seemed impossible to reach Norfolk by race day. It would be crushing to get this close and miss the race, so the Italians telegraphed the NAA asking for a short postponement. The Americans, determined as ever to hold the race in 1926, responded with a willingness to bend slightly to accommodate a now definite challenge, and put the race back to November 11. This sporting gesture, though they did not know it, sealed their doom. The British, pointing stiffly to the letter of the race rules, protested the short postponement but foolishly: since it favored the only challenger, it was in fact *their* only chance for the future.

On September 27 de Bernardi resumed his practice flights and three days later Ferrarin and Bacula reported to Schiranna for the first time. Although Ferrarin had no previous floatplane experience he approached his M.39 check-out professionally and within a week was fully qualified. While the coveted post of team leader remained vacant Ferrarin's aggressive personality tended to clash with de Bernardi's own strong ego, and to Castoldi's horror the two played a reckless competitive game of harrowing aerobatics in the racers. Ferrarin was the more experienced pilot but de Bernardi, older and senior in rank, was made team leader under the overall administrative direction of Major Aldo Guglielmetti.

Castoldi also had to reconcile conflicting technical reports from his two hot-blooded pilots. De Bernardi wanted less rudder but Ferrarin wanted more. Obviously they had been bothered by the directional instability, aggravated by a "free rudder" since any slight rudder deflection induced uncomfortable oscillations. Both pilots had mis-

interpreted the characteristic: Ferrarin thought he needed a larger rudder to control the aeroplane whereas de Bernardi thought he needed a smaller one to avoid exposure to the unwanted yaw. What was needed, however, was not control but stability. Castoldi knew at once the M.39 needed not a new rudder but more fin; when the rudder was held rigidly in place, effective fixed surface area was to some extent increased by the pilot. Castoldi enlarged the bottom fin but left the rudder itself unaltered.

Bacula completed only four flights before the team sailed, and Guasconi, who had been elevated to first reserve pilot, made only one. Before sailing the team was inspired by the soaring of a poet's rhapsody as well as by a sanguine, more mundane exigency. The scarlet M.39s bore a meaning to the Italians that went beyond the historic, and Gabriele D'Annunzio epitomized their deep emotional value with his send-off to *i tre rossi velivoli* — "the three red flying sails" — each of which, as Muzio Macchi carefully

explained, had its pontoon fuel tanks secretly filled with gallons of good red Italian chianti — to evade America's prohibition! On October 12 the team sailed from Genoa aboard the *Conte Rosso*, Italians again venturing forth to challenge the Americans on their home ground in the decade's only surviving high-speed classic. Muzio Macchi and Major Guglielmetti, having sailed earlier, arrived in the United States October 15 to make preparations, and eight days later the three racers, their team of pilots, and thirteen riggers and mechanics arrived. They were soon established with full facilities in a large hangar at the Naval Air Station, Hampton Roads, a vast improvement over the conditions of 1925. The race numbers 1, 3, and 5 were painted on the scarlet M.39s, their engines were mounted, and the incessant ground runs began. On November 3 de Bernardi made the first M.39 flight in the United States, taking off nicely in ship number 1, but within five minutes a strong backfire ignited fuel puddled in the cowl. De Bernardi

Pushing Ferrarin's M.39 under a veil of Norfolk rain, 1926 (MCT)

landed and tried to smother the flames with his leather jacket, but a United States Navy seaplane which hurried to his aid saved the day with its fire extinguisher. The racer's engine needed two new pistons and these were taken from the reserve engine. M.39 number 3, during runup, was still having carburetion problems.

Castoldi with his almost pathological suspicion of sabotage now doubted the fuel supply. Rejecting a tank-car load of fuel especially ordered by Fiat, he insisted on using fuel from the same source used by the Americans! He also demanded that the spark plugs be changed to the American brand (BG Midgets). Meanwhile the M.39 carburetors were at last properly tuned, and on November 9 Ferrarin was launched for a test flight in freshening gusts, his racer gleaming against a thrilling backdrop of great cloud floes to the west. Suddenly curtains of rain pelted down and the red Macchi was swallowed by gray. The ominous minutes ticked by, Castoldi frantic and helpless squinting into the wet gloom, but somehow Ferrarin finally found the slipway and his cool poise was hailed. "After such a trial the Italian aircraft can do without the navigability tests and all doubts about the ability of Italian pilots have been dispersed," reported one newspaper. Neither Americans nor Italians were giving any secrets away as to their speeds, and the mercurial moods of the two teams oscillated in a daily misphase. The Italians, who would read volumes in a facial expression, were heartened by Champion's mishap in the R3C-4 but put on guard by later reports of its achieving 256 mph, a doubtful report to be sure, but disturbingly plausible. The turbulent November weather took a turn for the worse and this further delayed the beginning of formal trials until late November 11, setting the speed race back in turn until November 13, but this served to increase the excitement. By this time the Italians had managed only six flights among them; Bacula had made only one.

At 4:15 P.M. on November 11 de Bernardi took off on his navigability trials, but after completing them successfully he was accidentally rammed by a Navy motor launch and his starboard float punctured. The Contest Committee ruled that the accident was not de Bernardi's fault and the float could be repaired without penalty. Schilt and Bacula finished their navigability trials, then Ferrarin, anxious for his racer's six-hour mooring-out test to be completed overnight when relatively calm water was assured, was pushed down the slipway to begin his trials at 5:15 P.M. The afternoon dusk of late autumn was pouring like opaque liquid across the landscape and Ferrarin's exhaust was beating a note of roughness, but he persisted in beginning the trials. When his engine quit far out on the course night had virtually fallen, and Ferrarin sat unlit and helpless, drifting in the busy path of huge ships that ceaselessly plied the Roads. Then, in the last faint glimmer of light, Ferrarin's M.39 was spotted by one of the U. S. Navy's most resourceful pilots, a man who became a living Navy institution, Chief Petty Officer (Aviation Pilot) Patrick J. "Pappy" Bryne, flying an ancient HS2L. Pappy landed alongside and while his gruff voice reassured Ferrarin, the Italian certainly could not understand one word of it; nor could he speak English. A massive black shape was sliding by a bit too close and Pappy backfired his engine, hoping the ship's pilot would see the flash. For the next two hours Pappy taxied his HS2L in circles around the M.39, occasionally backfiring his engine as a warning signal to ships, until launches finally located the M.39 and took it in tow. By 9 P.M. the Italian mechanics had opened the cowl and assessed the damage. The crankcase was cracked and there were several broken conrods. The reserve engine had already been partially cannibalized. It looked hopeless.

Drawing himself up straight, Commander Silvio Scaroni, the bemedaled

Handling M.39 racer in Hampton Roads. Ferrarin standing on pontoon. (Au)

Italian air attaché, an aviation pioneer in his own right with thirty confirmed victories in World War I combat, invoked his gravest tone. He looked each grimy mechanic in the eye and reminded them of Mussolini's order. There was no such thing as hopeless: the repairs must be completed. From the "bones of two" one engine shall be made. All night long the technicians worked, and throughout the next morning as well, several times cursing the job as impossible, becoming irritable, beginning to make little mistakes from the deadening fatigue. Not until 2 P.M. was the rebuilt engine finally mounted. Two hours later, as the sun sank low on the eve of the race, Ferrarin at last completed his navigability trials. His engine ran faultlessly.

As race day dawned Commander Scaroni sat with his nation's team to work out a plan of action for the race. The Americans' wrecked R3C-3 had been replaced with a slow but reliable Hawk fighter, a subtle threat because the Italians remembered only too vividly how five years before a nondescript M.7 won the race after all the specialized speedplanes dropped out. For this reason one M.39 must hold back and make absolutely sure to finish the distance. This task was given to Bacula, whose M.39 had the only low-compression engine of the team. His prop was set at low pitch as well, in part because of his derated engine, in part to help his takeoff — Bacula had yet to make a takeoff with a full fuel load. On the other hand, still ignorant of the Americans' true capability, Ferrarin and de Bernardi, who were flying the two high-compression M.39s, would push their craft much harder. De Bernardi's prop was set at the highest pitch of the three while Ferrarin's was set slightly lower; what this cost in prop performance Ferrarin

413

expected to be made up by a slightly higher rpm. Ferrarin's assigned takeoff time was five minutes before Cuddihy in the R3C-4, but all pilots were allowed fifteen minutes leeway; Ferrarin was to fake engine trouble in the hopes that the impatient American would depart on time. Then the Italian could follow Cuddihy aloft and, flying just behind him, assess the American's speed, hoping to have a slight reserve to use if de Bernardi, who would run wide open all the way, should falter. The two non-flying team members would be floating in a boat on the bay to give lap-by-lap hand signals. The Italian's major fear was Cuddihy's R3C-4. If Cuddihy dropped out they were to know at once in order to throttle back and increase their chances of completing the full distance. It was a neat plan which depended on total teamwork.[6]

By half-past two some 60,000 people had gathered on the air station and along Willoughby Spit, with tens of thousands more crowding every available vantage point along the course, which passed over Old Point Comfort and Newport News. The race would be timed by Odis A. Porter with an electric chronograph accurate to one four hundredth of a second. The first pilot, Bacula, was on the slipway warming up; soon he floated into Willoughby Bay and began his takeoff run. In less than half a minute, with very little spray, his M.39 rose cleanly, and the first of Italy's "three red meteors" was on the course. A few minutes later Ferrarin's charade worked as predicted and he was able to take off on Cuddihy's tail. Bacula by this time had already completed one lap and the crowd, unaware of his tactic, was surprised at his slow speed – just over

200 mph. In fact, Bacula was having minor problems with a loose fuel tap, which momentarily preoccupied his attention. Cuddihy's first-lap time, 20 mph better than Bacula, made the crowd cheer – but then Ferrarin flashed by in a crimson blur, slightly faster than Cuddihy. At last de Bernardi thundered by and his convincing speed was well out of Cuddihy's reach – if he lasted. The excitement increased lap by lap: there is no doubt that the 1926 edition was the most thrilling Schneider race ever flown.

On the third lap Ferrarin shot over Willoughby Bay at 200 feet streaming a long banner of greasy black smoke, noting with dismay that his oil pressure was dropping steadily. The ground crew's superhuman efforts the day before to rebuild his engine had been in vain – Ferrarin had to land with a broken oil pipe. He watched glumly as Cuddihy's blue-and-gold biplane receded rapidly toward the far horizon. What he did not know was that Cuddihy at that moment was involved in fruitless struggle with a balky fuel pump.

De Bernardi was flying loose turns, rounding the pylons some 200 yards out in a style not nearly as bold as Cuddihy's, and his engine was beginning to overheat. He lofted the M.39 to 600 feet, where he hoped to get cooler running for the remaining laps. His luck held, the temperature stabilized, and as de Bernardi at last hauled his racer around the final turn at Newport News, rolling out heading east over the broad olive mouth of the James River, the haze of Norfolk ahead on his right wing, he pointed the throbbing red snout of his Macchi toward the whitecaps below and boresighted the long piers of the Naval Operating Base with their forest of gray masts, the broad expanse of the Air Station just beyond. His thunder crescendoed, the exhilaration filled his throat, the temperature gauges rose, but almost at once the splash of color ahead blossomed into individual cars and people, hundreds of waving, cheering people, and de Bernardi hurtled low overhead

Mario de Bernardi being chaired after his 1926 Schneider triumph. Designer Mario Castoldi on left; Silvio Scaroni, wartime Italian ace and then Italian air attaché in the United States, on right. (UPI)

with a shattering whine at 260 mph, the winner!

In nine months the Italians pulled off a trick the British had given up as futile. The Italians were delirious with joy – it was said the Americans had not realized the hazards of the race until they saw de Bernardi being kissed by his mechanics and brother pilots! That evening to formalize *La Grande Vittoria alla Coppa Schneider*, de Bernardi addressed a telegram to Palazzo di Venezia in Rome which read simply, "*Your orders to win at all costs have*

been carried out." Four days later on November 17, despite his engine turning 100 rpm low, de Bernardi took his M.39 over the measured course four times to establish the new world speed record for seaplanes at 258·873 mph (his fastest downwind pass was measured at 272·132 mph, his fastest upwind was 243·232 mph). Later, accompanied by General Italo Balbo, Italian Air Minister, de Bernardi and Ferrarin dropped a wreath on Lake Varese to honor Centurione, their fallen comrade. Destiny later dealt

[6] The United States could not have been completely in the dark as to Italian strategy; they had not only provided the metal props used by the M.39s, but set the pitch to Italian order! Yet it is likely the Americans did not try to analyze the subtleties of how this factor might be applied against them.

de Bernardi in 1926 Schneider victory motor-cade, escorted by General Capillo (Au)

equal violence to most of those who remained. Sartori died in 1933, De Briganti in 1937, Bacula in 1938, and Ferrarin in 1941, all *caduto per incidenti di volo*; finally de Bernardi himself, in 1959 when he was sixty-seven years old, landed his light aeroplane after an aerobatic display for a holiday crowd at Rome. He parked the plane but did not cut the switch. When a curious mechanic went to find out why, he discovered de Bernardi slumped over. The old master's heart had failed, and like his comrades who had gone before, de Bernardi had died at the controls.

The last of the line: the final Schneider racer, Castoldi's magnificent twin-engine Macchi M.C.72, which in 1934 flew 709·209 kmh (faster than 440 mph), a world record still unsurpassed today for piston-engine seaplanes, and which remains almost one half century later fully 91 per cent of the current unlimited piston world speed record! (Au)

POSTSCRIPT

What then, after all, is the meaning of the speed seekers? True, their activity occurred during years usually dismissed, years when economic collapse, political confusion, and psychological wreckage were abroad in the world, years when life no longer seemed heroic and hedonistic masses clamored for materialism, years when the very foundations of European civilization trembled. But underneath the frantic pizzicato a deeper, more substantial note, just a tremor at first, began to gather strength, and the reluctant world was forced to acknowledge — and accommodate — the accelerating, intensifying transformation, the allegro of the aeroplane. No national political revolution has had as absolute an effect on mankind as that which descended on the frail wings of the aeroplane, forcing a complete overhaul in man's most basic techniques of defense and communication. And during the years of the speed seekers the aeroplane flexed its muscles. These years constitute a technical golden age no less profound simply because many have failed to notice.

Speed alone, of course, was not enough. Every new component, every new transfiguration of the aeroplane must be proven — and racing became the ultimate test. The measured course became for the speed seekers the proving and improving ground, the research lab, the birthplace of the unexpected and unpredictable. The alterations thus authored gave, in turn, more speed.

417

What we have discerned is man consolidating technology at an unprecedented rate. Is he to be faulted for grasping the attainable, seemingly disregarding tomorrow's consequences? Yet in truth such worship of the immediate reflects man's deepest nature. The increased pursuit of knowledge and its immediate application have been man's drive since primeval times, and there is no force capable of breaking it. How little man knew of 1930 in 1920 – and cannot the same be said of any decade in the twentieth century? The speed seekers proved, perhaps more vividly than any other group, that man's cardinal challenge is to improve his capacity for recognizing and accepting change.

Most people who lived during the years of the speed seekers together with their governments remained essentially ignorant of the implications that burgeoning industrialism imposed; instead they clung to and struggled to perpetuate an agrarian view of the world, skeptical and often hostile toward technology. Such root forces ultimately braked the speed seekers – and still work even today to disrupt technology. Nevertheless, since governments in the final analysis are motivated into effective activity not by political but by economic energy (a truism often only dimly perceived), and since technology in spite of various frictions inevitably becomes more complex, requiring ever greater investments to ensure the payoff, the government share of involvement inexorably grows in order to sustain an economically competitive posture – for only commercial technological success on a long-term basis can generate the resources to perpetuate the government. Paradoxically, however, state-controlled technology, because of inadequate self-evaluation, never produces results equivalent to commercially controlled technology. The speed seekers, at the apex of man's earliest realizations of these significant implications, enjoyed their most important successes as the result of the coalescing of government and commercial efforts; indeed, the future pursuit of technology will irresistibly lead to the coalescing of larger and larger commercial organizations and even governments themselves into super-national units with diminishing national identity, a situation which might have astounded even the speed seekers.

What can we say of these men who hastened twentieth-century technology by doubling in a half-dozen years a speed which had been but a dream for thousands, and doing it against a backdrop of penury, indifference, and frustration? They would have us say, rather than that there were great men among them, that they were a group of ordinary men who faced up to great challenge – a group of men who adhered to the conviction

la vitesse est l'aristocratie du mouvement.

Appendices

Calendars

1919

	January	May	September
S	5 12 19 26	4 11 18 25	7 14 21 28
M	6 13 20 27	5 12 19 26	1 8 15 22 29
T	7 14 21 28	6 13 20 27	2 9 16 23 30
W	1 8 15 22 29	7 14 21 28	3 10 17 24
T	2 9 16 23 30	1 8 15 22 29	4 11 18 25
F	3 10 17 24 31	2 9 16 23 30	5 12 19 26
S	4 11 18 25	3 10 17 24 31	6 13 20 27

	February	June	October
S	2 9 16 23	1 8 15 22 29	5 12 19 26
M	3 10 17 24	2 9 16 23 30	6 13 20 27
T	4 11 18 25	3 10 17 24	7 14 21 28
W	5 12 19 26	4 11 18 25	1 8 15 22 29
T	6 13 20 27	5 12 19 26	2 9 16 23 30
F	7 14 21 28	6 13 20 27	3 10 17 24 31
S	1 8 15 22	7 14 21 28	4 11 18 25

	March	July	November
S	2 9 16 23 30	6 13 20 27	2 9 16 23 30
M	3 10 17 24 31	7 14 21 28	3 10 17 24
T	4 11 18 25	1 8 15 22 29	4 11 18 25
W	5 12 19 26	2 9 16 23 30	5 12 19 26
T	6 13 20 27	3 10 17 24 31	6 13 20 27
F	7 14 21 28	4 11 18 25	7 14 21 28
S	1 8 15 22 29	5 12 19 26	1 8 15 22 29

	April	August	December
S	6 13 20 27	3 10 17 24 31	7 14 21 28
M	7 14 21 28	4 11 18 25	1 8 15 22 29
T	1 8 15 22 29	5 12 19 26	2 9 16 23 30
W	2 9 16 23 30	6 13 20 27	3 10 17 24 31
T	3 10 17 24	7 14 21 28	4 11 18 25
F	4 11 18 25	1 8 15 22 29	5 12 19 26
S	5 12 19 26	2 9 16 23 30	6 13 20 27

1921

	January	May	September
S	2 9 16 23 30	1 8 15 22 29	4 11 18 25
M	3 10 17 24 31	2 9 16 23 30	5 12 19 26
T	4 11 18 25	3 10 17 24 31	6 13 20 27
W	5 12 19 26	4 11 18 25	7 14 21 28
T	6 13 20 27	5 12 19 26	1 8 15 22 29
F	7 14 21 28	6 13 20 27	2 9 16 23 30
S	1 8 15 22 29	7 14 21 28	3 10 17 24

	February	June	October
S	6 13 20 27	5 12 19 26	2 9 16 23 30
M	7 14 21 28	6 13 20 27	3 10 17 24 31
T	1 8 15 22	7 14 21 28	4 11 18 25
W	2 9 16 23	1 8 15 22 29	5 12 19 26
T	3 10 17 24	2 9 16 23 30	6 13 20 27
F	4 11 18 25	3 10 17 24	7 14 21 28
S	5 12 19 26	4 11 18 25	1 8 15 22 29

	March	July	November
S	6 13 20 27	3 10 17 24 31	6 13 20 27
M	7 14 21 28	4 11 18 25	7 14 21 28
T	1 8 15 22 29	5 12 19 26	1 8 15 22 29
W	2 9 16 23 30	6 13 20 27	2 9 16 23 30
T	3 10 17 24 31	7 14 21 28	3 10 17 24
F	4 11 18 25	1 8 15 22 29	4 11 18 25
S	5 12 19 26	2 9 16 23 30	5 12 19 26

	April	August	December
S	3 10 17 24	7 14 21 28	4 11 18 25
M	4 11 18 25	1 8 15 22 29	5 12 19 26
T	5 12 19 26	2 9 16 23 30	6 13 20 27
W	6 13 20 27	3 10 17 24 31	7 14 21 28
T	7 14 21 28	4 11 18 25	1 8 15 22 29
F	1 8 15 22 29	5 12 19 26	2 9 16 23 30
S	2 9 16 23 30	6 13 20 27	3 10 17 24 31

1923

	January	May	September
S	7 14 21 28	6 13 20 27	2 9 16 23 30
M	1 8 15 22 29	7 14 21 28	3 10 17 24
T	2 9 16 23 30	1 8 15 22 29	4 11 18 25
W	3 10 17 24 31	2 9 16 23 30	5 12 19 26
T	4 11 18 25	3 10 17 24 31	6 13 20 27
F	5 12 19 26	4 11 18 25	7 14 21 28
S	6 13 20 27	5 12 19 26	1 8 15 22 29

	February	June	October
S	4 11 18 25	3 10 17 24	7 14 21 28
M	5 12 19 26	4 11 18 25	1 8 15 22 29
T	6 13 20 27	5 12 19 26	2 9 16 23 30
W	7 14 21 28	6 13 20 27	3 10 17 24 31
T	1 8 15 22	7 14 21 28	4 11 18 25
F	2 9 16 23	1 8 15 22 29	5 12 19 26
S	3 10 17 24	2 9 16 23 30	6 13 20 27

	March	July	November
S	4 11 18 25	1 8 15 22 29	4 11 18 25
M	5 12 19 26	2 9 16 23 30	5 12 19 26
T	6 13 20 27	3 10 17 24 31	6 13 20 27
W	7 14 21 28	4 11 18 25	7 14 21 28
T	1 8 15 22 29	5 12 19 26	1 8 15 22 29
F	2 9 16 23 30	6 13 20 27	2 9 16 23 30
S	3 10 17 24 31	7 14 21 28	3 10 17 24

	April	August	December
S	1 8 15 22 29	5 12 19 26	2 9 16 23 30
M	2 9 16 23 30	6 13 20 27	3 10 17 24 31
T	3 10 17 24	7 14 21 28	4 11 18 25
W	4 11 18 25	1 8 15 22 29	5 12 19 26
T	5 12 19 26	2 9 16 23 30	6 13 20 27
F	6 13 20 27	3 10 17 24 31	7 14 21 28
S	7 14 21 28	4 11 18 25	1 8 15 22 29

1925

	January	May	September
S	4 11 18 25	3 10 17 24 31	6 13 20 27
M	5 12 19 26	4 11 18 25	7 14 21 28
T	6 13 20 27	5 12 19 26	1 8 15 22 29
W	7 14 21 28	6 13 20 27	2 9 16 23 30
T	1 8 15 22 29	7 14 21 28	3 10 17 24
F	2 9 16 23 30	1 8 15 22 29	4 11 18 25
S	3 10 17 24 31	2 9 16 23 30	5 12 19 26

	February	June	October
S	1 8 15 22	7 14 21 28	4 11 18 25
M	2 9 16 23	1 8 15 22 29	5 12 19 26
T	3 10 17 24	2 9 16 23 30	6 13 20 27
W	4 11 18 25	3 10 17 24	7 14 21 28
T	5 12 19 26	4 11 18 25	1 8 15 22 29
F	6 13 20 27	5 12 19 26	2 9 16 23 30
S	7 14 21 28	6 13 20 27	3 10 17 24 31

	March	July	November
S	1 8 15 22 29	5 12 19 26	1 8 15 22 29
M	2 9 16 23 30	6 13 20 27	2 9 16 23 30
T	3 10 17 24 31	7 14 21 28	3 10 17 24
W	4 11 18 25	1 8 15 22 29	4 11 18 25
T	5 12 19 26	2 9 16 23 30	5 12 19 26
F	6 13 20 27	3 10 17 24 31	6 13 20 27
S	7 14 21 28	4 11 18 25	7 14 21 28

	April	August	December
S	5 12 19 26	2 9 16 23 30	6 13 20 27
M	6 13 20 27	3 10 17 24 31	7 14 21 28
T	7 14 21 28	4 11 18 25	1 8 15 22 29
W	1 8 15 22 29	5 12 19 26	2 9 16 23 30
T	2 9 16 23 30	6 13 20 27	3 10 17 24 31
F	3 10 17 24	7 14 21 28	4 11 18 25
S	4 11 18 25	1 8 15 22 29	5 12 19 26

1920

	January	May	September
S	4 11 18 25	2 9 16 23 30	5 12 19 26
M	5 12 19 26	3 10 17 24 31	6 13 20 27
T	6 13 20 27	4 11 18 25	7 14 21 28
W	7 14 21 28	5 12 19 26	1 8 15 22 29
T	1 8 15 22 29	6 13 20 27	2 9 16 23 30
F	2 9 16 23 30	7 14 21 28	3 10 17 24
S	3 10 17 24 31	1 8 15 22 29	4 11 18 25

	February	June	October
S	1 8 15 22 29	6 13 20 27	3 10 17 24 31
M	2 9 16 23	7 14 21 28	4 11 18 25
T	3 10 17 24	1 8 15 22 29	5 12 19 26
W	4 11 18 25	2 9 16 23 30	6 13 20 27
T	5 12 19 26	3 10 17 24	7 14 21 28
F	6 13 20 27	4 11 18 25	1 8 15 22 29
S	7 14 21 28	5 12 19 26	2 9 16 23 30

	March	July	November
S	7 14 21 28	4 11 18 25	7 14 21 28
M	1 8 15 22 29	5 12 19 26	1 8 15 22 29
T	2 9 16 23 30	6 13 20 27	2 9 16 23 30
W	3 10 17 24 31	7 14 21 28	3 10 17 24
T	4 11 18 25	1 8 15 22 29	4 11 18 25
F	5 12 19 26	2 9 16 23 30	5 12 19 26
S	6 13 20 27	3 10 17 24 31	6 13 20 27

	April	August	December
S	4 11 18 25	1 8 15 22 29	5 12 19 26
M	5 12 19 26	2 9 16 23 30	6 13 20 27
T	6 13 20 27	3 10 17 24 31	7 14 21 28
W	7 14 21 28	4 11 18 25	1 8 15 22 29
T	1 8 15 22 29	5 12 19 26	2 9 16 23 30
F	2 9 16 23 30	6 13 20 27	3 10 17 24 31
S	3 10 17 24	7 14 21 28	4 11 18 25

1922

	January	May	September
S	1 8 15 22 29	7 14 21 28	3 10 17 24
M	2 9 16 23 30	1 8 15 22 29	4 11 18 25
T	3 10 17 24 31	2 9 16 23 30	5 12 19 26
W	4 11 18 25	3 10 17 24 31	6 13 20 27
T	5 12 19 26	4 11 18 25	7 14 21 28
F	6 13 20 27	5 12 19 26	1 8 15 22 29
S	7 14 21 28	6 13 20 27	2 9 16 23 30

	February	June	October
S	5 12 19 26	4 11 18 25	1 8 15 22 29
M	6 13 20 27	5 12 19 26	2 9 16 23 30
T	7 14 21 28	6 13 20 27	3 10 17 24 31
W	1 8 15 22	7 14 21 28	4 11 18 25
T	2 9 16 23	1 8 15 22 29	5 12 19 26
F	3 10 17 24	2 9 16 23 30	6 13 20 27
S	4 11 18 25	3 10 17 24	7 14 21 28

	March	July	November
S	5 12 19 26	2 9 16 23 30	5 12 19 26
M	6 13 20 27	3 10 17 24 31	6 13 20 27
T	7 14 21 28	4 11 18 25	7 14 21 28
W	1 8 15 22 29	5 12 19 26	1 8 15 22 29
T	2 9 16 23 30	6 13 20 27	2 9 16 23 30
F	3 10 17 24 31	7 14 21 28	3 10 17 24
S	4 11 18 25	1 8 15 22 29	4 11 18 25

	April	August	December
S	2 9 16 23 30	6 13 20 27	3 10 17 24 31
M	3 10 17 24	7 14 21 28	4 11 18 25
T	4 11 18 25	1 8 15 22 29	5 12 19 26
W	5 12 19 26	2 9 16 23 30	6 13 20 27
T	6 13 20 27	3 10 17 24 31	7 14 21 28
F	7 14 21 28	4 11 18 25	1 8 15 22 29
S	1 8 15 22 29	5 12 19 26	2 9 16 23 30

1924

	January	May	September
S	6 13 20 27	4 11 18 25	7 14 21 28
M	7 14 21 28	5 12 19 26	1 8 15 22 29
T	1 8 15 22 29	6 13 20 27	2 9 16 23 30
W	2 9 16 23 30	7 14 21 28	3 10 17 24
T	3 10 17 24 31	1 8 15 22 29	4 11 18 25
F	4 11 18 25	2 9 16 23 30	5 12 19 26
S	5 12 19 26	3 10 17 24 31	6 13 20 27

	February	June	October
S	3 10 17 24	1 8 15 22 29	5 12 19 26
M	4 11 18 25	2 9 16 23 30	6 13 20 27
T	5 12 19 26	3 10 17 24	7 14 21 28
W	6 13 20 27	4 11 18 25	1 8 15 22 29
T	7 14 21 28	5 12 19 26	2 9 16 23 30
F	1 8 15 22 29	6 13 20 27	3 10 17 24 31
S	2 9 16 23	7 14 21 28	4 11 18 25

	March	July	November
S	2 9 16 23 30	6 13 20 27	2 9 16 23 30
M	3 10 17 24 31	7 14 21 28	3 10 17 24
T	4 11 18 25	1 8 15 22 29	4 11 18 25
W	5 12 19 26	2 9 16 23 30	5 12 19 26
T	6 13 20 27	3 10 17 24 31	6 13 20 27
F	7 14 21 28	4 11 18 25	7 14 21 28
S	1 8 15 22 29	5 12 19 26	1 8 15 22 29

	April	August	December
S	6 13 20 27	3 10 17 24 31	7 14 21 28
M	7 14 21 28	4 11 18 25	1 8 15 22 29
T	1 8 15 22 29	5 12 19 26	2 9 16 23 30
W	2 9 16 23 30	6 13 20 27	3 10 17 24 31
T	3 10 17 24	7 14 21 28	4 11 18 25
F	4 11 18 25	1 8 15 22 29	5 12 19 26
S	5 12 19 26	2 9 16 23 30	6 13 20 27

1926

	January	May	September
S	3 10 17 24 31	2 9 16 23 30	5 12 19 26
M	4 11 18 25	3 10 17 24 31	6 13 20 27
T	5 12 19 26	4 11 18 25	7 14 21 28
W	6 13 20 27	5 12 19 26	1 8 15 22 29
T	7 14 21 28	6 13 20 27	2 9 16 23 30
F	1 8 15 22 29	7 14 21 28	3 10 17 24
S	2 9 16 23 30	1 8 15 22 29	4 11 18 25

	February	June	October
S	7 14 21 28	6 13 20 27	3 10 17 24 31
M	1 8 15 22	7 14 21 28	4 11 18 25
T	2 9 16 23	1 8 15 22 29	5 12 19 26
W	3 10 17 24	2 9 16 23 30	6 13 20 27
T	4 11 18 25	3 10 17 24	7 14 21 28
F	5 12 19 26	4 11 18 25	1 8 15 22 29
S	6 13 20 27	5 12 19 26	2 9 16 23 30

	March	July	November
S	7 14 21 28	4 11 18 25	7 14 21 28
M	1 8 15 22 29	5 12 19 26	1 8 15 22 29
T	2 9 16 23 30	6 13 20 27	2 9 16 23 30
W	3 10 17 24 31	7 14 21 28	3 10 17 24
T	4 11 18 25	1 8 15 22 29	4 11 18 25
F	5 12 19 26	2 9 16 23 30	5 12 19 26
S	6 13 20 27	3 10 17 24 31	6 13 20 27

	April	August	December
S	4 11 18 25	1 8 15 22 29	5 12 19 26
M	5 12 19 26	2 9 16 23 30	6 13 20 27
T	6 13 20 27	3 10 17 24 31	7 14 21 28
W	7 14 21 28	4 11 18 25	1 8 15 22 29
T	1 8 15 22 29	5 12 19 26	2 9 16 23 30
F	2 9 16 23 30	6 13 20 27	3 10 17 24 31
S	3 10 17 24	7 14 21 28	4 11 18 25

CONVERSION TABLE

	Multiply	By	To Obtain
Distances	Nautical Miles[1]	1·8520	Kilometers
	Nautical Miles	1·1507771	Statute Miles
	Statute Miles[2]	1·6093472	Kilometers
	Statute Miles	·8689780	Nautical Miles
	Kilometers[3]	·62136996	Statute Miles
	Kilometers	·5399568	Nautical Miles
Dimensions[4]	Meters	3·2808333	Feet
	Feet	·3048006	Meters
	Millimeters[5]	·039370	Inches
	Inches[5]	25·40	Millimeters
	$m^{2(6)}$	10·76387	ft^2
	$ft^{2(6)}$	·09290341	m^2
Weights	Kilograms	2·2046223	Pounds
	Pounds	·45359243	Kilograms
Loadings[7]	kg/m^2	·2048169	lbs/ft^2
	obs/ft^2	4·8824089	kg/m^2
Propulsion	*Cheval* (CV)[8]	·986318	horsepower (hp)
	horsepower (hp)[8]	1·013872	*Cheval* (CV)
	Liters (swept volume)[9]	61·025027	cid (cubic inch displacement)
	cid (cubic inch displacement)[9]	·0163867	Liters (swept volume)
	Gallons (U.S.)	·83268	Gallons (Imp.)
	Gallons (Imp.)	1·20094	Gallons (U.S.)
	Gallons (U.S.)	3·785332	Liters
	Liters	·26417762	Gallons (U.S.)

Currency	as of:	25-X-1919	1-IX-1922	
	U.S. dollars	8·675	12·895	French francs
		·240	·224	English pounds
		10·327	22·702	Italian lire
	French francs	·115	·0775	U.S. dollars
		·0277	·0174	English pounds
		1·1904	1·761	Italian lire
	English pounds	4·168	4·463	U.S. dollars
		36·155	57·545	French francs
		43·042	101·312	Italian lire
	Italian lire	·0968	·044	U.S. dollars
		·840	·568	French francs
		·0232	·0099	English pounds

1 The basis for the nautical mile is the length of one minute of arc on the earth's surface at the equator. The international nautical mile is generally accepted to be 6,076·10333 feet (1,852 meters), and this is the basis for the conversions listed (although some references specify 6,076·11549 feet). Formerly, in the United States during the 1920s, the nautical mile was considered to be 6,080·20 feet (1·1516 statute mile; 1·853249 kilometer), and although this value occasionally lent confusion to the exact length of various air race courses, it is now obsolete. The course lengths specified herein have been verified in accordance with the accepted international values as listed in the conversion table. The term "knots" means nautical miles per hour, and although common in aviation today it was not widely used in aviation during the 1920s. The word originated with the knotted line sailing ships unreeled to measure their speed; the line was knotted every 47 feet 3 inches; the number of knots that passed the counter in twenty-eight seconds converted directly to the ship's speed in nautical miles per hour. It is improper to use the word "knot" unless one is speaking of speed — not distance.

2 The statute or land mile has a length of 5,280·000 feet. The basis for this length is too complex for a discussion here, but dates to Roman times. The statute mile was only rarely used to measure air race or speed courses; however, the term "mph" (miles per hour) is based on statute miles, and in the English-speaking countries this was the most common speed reference during the 1920s.

3 The kilometer is 1,000 meters, hence 3,280·8333 feet. Speed in kilometers per hour was the international reference for world speed records, and in this book the French convention common in the 1920s has been adopted, namely to abbreviate this speed measure as kmh.

4 To convert linear dimensions from metric to English:
(a) multiply meters by the conversion factor to obtain feet, but of course anything less than a whole foot will be expressed in decimal parts; thus
(b) the decimal part must be multiplied by 12 to arrive at inches — and decimal parts of an inch; this latter must then be
(c) multiplied by 16 to arrive finally at fractions of an inch in familiar 16ths.
Is it any wonder we are long overdue to convert to the metric system?
To convert feet and inches to metric:
(a) convert inches to millimeters (1 millimeter is ·001 meter);
(b) convert feet to meters;
(c) take care with the decimal point and simply add the results of (a) and (b).

5 Thus one meter is 39·3700 inches. Although the mathematically accurate reciprocal of this yields 25·40005 mm per inch, international agreement to round this off to 25·4 (as indicated) has been made official.

6 Some references indicate that in England the square meter was often accepted as precisely 10·76390 square feet — or ·00003 square feet more than the more widely accepted conversion value listed.

7 Weight per horsepower (kg/hp to lbs/hp and vice versa) can be converted directly by means of the conversions listed under *Weights*.

8 French or metric horsepower, sometimes called *force de cheval*, *cheval-vapeur*, or simply *cheval* (*cavalli* in Italy), abbreviated CV, is numerically equal to a rate of 75 kilogram-meters of work per second. The U.S. horsepower was originated by Boulton and Watt to state the power of their steam engine; they determined by experiment that, in English terms of measurement, a typical horse could be expected to sustain 22,000 foot-pounds of work per hour. For some obscure reason they arbitrarily increased this by 50 per cent, resulting in today's accepted definition of 33,000 ft-lb/hr, or 550 ft-lb/sec to express 1 hp. The metric value, long since out of favor, was much more common among European engine builders during the 1920s. A typical example is the Hispano-Suiza *modèle 42* engine, officially rated at 300CV — equivalent to 295·9 hp. These values were close enough, however, for the engine to be accepted as a 300-hp unit.

9 One cubic inch is 16·387162 cubic centimeters and 1,000 cubic centimeters are 61·0233792 cubic inches, but contain slightly less than 1 liter. The discrepancy arises from a small error in physical measurement when the metric system was established, namely that the maximum density of water — on which the liter is based — is ·999973 gram/cm^3 at 3·98° C. This small discrepancy leads to the conversion values listed.

APPENDIX 1 – Progress of Speed

■ Official (FAI homologated) World Maximum Speed Record *(Classe C: Avions a Moteur) (Plus grande vitesse sur base)*
▲ Official (FAI homologated) World Seaplane Speed Record *(Classe C bis (or C.2): Hydravions)*
In cases where absolute confirmation was not possible, figures are given in italics

Date	Speed	Pilot	Location	Aeroplane	Engine	Distance/Time		Notes
January 28, 1904	*108·414* kmh	Glenn Curtiss	Ormond Beach, Florida	(motorcycle)	—	10 st mi	:08:54·4	(1)
January 1906	*219·628* kmh	Glenn Curtiss	Ormond Beach, Florida	(motorcycle)	8-cyl.	1 st mi		(1)
■ November 12, 1906	41·292 kmh	Alberto Santos-Dumont	Bagatelle, France	Santos-Dumont 14 *bis*		220 meters		(2)
■ July 10, 1910	106·508 kmh	Leon F. Morane	Bétheny, Rheims, France	Bleriot XI *bis* (12 m²)	(3)	1 km		(3)
1911	*228·093* kmh	Burman	Germany	(Benz automobile)		1 km		(1)
■ September 29, 1913	203·850 kmh ■ 200·836 kmh	Marcel Prévost	Rheims, France	Deperdussin	(4)	1 km 200 km	:59:45·6	(4)
AUGUST 1914–NOVEMBER 1918 – WORLD WAR I								
April 26, 1918	*233·5* kmh	Sgt. Gianfelice-Gino	Langley Field, Virginia to Washington, D.C.	SVA	45 (2)	(145 st mi 1:00)		(5)
August 19, 1918	*262·5* kmh			Curtiss 18-T A-3325	17 (1)			(5) (6)
June 21, 1919	208·095 kmh	Gerald Gathergood	circuit around London	Air Co D.H.4R K-141	35 (1)	189 st mi	1:27:42·0	(7)
June *26*, 1919	261·629 kmh	Francesco Brack-Papa	Mirafiori, Turin, Italy	Fiat BR	47			(8)
September 2, 1919	249·307 kmh	Sadi Lecointe	circuit around Paris	Spad S.20 *bis*₁	4 (1)	200 km	:48:08·0	(9)
September 25, 1919	*265* kmh	Sadi Lecointe	Paris	Spad S.20 *bis*₁	4 (1)			(10)
October *20*, 1919	268·631 kmh	Count de Romanet	circuit around Paris	Nieuport 29V	4 (1)	190·3993 km	:42:31·6	(11)
November 15, 1919	229·621 kmh 232·468 kmh	Gerald Gathergood	Hendon, England	Air Co D.H.9R G-EAHT	35 (1)	100 km 200 km	:26:07·8 :51:37·2	(12)
November 20, 1919	*274* kmh	unknown	Montecelle (near Rome)	Marchetti *MVT*	*45 (2)*		*1:00*	(5)
December *16*, 1919	*307·225* kmh	Sadi Lecointe		Nieuport 29V	4 (1)	*1 km*		(13)
January 3, 1920	266·314 kmh	Sadi Lecointe	circuit around Paris	Nieuport 29V number 6	4 (1)	190·3993 km	:42:53·8	(14)
January 6, 1920 – FAI REOPENS OFFICIAL WORLD SPEED RECORD RECOGNITION; MAXIMUM SPEED DETERMINED BY 4 FLIGHTS OVER A 1-km COURSE								(15)
■ February 7, 1920	275·862 kmh	Sadi Lecointe	Villacoublay, France	Nieuport 29V number 6	4 (1)	1 km	*(average time* :13:05)	(16)
February 26, 1920	260·*830* kmh	Francesco Brack-Papa	Mirafiori, Turin, Italy	Fiat ARF	47			(17)
■ February 28, 1920	283·464 kmh	Jean Casale	Villacoublay, France	Spad S.20 *bis*₄	4 (1)	1 km	*(average time* :12·7)	(18)
March 3, 1920	*273* kmh	Francesco Brack-Papa	Mirafiori, Turin, Italy	Fiat ARF	47			(19)
March 4, 1920	276·888 kmh	Francesco Brack-Papa	Turin-Rome, Italy	Fiat ARF	47	623 km	2:15	(20)
March 21, 1920	259·803 kmh	F. P. Raynham	Martlesham Heath, Suffolk, England	Martinsyde Semiquaver G-EAPX	4 (2)	1 km		(21)
▲ April 25, 1920	211·395 kmh	Count de Romanet	Monaco–Cannes	Spad S.26	4 (2)	*80·577 km*	:22:52·2	(22)
May 1920	*222* kmh	Roland Rohlfs	Rockaway, New York	Curtiss 18-T A-3325	17 (1)	30,404·7 feet		(23)
May 3, 1920	279·923 kmh	Francesco Brack-Papa	Mirafiori, Turin, Italy	Fiat *ARF*	47			

Date	Speed	Pilot	Location	Aeroplane	Engine	Distance/Time		Notes
June 17, 1920	267·7 kmh	Leslie R. Tait-Cox	Martlesham Heath, England	Nieuport & General L.S.3 G-EASK	40 (2)	1 km		(24)
September 25, 1920	279·503 kmh	Sadi Lecointe	Villesauvage—La Marmogne (Gidy) France	Nieuport 29V (12·3 m²)	4 (1)	100 km	:21:28·0	(25)
September 28, 1920	274·537 kmh	Sadi Lecointe	Villesauvage—Gidy, France	Nieuport 29V (12·3 m²)	4 (1)	200 km	:43:42·6	(26)
☁ October 9, 1920	292·682 kmh	Count de Romanet	Buc, France	Spad S.20 *bis*₆	4 (2)	1 km	(average time :12·3)	(27)
October 9, 1920	293·877 kmh	Sadi Lecointe	Buc, France	Nieuport 29V (12·3 m²)	4 (1)	1 km	(average time :12·25)	(27)
■ October 10, 1920	296·694 kmh	Sadi Lecointe	Buc, France	Nieuport 29V (12·3 m²)	4 (1)	1 km	(average time :12·1)	(27)
■ October 20, 1920	302·529 kmh	Sadi Lecointe	Villacoublay, France	Nieuport 29V (12·3m²)	4 (1)	1 km	(average time :11·9)	
■ November 4, 1920	309·012 kmh	Count de Romanet	Buc, France	Spad S.20 *bis*₆	4 (3)	1 km	(average time :11·65) fastest :11·2	
November 27, 1920	*299·5* kmh	Corliss Moseley	Mitchel Field, New York	Verville VCP-R	24	1 km		(28)
■ December 12, 1920	313·043 kmh	Sadi Lecointe	Villacoublay, France	Nieuport 29V *bis* (*13·2 m²*) number 11	4 (*1*)	1 km	(average time :11·5; 1+2 :23·0; 3+4 :23·0) fastest :11·2	
September 25, 1921	*339* kmh	Sadi Lecointe	Villesauvage (Etampes) France	Nieuport-Delage sesquiplane number 6	4 (3)	1 km		(5)
■ September 26, 1921	330·275 kmh	Sadi Lecointe	Villesauvage (Etampes) France	Nieuport-Delage sesquiplane number 6	4 (3)	1 km	(average time :10·9)	
October 1, 1921	298·656 kmh	Francesco Brack-Papa	Villesauvage—Gidy, France	Fiat R.700	47	100 km	:20:05·4	(29)
October 1, 1921	281·272 kmh	Georges Kirsch	Villesauvage—Gidy, France	Nieuport-Delage sesquiplane number 7	4 (3)	200 km	:42:39·8	(29)
November 3, 1921	284·450 kmh	Bert Acosta	Omaha, Nebraska	Curtiss CR-1 A-6081	19 (1)	153·595 st mi	:52:08·4	(30)
November 22, 1921	297·5 kmh	Bert Acosta	Curtiss Field, Mineola, New York	Curtiss CR-1 *A-6081*	19 (1)	1 km		(31)
December 19, 1921	316·4 kmh	James H. James	Martlesham Heath, England	Gloucestershire Bamel G-EAXZ	35 (2)	1 km		(32)
April 30, 1922	*335* kmh	Bert Acosta	Curtiss Field, Mineola, New York	Curtiss Cactus-Kitten triplane	18 (2)			(5)
August 7, 1922	286·2 kmh	James H. James	circuit around London	Gloucestershire Bamel G-EAXZ	35 (2)	198 st mi	1:06:48·4	(33)
August 12, 1922	208·818 kmh 208·242 kmh	Henri Biard	Naples, Italy	Supermarine Sea Lion II G-EBAH	35 (2)	100 km 200 km	:28:41·4 :57:37·4	(34)
August 26, 1922	336·132 kmh	Francesco Brack-Papa	Mirafiori, Turin, Italy	Fiat R.700	47	1 km	:10·9 :10·3 :11·3 :10·4	(35)
■ September 21, 1922	341·239 kmh	Sadi Lecointe	Villesauvage (Etampes) France	Nieuport-Delage sesquiplane number 5	4 (3)	1 km	:10·4 :10·6 :10·4 :10·8	(36)
September 30, 1922	325·497 kmh	Sadi Lecointe	Villesauvage—Gidy, France	Nieuport-Delage sesquiplane number 5	4 (3)	100 km	:18:26·0	(37)
September 30, 1922	289·482 kmh	Fernand Lasne	Villesauvage—Gidy, France	Nieuport-Delage 29V (12·3 m²) number 4	4 (3)	200 km	:41:27·2	(37)

Date	Speed	Pilot	Location	Aeroplane	Engine	Distance/Time		Notes
October 2, 1922	353·1 kmh	Russell Maughan	Curtiss Field, Mineola, New York	Curtiss R-6 A.S.68564	20 (1)	*1 km*		(38)
October 3, 1922	324·610 kmh 330·971 kmh 339·007 kmh	James H. James	Villesauvage (Étampes) France	Gloucestershire Bamel G-EAXZ	35 (2)	1 km :11·6 :11·4 :11·0 :10·8 :10·4 :10·7 :11·2 :11·4 :10·4 :10·8 :10·4 :10·4		(39)
October 4, 1922	342·352 kmh	James H. James	Villesauvage (Étampes) France	Gloucestershire Bamel G-EAXZ	35 (2)	1 km :10·8 :09·8 :11·4 :10·2		(40)
October 8, 1922	354·774 kmh	Russell Maughan	Curtiss Field, Mineola, New York	Curtiss R-6 A.S.68564	20 (1)	1 km :10·4 *10·0* :10·2 :10·0		(41)
October 14, 1922	330·406 kmh 331·465 kmh	Russell Maughan	Selfridge Field, Mt. Clemens, Michigan	Curtiss R-6 A.S.68564	20 (1)	100 km :18:06·78 200 km :36:12·17		(42)
■ October 18, 1922	358·836 kmh	William Mitchell	Selfridge Field, Mt. Clemens, Michigan	Curtiss R-6 A.S.68563 A.S.68564 ■	20 (1)	1 km A.S.68563 A.S.68564 ■ :09·51 :09·47 :09·42 :09·17 :11·72 :11·45 :11·16 :10·95 :09·72 :09·45 :09·36 :09·25 :11·77 :11·35 :11·06 :10·76		(43)
▲ December 28, 1922	280·155 kmh	Alessandro Passaleva	Sesto Calende, Lago Maggiore, Italy	Savoia-Marchetti S.51 I-BAIU	4 (4)	1 km :12·8 :13·0 *:12·6* :13·0		(44)
December 31, 1922	348·028 kmh	Sadi Lecointe	Istres (Bouches-du-Rhône) France	Nieuport-Delage sesquiplane "Eugene Gilbert"	*13 (5)*	1 km 1+2 :20·2 3+4 :21·2		(45)
January 2, 1923	*348* kmh	Sadi Lecointe	Istres (Bouches-du-Rhône) France	Nieuport-Delage sesquiplane "Eugene Gilbert"	*13 (5)*	1 km		(5)
■ February 15, 1923	375·000 kmh	Sadi Lecointe	Istres (Bouches-du-Rhône) France	Nieuport-Delage sesquiplane "Eugene Gilbert"	*13 (5)*	1 km :09·2 :10·0 :09·4 :09·8		(46)
March 26, 1923	*376·408* kmh	Russell Maughan	Wright Field, Fairfield, Ohio	Curtiss R-6 A.S.68564	20 (2)	1 km *:09·80* or *:09·45*(?) :09·71 :09·54 :09·56		(47)
March 26, 1923	337·094 kmh 352·354 kmh	Lester Maitland	Wright Field, Fairfield, Ohio	Curtiss R-6 A.S.68563	20 (2)	1 km		
March 29, 1923	386·174 kmh	Lester Maitland	Wright Field, Fairfield, Ohio	Curtiss R-6 A.S.68563	20 (2)	1 km :10·58 :10·59 :08·40 :07·95 :10·39 :10·72 :09·58 :08·03		(48)
■ March 29, 1923	380·751 kmh	Russell Maughan	Wright Field, Fairfield, Ohio	Curtiss R-6 A.S.68564	20 (2)	1 km :10·66 :08·27 :10·50 :08·39		(49)
March *29*, 1923	270·060 kmh	Alex Pearson	Wright Field, Fairfield, Ohio	Verville-Sperry R-3	13 (5)	500 km *1:51:12·07*		(50)
April 1, 1923 – OFFICIAL WORLD MAXIMUM SPEED RECORD BASELINE LENGTH CHANGED FROM 1 km TO 3 km								(51)
July 30, 1923	*282·1 kmh*	Rutledge Irvine	Port Washington (Long Island Sound) N.Y.	Curtiss CR-3 A-6080	20 (3)	4·26 st mi		(52)
August 6, 1923	309·572 kmh.	Larry L. Carter	circuit around London	Gloster I G-EAXZ	35 (3)	200 st mi 1:02:23·0		(53)

Date	Speed	Pilot	Location	Aeroplane	Engine	Distance/Time			Notes
August 9, 1923	*291·1* kmh	A. W. Gorton	Philadelphia, Pennsylvania	Navy-Wright NW-2 A-6544	14				(54)
September 10, 1923	*383* kmh	Lawson H. Sanderson	Mitchel Field, New York	Wright F2W-1 A-6743	15 (1)	*2 st mi*			(55)
September 13, 1923	*392·92* kmh	Harold J. Brow	Mitchel Field, New York	Curtiss R2C-1 A-6691	21	*2 st mi*			(55)
September 16, 1923	*398·64* kmh	Lawson H. Sanderson	Mitchel Field, New York	Wright F2W-1 A-6743	15 (1)	*2 st mi*			(55)
September 16, 1923	*410* kmh	Alford Williams	Mitchel Field, New York	Curtiss R2C-1 A-6692	21	*2 st mi*			(55)
September 28, 1923	273·411 kmh	David Rittenhouse	Cowes, Isle of Wight, England	Curtiss CR-3 A-6081	20 (3)	200 km			(56)
October 6, 1923	392·379 kmh 392·154 kmh	Alford Williams	St. Louis, Missouri	Curtiss R2C-1 A-6692	21	100 km :15:17·48 200 km :30:36·01			(57)
October 14, 1923	360·01 kmh	W/O Devillers	Istres (Bouches-du-Rhône) France	Gourdou-Leseurre CT no. 1	42 (4)	50 km :09:15			(58)
November 2, 1923 ■	*414·314* kmh *416·193* kmh *417·590* kmh	Harold J. Brow Alford Williams Harold J. Brow	Mineola, New York	Curtiss R2C-1 A-6691 Curtiss R2C-1 A-6692 Curtiss R2C-1 A-6691	21	3 km			(59)
November 4, 1923 ■	423·771 kmh 427·592 kmh 429·025 kmh	Alford Williams Harold J. Brow Alford Williams	Mineola, New York	Curtiss R2C-1 A.6692 Curtiss R2C-1 A.6691 Curtiss R2C-1 A.6692	21	3 km W B ■W 26·0 26·2 25·5 25·0 25·0 25·0 26·2 25·5 25·2 24·8 24·4 25·0			
June 23, 1924	306·696 kmh	Sadi Lecointe	Istres (Bouches-du-Rhône) France	Nieuport-Delage 42 *sesquiplan de course*	6 (2)	500 km 1:37:49·0			(60)
August 3, 1924	*303·37* kmh	Alessandro Passaleva	Sesto Calende, Italy	Savoia-Marchetti S.51	4 (4)	3 km			(61)
September 4, 1924	*318* kmh	George T. Cuddihy	Philadelphia, Pennsylvania	Curtiss CR-3 A-6081	21				(62)
September 27, 1924	366·126 kmh *366·047* kmh	David Rittenhouse	Port Washington, Long Island, New York	Curtiss R2C-2 A-6692	21	4·26 st mi *200* km			(63)
▲ October 25, 1924	302·765 kmh	George T. Cuddihy	Bay Shore Park, Md.	Curtiss CR-3 A-6081	21	3 km *:36·09* *:35·52* *:35·70* *:35·38*			(64)
October 25, 1924	286·866 kmh 286·866 kmh 259·328 kmh	Ralph Ofstie	Bay Shore Park, Md.	Curtiss CR-3 A-6080	21	100 km :21:04·0 200 km :41:50·0 500 km *1:55:41·0*			(64)
November 8, 1924	393·340 kmh	Florentin Bonnet	Istres (Bouches-du-Rhône) France	Bernard (SIMB) V.2	5 (2)	3 km :29·4 :25·8 :31·0 :24·6			(65)
■ December 11, 1924	448·171 kmh	Florentin Bonnet	Istres (Bouches-du-Rhône) France	Bernard (SIMB) V.2	5 (2)	3 km :24·4 :24·0 :24·2 :23·8			(66)
June 11, 1925	*400* kmh +	Larry L. Carter	Cranwell, Lincs, England	Gloster II "Bluebird"	35 (4)	3 km			(67)
▲ September 13, 1925	364·924 kmh	Henri C. Biard	Southampton Water, England	Supermarine S.4	35 (5)	3 km :29·6 :30·0 :29·8 :29·0			(68)
September 18, 1925	*460* kmh	Alford Williams	Mineola, New York	Curtiss R3C-1	22	3 km			(69)
October 12, 1925	401·279 kmh 400·687 kmh	Cyrus Bettis	Mitchel Field, New York	Curtiss R3C-1	22	100 km *:14:57·13* 200 km :29:56·90			(70)

Date	Speed	Pilot	Location	Aeroplane	Engine	Distance/Time		Notes
October 18, 1925	312·464 kmh	Sadi Lecointe	Istres (Bouches-du-Rhône) France	Nieuport-Delage 42 *sesquiplan de course*	6 (2)	(300 km	:57:36·4)	(71)
Cctober 26, 1925	377·829 kmh 377·158 kmh	James Doolittle	Bay Shore Park, Maryland	Curtiss R3C-2	22	100 km 200 km	:15:52·81 :31:49·01	(72)
October 26, 1925	324·243 kmh	Hubert S. Broad	Bay Shore Park, Maryland	Gloster IIIA N.195	35 (5)	100 km	:18:30·28	(73)
▲ October 27, 1925	395·437 kmh	James Doolittle	Bay Shore Park, Maryland	Curtiss R3C-2	22	3 km		(74)
September 17, 1926	*414 kmh*	Mario De Bernardi	Schiranna, Lago Varese, Italy	Macchi M.39	48 (1)			(5)
October 27, 1926	*404·75 kmh*	Frank H. Conant II	Port Washington, (Long Island Sound), New York	Curtiss R3C-4	23	4·26 st mi		(5)
November 1926	*415·2 kmh*	George T. Cuddihy	Philadelphia, Pennsylvania	Curtiss R3C-3	25			(5)
November 13, 1926	399·423 kmh 399·118 kmh	Mario De Bernardi	Hampton Roads, Norfolk, Virginia	Macchi M.39 number 5	48 (1)	100 km 200 km	:15:01·30 :30:03·98	(75)
▲ November 17, 1926	416·618 kmh	Mario De Bernardi	Hampton Roads, Norfolk, Virginia	Macchi M.39 number 5	48 (1)	3 km		(76)

APPENDIX 2 – Race Tables

1920 JAMES GORDON BENNETT AVIATION CUP

HISTORY OF THE COMPETITION

Race	Date	Place	Winner	Aeroplane	Engine	Distance	Time	Speed	Representing
I	Aug. 28, 1909	Rheims, France	Glenn H. Curtiss	Curtiss biplane	Curtiss V-8 (50 hp)	20 km	0:15:50	75·492 kmh	USA
II	Oct. 29, 1910	Belmont, New York	Claude Grahame-White	Blériot XI bis	Gnôme rotary (100 hp)	100 km	1:01:04	98·552 kmh	ENGLAND
III	July 1, 1911	Eastchurch, England	Charles T. Weymann	Nieuport monoplane	Gnôme rotary (100 hp)	150 km	1:11:39	125·633 kmh	USA
IV	Sept. 9, 1912	Chicago, Illinois	Jules Védrines	Deperdussin	Gnôme rotary (160 hp)	200 km	1:10:56·8	169·700 kmh	FRANCE
V	Sept. 29, 1913	Rheims, France	Maurice Prévost	Deperdussin	Gnôme rotary (160 hp)	200 km	0:59:45·6	200·836 kmh	FRANCE

1914–1919 NO CONTEST

SEPTEMBER 28, 1920
(Aeroplanes required to be at Villesauvage Aerodrome, Étampes, by 0700 September 27 for "measurement and sealing.")

COURSE: 300 KM
(Over the plains of Beauce from Villesauvage Aerodrome, Étampes, to La Marmogne Farm near Gidy, and return; out-and-return distance 100 km; three out-and-return laps required. Landings and replenishments allowed. Starts allowed 0700–1900.)

PRIX: 10,000 FRANCS

Race No.	Aeroplane	Engine	Pilot	Take-off time	Lap times	Lap speeds	Place	Remarks
1	Verville VCP-R (USA)	24	Capt. Rudolph W. Schroeder USAS	1437			—	Retired on first lap due to excessive engine overheating, preignition, and "riching out" at high power settings. Its engine had highest compression in race. Aeroplane's *first* flight in France.
2	Dayton-Wright RB (USA)	11	Howard M. Rinehart	1411			—	Retired on first lap with broken control cable and jammed leading edge.
(3)	Curtiss-Cox "Texas Wildcat" (USA)	18 (1)	Roland Rohlfs	—				Crashed Sept. 26, 1920, at Étampes after its ferry flight from Villacoublay where it had been rebuilt as a biplane.
—	Curtiss-Cox "Cactus Kitten" (USA)	18 (1)	Clarence Coombs	—				Ineligible as fourth racer from a competing country. It was never uncrated in France.
4	Martinsyde "Semiquaver" G-EAPX (England)	4 (2)	Frederick P. Raynham	1636	0:25 plus	285·714 kmh for 50 km	—	Retired after one lap with broken oil pump. It did first 50 km in :10:30, the fastest 50 km time in the race. (This aeroplane had won 1920 Aerial Derby; smaller wings fitted after Aerial Derby crash.)
(5)	Nieuport & General L.S.3 "Goshawk" G-EASK (England)	40 (2)	L. R. Tait-Cox/ James H. James	—				Disqualified when it failed to arrive by 0700 Sept. 27. It did arrive on Sept. 28, flown by James.
(6)	Sopwith 107 "Rainbow" G-EAKI (England)	42 (1)	Harry G. Hawker	—				Withdrawn upon liquidation of the Sopwith firm in September, 1920.
7	Borel-Boccaccio (France)	4 (2)	M. Barault	—		*approx. 269 kmhE*		Eliminated at French trials held Sept. 25. Would have qualified but failed to pass between pylons on start; overturned on landing.

Race No.	Aeroplane	Engine	Pilot	Take-off time	Lap speeds	Lap times	Place	Remarks
8	Spad S.20 *bis*$_5$ (France)	4 (1)	Comte Bernard de Romanet	1342	(:23:16·2E) :22:52·0 :23:15·0 :52:59·6 1:39:06·6T	(257·879E) 262·391 kmh 258·065 113·222 181·616T	**2nd**	Sept. 25 elimination performance in parentheses. On third lap landed for adjustments to lubrication system; after approximately ½-hour on ground, resumed race. Oil gauge then burst, pilot drenched with oil.
9	Spad S.20 *bis*$_5$ (France)	4 (1)	Jean Casale	—	*(23:53·0E)*	(251·228E)		Sept. 25 elimination performance in parentheses. Eliminated from participation. (Casale was current world speed record holder.)
10	Nieuport 29V (12·3m²) (France)	4 (1)	Sadi Lecointe	1409	(:21:28·0E) :21:36·6 :22:06·0 :22:34·6 1:06:17·2T	(279·503E) 277·649 kmh 271·493 265·761 271·548T	**1st**	Sept. 25 elimination performance in parentheses; this was world 100 km closed-course record. 200 km record set during race. There is some evidence that included in times given are times of pylon turns, after crossing line inbound and before crossing line outbound: 7·6 seconds between laps 1 and 2, 3·2 seconds between laps 2 and 3. Official race performance based on figures listed. This aeroplane had special, clipped racing wings.
11	Nieuport 29V (13·2m²) (France)	4 (1)	Georges Kirsch	1337	(:22:18·0E) :21:29·0 :27:23·0	(269·058E) 279·286 kmh 219·111 (245·566 for 2 laps)	—	Sept. 25 elimination performance in parentheses. Retired on 3rd lap with oiled-up spark plugs. First lap time best 100-km time in the race. Had large wings.
—	Ansaldo A.1 "Balilla" (Italy)	45 (1)	not named	—				Italian hopeful. Withdrawn.
—	SVA "Special" (Italy)	45 (1)	not named	—				Italian hopeful. Withdrawn.

This was the third consecutive French victory.
The James Gordon Bennett Aviation Cup awarded to l'Aero-Club de France.

CONTEST CLOSED

1919/1920 PRIX HENRY DEUTSCH DE LA MEURTHE

AIR RACE AROUND PARIS

HISTORY OF THE COMPETITION

Holder	Date	Pilot	Aeroplane	Engine	Distance	Time	Speed
I II	May 1, 1912 Oct. 27, 1913	Emmanuel Helen Eugène Gilbert	Nieuport Deperdussin	Gnôme 70 hp Gnôme rotary 160 hp	200 km 200 km	1:35:43 1:13:25	125·370 kmh *162 kmh (sic)* (163·451 kmh)

CONDITIONS To be successful, a competitor must exceed the speed achieved by the current holder by 10%. Thus, the first post-war competitor must achieve at least 178 kmh. A year of competition was established by l'Aero-Club de France to be in effect from October 13, 1919 through October 31, 1920.

COURSE: 190.3993 KM For post-war competitions the circuit was redesignated:
Terrasse de St. Germain-en-Laye (Pavillon Henri IV)—Senlis (Cathedrale)—Meaux (Cathedrale)—Melun (Eglise Saint-Barthelemy)—start.

PRIX: 20,000 FRANCS M. Henry Deutsch de la Meurthe (Aero Club president) offered an *objet d'art* valued at 10,000 francs and three cash prizes worth 20,000 francs each to the first three holders.

Date	Aeroplane	Engine	Pilot	Take-off time	Time	Speed	Remarks
September 2, 1919	Spad-Herbemont S.20 *bis*₁	4 (1)	Sadi Lecointe	1021	0:48:08·0	249·307 kmh	Flight not recognized. Made over pre-war 200-km course. It was after this flight that post-war conditions were finalized.
October 13, 1919	Nieuport monoplane	*2*	Leth Jensen	1419	0:56:56·0	200·655 kmh	*Tentative holder.*
	Spad-Herbemont S.20 *bis*₂	4 (1)	Sadi Lecointe	first 1008 second 1313	— —	— —	Made two attempts. Retired once in fog. Retired second time at Juvisy with engine trouble.
	Gourdou-Leseurre monoplane	3 (2)	Maurice Rost	1155	—	—	Down in fog. Did not finish course.
October 14, 1919				1341	0:54:07·4	211·072 kmh	Needed 220 kmh; Rost's speed not enough to qualify.
	Nieuport 29V (13·2 m²)	4 (1)	Comte Bernard de Romanet	1406	—	—	Retired at Bourget, 20 km before finish line. This was the first appearance of the historic 29V racing aeroplane.
October 15, 1919	Gourdou-Leseurre monoplane	3 (2)	Maurice Rost	unk.	0:53:04·0	215·275 kmh	Again, Rost's speed insufficient.
	Spad-Herbemont S.20 *bis*₂	4 (1)	Sadi Lecointe	1025½	0:51:11·4	223·168 kmh	Speed enough to qualify; however, aeroplane not seen by control at Meaux, thus this flight not recognized.
				1529½	0:46:07·0	247·719 kmh	*Tentative holder.* Did Senlis-Meaux downwind at 323 kmh.
October 20, 1919				1518	0:45:20·0	252·000 kmh	Sadi raised his own record; accompanied by his mechanic, Bernard.
	Nieuport 29V	4 (1)	Comte Bernard de Romanet	1403	0:42:31·6	268·631 kmh	Needed 272·491 kmh to qualify. Speed on this flight insufficient to qualify for prix but was widely recognized as world speed record (unofficial). This flight may have been made *October 22.*
November 24, 1919	DEATH OF M. HENRY DEUTSCH DE LA MEURTHE						

Date	Aeroplane	Engine	Pilot	Take-off time	Time	Speed	Remarks
December 22, 1919	Martinsyde F.4 "Buzzard"	32	not named	—	—	—	Entered on this date by Royal Aero Club. Did not compete.
January 3, 1920	Nieuport 29V	4 (1)	Sadi Lecointe	0910	0:42:53·8	266·314 kmh	Flight made in 29V, race number 6. This was first time in which Lecointe-Nieuport combination proved to be the winner. *Holder of prix*.
January 24, 1920	Nieuport 29V	4 (1)	Sadi Lecointe	1504	—	—	Did not finish course. Previous record sufficient to retain prix.

Inasmuch as no other competitor attempted to improve on Sadi Lecointe's best speed by 10% within the deadline set, the *Prix* (the third of three cash awards) was homologated to Sadi Lecointe on August 3, 1920;

CONTEST CLOSED

431

1921 COUPE DEUTSCH DE LA MEURTHE

OCTOBER 1, 1921 Start between 0900 and 1800.
Article 1: "alightings, repairs, and replenishments are allowed."
Article 7: allows a second start if the first not proper; each start requires :30 warning.
The first Deutsch contest open to non-French competition.

COURSE: 300 KM Same course as that used for 1920 James Gordon Bennett Aviation Cup race.
PRIX: 20,000 FRANCS (*Objet d'art* worth 20,000 francs; 60,000 francs cash to be awarded in three annual installments of 20,000 francs each.)
Entries completely unrestricted; a speed race pure and simple.
Each nationality limited to three entries.

Race No.	Aeroplane	Engine	Pilot	Take-off time	Lap times	Lap speeds	Place	Remarks
1	Gloucestershire Mars I (Bamel) G-EAXZ	35 (2)	James Herbert James	1540	:22:09·6	270·758 kmh	—	Retired on 2nd lap due to fabric "lifting" on wings.
2	Fiat R.700	47	Francesco Brack-Papa	1023	:20:05·4	298·656 kmh	—	Retired on 2nd lap. Forced landing near Ruan (16 km from la Marmogne) with a fuel leak. (150 km in :30:19·4; approx. 184 mph.) Set 100 km closed-course speed record.
(3)	Lumiere-de Monge 5.1	4 (3)	Comte Bernard de Romanet	—				Crashed Sept. 23, 1921 in test flight as a monoplane. De Romanet killed.
(4)	Hanriot HD.22	4 (3)	Maurice Rost	—				Withdrawn Sept. 28, 1921 by Rene Hanriot.
5	Nieuport-Delage 29V (12·3 m²)	4 (3)	Fernand Lasne	1621	:23:09·8 :23:29·8 :23:17·8 1:09:57·4T	259·030 kmh 255·355 257·548 257·302T	2nd	This aeroplane won 1920 James Gordon Bennett Aviation Cup. New wings had been fitted.
6	Nieuport-Delage sesquiplan type 1921	4 (3)	Sadi Lecointe	0941			—	Crashed near Toury on first lap. Sadi Lecointe slightly injured. Time for first 50 km was :09:33·8, best 50-km performance in race.
7	Nieuport-Delage sesquiplan type 1921	4 (3)	Georges Kirsch	1651	:21:13·2 :21:26·6 :21:59·4 1:04:39·2T	282·752 kmh 279·807 272·851 278·408T	1st	First public appearance of Gustave Delage's lovely sesquiplane racer. Set 200 km closed-course speed record.

1922 COUPE DEUTSCH DE LA MEURTHE

SEPTEMBER 30, 1922 Same rules and course as for 1921 Coupe Deutsch; winner's speed must exceed 280 kmh to qualify for an award.

COURSE: 300 KM

PRIX: 20,000 FRANCS

Race No.	Aeroplane	Engine	Pilot	Take-off time	Lap times	Lap speeds	Place	Remarks
1	Gloucestershire Mars I (Bamel) G-EAXZ	35 (2)	James Herbert James	1424			—	Had smaller wings than those used in 1922 Aerial Derby. Retired on first lap after maps blew overboard. Second start not allowed since first had been proper. After race Bamel attacked—and equalled—world speed record.
—	Bristol 72 monoplane racer G-EBDR	42 (4)	Cyril F. Uwins	—				Withdrawn. Not ready.
2	Fiat R.700	47	Francesco Brack-Papa	first 1028	:20:43·6 :20:52·2 :20:51·4 1:02:27·2T	289·482 kmh 287·494 287·678 288·215T	—	First trial disallowed because aeroplane passed behind timekeepers on start.
				second 1438	:20:58·0	286·169 kmh	—	On second trial, retired on 2nd lap: force landed at la Marmogne with carburetor problems.
3	Spad-Herbemont S.58 "Louis Bleriot"	8 (2)	Jean Casale	1011	:24:21·8	246·272 kmh	—	Retired on 2nd lap with leaking radiator.
4	Nieuport-Delage 29V (12·3 m²)	4 (3)	Fernand Lasne	1035	:20:41·8 :20:45·4 :20:44·6 1:02:11·8T	289·902 kmh 289·064 289·250 289·405T	**1st**	Winner of 1920 Gordon Bennett, second in 1921 Coupe Deutsch. 200 km time a closed-course world record. Berthelin was alternate in case sesquiplane available for Lasne to fly.
5	Nieuport-Delage *sesquiplan type 1921 bis* "Eugene Gilbert"	4 (3)	Sadi Lecointe	1550	:18:26·0	325·497 kmh	—	Crash landed at beginning of 2nd lap after spark plug shot out of engine and pierced cowl; overturned; pilot unhurt. Did 50 km in :09:07·6 (328·707 kmh) 100 km time a closed course world record. This aeroplane won 1921 Coupe Deutsch.
6	Nieuport-Delage 37 type "course"	13 (5)	Sadi Lecointe	—				Built but never flew. Withdrawn. Sadi Lecointe reassigned after its withdrawal.
—	Simplex-Arnoux tailless monoplane	4 (3)	Georges Madon	—				Withdrawn. Damaged in trials.
—	Landwerlin-Berreur tailless monoplane	47	Charles Nungesser	—				Withdrawn. Not ready.

Prix awarded to Societé Nieuport-Astra.

CONTEST CLOSED

1919 AERIAL DERBY

AIR RACE AROUND LONDON

HISTORY OF THE COMPETITION

Race	Date	Place	Winner	Aeroplane	Engine	Distance	Time	Speed
I	June 8, 1912	Hendon	T. O. M. Sopwith	Blériot XI monoplane	Gnôme 70 hp	81 miles	1:23:08·4	58·46 mph
II	Sept. 20, 1913	Hendon	Gustav Hamel	Morane-Saulnier monoplane	Gnôme 80 hp	95 miles	1:15:49·0	75·18 mph
III	May 23, 1914	Hendon	William L. Brock (American)	Morane-Saulnier monoplane	Gnôme 80 hp	94·5 miles	1:18:54·0	71·86 mph
	1915–1918 – NO CONTEST							

JUNE 21, 1919

COURSE: 189 STATUTE MILES
Hendon Aerodrome N.W.9—Kempton Park (waterworks north of railroad station)—Epsom Race Course grandstand—West Thurrock (Wouldham Cement Works, factory chimney)— Epping (Parish church steeple)— Hertford (white cross in Hartham Meadow adjacent to railroad station north of town)—Hendon (pylon number 1 on aerodrome). Length 94·5 miles. TWO CIRCUITS REQUIRED. (Race numbers 6 and 13 not used.)

PRIZES: SPEED: 1st
Daily Mail gold trophy (200gn) and Shell Prize (100 sov); total value £710.
2nd
Shell Prize (100 sov); total value £500.

HANDICAP:
An artificial factor was applied to actual speeds to "manufacture" speeds of approximately 130 mph; separate prizes were awarded. The first three handicap winners received Shell Trophies and cash prizes of 100, 50 and 25 sovereigns respectively.

Race No.	Aeroplane	Engine	Pilot	Take-off time	Lap times	Lap speeds	Place speed	Place h'cap	Remarks
1	B.A.T. F.K.23 Bantam K-123	39 (1)	Clifford B. Prodger	1555			—	—	Retired at Fairlop with engine trouble on first lap. Prodger the only American in race. This Bantam had a long-span lower wing. 2nd prototype.
2	Grahame-White GWE-6 Bantam K-150 (G-EAFK)	1	Capt. P. R. T. Chamberlayne	1553	1:06:21·4	85·447 mph	—	—	Retired at Epsom with engine trouble on 2nd lap. Yellow fuselage, blue wings. 2nd prototype Bantam. Crashed 2 weeks later into a Hendon hangar; demolished.
(3)	B.A.T. F.K.27 K-143	39 (2)	not named	—					2-seater sport sesquiplane originally entered as number 3, but not completed; this would have been its 1st public appearance.
3	B.A.T. F.K.23 Bantam K-125	39 (1)	Major Christopher Draper, D.S.O.	1555½	0:48:58·6 0:48:08·4 1:37:07·0T	115·769 mph 117·781 mph 116·767T	4th	2nd	The "Skinned Bat" so-called because of its short-span lower wing. Black-and-white. A substitute for F.K.27 which was withdrawn.
(4)	Martinsyde F.4 Buzzard	32	not named	—					Original entry number 4; Air Ministry permission for its use withdrawn.
4	Avro 504K H-2586 (G-EAEV)	2	Lt. Col. G.L.P. Henderson M.C. A.F.C.	1552½	1:09:15·0 1:21:30·2 2:30:45·2T	81·877 mph 69·568 mph 75·222T	6th	7th	Avro landed at Hounslow on 2nd lap for "adjustments," then proceeded.
5	Grahame-White GWE-6A Bantam K-153	1	Major R. H. "Reggie" Carr A.F.C.	1553½			—	—	Carr a pre-war Hendon racing pilot. Landed at Hounslow with engine trouble on first lap.

Race No.	Aeroplane	Engine	Pilot	Take-off time	Lap times	Lap speeds	Place speed	Place h'cap	Remarks
7	AirCo D.H.4R K-141	35 (1)	Capt. Gerald Gathergood A.F.C.	1556½	0:44:51·4 0:42:50·6 1:27:42·0T	126·403 mph 132·343 mph 129·304T	**1st**	**5th**	Second lap speed the fastest achieved by any race competitor; "Scratch" in handicap.
8	AirCo D.H.4 2-seater K-142	33	Marcus D. Manton	1556	0:47:45·0 0:48:56·8 1:36:41·8T	118·743 mph 115·840 mph 117·274T	**3rd**	**4th**	Winner of special Grahame-White trophy.
9	AirCo D.H.9 3-seater K-109 (H-9277; G-EAAC)	36	Capt. H. J. Saint D.S.O.	1554½	0:56:19·4 0:55:35·6 1:51:55·0T	100·669 mph 101·991 mph 101·325T	**5th**	**6th**	Carried one passenger in race. This aeroplane made the first recognized commercial flight between London and Paris (Hendon-le Bourget) on July 15, 1919; pilot H. Shaw, one passenger, on charter for Aircraft Transport & Travel Co.
10	Martinsyde F.4 Buzzard K-152 (G-EAES)	32	Lt. Robert H. Nisbet	1557½	0:45:23·6 0:45:40·0 1:31:03·6T	124·908 mph 124·161 mph 124·533T	**2nd**	**3rd**	
11	Nieuport & General L.C.1 (no. 1) Nieuhawk K-151 (G-EAEQ)	40 (1)	L. R. Tait-Cox	1557	0:44:56·2	126·178 mph	—	—	Retired at West Thurrock with engine trouble on 2nd lap.
12	Bristol M.1C monoplane C-4964 (G-EAER)	2	Major C. H. Chichester-Smith D.S.O.	1554	0:57:48·0	98·097 mph	—	—	Retired at Hendon with engine trouble on 2nd lap. Only monoplane in the race.
14	Avro 543 Baby K-131 (G-EACQ)	31	Capt. H. A. Hamersley M.C.	1552	1:20:16·0 1:21:07·0 2:41:23·0T	70·639 mph 69·899 mph 70·267T	**7th**	**1st**	First public appearance of Avro Baby. Engine used built in 1909.
15	B.A.T. F.K.26 5-seater K-102 (G-EAAI)	33	Lt. C. Turner	—					First British aeroplane conceived and built as transport. Withdrawn. Damaged on Saturday morning before race.
16	B.A.T. F.K.23 Bantam	39 (1)	Capt. C. R. Vaughan	—					Withdrawn.
17	Sopwith R.M.1 Snapper K-149 (G-EAFJ)	40 (1)	Harry G. Hawker	—					Withdrawn. Originally Hawker was to fly a Sopwith monoplane (130 hp Clerget) with number 17; the Snapper was substituted, then withdrawn when the Air Ministry refused to let it fly.
18	Vickers Vimy Commercial	TWO 33	Capt. John Alcock D.S.O.	—					Withdrawn. Alcock was attending reception with King George V at Windsor in connection with first non-stop transatlantic flight made the previous week!

1920 AERIAL DERBY

JULY 24, 1920

COURSE: 200 STATUTE MILES Hendon Aerodrome N.W.9—Brooklands Aerodrome, Weybridge (large white cross in center of aerodrome and motor racing track)—Epsom race course grandstand—West Thurrock (Wouldham Cement Works; long, buff-colored building with white cross on roof adjacent to 5 factory chimneys) —Epping (Parish church steeple)—Hertford (large white cross in Hartham Meadow adjoining railroad station north of town)—Hendon (finish line in front of aerodrome enclosures). TWO CIRCUITS REQUIRED. Race number 9 not used.

PRIZES: SPEED: £500.
HANDICAP: £250, £100, and £50 respectively. Aeroplanes were started at different times, based on a handicap allowance calculated so that all would finish simultaneously.

Race No.	Aeroplane	Engine	Pilot	Take-off time	Lap times	Lap speeds	Place speed	Place h'cap	Remarks
1	Avro 543 Baby G-EACQ	31	H. J. L. "Bert" Hinkler	1415	1:23:33·2 1:22:12·8 2:45:46·0T	71·810 mph 72·981 mph 72·391T	8th	2nd	Same Baby that appeared in 1919 Aerial Derby.
2	Avro 543 Baby G-EAUG	31	Capt. H. A. Hamersley M.C.	1422	1:16:00·0 1:16:06·0 2:32:06·0T	78·947 mph 78·844 mph 78·895T	7th	1st	Newer specimen of same type that first appeared in 1919 Derby.
(3)	Spad S.29	1	Leth Jensen	—					Withdrew
4	De Havilland D.H. 14A G-EAPY	35 (1)	Flt.Lt. Frederick Sidney Cotton Passenger: Mr. Harwood	1515½	0:55:13·8	108·637 mph	—	—	Retired on 2nd lap with broken fuel line; aeroplane caught fire and tangled telephone lines on emergency landing. Cotton unhurt, passenger taken to hospital. Cotton attempted a flight from London to Capetown in this aeroplane, departing Feb. 4, 1920, but crashed enroute in Messina.
5	Sopwith Snipe G-EAUW	37	Capt. W. L. Jordan D.S.C. D.F.C.	1528	0:53:53·0 0:53:54·6 1:47:47·6T	111·352 mph 111·297 mph 111·324T	6th	5th	Privately owned; entered by Lt. Col. Frank K. McClean.
6	Sopwith Snipe G-EAUV	37	Flt.Lt. Walter H. Longton	1528	0:53:50·2	111·448 mph	—	—	Retired on 2nd lap; landed at Barnet out of fuel. (Privately owned.)
7	Sopwith Snipe G-EAUU	37	Flt.Lt. J. S. T. Fall	1528			—	—	Retired on 1st lap; landed at Epping with magneto trouble. (Privately owned.)
8	Avro 539A/1 Schneider G-EALG	36	Capt. Denis G. Westgarth-Heslam	1536½			—	—	Retired on 1st lap; landed at Abridge (past West Thurrock) with fuel system trouble. (Formerly a seaplane, entered in 1919 Schneider race.)
10	Nieuport & General L.C.1 (no. 2) Nieuhawk G-EAJY	40 (1)	James Herbert James	1544	0:44:21·4 0:46:06·0 1:30:27.4T	135·267 mph 130·152 mph 132·660T	2nd	4th	Single-seater similar to L.C.1. number 1 of 1919 Derby; James the number 2 pilot of "British-Nieuport."
11	Martinsyde F.6 2-seater G-EAPI	4 (2)	Robert H. Nisbet	1544½	0:46:30·0 0:46:43·4 1:33:13·4T	129·032 mph 128·415 mph 128·723T	4th	6th	This aeroplane later went to Canada where it flew through at least 1922 as a seaplane (G-CYEQ). First of three F.6s built.
12	Martinsyde F.4A Buzzard 2-seater G-EAPP	4 (2)	Sqd.Ldr. T. O'Brien Hubbard M.C.	1545½	0:52:20·2 0:51:19·8 1:43:40·0T	114·642 mph 116·891 mph 115·756T	5th	8th	First of three civil sporting 2-seaters. (Passenger carried in front of pilot.)
13	Sopwith 107 Rainbow G-EAKI	40 (2)	Harry G. Hawker	1547	0:41:31·0 0:42:12·0 1:23:43·0T	144·520 mph 142·180 mph 143·341T	—	—	Results disqualified because Hawker did not cross the finish line properly. This aeroplane had been a Jupiter-powered seaplane entry in the 1919 Schneider; had smaller wings than in 1919.

Race No.	Aeroplane	Engine	Pilot	Take-off time	Lap times	Lap speeds	Place speed	Place h'cap	Remarks
14	Bristol 32 Bullet G-EATS	42 (1)	Cyril F. Uwins	1548½	0:48:46·0 0:44:04·0 1:32:50·0T	123·035 mph 136·157 mph 129·264T	**3rd**	**7th**	
15	Martinsyde Semiquaver G-EAPX	4 (2)	Francis Thomas Courtney	1555	0:39:25·0 0:38:47·2 1:18:12·2T	152·220 mph 154·692 mph 153·446T	**1st**	**3rd**	Frederick P. Raynham was to have flown this aeroplane but Courtney took over. His 2nd lap was fastest of the race. After winning the race he crashed on landing; plane overturned, badly damaged, Courtney unhurt.
16	Nieuport & General L.S.3 Goshawk G-EASK	40 (2)	L. R. Tait-Cox	1556			—	—	Scratch entry. Retired on 1st lap; landed at Brooklands with engine trouble. Tait-Cox the number 1 pilot of "British-Nieuport," and L.S.3 the holder of British speed record.

1921 AERIAL DERBY

JULY 16, 1921

COURSE: 200 STATUTE MILES Same course as that used for 1920 Aerial Derby. TWO CIRCUITS REQUIRED.

PRIZES: **SPEED:** Trophy and £400.
HANDICAP: Trophies plus £200, £100, and £50 respectively.

Race No.	Aeroplane	Engine	Pilot	Take-off time assigned	Lap times	Lap speeds	Place speed	Place h'cap	Remarks
1	Avro 543 Baby 2-seater G-EAUM	31	Capt. T. Tully	15:32:36	1:21:31·0	73·605 mph	—	—	Disqualified on first lap for improper pylon turn; retired on second lap, landed at Brooklands.
2	Avro 543C Baby 1-seater G-EAXL	31	H. J. L. "Bert" Hinkler	15:40:54			—	—	Retired 1st lap; landed at Sidcup. New plane; had small wings (5 foot shorter span than 2-seater Baby.)
3	B.E. 2E	49 (1)	Capt. Alan Harper Curtis	(15:51:12)					Withdrew; was not satisfied with his handicap allowance of :57:06. Also, one cylinder developed a wobble on crankcase prior to race.
4	Sopwith Pup G-EAWV	1	Dring Lester Forestier-Walker	16:11:12			—	—	Retired first lap; pilot returned to Hendon feeling ill. Plane nosed up on landing. This was the last Pup on active war service in France.
5	Bristol 29 Tourer G-EAWB	36	Alan Samuel Butler	16:11:12	0:56:57·0 0:55:04·8 1:52:01·8T	105·356 mph 108·932 mph 107·114T	4th	3rd	A development of Bristol F.2B World War I fighter.
6	Avro 552 Viper G-EAPR	3 (5)	L. R. "Leslie" Tait-Cox	16:14:48	0:58:00·6 0:59:02·6 1:57:03·2T	103·430 mph 101·620 mph 102·517T	5th	5th	Standard Avro 504K except for Viper engine which replaced Le Rhône rotary. This aeroplane also raced in the first (1922) King's Cup race.
7	Sopwith Camel G-EAWN	38	Capt. Hubert S. Broad	16:18:15	1:03:15·2 1:02:14·8 2:05:30·0T	94·857 mph 96·391 mph 95·618T	6th	6th	Entered by Welsh Aviation Co. Ltd.
28	S.E.5A G-EAX?	3 (5)	Lt. Walter H. Longton D.F.C. A.F.C.	16:20:12	0:50:18·2 0:50:06·8 1:40:25·0T	119·276 mph 119·729 mph 119·502T	3rd	2nd	Earlier the same day this aeroplane had stood in reserve for the first Oxford—Cambridge air race; no time to repaint race number. Before that it had been in storage for two years, as had number 30.
30	S.E.5A G-EAXU	3 (5)	Frederick John Ortweiler	16:20:12	0:47:23·0 0:49:23·8 1:36:46·8T	126·627 mph 121·466 mph 123·993T	—	—	Disqualified for not rounding home pylon properly; otherwise would have won handicap by 6 seconds. This aeroplane earlier in the day had won the first Oxford—Cambridge air race, flown by W. S. Philcox for Cambridge; it still had light blue rudder (Cambridge colors.)
12	Nieuport & General L.C.1 (no. 2) Nieuhawk G-EAJY	40 (1)	Lt. J. Noakes A.F.C.	16:30:24	0:42:04·4	142·608 mph	—	—	On 2nd lap, ran out of fuel within sight of finish line! Noakes called "The Crazy Flier."
13	B.A.T. F.K.23 Bantam	39 (2)	Sqd. Ldr. Christopher Draper D.S.O.	(16:33:06)					Withdrew (B.A.T. firm ceased to exist.)
14	Martinsyde F.4A	4 (2)	Major S. H. "Tubby" Long D.S.O. M.C.	(16:33:06)					Withdrew. In accident prior to race. Entered by Col. C. E. C. Rabagliati.

Race No.	Aeroplane	Engine	Pilot	Take-off time assigned	Lap times	Lap speeds	Place speed	Place h'cap	Remarks
15	Martinsyde F.4 G-EAXB	4 (2)	Major E. L. "Leslie" Foot M.C.	16:36:00			—	—	Retired on 1st lap; returned to Hendon with leaky radiator just after starting.
16	Nieuport & General L.S.3 Goshawk G-EASK	40 (2)	Harry G. Hawker	(16:40:36)					Crashed on July 12, 1921. Hawker killed.
17	Bristol 32 Bullet G-EATS	42 (1)	Cyril F. Uwins	16:40:36	0:41:59·0 0:42:53·6 1:24:52·6T	142·914 mph 139·882 mph 141·382T	**2nd**	**4th**	Aeroplane had smaller wings than for 1920 Aerial Derby.
20	Martinsyde-Alula monoplane G-EAPX	4 (2)	Francis Thomas Courtney	(16:42:30)					Withdrew. This aeroplane had won the 1920 Aerial Derby as the "Semiquaver" biplane. It was the only monoplane entered in 1921, but was not ready to race.
21	Gloucestershire Mars-I Bamel G-EAXZ	35 (2)	James Herbert James	16:43:36	0:36:46·2 0:36:41·8 1:13:28·0T	163·177 mph 163·503 mph 163·339T	**1st**	**1st**	Bamel became Scratch entry upon withdrawal of Nieuport 29V bis.
(22)	Lumiere-de Monge 5.1	4 (3)	Comte Bernard de Romanet	(16:43:36)					Withdrew. Was to have flown in Aerial Derby as a monoplane. Called "Blanc Mange" by English. Suffered a collapsed wheel while being tested in France as biplane.
23	Avro 539B/1 Lion G-EAXM	35 (2)	Major D. G. Westgarth-Heslam	(16:43:36)					Withdrew. Same airframe entered in 1920 Aerial Derby, reconfigured to take Lion engine. Crashed on pre-race test flight. Westgarth-Heslam injured.
(24)	Nieuport-Delage 29V bis	4 (3)	Sadi Lecointe	(16:48:18)					Withdrew. Crashed in France on pre-race tests due to collapsed wheel. This aeroplane had been number 11 in 1920 Gordon Bennett; later had cockpit modified and set world speed record in December 1920.
—	Borel	4 (2)	M. Barault	—					Withdrew June 1921. (Possibly assigned 18 or 19.)
—	—	—	Capt. Proctor V.C.	—					Killed in "Aerial Derby trials." No details. (Possibly assigned 18 or 19.)

1922 AERIAL DERBY

AUGUST 7, 1922

COURSE: 198.0 STATUTE MILES Race now started from Waddon Aerodrome, Croydon, and flown clockwise (right turns) rather than counter-clockwise as in previous years. Turning points similar to previous years: From Croydon to Brooklands Aerodrome, Weybridge–Hertford–Epping–West Thurrock–Croydon. TWO CIRCUITS REQUIRED.

PRIZES: **SPEED:** Trophy and £300.

HANDICAP: 1st: Trophy and £150.   2nd: £75.   3rd: £50.

Race No.	Aeroplane	Engine	Pilot	Assigned take-off time	Lap times	Lap speeds	Place speed	Place h'cap	Remarks
1	Avro 543 Baby G-EAUM	31	H. J. L. "Bert" Hinkler	13:52:26	1:17:28·2 1:17:35·8 2:35:04·0T	76·675 mph 76·550 mph 76·612T	5th	—	Same Baby that won sealed handicap in 1919 Derby. No handicap place lower than 3rd awarded in 1922.
2	Bristol 77 monoplane G-EAVP	41	Larry L. Carter	14:27:51	0:55:18·6 0:54:42·2 1:50:00·8T	107·395 mph 108·586 mph 107·987T	4th	1st	
3	Martinsyde F.6 1-seater G-EBDK	3 (5)	Frederick P. Raynham	14:35:28	0:54:57·0 0:53:15·0 1:48:12·0T	108·098 mph 111·549 mph 109·797T	3rd	—	Flew in 1922 and 1923 King's Cup races as a 2-seater. Yellow with black trim; called "Mustardsyde."
4	De Havilland D.H.37 3 seater *Sylvia* G-EBDO	32	Alan S. Butler	(14:40:26) 1450	0:54:55·0	108·164 mph	—	—	Took off 10 minutes late due to magneto trouble. Knew after one lap that he could not place in handicap, so retired. Personal touring plane named after Butler's sister; in 1925 aeroplane was renamed *Lois* after his wife. Fitted with 4-blade prop, Arthur Hagg differential ailerons, painted black with gold wings, white lettering. Finished 5th in both 1922 and 1923 King's Cup races. Butler later Chairman of D.H. until 1950.
5	S.E.5A G-EAXQ	3 (5)	H. H. Perry	14:43:26	1:00:54·0	97·537 mph	—	—	Retired 2nd lap. Landed between West Thurrock and Bromley.
6	Martinsyde F.4 G-EATD	4 (2)	Capt. Rex H. Stocken	14:46:22			—	—	Retired first lap. Landed on Hounslow Heath with ignition trouble. (Bookmakers had him 1st in handicap.) Stocken employed by Aircraft Disposal Company (ADC).
7	Gloucestershire Mars III Sprawk 2-seater G-EAYN	37	L. R. Tait-Cox	14:43:07	0:57:37·0	103·095 mph	—	—	Retired 2nd lap. Aeroplane a Nieuport Nighthawk with Bentley engine, S.E.5 tail, 2-seats. In 1923 it was rebuilt with HLB airfoils, became Grouse. Later sold in Sweden.
8	Bristol 32 Bullet G-EATS	42 (3)	Rollo A. de Haga Haig	14:56:17	0:39:32·0 0:42:25·0 1:21:57·0T	150·253 mph 140·039 mph 144·966T	2nd	2nd	Over West Thurrock on 2nd lap de Haga Haig lost oil pressure; throttled back to 1000 rpm, landed straight in.
9	Gloucestershire Mars I Bamel G-EAXZ	35 (2)	James Herbert James	15:11:31	0:33:34·0 0:33:14·4 1:06:48·4T	176·961 mph 178·700 mph 177·827T	1st	3rd	James did Hertford-West Thurrock downwind at 246 mph. On landing aeroplane ran in among crowd. James ground-looped to stop, burst left tyre.
10	Bristol 72 monoplane G-EBDR	42 (4)	Cyril F. Uwins	(15:15:00)					Withdrawn. Should have been Scratch entry with Bamel :03:29·0 ahead. Not ready.

1923 AERIAL DERBY

AUGUST 6, 1923

COURSE: 200.0 STATUTE MILES Similar to that used for 1922 Derby. Croydon (start)—Brooklands Aerodrome, Weybridge—Hertford—West Thurrock—Croydon. TWO CIRCUITS REQUIRED. *No race numbers used.*

PRIZES: SPEED: 1st: Trophy and £100.   2nd: £25.
HANDICAP: 1st: Trophy and £100.   2nd: £50.   3rd: £25.

Aeroplane	Engine	Pilot	Assigned take-off time	Lap times	Lap speeds	Place speed	Place h'cap	Remarks
S.E.5A G-EBCA	49 (2)	"A. T. Renno" (Dr. E. D. Whitehead-Reid)	13:45:00	1:36:45·0 1:14:59·6 2:51:44·6T	62·016 mph 80·007 mph 69·872T	**9th**	**9th**	
Avro 543 Baby G-EAUM	31	H. J. L. "Bert" Hinkler	13:56:48	1:08:42·0	87·336 mph	—	—	Retired on 2nd lap at Hounslow. Hinkler's Baby had come to be known as "The Old Hen."
Sopwith Gnu G-EADB	2	J. R. King	14:07:45	1:10:30·0 1:17:41·6 2:28:11·6T	85·106 mph 77·227 mph 80·975T	**8th**	**7th**	
Boulton & Paul P.9 G-EBEQ	49 (1)	Flt.Lt. J. W. Woodhouse D.S.O. M.C.	14:10:03	1:05:07·0 1:06:05·0 2:11:12·0T	92·142 mph 90·794 mph 91·463T	**7th**	**3rd**	
Avro 504K G-EAMZ	38	W. M. W. Thomas	(14:23:36)					Withdrew. Thomas hurt his left knee in a motor-bike spill the day before the race.
Avro 552 Viper G-EAPR	3 (5)	H. A. Hamersley	14:29:24	0:54:46·0 0:55:10·0 1:49:56·0T	109·556 mph 108·761 mph 109·157T	**6th**	**1st**	
Martinsyde F.6 G-EBDK	3 (5)	Frederick P. Raynham	14:42:09	0:50:51·0 0:49:14·0 1:40:05·0T	117·994 mph 121·869 mph 119·900T	**5th**	**4th**	Raynham's engine ran rough for entire race. His F.6 was still a "bilious yellow."
De Havilland D.H.37 *Sylvia* 3-seater G-EBDO	32	Major Harold Hemming A.F.C.	14:43:01	0:51:24·0	116·732 mph	—	—	Retired 2nd lap. Landed at Romford. This aeroplane was later 3rd in both 1924 and 1925 King's Cup races; modified in 1926 with redesigned Puma engine, called Nimbus. On June 4, 1924 Hemming raced it at Bournemouth, stalled; plane destroyed, Hemming lost an eye. Aeroplane belonged to A. S. Butler whose investment saved De Havilland in October 1921.
De Havilland D.H.9A G-EBCG	33	H. H. Perry	14:47:08	0:46:22·0 0:47:18·0 1:33:40·0T	129·403 mph 126·850 mph 128·114T	**4th**	**2nd**	
De Havilland D.H.9A G-EBEZ	35 (1)	Francis T. Courtney	15:00:25			—	—	Retired first lap. Landed at Brooklands, "something wrong with tail."
De Havilland D.H.9A G-EBGX	35 (1)	Capt. C. D. Barnard	15:02:25	0:41:09·0 0:40:12·2 1:21:21·2T	145·808 mph 149·241 mph 147·505T	**3rd**	**6th**	
Sopwith 107 "Hawker" G-EAKI	42 (4)	Lt. Walter H. Longton D.F.C. A.F.C.	15:13:58	0:36:02·0 0:37:07·6 1:13:09·6T	166·512 mph 161·609 mph 164·024T	**2nd**	**8th**	Aeroplane renamed in honor of its former pilot. The only time the names *Sopwith* and *Hawker* were officially coupled together. One month later it was demolished in a crash during trials preparatory to the 1923 Schneider Trophy race.

Aeroplane	Engine	Pilot	Assigned take-off time	Lap times	Lap speeds	Place speed	Place h'cap	Remarks
Gloucestershire Gloster I G-EAXZ	35 (3)	Larry L. Carter	15:21:02	0:30:40·0 0:31:43·0 1:02:23·0T	195·652 mph 189·175 mph 192·359T	**1st**	**5th**	The rebuilt Bamel. Oil leak on last lap.
Bristol 32 Bullet G-EATS	42 (5)	Major E. L. Foot	—					Withdrawn after its pilot, Leslie Foot, was killed in crash of the Bristol 77 racer during the 1923 Grosvenor Cup race.

After this edition, a lack of prize money existed; this was coupled with a lack of sufficient numbers of new racing aeroplanes to warrant continuance. Therefore, in July 1924, the Royal Aero Club announced:

CONTEST CLOSED

442

1923 COUPE COMMODORE LOUIS D. BEAUMONT

OCTOBER 14, 1923

COURSE: 300 KM At Istres (Bouches-du-Rhône) near Marseilles.
Six laps of hexagonal 50-km circuit. Winner must exceed 290 km to receive *prix*.

PRIX: 75,000 FRANCS *Objet d'art* valued at 25,000 francs for constructor of winning aeroplane; 75,000 francs cash to winning pilot. (Not awarded in 1923.)

Aeroplane	Engine	Pilot	Remarks
Gourdou-Leseurre CT no. 1	42 (4)	Warrant-Officer Devillers	Only aeroplane to appear at starting line. When no other competitors appeared, its sponsor sportingly withdrew from formal competition; however Devillers made one 50-km circuit in :09:15 (some 324·324 kmh). It was never reentered in subsequent contests.
Nieuport-Delage 42 "monoplan no. 1"	6 (2)	Sadi Lecointe	Withdrawn.
Nieuport-Delage "sesquiplan no. 2"	13 (5)	Fernand Lasne	Withdrawn. This was the 1921 sesquiplane, fitted with wing radiators and otherwise modified. It held world speed record (375 kmh) set February 1923. Radiator capacity said to be insufficient to complete the 300 km distance at full throttle.
Nieuport-Delage "biplan no. 3"	4 (3)	not named.	Withdrawn.
Salmson-Béchéreau monoplane	9	not named.	Withdrawn.

Foreign competition failed to materialize; when this occurred all French competitors withdrew.

CONTEST POSTPONED

1924 COUPE COMMODORE LOUIS D. BEAUMONT

JUNE 23, 1924 (Scheduled June 22; postponed one day account weather.)

COURSE: 300 KM Same rules and course as for 1923 Coupe Beaumont.

PRIX: 75,000 FRANCS Supplementary regulations specified that at least two nations had to be represented.

Race No.	Aeroplane	Engine	Pilot	Take-off time	Lap times	Lap speeds	Place	Remarks
(1)	Gloucestershire Gloster I G-EAXZ	35 (3)	Larry L. Carter	—				Withdrawn in March 1924; new wings and wing radiators not ready in time.
(2)	Nieuport-Delage "sesquiplan no. 1"	13(5)	Fernand Lasne	—				Withdrawn on race day after Sadi Lecointe's winning performance. This was the type 1921 sesquiplane (modified) which set world speed record in February 1923.
3	Nieuport-Delage 42 "sesquiplan no. 2"	6 (2)	Sadi Lecointe	1108	:18:54·0 :19:22·6 :19:33·4 0:57:50·0T	317·460 kmh 309·651 306·801 311·239T	1st	After finishing the required 300 km, Sadi continued until he had covered 500 km to set the closed-course speed record for that distance (306.696 kmh in 1:37:49·0). Sadi also won 50,000 franc *Prix de M. Laurent-Eynac* given for bringing a major world speed record back to France.
4	Salmson-Bêchéreau monoplane	9	Lt. G. Fèrigoule	1800			—	Retired on 1st lap with radiator trouble. (Aeroplane employed special Lamblin wing radiators.)
5	Bernard (SIMB) V.1	8 (3)	Adjutant Florentin Bonnet	—				Overturned and demolished in a pre-race flight test, after its completion in May 1924.
—	Bernard (SIMB) V.2	5 (2)	not named	—				Withdrawn. Not ready in time.

1925 COUPE COMMODORE LOUIS D. BEAUMONT

OCTOBER 18, 1925

COURSE: 300 KM Same rules and course as for 1924 Coupe Beaumont.

PRIX: 75,000 FRANCS *Objet d'art* valued at 25,000 francs for constructor; similar for pilot; plus 75,000 francs cash for pilot.

Aeroplane	Engine	Pilot	Take-off time	Lap times	Lap speeds	Place	Remarks
Nieuport-Delage 42 *sesquiplan type course*	6 (2)	Sadi Lecointe	0800	0:57:36·4T	312·464 kmhT	**1st**	This aeroplane had won 1924 Coupe Beaumont. (Individual lap times/speeds unavailable.)
Salmson-Bêchéreau monoplane	9	Lt. G. Fèrigoule	FIRST 0730 SECOND 1015			___ ___	Retired due to radiator malfunction both times, on second attempt retired on third lap. (Individual lap times/speeds unavailable.)

Prix awarded to La Société Nieuport-Astra and Sadi Lecointe.

CONTEST CLOSED

1920 PULITZER

HISTORY OF THE COMPETITION

May 1919 (in conjunction with 2nd Pan American Aeronautic Convention): { Won by Mansell R. James in Sopwith Camel for best time in long distance flight: Atlantic City, New Jersey—Boston, Massachusetts. James disappeared on return to Atlantic City. No positive clues to this day. In 1920 the competition was changed to a closed-course speed race.

NOVEMBER 25, 1920 (Thanksgiving Day.)

COURSE: 116.0808 STATUTE MILES Mitchel Field, Long Island, New York. Triangle of 29·0202 miles, to be flown four times. (Original plan: triangle of 33 miles, 132 miles total.)

PRIZES: Samuel H. Valentine Prizes in the form of Liberty Bonds.

1st : Pilot: $1500 Liberty Bond plus Gold Plaque donated by Ralph Pulitzer.
Mechanic: $300 Liberty Bond.

2nd : Pilot: $750 Liberty Bond plus Silver Plaque donated by Ralph Pulitzer.
Mechanic: $150 Liberty Bond.

3rd : Pilot: $500 Liberty Bond plus Bronze Plaque donated by Ralph Pulitzer.
Mechanic: $100 Liberty Bond.

In addition, Liberty Bond prizes were awarded for each of 3 "Classes": De Havilland, Vought, and S.E.5.

CLASS PRIZE 1st : Pilot: $350 Liberty Bond.
Mechanic: $50 Liberty Bond

CLASS PRIZE 2nd : Pilot: $150 Liberty Bond.
Mechanic: $50 Liberty Bond.

(Aggregate total: $5100 in Liberty Bonds.)

ORGANIZATION: The race was conducted in 7 "Flights" and race numbers assigned accordingly:
Flight 1: 41—47 (Aero Club of America Contest Committee Invitation Class)
Flight 2:   1—9   (De Havilland Class)
Flight 3: 11—19 (De Havilland Class; number 13 omitted)
Flight 4: 21—26 (Vought Class)
Flight 5: 31—35 (S.E.5 Class)
Flight 6: 51—57
Flight 7: 61—65

Race No.	Aeroplane	Engine	Pilot	Take-off time	Lap times	Lap speeds	Place	Remarks
1	D.H.4 (Curtiss built)	10 (4)	2/Lt. Carl Eliason USAS		:14:11·73 :13:53·87 :14:00·11 :14:03·68 :56:09·39T	122·659 mph 125·287 124·356 123·830 124·026T	**7th**	Winner De Havilland Class Prize. Flight 2—Army entry. (Prize awarded to fastest entry in Flight 2, even though Flight 3 also included D.H. entries.)
2	D.H.4 (Dayton Wright built)	10 (1)	2/Lt. J. B. Wright USAS		:14:14·89 :14:11·00 :14:11·28 :14:15·03 :56:52·20T	122·206 mph 122·765 122·724 122·186 122·470T	**8th**	Second place: De Havilland Class Prize. Flight 2—Army entry. Ford built engine. B. Shoninger manufactured "Eagle" propeller.
3	D.H.4 (Fisher Body built)	10 (2)	Ltjg. V. C. Finch USN		:14:36·87 :14:35·60 :14:34·16 :14:46·31 :58:32·94T	119·142 mph 119·316 119·512 117·874 118·958T	**12th**	Flight 2—Navy entry. Lincoln built engine. Westmore propeller.
4	D.H.4 (U.S. built)	10 (7)	2/Lt. Ray W. Brown USAS	—				Flight 2—Army entry. Did not report.
5	D.H.4 (Fisher Body built)	10 (5)	1/Lt. Walter R. Lawson USAS		:14:57·35 :15:19·15 :15:14·54 :15:17·42 1:00:48·46T	116.424 mph 113·662 114·235 113·877 114·539T	**17th**	Flight 2—Army entry. Marmon built engine. "Imperial" propeller.

Race No.	Aeroplane	Engine	Pilot	Take-off time	Lap times	Lap speeds	Place	Remarks
6	D.H.4 (Curtiss built)	10 (1)	Capt. H. B. Mims USMC		:15:23·19 :15:28·69 :15:04·33 :14:53·13 1:00:49·34T	113·165 mph 112·495 115·524 116·974 114·511T	18th	Flight 2—Navy entry.
7	D.H.4 (U.S. built)	10 (4)	Major Davenport Johnson USAS		:14:48·80	117·544 mph	—	Flight 2—Army entry. Retired 2nd lap. Engine failed from undetermined causes; aeroplane badly damaged in forced landing. Ford built engine. Morris propeller.
8	D.H.4 (U.S. built)	10 (4)	Capt. Norbert Carolin USAS		:15:47·88 :15:49·18 :15:43·65 :15:18·51 1:02:39·22T	110·217 mph 110·066 110·711 113·742 111·164T	23rd	Flight 2—Army entry.
9	D.H.4 (U.S. built)	10 (7)	2/Lt. Merrill D. Mann USAS	—				Flight 2—Army entry. Did not report.
11	D.H.4 (U.S. built)	10 (1)	2/Lt. Lucas V. Beau USAS		:16:06·96 :14:57·86 :14:59·30 :14:57·50 1:01:01·62	108·042 mph 116·357 116·171 116·404 114·127T	19th	Flight 3—Army entry. Lincoln built engine. Eagle Corp. propeller.
12	D.H.4 (Fisher Body built)	10 (4)	2/Lt. Lawrence Claude USAS		:15:21·04 :14:49·04 :14:47·54 :14:59·11 :59:56·73	113·429 mph 116·205 117·710 116·196 116·186T	15th	Flight 3—Army entry. Ford built engine. Dayton-Wright propeller.
14	D.H.4 (Fisher Body built)	10 (3)	Lt. John P. Roullot USAS		:14:35·33 :14:15·95 :13:48·37 :13:26·93 :56:06·58T	119·352 mph 122·055 126·118 129·469 124·129T	6th	Flight 3—Army entry. Ford built engine. L.W.F. propeller.
15	D.H.4 (Curtiss built)	10 (4)	2/Lt. Reuben C. Moffat USAS		:15:29·02 :15:20·37 :15:49·23 :15:08·83 1:01:47·45T	112·455 mph 113·512 110·060 114·953 112·717T	21st	Flight 3—Army entry. Eagle Corp. propeller.
16	D.H.4 (Dayton-Wright built)	10 (4)	Lt. F. O. Rogers USMC		:15:42·16 :15:02·25	110·886 mph 115·791	—	Flight 3—Navy entry. Broken valve, piston, and connecting rod. Forced landing without further damage.
17	D.H.4 (U.S. built)	10 (5)	Capt. Horace N. Heisen USAS		:14:37·04 :14:26·07 :14:40·90 :14:31·27 :58:15·28T	119·120 mph 120·628 118·598 119·909 119·559T	11th	Flight 3—Army entry. McCook Field propeller.
18	D.H.4 (U.S. built)	10 (1)	Ltjg. D. L. Conly USN		:14:29·84 :14:25·47 :14:22·31 :14:23·14 :57:40·76T	120·106 mph 120·712 121·154 121·038 120·751T	10th	Flight 3—Navy entry. Ford built engine. Dayton-Wright propeller.
19	D.H.4 (U.S. built)	10 (5)	2/Lt. Charles M. Cummings USAS		:14:18·03 :14:18·63 :14:15·85 :14:15·61 :57:08·12T	121·759 mph 121·674 122·069 122·103 121·901T	9th	Flight 3—Army entry.

Race No.	Aeroplane	Engine	Pilot	Take-off time	Lap times	Lap speeds	Place	Remarks
21	Vought V.E.7	3 (7)	Ltjg. W. B. Gwyn USN		:14:55·07 :14:40·29 :14:52·31 :15:23·96 :59:51·63T	116·720 mph 118·680 117·081 113·071 116·351T	14th	Second place—Vought Class Prize. Flight 4—Navy entry. McCook Field propeller.
22	Vought V.E.7 (Naval Aircraft Factory built)	3 (8)	Ltjg. A. Laverents USN		:13:57·50 :13:55·64 :13:51·38 :13:54·67 :55:39·19T	124·744 mph 125·021 125·662 125·166 125·147T	5th	Winner—Vought Class Prize. Flight 4—Navy entry. S.E. propeller.
23	Vought V.E.7	3 (7)	2/Lt. Lawson H. Sanderson USMC		:15:08·32 :14:59·83 :14:59·92 :15:01·31 1:00:09·38T	115·018 mph 116·103 116·091 115·912 115·779T	16th	Flight 4—Navy entry. American Manufacturing Company propeller.
24	Vought V.E.7	3 (7)	2/Lt. W. V. Brown USMC		:15:05·52 :15:32·51 :15:35·08 :15:12·17 1:01:25·28T	115·373 mph 112·034 ·111·726 114·532 113·395T	20th	Flight 4—Navy entry. American Manufacturing Company propeller.
25	Vought V.E.7	3 (7)	Gunnery Sergeant J. K. Dunn USMC		:16:02·39 :15:36·25 :15:07·26 :15:04·48 1:01:50·38T	108·555 mph 111·586 115·152 115·506 112·628T	22nd	Flight 4—Navy entry American Manufacturing Company propeller.
26	Vought V.E.7	3 (7)	Ensign W. J. Daly USN		:18:32·59 :18:47·92 :18:51·63	93·900 mph 92·624 92·321	—	Flight 4—Navy entry. Retired on 4th lap; engine overheated. Forced landing without damage. McCook Field propeller.
31	S.E.5 (British built)	3 (7)	2/Lt. A. E. Simonin USAS		:14:57·34 :14:46·80 :15:05·66	116·425 mph 117·809 115·355	—	Flight 5—Army entry. (British propeller.) Lt. Lotha A. Smith originally assigned as pilot. Simonin, the new pilot, landed after only 3 laps, believing he had finished the race.
32	S.E.5 (British built)	3 (7)	2/Lt. S. M. Aimes USAS		:16:07·68 :15:51·51	107·962 mph 109·797	—	Flight 5—Army entry. S.E. propeller. Retired 3rd lap; returned to Mitchel Field with overheated engine.
33	S.E.5 (British built)	3 (7)	Capt. Felix Steinle USAS	—				Flight 5—Army entry. Did not start. Radiator overheated on ground.
34	S.E.5 (British built)	3 (7)	2/Lt. Fonda B. Johnson USAS		:15:04·23	115·538 mph	—	Flight 5—Army entry. Retired 2nd lap. Engine overheated. Returned to Mitchel Field.
35	S.E.5 (British built)	3 (9)	Capt. Maxwell Kirby USAS		:15:14·47 :14:46·04 :14:45·43 :14:56·73 :59:42·67T	114·244 mph 117·910 117·991 116·504 116·642T	13th	Winner—S.E.5 Class Prize. Flight 5—Army entry.
41	Thomas-Morse M.B.3 40093	13 (2)	Capt. Harold Evans Hartney USAS	1120	:11:52·31 :11:50·09 :11:48·80 :11:28·83 :47:00·03T	146·667 mph 147·126 147·394 151·667 148·187T	2nd	Winner—Aero Club of America Contest Committee Invitation Class Prize. Flight 1—Army entry. (First aeroplane aloft in race.) This was 2nd prototype of experimental batch of 5 M.B.3s built for Air Service evaluation in 1919; it was first M.B.3 to fly (February 21, 1919). McCook Field propeller.
42	Fokker D-VII (German built)	49 (3)	Major C. H. Wash USAS	—				Flight 1—Army entry. Withdrawn. Overturned in snow at Buffalo en route to race.

Race No.	Aeroplane	Engine	Pilot	Take-off time	Lap times	Lap speeds	Place	Remarks
43	Thomas-Morse M.B.3 *40094*	13 (2)	2/Lt. Leigh Wade USAS		:12:37·47	137·923 mph	—	Flight 1—Army entry. Retired 2nd lap. Returned to Mitchel Field with broken drift wire. One of 5 original 1919 M.B.3 prototypes.
44	Orenco model D	13 (2)	2/Lt. Oakley G. Kelly USAS	—				Flight 1—Army entry. Did not take off. Damaged in collision on Mitchel Field with race entry number 55 before start. Kelly had 3 teeth knocked out.
45	Orenco model D (Curtiss built)	13 (2)	1/Lt. St. Clair Streett USAS		:13:13·10 :13:16·67 :13:03·21 :12:44·04 :52:17·02T	131·727 mph 131·137 133·390 136·737 133·213T	4th	2nd place—Contest Committee Invitation Class Prize. Flight 1—Army entry. McCook Field propeller Fuel 20% benzol.
46	Loening M-81S Special A-5791	13 (1)	Lt. Benjamin G. Bradley USMC	1121	:12:38·51 :12:25·22 :12:35·14	137·734 mph 140·190 138·349	—	Flight 1—Navy entry. 2nd aeroplane aloft in race. Retired 4th lap: aluminum water connection cracked on 3rd lap; engine seized. Damage incurred on forced landing. (Had certain 3rd place in sight when mishap occurred.) Fuel 20% benzol. Hartzell propeller.
47	Sopwith Dolphin (British built)	13 (2)	2/Lt. Caleb V. Haynes USAS	—				Flight 1—Army entry. Did not report.
51	Loening M-80	13 (1)	Ltjg. P. E. Gillespie USN		:15:11·21	114·653 mph	—	Flight 6—Navy entry. Retired 2nd lap; returned to Mitchel Field with overheated engine.
52	Ansaldo SVA (Italian built)	45 (2)	Arthur W. Fox		:13:27·63 :15:21·07	129·357 mph 113·425	—	Flight 6—Entered by Eagle Flying Corporation. Retired 3rd lap. Pilot reported he could not see due to fogged goggles. LWF propeller.
53	Spad *S.13* (French built)	3 (4)	—	—				Flight 6—Army entry. Withdrawn. Capt. Maxwell Kirby originally assigned, but he switched to S.E.5 race no. 35.
54	Ansaldo SVA (Italian built)	45 (2)	2/Lt. Willis *P.* Taylor USAS		:14:54·64 :15:01·57 :14:43·36 :14:56·02* :59:35·59T*	116.776 mph 115·879 118·267 116·596* 116·873T*	—	Flight 6—Entered by Aero Import Co. Disqualified for cutting Lufbery Field pylon on last lap; * lap speed possibly in error due to cut pylon. Would have finished 13th otherwise. Ansaldo propeller.
55	Loening M-80	13 (1)	Ltjg J. E. Wolfer USN	—				Flight 6—Navy entry. Damaged in collision on Mitchel Field before start with number 44.
56	Ansaldo A.1 Balilla (Italian built)	45 (2)	Bert Acosta		:12:58·14 :13:04·05 :12:59·91 :12:55·52 :51:57·62T	134·260 mph 133·248 133·955 134·713 134·042T	3rd	Flight 6—Entered by Aero Import Company. Ansaldo propeller.
57	Morane-Saulnier AR (French built)	2	Charles Colt		:16:53·89 :16:36·24 :19:21·77 :20:24·43 1:13:16·33T	103·041 mph 104·867 89·925 85·324 95·054T	24th	Flight 6—Entered by Morane-Saulnier. Levasseur propeller.
61	Curtiss-Kirkham 18-T-1 Triplane A-3325	17 (1)	Lcdr. Willis B. Haviland USN		:12:35·32	138·316 mph	—	Flight 7—Navy entry. Retired 2nd lap with carburetor or fuel line trouble. Returned to Mitchel Field. Flew 4th fastest first lap. Curtiss propeller.
62	Curtiss-Kirkham 18-T-1 Triplane A-3326	17 (1)	2/Lt. W. D. Culbertson USMC		:11:03·34 :12:11·94 :12:18·18	157·495 mph 142·734 141·527	—	Flight 7—Navy entry. Retired on 4th lap with broken con-rod. Forced landing with no further damage. Flew fastest first lap in the race. Curtiss propeller.

Race No.	Aeroplane	Engine	Pilot	Take-off time	Lap times	Lap speeds	Place	Remarks
63	Verville VCP-R	24	1/Lt. Corliss C. Moseley USAS		:11:06·70 :11:00·37 :11:07·18 :11:15·32 :44:29·57T	156·701 mph 158·203 156·589 154·701 156·539T	**1st**	Flight 7—Army entry. Aeroplane had competed in 1920 Gordon Bennett two months before. Plagued with carburetion problems. Its Pulitzer performance was originally credited as 178 mph (time indicated, based on erroneous course length of 132 miles as originally planned). Fuel 50% benzol. McCook Field propeller. Last contestant to take off in race.
64	Young Special	unknown	O. Young	—				Flight 7—Privately entered. Did not report.
65	D.H.4 Hospital Plane (U.S. built)	10(1)	1/Lt. Eugene Hay Barksdale USAS		:15:05·90 :14:52·23	115·325 mph 117·092	—	Flight 7—Army entry. Retired 3rd lap. Reason unknown. Aeroplane all white with large red cross insignia.

450

1921 PULITZER

NOVEMBER 3, 1921
COURSE: 153.5955 STATUTE MILES Omaha, Nebraska.

5 laps of 30·7191 miles each. Course originally clockwise, to captive balloons on railroad track north of Calhoun, Nebraska and on southern outskirts of Loveland, Iowa. Changed to *counterclockwise* just before race. No captive balloons used. Race numbers assigned upon closing of entry list were subsequently changed by race time due to many non-starters.

PRIZES: 1st $3000. 2nd $2000. 3rd $1000.

Race No.	Aeroplane	Engine	Pilot	Take-off time	Lap times	Lap speeds	Place	Remarks
1	Thomas-Morse MB-7 A.S. 64373	13 (3)	Harold E. Hartney	1638			—	Entered privately by Thomas-Morse. Aeroplane crashed on first lap due to fuel pump failure; plane demolished, Hartney badly injured with broken hip, other injuries. Used 60% benzol fuel.
2	Thomas-Morse MB-6 A.S. 68539	13 (2)	Capt. John A. Macready USAS	1453	:11:31·2 :11:23·8 :11:28·2 :11:27·6 :11:29·6 :57:20·4T	159·995 mph 161·727 160·693 160·833 160·367 160·721T	3rd	Entered privately by Thomas-Morse. Used 60% benzol fuel. Macready was "The Altitude King," holder of current world altitude record set 2 months before. (The times :57:20·6 and :57:27·6 have been published erroneously.)
3	Curtiss-Cox "Cactus Kitten" triplane	18 (2)	Clarence B. Coombs	1446	:10:41·8 :10:43·0 :10:57·2 :10:52·0 :10:52·2 :54:06·2T	172·310 mph 171·989 168·273 169·615 169·563 170·336T	2nd	Entered by S. E. J. Cox. This was Coombs' first flight in this aeroplane; it was probably fastest on straightaway but difficult to maneuver. Red with silver wings, black struts. Used 50% benzol fuel. (Originally assigned race number 5.) (The time :54:07·6 has been published erroneously.)
4	Curtiss CR-1 A-6081	19 (1)	Bert Acosta	1440	:10:32·8 :10:24·4 :10:23·2 :10:22·4 :10:25·6 :52:08·4T	174·761 mph 177·112 177·453 177·681 176·772 176·750T	1st	Entered privately by Curtiss Co. Suffered broken flying wire; speed was unofficial world closed-course record. Used 50% benzol fuel. (Originally assigned race number 11.) (The times :52:09·2 and :52:09·6 have been published erroneously.)
27	Ansaldo A.1 Balilla	17 (3)	Lloyd Bertaud	1443	:12:36·8 :12:01·6 :12:19·2 :12:18·4 :12:17·4 1:01:33·4T	146·127 mph 153·255 149·606 149·768 149·971 149·711T	4th	Entered by Aero Import Co. 1819 Broadway, New York City. Race number retained from American Legion Air Derby held in Kansas City the day before (which this aeroplane/pilot won: *150* miles in 1:00:15·4 for some *149·361* mph). (Originally assigned race number 4.) Used 50% benzol fuel. (The times 1:01:31·4 and 1:01:31·6 have been published erroneously.) 4 blade Curtiss prop.
(6)	Ansaldo SVA-9	45 (1)	James Curran	1451	:17:38·0 :17:11·6	104·526 mph 107·201	—	Entered by Ralph C. Diggins Co., 140 N. Dearborn St. Chicago, Ill. Retired on 3rd lap with burned out rocker arms. Late arrival from Kansas City due to participation in American Legion meet. (Originally assigned race number 8.)
—	Curtiss-Cox "Texas Wildcat" monoplane	18 (2)	Charles B. D. Collyer	—				Entered by S. E. J. Cox. Withdrawn: disqualified because of high landing speed, although 75 mph landing speed restriction was *not* official in 1921. (Original race number assignment would probably have been 6 if it had qualified to race, although this is unconfirmed. Witnesses recall it was on display at Omaha, a bright red-orange color.)

Race No.	Aeroplane	Engine	Pilot	Take-off time	Lap times	Lap speeds	Place	Remarks
—	Thomas-Morse MB-3	13 (2)	Paul D. Wilson	—				Entered privately by Thomas-Morse, to be raced by their chief test pilot. Withdrawn. (Originally assigned race number 3.)
(7)	Ansaldo A.1 Balilla	45 (1)	Florian F. Manor	—				Entered by Lutz-Manor Co. Withdrawn. (Original race number assigned indicated.)
(9)	Spad S.13	3 (2)	Valentine Gephart	—				Entered by Valentine Gephart Co. Withdrawn. (Original race number assigned indicated.)
(10)	Miller Monoplane		Hugh S. Miller	—				Entered by Hugh S. Miller. Withdrawn. (Original race number assigned indicated.)
(12)	Ansaldo SVA-9	45 (1)	Earle F. White	—				Entered by C. B. Wrightsman, Kennedy Bldg., Tulsa, Oklahoma. Late arrival from Kansas City due to American Legion meet. Withdrawn from Pulitzer; White was declared winner of Larsen Efficiency Race on Nov. 5 in this aeroplane, number 8, later to be disqualified. (Original race number assigned indicated.)

1922 PULITZER

OCTOBER 14, 1922

COURSE: 250 KM At Selfridge Field, Mt. Clemens, Michigan.
Triangle 50 km in length to be covered 5 times. Race flown in three "heats". Take-off times: heat 1: 1300
(Race number gaps due to race number assignments for other events.)   heat 2: *1420*
     heat 3: 1545

LANDING SPEED RESTRICTION OF 75 mph MAXIMUM IMPOSED.

PRIZES: **1st** $1200.   **2nd** $600.   **3rd** $200.

Race No.	Aeroplane	Engine	Pilot	Take-off time	Lap times	Lap speeds	Place	Remarks
6	Aerial Engineering Corporation BR-2 "Bee-Line" A-6429	13 (5)	Lt. David Rittenhouse USN	—				Navy entry. Withdrawn. Pilot had no experience in aeroplane. Decided not to race. (Lamblin radiators.)
7	Thomas-Morse MB-7 A.S. 64374	13 (4)	Capt. Francis P. Mulcahy USMC	1300	:12:50·26 :13:53·02	233·687 kmh 216·081	—	Navy entry. Heat 1. Retired on 3rd lap with overheated engine despite jury-rigged radiator.
8	Curtiss CR-2 A-6080	20 (1)	Ltjg. Alford J. Williams USN	*1421½*	:09:58·68 :09:50·02 :09:53·01 :09:55·04 :09:57·96 :49:34·71T	300·661 kmh 305·074 303·536 302·501 301·023 302·551T (187·996 mphT)	**4th**	Navy entry. Heat 2. Lt. Frank C. Fechteler (son of RAdm. Augustus F. Fechteler) originally assigned as pilot, but he was killed Sept. 18, 1922, while surveying course in a Spad. Cactus Kitten triplane withdrawn and Al Williams reassigned to this aeroplane, after Oct. 1. This plane converted to D-12 engine and wing radiators in month prior to race. Fire extinguisher explosion during race made Williams "violently sick."
—	Curtiss-Cox TR "Navy Triplane" (Formerly Cactus Kitten)	18 (2)	—	—				Withdrawn. (Navy entry.) Available evidence suggests Al Williams was to fly this aeroplane in Pulitzer.
9	Wright NW-1 (Navy "X" Mystery Racer) A-6543	14	1/Lt. Lawson H. Sanderson USMC	*1422*	:10:02·37 :09:57·27 :10:04·47	298·820 kmh 301·371 297·782	—	Navy entry. Heat 2. Retired on 4th lap. Began losing oil; tried to continue. Ditched in Lake St. Clair when this became impossible.
—	Wright NW-1 (Navy "X" Mystery Racer) A-6544	14	—	—				Withdrawn. Not ready in time for race.
18	Aerial Engineering Corporation BR-1 "Bee-Line" A-6430	13 (5)	Lt. Steven W. Calloway USN	1300½	:11:24·83	262·839 kmh	—	Navy entry. Heat 1. Retired on 2nd lap upon rupture of oil gauge line and loss of oil. Its take-off marked first time public had seen retractable landing gear in a U.S. air race. Wing radiator-equipped.
40	Curtiss CR-2 A-6081	20 (1)	Lt. Harold J. Brow USN	*1421*	:09:36·44 :09:35·12 :09:34·22 :09:43·26 :09:38·15 :48:07·19T	312·261 kmh 312·978 313·469 308·610 311·338 311·722T (193·695 mphT)	**3rd**	Navy entry. Heat 2. Tail fairing strip came loose during race, causing Brow to lose control momentarily.

Race No.	Aeroplane	Engine	Pilot	Take-off time	Lap times	Lap speeds	Place	Remarks
42	Verville R-1 (VCP-1 High Speed Pursuit)	24	1/Lt. Corliss C. Moseley USAS	1546	:10:35·03 :10:27·19 :10:20·11 :10:21·43 :10:23·78 :52:07·54T	283·451 kmh 286·994 290·271 289·655 288·563 287·766T (178·809 mphT)	6th	Army entry. Heat 3. The same combination that won the 1920 Pulitzer. 1922 results, though out of the money, were 23 mph faster. Carried McCook number P-97. 1/Lt. Leigh Wade backup pilot.
43	Curtiss R-6 A.S. 68564	20 (1)	1/Lt. Russell L. Maughan USAS	1420½	:09:03·72 :09:03·06 :09:00·08 :09:05·31 :09:04·45 :45:16·62T	331·053 kmh 331·455 333·284 330·087 330·609 331·294T (205·856 mphT)	1st	Army entry. Heat 2. Second of two R-6s built; on its first flight October 2 it hit over 230 mph; set world speed record 4 days after race. Maughan's wife gave birth to a son during race. 1/Lt. Bushrod Hoppin backup pilot. Wood propeller EX-28904.
44	Curtiss R-6 A.S. 68563	20 (1)	1/Lt. Lester J. Maitland USAS	1420	:09:37·18 :09:20·31 :09:29·15 :09:10·55 :09:15·15 :46:52·34T	311·861 kmh 321·251 316·261 326·946 324·237 320·018T (198·850 mphT)	2nd	Army entry. Heat 2. Maitland had to use hand wobble fuel pump for much of race. 1/Lt. Caleb V. Haynes backup pilot. Wood prop. EX-28904.
45	Loening R-4 A.S. 68559	24	1/Lt. Ennis C. Whitehead USAS	1546½	:10:58·02 :10:53·93 :10:52·22 :11:05·42 :10:58·53 :54:48·12T	273·548 kmh 275·259 275·980 270·506 273·336 273·713T (170·077 mphT)	8th	Army entry. Heat 3. 1/Lt. George P. Tourtellot backup pilot.
46	Loening R-4 A.S. 68560	24	1/Lt. Lester D. Schulze USAS	1547	:11:47·22 :11:32·92 :11:32·73 :11:29·57 :11:37·29 :57:59·73T	254·518 kmh 259·770 259·841 261·032 258·142 258·641T (160.712 mphT)	9th	Army entry. Heat 3. 1/Lt. J. T. Hitchison backup pilot (Schulze later killed flying MB-3A number 54—Mitchell race winner— on a gunnery exercise.)
47	Thomas-Morse R-5 A.S. 68561	24	Capt. Frank O'Driscoll "Monk" Hunter USAS	1547½	:16:28·13 :11:21·76 :11:17·64 :11:38·25 :11:41·10 1:02:26·88T	182·162 kmh 264·023 265·628 257·787 256·739 240·200T (149·253 mphT)	11th	Army entry. Heat 3. Long-wing version of R-5. Rough-running engine and disorientation in haze cost time on first lap. 1/Lt. C. E. Crumrine backup pilot.
48	Thomas-Morse R-5 A.S. 68562	24	1/Lt. Clayton L. Bissell USAS	1548	:12:17·73 :12:17·23 :12:09·59 :11:38·38 :11:35·24 :59:58·17T	243·992 kmh 244·157 246·714 257·739 258·903 250·127T (155·421 mphT)	10th	Army entry. Heat 3. Short wing version of R-5. (Later assigned McCook number P-268.) 1/Lt. Thomas K. Matthews backup pilot.
49	Verville-Sperry R-3 A.S. 22-326	13 (5)	1/Lt. Eugene Hay Barksdale USAS	1301	:10:21·52 :10:19·26 :10:18·65 :10:18·66 :10:16·12 :51:34·21T	289·613 kmh 290·670 290·956 290·951 292·151 290·866T (180·735 mphT)	5th	Army entry. Heat 1. (Later assigned McCook number P-269.) 1/Lt. G. C. McDonald backup pilot.
50	Verville-Sperry R-3 A.S. 22-327	13 (5)	Capt. St. Clair Streett USAS	1548½	:11:36·41 :11:38·80 :11:13·18 :11:01·40	258·468 kmh 257·584 267·388 272·150	—	Army entry. Heat 3. Retired on last lap with broken oil line. 1/Lt. Valentine S. Miner backup pilot.

Race No.	Aeroplane	Engine	Pilot	Take-off time	Lap times	Lap speeds	Place	Remarks
51	Boeing MB-3A (Thomas-Morse design)	13 (3)	Capt. Albert M. Guidera USAS	1137½	:14:20·10 :13:37·67 :13:42·16 :13:08·39 :54:48·32T	209·278 kmh 220·138 218·935 228·313 218·957T (136·053 mphT)	2nd MITCHELL	Race numbers 51–56, originally entered in Pulitzer, were withdrawn "at last minute" to compete in the first John Lendrum Mitchell Trophy Race (4 laps, 200 km). Mitchell Race restricted to pilots of 1st Pursuit Group. Capt. Burt E. Skeel originally assigned to race #51; Guidera was his backup.
52	Boeing MB-3A (Thomas-Morse design)	13 (3)	1/Lt. Benjamin K. McBride USAS	1135½	:13:19·46 :13:32·57 :14:17·08 :14:14·00 :55:23·11T	225·152 kmh 221·519 210·015 210·773 216·665T (134·629 mphT)	4th MITCHELL	1/Lt. Walter H. Reid backup pilot.
53	Boeing MB-3A (Thomas-Morse design)	13 (3)	Capt. Hugh M. Elmendorf USAS	1137	:13:55·75 :14:20·54 :15:03·89 :16:28·59 :59:48·77T	215·375 kmh 209·171 199·139 182·078 200·626T (124·663 mphT)	5th MITCHELL	Capt. Vincent B. Dixon backup pilot.
54	Boeing MB-3A (Thomas-Morse design)	13 (3)	2/Lt. Donald F. Stace USAS	1135	:12:29·55 :12:27·18 :12:48·25 :12:40·75 :50:25·73T	240·144 kmh 240·906 234·299 236·609 237·959T (147·861 mphT)	1st MITCHELL	Stace received $400 from Dodge Bros. toward a new automobile. 1/Lt. Roy B. Mosher backup pilot.
55	Boeing MB-3A (Thomas-Morse design)	13 (3)	Capt. Oliver W. Broberg USAS	1136½	:13:49·61 :13:46·48 :13:39·29 :13:52·49 :55:07·87T	216·969 kmh 217·791 219·702 216·219 217·663T (135·249 mphT)	3rd MITCHELL	1/Lt. Hobart R. Yeaker backup pilot.
56	Boeing MB-3A (Thomas-Morse design)	13 (3)	1/Lt. James D. Summers USAS	1136	:13:35·04 :13:35·40	220·848 kmh 220·751	—	Retired on 3rd lap of Mitchell Race. 1/Lt. Roy W. Camblin backup pilot.
(57)	Dare variable-camber monoplane	10 (1)	Eddie Stinson	—				Withdrawn. The only civilian entry in Pulitzer. (Stinson finished 3rd in "On-to-Detroit" race in Junkers-Larsen J.L.6 all-metal monoplane.)
58	Verville-Sperry R-3 A.S. 22-328	13 (5)	1/Lt. Fonda B. Johnson USAS	1301½	:10:25·92 :10:35·97 :10:23·12 :10:18·32 :10:37·68 :52:21·01T	287·577 kmh 283·032 288·869 291·111 282·273 286·532T (178·042 mphT)	7th	Army entry. Heat 1. 1/Lt. Kenneth N. Walker backup pilot.
61	Boeing MB-3A (Thomas-Morse design)	13 (3)	1/Lt. Thomas K. Matthews USAS	—				Both withdrawn. (Army entries.) Hasty modification effort to enable two MB-3A's to complete 250 km Pulitzer distance at full throttle insufficient.
62	Boeing MB-3A (Thomas-Morse design)	13 (3)	1/Lt. George P. Tourtellot USAS	—				

1923 PULITZER

OCTOBER 6, 1923 (Postponed from October 3 due weather.)

COURSE: 200 KM Lambert Field, St. Louis, Missouri (Note Mitchell race results included. This event took place October 4.)
4 laps of 50 km triangle. Event number 8.

PRIZES: 1st $2000. **2nd** $1500. **3rd** $500.

Race No.	Aeroplane	Engine	Pilot	Take-off time	Lap times	Lap speeds	Place	Remarks
7	Wright F2W-1 A-6744	15 (1)	Lt. Steven W. Calloway USN	3-1	:08:02·64 :08:04·74 :08:06·54 :08:11·22 :32:25·14T	372·949 kmh 371·333 369·959 366·435 370·153T (230·002 mphT)	4th	Exact take-off time unknown. Notation 3-1 indicates first aeroplane to take-off in heat 3. This aeroplane had 60·1 gallon fuel supply, 3-blade metal prop.
8	Wright F2W-1 A-6743	15 (1)	1/Lt. Lawson H. Sanderson USMC	1431	:08:05·58 :08:07·73 :08:05·58 :08:05·70 :32:24·59T	370·691 kmh 369·057 370·691 370·599 370·258T (230·067 mphT)	3rd	Heat 1. 4000 foot starting dive. Aeroplane demolished on crash landing after race due to fuel exhaustion shortly after race completed. This aeroplane had 31·7 gallon fuel supply, 3-blade metal prop.
9	Curtiss R2C-1 A-6692	21	Ltjg. Alford J. "Al" Williams USN	2-1	:07:36·02 :07:41·46 :07:40·36 :07:38·17 :30:36·01T	394·720 kmh 390·066 390·998 392·867 392·155T (243·673 mphT)	1st	Heat 2. (Flew alone.) The R2C speed astonished the world (it set 100 and 200 km closed course records.) One month later Al Williams set world maximum speed record with this aeroplane; then it was converted into a seaplane. (Reed dural prop.)
10	Curtiss R2C-1 A-6691	21	Lt. Harold J. Brow USN	3-2	:07:41·44 :07:39·15 :07:43·61 :07:46·19 :30:50·39T	390·083 kmh 392·029 388·257 386·109 389·107T (241·779 mphT)	2nd	Heat 3. Engine overheated during race. Water boiled, rpm fell off. One month later Brow in this aeroplane briefly held world speed record (Nov. 2–4, 1923). Then this aeroplane went to Army as R-8 (sold by Navy for $1.00).
48	Verville-Sperry R-3 A.S.22-328	20 (1)	1/Lt. Alex Pearson USAS	2-2			—	Heat 2. Retired on 1st lap due to unbalanced Reed dural propeller which "sprung crankshaft" causing "extreme vibration."
49	Curtiss R-6 A.S.68563 (P-279)	21	1/Lt. Walter Miller USAS	3-3	:08:32·06 :08:31·18 :08:28·45 :08:32·04 :34:03·73T	351·521 kmh 352·126 354·017 351·535 352·297T (218·907 mphT)	5th	Heat 3. Aeroplane difficult to control; weak stability in pitch caused engine to cut out intermittently. 1/Lt. Lucas V. Beau backup pilot. Reed dural propeller D-27.
50	Curtiss R-6 A.S.68564 (P-278)	20 (2)	1/Lt. Johnny D. Corkille USAS	1432	:08:51·15 :08:31·96 :08:31·08 :08:32·71 :34:26·90T	338·887 kmh 351·590 352·195 351·076 348·348T (216·453 mphT)	6th	Heat 1. Violent 3000 foot dive to start. Glass came loose in pilot's goggles and helmet stripped by wind. This aeroplane the current world speed record holder; its race results here 10 mph better than 1922 winning speed. Original 1922 engine still installed. USAS birch propeller X-44499. 1/Lt. Harry Mills backup pilot.
—	Fiat R.700	47	Francesco Brack-Papa	—				Withdrawn September 1923.
—	Gloucestershire Gloster I G-EAXZ	35 (3)	Larry Carter	—				Withdrawn September 1923.
—	Nieuport-Delage sesquiplane	—	Sadi Lecointe	—				Withdrawn September 1923.

Race No.	Aeroplane	Engine	Pilot	Take-off time	Lap times	Lap speeds	Place	Remarks
53	Boeing MB-3A (Thomas-Morse design)	13 (4)	1/Lt. Thomas W. Blackburn	1300	:13:01·28 :13:21·81 :13:31·63 :12:56·35 :52:51·07T	230·391 kmh 224·492 221·776 231·854 227·053T (141·084 mphT)	3rd MITCHELL	Event 8A—the John L. Mitchell Trophy Race —was closely allied with the Pulitzer. Restricted to pilots of 1st Pursuit Group. Lt. Leland C. Hurd backup pilot.
54	Boeing MB-3A (Thomas-Morse design)	13 (4)	1/Lt. Thomas K. Matthews	1300½	:13:27·37 :14:00·10 :14:05·45	222·946 kmh 214·260 212·904	—	Retired on 4th lap; forced landing on Lambert Field due to failure of con-rod bearing. Lt. Hobart R. Yeager backup pilot.
55	Boeing MB-3A (Thomas-Morse design)	13 (4)	1/Lt. George P. Tourtellot USAS	1301	:12:57·47 :12:58·80 :12:58·96 :13:09·01 :52:04·24T	231·520 kmh 231·125 231·077 228·134 230·456T (143·198 mphT)	2nd MITCHELL	Lt. Arthur J. Liggett backup pilot. Ran out of gas near finish line but crossed line in full flight with dead motor!
56	Boeing MB-3A (Thomas-Morse design)	13 (4)	Capt. Vincent B. Dixon USAS	1301½	:13:18·92 :13:30·07 :13:22·33 :13:28·90 :53:40·22T	225·304 kmh 222·203 224·347 222·524 223·587T (138·930 mphT)	5th MITCHELL	Lt. Russell L. Meredith originally assigned. He was replaced by Dixon. Lt. Louis C. Simon backup pilot.
57	Boeing MB-3A (Thomas-Morse design)	13 (4)	1/Lt. J. Thad Johnson USAS	1302	:13:14·91 :13:13·56 :13:32·51 :13:33·20 :53:34·18T	226·441 kmh 226·826 221·536 221·348 224·007T (139·191 mphT)	4th MITCHELL	Lt. Edward M. Haight backup pilot.
65	Boeing MB-3A (Thomas-Morse design)	13 (4)	Capt. Burt E. Skeel USAS	1302½	:12:39·50 :12:46·96 :12:41·28 :12:47·21 :50:54·95T	236·998 kmh 234·693 236·444 234·616 235·683T (146·446 mphT)	1st MITCHELL	Lt. Frank O'D. Hunter backup pilot. Skeel's victory earned him privilege of flying Pulitzer racer in 1924.

1924 PULITZER

OCTOBER 4, 1924

COURSE: 200 KM   Wilbur Wright Field, Dayton, Ohio. 4 laps of hexagonal 50-km course. "Flying Start" (Event number 12).

PRIZES: **1st** $5,000 (Liberty Bonds).
2nd $2,500 (Liberty Bonds).
3rd $1,500 (Liberty Bonds).
4th $1,000 (Liberty Bonds).

Race No.	Aeroplane	Engine	Pilot	Take-off time	Lap times	Lap speeds	Place	Remarks
68	Curtiss R-6 A.S.68564 (P-278)	21	Capt. Burt E. Skeel USAS	1445			—	Crash on diving start. *Pilot killed.* Wood propeller USAS X-45101.
69	Curtiss R-6 A.S.68563 (P-279)	21	1/Lt. Wendell H. Brookley USAS	1445	:08:47·20 :08:40·94 :08:39·36 :08:39·05 :34:46·55T	341·426 kmh 345·529 346·580 346·787 345·067T (214·414 mphT)	**2nd**	Wood propeller USAS X-45101.
70	Verville-Sperry R-3 A.S.22-328 (P-362)	21	1/Lt. Harry H. Mills USAS		:08:41·37 :08:34·58 :08:33·89 :08:36·09 :34:25·93T	345·244 kmh 349·800 350·270 348·776 348·511T (216·554 mphT)	**1st**	Wood propeller USAS X-45101 (Winning speed of 215·72 mph has been published erroneously.)
71	Curtiss PW.8A A.S.23-1203 (P-364)	20 (3)	1/Lt. Rex K. Stoner USAS		:11:12·27 :11:03·13 :11:12·34 :10:56·42 :44:24·16T	267·750 kmh 271·440 267·722 274·215 270·254T (167·928 mphT)	**3rd**	Lt. Edwin Johnson mentioned; possibly originally assigned as pilot.
—	Curtiss R-8 A.S.23-1235 (P-354)	21	1/Lt. Alex Pearson USAS	—				Plane crashed Sept. 2, 1924 due to interplane strut failure. *Pilot killed.* (This was formerly Navy R2C-1 A-6691.)
—	Dewoitine racer	6 (2)	Sadi Lecointe	—				Withdrawn. Sadi, on retainer to Nieuport-Astra, was not allowed to fly Dewoitine. No Nieuport ready to race in U.S. Probably no French racer could meet Pulitzer 75 mph landing speed limit.

458

1925 PULITZER

OCTOBER 12, 1925 (Postponed from October 10 due weather.)

COURSE: 200 KM 4 laps of 50-km triangle; pylon locations: (1) Mitchel Field; (2) "2 miles north of Lindenhurst, east of St. Dominick Convent"; (3) "1½ miles northeast of Cold Spring [railroad] station."

PRIZES:
1st: $2,000 (Liberty Bonds).
2nd: $1,000 (Liberty Bonds).
3rd: $750 (Liberty Bonds).
4th: $250 (Liberty Bonds).

Race No.	Aeroplane	Engine	Pilot	Take-off time	Lap times	Lap speeds	Place	Remarks
40	Curtiss R3C-1 (Navy) A-6979	22	Ltjg Alford J. "Al" Williams USN	1514		392.182 kmh 390.894 388.480 377.649 388.971 T (241.695 mphT)	2nd	Heat 1. (NO RECORD OF LAP TIMES.) Williams lost speed lap by lap. Criticized for operating engine harshly. Lt. F. H. Conant USN backup pilot.
43	Curtiss R3C-1 (Army) (later A-7054 in USN)	22	1/Lt. Cyrus Bettis USAS	1516		398.812 kmh 401.436 400.309 402.289 400.687 T (248.975 mphT)	1st	Heat 1. World closed-course speed record (100 km only recognized.) Engine pitch *higher* than number 40 Lt. J. H. Doolittle USAS backup pilot.
	Curtiss P-1	20 (3)	2/Lt. Leo H. Dawson USAS	1600		274.07 kmh 273.59 272.78 273.27 273.43 T (169.9 mphT)	3rd	Heat 2. Heat 2 was run as a separate race, much more hotly competed than heat 1. (Dawson won two DSC in World War I.)
50	Curtiss PW.8B	20 (3)	1/Lt. Harmon Norton USMC	1600		272.46 kmh 271.82 262.97 279.70 271.66 T (168.8 mphT)	4th	Heat 2. Norton's aeroplane had been the John L. Mitchell Trophy winner earlier in the day, flown by 1/Lt. T. K. Matthews. Plane loaned to Navy for race. Race numbers assigned to Mitchell contestants were 46–55; PW.8s in heat 2 were all Mitchell competitors and retained their Mitchell race numbers.
	Curtiss PW.8B	20 (3)	Capt. Harvey W. Cook USAS	1600		268.76 kmh 269.24 269.40 270.05 269.40 T (167.4 mphT)	5th	Heat 2. Crash the previous Wednesday which gashed his forehead almost rendered Cook *hors d'combat*. Race postponement allowed him to recover. He was 7-victory ace with Rickenbacker's 94th Aero Sqd., had won two D.S.C.
	Curtiss PW.8B	20 (3)	Lt. George T. Cuddihy USN	1600		265.86 kmh 266.83 265.54	—	Heat 2. Retired on 4th lap with engine failure. Plane had been loaned to Navy for race.
—	Gloster-Napier II "Bluebird" G-EBJZ	35 (4)	Larry L. Carter	—				This aeroplane was being considered for entry in the Pulitzer. It crashed at Cranwell, Lincs, on its 4th test flight June 11, 1925. Plane demolished, Carter badly injured, later died.

After 1925, no further U.S. military interest in air racing as a means to improve Frontier technology.

CONTEST CLOSED

1922 CURTISS MARINE FLYING TROPHY

SYNOPSIS OF THE COMPETITION

Date	Location	Winner	Aeroplane	Engine	Distance	Time	Speed	Notes
1915	San Diego—San Juan, California. (several laps)	Major Oscar A. Brindley, USA	Martin military tractor hydroaeroplane		443·72 st mi	—	—	(1)
August 25, 1916	Newport News—Fishermans Is., Va.	Victor Carlstrom pass: C. B. Kirkham	Curtiss Twin JN hydroaeroplane A-93	TWO OXX-2 100 hp	661·44 st mi (goal: 700 mi/10 hr)	—	—	
October 26, 1917	Troy, New York—Port Washington, Long Island, New York	Caleb Bragg +1 passenger	Wright-Martin hydroaeroplane	3 (6)	296·92 st mi	—	—	
December 30, 1918	Pensacola, Florida	Lt. Thomas Clifford Rodman USMC	H-16 (carried 11 passengers)	TWO 10(1)	670 st mi	10 hours	—	(2)
1919, 1920, 1921	NO CONTEST	—	—	—	—	—	—	(3)
1923	NO CONTEST	—	—	—	—	—	—	
March 8, 1924	Miami, Florida	Lt. V. F. Grant, USN	Vought VE.7H (number 10)	12 (2)	200 km (8 × 25)	1:04:11·18	186·956 kmh (116·169 mph)	(4)
1925	NO CONTEST	—	—	—	—	—	—	
May 14, 1926	Anacostia, D.C. (off Haines Pt. in the Potomac R.)	Lt. Thomas P. Jeter, USN	Curtiss F6C-1		73·51 st mi	:33:41	130·94 mph	(5)
1927	NO CONTEST	—	—	—	—	—	—	
May 19, 1928	Anacostia, D.C.	Maj. Charles A. Lutz, USMC	Curtiss F6C-3 (twin pontoons)	29	100 st mi (5 × 20)	:38:04·2	157·604 mph	
May 25, 1929	Anacostia, D.C.	Lt. W. G. Tomlinson, USN	Curtiss XF7C-1	29	100 st mi		162·52 mph	
May 31, 1930	Anacostia, D.C.	Capt. Arthur H. Page, USMC	Curtiss F6C-3 A-7147 (twin pontoons)	20	100 st mi		164·08 mph	(6)

NOTES : (1) First award. Originally given for "largest flight made between sunrise and sunset in a seaplane flying between two points."
(2) Navy's first win in the event. The Aero Club of America announced the Trophy would be awarded "permanently".
(3) Plans announced to re-open competition; not carried out.
(4) "Free-for-all" high speed race.
(5) Nine entries. Distance may have been 80 st mi (in which case time and/or speed listed is uncertain).
(6) Last race; Trophy presented personally by Glenn Curtiss in one of his last public appearances before his death on July 23, 1930. Page's win set a Curtiss Marine Trophy speed record; his aeroplane was then modified (monoplane-landplane) for NAR in only three months. He was killed when the plane crashed during the 1930 NAR.

OCTOBER 8, 1922 (Originally scheduled 1400 October 7; postponed due weather.) New Deed of Gift, 1922, for High Speed.

COURSE: 160 STATUTE MILES Detroit River, Michigan.
Triangular course, 20 st mi; 8 laps required. Start and Finish in Detroit River between Memorial Park and Belle Isle.
Course: along Belle Isle south of Peach Isle to a barge moored off Canadian Shore, then across river mouth to Grosse Point waterworks, around Windmill Point, return to start.
On laps 5, 6, and 7 competitors required to land and taxi 1,200 feet through "Water Control" which included hairpin turn.
Each aeroplane had assigned colors. Colored flags displayed at 6 points around course. No scoreboards.

PRIZES: **1st:** Silver Trophy donated by Glenn Curtiss; $1,200. **2nd:** $600. **3rd:** $200.
SPECIAL: $300 for fastest competitor on laps 2, 3, and 4.

Race No.	Aeroplane	Engine	Pilot	Take-off time	Lap times	Lap speeds	Place	Remarks
1	Vought UO-1 A-6546	27 (2)	Capt. Francis P. Mulcahy USMC	—				*Purple* Catapult observation plane. Lcdr. Marc A. "Pete" Mitscher originally assigned. Withdrawn. Damaged wingtip and wingtip pontoon before race. (Span 34'1¾", weight 2608 lbs.)
(2)	Curtiss H-16	TWO 10 (1)	Lt. Rutledge Irvine USN	—				Plane stripped and two high-compression Liberties installed at the Naval Aircraft Factory. (Span 95'1", weight 10,900 lbs.) Withdrawn. Irvine reassigned to number 5.
3	Gallaudet D-4 A-2654	10 (1)	Lt. William Kenneth Patterson USN	1404	:11:00·35 :11:40·40 :11:41·24 :11:44·15 :11:43·96	109·033 mph 102·798 102·675 102·251 102·279	—	*Blue* Second of two D-4s, built by Edson Gallaudet in East Greenwich, R.I. Gear-driven propeller *amidships* behind wing on gear ring. Liberty engine installed at Norfolk especially for race. Retired on 6th lap with propeller fouled by debris thrown up in spray.
4	Curtiss 18-T-1 A-3326	19 (2)	1/Lt. Lawson H. Sanderson USMC	1405	:09:52·95 :09:46·81 :09:35·39 :09:34·16 :09:51·09 :10:19·00 :10:15·70	121·427 mph 122·697 125·133 125·401 121·809 116·317 116·940	—	*Yellow* 4-blade Charavay prop. Aeroplane had been in storage at Naval Aircraft Factory since 1920 Pulitzer. Would have won race but ran out of fuel within sight of finish line on last lap! Received special prize for greatest speed.
5	Curtiss 18-T-1 A-3325	19 (1)	Lt. Rutledge Irvine USN	1400	:14:08·73 :10:31·88 :10:34·49 :10:24·78 :10:38·32	84·833 mph 113·946 113·477 115·241 112·796	—	*Green* Aeroplane had been in storage at NAF since 1920 Pulitzer. Lt. T. B. Lee USN originally assigned. Retired on 6th lap: spectacular crash. On 5th lap left pontoon loosened during rough, cross-wind landing. It came adrift in flight impairing controllability. Irvine crash-landed in coal pile. Aeroplane fitted with pro-totype CD-12 (first Curtiss engine to pass 50-hour endurance test) and 4-blade Charavay propeller.
10	Vought VE-7H 2-seater *A-5971*	12 (2)	Lt. H. A. Elliott USN	1406	:10:56·19 :10:47·13 :10:40·04 :10:47·35 :10:57·42 :11:22·27 :11:28·15 :11:19·83 1:28:18·38T	109·724 mph 111·260 112·493 111·223 109·519 105·530 104·628 105·909 108·712T	**2nd**	*Gray* (VE-7H normally had engine 3 (2) or 3 (7); VE-7SF had 12 (1); VE-9H had 12 (2).) Elliott had flown Spads and SVA's on French and Italian Fronts.
11	Naval Aircraft Factory TS-2 A-6446	27 (1)	Lt. Harold J. Brow USN	1407	:11:17·54 :11:48·26 :11:47·32	106·267 mph 101·658 101·793	—	*Red* Aeroplane designed by J. C. Hunsaker, built at NAF. Standard high-lift wings (USA 27 airfoil). Retired on 4th lap minus all radiator water.

461

Race No.	Aeroplane	Engine	Pilot	Take-off time	Lap times	Lap speeds	Place	Remarks
12	Naval Aircraft Factory TS-1 *A-6248*	28 (1)	Lt. Steven W. Calloway USN	1402	:11:41·42 :11:24·20 :11:25·85 :11:35·97 :11:36·73	102·649 mph 105·232 104·979 103·453 103·340	—	*Brown* Aeroplane designed by J. C. Hunsaker, built by Curtiss. Engine forerunner of Whirlwind series. Standard high-lift wings (USA 27 airfoil). Retired on 6th lap after losing oil pressure.
14	Curtiss HA-2 A-4111	10 (*1*)	Ens. Alford J. "Al" Williams USN	—				*Black* 2-seater "Dunkirk fighter" reconditioned for race (upper wing raised, put on cabane; span 40', weight 3,906 lbs). Withdrawn. Not ready. (Had been in storage at NAS Norfolk.)
15	Naval Aircraft Factory TR-1 A-6303	28 (1)	Lt. A. W. Gorton USN	1403	:10:07·89 :10:08·66 :10:07·94 :10:17·51 :10:42·10 :10:58·50 :11:17·90 :11:32·67 1:25:13·17T	118·442 mph 118·293 118·433 116·597 112·132 109·339 106·210 103·946 112·650T	**1st**	*White* Basic TS type fitted with special Racing wings (modified RAF-15 airfoil).
16	Naval Aircraft Factory TR-3 A-6447	12 (2)	Lt. David Rittenhouse USN	1401	:10:28·00 :10:16·93 :10:21·75	114·650 mph 116·707 115·802	—	*Black and White check* Basic TS type fitted with special Racing wings (modified RAF-15 airfoil). Retired on 4th lap when prop. worked loose. TS/TR aeroplanes used 3 different engines (dash numbers -1, -2, -3) and 2 wing designs (S-standard; R-racing). Represented burgeoning Navy interest in speed seeking methods. This aeroplane went to 1923 Schneider as alternate aeroplane, greatly cleaned up.

1919 SCHNEIDER (CONTEST III)

SYNOPSIS OF THE COMPETITION

Contest	Date	Location	Winner	Aeroplane	Engine	Distance	Time	Speed	Representing
I	April 16, 1913	Monaco	Maurice Prévost	Deperdussin	Gnôme rotary 160 hp	280 km (28 × 10 km)	3:48:22	73·566 kmh (45·711 mph) (45·75 mph often published)	FRANCE
II	April 20, 1914	Monaco	C. Howard Pixton	Sopwith Schneider (Tabloid on pontoons)	Gnôme rotary 100 hp	*280 km (28 × 10 km)	2:00:13·4 *(pilot completed 300 km in 2:09:10·0)	139·739 kmh (86·830 mph) (86·78 mph often published)	ENGLAND
X	Sept. 26, 1927	Venice, Italy	Flt. Lt. Sidney Norman Webster RAF	Supermarine S.5 N-220 (number 4)	35 (6)	350 km (7 × 50 km)	:46:19·73	453·282 kmh (281·656 mph)	ENGLAND
XI	Sept. 7, 1929	Spithead (Calshot) England	Flying Officer H. R. D. Waghorn RAF	Supermarine S.6 N-247 (number 2)	Rolls-Royce R 1900 hp	350 km (7 × 50 km)	:39:42·39	528·880 kmh (328·630 mph)	ENGLAND
XII	Sept. 13, 1931	Spithead (Calshot) England	Flt. Lt. John N. Boothman RAF	Supermarine S.6B S-1595 (number 1)	Rolls-Royce R 2300 hp	350 km (7 × 50 km)	:38:22·18	547·307 kmh (340·080 mph) (fly-over)	ENGLAND

1915–1918 NO CONTEST

SEPTEMBER 10, 1919

COURSE: 200 NAUTICAL MILES
Bournemouth, England. (20nm triangle to be flown 10 times.) Race number assignment: 1 thru 6: ENGLAND/FRANCE alternate; 7 and after: all others.

PRIZE:
Trophy plus £1000 (or 25,000 francs). *Not awarded.*

Race No.	Aeroplane	Engine	Pilot	Take-off time	Lap times	Lap speeds	Place	Remarks
1	Fairey III-A G-EALQ (England)	35 (1)	Lt.Col. Vincent Nicholl, D.S.O., D.S.C.	1650			—	Retired on 1st lap because of fog. This aeroplane had been delivered in April 1917 to the RNAS as a Fairey model N.10. In 1919 it carried newspapers from Blackfriars to Thanet. Wingspan reduced from 46′ to 28′ for race (also became single-bay); designed by F. Duncanson.
2	Nieuport 29 (France)	4 (2)	Jean Casale	—				Badly damaged Sept. 7 upon striking buoy in Medina River estuary. Rebuilt by S. E. Saunders in 48 hours. Damaged again on Bournemouth beach; did not start. Short span wings; two long pontoons fitted, *en catamaran*.
(3)	Sopwith 107 Schneider G-EAKI (England)	42 (1)	Harry G. Hawker, O.B.E., A.F.C.	1700			—	Retired on 1st lap because of fog. No evidence that race number was affixed. Subsequently, Jupiter engine replaced by Dragonfly, and this aeroplane competed in 1920 Aerial Derby named Rainbow.
(4)	Nieuport 29 (France)	4 (2)	Henri Malard	—				Did not arrive in England. Forced down in English Channel on its way over; pilot not rescued for 24 hours! Long span wings; two short pontoons plus *flotteur de queue*
5	Supermarine Sea-Lion I G-EALP (England)	35 (1)	Sqd.Ldr. Basil D. Hobbs, D.S.O., D.F.C.	1655			—	Retired after 1st lap; landed on 1st lap at Swanage Bay in order to locate fogbound mark boat. On take-off he struck submerged object which rendered hull unseaworthy.

Race No.	Aeroplane	Engine	Pilot	Take-off time	Lap times	Lap speeds	Place	Remarks
6	Spad-Herbemont S.20 (France)	4 (2)	Sadi Lecointe	—				Damaged (leaks in pontoons). Did not start. Originally fitted with Forlanini pontoons which were discarded in favor of stepped pontoons. Top wing clipped prior to race by approximately 0·75 m per side.
7	SIAI (*Società Idrovolanti Alta Italia*)-Savoia S.13 *bis* (Italy)	44 (1)	*Sgt.* Guido Jannello	1705	*1:39T*	—	**Finish not credited**	Completed eleven improper laps. Not observed by official Swanage Mark Boat. (Only contestant who did not retire.) 4-blade prop. Total time of 1:47:11 has also been published; all times irrelevant, since Jannello did not fly prescribed course.
—	Avro 539/1 Schneider G-EALG (England—reserve)	36	Capt. H. A. Hamersley, M.C.	—				Reserve. (Eliminated from final team of 3 on Sept. 8, 1919.)
—	Rumored tentative Spanish entry	—	—	—				Withdrawn.
—	Rumored tentative Belgian entry	—	—	—				Withdrawn.

CONTEST ANNULLED

1920 SCHNEIDER (CONTEST IV)

SEPTEMBER 21, 1920
Competition originally scheduled for August 28, 29; postponed to September 18–21; race scheduled for September 20, postponed one day due to weather.

COURSE: 371.17KM
Venice, Italy. (*Intention* was to have a triangle of 20 nautical miles distance, to be flown 10 times for 200 nm total. 200 nm is 370·40 km. Total perimeter of triangle as flown *most probably* 37·117 km, but doubt exists. 37·556 km has also been published.)
Turning points: tethered balloons 50 m above surface.
Race number assignment unknown.

MANDATORY BALLAST OF 300 KILOGRAMS "COMMERCIAL WEIGHT" REQUIRED OF ALL ENTRANTS

PRIZES:
Trophy (value 25,000 francs). Royal Aero Club established prizes of £250, £150 and £100 for successful British competitors. These were not awarded. "Additional prizes of 50,000 francs" also mentioned. Unconfirmed.
The third of three prizes of 25,000 francs each (ART. 1, general regulations) would have been awarded this year.

Race No.	Aeroplane	Engine	Pilot	Take-off time	Lap times	Lap speeds	Place	Remarks
7	SIAI-Savoia S.12*bis* s/n 3011 (Italy)	46 (3)	*Comandante* Luigi Bologna		2:10:35T	170·544 kmhT (105·971 mphT)	1st	Speed based on course distance of 371·17 km and time as indicated. (If course distance was 375·56 km—possible but unlikely although this figure has been published—the speed was 172·561 kmh (107·224 mph), a speed published in accounts independent of the 375·56 km course length. In addition, the speed 172·484 kmh has been published, but this has incorrect relationship to time or either course length. Some doubt has been expressed as to the accuracy of the time indicated, yet it is most likely closest to the correct value. However there has been published unsubstantiated information which translates to a time of 2:26:17·2 which, if correct, yields only 152·237 kmh over a course distance of 371·17 km, an unlikely, too low speed.) Bologna was the only competitor who undertook the required navigability trials on *Sept. 19.* Speed contest set for *Sept. 20.* Bologna covered 5 laps in 1:15:24 but retired on lap 6 in squalls; he reflew entire distance on *Sept. 21.* Aeroplane fitted with 4-blade prop; had "Savoia" painted on side in large script letters. (*Sept. 18* has also been published as date of navigability trials.)
8	Societá Aeronautica Nieuport-Macchi (SANM) M.19 s/n 3098 (Italy)	47	Arturo Zanetti	—				Withdrawn. Only one built especially to meet the 300 kg ballast requirement. On its first flight in August 1920 it proved unstable. Modifications not completed before race. (Two M.19s planned; only one built.) (4-blade tractor propeller.)
9M	SANM (Macchi) M.12 s/n 23903 (Italy)	46 (1)	H. Giovanni De Briganti	—				Withdrawn. (Warren truss wings; twin boom; very wide hull. 2-blade pusher propeller.)
9S	SIAI-Savoia S.19 s/n 2002 (Italy)	46 (3)	Guido Jannello	—				Withdrawn. (4-blade tractor propeller.)
	SANM (Macchi) M.17 (Italy)	44 (1)	Arturo Zanetti	—				Withdrawn. (Substituted for M.19 when M.19 not ready.) M.17 design was derived from Macchi M.7; the first was destroyed at 1920 Monaco seaplane Rallye upon landing just after having won *Grand Prix* at 247 kmh; Zanetti slightly injured. Second M.17 not ready. The 300 kg ballast rule would have rendered M.17 performance poor.

Race No.	Aeroplane	Engine	Pilot	Take-off time	Lap times	Lap speeds	Place	Remarks
	Spad-Herbemont S.20 (France)	4 (2)	Jean Casale	—				Withdrawn "at the last minute."
	Nieuport 29 (France)	4 (2)	—	—				Withdrawn "at the last minute." No French aeroplanes were dispatched to Venice; French were preoccupied with Gordon Bennett race which they hosted—and won—one week later.
	Borel flying boat (France)	—	—	—				Withdrawn. Not ready.
	British flying boat (England)	—	—	—				Withdrawn. Not ready. No details.
	Rumored tentative Swiss entry. (Switzerland)	—	—	—				Existence unconfirmed and doubtful.

1921 SCHNEIDER (CONTEST V)

AUGUST 7, 1921
Navigability trials conducted August 6 at 1430; speed race held August 7 at 1000. Pre-race Italian eliminations conducted August 3 over an intended course of 150 km. (6 laps of Schneider course; therefore actual elimination distance 147·79 km; see below.)

COURSE: 212.8 NAUTICAL MILES
Venice, Italy. Triangular circuit of 13.30 nm to be covered 16 times. (Circuit length 24·632 kilometers, total distance 394·106 kilometers.)* Race number assignment made by Italian team leader, Collalti; numbers 13 and 17 not used.
Each competitor marked with colored distinguishing insignia, in which its race number was painted.
* Original regulations for 1921, approved by FAI, specified a course length of 200 nautical miles. Subsequent *Italian Intention* was to have a course length of 400 km, 16 laps of 25 km each. Their survey fell slightly short.

PRIZES:
1st: Trophy (value *25,000 francs*) *plus 10,000 lire*; **2nd**: half of all entrance fees *plus 3000 lire*;

3rd: one-third of all entrance fees *plus 1500 lire*; **4th**: remainder of all entrance fees, as per ART. 19, general regulations.

(Only first prize awarded; moreover winner received total amount of entrance fees (ART. 19).)

Race No.	Aeroplane	Engine	Pilot	Take-off time	Lap times	Lap speeds	Place	Remarks
1	Macchi M.7 *bis* (Italy)	44 (1)	H. Giovanni De Briganti	*1007*	See supplementary table *2:04:40·0T*	See supplementary table *189·677 kmhT* *(117·859 mphT)*	**1st**	RED RECTANGLE 3rd in pre-race Italian eliminations (:45:56·6; 193·007 kmh) For many years doubt has existed over De Briganti's time. Most published reports indicate a time of 2:04:29 and this has been widely accepted. Original documents recently brought to light reveal the time indicated here. The sum of the lap times yields the total time indicated; yet the Italians also published 2:04:39·8 (a discrepancy of $\frac{1}{5}$ second). It is impossible to now determine where any error in time measurement or addition occurred. This time no doubt is the basis for reports of 2:04:39, and perhaps through mis-copying, 2:04:29. (There has also been published a list of *clock times*; that is, that De Briganti completed lap 5 at 10:38:32·0 A.M., lap 10 at 11:17:27·4 A.M., lap 15 at 12:05:19·2 P.M., and lap 16 at 12:11:52·4 P.M. No take off time is given, and in any event these times yield incorrect (and highly unlikely) relationship to the lap times and M.7 performance.) If indeed his total time was *2:04:39·8*, the speed was *189·682 kmh (117·862 mph)*. The speed 192·518 kmh (119·625 mph) was published by the Italians, and has been to some extent accepted, but it is based on De Briganti having covered the *full intended* 400 km in 2:04:39·8, which he did not do.
2	Macchi M.18 (Italy)	44 (1)	Guzelloni	—				GREEN TRIANGLE Withdrawn. Did not compete in pre-race Italian eliminations.
3	Macchi M.18 I-AABU (Italy)	44 (1)	Alessandro Passaleva	—				YELLOW CIRCLE Withdrawn. Did not compete in pre-race Italian eliminations. Passaleva flew M.18 number 2 (see above) in *Gran Premio Venezia* on August 9. (Registry indicated may have belonged to number 2.)

Race No.	Aeroplane	Engine	Pilot	Take-off time	Lap times	Lap speeds	Place	Remarks
4	Macchi M. 19 s/n 3098 (Italy)	47	Arturo Zanetti	1011 or 1020	See supplementary table	See supplementary table		RED DIAMOND 1st in pre-race Italian eliminations (:41:43·6, 212·512 kmh). Although the 300 kg ballast requirement was dropped in 1921, the M.19 was nevertheless nominated for the race. It would have won the race if able to complete, but retired on 12th lap with failed crankshaft. Aeroplane caught fire. No serious injuries. Mechanic Pedetti aboard. (Had "large wing" and 4-blade propeller.)
5	Nieuport-Delage 29 (France)	4 (2)	Sadi Lecointe	—				WHITE RECTANGLE with BLUE CROSS During navigability trials August 6, this aeroplane buckled its float chassis upon "taking water" (on landing). Unable to race. Probably had same configuration as Casale's 1919 Nieuport although this is unconfirmed.
6	Savoia S.13 (Italy)	44 (1)	*Comandante* Giartosio	—				YELLOW STAR 9th in pre-race Italian eliminations (:53:19·2).
7	Savoia S.13 (Italy)	44 (1)	*Comandante* Luigi Bologna	—				RED CIRCLE 5th in pre-race Italian eliminations (:49:16·8).
8	Savoia S.13 (Italy)	44 (1)	*Comandante* Arcidiacono	—				GREEN RECTANGLE 6th in pre-race Italian eliminations (:50:26·8).
9	Savoia S.13 (Italy)	44 (1)	*Maresciallo* Minciotti	—				RED TRIANGLE 4th in pre-race Italian eliminations (:48:11·2).
10	Savoia S.13 (Italy)	44 (1)	*Maresciallo* Riccobello	—				GREEN DIAMOND 7th in pre-race Italian eliminations (:50:53·8).
11	Savoia S.13 (Italy)	44 (1)	*Maresciallo* Conforti	—				RED STAR 8th in pre-race Italian eliminations (:51:10·8).
12	Macchi M.7 (Italy)	44 (1)	*Maresciallo* Falaschi	—				GREEN STAR Withdrawn. Crashed prior to pre-race Italian eliminations.
14	Macchi M.7 (Italy)	44 (1)	*Maresciallo* Piero Corgnolino	1024	See supplementary table	See supplementary table	—	YELLOW RECTANGLE 2nd in pre-race Italian eliminations (:45:29·2, 194·945 kmh). Retired on last lap, fuel exhausted within 2 km of finish line; otherwise would have won.
15	Macchi M.7 (Italy)	44 (1)	*De Sie* or *Desio*	—				YELLOW TRIANGLE Withdrawn; did not compete in pre-race Italian eliminations.
16	Macchi M.7 (Italy)	44 (1)	Buonsembiante	—				GREEN CIRCLE Withdrawn; did not compete in pre-race Italian eliminations.
18	Savoia S.21 (Italy)	46 (1)	Guido Jannello	—				WHITE RECTANGLE with 4 VERTICAL RED BANDS Withdrawn. Did not compete in pre-race Italian eliminations. Jannello became ill prior to race and could not compete. S.21 was replaced by one of the old M.7s. (S.21 had very short top wing; was capable of 160 mph.) (Guarnieri was backup pilot. Engine trouble prevented participation.)

Race No.	Aeroplane	Engine	Pilot	Take-off time	Lap times	Lap speeds	Place	Remarks
19	Savoia S.22 (Italy)	TWO 44 (2)	Umberto Maddalena	—				WHITE RECTANGLE with 4 VERTICAL GREEN BANDS Withdrawn. Did not compete in pre-race Italian eliminations. Crashed before race during test flight, aeroplane demolished. Maddalena was entered in the Monaco seaplane Rallye April 1921 as pilot of this aeroplane. (Backup pilot Del Maschio.)
—	Pegna P.c.1 (Italy)							Design proposal only. Not completed. Monoplane with pivoted prop axis. (P.c.: *Pegna corsa*.)
—	Breguet flying boat (France)							Rumored French entry. Did not reach Venice.

SUPPLEMENTARY TABLE

Lap	1 – De Briganti		4 – Zanetti		14 – Corgnolino	
	Lap times	Lap speeds	Lap times	Lap speeds	Lap times	Lap speeds
1	:07:52.4	187.709 kmh	:07:06.4	207.959 kmh	:07:36.6	194.204 kmh
2	:07:48.4	189.312	:07:05.8	208.252	:07:36.4	194.290
3	:07:52.4	187.709	:07:03.8	209.235	:07:38.6	193.358
4	:07:46.2	190.205	:07:02.0	210.127	:07:40.4	192.602
5	:07:45.2	190.614	:07:02.0	210.127	:07:40.0	192.769
6	:07:46.0	190.287	:07:05.6	208.350	:07:40.4	192.602
7	:07:47.0	189.880	:07:10.4	206.026	:07:43.8	191.190
8	:07:53.0	187.471	:07:09.6	206.410	:07:41.4	192.184
9	:07:44.4	190.943	:07:04.8	208.742	:07:46.8	189.961
10	:07:46.4	190.124	:07:00.8	210.727	:07:47.0	189.880
11	:07:46.2	190.205	:07:02.0	210.127	:07:48.4	189.312
12	:07:45.2	190.614	RETIRED		:07:48.2	189.393
13	:07:46.2	190.205			:07:44.4	190.943
14	:07:47.8	189.555			:07:45.6	190.451
15	:07:45.4	190.532			:07:46.4	190.124
16	:07:47.8	189.555			RETIRED	

1922 SCHNEIDER (CONTEST VI)

AUGUST 12, 1922 (Competition dates advanced two weeks from August 24–26 to August 10–12.)

COURSE: 200.2 NAUTICAL MILES Naples Italy.
Triangle 15·4 nm (28·5208 km) in length to be flown 13 times. (Total distance 370·7704 km.) Race numbers I through 28 issued for several contests; 7–14 reserved for Schneider. Numbers 13 and 17 not used, just as in 1921.

PRIZES: 1st: Trophy plus half of all entry fees *plus 5000 lire*; 2nd: one-third of all entry fees; 3rd: remainder of entry fees (as per ART. 19, general regulations).

Race No.	Aeroplane	Engine	Pilot	Take-off time	Lap times	Lap speeds	Place	Remarks
7	Savoia-MVT (Marchetti-Vickers-Terni) S.50 s/n 2031 (Italy)	45 (3)	Guarnieri	—				Qualified for Italian first team, but crashed before race. Pilot killed. Engine may have produced up to 310 hp. Official race program indicates number 7 assigned. It has been suggested elsewhere but unconfirmed that the aeroplane bore number 8 which, after its crash, passed to the S.51. Serial listed was applied to landplane, probably retained when converted to seaplane.
8	Savoia S.51 I-BAIU (Italy)	4 (4)	Alessandro Passaleva	1617	See supplementary table 1:36:54·2T	See supplementary table 229·571 kmhT (142·649 mphT)	2nd	Fastest entry. *Capsized* during 6-hour navigability test. Had to be righted but England did not protest! During race its prop split from vibration. Four months later it set world seaplane speed record (over 280 kmh). (Race performance total times of 1:36:22 and 1:36:54·6 have been published in error.)
9	Macchi M.17 *bis* I-BAHG (Italy)	44 (1)	Arturo Zanetti	1611	See supplementary table 1:44:07·4T	See supplementary table 213·653 kmhT (132·757 mphT)	3rd	M.17 was entered in the 1920 Schneider but it could not take part that year due to 300 kg ballast requirement. Two M.17s built. One destroyed at Monaco in 1920. The second was modified in 1922 for the 1922 Schneider. (Race performance total times of 1:38:45 and 1:44:07 have been published in error.)
10	Macchi M.7 *bis* I-BAFV s/n 13206 (Italy)	44 (1)	Piero Corgnolino	1607	See supplementary table 1:51:27·0T	See supplementary table 199·607 kmhT (124·030 mphT)	4th	(Speeds of 123·7 mph and 123·9 mph have been published in error.)
—	Pegna P.c.2 (later Piaggio 2) MM 26 or 27 (Italy)	4 (4)	—	—				Pegna-Bonmartini-Cerroni founded May 1922 to build Pegna's high speed race designs; racer not completed by race time. Not issued race number.
11	CAMS 36 F-ESFB (France)	4 (2)	*Lieut. de Vaisseau de Corv.-Teste*	—				Both CAMS flying boats (numbers 11 and 12) were tractor types designed by R. Conflenti and built under license from Savoia. Owing to Italian rail strike, they were unable to reach Naples in time to compete.
12	CAMS 36 F-ESFA (France)	4 (2)	*Vroman*	—				Official race program lists Poirè as pilot. Apparently Vroman was substituted before race time. Pilot assignment irrelevant since aeroplanes unable to compete. (There is unsubstantiated evidence that CAMS performance was so poor they were "unable to leave water;" this is highly doubtful.)

Race No.	Aeroplane	Engine	Pilot	Take-off time	Lap times	Lap speeds	Place	Remarks
14	Supermarine Sea Lion II G-EBAH (England)	35 (2)	Henri C. Biard	1606	See supplementary table 1:34:51·6T	See supplementary table 234·516 kmhT (145·721 mphT)	**1st**	Modified from 1-seat amphibian *Sea King II*. *SS Philomel*, enroute Naples, diverted to Southampton to fetch racer—otherwise it would not have arrived in time! Could hit 160 mph on straightaway. Race performance set 100 km, 200 km closed-course seaplane speed records as well as first seaplane distance and duration records. Aeroplane had 4-blade propeller. (Note: sum of lap times published in Italian records yields 1:34:50·8, $\frac{4}{5}$ second less than Biard's officially accepted total time. This suggests one or more lap times are in error by an aggregate $\frac{4}{5}$ second; it is now impossible to pinpoint such errors. Other total times published elsewhere in error are 1:34:54·6 and 1:34:57·6.)

SUPPLEMENTARY TABLE

Lap	**14 – Biard** Lap times	Lap speeds	**8 – Passaleva** Lap times	Lap speeds	**9 – Zanetti** Lap times	Lap speeds	**10 – Corgnolino** Lap times	Lap speeds
1	:07:10·0	238·779 kmh	:07:31·8	227·257 kmh	:08:02·6	212·754 kmh	:08:39·2	197·756 kmh
2	:07:10·4 .	238·557	:07:34·0	226·156	:08:04·8	211·788	:08:38·0	198·214
3	:07:10·4	238·557	:07:32·0	227·157	:08:03·4	212·401	:08:36·6	198·751
4	:07:10·6	238·446	:07:18·8	233·990	:08:01·8	213·107	:08:34·4	199·601
5	:07:11·6	237·894	:07:27·6	229·390	:08:00·4	213·728	:08:31·6	200·694
6	:07:12·6	237·344	:07:31·0	227·660	:08:02·0	213·018	:08:34·2	199·679
7	:07:12·2	237·563	:07:26·6	229·903	:07:59·8	213·995	:08:31·8	200·615
8	:07:19·4	233·671	:07:30·2	228·065	:07:59·0	214·353	:08:29·4	201·560
9	:07:26·6	229·903	:07:27·8	229·287	:07:57·2	215·161	:08:34·0	199·757
10	:07:22·4	232·086	:07:29·0	228·675	:07:58·2	214·711	:08:31·0	200·929
11	:07:29·4	228·471	:07:27·2	229·595	:07:57·4	215·071	:08:34·8	199·446
12	:07:26·0 / :07:26·8*	230·213 / *229·801*	:07:21·4	232·612	:07:59·2	214·263	:08:36·2	198·905
13	:07:29·2	228·573	:07:16·8	235·062	:08:01·6	213·195	:08:35·8	199·059
T	1:34:51·6	234·516 kmh	1:36:54·2	229·571 kmh	1:44:07·4	213·653 kmh	1:51:27·0	199·607 kmh

* Upper figure listed in Italian source as lap time for lap 12; however there is the possibility this was misprinted. It is possible that lower figure is correct; if so, the total (as indicated) agrees with officially accepted total time.

1923 SCHNEIDER *(CONTEST VII)*

SEPTEMBER 28, 1923 (Competition ran September 27, 28.)
COURSE: 186 NAUTICAL MILES (344.472 KM) Cowes, Isle of Wight, England.
Triangle 37·20 nm (68·8944 km) to be covered 5 times.
Race numbers assigned: 1, 2: Italy; next three (3, 4, 5): USA; next three (6, 7, 8): England; next three (9, 10, 11); France. Each country's entries started together.
Interval between start of each country: 15 minutes. Competitors *must not* leave water until past start line.

PRIZE: Trophy.

Race No.	Aeroplane	Engine	Pilot	Take-off time	Lap times	Lap speeds	Place	Remarks
(1)	Macchi flying boat (Italy)	—	—	—				Withdrawn one week prior to race owing to both financial and political difficulties in Italy. The M.17 and M.19 designs were considered unsuitable as a basis for significant improvement. Coupled with weak position otherwise, Macchi was forced to withdraw. The S.51—which should have won in 1922 and which held current world seaplane speed record—was not sent due to lack of suitable updated engine.
(2)	Savoia S.51 (Italy)	—	—	—				
3	Curtiss CR-3 A-6080 (USA)	20 (3)	Lt. Rutledge Irvine USN	1101	:15:27·6 :14:43·0 :14:42·0 :14:43·0 :14:29·6 1:14:05·2T	267·378 kmh 280·883 281·202 280·883 285·211 278·975T (173·347 mphT)	2nd	Slow first laps due to take-off in direction opposite to course, causing lost time in turning to join proper course. Speeds published widely (e.g. 173·46 mph, etc.), are close but not exact due to excessive rounding-off during calculations.
4	Curtiss CR-3 A-6081 (USA)	20 (3)	Lt. David Rittenhouse USN	1101+	:15:06·4 :14:22·2 :14:24·8 :14:22·2 :14:11·0 1:12:26·6T	273·632 kmh 287·659 286·794 287·659 291·445 285·303T (177·279 mphT)	1st	No 6th lap flown by Rittenhouse as is sometimes reported. (Speed of 177·38 mph published; inexact due to excessive rounding off during calculations.)
5	Navy-Wright NW-2 A-6544 (USA)	14	Lt. A. W. Gorton USN	—				Crashed on trial flight Sept. 24, 1923 between Selsey Bill and Southsea Pier when engine blew up.
5	Naval Aircraft Factory TR-3A A-6447 (USA reserve)	12 (4)	Lt. Frank W. "Spig" Wead USN	—				This aeroplane a 1922 Curtiss Marine Trophy participant; vastly cleaned up for Schneider. Race number 5 affixed *after* crash of NW-2 (see above). Starting apparatus sheared on backfire when attempting to start engine for race. Did not race.
6	Blackburn Pellet G-EBHF (England)	35 (3)	Lcdr. Reginald W. Kenworthy	—				Crashed on take-off for navigability trials September 27, 1923. Aeroplane designed by F. A. Bumpus; used same engine that powered Gloster I racer to 1923 Aerial Derby victory.
7	Supermarine Sea Lion III G-EBAH (England)	35 (3)	Capt. Henri C. Biard	1115	:17:11·2 :16:13·8 :16:12·2 :16:09·8 :15:59·0 1:21:46·0T	240·516 kmh 254·693 255·112 255·743 258·623 252·772T (157·065 mphT)	3rd	Controversy over Biard's start. Initially he was disqualified for not crossing start line on water as required—this decision was reversed during race! This aeroplane was 1922 Schneider winner updated (had reduced wing span). Speed of 157·17 mph often published; inexact due to excessive rounding off during calculations.
(8)	Sopwith 107 Hawker G-EAKI (England)	42 (4)	Flt.Lt. Walter Longton	—				Turned over on forced landing during pre-race trials in early September while being flown as a landplane. Aeroplane demolished.

Race No.	Aeroplane	Engine	Pilot	Take-off time	Lap times	Lap speeds	Place	Remarks
9	CAMS 38 F-ESFD *(Chantiers Aéro-Maritimes de la Seine)* (France)	4 (3)	*Lt. de Vaisseau* Maurice Hurel	1130	:19:42·6	209·724 kmh	—	Retired on 2nd lap at Selsey Bill. While taxiing to starting line, Hurel shipped a sea damaging stabilizer and breaching longeron. Unaware of damage he took off but on 2nd lap his propeller hub worked loose and engine crankshaft seized. "Fair weather" ship with pusher prop, cockpit forward.
10	CAMS 36 *bis* F-ESFC (France)	4 (3)	*Lt. de Vaisseau* Georges E.M.C. Pelletier d'Oisy	—				Collided with moored observation yacht while taxiing to course. "Fair weather" ship with tractor prop, cockpit aft.
11	SICC-Latham No. 1 (L-1) F-ESEJ *(Société Industrielle de Caudebec-en-Caux)* (France)	TWO 7 (2)	Alphonse Duhamel	—				One of its tandem engines failed due to magneto trouble rendering it unable to start in speed race (it completed navigability trials). "Foul weather" ship.
—	SICC-Latham No. 2 (L-1) F-*ESEK* (France—reserve)	TWO 7 (2)	*Lt. de Vaisseau* Benoist	—				After flying from France to England on September 25, 1923, in gales it was damaged by handlers at Littlehampton. "Foul weather" ship. (Registration unconfirmed.)
—	Blanchard-Blériot C.1 monoplane F-ESEH *(Société Aeronautique Blanchard)* (France—reserve)	42 (7)	Capt. de Corv.-Teste	—				Reserve entry. Not dispatched to England. *Two* were entered in March 1923. The first completed achieved 220 kmh in tests; engine of second boosted to *550 hp* giving *280 kmh* but this 2nd aeroplane was damaged in a collision before it could be readied and sent to race.
—	Rumored Belgian entry	—	—	—				No details; unconfirmed.

1924 SCHNEIDER (NO CONTEST)

OCTOBER 27, 1924 (Schneider race *CANCELED*; substitute competitions held among US Navy competitors.)

COURSE: 350 KM Bay Shore Park (Baltimore) Maryland.
Triangle 50 km in length, to be flown 7 times.
Race number assignment: 1, 2: England; next three (3, 4, 5): Italy; next three (6, 7, 8): USA.

PRIZE: None awarded.

Race No.	Aeroplane	Engine	Pilot	Take-off time	Lap times	Lap speeds	Place	Remarks
(1)	Gloster-Napier II J.7504 (England)	35 (4)	Hubert S. Broad	—				Sank on its first test flight at Felixstowe Sept. 19, 1924. (Broad loaned by de Havilland.) (Backup pilot: Sqd.Ldr. Rea.) (Number J.7519 has also been published; doubtful.)
(2)	Supermarine Sea Urchin (England)	34 (3)	Henri C. Biard	—				Engine mounted in hull with exotic geared drive to propeller. Not completed. This was R. J. Mitchell's last racing flying boat design. (He embarked on float-equipped monoplanes.)
(3)	Pegna P.c.2 (Piaggio P.4) *MM 32 or 33* (Italy)	21	—	—				Withdrawn. Not completed. Low wing twin-float monoplane. (Allottment of race numbers uncertain.)
—	Pegna P.c.3 (Piaggio P.4) (Italy)	20 (3)	—	—				Low-wing twin-float monoplane. Very advanced design. Not completed "for administrative reasons" although construction almost finished. Not known whether registered as race entry. (Piaggio P.4 designation applied to both P.c.2 and P.c.3; P.c.: *Pegna corsa*.)
(4)	Macchi flying boat (Italy)	21	—	—				Monoplane flying boat. Withdrawn. Not ready. (Design was basis for 1925 M.33.)
(5)	C.R.D.A. *DGC.3* (Italy)	21	Frederico Guazzetti	—				Construction of racer *designed by* General Guidoni, then Director of Aircraft Manufacturing, may have been contracted to C.R.D.A. (*Cantieri Riuniti Dell' Adriatico*) in 1924. Designated DGC.3 (or *DGA.3*) it is reported to have had Curtiss tractor engine. It apparently sank twice during trials, *never flew*. (Unconfirmed.)
—	*Cantieri Navali Monfalcone* racer (Italy)	21	—	—				Biplane flying boat designed by R. Conflenti of Savoia. To be built at naval factory near Trieste. Withdrawn. Not ready.
—	Dornier (of Italy) S.4 (Italy)	21	—	—				Twin-float monoplane of advanced design. Not built owing to lack of grant from Italian government. Wind tunnel model completed. (Italy proposed a team of 3 plus 1 reserve; specific assignments uncertain.)
6	Curtiss R2C-2 A-6692 (USA)	21	Lt. David Rittenhouse USN	—				After race canceled, this aeroplane was held back for 1925. Its only flights in 1924 were contractor trials. It had won 1923 Pulitzer; converted to seaplane and did 227·5 mph unofficially on September 27, 1924 (Long Island Sound).
7	Wright F2W-2 A-6744 (USA)	15 (1)	Lt. A. W. Gorton USN	—				Crashed in Delaware River near Philadelphia, Pa., on test flight from NAF. October 11, 1924. Aeroplane badly damaged. Pilot unhurt.

Race No.	Aeroplane	Engine	Pilot	Take-off time	Lap times	Lap speeds	Place	Remarks
8	Curtiss CR-3 A-6081 (USA)	21	Lt. George T. Cuddihy USN	—			—	On October 25 Cuddihy in this aeroplane set world maximum seaplane speed record over 3 km: 302·7648 kmh. It also competed with its sister CR-3 over proposed Schneider course.
9	Curtiss CR-3 A-6080 (USA)	21	Lt. Ralph A. Ofstie USN	—		283·647 kmh 285·482 287·494 290·922 246·182 243·816 244·733 242·690 242·931 241·981	—	Over proposed Schneider course Ofstie in this aeroplane set seaplane closed-course speed records. Kept his speed high for first 200 km, then throttled back drastically to complete full 500 km. Times published (see Appendix 1) are close but do not yield exact speeds credited. ⌐100 km: 284·810 kmh, 176·972 mph 200 km: 286·853 kmh, 178·242 mph (although 286·866 kmh, 178·250 mph, was officially homologated for both 100 and 200 km); 350 km [not FAI]: 268·895 kmh, 167·083 mph ⌐500 km: 259·327 kmh, 161·138 mph. Backup pilots for USN team: Lt. Lester D. Hundt Boatswain Earl E. Reber Team Leader: Lt. Frank W. Wead
—	CAMS 45 (France)	5 (2)	—	—				Proposed French entry. Withdrawn in May 1924. Said to be "last racing seaplane design of Maurice Hurel"; no details.

No Competition Forthcoming; hence America made a sporting gesture: **CONTEST POSTPONED**

1925 SCHNEIDER (CONTEST VIII)

OCTOBER 26, 1925 (Originally scheduled for October 24; postponed due weather.)

COURSE: 350 KM Bay Shore Park (Baltimore) Maryland.
Triangle 50 km in length to be flown 7 times. { Race number assignment: 1–3 USA
{ (made by NAA) 4–5 England
6–7 Italy

PRIZE: Trophy.

Race No.	Aeroplane	Engine	Pilot	Take-off time	Lap times	Lap speeds	Place	Remarks
1	Curtiss R3C-2 A-6978 (USA)	22	Lt. Ralph A. Ofstie USN	1450+	:08:57·83 :08:30·14 :08:30·76 :08:21·48 :08:21·40	334·678 kmh 352·844 352·416 358·938 358·995	—	This aeroplane did not race in 1925 Pulitzer, but was put on floats from the start. It was the first R3C, the "dogship" and had the "freak" oil-less engine which produced 619 hp on bench test. Retired on 6th lap due to broken magneto shaft; landed 5 miles west of Huntingfield Point.
2	Curtiss R3C-2 A-6979 (USA)	22	Lt. George T. Cuddihy USN	1445+	:08:48·60 :08:25·80 :08:23·32 :08:21·37 :08:22·52 :08:22·49	340·522 kmh 355·872 357·625 359·016 358·195 358·216	—	Retired on 7th lap; engine overheated due to loss of oil; caught fire. Cuddihy had to wield hand extinguisher and land at once.
3	Curtiss R3C-2 (later A-7054 after Navy acquisition) (USA)	22	1/Lt. James H. Doolittle USAS	1438	:08:21·20 :07:58·85 :07:57·31 :07:57·04 :07:59·16 :07:56·94 :07:55·87T :56:06·37T	359·138 kmh 375·901 377·113 377·327 375·657 377·406 378·255 374·290T (232·573 mphT)	1st	This aeroplane won 1925 Pulitzer 12 days before. On October 27, 1925, Doolittle flew it to a new world seaplane speed record (245·713 mph). It was the last biplane to win the Schneider Trophy. During race it set seaplane closed-course world speed records: 100 km (laps 6 and 7) (234·772 mph) 200 km (laps 4, 5, 6, and 7) (234·355 mph) In U.S., the Trophy passed from Navy to Army!
4	Supermarine S.4 N-197 G-EBLP (England)	35 (5)	Henri C. Biard	—				This plane had posted world seaplane speed record (226·752 mph) at Southampton on Sept. 13, 1925, during flight tests. It crashed October 23, 1925 in pre-race trials at Baltimore. Though sometimes attributed to high speed stall, wing-aileron flutter was almost certainly a contributing factor. (Aeroplane did not carry either serial or registration marks.)
4	Gloster III-A N-194 (England—reserve)	35 (5)	H. J. L. "Bert" Hinkler	—				Inasmuch as only two English entries were official, race number 4 was affixed to this reserve Gloster *after* S.4 crash. Hinkler was Avro test pilot on loan to race team. On morning of October 26, during last-minute navigability trials, this aeroplane burst a float landing in a 3-foot chop.
5	Gloster III-A N-195 G-EBLJ (England)	35 (5)	Hubert S. Broad	1441	:09:35·71 :09:23·07 :09:14·97 :09:15·31 :09:19·86 :09:20·23 :09:21·80 1:05:30·95T	312·657 kmh 319·676 324·342 324·143 321·509 321·297 320·399 320·533T (199·170 mphT)	2nd	English team limited to 2 entries because of an oversight committed by RAeC in entry formalities. (Gloster III-A engines identical to S.4 engine.) Broad was de Havilland test pilot on loan to race team. Laps 3, 4 constituted English seaplane closed-course 100 km record. Air Ministry contract numbers N-194 and N-195 were not carried by aeroplanes at Baltimore. Often-published speed of 199·169 mph the result of excessive rounding off during calculations.

Race No.	Aeroplane	Engine	Pilot	Take-off time	Lap times	Lap speeds	Place	Remarks
6	Macchi M.33 *MM48* (Italy)	21	Riccardo Morselli	—				On the day for navigability trials ignition trouble prevented engine start. Since engines could not by then be "unsealed," Morselli was unable to compete.
7	Macchi M.33 *MM49* (Italy)	21	H. Giovanni De Briganti	1455+	:11:10·49 :11:57·93 :10:43·32 :10:43·83 :10:57·70 :11:02·91 :10:51·81 1:17:27·99T	268·460 kmh 250·721 279·799 279·577 273·681 271·530 276·154 271·085T (168·444 mphT)	**3rd**	M.33 was the first cantilever monoplane to successfully complete the race. Its speed was low due to course misunderstanding on 2nd lap when De Briganti flew a triangle 4 miles longer than required. Engine delivered less than normal rated power due to extensive teardown and study by Fiat prior to race; moreover, pilot did not open up because of wing flutter at high speed. It is known that M.33's bore serials MM48 and MM49; correlations with race numbers probable but unconfirmed.
—	Macchi M.27 (Italy)	*21* or *47*	—	—				Italian proposal. Not built.
—	Piaggio P.4 (Pegna P.c.3) (Italy)	*21*	—	—				Italian proposal; low-wing cantilever monoplane on twin floats. Not ready.
—	Curtiss R2C-2 A-6692 (USA—reserve)	21	Lt. Frank H. Conant II USN	—				USN reserve. Did not compete. (The 1923 Pulitzer winner.)
—	Gloster I J.7234 (England—reserve)	35 (2)	—	—				The old "Bamel" (1921, 1922, 1923 Aerial Derby winner) brought to Baltimore as reserve. It might have competed if it had been erected; insufficient time remained to qualify it for race after Hinkler's Gloster III-A was damaged.
—	Dornier	*21* or *47*	—	—				German-designed project. Plans to build it in Italy. Not built. (Possibly similar to Dornier S.4 design of 1924.)

1926 SCHNEIDER (CONTEST IX)

NOVEMBER 13, 1926 (Postponed from October 24 to November 11 at request of Italian Aero Club; repostponed due weather. Competition ran Nov. 12, 13.)

COURSE: 350KM Hampton Roads (Norfolk) Virginia.
Triangle 50 km in length to be flown 7 times.
Race number assignment: Italy/USA alternated. Pilots allowed 15 minutes leeway as to assigned start times.

PRIZE: Trophy.

Race No.	Aeroplane	Engine	Pilot	Take-off time	Lap times	Lap speeds	Place	Remarks
1	Macchi M.39 MM74 (Italy)	48 (2)	*Ten.* Adriano Bacula	1435 (1430 assigned)	:08:53·66 :08:34·45 :08:32·92 :08:22·31 :08:27·54 :08:38·83 :08:21·60 :59:51·31T	337·293 kmh 349·888 350·932 358·344 354·652 346·934 358·852 350·847T (218·006 mphT)	3rd	"Sacrifice" team member; *i.e.,* he flew slowly on purpose to insure finishing at all costs. Each M.39 had its propeller set at a different pitch; Bacula's was the finest (lowest pitch); his M.39 also had only low-compression engine of the Italian team.
2	Curtiss R3C-3 A-6978 (USA)	25	Lt. William G. "Red" Tomlinson USN	—				Packard engine installed at NAF (Philadelphia), cockpit breakaways removed. G.T. Cuddihy assigned; Tomlinson—team reserve pilot—was substituted at the *last minute*; aeroplane's first navigability trial was Tomlinson's first flight in R3C-3. Aeroplane wrecked on hard landing, November 12, 1926.
2	Curtiss F6C-3 Hawk A-7128 (USA—reserve)	21˜	Lt. William G. "Red" Tomlinson USN	1438 (1435 assigned)	:13:34·54 :13:10·83 :13:18·24 :13:37·81 :13:33·09 :14:03·57 :13:58·64 1:35:16·72T	220·984 kmh 227·609 225·496 220·100 221·378 213·379 214·633 220·406T (136·954 mphT)	4th	Standard service Hawk substituted after crackup of R3C-3; race number 2 then assigned.
3	Macchi M.39 MM75 (Italy)	48 (1)	*Capit.* Arturo Ferrarin	1447 (1440 assigned)	:07:56·69 :07:40·29 :07:50·77	377·604 kmh 391·058 382·352	—	On November 9 landed after first navigability trials with broken con-rod. Engine completely replaced between 10 p.m. Thursday and 2 p.m. Friday. He feigned engine trouble to delay start and follow Cuddihy to assess American's performance, but retired on 4th lap with broken oil line. (Propeller-medium pitch.)
4	Curtiss R3C-4 A-6979 (USA)	23	Lt. George T. Cuddihy USN	1446 (1445 assigned)	:08:01·21 :07:45·92 :07:44·11 :07:48·81 :07:41·87 :07:43·71	374·057 kmh 386·332 387·839 383·951 389·720 388·174	—	Lt. F. H. Conant originally assigned (on Oct. 27, 1926 he achieved 251·5 mph in this aeroplane during trials) but on Oct. 30, Conant *killed*. Lt. Carleton C. Champion, reserve pilot, substituted, but on eve of race Champion became conveniently "ill" and Cuddihy was assigned to R3C-4 at *last minute*. Retired on last lap due to failure of pontoon fuel wobble pump. His usable fuel was exhausted only 2 miles from finish.

Race No.	Aeroplane	Engine	Pilot	Take-off time	Lap times	Lap speeds	Place	Remarks

5	Macchi M.39 MM76
	
	(Italy)
		48 (1)	*Magg.* Mario de Bernardi	1500 (1450 assigned)	:07:47·11
					:07:32·69
					:07:30·05
					:07:32·63
					:07:31·20
					:07:30·10
					:07:32·44
					:52:56·22T
						385·348 kmh
						397·623
						399·956
						397·676
						398·936
						399·911
						397·843
						396·698T
						(246·496 mphT)
							1st	During race, established world closed-course seaplane speed records:
								  100 km (laps 5, 6) 248·189 mph
								  200 km (laps 3, 4, 5, 6) 248·000 mph
								de Bernardi flew wide turns, speed average might have been better with tighter turns. On November 17, 1926, de Bernardi raised world seaplane speed record to 258·874 mph at Norfolk. Prop coarse pitch for high speed. (Today this racer is in a Turin museum.)

6	Curtiss R3C-2 A-7054 (USA)	22	1/Lt. Christian Frank Schilt USMC	1501 (1455 assigned)	:08:18·93 :08:01·98 :08:00·23 :07:59·69 :08:01·63 :08:00·47 :08:01·03 :56:23·96T	360·772 kmh 373·459 374·820 375·242 373·731 374·633 374·197 372·345T (231·364 mphT)	**2nd**	This aeroplane—using the identical engine—had won 1925 Schneider. Flying wire broke during this race causing Schilt annoyance with mild aileron and wing flutter; engine 45 rpm low with reference to last pre-race test flight. (This aeroplane today is in USAF Museum, Dayton, Ohio.)
	Curtiss R2C-2 A-6692 (USA—reserve)	21	—	—				On Sept. 13, 1926 this aeroplane crashed in the Potomac *killing* 1/Lt. Harmon J. Norton USMC. The deaths of Conant and Norton wiped out 2/3 of the original team. U.S. team captain Lcdr. Homer C. Wick then was replaced by RAdm W. A. Moffett. Ltjg. J. J. Glenhart, originally on first team, dropped.
—	Supermarine S.5 (England)	35 (6)	—	—				Withdrawn. Delayed awaiting completion of Lion VII-B engine.
—	Gloster IV (England)	35 (6)	—	—				Withdrawn. Delayed awaiting completion of Lion VII-B engine.
—	Saunders (England)	34 (3)	—	—				Private designs of Samuel Saunders and Col. Whiston A. Bristow respectively. Both were low wing monoplanes; Royal Aero Club "persuaded" Saunders and Bristow to withdraw, which they did at club meeting March 19, 1926. This move the result of government pressure to avoid an unprepared challenge and embarrass an un-challenged U.S.A. into cancelling the race (as the U.S. did in 1924). Air Ministry specification 7/26 was written around Bristow's design which was sub-contracted to Short, where it became *Short Crusader* racer of 1927.
—	Bristow (England)	49 (4)	—	—				

APPENDIX 3
Aeroplane Specifications

FRANCE

	SPAD S.20 (basic)		SPAD S.20 (1919 Schneider)		SPAD S.20 (bis)				SPAD S.20 (bis5)		SPAD S.20 (bis6)	
					bis 1	bis 2	bis 3	bis 4				
AEROPLANE: (1)												
WING: ARRANGEMENT (2)	u	l	u	l	u	u	u	u	u	l	u	l
SPAN	9·72 m	8·69 m	7·19 m (20)	8·54 m	10·02 m	9·47 m	8·10 m	6·60 m	6·478 m	6·478 m	6·478 m	6·478 m
CHORD (3)	1·75 m	1·65 m	1·65 m	1·65 m					1·52 m	1·52 m	1·45 m	1·45 m
INCIDENCE (3)												
DIHEDRAL	0°	0°							3·5°	0°		
GAP (BIPLANE) (3)									1·25 m (29)		1·269 m	
STAGGER (BIPLANE)												
AREA (4)	30 m²		26 m² (21)		25 m²	23 m²	21·5 m²	16 m²	15·0 m²		15·2 m² (32)	
ADDITIONAL	(16)								(30)			
LENGTH: OVERALL	7·30 m		8·10 m (22)		7·30 m				7·18 m		7·50 m	
FUSELAGE			7·30 m (22)									
ADDITIONAL	(17)											
LANDING GEAR: TREAD	1·89 m		—									
ADDITIONAL			—									
SEAPLANES: ARRANGEMENT (5)	—		TP (23)	TP (24)	—				—		—	
PONTOON LENGTH	—		4·77 m	5·20 m	—				—		—	
PONTOON BEAM	—			0·710 m (26)	—				—		—	
DISTANCE BETWEEN PONTOON CENTERLINES	—			2·0 m	—				—		—	
ADDITIONAL	—		(25)		—				—		—	
HEIGHT: LEVEL POSITION-OVERALL	2·72 m			3·36 m	2·90 m				2·50 m		2·75 m	
ADDITIONAL				(27)								
EMPENNAGE: ARRANGEMENT (6)	h	v	h	v					h	v	h	v
SPAN (7)	3·242 m	1·23 m	3·242 m									
CHORD (8)		0·82mM										
CHORD-OVERALL												
AREA (8)									1·1 m²F 0·9 m²M	0·35 m²F ·40 m²M		
AREA-OVERALL									2·0 m²	0·75 m²		
ADDITIONAL												

480

FRANCE continued

AEROPLANE:	SPAD S.20 (basic) contd.	SPAD S.20 (1919 Schneider) contd.	SPAD S.20 (bis) contd.				SPAD S.20 (bis₅) contd.	SPAD S.20 (bis₆) contd.
WEIGHTS: EMPTY-OVERALL (Pa) (9)	867 kg	850 kg					890 kg	890 kg
AIRFRAME (Ps)							480 kg	512 kg
POWERPLANT (Pg) (10)							410 kg	378 kg
OTHER								
USEFUL-OVERALL (Pe)	439 kg	280 kg					160 kg	160 kg
PILOT	85 kg	85 kg					80 kg	80 kg
FUEL AND OIL (Pc) (9)	169 kg (18)	195 kg (28)					80 kg	80 kg
EQUIPMENT	185 kg	—						
OTHER	—	—						
GROSS WEIGHT (Pt)	1306 kg	1130 kg					1050 kg	1050 kg
LOADINGS: WING (11)	43·53	43·46					70·0	69·08
POWER (12)	4·35	3·77					3·28	3·18
ENGINE: (13)	4 (1)	4 (1)	4 (1)				4 (2)	4 (2) (33) 4 (3) (34)
PROPELLER: TYPE	Lumiere (19)						Lumiere	
DIAMETER	2·60 m						2·40 m	
ADDITIONAL							(31)	
QUANTITIES: FUEL								
OIL								
ADDITIONAL								
ACCESSORIES:								
PERFORMANCE: V max (14)		245 kmh	250 kmh	252 kmh	270 kmh	260 kmh		309·012 kmh (34)
V min (14)	107 kmh							
RATE OF CLIMB (S.L.)								
RATE OF CLIMB (ALTITUDE)								
TIME TO CLIMB								
CEILING (15)	8900 m							
ENDURANCE								
FACTOR OF SAFETY	+8							
ADDITIONAL								

APPENDIX 3
Aeroplane Specifications

FRANCE continued

AEROPLANE: (1)	SPAD S.26				SPAD S.58		NIEUPORT 29 (basic)		NIEUPORT 29 (1919 Schneider)			
	S.26 (35)		S.26 (bis)						number 2		number 4	
WING: ARRANGEMENT (2)	u	l	u	l	u	l	u	l	u	l	u	l
SPAN	(36)	8·69 m	10·42 m		8·688 m	8·688 m	9·78 m	9·78 m	8·0 m	8·0 m	9·78 m	9·78 m
CHORD (3)					1·65 m	1·65 m	1·5 m	1·5 m	1·5 m	1·5 m	1·5 m	1·5 m
INCIDENCE (3)												
DIHEDRAL									2°	0°	2°	0°
GAP (BIPLANE) (3)												
STAGGER (BIPLANE)												
AREA (4)	22 m²		32·5 m²		26·36 m²		26·84 m²		22·0 m²		26·5 m² (47)	
ADDITIONAL					(39)		(40)					
LENGTH: OVERALL	8·13 m		8·23 m		6·5 m		6·65 m		7·3 m			
FUSELAGE							5·45 m		6·6 m			
ADDITIONAL							(41)					
LANDING GEAR: TREAD	—								—			
ADDITIONAL	—								—			
SEAPLANES: ARRANGEMENT (5)	TP (23)				—		—		TP (23)		PQ	
PONTOON LENGTH					—		—					
PONTOON BEAM					—		—					
DISTANCE BETWEEN PONTOON CENTERLINES					—		—		2·8 m		2·8 m	
ADDITIONAL					—		—					
HEIGHT: LEVEL POSITION-OVERALL	3·16 m				2·8 m		2·56 m		3·1 m			
ADDITIONAL									(46)			
EMPENNAGE: ARRANGEMENT (6)							h	v				
SPAN (7)							3·2 m					
CHORD (8)							0·6 mM					
CHORD-OVERALL												
AREA (8)							2·04 m²F 1·70 m²M	0·35 m²F 0·80 m²M				
AREA-OVERALL							3·74 m²	1·15 m²				
ADDITIONAL												

APPENDIX 3
Aeroplane Specifications

FRANCE continued

AEROPLANE:	SPAD S.26 contd.		SPAD S.58 contd.	NIEUPORT 29 (basic) contd.	NIEUPORT 29 (1919 Schneider) contd.	
WEIGHTS: EMPTY-OVERALL (Pa) (9)	975 kg	1000 kg		741 kg (42)	905 kg	925 kg
AIRFRAME (Ps)						
POWERPLANT (Pg) (10)						
OTHER						
USEFUL-OVERALL (Pe)	195 kg	210 kg		369 kg		295 kg
PILOT	75 kg	75 kg				80 kg
FUEL AND OIL (Pc) (9)	120 kg (37)	120 kg (37)		169 kg		215 kg
EQUIPMENT		15 kg (38)				
OTHER				200 kg		
GROSS WEIGHT (Pt)	1170 kg	1210 kg	1200 kg	1110 kg (43)	1220 kg	1220 kg
LOADINGS: WING (11)	53·18	37·23	45·50	41·36	55·45	46·04
POWER (12)	3·66	3·78	2·67	3·70	4·21	4·21
ENGINE: (13)	4 (2)		8 (2)	4 (1)	4 (1)	
PROPELLER: TYPE				Lumiere		
DIAMETER				2·5 m		
ADDITIONAL						
QUANTITIES: FUEL	150 ltr			209 ltr (44)		
OIL	18 ltr			22 ltr		
ADDITIONAL						
ACCESSORIES:						
PERFORMANCE: V max (14)	211·395 kmh		250 kmh	236 kmh		
V min (14)				130 kmh		
RATE OF CLIMB (S.L.)						
RATE OF CLIMB (ALTITUDE)						
TIME TO CLIMB				(45)		
CEILING (15)		6500 m		8200 m		
ENDURANCE				2:00		
FACTOR OF SAFETY						
ADDITIONAL						

483

APPENDIX 3
Aeroplane Specifications

FRANCE continued

AEROPLANE: (1)	NIEUPORT 29V 1919–1920 (u)	(l)	NIEUPORT 29V 1920–1922 (u)	(l)	NIEUPORT-DELAGE (Sesquiplane) Type 1921 main	inferior	Type 1922/1923 main	inf.	NIEUPORT-DELAGE 37 (Type course) main	inf.	NIEUPORT-DELAGE 42 (Type course) main	inferior
WING: ARRANGEMENT (2)	u	l	u	l	main	inferior	main	inf.	main	inf.	main	inferior
SPAN	6·05m	6·05m	5·46m	6·0m	8·0m	1·5m	8·0m	1·5m	8·2m		9·5m	
CHORD (3)	1·2m	1·2m	1·2m	1·2m	1·5m		1·547m$_r$ Λ				1·7m$_r$ Λ	
INCIDENCE (3)												
DIHEDRAL			2°	0°	1·5°	0°		0°		0°		0°
GAP (BIPLANE) (3)			1·35m									
STAGGER (BIPLANE)			0·225m									
AREA (4)	13·2m²		12·3m²		11·0m²		11·0m²		12·7m²		15·5m²	
ADDITIONAL			(49)		(55)		(62)		(68)		(73)	
LENGTH: OVERALL	6·23m		6·2m		6·1m				7·08m		7·3m	
FUSELAGE									6·475m		6·055m	
ADDITIONAL			(50)		(56)				(69)		(74)	
LANDING GEAR: TREAD					1·5m							
ADDITIONAL												
SEAPLANES: ARRANGEMENT (5)	—				—				—		—	
PONTOON LENGTH	—				—				—		—	
PONTOON BEAM	—				—				—		—	
DISTANCE BETWEEN PONTOON CENTERLINES	—				—				—		—	
ADDITIONAL	—				—				—		—	
HEIGHT: LEVEL POSITION-OVERALL	2·4m		2·5m						2·5m			
ADDITIONAL					2·02m (57)						2·20m (75)	
EMPENNAGE: ARRANGEMENT (6)			h	v	h		v				h	v
SPAN (7)												
CHORD (8)												
CHORD-OVERALL												
AREA (8)			1·25m²F 0·75m²M	0·44m²F 0·45m²M	1·28m²F 0·72m²M		0·56m²F (58) 0·44m²M				1·8m²F 0·75m²M	0·70m²F 0·40m²M
AREA-OVERALL			2·00m²	0·89m²	2·00m²		1·00m²				2·55m²	1·10m²
ADDITIONAL												

APPENDIX 3
Aeroplane Specifications

FRANCE continued

AEROPLANE:	NIEUPORT 29V contd.			NIEUPORT-DELAGE (Sesquiplane) contd.		NIEUPORT-DELAGE 37 (Type course) contd.	NIEUPORT-DELAGE 42 (Type course) contd.
WEIGHTS: EMPTY-OVERALL (Pa) (9)	620 kg	690 kg		740 kg	769 kg	800 kg	1170 kg
AIRFRAME (Ps)		280 kg			395·5 kg (63)		520 kg
POWERPLANT Pg) (10)		410 kg			373·5 kg (63)		650 kg
OTHER							
USEFUL-OVERALL (Pe)	214 kg	246 kg		240 kg	245 kg	260 kg	270 kg
PILOT	72 kg	86 kg			86 kg		
FUEL AND OIL (Pc) (9)	72 kg	160 kg			159 kg (64)		170 kg
EQUIPMENT							
OTHER	70 kg						100 kg
GROSS WEIGHT (Pt)	834 kg	936 kg		980 kg	1014 kg	1060 kg	1440 kg
LOADINGS: WING (11)	63·18	76·10		89·09	92·18	83·46	92·90
POWER (12)	3·21	2·92		3·06	3·07	2·65	2·40
ENGINE: (13)	4 (1)	4 (51)		4 (3)	4 (3) (65)	13 (5)	6 (2)
PROPELLER: TYPE	Lumiere	Chauvière	Lumiere	Lumiere	Regy-Sabbah	Lumiere	
DIAMETER	2·4 m	2·45 m		2·3 m	2·3 m	2·41 m	
ADDITIONAL		(52)	(53)	(59)	(66)	(70)	
QUANTITIES: FUEL		200 ltr		173 ltr		200 ltr	
OIL		25 ltr		25 ltr		22 ltr	
ADDITIONAL				(60)		(71)	
ACCESSORIES:		(54)		(61)	(67)	(72)	
PERFORMANCE: Vmax (14)	266 kmh (48)	302 kmh	313 kmh	330·275 kmh	341·239 kmh (1922) 375 kmh (1923)		
Vmin (14)				150 kmh			
RATE OF CLIMB (S.L.)							
RATE OF CLIMB (ALTITUDE)							
TIME TO CLIMB							
CEILING (15)							
ENDURANCE	1:00			1:45	1:45		
FACTOR OF SAFETY							
ADDITIONAL							

APPENDIX 3
Aeroplane Specifications

FRANCE continued

	BERNARD (SIMB) C.1 (76)		BERNARD (SIMB) V.1		BERNARD (SIMB) V.2		LOUIS CLEMENT-MOINEAU RACER	BOREL-BOCCACCIO RACER		DE MONGE 5.1	
AEROPLANE: (1)	1922	1924			Oct. 1924	Dec. 11, 1924					(100)
WING: ARRANGEMENT (2)			test	racing				u	l	u	l
SPAN	10·2 m	11·0 m	10·5 m	*8·75 m*	9·904 m	9·10 m	8·5 m	7·1 m		8·0 m	6·0 m
CHORD (3)	2·1 m$_r$ / 1·58 m$_t$	2·3 m$_r$ Λ	1·96 m$_r$ / 1·26 m$_t$		1·64 m$_r$ Λ	1·64 m$_r$ Λ		0·9 m		2·6 m$_r$ / 1·4 m$_t$	1·0 m
INCIDENCE (3)					0°r	—0·5°r					
DIHEDRAL								2°	0°		
GAP (BIPLANE) (3)	—	—	—	—	—	—	—	1·1 m		1·1 m	
STAGGER (BIPLANE)	—	—	—	—	—	—	—				
AREA (4)	17·2 m²	19·2 m²	15·5 m²	*12·08 m²*	11·6 m²	10·8 m²	16·0 m²	13·0 m²		20 m²	
ADDITIONAL	(77)	(82)	(84)	(86)	(87)	(89)		(95)		(101)	
LENGTH: OVERALL	6·6 m	7·0 m	6·5 m		6·714 m	*6·8 m*	6·0 m	7·095 m		7·0 m	
FUSELAGE											
ADDITIONAL	(78)		(85)			(90)					
LANDING GEAR: TREAD	1·6 m				1·74 m		1·7 m				
ADDITIONAL											
SEAPLANES: ARRANGEMENT (5)	—		—		—		—	—		—	
PONTOON LENGTH	—		—		—		—			—	
PONTOON BEAM	—		—		—		—			—	
DISTANCE BETWEEN PONTOON CENTERLINES	—		—		—		—			—	
ADDITIONAL	—		—		—		—			—	
HEIGHT: LEVEL POSITION-OVERALL	2·75 m				2·32 m			2·4 m		2·75 m	
ADDITIONAL	(79)				(88)						
EMPENNAGE: ARRANGEMENT (6)	h	v	h	v	h	v	h	v	h	v	
SPAN (7)	3·2 m				3·3 m				*0·8 m*		
CHORD (8)											
CHORD-OVERALL											
AREA (8)	1·356 m²F / 1·29 m²M	0·36 m²F / 0·65 m²M	1·2 m²F / 1·0 m²M	0·43 m²F / 0·50 m²M				1·3 m²F / 1·0 m²M	0·4 m²F / 0·5 m²M		
AREA-OVERALL	2·646 m²	1·01 m²	2·2 m²	0·93 m²	*2·55 m²*			2·3 m²	0·9 m²		
ADDITIONAL		(83)						(94)			

APPENDIX 3
Aeroplane
Specifications

FRANCE continued

AEROPLANE:	BERNARD (SIMB) C.1 contd. (76)		BERNARD (SIMB) V.1 contd.		BERNARD (SIMB) V.2 contd.		LOUIS CLEMENT-MOINEAU RACER contd.	BOREL-BOCCACCIO RACER contd.	DE MONGE 5.1 contd.
WEIGHTS: EMPTY-OVERALL (Pa) (9)			900 kg		1000 kg	965 kg	580 kg	665 kg	
AIRFRAME (Ps)					510 kg	419 kg (91)		255 kg	
POWERPLANT (Pg) (10)					490 kg	546 kg (91)		410 kg	
OTHER									
USEFUL-OVERALL (Pe)			150 kg		172 kg	224 kg	90 kg	195 kg	
PILOT			80 kg		85 kg	82 kg		75 kg	
FUEL AND OIL (Pc) (9)			70 kg		87 kg	128 kg		120 kg	
EQUIPMENT						14 kg			
OTHER									
GROSS WEIGHT (Pt)	1200 kg	1250 kg	1050 kg		1172 kg	1189 kg	670 kg	860 kg (96)	950 kg
LOADINGS: WING (11)	69·77	65·10	67·74	86·92	101·03	110·09	41·88	66·15	47·50 (102)
POWER (12)	3·64	3·79	2·1		1·89	1·92	3·72	2·57	2·88
ENGINE: (13)	4 (3)		8 (3)		5 (2)		3 (1)	4 (2)	4 (3)
PROPELLER: TYPE					wood	Levasseur/Reed		Lumiere	Lumiere
DIAMETER			2·45 m					2·5 m	
ADDITIONAL								(97)	
QUANTITIES: FUEL	260 ltr	250 ltr							
OIL									
ADDITIONAL	(80)					(92)			
ACCESSORIES:						(93)		(98)	(103)
PERFORMANCE: V max (14)	315 kmh (EST)		420 kmh (EST)		448·171 kmh				330 kmh (EST)
V min (14)									120 kmh
RATE OF CLIMB (S.L.)									
RATE OF CLIMB (ALTITUDE)									
TIME TO CLIMB								(99)	
CEILING (15)	6000 m (EST)								7000 m
ENDURANCE							2:00		
FACTOR OF SAFETY	18 (81)								
ADDITIONAL									

APPENDIX 3
Aeroplane Specifications

FRANCE continued

	HANRIOT HD.22	SIMPLEX-ARNOUX RACER	LANDWERLIN-BERREUR RACER	GOURDOU-LESEURRE CT no. 1	SALMSON-BECHEREAU RACER 1923	SALMSON-BECHEREAU RACER 1924–1925	CAMS 36 (bis) F-ESFC u	CAMS 36 (bis) F-ESFC l	CAMS 38 F-ESFD u	CAMS 38 F-ESFD l
AEROPLANE: (1)										
WING: ARRANGEMENT (2)							u	l	u	l
SPAN	6·38 m	9·0 m	13·26 m	7·8 m	8·16 m	10·0 m	8·6 m	8·6 m	8·6 m	8·6 m
CHORD (3)	1·4 m	2·0 m$_r$ 1·8 m$_t$	1·675 m	Λ						
INCIDENCE (3)				(113)						
DIHEDRAL				0°	0°				0°	+
GAP (BIPLANE) (3)	—	—	—	—	—	—				
STAGGER (BIPLANE)	—	—	—	—	—	—				
AREA (4)	7·5 m²	16·3 m²	22·2 m²	12·2 m²	17·0 m²	19·0 m²	20·0 m²		18·8 m²	
ADDITIONAL	(104)	(109)	(114)	(116)	(117)				(121)	
LENGTH: OVERALL	5·71 m	4·25 m	6·0 m	7·2 m	7·92 m	8·0 m	8·321 m		8·32 m	
FUSELAGE										
ADDITIONAL	(105)	(110)			(118)					
LANDING GEAR: TREAD		1·55 m					—		—	
ADDITIONAL							—		—	
SEAPLANES: ARRANGEMENT (5)	—	—	—	—	—		FB		FB	
PONTOON LENGTH	—	—	—	—	—		—		—	
PONTOON BEAM	—	—	—	—	—		—		—	
DISTANCE BETWEEN PONTOON CENTERLINES	—	—	—	—	—		—		—	
ADDITIONAL	—	—	—	—	—		—		—	
HEIGHT: LEVEL POSITION-OVERALL	2·2 m			2·85 m	2·5 m		2·758 m		2·79 m	
ADDITIONAL	(106)									
EMPENNAGE: ARRANGEMENT (6)		h | v	h | v							
SPAN (7)		— |	— |							
CHORD (8)		— |	— |							
CHORD-OVERALL		— |	— |							
AREA (8)		— |	— |							
AREA-OVERALL		— |	— |							
ADDITIONAL		(111) |	(111) |							

APPENDIX 3
Aeroplane
Specifications

FRANCE continued

AEROPLANE:	HANRIOT HD.22 contd.	SIMPLEX-ARNOUX RACER contd.	LANDWERLIN-BERREUR RACER contd.	GOURDOU-LESEURRE CT no. 1 contd.	SALMSON-BECHEREAU RACER contd.		CAMS 36 (bis) F-ESFC contd.	CAMS 38 F-ESFD contd.
WEIGHTS: EMPTY-OVERALL (Pa) (9)	620 kg	800 kg (112)		675 kg	1350 kg		945 kg	941·2 kg
AIRFRAME (Ps)	170 kg			330 kg	600 kg			
POWERPLANT (Pg) (10)	450 kg			345 kg	750 kg			
OTHER								
USEFUL-OVERALL (Pe)	180 kg	180 kg		260 kg	350 kg		315 kg	313·1 kg
PILOT	80 kg	80 kg						
FUEL AND OIL (Pc) (9)	100 kg	100 kg		160 kg	250 kg		205 kg	205·0 kg
EQUIPMENT								
OTHER				100 kg	100 kg		110 kg	108·1 kg
GROSS WEIGHT (Pt)	800 kg (107)	980 kg	1320 kg (115)	935 kg	1700 kg	1620 kg	1260 kg	1254·3 kg
LOADINGS: WING (11)	106·67	60·12	59·46	76·64	100·0	85·26	63·0	66·72
POWER (12)	2·42	2·97	1·88	1·83	2·57	2·45	3·82	3·80
ENGINE: (13)	4 (3)	4 (3)	47	42 (4)	9		4 (3) (119)	4 (3)
PROPELLER: TYPE				Leseurre	4-blade			CAMS
DIAMETER								
ADDITIONAL								
QUANTITIES: FUEL	130 ltr	120 ltr						
OIL	25 ltr							
ADDITIONAL								
ACCESSORIES:								
PERFORMANCE: V max (14)	360 kmh (EST)	380 kmh (EST)		380 kmh			260 kmh (EST)	270 kmh (EST)
V min (14)	127 kmh (EST)	135 kmh (EST)		90 kmh₁			90 kmh / 110 kmh₁	90 kmh / 110 kmh₁
RATE OF CLIMB (S.L.)								
RATE OF CLIMB (ALTITUDE)								
TIME TO CLIMB							(120)	(122)
CEILING (15)				9000 m			6000 m	6000 m
ENDURANCE	1:00						2:00	2:00
FACTOR OF SAFETY				17			10	10
ADDITIONAL	(108)							

APPENDIX 3
Aeroplane Specifications

FRANCE cont.			U.S.A.								

	LATHAM N.1 F-ESEJ		BLANCHARD C.1 RACER F-ESEH	DAYTON-WRIGHT RB	VERVILLE VCP/R-1				CURTISS TEXAS WILDCAT AND CACTUS KITTEN			
AEROPLANE: (1)					1920 VCP-R		1922 R-1		1920		racing biplane	
WING: ARRANGEMENT (2)	u	l			u	l			test mono-plane	racing mono-plane	u	l
SPAN	12·4 m	12·4 m	12·25 m	21'2"	27'6"	28'2"	23'4"	23'4"	32'0"	25'0"	25'0"	20'6"
CHORD (3)				78"r / 48"t	72"r $42\frac{5}{64}$"t	66"r $42\frac{5}{64}$"t				48"	45"	30"
INCIDENCE (3)				1°r	−1·5°	−1°				0°		
DIHEDRAL					0°	0°				0°	0°	0°
GAP (BIPLANE) (3)			—	—					—	—	$32\frac{1}{2}$"	
STAGGER (BIPLANE)			—	—	18"r				—	—		
AREA (4)	50·0 m²		21·0 m²	102·74 ft²	228·5 ft²		222·68 ft²			90 ft²	145 ft²	
ADDITIONAL				(123)	(129)					(139)	(143)	
LENGTH: OVERALL	10·92 m		9·75 m	22'8"	24'2"		24'7"		$17'7\frac{3}{4}$"			
FUSELAGE									$17'0\frac{1}{2}$"			
ADDITIONAL				(124)	(130)				(140)			
LANDING GEAR: TREAD	—		—	$58\frac{1}{2}$"	$64\frac{3}{8}$"				$57\frac{1}{2}$"			
ADDITIONAL	—		—									
SEAPLANES: ARRANGEMENT (5)	FB		FB	—	—		—		—			
PONTOON LENGTH	—		—	—	—		—		—			
PONTOON BEAM	—		—	—	—		—		—			
DISTANCE BETWEEN PONTOON CENTERLINES	—		—	—	—		—		—			
ADDITIONAL	—		—	—								
HEIGHT: LEVEL POSITION-OVERALL	4·27 m		3·3 m	8'0"	8'8"		7'9"		7'7"			
ADDITIONAL				(125)					(141)			
EMPENNAGE: ARRANGEMENT (6)				h | v	h	v			h	v		
SPAN (7)				8'10"	10'	$55\frac{3}{16}$"			7'0"			
CHORD (8)					30"F / 25"M	$36\frac{1}{2}$"M			27"F / $11\frac{1}{4}$"M			
CHORD-OVERALL				40"	55"				$38\frac{1}{4}$"			
AREA (8)				14·6 ft²F / 9·6 ft²M | 3·0 ft²F / 7·91 ft²M	18 ft²F / 16 ft²M	9·5 ft²M						
AREA-OVERALL				24·2 ft² | 10·91 ft²	34 ft²							
ADDITIONAL				(126)	(131)							

490

	FRANCE cont.		U.S.A.				
	LATHAM N.1 F-ESEJ contd.	BLANCHARD C.1 RACER F-ESEH contd.	DAYTON-WRIGHT RB contd.	VERVILLE VCP/R-1 contd.		CURTISS TEXAS WILDCAT AND CACTUS KITTEN contd.	
AEROPLANE:							
WEIGHTS: EMPTY-OVERALL (Pa) (9)		950 kg	1400 lbs	*2450 lbs*		1816 lbs	
AIRFRAME (Ps)			660 lbs	*1105 lbs*			
POWERPLANT (Pg) (10)			740 lbs	*1345 lbs*			
OTHER							
USEFUL-OVERALL (Pe)		350 kg	450 lbs	*750 lbs*		591 lbs	
PILOT			175 lbs				
FUEL AND OIL (Pc) (9)		210 kg	275 lbs	*540 lbs* (132)			
EQUIPMENT							
OTHER		140 kg		*210 lbs* (133)			
GROSS WEIGHT (Pt)	2700 kg	1300 kg	1850 lbs	*3200 lbs* (134)	3394·5 lbs	2407 lbs	
LOADINGS: WING (11)	54·0	61·90	18·01	14·0	15·24	26·74	*16·60*
POWER (12)	3·33	2·60	7·4	*5·5*	5·32	5·73	
ENGINE: (13)	TWO 7 (2)	42 (7)	11	24 (135)	24	18 (1)	
PROPELLER: TYPE			Hartzell (127)	McCook		Curtiss wood	
DIAMETER			7′3″	9′2″		8′0″	
ADDITIONAL				(136)			
QUANTITIES: FUEL				89 gal		40 gal	
OIL				7 gal		8 gal	
ADDITIONAL				(137)			
ACCESSORIES:			(128)	(138)		(142)	
PERFORMANCE: V max (14)		*280 kmh* (EST)	*190 mph* (EST)	186 mph		*220 mph*	
V min (14)			64 mph₁			*95 mph*₁	
RATE OF CLIMB (S.L.)							
RATE OF CLIMB (ALTITUDE)							
TIME TO CLIMB							
CEILING (15)			15000′				
ENDURANCE			1:30	1:15		1:10	1:10
FACTOR OF SAFETY						6	4
ADDITIONAL							

APPENDIX 3
Aeroplane Specifications

U.S.A. continued

AEROPLANE: (1)	CURTISS TEXAS WILDCAT AND CACTUS KITTEN 1921/1922 racing triplane			CURTISS 18-T A-3325 A-3326 — 18-T-1 (landplane and seaplane)			18-T-2 seaplane	CURTISS CR A-6080 A-6081 — 1921 CR-1 (L-17-1)	1922 CR-2 (L-17-3)	1923–1924 CR-3 (H-17-4)	CURTISS R-6 A.S. 68563 A.S. 68564 1922–1924 (L-19-1)	
WING: ARRANGEMENT (2)	u	m	l	u	m	l	,,	u	l	,,	u	l
SPAN	20'0"	20'0"	20'0"	31'11"	31'11"	31'11"	40'7½"	22'8"	22'8"	,,	19'0"	19'0"
CHORD (3)	42"	36"	36"	42"	42"	42"	,,	48"	48"	,,	46"	46"
INCIDENCE (3)	0°	0°	0°	2·5°	2·5°	2·5°	,,	0°	0°	,,	0°	0°
DIHEDRAL	0°	0°	2·75°	0°	0°	0°	,,	0°	2°	,,	0°	0°
GAP (BIPLANE) (3)	32"		31"r	42"	35$\frac{9}{16}$"		,,	48"r 44"t		,,	45½"	
STAGGER (BIPLANE)	0"		0"	0"	0"		,,	15"		,,	7½"	
AREA (4)	179·5 ft²			287·42 ft²			400 ft²	168 ft²		,,	135·91 ft²	
ADDITIONAL	(144)			(149)			(149)	(160)			(170)	
LENGTH: OVERALL	19'3"			23'3$\frac{3}{16}$" (landplane)			28'3$\frac{7}{8}$"	21'0"$\frac{3}{8}$"		25'0"$\frac{3}{8}$"	18'10½"	
FUSELAGE												
ADDITIONAL				(150)				(161)			(171)	
LANDING GEAR: TREAD				59$\frac{1}{8}$"			—	60"		—	58$\frac{5}{8}$"	
ADDITIONAL							—			—		
SEAPLANES: ARRANGEMENT (5)	—			—			3P	—		TP	—	
PONTOON LENGTH	—			—				—		17'11"	—	
PONTOON BEAM	—			—				—			—	
DISTANCE BETWEEN PONTOON CENTERLINES	—			—				—		8'0"	—	
ADDITIONAL	—			—				—		(166)		
HEIGHT: LEVEL POSITION-OVERALL	8'6"			9'10$\frac{3}{8}$"			12'	8'4$\frac{1}{4}$"	8'10"	10'0"		
ADDITIONAL								(162)			(172)	
EMPENNAGE: ARRANGEMENT (6)	h		v	h		v	(159)	h	v	v	h	v
SPAN (7)	6'9½"		38½"	10'10½"		42"F		7'8"		(163)	7'0"	45"
CHORD (8)	17½"F 12"M		30"F 19"M	27½"F 18$\frac{7}{8}$"M		36"F 31$\frac{11}{16}$"M					33"F 14½"M	42"F 16½"M
CHORD-OVERALL	29½"		49"	46$\frac{3}{8}$"		67$\frac{11}{16}$"					47½"	58½"
AREA (8)				14·3 ft²F 13·02 ft²M		5·2 ft² 8·66 ft²		12·6 ft²F 9·2 ft²M			10·84 ft²F 6·56 ft²M	4·25 ft²F 4·97 ft²M
AREA-OVERALL				27·32 ft²		13·86 ft²		21·8 ft²	11·78 ft²	14·7 ft²	17·4 ft²	9·22 ft²
ADDITIONAL			(145)	(151)		(152)			(163)	(167)		(173)

APPENDIX 3
Aeroplane Specifications

U.S.A. continued

AEROPLANE:	CURTISS TEXAS WILDCAT AND CACTUS KITTEN contd.	CURTISS 18-T A-3325 A-3326 contd.		CURTISS CR A-6080 A-6081 contd.			CURTISS R-6 A.S.68563 A.S.68564 contd.
WEIGHTS: EMPTY-OVERALL (Pa) (9)	1936 lbs	1825 lbs		1728 lbs	1782 lbs	2119 lbs	1615·5 lbs
AIRFRAME (Ps)	834 lbs						
POWERPLANT (Pg) (10)	1102 lbs						
OTHER							
USEFUL-OVERALL (Pe)	470 lbs	1076 lbs		430 lbs	430 lbs	628 lbs	505·5 lbs
PILOT	165 lbs	330 lbs					180 lbs
FUEL AND OIL (Pc) (9)	305 lbs	445 lbs					325·5 lbs (174)
EQUIPMENT		301 lbs					
OTHER		(153)					
GROSS WEIGHT (Pt)	2406 lbs	2901 lbs	3972 lbs	2158 lbs	2212 lbs	2747 lbs	2121 lbs (175)
LOADINGS: WING (11)	13·40	10·09	9·93	12·85	13·17	16·35	15·61
POWER (12)	5·53	7·08	9·69	5·26	5·40	5·97	4·37
ENGINE: (13)	18 (2)	(154)	(154)	19 (1)	20 (1)	20 (3)	20 (1) (176)
PROPELLER: TYPE	Curtiss			Curtiss		Curtiss/Reed	(177)
DIAMETER	8'6"	9'0"		7'2"		8'9"	
ADDITIONAL		(155)	(155)				
QUANTITIES: FUEL	40 gal	67 gal		40 gal		67·5 gal	48 gal
OIL	*8 gal*	6 gal		5 gal		4 gal	4 gal
ADDITIONAL						(168)	
ACCESSORIES:	(146)	(156)		(164)			(178)
PERFORMANCE: V max (14)	*196 mph*	163 mph	*140 mph*	185·3 mph	198·8 mph	188 mph	240 mph
V min (14)	70 mph	58 mph		89 mph₁	66·2 mph	76 mph₁	75 mph₁
RATE OF CLIMB (S.L.)							
RATE OF CLIMB (ALTITUDE)							
TIME TO CLIMB	(147)	(157)		(165)		(169)	
CEILING (15)	*25000'*	34610'				22000'	
ENDURANCE	1:10			1:30		1:50	
FACTOR OF SAFETY				8		8	+10·5 −3·5
ADDITIONAL	(148)	(158)					

493

APPENDIX 3
Aeroplane Specifications

U.S.A. continued

AEROPLANE: (1)	CURTISS R2C A-6691 A-6692 — 1923 R2C-1 (R-8) (L-111-1) u	l	1924 R2C-2 (H-18-2)	CURTISS R3C A-6978 A-6979 A-7054 — 1925 R3C-1 (L-114-1) u	l	1925–1926 R3C-2	1926 R3C-3	1926 R3C-4	WRIGHT NW A-6543 A-6544 — 1922 NW-1 main	inf	1923 NW-2 u	l
WING: ARRANGEMENT (2)	u	l	,,	u	l	,,	,,	,,	main	inf	u	l
SPAN	22'0"	19'3"	,,	22'0"	20'0"	,,	,,	,,	30'6"	14'6"	27'11 11/16"	27'11 11/16"
CHORD (3)	56"	40"	,,	56"	40"	,,	,,	,,	63"	37"	63"	63"
INCIDENCE (3)	0°	0°	,,	0°	0°	,,	,,	,,	−1·5°	−1·5°	−1·5°	−1·5°
DIHEDRAL	0°	0°	,,	0°	0°	,,	,,	,,	1·5°	0°	2·5°	2·5°
GAP (BIPLANE) (3)	38"		,,	38"		,,	,,	,,	53"		72"	
STAGGER (BIPLANE)	11 1/4"		,,	11 1/4"		,,	,,	,,	12"		0"	
AREA (4)	144·25 ft²		,,	144·0 ft²		,,	,,	,,	180 ft²		266 ft²	
ADDITIONAL	(179)			(191)					(207)		(213)	
LENGTH: OVERALL	19'8 1/2"		22'7 3/8"	20'1 3/8"		22'7 3/8"			24'0"		28'4 1/4"	
FUSELAGE			20'1 3/8"								23'10 27/32"	
ADDITIONAL	(180)		(186)	(192)		(200)			(208)		(214)	
LANDING GEAR: TREAD	54"		—	55"		—			90"		—	
ADDITIONAL			—			—						
SEAPLANES: ARRANGEMENT (5)	—		TP	—		TP	TP	TP	—		TP	
PONTOON LENGTH	—		16'6"	—		16'8"			—		20'11 1/4"	
PONTOON BEAM	—			—		27"			—		32 1/2"	
DISTANCE BETWEEN PONTOON CENTERLINES	—		7'6"	—		7'6"			—		8'6"	
ADDITIONAL	—		(187)	—		(201)			—		(215)	
HEIGHT: LEVEL POSITION-OVERALL	6'9 1/4"		10'6"	6'9 1/2"		10'4"			11'7 3/16"			
ADDITIONAL	(181)		(188)	(193)		(202)			(209)			
EMPENNAGE: ARRANGEMENT (6)	h	v	v	h	v	v			h	v	h	v
SPAN (7)	8'2"	45 3/4"	50 3/4"	8'2"	45 3/4"	50 3/4"	,,	,,	10'2"		13'0"	62 3/16" (217)
CHORD (8)	36 3/4"F 16 1/2"M	36"F 16 1/2"M	36"F 21"M	36 3/4"F 16 1/2"M	36"F 16 1/2"M	36"F 21"M	,, ,,	,, ,,	33"F 18"M	25"M	29 1/4"F 19 1/2"M	52 5/8"F 25 3/4"M
CHORD-OVERALL	53 1/4"	52 1/2"	57"	53 1/4"	52 1/2"	57"	,,	,,	51"		48 3/4"	78 3/8"
AREA (8)	15·5 ft²F 8·5 ft²M	6·1 ft²F 6·6 ft²M	6·3 ft²F 7·0 ft²M	15·5 ft²F 8·5 ft²M	6·1 ft²F 6·6 ft²M	6·3 ft²F 7·0 ft²M	,,	,,				
AREA-OVERALL	24·0 ft²	12·7 ft²	13·3 ft²	24·0 ft²	12·7 ft²	13·3 ft²	,,	,,				
ADDITIONAL			(167)			(167)			(210)		(216)	

APPENDIX 3
Aeroplane
Specifications

	CURTISS R2C A-6691 A-6692 contd.		CURTISS R3C A-6978 A-6979 A-7054 contd.				WRIGHT NW A-6543 A-6544 contd.	
AEROPLANE:								
WEIGHTS: EMPTY-OVERALL (Pa) (9)	1691·8 lbs	2036 lbs	1792·0 lbs	2134·9 lbs			2480 lbs	3565 lbs
AIRFRAME (Ps)		898 lbs	644·8 lbs	957·5 lbs				
POWERPLANT (Pg) (10)		1096 lbs	1101·6 lbs (194)	1131·8 lbs				
OTHER		42 lbs	45·6 lbs	45·6 lbs				
USEFUL-OVERALL (Pe)	420·5 lbs	604 lbs	389·0 lbs	603·5 lbs			520 lbs	882 lbs
PILOT		180 lbs	180 lbs	180 lbs				
FUEL AND OIL (Pc) (9)		422 lbs	207·5 lbs	422·0 lbs			337 lbs (211)	636 lbs (211)
EQUIPMENT		2 lbs	1·5 lbs	1·5 lbs				
OTHER								
GROSS WEIGHT (PT)	2112·3 lbs (182)	2640 lbs	2181·0 lbs	2738·4 lbs	2800 lbs	2800 lbs	3000 lbs	4447 lbs
LOADINGS: WING (11)	14·64	18·30	15·15	19·02	19·4	19·4	16·67	16·72
POWER (12)	4·22	5·28	3·64	4·56	4·0	3·8	4·62	6·84
ENGINE: (13)	21		22		25	23	14	
PROPELLER: TYPE	Curtiss/Reed	Curtiss/Reed	Curtiss/Reed	Curtiss/Reed	Standard steel	Curtiss/Reed	Wood	Standard steel
DIAMETER	7'10"	8'4"	7'8"	8'4"		9'4"	9'0"	7'6"
ADDITIONAL	(183)	(189)	(195)	(203)		(206)		(218)
QUANTITIES: FUEL	40 gal	60 gal	42 gal	60 gal			56 gal	106 gal
OIL	3 gal	5 gal	4 gal	4 gal			4 gal	8·5 gal
ADDITIONAL		(190)	(196)					
ACCESSORIES:	(184)		(197)				(212)	
PERFORMANCE: Vmax (14)	266·59 mph	227·5 mph	285 mph	245·713 mph			209 mph	204 mph
Vmin (14)	74 mph	84 mph	73·5 mph	78·5 mph			71·2 mph₁	74 mph₁
RATE OF CLIMB (S.L.)								
RATE OF CLIMB (ALTITUDE)								
TIME TO CLIMB	(185)		(198)	(204)				
CEILING (15)	31800' (EST)		26400'	21200'				
ENDURANCE	:42	1:35	:50	1:11				
FACTOR OF SAFETY	13		12	10				
ADDITIONAL			(199)	(205)				

APPENDIX 3
Aeroplane
Specifications

U.S.A. continued

AEROPLANE: (1)	WRIGHT F2W A-6743 A-6744 1923 F2W-1		WRIGHT F2W A-6743 A-6744 1924 F2W-2		THOMAS-MORSE MB-3		THOMAS-MORSE MB-6 (R-2) A.S.68537-68539		THOMAS-MORSE MB-7 A.S.64373 A.S.64374	THOMAS-MORSE R-5 A.S.68561 A.S.68562	
WING: ARRANGEMENT (2)	u	l	u	l	u	l	u	l		long wing	short wing
SPAN	22'6"	22'6"	23'0"	23'0"	26'0"	24'6"	19'0"	19'0"	24'0"	29'0"	25'0"
CHORD (3)	54"	54"	50"	50"	63"	63"	57"	57"	66"r Λ	72"	
INCIDENCE (3)	−1·5°	−1·5°	−1°	−1°	(229)	+0°40'			+1°r	+3°r −2°t	
DIHEDRAL	0°	0°	0°	0°	3°	3°	+	+	5°	+2°	
GAP (BIPLANE) (3)	54½"		44⅜"		53¾"		49"		—	—	—
STAGGER (BIPLANE)	0"		0"		0"		0"		—	—	—
AREA (4)	174 ft²		170 ft²		250·5 ft²		157·11 ft²		112 ft²	174 ft²	150 ft²
ADDITIONAL	(219)		(224)		(230)				(242)	(250)	
LENGTH: OVERALL	21'4"		26'1 7/16"		20'0"		18'6"		18'6"	19'10"	
FUSELAGE			20'5¾"								
ADDITIONAL			(225)		(231)					(251)	
LANDING GEAR: TREAD	60"		—		57½"					60"	
ADDITIONAL			—								
SEAPLANES: ARRANGEMENT (5)	—		TP		—		—		—	—	
PONTOON LENGTH	—		20'6"		—						
PONTOON BEAM	—		32¾"		—						
DISTANCE BETWEEN PONTOON CENTERLINES	—		7'0"		—						
ADDITIONAL	—		(226)		—		—		—	—	
HEIGHT: LEVEL POSITION-OVERALL	7'11½"		10'10⅜"		8'5½"		7'10"		7'3"	8'6"	
ADDITIONAL					(232)						
EMPENNAGE: ARRANGEMENT (6)	h	v	v		h	v			h	v	h	v
SPAN (7)	8'7⅝"	46¾"	49 19/32"		8'10"	46½"				8'11" (252)	
CHORD (8)	35"F 18¾"M	49"F 23"M	49"F 31½"M		25½"F 23¼"M	36½"F 26"M				27"F 26"M	
CHORD-OVERALL	53¾"	72"	80½"		48¾"	62½"				49"	
AREA (8)	10·4 ft²F	7·9 ft²F 6·9 ft²M	7·9 ft²F 8·4 ft²M		10·25 ft²F 17·0 ft²M	2·045 ft²F 5·286 ft²M			5 ft²F		
AREA-OVERALL		14·8 ft²	16·3 ft²		27·25 ft²	7·331 ft²					
ADDITIONAL	(220)		(227)		(233)						

APPENDIX 3
Aeroplane Specifications

U.S.A. continued

	WRIGHT F2W A-6743 A-6744 contd.			THOMAS-MORSE MB-3 contd.	THOMAS-MORSE MB-6 (R-2) A.S.68537-68539 contd.	THOMAS-MORSE MB-7 A.S.64373 A.S.64374 contd.	THOMAS-MORSE R-5 A.S.68561 A.S.68562 contd.
AEROPLANE:							
WEIGHTS: EMPTY-OVERALL (Pa) (9)	2424 lbs	2468 lbs	3296 lbs	1505 lbs		1423 lbs	
AIRFRAME (Ps)							
POWERPLANT (Pg) (10)	1160 lbs						
OTHER							
USEFUL-OVERALL (Pe)	434 lbs	618 lbs	865 lbs	590 lbs		452 lbs	
PILOT	180 lbs	180 lbs	180 lbs			160 lbs	
FUEL AND OIL (Pc) (9)	254 lbs	438 lbs	685 lbs (228)			282 lbs	
EQUIPMENT						10 lbs	
OTHER	(221)					(243)	
GROSS WEIGHT (Pt)	2858 lbs	3086 lbs	4161 lbs	2095 lbs (234)	2023 lbs	1875 lbs	2850 lbs (253)
LOADINGS: WING (11)	16·42	17·74	24·48	8·36	12·88	16·74	16·38 19·0
POWER (12)	3·81	4·11	5·55	6·54	5·95	4·69	4·75
ENGINE: (13)	15 (1)			13 (2) (235)	13 (2)	13 (3) (244)	24
PROPELLER: TYPE	Standard steel		Standard steel	McCook	McCook	Thomas-Morse	
DIAMETER	7'8"		7'8"	7'6"		8'2"	8'5"
ADDITIONAL	(222)			(236)		(245)	(254)
QUANTITIES: FUEL	31·7 gal	60·1 gal	95 gal	65 gal		42 gal	66 gal
OIL	6·4 gal	9 gal	9 gal			5 gal	
ADDITIONAL	(221)			(237)		(246)	(255)
ACCESSORIES:	(223)			(238)	(241)	(247)	(256)
PERFORMANCE: V max (14)	247·7 mph		235 mph (EST)	163·68 mph		180·75 mph (248)	187·74 mph (257)
V min (14)	75 mph		90 mph	55 mph		60·5 mph	
RATE OF CLIMB (S.L.)	5000 fpm (EST)			1230 fpm			
RATE OF CLIMB (ALTITUDE)							
TIME TO CLIMB				(239)			
CEILING (15)	36300' (EST)			19500'			
ENDURANCE	:30			3:00 (240)			
FACTOR OF SAFETY						(249)	
ADDITIONAL							

U.S.A. continued

AEROPLANE: (1)	VERVILLE-SPERRY R-3 A.S.22-326 -327 -328		LOENING M-81 S RACER A-5791	LOENING R-4 A.S.68559 A.S.68560	BEE-LINE BR A-6429 A-6430		NAVY TS and TR		1923 TR-3A
	1922	1923–1924			A-6429	A-6430	1922		
WING: ARRANGEMENT (2)							u	l	u	l
SPAN	29'6"	30'7.2"	30'5$\frac{3}{8}$"	26'11"	28'1"	30'1"	25'0$\frac{5}{16}$"	25'0$\frac{5}{16}$"	23'0"
CHORD (3)	94"r 35.2"t	94"r 35.2"t	72"	84"	72"r 24"t	''	57"	57"	
INCIDENCE (3)	−1° r	−1° r			0°	''	0°	0°	
DIHEDRAL		0°			3.5°	''	0°	3°	
GAP (BIPLANE) (3)	—	—	—	—	—	—	66"r		
STAGGER (BIPLANE)	—	—	—	—	—	—	0"		
AREA (4)	144.3 ft²	146.5 ft²	148.0 ft²	174.0 ft²	104 ft²		225 ft²		
ADDITIONAL	(258)	(262)	(269)		(279)	(280)	(281)		
LENGTH: OVERALL	22'5"	23'6"	24'2$\frac{1}{2}$"	23'5$\frac{1}{2}$"	21'1$\frac{1}{4}$"		24'9$\frac{15}{16}$"		26'0"
FUSELAGE									
ADDITIONAL			(270)				(282)		
LANDING GEAR: TREAD		75"	55"				(69$\frac{1}{4}$") (283)		—
ADDITIONAL							—		—
SEAPLANES: ARRANGEMENT (5)	—	—	—	—	—	—	TP		
PONTOON LENGTH	—	—	—	—	—	—	16'6"		
PONTOON BEAM	—	—	—	—	—	—	26"		
DISTANCE BETWEEN PONTOON CENTERLINES	—	—	—	—	—	—	7'0"		
ADDITIONAL	—	—	—	—	—	—			
HEIGHT: LEVEL POSITION-OVERALL	7'1"		6'7"	7'7$\frac{1}{2}$"	6'4$\frac{1}{2}$"		9'6$\frac{13}{16}$"		9'3"
ADDITIONAL	(259)	(259)	(271)	(275)					
EMPENNAGE: ARRANGEMENT (6)	h	v	h	v	h	v			h	v
SPAN (7)	8'4"		8'4"	50"	8'10"				10'9$\frac{1}{2}$"	
CHORD (8)	29"F 20"M		29"F 20"M	44"F 20$\frac{1}{2}$"M	44$\frac{1}{2}$"F 20"M				27$\frac{1}{2}$"F 20"M	33$\frac{3}{4}$"F 20$\frac{1}{4}$"M
CHORD-OVERALL	49"		49"	64$\frac{1}{2}$"	64$\frac{1}{2}$"				47$\frac{1}{2}$"	54"
AREA (8)	13.5 ft²F 9.85 ft²M		11.8 ft²F 7.25 ft²M	4.95 ft²F 6.75 ft²M	16.0 ft²F 14.0 ft²M	7.0 ft²F 6.5 ft²M				
AREA-OVERALL	23.35 ft²		19.05 ft²	11.7 ft²	30 ft²	13.5 ft²				
ADDITIONAL			(263)	(264)						

APPENDIX 3
Aeroplane
Specifications

U.S.A. continued

AEROPLANE:	VERVILLE-SPERRY R-3 A.S.22-326 -327 -328 contd.		LOENING M-81 S RACER A-5791 contd.	LOENING R-4 A.S.68559 A.S.68560 contd.	BEE-LINE BR A-6429 A-6430 contd.		NAVY TS and TR contd.	
WEIGHTS: EMPTY-OVERALL (Pa) (9)	1892·5 lbs	2006 lbs	1450 lbs	2317 lbs	1635 lbs			
AIRFRAME (Ps)		912·5 lbs						
POWERPLANT (Pg) (10)		1093·5 lbs						
OTHER								
USEFUL-OVERALL (Pe)	488 lbs	472 lbs	400 lbs	733 lbs	421 lbs			
PILOT		180 lbs	150 lbs					
FUEL AND OIL (Pc) (9)		292 lbs	250 lbs					
EQUIPMENT								
OTHER								
GROSS WEIGHT (Pt)	2380·5 lbs	2478 lbs (265)	1850 lbs (272)	3050 lbs (276)	2056 lbs	2026 lbs	(284)	2129 lbs
LOADINGS: WING (11)	16·50	16·91	12·50	17·53	19·77		(284)	
POWER (12)	5·95	5·39	5·44	5·08	5·14	5·06	(284)	8·87
ENGINE: (13)	13 (5)	(266)	13 (1)	24	13 (4)		(285)	12 (3)
PROPELLER: TYPE	(260)	(267)	Hartzell					
DIAMETER			8'8"					
ADDITIONAL			(273)					
QUANTITIES: FUEL	49 gal	40 gal		72 gal	34 gal			
OIL	4·5 gal	4 gal		6·5 gal				
ADDITIONAL				(277)				
ACCESSORIES:		(268)	(274)					
PERFORMANCE: Vmax (14)	(261)	235 mph	160 mph (EST)	190 mph	177·1 mph	188·5 mph	130 mph	159 mph
Vmin (14)		73·2 mph		72 mph	70 mph			
RATE OF CLIMB (S.L.)								
RATE OF CLIMB (ALTITUDE)								
TIME TO CLIMB				(278)				
CEILING (15)	22900'				24500'	24600'		20700'
ENDURANCE								
FACTOR OF SAFETY	8·5							
ADDITIONAL								

499

APPENDIX 3
Aeroplane Specifications

GREAT BRITAIN

AEROPLANE: (1)	The BANTAMS				AVRO 539 G-EALG G-EAXM				AVRO BABY		MARTINSYDE SEMIQUAVER G-EAPX		
	B.A.T. F.K.23		Grahame-White		539/1		539A/1	539B/1					
WING: ARRANGEMENT (2)	u	l	u	l	u	l	"	"	u	l	u	l	Alula
SPAN	25'0"	25'0"	20'0"		25'6"	24'6"	"	"	25'0"	23'0"	20'2"		28'6"
CHORD (3)	47¼"	47¼"	54"	36"	54"	54"	"	"	48"	48"	58½"	48"	∧
INCIDENCE (3)									4·5°	4·5°			
DIHEDRAL	3°	3°	0°	+					3°	3°			
GAP (BIPLANE) (3)	39½"		36"r 33"t		54½"r 51"t		"	"	51"		48"		—
STAGGER (BIPLANE)					0"		"	"	18"		16"		—
AREA (4)	185 ft²		130 ft²		200 ft²		"	"	176·5 ft²		147 ft²		106·25 ft²
ADDITIONAL	(286)		(293)		(294)		"	"	(295)				
LENGTH: OVERALL	18'5"		16'6"		21'4"		18'1"	18'2"	20'0"		19'3"		
FUSELAGE													
ADDITIONAL	(287)								(296)				
LANDING GEAR: TREAD	84"				—		60"		60"		42"	72"	
ADDITIONAL					—								
SEAPLANES: ARRANGEMENT (5)	—		—		TP		—		—		—		
PONTOON LENGTH	—		—		14'0"		—		—		—		
PONTOON BEAM	—		—				—		—		—		
DISTANCE BETWEEN PONTOON CENTERLINES	—		—		7'0"		—		—		—		
ADDITIONAL	—								—				
HEIGHT: LEVEL POSITION-OVERALL	6'9"		6'0"		9'9"		8'6"		7'7"		7'2½"		
ADDITIONAL													
EMPENNAGE: ARRANGEMENT (6)	h	v	h	v	h	v	h	v	h	v			
SPAN (7)	9'2"		9'0"		9'6"	*	9'0"		7'6"	36"			
CHORD (8)									26¼"F 15"M	F-none 36"M			
CHORD-OVERALL									41¼"	36"			
AREA (8)	17·1 ft²F 6·3 ft²M	2·85 ft²F 4·4 ft²M	19·0 ft²F 10·0 ft²M	3·75 ft²F 5·5 ft²M	12·0 ft²F 8·0 ft²M	4·0 ft²F 5·25 ft²M			14·5 ft²F 7·75 ft²M	7·0 ft²M			
AREA-OVERALL	23·4 ft²	7·25 ft²	29 ft²	9·25 ft²	20 ft²	9·25 ft²			22·25 ft²	7·0 ft²			
ADDITIONAL										(297)			

APPENDIX 3
Aeroplane
Specifications

	The BANTAMS contd.		AVRO 539 G-EALG G-EAXM contd.			AVRO BABY contd.	MARTINSYDE SEMIQUAVER G-EAPX contd.	
AEROPLANE:								
WEIGHTS: EMPTY-OVERALL (Pa) (9)	*812 lbs*	640 lbs				630 lbs	1526 lbs	
AIRFRAME (Ps)							622 lbs	
POWERPLANT (Pg) (10)							904 lbs	
OTHER								
USEFUL-OVERALL (Pe)	348 lbs	355 lbs				340 lbs	500 lbs	
PILOT							180 lbs	
FUEL AND OIL (Pc) (9)							320 lbs	
EQUIPMENT								
OTHER	(288)							
GROSS WEIGHT (Pt)	*1160 lbs*	995 lbs				970 lbs (298)	2026 lbs	
LOADINGS: WING (11)	*6·27*	7·65				5·50 (298)	13·78	
POWER (12)	*6·82*	12·44				27·71 (298)	6·75	
ENGINE: (13)	39 (1)	1	36	36	35 (2)	31	4 (2)	
PROPELLER: TYPE	BAT							
DIAMETER	7'10½"	7'0"	8'6"	8'6"	10'0"	7'6"		
ADDITIONAL	(289)					(299)		
QUANTITIES: FUEL	22 gal	15 gal				8 gal		
OIL	2·5 gal					1·5 gal		
ADDITIONAL						(300)		
ACCESSORIES:						(301)		
PERFORMANCE: V max (14)	138 mph (290)	100 mph				82 mph	161·434 mph	
V min (14)	50 mph₁	40 mph				37 mph₁		
RATE OF CLIMB (S.L.)								
RATE OF CLIMB (ALTITUDE)								
TIME TO CLIMB	(291)					(302)		
CEILING (15)	26000'							
ENDURANCE	3:30 (292)	2:20				3:15		
FACTOR OF SAFETY								
ADDITIONAL								

GREAT BRITAIN continued

AEROPLANE: (1)	BRISTOL 77 G-EAVP	BRISTOL 32 G-EATS 1919–1920 u	l	1921–1922 u	l	BRISTOL 72 G-EBDR	"BRITISH NIEUPORT" L.C.1 No. 1 G-EAEQ u	l	No. 2 G-EAJY u	l	"BRITISH NIEUPORT" L.S.3 G-EASK u	l
WING: ARRANGEMENT (2)		u	l	u	l		u	l	u	l	u	l
SPAN	30'9"	31'2½"	29'2½"	22'0"	22'0"	25'2"	28'0"	28'0"	26'0"	26'0"	20'6"	20'6"
CHORD (3)	71"	71"	59"	54"	54"		63"	63"	63"	63"	46"	46"
INCIDENCE (3)	0°						2·75°	2·75°				
DIHEDRAL	2°	0°	0°	0°	4°		4°	4°			2°	2°
GAP (BIPLANE) (3)	—			54"		—	54"		54"		47½"	
STAGGER (BIPLANE)	—					—	19½"		19½"		0"	
AREA (4)	145 ft²	294·6 ft²					276 ft²		255 ft²		137·75 ft²	
ADDITIONAL	(303)	(308)					(310)		(318)		(320)	
LENGTH: OVERALL	20'4"	24'1"				21'7"	18'6"				18'9"	
FUSELAGE												
ADDITIONAL							(311)				(321)	
LANDING GEAR: TREAD							60"				60"	
ADDITIONAL												
SEAPLANES: ARRANGEMENT (5)	—	—				—	—				—	
PONTOON LENGTH	—	—				—	—				—	
PONTOON BEAM	—	—				—	—				—	
DISTANCE BETWEEN PONTOON CENTERLINES	—	—				—	—				—	
ADDITIONAL	—	—				—	—				—	
HEIGHT: LEVEL POSITION-OVERALL	8'0"	9'8"					9'6"				8'8"	
ADDITIONAL											(322)	
EMPENNAGE: ARRANGEMENT (6)	h | v						h	v			h	v
SPAN (7)	10'3" (h)						9'0"	52½"			7'6¼"	50½"
CHORD (8)							28"F / 17"M	44"F / 17½"M			29¾"F / 16"M	40"F / 22"M
CHORD-OVERALL							45"	61½"			45¾"	62"
AREA (8)	20 ft²F 15 ft²M (h) / 5·0 ft²F 4·5 ft²M (v)						18·0 ft²F / 10·0 ft²M	5·12 ft²F / 5·38 ft²M (312)			15·00 ft²F / 9·13 ft²M	5·0 ft²F / 5·4 ft²M
AREA-OVERALL	35 ft² (h) / 9·5 ft² (v)						28 ft²	10·5 ft²			24·13 ft²	10·4 ft²
ADDITIONAL											(323)	

APPENDIX 3
Aeroplane Specifications

GREAT BRITAIN continued

AEROPLANE:	BRISTOL 77 G-EAVP contd.	BRISTOL 32 G-EATS contd.	BRISTOL 72 G-EBDR contd.	"BRITISH NIEUPORT" L.C.1 contd.		"BRITISH NIEUPORT" L.S.3 G-EASK contd.
WEIGHTS: EMPTY-OVERALL (Pa) (9)	850 lbs	1700 lbs		1500 lbs	1420 lbs	
AIRFRAME (Ps)					725 lbs	
POWERPLANT (Pg) (10)					695 lbs	
OTHER						
USEFUL-OVERALL (Pe)	370 lbs	600 lbs		680 lbs	530 lbs	
PILOT					180 lbs	
FUEL AND OIL (Pc) (9)					350 lbs	
EQUIPMENT						
OTHER					(319)	
GROSS WEIGHT (Pт)	1220 lbs (304)	2300 lbs		2180 lbs	1950 lbs	
LOADINGS: WING (11)	8·41	7·81		7·90	7·65	
POWER (12)	12·2	5·35		7·39	6·61	
ENGINE: (13)	41	42 (309)	42 (4)	40 (1)		40 (2)
PROPELLER: TYPE						
DIAMETER	8'6"			9'0"		9'0"
ADDITIONAL	(305)			(313)		
QUANTITIES: FUEL	20 gal	50 gal		40 gal		
OIL	5 gal			4 gal		
ADDITIONAL				(314)		
ACCESSORIES:				(315)		
PERFORMANCE: Vmax (14)	130 mph (306)	160 mph		151 mph (316)		166·4 mph
Vmin (14)	49 mph₁	50 mph₁		58 mph₁		
RATE OF CLIMB (S.L.)						
RATE OF CLIMB (ALTITUDE)						
TIME TO CLIMB	(307)			(317)		
CEILING (15)				29000'		
ENDURANCE		2:00		3:00		
FACTOR OF SAFETY						
ADDITIONAL						

APPENDIX 3
Aeroplane
Specifications

GLOUCESTERSHIRE MARS-I "BAMEL"-GLOSTER I G-EAXZ · **GLOSTER II J.7504 J.7505**

AEROPLANE: (1)	Bamel original–1921		1921 Coupe Deutsch		1921 Dec.		1922	1923 Gloster I		1925 (J-7234)	Gloster II u	Gloster II l
WING: ARRANGEMENT (2)	u	l	u	l	u	l		u	l		u	l
SPAN	23'0"	23'0"	21'8"	21'8"	20'3"	20'3"		21'0"	21'0"		20'0"	20'0"
CHORD (3)	57"	57"	57"	57"	54½"	54½"		54½"	54½"			
INCIDENCE (3)	1·5°	1·5°	1·5°	1·5°	1·5°	1·5°						
DIHEDRAL	3°	3°	3°	3°	3°	3°						
GAP (BIPLANE) (3)	57"		57"		57"			54½"				
STAGGER (BIPLANE)	16"		16"		16"			16"				
AREA (4)	205 ft²		185 ft²		165 ft²			165 ft²			165 ft²	
ADDITIONAL	(324)		(330)		(331)						(343)	
LENGTH: OVERALL	22'0"							21'6"		25'2"	26'10"	
FUSELAGE										21'8"		
ADDITIONAL	(325)							(337)			(344)	
LANDING GEAR: TREAD	64½"										—	—
ADDITIONAL											—	—
SEAPLANES: ARRANGEMENT (5)	—									TP	TP	
PONTOON LENGTH	—									19'2"		
PONTOON BEAM	—									26½"		
DISTANCE BETWEEN PONTOON CENTERLINES	—											
ADDITIONAL	—									(340)		
HEIGHT: LEVEL POSITION-OVERALL	9'6"							9'2"		10'10"	11'0" (345)	
ADDITIONAL	(326)							(338)		(341)		
EMPENNAGE: ARRANGEMENT (6)	h	v					v			v		
SPAN (7)	9'0"	52½"					50"			52"		
CHORD (8)	28"F 17"M	44"F 17½"M					40"F 17"M			37"F 20"M		
CHORD-OVERALL	45"	61½"					57"			57"		
AREA (8)	18·0 ft²F 10·0 ft²M	5·12 ft²F 5·38 ft²M					6·65 ft²F 5·5 ft²M			5·0 ft²F 6·45 ft²M		
AREA-OVERALL	28 ft²	10·5 ft²					12·15 ft²			11·45 ft²		
ADDITIONAL	(327)						(333)			(342)		

504

APPENDIX 3
Aeroplane
Specifications

AEROPLANE:	GLOUCESTERSHIRE MARS-I "BAMEL"-GLOSTER I G-EAXZ contd.						GLOSTER II J.7504 J.7505 contd.	
WEIGHTS: EMPTY-OVERALL (Pa) (9)	1890 lbs			1973 lbs	1970 lbs	2440 lbs	1920 lbs	2500 lbs
AIRFRAME (Ps)								
POWERPLANT (Pg) (10)								
OTHER								
USEFUL-OVERALL (Pe)	660 lbs			677 lbs	680 lbs	680 lbs		
PILOT								
FUEL AND OIL (Pc) (9)								
EQUIPMENT								
OTHER							(346)	
GROSS WEIGHT (Pt)	2550 lbs	2504 lbs		2650 lbs (334)	2650 lbs	3120 lbs	2400 lbs	3100 lbs
LOADINGS: WING (11)	12·45	13·54		16·06	16·06	18·91	14·55	18·79
POWER (12)	5·67	5·56		5·89	4·73	5·57	3·90	5·04
ENGINE: (13)	35 (2)				35 (3)		35 (4)	
PROPELLER: TYPE	H. C. Watts							
DIAMETER	10'0"						9'10"	
ADDITIONAL	(328)						(347)	
QUANTITIES: FUEL	50 Imp gal			60 gal				
OIL				7 gal				
ADDITIONAL	(329)			(335)				
ACCESSORIES:								
PERFORMANCE: V max (14)			196·6 mph (332)	212·73 mph (336)		185 mph	260 mph (EST)	
V min (14)							79 mph (348)	
RATE OF CLIMB (S.L.)								
RATE OF CLIMB (ALTITUDE)								
TIME TO CLIMB					(339)			
CEILING (15)								
ENDURANCE								
FACTOR OF SAFETY								
ADDITIONAL								

APPENDIX 3
Aeroplane
Specifications

AEROPLANE: (1)	GLOSTER III N.194 N.195 1925 III-A		SOPWITH 107 G-EAKI Schneider		SOPWITH 107 G-EAKI Rainbow/Hawker		BLACKBURN PELLET G-EBHF		SUPERMARINE SEA LION I G-EALP		SUPERMARINE SEA LION II G-EBAH		SUPERMARINE SEA LION III G-EBAH	
WING: ARRANGEMENT (2)	u	l	u	l	u	l	u	l	u	l	u	l	u	l
SPAN	20'0"	20'0"	24'0"	24'0"	21'0"	21'0"	34'0"	29'6"	35'0"		32'0"	32'0"	26'0"	26'0"
CHORD (3)	50"	50"	61½"	61½"	61½"	61½"							68"	68"
INCIDENCE (3)	0°	0°												
DIHEDRAL	0°	5°									1·5°	3·5°	1·5°	3·5°
GAP (BIPLANE) (3)	48"r		54"		53"									
STAGGER (BIPLANE)	12"		−2½"		0"									
AREA (4)	152 ft²		221·75 ft²		210 ft²				360 ft²				285 ft²	
ADDITIONAL			(351)				(355)		(356)				(359)	
LENGTH: OVERALL	25'5"		21'6"		19'3"		28'7"		24'0"		24'9"		27'6"	
FUSELAGE	22'8"													
ADDITIONAL			(352)						(357)				(360)	
LANDING GEAR: TREAD	—		—				—		—		—		—	
ADDITIONAL	—		—				—		—					
SEAPLANES: ARRANGEMENT (5)	TP		TP		—		FB		FB		FB		FB	
PONTOON LENGTH	19'2"				—		—		—		—		—	
PONTOON BEAM	26½"				—		—		—		—		—	
DISTANCE BETWEEN PONTOON CENTERLINES	6'3"				—		—		—		—		—	
ADDITIONAL	(349)				—									
HEIGHT: LEVEL POSITION-OVERALL	9'8"						10'8"				12'0"			
ADDITIONAL														
EMPENNAGE: ARRANGEMENT (6)	h	v	h	v										
SPAN (7)			8'3"											
CHORD (8)														
CHORD-OVERALL			45"											
AREA (8)		11·1 ft²F / 5·4 ft²M	13·0 ft²F / 9·75 ft²M	3·75 ft²F / 4·25 ft²M										
AREA-OVERALL	26·5 ft²	16·5 ft²	22·75 ft²	8·0 ft²										
ADDITIONAL			(353)											

APPENDIX 3
Aeroplane Specifications

	GLOSTER III N.194 N.195 contd.	SOPWITH 107 G-EAKI contd.		BLACKBURN PELLET G-EBHF contd.		SUPERMARINE SEA LION contd.	
AEROPLANE:							
WEIGHTS: EMPTY-OVERALL (Pa) (9)	2028 lbs					2381 lbs	2403 lbs
AIRFRAME (Ps)							
POWERPLANT (Pg) (10)							
OTHER							
USEFUL-OVERALL (Pe)	659 lbs					782 lbs	827 lbs
PILOT							
FUEL AND OIL (Pc) (9)							
EQUIPMENT							
OTHER						(358)	(361)
GROSS WEIGHT (Pt)	2687 lbs (350)	2200 lbs		2800 lbs	2900 lbs	3163 lbs	3230 lbs
LOADINGS: WING (11)	17·68	9·92			8·06		11·33
POWER (12)	3·95	5·79			6·44	7·03	5·77
ENGINE: (13)	35 (5)	42 (1)	40 (2) (354)	35 (3)	35 (1)	35 (2)	35 (3)
PROPELLER: TYPE							
DIAMETER	7'9"					8'8"	8'8"
ADDITIONAL							
QUANTITIES: FUEL	54·75 Imp gal						
OIL	4·25 Imp gal						
ADDITIONAL							
ACCESSORIES:							
PERFORMANCE: Vmax (14)	225 mph	160 mph (EST)	175 mph (EST)		147 mph (EST)	155 mph (EST)	165 mph (EST)
Vmin (14)	80 mph					55 mph₁	63 mph₁
RATE OF CLIMB (S.L.)							
RATE OF CLIMB (ALTITUDE)							
TIME TO CLIMB						(362)	
CEILING (15)						23500'	
ENDURANCE					2:30		
FACTOR OF SAFETY							
ADDITIONAL							

APPENDIX 3
Aeroplane Specifications

AEROPLANE: (1)	GB cont. SUPERMARINE S.4 N.197	ITALY ANSALDO A.1 "BALILLA" original u	l	number 27 1921 Pulitzer u	l	ANSALDO SVA SVA-5 SVA-9 u	l	FIAT R.700 u	l	SAVOIA S.12 basic u	l	S.12 (bis) racing u	l
WING: ARRANGEMENT (2)		u	l	u	l	u	l	u	l	u	l	u	l
SPAN	30'7½"	7·68m	7·68m	26'0"	26'0"	9·18m	9·18m	10·6m	10·6m	15·07m		11·72m	
CHORD (3)	72"r 51½"t			60"	60"			1·65m	1·65m	2·2m	1·7m		
INCIDENCE (3)													
DIHEDRAL		0°	+	0°	1·5°			0°	1°				
GAP (BIPLANE) (3)	—			56"				1·65m					
STAGGER (BIPLANE)	—			0"				0					
AREA (4)	139ft²	21·2m²		230ft²		26·9m²		33·0m²		52·25m²		46·52m²	
ADDITIONAL	(363)	(368)		(375)		(380)		(389)					
LENGTH: OVERALL	26'7¾"	6·6m		22'6"		8·13m		7·85m		10·8m		10·0m	
FUSELAGE	25'0"												
ADDITIONAL	(364)	(369)						(390)				(401)	
LANDING GEAR: TREAD	—			64"		2·0m				—		—	
ADDITIONAL	—									—		—	
SEAPLANES: ARRANGEMENT (5)	TP	—		—		—		—		FB		FB	
PONTOON LENGTH	18'0"	—		—		—		—		—		—	
PONTOON BEAM	—									—		—	
DISTANCE BETWEEN PONTOON CENTERLINES	7'6"	—		—		—		—		—		—	
ADDITIONAL	(365)	—		—		—		—					
HEIGHT: LEVEL POSITION-OVERALL	11'8½"	2·53m		9'4"		3·2m		2·9m		3·8m		3·8m	
ADDITIONAL		(370)		(376)		(381)							
EMPENNAGE: ARRANGEMENT (6)	h / v			h	v								
SPAN (7)	8'2"			9'2"	44"								
CHORD (8)				24"F 25"M	36"F 24"M								
CHORD-OVERALL				49"	60"								
AREA (8)	15·8ft²F 9·5ft²M / 5·25ft²F 6·625ft²M												
AREA-OVERALL	25·3ft² / 11·875ft²												
ADDITIONAL													

APPENDIX 3 Aeroplane Specifications	GB cont. SUPERMARINE S.4 N.197 contd.	ITALY ANSALDO A.1 "BALILLA" contd.		ANSALDO SVA contd.		FIAT R.700 contd.	SAVOIA S.12 contd.	
AEROPLANE:								
WEIGHTS: EMPTY-OVERALL (Pa) (9)	2600 lbs	640 kg (371)	1823 lbs	665 kg	690 kg	1880 kg	1600 kg	1560 kg
⎰ AIRFRAME (Ps)						880 kg (391)		
⎱ POWERPLANT (Pg) (10)		282 kg				1000 kg (392)		
OTHER								
USEFUL-OVERALL (Pe)	591 lbs	245 kg	544 lbs	310 kg	300 kg	370 kg	1000 kg	800 kg
PILOT						75 kg		
FUEL AND OIL (Pc) (9)						295 kg (393)		
EQUIPMENT								
OTHER				(382)	(387)			
GROSS WEIGHT (Pt)	3191 lbs	885 kg	2367 lbs	975 kg	990 kg	2250 kg (394)	2600 kg	2360 kg
LOADINGS: WING (11)	22·96	41·75	10·29	36·25	36·80	68·18	49·76	50·73
POWER (12)	4·69	4·02	5·92	4·88	4·95	3·21	4·56	4·29
ENGINE: (13)	35 (5)	45 (372)	17 (3)	45 (372)		47	46 (2)	46 (3)
PROPELLER: TYPE		Ansaldo	Curtiss	Ansaldo		Rosatelli		
DIAMETER	8'0"	2·75 m				3·3 m		2·67 m
ADDITIONAL			(377)			(395)		(402)
QUANTITIES: FUEL	40 Imp gal		50 gal	(383)		360 ltr	487 ltr	
OIL	5 Imp gal					50 ltr		
ADDITIONAL	(366)		(378)			(396)		
ACCESSORIES:		(373)	(379)	(384)				
PERFORMANCE: Vmax (14)	226·752 mph (367)	225 kmh	170 mph	238 kmh	220 kmh	336·132 kmh (397)	215 kmh	222 kmh
Vmin (14)	90 mph₁		61 mph₁	65 kmh₁	72 kmh₁		120 kmh	
RATE OF CLIMB (S.L.)								
RATE OF CLIMB (ALTITUDE)								
TIME TO CLIMB		(374)		(385)	(388)	(398)	(400)	
CEILING (15)		7000 m		7620 m	4500 m			
ENDURANCE		3:30	1:30	4:00 (386)		1:20	4:00	
FACTOR OF SAFETY				10		12 (399)		
ADDITIONAL								

ITALY continued

AEROPLANE: (1)	SAVOIA S.13 basic u	S.13 basic l	S.13(bis) racing u	S.13(bis) racing l	SAVOIA S.21 u	S.21 l	SAVOIA S.50 (MVT) MM 11,12,13 u	S.50 l	SAVOIA S.51 I-BAIU u	S.51 l	MACCHI M.7 basic u	M.7 basic l	M.7(bis) racing-1921 u	M.7(bis) l
WING: ARRANGEMENT (2)	u	l	u	l	u	l	u	l	u	l	u	l	u	l
SPAN	11.08 m		8.10 m	7.30 m	5.1 m	7.69 m	8.4 m		10.0 m	4.0 m	9.95 m	9.10 m	7.75 m	
CHORD (3)	1.90 m	1.55 m									1.52 m	1.191 m		
INCIDENCE (3)											2°	2.5°		
DIHEDRAL					0°	2°	0°	5.5°			0°	3.5°		
GAP (BIPLANE) (3)											2.07 m			
STAGGER (BIPLANE)														
AREA (4)	32.89 m²		19.6 m²				21.5 m²		23.0 m²		23.5 m²		23.8 m²	
ADDITIONAL			(405)				(407)				(412)			
LENGTH: OVERALL	9.022 m		8.36 m		7.0 m		7.2 m		8.0 m		8.095 m		6.78 m	
FUSELAGE							6.5 m				7.5 m			
ADDITIONAL			(406)				(408)				(413)			
LANDING GEAR: TREAD	—	—	—		—		—		—		—		—	
ADDITIONAL	—	—	—		—		—		—		—		—	
SEAPLANES: ARRANGEMENT (5)	FB		FB		FB		TP		FB		FB		FB	
PONTOON LENGTH	—	—	—		—				—		—		—	
PONTOON BEAM	—	—	—		—				—		—		—	
DISTANCE BETWEEN PONTOON CENTERLINES	—		—		—				—		—		—	
ADDITIONAL											(414)			
HEIGHT: LEVEL POSITION-OVERALL	3.16 m		3.05 m		2.94 m		2.8 m		2.5 m		2.97 m			
ADDITIONAL											(415)			
EMPENNAGE: ARRANGEMENT (6)							h	v			h	v		
SPAN (7)											2.844 m	1.12 m		
CHORD (8)							F- none				0.6 mF 0.596 mM	0.616 mF 0.63 mM (417)		
CHORD-OVERALL											1.196 m	1.201 m (418)		
AREA (8)							F-none							
AREA-OVERALL											2.65 m²			
ADDITIONAL							(409)				(416)			

510

APPENDIX 3
Aeroplane
Specifications

AEROPLANE:	SAVOIA S.13 contd.		SAVOIA S.21 contd.	SAVOIA S.50 (MVT) MM 11, 12, 13 contd.	SAVOIA S.51 I-BAIU contd.	MACCHI M.7 contd.	
WEIGHTS: EMPTY-OVERALL (Pa) (9)	875 kg	730 kg	700 kg	650 kg	780 kg	775 kg	775 kg
AIRFRAME (Ps)							
POWERPLANT (Pg) (10)							
OTHER							
USEFUL-OVERALL (Pe)	475 kg	210 kg	200 kg	240 kg	300 kg	305 kg	255 kg
PILOT							75 kg
FUEL AND OIL (Pc) (9)							175 kg (421)
EQUIPMENT							5 kg
OTHER							
GROSS WEIGHT (Pt)	1350 kg	940 kg	900 kg	890 kg	1080 kg	1080 kg	1030 kg
LOADINGS: WING (11)	41·05	47·96		41·40	46·96	45·96	43·28
POWER (12)	5·19	3·62	2·73	3·56	3·6	4·15	3·68
ENGINE: (13)	44 (1)		46 (1)	45 (3)	4 (4)	44 (1)	
PROPELLER: TYPE							
DIAMETER		2·12 m					2·55 m
ADDITIONAL		(404)				(419)	
QUANTITIES: FUEL							
OIL							
ADDITIONAL							
ACCESSORIES:							
PERFORMANCE: V max (14)	206 kmh	243 kmh	290 kmh	264 kmh	280 kmh (411)	210 kmh	
V min (14)	110 kmh					90 kmh	
RATE OF CLIMB (S.L.)							
RATE OF CLIMB (ALTITUDE)							
TIME TO CLIMB	(403)			(410)		(420)	(422)
CEILING (15)			5000 m			6400 m	6500 m
ENDURANCE						4:00	3:00
FACTOR OF SAFETY			11				
ADDITIONAL							

APPENDIX 3
Aeroplane Specifications

ITALY continued

	MACCHI M.17 I-BAHG		MACCHI M.19		MACCHI M.33 MM48, 49		MACCHI M.39 MM74, 75, 76		PIAGGIO P.2 MM26, 27	PIAGGIO P.4 (PEGNA P.c.2)	PIAGGIO P.4 (PEGNA P.c.3)	DORNIER S.4 (proposal)
AEROPLANE: (1)												
WING: ARRANGEMENT (2)	u	l	u	l								
SPAN	8·74 m	7·86 m	15·86 m	11·35 m	10·0 m		9·26 m		10·4 m	10·108 m	9·35 m	8·8 m
CHORD (3)			1·799 m		Λ		1·68 m		2·2 m$_r$			1·85 m
INCIDENCE (3)							0					
DIHEDRAL							0					
GAP (BIPLANE) (3)					—		—		—	—	—	—
STAGGER (BIPLANE)					—		—		—	—	—	—
AREA (4)	17·0 m²		46·0 m²		15·0 m²		14·3 m²		20 m²	19·5 m²		
ADDITIONAL	(423)		(426)		(430)		(433)					
LENGTH: OVERALL	7·81 m		11·0 m		8·29 m		7·766 m		7·0 m	7·8 m	7·75 m	7·7 m
FUSELAGE	7·19 m		10·3 m		7·68 m		6·743 m			7·2 m	6·70 m	
ADDITIONAL	(424)		(427)		(431)						(440)	
LANDING GEAR: TREAD	—		—		—		—		—	—	—	—
ADDITIONAL	—		—		—		—		—	—	—	—
SEAPLANES: ARRANGEMENT (5)	FB		FB		FB		TP		—	TP	TP	TP
PONTOON LENGTH	—		—		—		6·0 m		—	5·02 m	5·91 m	5·4 m
PONTOON BEAM	—		—		—				—			
DISTANCE BETWEEN PONTOON CENTERLINES	—		—		—		2·54 m		—	2·2 m		1·8 m
ADDITIONAL					(432)		(434)		—			
HEIGHT: LEVEL POSITION-OVERALL	2·7 m		3·7 m		2·68 m		3·06 m		2·2 m		2·96 m	
ADDITIONAL	(425)											
EMPENNAGE: ARRANGEMENT (6)					h	v	h	v				h	v
SPAN (7)						1·56 m	3·05 m	1·588 m				2·6 m
CHORD (8)						0·61 mM	1·029 mF 0·406 mM	1·372 mF 0·406 mM				
CHORD-OVERALL					1·26 m		1·435 m	1·778 m				
AREA (8)												
AREA-OVERALL												
ADDITIONAL												

APPENDIX 3

Aeroplane Specifications

AEROPLANE:	MACCHI M.17 I-BAHG contd.	MACCHI M.19 contd.	MACCHI M.33 MM48, 49 contd.	MACCHI M.39 MM74, 75, 76 contd.	PIAGGIO P.2 MM26, 27 contd.	PIAGGIO P.4 (PEGNA P.c.2) contd.	PIAGGIO P.4 (PEGNA P.c.3) contd.	DORNIER S.4 (proposal) contd.
WEIGHTS: EMPTY-OVERALL (Pa) (9)	750 kg	2160 kg	975 kg	1300 kg	650 kg			
AIRFRAME (Ps)				888 kg				
POWERPLANT (Pg) (10)				412 kg				
OTHER								
USEFUL-OVERALL (Pe)	200 kg	500 kg	280 kg	315 kg	330 kg			
PILOT								
FUEL AND OIL (Pc) (9)								
EQUIPMENT								
OTHER								
GROSS WEIGHT (Pт)	950 kg	2660 kg (428)	1255 kg	1615 kg (435)	980 kg	2910 kg		
LOADINGS: WING (11)	55·88	57·83	83·67	112·94	49·0			
POWER (12)	3·65	3·91	3·14	2·02	3·27			
ENGINE: (13)	44 (1)	47	21	48 (436)	4 (4)		20(3)	
PROPELLER: TYPE				Reed				
DIAMETER	2·56 m	3·3 m		2·33 m				2·5 m
ADDITIONAL		(429)		(437)				
QUANTITIES: FUEL								
OIL								
ADDITIONAL								
ACCESSORIES:								
PERFORMANCE: V max (14)	245 kmh	230 kmh	320 kmh	416·617 kmh (438)	255 kmh			
V min (14)				132 kmh	110 kmh			
RATE OF CLIMB (S.L.)								
RATE OF CLIMB (ALTITUDE)								
TIME TO CLIMB					(439)			
CEILING (15)								
ENDURANCE					3:00			
FACTOR OF SAFETY								
ADDITIONAL								

APPENDIX 4 Aero Engines		Cylinder arrange-ment and cooling method	(1) Swept volume	(2) Bore	(2) Stroke	Gear ratio Engine: prop	(3) Valves per cylinder	Dry weight	Installed weight	Lbs/HP Dry weight: Rated (R) or Max (M) HP
FRENCH (8)										
1. LE RHONE 80 STAe 9C		Rotary-9 Air	10·910 ltr	105 mm	140 mm	direct	1i 1e	245 lbs	*282 lbs*	2·88M
2. LE RHONE J-110 STAe 9Jb		Rotary-9 Air	15·073 ltr	112 mm	170 mm	direct	1i 1e	324 lbs		2·94R
3. HISPANO-SUIZA	**(1)** *modele 34* STAe 8Aa	V-8 90° Water	11·762 ltr	120 mm	130 mm	direct	1i 1e	445 lbs	655 lbs	2·97R
	(2) *modele 34 bis* STAe 8Ab							485 lbs	*695 lbs*	2·69R
	(3) *modele 35* STAe 8Ba					geared 4:3		506 lbs		2·53R
	(4) *modele 35 bis* STAe 8Bc (13)							517 lbs		2·35R
	(5) WOLSELEY "VIPER"					direct				
	(6) WRIGHT-MARTIN model A					direct		438 lbs		2·92R
	WRIGHT-MARTIN **(7)** model E **(8)** **(9)**									
4. HISPANO-SUIZA	**(1)** *modele 42* STAe 8Fd (*8Fb*)	V-8 90 Water	18·472 ltr	140 mm	150 mm	direct	1i 1e	528 lbs	*810 lbs*	1·76R
	(2) *modele 42* STAe 8Fd (*8Fb*)							550 lbs		1·84R
	(3) *modele 42* STAe 8Fe (*8Fb*)							596 lbs		1·67M
	(4) ITALA									

Length	Width or diameter (4)	Height	Frontal area	Rated HP/Engine RPM (5)(6)	Nominal HP/Engine RPM (5)(6)	Maximum HP/Engine RPM (5)(6)	Fuel and oil consumption (7)	Carburetor	Magnetos	Spark plugs	Notes
36·1″	D36·0″	—		80/1200 c 4·33		85/1300 c 4·8 P 81	sfc 0·56 soc 0·19	no carburetor; mixing valve used	1 ADS 26 early		(9)
36·1″	D37·25″	—		110/1350 P 77			sfc 0·56 soc 0·19	none; mixing valve	LKVG	*Mosler*	
1·308 m	0·851 m	0·832 m		150/1450 c 4·8 P 114	*170/1700*	200/2000	sfc 0·52 soc 0·056 0·528 gph oil	1 Zenith 48 DC duplex	2 8-cylinder Dixie transverse *or* 2 1 A8S		(10)
		0·847 m		180/1700 c 5·3 P 122	*180/1540* *205/1800*	250/2240	sfc 0·53 0·793 gph oil	1 Zenith 58DC duplex			(11)
	0·851 m	0·847 m		200/2000 c 4·7 P 115	*200/1870* *210/2000*	*225/2200*	sfc 0·54 1·057 gph oil	1 Zenith 55 DC duplex			(12)
				220/2150 c 5·3 P 124	220/1970	238/2200	1·321 gph oil	1 Zenith 58 DC duplex			(14)
51·53″	33·46″	33·34″		210/2000 c 5·3				1 Zenith duplex	2 BTH QV.8 (15)		(16)
				150/1450 c 4·72 P 106	154/1500		sfc 0·51 soc 0·045	1 *Claudel-Hobson*			(17)
				180/*1700* c 5·33		230/2200		1 Stromberg	2 Dixie	AC	
								1 Zenith			
									2 Simms		
			4·75 sq ft	275/1800	260/1980 c 4·7		sfc 0·51 soc 0·027	1 Zenith 58 DC duplex	2 S.E.V.	Oleo	(18) (19)
				300/1800	290/1600 320/2000	335/2050			2 S.E.V. or BTH	*Oleo*	(20)
				300/1800 c 5·3 P 117	320/1900(21) 335/2000 c 5·3	357·7/1860 c 5·3 (22) P 125	*24 gph*	1 Zenith 65 DC duplex	2 S.E.V. or *2 8-cylinder Dixie transverse*	J.A.M.(23)	
											(24)

APPENDIX 4
Aero Engines

			Cylinder arrange-ment and cooling method	Swept volume (1)	Bore (2)	Stroke (2)	Gear ratio Engine: prop	Valves per cylinder (3)	Dry weight	Installed weight	Lbs/HP Dry weight: Rated (R) or Max (M) HP
5. HISPANO-SUIZA	**(1)**	*modele 50* STAe 12Ga	W-12 60° Water	27·708 ltr	140 mm	150 mm	direct	1i 1e	827 lbs		1·67M
	(2)	*modele 50* STAe 12Gb									1·34M
6. HISPANO-SUIZA	**(1)**	*modele 51* STAe 12Ha	V-12 60° Water	27·708 ltr	140 mm	150 mm	direct	1i 1e	*881 lbs*		1·96R
	(2)	*modele 51* STAe 12Hb									1·37M
7. LORRAINE-DIETRICH	**(1)**	*modele 13* STAe 12Da	V-12 60° Water	23·072 ltr	120 mm	170 mm	direct	1i 1e	383 kg	*558 kg*	2·28R
	(2)	*modele 13* STAe 12Db									2·05M
8. LORRAINE-DIETRICH	**(1)**	*modele 14* STAe 12E	W-12 60° Water	23·072 ltr	120 mm	170 mm	direct	1i 1e	*350 kg*		1·82M
	(2)	*modele 14²* STAe 12E		24·429 ltr	120 mm	180 mm			363·9 kg		1·84R
	(3)	*modele 14³* STAe 12E									
9. SALMSON C.M.18			Radial-18 (2 × 9) Water	37·552 ltr	125 mm	170 mm	direct	1i 1e	450 kg	*510 kg*	1·50M
U.S.A.											
10. LIBERTY	**(1)**		V-12 45° Water	1649·34 cid	5·00"	7·00"	direct	1i 1e	872 lbs	*1245 lbs*	2·18R
	(2)										
	(3)										
	(4)										
	(5)										
	(6)										
11. HALL-SCOTT L-6a			Vertical 6 in-line Water	824·67 cid	5·00"	7·00"	direct	1i 1e	502 lbs	630 lbs	2·51R

Length	Width or diameter [4]	Height	Frontal area	Rated HP/Engine RPM [5][6]	Nominal HP/Engine RPM [5][6]	Maximum HP/Engine RPM [5][6]	Fuel and oil consumption [7]	Carburetor	Magnetos	Spark plugs	Notes
				450/1800 c 5.3	450/1725	497/1800	sfc 0.51 soc 0.123 *31.5 gph*	3 Zenith	2		
						620/2200 c 6.0		3 Solex	2 S.E.V.	J.A.M.	(25)
1.77 m		*0.76 m*		450/1800 c 5.3	505/1800 520/1900	545/2000 c 5.3	sfc 0.51 *35 gph*	6 Solex	2		
					570/	620/2000 c 6.2					
				370/1650 c 5.25			sfc 0.52 soc 0.04 *27 gph*	2 Zenith 55 DI duplex	2 S.E.V. HL-1	Ponsot	
				370/1500 c 5.25	403/1700	410/1730					
				400/1650 c 5.0		422/1800 c 5.3 (26)	sfc 0.51 soc 0.026	2 Zenith 55 DI	2 S.E.V. HL-1	Ponsot	(27)
1.374 m	1.210 m	1.138 m		435/1800 c 5.0	450/1850 c 5.0		sfc 0.53 soc 0.044 *31 gph*	2 Zenith 60 DJ	2 S.E.V. H-12		(28)
				445/1800 c 5.3		500+ c 6.0					(29)
1.37 m	D 1.18 m	—	10.10 sq ft	500/1600 c 5.4	550/1700 c 5.4	660/1800 c 6.5	sfc 0.52 soc 0.187	2 Zenith 55 DC	2 Salmson-Billancourt 4G.18		(30)
69.1"	26.8"	43.0"	5.16 sq ft	400/1700	421/1700 c 5.42 P 119	430/1800 c 5.55 P 115	sfc 0.54 soc 0.037 *36 gph*	2 Zenith US-52 duplex	Delco battery ignition 1 twin Delco 8 volt generator	AC / Mosler / Goodnough / BG	(31)
									Dixie		
					400/1700 c 5.00 P 113				Delco	AC	(32)
			3.87 sq ft	200/1700 c 5.56 P 113		250/2200 c 6.55		2 Miller	1 Delco battery 8-volt ignition	AC	

517

APPENDIX 4
Aero Engines

			Cylinder arrangement and cooling method	Swept volume (1)	Bore (2)	Stroke (2)	Gear ratio Engine: prop	Valves per cylinder (3)	Dry weight	Installed weight	Lbs/HP Dry weight: Rated (R) or Max (M) HP
12.	WRIGHT E	**(1)** E-2	V-8 90° Water	717·78 cid	120 mm	130 mm	direct	1i 1e	485 lbs		2·21M
		(2) E-3 "Alert"							476 lbs		1·91M
		(3) E-4 "Tempest"							480 lbs		1·68M
		(4) E-4A									
13.	WRIGHT H	**(1)** Wright-Martin H	V-8 90° Water	1127·25 cid	140 mm	150 mm	direct	1i 1e	632 lbs		1·76M
		(2) H-2 "Hunter"							617 lbs		1·73M
		(3) H-2									
		(4) H-3 "Super Hunter"							610 lbs		
		(5) H-3									1·57R
14.	WRIGHT T-2		V-12 60° Water	1947·55 cid	5·75"	6·25"	direct	2i 2e	1110 lbs		1·71M
15.	WRIGHT T-3	**(1)** "Tornado"	V-12 60° Water	1947·55 cid	5·75"	6·25"	direct	2i 2e	1166 lbs		1·49M
		(2) T-3A									
16.	CURTISS OX-5		V-8 90° Water	502·60 cid	4·00"	5·00"	direct	1i 1e	377 lbs	445 lbs	4·20R
17.	CURTISS K-12	**(1)**	V-12 60° Water	1145·11 cid	4·50"	6·00"	geared 5:3	2i 2e	695 lbs		1·74R 1·49M
		(2)									
		(3)									

Length	Width or diameter (4)	Height	Frontal area	Rated HP/ Engine RPM (5)(6)	Nominal HP/ Engine RPM (5)(6)	Maximum HP/ Engine RPM (5)(6)	Fuel and oil consumption (7)	Carburetor	Magnetos	Spark plugs	Notes
49.13″				190/1800 c 5.32 P 116		220/2000	sfc 0.48	1 Stromberg			(33)
				200/1800 c 5.5 210/1800 c 6.5	225/1800 c 6.5	250/2275 c 5.5 270/2275 c 6.5		1 Stromberg	Splitdorf	BG	(34)
52.1″	33.6″	35.1″		200/1800	212/1800 c 5.32 P 122	285/2300 c 6.0	sfc 0.51 soc 0.026	1 Stromberg NA-D4 duplex	2 Splitdorf	BG	(35)
				240/2100		290		1 Stromberg			
				325/1800 c 5.32 P 127	315/1600 P 139 350/1900	360/2000	sfc 0.50	1 Stromberg NA-D6 (Army) NA-V6 (Navy)	2 Dixie type 800	AC	(36)
51.7″					326/1800 c 5.32	358/2000		1 Stromberg DA-D6			
					340/1900	400/2000			2 Simms		
51.7″				340/1800 c 5.5	333/1825 P 130	400/2000 c 6.5	sfc 0.46 soc 0.015	1 Stromberg	2 Dixie	BG IXA	(37)
				390/2100 c 6.0		407/ c 6.0 (38)					
66″ (40)	31.9″	42.4″		525/1800 c 5.3 600/2000 c 6.5		650/2000 c 6.5 ?/2250	sfc 0.482				(39)
68.8″ (40)	30.9″	42.4″	5.49 sq ft	600/1900 c 5.25 675/2000 c 6.5	680/2000 c 6.5 P 138.5	780/2200 c 6.5 P 140	sfc 0.548 soc. 0.065	2 Stromberg	2 Splitdorf	AC	(41)
				600/2000 c 5.3 P 122			sfc 0.52 soc 0.025				
55 3/8″	29 3/4	35 1/8		90/1400	90/1400 c 4.92	95/1450 P 111	sfc 0.60 soc 0.03 9 gph	1 Zenith 06DS duplex	1 Ericsson-Berling D-81-X2		(42)
68 5/16″ (43)	27 7/8″	40 1/8″ (43)		400/2500	396/2250 406/2420 c 5.66 (44) 465/2600 c 6.0 (45)	420/2650	sfc 0.55 soc 0.03	2 Ball & Ball DVA-3 duplex	2 Ericsson-Berling D-66-X4	Mosler	
									2 Berkshire	AC	
					415/2500 c 5.5 P 115	428/2550 c 5.5		2 Zenith duplex		Mosler	(46)

APPENDIX 4
Aero Engines

			Cylinder arrangement and cooling method	(1) Swept volume	(2) Bore	(2) Stroke	Gear ratio Engine: prop	(3) Valves per cylinder	Dry weight	Installed weight	Lbs/HP Dry weight: Rated (R) or Max (M) HP
18.	CURTISS C-12	(1)	V-12 60° Water	1145·11 cid	4·50"	6·00"	geared 5:3	2i 2e	680 lbs	830 lbs	1·59M
		(2)									
19.	CURTISS CD-12	(1)	V-12 60° Water	1145·11 cid	4·50"	6·00"	direct	2i 2e	700 lbs	922 lbs	1·67M
		(2)									
20.	CURTISS D-12	(1)	V-12 60° Water	1145·11 cid	4·50"	6·00"	direct	2i 2e	671 lbs	724 lbs	1·33M 1·55R
		(2)									
		(3)									
		(4)									
21.	CURTISS D-12A		V-12 60° Water	1209·63 cid	4·625"	6·00"	direct	2i 2e	670 lbs		1·33M
22.	CURTISS V-1400		V-12 60° Water	1399·93 cid	4·875"	6·250"	direct	2i 2e	660 lbs	1101·6 lbs 1131·8 lbs (60)	1·07M
23.	CURTISS V-1550		V-12 60° Water	1547·18 cid (63)	5·125"	6·250"	direct	2i 2e	700 lbs		0·95M
24.	PACKARD 1A-2025		V-12 60° Water	2025·45 cid	5·75"	6·50"	direct	2i 2e	880 lbs	1118 lbs	1·38M
25.	PACKARD 2A-1500		V-12 60° Water	1497·58 cid (67)	5·375"	5·50"	geared 2000:1015	2i 2e	880 lbs		1·26M
26.	PACKARD X-24		X-24 60° Water	2722·88 cid	5·375"	5·00"	direct	2i 2e	1402 lbs		1·12R

Length	Width or diameter (4)	Height	Frontal area	Rated HP/ Engine RPM (5) (6)	Nominal HP/ Engine RPM (5) (6)	Maximum HP/ Engine RPM (5) (6)	Fuel and oil consumption (7)	Carburetor	Magnetos	Spark plugs	Notes
56.5"	28.25"	34.75"	4.66 sq ft		338/1800 P 130	414/2250 (47)	33.8 gph 0.75 gph oil	2 Claudel-Hobson	2 Berkshire	Mosler	
		37.5"				427/2250 c 6.1		2 Ball & Ball		AC	
56.5"	28.25"	34.75"	4.66 sq ft	405/2000 c 6.1 385/2000 c 5.7 (49) P 135	372/2120 c 5.23 417/2100 c 6.09 (50)	420/2180 c 6.1 P 143	33.7 gph 0.41 gph oil	2 Ball & Ball 52 mm duplex (49)	2 Berkshire	AC	(48)
									2 Splitdorf SS-12	BG IXA	
56.75"	28.25"	34.75"	4.09 sq ft	375/2000 (51) 435/2300 c 5.3 P 135	450/2200 c 5.7 (51)	468/2700 c 5.3 (51) 507/2380 c 5.7	sfc 0.52 (52) soc 0.015	2 Zenith US 54 mm	2 Splitdorf SS-12		(53)
						500+/2560 (54)	38 gph	2 Stromberg NA-Y5 duplex		BG IXA	(55)
				470/2350 c 5.7(56)	478/2350 c 5.8 (57)						
				500/2300 c 6.0							(58)
55.75"	28.25"	36.10"			507/2300 c 5.8	520/2400		2 Stromberg NA-Y5 duplex	2 Splitdorf	BG IXA	(59)
58.5" (61)	26.0"	35.75"		500/2100 c 5.5	565/2400 c 6.25	520/2100 c 5.5 P 134 619/2525 c 6.25 665/ (62)	sfc 0.49 soc 0.018	2 Stromberg NA-V6 duplex	2 Splitdorf	BG Midget	
$60\frac{1}{16}$" (64)	26"	$35\frac{11}{16}$"		600/2400 525/2100 c 5.8	685/	736/2600 c 7.5	sfc 0.53 soc 0.015	2 Stromberg NA-Y6 duplex	2 Splitdorf VA	BG Midget	
				500/1800 (65)	578/1920 c 5.0 P 117(65)	638/ c 6.5 (65) 600/2000	sfc 0.52 soc 0.025	2 Packard	Delco battery ignition	AC	(66)
$69\frac{3}{16}$"	$27\frac{7}{8}$"	$38\frac{15}{32}$"	4.03 sq ft	525/2100 c 5.5 P 140 600/2500 c 6.0	650/2700	700/2800 c 7.6	sfc 0.52 soc. 0.025	2 Stromberg NA-Y6P duplex	2 Scintilla AG-12D	BG Midget	(68)
$77\frac{1}{2}$"	$28\frac{5}{16}$"	$44\frac{33}{64}$"	7.78 sq ft	1250/2700 c 6.0			sfc 0.55 soc 0.035	4 Stromberg NA-Y6P	4 Delco	BG Hornet	(69)

APPENDIX 4
Aero Engines

	Cylinder arrangement and cooling method	Swept volume (1)	Bore (2)	Stroke (2)	Gear ratio Engine: prop	Valves per cylinder (3)	Dry weight	Installed weight	Lbs/HP Dry weight: Rated (R) or Max (M) HP
27. AEROMARINE **(1)** U-8-D	V-8 60° Water	737·69 cid	4·25"	6·50"	direct	2i 2e	576 lbs		2·37M
(2) U-873	V-8 60° Water	873·61 cid	4·625"	6·50"	direct	2i 2e	499 lbs		1·73M
28. "WHIRLWIND" **(1)** Lawrence J-1	Radial-9 Air	787·26 cid	4·50"	5·50"	direct	1i 1e	478 lbs		1·99M
(2) Wright J-4									
(3) Wright J-5									
29. PRATT & WHITNEY "WASP"	Radial-9 Air	1343·81 cid	5·75"	5·75"	direct	1i 1e	650 lbs		1·53R
30. WRIGHT P-1 "CYCLONE"	Radial-9 Air	1654·05 cid	6·0"	6·5"	direct	1i 1e	832 lbs		1·85M
ENGLISH **31.** GREEN	Vertical 4 in-line Water	4·236 ltr	106 mm	120 mm	direct	1i 1e	185 lbs		4·62M
32. ROLLS-ROYCE FALCON Mark III	V-12 60° Water	867·08 cid	4·00"	5·75"	geared 95:56	1i 1e	723 lbs	912 lbs	3·29R
33. ROLLS-ROYCE EAGLE Mark VIII	V-12 60° Water	1240·54 cid	4·50"	6·50"	geared 5:3	1i 1e	933 lbs	1177 lbs	2·35M
34. ROLLS-ROYCE CONDOR **(1)** Mark III	V-12 60° Water	2111·25 cid	5·50"	7·50"	geared 1000:477	2i 2e	1310 lbs		1·82M
(2) Mark IV					direct		1154 lbs		1·65M
(3) Mark VIII					remote drive				

Length	Width or diameter	Height	Frontal area	Rated HP/Engine RPM [5][6]	Nominal HP/Engine RPM [5][6]	Maximum HP/Engine RPM [5][6]	Fuel and oil consumption [7]	Carburetor	Magnetos	Spark plugs	Notes
				180/1750 c 5·25	200/1800	228/1800 c 5·45	sfc 0·472 soc 0·011	Stromberg	Splitdorf	BG	
				260/1800 c 5·35		290/2000 c 6·35		Zenith			
39·4″	D 43·75″	—		200/1800 c 5·0 P 112 220/1800 c 5·3	212/1800 c 5·3	240/2000	sfc 0·60 soc 0·025	3 Stromberg NA-S4	2 Splitdorf	Mosler AC (71)	
								1 Stromberg NA-U5G	2 Scintilla	AC	(72)
40·2″	D 45·0″	—		220/1800 c 5·4			sfc 0·495 soc 0·015	1 Stromberg NA-T4	2 Scintilla AG-9D (73)		(74)
43⅜″	D 50⅝″	—		425/1900 c 5·25 P 140 (75)			sfc 0·52 soc 0·025	1 Stromberg NA-Y7A duplex	2 Scintilla AG-9D (73)	BG Hornet number 4	(76)
42·9″	D 47·25″	—		400/1650		450/1800					(77)
					35/1250	40/1350	sfc 0·44 soc 0·094	1 Zenith			
72·04″	37·24″	42·00″		220/1800	270/2000	285/2200 c 5·3 P 114	sfc 0·53 soc 0·026 18·5 gph	2 RRCH 38M duplex	2 Watford		(78)
75·98″	42·52″	48·03″		360/1800 c 5·22 (79)		398/2000 c 5·3 P 124	sfc 0·50 soc 0·028 25 gph	2 RRCH 42M duplex	4 Watford		(80)
69·34″ (81)	30·53″	43·24″	7·32 sq ft	600/1700	650/1900	720/2100 c 5·3 P 132	sfc 0·50 43 gph fuel 1·9 gph oil	2 Rolls-built Claudel-Hobson duplex	2 12-terminal BTH		(82)
						700/2100					
						800					(83)

APPENDIX 4
Aero Engines

	Cylinder arrangement and cooling method	Swept volume (1)	Bore (2)	Stroke (2)	Gear ratio Engine: prop	Valves per cylinder (3)	Dry weight	Installed weight	Lbs/HP Dry weight: Rated (R) or Max (M) HP
35. NAPIER LION **(1)** Mark Ia	W-12 60° Water	1461·14 cid	5·50"	5·125"	geared 44:29	2i 2e	890 lbs	1040 lbs	1·78M
(2) Mark II					geared 41:27		900 lbs		1·69M
(3) Mark III									
(4) Mark Va							960 lbs		1·56M
(5) Mark VII					direct		790 lbs		1·16M
(6) Mark VII-B					geared 2000:1532		928 lbs		
(7) Mark VII-D							1170 lbs		1·03M
36. SIDDELEY-DEASY "PUMA"	Vertical 6 in-line Water	18·825 ltr	145 mm	190 mm	direct	1i 2e	636 lbs	781 lbs	2·20M
37. BENTLEY B.R.2	Rotary-9 Air	24·938 ltr	140 mm	180 mm	direct	1i 1e	498 lbs	530 lbs	2·06M
38. CLERGET 9.B	Rotary-9 Air	12·893 ltr	120 mm	160 mm	direct	1i 1e	381 lbs		2·94M
39. A.B.C. "WASP" **(1)** Mark I	Radial-7 Air	654·05 cid	4·50"	5·875"	direct	1i 2e	320 lbs		1·88M
(2) Mark II		987·11 cid	4·75"	6·25"			352 lbs		1·76M
40. A.B.C. "DRAGONFLY" **(1)** Mark I	Radial-9 Air	1389·86 cid	5·50"	6·50"	direct	1i 2e	598 lbs		2·03R
(2) Mark Ia							635 lbs		2·02R
41. COSMOS (BRISTOL) "LUCIFER"	Radial-3 Air	486·89 cid	5·75"	6·25"	direct	2i 2e	324 lbs		2·32M

Length	Width or diameter [4]	Height	Frontal area	Rated HP/ Engine RPM [5] [6]	Nominal HP/ Engine RPM [5] [6]	Maximum HP/ Engine RPM [5] [6]	Fuel and oil consumption [7]	Carburetor	Magnetos	Spark plugs	Notes
57·0"	42·0"	36·75"	5·68 sq ft	450/	420/2000 c 5·0 469/2000 c 5·55	501/2100 P 123 [84]	sfc 0·48 soc 0·028 32 gph	1 Claudel-Hobson N.S.1 and 1 Claudel-Hobson N.S.2	2 BTH AV-12	KLG type F-10	[85]
				425/2000 c 5·0 450/2000 c 5·8	450/1925 c 5·55 P 122 525/2200 c 5·55	531/2200 c 5·8					[86]
				460/2000 c 5·8	480/2000 c 5·8 P 128	560/2380 c 6·5	sfc 0·49 soc 0·024				
			5·55 sq ft	500/2150	585/2400	633/2600 c 7·0	sfc 0·51 32 gph [87]				
61·75"			4·25 sq ft		530/2310 c 5·8 [88]	680/2600 c 8·0 P 142					[89]
					800						
					898/3300 c 10·0	1320/3600					[90]
69·88"	24·09"	43·62"	7·55 sq ft	250/1500 c 4·9 260/1500 c 5·4	246/1400 c 5·0 P 118	290/1700 c 5·4	sfc 0·55 soc 0·062 17 gph	2 Zenith	2 E.M.6		[91]
	D 42"	—	9·62 sq ft	230/1250		242/1350 c 5·3 P 95	sfc 0·69 soc 0·074 20 gph	none 1 "block-tube"	2 BTH ML		[92]
1·163 m	D 1·030 m	—			130/1250 c 4·56		sfc 0·60 soc 0·123				[93]
35·7"	D 42·2"	—		160/1650	170/1750 c 4·025 P 115		sfc 0·495 soc 0·019	2 A.B.C. 48 mm injectors	2 MLP P.L.7		[94]
					200/1800						
42·1"	D 50·5"	—			295/1600 c 4·025 P 114	320/1650 expected [95]	sfc 0·56 soc 0·020	2 A.B.C. H.C.8	2 BTH M.L.9		
					315/1600 c 4·42 P 110	340/1650 expected [95]			2 BTH 4-spark A.K.9		
				100/1600 c 4·8 P 102	133/1700	140/1870 c 5·3	sfc 0·557 soc 0·037 7·6 gph	1 Bristol-Claudel H.C.8	2 Thomson-Bennett		

APPENDIX 4
Aero Engines

		Cylinder arrangement and cooling method	Swept volume (1)	Bore (2)	Stroke (2)	Gear ratio Engine:prop	Valves per cylinder (3)	Dry weight	Installed weight	Lbs/HP Dry weight: Rated (R) or Max (M) HP
42. BRISTOL "JUPITER"	**(1)** I	Radial-9 Air	1752·79 cid	5·75"	7·50"	direct	2i 2e	*636 lbs*	698 lbs	1·28M
	(2) II					geared 37:24			757 lbs	*805 lbs*	1·68R
	(3) I-mark II					direct				
	(4) I-mark III									
	(5) IV									
	(6) V							730 lbs		1·43M
	(7) Gnôme-Rhône STAe 9Aa *bis*									
43. ARMSTRONG-SIDDELEY "JAGUAR"	**(1)** Mark I	Radial-14 (2 × 7) Air	1374·45 cid	5·00"	5·00"	direct	1i 1e	720 lbs		2·03M
	(2) Mark IV		1511·89 cid		5·50"			762 lbs		1·80M
ITALY **44.** ISOTTA-FRASCHINI	**(1)** V·6	Vertical 6 in-line Water	16·625 ltr	140 mm	180 mm	direct	1i 1e	*290 kg*	*325 kg*	2·36M
	(2) V·6 *bis*									
45. S.P.A.	**(1)** 6A	Vertical 6 in-line Water	14·600 ltr	135 mm	170 mm	direct	1i 1e	*256 kg*	282 kg	*2·51M*
	(2) 6A									
	(3) *6A.SS*		*15·036* ltr	137 mm	*170 mm*					
	(4) 6.2A		16·625 ltr	140 mm	180 mm			256 kg		2·26M

Length	Width or diameter[4]	Height	Frontal area	Rated HP/ Engine RPM [5][6]	Nominal HP/ Engine RPM [5][6]	Maximum HP/ Engine RPM [5][6]	Fuel and oil consumption [7]	Carburetor	Magnetos	Spark plugs	Notes
37·26″	D 52·50″	—	12·65 sq ft	400/1650	450/1800 c 5·0	500/2000 c 5·0 P 113	sfc 0·557 (96) soc 0·060 *27 gph fuel 1·25 gph oil*	3 Bristol Triplex Mark VI (97)	2 9-cylinder Thomson-Bennett		(98)
46·69″				450/1850							(99)
37·26″				380/1575					BTH AQ9		(100)
					490/1875	510/2000		*Zenith* (101)			(101)
				420/1700 c 5·0		*460/1870*	sfc 0·525 soc 0·040	3 Bristol Triplex (97)			(102)
				450/1900	{ 398/1575 424/1750 (103) { 435/1650 473/1825 490/1900 P 117 (104)	510/1870 c 6·3 (105)					
				380/1575 c 5·0	380/1615 c 5·0 435/1750	500 + *(550)* (high compression)	sfc 0·52 soc 0·033 *30 gph*	Zenith			(106)
41·0″	D 46·3″	—		330/1650 c 5·0		355/1750 c 5·0	sfc 0·52 *20·5 gph*				(107)
43·0″	D 44·0″		*10·55 sq ft*	385/1700 c 5·0	395/1700 P 123	425/1800 c 5·0	*sfc 0·45* soc 0·026 *29 gph*				
1·825 m	0·51 m	1·035 m		240	260/1650 *c 5·23* *P 108*	280/1750	*sfc 0·505* *soc 0·044*	2 Zenith or IF-55	2 6-spark A.M.6		(108)
					300						
1·55 m	0·53 m	0·99 m		190/1500	205/1600	225/1700 c 5·19 P 117	sfc 0·473 soc 0·033 *17 gph*	2 Zenith 48DC or Feroldi 55F	2 Marelli N.2 or A.M.6	*Mosler*	(109)
					210/1600			2 Zenith 48DF	2 Olivetti	KLG *BG*	(110)
					280						(111)
1·55 m	0·53 m	0·99 m			230/*1600* c 5·46	250/1600 c 5·78	sfc 0·507 soc 0·033	2 Zenith 55DC or Feroldi 55F	2 A.M.6		(112)

APPENDIX 4
Aero Engines

		Cylinder arrangement and cooling method	Swept volume [1]	Bore [2]	Stroke [2]	Gear ratio Engine: prop	Valves per cylinder [3]	Dry weight	Installed weight	Lbs/HP Dry weight: Rated (R) or Max (M) HP
46. ANSALDO-SAN GIORGIO	**(1)** 4E-28	V-12 60° Water	33·251 ltr	140 mm	180 mm	direct	2i 2e	475 kg	509 kg	2·43R
	(2) 4E-284							510 kg		1·97M
	(3) 4E-29									2·04R
47. FIAT A.14		V-12 60° Water	57.199 ltr	170 mm	210 mm	direct	2i 2e	1739 lbs	1970 lbs	2·10M
48. FIAT A.S.2	**(1)**	V-12 60° Water	31·403 ltr	140 mm	170 mm	direct	2i 2e	412 kg		1·03M
	(2)									
49. OTHER	**(1)**									
	(2)									
	(3)									
	(4)									

Length	Width or diameter	Height	Frontal area	(5) (6) Rated HP/ Engine RPM	(5) (6) Nominal HP/ Engine RPM	(5) (6) Maximum HP/ Engine RPM	(7) Fuel and oil consumption	Carburetor	Magnetos	Spark plugs	Notes
1·92 m	0·90 m	1·02 m		*430* c 5·2	475/1600		sfc 0·485 soc 0·033	Zenith 55DC	2 Dixie 120		(113)
				520/1650	*550/*	570/1800					
				550/1650							(114)
1·855 m	0·95 m	1·24 m	6·22 sq ft	*600/1500* *c 4·5* 685/1650 c 4·967 P 108	650/1550 c 4·967 P 94 750/1700	825/1800 c 4·967	sfc 0·47 soc 0·047	4 Fiat	4 Dixie 120	4/cylinder	(115)
1·584 m	0·72 m	0·948 m			800/2300 *c 6·0* *P 142*	882/2500 *c 6·2*		3	2 Marelli	BG Midget	(116)
						c 5·8					(117)
											(118)
											(119)
											(120)
											(121)

Notes to Appendices

Appendix 1—Progress of Speed

1 One of the early widely recognized speed achievements made in the twentieth century. Indicative of current state-of-the-art. As World War I opened, the aeroplane was not yet man's fastest vehicle!

2 The first aeroplane world maximum speed record recognized by the then thirteen-month-old FAI.

3 Gnôme 100-hp rotary engine. The first aeroplane speed record in excess of 100 kmh.

4 Gnôme twin-row 160-hp rotary engine. Record achieved during 1913 Gordon Bennett race, and was the first in excess of 200 kmh; it also climaxed a phenomenal string of nine consecutive speed records set during 1912–13 by Deperdussin racers. (The time and distance officially credited for the 1913 Gordon Bennett race are noted, although they agree only for a distance of 200·033 km.)

5 Unofficial – details unconfirmed.

6 Aeroplane on loan to Army; according to the press, it achieved 163 mph "with a full military load"; *Aviation* magazine reported its high speed as 151 mph. No other substantive details available.

7 1919 Aerial Derby victory.

8 Made with pilot plus two passengers in a flight "controlled by the Aero Club of Italy"; contemporary accounts say this flight "broke Sadi Lecointe's record of 143 mph," but no reliable account of Sadi's supposed "record" can be found. Brack-Papa's flight might have been made on June 27.

9 Unofficial French speed record, and the best recorded 200-kilometer closed-course performance to date, although this was a disallowed Prix Deutsch trial.

10 During the 1919 Prix Deutsch trials, Sadi Lecointe made several speed sprints, of which this is representative. On October 3 he was variously credited with some 290 kmh, unconfirmed.

11 This flight may have been made October 22; date unconfirmed.

12 English closed-course records (unofficial performances since FAI recognition would not come into effect until 1920). On one flight on this date Gathergood set thirteen English closed-course speed records. He was credited with covering 5 kilometers in 74·85 seconds (240·481 kmh); he did 232·57 kilometers in one hour, 201·56 kmh for two hours, and 400 kilometers (his longest measured distance) at the rate of 234·07 kmh.

13 Unofficial; few details available; apparently achieved with a strong tail wind. Flight may have taken place December 15, although the sixteenth is more probably correct. During this sprint in his new Prix Deutsch entry Sadi allegedly hit 364·5 kmh "during some seconds." Average speed of 307·555 kmh has also been published.

14 1919 Prix Deutsch winner.

15 Article 142 of the FAI Regulations specified that world maximum speed records would be flown over a straight course of 1 kilometer, two times in each direction, at a maximum altitude of 50 meters to be reached at a point 500 meters before entering each end of the course. Supplementary provisions specified the aeroplane must return to its starting point, must have made two safe landings recently before the flight of the record attempt; the speed would be determined from the average of the four speeds, which is the mathematically correct method but which was curiously not adhered to in several cases; and that a new record could be set only by exceeding the existing record by 4 kmh. In addition, closed-course speed records would be recognized over specified distances of 100 kilometers, 200 kilometers, 500 kilometers, 1,000 kilometers, etc., of which only the shorter distances are of interest here; thus, technically, only *component portions* of many of the various air races, which were often competed over different distances, could be considered as official speed records.

16 The first postwar official world maximum speed record. Sadi Lecointe had begun 1-kilometer trials February 1 when unofficially he averaged 273 kmh.

17 Made with pilot plus four passengers (distance and conditions unknown). A speed of 260·869 kmh has also been published for this flight. This aeroplane had been built for the 1919 transatlantic flight.

18 Individual times unknown; however, the two fastest passes totaled :25·0.

19 Made with pilot plus one passenger.

20 Made with pilot plus two passengers, one of whom was Gabriele D'Annunzio.

21 English speed record. Appears in English accounts as 161·434 mph (also variously credited as 259·75 kmh).

22 Frequently credited as the first postwar world seaplane speed record, established during the Prix Guynemer race.

23 Unofficial seaplane performance; the flight was timed in four passes over the approximately 5-nautical-mile speed course surveyed at Far Rockaway Naval Station, near what is today J. F. Kennedy International Airport; flight credited as 138 mph in U.S. press despite a crosswind which "cut 2 mph off speed." An accurate survey of the speed course exists, but not timers' sheets for the flight.

24 English speed record. Appears in English accounts as 166·4 mph.

25 100-kilometer closed-course record set during 1920 Gordon Bennett French team elimination trials.

26 200-kilometer closed-course record set during 1920 Gordon Bennett race.

27 Official world speed record trials were held for two days at the huge Buc aeronautic meeting; de Romanet set the first record; Sadi Lecointe followed later the same day but did not establish a new record since the previous mark

was not exceeded by 4 kmh; the next day, however, Sadi set a new record. The speeds homologated were based on the average of times — thus mathematically are slightly in error. (The average time given — :12·1 — yields 297·521 kmh, 0·3 per cent more than the speed homologated.)

28 U.S. record; severe carburetion problems precluded setting a new world speed record. This aeroplane had won the 1920 Pulitzer race two days before.

29 Closed-course record set during 1921 Coupe Deutsch race.

30 Although Acosta was widely credited with setting new closed-course records in his 1921 Pulitzer race performance, they remained unofficial since no one apparently bothered to compute the times for 100- and 200-kilometer distances as specified by the FAI.

31 Unsuccessful world speed record attempt; eight passes flown; fastest pass measured at 197·8 mph.

32 English speed record. Appears in English accounts as 196·6 mph.

33 1922 Aerial Derby victory; times were not computed over 100- and 200-kilometer distances for possible official closed-course world records. (English accounts say 177·85 mph. Distance not known precisely.)

34 First officially recognized 100- and 200-kilometer closed-course seaplane records, set during 1922 Schneider Trophy victory. The times and speeds in official FAI records are given although they do not jibe. The times given yield 209·132 kmh for 100 kilometers, 208·249 kmh for 200 kilometers. Biard also set the first officially recognized seaplane records for duration and distance.

35 World speed record attempt, nominally successful; however, the paper work necessary for homologation was not completed properly. The correct speed achieved, computed by averaging the four speeds, is indicated; erroneous values of 335·664 kmh based on an average time of 10·725 seconds, and 336·468 kmh were published.

36 The speed homologated in the FAI record book is indicated; this is based on averaging the times in *pairs*. The correct value (the average of the four speeds) is 341·315 kmh. The value 341·023 kmh has also been published.

37 Closed-course record established during the 1922 Coupe Deutsch race.

38 Unofficial; achieved on first flight of the second R-6. The average speed (219·4 mph in the U.S. press) is indicated; fastest pass was 233·704 mph (376·111 kmh.)

39 James made three attacks on the world speed record after failing to finish the Coupe Deutsch race three days before. The speeds credited by the French (based on averaging his times in pairs) were 324·349 kmh, 330·275 kmh, and 341·300 kmh respectively. The mathematically correct speed averages are given.

40 Correct average, based on average of four speeds, is indicated. The French credited James with 341·432 kmh, based on average of times in pairs. Interestingly, the average of James's four times is 10·55 seconds, precisely identical to the time average of Sadi Lecointe's world record flight of September 21, 1922. Although James had the edge it was not by the requisite 4 kmh, thus he had no record.

41 Although achieved over an electrically timed kilometer placed in a 10-mile straight run, this speed — made on an early test flight of the R-6 — was not homologated. U.S. sources, which published a speed of 220·458 mph (354·793 kmh), say the second run was made in "ten seconds flat" although French sources reported 10·2 seconds; yet they published 354·688 kmh. The correct speed average (based on lap times given) is indicated.

42 Closed-course records established during the 1922 Pulitzer race. (A small discrepancy exists in the officially recognized speed for 100 kilometers; the time given yields 331·254 kmh.)

43 General Mitchell made four attacks on the record, two in each R-6. The final speed record homologated is indicated; however, the correct speeds (average of the four speeds achieved) are 340·487, 348·173, 353·715, and 361·278 kmh (the world record flight) respectively.

44 World seaplane speed record; Passaleva made twelve passes over the

measured course; the last four were selected to constitute the record. The speed homologated is indicated, and is based on the average of the four times indicated (12·85 seconds). The average of the four corresponding speeds (i.e., the mathematically correct value) is 280·203 kmh. The time for the third pass has also been published as 12·8 seconds which would yield a speed average of 279·087 kmh, strongly suggesting a typographical error, but confusingly, there have also been published the following erroneous speeds related to this record: 280·255 kmh, 277·992 kmh, 172·716 mph, 174·07 mph, and 175·16 mph.

45 Unsuccessful world speed record attempt in the modified Coupe Deutsch sesquiplane before wing radiators were installed. Speed based on averaging times in pairs (times and thus speeds for individual passes unknown).

46 Achieved with new wing radiators installed. Average of the times in pairs yields the homologated speed indicated; average of the four speeds yields 375·407 kmh, the correct value. Other published references to this record have indicated, erroneously, 375·132 and 377·657 kmh.

47 Beginning March 21, Maughan and Maitland made repeated attacks on the record in order to establish the last recognized 1-kilometer world speed record. The times were averaged in pairs. Maughan's March 26 performance could not be homologated because of a blur on the time tape rendering the time of the first pass indefinite. (The speed indicated is based on a first pass time of :09·45; 376·336 kmh has also been published.)

48 Maitland's second attempt, his fastest; however, he "dove on the course," thus rendering his results inadmissible. The speed given is based on time average in pairs (second flight); the correct speed averages are 372·776 and 394·228 kmh respectively.

49 The homologated world speed record is indicated, based on averaging times in pairs; the correct speed is 386·240 kmh (240·010 mph); Maughan made twenty-four passes on his record flight.

50 Pearson's record flight may have taken place Saturday March 31 as many references indicate, but March 29 is more likely. USAF and FAI records indicate March 29. The time indicated was published; however, this equates to a speed of 269·781 kmh. (Other times — 1:51:12 and 1:50:12·7 — appear in references, probably typographical errors.) Yet the speed homologated would require a time of 1:51:05·19 (270·000 kmh has also been published; this would require 1:51:06·66), all providing yet another unresolvable discrepancy left over from the early records. Pearson broke the 500-kilometer record first set by Lucien Bossoutrot, who flew a 300-hp—powered Farman F.90 from Le Bourget on November 15, 1922 (3:35:36·4 for 139·158 kmh officially). On March 30, 1923, Lieutenant Batelier in a 370-hp Lorraine-powered Potez IV at Étampes did 184·207 kmh over 500 kilometers and claimed a new record. It was this flight — made apparently one day after Pearson's — that has caused the confusion in dates. But Batelier's performance was never homologated.

51 When the base line for world maximum speed records was lengthened to 3 kilometers, the requirement was also instituted that the new speed must exceed the existing record by 8 kmh to be homologated. Height over the course was still limited to 50 meters, and the height must not exceed 400 meters during the flight, a stipulation not always enforced. An attempt was made almost immediately to have the R-6 set the first world record over the new 3-kilometer distance. Lester Maitland was pilot. However, during speed trials between April 7 and May 3 the aeroplane was damaged twice and no new record was set. Sadi Lecointe, also, was at Istres with his Nieuport-Delage sesquiplane attempting unsuccessfully to be the first 3-kilometer recordman.

52 Seaplane speed record (175·3 mph) credited by press; unofficial. Actually the result of pre-Schneider false publicity to mislead competition. In fact, the two CR-3s were doing 197 mph and 201 mph (about 320 kmh) in sprints.

53 Aerial Derby victory; British closed-course record. (In English accounts, speed appears as 192·36 mph.)

54 Unofficial pre-race Schneider trials.

55 Speed trials of the new Pulitzer racers took place before they were shipped to St. Louis. Most used as markers two water towers, one at Mitchel Field, the other at Westbury 2 miles away. Almost from their very first flights the speeds leapfrogged: 238 mph (Wright F2W); 244·15 mph (Curtiss R2C – fastest pass allegedly 255 mph); 247·7 mph (Wright F2W); 255 mph (Curtiss R2C). On September 17 Al Williams flew an electrically timed kilometer at 398 kmh (247·5 mph) unofficially, his fastest lap allegedly 266 mph.

56 Closed-course seaplane record set during the 1923 Schneider victory. 273·411 kmh (169·889 mph) was homologated over 200 kilometers. For some unexplained reason *no* new seaplane 100-kilometer record was homologated! The speed for the entire race was 285·303 kmh. Why the 200-kilometer record homologated is so much slower is unexplained. (A speed of 284·850 kmh has also been published incorrectly.)

57 Closed-course records set during 1923 Pulitzer victory. This result led to the curious situation that the closed-course record exceeded the officially recognized maximum speed record! Williams was variously credited with a flight of 392·226 kmh on October 3, but this is unofficial and unconfirmed.

58 Achieved during fly-over of one lap of the Coupe Beaumont course; race canceled. (Time given for 50 kilometers yields only 324·324 kmh or 201·525 mph.)

59 Six spirited attacks on the world speed record made in two days as Brow and Williams swapped records. At the end of the first day Brow held the first homologated record above 400 kmh, as well as the first record homologated over the 3-kilometer distance. There is much conflicting information concerning the speeds achieved November 2 (time sheets are unavailable). Speed for the last flight of the day, which was homologated, as well as the most probable values for the other flights, are indicated. The U.S. press noted that November 2 results were 257·42 mph, 258·61 mph, and 259·47 mph (also 259·15 mph for the final figure, an error); Brow wrote in his personal flight logbook the remarks: ":30, speed trial 257 mph" for the first flight of November 2, and ":40, world's record 259·7" for the day's final flight. Other values published for Brow's first flight are 414·714 and 414·119 kmh, and for Williams' flight 416·300 kmh. Brow's record stood for forty-eight hours; on November 4 Williams in his first flight made twelve passes; his best four consecutive were numbers 5, 6, 7, and 8 (times indicated). Brow then made four passes. Finally Williams made six passes to establish the new homologated record (it exceeded Brow's November 2 result by more than 8 kmh). The speeds indicated and the record homologated were computed correctly by averaging the four speeds; erroneous November 4 speeds which were variously published include (for flight one) 420·077 kmh and 420·77 kmh; (for flight two) 426·325 kmh and 427·059 kmh; and (for flight three) 428·851 kmh and 429·055 kmh. The U.S. press also published 263·30 mph, 265·69 mph, and 266·59 mph respectively, which are close but not exact.

60 On the occasion of his 1924 Coupe Beaumont victory (six 50-kilometer laps), Sadi Lecointe flying the 14 m² racing Nieuport 42 continued for another four laps to set the new 500-kilometer closed-course record, breaking Pearson's March 1923 mark. Between June 12 and July 7, 1924, Sadi was engaged in attacks on the world speed record with this aeroplane, all unsuccessful. (Sadi's time for 500 kilometers has also been published as 1:37:47·2, apparently in error.)

61 Some accounts refer to this as the first seaplane world speed record over the new 3-kilometer distance; however, it was apparently not homologated; reason unknown, unless it was another case similar to Brack-Papa's of August 1922 of Italian pride refusing to submit to French scrutiny. Presumably the same aeroplane as that used for the December 28, 1922, record, fitted with a "high compression" engine.

62 Unofficial trials in preparation for Schneider race.

63 Rittenhouse's performance over 200 kilometers may have been made on a date other than September 27; it was never homologated. As for his widely heralded September 27 performance over 4·26 statute miles, contemporary accounts indicated 227·5 mph, fastest pass 242·5 mph (number of timed passes unknown).

64 Performances made at Baltimore Flying Meet, which replaced the canceled Schneider race. Although many references refer to October 26, the meet in fact was held Saturday, October 25. Cuddihy's 3-kilometer performance was homologated as the new record although it was less than Passaleva's alleged mark of August 3. Times given are unconfirmed. Speeds for the four passes were published in the United States as 185·946, 188·930, 187·977, and 189·665 mph respectively. (An average speed of 302·684 kmh has also been published but erroneously.) Ofstie's 100- and 200-kilometer figures in the official FAI record book as indicated are identical since it is illogical to have a 200-kilometer record faster than a 100-kilometer record; his correct performances (from the timers' sheets) are 284·810 (100 kilometers) and 286·853 (200 kilometers). In fact, Ofstie did his *second* 100 kilometers in :20:46·0 for 288·925 kmh. Other speeds published in error regarding these records are (for 100 kilometers) 286·075 kmh and 176·822 mph; (for 200 kilometers) 287·571 kmh, 178·250 and 178·262 mph.

65 Unsuccessful world speed record attempt. (The speed 389·890 kmh has also been published in error.)

66 The magnificent flight that effectively doubled man's World War I speed frontier and consolidated an aerodynamic watershed, made by the last landplane to establish the speed record until 1939! Bonnet was airborne for :13:20·4; he made six passes over the 3-kilometer course at a height of some 15 meters. Performances were timed to the nearest one fifth of a second; the first two were :25·0 and :24·2; the next four – which constituted the new record – are indicated. Clock times for the world speed record passes were:
   (1) 10:35:13·8 to 10:35:38·2 A.M.
   (2) 10:37:21·2 to 10:37:45·2 A.M.
   (3) 10:40:19·8 to 10:40:44·0 A.M.
   (4) 10:42:28·0 to 10:42:51·8 A.M.
The value homologated was the average of the four speeds and thus is mathematically correct. It converts to 278·48 mph, 241·993 knots.

67 World speed record trials. Speed achieved allegedly more than 250 mph. Aeroplane crashed.

68 World seaplane speed record; appears in English accounts as 226·752 mph; fastest lap 231·406 mph.

69 The first R3C-1 was flown by Jimmy Doolittle and Al Williams in unofficial speed trials. Doolittle was credited with 254 mph over one lap of the Pulitzer course; Williams was credited with 268 mph upwind, 302 mph downwind, and an average of 285 mph; his downwind figure – the first widely publicized mark above 300 mph – caused much worldwide press comment.

70 Closed-course 100-kilometer record set during 1925 Pulitzer race victory; 200-kilometer mark not homologated. (Time for 100 kilometers unconfirmed; other speeds published regarding this 100-kilometer performance are 401·336 kmh and 249·337 mph.)

71 1925 Coupe Beaumont victory.

72 Closed-course seaplane records achieved during 1925 Schneider victory.

73 British 100-kilometer closed-course seaplane speed record set during second place performance in 1925 Schneider race.

74 World seaplane speed record. In U.S. press, speed given as 245·713 mph.

75 Closed-course seaplane records achieved during 1926 Schneider victory.

76 World seaplane speed record; fastest upwind pass 243·232 mph (391·445 kmh); fastest downwind pass 272·132 mph (437·955 kmh). (Speed average of 416·280 kmh has also been published in error.)

Appendix 3—Aeroplane Specifications

1 All data in this table have been extensively researched and cross-checked. Often sources respected as "reliable" disagree on specific data; where such differences exist and reasonable confirmation is impossible, or where there may be doubt, the *most likely* figure is given in *italics*. Aeroplanes built to the metric system are given in metric, etc. The abbreviation m means meters; feet and inches are indicated by ' and " respectively. Aeroplane sequence of presentation follows the text.

2 *Monoplane* unless subscripted, in which case the following apply: for multiplanes, u: upper wing; m: mid-wing (in the case of triplanes); l: lower wing.

3 *Constant* chord, incidence, and gap unless subscripted, in which case the following apply: r: root; t: tip. If the wing was tapered and all chord dimensions are unknown, the symbol Λ is used.

4 The area given is the total wing area — the sum of all wings for multiplanes — including ailerons in all cases. The generally accepted convention during the 1920s was to consider only that portion of the wing actually exposed whereas modern convention considers wing area to be the total planform including that portion covered by the fuselage. The values listed, researched from contemporary documents, would reflect the earlier practice if applied.

5 Seaplane arrangement is indicated as follows: FB: flying boat; TP: twin pontoon; PQ: short twin pontoons with third, tail-mounted *flotteur de queue*; 3P: one main center-mounted pontoon with two smaller pontoons mounted at the wingtips.

6 Subscripts apply as follows: h: horizontal tail surfaces; v: vertical tail surfaces.

7 Refers to the maximum linear dimension parallel to the axis; lateral axis for horizontal surfaces, vertical axis for vertical surfaces.

8 Subscripts apply as follows: F: fixed surface (i.e., the horizontal stabilizer or vertical fin); M: movable surface (i.e., the elevator or rudder).

9 In general, convention as to the assignment of aeroplane weights followed the French practice. French weight abbreviations are identified by a capital P (*poids*); French subscripts with English equivalents are as follows:

P_s	*poids planeur* (airframe weight)	
$+ P_g$	*poids organes motopropulseurs* (powerplant weight; includes water weight for water-cooled engines)	
P_a	(or P_v) *poids avions a vide*, the sum of P_s and P_g; that is, the empty weight of the aeroplane	
$+ P_e$	(or P_u) *poids enlevé* (or *poids utile*; that is, the useful load carried; this includes the weight of pilot and all portable equipment, plus P_c — *poids combustible* — the weight of fuel and oil taken together)	
P	(or P_T) *poids total*, the sum of P_a and P_e; that is, the aeroplane's gross weight	

10 Powerplant weight included the weight of water if the engine was water-cooled (see P_g under note 9).

11 If aeroplane dimensions are metric, this figure is given in units kg/m²; if dimensions are English, units are lbs/ft². The figure listed is based on the fully loaded gross weight and wing area *as listed*.

12 If aeroplane dimensions are metric, this figure is given in units kg/hp; if dimensions are English, units are lbs/hp. The figure listed is based on the fully loaded gross weight and representative power (usually maximum power).

13 Entries refer to Appendix 4.

14 The terms V_{max} and V_{min} refer to the aeroplane's maximum and minimum velocity capability respectively. The V_{max} was the maximum speed either predicted, estimated, or demonstrated. The V_{min} is subscripted s if given as stall speed, l if given as landing speed (landing speed was generally some 20 to 40 per cent faster than stall speed). If no subscript is indicated, no such V_{min} discrimination was made in the original sources.

15 The aeroplane's absolute ceiling unless subscripted s, which then refers to the "service ceiling," a figure used sometimes to indicate the height at which the aeroplane's maximum rate-of-climb capability has diminished to 100 feet per minute.

16 Ailerons on lower wing only on all S.20 variants. Upper wing swept back 8°. Other S.20 (basic) versions had wings spanning 10·41 m, total area 33 m².

17 Length also given as 7·385 m; extra may be due to a larger prop boss. Fuselage *coque*: maximum width ·920 m, maximum depth 1·356 m.

18 The French P_c, which is weight of fuel *plus* oil.

19 Wood, two-blade.

20 Upper wing originally built with a span of 8·69 m; Sadi Lecointe clipped ·75 m from each tip.

21 Before wings clipped.

22 Over-all length including pontoons; fuselage length of 7·3 m includes prop boss.

23 Two wood pontoons, *flotteur redan* (stepped).

24 Two Forlanini pontoons.

25 Longitudinal distance nose of pontoon to step approximately *2·4 m*.

26 Diameter; pontoon was built as a symmetrical aerodynamic shape and had no step.

27 Vertical distance bottom of pontoon to top of upper wing 3·16 m; vertical distance pontoon center-line to thrust line 1·75 m.

28 Of which 165 kg was fuel.

29 At interplane strut.

30 Sweepback: 10° upper wing only. No cabane; upper wing root was dropped ·20 m below standard S.20 dimension to attach directly to fuselage. Ailerons on lower wing only; total aileron area 1·2 m². Airfoil a "nearly symmetrical" double-cambered section.

31 Wood, two blades; blade width ·25 m; pitch 2·9 m at $\frac{3}{4}$ radius.

32 Area given applies for October 9, 1920; area may have been reduced to *14·0 m²* by November 4, 1920.

33 October 9, 1920.

34 November 4, 1920.

35 The S.26 (S.20, 1920 Monaco type) had speed wings; S.26*bis* had altitude wings.

36 For speed-wing arrangement, upper wing span was considerably shorter than lower; exact specification unknown.

37 Fuel weight 105 kg, oil weight 15 kg.

38 Oxygen weight.

39 Ailerons on lower wing only; aileron span (each) 2·65 m; aileron chord ·28m; total aileron area 1·484 m².

40 Ailerons on lower wing only; aileron span (each) 3·86 m; aileron chord ·30 m; total aileron area 2·316 m². Airfoil thickness 97 mm; *plan d'essieux* (area of wing-shaped axle fairing contributing to over-all lift) ·25 m². Total wing area often given as 26·75 m², which includes the axle fairing area.

41 Length also published as 6·44 m; the fuselage length listed is that of the *coque* structure, which had a maximum diameter of ·98 m; diameter 1 m ahead of its rearmost extremity was ·43 m.

42 Empty weight also has been published as 761 kg, 800 kg, and 840 kg, almost certainly because of differences in installed combat equipment.

43 Gross weight also has been published as 1,104 kg, 1,179 kg, and 1,200 kg; see note 42.

44 Fuel distribution: 147 liters in fuselage tank, 62 liters in wing tank.

45 Climb to 1,000 m in :02:21; to 2,000 m in :04:37; to 5,000 m in :15:02; to 6,500 m in :25:01.

46 Vertical distance, bottom of pontoon to thrust line 2·1 m.

47 Since wheel axle fairing did not exist on seaplane, total area has been expressed as 26·5 m²; see note 40.

48 Achieved January 3, 1920.

49 Short upper wing dimensions listed. Area distribution: upper wing 6·3 m²; lower wing 6·0 m². The 13·2 m² version had equal-span wings (wing span given as 6·000 m in 1920). Airfoil used (data published in 1922): RA51 (Halbronn). Ailerons on lower wing only; total aileron area 1·23 m².

50 *Coque* dimensions: length 5·45 m; maximum diameter 0·98 m (identical to basic Nieuport 29C.1).

51 Engine installed: 1920 Gordon Bennett 4(1); 1921 Coupe Deutsch 4(2); 1922 Coupe Deutsch 4(3).

52 Chauvière model "Intégrale"; wood, two-blade, blade width ·20 m, pitch 2·8 m at ¾ radius, used in 1920 Gordon Bennett.

53 Used in 1922 Coupe Deutsch.

54 Radiators: two Lamblins; total radiating surface 25 m².

55 Wing area distribution: main wing 10 m²; inferior wing 1·0 m². Total aileron area 1·4 m².

56 *Coque* dimensions: length 5·45 m; maximum diameter 0·98 m. Thrust line located ·3 m below *coque* axis. Longitudinal distance forward extremity (prop boss) to wing leading edge 1·0 m; this was true for 1921, 1922, and 1923 versions. In 1923 over-all length was increased to 6·2 m; extra length due to enlarged rudder.

57 Figure listed is vertical distance ground level only to top of fuselage (level position).

58 Fixed vertical fin area distribution: 0·40 m² above longitudinal axis, 0·16 m² below. This data applies to 1921 and 1922 racing sesquiplanes; vertical tail was enlarged in 1923, precise dimensions unknown.

59 1921 propeller: Lumière wood, two-blade, pitch 3.0 m.

60 Tank locations: fuel tank behind engine, oil tank under fuel tank. In February 1923 the speed record sesquiplane carried smaller tanks: 139 liters fuel, 20 liters oil.

61 In 1921 cooling system consisted of two Lamblin type A-1 radiators (Lamblin's smallest current model) modified to have only 90 elements instead of the standard 130; this was said to have saved 14 kg total weight. Total water capacity 35 liters. Water header located inside fuselage above engine rear mounting.

62 Areas identical to 1921 sesquiplane although new, slightly tapered, square-tipped main wing fitted. Airfoil used in 1922: Göttingen 416.

63 Weight breakdown for racing/speed-record sesquiplane used in 1922–23 (these values are typical of aero technology in the early 1920s):

Pₛ (airframe):		Pg (powerplant):	
Wing	120·0 kg	Engine	250·0 kg
Struts	33·0 kg	Cooling water	35·0 kg
Landing gear with axle		Water feed tank	2·0 kg
and small wing	50·6 kg	Two radiators	28·0 kg
Two complete wheels	26·9 kg	One glass gascolater	0·45 kg
Fuselage with engine		Hoses	6·2 kg
bearers and fixed		Propeller	13·0 kg
tail unit	154·5 kg	Prop hub	10·85 kg
Rudder	3·0 kg	Fuel tank	18·0 kg
Elevator	4·6 kg	Oil tank with oil	
Tailskid	2·9 kg	radiator	10·0 kg
Total Pₛ	395·5 kg	Total Pg	373·5 kg

64 Of which, in the original weight schedule, 139 kg is attributed to fuel, 20 kg to oil.

65 In 1923 the sesquiplane *Eugène Gilbert* as modified for the world speed record may have used engine 13(5).

66 Propeller used in 1922 and 1923: Regy-Sabbah wood, two-blade, pitch 3·2 m.

67 In February 1923 the speed record sesquiplane employed Moreux wing radiators fitted to the bottom main wing surface only; total radiating surface 6·8 m².

68 Area distribution of main and inferior wings unknown; on *type chasse* area ratio (main: inferior) was 4·219:1; however, total wing area was 26·2 m², more than twice that of the *type course* racer. Racer airfoil was a Joukowski design, "very nearly symmetrical, but it had a slight bend downward at the trailing edge." Wing root was 9" thick at front spar.

69 Fuselage length figure refers to *coque*, which had a maximum width of 1·2 m, maximum depth of 1·5 m. Thrust line was located ·3 m below *coque* axis.

70 Propeller pitch 3·2 m.

71 Fuel tank located *behind* pilot; oil tank located *behind* fuel tank!

72 Cooling supplied by one very large Lamblin radiator. Two French-built A.M.-manufactured engine-driven fuel pumps were fitted to the American-made engine.

73 Area distribution: main wing 14 m²; inferior wing 1·5 m²; total aileron area 1·6 m².

74 Fuselage length figure refers to *coque*, which had a maximum width of 0·99 m, maximum depth of 1·22 m; longitudinal distance aeroplane forward extremity to main wing leading edge 1·5 m.

75 Figure listed is vertical distance ground level only to top of fuselage (level position); vertical distance ground level to thrust line 1·55 m.

76 Bernard official documents show this aeroplane as the type 3C.1; it has always been referred to as just the C.1.

77 Wing area listed obtained from original Bernard documents; total planform area (determined by modern convention) 18·768 m². Mean aerodynamic chord 1·84 m. Root airfoil 0·3 m (14·3 per cent) thick. Aileron span (each) 2·2 m; aileron chord 0·4 m.

78 Longitudinal distance c.g. to elevator hinge line 4·58 m.

79 Vertical distance ground level to thrust line (level position) 1·55 m. Height figure listed applies to both 1922 and 1924 versions.

80 Fuel tank location in lower part of wing at c.g.; oil tank location inside landing gear pylon.

81 Wing factor of safety (1922 version) listed; landing gear factor of safety 5.

82 Wing area listed obtained from original Bernard documents. Tip dimensions unavailable. Root airfoil 0·35 m (15·2 per cent) thick.

83 Empennage dimensions listed apply to 1922 version and probably to 1924 version as well although this is unconfirmed.

84 Mean aerodynamic chord 1·61 m.

85 Longitudinal distance c.g. to elevator hinge 4·35 m.

86 Smaller wing was built for world speed record attempt; not used.

87 Airfoil thickness ·265 m (16·2 per cent) at root. Radiator mounted on bottom surface of wing, spanning (on each side) approximately *1·65 m*; sixteen fins on 17 mm centers per element; six elements per wing.

88 Vertical distance ground level to thrust line (level position) 1·525 m.

89 Total radiator surface of December 1924 world speed record version is generally listed as 1·0 m² less than that of October 1924; this reduction was accomplished not in the wing (water cooling) radiator but by eliminating the belly-mounted Lamblin oil cooling radiator. The wings were clipped at Istres in preparation for the world speed record flight; this reduced both span and aileron area although exact aileron dimensions are unconfirmed.

90 C.g. located at 32 per cent of root chord (·525 m behind root leading edge). Longitudinal distance prop disc plane to c.g. 1·507 m.

91 Weight breakdown of world speed record aeroplane:

P_s (airframe):		P_g (powerplant):	
Wing	218 kg	Engine	391 kg
Fuselage with		Propeller with hub	33 kg
fixed surfaces	168 kg	Feed tank with	
Wheels	27 kg	tubes and filter	48 kg
Other	6 kg	Hoses	25 kg*
		Water radiator	18 kg
Total P_s	419 kg	Oil plus oil radiator	31 kg
		Total P_g	546 kg

*Includes 8·2 liters water.

(Note: Original data listed instruments, dashboard not as fixed equipment under empty weight but as 14 kg equipment in useful load.)

92 Fuel tank location amidships at c.g.; oil tank location behind engine. Lamblin-built radiators; radiating surface 5 m²; water flow rate 260 liters/minute per radiator.

93 Accessories: Letombe-Luchard self-starter; Dhainaut wheels; Palladium tires; TEL tachometer; Luterma plywood; Avionine linen cover.

94 No fixed vertical tail surfaces.

95 Wings noted for their large aspect ratio of 8. Ailerons on upper wing only; total aileron area 1·1 m².

96 Weight schedule listed almost certainly correct; also published is the following:

P_s (airframe)	290 kg	Pilot	80 kg
P_g (powerplant)	380 kg	P_c (fuel and oil)	100 kg
P_v (empty)	670 kg	P_u (useful)	180 kg
P_T (gross weight)	850 kg		

97 Lumière wood, two-blade; blade width ·20 m; pitch 2·9 m at $\frac{3}{4}$ radius.

98 Two Lamblin radiators used; total radiating surface 25 m².

99 Borel *avion de chasse* design similar to racer climbed 6,000 m in :06:53.

100 Lower wing removable.

101 Area distribution (obtained from French documents): upper wing 15 m²; lower wing (which had constant chord) 5 m². Total planform area (including portion covered by fuselage) would be: upper wing 16 m²; lower wing 6 m². Airfoil: St.-Cyr SC 40 (thin bi-convex with sharp leading edge).

102 As biplane; 63·33 as monoplane.

103 Equipped with Letombe compressed-air self-starter.

104 Airfoil: Technische Berichte Joukowski No. 430 (said to be similar to HD.3-165-2).

105 Figure probable but unconfirmed; over-all length may have been 5.93 m.

106 Height may have been 2·4 m (including radiators mounted on top).

107 Gross weight may have been as high as 830 kg.

108 The optimistic builders estimated *400 kmh* V_{max} with the landing gear retracted!

109 Airfoil: symmetrical bi-convex Prandtl (Göttingen) 411. Wing span has also been published as 8·0 m but this is almost certainly in error.

110 Dimension unconfirmed. Longitudinal distance aeroplane forward extremity to wing leading edge 1·0 m.

111 There was no horizontal tail.

112 The figure 700 kg has also been published.

113 Incidence values unknown; however, wingtip was decidedly washed-in (i.e., it had more incidence than wing root).

114 Constant-chord wings were swept forward 30°; the chord value listed is that measured parallel to aeroplane longitudinal axis; chord perpendicular to wing leading edge 1·45 m. Aspect ratio was 7·8, quite high for a swept cantilever structure. Airfoil: symmetrical bi-convex Prandtl (Göttingen) 410.

115 Gross weight may have been as high as 1,400 kg.

116 Airfoil: Joukowski thin profile.

117 Airfoil was 10 per cent thick.

118 Maximum diameter of *coque* was 1·2 m.

119 Engine listed used by 36 *bis* in 1923; CAMS 36 in 1922 used engine 4(2).

120 Climb to 2,000 m in :05:49.

121 Lower wing had positive dihedral (degree unconfirmed); ailerons on lower wing only.

122 Climb to 2,000 m in :05:25.

123 Wing span has also been published as 23', and by the French in at least three different inexact metric values; these all appear to be in error. Airfoil: Dayton-Wright special, maximum thickness approximately 5½" at root (7 per cent); aileron area 23·0 ft². Aspect ratio 4·36.

124 Length has also been published as 22'4", almost certainly in error.

125 Vertical distance ground line to thrust line (level position) 52"; ground line to top of fuselage at wing leading edge 82".

126 Rudder area includes ·85 ft² in balance. Area of two fixed fins added at the 1920 Gordon Bennett race unknown and not included.

127 Original Hartzell propeller removed and French-built Lumière propeller installed for 1920 Gordon Bennett race.

128 Accessories: Dayton-Wright radiator (tubes by U. S. Cartridge Company, Lowell, Massachusetts); radiator dimensions approximately 42" high, 18" wide; centrifugal water pump (flow rate 18·5 gpm). Dayton Wire Wheel Company wheels; Goodyear tires; J. C. Wood Elastic Company shock absorbers; instruments by Foxboro, National Cash Register Company, Sperry, and Waltham; E. I. du Pont de Nemours Company celluloid windows; National Veneer Products Company plywood; Valspar varnish finish by Valentine Co.

129 Area distribution: upper wing 127 ft², lower wing 101·5 ft². Airfoil: RAF-15. Ailerons on lower wing only; aileron span (each) $89\frac{13}{32}$"; total aileron area 37 ft². Ailerons had elephant-ear balances that overhung main wing structure by 12" on each side (lower main wing structure span 26'2"). Figures given are for small "racing wings"; a larger set of flight test wings was used briefly: span upper wing 32', lower wing 29', total area 269 ft².

130 Several other lengths have been published, but erroneously, apparently due to years of miscopying and perpetuating wrong information. *Coque* maximum width 40", maximum depth 50".

131 Horizontal stabilizer angle fixed at $+\frac{1}{2}$° to mean aerodynamic chord (0° to thrust line).

132 Fuel weight only.

133 Includes weight of pilot, oil, other non-fixed equipment.

134 Weight figures in existing data vary between: for empty weight 2,435 lbs and 2,485 lbs (the weight breakdown listed was obtained from French documents based on French measurement of aeroplane at the 1920 Gordon Bennett race); for gross weight 3,153 and 3,233 lbs. Also see note 135.

135 The VCP-1 experimental pursuit from which the racer was developed had a much lighter engine — type 13(1) — and its weights were: empty *2,000* lbs (available figures vary between 1,980 and 2,014 lbs); gross *2,650* lbs (variation between 2,617 and 2,669 lbs).

136 The VCP-1 used McCook Field ASED wood two-blade propeller design X-17157. The VCP-R racer was fitted with wood two-blade design X-19399, with diameter 9'0" (for use with "low-compression engine") or 9'2" (for use with "high-compression engine"); pitch $9'2\frac{3}{4}$".

137 Fuel distribution: 37-gal main tank in fuselage; 23-gal forward auxiliary tank; 15-gal rear auxiliary tank; two 7-gal tanks, one in each upper wing panel. (The VCP-1 had a 44-gal capacity: 37-gal main and one 7-gal reserve.) Total water capacity 13·75 gal.

138 Accessories: Goodyear Aero Cord tires (700 mm×100 mm); Van Sicklen tachometer; Taylor altimeter; Sperry airspeed indicator; Boyce water thermometer.

139 Airfoil Curtiss C-45. Aileron span (each) 7'0". Lateral distance between wing strut attachments 17'0".

140 Length figures unconfirmed due to paucity and unreliability of available original documents, but figures listed must be considered close to correct. Racing monoplane longitudinal distance from aeroplane forward extremity to elevator trailing edge also given as 16·83' (sic). Racing biplane longitudinal distance forward extremity to upper wing leading edge 54".

141 Vertical distance ground line to thrust line (level position) $52\frac{3}{4}$".

142 Accessories: Dunlop wheels; Palmer tires size $23\frac{3}{4}$" × 3" (installed in France).

143 Airfoil RAF-15. Ailerons on upper wing only: aileron span (each) 6'6"; aileron chord 9".

144 Ailerons on mid- and lower-wings. Airfoil: Sloan (13 per cent thick). Total wing area sometimes given as 175 ft²; actual planform area computed by modern convention yields in excess of 200 ft².

145 Empennage dimensions probably were identical to the 1920 version.

146 Accessories: Goodyear tires; Army type D tachometer; Foxboro altimeter; Sperry airspeed indicator.

147 Climb to 14,500' in ten minutes.

148 L/D given by manufacturer as 9.

149 Area distribution: upper wing 112 ft²; mid- and lower-wings each 87·71 ft². Airfoil: Sloan (13 per cent thick). Ailerons on mid- and lower-wings; aileron span (each) $7'10\frac{1}{2}$"; aileron chord $7\frac{1}{2}$"; total aileron area 21·58 ft². Prototype appeared initially with straight wings; subsequently wings on all 18-T variants were modified to incorporate 5° sweepback. Designation 18-T-1 signified one-bay interplane bracing; 18-T-2 signified two-bay interplane bracing; 18-T-2 wings were equal-span; wing data other than span unchanged.

150 Length $22'5\frac{9}{16}$" without prop.

151 Built-in angle of incidence of horizontal stabilizer +0·5°.

152 Rudder height 46".

153 Useful load includes pilot plus one passenger at 165 lbs each; 400 lbs fuel; 45 lbs oil.

154 Engine used in 1920 Pulitzer 17(1); in 1922 Curtiss Marine Trophy race A-3325 used 19(1) and A-3326 used 19(2). For the 1923 races engine 19(2) was used.

155 Prototype 18-T used wood prop, four-blade. In the 1920 Pulitzer the 18-Ts used two-blade wood props, diameter 9'0", pitch: 10'6" for A-3325, and $10'0\frac{3}{4}$" for A-3326. In 1922 and 1923 the props installed were four-blade, Charavay design, Hartzell-built.

156 Accessories: In 1920: Goodyear tires, 26"×4"; Victometer-Jones tachometer; Sperry airspeed indicator; Boyce water thermometer. In 1923 NAR: ballast load 236·59 lbs. Bush side radiators; Boyce Motometer thermometer (two); National Gauge thermometer (one); Johns-Manville tachometer; Foxboro airspeed indicator; Ajax tires 26"×4"; Valentine Company Valspar finish.

157 Climb to 13,125' in ten minutes.

158 V_max achieved August 19, 1918 with 18-T-1; maximum altitude achieved September 19, 1919 with 18-T-2. Range 550 miles at "economic" speed.

159 Empennage dimensions identical for both types with exception of seaplane, which had added vertical surface, dimensions unconfirmed.

160 Area distribution: upper wing 88 ft², lower wing 80 ft². Airfoil: Sloan (13 per cent thick); ailerons on lower wing only; aileron span (each) $10'2\frac{1}{4}$" (these were full-span ailerons); total aileron area 17·6 ft².

161 Longitudinal distances: lower wing leading edge back to c.g.: 7·76" fully loaded, 2·56" empty; lower wing leading edge to elevator hinge 14'2"; to rudder hinge $14'7\frac{1}{2}$"; from forward extremity (spinner tip) to upper wing leading edge $41\frac{5}{8}$"; to wheel center $48\frac{3}{8}$"; spinner length 15".

162 Vertical distance ground line to thrust line (level position) 62"; lower wing chord to thrust line 13"; thrust line to top of vertical tail $38\frac{1}{4}$".

163 Vertical surface area originally 9·6 ft² (prototype had low fin and rudder each with 4·8 ft² area). CR-3 vertical tail height 6" more than that of CR-2 (i.e., vertical distance thrust line to top of vertical tail on CR-3: $44\frac{1}{4}$").

164 Accessories: CR-1: two Lamblin radiators. CR-2: Curtiss wing radiators on top surface of upper wing only (eighteen elements); Goodyear tires (26" diameter); Army type D tachometer; Foxboro altimeter; Sperry airspeed indicator.

165 Climb to 16,500' in ten minutes.

166 Submerged displacement 4,670 lbs (approximately 170 per cent gross weight).

167 Horizontal tail dimensions unchanged.

168 Fuel distribution: fuselage tank 51·5 gal; 8-gal tank in each pontoon.

169 Climb to 14,300' in ten minutes.

170 Area distribution: upper wing 68·46 ft², lower wing 64·14 ft², axle fairing 3·31 ft². Airfoil Curtiss C-27. Ailerons on both upper and lower wings; aileron span (each) 40"; aileron chord $10\frac{1}{2}$"; total aileron area *9·25 ft²* (the figure 9·04 ft² has also been published).

171 *Coque* maximum width $28\frac{1}{2}$" (fuselage maximum width $32\frac{1}{2}$" including protruding exhaust stacks); maximum depth $38\frac{1}{2}$".

172 Height in three-point position 7'7"; vertical distance ground line to thrust line (level position) 54".

173 Rudder height above thrust line $37\frac{3}{4}$"; fin fixed 1° leading edge left to counteract torque. Horizontal tail dimensions unchanged.

174 Of which 303 lbs is fuel, 22·5 lbs oil.

175 In 1924 empty weight listed by USAS as 1,642 lbs, useful load 468 lbs, gross weight 2,110 lbs.

176 Engine listed used in 1922; in 1923 aeroplane A.S.68564 used engine 20(2), A.S.68563 used engine 21; in 1924 both aeroplanes used engine 21.

177 Propeller data: original 1922 prop: wood design EX-28904, diameter 7'4", coarse pitch (used by both racers); 1923 speed record props included in addition wood design X-44059 and Reed metal; 1923 Pulitzer props: racer number 50 used wood design X-44499, diameter 7'10", racer number 49 used Reed metal design D-27; 1924 Pulitzer props: wood design X-45101 (used by both racers).

178 Accessories: Goodyear tires 26"×3"; in 1923 Pulitzer: Army type C tachometer, Pioneer airspeed indicator, altimeter (none); in 1924 Pulitzer: Van Sicklen tachometer, Boyce thermometer.

179 Mean aerodynamic chord 50·3". Airfoil Curtiss C-62 (8·04 per cent thick). Ailerons on both upper and lower wings; upper wing aileron span (each) $39\frac{9}{32}$", aileron chord 12"; lower wing aileron span (each) $40\frac{1}{4}$", aileron chord $10\frac{1}{2}$"; total aileron area 9·8 ft². Total wing area of 148.25 ft² has also been published; figure listed obtained from official Curtiss documents. Fourteen wing radiator elements on both surfaces of upper wing; twelve elements on both surfaces lower wing; radiators formed from ·004" corrugated brass sheet.

180 Longitudinal distance forward extremity (spinner tip) to upper wing leading edge 50"; spinner length 17".

181 Vertical distance ground line to thrust line (level position) 53"; lower wing chord to thrust line $16\frac{3}{4}$".

182 Weight figures listed from original Curtiss documents; other weights published: empty 1,565 lbs, gross 2,071 lbs.

183 Reed type M-16 used in 1923 Pulitzer, diameter given as either *7'8"* or *7'10"*, latter figure more likely. Pitch 10'0".

184 Accessories: no battery or starter; B. F. Goodrich tires 26"×3"; Jones tachometer; Pioneer airspeed indicator; altimeter (none).

185 Climb to 5,000' in :01:36; to 10,000' in :03:36; to 15,000' in :05:48; to 20,900' in ten minutes. Manufacturer's calculated L/D: 9.

186 Longitudinal distances: lower wing leading edge aft to c.g. 10·38" fully loaded, c.g. to elevator hinge 11'10·4"; lower wing leading edge forward to mean aerodynamic chord leading edge 7·22".

187 Pontoon dimensions: nose of pontoon to step $9'11\frac{1}{4}$"; angle included in pontoon V-bottom 120°; angle of load water line to horizontal 2°40'. Total submerged displacement 4,454 lbs (approximately 171·5 per cent gross weight). Longitudinal distance step to c.g. $19\frac{3}{4}$".

188 Vertical distance thrust line to top of pontoons *52*".

189 Reed design EX-32600.

190 Capacities listed obtained from original preliminary design data; final disposition may have been fuel 64 gal, oil 4 gal.

191 Mean aerodynamic chord 48·6". Airfoil Curtiss C-80 (6 per cent thick). Ailerons on both upper and lower wings; aileron dimensions identical to those of R2C (see note 179). Wing planform almost identical to that of R2C except that lower wing had 9" longer span and upper wings had larger cutouts near fuselage (accounting for smaller over-all area and mean aerodynamic chord than R2C). Fourteen wing radiator elements on both surfaces upper and lower wings; total radiating surface 261 ft²; radiators formed from ·005" corrugated brass sheet provided by U. S. Cartridge Company, Lowell, Massachusetts. Usable water supply 12 gal; flow rate 75 gpm.

192 Longitudinal distance forward extremity (spinner tip) to upper wing leading edge 55½"; spinner length 17". C.g. location 31·8 per cent mean aerodynamic chord fully loaded; longitudinal distance c.g. to elevator hinge 11'10·4", to rudder hinge 12' 4·4".

193 Discrepancies exist in published figures for height; figure listed most likely; moreover, it corresponds closely to height of very similar R2C. Vertical distance ground line to thrust line (level position) 53"; lower wing chord to thrust line 16¾".

194 Includes 136·2 lbs radiator weight, 106 lbs water weight.

195 Curtiss-Reed type R forged steel design EX-32995, pitch 10'0".

196 One fuel tank in fuselage directly behind firewall, oil tank under engine crankcase; oil radiator water-cooled.

197 Accessories: Goodyear tires 26" diameter; Jones tachometer; Pioneer airspeed indicator; Boyce Motometer water thermometer; Boyce oil temperature gauge; National oil pressure gauge; U. S. Navy type B fuel pressure gauge; Waltham clock; Valspar finish.

198 Climb to 5,000' in :01:28; to 10,000' in :03:17; to 15,000' in :05:45.

199 Range 216 miles at full throttle (manufacturer's data).

200 C.g. location 33·2 per cent mean aerodynamic chord; longitudinal distance c.g to elevator hinge 11'9·8"; to rudder hinge 12'3·8". Longitudinal distance lower wing leading edge to step 30$\frac{1}{16}$"; to pontoon rear attach point 41½"; longitudinal distance between pontoon attach points 82$\frac{5}{16}$"; longitudinal distance step to c.g. 23¾".

201 Pontoon dimensions: nose of pontoon to step 9'11½"; angle included in pontoon V-bottom 120°.

202 Vertical distance thrust line to top of pontoon 52½"; to bottom of pontoon 75¼".

203 Curtiss/Reed type R forged steel design EX-32995-112; pitch 10'0".

204 Climb to 5,000' in :02:01; to 10,000' in :04:46; to 15,000' in :09:04.

205 Manufacturer's range: 290 miles at full throttle.

206 Prop diameter originally 9'1"; prop with diameter 9'4" fitted for 1926 Schneider race.

207 Airfoil M-80. Ailerons on main wing only; aileron span (each) 8'10"; total aileron area 21·0 ft². Lateral distance aeroplane center-line to main wing strut attach point 9'3".

208 Length figure close to exact but unconfirmed. Longitudinal distance forward extremity (spinner tip) to main wing leading edge 53"; c.g. location 31·4 per cent main wing chord; longitudinal distance c.g. to rudder hinge 15'9".

209 Vertical distance ground line to thrust line (level position) 78".

210 Angle of incidence of fixed horizontal stabilizer −3°.

211 Fuel weight only.

212 Tires 30"×5" high pressure. Two Lamblin radiators carried.

213 Airfoil M-80. Ailerons on both wings. Upper wing aileron span (each) 72$\frac{1}{16}$"; lower wing aileron span (each) 55$\frac{7}{16}$"; chord (all ailerons) 18"; total aileron area 24·0 ft². Wing overhang outboard of vertical pontoon struts 9'8$\frac{29}{32}$". Fifty wing radiator elements: on both surfaces of upper (thirty-two) and lower

(eighteen) wings; upper wing radiator span (each surface) 81" (lateral distance center-line to inboard edge 7½"); lower wing radiator span (each surface) 45" (lateral distance center-line to inboard edge 60").

214 Fuselage length listed is longitudinal distance from spinner tip to rearmost empennage extremity. Longitudinal distance spinner tip to wing leading edge 57$\frac{1}{32}$"; to rudder hinge 21'8$\frac{31}{32}$". Maximum fuselage width 33½". C.g. location 20·3" behind wing leading edge (fully loaded); longitudinal distance c.g. to elevator hinge 14'10$\frac{31}{32}$", to rudder hinge 15'4$\frac{17}{32}$".

215 Pontoon dimensions: nose of pontoon to step 12'2¼"; angle, load water line to horizontal 2·5°; angle included in pontoon V-bottom 120°; longitudinal distance c.g. to step 16$\frac{13}{32}$".

216 Angle of incidence of fixed horizontal stabilizer −0·5°.

217 Rudder dimension along hinge line.

218 NW-2 prototype originally fitted with two-blade wood prop similar to that used by NW-1; for 1923 Schneider race a three-blade forged dural, adjustable pitch prop was installed.

219 Airfoil Wright W-1 (modified M-80). Ailerons on both upper and lower wings; aileron span (each) 41"; aileron chord 17½"; total aileron area 16·4 ft². Sixty wing radiator elements: on both surfaces of upper (thirty-two) and lower (twenty-eight) wings; upper wing radiator span (each surface) 80½" (lateral distance center-line to inboard edge 6½"); lower wing radiator span (each surface) 71" (lateral distance center-line to inboard edge 16$\frac{7}{8}$"). Usable water capacity 8 gal; flow rate 70 gpm. Lateral distance aeroplane center-line to interplane strut 7'7$\frac{7}{8}$".

220 Horizontal stabilizer adjustable through incidence range of −3° to +1°. (−3° to 0° on F2W-2 seaplane.)

221 Aeroplane A-6743 useful load provided for only 206 lbs fuel; A-6744 carried 390 lbs fuel, as well as 44 lbs more installed equipment than its sister ship.

222 Prototype appeared with two-blade wood prop; for 1923 Pulitzer three-blade forged dural adjustable pitch props fitted to both F2W aeroplanes.

223 Accessories: no starter or battery; Goodyear Aero Cord tires 27"×4" high pressure.

224 Airfoil N-9 (modified Göttingen 398). Ailerons on both upper and lower wings; aileron span (each) 42$\frac{23}{32}$"; aileron chord 14$\frac{5}{16}$"; total aileron area 12·4 ft². Forty-eight wing radiator elements: on both surfaces of upper (twenty-four) and lower (twenty-four) wings. Lateral distance aeroplane center-line to interplane strut 7'8$\frac{1}{8}$".

225 Maximum fuselage width 32¾". Fuselage length dimension listed does not include spinner.

226 Pontoon dimensions: nose of pontoon to step 12'3$\frac{9}{16}$"; submerged displacement 7,100 lbs (170·6 per cent gross weight).

227 Horizontal tail dimensions unchanged; vertical tail dimensions listed apply to second (enlarged) rudder used by F2W-2.

228 Of which 617·5 lbs is fuel and 67·5 lbs oil.

229 Incidence varied laterally: from aeroplane center-line to attach point of the first (of two) interplane struts it was +3°; thereafter to tip it was 2°20'.

230 Airfoil RAF-15. Mean aerodynamic chord 63$\frac{3}{16}$". Differences exist in published data on chord. Best evidence is that Thomas-Morse–built MB-3s had chord of 63"; Boeing-built MB-3As had chord of 67". In any event, wing trailing edge was slightly curved in planform and scalloped as well, resulting in varying chord. Ailerons on upper wing only; aileron span (each) 76½"; aileron chord 28$\frac{5}{8}$"; total aileron area 22 ft². Wing area listed obtained from USAS official flight test data; however, other figures exist.

231 Differences in published length vary between 19'11" and 20'2". Fuselage maximum width 36"; maximum depth 45". Longitudinal distance c.g. to elevator hinge 12'7½"; to rudder hinge 13'5¼".

232 Vertical distance ground line to thrust line (level position) 56$\frac{13}{16}$".

233 MB-3A empennage dimensions:

	h	v
span	10'1"	—
chord	26"F	$35\frac{1}{2}$"F
	$14\frac{1}{4}$"M	$21\frac{3}{4}$"M
chord (overall)	$40\frac{1}{4}$"	$57\frac{1}{4}$"

234 Published data indicate numerous weight values for MB-3 variants. Indicated is the best available data relating to the MB-3s that participated in the 1920 Pulitzer race. In 1921 the Thomas-Morse–built MB-3 tested by Macready in March weighed 1,636 lbs empty (including engine 632 lbs, water 58 lbs); useful load was 912 lbs (including pilot 180 lbs, fuel 350 lbs, oil 37 lbs, military equipment 345 lbs) for a gross weight of 2,548 lbs.

235 Through 1920–21; in MB-3As engine 13(3) was used in 1922, and 13(4) in 1923.

236 McCook Field two-blade wood props used in 1920; in 1921 wood props with diameter 8'2", pitch $7'9\frac{3}{4}$" were used.

237 MB-3A: 45 gal.

238 Accessories: radiator: "cellular core," wing-mounted, length $20\frac{1}{4}$", width $7\frac{1}{2}$", radiating surface 160 ft², water capacity 5 gal, flow rate 40 gpm at 2·5 psi. In 1920 Pulitzer: Goodyear tires 30"×3"; Signal Corps type A tachometer; Signal Corps type D altimeter; airspeed indicator (none); Boyce type C water thermometer. In 1923 Mitchell (MB-3A): Goodyear tires 28"×4"; Van Sicklen tachometer; Taylor altimeter; Bristol airspeed indicator; Boyce Motometer thermometer.

239 MB-3 prototype: climb to 10,000' in :04:52; MB-3A: climb to 6,500' in :05:42; to 10,000' in :10:06; to 15,000' in :19:42; absolute ceiling 20,600' reached in :38:36.

240 MB-3A endurance 2:15.

241 Accessories: Goodyear tires; Van Sicklen tachometer; Tycos altimeter; Precision airspeed indicator.

242 Airfoil USA-27 (modified). Mean aerodynamic chord 60".

243 Figures apply to s/n 64374. (There is unconfirmed evidence that 64373 weighed 1,975 lbs gross.)

244 Engine listed used in 1921; engine 13(4) used in 1922.

245 Prop listed was used by 64373 in 1921 Pulitzer. Hartzell props also fitted.

246 Fuel distribution: main fuselage tank 33 gal; wing reserve tank 9 gal.

247 Accessories: Goodyear 30"×3" tires; Signal Corps tachometer; altimeter (none); U. S. Navy airspeed indicator (temporary installation for 1922 Pulitzer race only); Signal Corps water and oil thermometers and oil pressure gauge.

248 Achieved April 19, 1922.

249 Given by manufacturer as 9 with c.p. at 28 per cent mean aerodynamic chord; as 6 with c.p. at 48 per cent mean aerodynamic chord.

250 Airfoil USA-27 (modified; thickness *12·85 per cent*).

251 Length may have been 19'9".

252 Refers to elevators which had overhang aerodynamic balance; span of fixed horizontal stabilizer 6'9".

253 Gross weight may have been 2,750 lbs, at least on one version.

254 Pitch 7'0".

255 All fuel carried in wing center-section.

256 Accessories: tires 28"×3.5".

257 Achieved October 30, 1922.

258 Airfoil NACA 81 (modified; thickness 16·5 per cent or, for R-3, $15\frac{1}{2}$" thick at root). On original layout drawing (X-40216) both "clipped wing" (29'6" span) and long wing ($32'8\frac{1}{2}$" span) proposals were indicated; long wing version never built. (Span of racer version has also been published [unconfirmed] as 29'3".) Area has been given as 132·9 ft² but this neglected portion of planform covered by fuselage; planform area (computed by modern convention) is essentially the figure listed. Aileron trailing edge overhung wing trailing edge; aileron span (each) approximately *8'8"*.

259 Vertical distance ground line to thrust line (level position, aeroplane empty, gear fully extended) 59".

260 McCook Field props (s/n 22-1280 to 22-1283) and Hartzell birch props were fitted. Two types of Hartzell props were used: (1) diameter 8'3", pitch 8'4", (2) diameter 8'0", pitch $8'8\frac{1}{2}$".

261 162·8 mph (gear extended); 191·1 mph (gear retracted).

262 Airfoil remained NACA 81 modified to 16·5 per cent thickness. Mean aerodynamic chord 64·6". Tip geometry: tip radius $21\frac{1}{2}$"; actual wingtip extremity extended 15" outboard of developed tip. Longitudinal distance root leading edge to developed tip leading edge $36\frac{1}{2}$". Dihedral listed was taken at mean camber line; geometric dihedral of bottom wing surface (due to taper) 4·5°. Aileron span (each) 68"; total aileron area 9·3 ft². Wing radiators on both surfaces; element width 9"; ten elements on top wing surface, seven and a half elements on bottom; lateral distance radiator outboard edge to wingtip (both surfaces) 68". Wing span has also been published as 30'[0"] and 30'3"; figure listed is almost certainly correct.

263 Incidence of fixed horizontal stabilizer: 0°.

264 Vertical fin cambered to offset torque.

265 Weight figures listed most likely; empty weight has also been published as 2,032 lbs, gross as 2,503 lbs.

266 Engine 20(1) used in 1923; engine 21 used in 1924.

267 Prop used in 1923 Pulitzer was Curtiss/Reed model M-18, diameter 7'8". In 1924 Pulitzer McCook Field wood prop used.

268 Accessories: 1923: Booster-mag starter fitted; Goodyear tires 26"×4", wheels had 8" hub with internally sprung, Laddon shock absorbers. Van Sicklen tachometer; Taylor altimeter; Pioneer airspeed indicator; Boyce Motometer thermometer. In 1924: only change was Tycos altimeter replaced Taylor.

269 Total aileron area 8·4 ft². Wing overhang beyond strut attach point 7'6" each side.

270 Maximum fuselage width 25".

271 Height figure listed was taken at wings. Vertical distance ground line to thrust line (level position) 62"; thrust line to wheel center $48\frac{23}{32}$".

272 These are manufacturer's figures; pilot weight of 150 lbs is some 30 lbs less than service standard weight. Gross weight is given "in racing trim."

273 Loening data gives prop diameter as 8'8"; 1920 Pulitzer Contest Committee report lists prop with diameter 8'0" and pitch 8'3".

274 Accessories: Goodyear tires 26"×4"; U. S. Navy tachometer and thermometer; airspeed indicator (none).

275 Vertical distance ground line to top of fuselage (level position) $87\frac{1}{2}$".

276 Published data on R-4 gross weight varies between 2,700 lbs and 3,700 lbs for the final, "modified" version.

277 Fuel tank located behind pilot.

278 Climb to 10,000' in five minutes.

279 Airfoil Göttingen 387 (16 per cent thick).

280 A-6430 was fitted with wing radiators; forty-four elements (total), each $5\frac{1}{2}$" wide. A-6429 had two Lamblin radiators. Both aeroplanes had Lamblin oil radiators.

281 Wing geometry identical for TS and TR; TS airfoil USA-27 (S meant "standard wings"); TR airfoil modified RAF-15 (R meant "racing wings").

282 Longitudinal distance wing leading edge to elevator hinge $16'1\frac{1}{32}$"; to rudder hinge $16'3\frac{15}{16}$"; to c.g. 17·75" (fully loaded). (Vertical distance thrust line down to c.g. 10·82".)

283 For landplane versions. All TS and TR variants involved in air racing were seaplanes.

284 Gross weights and loadings:

	Gross weight	Wing loading	Power loading
TS-1	*2,025 lbs*	*9·0*	*8·44*
TS-2	*2,085 lbs*	*9·27*	*8·69*
TR-1	*1,790 lbs*	*7·96*	*7·46*
TR-3	*1,980 lbs*	*8·8*	*8·25*

Other weights published include, for TS-1, 2,123 lbs in 1920; for TS-2 2,460 lbs, presumably including military load (which was not carried in air racing events); and for TR-1 1,720 lbs.

285 Three engine types were allocated to the four TS and TR race participants in 1922:

aeroplane with dash number:	had engine:	
-1	28(1)	(i.e., TS-1, TR-1)
-2	27(1)	(i.e., TS-2)
-3	12(2)	(i.e., TR-3)

286 Area distribution: upper wing 95 ft², lower wing 90 ft². Ailerons on both upper and lower wings; total aileron area 18 ft².

287 Fuselage cross section area 8·7 ft².

288 Useful load in military configuration given by manufacturer as 525 lbs; this yields the gross weight value of 1,337 lbs which has been published. Other weights published: 833 lbs empty; 1,618 lbs gross.

289 Wood, two-blade, pitch 5'4".

290 Listed is speed demonstrated at sea level; credited V_{max} at 20,000': 121 mph.

291 Climb to 3,000' in :01:30; to 5,000' in :03:10; to 10,000' in :07:20; to 15,000' in :14:00; to 20,000' in :21:48.

292 At 75 per cent power at 15,000' (manufacturer's figures).

293 Ailerons on upper wings only; total aileron area 16 ft².

294 Ailerons on both upper and lower wings; total aileron area 22 ft².

295 Airfoil RAF-15. Ailerons on both upper and lower wings; aileron span (each) 63"; total aileron area 21 ft². Single-seat Baby had square wingtips.

296 Longitudinal distance forward extremity (prop boss) to upper wing leading edge 34"; upper wing leading edge to elevator hinge 14'11". (Figures apply to two-seater; single-seater was 30" shorter overall, but otherwise had identical dimensions. Engine mount on two-seater had been lengthened to balance passenger weight.)

297 No fixed vertical fin; rudder built in circular planform, diameter 36".

298 Weights for single-seater: empty 610 lbs; useful 215 lbs; gross 825 lbs. Loadings: wing 4·67 lbs/ft²; power 23·57 lbs/hp.

299 Propeller pitch 5'3".

300 Standard capacities for single-seater: fuel 6 gal; oil 1 gal.

301 Accessories: Palmer tires 600mm × 50mm; aeroplane carried tachometer, altimeter, airspeed indicator, radiator thermometer, oil pressure gauge, "cross-level" (sic), and "watch" (clock).

302 Climb to 1,000' in :02:15; to 5,000' in :11:00 (one-seater), :13:00 (two-seater); to 10,000' in :25:00 (one-seater), :35:00 (two-seater).

303 Total aileron area 18 ft².

304 This weight is equivalent to the M.1C (military monoplane) gross weight less 80 lbs "military load."

305 Wood, two-blade; pitch 8'11".

306 Credited V_{max} at 10,000': 117 mph (manufacturer's figure).

307 Climb to 5,000' in :03:30; to 10,000' in :09:00; to 15,000' in :19:00 (figures for M.1C with military load; model 77 racer performance was undoubtedly superior).

308 Ailerons on upper wing only. These dimensions refer only to 1920 version of Bullet. Reliable dimensions of clipped-wing version used in 1921 do not exist.

309 Engines used: 1920–21: 42(1); 1922: 42(3); 1923: 42(5).

310 Ailerons on both upper and lower wings; aileron span (each) 6'11·2"; aileron chord approximately 16"; total aileron area 37·2 ft².

311 Longitudinal distance forward extremity (propeller boss) to upper wing leading edge 26"; upper wing leading edge to elevator hinge 14'4". Maximum fuselage cross section area 10 ft². Over-all length figures in existing data vary between 18'0" and 18'9"; the original Nighthawk was 18'6" long and the most reliable existing technical data indicate that this is almost certainly the correct dimension for the two L.C.1 Nieuhawks.

312 Fixed vertical fin area distribution: above fuselage 3·44 ft², below fuselage 1·68 ft². Vertical span taken along extended rudder hinge line to top of rudder. Rudder chord listed does not include balance; with balance rudder chord is 24½".

313 Wood, two-blade; diameter also published as 9'6", pitch 7'0".

314 Three fuel tanks carried; location: one 16·5-gal tank in each fuselage side fairing; one 7-gal tank in upper wing center-section.

315 Accessories: Palmer aero tires 26" × 4".

316 Credited V_{max} at altitude: 140 mph at 10,000'; 121 mph at 20,000' (manufacturer's figures).

317 Climb to 5,000' in :03:00; to 10,000' in :07:00; to 20,000' in :20:00.

318 Wings clipped 2 feet in span on Nieuhawk No. 2. Although no separate sources confirm data other than that listed, it is most probable that all wing data indicated for L.C.1 No. 1 are also valid for No. 2.

319 Other weights published for one-seater: gross 2,120 lbs.

320 Wingtip planform: upper wing round, lower wing square. Wing area: Nieuport & General adhered to the convention then in vogue not to include portion covered by fuselage in total wing area; total planform area by modern convention is 151·97 ft². Ailerons on lower wing only; aileron span (each) 4'6"; aileron chord 15"; total aileron area 10·95 ft².

321 Fuselage cross section circular at engine firewall, diameter 44½".

322 Height measured to top of upper wing center-section (wingtips some 3" higher due to dihedral). Vertical distance ground line to thrust line (level position) 66".

323 Both horizontal and vertical tail dimensions were modified from straight Nighthawk; horizontal tail was provided with some 16 per cent less over-all area; rudder was enlarged to enhance the racer's flying qualities.

324 Wingtip planform on all versions of Bamel: upper wing round, lower wing square. Ailerons on lower wing only; total aileron area 18 ft².

325 Longitudinal distance forward extremity (spinner tip) to upper wing leading edge 47"; to wheel center 57"; to rear of cockpit 11'2½" (aft fuselage and tail adapted directly from Nighthawk); to rudder hinge 20'6½". Spinner length 10½". Maximum fuselage width 39".

326 Vertical distance thrust line to chord reference (bottom surface) of upper wing 33½"; of lower wing 23½". Horizontal tail chord 4" below thrust line. Vertical distance ground line to thrust line (level position) 72".

327 Empennage was Nighthawk for all 1921 activities of Bamel; also see note 312.

328 Wood, two-blade; pitch 9'6".

329 Both the fuel tank and cooling water tank (capacity 8·5 Imp. gal) were located in the cabane "hump."

330 Wing area listed was that widely reported by British accounts. The French, however, who measured the aeroplane on the occasion of its Coupe Deutsch participation, reported 18 m² (193·75 ft²), which corresponds more closely to the planform area yielded by manufacturer's span and chord dimensions.

331 This wing configuration remained until 1923, when the Bamel was totally overhauled to become Gloster I. It is reported – but not confirmed – that the Bamel's wing area was reduced even below this value for the 1922 Coupe Deutsch; the figure 160 ft² has been published, as well as 15·14 m² (163 ft²) by the French; if the wings were indeed clipped further for this race, no record of the reduced span exists. (Area distribution for 165 ft² version: upper wing 88 ft²; lower wing 77 ft².)

332 Achieved December 19, 1921.

333 Bamel's vertical tail planform was altered to S.E.5 style in 1922; area distribution of fixed vertical fin 4·75 ft² above fuselage, 1·9 ft² below fuselage. Horizontal tail surfaces were not substantially altered.

334 Weight not confirmed; published values for autumn 1922 vary from 2,557 lbs to the value listed.

335 These figures are given in U.S. gallons, converted from French 1922 measurements: fuel 227 liters, oil 27 liters, water 45 liters (twelve U.S. gal).

336 Achieved October 4, 1922 in France.
337 Length has also been published as 21'10"; figure listed is more probably correct. Longitudinal distance forward extremity (spinner tip) to upper wing leading edge *44"*; to rudder hinge *20'0"*; spinner length *10"*.
338 Vertical distance thrust line to chord reference (bottom surface) of upper wing *30½"*; of lower wing *24"*. Vertical distance ground line to thrust line (level position) *72"*
339 Climb to 20,000' in :12:24.
340 Gloster I tested several different pontoons, primarily those intended for use on Gloster II and Gloster III racers. Figures refer to typical May, Harden & May (a de Havilland subsidiary)—manufactured all-metal pontoons. Longitudinal distance nose of pontoon to step *9'8"* (dimensions unconfirmed; this dimension also varied).
341 Vertical distance thrust line to top of pontoon *68"*.
342 Gloster I adopted modified Gamecock style vertical tail when pontoons were fitted. Rudder chord listed does not include balance. Vertical fin area distributed approximately *3·45 ft²* above fuselage, *1·55 ft²* below fuselage. Any changes made to horizontal tail surfaces unknown.
343 Figures unconfirmed; much disparity in existing data exists. Wing areas of 150 ft² (13·93 m²) and 152 ft² have also been published, but the latter figure is Gloster III wing area; it appears that in many cases Gloster III dimensions may have been inadvertently (or otherwise) applied by latter-day historians to the vacuum existing for Gloster II; this may seem logical since the aeroplanes resembled each other, but must be considered at best inexact.
344 Reliable figures for landplane version do not exist. Wings and empennage were similar to Gloster I. Fuselage cross section has been given as 9·5 ft².
345 Applies to seaplane.
346 Weights and loadings listed to left apply to landplane; those on right apply to seaplane.
347 Pitch *15'11"*; propeller dimensions not confirmed.
348 Applies to landplane.
349 Pontoon dimensions: longitudinal distance nose of pontoon to step 19'8"; pontoon height 24".
350 Weights of Gloster III-B are: empty 2,278 lbs; useful load 684 lbs; gross weight 2,962 lbs.
351 Ailerons on both upper and lower wings; total aileron area 27 ft².
352 Over-all length (including pontoons) of 22'0" has also been published.
353 The probability is that these empennage dimensions were not altered throughout the aeroplane's existence.
354 Engine 40(2) was fitted for 1920 Aerial Derby, after which aeroplane was inactive until 1923, when it was refitted for racing with engine 42(4).
355 Few reliable details are known; it is known that area of lower wing was less than half that of upper wing; exact specifications other than those listed are unconfirmed.
356 Few reliable details exist regarding Sea Lion racers. The Sea Lion II was derived from the commercial Sea King II, a fact that has to some extent confused aero historians, and most published Sea Lion data apply in fact to the Sea King instead. It is virtually certain that the Sea Lion had a wing span essentially identical to the Sea King's, but a reduced wing chord. The preponderance of available evidence suggests the span was 32'0"; a span of 31'10" has also been indicated although this may apply to the Sea Lion III (unconfirmed). Sea King chord was 66"; exact Sea Lion chord remains unconfirmed although it was close to 60". Other Sea King wing dimensions (close but not necessarily identical to Sea Lion) are: gap 74½". Sea Lion II wing area was close to *340 ft²*.
357 The most likely length attributed to Sea Lion II is also the accepted Sea King II length.
358 Other weight values have been published, varying down to 2,850 lbs (excessively low).

359 Exact wing span unknown; it is reported to have been "noticeably shorter" than that of Sea Lion II. Area listed has been specifically attributed to Sea Lion III but is suspiciously close to Sea King II area of 284 ft² — although other Sea King wing dimensions were admittedly somewhat different.
360 Fuselage modifications for 1923 added significantly to aeroplane hull length.
361 Gross weight of 3,275 lbs has also been published.
362 Climb to 10,000' in :07:00.
363 Airfoil RAF-30. Some sources given span 30'6", area 136 ft².
364 Fuselage frontal area 8·45 ft². (Fuselage length listed is from forward extremity [spinner tip] to rearmost extremity on empennage. Some sources give over-all length 27'0".)
365 Total submerged buoyancy 4,950 lbs (approximately 155 per cent gross weight).
366 Water capacity 10 Imp. gal.
367 Achieved September 13, 1925.
368 Figures in existing data vary considerably for all dimensions of the A.1. The aeroplane — a pursuit — was originally built in metric, but because of a brief postwar popularity in the United States most available data are given in English measure (converted and rounded off) and thus must be considered to a great extent approximate. Wing span listed is accurate for 1918–20 versions.
369 According to some Italian documents length may have been 6·5 m, but this is doubtful.
370 Height has also been published as 2·85 m and 3·2 m in Italian documents; the latter figure almost certainly refers to larger SVA aeroplane.
371 This weight may include certain military equipment. Empty weight has also been published as 615 kg, more reasonable for a stripped, racing version.
372 Engine 45(1) was almost universally used through 1921; however, engine 45(2) was also used (see 1920 Pulitzer table, Appendix 2).
373 Accessories: 1920 Pulitzer: Pirelli tires 26" diameter; Jaeger tachometer; Fournier thermometer; airspeed indicator and altimeter (none).
374 Climb to 4,000 m in :13:00 (from Italian source); alternatively, climb to 6,500' in :05:30; to 16,000' in :16:00; to 20,000' in :25:00.
375 This was the "Americanized" version, which best available data suggest was slightly larger than original Italian version. Wing span has also been published as 25'0" (which is close to the original Italian value). Other listed dimensions may not be exact. Airfoil: modified Eiffel, Philips leading edge. Ailerons on upper wing only; aileron span (each) *6'4"*; aileron chord *19"*. Gap has also been published as 60". Wing area unconfirmed.
376 Height also published as 10'6" — but this almost certainly refers to larger SVA aeroplane. Height listed corresponds to 2·85 m (see note 370).
377 Wood, four-blade.
378 Fuel tank said to be jettisonable, located forward of pilot; auxiliary fuel tank in upper wing.
379 Confirmed accessories: Sperry altimeter.
380 Ailerons on upper wing only. In addition to the version listed, there was also a small-wing SVA-5 manufactured: span 7·91 m; area values in existing data vary between 24·2 m² and 24·5 m²; power: engine *44(1)*. The SVA-10 was a variant also powered by engine 44(1); its dimensions were: span 9·243 m (with lower wings of unequal length, a scheme to offset prop slipstream rotation, often mislabeled torque: the left lower wing was longer [center-line to tip 4·671 m with 15 ribs] than the right lower wing [center-line to tip 4·572 m with 14 ribs]; these dimensions have been confirmed, but it is not known if other SVA variants used similar asymmetric wings); length 8·18 m; total wing area 27·0 m²; empty weight 894 kg; useful load 400 kg; gross weight 1,294 kg.
381 Height figures in existing data vary widely; SVA-9 heights of 2·9 m, 2·8 m, and 2·72 m have been published, all of which appear to be insufficient.
382 SVA-5 gross weights in existing data vary between 925 kg and 1,000 kg; the figure listed is most likely closest to racing weight.

383 Figures in existing data vary between 40 and 75 gal; *50 gal* was a typical capacity for postwar versions.

384 Accessories: (1920) Pirelli tires; Jaeger tachometer.

385 Climb to 1,000 m in :02:40; to 2,000 m in :06:00; to 3,000 m in :09:00; to 4,000 m in :12:50; to 5,000 m in :18:00; to 6,000 m in :25:00.

386 Endurance figures, depending on fuel quantity, vary widely; wartime endurance was given as 7:30.

387 SVA-9 weights in existing data vary; empty weights of 730 kg and 775 kg, and gross weights of 1,000 and 1,160 kg have also been published; these values presumably include wartime military equipment not relevant — or installed — for air racing.

388 Climb to 3,000 m in 14:00.

389 Airfoil: *St.-Cyr SC 40* (thin bi-convex with sharp leading edge). Ailerons on upper wing only, equipped with "park bench" mass balances.

390 Length values in existing data vary widely, for some unaccountable reason all the way from 6·5 m to 8·2 m. The figure listed is almost certainly correct.

391 Total approximate; includes 270 kg attributed to wing.

392 Total approximate; includes for engine 790 kg, radiator 55 kg, cooling water 30 kg, propeller 78 kg, prop hub 8 kg.

393 Of which 270 kg is fuel, 25 kg oil.

394 Gross weight may have been 2,150 kg (possibly measured during flight test with 100 kg less fuel).

395 Wood, two-blade; prop profile identical to wing airfoil! Pitch published as both 3·1 m and 3·4 m; the latter figure was most likely used for air racing.

396 Fuel distribution: main tank 310 liters; feed tank 50 liters.

397 Achieved August 26, 1922.

398 Climb to 2,000 m in :05:45; to 3,000 m in :09:45; to 4,000 m in :13:45.

399 In a 25° bank (according to manufacturer).

400 Climb to 1,000 m in :03:30; to 2,000 m in :09:30; to 3,000 m in :17:00; to 4,000 m in :29:00.

401 Length 8·56 m without rudder.

402 Wood, four-blade.

403 Climb to 1,000 m in :04:30; to 2,000 m in :10:00; to 3,000 m in :17:00; to 4,000 m in :26:00; to 5,000 m in :45:00.

404 Wood, four-blade.

405 Dimensions of upper wing considerably less than those of lower wing; reliable data as to exact upper wing dimensions unavailable.

406 Other figures exist; length has been published as 7·6 m in error.

407 Wing warping was employed for lateral control; thus no ailerons were fitted. Lower wing dimensions were less than those of upper wing but exact values unavailable.

408 Length uncertain; the figure listed applies to over-all length of landplane but is unconfirmed. A figure of 5·5 m has been published as fuselage length without rudder and propeller.

409 No fixed horizontal stabilizer; "flying tail" elevator employed.

410 Climb to 1,000 m in :02:00; to 5,000 m in :11:00 (manufacturer's figures).

411 Achieved December 28, 1922.

412 Dimensions listed obtained from original Macchi blueprint and apply to I-BAFV (number 10 in 1922 Schneider). Area distribution: upper wing 14·5 m², lower wing 9·0 m². Both wings swept back 6°. Ailerons on upper wing only. Strut attach points: for upper wing, lateral distance aeroplane center-line to cabane strut ·96 m; to interplane strut 3·55 m; for lower wing, aeroplane center-line to interplane strut 3·15 m. Standard M.7 aeroplanes also came fitted with larger wings: upper and lower span unchanged; chord (upper) 1·67 m; chord (lower) 1·31 m; gap 1·968 m; stagger ·538 m; incidence (both) 2°; total area 26·0 m² with area distribution: upper wing 16 m², lower wing 10 m²; total aileron area 2·7 m².

413 Fuselage length listed is hull length without rudder. Hull maximum width 1·10 m; maximum depth ·90 m.

414 Longitudinal distance nose of hull to step 2·725 m.

415 Vertical distance bottom of step to top of vertical fin 2·41 m.

416 Incidence of fixed horizontal stabilizer +2°.

417 Above horizontal stabilizer.

418 Only above elevator.

419 Thrust line set +2° to longitudinal axis (i.e., prop pulling up).

420 Climb to 1,000 m in :02:45; to 2,000 m in :06:00; to 3,000 m in :09:30; to 4,000 m in :16:30.

421 Of which 155 kg is fuel, 20 kg oil.

422 Climb to 1,000 m in :02:30; to 5,000 m in :23:00.

423 Span values in existing data vary between 8·6 m and 8·8 m.

424 Over-all length values in existing published data include 7·0 m (in error) and 7·78 m; fuselage length listed is hull length without rudder.

425 Height values in existing data vary between 2·65 m and 2·75 m.

426 Upper wing span values in existing data vary down to 15·04 m but this is almost certainly in error; the figure listed was obtained from original Macchi documents. Most sources name total wing area as 485 ft² but factory drawings and other Italian documents indicate wing area was in fact 46 m² (495 ft²)

427 Over-all length may have been 11·4 m. Fuselage length listed is hull length without rudder. Maximum hull width 1·10 m.

428 Gross weight may have reached 2,770 kg.

429 Wood, four-blade.

430 Total planform area (by modern convention) 16·4 m²; mean aerodynamic chord 1·64 m. Wing was tapered in planform, thickness, and chord; average airfoil thickness 16 per cent; aspect ratio 6·1.

431 Length figures in existing data vary between 8·28 m and 8·34 m. Fuselage length listed is hull length without rudder; 7·76 m has also been published for this dimension but almost certainly in error.

432 Hull dimensions: longitudinal distance nose of hull to step 2·94 m; step location 34 per cent mean aerodynamic chord. Keel angle 8°.

433 Wings swept back *3°*. Wing area has been published as 15·5 m² and 14·5 m²; the figure listed was obtained from original Macchi documents and measurement of Macchi drawings confirms its essential correctness. Mean aerodynamic chord has been published as 1·8 m. Airfoil average thickness 10 per cent. Aileron span (each) *2·06 m.*

434 Pontoon dimensions: longitudinal distance nose of pontoon to step *3·143 m;* step location *45 per cent* mean aerodynamic chord. Total submerged displacement values vary in existing data; most probably correct figure is 2,720 kg (approximately 170 per cent gross weight). The figure 145 per cent gross weight has been indicated without confirmation, but in fact smaller pontoons with less reserve buoyancy were almost certainly not used until M.39 *successors* were built.

435 Depending on aeroplane, empty weight may have varied to 1,260 kg (according to original Macchi data); useful load to 350 kg (of which a minimum of approximately 185 kg fuel was required to complete the 350-km Schneider race); and gross weight to 1,575 kg.

436 Engine 48(1) used by two M.39 racers, 48(2) by the third in the 1926 Schneider race (see Appendix 2).

437 Original propeller almost certainly had the diameter listed (although other figures appear in existing data), with a blade angle of 33·5° at ¾ radius. For the 1926 Schneider the United States furnished Reed forged dural props, diameter *8'0".*

438 Achieved November 17, 1926.

439 Climb to 5,000 m in :16:00.

440 Cross section area 5·87 m².

Appendix 4—Aero Engine Specifications

1 cid: cubic inch displacement.
   ltr: liters.

2 For engines built to the metric system, dimensions are given in metric; etc.

3 i: inlet; e: exhaust.

4 D: diameter (for rotary and radial engines).

5 c: compression ratio;
   P: mean effective pressure acting on the piston, or brake mean effective pressure (bmep) given in pounds/square inch.

6 It is impossible to pinpoint any exact horsepower value for any given aero engine due to a multitude of variables, including the ever changing individual engine itself. Thus all horsepower listings are to a great extent approximate. Engines that passed formal endurance tests have official power ratings but these were relatively few. All other figures given were derived either from bench tests (but it is often impossible to say if the power was achieved for ten hours or ten seconds before something broke) or from manufacturers' assigned ratings (which were occasionally wishful thinking). *Rated power*, generally the value the manufacturer was able to achieve for continuous running and what his engine was advertised or guaranteed to deliver; *Nominal power*, what records indicate was actually delivered under conditions of stress in flight — the named power but not necessarily the maximum power; *Maximum power*, the highest power expected or actually achieved at least once (often in bench tests). Multiple listings include figures from multiple sources or from different points on a power curve.

7 sfc: specific fuel consumption (pounds/hp/hour);
   soc: specific oil consumption (pounds/hp/hour);
   gph: U.S. gallons per hour. Figures given were values usually achieved at nominal or rated power.

8 Most French aero engines when built were identified by the manufacturer's own "works designation," usually a number, less frequently a capital letter. In August 1917 the French government, by official decree, established an "appellation" (applied by the Service Technique Aéronautique, STAé) for all military aero engines then in use. This consisted of a capital letter preceded by a number — the number of cylinders — and followed sometimes by a small letter indicating variances in construction. When the manufacturer had used letters for his works designation, these were adopted directly in the official STAé appellation (e.g., LeRhône 9C, Salmson 18CM); but when the manufacturer had used sequential works numbers — as did Hispano and Lorraine — the STAé appellation (for engines adopted into military use) introduced the letter system beginning with A (prototypes were often disregarded). Thus, for example, a certain twelve-cylinder Lorraine, which was the manufacturer's *modèle 13*, became to the STAé the *12D* because it was the fourth military Lorraine, etc.

9 With compression 5·0, maximum power reached 90/1250.

10 The low-compression or so-called 150 Hispano-Suiza.

11 The high-compression or so-called 180 Hispano-Suiza. It is very doubtful if the 8A variants ever turned faster than 1,800 rpm in flight. Maximum figures come from U. S. bench test records.

12 The low-compression geared or so-called 200 Hispano-Suiza.

13 Type 8Bb low-compression development not pursued. Type 8Bd — a 200-hp low-compression (c4·7) version — not produced. Type 8Be — a 220-hp high-compression (c5·3) version — put into production.

14 The high-compression geared or so-called 220 Hispano-Suiza. Several gear ratios were used on 8B engines ranging from 2,000:750 for airship use, to 2,000:1,170 (*pour hydravions*), the lowest used on aeroplanes, down to 2,000:1,500 (*pour avions de chasse*) using 28:21 teeth, the type indicated here, and used for all high-speed applications.

15 BTH: British-Thomson-Houston.

16 Wolseley Company Ltd., tried to produce exact copies of the Hispano-Suiza *modèle 34* or 8Aa (which they called Python) and *modèle 35* or 8Ba (which they called Adder), but they had started Hispano manufacture late (1917) and soon dropped these early designs and attempted to copy the high-compression geared *modèle 35bis* or 8Bc; however, this effort met with many failures and put England's massive S.E.5A production program in jeopardy. Thus Wolseley initiated their own development — much as Wright-Martin had done in the United States — and evolved the Viper, a high-compression direct-drive adaptation which had no French equivalent. (The closest would have been a fast-running 8Ab.) In essence, as happened elsewhere, by copying and then improvising, they came up with a better engine than the original.

17 Hispano-Suiza *modèle 34* and *34bis* built under license by the Wright-Martin Aircraft Company, Simplex Works, New Brunswick, New Jersey. This design was improved into the model E, more powerful, and with cross-magneto drive and geared oil pump. Wright-Martin built 5,816 Hispanos; in all, some 28,977 Hispano-Suiza 11·762-liter aero engines were built worldwide during World War I.

18 The first Hispano-Suiza 300-hp design (the 8Fa rated at 300/2,000) was geared for fast running with both bore and stroke 140 mm, but the short-stroke pistons traveled into the crankcase, where they collected excessive oil, and the gears were too delicate for the high power. The engine was then redesigned into the longer-stroke, direct-drive *modèle 42* (the 8Fb rated at 300/1,800). (Hispano *modèle* numbers between 34 and 42 were applied to automobiles and other Hispano-Suiza designs, some proposals only).

19 The "type Marine" low-compression (c4·7; thus low-altitude) engine with high-lift cams (*grande levée de soupapes*). STAé designations 8Fd and 8Fg applied, for right-hand and left-hand rotation respectively. Otherwise engines were identical. (8Fc totally unknown.)

20 "Type Marine" variant, presumably with the common low-compression value of 4·7 although the horsepower figures listed (in French documents) seem unusually high. It has also been indicated but not confirmed that a compression of 4·9 was used in some applications. If so, the horsepower figures would seem more likely but the pistons would have been special, non-standard types not used elsewhere. Standard high compression was 5·3 — see listing for engine 4(3) — normally reserved in 1920 strictly for high altitude applications. Compression value unknown for the Hispano in the Martinsyde Semiquaver; likewise for models used in other Martinsydes (e.g., those entered in the 1920 Aerial Derby). S.E.V. magnetos used in French applications, BTH magnetos in English. Engines were typically referred to as 8Fb irrespective of exact type.

21 Nominal power attributed to engines used in the Spad S.20bis$_6$ in November 1920 and other French racers of 1921. In 1922 nominal powers of 350 hp were credited.

22 Achieved in a 1922 test using pure benzole as fuel and improved valve lifting. In 1922 the engine in the Nieuport-Delage sesquiplane was credited with 370/1,900 but this seems optimistic. The 360-hp version was used in the 1923 Schneider. Compression values higher than 5·3 were not used in France until after 1923.

23 Engines in the Nieuport-Delage sesquiplanes of 1921–22 used Oleo spark plugs.

24 Hispano-Suiza *modèle 42* built under license in Italy by Fabbrica Automobili Itala, a pre-World War I auto firm in Turin. (It remained in business until 1934.)

25 Data credited to engine in Bernard V.2 which set world speed record December 11, 1924. Compression of 6·2 not used in this 12Gb engine despite some references. This engine also used A.M. fuel pumps, a Letombe-Luchard compressed-air self-starter, and burned "710° benzole" (specific gravity 0·88) on the speed record flight.

26 Achieved on 1918 bench test of World War I prototype.

27 Short-stroke World War I prototype. Wrecked in 1918 test.

28 Low-compression (5·0) prototype of long-stroke 12E used in Spad 58 for 1922 Coupe Deutsch.

29 Company designation suffix uncertain. Second engine in production series of twenty-five was used in Bernard V.1 with high compression, burning pure benzole. The STAé 12Eb did not appear until 1925, but then became the first French aero engine to pass the government fifty-hour type test at a 450-hp rating.

30 Derived from the earlier Salmson model 18Z. For racing purposes, high compression (6·5) was used beginning in 1924.

31 The Army version used high compression. The engine was manufactured by several different firms. In all, some 22,094 Liberties were procured. The last military Liberty was retired September 13, 1935, at Kelly Field, San Antonio, Texas. High-compression version with BG spark plugs used by Navy entries in 1922 Curtiss Marine Trophy race. Race number 17 in 1920 Pulitzer used Mosler spark plugs.

32 Normal Navy version using low compression.

33 The E-2 was improved over the E by use of heavier cylinder sleeves and heads, inclined magneto bracket, triple-geared oil pump, shallow crankcase, and adjustable vertical shafts to overhead cams.

34 There existed an E-3 Standard and E-3 Alert, the latter typically used in air race entrants.

35 In March 1923 an E-4 passed the military 300-hour full-throttle test, running *573 hours at full throttle*. The E-4 used open-sleeve construction adapted to the Wright T-2. There existed E-4 Standard, E-4 Alert, and E-4 Tempest versions, the latter typically used in air racing. It is impossible to confirm that an E-4A in fact existed. The engine in the 1923 TR-3A Schneider reserve aeroplane was a specially tuned, high-compression E-4 credited with 290 hp; it is possible that "E-4A" may have been a spurious designation given to this E-4 "Gold Cup" engine.

36 Wright-Martin modified the Hispano-Suiza *modèle 42* by using a thicker cylinder head which permitted more heat expansion without warping; larger valve necks; more water around each exhaust valve; U.S.-built carburetor (the Strombergs as listed although a Claudel-Hobson was fitted to the early model installed in the 1920 Pulitzer entry race number 51); U.S.-built magnetos and other accessories; and improved pistons with the pin changed from fixed to floating. Nominal power listed achieved in Bureau of Standards bench test March 30, 1918.

37 H-3 engines had the added feature of adjustable valve timing. Wright pointed out that their eight-cylinder design produced virtually the same power as contemporary Curtiss twelve-cylinder engines (see 18 and 19) for a weight seventy pounds less. But Curtiss engines were generally smoother-running and more durable. H-3 s/n 6021, 6024, and 6031 were used in R-3 racers 22-326, -327, and -328 respectively in 1922. The high-compression version, which burned 50 per cent D.A.G. and 50 per cent benzole, was also used in the 1922 Bee-Line racers, and was called "Superfighter."

38 An H-3 was sent to France, where it was bench-tested at Chalais-Meudon, then installed in the Nieuport-Delage 37 racer for the 1922 Coupe Deutsch. After this aeroplane's demise, this engine was probably used in the 1923 Nieuport-Delage sesquiplane which set the world speed record in February 1923, although this is not confirmed. Accessories used on this American engine in France unknown. Unfortunately, quite recently, Chalais-Meudon historical documents were thoughtlessly destroyed.

39 In the 1922 Pulitzer the NW-1 used the second T-2 built; the second NW-1 racer used the first production T-2 (s/n 6140) in January 1923. The NW-2 as entered in the 1923 Schneider used T-2 s/n 6200; this engine blew up in a test flight at high rpm.

40 Includes prop boss; T-2, 57·4 inches from rearmost datum to prop flange inner face; similarly for the T-3, 55·8 inches.

41 T-3 s/n 6372 and 6373 were used in the 1923 Pulitzer to power Wright F2W racers A-6744 and A-6743 respectively.

42 The OX-2 was Curtiss' first 90-hp V-8. (The letter O was a sequential type designation; X originally meant "experimental." Henry Kleckler redesigned the rocker arms of Curtiss' own model O to make the first OX.) The OX-3 with concentric push-rod/pull-tube valve action soon followed, from which the world-famous OX-5 was developed. The OXX-2 with 4·25-inch bore (567·5 cid) giving 100 hp was developed simultaneously. This in turn led to the OXX-5 and 110-hp OXX-6, which had the same external installation dimensions as the OX-5, though it was not so widely used. (Height extended $17\frac{3}{4}$ inches above mounting bed.)

43 Length approximately 56 inches without rear-mounted crank and 7-inch prop boss. Height extended $24\frac{3}{16}$ inches above mounting bed.

44 Peak power achieved in early bench test of early K-12.

45 Power achieved by K-12 number 13 in a test January 11, 1919 (this was the engine used in the 18-T triplane piloted by Rohlfs which set the world altitude record).

46 Configuration after 1920.

47 Peak power achieved by the first C-12 in a bench test January 30, 1920.

48 In 1921 the second CD-12 was installed in CR-1 A-6080; the fourth CD-12 was installed in A-6081, which won the 1921 Pulitzer race. CD-12 with Navy bureau number 9673 was used in 18-T triplane A-3325 in the 1922 Curtiss Marine Trophy race.

49 Standard CD-12 low compression was 5·7; standard high compression was 6·1. The low-compression power listed was achieved during the first Navy test of the first CD-12 in April 1921, fitted with a Claudel-Hobson carburetor; the version offered for production had a Zenith carburetor. No production was begun. CD-12 number 1 was then modified and fitted with a Ball & Ball carburetor, perhaps after the 1921 Pulitzer. Stromberg carburetors were not fitted to the Curtiss V-12 engines until 1922.

50 The high-compression power was made with the third CD-12 burning 50 per cent benzole in a bench test August 5, 1921 (value listed slightly below peak power).

51 Rated power: low rating and normal rating listed. Nominal power: approximate power achieved in flight during the 1922 Pulitzer since the wood prop braked the engine. Maximum power: the highest power achieved in bench tests by the low-compression (5·3) engine is listed; the maximum power of the high-compression (5·7) engine in 1922 as listed was credited to a bench test of engine A.S.68869 (see note 53).

52 Using 50 per cent benzole and 50 per cent D.A.G. (domestic aviation gasoline) as in 1922 Pulitzer.

53 D-12s with Army s/n A.S.68869 and A.S.68870 were used in the R-6 racers A.S.68563 and A.S.68564 respectively in 1922. In the 1923 Pulitzer, engine A.S.68869 powered the Verville-Sperry R-3 A.S.22-328.

54 Bench test only.

55 R-6 A.S.68564 (P-278) retained D-12 A.S.68870 through 1923, but it was equipped with the new Stromberg carburetor for the 1923 world speed record flight.

56 Approximate power achieved in flight since the prop braked the engine. A mixture of 50 per cent Shell spirit and 50 per cent benzole was burned to win the 1923 Schneider, using this compression.

57 Power achieved by D-12 s/n 125 in bench tests between December 1923 and February 1924. Peak power somewhat higher. The so-called D-12HC (for high compression) variant used in the 1924 John L. Mitchell and 1925 Pulitzer races was similar and probably used a compression of 5·8.

58 Compressions of 6·0 and 6·1 were not used in D-12 engines until after McCook Field tests began in 1924. After 1925 the D-12 was offered until

1931 with normal compression 5·3 (later type certificated for civil use) and high compression 6·0 (military use only; no civil Approved Type Certificate [ATC]) in the following versions:

1925 D-12C rated 435/2300 weight 694 pounds. First example was Curtiss s/n 253; had improved fuel system and was often called V-1150-1.

1926 D-12D rated 460/2300 weight 680 pounds. First example was Curtiss s/n 377; used Stromberg NA-Y5D carburetor.

1927 D-12E rated 435/2300 weight 685 pounds. ATC number 10 applied for October 11, 1928, issued March 1, 1929. This version identical to D-12D except for camshafts, minor details, lower rating.

1927 D-12F rated 460/2300. Had modernized ignition using Scintilla VAG-12D magnetos; used Stromberg NA-Y5F carburetor. D-12M designation referred to engines later modified by Curtiss with no specific numerical sequence.

Between 1922 and 1932 1,169 D-12s were built. Early D-12s cost some $9,100; by 1932 a D-12E cost $4,852·50. Time between overhauls slightly more than two hundred hours.

59 D-12A Army s/n 23-147 was used in R-6 P-278 in 1924. Engine 23-152 was used in R-8 23-1235 (P-354) in 1924. Compression used for racing between 1923 and 1925 was 5·8; references to compression of 7·0 in U.S. racers in 1925 is unconfirmed. D-12A compression in 1925 Italian Macchi M.33 unknown, but probably fairly low.

60 The two weights refer to 1925 installation in Curtiss R3C-1 landplane and R3C-2 seaplane respectively.

61 The V-1400 was narrower and lighter than the D-12 because of an improved drive for the double overhead cams.

62 619 hp was the maximum power achieved by the "freak oil-less" engine in 1925 bench test, and is the basis for the power-weight value listed. 665 hp was apparently achieved in 1926 by the engine used in the Schneider Trophy.

63 The listed bore and stroke (from official Curtiss documents) yield the cid indicated, which no doubt is the basis for the designation V-1550; the *same* bore and stroke are published for the follow-on engine which earned fame as the Conqueror — yet most references to the Conqueror indicate 1,569 cid, and the Conqueror was called V-1570 by the military. This discrepancy in cid with identical bore/stroke has never been properly explained; it most probably came about because it was later recognized that slightly different strokes in fact exist between left and right cylinder banks due to different connecting rod configurations (in many V-12 designs the con-rods from left and right cylinder banks were fastened to the crankshaft differently). The difference would amount to an additional ·176 inch for one bank (six cylinders) on the Conqueror (i.e., stroke would be 6·426 inches on one side only).

64 56·75 inches without starter.

65 Low-compression (standard military) rating listed. The nominal and maximum powers listed were achieved during bench tests of the prototype (Packard s/n 225) on May 19, 1920. 600 hp was the maximum available for flight, but resulted in brutal overheating. Apparently compression of 6·5 was used in the 1920 Gordon Bennett.

66 In 1922 engines bearing Army s/n A.S.95036 and A.S.95038 were used in Thomas-Morse R-5 racers A.S.68561 and A.S.68562 respectively.

67 The listed bore and stroke (from official Packard documents) yield the cid indicated, no doubt the basis for the designation A-1500; yet a cid of 1,530 is often attributed to this series of engines. If accurate, the discrepancy most probably came about because of differences in con-rod configuration between left and right cylinder banks (see note 63). The difference would amount to an additional ·238 inch for one bank (six cylinders) on the 2A-1500 (i.e., stroke would be 5·738 inches on one side only).

68 The engine listed and used in the 1926 Schneider was the upright version employing Allison-built gears. Packard also built 1A-1500 and 3A-1500, ungeared and inverted versions of this engine, sometimes confused with the racing version. The basic A-1500 was awarded civil Approved Type Certificate number 18; price was $17,375 for the geared version.

69 An engine which resulted from marrying an upright and inverted V onto a common crankshaft — which was 7 inches in diameter! Built especially for Al Williams and used in his unsuccessful 1927 Vespa and 1929 Mercury Schneider racers. Swept volume commonly given as 2,775 cid (see note 67).

70 Aeromarine was a division of Detroit Cadillac Motor Car Company with facilities at Keyport, New Jersey. Their 150-hp B-66 (a 45-degree V-8) was an early engine; they then tried to improve on the Wright E series — the two Aeromarine engines listed were examples used in air racing — but in general the Aeromarine engines were not significantly better than the Wrights and the firm was unsuccessful in promoting them. High compression (6·35) was used in the 1922 Curtiss Marine Trophy race.

71 Mosler spark plugs on TS-1; AC spark plugs on TR-1 in 1922 Curtiss Marine Trophy race.

72 The J-1 was improved into the 442-pound, 220-hp J-3, which had a stronger crankshaft, larger prop hub, one carburetor instead of three. Further improvement — relocating accessories to the rear, etc. — led to the J-4, J-4A, and J-4B, for which the particulars listed were essentially identical. In 1926 civil Whirlwinds flew some 1·75 million miles.

73 The original Scintilla magnetos were made in Soleure, Switzerland; later by General Electric Company, American licensees, in Sidney, New York. The popular model AG-9D was made in Switzerland while the VAG-9D was the same model made in the United States. GE also held a license to build British BTH magnetos in the United States, but it was not exercised until after 1927.

74 The J-5 engine powered many famous long-distance flights, including Lindbergh's 1927 solo flight from New York to Paris.

75 Burning fuel containing 30 per cent benzole. Later rating of heavier (695 pound) Series C Wasp was 450/2100 (c5·25).

76 The first Wasps had a geared supercharger (gear ratio 5:1). New designs were laid down in 1929 from which, in 1935, the world-famous Twin-Wasp R-1830 — radial 14 cylinder (2 × 7), bore/stroke 5·50 inches/5·50 inches, c6·7, weight 1,403 pounds, rated 1050/2700 — was developed. The Twin-Wasp, like the Wasp, persisted for decades. It became virtually the standard Douglas DC-3 transport powerplant.

77 The P-1 had no supercharger; the P-2 of 1925–26 had one. The Cyclone introduced the rotary induction supercharger. The 1928 Cyclone had the same bore as the P-1 but a longer stroke (6·875 inches) giving 1,753 cid, same as the Bristol Jupiter. It used the same carburetor and accessories as those listed for the P&W Wasp (engine 29). With c5·0, p130, it delivered 525/1900 nominal, 560/2000 maximum, weighed 760 pounds, was 40·6 inches long, diameter 54·0 inches. The next Cyclone version, the slightly larger 575-hp R-1820, appeared in 1931 (bore/stroke 6·125 inches/6·875 inches yielding 1,823 cid); in 1932, weighing 940 pounds, and with c6·4 and 36 inches Hg manifold pressure, it was rated 715/1950 at sea level. The R-1820 was built by the hundreds of thousands — it powered dozens of famous planes including the B-17 and DC-3 — and *more than forty years later* was still running strong in Navy carrier operations in great numbers, delivering 1,525 hp.

78 The Falcon III was in wide use from 1917 until 1927. Maximum allowable rpm was 2,000 on Falcons I and II, increased to 2,200 and later 2,300 on Falcon III. Engine width 29 inches without exhaust manifold. (Martinsyde F.4 race number 4, entered and later withdrawn from the 1919 Aerial Derby, used a Falcon II; all other race entries in tables used the Mark III.)

79 Rated power 330/1700 using four Claudel-Hobson carburetors.

80 The Eagle IX appeared in 1923, was not so widely used as the Eagle VIII, which powered several of Britain's early long-range epic flights.

81 With no prop boss.

82 The Condor dates back to World War I, when it was designed to yield 600 hp. Earlier Condor marks employed different gearing ratios; most frequently used was 1000:553·7; occasionally 1000:666 was also used. Lower compression of 5·1 was also occasionally used. In 1923 the Condor was in the same class as the Wright T-3.

83 Planned for use in 1924 Schneider; never employed for air racing.

84 Achieved in bench tests March 1919.

85 First public display of the Lion came at the 1919 Aerial Derby in the winning AirCo D.H.4R using Lion I credited with 485/2100, compression 5·3. The Fairey III-A used a Lion I in the 1919 Schneider; the Sea Lion I racer used the Lion Ia as listed.

86 In 1921, Napier literature listed standard low compression as 5·0, high compression 5·8. Compression 5·55 was a military value used primarily for high-altitude applications, although the racers of 1921 used this compression. By 1923 only the low-compression version had been approved airworthy for civil use whereas high-compression variants – up to 6·5 – were by then used for speed seeking. The Lion that won the 1923 Aerial Derby aboard the Gloster I (compression 6·5) was removed and installed in the Blackburn Pellet racer for the 1923 Schneider.

87 With compression 5·8.

88 Achieved in bench test of direct-drive Lion VI (the first military direct-drive version) with Napier s/n E.75 during October 1924.

89 The Lion VII used in the Supermarine S.4 built for the 1925 Schneider was Napier s/n E.74. Some references say compression was 7·8 in this 1925 Lion VII, but 8·0 appears more likely.

90 Racing versions built in 1927 and 1929. Powers listed achieved in bench tests. Although the Lion VII was direct-drive (only the Lions VI, VII and VIII had no gears), the Mark VII-B developed in 1927 had a double reduction gear; by 1929 when the use of supercharging was inevitable, the Mark VII-D was hurriedly developed, fitted with a British-Thomson-Houston – built supercharger fraught with problems. Although high power was achieved in brief tests, the engine never raced.

91 Normal compression 4·9, boosted to 5·4 for racing.

92 Bentley rotaries were built by Humber of Coventry and Gwynne of Hammersmith. The early BR-1 was a smaller engine (bore/stroke 120mm/170mm yielding 19·227 liters swept volume, rated 150/1250, weighing 400 pounds) but the larger BR-2 was more widely used in postwar sporting aviation.

93 Designation follows standard French (STAé appellation) form. Engine was produced by Gwynne through 1921 as the 9J.

94 ABC engines were built by Walton Motors Ltd., Walton-on-Thames, formerly All-British Engine Company, Ltd., Hersham, Surrey, founded 1912 by Ronald Charteris. Wasp I in BAT Bantams variously credited with 170/1850.

95 Dragonfly engines seldom if ever achieved their maximum predicted power – and probably never in flight.

96 Using normal British aviation spirit with a specific gravity of 0·69.

97 Three carburetors in one housing; one set of controls.

98 Sopwith 107 racer used the prototype Cosmos Jupiter – the first built – in 1919 and 1920 until it was removed before the Gordon Bennett.

99 Although two geared versions were planned, only one geared prototype was built – the sole Jupiter II – which was exhibited at the 1920 Olympia Aero Show but afterward never seen again and in all probability quickly and quietly scrapped. As far as can be determined the proposed geared Jupiter III (to be rated 450/1850, geared 100:33) never got off the drawing board.

100 The *second* direct-drive version – hence the designation Jupiter I-Mark II (see Chapter 24). This was the first Jupiter to pass the fifty-hour type test in 1921; Fedden then took this Jupiter to the 1921 Paris Air Show, where it caused a sensation.

101 In 1922 this British-built Jupiter became the first version to pass the French fifty-hour type test. Improvements over the Jupiter I-Mark II were minor ones suggested by the 1921 British test. Bristol-built Jupiter I-Mark III with Bristol s/n 855 was used in the 1922 Bristol 72 monoplane racer and afterward powered the 1923 French Gourdou-Leseurre CT.1 Coupe Beaumont racer. After being sent to France, the engine was refitted with a Zenith-built carburetion system similar to that installed on Gnôme-Rhône Jupiters built under license.

102 Built to Air Ministry specification 37/23. It was the standard for the French-built Gnôme-Rhône Jupiter with STAé appellation 9Ab.

103 From bench tests of Bristol s/n 878 in April 1924.

104 From bench tests of s/n JX-1000 in March 1925.

105 From tests of Jupiter VI (similar to Jupiter V). Compression values: 6·3 (military high-altitude application); 5·3 (standard military); 5·0 (standard civil).

106 Jupiters built in France under license; STAé appellations applied:

    9Aa   low-compression model rated at 1,575 rpm in 1923
    9Ab   low-compression model rated at 1,700 rpm in 1924
    9Ac   high-compression model built in 1925
    9Ad   high-compression model built in 1926

The engine used in the Blanchard racer built for the 1923 Schneider was a special high-compression model designated 9Aa*bis*. All were direct-drive. (The first French-built geared Jupiter was the 9Ak of 1926.)

107 Jaguar I in 1919 had stroke of 5·00 inches; it was fairly widely used through 1921. Jaguar II and all subsequent Marks had longer stroke of 5·50 inches. Jaguar IV appeared in 1924.

108 The type V.6 (*not* its configuration) was built by II Fabbrica Automobili Isotta-Fraschini of Milan. After 1920, racing versions were credited with 260 hp typically.

109 Built by Società Piemontese Automobili (SPA), who abandoned aero engine construction after 1921, although the 6A was used by the hundreds in SVA types from 1917 for years thereafter.

110 Italian-built. (BG spark plugs were fitted to 1920 Pulitzer entry race number 54, otherwise KLG spark plugs were used.)

111 High compression for racing.

112 Bore considered too large to use high compression effectively.

113 4E-28 engine s/n 1003 powered Nieuport-Macchi M.12 23903 in 1920 Schneider race.

114 4E-29 engine s/n 1028 powered SIAI S.12*bis* number 3011; and 4E-29 engine s/n 1127 powered SIAI S.19 number 2002, both entered in 1920 Schneider. Ansaldo San Giorgio ceased aero engine production by 1924.

115 A-14 engine s/n 434 powered Macchi M.19 number 3098 entered in 1920 and 1921 Schneider. Version that powered Fiat R.700 racer in 1921 and 1922 Coupe Deutsch was called A-14S.

116 High-compression version.

117 Low-compression version; may have been as low as 5·3. Value listed unconfirmed but most likely.

118 RAF 1A. World War I vintage 90-hp V-8 engine similar to early Renaults.

119 Renault 80 hp.

120 Packard 1A-1237 300 hp; replaced German-built Mercedes in many captured Fokker D-VII pursuits, which were briefly but widely used in the United States. (Nominal power 366/1800, p 130; dry weight 740 pounds).

121 Bristol Mercury, air-cooled radial that *followed* the Jupiter (it had no resemblance to 1917 Mercury); it was later used in 1927 Short Crusader racer.

Photo captions credits code

Au	Author's collection
USAF	United States Air Force (includes Signal Corps, U.S. Air Service, Army Air Corps) – official photographs
USN	United States Navy official photographs
S	National Air Museum, Smithsonian Institution, Washington, D.C.
NA	The National Archives, Washington, D.C.
LC	The Library of Congress, Washington, D.C.
N	National Aeronautics and Space Administration (formerly NACA, the National Advisory Committee for Aeronautics), Washington, D.C.
U	Underwood
UPI	United Press International
F	Flight International magazine, London
H-S	Hawker-Siddeley Group, London
BAC	British Aircraft Corporation, Filton, Bristol
Real	Real Photographs Ltd., Victoria Station, Hoghton St., Southport, England
C	Curtiss Aeroplane and Motor Co. (manufacturer's photo)
MA	Musee de l'Air, Paris
MCT	Museo Caproni di Taliedo, Rome
M	Aer Macchi, Varese, Italy

INDEX

ABC, 351
  dickey car, 326
  Dragonfly engine, 123, 325, 327–8, 329, 348, 350, 524
  Gnat engine, 87, 325
  Wasp engine, 308, 325, 524
Abd-el-Krim, 128
Able, George, 259
ACA, *see* Aero Club of America
Academy of Model Aeronautics, 163
ACF, *see* Aéro Club de France
Acosta, Bert, 24, 32, 33, 39, 40, 43, 83, 120, 122, 182, 184, 186, 195–9, 201, 208, 229, 265, 267, 294–6, 384, 386, 424, 449, 451
Acoustic fatigue, 84
Adlershof (German engineer), 280
Aerial Advertising, 192
Aerial Age Weekly magazine, 24, 31
Aerial Derby, London, 45
  1912, 306, 348
  1919, 41, 308–9, 311, 315, 320, 327, 331, 348, 434
  1920, 42–3, 312, 314, 315, 317, 328, 349–51, 355, 358, 436
  1921, 43, 114, 143, 314, 322, 328, 332, 345, 359, 438
  1922, 44, 88, 316, 322, 333, 335, 361, 364, 440
  1923, 44, 322, 337–8, 351–2, 373, 441
Aerial Engineering Corporation, 294; *see also* Bee-Line racers
Aerial Experiment Association (AEA), 188
Aerial League of America, 24, 30
Aerial League of France, 49
Aerial Service Corporation, 252
Aero Club of America (ACA), 24, 28–33*passim*, 35, 45, 87, 161, 177, 198, 210, 265
  Invitation Class Prize 1920, 261
Aero Club of Canada, 23
Aéro Club de France (ACF), 21, 28, 48, 49, 114, 148, 182
Aero Club d'Italia, 50
Aero Club of Ithaca, 263
Aero Club of Texas, 28, 177
Aeroelasticity, 84, 86, 295, 319, 384
Aero Import Company, 302, 386
Aeromarine Airways, 192
Aeromarine Plane and Motor Company, 62
  U-873 engine, 297, 522
Aeronautical Digest, 221
Aeron/Reed, Germany, 74
Aeroplane, The, magazine, 30, 44, 53, 54, 145, 203, 325, 329, 332, 379
Aguinaldo, Emilio, 9
Aimes, S. M., 448
AirCo (Aircraft Manufacturing Company), 320, 323, 329
  D.H.4 ("Flaming Coffins"), 24, 31, 32, 134, 161, 164, 230, 237, 310, 320–1, 423
  D.H.4R, 320–2, 331, 435
  D.H.9, 86, 311, 322, 331, 351, 423, 435
  D.H.9A, 24
  D.H.9R, 322
  see also de Havilland
Air-cooled engines, 67–70, 355–8, 361

  radial, 68–70, 152–3, 296–9, 308, 356–7
  rotary, 67–8
Air Corps Act 1926, 19
Aircraft Industries Corporation, 176
Aircraft Investigating Board, 40
Aircraft Production Board, 60, 61
Air Enquiry Board, 368
Air Force Museum, Dayton, 242
Air Navigation Act 1919, 16
Airships, 19, 82
Air Survey Company, 316
Albany–New York *Scientific American* flight 1910, 195
Albatros fighter, 81
Alcoa, *see* Aluminium Company of America
Alcock, John, 25, 26, 41, 60, 309, 316, 348, 388, 435
Alemite valves, 69
Alexander, R. W., 53
Alitalia, 387
Allen, D. C., 192
Allison, James A., 72
Allison
  gear box, 285
  V-1710 engine, 72
Alula-Semiquaver, *see* Martinsyde
Alula wing, 319–20
Aluminium Company of America (Alcoa), 64, 82
  Alclad, 82
America, see Fokker
American Airways, 190
American Chemical Society, 168
American Flying Club, 23, 24, 30–1, 35
American Legion Air Derby 1921, 33, 196
America's Cup, 352
Anacostia, D. C., 37, 191, 202, 225, 241, 297
Anchorage Hotel, Washington, 18
Anglo-American Oil Company, 308
Annual American Legion Convention 1921, 32
Ansaldo, 302, 384–5
  A.1, 429, 449, 451–2, 508
  Balilla, 32, 196, 385–6
  BR bombers, 387
  SVA-series, 384–6, 388, 390, 449, 451–2, 508
Ansaldo (Bolzaneto, Borzoli, La Spezia), 385
Ansaldo-San Giorgio aero engines, 69, 394, 397, 528
Ansaldo-Turin, 385, 387
Antoinette, 78, 111, 315
Anzani, Alessandro, 68
Anzani engine, 73, 356
Apache, see Wright
Aquitania, 278
Archdeacon, Ernest, 45
Arcidiacono (pilot), 468
Armstrong-Siddeley
  Jaguar engine, 70, 526
Armstrong-Whitworth, Sir W. G., & Company, 81, 148, 307–8, 352
  B.E.2, 307–8
  F.K.1, 307
  F.K.3 "Little Ack," 307–8
Arnold, Bea, 18
Arnoux, René, 148–50, 151

Arnoux
  girouette de l'aviation, 148
  Stablavion, 148
  see also Simplex-Arnoux
Arrigoni (Italian designer), 396
Arrol-Johnston Ltd, 310
  BHP engine, 310–11
Arthur Hagg differential ailerons, 322
Astor, Vincent, 293
Astra, 148; *see also* Nieuport-Astra
Atlanta *Journal*, 29
Atlantic City, 29–30
Atlantic race, *see* Transatlantic flights
Automobile-Club de France, 45
Aviation magazine, 34, 221, 285
Avro, 43, 309–15, 316, 341
  Anson, 310
  Avian, 313
  Baby, 41, 42, 311–12, 435–6, 438, 440–1, 500
  "Racing Baby," 312, 500
  539B/1 Lion, 314
  The Old Hen, 312
  539/1 Puma racer, 310–11, 439, 464, 500
  Tudor, 310
  552 Viper, 438, 441
  "The Yellow Peril" triplane, 310
  504, 310, 314, 434, 441
  539A/1, 313–14, 436
Ayer, Bob, 303

Bacula, Adriano, 240, 241, 411–15, 478
Bailhache Judicial Committee, 325
Bairstow, Leonard, 86
Baker, Newton D., 11, 60
Balbo, Italo, 20, 390, 414
Balchen, Bernt, 198–9
Baldwin, Stanley, 7, 15, 16, 19
Balfour, Arthur, 14, 15
Balilla, *see* Ansaldo
Ball & Ball carburetors, 194
Ballooning, 27, 37, 45, 49
Ballot, Ernest, 59
Baltimore Flying Club, 53, 54
Baltimore seaplane meet 1924, 204
Balzer, Stephen M., 68
Bamel, *see* Gloucester Aircraft Company
Bane, Thurman, 18, 67, 278
Banks, F. R. "Rod," 72, 331
Baracca, Francesco, 390
Baracca Cup 1921, 390
Barault, M. (French pilot), 141–2, 428, 439
Barber, Horatio, 312
Baring, Maurice, 9
Barker, Billy, 24
Barksdale, Eugene H., 40, 274, 281–3, 293, 450, 454
Barnard, Franklin L., 365
Barnard, C. D., 441
Barnwell, Frank S., 79, 194, 353–4, 357–8, 361, 365
Barnwell, Richard H., 354
BAT (British Aerial Transport Company), 307–9
  Bantams F.K. 23, F.K. 26, F.K. 27, 307–9,

434–5, 438, 500
Basilisk, 308
  Skinned Bat, 308–9
Batelier, Lt., 283
Batter, Lt., 293
Bat Wing, 80
Baumann, Milton C., 162, 167
Baumhamer (Dutch engineer), 86
Bay Shore Park, Baltimore, 53, 54, 234, 341, 379, 409
Beacham, T. E., 74
Beardmore, 25, 310
  engines, 310
Beatty, David, 10, 11, 14, 15
Beau, Lucas "Vic," 213, 447
Beaumont, André (Jean Louis Camille de Conneau), 48
Beaumont, Louis D., 47–8, 49
Beaverbrook, Lord, 15
Bêchéreau, Louis, 81, 91–3, 129, 153–4, 170, 307
Beech, Irl, 38
Beech, Walter H., 36, 38
Bee-Line
  BR-1, 294–6, 453, 498
  BR-2, 453
  racers, 80, 88, 131, 252, 279, 282
Bell, Alexander Graham, 188
Bell, Larry, 24
Bell Aircraft, 275
  P-59 fighter, 275
Bellanca aeroplane, 40
Belleville washers, 123
Belmont, August, 32
Belmont Racetrack, 24, 182, 306
Bendix Trophy 1931, 235
Bennett, Floyd, 198
Bennett, James Gordon, 10, 26–8, 47
Benoist, Lt., 157–8, 473
Benson, Admiral, 12
Bentley
  B.R.2 rotary engine, 329, 333, 337, 524
Benz, 4
  140 hp engine, 301
Benzole, 66, 72, 117, 123, 124, 218, 236, 239, 265, 281, 331
Bernard, Adolphe, 79, 93, 129–30, 134, 135, 138
Bernard, Jean, 95, 113
Bernard (SIMB) (Société des Avions Bernard), 48, 77, 134, 229, 235
  A.B.3, 130
  airfoil, 80
  C.1, 83–4, 129–33, 486
  10C.1, 132
  12C.1, 132
  flush rivets, 84
  HV seaplanes, 138
  SAB, 130, 170
  V-racers, 134–5, 486
  V.1., 444
  V.2, 126, 134–8, 222, 287, 376, 426, 444, 486
  V.4, 138
Berreur, Georges A., 150
Bertaud, Lloyd W., 24, 33, 82, 196, 198, 302,

386, 451
Bettis, Cy, 40, 41, 54, 228, 229–32, 234, 426, 459
B.F. Sturtevant Airplane Company, 67, 163, 259, 288
Biard, Henri, 51–2, 53, 54, 84, 203, 341, 369–72, 374–5, 376, 378–80, 401–2, 424, 426, 471–2, 474, 476
Biddlecombe, C. H., 316
Billing, Noel P., 14, 367–8
Biplanes, 78–9, 80, 85, 86, 134
Bird, James, 368, 369, 372, 375, 378–9, 393
Bird of Paradise, *see* Fokker
Birkigt, Marc, 58, 59, 61–2, 93, 126, 129, 138, 330
Bishop, Courtlandt Field, 30
Bissell, Clayton L., 14, 18, 19, 271, 274, 278, 454
Bi-valve coque, 126
Bixby, Harold, 35
Blackburn, Robert, 7, 319–20, 372
Blackburn, Thomas W., 275, 457
Blackburn
  Pellet, 372–4, 472, 506
Blanchard-Blériot
  C.1, 157, 473, 490
Blashill, Al, 230
Blériot, Louis, 28, 49, 68, 78, 81, 92–3, 101, 106, 115, 129, 306
Blériot Aéronautique, 41, 78, 92, 305, 307, 348, 428, 434; *see also* Spad
  Mammoth transport, 106
Bliss, E. W., 358
Bliss, Harold N., 259
Blitzkrieg, 10
B.L.M. Motor Car Company, 296
Bloch, Marcel, *see* Dassault
Block, Harold C., 181–2
Blowes, A. W., 331
Bluebird, *see* Gloucestershire Aircraft Company
BMW (Bavarian Motor Works)
  engines, 82
Bocaccio, Paul, 141–2
"bodyless" speedplanes, 134
Boeing, William E., 70
Boeing Company, 213, 260, 261, 287
  MB-3A, 262, 268, 271, 273–4, 275, 455, 457
  Monomail, 88
  747, 166, 387
Boillot, Georges, 58
Bolas, Harold, 134
Bolling, Reynal C., 182, 321
Bolling Field, D. C., 72, 208
Bolling Mission, 320
Bologna, Luigi, 395, 396, 465, 468
Bombay peace demonstration 1919, 327
Bonaccini, Lt., 388
Bonaparte, Roland, 21
Bonnet, Florentin, 133, 135–6, 137–8, 222, 426, 444
Bonney, Leonard W., 192
Booth, Harry T., 80, 88, 192, 194, 205, 252–3, 294–6, 372, 404
Boothman, John N., 463
Borel, Gabriel, 28, 47, 81, 141, 439

Borel Flying Boat, 466
Borel-Bocaccio racer, 100, 141–2, 428, 486
Borra, Lt., 411
Bossoutrot, (French pilot), 73, 145
Boston *Globe*, 29
Botali & Clement radiators, 404
Boulet (mechanic), 106
Boulton & Paul, 81, 318
  P.9, 441
  P.10, 364
Bournemouth, England, 49, 50, 95–6, 110, 349, 352, 369, 392–3
Bournemouth Whitsun meeting 1927, 322
Boyd, T. A., 168, 293
Brack-Papa, Francesco, 25, 35, 36, 110, 117, 120, 383–4, 387–90, 423, 432, 433, 456
Bradley, Benjamin G., 196, 290, 449
Bradshaw, Granville, 325
Bragg, Caleb S., 31, 198, 460
Brancker, Sir W. Sefton, 16, 44, 56
Brandenburg seaplane fighters, 369
Branksome Towers Hotel, Bournemouth, 393
Brantes, Marquise de, 10
Brazil, J. P., 356
Brazil-Straker (Cosmos Company), 356, 357
  Cosmos engines, *see* Bristol
Br bombers, *see* Fiat
Bréguet, Jacques, 40
Bréguet, Louis, 28, 40, 49, 81, 130
Bréguet, 77, 117, 139
  14 bomber, 104, 128, 151
  "Coffeepot," 81
  19 *Jacqueline*, 40, 155
  941 STOL, 133
  Flying Boat, 469
Brenaime, Maurice, 49
Bridgman, Leonard, 44, 332
Brierley, Walter, 87
Brindley, Oscar A., 460
Bristol, 44, 47, 79, 344, 353–66
  Type 72, 433, 440, 502
  Badger, 357
  Badminton, 365
  Bulldog (Blenheim), 366
  Bullet (Type 32), 42, 358–61, 365, 437, 439–40, 442, 502
  F.2B Brisfit fighters, 60, 289, 329, 354–5, 358
  M.1 fighter, 354
  M.1C, 435
  M.1D (type 77), 86, 355, 364–5, 440, 502
  M.R.1 fighter, 354
  Scout, 354
  Tourer, 322, 438
  engines:
    Centaurus, 366
    Hercules, 357
    Jupiter, 44, 48, 88, 132, 152, 157, 325, 349–52, 357–9, 365
    Jupiter I—Mark III, 153, 337, 362, 526
    Lucifer, 327, 355, 364–5, 524
    Mercury, 344, 356–7, 366
    Orion (Jupiter VI), 365
    Pegasus, 358
Bristow, Whiston A., 56, 319, 365, 479

Britain First, 366
Britannia Trophy, 312, 313, 316, 358
British Advisory Committee on Aeronautics, 73
British and Colonial Airplane Company, 353, 354
British Deperdussin Company, 307, 392
British Empire Michelin Cup 1912, 347
British Marine Air Navigation Company, 375
British Nieuport (Nieuport and General
    Aircraft Company), 43, 325, 332, 358
    B.N.1, 325
    L.C.1 Nieuhawk, 326–7, 332, 435–6, 438, 502
    L.S.3 Goshawk, 28, 42, 43, 317, 328, 345, 424, 428, 437, 439, 502
    Nighthawk fighter, 325, 327, 329, 337
British Oil and Turpentine Company, 332
British Overseas Airways Corporation (BOAC), 375
British Powerboat Company, 375
Broad, Hubert S., 54, 234, 339–41, 342, 380, 427, 438, 474, 476
Broberg, Oliver W., 455
Brock, William A., 434
Brockworth Aerodrome, England, 86, 332, 333, 343
Brodie, Otto, 172
Brooklands, London, 146, 310, 328, 347, 351
Brookley, Wendell H., 214–15, 223, 293, 458
Brow, Harold J. "Hap," 192, 199–200, 219–23, 254, 255, 298, 426, 453, 456, 461
Brown, Arthur Whitten, 25, 26, 60, 309, 316, 348, 388
Brown, Donald, 70
Brown, G. H., 378
Brown, Ray W., 446
Brown, W. V., 448
BR racers, *see* Bee-Line racers
Bruce, Robert, 134
Bruner, S. G., 132–5, 136–8*passim*, 153
Bryan (scientist), 83
Buc, Paris, 102–4, 105–6, 114
Buchanan, J. S., 380
Buffum, Capt., 128
Bugatti, Ettore, 59, 145–6
Buhl (pilot), 196
Buhl-Verville Aircraft Company, 287
Bullet, see Bristol
Bumpus, Frank A., 372
Buonsembiante (Italian pilot), 51, 468
Bureau of Aeronautics (BuAer), 12, 37, 69, 244, 297, 299
Bureau of Aircraft Production, 169
Burgess, W. Starling, 148
Burman (German driver), 4, 423
Burnelli, Lawrence and Vincent, 40
Burney (English designer), 396
Burnside, Frank H., 260, 269
Burroughes, Hugh, 74–5, 323, 324–5, 329, 332, 340, 344
Burroughs & Wellcome, 347
Buscaylet-de Monge
    7.4, 145
    7.5, 145
Bush, Benjamin F., 35
Bush, W. H. "Joe," 203

Butler, Alan S., 44, 322, 438, 440
Byrd, Richard E., 198, 199, 208
Byrne, Patrick J. "Pappie," 241, 413

Cabot, Godfrey, 30, 39
Cactus Kitten, see Curtiss
Cain, Henry, 45
Caldwell, Frank W., 74
Callan, John L., 408
Callizo, Jean Marie, 118, 153
Calloway, Steven W., 253–5, 294, 296, 298, 453, 456, 461
Camel, see Sopwith
Camm, Sydney, 287, 316, 344, 352
Campbell, Ed, 266–7
CAMS (Chantiers Aéro-Maritime de la Seine), 405
    36 flying boat, 155–6, 158, 470, 473, 488
    38 flying boat, 156–7, 158, 159, 473, 488
    45 flying boat, 158, 475
Cantieri Navale di Monfalcone, 405
Cantilever tail, 132, 170, 205, 207, 343
Cantilever wing, 79–80, 82, 85–6, 122, 131, 134, 146, 147, 150, 164, 252, 277, 283, 287, 291, 294, 362, 376, 384, 395, 402–3, 405, 406, 410
Canots automobiles, 49
Canucks, 36
Capillo, General, 415
Cappannini, Gino, 386
Caproni, 386
Caproni/Reed, 74
Carburetors, 66, 171, 174–5
Carlstrom, Victor, 460
Carmier (engineer), 149
Carnegie, Sir Lancelot, 315
Carns (designer), 300
Cardin, Norbert, 447
Carpenter, Lt-Commander, 32
Carr, R. H. "Reggie," 307, 434
Carroll, Reggie S., 327
Carter, Larry L., 36, 44, 86, 337–9, 364, 425, 426, 440, 442, 444, 456, 459
Carter, Wilfred G., 349, 365
Casale, Jean, 423, 429, 433, 463, 466
Casalegno, Enrico, *see* Woodhouse, Henry
Case, Charles D., 178
Castoldi, Mario, 54, 405–6, 408–13, 415
Cattaneo, Giustino, 387
Caudron, René, 28, 326
    G.4, 98
CD-12 engine, *see* Curtiss
Centurione, Vittorio, 411, 414
Cesare, Oscar, 17
Cessna, Clyde, 38
CFR, *see* Cooperative Fuel Research
Chabonnat, M., 136
Chadbourne, Thomas, 69
Chadwick, Roy, 310
Chalais-Meudon, Paris, 46, 123
Chamberlayne, P. R. T., 306–7, 434
Chamberlin, Clarence D., 40, 198
Champes de Boishebert, Marquis des, 31
Champion, C. C., 70, 239–40, 413

Channel Islands, 369, 375, 378
Chantiers Aéro-Maritime de la Seine, *see* CAMS
Charaway propellers, 191
Charron (French driver), 27
Charteris, Ronald, 351
Chase Hotel, St Louis, 220
Chauvière propellers, 107
Cherub engines, 151
Chichester-Smith, C. H., 355, 435
Chrysler 80 roadster, 276
Churchill, Randolph, 10
Churchill, Winston, 7, 9, 11, 14, 19, 278, 347
Circuit-of-Britain air race, 48
Civil Aeronautics Administration, 192
Clarence Mackay Trophy 1926, 231
Clark, Virginius, 32, 74, 170
Clark Y airfoil, 170
Clarke, Alan, 29
Claude, Lawrence, 447
Claude Neon Lights, 192
Claudel, Henri, 66
Claudel-Hobson carburetors, 194, 330
Clémenceau, Georges, 6, 7
Clémenceau-Moineau racer, 486
Clergêt
    air-cooled radial engines, 296
    rotary engines, 68, 348, 524
Cleveland Air Races 1931, 235
Cleveland *Plain-Dealer*, 29
Clipper flying boats, 49
Coatalen, Louis, 59
Cobb, John, 332
Cobham, Alan, 322
Coe, C., 378
"Coffeepot," *see* Bréguet
Coffin, Howard E., 35, 37, 40, 41, 60, 70
Cohan, George M., 305
Coli, François, 108, 128, 135
Collier Trophy
    1915, 148
    1918, 285
    1921, 293
    1925, 74
Collyer, Charles B. D., 185, 451
Colt, Charles, 24, 449
Columbia, see Wright-Bellanca
Commercial Airplane Wing Syndicate, 319
Commissariato dell'Aeronautica, 405
Compagnie de Navigation Aérienne, 130
Conant, Frank H. "Hersey," 225, 234, 235, 238–9, 427, 477
Concorde, 84, 151
Concours International de Madrid 1923, 118
Conflenti, Raphael, 54, 154–6, 158, 393, 405
Conly, D. L., 447
Conforti (pilot), 468
Conover, W. N., 163
Consolidated Aircraft Company, 170, 260, 276
Conte Rosso, 412
Conte Verde, 54, 408
"Controllers," 147, 149, 151
Convair, 275, 303, 318
Cook, Frederick A., 26, 186–7
Cook, Harvey W., 459
Coolidge, Herbert, 7, 17–19*passim*, 55, 285
Coombs, Clarence B., 24, 181–2, 185–6, 196,

428, 451
Cooperative Fuel Research (CFR), 66
Coppens, Willy, 146
Corgnolino, Piero, 468, 470–1
Corkille, John D., 213, 456
Cornelius monoplane, 151
Cortinez, Lt., 355
Corrugation, 82
"Cosletizing," 82
Cosmos Company, (*see* Brazil-Straker)
    engines, 355, 364, 524; *see also* Bristol
Cotton, Sidney, 331, 436
Council of the Civil Aviation Organization
    (ICAO), 34
Coupe d'Aviation Maritime Jacques Schneider,
    see Schneider Trophy
Coupe Beaumont, 39
    1923, 88, 151, 153, 364, 443
    1924, 48–9, 127, 136, 138, 153–4, 338, 444
    1925, 128, 154, 445
Coupe Deutsch de la Meurthe, 27, 45
    1921, 46–7, 77, 80, 85, 104, 115–16, 120, 122, 143, 144–6, 244, 333, 335, 383, 388–9
    1922, 47, 105, 117, 123–5, 135, 149, 150, 336, 389–90
Coupe Internationale 1900–1905, 27, 329
Coupe Lamblin 1923, 136
Coupe Suzanne Deutsch de la Meurthe 1933, 93, 125
Coupe Zenith 1923, 136
Courtney, Frank T., 43, 44, 86, 309, 317–18, 319–20, 322, 343, 354, 365, 437, 439, 441
Couzinet, René, 138
Cox, George L., 187
Cox, Nellie, 178–9, 180–2*passim*, 186
Cox, S. E. J., 28, 177–8, 181–2, 184–7, 202, 252
Cox-Klemin Aircraft Company, 187
Cowes, England, 52, 110, 155, 158, 251, 299, 311, 373, 392
CRDA (Cantieri Riuniti dell'Adriatico), 405, 474
    D.G.C.3, 405
Creep fatigue, 84
Cresswell, Charles C., 263
Cricklewood, London, 325, 329
CR Italian fighters, 390
Crocco, General, 404
Crowell, Benedict, 11, 33, 35
Croydon, England, 42, 44, 335
    Whitsun Handicap 1922, 364
CR racers, *see* Curtiss
Cuddihy, George T., 204, 225, 233–4, 237, 240–1, 414, 426, 427, 459, 475–6, 478
Culbertson, W. D., 190, 449
Culver, J., 281
Cummings, Charles M., 447
Cunningham-Hall Aircraft Company, 275
Curran, James, 451
Curtiss, Alan Harper, 438
Curtiss, Glenn, 4, 22, 27, 29, 37, 39, 80, 180, 182, 184, 188, 189–91, 195, 196, 258–9, 294, 423, 428

Curtiss Aeroplane Company, 32, 33, 36, 38, 40, 44, 60–2 *passim*, 70, 74, 142, 169, 178, 244, 375
  aeroplanes:
    Cactus Kitten, 28, 181, 182, 184–7, 191, 196, 200, 424, 428, 490, 492
    CR racers, 186, 194–201, 209, 252, 294, 424, 451, 453, 492
    CR-3, 201–4, 225, 232, 234, 241, 249–50, 372, 379, 405, 407, 425, 426, 472, 475, 492
    CS torpedo, 243
    CT torpedo bomber, 194
    Eagle-2, 191
    F3C-1 (R3C), 227
    F6C, 460, 478
    F11C-3, 88
    Jenny, 36–8 *passim*, 169, 246, 259, 302
    NC, *see* Navy Curtiss
    Oriole, 24, 36, 38, 76, 181, 185
    P–1, 41, 78, 459
    P–2 fighters, 227
    P–6A, 78
    PW-8 Hawk, 39, 41, 67, 77, 209, 217, 235, 241, 413, 458–9
    R-6, 35, 38–9, 47, 65–6, 74, 77, 80, 124–5, 153, 205–6, 218, 219, 223, 253, 274, 283, 285, 293, 336, 425, 454, 456, 458, 492
    R-8, 223, 285, 458
    R2C, 127, 136, 153, 213–14, 217–24, 228, 232, 253–5, 257, 285, 333, 426, 494
    R2C-2 seaplanes, 224–5, 234, 237, 379
    R3C, 54–5, 56, 74, 225, 227–42, 342, 426, 427, 459, 476, 477, 479, 494
    R3C-2, 236, 240–2, 376, 379, 407, 409, 474, 477
    R3C-3, 237–8, 240–1, 413, 478
    R3C-4, 237–41, 413–14
    S-3 Scout, 184
    Texas Wildcat, 28, 79, 84, 180–1, 182–4, 185, 191, 252, 428, 451, 490, 492
    triplane 18-T, 63, 187, 189–92, 194, 246, 298, 451, 461
  airfoils:
    C-27, 206
    C-62, 80, 219
    C-80, 228
  engines:
    C-12, 64, 179, 191, 193, 196, 520
    CD-12, 64–5, 191–2, 193–4, 195, 196, 206, 228, 520
    D-12, 53, 55, 65–6, 69, 70–1, 93, 125, 199, 200, 202, 206, 209, 212–14, 217–18, 227, 236, 279, 283, 331, 390, 403, 405, 407, 520
    D-12A, 213, 214, 218, 224, 226, 285, 405, 407–8, 520
    K-12, 62–3, 64, 187–9, 194, 196, 386, 518
    OX, 36, 188, 356, 518
    V-1400, 71, 226–7, 228–9, 232, 234, 236, 311, 520
    V-1550, 236, 238, 239–40, 520
    V-1570 Conqueror, 236

    wetsleeve monobloc, 53, 62–3, 65, 74; *see also* Monobloc aero engine
  magnetos, 64
  propellers:
    R, 74, 228, 232
    Z-1, 73–4
    see also Reed propellers
  skin radiators, 76–7, 125, 135; *see also* Skin radiators
Curtiss Field, Long Island, 32, 40, 74, 186, 198, 208, 221–2, 227, 254
Curtiss-Kirkham engines,
  18-B Wasp, 188–9
  18-T, 188–92, 449
Curtiss Marine Trophy race 1922, 33, 37, 40, 191–2, 202, 246, 249, 294, 296, 298–9, 460
Curtiss-ply, 81, 195, 201, 206
Curtiss-Reed propellers, *see* Reed propellers
Curtiss-Reid Rambler, 364
Curtiss-Wright, 364
  Junior, 259
Cutler, Louis, 185

D-12 engine, *see* Curtiss
D.A.G. (Domestic Aviation Gasoline), 66
Daily Graphic, 323
Daily Mail, 25, 326
Daily Mail awards, 25, 306, 316, 347, 348, 388
Daily Mirror, 25
Daimler, Coventry, 329
Daimler, Gottfried, 4
Daly, W. J., 448
Daniels, Josephus, 11, 13
D'Annunzio, Gabriele, 7, 20, 385, 386, 388, 390, 412
Dare, Melvin E., 300–3
Dare Variable Camber monoplane, 300–3, 455
Dassault, Marcel, 93
Davis, Dwight F., 18, 40
Dawn to Dusk flight 1924, 209
Dawson, Leo H., 459
Dayton Engineering Laboratories Corporation (Delco), 60, 163, 168
Dayton-Wright Aeroplane Company, 60, 170
  RB, 28, 79, 88, 162–8, 278, 428, 490
De Bernardi, Mario, 241, 411–15, 427, 479
De Briganti, Giovanni "Nanni," 51, 54, 395, 398, 407–8, 415, 465, 467, 477
Decauville automobile, 59
De Conneau, *see* Beaumont
De Courcelles (French race driver), 113
Deeds, Edward A., 60–1, 69, 70, 161, 163, 289
DeGrandeville lamination, 72
De Havilland, Geoffrey, 320, 322, 323, 345, 347
De Havilland, 42, 322, 341
  Comet, 322
  D.H.4, 446–7, 450
  D.H.6 "Sky Hooks," 319, 329
  D.H.9A, 441
  D.H.14A, 436
  D.H.37, 322, 440–1
  D.H.80A Puss Moth *Karohi*, 313

  Moth, 322
  see also Airco; Hamilton propellers
De Havilland Hire Service, 322
Delage, Gustave, 47, 109, 113–14, 119, 122, 126, 244
Delage, Louis, 109
Delage automobiles, 109
  V-12, 109
Delahaye, 109
De Laval Steam Turbine Company, 67
De la Verne Machine Company, 296
Delco, *see* Dayton Engineering Laboratories Corporation
Delta wing, 148, 166
Demoiselle, 78
De Monge, Viscount Louis, 47, 72–3, 74, 84, 109, 122, 142–6
De Monge
  5.1, 84, 85, 142–5, 432, 439, 486
  5.2, 145
Denby, Edwin, 12, 17, 222
Denby, Mrs., 36
De Nieuport, Édouard and Charles, 87, 108; *see also* Nieuport
Deperdussin, Armand, 27, 91–2, 307
Deperdussin, 4, 27, 41, 46, 81, 83, 99, 124
  racing planes, 68, 81, 307, 423, 428, 430, 463
  rotary engine, 67
De Reuter, George Julius, 26
De Romanet, Marquis Bernard, 47, 74, 84, 98–104, 108, 110–11, 114, 122, 142, 143–5, 175, 320, 335, 393–4, 423–4, 429–30, 432, 439
Deschamps (French pilot), 145
Desoutter, Marcel, 309
Detroit Aerial Water Derby 1922, 33; *see also* Curtiss Marine Trophy race
Detroit Aviation Society, 35
Detroit *Free Press*, 211
"Detroit gang," 60
Detroit *News*, 29
Detroit River, 191
Deutsch de la Meurthe, Émile, 45
Deutsch de la Meurthe, Henry, 45–6, 47, 109
Devillers (French pilot) 152, 153, 426, 443
Dewar, Lord, 43
Dewoitine, 145, 458
Direct lift control (DLC), 300
Direzione Tecnica dell'Aeronautica Militare (DTAM), 384–5, 406
Dixon, Vincent B., 275, 457
Dodge Brothers, 274
Doolittle, James H., 40, 41, 54–5, 56, 78, 228–31, 234–5, 241, 242, 285, 303, 342–3, 379, 408, 427, 476
Dorman, Geoffrey, 44
Dormoy, Étienne, 170
Dornier, Claudius, 19, 82, 405
Dornier
  S.4 racer, 405, 474, 512
  Wal, 82
Douglas, Donald Wills, 24, 41
Douglas, Sholto, 9
Douglas
DC-3, 79

DC-8 jets, 37
mailplanes, 73
SDW-1, 255
transports, 295
World Cruisers, 13, 74
Douhet, Giulio, 19, 20
Dowding, Hugh, 354
Draper, Christopher, 308–9, 320, 434, 438
Dreadnought J.6986, 134
Drouhin (French pilot), 73
DT-4 seaplane, 237, 248, 250
Dubonnet, André, 126
Duesenberg engine, 299
Duhamel, Alphonse, 157–8, 473
Duhamel, Robert, 95
Dunlap, Lt., 281
Dunlop Tyre Company, 329
Dunn, Freddie, 354
Dunn, J. K., 448
Dunne, J. W., 148, 151
Dupré, George, 268
Duralumin, 73, 74, 82–4, 105, 110, 126, 130–1, 134, 135, 140, 144, 146, 195, 204, 207, 218, 254, 269, 274, 308, 316, 339
Durand, W. F., 67

Eagle engine, *see* Rolls-Royce
Eaker, Ira, 231
Eastern Air Lines, 196
Eaton, Samuel, 196
Edge, S. F., 329
Edward VIII, 44, 198–9
Eells, Fred, 188
Egaburn, Loulou, 98
Eiffel, A. G., 244
Elbe, Harry, 33
Eldbridge engine, 196
Eliason, Carl, 446
Elliott, H. A., 461
Ellor, James E., 67, 71
Elmendorf, Hugh M., 273–4, 455
Engines, *see* Air-cooled engines; Liquid-cooled engines
Ericson (referee), 341
Erlanger, Camille, 45
Esnault-Pelterie, Robert, 78, 87, 130
  R.E.P. engines, 78, 356
Établissement Lumière, 72–4, 142
Établissement Nieuport, *see* Nieuport
Étampes (Villesauvage Aerodrome), 27, 28, 47, 92, 99, 102, 105, 113, 124, 132, 144, 145, 172, 182–3, 318, 328, 336, 390
Ethyl alcohol, 72
Ethylene glycol, 77–8
Etrich, Ignaz and Igo, 148
Etrich
  Taube, 148, 319
"Eugene Gilbert," *see* Nieuport-Delage
European Circuit Air Race 1911, 48
Everling, E., 127
Ewen School, Hendon, 326
Excelsior Palace Hotel, Venice, 398
Eyre, Bill, 346

FAI (Fédération Aéronautique Internationale), 21–2, 30, 35, 36, 38, 43, 50–2 passim, 55, 126, 198, 210, 212, 328, 384, 388, 393, 409
Fairchild, 192
The City of New York, 185
Fairey, Charles Richard, 70, 148, 217, 227, 331, 373, 393
Fairey
III-A, 463
Fawn bomber, 70–1
Firefly fighter, 71
Fox, 71
Reed propeller, 74, 339, 343, 376
seaplane, 50, 331
Fall, J. S. T., 436
Farman, Henri, 28, 45
Farman planes, 387
Farnborough, see Royal Aircraft Establishment
Farnborough Air Show, 347
Faroux, Charles, 61
Farwell, F. O., 67
Fauvel, Charles, 150
F.2B fighter, see Bristol
Fechet, James E., 18
Fechteler, Augustus C., 199
Fechteler, Frank C., 199
Fedden, Roy, 68, 70, 349, 353, 355–8, 361, 365–6
Federal Trade Commission, 186
Felix engine, see Curtiss D-12 engine
Felixstowe, 338–40, 343
Fell, L. F. Rudstone, 71
Fergus Motors Company, 67
Ferigoule, G., 154, 444–5
Ferrarin, Arturo, 241, 385, 386–7, 400, 411–15, 478
Ferretti, Ettore, 411
Fetu (French pilot), 149
Fiat (Fabbrica Italiana Automobile Torino), 25, 36, 56, 387, 405, 407
aeroplanes:
ARF, 388, 423
BR bomber, 144, 387, 388, 390, 423
R.700, 388–90, 424, 432–3, 456, 508
speedplanes, 47, 120, 383–4
car: 15-liter, 59
engines:
A-10, 387
A-12, 387, 398, 528
A-20, 407
A-24, 407–8, 410
A.S.2, 411, 528
Filipa (Italian draftsman), 409
Fils de Alexandre Deutsch, Les, 45
Finch, V. C., 446
First Experimental Air Station, Australia, 361
Fisher, Jack, 13
Fisher Body Company, 169
Fiske, Bradley, 13
Flandin, P. E., 106
Fleet, Reuben H., 260
Flight magazine, 35, 52, 53, 71, 80, 317
Flush riveting, 84
Flutter, 28, 79, 84–6, 122, 138, 145, 180, 224, 241, 279, 280, 287, 292, 318, 335,

339, 380
Flying boats, 95, 394; see also Macchi; Savoia; Supermarine
Foch, Ferdinand, 7, 10, 20
Fokker, Tony, 79, 85, 87, 308, 309
Fokker, 86
D-VII, 24, 85, 208, 261, 385, 448
D-VIII, 79, 85, 86, 278
D-X parasol fighter, 85
E-1, 79
E-V, 85
Old Glory, 198
PW-5, 85
T-2, 264
tri-motor America, 198
tri-motor Bird of Paradise, 208
Folland, Henry P., 28, 42, 48, 54, 317, 322, 323–6, 328–9, 331–3, 335, 336, 339–41, 343–4, 345, 350, 373
Fonck, René, 98, 102, 231
Fontenelle Hotel, Omaha, 186
Foot, Leslie, 86, 320, 365, 439, 442
Ford, Edsel B., 35
Ford, Henry, 17, 83
Ford Motor Company, 41
"Tin Goose," 80, 82
Tri-Motor transports, 83, 172, 192, 196
Ford Museum, 168
Ford Reliability tours, 303
Forlanini floats, 95–6, 97, 404
Forrestier-Walker, Dring Lester, 438
Fossati, Mario, 387–8, 390
Foulois, Benjamin, 10, 12, 40, 302
Fowler, Harlan, 79
Fox, Arthur W., 449
Frankfurt, 14
French Air Corps, 20
Fried, Jerome A., 276
Frisbee (chef), 43
Froude Tank, La Spezia, 395
Fuels, 66, 71, 72, 168, 229
Fullam, William F. "Quarterdeck," 13, 17
Fulton, Hamilton, 319
Fulton Motor Company, 192
Funk, Rudy, 281

Gabard, E., 391
GAC, see Gloucestershire Aircraft Co.
Gallaudet, Edson F., 299–300
Gallaudet, 192
Bullet, 299
D-4, 299–300, 461
DB.1, 83
"Gallaudet Drive," 299
Galtier, Jean, 132
Gastambide & Levavasseur, 79
Gates, Richard, 43
Gathergood, Gerald, 41, 321–2, 423, 435
Geddes, Sir Eric, 14
Gee-Bee, 88, 235, 303
General Electric Company, 67
General Motors, 60, 72, 163, 168, 289
General Oil Company, 177, 186
General Steam Navigation Company, 370

George V, 11, 41, 44, 364, 369
Gephart, Valentine, 452
German Airship League, 21
Geyer, Harvey, 167
Gianfelice-Gino, Sgt., 423
Gianoli, Marcel, 132, 138
Gibson, A. H., 68, 168, 325
Gibson, G. and T. E., 332
Gibson, Harvey, 69
Gilbert, Eugène, 46, 430
Gillespie, P. E., 449
Gilman, N. H., 72
Gilmore, Bill, 32, 73, 178–9, 188, 194, 202, 205, 218, 219, 228, 229, 233, 237–8
Gipsy III engine, 313
Girouette de l'aviation, see Arnoux
Given, Fred, 244, 248
Glazebrook, C. T., 41
Glenn Curtiss Trophy, see Curtiss Marine Trophy race
Glidden, Charles J., 24, 31, 47, 303
Glidden Efficiency Trophy 1919, 24
Gliders, 316
Gloucestershire Aircraft Company (GAC), later Gloster, 47, 54, 75, 352
aeroplanes:
Bamel (Mars I), 43, 44, 47, 77, 125, 143, 145, 314, 331–2, 333–7, 339–40, 342–3, 359, 361, 424, 425, 432–3, 439–40, 504
Bluebird, 86, 338–9, 459
Gamecock fighter, 86
Gladiator, 324
Gloster I, 36, 44, 48, 335, 337–8, 339, 352, 373, 425, 442–3, 456, 477
Gloster II, 338–9, 426, 474, 504
Gloster IIIA, 427, 476, 506
Gloster IV, 80, 324, 343, 479
Gloster V, 344
Gloster VI, 331
Gorcock fighter, 86
Grebe, 75, 333, 337
Grouse I fighter, 333, 337
Mars fighters, 329, 331, 337
Mars III "Sprawk," 333, 440
Nightjar, 337
seaplane, 54
Sparrowhawk, 329
propellers, 343
H-S-B propeller, 74
Glues, 81
Gnôme-Rhône, 68, 126, 153, 358
rotary engine, 324, 347, 428, 430, 434, 463
Godoy, Capt., 355
Gold Bug Inn, Mineola, 39
Gooden, Frank, 326
Gordon Bennett Aeronautical Cup, 27, 37
Gordon Bennett Aviation Cup, 27, 92, 107
1909, 22, 27, 182, 306
1910, 306
1912, 49
1913, 79, 92, 124
1920, 28–9, 31, 38, 43, 47, 50, 76, 79, 81, 88, 99–102, 109, 111, 114, 116, 141, 142, 161, 166–7, 172–3, 182–3, 193, 318, 428

George V, 11, 41, 44, 364, 369
Gorton, A. W. "Jake," 192, 249–51, 255–7, 298, 426, 462, 472, 474
Goshawk, see British Nieuport
Göttingen airfoil, 124, 150, 255, 295, 387
Gourdou, Charles Édouard P., 151
Gourdou-Leseurre, 48, 118, 364
CT No. 1, 88, 151–3, 426, 430, 443, 488
type 13, 153
Goux, Jules, 58, 115
Gradis, M., 109
Grahame-White, Claude, 50, 305, 318, 428
Grahame-White Company, 305, 307
Bantams, 306–7, 434
Grahame-White School, Hendon, 87, 306, 369
Grampian Motor Company, 354
Grand Prix de l'Automobile-Club de France 1912, 59
Grand Prix d'Aviation 1921, 51
Grand Prix de Monaco 1920, 96, 111, 114, 394
Grand Prix des Voiturettes 1910, 58
Gran Premio d'Italia d'Aviazione, 115
Gran Premio Venezia 1921, 51
Grant, Charles Hampson, 87, 88, 162–3, 164, 166
Grant, Duncan, 163
Grant, Gertrude, 162–3
Grant, V. F., 460
Grant Fast Fighter, 87, 88
Granville, Zantford "Granny," 235
Greely, Adolphus W., 9
Green, Anna K., 180
Green, Carl, 86
Green, Fred M., 68, 69, 81, 277
Green engine, 311–12, 522
Grey, Charles G., 30, 44–5, 52, 55, 103–4, 203, 216, 234, 315, 325, 328, 329, 375
Greyhound, see Airco
Grieg, D'Arcy, 86
Grimes, H., 378
Grosvenor, Lord Edward, 44, 340, 365
Grosvenor Challenge Cup race
1923, 86, 365
1924, 313
Grumman, Leroy R., 32, 291
Grumman Aircraft Corporation, 202, 271
FF-1, 88
F8F, 22, 223
Hellcat fighters, 202
Gsell, Robert, 82
Guarnieri (Italian pilot), 51, 398, 401, 470
Guasconi, G., 411–12
Guazzetti, Frederico, 405, 411, 474
Guggenheim Medal 1960, 293
Guglielmetti, Aldo, 411–12
Guidera, Albert M., 455
Guidoni, A., 19, 54, 56, 385, 405, 407
Guidoni hydrofoils, 404
Gulfhawks, 223
Gulf Oil Corporation, 223
Gurney, Harlan "Bud," 37
Gwyn, W. B., 448

Hagg, Arthur, 322
Haig, Rollo de Haga, 337–8, 361, 440
Haines, Caleb V., 449
Halford, Frank B., 310, 322
Hall, Elbert J., 61, 166, 171
Hall, Melvin, 329
Hall, Randolph F., 259, 263, 265, 268, 271, 275–6
Hall, Theodore P., 276
Hall-Scott Automobile Company,
    L-6A engine, 166, 516
Hallett, George E. A., 61
Hamel, Gustav, 434
Hammersley, H. A., 311–12, 435–6, 441, 464
Hamilton, Thomas, 74, 75
Hamilton Aero Propeller Company, 74, 249–50, 254
Hamilton-Standard, 74
Handasyde, George, 79, 138, 315, 316, 319–20
Handasyde Aircraft Company, 319
Handley Page, Frederick, 81, 151
Handley Page, 79, 309
    bombers, 10
    slot, 319
Hanriot, Marcel, 28, 47, 146
Hanriot, René, 47, 133, 146–7
Hanriot, 83, 88, 404
    bombers, 128
    HD.1, 146
    HD.22 racer, 80, 82, 146–7, 151, 432, 488
    "Henrietta," 146
Harding, Warren G., 7, 12, 13, 17, 61, 244
Hargreaves, J., 368
Harmsworth, Alfred C. W., see Northcliffe, Lord
Harmsworth, Harold S., see Rothermere, Lord
Harris, Harold R., 86
Hart, Seth, 72
Harte, Richard, 147, 148
Hartney, Harold E., 10, 24, 32, 33, 35, 196, 261, 265, 266–7, 290, 448, 451
Hartzell propeller, 268, 279
Harvard Aeronautical Society, 87
Haviland, Willis B., 190, 449
Hawker, Harry G., 25, 28, 41–3passim, 306, 316, 328, 345–51, 428, 435–6, 439, 463
Hawker (H. G. Hawker Engineering Company), 316, 344, 351
    Hart, 71
    Hurricane, 66, 80, 287, 344, 352
    Sopwith Hawker, 351–2
Hawker-Siddeley, 352
Hawley, Alan R., 30
Haydn, Stone and Company, 318
Hazelhurst Field, 40, 181; see also Curtiss Field
H.C.8 carburetors, 325
Hearle, Frank, 321–2
Hearst, William R., 329
Heath, Spencer, 72
Heckstall-Smith, S., 325
Hedderwick, H. J., 306
Heinkel, 19
    He.70, 381
Heisen, Horace N., 447
Helen, Emmanuel, 430
Hele-Shaw, Dr., 74

Hell's Half-Acre, 38
Hemingway, Ernest, 21
Hemming, Harold, 322, 441
Henderson, 14
Henderson, Sir David, 324
Henderson, G. L. P., 434
Hendon, London, 41–3, 44, 308, 315, 328, 332, 345, 348, 350, 354
Henry, Ernest, 58–9
Henry, J. P., 167
Herbemont, André, A.-M., 92, 93–4, 95–6, 99–106, 108, 114, 170
Heron, Sam D., 68–9, 70, 71, 164, 325
Herring-Curtiss Company, 87, 259
Hill, Geoffrey, 151
Hill, Roderick, 151
Hinkler, Herbert J. L., 54, 311–13, 339–42, 365, 436, 438, 440–1, 476
Hispano-Kellner automobiles, 93
Hispano Suiza, 58, 59, 61, 69, 204, 314
    cars, 61, 126
    engines, 65, 66, 71, 229, 244, 310–11, 330, 376
        modèle 34 (V-8), 28, 61–2, 93, 139, 372, 514
        modèle 35, 514
        modèle 42, 62–3, 64, 73, 74, 93, 95, 100, 102, 105, 109, 110, 117, 120, 122, 124–5, 126, 130, 142, 143, 146, 155–6, 170, 260, 315, 316, 369, 514
        modèle 42 Marine, 98, 113
        modèle 50, 126, 134, 138, 158, 516
        modèle 51, 126, 134, 138, 516
Hitchison, Lt., 293
Hives, Ernest, 71, 72
HLB (High Lift Biplane) airfoil, 333
HMS Barham, 50
HMS Malaya, 393
Hoare, Sir Samuel J. G., 15, 17, 19, 55, 71
Hobbs, Basil, 369, 463
Hobbs, Leonard S. "Luke," 66
Hodgdon, Melvin W., 30
Hoff, Dr. W., 85
Holle, A. A., 147, 265, 319–20
Holt-Thomas, George, 323
Hoover, Herbert, 29
Hope, W. L., 313
Hopkinson, Bertram, 168
Hornet, 235
Hotel Cecil, London, 9
Hotel Montecello, Norfolk, 56
Hotel Pennsylvania, Long Island, 41
Hotel Ritz, 9
Howard, Clinton W., 215
HS2L flying boat, 241, 413
Hubbard, Frank, 228
Hubert, Jean, 130–2, 134–5, 136, 137–8
Hudson, Donald, 190, 235
Hudson-Frampton Motor Car Company, 35, 169
Hudson Motors, 60
Hughes, Charles E., 60, 171
Hughes, T. G., 192
Hunsaker, Jerome C., 32, 36, 37, 52, 55, 244, 246, 296
Hunter, Frank O'D. "Monk," 270–1, 274, 454
Hurel, Maurice, 156, 158, 159, 473

Hurricane, see Hawker
Hurst, McGeagh, 318
Hyde, James H., 10
Hydrofoils, 49, 395–6, 404
Hyduminium RR.58, 84

ICAO, see International Civil Aviation Organization
Icare, 49
Il domino dell'aria (Command of the Air), 19
Imperator, 182
Imperia Excelsior, 146
Imperial Airways, 365, 375
Imperial College of Science, 369
Imperial Japanese Navy, 329
Ince, Thomas H., 25
Indianapolis 500, 59, 72
Indianapolis Motor Speedway timer, 210
Institut Aérotechnique de Saint-Cyr, 45, 46, 141, 320
Institute of Aeronautical Engineers, 333; see also Royal Aeronautical Society
Instone Air Lines, 365
Internal-combustion engine, 57–9
International Aero Congress 1921, 32
International Aviation Reunion, Nice 1922, 390
International Civil Aviation Organization, 34
International Correspondence Schools, 187, 326
International Sporting Club of Monaco, 51
International Steel Wing Aircraft Syndicate, 134
Irvine, Rutledge, 191–2, 198, 202–4, 245, 249, 250, 425, 461, 472
Irwin, Bill, 178, 230, 239–40
Isaacs, Bernard, 43, 309
Isotta-Fraschini, 69
    engines, 385, 387, 392, 398, 405, 407, 526
Issy-les-Moulineaux, Paris, 46, 109, 118, 148, 306
Istres, France, 47, 48, 125, 127, 128, 136, 137, 153
Itala (Hispano-Suiza) engines, 402
Italian Grand Prix for motorcars, Brescia 1921, 115

Jackson, Ross, 293
Jacobs, Fernand, 21
Jacobs, Jim, 167
Jaguar, see Siddeley-Deasey
Jaille, Capt., 118
Jakobi, Ed, 301, 302
James, James H., 43, 125, 145, 326–7, 328, 332–3, 335–7, 424–5, 428, 432–3, 436, 439–40
James, Mansell R., 29–30
James Gordon Bennet Trophy, 27, 329
Jane's All the World's Aircraft, 44, 104
Jannello, Guido, 50, 51, 99, 392–3, 395–8passim, 400, 464–5, 468
Jatte, M., 58
Jeffery's Patent Waterproof Liquid Glue, 81
Jenny, see Curtiss
Jensen, Leth, 46, 95, 430, 436

Jeter, Thomas P., 460
Joffre, Jos. Jacques, 62
John L. Mitchell Trophy race,
    1922, 271–4
    1923, 214, 275
    1924, 231
Johnson, Basil, 71
Johnson, Claude, 59
Johnson, Davenport, 447
Johnson, Edward E., 223
Johnson, Fonda B., 281–3, 448, 455
Johnson, J. M., 170
Johnson, J. Thad, 275, 457
Johnson, Walter, 260
Johnston, T. J., 178–9
Jones, Charles S. "Casey," 36, 38, 76, 240
Jones, E. T., 67, 69
Jordon, W. L., 436
Joucques Aviation Company, 307
Joyce, James, 21
Junkers, Hugo, 79, 80, 82
Junkers, 19; 86
    fuel-injection pumps, 60
    J.1, 82
    J.10, 82
    J.L.6, 82, 192, 196, 302
Junor, Lt., 86
Jupiter engine, see Bristol

K-12 engine, see Curtiss
Kady, Arthur, 266–7
Kansas City meet 1921, 265
Karman, Theodore von, 83, 86
Kartveli, Alexander, 133
Keep, Stuart, 134
Kelleher, Capt., 272
Kellner, Jacques, 93
Kellner-Béchereau racer, 93, 109
Kellogg-Briand Pact 1928, 19
Kelly, E., 170
Kelly, Oakley G., 264, 290, 449
Kemble, Thomas S., 64
Kemp, Ronald, 310, 316
Kenworthy, Reginald W., 320, 373–4, 472
Kenwood, Lt.-Col., 128
Ketchum, Hallock, 238
Kettering, Charles F., 60, 71, 161, 163–4, 167, 168
Keyes, Roger, 11, 14
Keys, Clement M., 41, 53–5passim, 64, 70, 74, 178, 181, 191, 206, 208, 210, 217, 227
Keys, Conrad R., 181
Kilner, G., 172
Kincade, Harold T. "Doc," 266
King, J. R., 441
King's Cup race, 44, 45
    1922, 316, 322, 364–5
    1923, 316, 318, 322, 337, 375
    1924, 322, 374
    1925, 322
Kirby, Maxwell, 448
Kirkham, Charles B., 62–4, 65, 72, 88, 187–9, 191, 192, 195, 280
Kirkham, Clarence and Percy, 188

554

Kirkham Products Corporation, 192
    engines, 188
    racers, 236
    Vespa, 241
Kirsch, Georges, 28, 35, 102, 111, 113–14,
    122, 142, 389, 424, 429, 432
Klemin, Alexander, 81, 187
Kloor, I. A., 32
Koolhoven, Fritz "Kully," 92, 100, 218, 307–9
Korbel, Mario, 33
Kraeling, Harry, 74

Lachmann, 79
L'Aeronautica, 395
La Follette, Robert M., 285
La Gazetta dell'Aviazione, 204
Lahm, Frank P., 37, 48
Laird, Matty, 38
    Super Solution, 235
Lakehurst, New Jersey, 36
Lake Varese, 411, 414,
La Lorraine, 182
L'Alpino, 20
Lambert, Albert B., 35
Lambert Field, St. Louis, 35–7, 192
Lamblin, A., 75, 77
Lamblin
    lobster pot radiators, 54, 75–6, 77, 105, 110,
        117, 120, 122, 125, 132, 135, 137,
        143, 149, 153–4, 175, 194, 195, 246,
        248, 279, 284, 294–5, 333, 373, 388
    special radiators, 156–7, 376
Lancaster bomber, 310
Lanchester Motor Company, 329
Landing gear, 131, 153, 179, 253, 308, 314
    retractable, 87–8, 134, 135, 139–40, 146,
        147, 153, 164, 168, 277, 278, 280–1,
        282–3, 285, 287, 294–6, 362, 403
Landwerlin, Georges-Marie, 150
Landwerlin-Berreur tailless racer, 150–1, 433,
    488
Lang, Andrew, 331
Langley, Samuel P., 9, 68, 85
Langley Field, Virginia, 68, 268, 283
Larsen, John M., 196, 302
Lasne, Fernand, 115, 117, 124, 128, 389–90,
    424, 432–3, 443–4
Lassiter, William 17
Latham, Hubert, 111, 157
Latham flying boat racers, 157–8, 490
Laurent-Eynac, M., 20, 21, 71, 125–6, 128,
    136, 145
L'Auto, 52, 145
Laverents, A., 448
Law, Andrew Bonar, 15
Lawrence, Charles L., 32, 69, 296–7, 299
Lawrence,
    60-hp engine, 285
    J-1 engine, 269, 296–9
Lawrence Sperry Aircraft Company, see Sperry
Lawson, Walker R., 446
"Lazy Tong" mechanical starter, 223
League of Nations, 7, 13, 19
Leblanc, Alfred, 92

Le Bourget, 31, 46, 47, 328
Lecointe, Sadi, 28, 36, 38, 45–9passim, 85,
    95–6, 99, 100, 102–4, 107–8, 110–11,
    113–15, 117, 120–1, 124–5, 127–8,
    138, 145, 147, 154, 173, 319, 384,
    390, 392, 398, 423–7, 429–33, 439,
    443–5, 456, 458, 464, 468
Ledeboer, J. H., 41
Lees, Walter, 9
Legh, Peter, 308
Leighton, Bruce G., 69, 75, 297
Leitner, Henry, 73
Leitner-Watts propellers, 74, 373
Lejeune, John A., 268
Le Mans, 27
Lenoir, Joseph É., 58
LePère, 67, 118
    c.11, 263–4
LeRhône engines, 79, 269, 306, 354–5
    80, 514
    J-110, 514
Leseurre, Jean A., 151
Letombe self-starter, 143
Levasseur, Pierre, 72, 396
Levasseur
    L'Oiseau Blanc, 128, 135
    radiators, 130
    Reed propellers, 74, 134
Levavasseur, Léon, 80
    Monobloc, 80
Levey, Ethel, 305–6
Leviathan, 70, 198, 203, 204, 250, 253
Liberty Aircraft Products Corporation, 192
Liberty engines, 58, 65, 163, 170, 171, 252,
    299, 301, 320, 516
    cylinder, 63
    400-hp V-12, 61
    "Liberty six," 166
    supercharger, 67
    8, 123
Liberty Engine Builders' Trophy race 1923, 192
Lindbergh, Charles "Slim," 25, 37, 40, 69, 128,
    198, 223, 292, 299
Lind-Jackson, W., 378
Linton-Hope, Major, 367–8, 372
Lion engine, see Napier
Lippisch, Alexander, 150, 151
Lipton, Sir Thomas, 44
Liquid-cooled aero engines, 65–6, 70–1, 153–4,
    297, 410
Lloyd George, David, 6, 7, 9, 11, 14
Locarno Pact 1925, 19
Locatelli, Lt., 385, 388
Lockhart Mission, 169
Lockheed, 88
    F-104, 165
Lockheed Vega, Yankee Doodle, 185
Locklear, Ormer, 29
Loening, Albert P., 31, 291
Loening, Grover, 16, 32, 60, 163, 195, 288,
    291, 293
Loening, Mike, 293
Loening, 86, 236, 280
    air yachts, 293
    M-8 pursuit, 289
    M-80, 449

M-81S ("L Special") racer, 289–90, 449, 498
R-4, 274, 288, 290–3, 454, 498
L'Oiseau Blanc, see Levasseur
London Illustrated News, 13
London Morning Post, 108
Longchamps, E. F., 163
Longden, David, 329, 333, 340
Long, S. H. "Tubby," 438
Long Island Early Flyers Club, 37
Longton, Walter H. 'Scruffie," 352, 436, 438,
    441, 472
Lorraine-Dietrich, 71, 126
    500-hp engine, 134
    modèle 13 V-12 engine, 157, 516
    modèle 14 engine, 104–5, 135, 516
    modèle 15 engine, 104
Lory, Albert, 109
Louis Clément-Moineau racer, 88, 139–41
Louis Delage engine, 93
Love (scientist), 83
Low, A. R., 81
Ludendorff, Erich, 10
Luftwaffe, 19
Lumière, Georges, 142
Lumière brothers, 91
Lumière-de Monge racer, see De Monge, 5.1
Lumière propellers, 72–4, 100, 110, 122, 143,
    166, 167
Lutz, Charles A., 460
Lyautey, Louis, 128
Lympne airfield, 45, 328
Lysistrata, 26

MacArthur, Arthur, 9
MacArthur, Douglas, 9, 18–19
Macchi, Giulio, 394
Macchi, Muzio, 399, 405, 411, 412
Macchi, 50, 54, 240–1, 370, 405
    M.7, 51, 395, 398–400, 467–8, 470, 510
    M.12, 394–5
    M.17, 393–4, 395, 399–400, 405, 470, 512
    M.18, 401, 467
    M.19, 394–5, 398, 399, 405, 468, 512
    M.27, 407, 477
    M.33, 85, 406–9, 477, 512
    M.39, 56, 409–14, 427, 478–9, 512
Macchi-Castoldi, M. C. 72, 77, 78, 86, 285, 415
McBride, Benjamin K., 455
McCook Field, Dayton, 69, 71–4passim, 81, 85,
    86, 88, 163, 169–70, 175–6, 182,
    189, 194, 206, 211, 214, 223, 230,
    260, 263, 275, 279, 283, 292
McCook Field Museum, 176, 287
McCook Field propellers, 279, 281
McCook Field Structures Branch, 86, 187
Macdonald, James Ramsay, 7, 16, 19
MacFadden, Bernard, 163
McGraw, John, 201
Mackenzie-Grieve, Kenneth M., 25, 348
Macready, John A., 67, 86, 117, 118, 185,
    263–4, 266, 293, 451
MacRobertson England–Australia race 1934,
    313
Maddalena, Umberto, 394, 396–8, 469

Madon, Georges, 147, 148–50, 433
Magnetos, 158
Maitland, Lester, 16, 208–10, 211–12, 213,
    425, 454
Mallard, Henri, 110, 463
Mallinson, W. J., 324
Manchester Guardian, 332
Manly, Charles, 32, 68
Mann, Merrill D., 447
Manor, Florian F., 452
Manton, Marcus, 308, 435
Marcel Bloch type 700 fighter, 93
Marchetti, Alessandro, 51, 400–1, 405
    MVT, 423
Markey, Roscoe, 281
Mars fighters, see Gloucestershire Aircraft
    Company
Martin, Glenn L., 60, 161
Martin, Helmuth P., 315
Martin, James V., 87–8
Martin K-III Scout, 87, 88, 460
Martinsyde, 25, 358
    Alula monoplane, 439
    Atlantic (Raymor), 316
    F.4 Buzzard, 79, 315, 431, 434–6, 438–40
    F.4A, 315
    F.6, 316, 436, 440–1
    motorcycles, 319
    Semiquaver, 28, 42, 102, 265, 316–20, 423,
        428, 437, 500
Martlesham Heath, England, 317, 328, 331,
    335, 338, 340, 361
Martyn, A. W., 329, 333
Martyn & Company, H. H., 324, 328–9
Mary, 348
Mary (engineer), 125
Masiero, Guido, 386
Mass balancing, 86
Matthews, Thomas K., 275, 455, 457
Maughan, Russell, 24, 35, 40, 124, 208,
    209–10, 211–12, 213, 221, 274, 425,
    454
Maughan, Weston F., 210
May, David, 48
May, Harden and May pontoons, 339
Mayhew, 329
Maynard, Belvin W., 24, 32
Mead, George, 32, 69, 123, 203, 299
Mears, John H., 185
Menoher, Charles T., 11, 13, 16
Mercedes, 10, 60, 387
    engines, 58, 61, 65
    D-1, 387
    D-IVa, 387
Merlin engine, see Rolls-Royce
Messenger, see Sperry
Messerschmitt Me.109, 223
Metal Airscrew Company, 73
Metal construction, 81–4, 105
Metal fatigue, 105
Mica plugs, 67
Micarta, 73
Michelin, André, 115
Middle East, 14
Midgley, Thomas, 167, 168
Miller, Elizabeth T., 285

Miller, Hugh S., 452
Miller Monoplane, 452
Miller, Walter, 213–14, 456
Miller-Offenhauser, 59
Mills, Harry H., 213, 215, 285–6, 301, 458
Mims, H. B., 447
Mines Field (Los Angeles International), 185
Minneapolis *Tribune*, 39
Minnewaska, 54, 340, 379
Mirafiori Aerodrome, Turin, 110, 120, 383
Mirage, 93
MIT (Massachusetts Institute of Technology), 33, 38, 39, 228, 230, 244, 285
Mitchel, John P., 39
Mitchel Field, Long Island, 31–2, 39, 40, 55, 84, 174–5, 180, 219, 221, 247, 254, 261, 268, 280, 284, 293
Mitchell, John Lendrum, 9
Mitchell, John Lendrum, jr., 272–3
Mitchell, Reginald J., 54, 79, 234, 339, 368–9, 370, 372, 375–6, 378–81, 407, 410
Mitchell, William 7–9*passim*, 10–14, 16, 17–19, 22, 24, 32, 33, 35, 36, 40, 53, 55, 67, 69, 118, 125, 170–1, 174, 200, 205, 208, 210–11, 232, 260, 261, 271–3, 274, 275, 278–9, 283, 285, 288, 321, 329, 425
Mitchell Trophy race, *see* John L. Mitchell Trophy race
Mitscher, Marc A. "Pete," 37; 191, 200, 233, 246, 249, 254, 255
Mitsubishi/Reed, 74
Mock, Frank C., 66
Mödebeck, Major, 21
Model Airplane, 163
Model airplanes, 88, 163, 310
Moffat, Reuben C., 447
Moffet, William A., 11–12, 13, 16–18*passim*, 36, 40, 55, 56, 67, 70, 221, 222–3, 237, 240, 297, 298–9
Moineau, M. R., 139
Monaco Seaplane Rallye
  1920, 50, 96–9, 110–12, 393, 398, 399
  1921, 51, 396–7
Monobloc aero engine, 53, 61–2, 64, 72, 244, 310, 329–30, 332, 390, 407
  wetsleeve, 62, 65, 67, 71, 74, 171, 194, 226, 229, 236, 244
Monobloc aeroplane, *see* Levavasseur
Monocoques, 81, 93, 324
  metal, 81–4
  wood, 81, 82, 119, 135, 149, 170, 188, 195, 206, 253, 308, 339, 372
Monoplanes, 78–80, 85
  "bodyless," 134
  cantilever, 79–80, 122, 138; *see also* Cantilever wing
Montagu of Beaulieu, Lord, 374
Montague, Hugh, Viscount Trenchard, *see* Trenchard, "Boom"
Monte Carlo powerboat racing 1910, 49
Monteith, Charles N. "Monty," 287
Moore-Brabazon, J. T. C., 15
Morane, Leon F., 423
Morane, Robert, 28
Morane parasols, 151, 318

Morane-Saulnier, 81, 182, 434, 449
Moreux, G., 125
Moreux skin radiators, 135
Morgan, C. W. F., 316
Morrow, Dwight W., 40, 55
Morrow Board, 18, 19, 40, 55
Morse, Frank L., 259, 269
Morselli, Riccardo, 394, 407–8, 477
Mortane, M., 50
Mortimer Singer Prize 1913, 347
Moseley, Corliss C., 32, 173–6, 263, 424, 450, 454
Moss, Sanford A., 67, 118, 263
Moss turbo-supercharger, 172, 263
Motorcycles, 188
Mouillard (designer), 148
Mulcahy, Francis "Pat," 268, 274, 453, 461
Mulligan, Eddie, 203, 266, 268
Munk, Max, 151
Mussolini, Benito, 7, 19–20, 56, 232, 405, 409, 413

N-9 airfoil, 255
NAA, *see* National Aeronautic Association
NACA, *see* National Advisory Committee for Aeronautics
NACA 81 airfoil, 278
NACA ring cowl, 70
NAF, *see* Naval Aircraft Factory
Nakajima N.29, 118
Naon, Romulo, 29
Napier, Montagu S., 329, 331
Napier, 51, 69, 204, 329–30
  automobile, 329
  engines:
    Cub, 71
    Lion, 41, 71, 134, 234, 314, 320, 322, 329–32, 336, 338, 369, 371, 373, 390, 407, 524
    Lion Mark VII, 340, 342, 344, 378, 381, 524
Naples, Italy, 51–2, 155, 203, 399
National Advisory Committee for Aeronautics (NACA), 34, 67, 80, 244, 283, 293, 361
National Aeronautic Association (NAA), 35, 37–9*passim*, 41, 45, 55, 172, 210, 212, 221
National Aeronautic Association Convention 1924, 17
National Air Races (NAR), 33
  1923, 35–7, 192, 250, 275, 390
  1924, 39
  1925, 40–1, 74, 199, 237
  1926, 239
  1929, 78
National Air Transport, 70
National Cash Register Company, 37, 39, 60
National Defense Act (USA), 1920, 11
National Flying Meet, Curtiss Field 1922, 186
National Nautical School for Boys, Portishead, 355
National Physical Laboratory, Teddington, 376
Naval Academy, 233, 234, 238, 239, 244

Naval Aircraft Factory, Philadelphia, 204, 225, 235, 237, 248–9, 255, 257, 274, 296, 299
Naval Aviation Corps, 29
Naval Oil Reserve, Teapot Dome, 186
Navy Curtiss (NC flying boat), 25, 29, 37, 52, 74, 244, 348
Navy TS/TR aeroplanes, 296–9, 498
  TR-1, 297–8, 462
  TR-3, 297–8, 462
  TR-3A, 299, 472
  TS-1, 296–8, 461
  TS-2, 461
Navy-Wright, *see* Wright Aeronautical, NW racers
Newman, George, 50, 110, 374, 393
New York Aero Show 1920, 191
New York *American*, 10
New York *Evening Telegram*, 26
New York Giants, 201
New York *Herald*, 10, 26–7, 29, 187
New York *Times*, 17, 26, 41
New York–Toronto Derby 1919, 23–4, 182
New York *World*, 29, 35
Nicholl, Vincent, 463
Nicholls, Capt., 50, 393
Niedermeyer, Frederick W., 85
Nieuhawk, *see* British Nieuport
Nieuport, 4, 28, 36, 45, 48, 50, 73, 81, 95, 325, 336, 428, 430
  biplane racers, 46, 49, 100, 102, 103, 107–18
  29C-1, 110
  29G, 111–12
  29 seaplane racer, 112, 115
  29 standard, 111–12, 118, 136, 390, 463, 466
  29V (Vitesse), 75, 95, 108, 109–10, 111–17, 142, 193, 423–4, 482–4
  62, 138
Nieuport-Astra, 38, 47, 49, 109, 117, 118, 126, 128, 138
  propeller, 73
Nieuport-Delage, 79
  Bébé Scout, 109
  Eugène Gilbert, 121, 124–5, 136
  sesquiplane, 47, 77, 80, 85, 104, 115, 119–23, 124–5, 126, 146–7, 198, 211, 244, 389, 424–5, 432, 443–4, 456, 484
  29V, 116–17, 332, 429–31, 433, 439, 468
  37, 122–3, 433, 484
  40, 117–18, 126
  42, 126–8, 134, 154, 426–7, 443–5
Nieuport and General Aircraft Company, *see* British Nieuport
Nieuport-Macchi M.17, 99
Niles-Bement-Pond Tool Company, 70
Nimitz, Chester, 13
Nisbet, Robert H., 435–6
Nitti, 386
Noakes, J., 43, 327, 332, 438
Non-stop record flight 1924, 185
Noorduijn, R. B. C. "Bob," 308
Norfolk, Virginia, 55–6, 240–1, 412–13
North, J. D., 81, 82, 307

Northcliffe, Lord, 9, 25–6, 29, 44, 306, 316, 347, 348
Northolt, England, 320
Northrop, John, 151
Northrop transports, 295
Norton, Harmon J., 225, 237, 459
Noville, George, 198
Nungesser, Charles, 102, 128, 135, 145, 150, 222, 433
Nutt, Arthur, 64–5, 66, 193–4, 198, 206, 216, 218, 226–8*passim*, 236, 239–40, 242

O'Brien, Hubbard T., 436
Observer, The, 15
Octane rating, 66, 71, 168
Offertag, Fred, 267
Ofstie, Ralph A., 204, 233–4, 409, 426, 475–6
Ogilvie, Alec, 73
Ogilvie, C. P. B., 309, 327
Ogilvie & Partners, 319, 322
O'Gorman, Mervyn, 323
"Ohio hicks," 60–1, 69
Old Hen, The, *see* Avro
Old Welsh Harp Pub, 42, 315
Oleo strut, 87
Olympia Aero Show,
  1911, 81
  1920, 317
Olympiade 1920, 111
Olympic Congress 1905, 21
Omaha, Nebraska, 32–3, 43, 120, 122, 185–6, 196, 244, 263, 265–6
Omaha Aero Club, 32
Omaha *Daily News*, 32
Ombra, 50, 392–3
Openshaw, Laurence, 151, 352
Ordnance Engineering Company (Orenco), 182
  Model D, 449
Oriole, *see* Curtiss
Orlando, Vittorio, 6
Orlebar, A. H., 338
Orly, Paris, 143
Orteig, Raymond, 25
Ortweiler, Frederick J., 438
Ostfriesland, 14, 19
OX engine, *see* Curtiss
Oxford–Cambridge air race 1921, 43, 44

P-38, 292
P-51, 293
Packard, 60, 61, 69, 242, 301
  engines, 102, 170, 214
    A-1500, 236
    1A-2025, 171, 173–5, 236, 269, 274, 291, 520
    2A-1500, 236, 237, 520
    X-24, 242, 520
    X-2775, 236
  ST-1 torpedo bomber, 83
  touring car, 220
Page, Arthur H., 460
Paget, Louis, 151

Painleve, Paul, 144
Pall Mall Gazette, 14
Palmer wheels, 183
Pan-American Aeronautic Convention, Atlantic City 1919, 29, 302
Pan American World Airways, 276
Papa, M., 92
Parachutes, 224, 228
Paragon Propeller Company, 72
Parasol aeroplanes, 85, 151
Paris Air Show
   1919, 25, 88, 139, 358, 364, 388
   1920, 110
   1921, 72, 82, 130, 358
   1922–23, 83, 123, 129, 132–3, 145
   1924, 126, 137
Paris–Tokyo flight 1924, 40, 155
Parker, Major, 128
Parker, General, 209
Parnalls, 134
Passaleva, Alessandro, 401–2, 425–6, 467, 470–1
Patrick, Mason M., 13, 16, 17, 210, 211, 213, 235, 275, 285
Patterson, Frederick B., 37–9*passim*, 192
Patterson, William K., 461
Paulhan (French pilot), 306
Pearson, Alex, 38, 214, 223–4, 283–5, 293, 425, 456, 458
Peary, Robert E., 24, 26
Peaty, L. F., 347
Peaty, Muriel, 347
Pedetti (mechanic), 398
Pegna, Giovanni, 51, 54, 395, 402–5
Pegna,
   P.c.1, 395–6, 469
   P.c.2, 403, 470, 474
   P.c.3, 404, 474
   P.c.5, 304
   P.c.7, 404
   see also Piaggio-Pegna
Pegna-Bonmartini-Cerroni, 402
Pelican aerial lorry, 320
Pelletier d'Oisy, Georges E. M. C., 40, 155–6, 158, 473
Pemberton Billing Company, 367
Penang race course, 327
Penaud, Alphonse, 147
Perrin, H. E., 28, 41
Perroni, Pio and Mario, 384
Perry, H. H., 440–1
Pershing, "Black Jack," 10
Pétain, Henri, 20, 128
Peterson, C. G. "Pete," 244–5
Peugeot, Robert, 59
Peugeot engines, 58–9
   Charlatan V-8, 59
Pfalz fighter, 81
Philomel, 370
Phoebe, 24
Picasso, Pablo, 21
Picard (French pilot?), 150
Piccío, Colonel, 389

Picker, Lucien, 58
Picker-Moccand et Compagnie, 58
Pickett, H. B., 378
Piers Aeroplane Company, S.S., 296
Pilleverdier, Louis, 58, 59
Pixton, Howard C., 347, 463
Plate radiators, 76, 179, 189, 407–8
Platz, Reinhold, 85, 86
PN-9, 236
Poincaré, Raymond, 20, 21
Poiré, Lt., 155
Pollock, Major, 128
Ponnier monoplane, 92
Pontoons, 95, 201, 224, 228, 229, 232–3, 234, 236, 249, 297, 310, 339–40, 343, 349, 378, 395
   with skin radiators, 238, 410
Porter, Earl W., 32–3
Porter, Finlay R., 64, 65, 191, 193
Porter, Odis A., 56, 235, 414
Portsmouth, England, 52
Port Washington, Long Island, 202, 224
Post, Augustus, 30, 177, 182
Potter, William C., 289
Pouit, M. R., 146
Powell, A., 378
Prandtl, Ludwig, 80, 86
Pratt Trophy 1919, 308
Pratt & Whitney
   R-1830 Twin-Wasp engine, 66
   Wasp engine, 68, 70, 239, 366, 522
Preston, Howard E. "Joe," 325, 332
Prévost, Maurice, 4, 92, 423, 428, 463
Prier and Coanda monoplanes, 354
Prince of Wales, *see* Edward VIII
Prix Beaumont, *see* Coupe Beaumont
Prix Guynemer 1920, 96–7, 99, 111
Prix Henry Deutsch de la Meurthe
   1912, 45, 95
   1919, 45–6, 49, 94–5, 99, 108, 110, 430
   1920, 95, 108, 109, 112, 114, 430
   1921, 432
   1922, 433
Prodger, Clifford B., 309, 434
Prodger-Isaacs Syndicate, 309
Propellers, 72–5, 147, 396
   constant-speed, 75
   four-blade, 153, 322
   metal, 73–5, 218
   three-blade, 249–50
   wood, 72–3, 214, 218
Prudden, George H., 82
Prudential Securities Company, 177
Pterodactyl tailless plane, 151
Pulitzer, Herbert, 29, 31
Pulitzer, Joseph, 29
Pulitzer, Joseph Jr., 29, 35
Pulitzer, Ralph, 7, 29–31, 37, 40
Pulitzer races, 47, 125
   1920, 31, 173, 190, 261, 281, 290, 386, 446
   1921, 32–3, 43, 120, 122, 185–6, 196–8, 244, 263, 265–6, 295, 384, 386, 451
   1922, 33–5, 47, 65, 77, 80, 86, 88, 123, 125, 175–6, 199–201, 206, 208–10, 246–7, 252, 273–4, 278, 282–3, 293,

296, 300, 303, 453
   1923, 35–7, 48, 53, 74, 153, 213–14, 220–1, 232, 252–5, 284–5, 456
   1924, 37–9, 44, 214–15, 285–6, 458
   1925, 39, 40–1, 54, 55, 231–3, 459
Pulitzer Aviation Trophy, 29–30, 31, 33, 35, 37, 197
Puma engine, *see* Siddeley-Deasy
Punch, 26
Pup, *see* Sopwith
Puss Moth, *see* De Havilland
Pylon turn tactics, 230–1

Quadriplane, 308

R-3, *see* Verville
R-4, *see* Loening
R-5, *see* Thomas-Morse
R-6, *see* Curtiss
R2C, *see* Curtiss
R3C, *see* Curtiss
R-34, 25
R-101, 16
Radiators, 75–8, 140, 146, 166, 170, 240, 260, 270–1, 388
   flat-plate, 76, 179, 189, 407–8
   honeycomb, 75
   see also Lamblin radiators; skin radiators
RAE, *see* Royal Aircraft Establishment
RAeC, *see* Royal Aero Club
RAF, *see* Royal Air Force
RAF-15 airfoil, 80, 170, 182
RAF High Speed Flight, 231, 343
Rafwire, 332
Railton Mobil Special, 332
Ramage & Ferguson, 315
Rand-McNally road maps, 16
Rankine (engineer), 72
Rateau, Auguste, 66–7
Rateau supercharger, 118, 123, 278
Raynham, Freddie, 25, 28, 42, 310, 315–17, 318–19, 348, 423, 428, 440–1
RB racer, *see* Dayton-Wright
Read, Albert C. "Putty," 25
Reed, Sylvanus A., 73–4, 75
Reed propeller, 52, 54, 72, 73–4, 134, 136, 202, 206, 212, 213, 216, 217, 227, 228, 236, 279, 284, 411– *see also* Fairey
Regia Aeronautica, 20, 390, 401
Régy propeller, 117, 124, 125
Reid, Frank R., 18
Reid, Wilfred T., 361, 364, 404
Reissner, Hans, 82, 86
Renault, 69, 126
   air-cooled engine, 356
   300-hp engine, 73, 333
Rentschler, Frederick B., 69–70, 74, 245
Reynolds, George, 358
Reynolds number, 28, 80, 141
Rheims Aerodrome, 92
Rheims meeting 1909, 146, 305

Ricardo, Harry, 58, 168, 331
Richthofen, Manfred von, 78
Rickenbacker, Eddie, 10, 41, 196, 271
Rinehart, Howard M., 88, 161–4, 166–8, 428
Rittenhouse, David, 54, 202–4, 224, 250, 296, 298–9, 372, 379, 426, 453, 462, 472, 474
Robert, Roger, 138
Roberts, C. H. M., 13
Rockaway Beach, 25, 190
Rockne, Knute, 86
Rockwell, Capt., 128
Rockwell Field, California, 229–30
Rodgers, John, 18, 236
Rodman, Thomas Clifford, 460
Roe, Alliott Verdon, 25, 309–10, 314–15, 316, 339, 352; *see also* Avro
Roe, Humphrey, 310
Roe, S. Verdon, 309
Rogers, Fred O. "Tex," 268, 447
Rohlfs, Roland, 24, 61, 84, 114, 172, 178, 180, 182–4, 186, 187, 189, 190, 192, 196, 423, 428
Rohrbach, Adolf K., 19, 83
Rohrbach
   Roland, 81, 83
   Romar, 83
   Zeppelin-Staaken, 83
Rolls, Charles S., 41, 59
Rolls-Royce, 58–60*passim*, 67, 69, 331, 344, 381
   engines:
     Buzzard, 67, 71
     Condor VIII, 376, 522
     Eagle VIII, 25, 60, 71, 348, 522
     Eagle IX, 60, 375
     Falcon, 60, 71, 315, 356, 522
     Falcon III, 289, 316
     F-X, 71
     F-XI, 71
     Hawk, 60, 356
     Kestrel, 67, 71, 331
     Merlin, 72, 229, 242, 331, 383
     R, 72, 463
Rome–Tokyo flight 1920, 386, 411
Roosevelt, Franklin D., 11, 12, 14, 19, 29
Roosevelt, Quentin, 40
Roosevelt Field, Long Island, 40, 82, 180, 181
Rosatelli, Celestino, 144, 383–4, 385, 387–8, 406
Rost, Maurice, 146–7, 430, 432
Rotary engines, 67–8, 269
Rothermere, Lord, 9–10, 25, 366
Rovellet, John P., 447
Rounds, Edward W., 248, 255–6, 257
Rowe, Basil, 40, 276
Rowledge, Arthur J., 67, 71, 311, 330
Royal Aero Club (RAeC), 28, 36, 41, 43, 44–5, 50, 53–5*passim*, 59, 70, 110, 309, 312, 331, 351, 364, 371, 392–3
   Certificate of Performance, 337
   Schneider Trophy Committee, 340
Royal Aeronautical Society, 333, 380
Royal Aircraft Establishment (RAE), 67, 72, 78, 79, 82, 320, 376

Royal Aircraft Factory, Farnborough, 318, 320, 323–5, 330
  S.E.4, 283, 324
  S.E.5, 43, 66, 72, 438, 440–1, 448
Royal Air Force (RAF), 9–11passim, 14–15, 16–17, 20, 42, 44, 55, 71, 75, 337–8, 344, 354–5, 368
Royal Australian Air Force, 361
Royal Flying Corps (RFC), 9, 261, 312, 322, 354
Royal Marine Hotel, Cowes, 203
Royal Naval Air Service (RNAS), 9, 16, 306, 308, 341, 356, 369
Royal Navy, 11, 14–15, 60, 79, 203, 337, 368
Royce, Donald, 268
Royce, Frederick H., 59–60, 61, 71, 331, 368
Ruchonnet (designer), 81
Ruffy Baumann School, Hendon, 326
Russell, Frank, 178, 202, 239–40
Ryan, John D., 60, 289

S.4, S.5, S.6, see Supermarine
St-Cyr Aeronautical Institute, 28, 46, 141, 320
St Louis Aeronautic Corporation, 35
St Louis Air Board, 35
St Louis air meet 1923, see Pulitzer race 1923
St Louis Post-Dispatch, 29, 35
Saint, H. J., 435
Salisbury, Lord, 15
Salmond, Geoffrey, 19, 55, 56
Salmond, John, 19, 324
Salmson engines,
  AC.9, 153
  CM.9, 153
  CM.18, 153–4, 516
  Z.9, 153
  Z.18, 153
Salmson-Béchéreau, 48, 93, 139
  engines, 71, 109, 390
  racer, 153–4, 443–5, 488
Salmson-Canton-Unné engines, 139
Salmson-Moineau, 139
Salon Aéronautique, see Paris Air Show
Samuel H. Valentine prize, 28
Sanderson, Lawson H. "Sandy," 192, 245–8, 253–5, 298, 426, 448, 453, 456, 461
Sandino, Augusto, 237
San Remo–Cannes "Petite Croisière" race 1921, 396–7
Santoni, D. Lorenzo, 50, 155, 307, 392–3
Santos-Dumont, Alberto, 45, 423
Saratoga, 223
Sartori, Romeo, 411, 415
Saunders, Sam E., 52, 54, 56, 110, 251, 315, 373, 392, 479
Saunders-Roe, 315
Savage, J. C., 307, 332
Savoia, Umberto, 384, 392
Savoia, 54, 154–5, 392, 405
  S.12 and S.12 bis, 394–5, 396, 465, 508
  S.13, 50, 51, 392–3, 398, 464, 468, 510
  S.17, 50, 99, 393, 397
  S.19, 395, 400, 465
  S.21, 51, 396–8, 400, 468, 510

S.22, 396–8, 400, 469
S.50 MVT, 400–1, 470, 510
S.51, 425–6, 470, 472, 510
S.52 fighters, 401
SVA-series, 384–5
see also Marchetti-Savoia
Sayers, William H., 44, 53
Scadta (Avianca), 82
Scaroni, Silvio, 413–14
Schilt, Christian F., 237, 240, 241, 413, 479
Schiranna Air Station, 411
Schneider, Jacques, 49–50, 55, 95
Schneider Trophy seaplane races, 5, 17, 59
  1914, 347
  1919, 49, 50, 95–6, 97, 110, 112, 310–11, 349, 357, 369, 391–3, 463
  1920, 50, 99, 394–5, 465
  1921, 50–1, 115, 397–9, 467
  1922, 51–2, 155, 369–71, 399–400, 470
  1923, 36, 38, 48, 52–3, 65, 70, 74, 155–8, 201–4, 225, 250–2, 299, 372–3, 405, 472
  1924, 474
  1925, 54–5, 85, 225, 232–4, 313, 340–3, 379, 408–9, 476
  1926, 55–6, 225, 240–1, 411–14, 478
  1927, 80
  1931, 75, 231
Schneider Trophy, 20, 45, 49, 51–3passim, 55, 56, 71, 84, 88, 138, 154, 204, 214, 224–5, 231, 242, 331, 371, 391–2
Schofield, H. M., 365
School of Military Aeronautics, Berkeley, 229
Schreck, F. B. A., 138
Schroeder, Rudolph "Shorty," 24, 28, 39, 67, 171–2, 173, 180, 264, 289, 428
Schulze, Lester, 274, 291–3, 454
Schwarts, 149
Science Museum, 369
Scott, Charles W. A., 313
Scott, G. H., 16, 25
Scott, Sir Percy, 13
Scott-Paine, Hubert, 311, 367–8, 369–70, 375, 401–2
S.E.4 and S.E.5, see Royal Aircraft Factory
Seaplane Experimental Station, Felixstowe, 340
See, Léon, 149
Seely, J. E. B., 324
Seguin, Laurent, 67
Seguin rotary engine, 68
Selfridge Field, Detroit, 33–5, 124, 175, 199, 210, 214, 231, 246, 271, 273, 280, 282–3, 292, 301
Semi-monocoque, 314
Semiquaver, see Martinsyde
Semphill, Lord, 289, 329
Serck radiator, 369
Sesquiplane, 119, 245, 372, 401, 407; see also Nieuport-Delage
Seversky, Alexander P. "Sasha" de, 13, 88
Seward, William, 9
Shaw, B. Russell, 41, 235
Sheahan, Bernie W., 281
Shell Oil Company, 51, 235, 369
Shell Trophy 1919, 311
Shenandoah, 18, 36

"Sheradizing," 82
Sherbondy, E. H., 67
Short, Ellen, 17
Short, Oswald, 82, 155, 365
Short Brothers,
  Crusader seaplane racer, 313, 329, 365
  pontoons, 339
  Silver Streak, 82
SIAI (Società Idrovolanti Alta Italia), 50, 392, 394; see also Savoia
SICC-Latham,
  No. 1, 473
  No. 2, 473
Siddeley, John D., 81, 244, 311, 315
Siddeley-Deasy Motor Car Company, 68, 310, 356
  engines:
    Jaguar, 68, 69
    Jaguar II, 337
    Puma, 244, 310–11, 314, 322, 524
Siemens, 358
Sigrist, Frederick, 346–7, 350, 351, 352
Silichrome, 244
SIMB (Société Industrielle des Métaux et du Bois), see Bernard
Simms Station, Dayton, 39, 163
Simon, Robert, 192
Simonin, A. E., 448
Simons, Bob, 281, 284
Simple Aerodynamics and the Airplane, 287
Simplex-Arnoux tailless racer, 149–50, 433, 488
Simplex auto factory, 60, 69
Sims, William S., 13
Siskin fighter, 318
Skeel, Burt E. "Buck," 38, 39, 214–15, 223, 275, 457–8
Skin radiators, 54, 76–8, 125, 126, 135, 179, 199–200, 206, 207, 217, 238, 240, 249, 253, 255, 277, 279, 283–4, 294–5, 338, 339, 343, 410
Skyways (Mitchell), 19
Sky-Writing, 332
Sloan airfoil, 80, 184, 195, 206
Smith, Al, 19
Smith, Reggie, 333
Smith, Ross and Keith, 25
Smith Aero Instruments, 337
Smithsonian Museum, 194
Società Anonima Nieuport-Macchi (SANM), see Macchi
Società Bastianelli, 396
Società Italiana Transarea (SIT), 385
Société Aéranautique Blanchard, see Blanchard-Blériot
Société Anonyme des Moteurs Salmson, see Salmson
Société Avions Bernard, see Bernard
Société des Avions Simplex, see Simplex-Arnoux
Société Barriquand et Marre, 59
Société de Construction d'Appareils Aériens, 91
Société Industrielle de Caudebec-en-Caux (SICC-Latham), see Latham
Société Lorraine de Dietrich et Cie, see Lorraine
Société Moreux, 77
Société Trois B, 129

Society of Automotive Engineers, 60, 163, 242
Society of British Aircraft Constructors (SBAC), 50, 56, 70
Sodium-cooled valves, 71, 164
Sonderstrom AFB, 209
Sopwith, T. O. M. "Tommy," 8, 41, 71, 79, 306, 344, 346–7, 348, 351–2, 393, 434
Sopwith, 25, 28, 41, 258
  Bat Boat, 347
  Bee, 348
  Camel, 29–30, 43, 163, 325, 341, 348, 438
  Dolphin, 348, 449
  Gnu, 441
  Pup, 43, 348, 438
  107-Schneider-Rainbow-racer, 42, 349–51, 357, 428, 436, 463, 472, 506
  Snapper, 348–9, 435
  Snipe, 325, 348, 351–2, 436
  1½-Strutter, 318, 348
  Swallow, 348
  Tabloid, 79, 283, 347
  Transport (Atlantic), 348
Souther, Arthur F., 300
Southern Hotel, Baltimore, 379
SPA (Società Piedmontese Automobili) engines, 69, 385, 526
  6-2A, 400, 526
Spaatz, Tooey, 24
Spad, 4, 28, 47, 50, 92, 108, 170, 273
  Berlines, 98, 104
  Blériot Mammoth, 106
  S.13, 449, 452
  S.14 Canon, 93, 96
  S.20 pursuit, 45, 93–8, 99–103, 114, 142, 423–4, 429–30, 464, 466, 480–1
  S.26, 96, 98–9, 423, 482–3
  S.27, 94
  S.29, 436
  S.31, 96
  S.33, 94, 102
  S.45, 104
  S.51, 106
  S.58 Louis Blériot, 105–6, 433, 482
  S.61, 106
  S.81, 106
  Nr. 195, 24
Spad belts, 220
Spad-Herbemont planes, 81, 91–106, 110, 147; see also Spad
Sparrowhawk, see Gloucestershire Aircraft Company
Sperry, Elmer A., 32, 285
Sperry, Lawrence B., 36, 285
Sperry, 195, 279
  Messenger, 285, 295
Spin recovery, 302, 316
Spirit of St Louis, 299
Spitfires, see Vickers
Split-flap wings, 79; see also Wing flaps
SST (Supersonic Transports), 134
Stablavion, see Arnoux
Stace, Donald F., 273–4, 455
STAé (Service Technique Aéronautique), 104, 144, 149
Stag Lane, London, 322, 332, 345

Stainforth, George H., 344
Stalling, 151
Standards, 36
Standard Steel Propeller Company, 73, 74, 236;
  see also Hamilton-Standard
Stanley, H. N., 26
Stearman, Lloyd, 38
Steinle, Felix, 448
Stellite, 71
Stinson, Eddie, 38, 82, 184, 310–13, 455
Stinson,
  Detroiter, 303
  model R, 303
Stinson, Katherine, 172, 302
Stinson, Marjorie, 302
Stocken, Rex H., 440
Stoner, Rex K., 458
Stoppani, M., 385
Stout, William B., 80, 82, 83, 86, 196, 301
Stout ST-1, 303
Streett, St Clair "Wingbone," 13, 281–2, 449,
  454
Stressed skin, 83, 147, 301
Stromberg carburetors, 66, 211–12
  NA-Y5, 206
Stutz Bearcat, 12
Sturtevant, see B. F. Sturtevant Airplane
  Company
Sulzer Works, Ludwigshafen, 387
Summers, James D., 273, 455
Summers, "Mutt," 381
Sunbeam-Coatalen engine, 122
Sunbeam-Despujols III powerboat, 96
Sunbeam Motor Company, 352
  Arab engine, 123, 329
Sunbeam-Talbot, 59, 69
Supercharger, 66–7, 68, 71, 72, 117, 229,
  344, 405
  turbo-, 118, 123
Supermarine, 51, 367–81
  Baby, 369
  flying boats, 50, 203, 331
  motorboats, 369
  S.4, 54, 55, 77, 79, 84, 86, 232, 234,
    340–1, 375–81, 409, 426, 476, 508
  S.5, 380–1, 404, 463, 479
  S.6 series, 72, 75, 77, 86, 231, 242, 380–1,
    404, 410, 463
  Sea Eagle, 375
  Sea King, 368–9
  Sea Lion, 242, 311, 368–72, 401, 407, 424,
    463, 471, 472, 506
  seaplanes, 54, 311, 339
  Sea Urchin, 376, 474
Sweeney, Charles, 128
Swirbul, Leon "Jake," 271

Tailless aeroplanes, 147–51
Tait-Cox, Leslie R., 424, 428, 435, 437–8, 440
Talbott, Harold E., 60, 161
Talbott, Harold E. Jr., 60, 161, 163, 167
Taliaferro Field Test School, 208
Talon zipper, 238
TAT (TWA), 181

Taube aeroplane, see Etrich
Taylor, C. Fayette, 74, 435
Taylor, David W., 244
Taylor, Willis P., 449
Teapot Dome scandal, 186
Teste, Lt., 155, 157, 470, 473
Tetraethyl lead, 66, 72, 168
Texas Aero Club, 28
Texas Wildcat, see Curtiss
Thin-walled shell construction, 81, 83
Thomas, Benjamin D., 170, 258–9, 263, 265,
  268–70
Thomas, Oliver W., 259, 275
Thomas, René, 109
Thomas, William T., 188, 259, 275
Thomas Brothers School of Aviation, 260
Thomas-Morse, 32, 174, 244, 259
  MB-3, 86, 259–62, 267–8, 274, 448–9,
    452, 496
  MB-4, 260
  MB-6, 123, 262–3, 265–7, 451, 496
  MB-7, 263, 264–8, 274, 282, 451, 453, 496
  MB-9, 268–9
  MB-10, 269
  R-5 (TM-22), 83, 269–71, 274–5, 454, 496
  S-4 "Tommy Scout," 259
  S4E Space Eater, 40, 276
  TM-23, 276
Thompson, Jefferson DeMont, 30
Thompson Trophy, 41, 235
Thomson, B., 351
Thomson, Christopher B., 16
Those Magnificent Men in Their Flying Machines,
  26
Thurston, Albert P., 82
Thurston, Arthur L. "Mike," 73, 80, 88, 178,
  182, 189, 192, 194–5, 205, 252–3,
  279, 294–6, 404
Tiddlywinks, 50
Times, The, 25, 48, 53
Timing methods, 22, 56, 210
Timmer, Al, 167
"Tin Goose," see Ford
Tipton, William D., 35
Tirpitz, Alfred von, 14
Tomer, William 238
Tomlinson, William G. "Red," 240–1, 460, 478
Tophatters, 299
Tourtellot, George P., 275, 455, 457
Towers, John H., 25, 54, 203
Towne Manufacturing Company, 238
Tractor aeroplanes, 258–9
Transatlantic flights, 25, 26, 41, 60, 69, 198,
  309, 316, 318, 348
Transcontinental flights, 185, 230, 264
Transcontinental Reliability and Endurance
  Test 1919, 12, 24, 261
Transpacific flight 1927, 208
Trenchard, Hugh Montague "Boom" Viscount,
  7–10, 11, 14–17, 19, 55, 56, 71, 347,
  352, 354
Trenhaile, W., 333
Trier & Martin, 315
Triplanes, 78, 79, 184–7, 189–92
Triplex glass, 228
Trippe, Juan T., 276

Tucker, Harry J., 185
Tully, T., 438
Turner, C., 308
Turner, Percy, 333
Turner, Roscoe, 38
TWA, 181

United Aircraft and Transport Corporation, 70,
  74
United Air Lines, 37, 70, 172
USA-27 airfoil, 265, 269
US Air Commerce Act 1926, 55
US Air Mail, 61, 74, 321
US Air Service, 10–11, 13, 16, 18, 24, 37, 39,
  55, 67, 72, 88, 208, 211, 214, 216,
  261, 265, 285, 287, 321
US Air Service Engineering Division, 69, 169,
  171, 212, 287
  R-7, 293
US Army, 18, 28, 29, 31, 32, 36, 38, 40–1, 54,
  55, 69, 169, 170, 175–6, 194, 205–6,
  213–14, 218, 220, 223, 227–8, 234–5,
  264, 267
US Cartridge Company, 240
US Navy, 11–14, 17–18, 25, 29, 33, 36, 38,
  40–1, 52–5 passim, 69, 70, 82, 148,
  187, 189, 191, 193–5, 205, 206,
  213–14, 218–20, 223, 227–8, 232–4,
  236, 264, 264–5, 267, 289, 291,
  296–7
  Schneider team, 40, 202–4, 225, 255, 299
US Navy M-80 airfoil, 80
USS Akron, 19
USS Indiana, 13
USS Iowa, 14
USS Langley, 199
USS Lexington, 232
USS Mississippi, 233
USS Pittsburgh, 52, 203
USS Shawmut, 342
USS Washington, 17
Uwins, Cyril F., 42, 357–9, 362, 364, 433, 437,
  439–40

V.2, see Bernard
29V, see Nieuport
V-1400 engine, see Curtiss
Vane, Harry, 71, 329–31, 340, 371
Vanderbilt, Harold S., 192, 293
Vanderbilt Cup auto races, 40
Van Horn, R. E., 281
Variable camber wing, see Wing flaps
Varioplane, 319
Varioplane Company, 87
Vaughan, C. R., 435
Vaughan, Stanley, 230
Vaulx, Count Henri de la, 21
Vautier, André, 130
Védrines, Émile, 49, 92
Védrines, Jules, 428
Venice, Italy, 50–1, 115, 398
Verdun, 158

Verduzio, R., 56, 384, 387, 411
Versailles Treaty, 6–7, 28, 29, 307
Vertholen, Capt., 320
Verville, Alfred, 19, 80, 85, 88, 169–71, 175,
  259, 271, 278–80, 281, 283, 286,
  293, 295
Verville, 31, 32, 102, 404
  Messenger, see Sperry
  R-1, 175–6, 454
  R-3, 39, 80, 86, 88, 131, 215, 224, 277–87,
    292, 425, 454–6, 458, 498
  VCP, 170, 180, 279
  VCP-R, 81, 171–5, 261, 424, 428, 450, 490
Verville-Sperry, 38
VF-1, 299
Viale, S. M., 69
Vickers, 81, 258, 354
  machine guns, 110, 308
  R-80, 82
  Viking, 25
  Vimy, 25, 41, 60, 365, 435
Vickers-Armstrong, 381
  Spitfire, 66, 344, 381
Vickers La Spezia Works, 400
Vickers MVT, 400
Victor Emmanuel III, 19
Vieilles Tiges, 49, 146
Villa, Pancho, 163
Villacoublay Aerodrome, 92, 99, 110, 114, 115,
  118, 124, 182–3
Villesauvage Aerodrome, see Étampes
Vincent, Jesse G., 32, 60, 61, 67, 171, 175,
  236, 269
Voisin,
  bombers, 73
  fighters, 59
Vought, Chance M., 24, 32, 60
Vought, 244
  Corsair, 237
  fighter, 255
  UO-1, 461
  VE-7, 24, 460–1
VP propeller, 72, 74, 106, 324
Vroman (French pilot), 155
VTOLs, 133
Vuia, Trajan, 78

Wackett, Leonard J., 361
Waddon Aerodrome, 44, 335— see also
  Croydon
Wade, Leigh, 85, 261, 449
Wadsworth, James W., 12
Waghorn, H. R. D., 463
Wagner, Herbert A., 83
Wagner beam, 83
Wait, Bill, 77, 181, 184, 195–6, 205, 209, 210,
  218, 219, 228, 230–1, 232, 237,
  238–40, 242, 342
Wakefield Gold Medal, 70
Wakefield Oil Company, 51, 369
Waldon, Sidney D., 33, 60
Walker, Charles C., 322, 345
Walton Motor Company, 325
Waring, Sir Samuel, 307, 309, 324–5, 328

Waring & Gillow, 324
Warner, Edward P., 33–4, 38, 44, 52, 55
Washington Conference on Limitation of
    Armaments 1921, 13, 17, 278
War Production Board, 60, 293
Warren-truss, 384, 385, 388, 397
Wash, C. H., 448
Wasp engine, *see* Pratt & Whitney
Watts, H. C., 73, 332
Wayne, John, 202
Wead, Frank W. "Spig," 202, 250–1, 255–6,
    299, 472
Webster, Sidney Norman, 463
Weeks, John W., 12, 13, 17–18, 33
Wehrle, Howard F., 33, 266
Weick, Fred E., 70
Weiss José, 100, 147, 319
Weller, Capt., 128
Welsh Aviation Company, 341
Western Air Express, 73, 176
Western Air Lines, 209
Westervelt, G. C. "Scrappy," 257
Westgarth-Heslam, Denis G., 314, 436, 439
Westland, 372
Wetsleeve construction, *see* Curtiss; Monobloc
    aero engine
Weymann, Charles T., 111, 428
Whelan, Ben, 167
"Whistling Bill," 179
"Whistling Rufus," 189
White, Earle F., 452
White, Sir George Stanley, 353–4
White, Karl, 259, 268
White, Stanley, 357
Whitehead, Ennis, 273, 275, 291–3, 454
Whitehead-Reid, Dr., 44, 441
Whittaker, Wallace, 167
Whittemore-Hamm Company, 30
Wick, Homer, 56, 240
Wiencziers monoplane, 87
Wiggen, Albert, 69
Wilbur, Dwight, 17, 18
Wilbur Wright Field, *see* Wright Field
Wilgoos, Andrew, 69–70, 299
Wilkinson, George S., 331
Willard Hotel, Washington, 61
Williams, Al, 37, 41, 136, 187, 192, 200–1,
    219–23, 224, 228–32, 234, 236, 245,
    255, 285, 426, 453, 456, 459, 461
Williams, George M., 163, 167
Willys, John N., 60, 64, 181, 191
Willys Overland Corporation, 181
Wilm, Alfred, 82
Wilson, Charles B., 340–1, 378
Wilson, Eugene E., 12, 18, 69, 74, 187
Wilson, Henry, 11, 14
Wilson, Paul D., 260, 261, 265–6, 268–9, 452
Wilson, Woodrow, 7, 24, 171
Winans, W. R. R., 275
Wing flaps, 70, 162, 164, 165–6, 168, 301,
    376
Wing radiators, *see* Skin radiators
Winterhalter, Albert G., 11
Winton, Alex, 27
Withers (race starter), 203
Witmer, C., 170

Wolfer, J. E., 449
Wolseley Viper engine, 62, 314, 514
Wood, Gar, 301
Wood construction, 81, 82; *see also* Monocoque
Woodgate, C. F., 333
Woodhouse, Henry, 24, 30–1, 35, 47, 177
Woodhouse, J. W., 441
Woolson, Lionel M., 236
World altitude records, 67
    1919, 189, 331
    1920, 99, 172
    1921, 263–4
    1923, 118, 126
    1924, 153, 158
    1932, 358
World duration records, 73, 82, 198, 202, 302,
    316
World-Herald, 267
World speed records, 70, 78
    1913, 92
    1919, 388
    1920, 94, 99, 102–4, 110, 112–14*passim*,
      116, 120, 145, 175
    1921, 80, 120, 122, 198, 335, 393–4
    1922, 117, 120, 121, 124, 125, 208,
      210–11, 217, 283, 337
    1923, 37, 77, 121, 212, 217, 221–2, 283
    1924, 39, 49, 127, 136–8, 204, 210, 376
    1934, 285
    for seaplanes, 52, 99, 204, 232, 235, 249,
      379, 402, 414, 415
World War I, 4, 6, 9–10, 20, 29, 60, 61–2,
    66–7, 78, 81, 315, 354
World War II, 128, 133
Worseley, O. E., 343
Worthington, R. S., 292–3
Woyevodski (Russian designer), 134
Wright, Burdette S., 24
Wright, C. Anderson, 177
Wright, J. B., 446
Wright, Orville, 37, 60, 69, 79, 161–2, 212,
    288
Wright, Theodore P., 228, 238
Wright, Wilbur, 37
Wright Aeronautical Company, 36, 69, 70, 296
  aeroplanes:
    Apache, 70, 239
    F2W (TX), 213, 219, 251–7, 426, 456,
      474, 496
    model "B" boxkite, 163
    NW (Navy-X), 54, 73, 200, 243–57, 299,
      426, 453, 472, 494
  airfoil W-1, 253
  engines:
    Cyclone P-2, 70, 243, 522
    E-3, 297, 518
    E-4, 252, 299, 518
    H-series, 123, 264, 518
    H-2, 123, 259, 262, 268
    H-3, 123, 125, 210, 268, 269, 273–4,
      279–83, 294
    J-series, 299
    J-1, 257
    J-4, 69
    J-5 Whirlwind, 69, 243, 299, 522
    Tornado (T-series), 218, 220, 226, 243

    T-2, 243–4, 245, 248, 249–52, 311, 518
    T-3, 252, 253, 255, 518
    Typhoon, 252
Wright-Bellanca,
    Columbia, 198
Wright brothers, 25, 37, 45, 68, 78, 85, 130
Wright Field, Dayton, 37–9, 172, 180, 212,
    213, 223
Wright Flyer, 59, 87
Wright-Martin Aircraft Company, 60, 62, 69,
    163, 244, 289, 460
    Hispano engine, 123, 188, 259, 265, 289,
      514
Wright Memorial Trophy 1950, 293
Wright-Patterson AFB, *see* Wright Field
Wurtz, George, 230
Wyman-Gordon Company, 65

Yamamoto, C., 40
Yankee Doodle, *see* Lockheed Vega
Young, Brigham, 209, 450

Zahm, A. F., 170, 180
Zanetti, Arturo, 99, 394, 395, 398, 465, 468,
    470–1
Zanonia macrocarpa, 148
Zenith Carburetor Company, 93
  carburetors, 66, 124, 126, 194, 206
Zeppelin, 82
Zerbi, Tranquillo, 387, 388, 390, 407, 410–11
ZR-1, 36
Zuccarelli, Paolo, 58–9

Nieuport & General LS-3